The British Boxing Board of Control

BOXING
YEARBOOK
2004

LONSDALE
LONDON

Edited and compiled by
Barry J. Hugman

Queen Anne Press

First published in Great Britain in 2003 by
Queen Anne Press
a division of Lennard Associates Ltd
Mackerye End, Harpenden
Hertfordshire, AL5 5DR

A CIP catalogue record for this book
is available from the British Library

ISBN 1 85291 654 0

Typeset and designed by Typecast
8 Mudford Road, Yeovil, Somerset, BA21 4AA

Printed and bound in Great Britain by
Biddles

Front cover:
Ricky Hatton lands a right on Aldo Rios
in their WBU Light Welterweight World Championship fight
at the MEN Arena in Manchester.
(Alex Livesey/Getty Images)

Back cover:
Jimmy Vincent on his way to an 8th-round stoppage of David Walker
in their final eliminator for the British Welterweight title in Dagenham.
(Les Clark)

Contents

LONDON

Boxing Equipment At Its Best!

Enquiries should be made direct to Locus Sales Team at:
tel: 0141 876 4411   fax: 0141 876 4422   email: locus@tiscali.co.uk

Acknowledgements

Now in its 20th year, I would like to take time out and thank all of those who have helped to establish the *British Boxing Yearbook* - 'the Wisden of boxing' - as an essential work of reference for the sport and one that, in its own way, is just as important to the boxing public as is the weekly *Boxing News*.

As in previous years, I am indebted to the BBBoC's General Secretary, Simon Block, along with Lynne Conway, Helen Oakley and Donna Phillips, for their continued help and support in placing information at my disposal and being of assistance when required. Simon's assistant, Robert Smith, who is also the Southern Area Secretary and a former pro fighter of note, was again extremely helpful, as was another former well-known boxer, Dai Corp, the Welsh and Western Area Secretary who now works out of the Board's Cardiff office.

On a business front, I would like to thank the BBBoC and Bernard Hart, the Managing Director of the Lonsdale International Sporting Club, for his efforts in organising the annual British Boxing Board of Control Awards Luncheon where the book will be launched. Ably supported by Kymberley and Chas Taylor, the Awards Luncheon has been an ongoing function since 1984, when it was established to coincide with the launch of the first Yearbook. At the same time, I would like to acknowledge the support coming from Locus Sports, a long-established company of some 50 years standing in the sports equipment industry. Earlier in the year, Locus, based in Glasgow, acquired the Lonsdale Boxing Equipment contract. My thanks also go to Windsor Insurance Brokers Ltd for their continued support and to all of those who advertised within these pages.

Ron Olver has been with the *Yearbook* from day one and, as ever, remains a tower of strength with his help and support. Once again, despite it being another difficult year and suffering continued ill-health, Ron has produced the Directory of Ex-Boxers' Associations. A former Assistant Editor of both *Boxing News* and *Boxing World*, he is also well known as the British correspondent of the *Ring*; the author of *The Professionals*; for producing the boxing section within *Encyclopedia Britannica*; his work on *Boxing*, Foyles' library service; and as the former co-editor of the *Boxing News Annual*. His honorary work which includes being the Chairman of the BBBoC Charity Grants' Committee; the Vice-President of many ex-boxers' associations; the Public Relations Officer of the London Ex-Boxers' Association; membership of the Commonwealth Boxing Council as New Zealand's representative; and the International Hall of Fame – has, in recent years, seen him honoured by the Boxing Writers' Club, the BBBoC, and the Commonwealth Boxing Council. He has been further honoured by the Boxing Writers' Club, who have made him an Honorary Life Member. It was due to Ron's promptings that the ex-boxers' associations came into being as we now know them, and he will always be remembered by the *Boxing News* readership as the man responsible for the 'Old Timers' page, now in its 36th year.

Members of the *Yearbook* 'team' who wrote articles for this year's edition and who have recently been published, or are in the process of publishing their own books are: John Jarrett (*Gene Tunney: The Golden Guy Who Licked Jack Dempsey*); Bob Lonkhurst (*East End Idol, the biography of Terry Spinks*. At this moment, Bob is working on *Fen Tiger: The Success of Dave 'Boy' Green*, which is due out in the Spring), Ralph Oates (*The Heavyweight Boxing Quizbook*), Melanie Lloyd (*Sweet Fighting Man*. Melanie is currently working on *Sweet Fighting Man – Volume 11*) and Tracey Pollard (who is working on a book about the life and times of Brian London, the former British heavyweight champion). Also, we welcome Graeme Kent, who has written an article titled Victor McLaglen: The Fighting Film Star within these pages, is a well-established author with over 100 books and several hundred television and radio plays behind him.

Wynford Jones, the Class 'A' referee, who again came to my rescue when travelling to the Board's offices on a regular basis in order to collate vital data required for this publication, has produced an article titled: Johnny Owen Remembered. Other members of the Yearbook team are Bob Yalen, who covers boxing with ABC across the world and looks after the World Title Bouts' section; Harold Alderman, an unsung hero who has spent over 40 years researching the early days of boxing through to modern times, has extended the Early Gloved Championship Boxing section from 138 to 152lbs; Chris Kempson, who produces Highlights from the Amateur Season, is our man in the world of amateur boxing; Eric Armit, who is a leading authority on boxers' records throughout the world, is responsible for the A-Z of Current World Champions; and Derek O'Dell, a former amateur boxer, produces the Obituaries' section.

Regarding photographs, as in previous years the great majority were produced by Les Clark (he also writes the Boxing Quiz with a Few Below the Belt within these pages), who has possibly the largest library of both action and poses from British rings. If anyone requires a copy of a photo that has appeared in the *Yearbook* credited to Les, or requires a list, he can be reached at 352 Trelawney Avenue, Langley, Bucks SL3 7TS. Other photos were supplied by my good friends, Derek Rowe, Harry Goodwin, Paul Speak, Chris Bevan and Philip Sharkey. More help came in the shape of Larry Braysher, a well-known collector, who supplied several photos for the Obituaries' section.

Also, additional help came from Neil Blackburn (who yet again provided information to make the Obituaries' section as complete as possible); Mrs Enza Jacoponi, the Secretary of the European Boxing Union (EBU Championship data covering the past 12 months); Simon Block (Commonwealth and British Championship data); Patrick Myler (Irish amateur boxing information); Malcolm Collins and Peter Foley (general amateur boxing information); and Dai Corp, John Jarrett, Brian McAllister, Ken Morton, Les Potts, and Robert Smith (Area title data). Although the research on world title bouts since gloves continues to wind down, I would again like to praise the efforts of men such as Tracy Callis, Luckett Davis and John Hogg, who are always available to help track down old-time fighters' records from abroad.

Finally, my thanks go to Jean Bastin, who continued to produce a high standard of typesetting and design, and my wife, Jennifer, who looks after the proof reading.

Introduction

by Barry J. Hugman

Welcome to the 20th edition of the *British Boxing Yearbook*. The format hasn't changed dramatically over the years, as myself and the team continue to monitor and update the current goings on, while also continuing to research the past and pass on our findings.

Starting with the modern era, once again we have decided to stay with the way we produce Current British Based-Boxers: Complete Records. The decision to have one alphabet, instead of separating champions, being taken on the grounds that because there are so many champions these days – British, Commonwealth, European, IBF, WBA, WBC, WBO, and more recently WBU, IBO, WBF, etc, etc, and a whole host of Inter-Continental and International titles – it would cause confusion rather than what was really intended. If you wish to quickly locate whether or not a boxer fought during the past season (1 July 2002 to 30 June 2003) then the Boxers' Record Index at the back of the *Yearbook* is the place to look. Also, as in the very first edition, we chart the promotions in Britain throughout the season, thus enabling one to refer to the exact venue within a boxer's record.

Regarding our records, if a fighter is counted out standing up we have continued to show it as a stoppage rather than that of a kayo, as in fights where the referee dispenses with the count. Thus fights are recorded as count outs (the count being tolled with the fighter still on the canvas), retirements (where a fighter is retired on his stool or by his corner during a contest) and referee stopped contest. Of course, other types of decisions would take in draws, no contests, and no decisions. In these days of health and safety fears, more and more boxers are being counted out either standing up or when initially floored, especially when a referee feels that the man on the receiving end is unable to defend himself adequately or requires immediate medical attention. One of the reasons that we have yet to discriminate between cut-eye stoppages and other types of endings, is because a fighter who is stopped because of cuts is often on his way to a defeat in the first place. Thus, if you want to get a true reflection on the fight it is probably better to consult the trade paper, Boxing News, rather than rely on a referee's decision to tell you all you want to know; the recorded result merely being a guide.

Continuing the trend, there are always new articles to match the old favourites. Regular features such as Home and Away with British Boxers (John Jarrett), World Title Bouts During the Season (Bob Yalen), A-Z of Current World Champions (Eric Armit), Highlights from the Amateur Season (Chris Kempson), Directory of Ex-Boxers' Associations (Ron Olver), Obituaries (Derek O'Dell) and two regular quizzes (Ralph Oates and Les Clark), etc, being supported this year with interesting articles such as Lest We Forget (Bob Lonkhurst), Cathy

Brown: A Lady in Waiting (Ralph Oates), Tommy Farr versus Joe Louis: Reflections of a Fight (Melanie Lloyd), Johnny Owen Remembered (Wynford Jones), Phil Martin: The Enduring Legacy (Tracey Pollard) and Victor McLaglen: The Fighting Film Star (Graeme Kent).

Elsewhere, hopefully, you will find all you want to know about British (Area), Commonwealth, European and world title bouts that took place in 2002-2003, along with the amateur championships that were held in England, Scotland, Wales and Ireland, as well as being able to access details on champions from the past.

Historically, what was started several years ago under the heading of Early Gloved Boxing, was extended to 138lbs in the 2002 edition. Much of this work was due to Harold Alderman painstakingly piecing together results for the pre-Lonsdale Belt and named weight division period. There are still many who believe as gospel much of what was reported down the ages by 'respected' men such as Nat Fleischer, the owner of *The Ring Magazine* and the *Ring Record Book*, and then copied by numerous historians who failed to grasp what the sport was really like before the First World War. This year, we have extended Harold's work to 152lbs and, hopefully, we will try and complete the exercise in the 2005 edition.

Basically, boxing prior to the period in question was a shambles, following bare fists with an assortment of driving gloves, knuckle gloves, and two-ounce gloves, etc, until it arrived at what we recognise today. There were no Commissions, newspapermen becoming all powerful by naming their own champions at all kinds of weights, and in much of America the sport was illegal, no-decision contests rescuing it from being abolished. If you thought today was dire, then boxing prior to that period was almost impossible in all divisions bar the heavyweights. Because travel was difficult and news travelled slowly, fighters were able to move from town to town proclaiming themselves to be the best and 'ringers' constantly prevailed. With today's research being aided by access to early newspapers, and the use of computers, it is becoming clear that men like Fleischer 'took' the best fighters of the day and then 'fitted' them into the named weight divisions we now know so well. If that is still as clear as mud, then turn to the pages in question.

Abbreviations and Definitions used in the record sections of the Yearbook:
PTS (Points), CO (Count Out), RSC (Referee Stopped Contest), RTD (Retired), DIS (Disqualification), NC (No Contest), ND (No Decision).

British Boxing Board of Control Ltd: Structure

(Members of the World Boxing Council, World Boxing Association, International Boxing Federation, World Boxing Organisation, Commonwealth Boxing Council and European Boxing Union)

PRESIDENT	Leonard E. Read, QPM
CHAIRMAN	Lord Brooks of Tremorfa, DL
VICE CHAIRMAN	His Honour Alan Simpson, MA, Oxon
GENERAL SECRETARY	Simon Block
ADMINISTRATIVE STEWARDS	Charles Giles John Handelaar Dennis Lockton Nicky Piper Billy Walker*
REPRESENTATIVE STEWARDS	Geoff Boulter Bernard Connolly Paul Gooding* Dean Hollington* Ken Honniball Fred Kennedy* Kevin Leafe* Phil Lundgren Ron Pavett* Fred Potter Les Potts Brian Renney Dave Roden* John Williamson
STEWARDS OF APPEAL*	His Honour Brian Capstick, QC Geoffrey Finn William Tudor John Robert Kidby Prof. Andrew Lees Timothy Longdale, QC John Mathew, QC Colin Ross-Munroe, QC Peter Richards FRCS Robin Simpson, QC Nicholas Valios, QC
HONORARY STEWARDS*	Frank Butler, OBE Sir Henry Cooper, OBE, KSG Capt. Robert Graham, BEM Mary Peters, DBE Dr Oswald Ross Bill Sheeran
HEAD OFFICE	The Old Library Trinity Street Cardiff CF10 1BH Tel: 02920 367000 Fax: 02920 367019 E-mail: sblock@bbbofc.com Website: www.bbbofc.com

* Not directors of the company

AREA COUNCILS - AREA SECRETARIES

AREA NO 1 (SCOTLAND)
Brian McAllister
11 Woodside Crescent, Glasgow G3 7UL
Telephone 0141 3320392

AREA NO 2 (NORTHERN IRELAND)
John Campbell
8 Mount Eden Park, Belfast, Northern Ireland BT9 6RA
Telephone 02890 683310

AREA NO 3 (WALES)
Dai Corp
13 Hill Crest, Brynna, Llanharan, Pontyclun, Mid Glamorgan CF7 9SN
Telephone 01443 226465

AREA NO 4 (NORTHERN)
(Northumberland, Cumbria, Durham, Cleveland, Tyne and Wear, North Yorkshire [north of a line drawn from Whitby to Northallerton to Richmond, including these towns].)
John Jarrett
5 Beechwood Avenue, Gosforth, Newcastle upon Tyne NE3 5DH
Telephone 0191 285 6556

AREA NO 5 (CENTRAL)
(North Yorkshire [with the exception of the part included in the Northern Area - see above], Lancashire, West and South Yorkshire, Greater Manchester, Merseyside and Cheshire, Isle of Man, North Humberside.)
Richard Jones
1 Churchfields, Croft, Warrington, Cheshire WA3 7JR
Telephone 01925 765167

AREA NO 6 (SOUTHERN)
(Bedfordshire, Berkshire, Buckinghamshire, Cambridgeshire, Channel Islands, Isle of Wight, Essex, Hampshire, Kent, Hertfordshire, Greater London, Norfolk, Suffolk, Oxfordshire, East and West Sussex.)
Robert W. Smith
The Old Library, Trinity Street, Cardiff CF10 1BH
Telephone 02920 367000

AREA NO 7 (WESTERN)
(Cornwall, Devon, Somerset, Dorset, Wiltshire, Avon, Gloucestershire.)
Dai Corp
13 Hill Crest, Brynna, Llanharan, Pontyclun, Mid Glamorgan CF7 9SN
Telephone 01443 226465

AREA NO 8 (MIDLANDS)
(Derbyshire, Nottinghamshire, Lincolnshire, Salop, Staffordshire, Herefordshire and Worcestershire, Warwickshire, West Midlands, Leicestershire, South Humberside, Northamptonshire.)
Alec Kirby
105 Upper Meadow Road, Quinton, Birmingham B32
Telephone 0121 421 1194

Foreword

by Simon Block *(General Secretary, British Boxing Board of Control)*

In last year's Foreword I expressed my optimism about British Boxing and its future, and the beginning of this new season shows that optimism to be justified.

At the time of writing we have 23 tournaments booked for the month of September 2003, seven more than the same month last year, and there are plenty of top-level matches in the making, involving British boxers, both here and abroad, to whet the appetite. At world level, Lennox Lewis and Joe Calzaghe remain dominant, but Scott Harrison's defeat by Manuel Medina for the WBO feather-weight championship took most of us by surprise. Scott appeared to be making unstoppable progress, but I believe he has the grit and determination necessary to rebound from this loss and continue his onward march. At domestic level, there are some exciting matches in prospect, particularly in the heavyweight division and at the other end of the scale, the flyweight division. Ricky Hatton remains Britain's most exciting and popular boxer and is the very acceptable face of British boxing. Johnny Nelson, Howard Eastman, Jawaid Khaliq, Junior Witter, Alex Arthur and Michael Brodie are all still capable of further international honours and there is a wealth of young talent that has debuted in the last 12 months.

The women's sport has failed to develop in the way that some might have anticipated after Jane Couch's breakthrough into licensed professional boxing five years ago. There are, in fact, fewer active women boxers currently than there were two or three years ago. However, both Jane, currently promoting as well as boxing, and Cathy Brown remain our leading boxers, despite both suffering gutsy losses against the very best in the world in Lucia Rijka and Regina Halmich, respectively. Both are likely to be taking part in further international championship contests in the coming season.

Following our relocation from Jack Petersen House in London to The Old Library in the centre of Cardiff, I am pleased to report that the change has proved of no detriment to the operation of the Board and, if anything, the improved facilities of The Old Library have definitely leant themselves to an improvement in the efficiency of the Head Office. A number of licence holders have commented to me separately that they are pleased at the way they are dealt with promptly and courteously by our new staff, who have taken to their responsibilities with enthusiasm.

The reconstruction of the Board referred to in last year's Foreword has now been completed. The number of Directors has been reduced from 32 to 16, with eight of those Directors being elected, one from each of the eight Area Councils. There will still be up to 32 Stewards, as has always been the case, who will still carry out their functions of being the senior person from the Board in authority at ringside, to sit on tribunals and sub-committees and to represent the Board at tournaments and functions, both here and abroad, but only the 16 Directors will be responsible for the management of the Company.

Earlier in the year, on an historic occasion, I hosted a meeting, together with the Assistant General Secretary, Robert Smith, attended by our counterparts in the Amateur Boxing Associations of England and Wales, and Amateur Boxing Scotland. Our aim is to form a Joint Consultative Forum to help the development of the sport, amateur and professional, to represent the interests of the sport to Government, the media, etc, and to co-ordinate the medical safeguards and controls. Although each body will continue to administer the sport within its own jurisdiction, the Forum will exist to reconcile the difficulties and tensions that exist between the different disciplines and to promote a degree of harmony to ensure the development of amateur and professional boxing, which are, always have been, and always will be, inextricably linked.

The *Yearbook* shows this to be the case, covering both amateur and professional boxing, and this year's edition is no exception. I occasionally like to trawl through the amateur section of previous *Yearbooks* to remind myself of how today's professional stars got on in their amateur days and to see some of the matches which took place for cups or medals that today would cost thousands and, in some cases, millions of pounds to make.

Editor Barry Hugman and his boys have done a wonderful job for us again and I hope you find the book as useful, informative and enjoyable as I do.

British Boxing Board of Control Awards

The Awards, inaugurated in 1984 in the form of statuettes of boxers, and designed by Morton T. Colver, are supplied by Len Fowler Trophies of Holborn. Len was an early post-war light-heavyweight favourite. As in 2002, the Awards Ceremony, which has reverted back to a luncheon format, is due to be held this coming Autumn in London and will again be hosted by the Lonsdale International Sporting Club's Bernard Hart, the Managing Director of Lonsdale Sports Equipment Ltd, and sponsor of the Awards.

British Boxer of the Year: The outstanding British Boxer at any weight. 1984: Barrry McGuigan. 1985: Barry McGuigan. 1986: Dennis Andries. 1987: Lloyd Honeyghan. 1988: Lloyd Honeyghan. 1989: Dennis Andries. 1990: Dennis Andries. 1991: Dave McAuley. 1992: Colin McMillan. 1993: Lennox Lewis. 1994: Steve Robinson. 1995: Nigel Benn. 1996: Prince Naseem Hamed. 1997: Robin Reid. 1998: Carl Thompson. 1999: Billy Schwer. 2000: Glenn Catley. 2001: Joe Calzaghe. 2002: Lennox Lewis.

British Contest of the Year: Although a fight that took place in Europe won the 1984 Award, since that date, the Award, presented to both participants, has applied to the best all-action contest featuring a British boxer in a British ring. 1984: Jimmy Cable v Said Skouma. 1985: Barry McGuigan v Eusebio Pedroza. 1986: Mark Kaylor v Errol Christie. 1987: Dave McAuley v Fidel Bassa. 1988: Tom Collins v Mark Kaylor. 1989: Michael Watson v Nigel Benn. 1990: Orlando Canizales v Billy Hardy. 1991: Chris Eubank v Nigel Benn. 1992: Dennis Andries v Jeff Harding. 1993: Andy Till v Wally Swift Jnr. 1994: Steve Robinson v Paul Hodkinson. 1995: Steve Collins v Chris Eubank. 1996: P. J. Gallagher v Charles Shepherd. 1997: Spencer Oliver v Patrick Mullings. 1998: Carl Thompson v Chris Eubank. 1999: Shea Neary v Naas Scheepers. 2000: Simon Ramoni v Patrick Mullings. 2001: Colin Dunne v Billy Schwer. 2002: Ezra Sellers v Carl Thompson.

Overseas Boxer of the Year: For the best performance by an overseas boxer in a British ring. 1984: Buster Drayton. 1985: Don Curry. 1986: Azumah Nelson. 1987: Maurice Blocker. 1988: Fidel Bassa. 1989: Brian Mitchell. 1990: Mike McCallum. 1991: Donovan Boucher. 1992: Jeff Harding. 1993: Crisanto Espana. 1994: Juan Molina. 1995: Mike McCallum. 1996: Jacob Matlala. 1997: Ronald Wright. 1998: Tim Austin. 1999: Vitali Klitschko. 2000: Keith Holmes. 2001: Harry Simon. 2002: Jacob Matlala.

Special Award: Covers a wide spectrum, and is an appreciation for services to boxing. 1984: Doctor Adrian Whiteson. 1985: Harry Gibbs. 1986: Ray Clarke. 1987: Hon. Colin Moynihan. 1988: Tom Powell. 1989: Winston Burnett. 1990: Frank Bruno. 1991: Muhammad Ali. 1992: Doctor Oswald Ross. 1983: Phil Martin. 1994: Ron Olver. 1995: Gary Davidson. 1996: Reg Gutteridge and Harry Carpenter. 1997: Miguel Matthews and Pete Buckley. 1998: Mickey Duff and Tommy Miller. 1999: Jim Evans and Jack Lindsey. 2000: Henry Cooper. 2001: John Morris and Leonard 'Nipper' Read. 2002: Roy Francis and Richie Woodhall.

Sportsmanship Award: This Award recognises boxers who set a fine example, both in-and-out of the ring. 1986: Frank Bruno. 1987: Terry Marsh. 1988: Pat Cowdell. 1989: Horace Notice. 1990: Rocky Kelly. 1991: Wally Swift Jnr. 1992: Duke McKenzie. 1993: Nicky Piper. 1994: Francis Ampofo. 1995: Paul Wesley. 1996: Frank Bruno. 1997: Lennox Lewis. 1998: Johnny Williams. 1999: Brian Coleman. 2000: Michael Ayers and Wayne Rigby. 2001: Billy Schwer. 2002: Mickey Cantwell.

The 2002 'Special Award' went to Richie Woodhall (left) and Roy Francis (right). Presenting the award was the former BBBoC General Secretary, Ray Clarke, OBE

Les Clark

TARA BOXING PROMOTIONS & MANAGEMENT

Doughty's Gym, Princess Road, Shaw, Oldham OL2 7AZ
Tel/Fax: 01706-845753 (Office)   Tel: 01706-846762 (Gym)

Jack Doughty with left to right: Ady Lewis, Bobby Vanzie and Charles Shepherd

Trainer/Manager: JACK DOUGHTY
Trainers: Eamonn Vickers, Ray Ashton, Chris Fuller, Andy Jessiman, Maurice Core
Matchmaker: Richard Poxon M.C: Michael Pass

BOXERS

Shinny Bayaar - Flyweight
Choi Tseveenpurev - British Masters Featherweight Champion
Anjed Mahmood - S. Featherweight
Charles Shepherd - Former British, Commonwealth & IBO World
S. Featherweight Champion
Bobby Vanzie - Former British & Commonwealth Lightweight Champion
Mark Paxford - Welterweight
Gary Hadwin - Welterweight
Wayne Shepherd - L. Middleweight
Gary Dixon - Middleweight
Darren Stubbs - S. Middleweight

Cathy Brown: A Lady In Waiting

by Ralph Oates

American singer James Brown once had a most successful record called "This is a man's world" and the song's title could easily have been suitable in helping to describe the world of pugilism. Certainly, at one time, the 'Noble Art' was very much a male dominated sport by its very nature, the prospect of female involvement appearing remote to say the very least. Yet, this situation seems to be changing and I don't think that anyone could have failed to have noticed the ever increasing female participation in boxing.

In recent years, women have taken roles in various different areas of the sport. Tania Follett became the first woman in Britain to be licenced as a second and then, later, the first female boxing manager. Katherine Morrison also put her name in the record books by becoming the first Scottish lady promoter, not forgetting other lady promoters like Annette Conroy and Alma Ingle. Lisa Budd became the first woman MC, followed by Charlotte Russell. Judith Rollestone had the honour of being the first lady Administrative Steward for the British Boxing Board of Control, while Mary Peters, the famous Olympian, has, of course, been an Honorary Steward for some time now. The growth has been slow but steady, with the ladies even putting on the gloves to perform in the ring. In Britain, Jane Couch became the first lady boxer to be given a licence by The British Boxing Board of Control and has since enjoyed various forms of success. There is also Michelle Sutcliffe from Leeds, who has given a good account of herself, while meeting a host of top names, often on their own turf. The American, Christy Martin, nick-named 'The Coal Miner's Daughter', can, of course, be given credit for trailblazing the cause of women's boxing and has consequently developed into a major name. Later, Mia St. John, Lalia Ali (daughter of Muhammad Ali) and Jacqui Frazier Lyde (daughter of Joe Frazier) have kept the momentum going. When Lalia and Jacqui met it clearly caught the media's attention, which thus put the spotlight on female boxing. Part of the attraction of their match, which Lalia won on points over eight rounds, may well have been due to their respective illustrious fathers, notoriety, and their three tremendous encounters in the ring, but, nevertheless, the bout was given generous coverage by the media, which in turn helped the case for female boxing.

On this particular occasion the spotlight is on yet another lady boxer, Britain's WBF European flyweight champion, Cathy Brown, who for the last few years has made steady progress, improving her fistic education by meeting good-class opponents. Clearly, Cathy more than proved that she was for real when, in April this year, she was tested to the extreme when meeting Germany's defending champion, Regina Halmich, for the WIBF flyweight title. Regina is considered to be one of the best lady boxers in the world, so the task in front of Cathy was not an easy one. However, on the night in Schwerin, Cathy gave Halmich all the trouble she could handle, losing a disputed 10-round points decision. The performance Cathy produced in Germany enhanced her reputation greatly on the world stage. On behalf of the *Yearbook* I carried out the following interview with her.

(Ralph Oates) In which year were you born?
(Cathy Brown) 1970.
(RO) Where were you born?
(CB) In Leeds on a temporary basis so to speak, as I was adopted. My biological parents are Scottish. I was put in to an orphanage until my adopted parents collected me and took me to 'Geordie' land.
(RO) When did you come to London?
(CB) I came to London in 1991 when I was 21 years of age. I was then in search of a photographic career.
(RO) What made you decide to box?
(CB) I started kick boxing in 1991 and at that time it was just a hobby, but I became addicted to the dedicated training. I actually had my first ring fight after just three months and after that I was well and truly hooked. I had always loved boxing, but never had the opportunity to practice the skill to box until 1998. I was, in fact, approached by a promoter in 1999, who gave me a chance to fight on his show, hence my boxing career was born.
(RO) Have any other members of your family ever boxed?
(CB) No, I have to say none of my family have ever boxed or been interested in the sport.
(RO) How do your parents feel about your boxing career?
(CB) My parents hate my boxing career. I think they would prefer me to take up knitting or a career in administration. They still cannot understand that the sport is not just a hobby to me. My boxing career is the most important thing in my life at the moment.
(RO) Were you a big boxing fan before you decided to lace on the gloves?
(CB) I remember watching wrestling on TV as a child and loved it. My favourite being Big Daddy. I thought he was amazing. Then, later, as I got older, I started watching the Chuck Norris films and loved watching the fight scenes. I then became interested in all forms of combat, which, of course, included boxing. In fact I have grown to understand the various fighting arts. This in turn helps me to appreciate and enjoy the sport when in the role of a spectator.
(RO) What did you do before you came into boxing?
(CB) I was a forensic photographer. I studied for a degree in photography for four years and thus attained the said position. The job was basically photographing murder scenes and post mortems. I was also involved in sports event management for a few years.
(RO) What problems did you encounter at the start of your boxing career?
(CB) Chauvinism and not being taken at all seriously, which, I may add, is still occurring today. Trying to get promoters to take you seriously and thus put you on to their

shows is very difficult. This I find strange since I am a very good ticket seller and this in turn makes it good business sense to book me. I have even had certain referees refuse to handle my bouts, which annoys me. Everyone has a right to their own opinions but the world has moved on and women do now fight, and I think that critics should recognise this fact. Even commentators blatantly show they are very anti-women when it comes to boxing. All they want to talk about is how good you look in a dress and often demean your power and skill. Let anyone of them get into the ring with me for 10 rounds and then see if their opinions change after that. My heart is in boxing and I take my training very seriously, thus no one should criticise me for my dedication to the sport.

(RO) Have you ever had any moments of doubt and felt that in boxing you may have picked the wrong career?

(CB) No, not really. The more people try to make it difficult for me the more determined I become.

(RO) On average how many hours a week do you train?

(CB) I would say on average 20 hours a week, but this of course can vary.

(RO) Are you superstitious in any way before a contest?

(CB) No, I cannot say that I am in all truth.

(RO) You won your first championship in your third contest on 1 July 2000, defeating Jan Wild on points over six rounds for the vacant European WBF flyweight title. This must have been an exciting moment for you?

(CB) Yes it was exciting, since it was my first step on the ladder which I hope will take me to the very top.

(RO) How did you acquire the nick-name 'The Bitch'?

(CB) 'The Bitch' was born in the gym as like most boxers I have a dual personality. One inside the ring and one outside. I am a very approachable kind of person, but inside the ring I am determined to win and go all out for victory. On the whole, I am a very strong person and I needed something hard hitting and controversial for the media to get hold of and hence get my boxing skill noticed. The nick-name helps to draw attention to my boxing. This also helps to put womens' boxing on the map.

(RO) What is the best advice you've been given for life in general?

(CB) Life is just a ride; it's like a roller coaster, sometimes it's up, sometimes it's down, sometimes it's fast and sometimes slow, and it can get scary at times. However, when you have been on it for a while you realise it's just a ride and you need to enjoy it for what it is.

(RO) What is the best boxing advice you've been given to date?

(CB) Relax and enjoy your career as it will not go on forever and one day you can look back and admire everything you have achieved. Win or lose, it takes a strong, special person to put their feet inside the ring in the first place.

(RO) What annoys you most in boxing?

(CB) The lack of true recognition for talent and the over protection that some fighters are given.

(RO) What stance do you box in?

(CB) Orthodox.

(RO) How do you feel about boxing southpaws?

(CB) I think they should be shot at birth (Ha Ha).

(RO) You had your second professional contest in Belgium, stopping Veerle Braspenningsx in round six. Did you enjoy the experience of boxing abroad?

(CB) Yes I did, it was certainly an experience. The fans always try to unsettle you abroad, but I loved it and tend to fight even better in those situations, especially with the crowd booing and everything against you (decision wise). However, this only makes me even more determined to win and consequently I won the bout with Veerle by a stoppage in round six, which made this an even nicer experience.

(RO) Based on your experience, at this present time do you feel that women boxers are being taken more seriously in the sport than they were some years ago?

(CB) No, not really. Some people have come around, but there are still many out there who will never take us seriously as we are not supposed to be successful in a male-related sport.

(RO) Who has been your most difficult opponent so far?

(CB) Oksana Vasilieva, whom I fought in my sixth contest. In fact, I gave a great deal of weight away in this bout, but since Oksana was said to have had only two professional fights it was felt that I would be able to handle her without any undue problems. WRONG. It was a real battle all the way and I lost a four-round points decision, along with my undefeated record. I later found out that Oksana was a very experienced amateur with a reputed 54 bouts to her credit, so she really knew her way around the ring and was, in fact, a great deal more experienced than me.

(RO) Have you had any awkward moments in boxing to date?

(CB) Yes I did have an awkward moment when I fought Alina Shaternikova for the vacant WBF womens' flyweight title as I had trained to fight an orthodox boxer. However, once the bell went I found I was facing a southpaw, a shock situation which I had to deal with for 10 rounds before losing the decision on points. I will not go fully into this matter, but I was far from happy about the whole affair.

(RO) What changes, if any, would you like to see in boxing?

(CB) Many up-and-coming boxers are over protected. I would like to see some of them tested before they go for titles. Often title challenges are made by these fighters and they fail due to a lack of real competition at class level. In the long run this is bad for them and bad for boxing.

(RO) A number of male boxers fight on into middle age these days. How do you feel about that?

(CB) I think until a person has actually boxed for a period of time it's hard for them to comprehend just how difficult it is to give up the sport. To stop fighting is one of the hardest things to do. Very often it's a sport that an individual has practiced since an early age and once it's in your blood it's hard just to stop. So I can understand these fighters going on into middle age. Let's be honest, there are some great boxers in their middle age around today and they are performing well, often giving their younger counterparts a lesson or two. However, upon saying that, a fighter must know when it's time to call it a day. If he's

taking more punches than he previously did, along with other obvious signs of deterioration, then he or his team should take notice of these warning signs. The boxer's team should advise him accordingly, since at the end of the day the good health of the boxer is of the utmost importance.

(RO) Who is your favourite boxer?

(CB) Muhammad Ali, a truly remarkable boxer in every way. Ali not only had to fight his opponents inside the ring, but also do battle with racism outside of the ropes. I do have empathy with Ali's plight with regards to the latter issue, since I have to deal with sexism on many fronts. While it may be true to say that sexism isn't on the same level as racism, it is still a form of segregation.

(RO) What is your opinion about the various different boxing organisations? Do you think they serve boxing well, or do you think that one world champion in any one weight division is better for the sport?

(CB) To be frank, I hope that boxing does not become like kick-boxing, where there are far too many organisations producing world and European titles which do not mean a thing. I think in an ideal world there should be only one world champion in each weight division, but, sadly, I fear that there are too many politics, plus promoters, involved and, of course, TV deals wouldn't be made without a couple of different organisations. This, in turn, would mean that many of the boxers would not get good public exposure. Let's hope that for the good of the sport we do not see any more world organisations being formed. I think we have more than sufficient at the moment.

(RO) How do you feel boxers today compare with past boxers with regards to both skill and technique?

(CB) I think that trainers have improved their skills and technique over the years and, in turn, have produced some unique and, dare I say, some special talent. However, in the past, boxers used to fight 15 or 20 rounds in some cases with no gum shields, etc, and that really took some doing. So I have to say that I don't think that you can beat them

Cathy (right) on her way to defeating Oksana Vasilieva   Les Clark

for a true show of GRIT and even in today's modern world some of these fighters from the past would be difficult to defeat.

(RO) What is your answer to those who say women should not box?

(CB) Everyone is of course entitled to their own opinion, but I don't think that anybody has the right to hinder anyone's career decision. If I wish to box that is my decision and my right.

(RO) What has been your biggest disappointment so far in boxing?

(CB) My loss to Regina Halmich when challenging for the WIBF flyweight title on 26 April this year. I put her down for a count in the third round and really felt that I did enough to take the title. However, I was fighting in Germany on the champion's turf and knew that if I didn't knock her out I wouldn't take the title. I lost a 10-round points decision. On the other hand, I really enjoyed the fight and felt very strong, the strongest I have felt so far in my career, and was very proud of my performance.

(RO) If the opportunity came along to fight Regina again would you take it?

(CB) Without a shadow of a doubt.

(RO) What has been your proudest moment in boxing to date?

(CB) My first victory inside the distance, which took place in Belgium against Veerle Braspenningsx in February 2001. I won in round six and it gave me a great feeling.

(RO) You trained earlier this year in Miami. Did you learn a great deal from this experience?

(CB) Yes I did, Miami was an excellent experience. Training in the heat of the gym with no air conditioning was a true test of fitness, along with sprinting on the sand. I also had top quality sparring which stood me in good stead for the future.

(RO) Would you like to have a few bouts in America?

(CB) Yes I would love the opportunity to box in the States.

(RO) Who has been your biggest influence in boxing?

(CB) I would have to say myself and those who think I should not box and have attempted to make my pathway difficult. I have had to dig deep into myself to be where I am today and, at times, it's been really hard, but you find yourself reflecting on those hard times to keep you going. I would also like to add that my present trainer, Adam Booth, has made me believe in my strength and ability and has brought out the best in me.

(RO) I understand that you have only recently changed trainers?

(CB) That's right, I did, but it was the hardest decision I have had to make in boxing. I thought long and hard about the change and was aware that some felt that I was selfish to do so. However, this is a selfish sport and at the end of the day it's me who's taking the punches in the face and putting my health at risk. Nevertheless, there are times when you have to move on for whatever reason. I still respect my old trainer, Gary Inniss, and I would add that I have a great deal of admiration for him. Yet I must be honest and say that I know in my heart of hearts I did the

right thing in making the move when I did. I am pleased to say that I am working extremely well with Adam Booth, as his coaching suits me.

(RO) What advice would you give to any woman considering a career in boxing?

(CB) If you want to do it in your heart then pursue your dream, although the path along the way is really difficult. When the moments are hard, and there will be some very hard moments, really think about your own internal dedication and love for the sport. If you can give 200 per cent then go for it.

(RO) Do you have any favourite sports apart from boxing?

(CB) I love athletics, especially the sprints. Those who take part are such strong sports people physically. Watching them perform is an inspiration to me on low days.

(RO) Do you have any time for hobbies?

(CB) I wish. My schedule is so full that I have very little time for any kind of hobby.

(RO) What is your favourite kind of music?

(CB) Funk, Soul, R & B, Hip Hop, Garage etc, etc. Just as long as it is not Rock, as it kills my brain and gives me a headache.

(RO) Over the years there have been a number of boxing films made. Do you have a favourite?

(CB) No, not really. There hasn't been any good boxing films made since Rocky (Ha Ha). Although I loved Snatch, even though it was based on bare-knuckle fighting (is that still classed a boxing movie?). After due consideration, it's the only one I can think of that I liked.

(RO) What is your major ambition?

(CB) To hold a recognised world title and to be respected in the boxing industry.

(RO) When your boxing days come to an end, do you intend to stay in the sport in some other capacity?

(CB) I think it would kill me to come out of boxing altogether, so yes, I really would love to stay involved in boxing as long as possible.

It seems quite obvious to me that Cathy is a determined woman, who is devoted to the sport of boxing and clearly has the heart of a fighter in her soul. To say that she has a hard road to travel would be an understatement, since this is a fact that Cathy is more than aware of already and is indeed ready to face the various obstacles put in front of her. Yet, if true ability and courage is enough, then Cathy can succeed and thus become a major player in the world of womens' boxing. The fight game is a tough sport for men, let alone women, whereupon success with a good victory can be quickly followed by disappointment with an upset defeat. One day you are up the next day you are down. Certainly a fighter needs that vital ingredient called resilience in his or her make-up. After talking to Cathy, I feel she has this attribute and can, if the opportunity presents itself, one day win a major world title. At the moment it could be said that Cathy Brown is a lady in waiting. Waiting for that golden chance to come along, it could happen sooner rather than later. On behalf of the *Yearbook*, I wish Cathy the very best for the future.

Phil Martin: The Enduring Legacy

by Tracey Pollard

The 27th May 2004 marks the 10th anniversary of the death of Phil Martin. It is unlikely that anybody reading this book has not heard of Phil, which is quite remarkable when you consider that he was only 44 years old when he died and his highly-acclaimed stable of professional boxers was only four years old. During his tragically short career, Phil progressed from boxer to amateur coach and, finally, into that minefield of professional boxing as a trainer, manager and promoter, roles that he juggled simultaneously and successfully.

Ten years later Phil's legacy remains, not least in 'The Phil Martin Centre', the fitness centre named in his honour and home to his legendary 'Champs' Camp', but also in the shape of boxing promotions as we know them today. It is commonplace now to have multiple title fights and champions on a single promotion, but in 1991 when Phil staged a show featuring five British champions it was the first of its kind. Four of those champions were Phil's fighters and he very nearly went home with a fifth that night too!

But, perhaps, Phil's greatest legacy is the contribution he made towards the resurrection of the seriously deprived Moss Side district of Manchester, which had been devastated by riots. Phil helped to bring hope and respect to an area where previously there was none.

Phil did not have the advantage of coming from a boxing family, in fact he barely had a family at all and he certainly had very few advantages. He was born in Prestbury in Manchester under his real name, Philip

Phil in his pro fighting days　　　Harry Goodwin

Adelagun. His mother was from London, where they lived for a while, and his Nigerian father spent most of Phil's childhood in prison. Put into care at the age of two, he was shunted between council homes, relatives and foster homes until his father's release when he was 10. His father proved to be a domineering bully and among Phil's chores was staying awake to deliver his father's lunch to him at 3am in the morning. Not surprisingly, Phil left home at the first opportunity, when he was 14.

Two years later Phil met a 15-year-old typist called Audrey, who would later become his wife and his soulmate. Audrey's employer, John Bentham, was a solicitor and boxing enthusiast, who had set up some boxing equipment in the basement of his business, British Debt Services. He quickly established the BDS amateur boxing club and would become Phil's close friend and sponsor, while Phil would soon become a top-class amateur boxer, winning 112 of his 127 contests. Phil was only floored once during that time and was soon up on his feet on that occasion in Denmark. One of his losses was to John Conteh in the 1971 North-West Counties championships and he reached the English championship semi-finals in 1974, but lost on points. Like most amateurs, Phil dreamed of fighting in the Olympics, but he would have been 27 by then and he needed to earn some money to support Audrey and their five-year old daughter, Andrea.

Phil's first priority when he decided to turn pro was to change his name to Phil Martin in order to dissociate himself from his father. Trainer, Ken Daniels, remembers the day that Phil walked into The Lonsdale Club on Whitworth Street in Manchester, where Ken trained fighters for manager, Tommy Miller. "I knew as soon as he walked in that he was Phil Adelagun, a classy amateur, so when he asked me to train him I was pleased to accept." He recalls that the name-change worked to Phil's advantage in his first fight against Liverpool's Pat Thompson in London on December 2nd 1974. The referee rescued Thompson in the seventh and Pat later said: "The name fooled me, I had no idea how good he would be." The two would meet on a further three occasions, with Phil the victor each time. Their third contest, on 29 April 1975, just four months after the first, was for the vacant Central Area light-heavyweight title. This would be Phil's eighth fight with one loss on points to Harry White. "Phil was going up against good, good men," says Ken, "fighters like George Gray and Frankie Lucas. White was a very hard lad but Phil was too clever for him and should have been given the decision. Frankie 'The Animal' Lucas was also really good. A Nigel Benn type of fighter, he came tearing out in the first round and again in the second, but Phil stayed calm and used his brain. The next thing, Phil had him down and the referee stopped it in the fourth round." Lucas would go on to have two attempts at the middleweight title, losing to Kevin Finnegan and later to Tony Sibson.

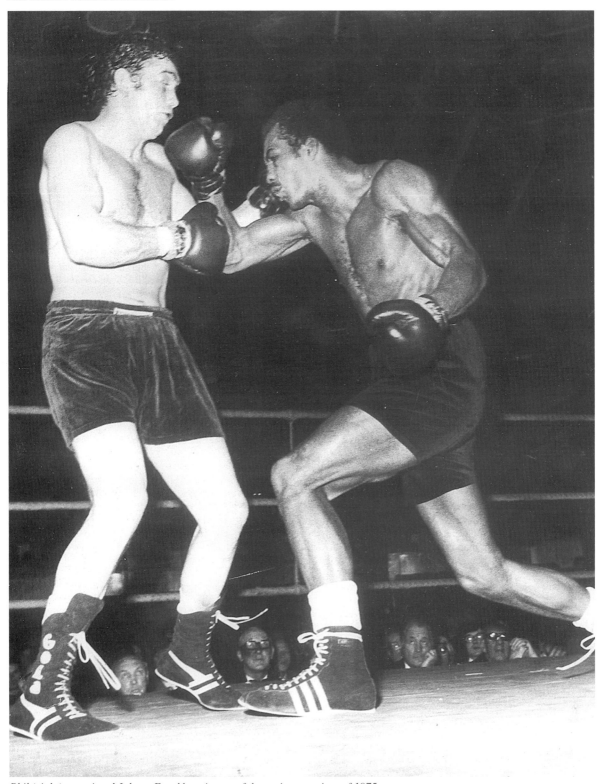

Phil (right) outpointed Johnny Frankham in one of the major surprises of 1975

Two fights later, Phil took the Central Area title with a clear points victory over Thompson. Journalist, Bob Cull, reported. "Martin had the class and the skill to keep the brave Thompson continually on the receiving end of a vicious left jab. It was one-way traffic, with Martin showing considerable coolness and style for a man with only seven professional fights behind him". It was an impressive win for Phil, but it was a fight in his home town six months later that really rocked the light-heavyweight division.

Johnny Frankham had lost his British title to Chris Finnigan the previous month and many considered that, after only 10 fights and one year as a professional, this was a colossal step-up for the 25-year-old Martin. Phil had only had one fight since winning the Area title, a return with Thompson (RSC 4), and he had been out of the ring for nearly six months for lack of opponents. However, Phil, who had quit his job as a motor mechanic to concentrate on his training, was confident. "You can take it from me", he told reporters, "if I catch Frankham with a big one he won't get up." Phil outpointed Frankham in one of the year's major boxing upsets and, despite taking some fierce punishment from the Reading gypsy, his longer reach and greater stamina won him the fight by five rounds to three, with two even. Graham Houston described Phil as the discovery of the year. Phil credited his wife as providing his inspiration. "Whenever I felt like packing up she encouraged me to keep going." Now he felt ready to take on Chris Finnegan for the British title.

But Phil would have to wait five months before he was granted his shot at the title vacated by Finnegan's enforced retirement. During that time, he notched up two further victories, against Danny Fontillio and Carl Watson. The Lonsdale Club was, in fact, a strip club and when the management decided to transform it into a gay bar, Tommy Miller rapidly removed his fighters to new premises. Phil made a lasting impression on the owner of the new gym, Barry Germain. "I remember watching him spar with Paul Sykes. I thought he was brave to get in there in the first place. Sykes was a heavyweight, a good three stone heavier than Phil and a violent man in and out of the ring. Paul was not what you would call a gentleman in sparring and so I was even more impressed when Phil came back again the next day and more than held his own. He was very intelligent too, with a dry sense of humour."

Phil fought Leicester's Tim Wood for the British light-heavyweight title at the World Sporting Club in London on 28 April 1976. He had come a long way in a short time and it was thought to be Wood's greater experience which won him the last two rounds of the fight and so won him the title. Going into the 14th round it was anybodys but, having carried the fight to his opponent and cut Wood's eye early in the fight, it looked like Phil might just have done enough. Referee, James Brimmell, scored the fight 147-146, giving Wood the 14th and 15th. Many at ringside disagreed.

Things didn't get any easier after the crushing disappointment of losing the title fight. Phil was now broke and looking for work. "It cost me a lot of money to train for the Wood fight," he said at the time, "I had to pack in my job to get in top condition and if one of my relatives had not given me £200 I would have been in big trouble." Fortunately, Phil and Ken Daniels weren't the only people who thought he was unlucky to lose the fight. A local firm stepped in with an offer to sponsor Phil so that he could push for a quick return. "Apparently two of the firm's directors were at the World Sporting club for the title fight and thought that I was unlucky to lose. They wanted the British title for Manchester, so they told me that they would pay me to carry on and that suited me down to the ground. I would have been forced to pack it in if this offer had not come along. But I'm ready to bounce back and with the backing I've got now the title is as good as won." But Phil didn't get a return. Instead, he had to wait six months and fight an eliminator with Bunny Johnson.

In only his 14th fight, Phil was once again taking on a former British champion. Johnson had won the British heavyweight title from Danny McAllinden the previous year. Although losing the title in his first defence, it was not before he had given Richard Dunn a tough 15 rounds. Despite that, Phil was confident and determined and in perfect condition for the fight. "Phil was winning the fight hands down," says Ken. "He was outboxing Johnson and then, just at the end of the ninth, on the bell, Johnson caught him with a sickening body shot. Phil was really hurt and I wondered if he'd been caught low, but nothing was said. Coming out for the 10th he had not recovered and the referee had to step in."

The new champion would defend successfully against Rab Affleck and Dennis Andries before forfeiting the title, but for Phil it was a turning point in his career. He left manager, Tommy Miller, to join Micky Duff, who had offered to manage him and put him with trainer, George Francis. "I am not a philanthropist," Duff said. "If I didn't think that Phil had it in him to become British champion at least, I wouldn't have wanted to manage him or invite him to London." Phil was delighted with Duff's offer. He had fought twice since the Johnson defeat, beating Michael Dylbatta and Yannick Dafour in France and had worked out that after tax and expenses he had only earned £2,000 in three years in the ring. But he couldn't bear to leave Manchester and live in London.

He had four fights under Duff, but with Ken Daniels obliged to train only Tommy Miller's fighters, Phil discovered the difficulty in finding a Manchester trainer with a London manager. After travelling to Europe for three of his fights and losing two of them, he finished with losses to Rab Affleck, Louis Perguad and Ennio Cornetti and a win over Harold Skog. But he was not disillusioned. "He had lost heart with managers and promoters, that side of it more than boxing itself," recalls Audrey, Phil had never had a fight outside the ring. "I'd rather walk away," he once said. "I don't think I've got anything to prove," but he couldn't walk away from boxing.

Having helped to coach the amateurs when he boxed at the BDS, he told Audrey he wanted to do that again. "We found a building in Moss Side that was big enough for a ring, and, although we had to share it, it was an instant

HAROLD GURTON / PHIL MARTIN PROMOTION

BOXING
SUNDAY JULY 25TH

SENGLAND

KARL THOMPSON
BRITISH CRUISEWEIGHT CHAMPION
WBC INTERCONTINENTAL CHAMPION
8 X 3 MINUTE ROUNDS

PAUL BURKE
BRITISH LIGHTWEIGHT CHAMPION
8 X 3 MINUTE ROUNDS

MAURICE HARDCORE
BRITISH LIGHTHEAVYWEIGHT CHAMPION
8 X 3 MINUTE ROUNDS

FRANK GRANT
BRITISH MIDDLEWEIGHT CHAMPION
8 X 3 MINUTE ROUNDS

Vs USA

12 x 3 Minute Rounds BRITISH SUPERFEATHERWEIGHT CHAMPIONSHIP

STEVE WALKER   NEIL HADDOCK

Vs

CHALLENGER
CHAMPS CAMP MOSS SIDE

CHAMPION
WALES

STEVE THE VIKING FOSTER
CHAMPS CAMP SALFORD
8 X 3 MINUTE ROUNDS

**UNDEFEATED
NICK BOYD**
CHAMPS CAMP BOLTON
6 X 2 MINUTE ROUNDS

**UNDEFEATED
ERIC NOI**
CHAMPS CAMP MIDDLETON
6 X 3 MINUTE ROUNDS

**UNDEFEATED
MAGIC MARIO CULPEPPER**
CHAMPS CAMP MOSS SIDE
6 X 2 MINUTE ROUNDS

Venue: OLDHAM SPORTS CENTRE, LORD ST., OLDHAM. Doors Open at 3.00 Boxing Commences: 4.00
Tickets: £15.00 · Ringside - £25 · Special Ringside - £35
Available from: CHAMPS CAMP (061) 226 4540 · HMV BOX OFFICE (061) 824 2810 · NICK BOYD (0204) 75406 · FRANK GRANT (0274) 736045
PAUL BURKE (0772) 798494/700081 · STEVE FOSTER (061) 737 9427 · CARL THOMPSON (061) 205 1346 · MAGIC MARIO (0860) 293700
STEVE WALKER (061) 434 4707 · MAURICE HARDCORE (061) 448 0031. 678 8833 TICKETS

success. The attendance doubled on every one of those first nights. He was young for a trainer and good at what he did, studying training and diets and trying everything on himself first. He got a degree in physiology and sports and studied boxing as a skill." Audrey had attended every one of Phil's amateur and professional fights in this country and she was by his side as he created the Moss Side amateur boxing club. "The club became very well known and when people arrived for a show, it created a buzz in the hall." The club was very successful and during the season of 1993, for example, they won 27 of their 31 matches. Phil took the curious youngsters who wandered in and moulded them into successful amateur boxers.

"The membership was very mixed, black and white, but there was tremendous camaraderie", remembers Audrey. "Phil made them all feel part of the team. If one trained for a fight, they all trained for that fight. The success was for everybody. Phil made them believe in themselves and they were made to believe that they could achieve anything, not just in boxing, many of them going on to become successful in other fields. They all called him 'Dad'. They had great respect for him. They will all tell you the same." Ken Daniels remembers Phil inviting him to the gym. "He said he had a talented young boxer who wanted to turn pro and he asked me to tell him what I thought of him, which I thought was nice. He was trying to talk him out of it because the lad was clever and had a degree and he wasn't sure that he should encourage him to box. The lad was determined though and young Tony Ekubia went on to be a very successful pro."

Maurice Core was another of those young amateurs. He won 62 of his 67 fights, becoming the Northern Counties champion and reaching the National Boys' Clubs finals and the finals of the ABAs. "Phil got us fit," he says. "There were all these talented England stars and such, but we were winning because of our training. Phil could see when we would win, who we could beat and he took all the worry off us."

Phil had great ideas for his club and when he found bigger premises he took the lads along, but they weren't very impressed. It was the shell of a room left charred and gutted by the riots. "Phil was excited," Maurice remembers. "But all we could see was this dump full of rubble and bricks and snakes." Snakes? "Yeah, all the animals had escaped from the pet shop next door. We caught five in the end and there are photos of us holding all these snakes. We all helped out with the plastering and everything."

They transformed it into one of the most modern gyms in Britain. Phil also ran an employment training centre from the premises. "I can sympathise with any youngster who has a hard life," said Phil. "My dad was in prison for so long I never saw him until I was 12. At 15 I was reduced to going down to my local police station and asking them to find me somewhere to live. Boxing was my escape. I preach the same creed over and over again and I tell the kids to ignore what people outside say about Moss Side youngsters. I also tell them they are as good as anybody else. I am proud that nobody notices whether you are black or white when you walk in 'Champs Camp'. It all started when I put the £3,000 I had saved from my boxing career into getting all this off the ground."

Maurice Core, Ensley Bingham, Frank Eubank, Ossie Maddix and Paul Burke were among the amateurs trained by Phil, who now became 'Champs Camp' pros. Frank Grant, Eric Noi, Carl Thompson and John Green were just some of the many fighters who joined them. "Phil had a way of making you feel safe," says Maurice. "I never once went into a fight worried. All I had to do was train, everything else was done for me. Everyone felt safe with him, that's why we called him 'Dad'." Eric Noi said something similar. "I always felt so protected. I didn't think I could lose with Phil there."

Having seen all of Phil's fights, Audrey now tried to get to all of his fighters' fights and she was very much involved in the gym. She describes how Phil envisioned a fitness centre that was also open to the general public, even women! "He wanted rows of treadmills and rowing machines. I'd never heard of anything like that. I don't know if they had anything in London even, but it was a shock to Moss Side!" Trainer, Billy Graham, became a part of the 'Champs Camp' team, although they later parted acrimoniously. He was stunned when he first visited his old stablemate. "I'd never seen a gym like that in my life. The amateur gym I used had pigeons flying inside, while the first pro/gym I trained in was a strip club. At 'Champs Camp' they even had a cleaner!"

Harold Gorton had followed Phil's amateur career and had known him ever since. They were great friends and would become partners. "I recognised that he was something out of the ordinary with his training methods. We talked about the only way forward, his lads having beaten most of their opponents from the Southern area. We both realised that very soon we wouldn't get fights for them. The only way forward was to promote ourselves." When Phil received phone calls asking for a certain fighter, he would say: "I haven't seen him for a couple of months. The last time I saw him he was really overweight. I'll see if I can find him." The fighter was, of course, in the gym working hard as all the lads were. They all abided by Phil's motto: 'Fail to prepare, prepare to fail'. "The gym was like a fight factory, it had a great atmosphere," said Harold. Maurice remembers how Phil would put them in the small ring with Eddie Smith. "Everyone was scared of Eddie, but he probably got us where we are. Tony Ekubia was the worst for sparring. He had no concept of soft-sparring, he just tried to kill everybody." But Phil's fighters soon earned a reputation that left nobody in any doubt as to their abilities, so he staged his own promotions.

When Phil visited Bowlers Sports and Exhibition centre in Manchester, in his capacity as an employment training officer, he met the Managing Director and former first-class cricketer, Jack Simmons. Phil had found work for hundreds of youngsters in the previous two years and the meeting led to a show being staged there. "Phil has a name for fairness in the city," said Jack. "When some managers become promoters they forget to look after their fighters properly, but Phil Martin's fighters still get that

superb personal supervision of his." "Phil just wanted fairness," Audrey says. "Although it was okay for these people to make money, he just felt that greed was unnecessary." Steve Bunce recently recounted a tale confirmed by Howard. In brief, Phil discovered that the manager who had brought his fighters over from America for one of Phil's shows had only given them a fraction of their wages. Furious, Phil and a couple of friends bundled the chap into the back of a van, made their opinion of him perfectly clear, extracted the fighters' wages and left him stranded. This was classic Phil Martin. He didn't let the business of promoting allow him to lose sight of his original goal. "I can tell you what still motivates me – even as a promoter. The knowledge that no Manchester lad in my lifetime has ever done really well out of being a professional boxer. Lads from other cities do alright for themselves, especially if they are from London. Yet, over the years, the boxing business has only looked on Manchester as the place their big name fighters get stiffs laid on from. Well all that has got to change." And it did.

He next staged two ground-breaking promotions featuring fighters brought over from America against his fighters from 'Champs Camp', including his four British champions. 1992 had been the year of the underdog – Phil's underdogs. Phil finally brought that British light-heavyweight title to Manchester when Maurice Core took it from Belfast's tough Noel Magee in September, while Frank 'The Terminator' Grant terminated the reign of middleweight champ, Herol 'Bomber' Graham, earlier that same month. Graham hadn't been beaten by a British boxer for 14 years. Carl Thompson had already smashed Steve Lewsam in June to become the British cruiserweight champion and, in September, he took the international crown from Arthur 'Stormy' Weathers. Paul Burke waited until 1993 to take the British and Commonwealth lightweight titles from Billy Schwer. "I always used to say that we would have at least three or four champions out of the crop," said Harold, "but I didn't think it would happen so quickly."

But Phil was becoming disillusioned with the gloveless side of the sport and was even considering a return to the amateurs, although he felt he would want to oversee the careers of Maurice Core and Tony Ekubia. When he started to feel over-tired in the winter of 1993 it was put down to stress. By February he felt ill enough to consult a doctor, who told him that he was indeed very ill. But it was March before he was told it was cancer. Phil and Audrey had three children, Andrea, 24, Carlos, 14, and Mario, who was just four years old.

Word soon got around, but Phil was still coming into the gym and going on the pads although he wasn't well enough, Audrey having been told that he only had two weeks left. Phil tried to organise everything in the gym. In fact, he was still making matches on the phone two days before he died. He tried to make plans for Maurice. "He thought it would be best for me to go to Denmark, but I didn't want to go. I knew things would never be the same again, we used to go everywhere together. I kept making excuses and said I couldn't afford the ticket. When I visited him he was in bed and he had bought me a ticket so now I had to go. I hadn't been there long when I received a phone call telling me I should get back as soon as possible. The journey was a nightmare and I was diverted all over Europe. I phoned Audrey to tell her I was stuck at the airport, waiting for a plane and she said: "Oh, Maurice, haven't you heard? I'm afraid it's too late."

Phil died on 27 May 1994, holding Audrey's hand, surrounded by his family and friends and his extended family of boxers.

'Champs Camp' was renamed 'The Phil Martin Centre' and today Maurice Core is himself a trainer, passing on the things he learned from Phil. 'Champs Camp' fighters now include Michael Brodie, Carl Thompson, Chris Barnett and Michael Jones. Audrey had to endure unthinkable tragedy, losing her father and mother in the years following Phil's death and also her daughter, Andrea, who died to a cancer as rapid, if not more vicious than Phil's. Andrea was 31 and left two little girls aged two and four.

When Phil talked about 'Champs Camp' in February 1991, he probably didn't realise that he was describing a legacy that would live on after his death. "What I had to contend with after the riots was the image portrayed of Moss Side youngsters on television. A land of no hope for all those in it. The figures now tell a different story. Nowhere in Britain can compare with what the community of Moss Side has achieved here. I would say that 75 per cent of the youngsters who come here have either become professional boxers, or have gone into regular full-time employment."

This was written about Phil in July of 1993. "For the sake of the people he doesn't line his pocket, he has chosen between investing in profit and investing in people. He has invested in people and they have grown in stature and worth beyond most expectations."

Maruice Core, who now runs the 'Champs Camp'

Harry Goodwin

Johnny Owen Remembered

by Wynford Jones

Johnny Owen was yet another of the champions produced by the Merthyr Valley. Born on 7 January 1956, he began his boxing career as an amateur, aged 10, at the Courthouse Club, before moving on to the Hoover Boxing Club where he was guided by Don James, who transformed his style. He lost only 18 out of 122 contests and was an ABA junior champion, representing Wales on seven occasions.

When Johnny decided to turn professional he chose Dai Gardiner as his mentor and thus began a meteoric rise to boxing fame. A few days after obtaining his professional licence, in September 1976, he was in action against Cardiff's George Sutton at the Pontypool Leisure Centre. This contest was considered a stiff test for Owen, but he completely outboxed Sutton to take an eight-round points decision. For his second contest Johnny had to travel to Derry to meet Neil McLaughlin and many thought Johnny to be unlucky to have been given a draw, but, in two subsequent meetings with the Irishman, he established his superiority.

On 29 March 1977, Johnny was matched with George Sutton for the vacant Welsh bantamweight title, the contest taking place at the Ebbw Vale Leisure Centre. This was a superb contest with Johnny taking the 10-round decision and his first professional title. The Welsh Area Council had originally been reluctant to allow Johnny to be matched for the title so soon in his professional career, but this performance must surely have dispelled any remaining doubts. This result led to Johnny being matched with John Kellie in an eliminator for the British bantamweight title, and with a superb display of power punching he forced referee, Wally Thom, to intervene during the sixth round.

I had the privilege of refereeing his next contest, with the Irishman, Terry Hanna, at the Ebbw Vale Leisure Centre on 16 June 1977. I was impressed by Johnny's boxing ability and also by his punching power. It took him four rounds to wear down his game opponent, but at that point I was forced to intervene.

On 29 November, Johnny was matched with Paddy Maguire for the British title at London's National Sporting Club, matchmaker Les Roberts securing the contest with a bid of £7,070. With tickets priced at £25, this was to be boxing's contribution to the fund raising for the Silver Jubilee year. Wales has produced many fine champions over the years but, at this time, the only one at bantamweight had been Bill Beynon, who in 1913 beat Digger Stanley at the old NSC to take the title. Now it was time for Johnny Owen to add his name to the list of champions. In Maguire, Johnny was up against a tough fighter who, in 34 previous contests, had garnered a wealth of experience all over the world. But, in spite of the imbalance in experience, the Merthyr man boxed coolly and took charge from the start. He wore down his opponent and with Maguire bleeding from an eyebrow wound, Sid Nathan stopped the contest in the 11th round. The shy, modest and deceptively frail-looking Merthyr man was now bantamweight champion of Great Britain and was presented with the Lonsdale Belt by the Duke of Gloucester.

Fresh from his British title win over Maguire, Johnny began 1978 with an eight-round stoppage win over Alan Oag at Aberavon and followed up by beating Antonio Medina on points over eight rounds at Middlesborough, before being matched with fellow Welshman, Wayne Evans, in a defence of his British title. This contest was staged at Ebbw Vale Leisure Centre on 6 April and turned out to be magnificent. Evans was a tough challenger, but had no answer to Johnny's non-stop attacks. When the referee, Jim Brimmell, intervened in the 10th round, Johnny was dominating the contest.

He extended his unbeaten run with wins over Dave Smith, Davy Larmour and Wally Angliss and was then matched with the Australian, Paul Ferreri, for the Commonwealth bantamweight title. The contest took place on 2 November and was promoted by Heddwyn Taylor at Ebbw Vale Leisure Centre. This was a magnificent battle, with Johnny taking the decision of referee Roland Dakin after 15 hard-fought rounds. For the first time in his career, Johnny was behind in this contest and he showed great character as he came battling through in the later stages to edge out Ferreri. I was sitting in Ferreri's corner and during the last round, Dennie Mancini, who was assisting in Ferreri's corner turned to my refereeing colleague, Jim Brimmell, and conceded, "Your man's won, Jim." Ferreri must have found Owen's attacking, strength and sheer fitness quite daunting.

Following this win, Johnny was kept waiting for a tilt at the European title, but, on 3 March 1979, his contest with the champion, Juan Francisco Rodriguez, materialised. It was staged in Almeria, Spain, and Johnny was clearly the victim of a hometown decision, just like so many other British boxers on previous visits to Spain. Thus, the 'unbeaten' tag was lost, but he was not too despondent.

Johnny kept busy with wins over Lee Graham and Frenchman Guy Caudron and, on 13 June, made the Lonsdale Belt his own property when Dave Smith retired after 12 rounds at Caerphilly. Yet another meeting with Neil McLaughlin followed and Johnny rounded off the year with wins over Jose Luis Garcia and Davey Vasquez at Ebbw Vale. He then opened 1980 with a fifth-round win over fellow Welshman, Glyn Davies, at the National Sporting Club, while in February he was matched with Juan Francisco Rodriguez once more for the European title. This time the contest was set for Ebbw Vale and it turned out to be a tough battle over 12 rounds, with Johnny taking the title on points. This was not a sparkling contest, but was characterised by Johnny's superb fitness. He kept up a sustained attack from the first bell and never took a

backward step. He was now the British, Commonwealth and European bantamweight champion.

Johnny had known for some time that he would have to defend his British title against John Feeney of Hartlepool and this contest was to have taken place at Wembley in March, but because of problems over other contests on the bill, such as Alan Minter's return with Vito Antuofermo, the contest did not take place until 28 June, meaning that Johnny had been out of the ring for four months. However, over 15 rounds, Johnny emerged as a comfortable winner, on this, his first appearance on a major commercial show in London.

Following this contest, matchmaker Mickey Duff sought a world title chance for Johnny and his fateful meeting with Lupe Pintor was eventually set for 19 September. I last saw Johnny at the Eisteddfod Pavilion at Gowerton in August on the night when Colin Jones successfully defended his British welterweight title against Peter Neal. Johnny was anxiously awaiting his clash with Pintor but could barely believe it was about to happen. He had earned his opportunity and was there on merit. The result of the contest ultimately seems irrelevant. The record books record the cold facts: Lost. co.12. What they do not record is the great battle which Johnny put up when taking the early part of the contest to Pintor, while showing great strength, courage, determination and fitness. In the ninth round, Johnny went to the canvas from a heavy punch, and from this point on Pintor's power was beginning to tell. From the television pictures, Johnny seemed very tired when he went down again in the 12th round. Courage and pride brought him to his feet only for him to be floored again for the last time. Hindsight suggests that maybe he should have been protected from his own remarkable qualities, but we know from the third Ali-Frazier contest that boxers often take themselves to the limits of their very being. The referee for the contest was Marty Denkin of California and his post fight observations leave me cold. He stated: "This is the first time there has ever been an incident like this in a fight I've been involved in." In the 12th round it was a little like a police officer examining a drunk driver when I looked at Owen, but he said to me: "I'm alright sir, I can carry on and I let him."

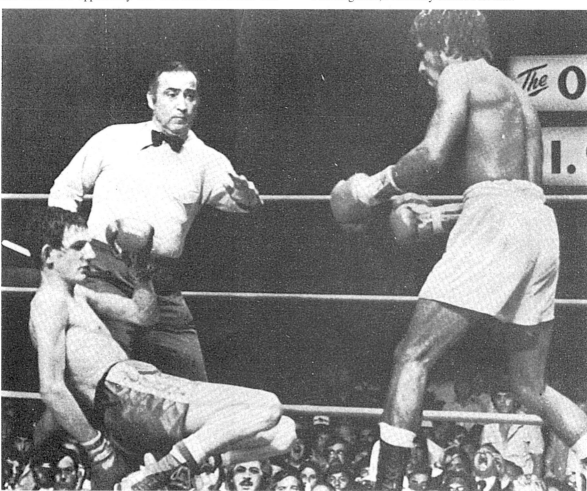

Final action from the Pintor v Owen fight in September 1980

No one will need to be reminded that a drunk driver is not left in charge of his vehicle and there is a case for arguing that the same standard should have applied here, regardless of the fact that a world title was at stake. Johnny Owen battled for his life for several weeks and finally lost the biggest fight of all on 4 November 1980. His body was brought back to Merthyr, with the funeral to be held at the High Street Baptist Chapel on Tuesday 11 November, followed by internment at Pant Cemetery.

On the day of the funeral, Merthyr was cold, damp, covered by a thick blanket of grey cloud and with snowflakes in the air, which seemed appropriate for a town well used to its share of tragedy. The chapel was packed to capacity and everyone sat there in silence waiting for the service to begin. Johnny's coffin was draped in the Welsh flag and there was an overwhelming sadness about the whole occasion. Hundreds of people stood outside the chapel and lined the lower part of the High Street as the cortege left for the cemetery where a huge crowd had gathered and our young champion was laid to rest to the strains of one of the great Welsh hymns, *Cwm Rhondda*. Following the service I stepped up to the grave with my father and we held hands as we paid our silent tribute, both battling against tears. As we turned away I remember squeezing his hand, words were impossible. We immediately came face to face with Les Roberts, the matchmaker of London's famous National Sporting Club, who had played such a big part in Johnny's career. Les, a dour Yorkshireman, never short of a word and usually quite outspoken, was similarly choked, as were so many of boxing's toughest characters. Such was the effect of this tragedy. Journalists Ken Jones and Hugh McIlvanney had said that they both had bad vibes regarding this contest from the outset, and this was the ultimate outcome. John Arlott, the famous cricket writer and broadcaster, referred to Johnny, when he made the presentation for the BBC Sports Personality of the Year just weeks after Johnny's death, when he said: "We take sport too seriously and life too lightly". However, Johnny's situation was put at its best by McIlvanney, who wrote in the *Observer*, that the tragedy was that "he was articulate in the most dangerous language".

Following the injury to Johnny, an Appeal Fund was launched and donations arrived from all over the world. In the end, this turned out to be of little use to Johnny personally, but the people of the area benefited considerably when it was decided to donate the remainder of the money to the Prince Charles Hospital. The paediatric unit received £100,000 and was able to purchase much needed equipment, thus helping many babies who might not otherwise have survived, and a plaque placed at the hospital acknowledges this contribution from the Appeal Fund.

The years which have elapsed since Johnny's death have seen significant developments in the medical aspects of the sport and we should be thankful for this, but we should also be grateful for the fact that we shared in the career of this remarkable fighting man.

I shall always remember Johnny's smile and the twinkle in his eye, and we should not lose sight of the fact that the ring was undoubtedly his kingdom.

Lupe Pintor was stopped by Wilfredo Gomez (left) in an unsuccessful WBC super-bantamweight title challenge on 3 December 1982

The Johnny Owen statue in Merthyr town centre was unveiled by none other than Lupe Pintor on 2 November 2002

Wynford Jones

Lest We Forget

by Bob Lonkhurst

When Michael Watson crossed the finishing line to complete the 2003 London Marathon, it marked the most remarkable comeback in boxing history. Courage, determination and an intense period of training prepared him for the gruelling event, in which he walked the route over the course of six days. His aim was to raise £100,000 for the Brain and Spine Foundation.

A life-long Arsenal supporter, Michael was a guest of the club for their home game against Everton on 23 March. In an interview with a club reporter, he said: "Attempting the marathon has given me an aim and an incentive. It's like I am preparing for a fight again. It's given me a goal – something to work towards."

The events following Watson's fight with Chris Eubank at Tottenham in 1991, have been well documented. Nevertheless, it is important to remember that he was in a coma for 40 days, spent a further four months in intensive care and eight months rehabilitation. In the years which followed, his progress was extremely slow, but never once did he give up hope.

Whilst Michael's story epitomises the dangers of boxing, he has thankfully made a recovery, albeit not a complete one. Other fighters over recent decades were less fortunate, and this story is intended as a reflection on their careers to ensure that they will always be remembered.

Injuries sustained by Michael Watson and others effect everyone within boxing, and inevitably bring about repeated calls for the sport to be banned. Although such calls have been more frequent in recent years, boxing has always had its detractors. Back in 1956, Dr Edith Summerskill (later Baroness), published a hard hitting book entitled *The Ignoble Art*. At the time she was the sport's most committed opponent, and campaigned long and hard to get it banned. Her persistency brought rebuke from many people connected with boxing, not least former British heavyweight champion, Tommy Farr.

In May 1963, Tommy spoke out angrily. "I boxed at every weight from paper to heavy," he remarked, "if she or her doctors can find anything wrong with my faculties, I shall be surprised. I think the honourable lady likes publicity. She would do well to turn her attentions to something else. Boxing has been a whip donkey for too long – why not try motor racing?" Farr certainly did have his faculties, despite having fought almost 200 battles. When he died in 1986 at the age of 73, he was an educated, alert and dignified man. Cancer was the cause of his death, not boxing. Tommy's words, however, do have a ring of truth about them. Whilst it would be unwise and unprofessional to ignore the advice of the British Medical Council, many opponents of boxing are on a publicity crusade. Rarely do they consult with fighters, or consider aspects of the other side.

In defending the sport against those who seek to have it banned, it is important to remember some of the young men who lost their lives pursuing their dreams of becoming champions in the ring. They had many things in common, not least, courage. Most came from under privileged areas, and fought because it was what they did best. All died participating in a sport they loved.

At Canning Town in London's east end, just a stone's throw from the old docks, stands the Peacock gymnasium. Immediately outside the front entrance is a monument, designed and erected in memory of Bradley Stone, a young east-end fighter who died on 28 April 1994, following his contest with Ritchie Wenton for the British super-bantamweight title.

Born on 27 May 1970, Bradley was a good amateur, reaching the London ABA featherweight final in 1989. Under the management of Jimmy Tibbs, he developed into a fine prospect as a professional, building an undefeated run of 18 contests (one draw) over four years. His finest performance was at Wembley in September 1993, when he stopped the late Tony Silkstone in three rounds in a final eliminator for the British title. At that stage Bradley's career started to fall apart. In what was thought to be a routine warm-up for his British title contest, he was soundly beaten in five rounds by an Algerian, Boualem Belkif, at York Hall in March 1994. Just seven weeks later, he was dead.

On 26 April, Stone met Wenton at the York Hall. Although he was stopped in the 10th round of a hard, close contest, he did not appear to be in particular distress. In fact, it was a contest where neither boxer appeared to have taken undue punishment. Bradley left the ring unaided, returned to his dressing room, and there talked normally to doctors, reporters and Board of Control officials. He later went to his girlfriend's house, but, at 2.30am, he collapsed

Michael Watson   Derek Rowe

and was taken to the Royal London Hospital. There he underwent surgery to remove a blood clot from his brain. His injuries were so severe that he never recovered and died two days later at the age of 24.

Although he was the first professional boxer to die from ring injuries in Britain since 1986, there were the usual "ban boxing" calls. Amongst the many debates which followed, some interesting figures were published of fatal accidents which had occurred in sport between 1986 and 1994; watersports - 412, motor sports - 87, air sports - 82, climbing - 65, horse riding - 31, athletics - 28, pedal cycling - 20, boxing - 1. Bradley Stone, in fact, died during a week when two motor racing drivers lost their lives during high-speed accidents. A top jockey also sustained serious injuries, yet there was little, if any, adverse criticism regarding the safety of those sports. Brought up in an extremely tough area, Bradley was a young man who loved boxing. He was never happier, or prouder, than the night he climbed into the York Hall ring to fight for the Lonsdale belt. He died chasing his dream.

Apart from being a promising young fighter, Bradley also possessed tremendous natural talent as an actor. In 1993, he played a leading role in Ron Pick's fine documentary, *Fighters*. More performances were planned.

I vividly recall talking to Stone at length one evening at the producer's studio where we attended a private showing of the film. "You know Bob, boxing is my life," he said proudly. "Without it, I would have nothing. I would either be on drugs or inside." He made no secret of the fact that

Barry McGuigan, in his fighting days, still remembers Young Ali
Derek Rowe

boxing gave him dignity and respect. He was convinced that if he could win the British title, it would mean so much to many of the kids he grew up with who were experiencing difficulties in life. Sadly, that dream was never fulfilled.

Bradley's funeral at Ascension Church, Custom House, on 9 May 1994, was one of the most moving events I have ever attended. The warmth of the east-end people, and those from the boxing fraternity, made me proud to have known Bradley Stone. His memory lives on because he died pursuing his dream as a professional fighter.

Young Ali, a 23-year-old Nigerian boxer, came to London in 1982 to meet exciting featherweight prospect, Barry McGuigan, at the World Sporting Club. He was a late replacement for Steve Farnsworth. Born Asymin Mustapha, Ali was bantamweight champion of Nigeria and West Africa and had won 18 of 20 contests. Recently, however, he had been stopped in 11 rounds by Stix McLeod of Zimbabwe for the All-African featherweight title in Lagos, but he was still regarded as a contender for the Commonwealth title held by Azumah Nelson.

Against McGuigan on 14 June, Young Ali never stopped trying in a lively, entertaining contest. Wearing trunks in the Nigerian colours, he started aggressively, winning the opening round with solid jabs and fast hooks, but, despite having plenty of skill, he did not have the power to hold Barry off for long. Going into the sixth round, McGuigan was ahead, although his big punches had not appeared to trouble the game Nigerian. Suddenly, the Irishman crashed two explosive rights to the jaw and Ali crashed to the floor. He was counted out, face downwards, after two minutes, 47 seconds of the round. After looking to be in trouble for sometime, the Nigerian appeared to recover and left the ring unaided. On route to the dressing room, however, he collapsed, was rushed to hospital, and never regained consciousness.

Young Ali was on a life-support machine at the Middlesex Hospital for several months. Every evening Barry McGuigan's father telephoned for news of his condition. Barry himself was so devastated that he didn't box for four months. In November 1982, Ali was flown back to Lagos, but on 13 December news reached Britain through a press agency that he had died three days earlier. His family had authorised the life-support machine to be switched off when it became clear that recovery was not possible. When he heard the news, McGuigan broke down and asked to be left alone. He became a virtual recluse and seriously considered retiring from boxing. In April 1983 however, he resumed his career, and almost three years to the day after beating Ali, took the world featherweight title from Eusebio Pedroza. It was a magnificent victory, and in an interview shortly afterwards he touched the hearts of the world-wide television audience. Asked by Harry Carpenter how he felt, Barry emotionally replied: "I dedicate this world title to Young Ali. At least he wasn't beaten by a nobody, but by a world champion. Now this championship is his." It was a moving statement, but typical of the men who participate in this hard and controversial sport. The fact that Young Ali's death was a tragic accident was no

consolation to Barry. He had prayed continually for the young Nigerian, and continued to do so long after he became world champion.

Johnny Owen from Merthyr was another young man who lived for boxing, but lost his life pursuing a dream. A story of his misfortune appears elsewhere in this book, but it is worth recalling the tribute paid to him in 1980 by the then Chairman of the British Boxing Board of Control, Alexander Elliott:

> Johnny was certainly one of the most dedicated of British boxers. Boxing was his life, and his commitment to the sport, and his determination to succeed, were legend.
>
> He single-mindedly devoted himself to the achievement of the highest of all honours, and it is all the more cruel that he should be struck down at the very peak of his career, having come so close to realising that prize. His loss to British boxing cannot be overstated, but as and when the questions are asked, we should be reminded, although it is no consolation, that he was taken from us doing the one thing that he loved above all.

The Johnny Owen story is still very fresh in our memories, a statue of him having been unveiled last year at Merthyr by Lupe Pintor. The attendance of the former world champion from Mexico was itself an act of great courage and humanity that was appreciated by everyone present. I will never forget the moment when he and Johnny's father, Dick, embraced warmly in front of the statue amid the pouring rain. Tears streamed down their faces at a ceremony which could surely only happen in boxing.

Steve Watt was born in Glasgow on 26 January 1956, but moved to London at the age of 12. He developed into a good amateur, winning the London NW Divs welterweight championship in 1981, having been runner-up in 1979. In the London finals, Watt faced 18-year-old Rocky Kelly (Hogarth), who was already being described as the sensation of the championships. In a great fight, Steve battled hard, but Kelly was too good and took a unanimous decision.

The following year Steve became London champion, following fine wins over Mickey Hughes, Jimmy Mitchell, Lloyd Morgan, (NW Divs final), Courtney Phillips and Mark Mills in the London final at the Royal Albert Hall. He attributed his run of success to the fact that he had moved to Hayes Amateur Boxing Club, and trained under the legendary Dicky Gunn, who had looked after the Olympic gold medallist, Chris Finnegan.

Watt's exciting run in the 1982 ABA championships

Rod Douglas (left) seen in his last fight, an unsuccessful British middleweight title challenge against Herol Graham in October 1989

came to a halt when he was outpointed by Chris Pyatt in the semi-finals at Gloucester. His good form did, however, earn him a place in the London ABA team which faced Finland at Helsinki in October. Although they lost the match 6-4, Steve won a unanimous decision over Lasse Friman.

Steve turned professional in 1983 and won his first eight contests, six inside the distance. His first set-back came in February 1985, when he lost in three rounds to John Ridgeman, due to a badly cut eye. The highlight of his paid career came in October that year when he won the Scottish welterweight title, stopping Tommy McCallum in five rounds. It was what he had wanted more than anything else. Six months later, on Friday 13th March 1986, Steve faced his old foe, Rocky Kelly, who since turning professional had won 22 of his 26 fights. Before a packed house at the London West Hotel, Fulham, they engaged in a breath-taking battle of raw courage, testing each other to the limit. Watt was the better boxer for much of the fight, but then tried to match Kelly in a 'street fight'. Rocky was better equipped for such combat and gradually wore Steve down. The end came after two minutes, seven seconds of the 10th and final round when the referee, Syd Nathan, stepped in to rescue Watt. Instinctively, he protested, but after the fight he collapsed and lapsed into a coma. He never regained consciousness.

As Steve lay in hospital, Rocky sat at his bedside. Despite rumours to the contrary, there was genuine respect between these two real hard men from West London. Any reports to the contrary had been for publicity purposes only. Steve died at Charing Cross hospital on 16 March 1986, aged 30. With his family's consent, his heart, liver and kidneys were donated to transplant surgery. A model professional, Steve amassed 11 victories from 13 contests. Fate surely deprived him of a major title.

Scottish bantamweight, James Murray, knew all about poverty. He came from the deprived village of Newmains just outside Wishaw, which suffered huge unemployment following the closure of the local colliery and steelworks. He led a simple life, working as a gardener for the local council, but had the burning desire to become a champion in the ring. As an amateur, James was trained by the former world flyweight champion, Walter McGowan, at the Royal Albert club. After just five contests he reached the flyweight semi-finals of the 1989 Scottish championships. Aged 19, he faced an experienced Drew Docherty, four years his elder, who had won titles in each of the previous five seasons. Always up against it, James did not have the experience, and was stopped in the third round.

After turning professional in March 1993, James won his first five contests before losing on points to Paul Webster at the York Hall, in his first ever fight outside Scotland. It was a temporary set-back, and 10 consecutive victories followed, including a points decision over Shaun Anderson in November 1994 for the vacant Scottish bantamweight title. Two months later, James successfully defended it, when stopping Louis Veitch in three rounds.

After victories over Ady Benton (rsc 7) and Danny Ruegg (pts), Murray challenged Drew Docherty for the British bantamweight title at the Hospitality Inn, Glasgow, on 13 October 1995. It was a fascinating contest, with Docherty having lost two of 17 professional contests and Murray just one of 16. Although Drew had held the title since 1992, James was a slight pre-fight favourite.

Murray seemed to be heading for victory during the early stages of the contest, Docherty taking a count of 'three' in the opening round and another short count in the sixth. Although James sustained a gashed left eye in round three and a cut on the bridge of the nose in the sixth, he looked to be in front by the end of the eighth. During round nine, however, he began to fade, in what was becoming a desperate battle of supremacy. The 10th was a bitter round. Both men bled from the nose, whilst Murray's left eye was closing rapidly. The fight ended dramatically after 2.26 seconds of the final round when James went to the canvas for the first and only time in his career, amateur or professional. He fell into unconsciousness and never recovered.

James Murray died at the Southern General Hospital, Glasgow, at 8.50am on Sunday 15 October 1995. A man of extreme courage and compassion, he had requested that his organs be donated to a local transplant unit in Glasgow. Within a very short time of James' death, his father made it clear that the family had no wish to see boxing banned. "No way," he remarked courageously. "The people who call for bans don't know boxing, you have got to be involved in boxing to know it."

Although the death of James Murray was the fourth in a British ring since Johnny Owen in 1980, it was the first in Scotland for 40 years. The last was when 18-year-old Willie McStay died after an amateur contest in Glasgow.

Whilst ring contributed fatalities are devastating, it is the right of every young man to be a boxer. The sport is properly organised, controlled and regulated. There are strict medical controls in place, and substantial improvements have been made over recent years, and will no doubt continue to be made.

The careers of Bradley Stone, Young Ali, Johnny Owen, Steve Watt and James Murray will live in the memories of fight fans for ever, as will those of other young men such as Michael Watson, Carl Wright, Mark Gault, Spencer Oliver, Paul Ingle, Rod Douglas and Chris Henry, who survived horrendous injuries. In pursuing their dreams, they fought for honour, and in doing so displayed a degree of courage which most of us will never possess. They entertained those of who are passionate about the sport, yet died doing what they did best. May they never be forgotten.

The Dave Green book will be entitled
FEN TIGER – The success of Dave 'Boy' Green.
To be published in the spring.
A biography of Eric Boon will follow.

Tommy Farr versus Joe Louis: Reflections of a Fight

by Melanie Lloyd

"For one glorious hour of triumph but not of victory, fame lifted me upon the shoulders of men." Tommy Farr (1950).

Tommy Farr is one of Britain's most well respected and fondly remembered heavyweights. This is the story of his famous challenge for the undisputed heavyweight championship of the world against Joe Louis. Their 15-round battle, which happened on 30 August 1937 in New York's Yankee Stadium, is often talked about by the British boxing fraternity and, although the fight was well before my time, it is one of my special favourites.

Going back to his early days, life never provided an easy road for Tommy Farr. His mother died when she was 32 years old and his father, himself a bare-knuckle boxer, wasted away in his bed, having been paralysed in a mining accident. But there was an ever present guiding light in Tommy's life in the shape of an old coal miner who had one leg, a head full of wisdom, a sharp turn of phrase and the tendency to swear vociferously in Welsh whenever he got really fiery. His name was Joby Churchill and he had been Tommy's father figure since the Tonypandy tearaway was a boy. As Tommy grew up and turned to fighting for money in a serious way, Joby's protective advice and shrewd betting methods kept his charge on the straight and narrow and in the black in the bank. Together they rode the rough seas of a hard career, and every punch that Tommy took, Joby took it with him from the sidelines.

Having won the Welsh light-heavyweight and heavyweight titles, Tommy won the British and Empire heavyweight championship against Ben Foord in March 1937. Along the way, he alienated himself from quite a few of his contemporaries with his plain speaking qualities that the man himself identified as 'petulance,' 'outspokenness' and 'mulishness.' He certainly was never one to call a spade 'a long handled gardening implement,' and that is a fact. But he only spoke out when he genuinely felt that an injustice had been done and, if he worried about the consequences, he did so after the event.

After winning the British title, Tommy's next fight was against Max Baer. He was strongly ranked the outsider against America's charming 'Clown Prince', but he won on points over 12 rounds at Harringay Arena. In June 1937, Tommy demolished 'The German Tiger,' Walter Neusel, in three rounds, again at Harringay. Incidentally, prior to this fight, Tommy offered to fight Neusel in the car park of the Star and Garter in Windsor after a heated exchange of words.

A week after Tommy's victory over Neusel, Joe Louis won the world heavyweight title against James Braddock in Chicago, stopping 'The Cinderella Man' in eight rounds. There were many contrasts between Tommy and Joe. For instance, whilst Tommy was freely speaking his mind to anybody who cared to listen, Joe was being told never to smile when he knocked down a white man. When Tommy was revelling in his boxing success story, Joe was keeping a low profile, confined to keeping his own council by the intolerant attitudes of a large proportion his own countrymen. While Tommy enjoyed the undivided love and devotion of Joby Churchill, the main man in Joe's life was his trainer, Jack Blackburn, who had initially agreed with Joe's managers, John Roxborough and Julian Black, to train Joe for four weeks, reasoning that training black boxers was a waste of time because of the lack of opportunities they would be offered. Blackburn stayed with Joe for the rest of his life – he died when Joe was 27 – and it is a testimony to their friendship that Joe named his son Jackie after his loyal trainer.

Generally speaking, segregation was everywhere in America, but Joe knew how to play the game and was the antithesis to Jack Johnson, who won his title in 1908 against Tommy Burns. Johnson could never keep the wide grin off his face as he battered every 'White Hope' that they placed before him and he wore white women like bracelets. Joe Louis was the first black man who had actually been allowed to fight for the world heavyweight title since Johnson lost his crown to Jess Willard in 1915. And the quietly spoken and publicly unassuming 'Brown Bomber' was never allowed to forget that. Although he was widely respected all around the world, this was a time when the Klu Klux Klan were openly marching upon the White House. Joe was to become highly influential in the fight for tolerance, acceptance and freedom in an equal world, but in return he had to obey the rules - rules written by white people for white people. Joe Louis was very much aware that his success story had given the Negro population of the ghettos something to celebrate. And so he kept things sweet. Incidentally, Jack Johnson was one of the many celebrities at the ringside for his fight against Farr.

Meanwhile, a fight was made between Tommy and another German, Max Schmeling, who had caused a sensation in June 1936 by knocking Joe Louis out in the 12th round at the Yankee Stadium. Now that Joe was the world heavyweight champion, the fight between Tommy and Max was to be seen as a box-off, the winner to challenge Joe for his title. The contracts were signed but this fight never took place. Everybody involved had their own version of why it never happened. Basically it all came down to politics. For Tommy's part, the American promoter, Mike Jacobs, sent his representative, Sol Strauss, to Britain to negotiate with Tommy on a fight with Louis, and the subsequent freezing out of Max Schmeling. Tommy agreed. He signed the contract and was immediately whisked off to Paris, perhaps as a means of keeping him away from any influences that might have swayed his decision, particularly those acting on behalf of Max Schmeling. Whilst in Paris, Tommy was wined and dined and swept off his feet by avid media courtship and an

endless run of social niceties. He was also separated from those who he had always held close, most importantly, Joby Churchill. From Paris, Tommy travelled to New York on the Queen Mary.

As Tommy stepped on to American soil he was engulfed by the newspaper boys and film cameras. Everybody wanted the story of this Welshman, who had the audacity to believe that he was capable of sharing a ring

Tommy Farr in fighting pose

with Joe Louis. It was not long before Tommy felt suffocated by the relentless pace and the stifling heat of New York – it was too much of a culture shock, so Mike Jacobs had him installed into a luxurious training camp 50 miles away at the city of Long Branch, New Jersey. There Tommy was treated like royalty by those around him. He was given the freedom of the city and even took afternoon tea with a millionairess, who was eager to understand the concept of the prize fighter. The press pack hounded him on a daily basis and Tommy was starting to get hot under the collar about some of the fictitious facts they printed about him in the newspapers. He did not understand that this was how the American media worked and promoter, Mike Jacobs, was seeing to it that Tommy Farr was getting the full treatment. However, the journalist who really upset Tommy was a reporter, who, whilst being interviewed on American national radio, opined that Tommy had as much chance of beating Joe Louis as Shirley Temple.

Tommy only felt the sweet sensation of relief when Joby Churchill arrived on the scene. And you can well imagine what the newspaper reporters made of him! He was hailed as "The Druid at Long Branch," "Captain Cuttle," and "The wooden legged bard from Tonypandy." One famous columnist, Dan Parker, chronicled Joby's arrival, noting that the one piece of luggage that Joby had brought with him was a small satchel in which he carried one spare suit, one spare pair of boots, four shirts and one collar (rubber variety). "But," wrote Parker, "Joby's no sucker… He's different, a breath of mountain air."

Jacobs kept the publicity coming thick and fast. He knew that this fight needed to be forcefully sold to the Americans, particularly the boxing-wise New Yorkers. The word on the street was that Tommy would not and could not last more than six rounds. Publicity stunts were the order of the day, including a staged argument with Max Baer at Tommy's training camp that very nearly backfired, and a visit from Jack Dempsey who wished Tommy all the best for the film cameras and afterwards told the reporters, "He's the kind of guy who would not blink if the roof fell in."

Meanwhile, Joe was getting plenty of coverage from his training camp at Pompton Lakes. In one head-to-head filming session between the two camps, Louis declared, "I think I will win because I am training hard for my faith. I will be in the best of condition because I want to keep the heavyweight championship of the world in the United States. Tommy Farr, what makes you think you will win?" And Tommy replied from his own camp, "I'm 23, the same age as you, and I've had over three thousand rounds of actual fighting and never taken the count. You've had less than two hundred rounds of boxing and you've been knocked out. All Britishers the world over can rely on my manager and me to win, or die in the attempt."

Despite Tommy's earlier frustrations with the newspaper reporters, he was beginning to appear relaxed in front of the cameras and the microphones. His words flowed and he came across as very polite and charming. During an interview on American national radio with Clem McCarthy, a top sports reporter (mainly known for his racing commentaries), the gravel voiced McCarthy asked about Tommy's tough beginnings and life in the boxing booths. "Did you get a weekly wage in those booths?" asked McCarthy. "Yes, about $2," came Tommy's reply. "$2 a week!" exclaimed McCarthy. "Yes." "Oh, for goodness sake! Can you do anything with $2 in Wales?" Tommy chuckled, "Well you can buy some cigarettes, and go to the pictures now and then." McCarthy sounded like he couldn't believe what he was hearing. "Well, tell me something Tommy, if somebody beat you, how much did the man who beat you get?" "Well, he'd get a pound and I wouldn't get no supper!"

Despite all the hype surrounding the fight, the New Yorkers remained unconvinced as to it's validity. On the day of the official weigh-in at New York's State Commission Building, Mike Jacobs suddenly burst in and dramatically announced that the fight had been postponed until the following Monday, another four days. He blamed it on the weather, but, in truth, it was poor ticket sales that caused the delay. Jacobs gambled that if he waited until after the Saratoga Races were over he would have a far healthier attendance. When fight night arrived, approximately thirty-two thousand spectators took their seats in the Yankee Stadium.

Meanwhile, back in Britain the excitement had built to pressure cooker level. This was not the first transatlantic radio broadcast, but it was by far the most important to date, and on a larger scale than ever before. When the night of the fight arrived millions of British people rose from their beds in the early hours of the morning to tune in and listen to the BBC broadcast. Barry Hugman told me that his parents were on a Mediterranean cruise at the time and his father listened from the ship radio. My own dad got out of bed to sit in the kitchen with a cup of tea and listen to the fight with his father and his older brother at their home in the Glamorgan village of Glyn Neath. In fact, I think I have yet to meet any boxing fan who is old enough that did not listen to this fight as it happened. In the Welsh Valleys the people went up into the hills and mountains and lit campfires and sat together to listen to the fight. Many of these were miners who would have to be back at the coalfaces to report for duty by six o'clock the following morning, as indeed were my grandfather and uncle. In Tommy's home town of Tonypandy, a thousand people, men and women filed in to the Judges Hall to listen to the fight. Outside the hall another seven thousand stood and listened on speakers. And for the miners who had to work the pits that night, messages were sent to the coalface every three minutes, keeping them in the picture, round by round. In one tinplate factory, a nightshift worker took a radio with him so that he and his workmates could listen to the fight. He was discovered and sacked on the spot, which caused a mass walkout. So strong was the feeling, so tangible was local belief that 'their boy' was going to cut the mustard.

The moment arrived. Louis was favourite to win at four-to-one. The pundits had declared that this was going to be merely a routine defence of Louis' newly-won title - but nobody gave a copy of the script to the boy from

Tonypandy. This was the moment that he had been working for all his life, from his very first fight for money on the Welsh mountainside at the age of 12, and Tommy Farr had come to fight. The gladiators stepped through the ropes. The atmosphere was electric. The New York police department had placed a thousand officers on duty that night in and around the stadium.

The first bell went and the boxers came out, trading jabs, matching speed and strength, sizing each other up. Tommy started as he meant to go on, coming forward, punctuating his performance with some good body shots. Joe was patient and accurate. In the second, Joe remained calm and calculating, throwing lots of searching, powerful jabs, many on the counter, while Tommy was aggressive, leaping in with hooks and jabs to head and body, always looking to get on the inside, but Joe kept his defences tight. By the time Tommy returned to his stool he was bleeding. Joe built up his assault at the start of the third, aiming to further damage Tommy's face, and then Tommy came swarming forward and threw a big right hand over the top. The punch landed and Joe took it well and danced away to his left, going back to work behind his jab before unloading with a big right hand over the top of one of Tommy's jabs. At the end of the round Tommy's face was a mask of

blood, but he reached out to Joe as they returned to their corners, touching his opponent on the arm. Back on his stool now, Tommy Farr was a sorry sight. Both eyes were cut, and even worse, he had caught one of his fingers on a loose piece of cotton inside his right-hand glove. The finger had been dislocated. This, he kept to himself. He was afraid that if Joby got to know about it, his loyal pal would have a heart attack. Tommy continued to aim for the body in the fourth, while Joe continued to snap out that hurtful jab, regularly letting go with his right cross. To give some idea of the power of Joe's punches, Jimmy Braddock, after losing his world title to him, described Joe's left as, "Somebody jamming an electric light bulb in your face, and screwing it." Braddock described Joe's right as, "Like something nailing you with a crowbar." Tommy stayed springy on his legs as he leapt forward with hooks and jabs. They touched gloves at the end of the round before returning to their corners. Joe continued with his measured approach in the fifth. The American's gloves were finding Tommy's damaged features with ferocious regularity now, and yet Tommy still kept coming forward, always attacking, always the aggressor, often beating Joe to the punch.

The sixth round came, the one where Tommy was

Farr (left) and Louis exchange left jabs

supposed to get stopped. The Welshman landed with a terrific left hook to Joe's jaw in the opening seconds, and followed through with a pucker right upper-cut and another hook. At this stage, the crowd were really starting to sit up and take notice of the boy from Tonypandy. Tommy stayed busy and Joe stayed cagey. Tommy bobbed and weaved and leapt out of his crouching style to score with shots up and down. It was a great round for him and as they returned to their corners, he patted Joe fondly on the shoulder. Joe kept his jab working overtime in the seventh and then he moved to the side and as Tommy surged forward Joe caught him with a left uppercut on the way in. Joe stepped in then, catching Tommy up in a blizzard of leather, throwing punches from all angles. Tommy soaked it up, fending off the blows with his elbows, his face was a mess and he grimaced as Joe landed with a left hook to his stomach. Tommy did his best to negate Joe's attack by crowding in close, throwing what he could from the inside. Just as the sixth had been a great round for Tommy, the seventh was an excellent round for Joe. As the bell rang to end the round and the fighters returned to their stools the crowd looked on in amazement. They could not believe that Tommy Farr was still there, still in this fight. Whatever happened now, he had already gone further than they said he would.

The bloodthirsty element of the crowd waited expectantly for Joe to finish Tommy off in the eighth, but they would have a long wait. Tommy's eyes were closing but he was still well in the fight and as Joe's jab continued to snake out, picking, hurting, tearing, suddenly Tommy turned it on and got through with a ramrod jab of his own, straight through Joe's defence it went. Joe's legs wobbled and his knees sagged for a second. The crowd cried out in wonder as Tommy piled in to capitalize on his success. The New Yorkers could not believe this Welshman and as the commentary came across the airwaves back in Britain, the millions who were behind Tommy Farr were ecstatic. And as for the proud Valley men gathered around the campfires, they could barely contain themselves. "Oh Tommy Farr is putting up a grand scrap," declared the radio announcer. Then Joe pulled it back together and by the end of the round it was the Brown Bomber who was in command. As they returned to their corners, this time it was a fond ruffle of Joe's hair that came from Tommy. Tommy surged forward in the ninth and he paid the price as Joe's gloves found their target, for his sight was severely impaired by his injuries. But he got through and scored with a hard right hook and, as Joe backed to the ropes, Tommy bulled forward, but against a boxer of Louis' calibre the shots were not effective enough. Although Tommy had plenty of bounce left, Joe remained in control. The bell went and this time Tommy patted Joe on the shoulder.

Joe Louis (right) always reckoned that his fight with Britain's Tommy Farr was one of his most difficult defences

Tommy attempted a game of peak-a-boo at the start of the 10th but Joe would not be goaded. Tommy once again turned aggressor and the crowd roared as he scored with a left jab, right hook, left hook combination. Joe's right eye was swollen underneath now as he carefully picked his shots on the counter, always scoring. The 11th round began and Joe's jab kept pumping out, getting stronger and meaner as the fight progressed, but Tommy Farr was not a man to let a few piffling little things like a dislocated finger, two closing eyes, a 'light-bulb' left and a 'crowbar' right put him off. He was still there, still coming forward, still right in Joe's face. Every time Tommy scored the crowd cheered. And cheer they did when Tommy managed to get through with a big right hand, and then he scored three jabs in succession while coming forward, his feet off the floor. His glove touched Joe's biceps as he returned to his stool.

Tommy came out for the 12th with panda eyes, making persistent attempts to get inside to Joe's body, but Joe's punches were by far the more dangerous as he piled up the points. He earned a ruffle of his hair from his Welsh rival as he returned to his corner. The 13th round came and went with comparatively speaking, little fuss or bother. Tommy was starting to show signs of tiring, his workrate had dropped considerably. He tried for a fight in the final seconds but Joe neatly turned him around off the ropes as the bell went. Joe came out for the finish in the 14th, his punches were snappy and painful and that jab never stopped searching for an opening, for the 'crowbar right' to do it's thing, but Tommy kept his defence tight and Joe could not penetrate. Tommy pawed away with his jab, and as he tried for a few right-hand bombs he was still energetic enough to duck and crouch, making himself hard to catch.

When the 15th and final round arrived, Tommy had already answered the call and his advance had to be checked by the referee, Arthur Donovan. The bell sounded. They raised their fists high in the air and touched gloves. And they were off again. Tommy ploughed forward with a two-handed attack, while Joe kept him back behind his jab. Tommy's jab was a tired action now and he kept his right hand cocked at his side for the most part, saving it for the last part of the round, for one big last push when he let his right go again and again. But Joe had this marvellous ability to move his head back ever so slightly to miss a shot, and yet Tommy was always there, always fighting, right up until the last bell, sometimes blindly – always bravely.

Before the decision was announced respect for Tommy Farr was alive in the air. In Tommy's corner they were jumping for joy, so sure were they that their man had taken the title. The radio commentary had given the impression that Tommy was going to win it. The campfire crowds were ecstatic. Cheering for Tommy Farr could be heard in millions of homes across Britain. But celebrations were premature. The MC stepped forward and took the microphone. "The winner, and still the champion, Louis."

There were as many boos as cheers at the Yankee Stadium, but as soon as Tommy had overcome his initial disappointment, he was across the ring to offer congratulations to the victor. This was indeed a close fight, and Tommy's aggression was a strong match for Joe's powerful and accurate countering and jabbing. But if I am to be honest, and I will probably make myself very unpopular now – particularly with my Welsh counterparts, from watching the tape over and over again, I think Joe Louis won clearly.

That night Tommy sent a message across the airwaves to his fans, explaining that he had done his best and although he felt that the cuts under his eyes had let him down, he was happy that he had put on a good show and he was looking forward to seeing them all soon, particularly his brothers and sisters. The day after the fight, one of the first messages of congratulation that Tommy received came from Joe Louis at his training camp at Pompton Lakes. Later that day Tommy gave a press conference and spoke in front of the film cameras. He was wearing a dressing gown and his brave showing belied the pain that he must have felt. His face, however, told it's own story. The terrible scars beneath both eyes were only the tip of the iceberg. But his words were typical of the man, "Well, I think it was a great fight, a very clean fight, and a very hard fight. And I hope that all the ones that seen it, they enjoyed it as much as I did. Because I enjoyed every minute of it."

Joe Louis died in April 1981 and Tommy Farr on St David's Day, 1986. But they had been re-united many times as they grew older. Because after the final bell, when their fight was over, Tommy and Joe enjoyed a bond that was never to be broken. An instance that, to my mind, sums up the friendship between them occurred in September 1966. They attended an evening together at the Pigalle Sporting Club in Piccadilly and, while they were there, they announced that they were looking for a heavyweight boxer to help groom into a world champion. What a lucky boy he would have been. During the evening films were shown of some of Joe's victories, including the one over Tommy. When asked about what he thought of the fight after nearly 30 years had passed Tommy replied, "I still feel sore now. I thought my nose was going to start bleeding in the middle of the film!"

*****

Melanie Lloyd's first book *'Sweet Fighting Man'* was published by SportsBooks Limited in November 2002. In a series of interviews with professional British boxers, each of her 'victims' as Melanie has fondly christened them, tells his own story in his own words giving an in depth insight into his world. Boxing News called it, *'A superb read… Lloyd has got them talking as only a woman can. That is, they have opened their hearts.'* Sweet Fighting Man can be purchased from all good bookshops (you might have to order it), or from sfm@sportsbooks.ltd.uk. Alternatively, telephone 07930 918 281. Melanie is currently working on *'Sweet Fighting Man – Volume II'*, which she hopes to complete by the end of next year.

Victor McLaglen: The Fighting Film Star

by Graeme Kent

Burly Victor McLaglen became well-known as an Oscar-winning film star for his role as Nolan in John Ford's 1935 masterpiece, *The Informer*, but long before this the London-born giant had achieved fame as the first heavyweight to go into the ring with the legendary black champion Jack Johnson after the latter had taken the world heavyweight title from Tommy Burns at Rushcutter's Bay in Australia in 1908.

When he fought Johnson, McLaglen was a 22-year-old English soldier-of-fortune, and the son of a South African bishop. For the past three years he had been working his way optimistically around North America in a variety of menial jobs and his fighting record was negligible. He was matched against Johnson as a last-minute substitute because the champion and his connections knew that the burly youngster had no chance.

McLaglen claimed to have been born in Tunbridge Wells in 1886, one of eight brothers and a sister, although his birth certificate gives the less salubrious east-end of London as his birthplace. He had been brought up in South Africa, where his father worked as a minister, and later became Bishop of Claremont. The family then returned to England at the time of the Boer War. One of McLaglen's older brothers, Fred, joined the colours and left for Cape Town.

The 14-year-old McLaglen dearly wanted to follow him, but his father forbade it. However, McLaglen, who captained the Tower Hamlets schools' football team and was tall and looked older than his years, ran away from home. He lied about his age and joined the Life Guards, in the anticipation of being sent to the war. The attestation book of the 1st Lifeguards for this period records that he enlisted on the 30th July, 1901. He gave his age as 19, his trade as engineer, and claimed to have been born in Stepney, London. His complexion was dark and his eyes hazel.

To his chagrin, Trooper McLaglen, instead of fighting the Boers, found himself spending most of his time on guard duty outside Windsor Castle. It was here that he first learnt to box and took part in his regimental heavyweight championships, fighting grown men.

Like many boxers afterwards McLaglen found that boxing was a passport to a relatively easy life in the Army and he was excused many of the fatigues that fell to the lot of his less athletic comrades. He was still only a boy, fighting men, and it was during this period that he began to accumulate some of the battered features which were to serve him well as a 'heavy' in his later Hollywood pictures.

The Boer War ended without the need for McLaglen's services. After three years of home soldiering, bored and disillusioned and still, at 17, too young to serve, he was at last discovered by his father, who promptly informed the authorities that his wayward son, at 17, was still under-age and would have to be discharged immediately. The Life Guards agreed and McLaglen was released. The official reason given was 'Discharged in consequence of him having made a miss-statement as to his age on enlistment'. McLaglen's service conduct summary was adjudged to have been very good.

Army service had not made McLaglen lose his taste for adventure. 'By this time, my brothers, all of whom were as tall as I, had scattered all over the world,' he recounted. 'I decided I wanted to go to Canada.'

When he was 18, McLaglen crossed the Atlantic steerage and found work as a farm hand at 10 dollars a month in Ontario in central Canada. He had not been there long when he heard of a silver strike at Cobalt, not too far away. McLaglen abandoned the farm at once and joined in the rush.

McLaglen was among the hundreds of hopefuls who arrived among the first wave of prospectors. There was nothing in the region but snow, ice and flat rock. The mining camp sprung up on every level surface to be found in the region, being called Cobalt after the mineral found lying interleaved with the silver deposits in the ground.

From the beginning, Cobalt was known as that most cherished of institutions, a 'poor man's mining camp.'

Victor in fighting pose

Because the silver veins lay so close to the surface, it could be mined with a pickaxe and shovel. An historian described the first shipments out as 'slabs of native metal stripped off the walls of the vein like boards from a barn.'

McLaglen joined up with several other prospectors and started digging some way from the centre of the region. Although he was only 19, he had achieved his full growth, being a muscular six feet, three inches at a weight of 195 pounds and fully able to hold his own with his companions at digging or fighting off potential claim-jumpers.

For months they toiled under conditions of great hardship, but eventually they found silver and started to pile it up. It was then that McLaglen encountered his first great setback. It was discovered that he had no right to the claim. He was always vague about the exact details. The most that he would ever say about the event was, 'I was deliberately cheated out of my share of the silver after I had worked a year. We had found the ore, but I had failed to sign certain papers that would have entitled me to my share.'

Whether McLaglen was defrauded by his partners is not certain, although they would have been brave men to have attempted to cheat such a husky youngster. It is more likely that he fell foul of mining bureaucracy. What was happening on a large scale in the region was the application of a regulation that a valuable mineral had to be found on the site before a claim could be registered. Many miners found that their claims did not belong to them because they had registered them before striking lucky, and this probably had been McLaglen's misfortune.

Whatever the cause, in 1905 the disillusioned 20-year-old was broke and in urgent need of money. For shelter he built himself a wooden shack on the shores of Lake Timiskamig. By this time Cobalt had become a boom town. Major mining companies and syndicates were moving in to work alongside the fortune hunters. At its peak ten thousand people were living in the town.

The tough miners were in urgent need of forms of relaxation on which to spend the fortunes some of them were accruing almost overnight. Saloons and brothels flourished, taking in thousands of dollars a week. One popular form of entertainment was the arrival of battered but experienced professional boxers and wrestlers, willing to take on all comers for a price. These were familiar sights in mining camps.

After a professional wrestler had come to Cobalt, the down-and-out McLaglen accepted the man's challenge and defeated him before a large audience of miners. He won only a few dollars, but many of the miners had bet on him to win, a sign that the young giant already had something of a reputation as a fighter. After McLaglen's success the winning punters passed the hat for him, and he ended up with almost $500, more money than he had ever seen before.

For a man of his strength and size, fighting seemed an easier option than mining and it was then that McLaglen took the decision to become a professional – challenging anyone in the area at wrestling or fighting, either with the gloves or bare fists. Among the tough but untutored prospectors he proved a real handful, taking a share of the gate money for his bouts from any local entrepreneur who cared to make the arrangements.

Things were going so well that McLaglen sent for his brother Fred, the sibling who had fired his incipient wanderlust by going off to fight the Boers. By this time Fred had engaged in a few boxing matches himself and was able to impact such skills as he had to his brother and act as his sparring partner. It was during this period that McLaglen developed his main training exercise. He would saw logs of wood at chest-height for long periods. He never became a skilful boxer but he was strong, and his exercise routines helped him to develop a fair right-hand punch.

For a time, he and Fred toured the thriving mining areas, challenging all-comers at boxing or wrestling and when no one accepted their challenges they put on exhibitions of both sports. Before long, Fred tired of the rough-and-ready conditions of Ontario decided to try his luck further south, in the USA. Before he left, he saw McLaglen fixed up as a professional wrestler with a touring circus, where the young man accepted challenges from the audience, paying $25 to anyone who could last three rounds with him. McLaglen's main venue was the Happy Land Park in Winnipeg. Here his most notorious and highly publicised feat was to defeat an entire football team in the ring, taking its members on one at a time.

This job did not pay very well and although it got him away from the dangers and hardships of the mining camps, McLaglen soon became fed up with it. He quite liked the ambience and relatively easy way of show business life, but aspired to something a little higher up the evolutionary scale than the small circus with its cowed animal acts and unfunny slapstick clowns. At some time during this period he worked as a barman and then as a railway policeman, driving hobos from the sidings and dissuading them from riding the rods.

Next, with a partner, he put together a physical culture and strong man act, clad in silver paint, involving displays of muscle-flexing and strength, including the lifting of impressive weights, which were perhaps not quite as heavy as they looked. McLaglen's speciality at this point, and one he was rather proud of, was to lie in a wrestler's bridge on the stage with an anvil balanced on his chest, while his partner used a sledgehammer to break a rock placed on top of the anvil. The act called itself the Great Romanos and the two men started looking for more work.

At least the bishop's son got to see more of North America as he moved round the country with the act. By now he was beginning to supplement his income by boxing in properly organised professional tournaments, usually picking up bouts in towns along the route of the circuit, or during weeks when he had no theatrical bookings. He is recorded as engaging in three bouts in the Washington area during this period. He lost to Phil Schlossberg, outpointed Emil Shock and knocked out Curley Carr, all of them complete unknowns. The fight manager, Doc Kearns, who met McLaglen at this time, described him as 'a big-chested youngster with a booming laugh who could fight like a tiger.'

By 1907, aged 21, he was based at Tacoma in Washington and taking part in wrestling matches as well as boxing contests. Then, as now, wrestling was mostly an affair of fixed and choreographed matches, but McLaglen was obviously already showing signs of latent thespian ability. On 4 November, 1907, *The Tacoma Daily Ledger* reported: 'In the fiercest and at the same time very cleanest wrestling match ever seen in Tacoma, Dr. B.F. Roller of Seattle last night twice pinned "Sharkey" McLaglen, the South African champion, to the mat and won the bout after a 42-minute struggle before an assembly of 800 appreciative lovers of sports at the Savoy Theatre.'

During this stage of his career, McLaglen often claimed to be South African, although as he had left the continent when he was a boy there was no way in which he could have been the champion of that country. As for his ring appellation, perhaps it was supposed to imply a lifetime of fighting off-shore sharks.

McLaglen never bothered to keep a complete record of his contests, a sign that he did not take boxing very seriously. He was a self-avowed 'pork-and-beaner', someone who often fought only for his next meal. When he could, on his travels he would challenge a local champion purely as a means of garnering publicity for his vaudeville act when he arrived at a new town. This meant, of course, that he was always up against the district favourite, something that never particularly bothered him, even

though he was only just out of his teens: 'I always liked a mixed reception,' claimed. 'The knowledge that some of the fans were against me, always inspired me to do my best.'

The fight with Jack Johnson came out of the blue. McLaglen just happened to be available when the champion's original opponent, Denver Ed Martin, dropped out. The fact that Martin had been selected as an opponent in the first place was a sign that Johnson was not being fed with 'a live one', so early in his reign. The black boxer's recent record was spotty in the extreme. Once he had been a leading heavyweight, noted for his footwork, but that had been a decade earlier.

Martin had already met Johnson twice. In 1903 in Los Angeles, he had gone 20 rounds with the up-and-coming Galveston man, for the so-called Coloured Heavyweight Championship, a synthetic title dreamt up by Californian sports writers. Martin had held his own with the younger man for the first 10 rounds, but had then been floored several times, leaving Johnson to run out an easy winner. A year later they had met again. By now Johnson had improved considerably and Martin had gone back commensurately and was knocked out in the second round.

Since then, over a period of five years, Martin had almost drifted out of the game, fighting on average only once a year, with a solitary win to his name. He had been resurrected on this occasion merely to provide an easy

This rare picture shows Victor (left) posing with the legendary Jack Johnson after their exhibition bout in Vancouver

opponent for Johnson, who had barely trained since winning the championship. No reason was given for his late withdrawal from the exhibition, it merely being announced that Martin had been called away unexpectedly to Seattle.

When the black fighter pulled out of the fight, there was consternation in the Johnson camp. Every seat in the Vancouver Athletic Club had been sold and Johnson had already collected his share of the box-office receipts. They had to get someone to sit in the opposite corner and it did not matter who this was. In boxing parlance, the only stipulation was that the opponent should at least have a faint pulse beat.

It was then that Victor McLaglen appeared, swaggering, charismatic, capable of engendering his own headlines, with a few fights behind him and showing absolutely no sign of being able to bother Jack Johnson in the ring in the slightest. He was made for the part and was quickly imported from his temporary home in Tacoma.

At the time, Johnson had other things on his mind. Arriving from Australia by way of Hawaii, because of his colour he had been refused admittance to half a dozen hotels in Victoria and was dossing down in a cheap lodging house on the waterfront. To make matters worse, he had decided in future to look after his own affairs and was in the messy process of dispensing with the services of his indignant manager, Sam Fitzpatrick, one of at least eight managers Johnson was to employ over the course of his career. The forthcoming fight was merely the beginning of a long process for Johnson of cashing in on his championship with a minimum of effort.

The bout was billed as a no-contest affair, which meant that McLaglen would have to knock Johnson out to win, a most unlikely eventuality. Because of this it was not billed as a world championship defence. In fact it was little more than a glorified exhibition match, designed to show Johnson off to the Canadian audience.

The British fighter was well aware that he had little or no chance against the champion, but not only would the money offered be useful, McLaglen knew that the fame that would ensue would carry over into his show-business career. From now on, no matter what the result, he would always be known as the first man to fight Johnson after the latter became champion, an item which soon found its way into his billing matter on the halls. And anyway, there was always the chance, no matter how faint, that he might just manage to connect on Johnson with one lucky sucker punch.

Such was Johnson's fame, even this early in his career as a title-holder, that the fight was a sell out. McLaglen recorded later that engrossed spectators were practically hanging from the rafters. It mattered not that local newspapers were sniffily dismissing the challenger as an unknown.

The evening's entertainment began with Johnson, resplendent in white tie and tails, being introduced to the enthusiastic audience from the ring. He made a short speech, complimenting the citizens of Vancouver for being fair-minded and good sports. He paid a tribute to Canada's

former champion, Tommy Burns, as 'that great, game little fellow'. Johnson concluded his peroration by announcing that he was ready and waiting to meet the ex-champion, James J. Jeffries, at any time, adding: 'No matter where or when I fight I will be trying, and if I am beaten it will be by a better man.'

Johnson then left to change into his fighting gear, while McLaglen entered the ring to wait for him. Nervous as he was at the time, years later McLaglen was able to describe the preambles to the fight vividly. Upon the champion's return, he recalled, Johnson was wearing bright blue trunks and received a warm welcome from the spectators. The champion's weight was announced as 211 pounds, while McLaglen was almost a stone lighter, at 198 pounds.

The fight itself was to prove an anti-climax. Johnson felled McLaglen with almost the first punch he threw. The two men broke from an early clinch and Johnson shot a hard straight left to his opponent's body. Entering into the spirit of the event, McLaglen had been smiling at the time, but the grin turned to a grimace of agony. The Englishman backed away slowly, then his legs buckled and he sank to his knees, his body doubled up and his forehead resting on the canvas. When McLaglen staggered to his feet at the count of nine, already all the fight had been knocked out of him.

The next day, the Vancouver *Daily Post* reported contemptuously of the white heavyweight's reaction. 'For the rest of the bout he was looking for a soft spot to fall. As McLaglen (*sic*) had no business in the ring in the first place, not having the speed to cope with the shifty black, he made but a sorry showing thereafter.'

Onlookers were struck by Johnson's sheer strength in throwing the burly McLaglen around at will, and commented on the fact that the champion did not move his feet much, being content to occupy the centre of the ring and force McLaglen to circle warily around him. The champion impressed with his ability to tie his opponent up in a clinch, using only one hand, while walloping McLaglen with his free fist. Above all, Johnson's hand-speed was marvelled at; when he delivered combinations of punches the effect was little more than a blur.

Satisfied that he had little to beat, Johnson toyed lazily with his big opponent throughout the rest of the bout and resorted to his custom of talking idly to ringsiders as he held the sweating, swinging Englishman off. The champion did not sit down between rounds and was heard discussing the latest fashions in male costume jewellery with an acquaintance seated close to the ring.

For his part, once the initial effects of Johnson's body punch had worn off, McLaglen did his best to land a haymaker, gaining slightly in confidence as the bout went on. 'I tried my best to rattle him in the last two rounds,' he wrote later, 'conscious of the immortality that would be mine were I lucky enough to slip him a sleeper.' Better men than McLaglen had tried unsuccessfully to do that and would continue to do so for the remainder of the champion's reign.

The Vancouver fight made so little impression on the champion that, like the *Daily Post* reporter, he could not

even spell McLaglen's name correctly and had forgotten that there had been no referee's decision when, years later, he mentioned the episode in his autobiography. 'Between stage appearances I had some minor ring affairs,' he wrote dismissively. 'One of these was with Victor MacLaghlen (*sic*) in Vancouver, 10 March, 1909, which I won in six rounds.'

Boxing had not finished with McLaglen yet, nor had he completely disassociated himself from the periphery of the 'White Hope' campaign. After the Johnson bout, he returned to the Pantages circuit with the Great Romanos, this time linked with his brother, Arthur, as his partner and when stage work dried up they would take work with circuses between engagements. McLaglen was never a top of the bill ace, but his unexpected six rounds with Jack Johnson had given him, as he had anticipated, a certain amount of fame in the sticks.

He was never shy of cashing in on the attendant publicity, giving interviews to local newspapers all along the Pantages route, not unexpectedly allowing himself the best of it for the press stories. What had in reality been an extremely one-sided exhibition bout was transmogrified for the public into a thrillingly close encounter, with McLaglen, in his version, taking the champion to the wire.

His favourite publicity-seeking ploy for the act was to turn up at a gymnasium in whichever city he was appearing that week, and noisily challenge the best-known local heavyweight to a bout. The fact that it would be almost impossible to arrange and stage such a contest in the seven days that he was in the vicinity was not lost on the strong man, but he usually managed to have a few journalists waiting in the gymnasium to take down the affronted reaction of the local hopeful.

In Springfield, Missouri, in 1911, it all went horribly wrong. The local fistic hero was a heavyweight called Joe Cox and in the hope of getting the customary headlines, McLaglen swaggered along to the town gymnasium, accompanied by a coterie of reporters, and noisily challenged Cox.

Unfortunately for the Englishman, a wily local promoter called Billy McCarney had joined in the managerial scramble to find a 'White Hope'. He had a secret prospect hidden away and was planning to match his hopeful with Cox in the near future. His heavyweight's name was Jess Willard, known as the Pottawatamie Giant, a man of six feet, five inches in height and weighing 250 pounds. Willard was slow and clumsy and, at this stage, almost completely untutored in the fistic arts. However, he was terribly strong and the possessor of a hard and extremely long left jab. He had won a few contests, but so far he had been kept under wraps and the ingenuous McLaglen had not heard of him.

Knowing of McLaglen's inglorious fighting record, tongue-in-cheek, McCarney proposed that McLaglen fight a few rounds with Willard in the gym first. If he acquitted himself well, promised the promoter, he would consider matching the Englishman against Joe Cox in a public contest.

It was not what McLaglen had been expecting, but he agreed to come back later and face Willard. As soon as the Englishman had left, McCarney spread the word that his giant was about to be let loose on a mug, albeit one who had fought the world champion only a couple of years earlier. When McLaglen returned, he found to his amazement that the gymnasium was packed to capacity. McCarney had charged 50 cents a head for eager locals to witness the slaughter. When he saw Willard for the first time, McLaglen must have wondered if he had been taken for a sucker. The former cowboy had to duck his head to get through the door and the breadth of his shoulders seemed to blot out the sunlight streaming in through the window.

Nevertheless, the Bishop's son did his best. He bundled in gamely to Willard, only to discover that there seemed no way past the big man's telescopic left jab. When Willard finally unloaded a couple of devastating rights in the fourth round, McLaglen realised how badly he had been had. He quit on the spot, and reeled bloodily away from the gymnasium, to the jeers of the spectators.

It was not quite the end of Victor McLaglen's boxing career. Over the next few years, whenever he was out of work and had to keep the wolf from the door, he would summon up his resolve and grimly return to the ring. He had four fights in New York in 1913, winning three and being knocked out in the fourth. To his credit, one of his victories was over a very useful second-rank heavyweight called Dan 'Porky' Flynn. During the course of a long career, Flynn fought a number of top 'White Hopes', including Carl Morris, Gunboat Smith, Boer Rodel and Battling Levinsky. He knocked out Rodel and went the distance with the others, so this victory by McLaglen was easily the Englishman's outstanding ring achievement.

By now he was 26 and tiring of fighting. Counting his early Army days, he had been in the ring, on and off, for 10 years and had got nowhere and the theatrical bookings were beginning to dry up as well. McLaglen and Arthur had had enough. 'We got tired of that,' he explained simply, 'so we shipped for Hawaii. From there we went to the Fiji islands, Tahiti and Australia.'

Attempts to dive for pearls in the South Sea islands failed, so they moved on to Australia. Arthur McLaglen had been there before. In 1910, he had fought three two-round exhibition contests with the former world heavyweight champion, Bob Fitzsimmons. However, as soon as they landed they heard of a gold strike in the interior and ignoring his unpleasant prospecting experiences in Canada, McLaglen promptly joined in the gold rush with his brother. On one occasion they almost died of thirst and starvation.

They next set sail for South Africa. By this time McLaglen was practically down and out, as he and Arthur had made no money in Australia. On reaching South Africa, the first thing they heard was that war had broken out in Europe. The news did not displease the McLaglens. None of them was averse to fighting, and at least military life promised the prospect of regular meals and adventure. 'We left immediately for London to enlist and glad to get the chance,' McLaglen said.

News of the war had brought home all the McLaglen brothers old enough to fight, Victor, Lewis, Leopold, Clifford, Arthur and Fred. They arrived, broke but optimistic, from such remote places as China, Canada and South Africa. They were all a little weary and shop-soiled.

Fred had been fighting in the USA, without a great deal of success and by the time he reached England again, he had opposed and been knocked out by such white heavyweight prospects as Dan Dailey, Al Reich, Carl Morris and Gunboat Smith. Doc Kearns had seen Fred fight during this period and had described him succinctly as a one-punch fighter. 'One punch on the whiskers and he folded.'

To make matters worse, Fred had to put up with a considerable amount of ribbing when he met up with Victor in London. In one of his last bouts in the USA, in January 1914, Fred had been knocked out in two rounds by Porky Flynn, one of Victor's occasional victims.

Fred's story had an unhappy ending. All six brothers enlisted and went off to fight, but only five of them returned in 1918, Fred being killed while serving in East Africa.

Victor McLaglen was commissioned and spent a few months as a recruiting officer in London. In 1915 he managed to squeeze in one more bout, defeating Dan McGoldrick on a technical knockout in five rounds. His military career after this is obscure and there are no traces of him in the military archives of the Cheshire and Middlesex regiments, or the Irish Fusiliers, three of the units in which he claimed to have served.

In interviews, McLaglen also told reporters that he had been posted to the Middle East where he saw action against the Turks at Sind, Judalia and Sheik Saad, and to have been promoted to captain for bravery. Again there are no official records of his having been present at such engagements.

He does resurface briefly. At the end of the war, by virtue of his impressive size, battered face and fighting background, he was appointed Assistant Provost Marshal of Baghdad, responsible for the discipline of both the troops stationed in the town and the Arabs who lived there. The job was no sinecure. He was involved in a number of brawls, trying to separate fighting soldiers and Arabs, and claimed to have been stabbed twice and to have survived an attempt to kill him with poisoned dates.

In 1919 he was out of the Army, unemployed again, penniless and by this time married. He was also 32 years old, past it for most heavyweights, especially less able ones who had taken as many ring beatings as he had. Nevertheless, as he had done so many times before, McLaglen made one last effort to restore his fortunes by entering the ring.

He was matched with the up-and-coming Frank Goddard, a future British heavyweight champion, although his title tenure of only three weeks set a British record. Goddard's other claim to fame was that he had been banned from one training camp because his language was too bad for the other boxers, and from another for throwing a plum pudding at a portrait of Queen Victoria hanging on the wall.

The former 'White Hope' was billed as Captain Victor McLaglen, and much was made in the publicity build-up to his bout with Jack Johnson 10 years before. McLaglen was no match for his younger opponent who, as a former humble trooper, must have relished the prospect of hitting an officer with impunity, and McLaglen was knocked out in three rounds in what would be his last fight.

However, boxing continued to be good to McLaglen. Some time after his fight with Frank Goddard, and at a loose end, he was hanging around the National Sporting Club, a meeting place for wealthy and influential patrons of the noble art. Here he happened to bump into I. B. Davidson, a film producer, who was looking for a brawny, tough-looking character to play a prize fighter called Alf Truscott in a silent costume melodrama entitled *The Call of the Road*. McLaglen, still bearing the marks of the Goddard fight, certainly looked the part and was never one to turn down a challenge. To his surprise, not only did he enjoy making films he was actually rather good at it.

He was cast as an action hero in a number of British films and was then recruited by Hollywood, where he became a considerable hit in silent movies. His career in talkies was given a boost when he won an Oscar as Nolan, an informer betraying a comrade for the price of a boat-fare to America, in the Irish-set *The Informer*.

Victor McLaglen's finest hour came many years after he had left the fight game behind him, when, at the age of 49, he had been presented with the Best Actor Oscar at the 1935 Hollywood ceremonies. The award was to prove a professional lifeline to the former soldier-of-fortune, but he never regarded it very highly. 'Acting never appealed to me, and I was dabbling in it solely as a means of making money.' He had better things to remember. Towards the end of his long and rather incredible life, he once went on record as saying rather wistfully: 'The only thing which ever thrilled me was boxing.'

Victor, the actor

Home and Away with British Boxers During 2002-2003

by John Jarrett

JULY

There was a time when a heavyweight standing six-two in his socks and hitting the scales around 16 stones was big enough for anything, but not anymore. Dominic Negus found that out when he answered the bell against Audley Harrison at Wembley Conference Centre. At six-five, the former Olympic super-heavyweight champion came in half-a-pound over 18 stones. Big fella!

Harrison was too big for Dominic, as the one-time 'Milky Bar Kid' bit off more than he could chew in a bad-tempered six-threes. Audley came out with the 59-55 points decision and Negus was fortunate in not being disqualified in the fourth round, when he deliberately butted Harrison after being punched on to his haunches.

In taking his sixth straight professional win, Audley handled a tough, aggressive, opponent competently enough, although at times he seemed to tire from the pace and should perhaps have been expected to stop the Romford man, a loser inside against Bruce Scott and Kevin Mitchell when boxing at cruiserweight. But Audley brushed aside criticism at the final bell, even from his BBC paymasters, insisting he was on the right road to the world championship. Time will tell.

In an eight rounder on the Wembley card, the Walthamstow heavyweight, Mark Potter, did what Harrison couldn't do when stopping game Derek McCafferty in round six. The Peterborough puncher had gone the six rounds distance with Audley in his second pro outing and never looked in trouble. Derek was in trouble against Potter, who beat him for the third time.

Former WBC super-middleweight champion, Glenn Catley, struggled to beat a Russian southpaw, Vage Kocharyan, on a decision in his first contest on home soil in three-and-a-half years, taking his pro log to 27-6 (19). A possible fight down the road for the Bristol man could be with Robin Reid who retained his WBF super-middleweight title in a tough 12 rounds with Argentina's Francisco Mora.

The handsome Reid, who could be boxing's poster boy, dropped his challenger twice in taking a unanimous decision and retaining his title for the fifth time. But Robin, a former WBC champion, at 31, is aching for a 'Big Fight' before he hangs them up. I saw him give unbeaten Joe Calzaghe one of his toughest fights, one of only three defeats suffered by the Runcorn man in 36 pro bouts.

Dagenham super-featherweight, Nicky Cook, ran his unbeaten string to 18-0, but knew he had a fight on his hands with Andrei Devyataykin, a tough Russian lightweight. Cook came out with a cut on his right eye, but did enough to take the decision.

In an eight-year professional career taking in 30 bouts (24-4-2), Coventry's Dean Pithie had managed to win a couple of those 'Second Division' titles, while running Michael Gomez to a close finish for the British super-featherweight title. Now he was fighting Alex Moon for the Liverpool man's Commonwealth championship in front of the hometown fans and Dean was determined to go for broke. He did it, fending off a strong finish by Moon to take the decision and the title. 'I'm back,' announced the delighted new champion, 'and I'm here to stay.' Still only 28, Dean could make a few bob yet.

Forget the heavyweights! The fight Britain wants to see is Ricky Hatton versus Junior Witter at light-welterweight and if there is a title of some sort in the pot by the time they meet, so much the better. It doesn't matter. The fight is the thing. Waiting for it to happen, Witter put his slick skills on show in London at the Grosvenor House Hotel, where Frank Warren staged a star-studded benefit night for Michael Watson. Hatton was ringside to see the Bradford southpaw annihilate Ghana's Laatekwei Hammond inside two rounds for the vacant Commonwealth title. The visitor was down three times, as Junior showed he was ready for the big boys, especially Ricky Hatton!

It was all going great for Steve Roberts. Undefeated in 29 pro fights, the West Ham southpaw had won the Southern Area light-middleweight title, the WBF super-middleweight title, then dropped back to win the WBF light-middle championship. Making his 10th defence of this title at Nottingham, Steve was expected to blow away Russia's Andrei Pestriaev. But it all went horribly wrong and Steve was almost blown away in a torrid, for him, eighth round. He survived but was fighting a losing battle and, at the final bell, the veteran Pestriaev was the new champ!

Nottingham's IBO welterweight champion, Jawaid Khaliq, sent his fans home happy as he turned back the challenge of Jose Rosa, a dumpy Dominican, getting off the deck in the fifth to take the unanimous decision. Nicky Booth kept his Commonwealth bantamweight title with a fifth-round knockout of Moses Kinyua, a game little fellow from Kenya.

Nicky's older brother Jason, the British and Commonwealth flyweight champion, was ringside to cheer Nicky on, having recently been hospitalised following a vicious attack in the city. He was found unconscious in a pool of blood with a gash in the back of his head.

The ring career of British and Commonwealth super-bantamweight champion, Michael Alldis, was in jeopardy after a police car ran into the back of his car. Suffering neck pains from whiplash and severe headaches caused by the crash, the 34-year-old Alldis was looking to take action against Sussex police.

AUGUST

You just never know when the big chance is going to come along in this game. The trick is to be ready when it does. Three times British lightweight champion, Bobby Vanzie, was ready to travel to Italy to fight Sandro Casamonica for the vacant European title and three times

the Italians called the fight off. So Bobby said the hell with it and the promoters, with just ten days to go, offered the chance to David Burke. The Liverpool lad already had himself a Commonwealth title shot coming up so declined the offer.

Enter Jason Cook. The Maesteg fighter had put 18 fights in the book (one defeat) in a six-year pro career, with a year out as a guest of Her Majesty. There was nothing wrong about Jason's boxing pedigree. In 1993 he was British ABA champion and took silver a year later at the Commonwealth Games. Did he want the fight with Casamonica in Italy? The answer was a definite YES!

Jason had heard the old cliche about having to score a knockout to get a draw in Italy and in the third round it looked like the Welsh lad wouldn't even have to worry about a dodgy decision, taking home his biggest ever purse and little else for his short break in the sunshine of San Mango d'Aquino.

Casamonica smashed over a right hand and Cook dropped with a thud. The crowd went crazy as Jason beat the count and Sandro moved in for the finish. But Mr Cook was far from finished. He weathered the storm and suddenly hurt the Italian veteran with a left hook, then another bomb exploded on the Italian's chin and he was out before he hit the floor. The referee didn't even bother counting and Jason Cook was the new lightweight champion of Europe, only the second Welshman to win this title since the great Freddie Welsh, and that was 88 years ago! Dreams do come true in this business.

The king was in his castle and some six thousand of his subjects turned out to pay homage. WBO super-middle-weight king, Joe Calzaghe, was jousting with Puerto Rico's Miguel Jiminez at Cardiff Castle with 'King Joe' unbeaten in 33 duels and ready to give the big holiday crowd another victory.

Well Joe got his win, retaining his championship with a lop-sided decision over an opponent more intent on survival than success, but when the king got back to his counting house he had to use his right hand to count his handsome purse, having damaged his left hand in the second round when trying to knock out the tough invader.

The champion, in turning back his 11th challenger, was disappointed. He had hoped to make a good impression on the American TV audience and move nearer a mega-fight with Bernard Hopkins or Roy Jones. But those fights are never going to happen. Nor is a title unification fight with Germany's Sven Ottke, not in the world of the 'Alphabet Boys'. You stay in your backyard and I'll stay in mine! We're all making money, aren't we? Be happy. Next challenger please!

Ring announcers will always be grateful to Iranian-born Mehrdud Takalobigashi for changing his name to plain old Takaloo for boxing purposes. He was on the Cardiff bill defending his WBU light-middleweight title against Daniel Santos, who was putting his WBO belt into the pot as well.

Takaloo had sparred Calzaghe preparing for this fight and he told reporters, 'If Santos beats me it's because he's a better fighter.' The Puerto Rican southpaw did beat

Takaloo, by a unanimous decision, and it was because he was a better fighter, despite Takaloo's claims that Santos was a dirty fighter. The Margate man was cut by the right eye in a clash of heads in the first round, but did score the only knockdown, in the fourth round, and will have learned a lot from this encounter.

Tuning up for a crack at the vacant British super-featherweight title against fellow Scot, Willie Limond, Edinburgh's unbeaten Alex Arthur barely worked up a decent sweat when knocking out Pavel Potipko in 100 seconds of round one. Now 12-0 (10) Arthur said, 'I can see myself stopping him (Limond) in five rounds. Winning a Lonsdale Belt has been a dream of mine.'

Southern Area welterweight champion, David Walker, was signed to defend his title against Brett James and they gave the York Hall fans a preview of what was to come. Walker was in devastating form as he destroyed Robert Burton, a southpaw, inside two rounds, while James, from St Pancras, was forced to go the six rounds with the Birmingham stayer, Brian Coleman, who survived two knockdowns in the third round.

A former brilliant amateur star, Nottingham's Carl Froch had a walkover against mismatched Darren Covill at super-middle, all finished at 2.03 of the first. Froch needs to step up in class, even though this was only his third pro outing, all wins. It was 1959 when I first met Tommy Miller, at the New St James's Hall in Newcastle. Tommy had a winner that night as Brian Husband beat the British welter champ, Tommy Molloy, over eight rounds. Now 86 and Britain's oldest working licence holder, Tommy was feted with a dinner at the Shay Social Club at Halifax FC.

The Derby Storm Arena was jam-packed with Damon Hague's rabid supporters and the local hero didn't let them down, hammering Andrew Facey to a fifth-round knockout, but not before taking a few shots along the way from his Sheffield rival. Damon dropped his man twice in the second round with solid rights to the head, but Facey boxed his way back in the fourth and it was all even going into the fifth. But Hague, his fans roaring him on, smashed in another big right and Facey was done for the night and off to hospital with a fractured cheekbone. The fight was a final eliminator for the WBF middleweight title.

SEPTEMBER

Even Clinton Woods didn't think he could win. Why should he? Nobody else thought he could win. Thousands of miles from his Sheffield home, Woods was going in with 'Superman', 12 rounds or less, for the world light-heavyweight championship. The contest was scheduled for Portland, Oregon, but it might as well have been in Timbuktu! All that way to fight the man most pundits concede to be the greatest fighter, pound for pound, in the world today, a guy called Roy Jones. Stracey over Napoles. It happened. Honeyghan over Curry. It happened. But Woods over Jones? We couldn't see this one, not even with field glasses! Hey, you couldn't blame Clinton for jumping at the chance and in this one you knew it wasn't just the mega payday the Yorkshire lad was after. It was a fighter's dream.

Well, dreams don't always come true. They didn't this time as the gallant Woods was stopped inside six rounds, still on his feet but being picked apart by a superb champion, a man whose sole defeat (disqualification) in 47 pro fights was immediately avenged. Woods had swept the board, winning British, Commonwealth, and European titles, but they were in a different world to the one ruled by Roy Jones.

There was a time in British boxing when blood relatives were not allowed in a fighter's corner. On a Saturday night in Manchester's huge MEN Arena, London-born Stephen Smith was wishing that rule was still on the books. Smith was challenging the local hero, Ricky Hatton, for his WBU light-welterweight title, a tough assignment. It got even tougher in the first round when Stephen took a count and there was already blood on his face when he went to his stool.

Things got worse in the second round. Much worse. Stronger, hitting harder, Hatton dumped Smith for a second time and Stephen was bleeding from a nasty cut over his right eye, Hatton's elbow catching him before he went down. Then all hell broke loose! As Mickey Vann took up the count, Darkie Smith, Stephen's father and trainer, charged into the ring to remonstrate with the third man, shoving him as he did so. After ordering Darkie to leave the ring, Vann spread his arms wide. The fight was over, Smith was disqualified, Hatton the winner and still champion.

'Tonight I saw Stephen nutted twice,' said Darkie afterwards, 'and everyone saw him (Hatton) walk forwards and smack Stephen with the elbow. What do you do?' What you don't do is enter the ring during a round and shove the referee. That was the reaction of a father. It was not the reaction of a professional trainer. Maybe they should have left that rule about blood relatives in the book after all.

Anthony Farnell gained revenge over Ruben Groenewald for a narrow defeat in a gruelling fight three months previously, when the South African picked up the vacant WBU middleweight belt. The loss didn't sit well with the Manchester man and he made no mistake this time in another hard bout, a split decision giving him the title. At York Hall, Danny Williams won the Lonsdale Belt outright as he kept his British and Commonwealth heavyweight titles against the determined challenge of Keith Long, who was still pitching leather at the final bell. It was a fine performance from the champion, but can have done little for Danny's image on the world scene, letting a 34-year-old in only his tenth contest take him to the limit.

Still hoping for another shot at Danny is former champion, Julius Francis, who gave Williams his only defeat in 1999. Danny has since knocked out Francis in a defence of his titles, but Julius was looking for the champ after racking up an impressive sixth-round knockout over Steffen Nielsen in Randers. Newark super-bantam, Esham

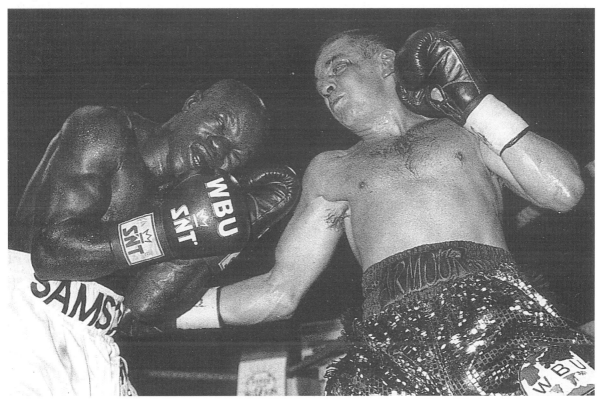

John Armour (right) digs in a right to Francis Ampofo's body on his way to a hat-trick of wins over his game opponent

Les Clark

45

Pickering, was not so lucky in Gran Canaria where he looked a winner over the unbeaten Spaniard, Alejandro Monzon, only for the judges to score a split decision for Monzon. At stake was the meaningless vacant Trans-continental WBA title. Big deal!

It was action all the way at Brentwood's International Centre where John Armour retained his WBU bantam-weight title against Francis Ampofo for the third time in three tremendous battles. Following the contest, the little Ghanian-born Londoner decided that it was one fight too many and announced his retirement. In 28 fights he finished 17-11 and was a former Commonwealth flyweight champion, undefeated British fly champion, and IBO Inter-Continental bantamweight titleholder. Whoever it was said good stuff comes in little bundles must have had Francis in mind. Good fighter, lovely fellow.

In another WBU title bout, Colin 'Dynamo' Dunne failed to live up to his nickname and needed a strong finish to retain his lightweight title for the seventh time with a majority decision over an awkward Colombian, Esteban Morales. Nicky Booth met a tartar in the smart-boxing Canadian, Steve Molitor, who was a comfortable points winner and took the Commonwealth bantamweight title home with him. The visitor was a revelation, dropping Booth in the opener and giving him a boxing lesson the rest of the way. A southpaw, Steve stayed unbeaten at 13-0-1.

Wayne McCullough was a happy man, and the fight hadn't even started! The man from Belfast, via Las Vegas, was back in a British ring for the first time since March 1994 ready to take on the world. This night at York Hall he just had to take care of the willing South African, Johannes Maisa, a buzzsaw calling himself 'The Hurricane!' The storm had abated in round four and the referee stopped it to give Wayne his comeback win. Bring on Scott Harrison!

Gary Hibbert had been sparring with David Burke as the Liverpool southpaw prepared for his Commonwealth lightweight title challenge to James Armah. But when Armah pulled out and gave up the title, Hibbert ended up fighting for the vacant championship at the Everton Park Sports Centre. Burke was in command, dropping Gary in the third and again in round 10 before the referee called it off.

OCTOBER

It was 'Scotland the Brave' at Renfrew's jam-packed Braehead Arena when Scott Harrison challenged Julio Pablo Chacon for the WBO featherweight title, in bidding to become the first Scot to grab at least a slice of the world nine-stone diadem. The tough champion, from Argentina, had lost only two bouts of 46 with 31 inside wins and had defended his title twice since winning it. He wouldn't go easy.

Well, this fellow from Cambuslang wasn't a bad fighter.

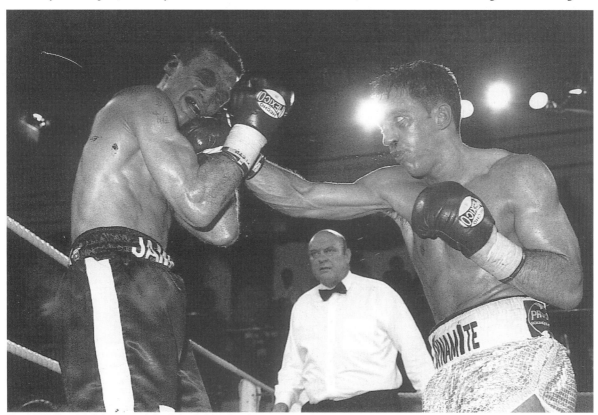

David Walker (right) successfully defended his Southern Area welterweight title with a fourth-round stoppage win over Brett James

Les Clark

Just turned 25, he was 17-1-1 going in and had won British and Commonwealth titles, the IBO Inter-Continental and WBO Interim belt. He was ready. Harrison set the crowd alight as he turned loose a relentless attack that left the clever Chacon nowhere to go and, at the final bell, it was indeed 'Scotland the Brave'. Harrison had arrived in the big time! Edinburgh box-fighter, Alex Arthur, won the vacant British super-featherweight title with a splendid fourth-round knockout of the Dewsbury southpaw, Steve Conway, a late substitute for the injured Willie Limond. Taking his pro log to 13-0, 11 inside, Arthur was in a different class and looks a boy to watch.

On the Renfrew bill, Lucky Samba, a South African based in London, was out of luck when matched with Bradford's Junior Witter and the British and Commonwealth light-welterweight champion toyed with his man before it was stopped in round two. Of course the fight everyone is waiting for is Witter versus Hatton, a fight reportedly inked into Hatton's contract with Frank Warren. Watch this space!

Maesteg's Jason Cook had upset the odds when winning the European lightweight title on a knockout in Italy and now he was showing the hometown fans how he did it, on the first show in his hometown since 1964. Coming out of the other corner was Nasser Lakrib, a Frenchman out of his depth. By the fifth round, Lakrib was out of the fight, hammered defenceless by the new Welsh hero.

On the Maesteg bill, Liverpool super-middleweight, Tony Dodson, was not so lucky as he blew his WBF Inter-Continental belt when stopped by tough Pole, Albert Rybacki, inside nine rounds. Leading after eight rounds, Dodson deflected a right to the body which landed below the belt and dropped him in pain. He beat the count but could not hold off the Pole, who hammered away to bring the referee's intervention.

In Hartlepool, the local favourite, Michael Hunter, drove Frankie DeMilo before him for 12 rounds at the Jester's Centre Go-Cart arena and roared across the line a unanimous winner of the vacant WBF super-bantamweight championship, taking his record to 12-0-1 and bringing the first 'world' title to his hometown.

If you have to be in the wrong part of town one dark night you could do worse than take Tony Oakey with you. You could be safely home by the time Tony has sorted out the bad guys. In the boxing ring, this tough puncher from Pompey was still undefeated in 16 pro fights and the crowd at York Hall raised the roof as he hammered away at the gritty Estonian, Andrei Kaersten, to retain his WBU light-heavyweight title with a unanimous decision. Tony had to climb off the deck twice to fight his way to victory. Commonwealth welterweight champion, James Hare, is a good looking kid and he looked good defeating awkward Zimbabwean challenger, Farai Musiiwa, at the Sports Centre in Huddersfield. Hare was never in danger against his six-foot rival, bringing him down to the canvas in the fourth and when James decked his man twice in the eighth it was called off.

The Eastman brothers were on the bill at York Hall, with British, Commonwealth and European middleweight champion, Howard, stepping out for the first time since losing a world title challenge to William Joppy, dropping down the scale to face Chardan Ansoula, who was dropped, cut, and stopped in just 63 seconds! Brother Gilbert came back after three years to outpoint Ojay Abrahams in a four.

The Audley Harrison road show moved into Liverpool for the Sydney Olympic gold medallist's seventh professional outing. Chosen for the role of the fall guy was Wade Lewis from Alabama, who claimed a record of 11-3 with 10 stoppages. Lewis never looked like hitting Harrison, never mind beating him, and was on his way to the showers after 43 seconds of round two. Audley floored his man in the first and twice in the second before the referee, and the fans, had seen enough.

Dagenham's unbeaten Nicky Cook moved to 19-0 with a fine victory over Gary Thornhill, stopping the Liverpool man in the seventh round to retain his WBF Inter-Continental super-featherweight title after an evenly contested bout.

A flyweight tidbit down the road is a meeting of Peter Culshaw and Damaen Kelly. Both lads were showcased on the Harrison bill, with WBF champion, Kelly, outpointing the Filipino, Jovy Oracion, while WBU kingpin, Culshaw, beat another Filipino in Celso Dangud, also over eight non-title rounds.

Defending his Southern Area lightweight title at York Hall, Luton's Graham Earl kept his crown and his unbeaten record (16-0) with a points decision over Chill John of Brighton and was looking for British champion, Bobby Vanzie, having already won an eliminator. Vanzie was on the same bill, but was far from impressive in beating Andrei Devyataykin of Russia over eight untidy rounds.

David Walker was on another York Hall bill to give Brett James a shot at his Southern Area welterweight title. The Hampstead man was unbeaten in 12 fights (two draws), but was up against a strong champion who was out to hang on to his undefeated tag in 15 bouts (one draw) with seven stoppages. David lived up to his 'Kid Dynamite' nickname, having Brett in trouble in the second and the fourth before it was stopped.

In Cape Town, Henry Akinwande stopped Sam Ubokane in the seventh round, but the former WBO Commonwealth and European champion looked awful doing so.

NOVEMBER

Many fighters win some sort of world title, which is not too difficult in today's market, but to take that one step further towards 'Hall of Fame' stature, they need a career-defining fight. For Michael Brodie that dream contest was to be Naseem Hamed. Michael had won all sorts of titles since turning pro in 1994; British, Commonwealth, European super-bantamweight and, in his last fight, the WBF featherweight championship. But as he prepared to defend that honour against Mexico's Luis Fuentes in the Manchester suburb of Altrincham, they were still talking about the Naz fight. Talking, that's all! But Naz wasn't even in serious training and there was speculation he may

not fight again, so Brodie did what he does best, got in there and fought. He had to against this kid from Mexico, a cool 21-year-old who outboxed Michael for much of the first half of the bout. Brodie clinched victory (now 34-1) over the last half with his ring savvy, experience and solid body punching, but he came out of the ring with both eyes swollen and bruised after another hard day at the office.

In the fight of the night, Liverpool's Gary Ryder upset the odds to grab Wayne Rigby's WBF light-welterweight title in only his 10th fight, but as always Mr Rigby battled all the way to the final bell. Wayne has been in some titanic struggles, none more so than his memorable two-fight series with Michael Ayers, and he found himself in another here with Ryder. Gary was the same age, 30, but he was fresh and hadn't been in the wars like Rigby. Maybe that made the difference.

In another title bout on the bill, Brian Magee retained his IBO super-middleweight title with an easy decision over America's Jose Spearman, a reluctant partner in what turned out to be a boring spectacle dragged out over 12 rounds. The Belfast southpaw, a class act in the amateurs and unbeaten as a money fighter, now 17-0, will want to forget this one in a hurry and hope his fans do too.

Another fighter looking to forget his latest effort was Johnny Nelson, who retained his WBO cruiserweight title over the Panamanian challenger, Guillermo Jones, thanks to two myopic judges who allowed the Sheffield man to stay champion on a drawn decision at Derby's Storm Arena. The storm came when the verdict was announced and even Nelson's promoter, Frank Warren, admitted he thought Johnny lost it. Nelson can do it all, but every now and then he does it like this. Poor Jones. In two previous world title challenges, at light-middle, he had drawn and lost a split decision. So this was third time UNLUCKY!

In stark contrast to his stablemate, Nelson, Junior Witter turned in a ruthless demolition job on unfortunate Italian, Giuseppe Lauri, to win their WBO light-welterweight title final eliminator after 81 seconds of round two, referee Mickey Vann stopping it after Lauri had been down twice (officially) and was being taken apart. The Bradford switch-hitter was doubly pleased with himself as Ricky Hatton had taken five rounds to dispose of Lauri, in September 2000.

Wayne McCullough eased to his second comeback victory over outclassed Russian, Nikolai Eremeev, whose corner waved the towel with five seconds left in the fourth round of their contest at Belfast's Maysfield Sports Centre. The 'Pocket Rocket' is no longer the fighter he was when ruling the WBC bantamweight division, but, at 32, he was looking for a big fight, hopefully with newly-crowned WBO featherweight champ, Scott Harrison.

The British welterweight champion, Neil Sinclair, put

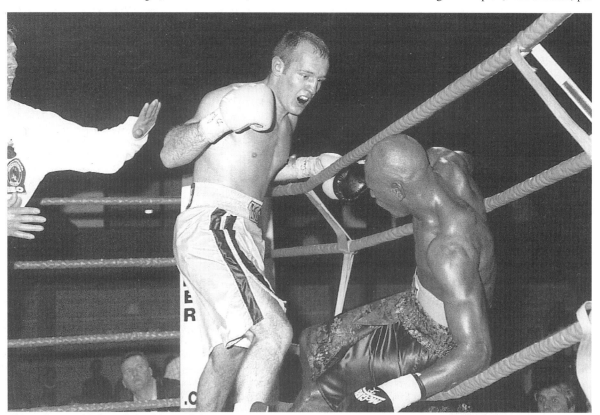

Although not at his best, Brian Magee (left) was an easy winner over America's Jose Spearman when retaining the IBO super-middleweight title

Les Clark

another notch on his Lonsdale Belt with an easy victory over Paul Knights, the third man calling it off after 67 seconds of the second round with the Redhill challenger in trouble after having been decked. The former Southern Area champion had accepted the contest on a week's notice after the job was turned down by James Hare and Harry Dhami.

Former undefeated WBU flyweight champion, Peter Culshaw, moved up a division to capture the vacant WBF super-flyweight title with a comprehensive points beating of the lanky South African southpaw, Ncedo Cecane, over 12 absorbing rounds at Liverpool Olympia, watched by Damaen Kelly, who must have been wondering if his long-awaited meeting with Culshaw was still on the cards. If it is, Kelly is adamant it will have to be at flyweight.

The big fight in Atlantic City was the much-anticipated rematch between Arturo Gatti and Mickey Ward so there was a good crowd on hand to see Audley Harrison's fight with America's Shawn Robinson on the undercard. It was hardly a fight as Robinson, dwarfed by Harrison, was crushed at 2.09 of round one. Opposition aside, it was a successful debut for Audley on American soil.

Brothers in arms! At Nottingham, the local favourites, Jason and Nicky Booth, saw non-title action, with British and Commonwealth flyweight boss, Jason, stopping Russia's Kakhar Sabitov in six rounds, while British bantamweight champ, Nicky, racked up a meaningless

three rounds stoppage of Estonia's Sergei Tasimov. Next day, on manager Jack Doughty's bill at Shaw, Charles and Wayne Shepherd were victorious, with the former IBO super-featherweight titleholder, Charles, making a come-back at the expense of Nottingham veteran, Nigel Senior, while Wayne gave Sam Gorman his first pro defeat over six rounds.

Nottingham's Jawaid Khaliq disappointed everyone with a lacklustre points win (split decision) in front of the hometown fans, defeating Ukrania's Roman Dzuman to hang on to his IBO welterweight championship. With so many 'world champions' on the scene today, quality suffers for quantity, and it is the same when it comes to finding suitable challengers. Earl Foskin, a 35-year-old Jamaican lasted all of 87 seconds against James Hare for his Commonwealth welterweight title. Poor stuff.

DECEMBER

Frank Warren's wonderboys, Joe Calzaghe and Ricky Hatton, sold out the Telewest Arena in Newcastle, but the 10,000 crowd were less than impressed with the level of opposition, albeit substitutes, served up for the main events. Tocker Pudwill was a household name in his own household back in North Dakota, but was no match for the unbeaten Calzaghe, who retained his WBO super-middle-weight title for the 12th time with a two-rounds stoppage. The American had in fact gone 12 rounds with Sven Ottke,

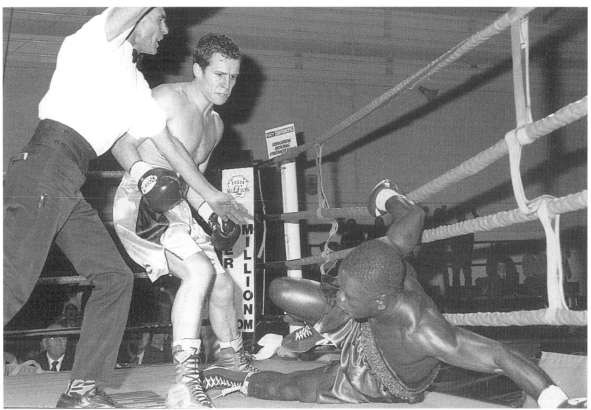

James Hare seen on his way to an 87-second stoppage win over the unfortunate Jamaican, Earl Foskin   Les Clark

but there was no way he was going to duplicate that feat with Calzaghe, who decked his man three times in the first before it was halted 39 seconds into round two after another knockdown.

Hatton's fans saw a bit more of their man against Joe Hutchinson, a southpaw from Indianapolis who had been in with guys like Arturo Gatti, and Hector Camacho junior. He took the 'Manchester Hitman' into the fourth round before going down from a crippling left to the body that drove all the fight out of him. It was 31-0 for Ricky as he retained his WBU light-welterweight championship for the eighth time, but Hatton, like Calzaghe, is pining for a mega-fight. Some day…

Edinburgh's Alex Arthur gave Carl Greaves a shot at his British super-featherweight title in the Newcastle ring and didn't put a punch wrong in stopping the Newark challenger in round six to run his unbeaten pro log to 14-0, 12 inside. Carl fought out of his skin, but could not make an impression on the cool Scot and he was catching everything when it was called off.

Hartlepool's new WBF super-bantamweight champion, Michael Hunter, had a good workout on the Calzaghe bill when he made it three out of three over Birmingham's Tony Hanna in a non-title eight rounder. The Brummie, a 10-year professional with 75 fights behind him, is regularly beaten but never beaten up. He is a survivor.

If you can't find a promoter, get a licence and do it yourself! That was the way for Jane Couch as she staged a Christmas dinner show that packed the ballroom of

A return match saw Richard Williams (left) stop Paul Samuels in the 10th round of an IBO light-middleweight title defence   Les Clark

Bristol's Thistle Hotel to see the locally-based 34-year-old take the vacant WBF light-welterweight championship with a lop-sided 10 rounds decision over Bulgaria's Borislava Goranova. It was Jane's 22nd money fight and her third title, having already won belts at lightweight and welter.

When they met in June, Richard Williams retained his IBO light-middleweight title over Paul Samuels on a technical draw, after suffering cuts in an accidental clash of heads. Six months later they were doing it again, at the Brentwood International Centre, and this time Williams left nothing to chance. The Welshman gave a good account of himself and was still in contention going into the 10th round. He almost made it to the bell, but was cut down with a searing right hook to the jaw and was counted out with one second left in the round.

Defending his WBU lightweight title against Liverpool rival, David Burke, Colin Dunne had lost only one of his 39 fights and had retained his title seven times in a five-year reign. At 32, the Holloway-based champion still looked good for a few more, but the Commonwealth titleholder, Burke, had other ideas. The 27-year-old southpaw sent Dunne to the canvas in the third round for a disputed knockdown and withstood Colin's attacks to finish a grand contest with a split-decision victory.

Colin Lynes racked up his 21st straight victory when he stopped New York's Richard Kiley to win the vacant IBO Inter-Continental light-welterweight title on the Brentwood bill. The Hornchurch lad was winning handily when he smashed Kiley to the canvas in the ninth round and the referee waved it off without starting a count. The American protested the stoppage, but he was trailing badly and looked in for more leather over the final three rounds.

They call David Walker 'Kid Dynamite' and at 26 he seemed to have it all going for him. Unbeaten in 16 pro fights (one draw), the Sidcup welterweight had won an ABA title and was the Southern Area champion. Now he was fighting Jimmy Vincent in a British title final eliminator at the Goresbrook Leisure Centre and the cards looked stacked against the 34-year-old Birmingham fighter.

But Vincent was up for this one, coming to the ring in superb condition for his big chance. Walker would admit he hadn't trained as he should have and he learned a bitter lesson. The Midland veteran covered well against the early storm as Walker tried to take him out, decked David in the fourth with a left hook, and roared on to victory in the eighth round, the referee stopping the fight with Walker defenceless.

On the Goresbrook bill, Nottingham super-middleweight, Carl Froch, impressed as he demolished Midland Area champion, Mike Duffield, in just 74 seconds to claim his fifth pro win, while the British and Commonwealth middleweight champion, Howard Eastman, looking to get his European title back, warmed up with a victory over Hussain Osman, who was pulled out by the corner after four rounds. The Battersea Bomber had cut the Syrian's left eye and boxed at his own pace against a rugged opponent.

Hartlepool southpaw, Alan Temple, reached the end of the road as Darren Melville knocked him down three times for a clear points win at Millwall to convince Alan it was

time to call it a day. After winning two ABA titles (feather and light-welter), Alan spent eight years putting 30 fights (13-17) in the book against the best in the business and boxed in three British title eliminators at lightweight.

Rising stars, Roman Greenberg and David Haye, look like boys to watch. Haye, in world class as an amateur heavyweight, won his cruiser debut at York Hall against Hull veteran, Tony Booth, in two rounds, while Greenberg, the London Israeli heavyweight, took his pro log to 6-0, easily beating Derek McCafferty.

JANUARY

I don't know what Noel Wilders got for Christmas but at least he had a Happy New Year. He had a birthday on the 4th January (28) and then he was going to fight for the European bantamweight title in the beautiful French city of Nice and that had to be better than a cold day in Castleford. 'Noel's from Castleford,' said veteran manager, Trevor Callighan, 'and no one's ever done any favours for folk from there.'

Well, things were looking up for this forgotten hero of British boxing. Noel Wilders had won an ABA championship. He had won the Central Area bantamweight title, won two eliminators for the British title and in October 1999 I had watched him outbox feisty little Francis Ampofo to become British champion. He had defended the title, then won the IBO version and defended that one. And

he was still unbeaten in 22 professional contests when he went off to Nice with Callighan and Michael Marsden, his trainer. Good luck, kid.

Noel didn't need luck in the ring with the local hero, Fabien Guillerme; his consummate boxing skills were enough to subdue the energetic efforts of the Frenchman. Where Noel needed luck was when the officials added up their tallies. He had won it, but only just. After 12 rounds, the scorecards were 116-112, and 115-113 twice, yet the British sportscaster, Steve Holdsworth, had Noel a lop-sided winner at 120-109. Just as well it wasn't a close fight!

Two European titles in one night! While Noel was doing his thing in Nice, Howard Eastman was doing his in Nottingham, punching another Frenchman, Christophe Tendil, into fourth round submission (broken jaw) to regain the European middleweight title and take his pro log to 35-1.

In another middleweight fight at the Ice Centre, the vacant WBF title was at stake as well as two unbeaten records when Wayne Pinder (18-0-1) clashed with Damon Hague (21-0-1), 12 rounds or less. The aggressive Hague, a big ticket seller, took the fight to his Manchester rival which suited Pinder, the boxer of the two, and he picked the favourite off, chipping away until Hague could take no more. A burst of leather in the seventh round sent Damon slumping into the ropes and to the deck with John Coyle waving it all over without a count. The paramedics were

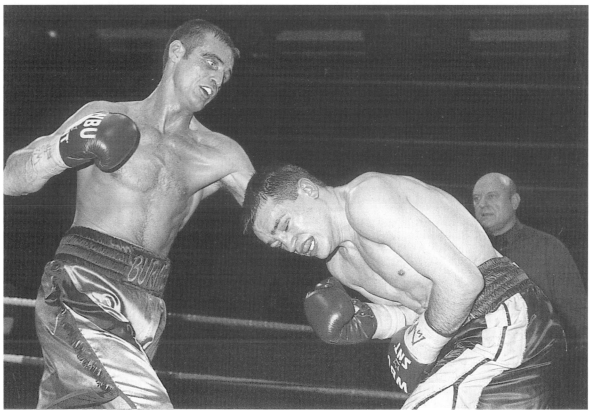

Colin Dunne (right) finally lost his grip on the WBU lightweight title when outpointed by David Burke Les Clark

51

quickly into the ring and fortunately the Derby lad was soon on his feet.

Darlington's undefeated (20-0-1) Oscar Hall didn't put a glove wrong in taming former British title challenger, Alan Bosworth, over 10 rounds of their British light-welter eliminator and looked like he might finally be making a move on the big boys after four-and-a-half years boxing six rounders down the bill. In Oscar's only big fight, going into this one, he beat Dean Nicholas (disq 9) to win the Northern Area welterweight title. His form against Bosworth was a revelation.

Jason Cook won his big fight at Bridgend, beating the Italian veteran, Stefano Zoff, on a split decision after 12 gruelling rounds. But the Welshman had already lost his European lightweight title when he climbed into the ring, lost on the scales when he came in at 9st 10½lbs. 'It's my own silly fault,' admitted Jason. 'I lost my title through stupidity.'

Zoff would have been declared champion had he won the fight, but at least Cook denied him that honour, battling it out to the final bell with the Italian who was a former European titleholder at feather and light as well as a former WBA champ. The 36-year-old challenger dropped Jason to a knee in the opener, but Cook repaid the compliment in the sixth round of a fight that was becoming untidy. Zoff

took the 10th and 11th over a tiring Cook, but Jason dug down to pull it out. Pity about the title.

Putting the expected defeat by Roy Jones behind him, Clinton Woods got back to business with a third-round stoppage over the squat Argentinian, Sergio Martin Beaz, in front of his hometown supporters at Sheffield's Ponds Forge Leisure Centre and was after a fight with the undefeated WBO champion, Dariusz Michalczewski. Even in Germany it would be better than that Jones fellow!

Heavyweight action saw Michael Sprott do himself a bit of good when he stopped former British champion, Michael Holden, inside four rounds on the Sheffield bill, while former Audley Harrison victim, Mark Krence, powered his way to a fourth-round victory over Petr Horacek, taking his record to 14-1. London-based Israeli, Roman Greenberg, turned up the heat to knock out Piotr Jurczyk in just 80 seconds. Former amateur star, David Haye, isn't a heavyweight yet, but he will be. Just 21, Haye weighed 13st 8¼lbs and it was enough to see off a limited Frenchman, Saber Zairi, in four rounds.

Life didn't get any easier for British lightweight champion, Bobby Vanzie, when he switched promoters from Tommy Gilmour to Frank Warren. He laboured to beat two Russian imports and crashed to ignominious defeat at the fast hands of 20-year-old Yuri Romanov, who

Howard Eastman (left) regained the European middleweight title he never lost in the ring when forcing the Frenchman, Christophe Tendil, out of the fight with a broken jaw

Les Clark

bounced the weight-weakened Bradford southpaw off the canvas five times before the bout was halted in round eight. Romanov retained his WBO Inter-Continental title, in case you're interested.

Anthony Farnell is proud to be WBU middleweight champion, no matter what anybody else thinks of his title, and he turned in a champion-like performance to punch the resistance out of Russia's Nikolai Talalakin, who stayed on his stool after the 10th round, by which time he was a well beaten boxer, with eye damage and had been put down three times.

FEBRUARY

Two of our lads went over to Germany this month but came home empty-handed. Glenn Catley lost his rematch with Haussler and a week later Danny Williams was crushed by Sinan Samil Sam. Back to the gym, boys!

Catley had looked forward to the return with Danilo Haussler for the European super-middleweight title after losing the first bout a year previously. 'Glenn definitely won,' was manager Chris Sanigar's verdict, furious at the majority decision that allowed the German to keep his title. The EBU ordered the rematch after judges at a seminar watched the fight tapes and every one scored it a win for Catley!

So the Bristol Boys were off again, this time to Chemnitz in East Germany. Haussler had put two defences in the book since their first fight, taking his record to 20-0, while Glenn had boxed only once, 27 wins against six defeats. But his challenge was all over in round five, with Danilo winning on a technical decision, the cut he sustained in the first round prompting the referee to call a halt and go to the scorecards. Haussler was ahead on all three cards, winner and still champion!

European heavyweight champion, Sinan Samil Sam, had looked less than impressive in stopping nine of his 16 victims but he was up for this one with British and Commonwealth titleholder, Williams, showing a good chin and a big right hand. It was enough to finish Williams in round six of their Berlin match. Danny was under pressure through the first two rounds, but improved in round three. In the fourth he had a new experience; Sam landed a big right hook and Williams was down for the first time in his career. Danny beat the count but was floored again before the bell. He got through the fifth with a standing count but was rocking badly in the sixth and his trainer, Jim McDonnell, threw the towel in. The referee accepted the retirement as Danny told reporters, 'I'm shocked. He raised his game tonight and could really punch.'

British title action saw Jamie McKeever capture the featherweight title vacated by Scott Harrison, with a crushing sixth-round stoppage of his Merseyside rival,

Having won the WBU middleweight title, Anthony Farnell (left) made a successful first defence when forcing Russia's Nikolai Talalakin to retire at the end of the 10th round

Les Clark

Tony Mulholland, at the Everton Park Sports Centre. These two had fought a bloody 10-round war for the Central Area title five months previously, with Birkenhead's McKeever shading it. This time he made no mistake, taking charge of the ring in the first and powering his way to victory in the sixth, vicious body shots finishing the Liverpool man. At 30, Tony remembered the 27 stitches it took to close his wounds in the first bout, and tried to box the younger man off. But McKeever would not be denied and, at 23, he took the Lonsdale Belt home with him. Champion!

Another young man going for a British title was 21-year-old Welshman, Bradley Pryce, but he found the task beyond him as the welterweight champion, Neil Sinclair, outboxed and outpunched his challenger for an eighth-round stoppage at Belfast's Odyssey Arena. Victory was sweetened for the man from Northern Ireland as he won the Lonsdale Belt outright. With trainer, Enzo Calzaghe, and his world champion son, Joe, in the corner, Pryce boxed well through the first four rounds, took a belting in round five and stayed out of trouble until the eighth when it all went pear-shaped. Sinclair dropped Pryce with a solid left hook and he never got over it. Enzo threw the towel in as the third man was moving to stop it.

On the same bill, former British light-welterweight champion, Mark Winters, stopped a game David Kehoe inside two rounds and was looking for another title shot with his eye on the lightweight division. Dublin's Jim Rock wore his pink pants into the ring for the vacant WBU light-middleweight championship fight, but they didn't help him against Takaloo, who ended matters in the ninth round with a booming right to the jaw to regain his old title. The Iranian, aged five when brought to Margate by his parents, has another battle on his hands. To stay in Britain!

A young man in a hurry was Luton's Southern Area lightweight champion, Graham Earl, who clocked up his 17th straight win when he destroyed any future title ambitions that Steve Murray might have still had. In a contest that not only involved the Area title, but also carried a final eliminator for the British title label, Murray, trying to get back in contention following a bad defeat at the hands of Yuri Romanov in September, was rescued by Larry O'Connell at 2.02 of the second round. Having already been decked earlier in the round, the man from Harlow was not returning fire and it was a sensible decision. As for the confident Earl, who even surprised his management team with the speed of his victory, he could look forward with some optimism to a fight against Bobby Vanzie for the British championship.

The poor standard of Commonwealth title challengers was again spotlighted when Duncan Karanja (Kenya) and Frans Hantindi (Namibia) were taken apart by Esham Pickering and James Hare, respectively. At Brentford,

In making his third defence of the Southern Area lightweight title, Graham Earl (left) destroyed Steve Murray and put himself first in line for a crack at Bobby Vanzie and the British title

Les Clark

Pickering, not noted as a puncher, knocked out Karanja in the fifth after decking him twice en-route to claiming the vacant super-bantamweight title, while Hare, a good fighter who can box and punch, destroyed Hantindi in a mere 74 seconds to retain his welterweight title in Huddersfield. The Namibian had been down three times before the end!

On the Huddersfield bill, Spencer Matsangura came from Zimbabwe to contest the vacant flyweight title with the smart local, Dale Robinson, who dropped his man twice to take a comfortable decision. Probably the best of the invaders from the African continent was Misheck Kondwani, who gave Nicky Cook a tough night in Brentford before the Dagenham featherweight took the decision and the vacant title.

The nominal main event at Brentford saw Audley Harrison take his pro log to 9-0 as his first scheduled eight rounder ended when America's Rob Calloway couldn't come up for the fifth round, claiming a damaged jaw. The man from Missouri was dwarfed by the Olympic champion, who came in three stones heavier at 17st 12$\frac{1}{2}$lbs and he was never able to make any kind of impression.

Liverpool's Commonwealth light-middleweight champion, Michael Jones, wanted to give his right elbow a good workout after an operation and 34-year-old Warley veteran, Howard Clarke, gave him what he wanted in a brisk six rounder at the Everton Park Sports Centre. Michael got his win, now 17-0, and Howard got another payday. Delroy Leslie had been WBF middleweight champ, held two Southern Area titles, and won 28 of 35 bouts in a 10-year career. However, John 'Boy' Humphrey convinced Delroy it was time to go when crushing him inside two rounds at Norwich to retain his Southern Area light-middleweight title.

MARCH

Some fighters are just too game for their own good. They don't know when they are beaten, or if they do they refuse to accept it. Some years down the line, long past when the gloves are put away, will it be worth being able to say you were never knocked out, always went the distance? Will people recall that your manager or your corner team was as game as you were, and shake their head as you walk off, your head shaking?

Many observers of the 12-round beating absorbed by Wayne McCullough at the thudding fists of Scott Harrison at Renfrew's Braehead Arena were of the opinion that the former WBC bantamweight champion should have been taken out of the contest anytime from round eight onwards. Either by his corner, his manager (his wife), or the referee, Mr John Coyle.

The scoring reflected the one-sided nature of the fight, with 120-108, 119-109, and 119-108, all in favour of Harrison, who took his record to 19-1-1 in retaining his WBO featherweight championship for the first time with a powerful performance that marked him as one of our better fighters, one almost ready for the likes of Erik Morales, Johnny Tapia, and Marco Antonio Barrera.

Is the other Harrison, heavyweight Audley, one of our better fighters? Well, he thinks he is, and when a man is as big as the former Olympic super-heavyweight champion, you don't argue with him. Ratko Draskovic was the 10th guy to lose an argument with Harrison in the professional ring, but the 37-year-old East European went the eight rounds distance and was still snorting defiance at the final bell. At least Harrison was able to test his stamina against a fellow who had never been stopped, as he completed his 10-fight television contract with the BBC, which earned him one million pounds! Auntie may want more for her money next time.

The gamble of Dean Francis and manager-trainer, Chris Sanigar, backfired in the Wembley ring when the Basingstoke fighter was beaten over 12 rounds by Matthew Barney for the vacant British super-middleweight championship. The gamble was not about money, it was a gamble on being able to win this fight virtually with one hand! Call it arrogance if you like.

Francis had suffered a dislocated right shoulder some four years previously and, despite two operations, was no longer a fully-equipped fighter. In this fight with Barney, his right hand was a passenger, as well it must have been in training for a championship contest of 12 rounds.

Francis admitted as much afterwards, being quoted as saying, 'If I'd had longer to train with the one hand, it might have been different.' He thought he could beat Barney with one hand, and he couldn't. Matthew got what he deserved, and so, too, did Dean Francis.

Liverpool's Peter Culshaw put his WBF super-flyweight championship on the line for Wandee Chareon from Thailand and boxed his way to a comfortable decision on all three cards. It was win number 24 against one loss for Peter. Whether or not the eagerly-awaited meeting with Damaen Kelly ever takes place now that the tall Scouser has stepped up a division we will just have to wait and see.

Another fight to be savoured is the all-Scottish encounter between Edinburgh's Alex Arthur and Glasgow's Willie Limond. Both lads were showcased on the Renfrew bill with Arthur turning in a superb performance to stop South Africa's Patrick Malinga in six rounds to pick up the WBA International super-featherweight belt, while Limond knocked out Walsall's Jimmy Beech in round four with a left hook to the body. Willie took his pro log to 18-0 (6), while Arthur stayed undefeated after stopping 13 of his 15 professional opponents.

Mixed fortunes for Jawaid Khaliq and David Starie in South Africa. Nottingham's Khaliq produced a sensational victory over Jan Bergman to retain his IBO welterweight title, surviving heavy knockdowns in rounds five and six to drop Bergman later in that round and finish him in the seventh. Jan had also been down in the second. Now 32, the former WBU champion's future could all be behind him. There was a shock for Commonwealth super-middleweight champion, Starie, who dropped his title in a bloody encounter with Andre Thysse. The South African had height and reach advantages and his awkward style troubled Starie, who was gashed over the left eye going into round eight. Then Thysse came off worse in a clash of

heads and a bad cut on his forehead. The injury spurred him to violent action and Starie was floored twice in the ninth and struggled to last to the final bell. By then the title had gone, Thysse being an upset winner after just 15 fights, with one defeat.

They love Tony Oakey down there in Portsmouth and he didn't let them down as he outfought Neil Linford over 12 rounds to hang on to his WBU light-heavyweight title for the third time, taking his record to 18-0. These two used to spar together, but there was no love lost when the bell heralded round one and at the final bell Oakey's phenomenal workrate ensured he went home with his belt.

It was a fight too far for Liverpool's Gary Ryder when going against Pablo Sarmiento at York Hall. In 47 fights the Argentinian had beaten Billy Schwer for the IBO light-welter title and retained here against Michael Ayers. In winning 10 fights, Gary had won the WBF title, but wasn't equipped to handle Sarmiento and was stopped in the eighth on a cut eye. Another British lad on the bill lost his unbeaten record (21-0) when Colin Lynes dropped his IBO Inter-Continental light-welterweight title to South Africa's Samuel Malinga. Lynes had been down in the seventh and was marked up badly when his corner pulled him out after the eighth.

APRIL

It was a big one for Ricky Hatton and he won it big! Vince Phillips, although 39, was still a force to reckon with and he was the only pro to beat Hatton's eventual target, the Russian-born world champ, Kostya Tszyu, even if it was six years ago. But the veteran American, himself a former IBF champion (he took the title off Tszyu), did well to finish the 12 rounds against the unstoppable 'Manchester Hitman'. Despite a bad cut over his right eye sustained in the opening round, the local hero, with a packed 14,000 MEN Arena crowd threatening to dislodge the roof, Ricky hammered his way to victory number 32 (24 inside) to stamp his mark on the world scene. Phillips almost didn't make it into the ring that night. He almost didn't make it into the country! Back in Arkansas, Vince owed $18,000 in child maintenance payments, his passport had expired and he was between managers. He only arrived in the UK on the Wednesday before the Saturday fight and just hours before he was due in the ring, he threatened to walk out unless more money was forthcoming. By that time the promoter, Frank Warrren, was considering a career change into international tiddlywinks and to hell with the whole fight business!

Warren even brought Aldo Rios in from Argentina as a stand-by opponent but, at the appointed hour, actually

Boxing on home turf, Jason Booth (right) had his hands full with the South African, Lindi Memani, before coming home on points

Les Clark

some 20 minutes after, it was Vince Phillips who walked to the ring and he fought like a true professional in trying to rip the WBU light-welterweight crown from Hatton's head. But when Ricky gets in the ring, he has tunnel vision, his eyes fixed on the finish line and, so far, he has finished in front. His biggest domestic rival is Junior Witter and the Bradford southpaw beat Belgium's Jurgen Haeck in the chief support to add the European Union belt to his British and Commonwealth titles. The visitor's left eye was a mess when his corner pulled him out after four rounds.

Manchester favourite, Anthony Farnell, lost his WBU middleweight title as Wayne Elcock outboxed him to take the unanimous decision, decking him in the fifth to cement his victory. It was only the Birmingham man's 11th pro outing and, at 29, he is something of a late developer. But he is developing!

Former British super-featherweight champion, Michael Gomez, is punching his way back and racked up his third straight win over the limited Bulgarian, Vladimir Borov, who was stopped with a cut eye in round three. Promising local welterweight, David Barnes, took his pro log to 12-0 with a points win over Ukrainia's Viktor Fesetchko, but the lad has seen better nights.

Commonwealth super-featherweight champion, Dean Pithie, had hoped to defend his title in his Coventry home-town, but when he stepped out against Glasgow's Craig Docherty it was at York Hall and maybe that made the difference. What actually made the difference though was the thudding left hook to the body that dropped Dean in the eighth round and made the points score academic. The Scot, aware that two of Dean's four defeats were from body shots, used the same formula and went home a champion.

Up at heavyweight, Michael Holden used to be a champion, but he lost another one when beaten by Poland's Albert Sosnowski, no disgrace against a man with only one defeat in 28 fights. The Brixton bomber, Ted Bami, hammered out a ninth-round stoppage win over Hungaria's Laszlo Herczeg on the York Hall show to win the vacant WBF light-welterweight title, taking his record to 12-1, and putting his name in the frame for something big.

Sinan Samil Sam, the 'Terrible Turk', who rules heavyweight Europe, feasted on another member of Britain's beef trust when he dropped Julius Francis twice in round seven for the finish, even if the former British champ had done well to that point.

On the same night, in Brentford, Sam's last victim, Danny Williams, won his comeback fight when he blitzed the Australian veteran, Bob Mirovic, in the fourth round to retain his Commonwealth title. On the world scene, Mirovic is so far off he is on another planet, yet for three rounds he was in with a chance, not because he was good, rather because Danny was so bad. Mark his report card, 'Needs to do better!'

Maybe the new face of heavyweight boxing in Britain is that of big Matt Skelton from Bedford who made it five out of five with a second-round knockout over Russia's Alexei Varakin at York Hall. His manager, Frank Maloney, is high on the big fellow and is already looking for Audley Harrison.

Brothers, Howard and Gilbert Eastman, met with mixed fortunes at the Nottingham Ice Arena where Howard retained his British, Commonwealth and European middleweight titles with a third-round stoppage of willing Plymouth southpaw, Scott Dann, to make the Lonsdale Belt his own property. At light-middleweight, Gilbert also finished work that night in round three, but he was a loser against Sheffield's Andrew Facey.

Nottingham's champion brothers, Nicky and Jason Booth, went home winners after a night in the town's Harvey Hadden Centre. Nicky had his work cut out when defending his British bantamweight title against Finchley's Jamie Yelland, who was still punching at the final bell. The British flyweight titleholder, Jason, had his hands full with another South African in Lindi Memani, who offered stubborn resistance to lose on points, surviving a knockdown in the final round of an eight.

It's an ill wind etc, etc. Jamie Moore jumped at the chance to fight Liverpool's unbeaten Michael Jones for his Commonwealth, and the vacant British light-middleweight titles, when Paul Samuels pulled out. Moore boxed out of his skin to take the decision and the titles, becoming the first Salford fighter to win a British championship in over a century!

MAY

The fight with Matthew Ellis at venerable old York Hall brought out the best and the worst in Audley Harrison. As a performance it was one of his best since turning pro after bringing the gold home from Sydney. Blackpool's Ellis was five inches shorter and 32 pounds lighter, but he gave Harrison a fight in a lively opening round, waking Audley up to the fact that he had a tiger by the tail. He was all business in the second round and it was stopped after Ellis had been sent crashing to the boards three times. Good fight. What followed was not so good.

With Herbie Hide stuck in a ringside seat and big Frank Bruno on hand, himself already talking about a comeback at 41, Harrison took the mike and started a promotional spiel, which unfortunately backfired. Badly! Audley wanted Hide removed from ringside where the BBC had, or had not, invited him to join their commentary team... Herbie, a loose cannon with a history of controversial incidents, pushed, or did not, push a woman to the floor... security was inadequate, and there was a nasty disturbance in which chairs were thrown and people were injured.

There had to be a Board of inquiry, of course, and Jess Harding, the promoter, was fined £1,000 with £600 costs, Harrison was fined £1,000 with £600 costs and Hide was fined £500 with £300 costs. And, hopefully, some lessons were learned.

Like Audley Harrison, the Commonwealth featherweight champion, Nicky Cook, had a rough opening round with his challenger, David Kiilu, before getting rid of his man in round two. The tall Kenyan took the first and the champion had a cut under his right eye going to his stool. But Nicky was all business in the second and two sickening rights to the body finished Kiilu, who lost for the third time against 15 wins and a draw. The undefeated Cook, from

Dagenham, took his score to 21-0, 13 inside, and was looking for a shot at the European title.

On another night at York Hall, Takaloo had a tougher job than expected when defending his WBU light-middleweight title against Jose Rosa, from the Dominican Republic, but based in Argentina. The Margate Iranian dumped Rosa heavily in the opening minute with a sizzling left hook. Jose beat the count, but when Takaloo tried to finish him he damaged his right hand on the visitor's hard head. From then on, the champion played it safe and boxed his way to a unanimous decision.

Football had 'Roy of the Rovers', now boxing has 'Roy from Liverpool' in Roy Rutherford, a 29-year-old featherweight from Coventry who had boxed only once in a year-and-a-half. On two weeks notice, Roy was offered the chance to meet the British champion, Jamie McKeever, for his title at Everton Park Sports Centre. Yes please! It was not a good night for Jamie; he damaged his left hand, was cut by the right eye, and was floored, all inside three rounds! But he carried on to the end when he saw his Lonsdale Belt being fastened around the slim waist of Roy Rutherford, Britain's new featherweight champion.

When Roy gets around to defending his new title, he may find Dazzo Williams in the other corner. The Hereford-based cockney powered his way to a thrilling victory in a title eliminator, edging out Rugely's Steve Chinnock over 10 gruelling rounds that saw both lads on the deck and Dazzo finishing with both eyes banged up.

South African veteran, Zolile Mbityi, had failed in previous title tilts at Peter Culshaw and Damaen Kelly and now, at 33, he was back to try again, this time against new Commonwealth flyweight champion, Dale Robinson, in Huddersfield. The Yorkshireman was undefeated in 12 pro contests. He was also 10 years younger than Zolile and this told over the closing rounds as Robinson boxed his way to a 115-113 points victory. He's getting there.

Former Southern Area welterweight champion, David Walker, bounced back at light-middleweight to rack up a brutal knockout of John 'Boy' Humphrey at Dagenham's Goresbrook Leisure Centre. The fight was for Humphrey's Southern Area title and was also recognised as a title eliminator for the British championship. Since losing his own title to Jimmy Vincent on a shock kayo, Walker had won two at the higher weight without impressing. His second round annihilation of the Newmarket man was impressive, and it looked like 'Kid Dynamite' was back on track.

In September 2001, Herbie Hide was flattened inside two violent rounds by veteran Zambian, Joseph Chingangu. On the Dagenham bill, the former British and WBO heavyweight champion destroyed his conqueror in just 2.33

After damaging his right hand in the first session, Takaloo (right), defending the WBU light-middleweight title, had to content himself with a points win over a durable opponent in Jose Rosa

Les Clark

of a wild first round and was looking for a fight with the man he calls 'Audrey' Harrison. Maybe one day...

Stephen Smith returned to boxing after the fight he would rather forget, the night his father entered the ring thus ending his challenge to Ricky Hatton. Stephen had said he would quit the sport but now he was back and still with something to offer, taking an eight-rounds decision over fellow-southpaw, Jon Honney, and his log to 32-2.

Miami in May is nice and for Russian-born British-based Israeli heavyweight, Roman Greenberg, it was even nicer with a couple of undemanding wins, stopping Tracy Williams and Troy Beets a couple of weeks apart. Williams stayed on his stool after two rounds, claiming a broken nose, while Beets was stopped in the third, indicating to the referee that one of his ears wasn't working properly. Greenberg is now 11-0.

At Clevedon, Jane Couch, the self-styled 'Fleetwood Assassin,' worked hard to take the eight-round decision over Ukrainia's Larisa Berezenko to take her log to 20-4.

Former British welterweight champion, Derek Roche, was too good for Welsh title-holder, Jason Williams, who was floored twice in round two before it was called off by the referee.

JUNE

When Lennox Lewis annihilated Mike Tyson, like most of you reading this, I said, 'Okay, that's it, you're 'The Man', walk away, there's nothing more to prove, nobody else to fight. Even the Americans admit you're the best, a worthy heavyweight champion of the world. Exit stage left.'

Lennox didn't listen. He didn't listen to his mother, Violet. He didn't listen to his trainer, Emanuel Steward. So he sure as hell wasn't going to listen to me! Or you! This month, in Los Angeles, after he had beaten Vitali Klitschko, there must have been a time when Lennox wished he had walked away after the Tyson fight. But he didn't. He agreed to fight Kirk Johnson, which probably wouldn't have stretched him too much, but with two weeks to go Johnson pulled out with an injury and Lewis was in with Vitali Klitschko, who was in training for another fight.

That night at the Staples Centre, the champ was overweight, his work was sloppy and he was in trouble. Klitschko was a giant at six-foot-seven, his ramrod fists had stopped 31 of 32 victims, and he was hitting Lewis more than Lewis was hitting him. Vitali won the first two rounds and people were sitting up and taking notice, this big guy looks good! He didn't look so good in the third round when a big right hand opened a horrific gash under his left eyebrow.

Now it was a fight and the giant Ukrainian was winning it! But his face was a mess, bloody from the big cut and two more on his left cheek, and in the sixth a Lewis uppercut tore his mouth open. As the round ended, the doctor took a look at the damage and indicated to the referee that this fight was over. Lennox Lewis was the winner and still champion of the world. But the cheers of the crowd were for the beaten challenger, Vitali Klitschko,

and back home we were all saying, 'Lennox, you should have listened to us.' Maybe he wished he had!

WBO super-middleweight champion, Joe Calzaghe, set Cardiff's International Arena alight with a blazing two-round stoppage of former WBA champ, Byron Mitchell, to retain his title for the umpteenth time and take his unbeaten record to 36-0 (29 inside) in his 10-year pro career. But this is probably as good as Joe is going to get because the fights he wants aren't going to happen. Sven Ottke? Maybe, if Joe goes to Germany and takes less money. Bernard Hopkins? Maybe, if Joe goes to America and Hopkins gets all the money! Well, Joe is a mere 31. Hopkins is 38, Ottke is 36. They can't go on forever.

The way Calzaghe fought Mitchell he looks good for another 10 years. He outpunched the man from Alabama in the first round and stepped up a gear coming out for round two. But Mitchell set himself, loaded up on his punches, and a solid right hook smacked against Joe's chin and he went down for the first time in his career, amateur and pro. As the 5,000 fans held their breath, Calzaghe got quickly to his feet to take the mandatory eight count, then stormed into Mitchell with renewed fury to drop him for a count. No sooner was the American on his feet then Joe was on him and, as he staggered back into the ropes, Mitchell was pulled out by the referee.

In the chief support, Swansea's Enzo Maccarinelli survived a brutal knockdown in the first round to hammer his way to a fourth-round knockout victory over former British and Commonwealth cruiser champion, Bruce Scott, taking his log to 14-1 and winning the vacant WBU title. At 6ft 4in, the powerful Welsh boy is a tall order for anyone.

Joe Calzaghe may not have to worry about Sven Ottke. After retaining his IBF/WBA titles against David Starie in Magdeburg, the veteran told his fans, 'I may box again, but this may be my last time.' Sven looked favoured by the unanimous decision that gave him victory and had Starie tried a little harder, the former British and Commonwealth champion may well have upset the odds and come home a winner.

Like Joe Calzaghe, the Manchester featherweight, Michael Brodie, is another fighter looking for that big fight to define his career. The one he wanted was Naseem Hamed, but that one isn't going to happen. A pity, because Brodie is a good fighter. He proved it again in front of the hometown fans although not enough of them turned out to fill the MEN Arena. They missed a good fight as Michael beat tough Argentinian, Juan Cabrera, over 12 rounds to win the vacant IBO championship and take his record to 35-1 and that one defeat, to Willie Jorrin for the WBC super-bantam belt, was questionable to say the least.

In a clash of southpaws at Sheffield, Noel Wilders lost his hold on the European bantamweight title when he was ruthlessly stopped in seven rounds by tough David Guerault. The Frenchman was given *cart blanche* by the Spanish referee as he roughed up the Yorkshire lad, who was a mess when it was stopped.

Liverpool southpaw, David Burke, was out of luck going for the vacant European lightweight title in Trieste

where the Italian veteran, Stefano Zoff, came out with the decision. In supporting bouts, Derek Roche survived a rough six rounds to beat awkward Silvio Rojas and Hartlepool's WBF super-bantam boss, Michael Hunter, enjoyed his first pro job abroad as he stopped Afrim Mustafa inside five rounds. James Hare moved to 27-0-1 and picked up the vacant WBF welterweight belt in Manchester when he romped to a decision over the gritty Ukrainian, Roman Dzuman, who survived a second round knockdown. Southpaw, Sergio Martinez, took the IBO light-middleweight title home with him to Argentina after upsetting Richard Williams on a unanimous decision. Floored himself in rounds three and 11, Martinez fought back to deck Williams and almost stop him in the final round. Brian Magee retained his IBO super-middleweight title for the fourth time with a fine 10th-round stoppage over South African, Andre Thysse, the conqueror of David Starie.

John Jarrett's new book titled, *Gene Tunney: The Golden Guy Who Licked Jack Dempsey Twice* is now on sale at £16.95 from all good bookshops. A much needed superb biography on one of the great champions, in hardback, there are 285 pages, including an index, and eight pages of b/w grainy photographs. Published by Robson Books, it is a must for boxing fans everywhere.

Facts and Figures, 2002-2003

There were 601 (612 in 2001-2002) British-based boxers who were active between 1 July 2002 and 30 June 2003, spread over 198 (185 in 2001-2002) promotions held in Britain, not including the Republic of Ireland, during the same period. The 601 fighters active during 2002-2003 comprised 470 men already holding licenses, or having been re-licensed, and 131 (111 in 2001-2002) new professionals. These figures include four women – Cathy Brown, Jane Couch, Laura Norton and Juliette Winter - and six foreign-born boxers – Charden Ansoula, Patrick Cito, Varuzhan Davtyan, Ossie Duran, Cristian Hodorogea and Choi Tseveenpurev – who began their careers elsewhere but are now domiciled in Britain.

Unbeaten During Season (Minimum Qualification: 6 Contests)

8: Roman Greenberg. 7: Adnan Amar, Tony Moran. 6: Steve Foster, Carl Froch, Audley Harrison, Lee McAllister, Matt Skelton, Jeff Thomas (1 draw).

Longest Unbeaten Sequence (Minimum Qualification: 10 Contests)

36: Joe Calzaghe. 32: Ricky Hatton. 27: James Hare (1 draw). 23: Oscar Hall (1 draw). 22: Thomas McDonagh (2 draws). 21: Nicky Cook. 20: Steven Bendall, Gavin Rees. 19: Michael Jennings, Brian Magee. 18: Graham Earl, Willie Limond, Tony Oakey. 16: Jawaid Khaliq, John McDermott. 14: Elvis Michailenko (1 draw). 15: Alex Arthur, Jason Cook, Michael Hunter (1 draw). 14: Kevin Lear. 13: Dale Robinson. 12: David Barnes, Peter Culshaw. 11: Wayne Elcock, Roman Greenberg, Audley Harrison, Andrew Lowe, Enzo Maccarinelli, Lawrence Murphy (1 draw), Ajose Olusegun, Junior Witter. 10: Ted Bami, Steve Foster, Tony Moran, Young Muttley.

Most Wins During Season (Minimum Qualification: 6 Contests)

8: Roman Greenberg. 7: Adnan Amar, Andy Halder, Tony Moran. 6: Steve Foster, Carl Froch, Audley Harrison, Lee McAllister, Matt Skelton.

Most Contests During Season (Minimum Qualification: 10 Contests)

19: Pete Buckley. 17: Paul Bonson, Daniel Thorpe. 14: Dave Clarke, Ernie Smith. 13: Keith Jones, Jason Nesbitt, Joel Viney. 12: Tony Booth, Arv Mittoo. 11: Leigh Wicks. 10: Darren Ashton, Jason Collins, Mark Phillips.

Most Contests During Career (Minimum Qualification: 50 Contests)

203: Pete Buckley. 145: Brian Coleman. 125: Tony Booth. 90: Keith Jones. 88: Paul Bonson. 86: Nigel Senior, Karl Taylor. 83: Arv Mittoo. 82: Anthony Hanna. 79: Leigh Wicks. 72: Darren Ashton, Michael Pinnock. 71: Harry Butler. 70: Paul Wesley. 69: Wayne Shepherd. 68: Ojay Abrahams. 67: Howard Clarke. 63: Ernie Smith, Gary Williams. 60: David Kirk. 57: Dave Hinds. 56: Johnny Nelson. 53: Carl Allen.

Stop Press: Results for July/August 2002

The International Centre, Brentwood – 5 July (Promoter: Matchroom/Prince Promotions)

Nathan Sting w rtd 11 John Armour (WBU Bantamweight Title). Kevin Bennett w rsc 2 Colin Dunne. Mark Payne w pts 6 Marc Callaghan. Kevin Anderson w co 2 Mohamed Bourhis. Albsert Sosnowski w rsc 2 Jason Brewster. Barry Morrison w rsc 3 Cristian Hodorogea. Darren Rhodes w rsc 3 Darren Bruce. Steve Conway w rsc 4 Dariusz Snarski. Allan Foster w pts 4 Ojay Abrahams. Michael Lomax w pts 4 Ernie Smith.

Dessau, Germany – 5 July

Dirk Dzemski w pts 12 Allan Gray (NBA Middleweight Title)

Dolphin Leisure Centre, Darlington – 11 July (Promoter: Garside)

Oscar Hall w pts 8 William Webster. Isaac Ward drew 4

Rocky Dean. Ben Coward w pts 6 Dave Pearson. Franny Jones w rsc 2 Gary Cummings. Lee McAllister w rtd 2 John-Paul Ryan.

Braehead Arena, Renfrew – 12 July (Promoter: Sports Network)
Manuel Medina w pts 12 Scott Harrison (WBO Featherweight Title). Alex Arthur w rsc 8 Willie Limond (British S.Featherweight Title). Esham Pickering w rsc 4 Brian Carr (British & Commonwealth S.Bantamweight Titles). Kevin McIntyre w pts 4 Paul Denton. Steve Foster w rtd 3 David McIntyre. Lawrence Murphy w pts 4 Jason Collins. Gary Young w pts 4 Lee Williamson. Colin Bain w pts 4 Gareth Wiltshaw. George Telfer w pts 4 Pete Buckley.

Beverley Hills, Los Angeles, California – 15 July
David Haye w rsc 1 Vance Wynn.
Bescot Stadium, Walsall – 17 July (Promoter: Bradley)
Peter Jackson w pts 10 Mike Duffield (Midlands Area S.Middleweight Title). Dean Hickman w pts 6 Lee McAllister. Young Muttley w pts 4 Tony Montana.

Goresbrook Leisure Centre, Dagenham – 17 July (Promoter: Sports Network)
Graham Earl w pts 12 Bobby Vanzie (British Lightweight Title). David Barnes w pts 12 Jimmy Vincent (British Welterweight Title). Matt Skelton w rsc 4 Antoine Palatis. Matthew Hatton w rsc 1 Jay Mahoney. Kevin Mitchell w co 1 Stevie Quinn. Haider Ali w pts 4 Jason Nesbitt. Martin Power w pts 6 Darren Cleary. Gokhan Kazaz w pts 4 Joel Ani.

York Hall, Bethnal Green, London – 22 July (Promoter: Maloney)
Bobby Banghar w pts 6 Karim Hussine. Chas Simmonds w pts 6 Pete Buckley. Gary Woolcombe w pts 6 Arv Mittoo. Ashley Theophane w pts 6 Brian Coleman. Rob Jeffries w pts 6 Jaz Virdee.

Making the second defence of his newly won European middleweight title, Howard Eastman (right) forced the Frenchman, Hacine Cherifi, to quit at the end of the eighth

Les Clark

The Sports Village, Norwich – 25 July (Promoter: Hennessy Sports)
Howard Eastman w rtd 8 Hacine Cherifi (European Middleweight Title). David Walker w rsc 4 Spencer Fearon (Southern Area L.Middleweight Title). Alan Bosworth w rsc 5 Gavin Down (British Title Eliminator & British Masters L.Welterweight Title). Steven Spartacus w co 3 Simeon Cover (British Masters L.Heavyweight Title). Lenny Daws w rtd 2 Karl Taylor. Ryan Rhodes w rsc 5 Alan Gilbert. Gilbert Eastman w rsc 1 Jason Collins. Jackson Williams w pts 4 Paul Rushton. Danny Smith w pts 4 William Webster. Daniel Cadman w pts 4 Leigh Wicks.

The Pavilions, Plymouth – 26 July (Promoter: Matchroom/Prince Promotions)
Samuel Malinga w rsc 3 Ted Bami (WBF L.Welterweight Title). Adrian Stone w rsc 4 Farai Musiiwa. Scott Dann w rsc 2 Kreshnik Qato. Michael Hunter w rsc 1 Rocky Dean. Jon Honney w pts 6 Michael Ayers. Tony Dodson w rtd 3 Varuzhan Davtyan. Kelly Oliver w pts 4 Tony Booth. Danie Venter w rsc 1 Collice Mutizwa. Andrew Ferrans drew 4 Baz Carey. Simon Goodwin w pts 4 Marcus Lee.

Octagon Centre, Sheffield – 31 July (Promoter: Hobson)
Denzil Browne w rsc 6 Phill Day. Mark Brookes w pts 6 Hastings Rasani. Amer Khan w pts 6 Michael Pinnock. Paul Owen w pts 6 Patrick Cito.

York Hall, Bethnal Green, London – 1 August (Promoter: Lion Promotions)
Charles Adamu w pts 12 Matthew Barney (Commonwealth S.Middleweight Title). Michael Sprott w rsc 1 Colin Kenna (Southern Area Heavyweight Title). Brett James w pts 10 Sammy Smith (Southern Area Welterweight Title). Mark Krence w pts 4 Dereck McCafferty. David Haye w co 1 Greg Scott-Briggs. Dave Stewart w rtd 2 Norman Dhalie. Ryan Walls w pts 4 Darren Ashton. Mark Alexander w pts 4 Arv Mittoo. Arthur Shekhmurzov w pts 6 Howard Clarke. Pete Buckley w pts 4 Jas Malik.

Copley Centre, Stalybridge – 3 August (Promoter: Ingle)
Donovan Smillie w pts 6 William Webster. Ali Nuumembe w pts 6 Lee Williamson. Lee McAllister w pts 4 Brian Coleman. Jonathan Woollins w rsc 1 Chris Duggan. Joel Viney w pts 6 Daniel Thorpe.

Brockton, Mass, USA – 9 August
Kevin McBride w co 1 Lenzie Morgan.

Everton Park Sports Centre, Liverpool – 29 August (Promoter: Vaughan)
Paul Smith w pts 4 Patrick Cito. Gary Thornhill w rsc 1 Jason Nesbitt. Steve Mullin w pts 6 Peter Allen. Carl Wall w pts 6 Jimi Hendricks. Ali Nuumbembe w pts 6 Ernie Smith. Derry Matthews w rtd 2 Marty Kayes.

EVANS-WATERMAN PROMOTIONS

Licensed to the British Boxing Board of Control

Members of the Professional Boxing Promoters' Association

**88 WINDSOR ROAD
BRAY, MAIDENHEAD
BERKS SL6 2DJ
Tel: 01628 623640 Fax: 01628 684633 Mobile: 07768 954643**

e-mail: jimbox@tinyworld.co.uk

CURRENT LIST

HEAVYWEIGHTS		
Roman Greenberg	–	6-8 Rounds
Jacklord Jacobs	–	6-8 Rounds
Keith Fletcher	–	4-6 Rounds

CRUISERWEIGHTS		
Tommy Eastwood	–	6-8 Rounds
Shpetim Hoti	–	4-6 Rounds
Matthew Ellis	–	6-8-10 Rounds

LIGHT-HEAVYWEIGHTS		
Jamie Hearn	–	6-8 Rounds
Peter Haymer	–	6-8 Rounds
Egbui "Abs" Ikeagwo	–	4-6 Rounds

SUPER-MIDDLEWEIGHT		
Gareth Lawrence	–	4-6 Rounds Debut

MIDDLEWEIGHTS		
Matthew Barr	–	6-8 Rounds
Alan Gilbert	–	6-8 Rounds
Dean Powell	–	6-8 Rounds
Mo	–	4-6 Rounds

LIGHT-MIDDLEWEIGHTS		
Geard Ajetovic	–	6-8 Rounds
Scott Spencer	–	4-6 Rounds
Rocky Muscus	–	4-6 Rounds

WELTERWEIGHT		
Robert Lloyd-Taylor	–	6-8 Rounds

LIGHT-WELTERWEIGHT		
Nathan Ward	–	6-8 Rounds

LIGHTWEIGHTS		
Jon Honney	–	6-8-10 Rounds
Chris McDonagh	–	4-6 Rounds
Colin Wilson	–	4-6 Rounds Debut

SUPER-FEATHERWEIGHT		
No-No Junior	–	6-8 Rounds

JIM EVANS STABLE OF TRAINERS:-

Johnny Bloomfield
Darren Whitman
James Cook
Johnny Eames

WEST LONDON'S FASTEST RISING STABLE

Diary of British Boxing Tournaments, 2002-2003

Tournaments are listed by date, town, venue and promoter, and cover the period 1 July 2002 – 30 June 2003

Code: SC = Sporting Club

Date	Town	Venue	Promoters
08.07.02	Mayfair	Grosvenor House Hotel	Sports Network
10.07.02	Wembley	Conference Centre	Harding
12.07.02	Southampton	The Guildhall	Bishop
13.07.02	Coventry	The Skydome	Matchroom/Prince Promotions
13.07.02	Wolverhampton	Light Bar	Bradley
20.07.02	Bethnal Green	York Hall	Sports Network
21.07.02	Salford	The Willows	Viking Promotions
27.07.02	Nottingham	Harvey Hadden Leisure Centre	Matchroom
03.08.02	Blackpool	Norbreck Castle Hotel	Garside
03.08.02	Derby	Storm Centre	Evans-Waterman Promotions
17.08.02	Cardiff	The Castle	Sports Network
23.08.02	Bethnal Green	York Hall	Burns/Hennessy Sports
06.09.02	Bethnal Green	York Hall	Lion Promotions
06.09.02	Glasgow	Thistle Hotel	Morrison
07.09.02	Liverpool	Everton Park Sports Centre	Matchroom/Prince Promotions
08.09.02	Wolverhampton	Light Bar	Bradley
14.09.02	Newark	Grove Leisure Centre	Dalton
14.09.02	Bethnal Green	York Hall	Sports Network
15.09.02	Swansea	Leisure Centre	Boyce
17.09.02	Bethnal Green	York Hall	Lion Promotions
21.09.02	Brentwood	International Centre	Matchroom/Prince Promotions
21.09.02	Norwich	Sports Village	Ingle
22.09.02	Southwark	Elephant & Castle Leisure Centre	Maloney
23.09.02	Glasgow	Holiday Inn	St Andrew's SC
23.09.02	Cleethorpes	Winter Gardens	Dalton
26.09.02	Fulham	Paragon Hotel	Jacobs
26.09.02	Hull	Willerby Manor Hotel	Pollard
27.09.02	Bracknell	Sports Centre	Evans-Waterman Promotions
28.09.02	Manchester	MEN Arena	Sports Network
28.09.02	Wakefield	Light Waves Leisure Centre	Prince Promotions
29.09.02	Shrewsbury	Butter Market Nightclub	Cowdell
03.10.02	Sunderland	Marriott Hotel	Conroy
05.10.02	Chesterfield	Queens Park Sports Centre	Ingle/Hobson
05.10.02	Coventry	AT 7 Centre	Capitol Promotions
05.10.02	Liverpool	Olympia	Harding
05.10.02	Huddersfield	Leisure Centre	Matchroom/Prince Promotions
06.10.02	Rhyl	The Marina	P. Williams
07.10.02	Birmingham	Burlington Hotel	Cowdell
08.10.02	Glasgow	Hilton Hotel	Evans-Waterman Promotions
10.10.02	Stoke	Kings Hall	Brogan
10.10.02	Piccadilly	Cafe Royal	National SC
12.10.02	Bethnal Green	York Hall	Sports Network
15.10.02	Bethnal Green	York Hall	Evans-Waterman Promotions
18.10.02	Hartlepool	Jesters Leisure Centre	Garside
19.10.02	Renfrew	Braehead Arena	Sports Network
19.10.02	Norwich	Sports Village	Peacock Promotions
20.10.02	Southwark	Elephant & Castle Leisure Centre	Honeyghan
21.10.02	Cleethorpes	Winter Gardens	Frater
21.10.02	Glasgow	Holiday Inn	St Andrew's SC
25.10.02	Millwall	Britannia Hotel	Peacock Promotions
25.10.02	Bethnal Green	York Hall	Hennessy Sports
25.10.02	Cotgrave	Welfare Centre	Loftus

26.10.02	Maesteg	Sports Centre	Matchroom/Prince Promotions
26.10.02	Wigan	Robin Park Centre	Veitch
27.10.02	Southwark	Elephant & Castle Leisure Centre	Maloney
30.10.02	Leicester Square	Equinox Nightclub	World Sports Organisation/Pyle
01.11.02	Preston	The Guildhall	P. Williams
02.11.02	Belfast	Maysfield Leisure Centre	Sports Network
02.11.02	Wolverhampton	Light Bar	Bradley
08.11.02	Doncaster	The Dome	Rushton
09.11.02	Altrincham	Leisure Centre	Matchroom/Prince Promotions
12.11.02	Leeds	Elland Road (Leeds United FC)	Spratt
16.11.02	Nottingham	Harvey Hadden Leisure Centre	Matchroom/Prince Promotions
16.11.02	Coventry	Leofric Hotel	Capitol Promotions
17.11.02	Shaw	Tara Sports & Leisure Centre	Tara Promotions
17.11.02	Bradford	Hanover International Hotel	Ingle
18.11.02	Glasgow	Holiday Inn	St Andrew's SC
20.11.02	Leeds	Irish Centre	Walker
21.11.02	Hull	City Hall	Pollard
23.11.02	Derby	Storm Arena	Sports Network
27.11.02	Mayfair	Hilton Hotel	Evans-Waterman Promotions
28.11.02	Finchley	Kinloss Suite	Evans-Waterman Promotions
29.11.02	Hull	Myton Suite	Hull & District SC
29.11.02	Liverpool	Olympia	Harding
30.11.02	Liverpool	Everton Park Sports Centre	Matchroom/Prince Promotions
30.11.02	Newark	Grove Leisure Centre	Dalton
30.11.02	Coventry	AT 7 Centre	Capitol Promotions
02.12.02	Bradford	Hilton Hotel	Yorkshire Executive SC
02.12.02	Leeds	Le Meridien Hotel	Walker
02.12.02	Leicester	Ramada Jarvis Hotel	Griffin
03.12.02	Bethnal Green	York Hall	Evans-Waterman Promotions
03.12.02	Shrewsbury	Albrighton Hotel	Cowdell
05.12.02	Sunderland	Marriott Hotel	Conroy
05.12.02	Sheffield	Moat House Hotel	Hobson
07.12.02	Brentwood	International Centre	Matchroom/Prince Promotions
08.12.02	Bethnal Green	York Hall	Maloney
08.12.02	Bristol	Thistle Grand Hotel	Couch
08.12.02	Glasgow	Thistle Hotel	Morrison
09.12.02	Nottingham	Holiday Inn	Loftus
09.12.02	Birmingham	Burlington Hotel	Cowdell
11.12.02	Hull	Willerby Manor Hotel	Pollard
12.12.02	Leicester Square	Equinox Nightclub	World Sports Organisation/Pyle
14.12.02	Newcastle	Telewest Arena	Sports Network
16.12.02	Cleethorpes	Winter Gardens	Dalton
20.12.02	Bracknell	Leisure Club	Evans-Waterman Promotions
21.12.02	Dagenham	Goresbrook Leisure Centre	Hennessy Sports
21.12.02	Millwall	Britannia Hotel	Peacock Promotions
22.12.02	Salford	The Willows	Viking Promotions
08.01.03	Aberdare	Sobell Sports Centre	Boyce
18.01.03	Preston	The Guildhall	Sports Network
20.01.03	Glasgow	Holiday Inn	St Andrew's SC
24.01.03	Sheffield	Ponds Forge Leisure Centre	Evans-Waterman Promotions/Hobson
25.01.03	Bridgend	Recreation Centre	Matchroom/Prince Promotions
28.01.03	Nottingham	Ice Rink	Hennessy Sports
30.01.03	Piccadilly	Cafe Royal	National SC
01.02.03	Belfast	Odssey Arena	Sports Network
03.02.03	Bradford	Hilton Hotel	Yorkshire Executive SC
08.02.03	Liverpool	Everton Park Sports Centre	Matchroom/Prince Promotions
08.02.03	Brentford	Fountain Leisure Centre	Harding
08.02.03	Norwich	Sports Village	Peacock Promotions
09.02.03	Bradford	Hanover International Hotel	Ingle

10.02.03	Sheffield	Intake Embassy Club	Rhodes
15.02.03	Wembley	Conference Centre	Sports Network
15.02.03	Wolverhampton	Light Bar	Bradley
16.02.03	Salford	The Willows	Viking Promotions
17.02.03	Glasgow	Holiday Inn	St Andrew's SC
18.02.03	Bethnal Green	York Hall	Maloney
21.02.03	Doncaster	The Dome	Rushton
22.02.03	Huddersfield	Leisure Centre	Matchroom/Prince Promotions
23.02.03	Shrewsbury	Butter Market Nightclub	Cowdell
23.02.03	Streatham	Caesar's Nightclub	Pyle
23.02.03	Aberystwyth	Arts Centre	G. Williams
24.02.03	Birmingham	Burlington Hotel	Cowdell
26.02.03	Bristol	Marriott Hotel	Couch
27.02.03	Sunderland	Marriott Hotel	Conroy
28.02.03	Irvine	Volunteer Rooms	St Andrew's SC
05.03.03	Bethnal Green	York Hall	Hennessy Sports
14.03.03	Glasgow	Thistle Hotel	Morrison
06.03.03	Bristol	Ashton Gate (Bristol City FC)	Sanigar
08.03.03	Coventry	AT 7 Centre	Capitol Promotions
08.03.03	Bethnal Green	York Hall	Matchroom/Prince Promotions
09.03.03	Shaw	Tara Leisure Centre	Tara Promotions
16.03.03	Nottingham	Victoria Leisure Centre	Ingle
17.03.03	Southampton	The Guildhall	Bishop
17.03.03	Glasgow	Holiday Inn	St Andrew's SC
18.03.03	Reading	Rivermead Leisure Centre	Evans-Waterman Promotions/Hobson
20.03.03	Queensway	Porchester Hall	Jacobs
21.03.03	Longford	Heathrow Thistle Hotel	Currivan
21.03.03	West Bromwich	Gala Baths	Bradley
22.03.03	Renfrew	Braehead Arena	Sports Network
22.03.03	Coventry	Leofric Hotel	Capitol Promotions
24.03.03	Barnsley	The Metrodome	Koncrete Promotions
28.03.03	Millwall	Britannia Hotel	Peacock Promotions
29.03.03	Portsmouth	Mountbatten Centre	Sports Network
29.03.03	Wembley	Conference Centre	Harding
03.04.03	Hull	Willerby Manor Hotel	Pollard
05.04.03	Manchester	MEN Arena	Sports Network
05.04.03	Coventry	Leofric Hotel	Coventry SC
05.04.03	Belfast	Ulster Hall	McCausland
08.04.03	Bethnal Green	York Hall	Maloney
10.04.03	Clydach	Manor Park Country House	Boyce
12.04.03	Bethnal Green	York Hall	Matchroom/Prince Promotions
12.04.03	Norwich	Sports Village	Ingle
13.04.03	Bradford	Pennington's Nightclub	Ingle
13.04.03	Streatham	Caesar's Nightclub	Pyle
14.04.03	Glasgow	Holiday Inn	St Andrew's SC
16.04.03	Nottingham	Ice Rink	Hennessy Sports
17.04.03	Hull	The Stadium	Pollard
19.04.03	Liverpool	Everton Park Sports Centre	Matchroom/Prince Promotions
26.04.03	Brentford	Fountain Leisure Centre	Lion Promotions
28.04.03	Cleethorpes	Winter Gardens	Frater
28.04.03	Nottingham	Harvey Hadden Leisure Centre	Matchroom/Prince Promotions
07.05.03	Ellesmere Port	Civic Centre	P. Williams
08.05.03	Widnes	Kingsway Leisure Centre	Sports Network
09.05.03	Doncaster	The Dome	Rushton
09.05.03	Longford	Heathrow Thistle Hotel	Currivan
10.05.03	Huddersfield	Leisure Centre	Matchroom/Prince Promotions
12.05.03	Birmingham	Burlington Hotel	Cowdell
12.05.03	Southampton	The Guildhall	Bishop
13.05.03	Leeds	Elland Road (Leeds United FC)	Spratt

15.05.03	Clevedon	Hand Stadium	Couch
15.05.03	Mayfair	Marriott Hotel	Maloney
16.05.03	Glasgow	Thistle Hotel	Morrison
17.05.03	Liverpool	Everton Park Sports Centre	Matchroom/Prince Promotions
24.05.03	Sheffield	Concorde Centre	Rhodes
24.05.03	Bethnal Green	York Hall	Sports Network
27.05.03	Dagenham	Goresbrook Leisure Centre	Hennessy
29.05.03	Sunderland	Marriott Hotel	Conroy
31.05.03	Barnsley	The Metrodome	Koncrete Promotions
31.05.03	Bethnal Green	York Hall	Harding
02.06.03	Glasgow	Holiday Inn	St Andrew's SC
02.06.03	Cleethorpes	Winter Gardens	Dalton
03.06.03	Bethnal Green	York Hall	Maloney
06.06.03	Norwich	Sports Village	Featherby
06.06.03	Hull	KC Sports Stadium Banqueting Hall	Hull & District SC
07.06.03	Coventry	AT 7 Centre	Capitol Promotions
08.06.03	Nottingham	Victoria Leisure Centre	Ingle
08.06.03	Shaw	Tara Sports & Leisure Centre	Tara Promotions
09.06.03	Bradford	Hilton Hotel	Yorkshire Executive SC
10.06.03	Sheffield	Ponds Forge Leisure Centre	Evans-Waterman Promotions/Hobson
13.06.03	Bristol	Ashton Gate (Bristol City FC)	Sanigar
13.06.03	Queensway	Porchester Hall	Merton
15.06.03	Bradford	Pennington's Nightclub	Ingle
20.06.03	Gatwick	Effingham Park Hotel	Pyle
20.06.03	Liverpool	Everton Park Sports Centre	Vaughan
21.06.03	Manchester	MEN Arena	Matchroom/Prince Promotions
28.06.03	Cardiff	International Arena	Sports Network
30.06.03	Shrewsbury	Lord Hill Hotel	Bradley

Active British-Based Boxers: Career Records

Shows the complete record for all British-based boxers who have been active between 1 July 2002 and 30 June 2003. Names in brackets are real names, where they differ from ring names, and the first place name given is the boxer's domicile. Boxers are either shown as being self-managed or with a named manager, the information being supplied by the BBBoC shortly before going to press. Also included are foreign-born fighters who made their pro debuts in Britain, along with others like Charden Ansoula (Congo), Patrick Cito (Congo), Varuzhan Davtyan (Armenia), Ossie Duran (Ghana), Cristian Hodorogea (Romania) and Choi Tseveenpurev (Mongolia), who, although starting their careers elsewhere, now hold BBBoC licenses.

Ojay Abrahams

Watford. *Born* Lambeth, 17 December, 1964
Middleweight. Former British Masters
Middleweight Champion. Ht. 5'8½"
Manager A. Ayling

21.09.91	Gordon Webster W RSC 3 Tottenham
26.10.91	Mick Reid W RSC 5 Brentwood
26.11.91	John Corcoran W PTS 6 Bethnal Green
21.01.92	Dave Andrews DREW 6 Norwich
31.03.92	Marty Duke W RSC 2 Norwich
19.05.92	Michael Smyth L PTS 6 Cardiff
16.06.92	Ricky Mabbett W PTS 6 Dagenham
13.10.92	Vince Rose L RSC 3 Mayfair
30.01.93	Vince Rose DREW 6 Brentwood
19.05.93	Ricky Mabbett L RSC 4 Leicester
18.09.93	Ricky Mabbett L PTS 6 Leicester
09.12.93	Nick Appiah W PTS 6 Watford
24.01.94	Errol McDonald W RSC 2 Glasgow
09.02.94	Vince Rose W PTS 6 Brentwood
23.05.94	Spencer McCracken L PTS 6 Walsall
11.06.94	Darren Dyer W RSC 1 Bethnal Green
29.09.94	Gary Logan L PTS 10 Bethnal Green
	(Southern Area Welterweight Title Challenge)
13.12.94	Geoff McCreesh L PTS 6 Potters Bar
11.02.95	Gary Murray L PTS 8 Hamanskraal, South Africa
17.07.95	Andreas Panayi L PTS 8 Mayfair
02.10.95	Larbi Mohammed L RTD 5 Mayfair
08.12.95	Jason Beard W CO 2 Bethnal Green
09.04.96	Kevin Thompson W RSC 3 Stevenage
07.05.96	Harry Dhami L RSC 5 Mayfair
	(Vacant Southern Area Welterweight Title)
12.11.96	Spencer McCracken L PTS 8 Dudley
22.04.97	Paul King W RSC 4 Bethnal Green
29.05.97	Paul Ryan L RSC 3 Mayfair
30.06.97	Ahmet Dottuev L RSC 4 Bethnal Green
08.11.97	Anthony McFadden L PTS 8 Southwark
24.03.98	Leigh Wicks W PTS 6 Bethnal Green
28.04.98	Jim Webb W RSC 2 Belfast
10.09.98	Delroy Leslie L PTS 10 Acton
	(Vacant Southern Area L. Middleweight Title)
19.12.98	Michael Jones L PTS 6 Liverpool
23.01.99	Wayne Alexander L DIS 1 Cheshunt
	(Vacant Southern Area L. Middleweight Title)
01.05.99	Wayne Alexander L RSC 3 Crystal Palace
26.06.99	Geoff McCreesh L PTS 8 Millwall
05.10.99	Hussain Osman L PTS 4 Bloomsbury

23.10.99	Paul Samuels L PTS 8 Telford
18.01.00	Howard Eastman L RSC 2 Mansfield
23.03.00	Pedro Thompson DREW 6 Bloomsbury
08.04.00	Anthony Farnell L PTS 8 Bethnal Green
16.05.00	Ryan Rhodes L PTS 6 Warrington
23.05.00	Alexandru Andrei L PTS 6 Paris, France
04.07.00	Lester Jacobs L PTS 4 Tooting
21.09.00	Harry Butler W PTS 6 Bloomsbury
07.10.00	Kofi Jantuah L RTD 3 Doncaster
25.11.00	Donovan Smillie W RSC 2 Manchester
16.12.00	Marlon Hayes L RTD 6 Sheffield
15.01.01	Gordon Behan DREW 6 Manchester
24.02.01	Ruben Groenewald L PTS 6 Bethnal Green
22.04.01	Harry Butler W PTS 6 Streatham
17.05.01	Lee Murtagh W RSC 2 Leeds
	(Vacant British Masters L. Middleweight Title)
21.06.01	Charden Ansoula L PTS 4 Earls Court
28.07.01	Gary Logan L RSC 4 Wembley
10.12.01	Jimmy Vincent L PTS 10 Birmingham
	(British Masters L. Middleweight Title Challenge)
28.01.02	Ian Cooper W PTS 6 Barnsley
16.03.02	John Humphrey L PTS 10 Bethnal Green
	(Vacant Southern Area L. Middleweight Title)
13.04.02	Mihaly Kotai L PTS 6 Liverpool
20.04.02	Freeman Barr L PTS 8 Cardiff
10.05.02	Carl Froch L RSC 1 Bethnal Green
15.06.02	Sam Soliman L PTS 4 Tottenham
17.08.02	Wayne Elcock L PTS 4 Cardiff
17.09.02	David Starie L RSC 4 Bethnal Green
25.10.02	Gilbert Eastman L PTS 4 Bethnal Green
12.12.02	Allan Gray L PTS 10 Leicester Square
	(Southern Area Middleweight Title Challenge. Vacant WBF International Middleweight Title)
05.03.03	David Walker L PTS 6 Bethnal Green
19.04.03	Geard Ajetovic L PTS 4 Liverpool
12.05.03	Jason Collins L PTS 10 Birmingham
	(Vacant British Masters S. Middleweight Title)

Career: 68 contests, won 19, drew 4, lost 45.

Geard Ajetovic

Prescot. *Born* Beocin, Yugoslavia, 28 February, 1981
L. Middleweight. Ht. 5'8½"
Manager G. Storey

19.04.03	Ojay Abrahams W PTS 4 Liverpool
17.05.03	Jason Samuels W PTS 4 Liverpool

Career: 2 contests, won 2.

Henry Akinwande

Dulwich. *Born* London, 12 October, 1965
WBN & IBF Inter-Continental
Heavyweight Champion. Former
Undefeated WBC FeCarBox Heavyweight
Champion. Former Undefeated WBO,
European & Commonwealth Heavyweight
Champion. Ht. 6'7"
Manager Self

04.10.89	Carlton Headley W CO 1 Kensington
08.11.89	Dennis Bailey W RSC 2 Wembley
06.12.89	Paul Neilson W RSC 1 Wembley
10.01.90	John Fairbairn W RSC 1 Kensington
14.03.90	Warren Thompson W PTS 6 Kensington
09.05.90	Mike Robinson W CO 1 Wembley
10.10.90	Tracy Thomas W PTS 6 Kensington
12.12.90	Francois Yrius W RSC 1 Kensington
06.03.91	J. B. Williamson W RSC 2 Wembley
06.06.91	Ramon Voorn W PTS 8 Barking
28.06.91	Marshall Tillman W PTS 8 Nice, France
09.10.91	Gypsy John Fury W CO 3 Manchester
	(Elim. British Heavyweight Title)
06.12.91	Tim Bullock W CO 3 Dussledorf, Germany
28.02.92	Young Joe Louis W RSC 3 Issy les Moulineaux, France
26.03.92	Tucker Richards W RSC 2 Telford
10.04.92	Lumbala Tshimba W PTS 8 Carquefou, France
05.06.92	Kimmuel Odum W DIS 6 Marseille, France
18.07.92	Steve Garber W RTD 2 Manchester
19.12.92	Axel Schulz DREW 12 Berlin, Germany
	(Vacant European Heavyweight Title)
18.03.93	Jimmy Thunder W PTS 12 Lewisham
	(Vacant Commonwealth Heavyweight Title)
01.05.93	Axel Schulz W PTS 12 Berlin, Germany
	(Vacant European Heavyweight Title)
06.11.93	Frankie Swindell W PTS 10 Sun City, South Africa
01.12.93	Biagio Chianese W RSC 4 Kensington
	(European Heavyweight Title Defence)
05.04.94	Johnny Nelson W PTS 10 Bethnal Green
23.07.94	Mario Schiesser W CO 7 Berlin, Germany
	(European Heavyweight Title Defence)
08.04.95	Calvin Jones W CO 2 Las Vegas, USA
22.07.95	Stanley Wright W RSC 2 Millwall
16.12.95	Tony Tucker W PTS 10 Philadelphia, USA
27.01.96	Brian Sergeant W RSC 1 Phoenix, USA
23.03.96	Gerard Jones W DIS 7 Miami, USA
29.06.96	Jeremy Williams W CO 3 Indio, USA
	(Vacant WBO Heavyweight Title)

09.11.96 Alexander Zolkin W RSC 10 Las Vegas, USA
(WBO Heavyweight Title Defence)
11.01.97 Scott Welch W PTS 12 Nashville, USA
(WBO Heavyweight Title Defence)
12.07.97 Lennox Lewis L DIS 5 Lake Tahoe, USA
(WBC Heavyweight Title Challenge)
13.12.97 Orlin Norris W PTS 12 Pompano Beach, USA
(Final Elim. WBA Heavyweight Title)
06.03.99 Reynaldo Minus W RSC 2 St Paul, USA
15.05.99 Najeed Shaheed W RSC 9 Miami, USA
22.02.00 Chris Serengo W RSC 1 Capetown, South Africa
25.05.00 Russull Chasteen W CO 5 Tunica, USA
08.12.00 Ken Craven W CO 1 Tallahassee, USA
(Vacant WBC FeCarBox Heavyweight Title)
17.03.01 Peter McNeeley W CO 2 Tallahassee, Florida, USA
16.06.01 Maurice Harris W CO 1 Cincinnati, USA
17.11.01 Oliver McCall L CO 10 Las Vegas, Nevada, USA
08.03.02 Curt Paige W RSC 1 Kissimmee, Florida, USA
29.10.02 Sam Ubokane W RSC 7 Capetown, South Africa
10.12.02 Roman Sukhoterin W PTS 12 Constanta, Romania
(WBN Inter-Continental Heavyweight Title Challenge)
31.05.03 Timo Hoffmann W PTS 12 Frankfurt, Germany
(IBF Inter-Continent Heavyweight Title Challenge)
Career: 47 contests, won 44, drew 1, lost 2.

Mark Alexander

Finsbury Park. *Born* Hackney, 18 November, 1975
Featherweight. Ht. 5'9½"
Manager T. Sims

10.04.01 Steve Hanley W PTS 4 Wembley
31.07.01 Damien Dunnion W PTS 4 Bethnal Green
19.12.01 Dazzo Williams L PTS 6 Coventry
15.05.03 Buster Dennis W PTS 4 Mayfair
Career: 4 contests, won 3, lost 1.

Wayne Alexander

Croydon. *Born* Tooting, 17 July, 1973
Middleweight. Former Undefeated British & European L.Middleweight Champion.
Former Undefeated Southern Area L.Middleweight Champion. Ht. 5'8¾"
Manager F. Warren

10.11.95 Andrew Jervis W RTD 3 Derby
13.02.96 Paul Murray W PTS 4 Bethnal Green
11.05.96 Jim Webb W RSC 2 Bethnal Green
13.07.96 John Janes W RSC 3 Bethnal Green
05.06.97 Prince Kasi Kaihau W CO 4 Bristol
29.11.97 John Janes W RSC 1 Norwich
21.03.98 Darren Covill W RSC 2 Bethnal Green
09.05.98 Pedro Carragher W CO 2 Sheffield
14.07.98 Lindon Scarlett W RSC 5 Reading
05.12.98 Jimmy Vincent W RSC 3 Bristol
23.01.99 Ojay Abrahams W DIS 1 Cheshunt
(Vacant Southern Area L. Middleweight Title)
01.05.99 Ojay Abrahams W RSC 3 Crystal Palace

07.08.99 George Richards W RSC 2 Dagenham
19.02.00 Paul Samuels W RSC 3 Dagenham
(Vacant British L. Middleweight Title)
12.08.00 Paul Denton W RSC 1 Wembley
10.02.01 Harry Simon L RSC 5 Widnes
(WBO L. Middleweight Title Challenge)
28.07.01 Viktor Fesetchko W PTS 8 Wembley
17.11.01 Joe Townsley W RSC 2 Glasgow
(British L. Middleweight Title Defence)
19.01.02 Paolo Pizzamiglio W RSC 3 Bethnal Green
(Vacant European L. Middleweight Title)
18.01.03 Viktor Fesetchko W PTS 6 Preston
Career: 20 contests, won 19, lost 1.

Haider Ali

Leyton. *Born* Quetta, Pakistan, 12 November, 1979
S. Featherweight. Ht. 5'8½"
Manager F. Warren

24.05.03 Buster Dennis W PTS 4 Bethnal Green
Career: 1 contest, won 1.

Haider Ali   Les Clark

Carl Allen

Wolverhampton. *Born* Wolverhampton, 20 November, 1969
Lightweight. Former Undefeated Midlands Area S. Bantamweight Champion.
Ht. 5'7¼"
Manager Self

26.11.95 Gary Jenkinson W PTS 6 Birmingham
29.11.95 Jason Squire L PTS 6 Solihull
17.01.96 Andy Robinson L PTS 6 Solihull
13.02.96 Ervine Blake W RSC 5 Wolverhampton
21.02.96 Ady Benton L PTS 6 Batley

29.02.96 Chris Jickells W PTS 6 Scunthorpe
27.03.96 Jason Squire DREW 6 Whitwick
26.04.96 Paul Griffin L RSC 3 Cardiff
30.05.96 Roger Brotherhood W RSC 5 Lincoln
26.09.96 Matthew Harris W PTS 10 Walsall
(Midlands Area S. Bantamweight Title Challenge)
07.10.96 Emmanuel Clottey L RTD 3 Lewisham
21.11.96 Miguel Matthews W PTS 8 Solihull
30.11.96 Floyd Havard L RTD 3 Tylorstown
29.01.97 Pete Buckley W PTS 8 Stoke
11.02.97 David Morris DREW 8 Wolverhampton
28.02.97 Ian McLeod L RTD 3 Kilmarnock
21.05.97 David Burke L PTS 4 Liverpool
30.06.97 Duke McKenzie L PTS 8 Bethnal Green
12.09.97 Brian Carr L PTS 8 Glasgow
04.10.97 Sergei Devakov L PTS 6 Muswell Hill
03.12.97 Chris Lyons W PTS 8 Stoke
21.05.98 Roy Rutherford L PTS 6 Solihull
09.06.98 Scott Harrison L RSC 6 Hull
30.11.98 Gary Hibbert L PTS 4 Manchester
09.12.98 Chris Jickells W RSC 3 Stoke
04.02.99 Mat Zegan L PTS 4 Lewisham
17.03.99 Craig Spacie W PTS 8 Stoke
08.05.99 Phillip Ndou L RSC 2 Bethnal Green
14.06.99 Pete Buckley W PTS 6 Birmingham
22.06.99 David Lowry L PTS 4 Ipswich
11.10.99 Lee Williamson L PTS 6 Birmingham
19.10.99 Tontcho Tontchev L CO 2 Bethnal Green
20.12.99 Nicky Cook L CO 3 Bethnal Green
08.02.00 Lee Williamson W PTS 8 Wolverhampton
29.02.00 Bradley Pryce L PTS 4 Widnes
28.03.00 Lee Williamson W PTS 8 Wolverhampton
16.05.00 Bradley Pryce L RSC 3 Warrington
24.06.00 Michael Gomez L CO 2 Glasgow
10.10.00 Steve Hanley W PTS 8 Brierley Hill
05.02.01 Lee Meager DREW 6 Hull
12.03.01 Pete Buckley W PTS 6 Birmingham
27.03.01 Pete Buckley W PTS 8 Brierley Hill
15.09.01 Esham Pickering L PTS 6 Derby
17.11.01 Steve Conway L PTS 8 Dewsbury
08.12.01 Esham Pickering L PTS 8 Chesterfield
07.02.02 Mark Bowen L PTS 6 Stoke
20.04.02 Esham Pickering L PTS 6 Derby
21.07.02 Eddie Nevins L PTS 4 Salford
07.09.02 Colin Toohey DREW 6 Liverpool
26.10.02 Dazzo Williams W RSC 2 Maesteg
02.12.02 Esham Pickering L PTS 6 Leicester
28.01.03 Lee Meager L PTS 8 Nottingham
09.05.03 Jeff Thomas DREW 6 Doncaster
Career: 53 contests, won 17, drew 5, lost 31.

Peter Allen

Birkenhead. *Born* Birkenhead, 13 August, 1978
Lightweight. Ht. 5'5"
Manager T. Miller

30.04.98 Sean Grant L PTS 6 Pentre Halkyn
21.06.98 Garry Burrell W PTS 6 Liverpool
20.09.98 Simon Chambers L PTS 6 Sheffield
16.11.98 Stevie Kane W PTS 6 Glasgow
07.12.98 Simon Chambers L PTS 6 Bradford
28.02.99 Amjid Mahmood L PTS 6 Shaw
12.03.99 Marc Callaghan L PTS 4 Bethnal Green
15.09.99 Steve Brook L PTS 6 Harrogate
07.10.99 Nicky Wilders L PTS 6 Sunderland

18.10.99 Mark Hudson L PTS 6 Bradford
15.11.99 Craig Docherty L RSC 1 Glasgow
09.12.01 Jeff Thomas L PTS 6 Blackpool
01.03.02 Andrew Ferrans L PTS 8 Irvine
15.03.02 Ricky Burns L PTS 6 Glasgow
17.04.02 Andrew Smith W PTS 6 Stoke
24.06.02 Tasawar Khan L PTS 6 Bradford
14.09.02 Carl Greaves L PTS 6 Newark
08.10.02 Andrew Ferrans L PTS 8 Glasgow
21.10.02 Tony McPake L PTS 6 Glasgow
17.11.02 Choi Tseveenpurev L RSC 4 Shaw
16.02.03 Darryn Walton L PTS 6 Salford
31.05.03 Mally McIver L PTS 6 Barnsley
Career: 22 contests, won 3, lost 19.

Peter Allen   Les Clark

Leigh Alliss

Stroud. *Born* Stroud, 11 September, 1975
L. Heavyweight. Ht. 5'9½"
Manager N. Christian

06.03.03 Ovill McKenzie L PTS 4 Bristol
12.05.03 Mark Phillips W PTS 6 Southampton
13.06.03 Egbui Ikeagbu W PTS 6 Bristol
Career: 3 contests, won 2, lost 1.

Adnan Amar

Nottingham. *Born* Nottingham, 17
February, 1983
L. Welterweight. Ht. 5'9"
Manager J. Ingle

11.06.01 Steve Hanley W PTS 4 Nottingham
13.11.01 Duncan Armstrong W PTS 6 Leeds
21.10.02 Jason Gonzales W PTS 6 Cleethorpes
23.02.03 Arv Mittoo W PTS 6 Shrewsbury
16.03.03 Gareth Wiltshaw W PTS 6 Nottingham
16.04.03 Dave Cotterill W PTS 4 Nottingham
28.04.03 Ernie Smith W PTS 6 Cleethorpes
12.05.03 Pedro Thompson W RSC 4
          Birmingham
08.06.03 David Kirk W PTS 6 Nottingham
Career: 9 contests, won 9.

Francis Ampofo   Les Clark

Francis Ampofo

Bethnal Green. *Born* Ghana, 5 June, 1967
Bantamweight. Former IBO Inter-
Continental Bantamweight Champion.
Former Undefeated British Flyweight
Champion. Former Commonwealth
Flyweight Champion. Ht. 5'1½"
Manager D. Powell

30.01.90 Neil Parry W PTS 6 Bethnal Green
06.03.90 Robbie Regan L PTS 6 Bethnal Green
29.05.90 Eric George W RSC 3 Bethnal Green
12.09.90 Eric George W CO 2 Bethnal Green
26.03.91 Ricky Beard W PTS 8 Bethnal Green
22.06.91 Neil Johnston W RSC 2 Earls Court
03.09.91 Robbie Regan W RSC 11 Cardiff
          (British Flyweight Title Challenge)
17.12.91 Robbie Regan L PTS 12 Cardiff
          (British Flyweight Title Defence)
25.02.92 Ricky Beard W PTS 8 Crystal Palace
16.06.92 Shaun Norman RSC 4 Dagenham
22.12.92 James Drummond W PTS 12 Mayfair
          (Vacant British Flyweight Title)
17.02.93 Alberto Cantu W RSC 5 Bethnal Green
29.06.93 Albert Musankabala W RSC 3 Mayfair
          *(Vacant Commonwealth Flyweight
          Title)*
11.06.94 Jacob Matlala L RTD 9 Bethnal Green
          (WBO Flyweight Title Challenge)
20.09.94 James Drummond W RSC 3
          Musselburgh
          (British Flyweight Title Defence)
20.12.94 Daren Fifield W RSC 2 Bethnal Green
          *(British Flyweight Title Defence.
          Commonwealth Flyweight Title
          Challenge)*
06.03.95 Danny Ward L CO 12 Mayfair
          *(Commonwealth Flyweight Title
          Defence)*
27.11.96 Rowan Williams W PTS 6 Bethnal
          Green
08.04.97 Vince Feeney L PTS 10 Bethnal Green
          *(Vacant Southern Area Bantamweight
          Title)*

19.09.97 Gary Hickman W RSC 2 Southend
25.10.97 Paul Lloyd L PTS 12 Queensferry
          *(Commonwealth Bantamweight Title
          Challenge. Vacant British
          Bantamweight Title)*
08.09.98 Graham McGrath W RTD 3 Bethnal
          Green
25.01.99 Shaun Anderson W RSC 9 Glasgow
          *(Vacant IBO Inter-Continental
          Bantamweight Title)*
30.10.99 Noel Wilders L PTS 12 Peterlee
          (Vacant British Bantamweight Title)
01.04.00 Ady Lewis L PTS 12 Bethnal Green
          *(Vacant British & Commonwealth
          Bantamweight Titles)*
09.12.00 John Armour L PTS 12 Southwark
          (Vacant WBU Bantamweight Title)
11.05.02 John Armour L PTS 12 Dagenham
          (WBU Bantamweight Title Challenge)
21.09.02 John Armour L PTS 12 Brentwood
          (WBU Bantamweight Title Challenge)
Career: 28 contests, won 17, lost 11.

(Terry) Junior Anderson

Southampton. *Born* Leeds, 23 May, 1974
Bantamweight. Ht. 5'8"
Manager P. Rees

17.03.03 Neil Read L CO 2 Southampton
Career: 1 contest, lost 1.

Kevin Anderson

Methil. *Born* Kirkcaldy, 26 April, 1980
Welterweight. Ht. 5'8"
Manager T. Gilmour

12.04.03 Paul McIlwaine W RSC 2 Bethnal
          Green
19.04.03 Piotr Bartnicki W RSC 2 Liverpool
17.05.03 Georges Dujardin W RSC 1 Liverpool
Career: 3 contests, won 3.

Kevin Anderson   Les Clark

Simon Andrews

Plymouth. *Born* Birmingham, 24 April, 1970
S. Middleweight. Ht. 5'9½"
Manager Self

19.09.95 J. P. Matthews L RSC 3 Plymouth
13.11.95 Carl Winstone L PTS 6 Barnstaple
03.12.95 Jason Hart L PTS 6 Southwark
12.02.96 Neville Smith L RSC 3 Heathrow
04.04.96 Jetty Williams W PTS 6 Plymouth
10.05.96 Graham Townsend L RSC 5 Wembley
18.10.96 Gareth Thomas W RSC 5 Barnstaple
07.11.96 Gary Reyniers DREW 6 Battersea
10.12.96 Gareth Thomas W RSC 4 Plymouth
15.02.97 Neville Smith L PTS 4 Tooting
19.04.97 Peter Vosper L PTS 10 Plymouth
(Vacant Western Area L. Heavyweight Title)
12.07.97 Markus Beyer L RSC 5 Earls Court
02.12.97 Gary Reyniers L PTS 6 Windsor
24.02.98 Alex Mason L PTS 6 Edgbaston
24.03.98 Gordon Behan L RSC 6 Wolverhampton
24.09.98 Alex Mason L PTS 8 Edgbaston
17.03.99 Matthew Barney L RTD 4 Kensington
03.10.99 Damon Hague L PTS 6 Chesterfield
20.11.99 Damon Hague L RSC 4 Grantham
27.02.00 Matt Mowatt L PTS 6 Plymouth
29.03.00 Gareth Hogg L RSC 5 Piccadilly
02.06.00 Steven Bendall L RSC 5 Ashford
25.02.01 Joe Brame L RSC 5 Streatham
12.05.01 Freddie Yemofio W PTS 4 Plymouth
30.09.01 Darren Dorrington L RSC 4 Bristol
(Western Area S. Middleweight Title Challenge)
12.12.01 Mark Phillips L PTS 6 Clydach
16.03.02 Mike Thompson L PTS 4 Northampton
13.04.02 Peter Jackson L PTS 4 Wolverhampton
27.07.02 Jason McKay L RSC 3 Nottingham
29.09.02 Roddy Doran L PTS 6 Shrewsbury
Career: 30 contests, won 4, drew 1, lost 25.

Joel Ani   Les Clark

Joel Ani

Tottenham. *Born* Nigeria, 6 February, 1972
Middleweight. Ht. 5'8"
Manager B. Lawrence

22.10.92 Danny Quacoe W CO 1 Bethnal Green
03.02.93 Kevin Adamson L RSC 6 Earls Court
29.03.93 George Wilson W PTS 6 Mayfair
06.05.93 Korso Aleain W RSC 2 Bayswater
23.06.93 Steve McGovern L PTS 6 Edmonton
02.10.98 Gareth Lovell DREW 6 Cheshunt
11.12.98 Mark Richards L DIS 3 Cheshunt
26.02.99 David Baptiste L RSC 5 Longford
26.09.02 Harry Butler W PTS 4 Fulham
25.10.02 Craig Lynch L PTS 6 Millwall
01.02.03 Mickey Quinn L PTS 4 Belfast
23.02.03 Michael Thomas W DIS 1 Streatham
17.05.03 Graham Delehedy L RSC 4 Liverpool
Career: 13 contests, won 5, drew 1, lost 7.

Charden Ansoula

St Pancras. *Born* Brazzaville, Congo, 23 February, 1978
Middleweight. Ht. 5'11"
Manager T. Follett

12.12.97 Antonio de Brito W PTS 4 St Nazaire, France
28.03.98 Max Hannequart W PTS 4 St Martin de Crau, France
16.05.98 Kuvanych Toygonbayev L PTS 4 Paris, France
13.10.98 Mohamed Boutalakht L PTS 6 Guilherand-Granges, France
02.04.99 John Ameline W RSC 5 Lisieux, France
12.06.99 Antonio de Brito L RSC 3 Mont de Marsan, France
11.12.99 Zdenek Zubko W RSC 2 Ciudad Real, Spain
21.03.00 Jason Collins L PTS 6 Telde, Gran Canaria, Spain
24.07.00 Julio Cesar Soto W PTS 6 Villafranca, Spain
24.05.01 Jed Tytler W RSC 2 Kensington
21.06.01 Ojay Abrahams W PTS 4 Hammersmith
04.10.01 Maurice Forbes W PTS 4 Finsbury
16.03.02 Darren Williams W CO 5 Northampton
31.05.02 Alex Hilton W RSC 1 Bucharest, Romania
15.06.02 Delroy Mellis W RSC 5 Tottenham
17.09.02 Valery Odin W PTS 6 Bethnal Green
25.10.02 Howard Eastman L RSC 1 Bethnal Green
Career: 17 contests, won 12, lost 5.

John Armour

Chatham. *Born* Chatham, 26 October, 1968
WBU Bantamweight Champion. Former Undefeated European & Commonwealth Bantamweight Champion. Ht. 5'4¾"
Manager Self

24.09.90 Lupe Castro W PTS 6 Lewisham
31.10.90 Juan Camero W RSC 4 Crystal Palace
21.01.91 Elijro Mejia W RSC 1 Crystal Palace
30.09.91 Pat Maher W CO 1 Kensington
29.10.91 Pete Buckley W PTS 6 Kensington
14.12.91 Gary Hickman W RSC 6 Bexleyheath
25.03.92 Miguel Matthews W PTS 6 Dagenham
30.04.92 Ndabe Dube W RSC 12 Kensington
(Vacant Commonwealth Bantamweight Title)
17.10.92 Mauricio Bernal W PTS 8 Wembley
03.12.92 Albert Musankabala W RSC 5 Lewisham
(Commonwealth Bantamweight Title Defence)
28.01.93 Ricky Romero W CO 1 Southwark
10.02.93 Morgan Mpande W PTS 12 Lewisham
(Commonwealth Bantamweight Title Defence)
09.06.93 Boualem Belkif W PTS 10 Lewisham
01.12.93 Karl Morling W CO 3 Kensington
14.01.94 Rufus Adebayo W RSC 7 Bethnal Green
(Commonwealth Bantamweight Title Defence)
23.09.94 Shaun Anderson W RSC 11 Bethnal Green
(Commonwealth Bantamweight Title Defence)
14.02.95 Tsitsi Sokutu W RSC 7 Bethnal Green
(Commonwealth Bantamweight Title Defence)
19.04.95 Antonio Picardi W RSC 8 Bethnal Green
(Vacant European Bantamweight Title)
19.05.95 Matthew Harris W RSC 3 Southwark
29.11.95 Redha Abbas W CO 5 Bethnal Green
(European Bantamweight Title Defence)
17.12.96 Lyndon Kershaw W RSC 8 Bethnal Green
29.01.97 Petrica Paraschiv W PTS 12 Bethnal Green
(Vacant Interim WBC International Bantamweight Title)
20.05.97 Anatoly Kvitko W RSC 8 Gillingham
28.11.97 Ervine Blake W PTS 10 Bethnal Green
12.12.98 Carlos Navarro L RSC 4 Southwark
(WBU S. Bantamweight Title Challenge)
19.06.99 Mohamed Ouzid W RSC 5 Dublin
25.07.00 Alexander Tiranov W PTS 8 Southwark
09.12.00 Francis Ampofo W PTS 12 Southwark
(Vacant WBU Bantamweight Title)
01.12.01 Ian Turner W PTS 8 Bethnal Green
11.05.02 Francis Ampofo W PTS 12 Dagenham
(WBU Bantamweight Title Defence)
21.09.02 Francis Ampofo W PTS 12 Brentwood
(WBU Bantamweight Title Defence)
Career: 31 contests, won 30, lost 1.

John Armour   Les Clark

(Shaun) Lee Armstrong

Huddersfield. *Born* Hartlepool, 18 October, 1972
Central Area L. Middleweight Champion. Former Undefeated Central Area S.Featherweight Champion. Ht. 5'8"
Manager C. Aston

26.04.96	Daryl McKenzie W RSC 4 Glasgow	
10.05.96	Charlie Rumbol W PTS 6 Wembley	
23.05.96	Ian Richardson W PTS 6 Queensferry	
04.10.96	Michael Gibbons L RSC 3 Wakefield	
18.11.96	Garry Burrell W PTS 6 Glasgow	
20.02.97	Carl Greaves W RSC 4 Mansfield	
10.04.97	Chris Lyons W PTS 6 Sheffield	
28.04.97	Hugh Collins W RTD 5 Glasgow	
26.06.97	Garry Burrell W PTS 6 Sheffield	
06.10.97	Roger Sampson L PTS 6 Bradford	
13.11.97	Graeme Williams W PTS 6 Bradford	
30.11.97	Gary Jenkinson W PTS 6 Shaw	
06.02.98	Nigel Leake W PTS 6 Wakefield	
05.04.98	John T. Kelly W PTS 4 Shaw	
21.05.98	Pete Buckley W PTS 6 Bradford	
14.06.98	Pete Buckley W PTS 6 Shaw	
23.10.98	Nigel Leake W RSC 3 Wakefield	

(Vacant Central Area S. Featherweight Title)

11.12.98	Ian McLeod L RSC 8 Prestwick	

(IBO Inter-Continental S. Featherweight Title Challenge)

21.02.99	Bobby Lyndon W RSC 5 Bradford	
03.04.99	John T. Kelly L PTS 6 Carlisle	
25.04.99	Chris Lyons W PTS 8 Leeds	
02.10.99	Jamie McKeever DREW 6 Cardiff	
14.11.99	Keith Jones W PTS 6 Bradford	
11.12.99	Jason Dee L RSC 4 Merthyr	
21.02.00	Gary Flear W PTS 8 Glasgow	
27.03.00	Sebastian Hart L CO 4 Barnsley	
24.09.00	Dave Travers W PTS 6 Shaw	
23.10.00	Craig Docherty DREW 8 Glasgow	
10.12.01	Arv Mittoo W PTS 6 Bradford	
27.04.02	Keith Jones W PTS 6 Huddersfield	
09.05.02	Richard Inquieti L RSC 5 Sunderland	
22.02.03	Gavin Wake W PTS 10 Huddersfield	

(Vacant Central Area L. Middleweight Title)

Career: 32 contests, won 23, drew 2, lost 7.

Lee Armstrong   Les Clark

Alex Arthur

Edinburgh. *Born* Edinburgh, 26 June, 1978
British & WBA Inter-Continental S.Featherweight Champion. Former Undefeated IBF & WBO Inter-Continental S. Featherweight Champion. Ht. 5'9"
Manager F. Warren/F. Maloney

25.11.00	Richmond Asante W RSC 1 Manchester	
10.02.01	Eddie Nevins W RSC 1 Widnes	
26.03.01	Woody Greenaway W RTD 2 Wembley	
28.04.01	Dafydd Carlin W PTS 4 Cardiff	
21.07.01	Rakhim Mingaleev W PTS 4 Sheffield	
15.09.01	Dimitri Gorodetsky W RSC 1 Manchester	
27.10.01	Alexei Slyautchin W RSC 1 Manchester	
17.11.01	Laszlo Bognar W RSC 3 Glasgow	
19.01.02	Vladimir Borov W RSC 2 Bethnal Green	

Alex Arthur   Les Clark

11.03.02 Dariusz Snarski W RSC 10 Glasgow
(*Vacant IBF Inter-Continental
S.Featherweight Title*)
08.06.02 Nikolai Eremeev W RTD 5 Renfrew
(*Vacant WBO Inter-Continental
S.Featherweight Title*)
17.08.02 Pavel Potipko W CO 1 Cardiff
19.10.02 Steve Conway W CO 4 Renfrew
(*Vacant British S. Featherweight
Title*)
14.12.02 Carl Greaves W RSC 6 Newcastle
(*British S.Featherweight Title
Defence*)
22.03.03 Patrick Malinga W RSC 6 Renfrew
(*Vacant WBA Inter-Continental
S.Featherweight Title*)
Career: 15 contests, won 15.

Jamie Arthur

Cwmbran. *Born* Aberdeen, 17 December,
1979
Lightweight. Ht. 5'9"
Manager F. Warren

22.03.03 Daniel Thorpe W PTS 4 Renfrew
28.06.03 James Gorman W PTS 4 Cardiff
Career: 2 contests, won 2.

Richmond Asante

East Ham. *Born* Ghana, 7 July, 1976
Featherweight. Ht. 5'5¹/₂"
Manager Self

25.11.00 Alex Arthur L RSC 1 Manchester
18.02.01 Gareth Wiltshaw W PTS 4 Southwark
01.04.01 Stevie Quinn L PTS 4 Southwark
03.06.01 Steve Gethin W PTS 4 Southwark
09.09.01 Mickey Coveney L PTS 4 Southwark
26.01.02 Marc Callaghan L PTS 4 Dagenham
27.04.02 Jesse James Daniel W PTS 6
Huddersfield
12.12.02 Mickey Bowden L PTS 6 Leicester
Square
Career: 8 contests, won 3, lost 5.

Darren Ashton

Stoke. *Born* Stoke, 26 February, 1969
Cruiserweight. Former Undefeated
Midlands Area L. Heavyweight &
S. Middleweight Champion. Ht. 6'1"
Manager Self

13.10.93 Tony Colclough W RSC 1 Stoke
08.12.93 Nigel Rafferty W PTS 6 Stoke
23.03.94 L. A. Williams W PTS 6 Stoke
23.05.94 Nigel Rafferty W PTS 6 Walsall
30.11.94 Carlos Christie L PTS 6 Solihull
04.03.95 John Wilson NC 3 Livingston
06.05.95 Dale Nixon W RSC 4 Shepton Mallet
13.05.95 Stefan Wright W PTS 6 Glasgow
11.10.95 Neil Simpson L RSC 3 Solihull
17.11.95 Mark Baker L RSC 1 Bethnal Green
12.01.96 Frederic Alvarez L PTS 6 Copenhagen,
Denmark
27.05.96 Harri Hakulinen L PTS 4 Helsinki,
Finland
09.07.96 Chris Johnson L RSC 1 Bethnal
Green
08.02.97 Paul Bowen L PTS 4 Millwall
04.04.97 Mark Snipe W RSC 2 Brighton
26.06.97 Clinton Woods L PTS 6 Sheffield

02.09.97 Adrian Strachan W PTS 4 Southwark
15.09.97 Darren Dorrington W DIS 2 Bristol
21.11.97 Stuart Fleet W RSC 4 Hull
(*Vacant Midlands Area
S. Middleweight Title*)
07.02.98 Sven Hamer L RSC 6 Cheshunt
27.03.98 Toks Owoh L RSC 2 Telford
16.05.98 Ali Forbes L PTS 6 Chigwell
23.05.98 Howard Eastman L RSC 4 Bethnal
Green
23.09.98 Bobby Banghar L RSC 2 Bloomsbury
13.11.98 Graham Townsend L DIS 6 Brighton
30.11.98 Mervyn Penniston-John L PTS 4
Manchester
19.12.98 Ole Klemetsen L RSC 2 Liverpool
11.02.99 Alex Mason W PTS 10 Dudley
(*Vacant Midlands Area L. Heavyweight
Title*)
13.03.99 Glenn Williams L PTS 4 Manchester
17.05.99 Tony Booth L PTS 6 Cleethorpes
04.06.99 Lee Osie Manuel L RSC 5 Vigo, Spain
(*Transcontinental L. Heavyweight Title
Challenge*)
31.07.99 Darren Corbett L RSC 2 Carlisle
09.10.99 Glenn Williams L PTS 6 Manchester
28.10.99 Warren Stowe W PTS 6 Burnley
04.12.99 Mike Gormley L PTS 4 Manchester
21.02.00 Tony Oakey L PTS 4 Southwark
04.03.00 Neil Linford L PTS 6 Peterborough
20.03.00 Brian Magee L RTD 5 Mansfield
29.05.00 Roy Finlay L PTS 4 Manchester
21.10.00 Tony Oakey L PTS 4 Wembley
31.10.00 Konstantin Schvets L RSC 1
Hammersmith
30.11.00 Neil Linford L PTS 4 Peterborough
08.12.00 Delroy Leslie L RTD 3 Crystal Palace
27.01.01 Peter Haymer L PTS 4 Bethnal Green
17.02.01 Faisal Mohammed L RSC 1 Bethnal
Green
28.03.01 Michael Pinnock DREW 6 Piccadilly
20.04.01 Tony Griffiths W PTS 4 Millwall
28.04.01 Enzo Maccarinelli L CO 1 Cardiff
27.05.01 Lee Whitehead W RSC 2 Manchester
15.06.01 Garry Delaney L RTD 4 Millwall
(*Vacant British Masters Cruiserweight
Title*)
13.09.01 Mark Brookes L PTS 4 Sheffield
20.09.01 Tony Strong W PTS 4 Blackfriars
09.10.01 Nathan King L PTS 6 Cardiff
27.10.01 Steven Spartacus L PTS 4 Manchester
19.11.01 Billy McClung L PTS 6 Glasgow
19.01.02 Steven Spartacus L PTS 4 Bethnal
Green
10.02.02 Blue Stevens L PTS 4 Southwark
02.03.02 Pinky Burton L PTS 6 Wakefield
18.03.02 Paul Bowen L PTS 6 Crawley
20.04.02 Andrew Facey L PTS 6 Derby
28.04.02 Scott Baker L RSC 6 Southwark
13.06.02 John Killian L PTS 4 Leicester Square
05.10.02 Mark Brookes L PTS 4 Chesterfield
30.10.02 John Killian L PTS 4 Leicester Square
16.11.02 Phill Day DREW 4 Coventry
14.12.02 Michael Thompson L PTS 4
Newcastle
08.01.03 Gareth Hogg L RSC 2 Aberdare
16.02.03 Alan Page L PTS 4 Salford
16.03.03 Carl Wright DREW 6 Nottingham
03.04.03 Jamie Warters L PTS 6 Hull
09.05.03 Ryan Walls L PTS 6 Longford
31.05.03 Courtney Fry L PTS 4 Bethnal Green
Career: 72 contests, won 15, drew 3, lost 53, no
contest 1.

Wayne Asker

Bury St Edmunds. *Born* Bury St Edmunds,
20 November, 1975
Middleweight. Ht. 5'9"
Manager Self

02.07.98 Dennis Griffin W PTS 4 Ipswich
03.10.98 Delroy Mellis W PTS 6 Crawley
19.01.99 David Baptiste W PTS 6 Ipswich
09.05.99 Hussan Osman L PTS 4 Bracknell
22.06.99 David Baptiste L PTS 4 Ipswich
28.03.01 Dean Ashton W PTS 6 Piccadilly
08.12.01 Leigh Wicks W PTS 4 Dagenham
10.02.02 Ruben Groenewald L PTS 10
Southwark
(*Vacant British Masters
S.Middleweight Title*)
15.06.02 Donovan Smillie DREW 6 Norwich
21.09.02 Jason Collins DREW 6 Norwich
08.12.02 Gary Logan L PTS 6 Bethnal Green
03.06.03 Matthew Tait L RSC 7 Bethnal Green
Career: 12 contests, won 5, drew 2, lost 5.

Wayne Asker   Les Clark

Paul Astley

Treharris. *Born* Stoke, 3 September, 1976
Middleweight. Ht. 6'0"
Manager P. Boyce

08.01.03 Chris Steele W PTS 4 Aberdare
25.01.03 Jason Samuels L CO 1 Bridgend
Career: 2 contests, won 1, lost 1.

(Raymond) Sugar Ray Atherton

Liverpool. *Born* Liverpool, 26 April, 1970
Middleweight. Ht. 5'7"
Manager T. Gilmour

05.04.03 Tommy Tolan L RSC 2 Belfast
Career: 1 contest, lost 1.

Martyn Bailey

Wrexham. *Born* Wrexham, 16 January, 1976
British Masters Middleweight Champion.
Ht. 5'8"
Manager Self

07.10.99	John Marsden W PTS 6 Sunderland
27.11.99	Lee Molloy L RSC 2 Liverpool
18.02.00	Donovan Davey W PTS 6 Pentre Halkyn
06.03.00	Richard Inquieti L RSC 5 Bradford
05.05.00	Richard Inquieti W PTS 6 Pentre Halkyn
22.09.00	David Smales W RSC 3 Wrexham
28.11.00	Paul Martin W PTS 6 Brierley Hill
04.02.01	Pedro Thompson W PTS 6 Queensferry
08.04.01	Peter Dunn W PTS 6 Wrexham
10.06.01	Robert Burton DREW 6 Ellesmere Port
08.10.01	Reagan Denton L PTS 4 Barnsley
21.10.01	Wayne Shepherd W PTS 6 Pentre Halkyn
16.11.01	Robert Burton DREW 4 Preston
08.03.02	Danny Moir W PTS 6 Ellesmere Port
29.04.02	Paul Lomax DREW 6 Bradford
01.11.02	Tony Byrne W PTS 6 Preston
02.12.02	Lee Murtagh W RSC 6 Leeds
	(British Masters Middleweight Title Challenge)
07.05.03	Paul Lomax W RTD 3 Ellesmere Port
	(British Masters Middleweight Title Defence)

Career: 18 contests, won 12, drew 3, lost 3.

Colin Bain

Glasgow. *Born* Hawick, 10 August, 1978
Lightweight. Ht. 5'8"
Manager K. Morrison

14.03.03	Dafydd Carlin W PTS 6 Glasgow
16.05.03	Martin Hardcastle W PTS 6 Glasgow

Career: 2 contests, won 2.

Mark Baker

Sidcup. *Born* Farnborough, 14 July, 1969
L. Heavyweight. Former Undefeated WBF
L. Heavyweight Champion. Former
Undefeated Southern Area Middleweight
Champion. Ht. 5'9½"
Manager Self

07.09.92	Jason McNeill W RSC 2 Bethnal Green
15.10.92	Graham Jenner W RTD 4 Lewisham
03.12.92	Adrian Wright W RSC 1 Lewisham
10.02.93	Paul Hanlon W RSC 2 Lewisham
26.04.93	Karl Mumford W CO 1 Lewisham
15.06.93	Alan Baptiste W PTS 6 Hemel Hempstead
14.01.94	Karl Barwise L PTS 6 Bethnal Green
11.03.94	Graham Jenner W RSC 2 Bethnal Green
26.04.94	Jerry Mortimer W PTS 6 Bethnal Green
23.09.94	Alan Baptiste W RSC 1 Bethnal Green
17.10.94	Steve Thomas W RSC 5 Mayfair
27.10.94	Chris Richards W PTS 6 Milwall
13.12.94	Stinger Mason W RSC 4 Ilford

20.01.95	Mark Dawson W RSC 3 Bethnal Green
17.11.95	Darren Ashton W RSC 1 Bethnal Green
13.01.96	Mark Dawson W RSC 3 Halifax
05.03.96	Sven Hamer W PTS 10 Bethnal Green
	(Vacant Southern Area Middleweight Title)
14.10.96	John Duckworth W RSC 6 Mayfair
27.03.97	Heath Todd W RSC 5 Dubai
30.06.97	Mark Delaney W PTS 10 Bethnal Green
	(Elim. British S. Middleweight Title)
08.10.97	Robert Peel W RSC 5 Poplar
06.12.97	Clinton Woods L PTS 12 Wembley
	(Vacant Commonwealth S. Middleweight Title)
07.03.98	Dean Francis L RSC 12 Reading
	(British & WBO Inter-Continental S. Middleweight Title Challenges)
04.02.99	Danny Juma W PTS 6 Lewisham
29.04.99	Errol McDonald W PTS 10 Bethnal Green
22.06.99	David Starie L PTS 12 Ipswich
	(British & Commonwealth S. Middleweight Title Challenges)
09.03.00	Ali Forbes W PTS 12 Bethnal Green
	(Vacant WBF L. Heavyweight Title)
22.05.00	Neil Simpson L PTS 12 Coventry
	(Vacant British & Commonwealth L. Heavyweight Titles)
09.12.00	Paul Bonson W PTS 6 Southwark
20.01.01	Andy Manning W PTS 8 Bethnal Green
05.02.01	Howard Eastman L RTD 5 Hull
10.04.01	Tony Booth W PTS 4 Wembley
22.09.02	Radcliffe Green W PTS 6 Southwark

Career: 33 contests, won 27, lost 6.

Scott Baker

Walthamstow. *Born* Londonderry, 29
August, 1977
Cruiserweight. Ht. 6'2"
Manager Self

22.06.99	Adam Cale W PTS 4 Ipswich
13.09.99	Georgie Stevens L PTS 4 Bethnal Green
01.10.99	Jason Brewster W RTD 5 Cleethorpes
16.06.00	Adam Cale W PTS 4 Bloomsbury
08.09.00	Mark Dawson L RSC 3 Hammersmith
03.02.01	Slick Miller L RSC 4 Brighton
16.12.01	Jimmy Steel W PTS 4 Southwark
28.04.02	Darren Ashton W RSC 6 Southwark
03.06.03	Marcus Lee L RSC 3 Bethnal Green

Career: 9 contests, won 5, lost 4.

Vince Baldassara

Clydebank. *Born* Clydebank, 6 November,
1978
Welterweight. Ht. 5'11"
Manager B. Winter

14.03.03	George Telfer L PTS 4 Glasgow

Career: 1 contest, lost 1.

Ted Bami (Minsende)

Brixton. *Born* Zaire, 2 March, 1978
WBF L. Welterweight Champion. Ht. 5'7"
Manager B. Hearn

26.09.98	Des Sowden W RSC 1 Southwark
11.02.99	Gary Reid W RSC 2 Dudley
10.03.00	David Kehoe W PTS 4 Bethnal Green

08.09.00	Jacek Bielski L RSC 4 Hammersmith
29.03.01	Keith Jones W PTS 4 Hammersmith
05.05.01	Francis Barrett W PTS 6 Edmonton
31.07.01	Lance Crosby W PTS 6 Bethnal Green
19.03.02	Michael Smyth W CO 4 Slough
23.06.02	Keith Jones W RSC 4 Southwark
17.08.02	Bradley Pryce W RSC 6 Cardiff
26.10.02	Adam Zadworny W PTS 4 Maesteg
07.12.02	Sergei Starkov W PTS 4 Brentwood
08.03.03	Andrei Devyataykin W RSC 1 Bethnal Green
12.04.03	Laszlo Herczeg W RSC 9 Bethnal Green
	(Vacant WBF L.Welterweight Title)

Career: 14 contests, won 13, lost 1.

Ted Bami   Les Clark

(David) Dai Bando (Tams)

Bargoed. *Born* Newport, 20 January, 1978
L. Welterweight. Ht. 5'8"
Manager C. Sanigar

13.07.02	Dean Hickman L RSC 1 Wolverhampton
02.11.02	Jatinder Lal Drew 6 Wolverhampton
28.11.02	Keith Porter L PTS 4 Finchley
16.04.03	Ali Nuumbembe L PTS 4 Nottingham

Career: 4 contests, drew 1, lost 3.

David Barnes (Smith)

Manchester. *Born* Manchester, 16 January,
1981
Welterweight. Ht. 5'8½"
Manager F. Warren/B. Hughes

07.07.01	Trevor Smith W RSC 2 Manchester
15.09.01	Karl Taylor W PTS 4 Manchester
27.10.01	Mark Sawyers W RSC 2 Manchester
15.12.01	James Paisley W RTD 2 Wembley
09.02.02	David Kirk W RTD 1 Manchester

04.05.02 David Baptiste W CO 3 Bethnal Green
01.06.02 Dimitri Protkunas W RSC 1 Manchester
28.09.02 Sergei Starkov W PTS 6 Manchester
12.10.02 Rusian Ashirov W PTS 6 Bethnal Green
14.12.02 Rozalin Nasibulin W RSC 3 Newcastle
18.01.03 Brice Faradji W PTS 6 Preston
05.04.03 Viktor Fesetchko W PTS 8 Manchester
Career: 12 contests, won 12.

Chris Barnett

Manchester. *Born* Coventry, 15 July, 1973
Lightweight. Former Undefeated IBO
International L. Welterweight Champion.
Ht. 5.5½"
Manager J. Trickett

18.02.95 Wayne Jones W RSC 5 Shepton Mallet
24.11.95 Brian Coleman W PTS 6 Manchester
09.04.96 Charlie Paine W RSC 2 Salford

25.10.96 John Smith W PTS 6 Mere
22.12.96 Wayne Shepherd W PTS 6 Salford
18.01.97 Kid McAuley W RTD 3 Manchester
24.02.97 Jay Mahoney L PTS 6 Manchester
20.03.97 Mike Watson W RSC 2 Salford
08.05.98 David Kirk W PTS 6 Manchester
17.07.98 Ivan Walker W RSC 1 Mere
17.10.98 Trevor Smith W RSC 4 Manchester
10.07.99 Karim Bouali DREW 6 Southwark
09.10.99 Mick Mulcahy W RSC 2 Manchester
27.11.99 Glenn McClarnon W PTS 12 Liverpool
(Vacant IBO International L. Welterweight Title)
29.02.00 Victor Barinov L PTS 8 Manchester
19.08.00 Newton Villareal L RSC 3 Brentwood
(IBO L.Welterweight Title Challenge)
06.10.01 Jason Dee W DIS 5 Manchester
26.11.01 Viktor Baranov L PTS 6 Manchester
28.05.02 James Armah L PTS 8 Liverpool
09.11.02 Anthony Maynard L PTS 6 Altrincham
19.04.03 Gary Hibbert L RSC 7 Liverpool
Career: 21 contests, won 13, drew 1, lost 7.

Matthew Barney

Southampton. *Born* Fareham, 25 June, 1974
British & IBO Inter-Continental
S.Middleweight Champion. Former
Undefeated Southern Area & British
Masters S.Middleweight Champion.
Ht. 5'10¾"
Manager E. Maloney

04.06.98 Adam Cale W PTS 6 Barking
23.07.98 Adam Cale W PTS 6 Barking
02.10.98 Dennis Doyley W PTS 4 Cheshunt
22.10.98 Kevin Burton W PTS 6 Barking
07.12.98 Freddie Yemofio W PTS 4 Acton
17.03.99 Simon Andrews W RTD 4 Kensington
09.05.99 Gareth Hogg W PTS 4 Bracknell
20.05.99 Bobby Banghar W RSC 5 Kensington
(British Masters S. Middleweight Final)
05.06.99 Paul Bowen DREW 10 Cardiff
(Southern Area S. Middleweight Title Challenge)
20.08.99 Adam Cale W PTS 4 Bloomsbury
05.10.99 Delroy Leslie L PTS 10 Bloomsbury
(Vacant Southern Area Middleweight Title)
15.04.00 Mark Dawson W PTS 6 Bethnal Green
06.05.00 Jason Hart W PTS 10 Southwark
(Vacant Southern Area S. Middleweight Title)
30.09.00 Neil Linford L PTS 10 Peterborough
(Elim. British S. Middleweight Title)
02.02.01 Darren Covill W PTS 6 Portsmouth
16.03.01 Matt Mowatt W RSC 1 Portsmouth
(British Masters S. Middleweight Title Defence)
14.07.01 Robert Milewics W PTS 8 Wembley
20.10.01 Jon Penn W RSC 4 Portsmouth
26.01.02 Hussain Osman L RTD 9 Dagenham
(Vacant IBO Inter-Continental S.Middleweight Title. Southern Area S.Middleweight Title Defence)
08.04.02 Hussain Osman W PTS 12 Southampton
(IBO Inter-Continental & Southern Area S. Middleweight Title Challenges)
22.09.02 Paul Owen W CO 7 Southwark
(Vacant British Masters S.Middleweight Title)

David Barnes   Les Clark

20.10.02 Chris Nembhard W PTS 10 Southwark
   (*Southern Area S. Middleweight Title
   Defence*)
29.03.03 Dean Francis W PTS 12 Wembley
   (*Vacant British S.Middleweight Title*)
Career: 23 contests, won 19, drew 1, lost 3.

Matthew Barr

Walton. *Born* Kingston, 22 May, 1977
Middleweight. Ht. 5'11"
Manager Self

02.12.97 Keith Palmer L RSC 3 Windsor
23.02.98 Martin Cavey W RSC 1 Windsor
14.05.98 Gerard Lawrence L RSC 1 Acton
29.10.98 Sonny Thind W RSC 2 Bayswater
20.05.99 Paul Knights L RSC 1 Barking
31.10.99 Allan Gray W PTS 4 Raynes Park
25.02.00 John Humphrey W RSC 1 Newmarket
06.05.00 Ernie Smith W PTS 4 Southwark
22.10.00 Ernie Smith W PTS 4 Streatham
23.11.00 Harry Butler W PTS 4 Bayswater
23.11.01 John Humphrey L RSC 2 Bethnal
   Green
13.09.02 Brian Knudsen W PTS 6 Randers,
   Denmark
29.03.03 Lee Hodgson W RSC 1 Wembley
Career: 13 contests, won 9, lost 4.

Francis Barrett

Wembley. *Born* Galway, 7 February, 1977
Southern Area L. Welterweight Champion.
Ht. 5'7"
Manager Self

12.08.00 Mohamed Helel W PTS 4 Wembley
23.09.00 Trevor Smith W RSC 1 Bethnal Green
21.10.00 Keith Jones W PTS 4 Wembley
24.02.01 David White W PTS 4 Bethnal Green
10.03.01 Karl Taylor W RSC 3 Bethnal Green
26.03.01 Tony Montana W PTS 4 Wembley
05.05.01 Ted Bami L PTS 6 Edmonton
22.09.01 Gary Reid W PTS 4 Bethnal Green
19.01.02 Dafydd Carlin W PTS 4 Bethnal Green
25.05.02 David Kirk W PTS 6 Portsmouth
25.10.02 Darren Covill W PTS 4 Bethnal Green
21.12.02 Keith Jones W PTS 6 Dagenham
05.03.03 Jon Honney W PTS 10 Bethnal Green
   (*Vacant Southern Area L.Welterweight
   Title*)
27.05.03 Silence Saheed L RSC 1 Dagenham
Career: 14 contests, won 12, lost 2.

Ryan Barrett

Thamesmead. *Born* London, 27 December,
1982
Lightweight. Ht. 5'10"
Manager M. Roe

13.06.02 Gareth Wiltshaw W PTS 4 Leicester
   Square
06.09.02 Jason Gonzales W PTS 4 Bethnal Green
12.12.02 Martin Turner W RSC 1 Leicester
   Square
08.03.03 David Vaughan DREW 4 Bethnal Green
Career: 4 contests, won 3, drew 1.

(Shinebayer) Shinny Bayaar
(Sukhbaatar)

Carlisle. *Born* Mongolia, 27 August, 1977
Flyweight. Ht. 5'0"
Manager J. Doughty

10.10.01 Damien Dunnion L PTS 8 Stoke
09.12.01 Delroy Spencer W PTS 4 Shaw
17.11.02 Anthony Hanna W PTS 6 Shaw
20.03.03 Sunkanmi Ogunbiyi L PTS 4
   Queensway
08.06.03 Darren Cleary W RSC 2 Shaw
Career: 5 contests, won 3, lost 2.

Gary Beardsley

Belper. *Born* Belper, 18 July, 1968
Middleweight. Former Undefeated British
Masters Middleweight Champion. Ht. 5'10"
Manager Self

09.02.95 Shaun Stokes W RSC 3 Doncaster
01.03.95 Eddie Haley W RSC 1 Glasgow
06.03.95 Stefan Scriggins L PTS 6 Leicester
15.03.95 Jamie Gallagher W PTS 6 Stoke
20.10.95 Dewi Roberts W PTS 6 Mansfield
22.11.95 Richard Swallow DREW 6 Sheffield
06.12.95 John Smith W PTS 8 Stoke
06.02.96 Georgie Smith L RSC 1 Basildon
22.03.96 Mark Legg W PTS 6 Mansfield
09.12.96 Derek Roche L RSC 2 Bradford
16.01.97 Steve Levene L PTS 6 Solihull
29.01.97 Howard Clarke L PTS 6 Stoke
20.11.99 William Webster W PTS 6 Grantham
18.01.00 Mike Duffield W RTD 2 Mansfield
09.04.00 Matt Mowatt W PTS 6 Alfreton
01.07.00 Wayne Pinder L PTS 4 Manchester
19.11.00 Matt Mowatt W PTS 10 Chesterfield
   (*Vacant British Masters Middleweight
   Title*)
08.12.00 Cornelius Carr L PTS 4 Crystal Palace
25.02.01 William Webster W PTS 6 Derby
30.11.02 Michael Monaghan L PTS 6 Newark
28.01.03 Matthew Thirlwall W PTS 6
   Nottingham
05.03.03 Howard Eastman L RSC 2 Bethnal
   Green
16.04.03 Matthew Thirlwall L PTS 6
   Nottingham
31.05.03 Hussain Osman L RSC 5 Bethnal
   Green
Career: 24 contests, won 12, drew 1, lost 11.

Lee Bedell

Sheffield. *Born* Sheffield, 9 February, 1970
L. Welterweight. Ht. 5'6½"
Manager G. Rhodes

10.02.03 Paul Rushton W RSC 3 Sheffield
08.04.03 Chas Simmonds L PTS 4 Bethnal
   Green
24.05.03 Jamie Hill W RSC 3 Sheffield
03.06.03 Ashley Theophane L RSC 4 Bethnal
   Green
Career: 4 contests, won 2, lost 2.

Jimmy Beech

Walsall. *Born* Walsall, 19 January, 1979
S. Featherweight. Ht. 5'7"
Manager Self

23.06.99 Ike Halls W RTD 2 West Bromwich
03.09.99 Tom Wood W PTS 6 West Bromwich
07.04.00 Willie Limond L RSC 2 Glasgow
28.01.01 Lenny Hodgkins W PTS 6
   Wolverhampton
16.11.01 Pete Buckley W PTS 6 West
   Bromwich
23.11.01 Henry Castle L PTS 4 Bethnal Green
07.02.02 Dave Cotterill W PTS 6 Stoke

25.02.02 Mickey Bowden W PTS 4 Slough
09.03.02 Tony Mulholland L PTS 6 Manchester
05.05.02 James Rooney W RSC 5 Hartlepool
25.05.02 Henry Castle L PTS 4 Portsmouth
07.09.02 Ricky Eccleston W RSC 3 Liverpool
28.09.02 Michael Gomez L RSC 4 Manchester
14.12.02 Gavin Rees L PTS 4 Newcastle
22.03.03 Willie Limond L CO 4 Renfrew
28.04.03 Tony McPake L PTS 6 Nottingham
27.05.03 Billy Corcoran W PTS 6 Dagenham
Career: 17 contests, won 9, lost 8.

Steve Bell

Ashton under Lyne. *Born* Manchester, 11
June, 1975
S. Featherweight. Ht. 5'10"
Manager F. Warren/T. Jones

08.05.03 Jus Wallie DREW 4 Widnes
Career: 1 contest, drew 1.

Steve Bell   Les Clark

Steven Bendall

Coventry. *Born* Coventry, 1 December,
1973
IBO Inter-Continental Middleweight
Champion. Former Undefeated WBU Inter-
Continental Middleweight Champion.
Ht. 6'0"
Manager Self

15.05.97 Dennis Doyley W RSC 2 Reading
13.09.97 Gary Reyniers W PTS 4 Millwall
27.02.99 Israel Khumalo W PTS 4 Oldham
02.07.99 Darren Covill W RTD 3 Bristol
24.09.99 Sean Pritchard W PTS 6 Merthyr
03.12.99 Ian Toby W PTS 6 Peterborough
07.04.00 Des Sowden W RSC 3 Bristol
02.06.00 Simon Andrews W RSC 5 Ashford
08.09.00 Jason Barker W PTS 6 Bristol
03.11.00 Eddie Haley W RSC 1 Ebbw Vale
01.12.00 Peter Mitchell W PTS 8 Peterborough
22.08.01 Bert Bado W RSC 1 Hammanskraal,
   South Africa

29.09.01 Alan Gilbert W RTD 3 Southwark
08.12.01 Jason Collins W PTS 12 Dagenham
(Vacant WBU Inter-Continental Middleweight Title)
02.03.02 Ahmet Dottouev W RTD 4 Brakpan, South Africa
(WBU Inter-Continental Middleweight Title Defence)
26.04.02 Viktor Fesetchko W RSC 10 Coventry
(Vacant IBO Inter-Continental Middleweight Title)
13.07.02 Phillip Bystrikov W RSC 5 Coventry
06.09.02 Tomas da Silva W RSC 8 Bethnal Green
24.01.03 Lee Blundell W RSC 2 Sheffield
(IBO Inter-Continental Middleweight Title Defence)
26.04.03 Mike Algoet W PTS 12 Brentford
(IBO Inter-Continental Middleweight Title Defence)
Career: 20 contests, won 20.

Steven Bendall   Les Clark

Kevin Bennett

Hartlepool. *Born* Birmingham, 15 August, 1975
L. Welterweight. Ht. 5'7"
Manager M. Marsden

01.12.99 Karim Bouali W PTS 4 Yarm
28.03.00 Les Frost W RSC 2 Hartlepool
25.06.00 Steve Hanley W PTS 6 Wakefield
23.07.00 Gary Reid W RSC 4 Hartlepool
28.10.00 Gary Harrison W RTD 2 Coventry
27.11.00 Keith Jones W PTS 4 Birmingham
23.01.01 Tommy Peacock W RSC 5 Crawley
03.03.01 Iain Eldridge W PTS 6 Wembley
08.05.01 Keith Jones W PTS 6 Barnsley
04.06.01 Gary Ryder L RSC 6 Hartlepool
20.10.01 Paul Denton W PTS 4 Portsmouth
03.11.01 Mark Ramsey W PTS 6 Glasgow
26.01.02 Glenn McClarnon L PTS 8 Dagenham
18.05.02 Colin Lynes L RSC 4 Millwall
21.03.03 Keith Jones W PTS 4 West Bromwich
21.06.03 Zoltan Surman W RSC 4 Manchester
Career: 16 contests, won 13, lost 3.

Jim Betts

Scunthorpe. *Born* Tickhill, 6 October, 1977
Bantamweight. Former Undefeated British Masters Flyweight Champion. Ht. 5'6½"
Manager M. Marsden

26.03.98 Des Gargano W PTS 6 Scunthorpe
13.05.98 David Jeffrey W RSC 3 Scunthorpe
05.06.98 Chris Price W PTS 6 Hull
11.09.98 Marty Chestnut W PTS 6 Newark
16.10.98 Marty Chestnut W PTS 6 Salford
28.11.98 Ola Dali W PTS 4 Sheffield
17.05.99 Dave Travers W RTD 4 Cleethorpes
17.07.99 Ross Cassidy W RSC 1 Doncaster
27.09.99 Graham McGrath W PTS 6 Cleethorpes
19.02.00 Chris Price W PTS 6 Newark
19.06.00 Chris Price W PTS 4 Burton
30.08.00 David Coldwell W RSC 2 Scunthorpe
(Vacant British Masters Flyweight Title. Elim. British Flyweight Title)
26.02.01 Chris Emanuele L PTS 6 Nottingham
08.05.01 Sean Grant W RSC 1 Barnsley
11.06.01 Daniel Ring W PTS 6 Nottingham
15.09.01 Nicky Booth L RSC 7 Nottingham
(British & Commonwealth Bantamweight Title Challenges)
18.03.02 Ian Turner W RTD 4 Crawley
18.05.02 Gareth Payne W PTS 6 Millwall
27.07.02 Colin Moffett W RSC 3 Nottingham
Career: 19 contests, won 17, lost 2.

Paul Billington

Warrington. *Born* Billinge, 1 March, 1972
L. Heavyweight. Ht. 5'10"
Manager T. Miller

14.09.02 Michael Monaghan L RSC 4 Newark
29.05.03 Karl Wheeler L PTS 6 Sunderland
Career: 2 contests, lost 2.

Lee Blundell

Wigan. *Born* Wigan, 11 August, 1971
WBF Inter-Continental Middleweight Champion. Former Undefeated Central Area L. Middleweight Champion. Ht. 6'2"
Manager L. Veitch

25.04.94 Robert Harper W RSC 2 Bury
20.05.94 Freddie Yemofio W RSC 6 Acton
08.09.94 Gordon Blair W DREW 6 Glasgow
07.12.94 Kesem Clayton W RTD 2 Stoke
18.02.95 Glenn Catley L RSC 6 Shepton Mallet
11.12.95 Martin Jolley W PTS 6 Morecambe
16.03.97 Martin Jolley W PTS 6 Shaw
08.05.97 Paul Jones L RSC 4 Mansfield
19.09.99 Dean Ashton W RSC 4 Shaw
28.10.99 Jason Collins W DREW 6 Burnley
06.12.99 Danny Thornton W PTS 6 Bradford
05.03.00 Ian Toby W RTD 3 Shaw
21.05.00 Phil Epton W RSC 2 Shaw
30.11.00 Danny Thornton W RSC 8 Blackpool
(Vacant Central Area L.Middleweight Title)
08.03.01 Paul Wesley W RSC 3 Blackpool
03.04.01 Spencer Fearon W PTS 6 Bethnal Green
26.07.01 Harry Butler W RSC 4 Blackpool
15.09.01 Anthony Farnell L RSC 2 Manchester
(Vacant WBO Inter-Continental L.Middleweight Title)
09.12.01 Neil Bonner W RSC 3 Blackpool

16.03.02 Ryan Rhodes W RSC 3 Bethnal Green
(Vacant WBF Inter-Continental Middleweight Title)
03.08.02 Alan Gilbert W RSC 6 Blackpool
(WBF Inter-Continental Middleweight Title Defence)
26.10.02 Darren McInulty W RSC 1 Wigan
(WBF Inter-Continental Middleweight Title Defence)
24.01.03 Steven Bendall L RSC 2 Sheffield
(IBO Inter-Continental Middleweight Title Challenge)
Career: 23 contests, won 17, drew 2, lost 4.

Neil Bonner

Abergele. *Born* Enfield, 13 October, 1975
Middleweight. Ht. 5'9"
Manager Self

22.09.00 Drea Dread W RSC 4 Wrexham
03.11.00 James Lee L PTS 4 Ebbw Vale
04.02.01 Richard Inquieti W PTS 6 Queensferry
26.08.01 Colin McCash W RSC 1 Warrington
09.09.01 Peter Jackson L PTS 6 Hartlepool
21.10.01 Matt Scriven NC 1 Glasgow
09.12.01 Lee Blundell L RSC 3 Blackpool
08.03.02 Paul Buchanan L PTS 6 Ellesmere Port
19.04.02 Lee Murtagh L PTS 6 Darlington
11.05.02 Darrell Grafton L PTS 6 Chesterfield
08.06.02 Joe Townsley L PTS 6 Renfrew
06.10.02 Wayne Shepherd W PTS 6 Rhyl
01.11.02 Dean Cockburn L RSC 2 Preston
24.05.03 Dean Walker L PTS 6 Sheffield
Career: 14 contests, won 4, lost 9, no contest 1.

Paul Bonson

Featherstone. *Born* Castleford, 18 October, 1971
Cruiserweight. Former Central Area L. Heavyweight Champion. Ht. 5'10"
Manager Self

04.10.96 Michael Pinnock W PTS 6 Wakefield
14.11.96 Michael Pinnock DREW 6 Sheffield
22.12.96 Pele Lawrence DREW 6 Salford
20.04.97 Shamus Casey W PTS 6 Leeds
26.06.97 Andy Manning L PTS 6 Sheffield
19.09.97 Mike Gormley W PTS 6 Salford
03.10.97 Rudi Marcussen L PTS 4 Copenhagen, Denmark
03.12.97 Alex Mason DREW 6 Stoke
14.12.97 Willie Quinn L RSC 4 Glasgow
15.01.98 Alex Mason L PTS 6 Solihull
13.02.98 Peter Mason L PTS 4 Seaham
23.02.98 Martin McDonough W PTS 6 Windsor
07.03.98 Michael Bowen L PTS 6 Reading
14.03.98 Alain Simon L PTS 6 Pont St Maxence, France
08.04.98 Tim Brown DREW 4 Liverpool
21.05.98 Mark Hobson L PTS 6 Bradford
21.06.98 Kenny Rainford L PTS 6 Liverpool
01.09.98 Roberto Dominguez L PTS 8 Vigo, Spain
23.10.98 Rob Galloway W PTS 6 Wakefield
16.11.98 Chris P. Bacon L PTS 8 Glasgow
11.12.98 Robert Zlotkowski L PTS 4 Prestwick
20.12.98 Glenn Williams L PTS 6 Salford
24.04.99 Kenny Gayle DREW 4 Peterborough
29.05.99 Dave Johnson L PTS 6 South Shields
19.06.99 Sebastiaan Rothmann L PTS 8 Dublin
12.07.99 Jim Twite L PTS 4 Coventry
07.08.99 Juan Perez Nelongo L PTS 8 Arona, Tenerife

11.09.99 Mark Hobson L PTS 4 Sheffield
02.10.99 Enzo Maccarinelli L PTS 4 Cardiff
16.10.99 Robert Zlotkowski L PTS 6 Bethnal Green
27.10.99 Peter McCormack W PTS 6 Birmingham
04.12.99 Glenn Williams W PTS 4 Manchester
11.12.99 Chris Davies L PTS 4 Merthyr
05.02.00 Paul Maskell L PTS 4 Bethnal Green
11.03.00 Tony Dodson L PTS 4 Kensington
26.03.00 Wayne Buck L PTS 8 Nottingham
29.04.00 Cathal O'Grady L PTS 4 Wembley
13.05.00 Mark Hobson L PTS 4 Barnsley
25.06.00 Andy Manning W PTS 10 Wakefield
(Vacant Central L.Heavyweight Title)
08.09.00 Robert Milewicz L PTS 4 Hammersmith
21.10.00 Jon Penn L PTS 6 Sheffield
12.11.00 Glenn Williams L PTS 10 Manchester
(Central Area L.Heavyweight Title Defence)
24.11.00 Alex Mason L PTS 6 Darlington
09.12.00 Mark Baker L PTS 6 Southwark
23.01.01 Calvin Stonestreet W PTS 4 Crawley
03.02.01 Tony Dodson L PTS 4 Manchester
18.02.01 Butch Lesley L PTS 6 Southwark
13.03.01 Konstantin Schvets L PTS 6 Plymouth
07.04.01 Rob Hayes-Scott L PTS 4 Wembley
26.04.01 Mike White L PTS 6 Gateshead
17.05.01 Clint Johnson W PTS 6 Leeds
24.05.01 Sven Hamer L PTS 4 Kensington
04.06.01 Joe Gillon DREW 6 Glasgow
11.06.01 Darren Chubbs L PTS 4 Nottingham
21.06.01 Michael Pinnock W PTS 6 Sheffield
27.07.01 Clinton Woods L PTS 6 Sheffield
09.09.01 Eamonn Glennon W PTS 6 Hartlepool
28.09.01 Elvis Michailenko L PTS 6 Millwall
13.11.01 Tony Moran W PTS 6 Leeds
23.11.01 Elvis Michailenko L PTS 6 Bethnal Green
06.12.01 Shaun Bowes W RSC 5 Sunderland
16.12.01 Tommy Eastwood L PTS 4 Southwark
26.01.02 Dominic Negus L PTS 4 Bethnal Green
10.02.02 Butch Lesley L PTS 4 Southwark
25.02.02 Roman Greenberg L PTS 6 Slough
15.03.02 Michael Thompson L PTS 6 Spennymoor
22.03.02 Mark Smallwood L PTS 6 Coventry
19.04.02 Michael Thompson L PTS 6 Darlington
11.05.02 Mark Brookes L PTS 4 Chesterfield
15.06.02 Peter Haymer L PTS 4 Tottenham
23.06.02 Scott Lansdowne W PTS 4 Southwark
13.07.02 Jason Brewster W PTS 6 Wolverhampton
27.07.02 Albert Sosnowski L PTS 4 Nottingham
08.09.02 Varuzhan Davtyan L PTS 4 Wolverhampton
22.09.02 Neil Linford L PTS 6 Southwark
29.09.02 Tony Dowling L PTS 6 Shrewsbury
12.10.02 Andrew Lowe L PTS 4 Bethnal Green
25.10.02 Carl Froch L PTS 6 Bethnal Green
30.11.02 Robert Norton L PTS 6 Coventry
14.12.02 Nathan King W PTS 4 Newcastle
18.01.03 Enzo Maccarinelli L PTS 4 Preston
08.02.03 Steven Spartacus L PTS 6 Norwich
05.03.03 Marcus Lee W PTS 4 Bethnal Green
18.03.03 Mark Krence L PTS 4 Reading
28.03.03 Eric Teymour L PTS 6 Millwall
19.04.03 Tony Moran L PTS 4 Liverpool
12.05.03 Colin Kenna L PTS 6 Southampton
10.06.03 Lee Swaby L PTS 4 Sheffield
Career: 88 contests, won 18, drew 6, lost 64.

Jason Booth

Nottingham. *Born* Nottingham, 7 November, 1977
British Flyweight Champion. Former Undefeated Commonwealth Flyweight Champion. Ht. 5'4"
Manager M. Shinfield

13.06.96 Darren Noble W RSC 3 Sheffield
24.10.96 Marty Chestnut W PTS 6 Lincoln
27.11.96 Jason Thomas W PTS 4 Swansea
18.01.97 David Coldwell W PTS 4 Swadlincote
07.03.97 Pete Buckley W PTS 6 Northampton
20.03.97 Danny Lawson W RSC 3 Newark
10.05.97 Anthony Hanna W PTS 6 Nottingham
19.05.97 Chris Lyons W PTS 6 Cleethorpes
31.10.97 Mark Reynolds W PTS 6 Ilkeston

31.01.98 Anthony Hanna W PTS 6 Edmonton
20.03.98 Louis Veitch W CO 2 Ilkeston
(Elim. British Flyweight Title)
09.06.98 Dimitar Alipiev W RSC 2 Hull
17.10.98 Graham McGrath W RSC 4 Manchester
07.12.98 Louis Veitch W RSC 5 Cleethorpes
08.05.99 David Guerault L PTS 12 Grande Synthe, France
(European Flyweight Title Challenge)
12.07.99 Mark Reynolds W RSC 3 Coventry
16.10.99 Keith Knox W RSC 10 Belfast
(British & Commonwealth Flyweight Title Challenges)
22.01.00 Abie Mnisi W PTS 12 Birmingham
(Commonwealth Flyweight Title Defence)

Jason Booth   Les Clark

01.07.00 John Barnes W PTS 6 Manchester
13.11.00 Ian Napa W PTS 12 Bethnal Green
(British & Commonwealth Flyweight Title Defences)
26.02.01 Nokuthula Tshabangu W CO 2 Nottingham
(Commonwealth Flyweight Title Defence)
30.06.01 Alexander Mahmutov L PTS 12 Madrid, Spain
(European Flyweight Title Challenge)
23.02.02 Jason Thomas W PTS 6 Nottingham
01.06.02 Mimoun Chent L TD 8 Le Havre, France
(Vacant European Flyweight Title)
16.11.02 Kakhar Sabitov W RSC 6 Nottingham
28.04.03 Lindi Memani W PTS 8 Nottingham
Career: 26 contests, won 23, lost 3.

Nicky Booth   Les Clark

Nicky Booth

Nottingham. *Born* Nottingham, 21 January, 1980
British Bantamweight Champion. Former Commonwealth Bantamweight Champion.
Ht. 5'5"
Manager M. Shinfield

26.02.98 Shane Mallon W RSC 4 Hull
15.05.98 Marty Chestnut W PTS 6 Nottingham
14.07.98 Ian Napa L PTS 6 Reading
11.09.98 Anthony Hanna DREW 6 Cleethorpes
25.11.98 Anthony Hanna L PTS 6 Clydach
30.04.99 Delroy Spencer W PTS 6 Scunthorpe
06.06.99 Delroy Spencer W PTS 4 Nottingham
20.09.99 Russell Laing W PTS 8 Glasgow
03.12.99 David Jeffrey W PTS 4 Peterborough
03.03.00 Shaun Anderson W PTS 6 Irvine
22.05.00 Gareth Payne W PTS 4 Coventry
24.09.00 Gary Ford W PTS 6 Shaw
09.10.00 Tommy Waite W PTS 12 Liverpool
(British & Commonwealth Bantamweight Title Challenges)
26.02.01 Ady Lewis W RSC 7 Nottingham
(British & Commonwealth Bantamweight Title Defences)
11.06.01 Kevin Gerowski W RSC 4 Nottingham
14.07.01 Jose Sanjuanelo W RSC 9 Wembley
(Vacant IBO Bantamweight Title)
15.09.01 Jim Betts W RSC 7 Nottingham
(British & Commonwealth Bantamweight Title Defences)
23.02.02 Stephen Oates W RSC 7 Nottingham
(British & Commonwealth Bantamweight Title Defences)
27.07.02 Moses Kinyua W CO 5 Nottingham
(Commonwealth Bantamweight Title Defence)
21.09.02 Steve Molitor L PTS 12 Brentwood
(Commonwealth Bantamweight Title Defence)
16.11.02 Sergei Tasimov W RSC 3 Nottingham
28.04.03 Jamie Yelland W PTS 12 Nottingham
(British Bantamweight Title Defence)
Career: 22 contests, won 17, drew 1, lost 4.

Tony Booth

Hull. *Born* Hull, 30 January, 1970
Cruiserweight. Former Undefeated British Masters L. Heavyweight Champion.
Former Undefeated British Central Area Cruiserweight Champion. Ht. 5'11¾"
Manager Self

08.03.90 Paul Lynch L PTS 6 Watford
11.04.90 Mick Duncan W PTS 6 Dewsbury
26.04.90 Colin Manners W PTS 6 Halifax
16.05.90 Tommy Warde W PTS 6 Hull
05.06.90 Gary Dyson W PTS 6 Liverpool
05.09.90 Shaun McCrory L PTS 6 Stoke
08.10.90 Bullit Andrews W RSC 3 Cleethorpes
23.01.91 Darron Griffiths DREW 6 Stoke
06.02.91 Shaun McCrory L PTS 6 Liverpool
06.03.91 Billy Brough L PTS 6 Glasgow
18.03.91 Billy Brough W PTS 6 Glasgow
28.03.91 Neville Brown L PTS 6 Alfreton
17.05.91 Glenn Campbell L RSC 2 Bury
(Central Area S. Middleweight Title Challenge)
25.07.91 Paul Murray W PTS 6 Dudley
01.08.91 Nick Manners DREW 8 Dewsbury
11.09.91 Jim Peters L PTS 8 Hammersmith
28.10.91 Eddie Smulders L RSC 6 Arnhem, Holland
09.12.91 Steve Lewsam L PTS 8 Cleethorpes
30.01.92 Serg Fame W PTS 6 Southampton
12.02.92 Tenko Ernie W RSC 4 Wembley
05.03.92 John Beckles W RSC 6 Battersea
26.03.92 Dave Owens W PTS 6 Hull
08.04.92 Michael Gale L PTS 8 Leeds
13.05.92 Phil Soundy W PTS 6 Kensington
02.06.92 Eddie Smulders L RSC 1 Rotterdam, Holland
18.07.92 Maurice Core L PTS 6 Manchester
07.09.92 James Cook L PTS 8 Bethnal Green
30.10.92 Roy Richie DREW 6 Istrees, France
18.11.92 Tony Wilson DREW 8 Solihull
25.12.92 Francis Wanyama L PTS 6 Izegem, Belgium
09.02.93 Tony Wilson W PTS 8 Wolverhampton

01.05.93 Ralf Rocchigiani DREW 8 Berlin, Germany
03.06.93 Victor Cordoba L PTS 8 Marseille, France
23.06.93 Tony Behan W PTS 6 Gorleston
01.07.93 Michael Gale L PTS 8 York
17.09.93 Ole Klemetsen L PTS 8 Copenhagen, Denmark
07.10.93 Denzil Browne DREW 8 York
02.11.93 James Cook L PTS 8 Southwark
12.11.93 Carlos Christie W PTS 6 Hull
28.01.94 Francis Wanyama L RSC 2 Waregem, Belgium
(Vacant Commonwealth Cruiserweight Title)
26.03.94 Torsten May L PTS 6 Dortmund, Germany
21.07.94 Mark Prince L RSC 3 Battersea
24.09.94 Johnny Held L PTS 8 Rotterdam, Holland
07.10.94 Dirk Wallyn L PTS 6 Waregem, Belgium
27.10.94 Dean Francis L CO 1 Bayswater
23.01.95 Jan Lefeber L PTS 8 Rotterdam, Holland
07.03.95 John Foreman L PTS 6 Edgbaston
27.04.95 Art Stacey W PTS 10 Hull
(Vacant Central Area Cruiserweight Title)
04.06.95 Montell Griffin L RSC 2 Bethnal Green
06.07.95 Nigel Rafferty W RSC 7 Hull
22.07.95 Mark Prince L RSC 2 Millwall
06.09.95 Leif Keiski L PTS 8 Helsinki, Finland
25.09.95 Neil Simpson W PTS 8 Cleethorpes
06.10.95 Don Diego Poeder L RSC 2 Waregem, Belgium
11.11.95 Bruce Scott L RSC 3 Halifax
16.12.95 John Marceta L RSC 2 Cardiff
20.01.96 Johnny Nelson L RSC 2 Mansfield
15.03.96 Slick Miller W PTS 6 Hull
27.03.96 Neil Simpson L PTS 6 Whitwick
17.05.96 Mark Richardson W RSC 2 Hull
13.07.96 Bruce Scott L PTS 8 Bethnal Green
03.09.96 Paul Douglas L PTS 4 Belfast
14.09.96 Kelly Oliver L RSC 2 Sheffield
06.11.96 Martin Jolley W PTS 4 Hull
22.11.96 Slick Miller W RSC 5 Hull
11.12.96 Crawford Ashley L RSC 1 Southwark
18.01.97 Kelly Oliver L RSC 4 Swadlincote
27.02.97 Kevin Morton L PTS 6 Hull
25.03.97 Nigel Rafferty DREW 8 Wolverhampton
04.04.97 John Wilson L PTS 6 Glasgow
16.04.97 Robert Norton L RSC 4 Bethnal Green
15.05.97 Phill Day W PTS 4 Reading
11.09.97 Steve Bristow L PTS 4 Widnes
22.09.97 Martin Langtry W PTS 6 Cleethorpes
04.10.97 Bruce Scott W PTS 8 Muswell Hill
28.11.97 Martin Jolley W PTS 6 Hull
15.12.97 Nigel Rafferty W PTS 6 Cleethorpes
06.03.98 Peter Mason W RSC 3 Hull
09.06.98 Crawford Ashley L RSC 6 Hull
(British L. Heavyweight Title Challenge. Vacant Commonwealth L. Heavyweight Title)
18.07.98 Omar Sheika W PTS 8 Sheffield
26.09.98 Toks Owoh L PTS 6 Norwich
29.10.98 Nigel Rafferty W PTS 8 Bayswater
14.12.98 Sven Hamer L PTS 6 Cleethorpes
05.01.99 Ali Saidi W RSC 4 Epernay, France
17.05.99 Darren Ashton W PTS 6 Cleethorpes
12.07.99 Neil Simpson L PTS 10 Coventry
(Elim. British L. Heavyweight Title)
27.09.99 Adam Cale W PTS 6 Cleethorpes

16.10.99 Cathal O'Grady L CO 4 Belfast
18.01.00 Michael Sprott L PTS 6 Mansfield
12.02.00 Thomas Hansvoll L PTS 6 Sheffield
29.02.00 John Keeton L RSC 2 Widnes
09.04.00 Greg Scott-Briggs W PTS 10 Alfreton
(Vacant British Masters L. Heavyweight Title)
15.05.00 Michael Pinnock W PTS 6 Cleethorpes
19.06.00 Toks Owoh L RSC 3 Burton
08.09.00 Dominic Negus W PTS 6 Bristol
30.09.00 Robert Norton L RSC 3 Peterborough
31.10.00 Firat Aslan L RSC 2 Hammersmith
11.12.00 Mark Krence L PTS 6 Sheffield
05.02.01 Denzil Browne L RSC 5 Hull
(Vacant Central Area Cruiserweight Title)
01.04.01 Kenny Gayle DREW 4 Southwark
10.04.01 Mark Baker L PTS 4 Wembley
16.06.01 Butch Lesley L RSC 3 Dagenham
09.09.01 Tommy Eastwood L PTS 4 Southwark
22.09.01 Peter Haymer L PTS 4 Bethnal Green
15.10.01 Colin Kenna L PTS 6 Southampton
01.11.01 Terry Morrill W RSC 7 Hull
24.11.01 Matt Legg L PTS 4 Bethnal Green
16.12.01 Blue Stevens L PTS 4 Southwark
19.01.02 John McDermott L RSC 1 Bethnal Green
20.04.02 Enzo Maccarinelli L PTS 4 Cardiff
28.04.02 Scott Lansdowne W RSC 4 Southwark
10.05.02 Paul Buttery L PTS 4 Preston
23.06.02 Neil Linford L RSC 5 Southwark
03.08.02 Mark Krence L PTS 4 Derby
17.08.02 Enzo Maccarinelli L RTD 2 Cardiff
23.09.02 Slick Miller W PTS 6 Cleethorpes
05.10.02 Phill Day W PTS 4 Coventry
19.10.02 James Zikic L PTS 4 Norwich
27.10.02 Hughie Doherty L PTS 4 Southwark
21.11.02 Jamie Warters W PTS 8 Hull
28.11.02 Roman Greenberg L PTS 4 Finchley
08.12.02 David Haye L RTD 2 Bethnal Green
30.01.03 Mohammed Benguesmia L RTD 4 Algiers, Algeria
05.04.03 Jason Callum L PTS 6 Coventry
17.05.03 Tony Moran L PTS 6 Liverpool
Career: 125 contests, won 41, drew 8, lost 76.

Alan Bosworth

Northampton. *Born* Northampton, 31 December, 1967
L. Welterweight. Ht. 5'7"
Manager Self

17.10.95 Simon Hamblett W RSC 2 Wolverhampton
29.10.95 Shaun Gledhill W PTS 6 Shaw
16.11.95 Brian Coleman W PTS 6 Evesham
23.11.95 David Thompson W RSC 4 Tynemouth
13.01.96 Jason Blanche W PTS 6 Halifax
31.01.96 Arv Mittoo W PTS 6 Stoke
16.02.96 John Docherty W PTS 6 Irvine
24.03.96 Scott Walker DREW 6 Shaw
16.05.96 Yifru Retta W PTS 6 Dunstable
07.03.97 Wayne Rigby L RSC 5 Northampton
09.09.97 Colin Dunne L RSC 8 Bethnal Green
31.10.98 Alan Temple L PTS 6 Basingstoke
26.02.99 Des Sowden W PTS 6 Longford
13.03.99 Paul Burke L PTS 6 Manchester
24.04.99 Jan Bergman L RSC 6 Munich, Germany
02.07.99 Keith Jones W PTS 6 Bristol
24.09.99 Woody Greenaway L PTS 6 Merthyr
03.12.99 Darren Underwood W CO 5 Peterborough
20.01.00 Brian Coleman W PTS 6 Piccadilly

24.03.00 Allan Vester L PTS 12 Aarhus, Denmark
(IBF Inter-Continental L. Welterweight Title Challenge)
28.04.00 George Scott L PTS 8 Copenhagen, Denmark
02.06.00 Mohamed Helel W PTS 6 Ashford
25.07.00 Shea Neary L PTS 10 Southwark
01.12.00 David Kirk DREW 8 Peterborough
13.03.01 Eamonn Magee L RSC 5 Plymouth
23.06.01 Keith Jones W PTS 6 Peterborough
23.11.01 Daniel James W RSC 7 Bethnal Green
(Elim. British L.Welterweight Title)
16.03.02 Junior Witter L RSC 3 Northampton
(Vacant British L.Welterweight Title)
28.09.02 Eamonn Magee L RSC 5 Manchester
28.01.03 Oscar Hall L PTS 10 Nottingham
(Elim. British L. Welterweight Title)
Career: 30 contests, won 15, drew 2, lost 13.

Ivan Botton

Newark. *Born* Nottingham, 8 October, 1979
L. Heavyweight. Ht. 6'1¼"
Manager Self

20.03.00 Dean Ashton W RSC 2 Mansfield
11.05.00 Matthew Pepper W RSC 4 Newark
29.01.01 Michael Pinnock L PTS 4 Peterborough
02.06.01 Adam Cale W PTS 4 Wakefield
20.04.02 Adam Cale DREW 4 Wembley
11.05.02 Dave Clarke W PTS 6 Newark
14.09.02 Simeon Cover W PTS 6 Newark
08.06.03 Simeon Cover L PTS 6 Nottingham
Career: 8 contests, won 5, drew 1, lost 2.

Ivan Botton   Les Clark

Mickey Bowden

Forest Hill. *Born* Lewisham, 30 June, 1975
Featherweight. Ht. 5'8"
Manager J. Rooney

25.02.99 Kevin Gerowski W PTS 4 Kentish Town
09.05.99 Graham McGrath W RSC 4 Bracknell

79

07.08.99	Brendan Bryce W PTS 4 Dagenham
26.05.01	Anthony Hanna W PTS 4 Bethnal Green
25.02.02	Jimmy Beech L PTS 4 Slough
25.04.02	Nelson Valez L PTS 4 Las Vegas, Nevada, USA
30.10.02	Anthony Hanna W PTS 4 Leicester Square
12.12.02	Richmond Asante W PTS 6 Leicester Square

Career: 8 contests, won 6, lost 2.

Mark Bowen

Bilston. *Born* Wolverhampton, 11 September, 1974
Lightweight. Ht. 5'7"
Manager Self

08.03.01	Woody Greenaway DREW 6 Stoke
18.08.01	Mally McIver W RSC 1 Dewsbury
07.02.02	Carl Allen W PTS 6 Stoke
17.04.02	Craig Spacie W PTS 8 Stoke
03.12.02	Jason Nesbitt W PTS 6 Shrewsbury
15.02.03	Danny Hunt L RSC 1 Wembley

Career: 6 contests, won 4, drew 1, lost 1.

Jason Brewster

Coseley. *Born* Wolverhampton, 6 February, 1971
Heavyweight. Ht. 6'1"
Manager Self

23.06.99	Mark Williams DREW 6 West Bromwich
03.09.99	Adam Cale W PTS 6 West Bromwich
01.10.99	Scott Baker L RTD 5 Cleethorpes
18.02.00	Nigel Rafferty L PTS 6 West Bromwich
11.05.00	Tony Dowling L RSC 2 Newark
09.06.00	Paul Richardson L PTS 6 Blackpool
10.09.00	Adam Cale W PTS 4 Walsall
06.11.00	Nigel Rafferty W PTS 8 Wolverhampton
13.11.00	Mark McManus L RTD 2 Bethnal Green
01.04.01	Paul Richardson L RSC 4 Wolverhampton
20.05.01	Kevin Burton W PTS 6 Wolverhampton
07.09.01	Slick Miller W PTS 6 West Bromwich
24.09.01	Lee Nicholson W PTS 6 Cleethorpes
15.12.01	Butch Lesley L RSC 1 Chigwell
17.02.02	Lee Nicholson W PTS 6 Wolverhampton
13.07.02	Paul Bonson L PTS 6 Wolverhampton
05.10.02	Tony Moran L PTS 4 Liverpool
14.12.02	John McDermott L RSC 1 Newcastle
15.02.03	Phill Day L PTS 6 Wolverhampton

Career: 19 contests, won 7, drew 1, lost 11.

Michael Brodie

Manchester. *Born* Manchester, 10 May, 1974
IBO & WBF Featherweight Champion. Former Undefeated British, European & Commonwealth S. Bantamweight Champion. Ht. 5'6"
Manager J. Trickett

03.10.94	Graham McGrath W RSC 5 Manchester
20.10.94	Chip O'Neill W CO 3 Middleton

28.11.94	Muhammad Shaffique W CO 2 Manchester
13.12.94	Pete Buckley W PTS 6 Potters Bar
16.02.95	G. G. Goddard W PTS 6 Bury
03.04.95	Garry Burrell W RSC 4 Manchester
05.05.95	G. G. Goddard W PTS 6 Swansea
17.05.95	Ian Reid W RSC 3 Ipswich
10.06.95	Chris Clarkson W PTS 6 Manchester
14.11.95	Niel Leggett W CO 1 Bury
25.11.95	Karl Morling W RSC 1 Dagenham
18.12.95	Marty Chestnut W RTD 3 Mayfair
26.02.96	Bamana Dibateza W PTS 6 Manchester
13.04.96	John Sillo W CO 1 Liverpool
07.05.96	Elvis Parsley W RSC 1 Mayfair
06.07.96	Colin Innes W RSC 2 Mayfair
19.09.96	Ervine Blake W RSC 4 Manchester
09.11.96	Miguel Matthews W PTS 6 Manchester
22.03.97	Neil Swain W RSC 10 Wythenshawe *(Vacant British S. Bantamweight Title)*
30.08.97	Pete Buckley W PTS 8 Cheshunt
01.11.97	Wilson Docherty W CO 4 Glasgow *(British S. Bantamweight Title Defence. Vacant Commonwealth S. Bantamweight Title)*
31.01.98	Brian Carr W RSC 10 Edmonton *(British & Commonwealth S. Bantamweight Title Defences)*
23.05.98	Simon Ramoni W PTS 12 Bethnal Green *(Commonwealth S. Bantamweight Title Defence)*
17.10.98	Sergei Devakov W PTS 12 Manchester *(European S. Bantamweight Title Challenge)*
13.03.99	Salim Medjkoune W RSC 9 Manchester *(European S. Bantamweight Title Defence)*
31.07.99	Serge Poilblan W RSC 12 Carlisle *(European S. Bantamweight Title Defence)*
01.10.99	Drew Docherty W RSC 6 Bethnal Green *(European S. Bantamweight Title Defence)*
26.02.00	Salim Medjkoune W RSC 9 Carlisle *(European S. Bantamweight Title Defence)*
01.07.00	Mustapha Hame W CO 4 Manchester *(European S.Bantamweight Title Defence)*
09.09.00	Willie Jorrin L PTS 12 Manchester *(Vacant WBC S.Bantamweight Title)*
03.02.01	Sergio Aguila W RSC 4 Manchester
06.10.01	Frederic Bonifai W RSC 5 Manchester
26.11.01	Sean Fletcher W CO 2 Manchester
18.05.02	Pastor Maurin W PTS 12 Millwall *(Vacant WBF Featherweight Title)*
09.11.02	Luis Fuente W PTS 12 Altrincham *(WBF Featherweight Title Defence)*
21.06.03	Juan Cabrera W PTS 12 Manchester *(Vacant IBO Featherweight Title)*

Career: 36 contests, won 35, lost 1.

Mark Brookes

Swinton. *Born* Doncaster, 1 December, 1979
L. Heavyweight. Ht. 6'0"
Manager D. Hobson

21.10.00	Rob Galloway W RSC 5 Sheffield
11.12.00	Jimmy Steel W PTS 6 Sheffield
24.03.01	Matthew Pepper W RSC 1 Sheffield
18.06.01	Clint Johnson W PTS 6 Bradford

27.07.01	Michael Pinnock W PTS 4 Sheffield
13.09.01	Darren Ashton W PTS 4 Sheffield
22.09.01	Valery Odin L PTS 4 Canning Town
15.12.01	Clint Johnson W PTS 4 Sheffield
11.05.02	Paul Bonson W PTS 4 Chesterfield
05.10.02	Darren Ashton W PTS 4 Chesterfield
05.12.02	Simeon Cover W RSC 3 Sheffield
18.03.03	Peter Haymer L PTS 6 Reading
10.06.03	Michael Pinnock W PTS 4 Sheffield

Career: 13 contests, won 11, lost 2.

Cathy Brown

Peckham. *Born* Leeds, 28 July, 1970
WBF European Flyweight Champion. Ht. 5'2"
Manager A. Booth

31.10.99	Veerle Braspenningsx W PTS 5 Raynes Park
05.02.00	Veerle Braspenningsx W RSC 6 Sint-Truiden, Belgium
01.07.00	Jan Wild W PTS 6 Southwark *(Vacant WBF European Flyweight Title)*
31.10.00	Viktoria Vargal W RSC 3 Hammersmith
28.02.01	Marietta Ivanova W PTS 4 Kensington
26.04.01	Oksana Vasilieva L PTS 4 Kensington
16.06.01	Romona Gughie W RSC 3 Wembley
22.11.01	Audrey Guthrie W PTS 6 Mayfair *(WBF European Flyweight Title Defence)*
13.12.01	Ilina Boneva W RSC 5 Leicester Square
13.03.02	Svetla Taskova W PTS 4 Mayfair
13.06.02	Alina Shaternikova L PTS 10 Leicester Square *(Vacant WBF Womens Flyweight Title)*
30.10.02	Monica Petrova W PTS 6 Leicester Square
20.03.03	Juliette Winter L PTS 4 Queensway
26.04.03	Regina Halmich L PTS 10 Schwerin, Germany *(WIBF Flyweight Title Challenge)*

Career: 14 contests, won 10, lost 4.

Darren Bruce

Grays. *Born* Orsett, 1 December, 1972
Welterweight. Former Undefeated IBO Inter-Continental Welterweight Champion. Ht. 5'11"
Manager B. Hearn

28.11.97	Noel Henry W RSC 1 Bethnal Green
27.01.98	Darren McInulty W PTS 4 Bethnal Green
11.03.98	Kevin Lang W RSC 6 Bethnal Green
02.05.98	Harry Butler W RSC 6 Kensington
05.06.98	Leigh Wicks W PTS 6 Southend
08.09.98	Darren McInulty W CO 1 Bethnal Green
31.10.98	Shaun O'Neill W RSC 1 Southend
06.11.98	Delroy Mellis W RTD 3 Mayfair
11.12.98	John Green W RSC 1 Cheshunt
26.02.99	George Richards W PTS 6 Coventry
27.04.99	Dennis Berry W RSC 3 Bethnal Green
29.06.99	Frederic Noto L PTS 10 Bethnal Green
16.10.99	Charlie Kane W RTD 5 Bethnal Green *(Vacant IBO Inter-Continental Welterweight Title)*
05.02.00	Michael Smyth W CO 5 Bethnal Green *(IBO Inter-Continental Welterweight Title Defence)*

11.03.00   Mark Ramsey DREW 6 Kensington
02.12.00   Willy Wise L PTS 12 Bethnal Green
(Vacant IBO Welterweight Title)
14.07.01   Mark Ramsey L PTS 6 Wembley
29.06.02   Peter Dunn W PTS 6 Brentwood
21.09.02   Derek Roche L PTS 8 Brentwood
07.12.02   Piotr Bartnicki L RSC 3 Brentwood
19.04.03   Andrzej Butowicz W PTS 6 Liverpool
Career: 21 contests, won 15, drew 1, lost 5.

Pete Buckley

Birmingham. *Born* Birmingham, 9 March, 1969
L. Welterweight. Former Undefeated Midlands Area S. Featherweight Champion. Former Midlands Area S. Bantamweight Champion. Ht. 5'8"
Manager Self

04.10.89   Alan Baldwin DREW 6 Stafford
10.10.89   Ronnie Stephenson L PTS 6 Wolverhampton
30.10.89   Robert Braddock W PTS 6 Birmingham
14.11.89   Neil Leitch W PTS 6 Evesham
22.11.89   Peter Judson W PTS 6 Stafford
11.12.89   Stevie Woods W PTS 6 Bradford
21.12.89   Wayne Taylor W PTS 6 Kings Heath
10.01.90   John O'Meara W PTS 6 Kensington
19.02.90   Ian McGirr L PTS 6 Birmingham
27.02.90   Miguel Matthews DREW 6 Evesham
14.03.90   Ronnie Stephenson DREW 6 Stoke
04.04.90   Ronnie Stephenson L PTS 8 Stafford
23.04.90   Ronnie Stephenson W PTS 6 Birmingham
30.04.90   Chris Clarkson L PTS 8 Mayfair
17.05.90   Johnny Bredahl L PTS 6 Aars, Denmark
04.06.90   Ronnie Stephenson W PTS 8 Birmingham
28.06.90   Robert Braddock W RSC 5 Birmingham
01.10.90   Miguel Matthews W PTS 8 Cleethorpes
09.10.90   Miguel Matthews L PTS 8 Wolverhampton
17.10.90   Tony Smith W PTS 6 Stoke
29.10.90   Miguel Matthews W PTS 8 Birmingham
21.11.90   Drew Docherty L PTS 8 Solihull
10.12.90   Neil Leitch W PTS 8 Birmingham
10.01.91   Duke McKenzie L RSC 5 Wandsworth
18.02.91   Jamie McBride L PTS 8 Glasgow
04.03.91   Brian Robb W RSC 7 Birmingham
26.03.91   Neil Leitch DREW 8 Wolverhampton
01.05.91   Mark Geraghty W PTS 8 Solihull
05.06.91   Brian Robb W PTS 10 Wolverhampton
(Vacant Midlands Area S. Featherweight Title)
09.09.91   Mike Deveney L PTS 8 Glasgow
24.09.91   Mark Bates W RTD 5 Basildon
29.10.91   John Armour L PTS 6 Kensington
14.11.91   Mike Deveney L PTS 6 Edinburgh
28.11.91   Craig Dermody L PTS 6 Liverpool
19.12.91   Craig Dermody L PTS 6 Oldham
18.01.92   Alan McKay DREW 8 Kensington
20.02.92   Brian Robb W RSC 5 Oakengates
(Midlands Area S. Featherweight Title Defence)
27.04.92   Drew Docherty L PTS 8 Glasgow
15.05.92   Ruben Condori L PTS 10 Augsburg, Germany
29.05.92   Donnie Hood L PTS 8 Glasgow

07.09.92   Duke McKenzie L RTD 3 Bethnal Green
12.11.92   Prince Naseem Hamed L PTS 6 Liverpool
19.02.93   Harald Geier L PTS 12 Vienna, Austria
(Vacant WBA Penta-Continental S. Bantamweight Title)
26.04.93   Bradley Stone L PTS 8 Lewisham
18.06.93   Eamonn McAuley L PTS 6 Belfast
01.07.93   Tony Silkstone L PTS 8 York
06.10.93   Jonjo Irwin L PTS 8 Solihull
25.10.93   Drew Docherty L PTS 8 Glasgow
06.11.93   Michael Alldis L PTS 8 Bethnal Green
30.11.93   Barry Jones L PTS 4 Cardiff
19.12.93   Shaun Anderson L PTS 6 Glasgow
22.01.94   Barry Jones L PTS 6 Cardiff
29.01.94   Prince Naseem Hamed L RSC 4 Cardiff
10.03.94   Tony Falcone L PTS 4 Bristol
29.03.94   Conn McMullen W PTS 6 Bethnal Green
05.04.94   Mark Bowers L PTS 6 Bethnal Green
13.04.94   James Murray L PTS 6 Glasgow
06.05.94   Paul Lloyd L RTD 4 Liverpool
03.08.94   Greg Upton L PTS 6 Bristol
26.09.94   John Sillo L PTS 6 Liverpool
05.10.94   Matthew Harris L PTS 6 Wolverhampton
07.11.94   Marlon Ward L PTS 4 Piccadilly
23.11.94   Justin Murphy L PTS 4 Piccadilly
29.11.94   Neil Swain L PTS Cardiff
13.12.94   Michael Brodie L PTS 6 Potters Bar
20.12.94   Michael Alldis L PTS 8 Bethnal Green
10.02.95   Matthew Harris W RSC 6 Birmingham
(Midlands Area S. Bantamweight Title Challenge)
23.02.95   Paul Ingle L PTS 8 Southwark
20.04.95   John Sillo L PTS 6 Liverpool
27.04.95   Paul Ingle L PTS 8 Bethnal Green
09.05.95   Ady Lewis L PTS 4 Basildon
23.05.95   Spencer Oliver L PTS 6 Potters Bar
01.07.95   Dean Pithie L PTS 4 Kensington
21.09.95   Patrick Mullings L PTS 6 Battersea
29.09.95   Marlon Ward L PTS 4 Bethnal Green
25.10.95   Matthew Harris L PTS 10 Telford
(Midlands Area S. Bantamweight Title Defence)
08.11.95   Vince Feeney L PTS 8 Bethnal Green
28.11.95   Barry Jones L PTS 6 Cardiff
15.12.95   Patrick Mullings L PTS 4 Bethnal Green
05.02.96   Patrick Mullings L PTS 8 Bexleyheath
09.03.96   Paul Griffin L PTS 4 Millstreet
21.03.96   Colin McMillan L RSC 3 Southwark
14.05.96   Venkatesan Deverajan L PTS 4 Dagenham
29.06.96   Matt Brown W RSC 1 Erith
03.09.96   Vince Feeney L PTS 4 Bethnal Green
28.09.96   Fabrice Benichou L PTS 8 Barking
09.10.96   Gary Marston DREW 8 Stoke
06.11.96   Neil Swain L PTS 4 Tylorstown
29.11.96   Alston Buchanan L PTS 8 Glasgow
22.12.96   Brian Carr L PTS 6 Glasgow
11.01.97   Scott Harrison L PTS 4 Bethnal Green
29.01.97   Carl Allen L PTS 8 Stoke
12.02.97   Ronnie McPhee L PTS 6 Glasgow
25.02.97   Dean Pithie L PTS 4 Sheffield
07.03.97   Jason Booth L PTS 6 Northampton
20.03.97   Thomas Bradley W PTS 6 Newark
08.04.97   Sergei Devakov L PTS 6 Bethnal Green
25.04.97   Matthew Harris L PTS 6 Cleethorpes
08.05.97   Gregorio Medina L RTD 2 Mansfield

13.06.97   Mike Deveney L PTS 6 Paisley
19.07.97   Richard Evatt L PTS 4 Wembley
30.08.97   Michael Brodie L PTS 8 Cheshunt
06.10.97   Brendan Bryce W PTS 6 Piccadilly
20.10.97   Kelton McKenzie L PTS 6 Leicester
20.11.97   Ervine Blake L PTS 8 Solihull
06.12.97   Danny Adams L PTS 4 Wembley
13.12.97   Gary Thornhill L PTS 6 Sheffield
31.01.98   Scott Harrison L PTS 4 Edmonton
05.03.98   Steve Conway L PTS 6 Leeds
18.03.98   Ervine Blake L PTS 8 Stoke
26.03.98   Graham McGrath W RTD 4 Solihull
11.04.98   Salim Medjkoune L PTS 6 Southwark
18.04.98   Tony Mulholland L PTS 4 Manchester
27.04.98   Alston Buchanan L PTS 8 Glasgow
11.05.98   Jason Squire W RTD 2 Leicester
21.05.98   Lee Armstrong L PTS 6 Bradford
06.06.98   Tony Mulholland L PTS 6 Liverpool
14.06.98   Lee Armstrong L PTS 6 Shaw
21.07.98   David Burke L PTS 6 Widnes
05.09.98   Michael Gomez L PTS 6 Telford
17.09.98   Brian Carr L PTS 6 Glasgow
03.10.98   Justin Murphy L PTS 6 Crawley
05.12.98   Lehlohonolo Ledwaba L PTS 8 Bristol
19.12.98   Acelino Freitas L RTD 3 Liverpool
09.02.99   Chris Jickells L PTS 6 Wolverhampton
16.02.99   Franny Hogg L PTS 6 Leeds
26.02.99   Richard Evatt L RSC 5 Coventry
17.04.99   Martin O'Malley L RSC 3 Dublin
29.05.99   Richie Wenton L PTS 6 Halifax
14.06.99   Carl Allen L PTS 6 Birmingham
26.06.99   Paul Halpin L PTS 4 Millwall
15.07.99   Salim Medjkoune L PTS 6 Peterborough
07.08.99   Steve Murray L PTS 6 Dagenham
12.09.99   Kevin Gerowski L PTS 6 Nottingham
20.09.99   Mat Zegan L PTS 6 Peterborough
02.10.99   Jason Cook L PTS 4 Cardiff
09.10.99   Brian Carr L PTS 6 Manchester
19.10.99   Gary Steadman L PTS 4 Bethnal Green
27.10.99   Miguel Matthews W PTS 8 Birmingham
20.11.99   Carl Greaves L PTS 10 Grantham
(British Masters S. Featherweight Title Challenge)
11.12.99   Gary Thornhill L PTS 6 Liverpool
29.01.00   Bradley Pryce L PTS 4 Manchester
19.02.00   Gavin Rees L PTS 4 Dagenham
29.02.00   Tony Mulholland L PTS 4 Widnes
20.03.00   Carl Greaves L PTS 8 Mansfield
27.03.00   James Rooney L PTS 4 Barnsley
08.04.00   Delroy Pryce L PTS 4 Bethnal Green
17.04.00   Franny Hogg L PTS 8 Glasgow
11.05.00   Craig Spacie L PTS 4 Newark
25.05.00   Jimmy Phelan DREW 6 Hull
19.06.00   Delroy Pryce L PTS 4 Burton
01.07.00   Richard Evatt L PTS 4 Manchester
16.09.00   Lee Meager L PTS 4 Bethnal Green
23.09.00   Gavin Rees L PTS 4 Bethnal Green
02.10.00   Brian Carr L PTS 4 Glasgow
14.10.00   Gareth Jordan L PTS 4 Wembley
13.11.00   Kevin Lear L PTS 6 Bethnal Green
24.11.00   Lee Williamson L PTS 6 Hull
09.12.00   Leo O'Reilly L PTS 4 Southwark
15.01.01   Eddie Nevins L PTS 4 Manchester
23.01.01   David Burke L PTS 4 Crawley
31.01.01   Tony Montana L PTS 6 Piccadilly
19.02.01   Kevin England W PTS 6 Glasgow
12.03.01   Carl Allen L PTS 6 Birmingham
19.03.01   Duncan Armstrong L PTS 6 Glasgow
27.03.01   Carl Allen L PTS 8 Brierley Hill
05.05.01   Danny Hunt L PTS 4 Edmonton
09.06.01   Gary Thornhill L PTS 4 Bethnal Green

21.07.01	Scott Miller L PTS 4 Sheffield
28.07.01	Kevin Lear L PTS 4 Wembley
25.09.01	Ricky Eccleston L PTS 4 Liverpool
07.10.01	Nigel Senior L PTS 6 Wolverhampton
31.10.01	Woody Greenaway L PTS 6 Birmingham
16.11.01	Jimmy Beech L PTS 6 West Bromwich
01.12.01	Chill John L PTS 4 Bethnal Green
09.12.01	Nigel Senior W PTS 6 Shaw
26.01.02	Scott Lawton L PTS 4 Bethnal Green
09.02.02	Sam Gorman L PTS 6 Coventry
23.02.02	Alex Moon L PTS 4 Nottingham
04.03.02	Leo Turner L PTS 6 Bradford
11.03.02	Martin Watson L PTS 4 Glasgow
26.04.02	Scott Lawton L PTS 4 Coventry
10.05.02	Lee Meager L PTS 6 Bethnal Green
08.06.02	Bradley Pryce L RSC 1 Renfrew
20.07.02	Jeff Thomas L PTS 4 Bethnal Green
23.08.02	Ben Hudson DREW 4 Bethnal Green
06.09.02	Dave Stewart L PTS 6 Bethnal Green
14.09.02	Peter McDonagh L PTS 4 Bethnal Green
20.10.02	James Paisley L PTS 4 Southwark
12.11.02	Martin Hardcastle DREW 6 Leeds
29.11.02	Daniel Thorpe L PTS 6 Hull
09.12.02	Nicky Leech L PTS 6 Nottingham
16.12.02	Joel Viney L PTS 6 Cleethorpes
28.01.03	Billy Corcoran L PTS 6 Nottingham
08.02.03	Colin Toohey L PTS 6 Liverpool
15.02.03	Terry Fletcher L PTS 4 Wembley
22.02.03	Dean Lambert L PTS 4 Huddersfield
05.03.03	Billy Corcoran L PTS 6 Bethnal Green
18.03.03	Nathan Ward L PTS 4 Reading
05.04.03	Baz Carey L PTS 4 Manchester
15.05.03	Mike Harrington W PTS 4 Clevedon
27.05.03	Dave Stewart L PTS 4 Dagenham
07.06.03	Rimell Taylor DREW 6 Coventry

Career: 203 contests, won 29, drew 10, lost 164.

(Andrew) Stefy Bull (Bullcroft)

Doncaster. *Born* Doncaster, 10 May, 1977
L. Welterweight. Former Undefeated
Central Area Featherweight Champion.
Ht. 5'10"
Manager J. Rushton

30.06.95	Andy Roberts W PTS 4 Doncaster
11.10.95	Michael Edwards W PTS 6 Stoke
18.10.95	Alan Hagan W RSC 1 Batley
28.11.95	Kevin Sheil W PTS 6 Wolverhampton
26.01.96	Robert Grubb W PTS 6 Doncaster
12.09.96	Benny Jones W PTS 6 Doncaster
15.10.96	Kevin Sheil DREW 6 Wolverhampton
24.10.96	Graham McGrath W PTS 6 Birmingham
17.12.96	Robert Braddock W RSC 4 Doncaster *(Vacant Central Area Featherweight Title)*
10.07.97	Carl Greaves W PTS 6 Doncaster
11.10.97	Dean Pithie L RSC 11 Sheffield *(Vacant WBO Inter-Continental S. Featherweight Title)*
19.03.98	Chris Lyons W RSC 4 Doncaster
08.04.98	Alex Moon L RSC 3 Liverpool
31.07.99	Jason Dee L RSC 4 Carlisle
09.05.03	Joel Viney W RTD 3 Doncaster
02.06.03	Jason Nesbitt W PTS 6 Cleethorpes

Career: 16 contests, won 12, drew 1, lost 3.

David Burke

Liverpool. *Born* Liverpool, 3 February, 1975
WBU Lightweight Champion. Former
Undefeated Commonwealth Lightweight
Champion. Ht. 5'9"
Manager B. Hearn

01.03.97	Ervine Blake W PTS 4 Liverpool
21.05.97	Carl Allen W PTS 4 Liverpool
26.09.97	Rudy Valentino W PTS 4 Liverpool
12.03.98	Bamana Dibateza W PTS 6 Liverpool
08.04.98	John O. Johnson W RSC 1 Liverpool
23.05.98	Mike Deveney W PTS 6 Bethnal Green
21.07.98	Pete Buckley W PTS 6 Widnes
24.10.98	Gary Flear W PTS 6 Liverpool
12.12.98	Justin Murphy W RSC 4 Southwark
05.03.99	Alan Temple W PTS 8 Liverpool
15.05.99	Marian Leonardu L RSC 3 Blackpool
19.06.99	Chris Williams W RTD 1 Dublin
13.12.99	Chris Jickells W PTS 6 Glasgow
09.03.00	Woody Greenaway W RSC 2 Liverpool
23.01.01	Pete Buckley W PTS 4 Crawley
03.02.01	Keith Jones W PTS 4 Manchester
03.03.01	Marco Fattore W RSC 1 Wembley
24.04.01	Jason Dee W RSC 1 Liverpool
26.05.01	Matthew Zulu W PTS 6 Bethnal Green
25.09.01	Richard Howard W PTS 6 Liverpool
09.03.02	Anthony Maynard W PTS 6 Manchester
07.09.02	Gary Hibbert W RSC 10 Liverpool *(Vacant Commonwealth Lightweight Title)*

David Burke　　　　　　　　　　　　　Les Clark

07.12.02 Colin Dunne W PTS 12 Brentwood
 (WBU Lightweight Title Challenge)
07.06.03 Stefano Zoff L PTS 12 Trieste, Italy
 (Vacant European Lightweight Title)
Career: 24 contests, won 22, lost 2.

Matthew Burke
Stratford. *Born* London, 7 October, 1980
Featherweight. Ht. 5'11¼"
Manager B. Hearn

29.06.02 Joel Viney W PTS 4 Brentwood
21.09.02 Andy Robinson W PTS 4 Brentwood
07.12.02 John Simpson L PTS 4 Brentwood
Career: 3 contests, won 2, lost 1.

Ricky Burns
Coatbridge. *Born* Bellshill, 13 April, 1983
L. Welterweight. Ht. 5'10"
Manager R. Bannan/K. Morrison

20.10.01 Woody Greenaway W PTS 4 Glasgow
15.03.02 Peter Allen W PTS 6 Glasgow
08.06.02 Gary Harrison W RSC 1 Renfrew
06.09.02 Ernie Smith W PTS 6 Glasgow
19.10.02 Neil Murray W RSC 2 Renfrew
08.12.02 No No Junior W PTS 8 Glasgow
Career: 6 contests, won 6.

Pinky Burton
Sheffield. *Born* Perth, 13 December, 1979
L. Heavyweight. Ht. 5'11½"
Manager T. Gilmour/C. Aston

28.04.01 Nathan King L PTS 4 Cardiff
28.01.02 Rob Galloway W RSC 4 Barnsley
02.03.02 Darren Ashton W PTS 6 Wakefield
17.02.03 Eamonn Glennon W PTS 6 Glasgow
24.03.03 Michael Pinnock W PTS 4 Barnsley
02.06.03 Ovill McKenzie W PTS 8 Glasgow
Career: 6 contests, won 5, lost 1.

Robert Burton
Barnsley. *Born* Barnsley, 1 April, 1971
Central Area Welterweight Champion.
Ht. 5'9"
Manager T. Schofield

05.02.01 Gavin Pearson W RSC 3 Bradford
23.02.01 Scott Millar W CO 5 Irvine
20.03.01 Peter Dunn W PTS 6 Leeds
08.05.01 Arv Mittoo W PTS 4 Barnsley
10.06.01 Martyn Bailey DREW 6 Ellesmere Port
08.10.01 Gavin Pearson W RSC 2 Barnsley
16.11.01 Martyn Bailey DREW 4 Preston
24.11.01 Peter Dunn L PTS 6 Wakefield
28.01.02 Peter Dunn W RSC 8 Barnsley
 (Vacant Central Area Welterweight Title)
23.08.02 David Walker L RSC 2 Bethnal Green
19.10.02 John Humphrey L RTD 4 Norwich
09.02.03 Donovan Smillie L PTS 6 Bradford
24.03.03 Andy Halder L PTS 6 Barnsley
31.05.03 David Keir W RSC 9 Barnsley
 (Central Area Welterweight Title Defence)
Career: 14 contests, won 7, drew 2, lost 5.

Harry Butler
Worcester. *Born* Wisbech, 12 August, 1977
S. Middleweight. Ht. 5'8"
Manager Self

19.07.97 Takaloo L RSC 1 Wembley
30.08.97 Patrick Pasi L PTS 4 Cheshunt
26.09.97 Darren Williams L PTS 6 Port Talbot
21.10.97 John Green L PTS 6 Yarm
15.11.97 Michael Jones L PTS 4 Bristol
02.12.97 Ross McCord W RSC 3 Swansea
13.12.97 Hercules Kyvelos L PTS 4 Sheffield
06.01.98 Alan Gilbert L PTS 4 Brighton
13.02.98 Gareth Hogg L RSC 3 Weston super Mare
14.03.98 Sonny Thind L PTS 4 Bethnal Green
03.04.98 Jon Foster L PTS 6 Ebbw Vale
18.04.98 Anthony Farnell L PTS 6 Manchester
02.05.98 Darren Bruce L RSC 6 Kensington
04.06.98 Adrian Houldey L PTS 6 Dudley
14.06.98 Gerard Lawrence L PTS 6 Golders Green
08.08.98 Sonny Pollard W RSC 4 Scarborough
05.09.98 Jawaid Khaliq L PTS 4 Telford
26.09.98 James Lowther L RSC 6 York
21.11.98 Brian Knudsen L RSC 4 Southwark
18.02.99 Clive Johnson L PTS 6 Barking
05.03.99 Paul Burns L RSC 5 Liverpool
23.04.99 Jason Williams L RSC 7 Clydach
26.06.99 Lawrence Murphy L RSC 1 Glasgow
19.09.99 Mick Mulcahy L PTS 6 Shaw
14.10.99 Lester Jacobs L PTS 6 Bloomsbury
06.11.99 Junior Witter L PTS 6 Widnes
06.12.99 Malcolm Melvin L PTS 8 Birmingham
20.12.99 Richard Williams L RSC 1 Bethnal Green
26.02.00 Jason Cook L PTS 6 Swansea
13.03.00 Christian Brady L PTS 6 Birmingham
20.03.00 Jamie Moore L RSC 2 Mansfield
15.05.00 Ernie Smith W PTS 6 Birmingham
26.05.00 Barry Connell L PTS 4 Glasgow
21.09.00 Ojay Abrahams L PTS 6 Bloomsbury
07.10.00 Michael Alexander L PTS 6 Doncaster
26.10.00 Matthew Ashmole W PTS 6 Clydach
23.11.00 Matthew Barr L PTS 4 Bayswater
30.11.00 Shpetim Hoti W PTS 4 Bloomsbury
11.12.00 Jimmy Vincent L PTS 6 Birmingham
28.01.01 Peter Jackson L PTS 6 Wolverhampton
10.02.01 Thomas McDonagh L PTS 6 Widnes
24.02.01 Spencer Fearon L PTS 4 Bethnal Green
09.03.01 John Humphrey L RSC 1 Millwall
22.04.01 Ojay Abrahams L PTS 6 Streatham
05.05.01 Liam Lathbury L PTS 6 Brighton
19.05.01 Delroy Leslie L PTS 6 Wembley
21.06.01 Shpetim Hoti W PTS 4 Earls Court
04.07.01 Darren Covill W RSC 4 Bloomsbury
26.07.01 Lee Blundell L PTS 4 Blackpool
20.09.01 Ruben Groenewald L PTS 4 Blackfriars
08.10.01 Roddy Doran L PTS 6 Birmingham
20.10.01 Ty Browne L PTS 6 Portsmouth
31.10.01 Roddy Doran DREW 6 Birmingham
16.11.01 Mark Richards L PTS 6 West Bromwich
23.11.01 Erik Teymour L RSC 2 Bethnal Green
26.01.02 Jamie Moore L RSC 3 Dagenham
04.03.02 Malcolm Melvin L PTS 8 Birmingham
15.03.02 Tom Cannon L PTS 6 Glasgow
24.04.02 Jim Rock L PTS 6 Dublin
11.05.02 Jason McKay L PTS 4 Dagenham
01.06.02 Mickey Quinn L PTS 4 Manchester
15.06.02 Darren Rhodes L PTS 4 Leeds
23.08.02 Matthew Thirlwall L RSC 3 Bethnal Green
26.09.02 Joel Ani L PTS 4 Fulham
06.10.02 Craig Winter L PTS 6 Rhyl
20.11.02 Dean Cockburn L PTS 6 Leeds
03.12.02 Roddy Doran L PTS 6 Shrewsbury
22.12.02 Alan Page L RSC 1 Salford

24.02.03 Hamid Jamali L PTS 6 Birmingham
21.03.03 Sam Price L PTS 4 Longford
29.03.03 Courtney Fry L RSC 3 Wembley
Career: 71 contests, won 7, drew 1, lost 63.

Paul Butlin
Oakham. *Born* Oakham, 16 March, 1976
Heavyweight. Ht. 6'1½"
Manager A. Phillips

05.10.02 Dave Clarke W PTS 4 Coventry
16.11.02 Gary Williams W RSC 1 Coventry
09.12.02 Slick Miller W PTS 6 Nottingham
08.03.03 Dave Clarke W PTS 6 Coventry
19.04.03 Paul Buttery L RSC 3 Liverpool
Career: 5 contests, won 4, lost 1.

Paul Buttery
Preston. *Born* Preston, 12 May, 1977
Heavyweight. Ht. 6'2½"
Manager T. Gilmour

03.02.01 Luke Simpkin L RSC 1 Manchester
24.04.01 Dave Faulkner W CO 1 Liverpool
16.11.01 Eamonn Glennon W RSC 1 Preston
10.05.02 Tony Booth W PTS 4 Preston
01.11.02 Colin Kenna DREW 6 Preston
19.04.03 Paul Butlin W RSC 3 Liverpool
17.05.03 Collice Mutizwa W RSC 1 Liverpool
Career: 7 contests, won 5, drew 1, lost 1.

Paul Buttery   Les Clark

Tony Byrne
Preston. *Born* Preston, 17 November, 1978
L. Middleweight. Ht. 5'7"
Manager Self

10.06.01 Paul Lomax W PTS 6 Ellesmere Port
16.11.01 Gary Jones W PTS 6 Preston
09.12.01 Paul Lomax W PTS 6 Blackpool
08.02.02 Jamie Logan W RTD 3 Preston
08.03.02 Andrei Ivanov W PTS 6 Ellesmere Port
10.05.02 Scott Millar W RSC 2 Preston
01.11.02 Martyn Bailey L PTS 6 Preston
Career: 7 contests, won 6, lost 1.

Adam Cale

Worcester. *Born* Worcester, 11 April, 1972
Cruiserweight. Ht. 6'2"
Manager Self

04.06.98	Matthew Barney L PTS 6 Barking	
23.07.98	Matthew Barney L PTS 6 Barking	
07.10.98	Kevin Burton W PTS 6 Stoke	
31.10.98	Faisal Mohammed L RSC 2 Basingstoke	
09.02.99	Kevin Burton W PTS 8 Wolverhampton	
26.02.99	Neil Simpson L RSC 3 Coventry	
27.05.99	Carl Smallwood L PTS 6 Edgbaston	
06.06.99	Wayne Buck L PTS 6 Nottingham	
22.06.99	Scott Baker L PTS 4 Ipswich	
20.08.99	Matthew Barney L PTS 4 Bloomsbury	
03.09.99	Jason Brewster L PTS 6 West Bromwich	
20.09.99	Kenny Gayle L PTS 4 Peterborough	
27.09.99	Tony Booth L PTS 6 Cleethorpes	
11.10.99	Stevie Pettit L PTS 6 Birmingham	
20.10.99	Stevie Pettit L PTS 6 Stoke	
08.12.99	Nigel Rafferty L RSC 6 Stoke	
12.02.00	Tony Dowling L PTS 4 Sheffield	
26.02.00	Chris Davies L RSC 4 Swansea	
18.05.00	Elvis Michailenko L PTS 4 Bethnal Green	
16.06.00	Scott Baker L PTS 4 Bloomsbury	
10.09.00	Jason Brewster L PTS 4 Walsall	
21.10.00	Scott Lansdowne L RSC 5 Sheffield	
25.11.00	Peter Haymer L RSC 1 Manchester	
22.04.01	Radcliffe Green L CO 5 Streatham	
02.06.01	Ivan Botton L PTS 4 Wakefield	
26.07.01	Eamonn Glennon L PTS 6 Blackpool	
26.08.01	Peter Merrall L PTS 6 Warrington	
09.09.01	Rob Hayes-Scott L RSC 1 Southwark	
01.11.01	Mark Ellwood L PTS 6 Hull	
16.11.01	Gary Thompson L PTS 6 Preston	
22.11.01	Tony Strong L CO 1 Mayfair	
27.01.02	Oneal Murray L PTS 6 Streatham	
12.02.02	Tommy Eastwood L PTS 4 Bethnal Green	
08.03.02	Spencer Wilding L PTS 6 Ellesmere Port	
19.03.02	Blue Stevens L RSC 4 Slough	
20.04.02	Ivan Botton DREW 4 Wembley	
02.06.02	Darren Stubbs L RSC 6 Shaw	
07.09.02	Tony Moran L PTS 4 Liverpool	
26.09.02	Brian Gascoigne L PTS 4 Fulham	
05.10.02	Carl Wright L PTS 6 Coventry	
29.11.02	Tony Moran L RSC 1 Liverpool	

Career: 41 contests, won 2, drew 1, lost 38.

Marc Callaghan

Barking. *Born* Barking, 13 November, 1977
S. Bantamweight. Ht. 5'6"
Manager B. Hearn

08.09.98	Kevin Sheil W PTS 4 Bethnal Green	
31.10.98	Nicky Wilders W RSC 1 Southend	
12.01.99	Nicky Wilders W RTD 2 Bethnal Green	
12.03.99	Peter Allen W PTS 4 Bethnal Green	
25.05.99	Simon Chambers L RSC 1 Mayfair	
16.10.99	Nigel Leake W PTS 4 Bethnal Green	
20.12.99	Marc Smith W PTS 4 Bethnal Green	
05.02.00	Steve Brook W RSC 2 Bethnal Green	

01.04.00	John Barnes W PTS 4 Bethnal Green	
19.08.00	Anthony Hanna W PTS 4 Brentwood	
09.10.00	Jamie McKeever L PTS 6 Liverpool	
04.11.00	Nigel Senior W RSC 4 Bethnal Green	
03.03.01	Anthony Hanna W PTS 6 Wembley	
26.05.01	Roy Rutherford L RSC 3 Bethnal Green	
01.12.01	Nigel Senior L CO 1 Bethnal Green	
26.01.02	Richmond Asante W PTS 4 Dagenham	
18.03.02	Michael Hunter DREW 6 Crawley	
11.05.02	Andrew Ferrans W PTS 6 Dagenham	
21.09.02	Steve Gethin W PTS 6 Brentwood	
07.12.02	Stevie Quinn L PTS 4 Brentwood	
08.03.03	Dazzo Williams L PTS 8 Bethnal Green	

Career: 21 contests, won 14, drew 1, lost 6.

Marc Callaghan   Les Clark

Jason Callum

Coventry. *Born* Coventry, 5 April, 1977
Heavyweight. Ht. 6'3"
Manager O. Delargy

05.04.03   Tony Booth W PTS 6 Coventry
Career: 1 contest, won 1.

Joe Calzaghe

Newbridge. *Born* Hammersmith, 23 March, 1972
WBO S. Middleweight Champion. Former Undefeated British S. Middleweight Champion. Ht. 5'11"
Manager F. Warren

01.10.93	Paul Hanlon W RSC 1 Cardiff	
10.11.93	Stinger Mason W RSC 1 Watford	
16.12.93	Spencer Alton W RSC 2 Newport	
22.01.94	Martin Rosamond W RSC 1 Cardiff	
01.03.94	Darren Littlewood W RSC 1 Dudley	
04.06.94	Karl Barwise W RSC 1 Cardiff	
01.10.94	Mark Dawson W RSC 1 Cardiff	
30.11.94	Trevor Ambrose W RSC 2 Wolverhampton	
14.02.95	Frank Minton W CO 1 Bethnal Green	
22.02.95	Bobbi Joe Edwards W PTS 8 Telford	

19.05.95	Robert Curry W RSC 1 Southwark	
08.07.95	Tyrone Jackson W RSC 4 York	
30.09.95	Nick Manners W RSC 4 Basildon	
28.10.95	Stephen Wilson W RSC 8 Kensington	
	(Vacant British S. Middleweight Title)	
13.02.96	Guy Stanford W RSC 1 Cardiff	
13.03.96	Anthony Brooks W RSC 2 Wembley	
20.04.96	Mark Delaney W RSC 5 Brentwood	
	(British S. Middleweight Title Defence)	
04.05.96	Warren Stowe W RTD 2 Dagenham	
15.05.96	Pat Lawlor W RSC 2 Cardiff	
21.01.97	Carlos Christie W CO 2 Bristol	
22.03.97	Tyler Hughes W CO 1 Wythenshawe	
05.06.97	Luciano Torres W RSC 3 Bristol	
11.10.97	Chris Eubank W PTS 12 Sheffield	
	(Vacant WBO S. Middleweight Title)	
24.01.98	Branco Sobot W RSC 3 Cardiff	
	(WBO S. Middleweight Title Defence)	
25.04.98	Juan Carlos Gimenez W RTD 9 Cardiff	
	(WBO S. Middleweight Title Defence)	
13.02.99	Robin Reid W PTS 12 Newcastle	
	(WBO S. Middleweight Title Defence)	
05.06.99	Rick Thornberry W PTS 12 Cardiff	
	(WBO S. Middleweight Title Defence)	
29.01.00	David Starie W PTS 12 Manchester	
	(WBO S, Middleweight Title Defence)	
12.08.00	Omar Sheika W RSC 5 Wembley	
	(WBO S.Middleweight Title Defence)	
16.12.00	Richie Woodhall W RSC 10 Sheffield	
	(WBO S. Middleweight Title Defence)	
28.04.01	Mario Veit W RSC 1 Cardiff	
	(WBO S. Middleweight Title Defence)	
13.10.01	Will McIntyre W RSC 4 Copenhagen, Denmark	
	(WBO S. Middleweight Title Defence)	
20.04.02	Charles Brewer W PTS 12 Cardiff	
	(WBO S. Middleweight Title Defence)	
17.08.02	Miguel Jimenez W PTS 12 Cardiff	
	(WBO S.Middleweight Title Defence)	
14.12.02	Tocker Pudwill W RSC 2 Newcastle	
	(WBO S. Middleweight Title Defence)	
28.06.03	Byron Mitchell W RSC 2 Cardiff	
	(WBO S.Middleweight Title Defence)	

Career: 36 contests, won 36.

Joe Calzaghe   Les Clark

Tom Cannon

Coatbridge. *Born* Bellshill, 18 March, 1980
Middleweight. Ht. 5'11¹/₂"
Manager R. Bannon/K. Morrison

15.06.01	Valery Odin L PTS 4 Millwall	
20.10.01	Andrew Lowe L PTS 4 Glasgow	
26.01.02	Arthur Chekmuroz DREW 4 Bethnal Green	
15.03.02	Harry Butler W PTS 6 Glasgow	
08.06.02	Ty Browne W PTS 4 Renfrew	
06.09.02	Gary Dixon W PTS 6 Glasgow	
21.10.02	Dean Cockburn DREW 4 Glasgow	

Career: 7 contests, won 3, drew 2, lost 2.

(Barry) Baz Carey

Coventry. *Born* Coventry, 11 March, 1971
S. Featherweight. Ht. 5'4¹/₂"
Manager A. Phillips

19.12.01	J.J. Moore L PTS 4 Coventry
18.01.02	J.J. Moore DREW 4 Coventry
25.02.02	Chris McDonagh L PTS 6 Slough
19.03.02	Ilias Miah W PTS 6 Slough
21.09.02	Jackson Williams L PTS 6 Norwich
10.10.02	Dean Scott W RSC 2 Stoke
19.10.02	Lee McAllister L PTS 4 Renfrew
21.11.02	Chris Hooper L RTD 3 Hull
22.03.03	Dave Hinds W PTS 6 Coventry
05.04.03	Pete Buckley W PTS 4 Manchester
12.05.03	Matthew Marshall L PTS 6 Southampton
07.06.03	Joel Viney W PTS 6 Coventry

Career: 12 contests, won 5, drew 1, lost 6.

Dafydd Carlin

Belfast. *Born* Brecon, 2 August, 1978
Northern Ireland Lightweight Champion.
Ht. 5'6"
Manager A. Wilton

01.04.01	Paddy Folan W PTS 4 Southwark
28.04.01	Alex Arthur L PTS 4 Cardiff
03.06.01	Dave Hinds W PTS 4 Southwark
22.09.01	Danny Hunt L PTS 4 Bethnal Green
15.12.01	Matthew Hatton L PTS 6 Wembley
19.01.02	Francis Barrett L PTS 4 Bethnal Green
12.02.02	Scott Miller L PTS 4 Bethnal Green
20.04.02	Bradley Pryce L RSC 8 Cardiff
12.10.02	Ross Minter L RSC 1 Bethnal Green
08.12.02	Ben Hudson L PTS 6 Bethnal Green
01.02.03	Robbie Murray L PTS 4 Belfast
18.02.03	Peter McDonagh W PTS 4 Bethnal Green
14.03.03	Colin Bain L PTS 6 Glasgow
05.04.03	Gary Hamilton W PTS 10 Belfast
	(Vacant Northern Ireland Lightweight Title)

Career: 14 contests, won 4, lost 10.

Brian Carr

Moodiesburn. *Born* Glasgow, 20 June, 1969
Scottish Featherweight Champion. Former
Commonwealth S. Bantamweight
Champion. Ht. 5'6"
Manager K. Morrison

18.12.94	Fred Reeve W CO 2 Glasgow
21.01.95	Shaun Anderson W PTS 6 Glasgow
04.03.95	G. G. Goddard W PTS 8 Livingston
13.05.95	Paul Wynn W RTD 2 Glasgow
08.06.95	Abdul Manna W PTS 6 Glasgow

13.10.95	Muhammad Shaffique W PTS 6 Glasgow
17.12.95	Abdul Mannon W PTS 8 Glasgow
16.03.96	Chip O'Neill W PTS 4 Glasgow
26.04.96	Mike Deveney W PTS 10 Glasgow
	(Vacant Scottish Featherweight Title)
20.09.96	Fred Reeve W RSC 3 Glasgow
06.11.96	Mike Deveney W PTS 10 Glasgow
	(Scottish Featherweight Title Defence)
22.12.96	Pete Buckley W PTS 6 Glasgow
04.04.97	Lyndon Kershaw W PTS 10 Glasgow
	(Elim. British S. Bantamweight Title)
05.07.97	Kevin Sheil W RSC 5 Glasgow
12.09.97	Carl Allen W PTS 6 Glasgow
01.11.97	Steve Conway W PTS 6 Glasgow
31.01.98	Michael Brodie L RSC 10 Edmonton
	(British & Commonwealth S. Bantamweight Title Challenges)
17.09.98	Pete Buckley W PTS 6 Glasgow
06.02.99	Patrick Mullings L PTS 12 Halifax
	(Vacant British S. Bantamweight Title)
27.02.99	Fondil Madani W CO 3 Bethnal Green
09.04.99	Keith Jones W PTS 8 Glasgow
26.06.99	Cassius Baloyi L RTD 9 Glasgow
	(WBU Featherweight Title Challenge)
09.10.99	Pete Buckley W PTS 6 Manchester
12.11.99	Harry Woods W PTS 6 Glasgow
11.12.99	Lee Williamson DREW 6 Liverpool
18.03.00	Nedal Hussein L PTS 12 Glasgow
	(Vacant Commonwealth S. Bantamweight Title)
26.05.00	Ian Turner W PTS 6 Glasgow
24.06.00	Dave Hinds W PTS 4 Glasgow
02.10.00	Pete Buckley W PTS 4 Glasgow
03.11.01	Mishek Kondwani W PTS 12 Glasgow
	(Vacant Commonwealth S.Bantamweight Title)
18.03.02	Michael Alldis L PTS 12 Crawley
	(Vacant British S. Bantamweight Title. Commonwealth S. Bantamweight Title Defence)
22.03.03	John Mackay L PTS 8 Renfrew

Career: 32 contests, won 25, drew 1, lost 6.

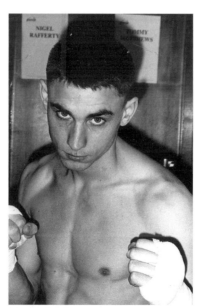

Henry Castle   Les Clark

Henry Castle

Salisbury. *Born* Southampton, 7 February, 1979
Featherweight. Ht. 5'6¹/₄"
Manager K. Sanders

29.01.01	Jason Nesbitt W CO 6 Peterborough
26.03.01	Eddie Nevins W RSC 2 Peterborough
23.11.01	Jimmy Beech W PTS 4 Bethnal Green
11.03.02	David Lowry W RSC 1 Glasgow
20.04.02	Jason Nesbitt W PTS 4 Cardiff
25.05.02	Jimmy Beech W PTS 4 Portsmouth
17.08.02	Joel Viney W RSC 1 Cardiff
23.11.02	John Mackay L RTD 8 Derby
29.03.03	Jus Wallie L RSC 2 Portsmouth

Career: 9 contests, won 7, lost 2.

Glenn Catley

Bristol. *Born* Sodbury, 15 March, 1972
S.Middleweight. Former WBC
S.Middleweight Champion. Former
Undefeated IBF & WBO Inter-Continental
S.Middleweight Champion. Former
Undefeated British Middleweight
Champion. Former WBC International
Middleweight Champion. Ht. 5'8"
Manager C. Sanigar/F. Warren

27.05.93	Rick North W PTS 4 Bristol
26.06.93	Chris Vassiliou W CO 2 Keynsham
31.08.93	Marty Duke W RSC 2 Croydon
13.09.93	Barry Thorogood W PTS 4 Bristol
03.11.93	Marty Duke W RSC 1 Bristol
13.12.93	Shamus Casey W PTS 4 Bristol
10.03.94	Mark Cichocki W PTS 6 Bristol
23.03.94	Carlo Colarusso L RSC 5 Cardiff
25.04.94	Chris Davies W RSC 1 Bristol
02.07.94	Martin Jolley W RSC 1 Keynsham
22.11.94	Kirkland Laing W RSC 5 Bristol
18.02.95	Lee Blundell W RSC 6 Shepton Mallet
06.05.95	Mark Dawson W RSC 5 Shepton Mallet
28.07.95	Kevin Adamson W CO 1 Bristol
02.09.95	Quinn Paynter W RSC 1 Wembley
30.09.95	John Duckworth W RSC 3 Cardiff
28.10.95	Carlos Christie W PTS 8 Bristol
10.11.95	Carlos Christie W CO 3 Bristol
16.12.95	Peter Vosper W RSC 2 Cardiff
26.04.96	Lee Crocker W RSC 2 Cardiff
19.10.96	Paul Wesley W RSC 7 Bristol
21.01.97	George Bocco W RTD 4 Bristol
	(Vacant WBC International Middleweight Title)
05.06.97	Andras Galfi L RSC 7 Bristol
	(WBC International Middleweight Title Defence)
17.01.98	Neville Brown W RTD 8 Bristol
	(British Middleweight Title Challenge)
05.09.98	Richie Woodhall L PTS 12 Telford
	(WBC S. Middleweight Title Challenge)
24.10.98	Andras Galfi W PTS 12 Bristol
	(Vacant WBO Inter-Continental S. Middleweight Title)
05.12.98	Andrew Flute W RSC 5 Bristol
	(Vacant IBF Inter-Continental S. Middleweight Title)
10.12.99	Eric Lucas W RSC 12 Montreal, Canada
	(Final Elim. WBC S. Middleweight Title)
06.05.00	Markus Beyer W RSC 12 Frankfurt, Germany
	(WBC S. Middleweight Title Challenge)

01.09.00 Dingaan Thobela L CO 12 Brakpan,
South Africa
(WBC S.Middleweight Title Defence)
10.07.01 Eric Lucas L RSC 7 Montreal, Canada
(Vacant WBC S.Middleweight Title)
09.03.02 Danilo Haeussler L PTS 12 Frankfurt,
Germany
*(European S. Middleweight Title
Challenge)*
10.07.02 Vage Kocharyan W PTS 8 Wembley
01.02.03 Danilo Haussler L TD 5 Chemnitz,
Germany
*(European S. Middleweight Title
Challenge)*

Career: 34 contests, won 27, lost 7.

Simon Chambers

Sheffield. *Born* Sheffield, 14 September,
1971
Featherweight. Ht. 5'4½"
Manager Self

27.04.98 Stevie Kane W PTS 6 Glasgow
01.06.98 Garry Burrell L PTS 6 Glasgow
08.06.98 Steve Saville L RSC 2 Birmingham
20.09.98 Peter Allen W PTS 6 Sheffield
17.10.98 Eddie Nevins L RSC 4 Manchester
07.12.98 Peter Allen W PTS 6 Bradford
22.01.99 Maurycy Gojko L PTS 4 Carlisle
23.02.99 Keith Jones DREW 4 Cardiff
19.04.99 Bobby Lyndon W RSC 3 Bradford
06.05.99 John Barnes L PTS 6 Sunderland
25.05.99 Marc Callaghan W RSC 1 Mayfair
07.06.99 Craig Docherty L PTS 6 Glasgow
15.07.99 Graham Earl L CO 6 Peterborough
23.09.02 John Simpson L RSC 1 Glasgow
29.11.02 Gary Davis L RSC 2 Liverpool
16.02.03 John-Paul Ryan W RSC 2 Salford
28.02.03 Andrew Ferrans L RSC 7 Irvine
14.04.03 John Simpson L PTS 6 Glasgow
24.05.03 Martin Hardcastle L RSC 2 Sheffield

Career: 19 contests, won 6, drew 1, lost 12.

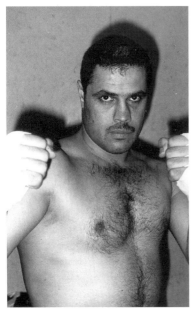

Ahmad Cheleh   Les Clark

Ahmad Cheleh (Chleh)

Dewsbury. *Born* Damascus, Syria, 5
January, 1976
Heavyweight. Ht. 6'0"
Manager T. Schofield

30.11.02 Dave Clarke L RSC 1 Liverpool
25.01.03 Scott Gammer L CO 1 Bridgend

Career: 2 contests, lost 2.

Stephen Chinnock

Rugeley. *Born* Lichfield, 4 December, 1975
Midlands Area Featherweight Champion.
Ht. 5'10"
Manager Self

10.09.00 Neil Read W RSC 5 Walsall
06.11.00 Jason Nesbitt W PTS 6 Wolverhampton
27.11.00 Jason White W PTS 4 Birmingham
20.05.01 Gareth Wiltshaw W PTS 6
Wolverhampton
07.10.01 Kevin Gerowski W PTS 10
Wolverhampton
*(Vacant Midlands Area Featherweight
Title)*
18.01.02 John Mackay W PTS 4 Coventry
13.04.02 Neil Read W CO 3 Wolverhampton
*(Midlands Area Featherweight Title
Defence)*
08.09.02 Nigel Senior W PTS 6 Wolverhampton
17.05.03 Dazzo Williams L PTS 10 Liverpool
(Elim. British Featherweight Title)

Career: 9 contests, won 8, lost 1.

(Patoma) Patrick Cito (Sitho)

Birmingham. *Born* Congo, 15 September,
1976
S. Middleweight. Ht. 5'9"
Manager N. Nobbs

11.02.94 Maneno Oswald L CO 6 Dar-es-
Salaam, Tanzania
22.02.97 Rashid Matumla L PTS 10 Tanga,
Tanzania
07.12.97 Joseph Marwa L PTS 10 Dar-es-
Salaam, Tanzania
12.09.98 Jong-Myung Kim W CO 3 Nairobi,
Kenya
28.04.99 Mondi Mbonambi L RSC 3 Benoni,
South Africa
03.10.99 John Tshabalala L PTS 6
Johannesburg, South Africa
29.10.99 Johan Sinden DREW 6 Guateng, South
Africa
28.11.99 Johnson Tshuma L PTS 8 Peddie,
South Africa
25.06.00 Mack Rarzar W CO 1 Johannesburg,
South Africa
05.10.00 Tyrone Churchill W RSC 2
Johannesburg, South Africa
12.11.00 Renier Dorfling L RSC 1 Mpumalanga,
South Africa
29.08.01 William Gare L PTS 8 Gaborone,
South Africa
08.05.03 Matthew Hall L PTS 4 Widnes
31.05.03 Ryan Kasprzycki W RSC 2 Barnsley
08.06.03 Alan Page L RSC 3 Shaw

Career: 15 contests, won 4, drew 1, lost 10.

Dave Clarke

Blackpool. *Born* Dover, 20 June, 1976
Heavyweight. Ht. 6'1"
Manager L. Veitch

22.11.01 Roman Greenberg L RSC 5 Paddington
11.02.02 Colin Kenna L RSC 4 Southampton
15.03.02 Shaun Bowes L PTS 6 Spennymoor
24.03.02 Tommy Eastwood L PTS 6 Streatham
11.05.02 Ivan Botton L PTS 6 Newark
03.06.02 Tony Moran L PTS 6 Glasgow
25.06.02 Carl Wright L PTS 6 Rugby
20.07.02 Matt Legg L RSC 2 Bethnal Green
05.10.02 Paul Butlin L PTS 4 Coventry
12.10.02 Enzo Maccarinelli L RSC 2 Bethnal
Green
20.11.02 Costi Marin W RSC 2 Leeds
30.11.02 Ahmad Cheleh W RSC 1 Liverpool
05.12.02 Roman Greenberg L RSC 1 Sheffield
08.01.03 Scott Gammer L PTS 4 Aberdare
08.03.03 Paul Butlin L PTS 6 Coventry
17.03.03 Costi Marin W PTS 6 Glasgow
24.03.03 Neil Dawson L PTS 4 Barnsley
13.04.03 Oneal Murray W PTS 4 Streatham
28.04.03 Shane Woollas L PTS 6 Cleethorpes
15.05.03 Matt Skelton L RSC 1 Mayfair
28.06.03 Scott Gammer L RSC 1 Cardiff

Career: 21 contests, won 4, lost 17.

Howard Clarke

Warley. *Born* London, 23 September, 1967
Middleweight. Ht. 5'10"
Manager Self

15.10.91 Chris Mylan W PTS 4 Dudley
09.12.91 Claude Rossi W RSC 3 Brierley Hill
04.02.92 Julian Eavis W PTS 4 Alfreton
03.03.92 Dave Andrews W RSC 3 Cradley
Heath
21.05.92 Richard O'Brien W CO 1 Cradley
Heath
29.09.92 Paul King W PTS 6 Stoke
27.10.92 Gordon Blair L RSC 4 Cradley Heath
16.03.93 Paul King W PTS 6 Edgbaston
07.06.93 Dean Bramhald W RTD 2 Walsall
29.06.93 Paul King W PTS 6 Edgbaston
06.10.93 Julian Eavis L PTS 8 Solihull
30.11.93 Julian Eavis W PTS 8 Wolverhampton
08.02.94 Nigel Bradley W RTD 6
Wolverhampton
18.04.94 Andy Peach W PTS 6 Walsall
28.06.94 Dennis Berry L RSC 3 Edgbaston
12.10.94 Julian Eavis W PTS 8 Stoke
25.10.94 Andy Peach W RSC 3 Edgbaston
02.11.94 Julian Eavis W PTS 8 Birmingham
29.11.94 Julian Eavis W PTS 6 Cannock
07.12.94 Peter Reid W PTS 8 Stoke
25.01.95 Dennis Berry L PTS 8 Stoke
08.03.95 Andrew Jervis W PTS 6 Solihull
11.05.95 David Bain W RSC 1 Dudley
20.09.95 Michael Smyth DREW 6 Ystrad
02.10.95 Nigel Wenton L PTS 6 Mayfair
02.12.96 Martin Smith L PTS 8 Birmingham
29.01.97 Gary Beardsley W PTS 6 Stoke
11.02.97 Prince Kasi Kaihau L RSC 4
Wolverhampton
19.03.97 Mark Cichocki W PTS 6 Stoke
15.04.97 Prince Kasi Kaihau W PTS 6
Edgbaston
30.04.97 Allan Gray W PTS 8 Acton
22.05.97 Michael Alexander W RSC 3 Solihull
21.06.97 Paul Samuels L PTS 8 Cardiff
09.09.97 Harry Dhami L PTS 8 Bethnal Green
05.11.97 Andras Galfi W PTS 8 Tenerife
27.01.98 Mack Razor L PTS 8 Hammanskraal,
South Africa
23.03.98 Lindon Scarlett DREW 6 Crystal
Palace
18.07.98 Jason Papillion W PTS 8 Sheffield

13.03.99	Fernando Vargas L RSC 4 New York City, USA
	(IBF L. Middleweight Title Challenge)
05.11.99	Michael Rask L PTS 12 Aalberg, Denmark
	(WBA Inter-Continental L. Middleweight Title Challenge)
29.05.00	Anthony Farnell L PTS 12 Manchester
	(WBO Inter-Continental L. Middleweight Title Challenge)
12.08.00	Takaloo L PTS 12 Wembley
	(Vacant IBF Inter-Continental L.Middleweight Title)
04.11.00	Richard Williams L CO 4 Bethnal Green
16.12.00	Ryan Rhodes L PTS 6 Sheffield
03.02.01	Michael Jones L PTS 4 Manchester
26.02.01	Jawaid Khaliq L PTS 6 Nottingham
07.04.01	Gary Lockett L RSC 2 Wembley
06.05.01	Ian Cooper L PTS 6 Hartlepool
04.06.01	James Docherty L PTS 6 Hartlepool
14.07.01	Gary Lockett L CO 1 Wembley
15.09.01	Thomas McDonagh L PTS 6 Manchester
10.11.01	Ossie Duran L PTS 6 Wembley
26.11.01	Wayne Pinder L PTS 6 Manchester
16.12.01	Erik Teymour L PTS 6 Southwark
27.01.02	Paul Samuels L PTS 6 Streatham
03.03.02	Lee Murtagh NC 2 Shaw
20.04.01	Wayne Elcock L PTS 4 Cardiff
25.05.02	Ross Minter W RSC 2 Portsmouth
08.06.02	Alexander Vetoux L RSC 4 Renfrew
27.07.02	Mihaly Kotai L RSC 1 Nottingham
08.12.02	Matthew Tait L PTS 6 Bethnal Green
21.12.02	Matthew Thirlwall L PTS 6 Dagenham
25.01.03	Paul Samuels L PTS 6 Bridgend
08.02.03	Michael Jones L PTS 6 Liverpool
05.03.03	Gilbert Eastman L PTS 6 Bethnal Green
05.04.03	Paul Smith L PTS 4 Manchester
21.06.03	Wayne Pinder L PTS 4 Manchester

Career: 67 contests, won 27, drew 2, lost 37, no contest, 1.

Howard Clarke Les Clark

Darren Cleary

Salford. *Born* Salford, 28 February, 1980
Bantamweight. Ht. 5'5"
Manager S. Foster/S. Wood

27.05.01	Marty Kayes W PTS 4 Manchester
07.07.01	Marty Kayes W PTS 4 Manchester
18.03.02	Jamil Hussain DREW 4 Crawley
27.04.02	Jamil Hussain DREW 4 Huddersfield
11.05.02	Jimbo Rooney W PTS 4 Dagenham
08.07.02	Martin Power L PTS 4 Mayfair
21.12.02	Rocky Dean L PTS 4 Millwall
08.06.03	Shinny Bayaar L RSC 2 Shaw

Career: 8 contests, won 3, drew 2, lost 3.

Darren Cleary Les Clark

Neil Cleaver (Karisa)

Birkenhead. *Born* Birkenhead, 16 June, 1974
Heavyweight. Ht. 6'3"
Manager D. Isaaman

28.04.03	Costi Marin L RSC 2 Nottingham

Career: 1 contest, lost 1.

Dean Cockburn

Doncaster. *Born* Doncaster, 28 March, 1979
Middleweight. Ht. 5'9½"
Manager T. O'Neill

17.09.01	Mark Chesters W RSC 4 Glasgow
17.11.01	Paul Wesley W PTS 4 Glasgow
25.03.02	Paul Buchanan L PTS 6 Sunderland
21.06.02	Darren Stubbs W RSC 1 Leeds
08.10.02	Jason McKay L PTS 4 Glasgow
21.10.02	Tom Cannon DREW 4 Glasgow
01.11.02	Neil Bonner W RSC 2 Preston
20.11.02	Harry Butler W PTS 6 Leeds
17.03.03	Barry Thorogood W PTS 4 Southampton
10.05.03	George Robshaw L PTS 6 Huddersfield

Career: 10 contests, won 6, drew 1, lost 3.

Brian Coleman

Birmingham. *Born* Birmingham, 27 July, 1969
L. Middleweight. Ht. 5'11"
Manager Self

21.11.91	Jamie Morris DREW 6 Stafford
11.12.91	Craig Hartwell DREW 6 Leicester
22.01.92	John O. Johnson L PTS 6 Stoke
20.02.92	Davy Robb L PTS 6 Oakengates
31.03.92	Blue Butterworth L PTS 6 Stockport
17.05.92	Korso Aleain L RSC 5 Harringay
17.09.92	Nicky Bardle L RSC 4 Watford
21.10.92	Jason Barker W PTS 6 Stoke
10.12.92	A. M. Milton DREW 4 Bethnal Green
31.03.93	A. M. Milton L PTS 4 Bethnal Green
26.04.93	Jason Beard L PTS 6 Lewisham
06.05.93	Mark Allen W PTS 6 Walsall
18.05.93	Sean Metherell DREW 6 Kettering
27.05.93	Blue Butterworth L PTS 6 Burnley
23.06.93	Jonathan Thaxton L PTS 8 Gorleston
11.08.93	Steve Howden L RSC 4 Mansfield
13.09.93	Mick Hoban L PTS 6 Middleton
01.12.93	A. M. Milton L PTS 4 Bethnal Green
08.12.93	Chris Pollock W PTS 6 Stoke
16.12.93	Mark Newton L PTS 6 Newport
11.01.94	Paul Knights L RSC 4 Bethnal Green
08.02.94	Andy Peach W PTS 6 Wolverhampton
18.02.94	Cam Raeside L PTS 6 Leicester
08.03.94	Chris Pollock L PTS 6 Edgbaston
29.03.94	P. J. Gallagher L PTS 6 Bethnal Green
14.04.94	Cham Joof L CO 3 Battersea
02.06.94	Scott Walker L CO 1 Middleton
12.09.94	Shabba Edwards L PTS 6 Mayfair
19.09.94	Mark Breslin L CO 1 Glasgow
09.11.94	Kenny Scott L PTS 6 Stafford
23.11.94	Billy McDougall W PTS 4 Piccadilly
29.11.94	Warren Stephens W PTS 6 Wolverhampton
09.12.94	Danny Stevens L RTD 2 Bethnal Green
24.01.95	Wayne Jones L PTS 6 Piccadilly
07.02.95	Alan Temple L PTS 6 Ipswich
23.02.95	Darren Covill L PTS 4 Southwark
16.03.95	Paul Knights L RSC 2 Basildon
02.07.95	Tommy Lawler L PTS 4 Dublin
08.09.95	George Naylor L PTS 6 Liverpool
27.09.95	Allan Gray L PTS 6 Bethnal Green
20.10.95	Mikael Nilsson L PTS 4 Ipswich
02.11.95	Marco Fattore W PTS 6 Mayfair
16.11.95	Alan Bosworth L PTS 6 Evesham
24.11.95	Chris Barnett L PTS 6 Manchester
02.12.95	Neil Sinclair L RTD 1 Belfast
20.01.96	James Hare L PTS 6 Mansfield
29.01.96	Dave Fallon L PTS 6 Piccadilly
13.02.96	Martin Holgate L PTS 4 Bethnal Green
21.02.96	Marco Fattore W PTS 6 Piccadilly

87

13.03.96 Paul Samuels L PTS 6 Wembley
03.04.96 Ian Honeywood L PTS 6 Bethnal
Green
20.04.96 Ray Robinson L PTS 6 Brentwood
24.05.96 Scott Dixon L PTS 8 Glasgow
08.06.96 Mark Winters L PTS 4 Newcastle
06.07.96 Nick Boyd L PTS 4 Manchester
16.08.96 Charlie Paine W PTS 6 Liverpool
27.08.96 Dave Brazil L PTS 6 Windsor
19.09.96 Ricky Sackfield L RSC 3 Manchester
27.09.96 Nicky Bardle L PTS 4 Stevenage
08.10.96 Marcus McCrae W PTS 6 Battersea
09.11.96 Mark Haslam L PTS 6 Manchester
27.11.96 Bernard Paul L PTS 6 Bethnal Green
09.12.96 Wayne Windle L PTS 6 Chesterfield
18.01.97 Paul Burke L PTS 6 Manchester
19.02.97 Anthony Campbell L PTS 6 Acton
25.03.97 Craig Stanley DREW 4 Lewisham
03.04.97 Kevin McCarthy L PTS 6 Wembley
22.04.97 Georgie Smith L PTS 6 Bethnal Green
19.05.97 John O.Johnson DREW 6 Cleethorpes
02.06.97 Steve McLevy W RSC 3 Glasgow
02.08.97 Junior Witter L PTS 4 Barnsley
13.09.97 Jason Rowland L PTS 8 Millwall
04.10.97 Everald Williams L PTS 4 Muswell
Hill
24.10.97 Anthony Maynard L CO 1 Birmingham
27.01.98 Kevin McCarthy L PTS 6 Streatham
23.02.98 Kevin McKillan L PTS 6 Salford
05.03.98 Junior Witter L PTS 6 Leeds
24.03.98 Jon Harrison DREW 6 Wolverhampton
03.04.98 Peter Nightingale L PTS 6 West
Bromwich
23.04.98 Marc Smith W PTS 6 Edgbaston
06.05.98 Stuart Rimmer L PTS 6 Blackpool
18.05.98 Steve Conway L PTS 6 Cleethorpes
26.05.98 Rimvidas Billius L PTS 4 Mayfair
06.06.98 Jamie McKeever L PTS 4 Liverpool
18.06.98 Shaun Stokes L PTS 6 Sheffield
12.09.98 Graham Earl L PTS 4 Bethnal Green
03.10.98 Peter Nightingale L PTS 6 West
Bromwich
12.10.98 Christian Brady L PTS 6 Birmingham
22.10.98 Colin Lynes L RSC 2 Barking
25.11.98 Arv Mittoo W PTS 6 Clydach
07.12.98 Gavin Down L PTS 6 Manchester
21.01.99 Dennis Griffin W PTS 6 Piccadilly
06.02.99 Tontcho Tontchev L PTS 6 Halifax
26.02.99 Peter Nightingale L PTS 6 West
Bromwich
08.03.99 Sammy Smith W PTS 8 Birmingham
25.03.99 Ernie Smith W PTS 6 Edgbaston
03.04.99 Ricky Hatton L CO 2 Kensington
27.05.99 Ernie Smith L PTS 6 Edgbaston
04.06.99 Steve Conway L PTS 6 Hull
26.06.99 Steve Murray L PTS 6 Millwall
07.08.99 Jonathan Thaxton L PTS 6 Dagenham
13.09.99 Bobby Vanzie L PTS 6 Bethnal Green
27.09.99 Steve Conway L PTS 6 Leeds
24.10.99 Peter Nightingale L PTS 10
Wolverhampton
*(Midlands Area Welterweight Title
Challenge)*
06.11.99 Jacek Bielski L PTS 4 Bethnal Green
22.11.99 Sonny Thind W RSC 5 Piccadilly
30.11.99 Ernie Smith W PTS 8 Wolverhampton
11.12.99 Oscar Hall L PTS 6 Liverpool
20.01.00 Alan Bosworth L PTS 6 Piccadilly
12.02.00 Shaun Stokes W PTS 4 Sheffield
24.02.00 Ernie Smith L PTS 6 Edgbaston
09.03.00 Paul Burns L PTS 6 Liverpool
25.03.00 Michael Jennings L PTS 6 Liverpool
16.05.00 Michael Jennings L PTS 6 Warrington
25.05.00 Lee Molyneux L PTS 6 Peterborough

19.06.00 Gavin Down L PTS 4 Burton
19.08.00 Glenn McClarnon L PTS 6 Brentwood
25.09.00 Derek Roche L PTS 6 Barnsley
14.10.00 Colin Lynes L PTS 6 Wembley
31.10.00 Ivan Kirpa L RSC 3 Hammersmith
02.12.00 John Tiftik L PTS 4 Chigwell
11.12.00 Lee Bird W CO 4 Cleethorpes
23.01.01 Paul Knights L PTS 6 Crawley
03.02.01 Darren Spencer L PTS 6 Manchester
10.02.01 Carl Wall L RSC 1 Widnes
17.03.01 Bradley Pryce L PTS 4 Manchester
26.03.01 Ross Minter L PTS 4 Wembley
28.04.01 Ismail Khalil L PTS 4 Cardiff
08.05.01 Gavin Wake L PTS 4 Barnsley
21.05.01 Ernie Smith L PTS 6 Birmingham
09.06.01 Matthew Hatton L RTD 2 Bethnal
Green
08.12.01 Gavin Down L RSC 1 Chesterfield
23.02.02 Young Muttley L PTS 4 Nottingham
22.03.02 Sam Gorman L PTS 6 Coventry
26.04.02 Andy Egan L PTS 6 Coventry
08.06.02 Ronnie Nailen L PTS 4 Renfrew
23.08.02 Brett James L PTS 6 Bethnal Green
28.09.02 Thomas McDonagh L RSC 1
Manchester
18.02.03 Ben Hudson L PTS 6 Bethnal Green
09.03.03 Wayne Shepherd L PTS 6 Shaw
22.03.03 Andy Egan L PTS 6 Coventry
05.04.03 Matthew Hall L RSC 1 Manchester
09.05.03 Sammy Smith L PTS 6 Longford
31.05.03 Terry Fletcher L PTS 4 Barnsley
15.06.03 Lee McAllister L PTS 6 Bradford
Career: 145 contests, won 22, drew 7, lost 116.

Jason Collins

Walsall. *Born* Walsall, 5 December, 1972
Middleweight. Former Undefeated British
Masters S. Middleweight Champion.
Ht. 5'9"
Manager Self

18.02.99 Biagio Falcone L PTS 6 Glasgow
17.03.99 Stuart Harper W RSC 2 Stoke
06.06.99 Jon Foster DREW 6 Nottingham
15.08.99 Matt Galer W PTS 6 Derby
28.10.99 Lee Blundell DREW 6 Burnley
20.11.99 Dennis Berry L PTS 6 Grantham
14.12.99 Jorge Araujo L PTS 6 Telde, Gran
Canaria, Spain
15.01.00 Martin Jolley W RTD 1 Doncaster
18.02.00 Oscar Hall DREW 6 West Bromwich
27.02.00 Jawaid Khaliq L PTS 6 Leeds
05.03.00 Wayne Shepherd W PTS 6 Shaw
21.03.00 Sharden Ansoula W PTS 6 Telde, Gran
Canaria
21.05.00 Neville Brown L RSC 2 Derby
08.07.00 Darren Rhodes DREW 4 Widnes
04.09.00 Darren Rhodes W PTS 4 Manchester
01.10.00 Juergen Braehmer L CO 1 Hamburg,
Germany
13.11.00 Takaloo L RSC 2 Bethnal Green
16.12.00 Louis Swales DREW 4 Sheffield
27.01.01 Spencer Fearon W PTS 4 Bethnal
Green
26.03.01 P.J. Maxwell W PTS 4 Wembley
20.04.01 Jim Rock L PTS 6 Dublin
08.06.01 Leigh Wicks W PTS 4 Hull
21.06.01 Lester Jacobs L CO 9 Earls Court
(WBF Middleweight Title Challenge)
07.09.01 Delroy Mellis W DIS 5 Bethnal Green
22.09.01 Ian Cooper L PTS 10 Newcastle
*(Vacant British Masters Middleweight
Title)*

27.10.01 Ryan Rhodes L PTS 4 Manchester
17.11.01 Gerard Murphy L PTS 4 Glasgow
08.12.01 Steven Bendall L PTS 12 Dagenham
*(Vacant WBU Inter-Continental
Middleweight Title)*
12.02.02 Delroy Leslie L RSC 1 Bethnal Green
18.03.02 Andrew Buchanan W PTS 4 Crawley
01.06.02 Wayne Elcock L RSC 2 Manchester
17.08.02 Jeff Lacy L CO 1 Cardiff
21.09.02 Wayne Asker DREW 6 Norwich
10.10.02 Mike Duffield W PTS 4 Piccadilly
25.10.02 Matthew Thirlwall L RSC 5 Bethnal
Green
23.11.02 Wayne Elcock L RSC 1 Derby
24.02.03 Michael Monaghan L PTS 8
Birmingham
20.03.03 Kreshnik Qato L PTS 4 Queensway
29.03.03 Gary Lockett L CO 1 Portsmouth
12.05.03 Ojay Abrahams W PTS 10
Birmingham
*(Vacant British Masters
S.Middleweight Title)*
06.06.03 Danny Thornton L PTS 10 Hull
*(Vacant Central Area Middleweight
Title)*
Career: 41 contests, won 13, drew 6, lost 22.

Jason Collins   Les Clark

Barry Connell

Glasgow. *Born* Glasgow, 25 July, 1979
S. Middleweight. Ht. 6'1"
Manager K. Morrison

24.02.00 Colin Vidler W PTS 6 Glasgow
07.04.00 Ernie Smith W PTS 6 Glasgow
26.05.00 Harry Butler W PTS 4 Glasgow
14.03.03 Paul Owen W PTS 6 Glasgow
22.03.03 Simeon Cover W PTS 4 Renfrew
16.05.03 Martin Thompson DREW 4 Glasgow
Career: 6 contests, won 5, drew 1.

Tony Conroy

Coventry. *Born* Coventry, 18 December,
1977
Midlands Area Welterweight Champion.
Ht. 5'9"
Manager A. Phillips

22.10.99	Mark Halstead W PTS 4 Coventry
24.02.00	Dave Gibson W PTS 4 Edgbaston
22.05.00	Dave Hinds W PTS 4 Coventry
28.10.00	Chris Hall W RSC 1 Coventry
02.01.01	Woody Greenaway W PTS 4 Coventry
25.06.02	Robin Thomas W RSC 1 Rugby
13.07.02	Woody Greenaway W RSC 3 Coventry
05.10.02	Keith Jones L RSC 4 Coventry
30.11.02	Karl Taylor W PTS 4 Coventry
08.03.03	Jimmy Gould L PTS 4 Coventry
22.03.03	Pedro Thompson W PTS 6 Coventry
07.06.03	Richard Swallow W RSC 5 Coventry
	(Vacant Midlands Area Welterweight Title)

Career: 12 contests, won 10, lost 2.

Tony Conroy　　　　　　　　　　Les Clark

Steve Conway

Dewsbury. *Born* Hartlepool, 6 October, 1977
S. Featherweight. Ht. 5'8"
Manager Self

21.02.96	Robert Grubb W PTS 6 Batley
24.04.96	Ervine Blake W PTS 6 Solihull
20.05.96	Chris Lyons W PTS 6 Cleethorpes
30.05.96	Ram Singh W PTS 6 Lincoln
03.02.97	Jason Squire W PTS 6 Leicester
11.04.97	Marc Smith W PTS 4 Barnsley
22.09.97	Arv Mittoo W PTS 6 Cleethorpes
09.10.97	Arv Mittoo W PTS 6 Leeds
01.11.97	Brian Carr L PTS 6 Glasgow
14.11.97	Brendan Bryce W PTS 6 Mere
04.12.97	Kid McAuley W RSC 5 Doncaster
15.12.97	Nicky Wilders W PTS 6 Cleethorpes
05.03.98	Pete Buckley W PTS 6 Leeds
25.04.98	Dean Phillips W PTS 6 Cardiff
09.05.98	Gary Flear W PTS 4 Sheffield
18.05.98	Brian Coleman W PTS 6 Cleethorpes
05.09.98	Benny Jones W PTS 4 Telford
19.12.98	Gary Thornhill L RSC 9 Liverpool
	(WBO Inter-Continental S. Featherweight Title Challenge)
04.06.99	Brian Coleman W PTS 6 Hull
27.09.99	Brian Coleman W PTS 6 Leeds
27.02.00	Chris Price W RTD 3 Leeds
21.03.00	Pedro Miranda L RSC 3 Telde, Gran Canaria
15.07.00	Arv Mittoo W PTS 6 Norwich
20.10.00	Junior Witter L RTD 4 Belfast
25.02.01	Ram Singh W RSC 2 Derby

02.06.01	Jimmy Phelan W PTS 4 Wakefield
18.08.01	Keith Jones W PTS 8 Dewsbury
17.11.01	Carl Allen W PTS 8 Dewsbury
27.04.02	Steve Robinson W PTS 8 Huddersfield
05.10.02	Rakheem Mingaleev W RSC 4 Huddersfield
19.10.02	Alex Arthur L CO 4 Renfrew
	(Vacant British S. Featherweight Title)

Career: 31 contests, won 26, lost 5.

Jason Cook

Maesteg. *Born* Maesteg, 27 February, 1975
Welsh L. Welterweight Champion. Former
Undefeated European Lightweight
Champion. Ht. 5'9"
Manager B. Hearn

11.10.96	Brian Robb W RSC 2 Mayfair
27.11.96	Andrew Reed W RSC 3 Bethnal Green
27.05.97	Marc Smith W PTS 4 Mayfair
31.10.97	Marc Smith W PTS 4 Mayfair
24.01.98	David Kirk W RSC 3 Cardiff
26.05.98	Trevor Smith L RSC 1 Mayfair
23.02.99	Darren Woodley W RSC 4 Cardiff
28.05.99	Dave Hinds W RSC 1 Liverpool
02.10.99	Pete Buckley W PTS 4 Cardiff
11.12.99	Woody Greenaway W RSC 1 Merthyr
	(Vacant Welsh L. Welterweight Title)
26.02.00	Harry Butler W PTS 6 Swansea
17.04.00	Andrei Sinepupov W RTD 3 Birmingham
12.05.00	Keith Jones W PTS 10 Swansea
	(Welsh L. Welterweight Title Defence)
09.10.00	Assen Vasilev W PTS 6 Liverpool

Jason Cook　　　　　　　　　　Les Clark

17.02.01 Dariusz Snarski W PTS 8 Kolbrzeg, Poland
18.03.02 Nono Junior W RSC 1 Crawley
11.05.02 Andrei Devyataykin W PTS 6 Dagenham
29.06.02 Viktor Baranov W PTS 6 Brentwood
03.08.02 Sandro Casamonica W RSC 3 San Mango D'Aquino, Italy
(Vacant European Lightweight Title)
26.10.02 Nasser Lakrib W RSC 5 Maesteg
(European Lightweight Title Defence)
25.01.03 Stefano Zoff W PTS 12 Bridgend
Career: 21 contests, won 20, lost 1.

Nicky Cook

Dagenham. *Born* Stepney, 13 September, 1979
Commonwealth Featherweight Champion. Former Undefeated WBF Inter-Continental S. Featherweight Champion. Ht. 5'6½"
Manager J. Harding

11.12.98 Sean Grant W CO 1 Cheshunt
26.02.99 Graham McGrath W CO 2 Coventry
27.04.99 Vasil Paskelev W CO 1 Bethnal Green
25.05.99 Wilson Acuna W PTS 4 Mayfair
12.07.99 Igor Sakhatarov W PTS 4 Coventry

Nicky Cook   Les Clark

20.08.99 Vlado Varhegyi W PTS 4 Bloomsbury
27.11.99 John Barnes W PTS 6 Liverpool
20.12.99 Carl Allen W CO 3 Bethnal Green
10.03.00 Chris Jickells W RSC 1 Bethnal Green
27.05.00 Anthony Hanna W PTS 6 Mayfair
16.06.00 Salem Bouaita W PTS 6 Bloomsbury
04.11.00 Vladimir Borov W RSC 1 Bethnal Green
08.12.00 Rakhim Mingaleev W PTS 8 Crystal Palace
19.05.01 Foudil Madani W RSC 1 Wembley
28.11.01 Woody Greenaway W RSC 3 Bethnal Green
19.12.01 Marcelo Ackermann W RSC 3 Coventry
(Vacant WBF Inter-Continental S.Featherweight Title)
20.04.02 Jackie Gunguluza W RTD 4 Wembley
(WBF Inter-Continental S.Featherweight Title Defence)
10.07.02 Andrei Devyataykin W PTS 8 Wembley
05.10.02 Gary Thornhill W RSC 7 Liverpool
(WBF Inter-Continental S.Featherweight Title Defence)
08.02.03 Mishek Kondwani W RSC 12 Brentford
(Vacant Commonwealth Featherweight Title)
31.05.03 David Kiilu W CO 2 Bethnal Green
(Commonwealth Featherweight Title Defence)
Career: 21 contests, won 21.

Danny Cooper

Southampton. *Born* Southampton, 11 July, 1967
L. Middleweight. Ht. 5'6½"
Manager Self

12.04.86 Barry Bacon W PTS 6 Isle of Man
30.04.86 Mark Broome W CO 6 Edmonton
02.12.86 Tony Ekubia L RSC 4 Southend
14.03.88 Tony Whitehouse W RSC 1 Mayfair
18.05.88 Young Gully W RSC 4 Portsmouth
24.11.88 Steve Phillips W PTS 6 Southampton
02.03.89 Glyn Mitchell L PTS 6 Southampton
09.05.89 Eamonn Payne W PTS 6 Southend
25.10.90 B.F. Williams W PTS 6 Battersea
16.12.91 Ron Shinkwin W PTS 6 Southampton
17.03.03 Danny Gwilym W PTS 6 Southampton
12.05.03 Rocky Muscas W PTS 6 Southampton
Career: 12 contests, won 10, lost 2.

Steve Cooper

Worcester. *Born* Worcester, 19 November, 1977
Welterweight. Ht. 5'8½"
Manager P. Cowdell

09.12.02 Darren Goode W CO 3 Birmingham
Career: 1 contest, won 1.

Darren Corbett

Belfast. *Born* Belfast, 8 July, 1972
IBO Inter-Continental L. Heavyweight Champion. Former Commonwealth, IBO Inter-Continental & All-Ireland Cruiserweight Champion. Ht. 5'11"
Manager Self

10.12.94 David Jules W RSC 1 Manchester
13.12.94 Carl Gaffney W RSC 1 Potters Bar
21.02.95 Steve Garber W PTS 6 Sunderland
18.03.95 Gary Williams DREW 6 Millstreet
14.04.95 Dennis Bailey W RSC 2 Belfast
27.05.95 R. F. McKenzie L PTS 6 Belfast
26.08.95 Nigel Rafferty W PTS 6 Belfast
07.10.95 Nigel Rafferty W PTS 6 Belfast
02.12.95 Bobbi Joe Edwards W PTS 6 Belfast
07.05.96 Cliff Elden W RSC 1 Mayfair
28.05.96 Darren Fearn W RSC 1 Belfast
03.09.96 Chris Woollas W RSC 7 Belfast
05.11.96 Ray Kane W RSC 5 Belfast
*(Vacant All-Ireland Cruiserweight
Title)*
17.12.96 Chris Woollas W RSC 1 Doncaster
28.01.97 Nigel Rafferty W PTS 10 Belfast
*(All-Ireland Cruiserweight Title
Defence)*
29.04.97 Noel Magee W CO 2 Belfast
*(All-Ireland Cruiserweight Title
Defence)*
02.06.97 Chris Okoh W RSC 3 Belfast
*(Commonwealth Cruiserweight Title
Challenge)*
17.10.97 Hector Sanjuro W PTS 6 Ledyard,
USA
20.12.97 Robert Norton W PTS 12 Belfast
*(Commonwealth Cruiserweight Title
Defence)*
21.02.98 Dirk Wallyn W PTS 10 Belfast
28.04.98 Konstantin Ochrej W RSC 4 Belfast
*(Vacant IBO Inter-Continental
Cruiserweight Title)*
26.05.98 Roberto Dominguez W CO 1 Mayfair
*(IBO Inter-Continental Cruiserweight
Title Defence)*
28.11.98 Bruce Scott L RSC 10 Belfast
*(Commonwealth Cruiserweight Title
Defence. Vacant British Cruiserweight
Title)*
10.04.99 Stephane Allouane L RSC 9
Manchester
*(Vacant IBO Inter-Continental
Cruiserweight Title)*
31.07.99 Darren Ashton W RSC 2 Carlisle
14.12.99 Neil Simpson W PTS 12 Coventry
*(Vacant IBO Inter-Continental
L. Heavyweight Title)*
25.03.00 Lennox Lewis W RSC 2 Liverpool
*(IBO Inter-Continental L. Heavyweight
Title Defence)*
16.06.01 Tyler Hughes W RSC 1 New York
City, USA
16.11.01 Radcliffe Green W PTS 8 Dublin
05.04.03 Clint Johnson W RSC 4 Belfast
Career: 30 contests, won 26, drew 1, lost 3.

Billy Corcoran

Wembley. *Born* Galway, 18 November,
1980
Lightweight. Ht. 5'7³/₄"
Manager R. McCracken

23.08.02 Jason Nesbitt W PTS 4 Bethnal Green
25.10.02 Jason Nesbitt W RSC 2 Bethnal Green
21.12.02 Daniel Thorpe W CO 2 Dagenham
28.01.03 Pete Buckley W PTS 6 Nottingham
05.03.03 Pete Buckley W PTS 6 Bethnal Green
16.04.03 Mark Payne DREW 4 Nottingham
27.05.03 Jimmy Beech L PTS 6 Dagenham
Career: 7 contests, won 5, drew 1, lost 1.

Billy Corcoran   Les Clark

Dave Cotterill

Hemsworth. *Born* Pontefract, 25 April,
1977
S. Featherweight. Ht. 5'8"
Manager S. Butler

26.10.00 Leo Turner L PTS 6 Stoke
04.11.00 Scott Spencer L PTS 4 Bethnal Green
30.11.00 Joel Viney W RSC 1 Blackpool
05.12.00 Duncan Armstrong W PTS 6
Nottingham
23.02.01 Andrew Ferrans W RSC 2 Irvine
30.04.01 Andrew Ferrans L RSC 1 Glasgow
18.06.01 Nigel Senior W PTS 6 Bradford
08.10.01 James Rooney L RSC 4 Barnsley
24.11.01 Dave Curran W PTS 6 Wakefield
07.02.02 Jimmy Beech L PTS 6 Stoke
08.03.02 Lee Holmes L PTS 6 Ellesmere Port
22.03.02 Gary Greenwood L PTS 6 Coventry
31.05.02 Lance Crosby L RSC 1 Hull
16.04.03 Adnan Amar L PTS 4 Nottingham
Career: 14 contests, won 5, lost 9.

Jane Couch

Fleetwood. *Born* Fleetwood, 12 August,
1968
WBF L. Welterweight Champion. Former
Undefeated WBF Lightweight Champion.
Former Undefeated WIBF & WBF
Welterweight Champion. Ht. 5'7"
Manager Tex Woodward

30.10.94 Kalpna Shah W RSC 2 Wigan
29.01.95 Fosteres Joseph W PTS 6 Fleetwood
18.04.95 Jane Johnson W RSC 4 Fleetwood
01.07.95 Julia Shirley W PTS 6 Fleetwood
24.05.96 Sandra Geiger W PTS 10 Copenhagen,
Denmark
(WIBF Welterweight Title Challenge)
01.03.97 Andrea Deshong W RSC 7 New
Orleans, USA
(WIBF Welterweight Title Defence)
24.08.97 Leah Mellinger W PTS 10 Connecticut,
USA
(WIBF Welterweight Title Defence)
24.10.97 Dora Webber L PTS 6 Mississippi,
USA
10.01.98 Dora Webber L PTS 10 Atlantic City,
USA
25.11.98 Simone Lukic W RSC 2 Streatham
20.02.99 Marisch Sjauw W PTS 10 Thornaby
*(WIBF Welterweight Title Defence.
Vacant WBF Welterweight Title)*
01.04.99 Heike Noller W PTS 8 Birmingham
31.10.99 Sharon Anyos W PTS 10 Raynes Park
(Vacant WBF Lightweight Title)
09.03.00 Michelle Straus W RSC 3 Bethnal
Green
01.07.00 Galina Gumliska W RSC 6 Southwark
(WBF Lightweight Title Defence)
19.08.00 Liz Mueller L PTS 6 Mashantucket,
Connecticut, USA
16.06.01 Viktoria Oleynikov W PTS 4 Wembley
31.07.01 Shakurah Witherspoon W PTS 4
Montego Bay, Jamaica
16.12.01 Tzanka Karova W RSC 3 Bristol
21.06.02 Sumya Anani L RSC 4 Waco, Texas,
USA
(Vacant WIBA L. Welterweight Title)
03.08.02 Borislava Goranova W PTS 6
Blackpool

Jane Couch (left)   Les Clark

08.12.02 Borislava Goranova W PTS 10 Bristol
(Vacant WBF L.Welterweight Title)
26.02.03 Borislava Goranova W RSC 7 Bristol
15.05.03 Larisa Berezenko W PTS 8 Clevedon
21.06.03 Lucia Rijker L PTS 8 Los Angeles,
California, USA
Career: 25 contests, won 20, lost 5.

Simeon Cover

Worksop. *Born* Clapton, 12 March, 1978
S. Middleweight. Ht. 5'11"
Manager D. Ingle

28.03.01 Danny Smith L PTS 6 Piccadilly
18.08.01 Rob Stevenson W PTS 6 Dewsbury
24.09.01 Colin McCash L PTS 6 Cleethorpes
01.11.01 Rob Stevenson L PTS 6 Hull
16.11.01 Jon O'Brien L PTS 6 Dublin
24.11.01 Darren Rhodes L RSC 5 Wakefield
31.01.02 Shpetim Hoti W PTS 6 Piccadilly
13.04.02 Earl Ling L CO 4 Norwich
13.05.02 Roddy Doran DREW 8 Birmingham
02.06.02 Gary Dixon W PTS 6 Shaw
03.08.02 Mike Duffield W RSC 2 Derby
14.09.02 Ivan Botton L PTS 6 Newark
05.12.02 Mark Brookes L RSC 3 Sheffield
15.02.03 Peter Jackson W RSC 2
Wolverhampton
23.02.03 Roddy Doran L PTS 10 Shrewsbury
*(Vacant British Masters
S.Middleweight Title)*
22.03.03 Barry Connell L PTS 4 Renfrew
12.04.03 Danny Smith L CO 5 Norwich
08.06.03 Ivan Botton W PTS 6 Nottingham
Career: 18 contests, won 6, drew 1, lost 11.

Darren Covill

Welling. *Born* Welling, 11 April, 1970
Middleweight. Ht. 5'8"
Manager Self

23.02.95 Brian Coleman W PTS 4 Southwark
19.05.95 Allan Gray L PTS 6 Southwark
04.06.95 Dick Hanns-Kat W RSC 3 Bethnal
Green
14.09.95 Gavin Barker W CO 1 Battersea
21.09.95 Shaun Stokes L PTS 6 Sheffield
22.11.95 Jason Barker L PTS 4 Sheffield
05.02.96 Jason Barker W RSC 1 Bexleyheath
21.03.96 Paul Miles L PTS 4 Southwark
11.07.97 Leigh Wicks W RSC 2 Brighton
26.09.97 Jason Williams L PTS 6 Port Talbot
08.10.97 Steve Roberts L PTS 6 Poplar
08.11.97 David Baptiste W PTS 4 Southwark
06.12.97 Ali Khattab L PTS 4 Wembley
31.01.98 Paolo Roberto L PTS 6 Edmonton
13.02.98 John Docherty W RSC 1 Barrhead
21.03.98 Wayne Alexander L RSC 2 Bethnal
Green
04.06.98 Darren McInulty DREW 6 Barking
10.09.98 Cornelius Carr L RTD 2 Acton
25.11.98 Leigh Wicks L PTS 4 Streatham
16.01.99 Anthony McFadden L RSC 2 Bethnal
Green
18.02.99 Adrian Stone L RSC 2 Barking
24.03.99 Lester Jacobs L RSC 2 Bayswater
02.07.99 Steven Bendall L RTD 3 Bristol
27.02.00 Gareth Hogg L RSC 3 Plymouth
02.02.01 Matthew Barney L PTS 6 Portsmouth
24.03.01 Allan Foster L RTD 3 Sheffield
12.05.01 Hughie Doherty L PTS 4 Plymouth
04.07.01 Harry Butler L RSC 4 Bloomsbury
20.09.01 Lester Jacobs L CO 2 Blackfriars

22.11.01 Dean Powell L PTS 4 Mayfair
08.12.01 Tomas da Silva L PTS 4 Millwall
15.12.01 Reagan Denton L PTS 4 Sheffield
27.03.02 John Tiftik W RSC 2 Mayfair
25.04.02 Brendan Rollinson L PTS 4 Hull
21.05.02 Elroy Edwards L PTS 4 Custom House
13.07.02 Conroy McIntosh L PTS 4
Wolverhampton
21.07.02 Wayne Pinder L CO 2 Salford
23.08.02 Carl Froch L RSC 1 Bethnal Green
10.10.02 Freddie Yemofio L PTS 4 Piccadilly
25.10.02 Francis Barrett L PTS 4 Bethnal Green
21.12.02 William Webster L PTS 4 Dagenham
Career: 41 contests, won 8, drew 1, lost 32.

Ben Coward

Swinton. *Born* Barnsley, 16 November,
1976
S. Middleweight. Ht. 5'9"
Manager H. Rainey

26.11.97 Pete Stanway W PTS 6 Sheffield
06.02.98 Brian Stanway L RSC 1 Wakefield
15.12.98 Shaun O'Neill L RSC 5 Sheffield
02.06.03 Steve Scott DREW 6 Cleethorpes
Career: 4 contests, won 1, drew 1, lost 2.

Jamie Coyle

Stirling. *Born* Stirling, 24 August, 1976
L. Middleweight. Ht. 6'0"
Manager T. Gilmour

02.06.03 Richard Inquieti W RSC 2 Glasgow
Career: 1 contest, won 1.

Peter Culshaw

Liverpool. *Born* Liverpool, 15 May, 1973
WBF S.Flyweight Champion. Former
Undefeated WBU International S.
Flyweight Champion. Former
Commonwealth Flyweight Champion.
Former Undefeated WBU & Central Area
Flyweight Champion. Ht. 5'6"
Manager Self

02.07.93 Graham McGrath W PTS 6 Liverpool
28.09.93 Vince Feeney W PTS 6 Liverpool
11.12.93 Nick Tooley W RSC 1 Liverpool
25.02.94 Des Gargano W PTS 6 Chester
06.05.94 Neil Swain W PTS 6 Liverpool
26.09.94 Daryl McKenzie W PTS 6 Liverpool
20.04.95 Rowan Williams W CO 6 Liverpool
29.09.95 Maxim Pougatchev DREW 8
Liverpool
05.03.96 Louis Veitch W RSC 3 Barrow
*(Central Area Flyweight Title
Challenge)*
13.04.96 Lyndon Kershaw W RSC 3 Liverpool
25.06.96 Danny Ward W RSC 3 Stevenage
*(Commonwealth Flyweight Title
Challenge)*
27.09.96 James Wanene W RSC 7 Stevenage
*(Commonwealth Flyweight Title
Defence)*
02.08.97 Jason Thomas W PTS 8 Barnsley
11.09.97 Ady Lewis L RSC 8 Widnes
*(Commonwealth Flyweight Title
Defence. British Flyweight Title
Challenge)*
12.03.98 Foudil Madani W RSC 4 Liverpool
*(Vacant WBU International
S. Flyweight Title)*

24.10.98 Mzukisi Marali W RSC 7 Liverpool
(Vacant WBF Flyweight Title)
05.03.99 Zolile Mbityi W PTS 12 Liverpool
(WBU Flyweight Title Defence)
15.05.99 Adrian Ochoa W RSC 9 Blackpool
(WBU Flyweight Title Defence)
09.03.00 Oscar Andrade W PTS 12 Liverpool
(WBU Flyweight Title Defence)
24.05.00 Jake Matlala W PTS 12 Carnival City,
South Africa
(WBU Flyweight Title Defence)
11.11.00 Dimitar Alipiev W CO 1 Belfast
(WBU Flyweight Title Defence)
09.06.01 Ian Napa W RSC 8 Bethnal Green
(WBU Flyweight Title Defence)
06.04.02 Sergei Tasimov W RSC 2 Copenhagen,
Denmark
05.10.02 Celso Dangud W PTS 8 Liverpool
29.11.02 Ncedo Cecane W PTS 12 Liverpool
(Vacant WBF S. Flyweight Title)
29.03.03 Wandee Chareon W PTS 12 Wembley
(WBF S. Flyweight Title Defence)
Career: 26 contests, won 24, drew 1, lost 1.

Peter Culshaw   Les Clark

Gary Cummings

Sheffield. *Born* Sheffield, 11 November,
1972
Welterweight. Ht. 5'9"
Manager J. Ingle

13.04.03 Wasim Hussain W RSC 2 Bradford
17.04.03 Dave Hill W CO 5 Hull
06.06.03 Danny Smith L PTS 6 Norwich
Career: 3 contest, won 2, lost 1.

Dave Curran

Doncaster. *Born* Tipperary, 15 January,
1977
Lightweight. Ht. 5'7¾"
Manager T. Petersen

24.11.01 Dave Cotterill L PTS 6 Wakefield
29.04.02 Mark Hudson W RSC 1 Bradford
28.05.02 Martin Hardcastle L RSC 3 Leeds
26.10.02 Jeff Thomas L RSC 6 Wigan
Career: 4 contests, won 1, lost 3.

Scott Dann

Plymouth. *Born* Plymouth, 23 July, 1974
Middleweight. Former Undefeated IBO
Inter-Continental Middleweight Champion.
Ht. 5'10½"
Manager C. Sanigar

15.11.97	Jon Rees W RSC 1 Bristol
25.04.98	Israel Khumalo W RSC 3 Cardiff
30.05.98	Michael Alexander W PTS 4 Bristol
14.07.98	Richard Glaysher W RSC 1 Reading
24.10.98	James Donoghue W PTS 6 Bristol
27.02.00	James Donoghue W RSC 1 Plymouth
07.04.00	Martin Jolley W RSC 2 Bristol
08.09.00	Sean Pritchard W RSC 5 Bristol
06.10.00	Peter Mitchell W RSC 3 Maidstone
03.11.00	Anthony Ivory W PTS 8 Ebbw Vale
13.03.01	Jason Hart W RSC 2 Plymouth
12.05.01	Elvis Adonesi W CO 7 Plymouth
	(Vacant IBO Inter-Continental Middleweight Title)
13.09.01	Jon Penn L RSC 5 Sheffield
10.05.02	Mark Phillips W PTS 6 Bethnal Green
10.07.02	Mark Phillips W PTS 4 Wembley
29.11.02	Delroy Leslie W RSC 1 Liverpool
	(Final Elim. British Middleweight Title)
16.04.03	Howard Eastman L RSC 3 Nottingham
	(British, Commonwealth & European Middleweight Title Challenges)

Career: 17 contests, won 15, lost 2.

Tomas da Silva

Canning Town. *Born* Sao Luiz Maranhao,
Brazil, 19 May, 1976
L. Middleweight. Ht. 5'11"
Manager A. Bowers

22.09.01	Conroy McIntosh W PTS 4 Canning Town
03.11.01	Ryan Kerr L PTS 4 Glasgow
16.11.01	Tommy Tolan W RSC 6 Dublin
08.12.01	Darren Covill W PTS 4 Millwall
16.12.01	Duje Postenjak L PTS 6 Glasgow
09.02.02	Thomas McDonagh DREW 4 Manchester
18.02.02	Biagio Falcone W RSC 3 Glasgow
19.04.02	Mark Graversen L PTS 6 Aarhus, Denmark
06.09.02	Steven Bendall L RSC 8 Bethnal Green
27.10.02	Matthew Tait L PTS 6 Southwark
03.12.02	Dean Powell L PTS 4 Bethnal Green
18.01.03	Thomas McDonagh L PTS 4 Preston
05.04.03	Ciaran Healy L PTS 4 Belfast

Career: 13 contests, won 4, drew 1, lost 8.

Chris Davies

Blaenclydach. *Born* Pontypridd, 24 August,
1974
L. Heavyweight. Ht. 5'9"
Manager T. Gilmour

27.04.94	Craig Joseph L PTS 6 Solihull
25.05.94	Glenn Catley L RSC 1 Bristol
29.05.96	Mark Hickey W RSC 1 Ebbw Vale
19.07.96	Michael Pinnock W PTS 6 Ystrad

31.08.96	James Branch L PTS 4 Dublin
02.10.96	Neil Simpson L PTS 4 Cardiff
02.10.99	Carl Nicholson W CO 1 Cardiff
22.10.99	Jim Twite W CO 1 Coventry
30.10.99	Ganny Dovidovas W PTS 4 Southwark
11.12.99	Paul Bonson W PTS 4 Merthyr
26.02.00	Adam Cale W RSC 4 Swansea
18.03.00	Neville Brown W RSC 2 Glasgow
11.04.00	Lee Manuel Ossie L PTS 10 Vigo, Spain
12.06.00	Cathal O'Grady W RSC 1 Belfast
29.01.01	Peter Oboh L RSC 8 Peterborough
	(Elim. Commonwealth L. Heavyweight Title)
07.09.01	Mark Williams W RSC 4 Bethnal Green
20.10.01	Tony Oakey L PTS 12 Portsmouth
	(Commonwealth L. Heavyweight Title Challenge)
26.10.02	Valery Odin W PTS 6 Maesteg
30.11.02	Sergei Karanevich W PTS 6 Liverpool

Career: 19 contests, won 12, lost 7.

Gary Davis (Harding)

St Helens. *Born* Liverpool, 17 October,
1982
S. Bantamweight. Ht. 5'6"
Manager F. Maloney/F. Warren

01.06.02	Steve Gethin L RSC 2 Manchester
05.10.02	Jason Thomas W RSC 5 Liverpool
29.11.02	Simon Chambers W RSC 2 Liverpool

Career: 3 contest, won 2, lost 1.

Varuzhan Davtyan

Birmingham. *Born* Armenia, 11 August,
1972
L. Heavyweight. Ht. 5'8½"
Manager Self

Previous record unknown

09.03.02	Tony Dodson W PTS 6 Manchester
09.05.02	Rasmus Ojemaye W RSC 3 Leicester Square
29.06.02	Elvis Michailenko L PTS 6 Brentwood
08.09.02	Paul Bonson W PTS 4 Wolverhampton
05.10.02	Mark Hobson L RSC 3 Huddersfield
30.11.02	Eric Teymour L PTS 6 Liverpool
14.12.02	Tomasz Adamek L RTD 4 Newcastle
05.03.03	Carl Froch L RSC 5 Bethnal Green
17.05.03	Jason McKay L PTS 6 Liverpool
24.05.03	Eric Teymour L PTS 4 Bethnal Green
28.06.03	Nathan King L PTS 4 Cardiff

Career: 11 contests, won 3, lost 8.

Lenny Daws

Morden. *Born* Carshalton, 29 December,
1978
Welterweight. Ht. 5'10½"
Manager R. McCracken

16.04.03	Danny Gwilym W RSC 2 Nottingham
27.05.03	Ben Hudson W RSC 2 Dagenham

Career: 2 contests, won 2.

Neil Dawson

Rotherham. *Born* Rotherham, 1 July, 1980
Cruiserweight. Ht. 6'4"
Manager T. Gilmour/C. Aston

12.11.02	Eamonn Glennon W PTS 6 Leeds
24.03.03	Dave Clarke W PTS 4 Barnsley

Career: 2 contests, won 2.

Phill Day

Banbury. *Born* Swindon, 5 November, 1974
Cruiserweight. Ht. 5'11½"
Manager A. Phillips

07.07.95	Tim Redman L RSC 2 Cardiff
21.09.95	John Pettersson L RSC 4 Battersea
10.11.95	L. A. Williams W PTS 6 Bristol
21.02.96	Carl Heath L PTS 6 Piccadilly
18.10.96	David Jules W RSC 1 Barnstaple
09.12.96	Naveed Anwar W PTS 6 Bristol
24.03.97	Jim Pallatt W CO 1 Bristol
15.05.97	Tony Booth L PTS 4 Reading
17.01.98	Richie Chapman W PTS 4 Bristol
07.03.98	Lee Swaby W PTS 4 Reading
16.04.98	Cliff Elden W RSC 3 Mayfair
30.05.98	Chris P. Bacon L RSC 4 Bristol
05.10.02	Tony Booth L PTS 4 Coventry
16.11.02	Darren Ashton DREW 4 Coventry
15.02.03	Jason Brewster W PTS 6 Wolverhampton
18.03.03	David Haye L RSC 2 Reading
17.04.03	Jamie Warters DREW 6 Hull
10.06.03	Carl Thompson L CO 4 Sheffield

Career: 18 contests, won 8, drew 2, lost 8.

Phill Day   Les Clark

Rocky Dean

Thetford. *Born* Bury St Edmonds, 17 June,
1978
S. Bantamweight. Ht. 5'5"
Manager Self

14.10.99	Lennie Hodgkins W PTS 6 Bloomsbury
30.10.99	Lennie Hodgkins W PTS 6 Southwark
18.05.00	Danny Lawson W RSC 1 Bethnal Green
29.09.00	Anthony Hanna W PTS 4 Bethnal Green
10.11.00	Chris Jickells L RSC 1 Mayfair
19.04.02	Peter Svendsen W PTS 6 Aarhus, Denmark
19.10.02	Sean Grant W RSC 3 Norwich
21.12.02	Darren Cleary W PTS 4 Millwall
08.02.03	Steve Gethin DREW 4 Norwich

Career: 9 contests, won 7, drew 1, lost 1.

Graham Delehedy

Liverpool. *Born* Liverpool, 7 October, 1978
L. Middleweight. Ht. 5'8"
Manager T. Gilmour

17.05.03 Joel Ani W RSC 4 Liverpool
Career: 1 contest, won 1.

(Mtabingwa) Frankie DeMilo

Bristol. *Born* Rwanda, 6 April, 1974
British Masters & Western Area S.
Bantamweight Champion. Ht. 5'7½"
Manager C. Sanigar

26.02.99 Danny Lawson W PTS 6 Longford
17.03.99 Daniel Ring W RSC 2 Kensington
02.07.99 Graham McGrath W PTS 4 Bristol
24.09.99 Jason Thomas L RSC 2 Merthyr
22.11.99 Anthony Hanna W PTS 6 Piccadilly
03.12.99 Ian Turner W PTS 6 Peterborough
20.01.00 David Jeffrey W RSC 8 Piccadilly
　　　　　(Vacant Western Area S. Bantamweight Title)
29.03.00 Jason Thomas W RSC 8 Piccadilly
　　　　　(Vacant British Masters S. Bantamweight Title)
02.06.00 Kevin Gerowski W RSC 7 Ashford
　　　　　(British Masters S. Bantamweight Title Defence)
08.09.00 Harry Woods W RTD 6 Bristol
　　　　　(British Masters S.Bantamweight Title Defence)
03.11.00 Ian Turner W PTS 10 Ebbw Vale
　　　　　(British Masters S.Bantamweight Title Defence)
12.05.01 John Barnes W PTS 10 Plymouth
　　　　　(British Masters S. Bantamweight Title Defence)
30.09.01 Sean Green W PTS 6 Bristol
16.12.01 Rakhim Mingaleev W PTS 6 Bristol
08.02.02 Francisco Tejedor W PTS 6 Copenhagen, Denmark
14.06.02 Jadgar Abdulla L PTS 4 Copenhagen, Denmark
18.10.02 Michael Hunter L PTS 12 Hartlepool
　　　　　(Vacant WBF S. Bantamweight Title)
Career: 17 contests, won 14, lost 3.

Buster Dennis　　　　　Les Clark

(Dennis) Buster Dennis (Mwanze)

Canning Town. *Born* Mawokota, Uganda,
31 December, 1981
S. Bantamweight. Ht. 5'0"
Manager A. Bowers

28.03.03 Vitali Makarov W RSC 2 Millwall
03.04.03 Chris Hooper L RSC 1 Hull
15.05.03 Mark Alexander L PTS 4 Mayfair
24.05.03 Haider Ali L PTS 4 Bethnal Green
Career: 4 contests, won 1, lost 3.

Paul Denton (Ramsey)

Birmingham. *Born* Birmingham, 12 April,
1970
Welterweight. Ht. 5'10"
Manager Self

18.03.93 Mark O'Callaghan W RSC 4 Lewisham
29.04.93 Dave Maj DREW 6 Mayfair
11.08.93 Billy McDougall W PTS 6 Mansfield
01.10.93 Ferid Bennecer W CO 3 Waregem, Belgium
01.12.93 Brian Hickey W CO 1 Kensington
28.01.94 Youssef Bakhouche L PTS 6 Waregem, Belgium
07.05.94 Viktor Fesetchko L PTS 6 Dnepropetrousk, Ukraine
23.09.94 Roy Rowland W RSC 5 Bethnal Green
03.01.95 Patrick Charpentier L RSC 4 Epernay, France
25.02.95 Paul Ryan L RSC 4 Millwall
25.11.95 Michael Carruth L PTS 8 Dublin
03.02.96 George Naylor W RSC 3 Liverpool
26.04.96 Ross Hale W RSC 4 Cardiff
15.11.96 Frank Olsen L RSC 4 Nestved, Denmark
14.03.97 Mark Winters L PTS 8 Reading
13.06.97 Alan McDowall DREW 6 Paisley
21.03.98 Naas Scheepers L PTS 8 Hammanskraal, South Africa
19.09.98 Neil Sinclair L RSC 1 Dublin
19.12.98 Ricky Hatton L RSC 6 Liverpool
16.02.99 Steve Tuckett L PTS 6 Leeds
27.02.99 Michael Carruth L RSC 5 Bethnal Green
27.05.00 Jacek Bielski L PTS 6 Mayfair
19.06.00 Oscar Hall L PTS 4 Burton
08.07.00 Michael Jennings L PTS 6 Widnes
12.08.00 Wayne Alexander L RSC 1 Wembley
02.10.00 Kevin McIntyre L PTS 6 Glasgow
18.11.00 Pavel Melnikov L PTS 4 Dagenham
01.12.00 Paul Dyer L PTS 4 Peterborough
11.12.00 Michael Jennings L PTS 4 Widnes
17.02.01 David Walker L PTS 4 Bethnal Green
26.02.01 James Hare L PTS 4 Nottingham
07.04.01 Brett James L PTS 4 Wembley
24.04.01 Paul Burns L PTS 4 Liverpool
08.05.01 Derek Roche L PTS 6 Barnsley
27.05.01 Jamie Moore L RSC 3 Manchester
07.07.01 Thomas McDonagh L PTS 6 Manchester
20.10.01 Kevin Bennett L PTS 4 Portsmouth
26.11.01 James Hare L RTD 4 Manchester
09.02.02 Matthew Hatton L PTS 6 Manchester
02.03.02 Ross Minter L PTS 6 Bethnal Green
10.05.02 Leo O'Reilly L PTS 6 Bethnal Green
14.12.02 Matthew Hatton L PTS 6 Newcastle
05.03.03 Costas Katsantonis L PTS 6 Bethnal Green
08.04.03 Jason Rowland L PTS 6 Bethnal Green
24.05.03 Matthew Macklin L PTS 6 Bethnal Green
Career: 45 contests, won 7, drew 2, lost 36.

Reagan Denton

Sheffield. *Born* Sheffield, 26 June, 1978
S. Middleweight. Ht. 5'11"
Manager Self

15.05.99 Pedro Thompson W PTS 4 Sheffield
15.11.99 Colin Vidler W PTS 4 Bethnal Green
25.09.00 William Webster W PTS 4 Barnsley
08.10.01 Martyn Bailey W PTS 4 Barnsley
15.12.01 Darren Covill W PTS 4 Sheffield
24.03.03 Dave Pearson W PTS 6 Barnsley
Career: 6 contests, won 6.

Norman Dhalie

Birmingham. *Born* Birmingham, 24 March,
1971
Welterweight. Ht. 5'7"
Manager Self

06.04.92 Karl Morling L PTS 6 Northampton
27.04.92 Wilson Docherty L RSC 2 Glasgow
02.07.92 John White L RSC 6 Middleton
29.09.92 Gary Marston DREW 6 Stoke
07.10.92 Jacob Smith W PTS 6 Sunderland
03.12.92 Bradley Stone L CO 4 Lewisham
26.01.93 Neil Smith L PTS 4 Leicester
13.02.93 John White L CO 2 Manchester
20.04.93 Bobby Guynan L PTS 6 Brentwood
29.04.93 Kevin Toomey L PTS 6 Hull
23.05.93 Mike Anthony Brown W PTS 4 Brockley
09.06.93 Joey Moffat L RTD 4 Liverpool
30.09.93 Simon Frailing W PTS 6 Hayes
06.10.93 Kevin McKillan L RSC 1 Solihull
06.12.93 Colin Innes W PTS 6 Bradford
16.12.93 Peter Till L PTS 8 Walsall
19.01.94 John Naylor L RSC 3 Stoke
21.02.94 Hugh Collins L RTD 4 Glasgow
14.04.94 Mike Anthony Brown L PTS 6 Battersea
28.04.94 John Stovin DREW 6 Hull
06.05.94 Sugar Gibiliru L RTD 5 Liverpool
02.09.94 Dave Fallon L DIS 4 Spitalfields
28.09.94 Tanveer Ahmed L CO 5 Glasgow
24.11.94 Tony Foster L RTD 7 Hull
17.02.95 Paul Knights L RTD 5 Crawley
16.06.95 George Naylor L PTS 6 Liverpool
25.10.95 Joe Donohoe W PTS 6 Stoke
20.12.95 J. T. Williams L CO 2 Usk
16.03.96 Robbie Sivyer L CO 4 Barnstaple
15.10.96 Wayne Windle W PTS 6 Wolverhampton
02.12.96 Andy Robinson W PTS 6 Birmingham
06.10.97 Vic Broomhead W PTS 6 Birmingham
14.10.97 Chris Pegg W RSC 5 Wolverhampton
11.11.97 Vic Broomhead W PTS 6 Edgbaston
02.03.98 Wayne Windle W PTS 6 Birmingham
23.04.98 Thomas Bradley L CO 5 Edgbaston
27.05.99 Carl Tilley W RSC 1 Edgbaston
04.03.02 Nicky Leech L PTS 6 Birmingham
23.11.02 Terry Fletcher L CO 2 Derby
09.02.03 Nadeem Siddique L PTS 4 Bradford
08.06.03 Jeff Thomas L PTS 6 Shaw
Career: 41 contests, won 12, drew 2, lost 27.

Craig Dickson

Glasgow. *Born* Glasgow, 6 March, 1979
L. Middleweight. Ht. 5'11"
Manager T. Gilmour

21.10.02 Paul Rushton W RSC 2 Glasgow
18.11.02 Ernie Smith W PTS 6 Glasgow
17.02.03 Jon Hilton W RSC 2 Glasgow
14.04.03 Richard Inquieti W PTS 4 Glasgow
Career: 4 contests, won 4.

Mark Dillon

Belfast. *Born* Dublin, 21 September, 1975
L. Middleweight. Ht. 5'8"
Manager B. Hearn

30.11.02 Lee Williamson L PTS 4 Liverpool
Career: 1 contest, lost 1.

Mark Dillon   Les Clark

Haroon Din

Sheffield. *Born* Middlesbrough, 21 May, 1978
S. Featherweight. Ht. 5'8"
Manager Self

21.09.98 Les Frost L PTS 6 Cleethorpes
14.12.98 Les Frost L RSC 1 Cleethorpes
02.05.99 Amjid Mahmood W PTS 6 Shaw
20.05.00 Dave Travers W PTS 6 Leicester
24.06.00 Willie Limond L PTS 4 Glasgow
30.08.00 Leon Dobbs W CO 1 Scunthorpe
19.11.00 Carl Greaves L RSC 4 Chesterfield
24.09.01 Nigel Senior W PTS 6 Cleethorpes
17.12.01 Nigel Senior W PTS 6 Cleethorpes
31.01.02 Ilias Miah W RSC 3 Piccadilly
20.04.02 Gareth Wiltshaw W PTS 6 Derby
17.11.02 Gareth Wiltshaw W PTS 6 Bradford
05.04.03 Andy Morris L RSC 1 Manchester
Career: 13 contests, won 8, lost 5.

Gary Dixon

Carlisle. *Born* Carlisle, 2 November, 1974
S. Middleweight. Ht. 5'10½"
Manager J. Doughty

18.03.01 Jamie Logan W PTS 6 Shaw
10.05.01 Paul Owen L RSC 3 Sunderland
26.07.01 Michael Thompson W PTS 6 Blackpool
23.09.01 Mark Sawyers DREW 6 Shaw
09.12.01 Danny Wray W RSC 4 Shaw
03.03.02 William Webster W PTS 6 Shaw
02.06.02 Simeon Cover L PTS 6 Shaw
06.09.02 Tom Cannon L PTS 6 Glasgow
17.11.02 Conroy McIntosh L RSC 2 Shaw
09.03.03 Mike Duffield W PTS 6 Shaw
Career: 10 contests, won 5, drew 1, lost 4.

Scott Dixon   Les Clark

Scott Dixon

Hamilton. *Born* Hamilton, 28 September, 1976
L. Middleweight. Former Undefeated WBO Inter-Continental L. Middleweight Champion. Former Undefeated Commonwealth Welterweight Champion. Former Undefeated WBB & Scottish Welterweight Champion. Ht. 5'9"
Manager Self

13.10.95 Andrew Smith W PTS 4 Glasgow
17.12.95 Martin Evans W RSC 4 Glasgow
12.02.96 Colin Innes W PTS 6 Glasgow
16.03.96 Ian Richardson W PTS 4 Glasgow
26.04.96 Andy Green W RSC 5 Glasgow
24.05.96 Brian Coleman W PTS 8 Glasgow
20.09.96 Alan Temple W PTS 6 Glasgow
06.11.96 Rocky Ferrari DREW 6 Glasgow
22.12.96 Marc Smith W PTS 6 Glasgow
04.04.97 Jimmy Phelan W PTS 6 Glasgow
16.05.97 Dean Bramhald W PTS 6 Glasgow
13.06.97 Chris Price W PTS 6 Paisley
05.07.97 Mark McGowan W PTS 4 Glasgow
12.09.97 Gerard Murphy W PTS 8 Glasgow
01.11.97 Nigel Bradley W PTS 4 Glasgow
12.11.97 John Green DREW 8 Glasgow
14.12.97 Tony Walton W PTS 6 Glasgow
27.02.98 Chris Saunders W PTS 10 Glasgow
    (*Elim. British Welterweight Title*)
19.09.98 Michael Carruth L PTS 12 Dublin
    (*Vacant WAA Welterweight Title*)
13.11.98 Lee Molyneux W PTS 4 Brighton
26.02.99 Edwin Murillo W CO 6 Bethnal Green
    (*WBB Welterweight Title Challenge*)
07.06.99 Mark Ramsey W PTS 8 Glasgow
22.10.99 Derek Roche L PTS 12 Coventry
    (*British Welterweight Title Challenge*)
05.02.00 Sean Sullivan W PTS 12 Bethnal Green
    (*Vacant Commonwealth Welterweight Title*)
06.06.00 Charlie Kane W RSC 6 Motherwell
    (*Commonwealth Welterweight Title Defence. Vacant Scottish Welterweight Title*)

24.06.00 Leith Wicks W PTS 4 Glasgow
19.08.00 Steve Roberts L RSC 9 Brentwood
    (*Vacant WBF L. Middleweight Title*)
25.11.00 Anthony Farnell L RSC 7 Manchester
    (*WBO Inter-Continental L. Middleweight Title Challenge*)
20.03.01 Wayne Shepherd W PTS 6 Glasgow
27.04.01 Anders Styve L PTS 4 Aalborg, Denmark
18.05.01 Ruben Varon W RSC 5 Guadalajara, Spain
07.07.01 Jamie Moore W CO 5 Manchester
    (*Vacant WBO Inter-Continental L.Middleweight Title*)
22.09.01 Takaloo L CO 1 Bethnal Green
    (*WBU L.Middleweight Title Challenge*)
15.03.02 Michael Rask L PTS 8 Vilborg, Denmark
17.05.03 Marcus Portman L PTS 6 Liverpool
Career: 35 contests, won 25, drew 2, lost 8.

Terry Dixon

Harlesden. *Born* London, 29 July, 1966
Cruiserweight. Ht. 5'11"
Manager J. Oyebola

21.09.89 Dave Mowbray W RSC 1 Southampton
30.11.89 Brendan Dempsey W RSC 8 Barking
08.03.90 Cordwell Hylton W PTS 8 Watford
06.04.90 Prince Rodney W RSC 7 Stevenage
23.10.90 Dennis Bailey W PTS 6 Leicester
07.03.91 Carl Thompson L PTS 8 Basildon
22.04.91 Everton Blake L RSC 8 Mayfair
25.03.92 Mark Bowen W RTD 1 Kensington
27.04.92 Ian Bulloch W RSC 4 Mayfair
17.10.92 Darren McKenna L RSC 3 Wembley
04.10.93 Steve Yorath W RSC 4 Mayfair
03.08.94 Chemek Saleta L PTS 8 Bristol
09.05.02 Kevin Barrett DREW 4 Leicester Square
30.10.02 Leighton Morgan W RSC 1 Leicester Square
29.03.03 Mal Rice W PTS 4 Wembley
Career: 15 contests, won 10, drew 1, lost 4.

Craig Docherty

Glasgow. *Born* Glasgow, 27 September, 1979
Commonwealth S. Featherweight Champion. Ht. 5'7"
Manager T. Gilmour

16.11.98 Kevin Gerowski W PTS 6 Glasgow
22.02.99 Des Gargano W PTS 6 Glasgow
19.04.99 Paul Quarmby W RSC 4 Glasgow
07.06.99 Simon Chambers W PTS 6 Glasgow
20.09.99 John Barnes W PTS 6 Glasgow
15.11.99 Peter Allen W RSC 1 Glasgow
24.01.00 Lee Williamson W PTS 6 Glasgow
19.02.00 Steve Hanley W PTS 6 Prestwick
05.06.00 Sebastian Hart W RSC 1 Glasgow
23.10.00 Lee Armstrong DREW 8 Glasgow
22.01.01 Nigel Senior W RSC 4 Glasgow
20.03.01 Jamie McKeever W RSC 3 Glasgow
11.06.01 Rakhim Mingaleev W PTS 8 Nottingham
27.10.01 Michael Gomez L RSC 2 Manchester
    (*British S.Featherweight Title Challenge*)
18.03.02 Joel Viney W CO 1 Glasgow
13.07.02 Dariusz Snarski W PTS 6 Coventry
25.01.03 Nikolai Eremeev W PTS 6 Bridgend
12.04.03 Dean Pithie W CO 8 Bethnal Green
    (*Commonwealth S. Featherweight Title Challenge*)
Career: 18 contests, won 16, drew 1, lost 1.

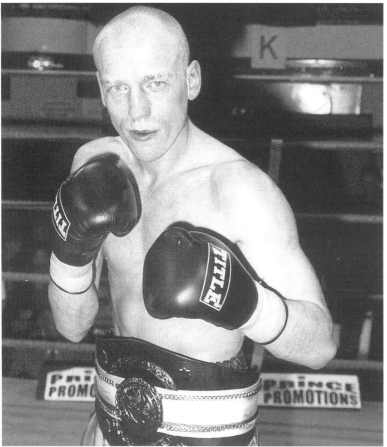

Craig Docherty   Les Clark

Tony Dodson

Liverpool. *Born* Liverpool, 2 July, 1980
Central Area S.Middleweight Champion.
Former WBF Inter-Continental
S.Middleweight Champion. Ht. 6'0½"
Manager B. Hearn

31.07.99	Michael McDermott W RTD 1 Carlisle
02.10.99	Sean Pritchard W RSC 3 Cardiff
22.01.00	Mark Dawson W PTS 4 Birmingham
11.03.00	Paul Bonson W PTS 4 Kensington
19.08.00	Jimmy Steel W RSC 3 Brentwood
09.09.00	Danny Southam W RSC 2 Manchester
09.10.00	Elvis Michailenko DREW 6 Liverpool
03.02.01	Paul Bonson W PTS 4 Manchester
25.09.01	Paul Wesley W PTS 6 Liverpool
13.10.01	Roman Divisek W CO 1 Budapest, Hungary
10.11.01	Valery Odin W RSC 4 Wembley
10.12.01	Jon Penn W RSC 2 Liverpool
	(Vacant Central Area S.Middleweight Title)
23.02.02	Jason Hart W RSC 2 Nottingham
09.03.02	Varuzhan Davtyan L PTS 6 Manchester
13.04.02	Brian Barbosa W PTS 8 Liverpool
07.09.02	Mike Algoet W PTS 10 Liverpool
	(Vacant WBF Inter-Continental S.Middleweight Title)
26.10.02	Albert Rybacki L RSC 9 Maesteg
	(WBF Inter-Continental S.Middleweight Title Defence)
19.04.03	Pierre Moreno L RSC 9 Liverpool
	(Vacant WBF Inter-Continental S.Middleweight Title)

Career: 18 contests, won 14, drew 1, lost 3.

Hughie Doherty

Wellingborough. *Born* Greenwich, 25 July, 1982
L. Heavyweight. Ht. 5'10"
Manager K. Sanders

29.01.01	Tommy Matthews W PTS 4 Peterborough
12.05.01	Darren Covill W PTS 4 Plymouth
27.10.02	Tony Booth W PTS 4 Southwark

Career: 3 contests, won 3.

Tony Doherty

Chadderton. *Born* London, 8 April, 1983
Welterweight. Ht. 5'8"
Manager F. Warren/B. Hughes

08.05.03	Karl Taylor W PTS 4 Widnes
28.06.03	Paul McIlwaine W RSC 1 Cardiff

Career: 2 contest, won 2.

Roddy Doran

Shrewsbury. *Born* Shrewsbury, 15 March, 1972
Middleweight. Former Undefeated British
Masters S. Middleweight Champion.
Ht. 5'11"
Manager D. Bradley

08.10.01	Harry Butler W PTS 6 Birmingham
31.10.01	Harry Butler DREW 6 Birmingham
11.02.02	Freddie Yemofio W PTS 8 Shrewsbury
15.04.02	William Webster W PTS 8 Shrewsbury
13.05.02	Simeon Cover DREW 8 Birmingham
29.09.02	Simon Andrews W PTS 6 Shrewsbury
03.12.02	Harry Butler W PTS 6 Shrewsbury
23.02.03	Simeon Cover W PTS 10 Shrewsbury
	(Vacant British Masters S.Middleweight Title)
30.06.03	Mark Phillips W PTS 6 Shrewsbury

Career: 9 contests, won 7, drew 2.

Darren Dorrington

Bristol. *Born* Bristol, 24 July, 1968
Middleweight. Western Area
S. Middleweight Champion. Ht. 5'11"
Manager C. Sanigar

13.09.93	Justin Smart DREW 4 Bristol
03.11.93	Russell Washer W PTS 4 Bristol
20.01.94	Shamus Casey W PTS 6 Battersea
29.01.94	Barry Thorogood DREW 6 Cardiff
10.03.94	Ray Price W RSC 6 Bristol
25.05.94	Steve Thomas W PTS 4 Bristol
02.07.94	Paul Murray W RSC 3 Keynsham
03.08.94	Gary Pemberton W CO 4 Bristol
07.10.94	Peter Vosper W RSC 6 Taunton
	(Vacant Western Area S. Middleweight Title)
27.10.94	Russell Washer W PTS 8 Bayswater
22.11.94	Robert Allen L RSC 5 Bristol
21.03.95	Lee Crocker L PTS 6 Swansea
19.06.96	Peter Vosper W RSC 3 Bristol
09.12.96	Ernie Loveridge W PTS 6 Bristol
21.01.97	Peter Mitchell W RSC 5 Bristol
24.03.96	Peter Mitchell W RSC 7 Bristol
05.06.97	Paul Carr W PTS 6 Bristol
15.09.97	Darren Ashton L DIS 2 Bristol
11.10.97	Jason Matthews L RSC 7 Sheffield
	(WBO Inter-Continental Middleweight Title Challenge)
17.01.98	Rob Stevenson W RSC 3 Bristol
30.03.98	Bruno Girard L PTS 8 Tenerife
30.05.98	Jason Hart W RTD 2 Bristol
14.07.98	Adrian Riley W RTD 2 Reading
24.10.98	Jimmy Vincent DREW 6 Bristol
02.07.99	Elvis Adonesi L RTD 11 Bristol
	(Vacant WBU Inter-Continental L. Middleweight Title)
07.04.00	Elvis Adonesi L PTS 12 Bristol
	(Vacant WBU Inter-Continental Middleweight Title)
30.09.01	Simon Andrews W RSC 4 Bristol
	(Western Area S.Middleweight Title Defence)
16.12.01	16/12/01 Viktor Fesetchko L PTS 10 Bristol
	(Vacant WBF European Middleweight Title)
06.03.03	Mark Phillips W PTS 8 Bristol
13.06.03	Dale Nixon W RSC 5 Bristol

Career: 30 contests, won 19, drew 3, lost 8.

(Genadijus) Ganny Dovidovas

Beckton. *Born* Lithuania, 29 October, 1974
S. Middleweight. Ht. 6'1"
Manager C. Smith

26.02.99	Jimmy Steel W PTS 6 Bethnal Green	
30.09.99	Peter Mason W RSC 3 Kensington	
14.10.99	Anthony Wright W PTS 6 Bloomsbury	
30.10.99	Chris Davies L PTS 4 Southwark	
26.11.99	Reece McAllister W RSC 1 Bayswater	
25.02.00	Jason Barker DREW 4 Newmarket	
09.03.00	Ossie Duran W PTS 4 Bethnal Green	
20.05.00	Paul Jones L PTS 6 Rotherham	
03.11.00	Juan Francisco Galvez L PTS 8 Erandio, Spain	
31.05.02	Marian Diaconu L CO 3 Bucharest, Romania	
13.07.02	Mark Smallwood L RSC 3 Coventry	

Career: 11 contests, won 5, drew 1, lost 5.

Ganny Dovidovas   Les Clark

Tony Dowling

Lincoln. *Born* Lincoln, 5 January, 1976
Cruiserweight. Ht. 6'2"
Manager J. Ashton

22.03.96	Slick Miller W RSC 4 Mansfield	
30.05.96	Nigel Rafferty W PTS 6 Lincoln	
29.07.96	Albert Call L RSC 4 Skegness	
12.02.00	Adam Cale W PTS 4 Sheffield	
20.03.00	Danny Southam W PTS 4 Mansfield	
11.05.00	Jason Brewster W RSC 2 Newark	
08.07.00	Slick Miller W PTS 4 Widnes	
09.09.00	Lee Swaby L RSC 9 Newark	
	(Vacant British Masters Cruiserweight Title)	
20.04.01	Cathal O'Grady L RSC 1 Dublin	
15.09.01	Michael Pinnock W PTS 6 Derby	
20.10.01	Garry Delaney L RSC 6 Glasgow	
11.05.02	Gary Thompson W RSC 3 Newark	
29.09.02	Paul Bonson W PTS 6 Shrewsbury	
30.11.02	Scott Lansdowne L RSC 2 Newark	
	(Vacant Midlands Area Cruiserweight Title)	

Career: 14 contests, won 9, lost 5.

Gavin Down

Chesterfield. *Born* Chesterfield, 2 February, 1977
British Masters L.Welterweight Champion. Former Undefeated Midlands Area L.Welterweight Champion. Ht. 5'9"
Manager J. Ingle

21.09.98	Peter Lennon W RSC 1 Cleethorpes	
27.11.98	Trevor Tacy L PTS 6 Nottingham	
07.12.98	Brian Coleman W PTS 6 Manchester	
26.02.99	Brian Gifford W PTS 6 West Bromwich	
27.03.99	Lee Molyneux W PTS 4 Derby	
15.05.99	Les Frost W RSC 1 Sheffield	
27.06.99	Lee Molyneux W PTS 6 Alfreton	
03.10.99	Ernie Smith W RSC 1 Chesterfield	
28.11.99	Dave Gibson W PTS 6 Chesterfield	
09.04.00	Sammy Smith W PTS 6 Alfreton	
21.05.00	Arv Mittoo W PTS 6 Derby	
19.06.00	Brian Coleman W PTS 4 Burton	
13.08.00	Lee Bird W PTS 6 Nottingham	
30.08.00	Ram Singh W PTS 6 Scunthorpe	
04.11.00	Sebastian Hart W RSC 4 Derby	
19.11.00	David Kirk W PTS 10 Chesterfield	
	(Vacant British Masters L. Welterweight Title)	
11.12.00	Dave Gibson W RSC 5 Cleethorpes	
25.02.01	Jay Mahoney W RSC 1 Derby	
01.04.01	Steve Saville W RSC 3 Alfreton	
	(Vacant Midlands Area L. Welterweight Title)	
16.06.01	Arv Mittoo W PTS 6 Derby	
21.07.01	Tommy Peacock W RSC 1 Sheffield	
15.09.01	Lee Williamson W PTS 6 Derby	
08.12.01	Brian Coleman W RSC 1 Chesterfield	
12.02.02	Bradley Pryce L RSC 9 Bethnal Green	
	(Vacant IBF Inter-Continental L.Welterweight Title)	
11.05.02	Woody Greenaway W RSC 3 Chesterfield	
05.10.02	Daniel Thorpe W RSC 2 Chesterfield	
19.10.02	Daniel James W RTD 5 Norwich	
28.01.03	Tony Montana W PTS 4 Nottingham	

Career: 28 contests, won 26, lost 2.

Mike Duffield

Cleethorpes. *Born* Cleethorpes, 9 April, 1969
Midlands Area S. Middleweight Champion. Ht. 6'2½"
Manager Self

22.09.97	Ian Toby L PTS 6 Cleethorpes	
21.10.97	Ian Toby W PTS 6 Yarm	
14.11.97	Mike Gormley L RSC 2 Mere	
15.12.97	Jon Penn L RSC 2 Cleethorpes	
16.03.98	Matt Galer L PTS 6 Nottingham	
28.04.98	Gary Reyniers DREW 6 Brentford	
18.05.98	Carlton Williams W PTS 6 Cleethorpes	
17.07.98	Mike White W PTS 6 Mere	
21.09.98	Phil Ball W RSC 2 Cleethorpes	
26.11.98	Gordon Behan L RSC 3 Edgbaston	
	(Vacant Midlands Area Middleweight Title)	
18.02.99	Lawrence Murphy L RSC 2 Glasgow	
29.05.99	Eddie Haley L RSC 6 South Shields	
28.11.99	Martin Jolley W PTS 6 Chesterfield	
18.01.00	Gary Beardsley L RTD 2 Mansfield	
15.05.00	William Webster L PTS 6 Birmingham	
15.07.00	Earl Ling L PTS 6 Norwich	
30.08.00	Matthew Pepper W RSC 4 Scunthorpe	
04.11.00	Damon Hague L RSC 3 Derby	
	(Vacant WBF European S. Middleweight Title)	

20.04.02	Donovan Smillie W PTS 4 Derby	
31.05.02	Jamie Wilson W PTS 6 Hull	
03.08.02	Simeon Cover L RSC 2 Derby	
08.09.02	Peter Jackson L PTS 4 Wolverhampton	
21.09.02	Danny Smith L PTS 6 Norwich	
10.10.02	Jason Collins L PTS 4 Piccadilly	
02.11.02	Peter Jackson W PTS 10 Wolverhampton	
	(Vacant Midlands Area S.Middleweight Title)	
21.12.02	Carl Froch L RSC 1 Dagenham	
09.03.03	Gary Dixon L PTS 6 Shaw	
17.04.03	Mark Ellwood L PTS 10 Hull	
	(Vacant British Masters L.Heavyweight Title)	
15.06.03	Donovan Smillie L RSC 3 Bradford	
	(Vacant British Masters S.Middleweight Title)	

Career: 29 contests, won 9, drew 1, lost 19.

Mike Duffield   Les Clark

Ciaran Duffy

Leeds. *Born* Donegal, 11 September, 1980
L. Middleweight. Ht. 5'11"
Manager Self

03.11.01	Wayne Shepherd W PTS 6 Glasgow	
03.12.01	Pedro Thompson W PTS 6 Leeds	
22.04.02	Richard Inquieti W PTS 6 Glasgow	
20.11.02	Dave Pearson DREW 6 Leeds	
17.03.03	Danny Moir W PTS 6 Glasgow	

Career: 5 contests, won 4, drew 1.

Chris Duggan

Coatbridge. *Born* Glasgow, 26 May, 1981
Welterweight. Ht. 5'10½"
Manager P. Cowdell

03.02.01	Ty Browne L RSC 1 Brighton	
27.07.01	Dean Walker L RSC 4 Sheffield	
10.12.01	Carl Walton W PTS 6 Birmingham	
15.04.02	Arv Mittoo W PTS 6 Shrewsbury	
13.05.02	Lee Williamson L RSC 3 Birmingham	
09.06.03	Mally McIver L RSC 3 Bradford	

Career: 6 contests, won 2, lost 4.

Peter Dunn

Pontefract. *Born* Doncaster, 15 February, 1975
Welterweight. Ht. 5'8"
Manager Self

08.12.97	Leigh Daniels W PTS 6 Bradford
15.05.98	Peter Lennon W PTS 6 Nottingham
18.09.98	Jan Cree L RSC 5 Belfast
23.10.98	Bobby Lyndon W PTS 6 Wakefield
03.12.98	Craig Smith L RSC 3 Sunderland
17.03.99	Des Sowden W PTS 6 Kensington
15.05.99	Ray Wood DREW 4 Blackpool
29.05.99	Dean Nicholas L PTS 6 South Shields
01.10.99	Jon Honney L PTS 4 Bethnal Green
18.10.99	Jan Cree W PTS 6 Glasgow
26.11.99	Gavin Pearson DREW 6 Wakefield
18.02.00	John T. Kelly L PTS 6 Pentre Halkyn
11.03.00	Iain Eldridge L RSC 2 Kensington
18.09.00	Joe Miller L PTS 6 Glasgow
26.10.00	Ram Singh W PTS 6 Stoke
27.11.00	Young Muttley L RSC 3 Birmingham
22.02.01	Darren Spencer W PTS 6 Sunderland
03.03.01	Glenn McClarnon L PTS 4 Wembley
20.03.01	Robert Burton L PTS 6 Leeds
08.04.01	Martyn Bailey L PTS 6 Wrexham
17.05.01	Gavin Pearson L PTS 6 Leeds
25.09.01	Darren Spencer L PTS 4 Liverpool
06.10.01	Lee Byrne L RSC 4 Manchester
13.11.01	Richard Inquieti DREW 6 Leeds
24.11.01	Robert Burton W PTS 6 Wakefield
28.01.02	Robert Burton L RSC 8 Barnsley
	(Vacant Central Area Welterweight Title)
23.03.02	Colin Lynes L PTS 4 Southwark
19.04.02	Oscar Hall L PTS 6 Darlington
28.05.02	Matt Scriven L PTS 8 Leeds
29.06.02	Darren Bruce L PTS 6 Brentwood
28.09.02	Surinder Sekhon L PTS 6 Wakefield

Career: 31 contests, won 8, drew 3, lost 20.

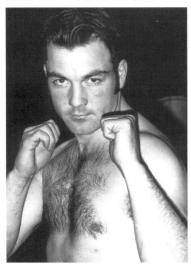

Peter Dunn   Les Clark

Colin Dunne

Holloway. *Born* Liverpool, 19 September, 1970
Lightweight. Former WBU Lightweight Champion. Former Undefeated WBF & Southern Area Lightweight Champion. Ht. 5'6"
Manager T. Toole

07.12.93	Mark O'Callaghan W RSC 1 Bethnal Green
14.01.94	Wayne Jones W RSC 3 Bethnal Green
04.03.94	Malcolm Thomas W CO 1 Bethnal Green
26.04.94	Steve Burton W CO 2 Bethnal Green
17.05.94	Phil Found W PTS 6 Kettering
23.09.94	Steve Howden W CO 1 Bethnal Green
11.10.94	Jimmy Phelan W PTS 6 Bethnal Green
09.11.94	Mark O'Callaghan W RSC 2 Millwall
09.12.94	David Thompson W RSC 3 Bethnal Green
20.01.95	Chris Aston W RSC 4 Bethnal Green
03.03.95	Marco Fattore W RSC 3 Bethnal Green
19.04.95	Rudy Valentino W PTS 6 Bethnal Green
12.05.95	Chris Aston W RSC 4 Bethnal Green
27.09.95	Steve Howden W RSC 4 Bethnal Green
28.10.95	Chris Clarkson W RSC 4 Kensington
08.12.95	Jonathan Thaxton W RSC 5 Bethnal Green
	(Vacant Southern Area Lightweight Title)
05.03.96	Rudy Valentino W RSC 4 Bethnal Green
03.04.96	Kino Rodriguez W RSC 2 Bethnal Green
10.05.96	Lajos Nagy W RSC 5 Wembley
03.07.96	Marian Stoica W PTS 8 Wembley
24.10.96	Bamana Dibateza W PTS 8 Wembley
20.11.96	Michael Ayers L RSC 9 Wembley
	(British Lightweight Title Challenge)
24.04.97	Lewis Reynolds W CO 4 Mayfair
	(Southern Area Lightweight Title Defence)
30.06.97	Demir Nanev W RSC 8 Bethnal Green
09.09.97	Alan Bosworth W RSC 8 Bethnal Green
28.11.97	Zoltan Kalocsai W PTS 12 Bethnal Green
	(Vacant WBU Lightweight Title)
23.05.98	Emmanuel Clottey W PTS 12 Bethnal Green
	(WBU Lightweight Title Defence)
21.07.98	Affif Djelti W PTS 12 Widnes
	(WBU Lightweight Title Defence)
12.12.98	Sedat Puskullu W RSC 3 Southwark
27.02.99	Phillip Holiday W PTS 12 Bethnal Green
	(WBU Lightweight Title Defence)
13.07.00	Leonti Voronchuk W CO 4 Bethnal Green
25.07.00	Rakhim Mingaleev W RTD 5 Southwark
14.10.00	Billy Schwer W PTS 12 Wembley
	(WBU Lightweight Title Defence)
16.06.01	Barrie Kelley W CO 3 Dagenham
07.09.01	Sergei Starkov W RSC 3 Bethnal Green
10.11.01	Alan Temple W RSC 7 Wembley
26.01.02	Martin Jacobs W PTS 12 Dagenham
	(WBU Lightweight Title Defence)
18.05.02	Wayne Rigby W RTD 10 Millwall
	(WBU Lightweight Title Defence. Vacant WBF Lightweight Title)
21.09.02	Esteban Morales W PTS 12 Brentwood
	(WBU Lightweight Title Defence)
07.12.02	David Burke L PTS 12 Brentwood
	(WBU Lightweight Title Defence)

Career: 40 contests, won 38, lost 2.

Colin Dunne   Les Clark

(Osumanu) Ossie Duran (Yahaya)

London. *Born* Accra, Ghana, 23 April, 1977
WBF European Welterweight Champion. Former Undefeated Ghanaian Lightweight Champion. Ht. 5'10"
Manager Self

28.08.96	Dick Dotse W RSC 4 Togo
20.09.96	Victor Abbey W RSC 2 Ivory Coast
30.11.96	David Allotey W PTS 8 Accra, Ghana
28.12.96	Neuziwere Apolo W RSC 1 Accra, Ghana
05.03.97	Ike Obi L PTS 10 Nigeria
26.04.97	Abas de Souza W RSC 6 Benin
28.06.97	Tony Danso DREW 12 Accra, Ghana
	(Ghanaian Lightweight Title Challenge)
06.09.97	Iron Cutter W RSC 2 Accra, Ghana
04.10.97	Tony Danso W PTS 12 Accra, Ghana
	(Ghanaian Lightweight Title Challenge)
06.06.98	David Tetteh L PTS 12 Accra, Ghana
	(Commonwealth Lightweight Title Challenge)
09.03.00	Ganny Dovidovas L PTS 4 Bethnal Green
19.04.00	Vincent Nobela W PTS 6 Kensington
28.09.00	Mark Ramsey W RSC 2 Kensington
31.10.00	Yuri Tsarenko W PTS 4 Hammersmith
28.02.01	David Kirk W PTS 8 Kensington
	(Vacant WBF European Welterweight Title)
26.04.01	Geoff McCreesh W PTS 6 Kensington
10.11.01	Howard Clarke W PTS 6 Wembley
13.12.01	Delroy Mellis W PTS 10 Leicester Square
	(WBF European Welterweight Title Defence)
22.02.03	Glenn McClarnon W RSC 2 Huddersfield
19.06.03	Sergei Styopkin L PTS 12 Podolsk, Russia
	(IBF Inter-Continental Welterweight Title Challenge)

Career: 20 contests, won 15, drew 1, lost 4.

Graham Earl

Luton. *Born* Luton, 26 August, 1978
Southern Area Lightweight Champion.
Ht. 5'5¾"
Manager F. Maloney

02.09.97	Mark O'Callaghan W RSC 2 Southwark
06.12.97	Mark McGowan W PTS 4 Wembley
11.04.98	Danny Lutaaya W RSC 2 Southwark
23.05.98	David Kirk W PTS 4 Bethnal Green
12.09.98	Brian Coleman W PTS 4 Bethnal Green
10.12.98	Marc Smith W RSC 1 Barking
16.01.99	Lee Williamson W RSC 4 Bethnal Green
08.05.99	Benny Jones W PTS 6 Bethnal Green

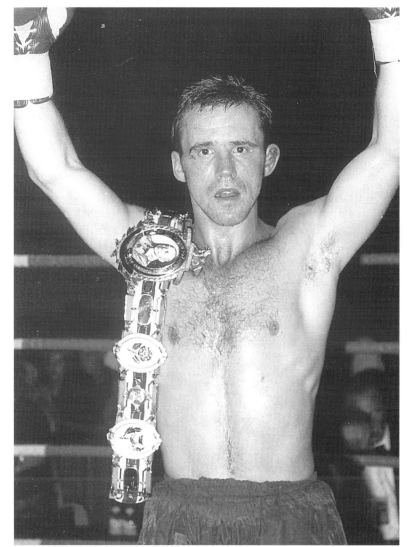

Graham Earl   Les Clark

15.07.99	Simon Chambers W CO 6 Peterborough
04.03.00	Ivo Golakov W RSC 1 Peterborough
29.04.00	Marco Fattore W PTS 6 Wembley
21.10.00	Lee Williamson W RSC 3 Wembley
10.03.01	Brian Gentry W RSC 8 Bethnal Green
	(Vacant Southern Area Lightweight Title)
22.09.01	Liam Maltby W CO 1 Bethnal Green
	(Southern Area Lightweight Title Defence)
15.12.01	Mark Winters W PTS 10 Wembley
	(Elim. British Lightweight Title)
12.10.02	Chill John W PTS 10 Bethnal Green
	(Southern Area Lightweight Title Defence)
15.02.03	Steve Murray W RSC 2 Wembley
	(Southern Area Lightweight Title Defence. Final Elim. British Lightweight Title)
24.05.03	Nikolai Eremeev W PTS 8 Bethnal Green

Career: 18 contests, won 18.

Gilbert Eastman

Battersea. *Born* Guyana, 16 November, 1972
L. Middleweight. Ht. 5'10"
Manager Self

22.04.96	Wayne Shepherd W PTS 4 Crystal Palace
09.07.96	Costas Katsantonis W RSC 1 Bethnal Green
11.01.97	Mike Watson W RSC 1 Bethnal Green
25.03.97	Danny Quacoe W RSC 3 Lewisham
30.08.97	Karl Taylor W PTS 4 Cheshunt
08.11.97	Ray Newby W PTS 6 Southwark
14.02.98	Cam Raeside W RSC 5 Southwark
21.04.98	Dennis Berry W RSC 6 Edmonton
23.05.98	Shaun O'Neill W RSC 1 Bethnal Green
12.09.98	Everald Williams W RTD 5 Bethnal Green
21.11.98	Lindon Scarlett W RTD 3 Southwark
06.03.99	Kofi Jantuah L RSC 11 Southwark
	(Commonwealth Welterweight Title Challenge)
25.10.02	Ojay Abrahams W PTS 4 Bethnal Green
21.12.02	Pedro Thompson W RSC 2 Dagenham
05.03.03	Howard Clarke W PTS 6 Bethnal Green
16.04.03	Andrew Facey L RSC 3 Nottingham

Career: 16 contests, won 14, lost 2.

Howard Eastman

Battersea. *Born* New Amsterdam, Guyana, 8 December, 1970
British, European & Commonwealth Middleweight Champion. Former Undefeated IBO Inter-Continental & WBA Inter-Continental Middleweight Champion. Former Undefeated Southern Area Middleweight Champion. Ht. 5'11"
Manager Self

06.03.94	John Rice W RSC 1 Southwark
14.03.94	Andy Peach W PTS 6 Mayfair
22.03.94	Steve Phillips W RSC 5 Bethnal Green
17.10.94	Barry Thorogood W RSC 6 Mayfair
06.03.95	Marty Duke W RSC 1 Mayfair
20.04.95	Stuart Dunn W RSC 2 Mayfair
23.06.95	Peter Vosper W RSC 1 Bethnal Green
16.10.95	Carlo Colarusso W RSC 1 Mayfair
29.11.95	Brendan Ryan W RSC 2 Bethnal Green
31.01.96	Paul Wesley W RSC 1 Birmingham
13.03.96	Steve Goodwin W RSC 5 Wembley
29.04.96	John Duckworth W RSC 5 Mayfair
11.12.96	Sven Hamer W RSC 10 Southwark
	(Vacant Southern Area Middleweight Title)
18.02.97	John Duckworth W CO 7 Cheshunt
25.03.97	Rachid Serdjane W RSC 7 Lewisham
14.02.98	Vitali Kopitko W PTS 8 Southwark
28.03.98	Terry Morrill W RTD 4 Hull
23.05.98	Darren Ashton W RSC 4 Bethnal Green
30.11.98	Steve Foster W RSC 7 Manchester
	(Vacant British Middleweight Title)
04.02.99	Jason Barker W RSC 6 Lewisham
06.03.99	Jon Penn W RSC 3 Southwark
	(Vacant IBO Inter-Continental S. Middleweight Title)
22.05.99	Roman Babaev W RSC 6 Belfast
	(WBA Inter-Continental Middleweight Title Challenge)
10.07.99	Teimouraz Kikelidze W RSC 6 Southwark
	(WBA Inter-Continental Middleweight Title Defence)

13.09.99	Derek Wormald W RSC 3 Bethnal Green	

(British Middleweight Title Defence)

13.11.99 Mike Algoet W RSC 8 Hull
(WBA Inter-Continental Middleweight Title Defence)
18.01.00 Ojay Abrahams W RSC 2 Mansfield
04.03.00 Viktor Fesetchko W RTD 4 Peterborough
29.04.00 Anthony Ivory W RTD 6 Wembley
25.07.00 Ahmet Dottouev W RTD 5 Southwark
(WBA Inter-Continental Middleweight Title Defence)
16.09.00 Sam Soliman W PTS 12 Bethnal Green
(Commonwealth Middleweight Title Challenge)
05.02.01 Mark Baker W RTD 5 Hull
10.04.01 Robert McCracken W RSC 10 Wembley
(British & Commonwealth Middleweight Title Defences. Vacant European Middleweight Title)
17.11.01 William Joppy L PTS 12 Las Vegas, Nevada, USA
(Vacant WBA Interim Middleweight Title)

25.10.02 Chardan Ansoula W RSC 1 Bethnal Green
21.12.02 Hussain Osman W RTD 4 Dagenham
28.01.03 Christophe Tendil W RTD 4 Nottingham
(Vacant European Middleweight Title)
05.03.03 Gary Beardsley W RSC 2 Bethnal Green
16.04.03 Scott Dann W RSC 3 Nottingham
(British, Commonwealth & European Middleweight Title Defences)

Career: 38 contests, won 37, lost 1.

Tommy Eastwood

Epsom. *Born* Epsom, 16 May, 1979
Cruiserweight. Ht. 5'11½"
Manager F. Maloney

09.09.01 Tony Booth W PTS 4 Southwark
16.12.01 Paul Bonson W PTS 4 Southwark
12.02.02 Adam Cale W PTS 4 Bethnal Green
24.03.02 Dave Clarke W PTS 6 Streatham
23.06.02 Brodie Pearmaine W PTS 4 Southwark
24.01.03 Lee Swaby L PTS 6 Sheffield

Career: 6 contests, won 5, lost 1.

Howard Eastman　　　　　　　　　　　　Les Clark

Ricky Eccleston

Liverpool. *Born* Liverpool, 22 September, 1981
Lightweight. Ht. 5'8½"
Manager B. Hearn

01.07.00 Dave Hinds W PTS 4 Manchester
09.09.00 Billy Smith W PTS 4 Manchester
09.10.00 Nigel Senior W PTS 4 Liverpool
27.11.00 Dave Hinds W PTS 4 Birmingham
03.02.01 Steve Hanley W PTS 4 Manchester
24.04.01 Gary Flear W PTS 4 Liverpool
25.09.01 Pete Buckley W PTS 4 Liverpool
27.10.01 Gary Flear W PTS 4 Manchester
28.05.02 David Kehoe W RSC 4 Liverpool
07.09.02 Jimmy Beech L RSC 3 Liverpool
08.02.03 Mark Haslam W PTS 6 Liverpool

Career: 11 contests, won 10, lost 1.

Chris Edwards

Stoke. *Born* Stoke, 6 May, 1976
Flyweight. Ht. 5'3"
Manager Self

03.04.98 Chris Thomas W RSC 2 Ebbw Vale
21.09.98 Russell Laing L PTS 6 Glasgow
26.02.99 Delroy Spencer L PTS 6 West Bromwich
17.04.99 Stevie Quinn L RSC 4 Dublin
19.10.99 Lee Georgiou L RSC 2 Bethnal Green
03.12.99 Daniel Ring L PTS 4 Peterborough
15.05.00 Paddy Folan L PTS 6 Bradford
07.10.00 Andy Roberts W PTS 4 Doncaster
27.11.00 Levi Pattison W PTS 4 Birmingham
16.03.01 Jamie Evans L PTS 6 Portsmouth
03.06.01 Darren Taylor DREW 6 Hanley
08.10.01 Levi Pattison L PTS 4 Barnsley
06.12.01 Neil Read W PTS 8 Stoke
10.10.02 Neil Read W PTS 6 Stoke
13.06.03 Lee Haskins L PTS 6 Bristol

Career: 15 contests, won 5, drew 1, lost 9.

Elroy Edwards

Brixton. *Born* Jamaica, 12 October, 1971
L. Middleweight. Ht. 5'9½"
Manager B. Baker

21.05.02 Darren Covill W PTS 4 Custom House
27.10.02 Justin Hudson W RSC 3 Southwark
08.01.03 Taz Jones L PTS 6 Aberdare
22.02.03 Reggie Robshaw L PTS 4 Huddersfield
21.03.03 Lee Hodgson L RSC 3 Longford
20.06.03 Paul Smith L RSC 2 Liverpool

Career: 6 contests, won 2, lost 4.

Greg Edwards

Hereford. *Born* Hereford, 26 June, 1978
S. Featherweight. Ht. 5'7"
Manager D. Gardiner

28.01.02 Chris Hooper L RSC 2 Barnsley
27.03.02 Jason Nesbitt L RSC 5 Mayfair
15.09.02 Daleboy Rees L PTS 4 Swansea
23.09.02 Andrew Ferrans L RTD 4 Glasgow

Career: 4 contests, lost 4.

Andy Egan

Coventry. *Born* Coventry, 16 September, 1977
Welterweight. Ht. 5'8¾"
Manager A. Phillips

02.01.01 Gareth Jones L PTS 4 Coventry

19.12.01 Brian Gifford W RSC 1 Coventry
18.01.02 Marcus Portman L PTS 4 Coventry
09.02.02 Tony Smith W PTS 4 Coventry
26.04.02 Brian Coleman W PTS 6 Coventry
30.11.02 Wayne Wheeler W RSC 1 Coventry
22.03.03 Brian Coleman W PTS 6 Coventry
07.06.03 Lee Williamson W PTS 6 Coventry
Career: 8 contests, won 6, lost 2.

Wayne Elcock

Birmingham. *Born* Birmingham, 12
February, 1974
WBU Middleweight Champion. Ht. 5'9¹/₂"
Manager F. Maloney

02.12.99 William Webster W PTS 6 Peterborough
04.03.00 Sonny Pollard W RSC 3 Peterborough
07.07.01 Darren Rhodes W PTS 4 Manchester
09.10.01 Valery Odin W PTS 4 Cardiff
02.03.02 Charles Shodiya W RSC 1 Bethnal
Green
20.04.02 Howard Clarke W PTS 4 Cardiff
01.06.02 Jason Collins W RSC 2 Manchester
17.08.02 Ojay Abrahams W PTS 4 Cardiff
23.11.02 Jason Collins W RSC 1 Derby
15.02.03 Yuri Tsarenko W PTS 10 Wembley
05.04.03 Anthony Farnell W PTS 12 Manchester
(*WBU Middleweight Title Challenge*)
Career: 11 contests, won 11.

Wayne Elcock   Les Clark

Iain Eldridge

Watford. *Born* Watford, 26 February, 1975
L. Welterweight. Ht. 5'8"
Manager Self

18.11.99 Des Sowden W RSC 4 Mayfair
21.02.00 Lee Sharp L PTS 6 Glasgow
11.03.00 Peter Dunn W RSC 2 Kensington
22.07.00 Ross McCord W RSC 2 Watford
19.08.00 Karl Taylor W PTS 4 Brentwood
03.03.01 Kevin Bennett L PTS 6 Wembley

23.11.01 Costas Katsantonis L RSC 1 Bethnal
Green
(*Vacant Southern Area L.Welterweight
Title*)
15.10.02 Wayne Wheeler DREW 4 Bethnal
Green
25.10.02 Lee Meager L RSC 5 Bethnal Green
03.12.02 Cristian Hodorogea L PTS 4 Bethnal
Green
Career: 10 contests, won 4, drew 1, lost 5.

Matthew Ellis

Blackpool. *Born* Oldham, 12 April, 1974
Heavyweight. Ht. 5'11³/₄"
Manager Self

03.02.96 Laurent Rouze W CO 1 Liverpool
01.04.96 Ladislav Husarik W RTD 4 Den Bosch,
Holland
06.09.96 Darren Fearn W RSC 6 Liverpool
26.10.96 Daniel Beun W RSC 1 Liverpool
01.03.97 Yuri Yelistratov L RSC 5 Liverpool
20.07.97 Ricardo Phillips W PTS 4 Indio, USA
26.09.97 Albert Call DREW 6 Liverpool
12.03.98 Yuri Yelistratov W RSC 1 Liverpool
21.07.98 Chris Woollas W RSC 5 Widnes
24.10.98 Peter Hrivnak W RSC 1 Liverpool
12.12.98 Harry Senior W PTS 8 Southwark
27.02.99 Michael Murray W PTS 8 Bethnal
Green
15.05.99 Biko Botowamungu W PTS 8
Blackpool
27.05.00 Alex Vasiliev W CO 4 Southwark
16.09.00 Dimitri Bakhtov W PTS 4 Bethnal
Green
18.11.00 Chris Woollas W PTS 4 Dagenham
17.02.01 Alexei Osokin W PTS 8 Bethnal Green
12.07.01 Ronnie Smith W PTS 6 Houston,
Texas, USA
22.09.01 Colin Abelson W CO 1 Bethnal Green
02.03.02 Dennis Bakhtov L RSC 5 Bethnal Green
(*WBC International Heavyweight Title
Challenge*)
29.03.03 Derek McCafferty W PTS 4 Wembley
31.05.03 Audley Harrison L RSC 2 Bethnal
Green
Career: 22 contests, won 18, drew 1, lost 3.

Mark Ellwood

Hull. *Born* Hull, 13 June, 1963
British Masters L. Heavyweight Champion.
Ht. 5'9¹/₂"
Manager S. Pollard

01.11.01 Adam Cale W PTS 6 Hull
25.04.02 Mark Phillips W PTS 6 Hull
26.09.02 Shpetim Hoti W PTS 6 Hull
21.11.02 Martin Thompson W PTS 6 Hull
11.12.02 William Webster W PTS 6 Hull
17.04.03 Mike Duffield W PTS 10 Hull
(*Vacant British Masters L.Heavyweight
Title*)
Career: 6 contests, won 6.

(Christoforo) Chris Emanuele

Nuneaton. *Born* Nuneaton, 26 November,
1973
Former British Masters Bantamweight
Champion. Ht. 5'5³/₄"
Manager A. Phillips

08.12.97 Marty Chestnut W PTS 6 Leicester
17.01.98 Stephen Oates L RSC 4 Bristol

18.05.98 Anthony Hanna L RSC 3 Cleethorpes
11.09.98 Dave Travers L RSC 2 Newark
27.11.98 Terry Gaskin W PTS 6 Nottingham
21.02.99 Paddy Folan DREW 6 Bradford
17.05.99 Daniel Ring DREW 6 Cleethorpes
17.07.99 Andy Roberts W PTS 4 Doncaster
26.11.99 Paddy Folan W RSC 5 Wakefield
11.03.00 Jamie Yelland L PTS 4 Kensington
17.04.00 Tommy Waite L PTS 6 Bradford
20.05.00 Sean Grant W RSC 5 Rotherham
06.06.00 Shaun Anderson L PTS 6 Motherwell
08.07.00 Tiger Singh W RSC 1 Rotherham
13.07.00 Lee Georgiou W CO 1 Bethnal Green
01.10.00 Michael Hunter L PTS 6 Hartlepool
28.10.00 Gareth Payne L CO 1 Coventry
26.02.01 Jim Betts W PTS 6 Nottingham
17.03.01 Stephen Oates L PTS 8 Manchester
30.04.01 John Barnes L PTS 4 Glasgow
15.06.01 John Mackay W RSC 4 Millwall
21.07.01 Noel Wilders L PTS 6 Sheffield
15.09.01 Colin Moffett W RSC 4 Nottingham
17.11.01 Jason Thomas W RSC 1 Coventry
09.02.02 Sean Green W RSC 6 Coventry
(*Vacant British Masters Bantamweight
Title*)
22.03.02 Choi Tseveenpurev L PTS 4 Coventry
26.04.02 Gareth Payne L RSC 3 Coventry
(*British Masters Bantamweight Title
Defence*)
24.03.03 Jason Thomas L PTS 4 Barnsley
Career: 28 contests, won 12, drew 2, lost 14.

Richard Evatt

Coventry. *Born* Coventry, 26 August, 1973
S. Featherweight. Former IBO Inter-
Continental Featherweight Champion. Ht. 5'6"
Manager Self

18.12.95 Kevin Sheil W RSC 1 Mayfair
06.02.96 Joe Donohoe W RSC 2 Basildon
09.04.96 Fred Reeve W RSC 1 Stevenage
20.04.96 Wayne Jones W RSC 2 Brentwood
04.05.96 Miguel Matthews W PTS 6 Dagenham
27.11.96 Brian Robb W RSC 2 Bethnal Green
17.12.96 Andy Robinson W RSC 2 Doncaster
08.03.97 Brian Robb W CO 3 Brentwood
19.07.97 Pete Buckley W PTS 4 Wembley
19.09.97 Demir Nanev W RSC 1 Southend
18.11.97 Rudy Valentino W RSC 3 Mansfield
27.01.98 Hendrik Makolane W RSC 1 Bethnal
Green
23.02.98 Mzukisi Oliphant W RSC 7 Glasgow
(*Vacant IBO Inter-Continental
Featherweight Title*)
11.12.98 John T. Kelly W RSC 2 Cheshunt
12.01.99 Keith Jones W CO 3 Bethnal Green
13.02.99 Smith Odoom L PTS 12 Jastrzebie,
Poland
(*IBO Inter-Continental Featherweight
Title Defence*)
26.02.99 Pete Buckley W RSC 5 Coventry
10.04.99 Junior Jones L RSC 11 Manchester
(*Vacant IBO Featherweight Title*)
22.10.99 Mick O'Malley L RTD 1 Coventry
(*Vacant Commonwealth
S. Featherweight Title*)
17.04.00 Isaac Sebaduka L RSC 2 Birmingham
01.07.00 Pete Buckley W PTS 4 Manchester
19.08.00 Keith Jones W PTS 6 Brentwood
28.10.00 Roy Rutherford W PTS 10 Coventry
07.04.01 Rakhim Mingaleev W PTS 4 Wembley
16.11.02 Craig Spacie L RSC 2 Nottingham
Career: 25 contests, won 20, lost 5.

Andrew Facey

Sheffield. *Born* Wolverhampton, 20 May, 1972
S. Middleweight. Former Undefeated Central Area Middleweight Champion.
Ht. 6'0"
Manager J. Ingle

06.12.99	Peter McCormack W CO 2 Birmingham
09.06.00	Matthew Pepper W RSC 1 Hull
04.11.00	Earl Ling W PTS 6 Derby
11.12.00	Gary Jones W PTS 6 Cleethorpes
10.02.01	Louis Swales W RSC 3 Widnes
17.03.01	Darren Rhodes L PTS 4 Manchester
24.03.01	Matthew Tait W PTS 4 Chigwell
16.06.01	Earl Ling DREW 6 Derby
09.12.01	Michael Pinnock W PTS 6 Shaw
02.03.02	Darren Rhodes W RSC 6 Wakefield
	(Vacant Central Area Middleweight Title)
20.04.02	Darren Ashton W PTS 6 Derby
13.04.02	Leigh Wicks W PTS 6 Norwich
03.08.02	Damon Hague L CO 5 Derby
	(Final Elim. WBF Middleweight Title)
25.10.02	William Webster W PTS 4 Cotgrave
16.04.03	Gilbert Eastman W RSC 3 Nottingham

Career: 15 contests, won 12, drew 1, lost 2.

Anthony Farnell

Manchester. *Born* Manchester, 1 July, 1978
Middleweight. Former WBU Middleweight Champion. Former Undefeated WBO Inter-Continental L. Middleweight Champion.
Ht. 5'10"
Manager F. Warren/T. Jones

03.05.97	Lee Molyneux W PTS 4 Manchester
02.08.97	Martin Renaghan W RSC 3 Barnsley
20.09.97	Dominique van der Steene W CO 1 Aachen, Germany
13.12.97	Paul Scott W RSC 3 Sheffield
24.01.98	Steve Brumant W PTS 4 Cardiff
21.03.98	Hughie Davey W PTS 6 Bethnal Green
18.04.98	Harry Butler W PTS 6 Manchester
09.05.98	David Thompson W CO 1 Sheffield
18.07.98	Lee Molyneux W CO 3 Sheffield
05.09.98	Darren Williams W RTD 4 Telford
31.10.98	Mark Richardson W PTS 6 Atlantic City, USA
28.11.98	George Richards W RSC 7 Sheffield
19.12.98	Koba Kulu W RTD 5 Liverpool
27.02.99	Koba Kulu W RSC 1 Oldham
01.05.99	Alan Gilbert W RSC 8 Crystal Palace
29.05.99	John Long W RSC 6 Halifax
	(Vacant WBO Inter-Continental L. Middleweight Title)
07.08.99	Israel Ponce W RSC 3 Atlantic City, USA
09.10.99	Javier Santibanez W CO 1 Manchester
	(WBO Inter-Continental L. Middleweight Title Defence)
27.11.99	Marino Monteyne W CO 6 Lubeck, Germany
29.01.00	Ian Toby W RSC 3 Manchester
08.04.00	Ojay Abrahams W PTS 8 Bethnal Green

29.05.00	Howard Clarke W PTS 12 Manchester
	(WBO Inter-Continental L. Middleweight Title Defence)
04.09.00	Juan Carlos Sanchez W PTS 12 Manchester
	(WBO Inter-Continental L. Middleweight Title Defence)
25.11.00	Scott Dixon W RSC 7 Manchester
	(WBO Inter-Continental L. Middleweight Title Defence)
15.01.01	Sergio Acuna W PTS 12 Manchester
	(WBO Inter-Continental L. Middleweight Title Defence)
17.03.01	Shakir Ashanti W RSC 2 Manchester
	(WBO Inter-Continental L. Middleweight Title Defence)
07.07.01	Takaloo L RSC 1 Manchester
	(Vacant WBU L.Middleweight Title)

15.09.01	Lee Blundell W RSC 2 Manchester
	(Vacant WBO Inter-Continental L.Middleweight Title)
27.10.01	Pavel Melnikov W RSC 12 Manchester
	(WBO Inter-Continental L. Middleweight Title Defence)
09.02.02	Matt Galer W RSC 3 Manchester
01.06.02	Ruben Groenewald L PTS 12 Manchester
	(Vacant WBU Middleweight Title)
28.09.02	Ruben Groenewald W PTS 12 Manchester
	(WBU Middleweight Title Challenge)
18.01.03	Nikolai Talalakin W RTD 10 Preston
	(WBU Middleweight Title Defence)
05.04.03	Wayne Elcock L PTS 12 Manchester
	(WBU Middleweight Title Defence)

Career: 34 contests, won 31, lost 3.

Anthony Farnell   Les Clark

Spencer Fearon

Forest Hill. *Born* London, 20 December, 1973
Middleweight. Ht. 6'0"
Manager Self

28.06.97	Mark Sawyers W PTS 4 Norwich
13.09.97	Danny Quacoe W PTS 4 Millwall
21.03.98	Perry Ayres W PTS 4 Bethnal Green
16.05.98	Danny Quacoe W PTS 4 Bethnal Green
26.09.98	Rob Stevenson W CO 2 Norwich
14.11.98	Prince Kasi Kaihau W CO 5 Cheshunt
23.01.99	George Richards L PTS 6 Cheshunt
08.04.00	Leigh Wicks W PTS 4 Bethnal Green
12.08.00	Freddie Yemofio W RSC 4 Wembley
23.09.00	Matthew Bowers W RSC 2 Bethnal Green
27.01.01	Jason Collins L PTS 4 Bethnal Green
24.02.01	Harry Butler W PTS 4 Bethnal Green
03.04.01	Lee Blundell L PTS 6 Bethnal Green
03.06.01	Gary Logan L RSC 2 Southwark
	(Vacant Southern Area Middleweight Title)
08.02.03	Leigh Wicks W PTS 6 Brentford

Career: 15 contests, won 11, lost 4.

Andrew Ferrans

New Cumnock. *Born* Irvine, 4 February, 1981
S. Featherweight. Ht. 5'9"
Manager T. Gilmour

19.02.00	Chris Lyons W PTS 6 Prestwick
03.03.00	Gary Groves W RSC 1 Irvine
20.03.00	John Barnes DREW 6 Glasgow
06.06.00	Duncan Armstrong W PTS 6 Motherwell
18.09.00	Steve Brook W PTS 6 Glasgow
20.11.00	Duncan Armstrong W PTS 6 Glasgow
23.02.01	Dave Cotterill L RSC 2 Irvine
30.04.01	Dave Cotterill W RSC 1 Glasgow
04.06.01	Jason Nesbitt W RSC 2 Glasgow
17.09.01	Gary Flear W PTS 8 Glasgow
10.12.01	Jamie McKeever L PTS 6 Liverpool
21.01.02	Joel Viney W PTS 8 Glasgow
01.03.02	Peter Allen W PTS 8 Irvine
13.04.02	Tony Mulholland L PTS 4 Liverpool
11.05.02	Marc Callaghan L PTS 6 Dagenham
23.09.02	Greg Edwards W RTD 4 Glasgow
08.10.02	Peter Allen W PTS 8 Glasgow
18.11.02	Joel Viney W PTS 6 Glasgow
30.11.02	Colin Toohey L PTS 6 Liverpool
28.02.03	Simon Chambers W RSC 7 Irvine
28.04.03	Craig Spacie L PTS 6 Nottingham

Career: 21 contests, won 14, drew 1, lost 6.

Gary Firby

Gateshead. *Born* Gateshead, 5 October, 1979
Middleweight. Ht. 5'10"
Manager T. Conroy

09.12.01	Mark Chesters W PTS 6 Blackpool
21.01.02	Mark Chesters W RSC 1 Glasgow
21.02.02	Craig Lynch L RSC 3 Sunderland
09.05.02	Ian Thomas DREW 6 Sunderland
03.10.02	Dave Pearson L CO 3 Sunderland

Career: 5 contests, won 2, drew 1, lost 2.

Terry Fletcher

Bradford. *Born* Leeds, 20 March, 1982
Welterweight. Ht. 5'10"
Manager F. Warren/F. Maloney

23.11.02	Norman Dhalie W CO 2 Derby
15.02.03	Pete Buckley W PTS 4 Wembley
31.05.03	Brian Coleman W PTS 4 Barnsley

Career: 3 contests, won 3.

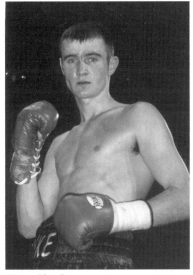

Terry Fletcher   Les Clark

(Patrick) Paddy Folan (Powders)

Huddersfield. *Born* Birmingham, 25 June, 1972
Featherweight. Ht. 5'7"
Manager C. Aston

25.10.98	Waj Khan W PTS 6 Shaw
26.11.98	Daniel Ring DREW 6 Bradford
07.12.98	Kevin Gerowski L PTS 6 Bradford
21.02.99	Chris Emanuele DREW 6 Bradford
19.04.99	Gary Groves L CO 1 Bradford
19.09.99	Gary Ford L PTS 6 Shaw
14.11.99	Shane Mallon W PTS 6 Bradford
26.11.99	Chris Emanuele L RSC 5 Wakefield
05.03.00	Gary Ford L PTS 6 Shaw
15.05.00	Chris Edwards W PTS 6 Bradford
25.06.00	Levi Pattison L PTS 6 Wakefield
30.11.00	Neil Read W PTS 6 Blackpool
07.12.00	John-Paul Ryan L PTS 6 Stoke
11.02.01	Michael Hunter L RSC 6 Hartlepool
20.03.01	Sean Grant DREW 6 Leeds
01.04.01	Dafydd Carlin L PTS 4 Southwark
09.04.01	Sean Grant L PTS 6 Bradford
10.06.01	Lee Holmes L PTS 6 Ellesmere Port
31.07.01	Jamie Yelland L RSC 5 Bethnal Green
22.10.01	Sean Grant L PTS 6 Glasgow
19.11.01	Gary Groves W PTS 6 Glasgow
09.12.01	Joel Viney L PTS 6 Blackpool
21.02.02	Gypsy Boy Mario W PTS 6 Sunderland
02.03.02	Sean Hughes L PTS 6 Wakefield
28.05.02	John Paul Ryan L PTS 6 Leeds
24.06.02	Gary Groves W RSC 2 Bradford
20.07.02	Steve Foster L CO 1 Bethnal Green
05.10.02	Sean Hughes L PTS 4 Huddersfield

Career: 28 contests, won 7, drew 3, lost 18.

Allan Foster

Northampton. *Born* Kilmarnock, 8 November, 1973
S. Middleweight. Ht. 5'11"
Manager T. Gilmour

03.12.99	Steve Timms W RSC 4 Peterborough
05.03.00	Richie Jenkins W RSC 6 Peterborough
02.06.00	Leigh Wicks W PTS 4 Ashford
06.10.00	Paul Johnson W PTS 4 Maidstone
01.12.00	Michael Pinnock W PTS 4 Peterborough
17.02.01	Tommy Matthews W PTS 4 Bethnal Green
24.03.01	Darren Covill W RTD 3 Sheffield
31.07.01	Mark Snipe W PTS 6 Bethnal Green
16.03.02	Alan Jones DREW 6 Northampton
08.10.02	Clint Johnson W PTS 6 Glasgow

Career: 10 contests, won 9, drew 1.

Allan Foster   Les Clark

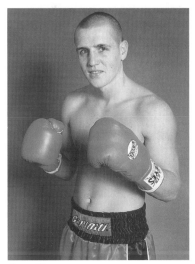

Steve Foster   Paul Speak

Steve Foster

Salford. *Born* Salford, 16 September, 1980
S. Bantamweight. Ht. 5'6"
Manager S.Foster/S.Wood/F.Warren

15.09.01	Andy Greenaway W PTS 4 Manchester
27.10.01	Gareth Wiltshaw W PTS 4 Manchester
02.03.02	Andy Greenaway W RSC 1 Bethnal Green
04.05.02	Gareth Wiltshaw W PTS 4 Bethnal Green
08.07.02	Ian Turner W RSC 1 Mayfair
20.07.02	Paddy Folan W CO 1 Bethnal Green
28.09.02	Jason White W RSC 3 Manchester
14.12.02	Sean Green W RSC 3 Newcastle
22.03.03	David McIntyre W PTS 4 Renfrew
24.05.03	Henry Janes W PTS 6 Bethnal Green

Career: 10 contests, won 10.

Dean Francis

Basingstoke. *Born* Basingstoke, 23 January, 1974
S. Middleweight. Former Undefeated British, European & WBO Inter-Continental S. Middleweight Champion. Ht. 5'10½"
Manager C. Sanigar

28.05.94	Darren Littlewood W PTS 4 Queensway
17.06.94	Martin Jolley W PTS 6 Plymouth
21.07.94	Horace Fleary W RSC 4 Tooting
02.09.94	Steve Osborne W RTD 4 Spitalfields
27.10.94	Tony Booth W CO 1 Bayswater
22.11.94	Darron Griffiths W RTD 1 Bristol
30.03.95	Paul Murray W RSC 2 Bethnal Green
25.05.95	Hunter Clay W RSC 8 Reading
16.06.95	Paul Murray W RTD 3 Southwark
20.10.95	Zafarou Ballogou L RSC 10 Ipswich
	(WBC International S. Middleweight Title Challenge)
16.12.95	Kid Milo W RSC 3 Cardiff
13.02.96	Mike Bonislawski W RSC 2 Bethnal Green
26.04.96	Neil Simpson W RSC 3 Cardiff
08.06.96	John Marceta W RSC 8 Newcastle
14.09.96	Larry Kenny W RSC 2 Sheffield
19.10.96	Rolando Torres W RSC 4 Bristol
	(Vacant WBO Inter-Continental S. Middleweight Title)
14.03.97	Cornelius Carr W RSC 7 Reading
	(WBO Inter-Continental S. Middleweight Title Defence)
15.05.97	Kit Munro W RSC 2 Reading
	(WBO Inter-Continental S. Middleweight Title Defence)
19.07.97	David Starie W RSC 6 Wembley
	(British S. Middleweight Title Challenge)
19.12.97	Frederic Seillier W RSC 9 Millwall
	(Vacant European S. Middleweight Title)
07.03.98	Mark Baker W RSC 12 Reading
	(British & WBO Inter-Continental S. Middleweight Title Defences)
22.08.98	Xolani Ngemntu W CO 2 Hammanskraal, South Africa
	(WBO Inter-Continental S. Middleweight Title Defence)
31.10.98	Undra White L RTD 4 Basingstoke
	(Vacant IBO Inter-Continental S. Middleweight Title)
20.04.02	Mondili Mbonambi W PTS 8 Wembley
29.03.03	Matthew Barney L PTS 12 Wembley
	(Vacant British S. Middleweight Title)

Career: 25 contests, won 22, lost 3.

Julius Francis

Woolwich. *Born* Peckham, 8 December, 1964
Heavyweight. Former Undefeated Commonwealth Heavyweight Champion. Former British Heavyweight Champion. Former Undefeated Southern Area Heavyweight Champion. Ht. 6'2"
Manager Self

23.05.93	Graham Arnold W RSC 5 Brockley
23.06.93	Joey Paladino W CO 4 Edmonton
24.07.93	Andre Tisdale W PTS 4 Atlantic City, USA
28.08.93	Don Sargent W RSC 2 Bismark, USA
01.12.93	John Keeton W PTS 4 Bethnal Green
27.04.94	Manny Burgo W PTS 4 Bethnal Green
25.05.94	John Ruiz L CO 4 Bristol
12.11.94	Conroy Nelson W RSC 4 Dublin
23.11.94	Gary Charlton W RSC 1 Piccadilly
23.02.05	Damien Caesar W RSC 8 Southwark
	(Vacant Southern Area Heavyweight Title)
27.04.95	Keith Fletcher W PTS 10 Bethnal Green
	(Southern Area Heavyweight Title Defence)
25.05.95	Steve Garber W PTS 8 Reading
01.07.95	Scott Welch L RSC 10 Kensington
	(Southern Area Heavyweight Title Defence. Final Elim. British Heavyweight Title)
24.10.95	Neil Kirkwood W RSC 7 Southwark
30.11.95	Nikolai Kulpin L PTS 10 Saratov, Russia
05.02.96	Michael Murray L PTS 10 Bexleyheath
	(Elim. British Heavyweight Title)
09.04.96	Damien Caesar W CO 1 Stevenage
	(Vacant Southern Area Heavyweight Title)
07.05.96	Darren Fearn W PTS 8 Mayfair
09.07.96	Mike Holden W PTS 10 Bethnal Green
28.09.96	James Oyebola W RSC 5 Barking
	(Southern Area Heavyweight Title Defence)
15.02.97	Zeljko Mavrovic L RSC 8 Vienna, Austria
	(European Heavyweight Title Challenge)
30.06.97	Joseph Chingangu W PTS 12 Bethnal Green
	(Vacant Commonwealth Heavyweight Title)
27.09.97	Garry Delaney W RSC 6 Belfast
	(Commonwealth Heavyweight Title Defence. Vacant British Heavyweight Title)
28.02.98	Axel Schulz L PTS 12 Dortmund, Germany
18.04.98	Vitali Klitschko L RSC 2 Aachen, Germany
30.01.99	Pele Reid W RSC 3 Bethnal Green
	(British & Commonwealth Heavyweight Title Defences)
03.04.99	Danny Williams W PTS 12 Kensington
	(British & Commonwealth Heavyweight Title Defences)
26.06.99	Scott Welch W PTS 12 Millwall
	(British & Commonwealth Heavyweight Title Defences)
29.01.00	Mike Tyson L RSC 2 Manchester
13.03.00	Mike Holden L PTS 12 Bethnal Green
	(British Heavyweight Title Defence)

03.04.01	Mike Holden W PTS 12 Bethnal Green
	(Final Elim. British Heavyweight Title)
28.07.01	Danny Williams L CO 4 Wembley
	(British & Commonwealth Heavyweight Title Challenges)
10.05.02	Luke Simpkin DREW 6 Millwall
13.09.02	Steffen Nielsen W CO 6 Randers, Denmark
26.04.03	Sinan Samil Sam L RSC 7 Schwerin, Germany
	(European Heavyweight Title Challenge)
13.06.03	Steffen Nielsen L PTS 10 Aalborg, Denmark
	(Vacant European Union Heavyweight Title)

Career: 36 contests, won 23, drew 1, lost 12.

Carl Froch

Nottingham. *Born* Nottingham, 2 July, 1977
S. Middleweight. Ht. 6'4"
Manager R. McCracken

16.03.02	Michael Pinnock W RSC 4 Bethnal Green
10.05.02	Ojay Abrahams W RSC 1 Bethnal Green
23.08.02	Darren Covill W RSC 1 Bethnal Green
25.10.02	Paul Bonson W PTS 6 Bethnal Green
21.12.02	Mike Duffield W RSC 1 Dagenham
28.01.03	Valery Odin W RSC 6 Nottingham
05.03.03	Varuzhan Davtyan W RSC 5 Bethnal Green
16.04.03	Michael Monaghan W RSC 3 Nottingham

Career: 8 contests, won 8.

Carl Froch   Les Clark

Courtney Fry

Wood Green. *Born* Enfield, 19 May, 1975
L. Heavyweight. Ht. 6'1½"
Manager H. Holland

29.03.03	Harry Butler W RSC 3 Wembley
31.05.03	Darren Ashton W PTS 4 Bethnal Green

Career: 2 contests, won 2.

Scott Gammer

Pembroke Dock. *Born* Pembroke Dock, 24 October, 1976
Heavyweight. Ht. 6'2"
Manager P. Boyce

15.09.02	Leighton Morgan W RSC 1 Swansea
26.10.02	James Gilbert W RSC 1 Maesteg
08.01.03	Dave Clarke W PTS 4 Aberdare
25.01.03	Ahmad Cheleh W CO 1 Bridgend
28.06.03	Dave Clarke W RSC 1 Cardiff

Career: 5 contests, won 5.

Brian Gascoigne

Sutton in Ashfield. *Born* Kirkby in Ashfield, 4 June, 1970
Cruiserweight. Ht. 6'5"
Manager M. Shinfield

23.11.98	Lennox Williams W RSC 3 Piccadilly
30.04.99	Shane Woollas DREW 6 Scunthorpe
03.10.99	Lee Swaby DREW 6 Chesterfield
06.12.99	Mark Hobson L RSC 3 Bradford
09.04.00	Nigel Rafferty W PTS 6 Alfreton
25.06.00	Danny Southam L RSC 4 Wakefield
04.12.00	Huggy Osman L PTS 6 Bradford
10.04.01	Kevin Barrett L RSC 1 Wembley
26.09.02	Adam Cale W PTS 4 Fulham
17.02.03	Tony Moran L RSC 1 Glasgow
31.05.03	Nate Joseph W RTD 1 Barnsley
02.06.03	Costi Marin W PTS 6 Glasgow

Career: 12 contests, won 5, drew 2, lost 5.

Steve Gethin

Walsall. *Born* Walsall, 30 July, 1978
S. Bantamweight. Ht. 5'9"
Manager Self

03.09.99	Ike Halls W RSC 3 West Bromwich
24.10.99	Ricky Bishop W RSC 4 Wolverhampton
22.01.00	Sebastian Hart L PTS 4 Birmingham
10.09.00	Nigel Senior DREW 6 Walsall
03.06.01	Richmond Asante L PTS 4 Southwark
28.11.01	Mickey Coveney L PTS 4 Bethnal Green
09.12.01	Gary Groves W PTS 6 Shaw
17.02.02	Gary Groves W PTS 6 Wolverhampton
01.06.02	Gary Davis W RSC 2 Manchester
21.09.02	Marc Callaghan L PTS 6 Brentwood
02.12.02	Neil Read W RTD 3 Leicester
14.12.02	Isaac Ward L PTS 4 Newcastle
08.02.03	Rocky Dean DREW 4 Norwich
15.02.03	Anthony Hanna W PTS 6 Wolverhampton
08.05.03	Derry Matthews L RSC 3 Widnes

Career: 15 contests, won 7, drew 2, lost 6.

Andy Gibson

Larne. *Born* Larne, 6 June, 1979
L. Middleweight. Ht. 5'11"
Manager T. Gilmour

23.09.02	Jason Samuels W PTS 4 Glasgow
03.10.02	Danny Moir W RTD 4 Sunderland
18.11.02	Andy Halder W PTS 4 Glasgow
20.01.03	Richard Inquieti W RSC 5 Glasgow

Career: 4 contests, won 4.

Alan Gilbert

Crawley. *Born* Bromley, 17 November, 1970
Middleweight. Ht. 5'11"
Manager Self

02.12.97	Martin Cavey W RSC 1 Windsor
06.01.98	Harry Butler W PTS 4 Brighton
23.02.98	Jon Harrison W PTS 6 Windsor
21.04.98	Paul Henry L PTS 4 Edmonton
08.08.98	Lee Murtagh L PTS 4 Scarborough
03.10.98	C. J. Jackson W RSC 3 Crawley
25.02.99	Justin Simmons W RSC 5 Kentish Town
01.05.99	Anthony Farnell L RSC 8 Crystal Palace
07.08.99	Wayne Shepherd DREW 8 Dagenham
	(Vacant British Masters
	L. Middleweight Title)
11.03.00	Michael Jones L RTD 3 Kensington
12.06.00	Jim Rock L PTS 6 Belfast
22.07.00	Delroy Mellis L RSC 3 Watford
	(Vacant Southern Area L.Middleweight Title)
23.01.01	Delroy Mellis L RSC 3 Crawley
	(Southern Area L. Middleweight Title Challenge)
29.09.01	Steven Bendall L RTD 3 Southwark
10.02.02	Allan Gray DREW 4 Southwark
28.04.02	Allan Gray L PTS 10 Southwark
	(Vacant Southern Area Middleweight Title)
03.08.02	Lee Blundell L RSC 6 Blackpool
	(IBF Inter-Continental Middleweight Title Challenge)
15.10.02	Dean Powell W PTS 4 Bethnal Green
28.04.03	Ben Ogden L RSC 1 Nottingham
20.06.03	Leigh Wicks W PTS 4 Gatwick

Career: 20 contests, won 7, drew 2, lost 11.

Alan Gilbert   Les Clark

Eamonn Glennon

Blackpool. *Born* Blackpool, 12 February, 1970
Cruiserweight. Ht. 5'10"
Manager Self

06.12.99	Rob Galloway W PTS 6 Bradford
02.03.00	Rob Galloway W PTS 6 Blackpool
09.06.00	Mark Dawson L PTS 6 Blackpool
25.09.00	Dave Faulkner W PTS 4 Barnsley

08.12.00	Darren Chubbs L PTS 4 Crystal Palace
27.01.01	John McDermott L RSC 1 Bethnal Green
10.03.01	Danny Percival L PTS 4 Bethnal Green
22.04.01	Colin Kenna L PTS 4 Streatham
30.04.01	Lee Swaby L PTS 6 Glasgow
26.07.01	Adam Cale W PTS 6 Blackpool
09.09.01	Paul Bonson L PTS 6 Hartlepool
29.09.01	Dominic Negus L PTS 6 Southwark
09.10.01	Enzo Macarinelli L RSC 2 Cardiff
16.11.01	Paul Buttery L RSC 1 Preston
15.12.01	Mark Krence L RSC 2 Sheffield
10.05.02	Tony Moran L RTD 1 Preston
24.06.02	Lee Mountford W PTS 6 Bradford
21.07.02	Lee Whitehead L PTS 6 Salford
03.08.02	Lee Whitehead W PTS 6 Blackpool
12.11.02	Neil Dawson L PTS 6 Leeds
05.12.02	Lee Swaby L PTS 4 Sheffield
16.12.02	Michael Pinnock DREW 6 Cleethorpes
03.02.03	Lee Mountford DREW 6 Bradford
17.02.03	Pinky Burton L PTS 6 Glasgow
13.04.03	Nate Joseph L PTS 6 Bradford
28.04.03	Chris Woollas L PTS 6 Cleethorpes

Career: 26 contests, won 6, drew 2, lost 18.

Michael Gomez (Armstrong)

Manchester. *Born* Dublin, 21 June, 1977
S.Featherweight. Former Undefeated WBO Inter-Continental & British S.Featherweight Champion. Former WBO Inter-Continental S.Featherweight Champion. Former Undefeated Central Area & IBF Inter-Continental Featherweight Champion.
Ht. 5'5"
Manager F. Warren

10.06.95	Danny Ruegg W PTS 6 Manchester
15.09.95	Greg Upton L PTS 4 Mansfield
24.11.95	Danny Ruegg L PTS 4 Manchester
19.09.96	Martin Evans W RSC 1 Manchester
09.11.96	David Morris W PTS 4 Manchester
22.03.97	John Farrell W RSC 2 Wythenshawe
03.05.97	Chris Williams L PTS 4 Manchester
11.09.97	Wayne Jones W RSC 2 Widnes
18.04.98	Benny Jones W PTS 4 Manchester
16.05.98	Craig Spacie W RSC 3 Bethnal Green
05.09.98	Pete Buckley W PTS 6 Telford
14.11.98	David Jeffrey W RSC 1 Cheshunt
19.12.98	Kevin Sheil W RSC 4 Liverpool
13.02.99	Dave Hinds W PTS 6 Newcastle
27.02.99	Chris Jickells W RSC 5 Oldham
	(Vacant Central Area Featherweight Title)
29.05.99	Nigel Leake W RSC 2 Halifax
	(Vacant IBF Inter-Continental Featherweight Title)
07.08.99	William Alverzo W PTS 6 Atlantic City, USA
04.09.99	Gary Thornhill W RSC 2 Bethnal Green
	(Vacant British S. Featherweight Title)
06.11.99	Jose Juan Manjarrez W PTS 12 Widnes
	(WBO Inter-Continental S. Featherweight Title Defence)
11.12.99	Oscar Galindo W RSC 11 Liverpool
	(WBO Inter-Continental S. Featherweight Title Defence)
29.01.00	Chris Jickells W RSC 4 Manchester
29.02.00	Dean Pithie W PTS 12 Widnes
	(British S. Featherweight Title Defence)
24.06.00	Carl Allen W CO 2 Glasgow

08.07.00 Carl Greaves W CO 2 Widnes
(British S. Featherweight Title Defence)
19.10.00 Awel Abdulai W PTS 8 Harrisburg, USA
11.12.00 Ian McLeod W PTS 12 Widnes
(British S.Featherweight Title Defence)
10.02.01 Laszlo Bognar L RSC 9 Widnes
(WBO Inter-Continental S. Featherweight Title Defence)
07.07.01 Laszlo Bognar W RSC 3 Manchester
(WBO Inter-Continental S. Featherweight Title Challenge)
27.10.01 Craig Docherty W RSC 2 Manchester
(British S.Featherweight Title Defence)
01.06.02 Kevin Lear L RTD 8 Manchester
(Vacant WBU S. Featherweight Title)
28.09.02 Jimmy Beech W RSC 4 Manchester
18.01.03 Rakhim Mingaleev W RTD 4 Preston
05.04.03 Vladimir Borov W RSC 3 Manchester
Career: 33 contests, won 28, lost 5.

Michael Gomez   Paul Speak

Jason Gonzales

Birmingham. *Born* Birmingham, 5 January, 1970
Lightweight. Ht. 5'6"
Manager Self

22.11.01 Chris McDonagh L PTS 6 Paddington
10.12.01 Daniel Thorpe L RSC 2 Birmingham
09.02.02 Gary Greenwood L PTS 6 Coventry
28.04.02 Albi Hunt L PTS 6 Southwark
15.06.02 Jackson Williams L PTS 6 Norwich
23.06.02 James Paisley L PTS 6 Southwark
06.09.02 Ryan Barrett L PTS 4 Bethnal Green
10.10.02 Jackson Williams L PTS 4 Piccadilly
21.10.02 Adnan Amar L PTS 6 Cleethorpes
Career: 9 contests, lost 9.

Darren Goode

Plymouth. *Born* Plymouth, 26 February, 1975
L. Welterweight. Ht. 5'8"
Manager N. Christian

27.09.02 Nathan Ward L RSC 1 Bracknell
02.11.02 Dean Hickman L RSC 2 Wolverhampton
09.12.02 Steve Cooper L CO 3 Birmingham
18.02.03 Chas Simmonds L RSC 2 Bethnal Green
15.05.03 Chris Long L RSC 1 Clevedon
Career: 5 contests, lost 5.

Darren Goode   Les Clark

Craig Goodman

Nottingham. *Born* Nottingham, 2 January, 1980
Middleweight. Ht. 5'7"
Manager J. Gill

01.10.99 Sonny Thind L PTS 6 Bethnal Green
18.10.99 David Smales L PTS 6 Glasgow
01.12.99 David Smales L PTS 6 Stoke
13.12.99 Richard Holden L PTS 6 Cleethorpes
19.02.00 Richard Holden L PTS 6 Newark
26.03.00 John Marsden L PTS 6 Nottingham
17.04.00 Alan Kershaw L PTS 6 Bradford
20.05.00 Chris Hall L PTS 6 Rotherham
07.05.03 Omar Gumati L PTS 6 Ellesmere Port
Career: 9 contests, lost 9.

James Gorman

Belfast. *Born* Belfast, 1 August, 1979
L. Welterweight. Ht. 5'8"
Manager A. Wilton

28.06.03 Jamie Arthur L PTS 4 Cardiff
Career: 1 contest, lost 1.

Sam Gorman

Alfreton. *Born* Nuneaton, 19 October, 1981
Welterweight. Ht. 5'9"
Manager J. Weaver

17.11.01 Shaune Danskin W RSC 3 Coventry
09.02.02 Pete Buckley W PTS 6 Coventry
22.03.02 Brian Coleman W PTS 6 Coventry
25.06.02 Pedro Thompson W PTS 6 Rugby
17.11.02 Wayne Shepherd L PTS 6 Shaw
Career: 5 contests, won 4, lost 1.

Jimmy Gould

West Bromwich. *Born* Wolverhampton, 8 July, 1977
Welterweight. Ht. 5'10"
Manager Self

23.06.99 Benny Jones W PTS 6 West Bromwich
03.09.99 Dave Travers W PTS 6 West Bromwich
06.11.00 Jon Honney W PTS 6 Wolverhampton
28.01.01 David White W PTS 6 Wolverhampton
20.05.01 Keith Jones W PTS 6 Wolverhampton
07.09.01 Woody Greenaway W PTS 6 West Bromwich
07.10.01 Steve Hanley W PTS 6 Wolverhampton
13.04.02 Keith Jones W PTS 8 Wolverhampton
25.05.02 Raymond Narh L RSC 3 Portsmouth
08.09.02 Tony Montana L PTS 8 Wolverhampton
08.03.03 Tony Conroy W PTS 4 Coventry
08.05.03 Michael Jennings L RTD 6 Widnes
(Vacant WBU Inter-Continental Welterweight Title)
Career: 12 contests, won 9, lost 3.

Jimmy Gould   Les Clark

Darrell Grafton

Chesterfield. *Born* Chesterfield, 14 July, 1974
Welterweight. Ht. 5'10"
Manager M. Shinfield

11.06.01 Chris Steele W RSC 1 Nottingham
15.09.01 Ram Singh W DIS 5 Nottingham

22.10.01 Emmanuel Marcos W RSC 2 Glasgow
10.12.01 Prince Kasi Kaihau W RSC 5 Nottingham
23.02.02 Jon Honney W RTD 1 Nottingham
11.05.02 Neil Bonner W PTS 6 Chesterfield
24.03.03 Ernie Smith W PTS 6 Barnsley
28.04.03 David Keir W DIS 5 Nottingham
Career: 8 contests, won 8.

Danny Grainger

Chesterfield. *Born* Chesterfield, 1 September, 1979
L. Heavyweight. Ht. 5'11"
Manager J. Ingle

05.10.02 Jamie Wilson W PTS 6 Chesterfield
21.10.02 Jamie Wilson W PTS 6 Cleethorpes
29.11.02 Gary Jones W PTS 6 Hull
08.06.03 Darren Stubbs W RSC 2 Shaw
Career: 4 contests, won 4.

Sean Grant   Les Clark

Sean Grant

Newton Aycliffe. *Born* Bishop Auckland, 18 January, 1971
Featherweight. Ht. 5'6"
Manager Self

04.12.97 John Barnes L PTS 6 Sunderland
03.02.98 Graham McGrath W PTS 6 Yarm
30.04.98 Peter Allen W PTS 6 Pentre Halkyn
18.07.98 Noel Wilders L RSC 4 Sheffield
19.09.98 Willie Valentine L PTS 4 Dublin
11.12.98 Nicky Cook L CO 1 Cheshunt
29.05.99 Gary Groves W PTS 6 South Shields
29.06.99 Barry Waite L RSC 3 Bethnal Green
16.10.99 David Lowry L RSC 1 Belfast
13.12.99 Jesse James Daniel L RSC 5 Cleethorpes
22.01.00 Gareth Payne L RSC 1 Birmingham
20.05.00 Chris Emanuele L RSC 5 Rotherham
23.07.00 Michael Hunter L PTS 6 Hartlepool
20.10.00 Stevie Quinn L RSC 2 Belfast
20.03.01 Paddy Folan DREW 6 Leeds
09.04.01 Paddy Folan W PTS 6 Bradford

08.05.01 Jim Betts L RSC 3 Barnsley
09.06.01 Martin Power L PTS 4 Bethnal Green
22.10.01 Paddy Folan W PTS 6 Glasgow
17.11.01 Jesse James Daniel L RSC 1 Dewsbury
08.02.02 Lee Holmes L CO 5 Preston
15.06.02 Noel Wilders L RSC 3 Leeds
19.10.02 Rocky Dean L RSC 3 Norwich
Career: 23 contests, won 5, drew 1, lost 17.

Allan Gray   Les Clark

Allan Gray

Putney. *Born* Roehampton, 4 August, 1971
WBF International & Southern Area Middleweight Champion. Ht. 5'9"
Manager Self

19.05.95 Darren Covill W PTS 6 Southwark
23.06.95 Wayne Jones W PTS 6 Bethnal Green
27.09.95 Brian Coleman W PTS 6 Bethnal Green
28.10.95 John O. Johnson W PTS 6 Kensington
29.11.95 Justin Simmons L PTS 6 Bethnal Green
08.12.95 Mike Watson W PTS 8 Bethnal Green
15.03.96 Mike Watson DREW 6 Dunstable
29.04.96 Mike Watson W PTS 6 Mayfair
03.07.96 Jon Harrison W PTS 6 Wembley
24.10.96 Costas Katsantonis W PTS 6 Mayfair
29.01.97 Gary Hiscox W PTS 6 Bethnal Green
19.02.97 Costas Katsantonis W PTS 6 Acton
30.04.97 Howard Clarke L PTS 8 Acton
27.01.98 Peter Nightingale W PTS 6 Streatham
26.09.98 Harry Dhami L PTS 10 Southwark
(Southern Area Welterweight Title Challenge)
16.02.99 Lee Bird W PTS 6 Brentford
31.10.99 Matthew Barr L PTS 4 Raynes Park
15.04.00 Jim Rock L PTS 10 Bethnal Green
(Vacant All-Ireland L. Middleweight Title)
22.10.00 Delroy Mellis L RSC 6 Streatham
(Southern Area L.Middleweight Title Challenge)
28.10.01 Leigh Wicks W PTS 4 Southwark
16.12.01 Leigh Wicks W PTS 4 Southwark
10.02.02 Alan Gilbert DREW 4 Southwark

28.04.02 Alan Gilbert W PTS 10 Southwark
(Vacant Southern Area Middleweight Title)
12.12.02 Ojay Abrahams W PTS 10 Leicester Square
(Southern Area Middleweight Title Defence. Vacant WBF International Middleweight Title)
Career: 24 contests, won 16, drew 2, lost 6.

Carl Greaves

Carl Greaves   Les Clark

Newark. *Born* Nottingham, 12 June, 1976
WBF S. Featherweight Champion. Former Undefeated British Masters & Midlands Area S. Featherweight Champion. Ht. 5'7"
Manager Self

22.03.96 Paul Hamilton W PTS 6 Mansfield
30.05.96 Kevin Sheil W PTS 6 Lincoln
02.10.96 Robert Grubb W PTS 8 Stoke
01.11.96 Benny Jones W PTS 6 Mansfield
26.11.96 Danny Ruegg W RTD 4 Sheffield
04.12.96 Des Gargano W PTS 6 Stoke
20.02.97 Lee Armstrong L RSC 4 Mansfield
10.04.97 Kevin Sheil W PTS 6 Sheffield
08.05.97 Benny Jones L RSC 4 Mansfield
10.07.97 Stefy Bull L PTS 6 Doncaster
18.08.97 Graham McGrath W PTS 6 Nottingham
06.10.97 Ervine Blake L PTS 10 Birmingham
(Vacant Midlands Area S. Featherweight Title)
30.10.97 Graham McGrath W PTS 6 Newark
18.11.97 Garry Burrell W CO 4 Mansfield
07.05.98 John T. Kelly W PTS 6 Sunderland
14.10.98 Andy Robinson W PTS 6 Stoke
02.12.98 Graham McGrath W PTS 6 Stoke
18.03.99 Ernie Smith W PTS 6 Doncaster
27.06.99 Chris Jickells W PTS 10 Alfreton
(British Masters S. Featherweight Final)

20.11.99 Pete Buckley W PTS 10 Grantham
(British Masters S. Featherweight Title Defence)
18.01.00 Keith Jones W PTS 6 Mansfield
19.02.00 Marc Smith W PTS 6 Newark
20.03.00 Pete Buckley W PTS 4 Mansfield
11.05.00 Marco Fattore W PTS 8 Newark
08.07.00 Michael Gomez L CO 2 Widnes
(British S. Featherweight Title Challenge)
09.09.00 Dave Hinds W PTS 6 Newark
19.11.00 Haroon Din W RSC 4 Chesterfield
24.03.01 Nigel Senior W CO 6 Newark
(Vacant Midlands Area S. Featherweight Title)
16.06.01 Dave Hinds W PTS 6 Derby
11.05.02 Wayne Wheeler W RSC 1 Newark
14.09.02 Peter Allen W PTS 6 Newark
14.12.02 Alex Arthur L RSC 6 Newcastle
(British S. Featherweight Title Challenge)
16.04.03 Ben Odamattey W PTS 12 Nottingham
(Vacant WBF S.Featherweight Title)

Career: 33 contests, won 27, lost 6.

(Roger) Radcliffe Green

Balham. *Born* Jamaica, 24 November, 1973
L. Heavyweight. Ht. 5'9½"
Manager I. Akay

26.03.01 Peter Haymer L PTS 4 Wembley
22.04.01 Adam Cale W CO 5 Streatham
03.06.01 Rob Hayes-Scott W RSC 4 Southwark
21.07.01 John Keeton L PTS 4 Sheffield
28.10.01 Michael Pinnock W PTS 4 Southwark
16.11.01 Darren Corbett L PTS 8 Dublin
10.02.02 Valery Odin L PTS 6 Southwark
20.04.02 Nathan King L PTS 6 Cardiff
04.05.02 Andrew Lowe L PTS 4 Bethnal Green
22.09.02 Mark Baker L PTS 6 Southwark
27.10.02 Neil Linford DREW 10 Southwark
(Vacant British Masters L.Heavyweight Title)
08.02.03 Eric Teymour L RTD 1 Norwich
29.03.03 Andrew Lowe L PTS 10 Wembley
(Vacant Southern Area L. Heavyweight Title)

Career: 13 contests, won 3, drew 1, lost 9.

Sean Green

Doncaster. *Born* Doncaster, 2 November, 1977
S. Bantamweight. Ht. 5'6"
Manager J. Rushton

17.12.96 Willie Smith W PTS 6 Doncaster
17.02.97 Jason Whitaker W PTS 6 Bradford
24.02.97 Neil Armstrong L PTS 6 Glasgow
08.05.97 Ross Cassidy DREW 6 Mansfield
27.09.97 Tommy Waite W RSC 3 Belfast
24.10.97 Graham McGrath DREW 6 Birmingham
04.12.97 Jason Thomas DREW 4 Doncaster
21.01.98 Graham McGrath W PTS 6 Stoke
19.03.98 Steve Williams L PTS 6 Doncaster
06.05.98 Louis Veitch W PTS 6 Blackpool
10.10.98 Ian Napa L PTS 6 Bethnal Green
09.12.98 Graham McGrath W PTS 6 Stoke
21.05.99 Chris Jickells W PTS 6 Glasgow

01.06.99 Samir Laala L RSC 3 Levallois, France
27.10.99 Graham McGrath W PTS 6 Birmingham
30.11.99 Phil Lashley W PTS 6 Wolverhampton
13.12.99 Kevin Gerowski L PTS 6 Cleethorpes
15.01.00 Levi Pattison W PTS 4 Doncaster
07.10.00 Hussein Hussein L RSC 1 Doncaster
02.12.00 Danny Costello L PTS 4 Chigwell
16.06.01 Danny Costello W RSC 3 Dagenham
30.09.01 Frankie DeMilo L PTS 6 Bristol
09.02.02 Chris Emanuele L RSC 6 Coventry
(Vacant British Masters Bantamweight Title)
23.09.02 Joel Viney W PTS 6 Cleethorpes
08.11.02 Anthony Hanna W PTS 6 Doncaster
14.12.02 Steve Foster L RSC 3 Newcastle

Career: 26 contests, won 13, drew 3, lost 10.

(Paul) Woody Greenaway

Gelligaer. *Born* Gelligaer, 5 February, 1972
Lightweight. Ht. 5'7"
Manager Self

23.07.98 Terry Butwell W PTS 6 Barking
17.09.98 Pat Larner L RSC 3 Brighton
13.11.98 Daniel James L PTS 4 Brighton
24.11.98 Ernie Smith W PTS 6 Wolverhampton
07.12.98 Barry Hughes W PTS 6 Acton
14.12.98 Steve Saville W PTS 6 Birmingham
23.02.99 Jason Dee L CO 6 Cardiff
03.04.99 Steve Murray L CO 2 Kensington
26.06.99 Nwajcvenki Sambo L PTS 6 Glasgow
15.07.99 Koba Gogoladze L RSC 2 Peterborough
24.09.99 Alan Bosworth W PTS 6 Merthyr
22.10.99 Roy Rutherford L PTS 4 Coventry
06.11.99 Jason Hall L RSC 5 Bethnal Green
11.12.99 Jason Cook L RSC 1 Mayfair
(Vacant Welsh L. Welterweight Title)
26.02.00 Ross McCord W PTS 4 Swansea
09.03.00 David Burke L RSC 2 Liverpool
19.04.00 No No Junior L PTS 4 Kensington
12.05.00 Dave Tatton L PTS 4 Swansea
30.05.00 Manzo Smith L PTS 4 Kensington
09.09.00 Gary Hibbert L RSC 2 Manchester
26.10.00 Barrie Kelley L PTS 6 Clydach
06.11.00 Steve Saville L CO 5 Wolverhampton
12.12.00 Ross McCord W PTS 6 Clydach
02.01.01 Tony Conroy L PTS 4 Coventry
05.02.01 Leo O'Reilly L CO 1 Hull
08.03.01 Mark Bowen DREW 6 Stoke
16.03.01 Jon Honney L PTS 6 Portsmouth
26.03.01 Alex Arthur L RTD 2 Wembley
27.04.01 Dave Stewart L PTS 6 Glasgow
05.05.01 Chill John L PTS 6 Brighton
19.05.01 Mark Hawthorne L PTS 4 Wembley
02.06.01 Lance Crosby L PTS 6 Wakefield
11.06.01 Anthony Maynard L PTS 4 Nottingham
21.06.01 Ajose Olusegun L RSC 1 Earls Court
31.07.01 Costas Katsantonis L RSC 4 Bethnal Green
07.09.01 Jimmy Gould L PTS 6 West Bromwich
15.09.01 Andy McLean L RSC 3 Manchester
20.10.01 Ricky Burns L PTS 4 Glasgow
31.10.01 Pete Buckley W PTS 6 Birmingham
17.11.01 Dean Pithie L PTS 6 Coventry
28.11.01 Nicky Cook L RSC 3 Bethnal Green
19.01.02 Nigel Wright L CO 2 Bethnal Green

15.03.02 Barry Hughes L PTS 8 Glasgow
11.05.02 Gavin Down L RSC 3 Chesterfield
13.07.02 Tony Conroy L RSC 3 Coventry

Career: 45 contest, won 8, drew 1, lost 36.

Roman Greenberg

Maidenhead. *Born* Russia, 18 May, 1982
Heavyweight. Ht. 6'2½"
Manager J. Evans

22.11.01 Dave Clarke W RSC 5 Paddington
25.02.02 Paul Bonson W PTS 6 Slough
25.04.02 Jakarta Nakyru W RSC 4 Las Vegas, Nevada, USA
28.11.02 Tony Booth W PTS 4 Finchley
05.12.02 Dave Clarke W RSC 1 Sheffield
20.12.02 Derek McCafferty W PTS 4 Bracknell
24.01.03 Piotr Jurczk W CO 1 Sheffield
04.03.03 Calvin Miller W RSC 2 Miami, Florida, USA
18.03.03 Gary Williams W RSC 1 Reading
15.05.03 Tracy Williams W RTD 2 Miami, Florida, USA
29.05.03 Troy Beets W RSC 3 Miami, Florida, USA

Career: 11 contests, won 11.

Gary Greenwood

Hinckley. *Born* Leicester, 9 December, 1974
Lightweight. Ht. 5'8"
Manager O. Delargy

09.03.00 Ray Wood W PTS 4 Liverpool
03.12.00 Tony Montana DREW 6 Shaw
13.02.01 Dave Travers W PTS 6 Brierley Hill
10.05.01 Brian Gifford W PTS 6 Sunderland
23.06.01 Jay Mahoney L PTS 4 Peterborough
17.11.01 Nigel Senior W PTS 6 Coventry
09.02.02 Jason Gonzales W PTS 6 Coventry
22.03.02 Dave Cotterill W PTS 6 Coventry
02.06.02 Mally McIver W RSC 1 Shaw
13.07.02 Gary Reid W RSC 5 Coventry
10.10.02 Stuart Rimmer W RSC 1 Stoke
30.11.02 Nigel Senior W PTS 4 Coventry
23.02.03 Ernie Smith W PTS 4 Shrewsbury
05.04.03 Keith Jones DREW 8 Coventry

Career: 14 contests, won 11, drew 2, lost 1.

Omar Gumati

Chester. *Born* Chester, 18 May, 1984
L. Middleweight. Ht. 5'9"
Manager M. Goodall

07.05.03 Craig Goodman W PTS 6 Ellesmere Port

Career: 1 contest, won 1.

Danny Gwilym

Bristol. *Born* Bristol, 15 January, 1975
L. Middleweight. Ht. 5'7"
Manager T. Woodward

16.12.01 Wayne Wheeler L RSC 2 Bristol
11.02.02 James Lee L PTS 6 Southampton
12.07.02 Mo W PTS 6 Southampton
26.02.03 Wasim Hussain W PTS 6 Bristol
17.03.03 Danny Cooper L PTS 6 Southampton
16.04.03 Lenny Daws L RSC 2 Nottingham

Career: 6 contests, won 2, lost 4.

H

Gary Hadwin

Carlisle. *Born* Carlisle, 10 February, 1969
Welterweight. Ht. 5'9"
Manager J. Doughty

02.06.02 Andrei Ivanov L PTS 6 Shaw
08.11.02 Jason Rushton L CO 4 Doncaster
Career: 2 contests, lost 2.

Damon Hague   Les Clark

Damon Hague (Wheatley)

Derby. *Born* Derby, 29 October, 1970
WBF Middleweight Champion. Former
Undefeated WBF European & Midlands
Area S.Middleweight Champion. Ht. 6'0"
Manager D. Ingle

27.11.98 Jimmy Steel DREW 6 Nottingham
14.12.98 Dean Ashton W PTS 6 Cleethorpes
26.02.99 Adrian Houldey W RSC 5 West
          Bromwich
27.03.99 Mark Owens W RSC 2 Derby
15.05.99 Michael Pinnock W PTS 4 Sheffield
27.06.99 Mark Owens W RSC 5 Alfreton
15.08.99 Ian Toby W PTS 6 Derby
03.10.99 Simon Andrews W PTS 6 Chesterfield
20.11.99 Simon Andrews W RSC 4 Grantham
15.01.00 Matthew Pepper W CO 1 Doncaster
09.04.00 Matthew Pepper W RSC 3 Alfreton
21.05.00 Martin Jolley W PTS 6 Derby
19.06.00 William Webster W PTS 4 Burton
13.08.00 Martin Jolley W RTD 1 Nottingham
04.11.00 Mike Duffield W RSC 3 Derby
          (Vacant WBF European
          S. Middleweight Title)
25.02.01 Rob Stevenson W PTS 8 Derby
16.06.01 Dean Ashton L DIS 1 Derby

21.07.01 Leigh Wicks W PTS 4 Sheffield
15.09.01 Dean Ashton W RTD 2 Derby
          (Vacant Midlands Area S.Middleweight
          Title)
08.12.01 Rob Stevenson W RSC 7 Chesterfield
20.04.02 Jimmy Steel W PTS 6 Derby
03.08.02 Andrew Facey W CO 5 Derby
          (Final Elim. WBF Middleweight Title)
23.11.02 Leigh Wicks W PTS 6 Derby
28.01.03 Wayne Pinder L RSC 7 Nottingham
          (Vacant WBF Middleweight Title)
16.04.03 Wayne Pinder W RSC 2 Nottingham
          (WBF Middleweight Title Challenge)
Career: 25 contests, won 22, drew 1, lost 2.

Andy Halder

Coventry. *Born* Coventry, 22 August, 1973
Middleweight. Ht. 5'11"
Manager J. Weaver

13.07.02 Martin Scotland W PTS 4 Coventry
05.10.02 Andrei Ivanov W PTS 6 Coventry
25.10.02 Jon Hilton W PTS 6 Cotgrave
18.11.02 Andy Gibson L PTS 4 Glasgow
30.11.02 Conroy McIntosh W PTS 4 Coventry
24.01.03 Chris Steele W PTS 4 Sheffield
08.03.03 Conroy McIntosh W PTS 4 Coventry
24.03.03 Robert Burton W PTS 6 Barnsley
10.06.03 P.J.Maxwell L RSC 1 Sheffield
Career: 9 contests, won 7, lost 2.

Andy Halder   Les Clark

Ceri Hall

Loughor. *Born* Swansea, 25 March, 1980
L. Welterweight. Ht. 5'10"
Manager P. Boyce

15.09.02 Martin Turner W RSC 1 Swansea
10.04.03 Silence Saheed DREW 4 Clydach
Career: 2 contests, won 1, drew 1.

Jason Hall

Hanwell. *Born* Perivale, 19 November, 1975
Lightweight. Ht. 5'8¹/₂"
Manager F. Maloney

19.04.97 Johannes Musa W RSC 3 Las Vegas,
          USA
06.06.97 Raul Basulto L RSC 10 Las Vegas,
          USA
30.07.97 Mark Chang w pts 4 Las Vegas, USA
27.06.98 Andrew Poulos W PTS 4 Vancouver,
          Canada
29.06.99 Brendan Ahearne W PTS 6 Bethnal
          Green
20.08.99 Keith Jones W PTS 6 Bloomsbury
05.10.99 John Paul Temple W PTS 6 Bloomsbury
06.11.99 Woody Greenaway W RSC 5 Bethnal
          Green
10.03.00 Arv Mittoo L RSC 3 Bethnal Green
18.02.01 Marco Fattore W PTS 6 Southwark
01.04.01 Gary Flear W PTS 8 Southwark
28.04.01 Bradley Pryce L PTS 12 Cardiff
          (Vacant WBO Inter-Continental
          Lightweight Title)
15.12.01 Steve Murray L RSC 4 Wembley
          (Elim. British Lightweight Title)
22.09.02 Chill John W PTS 6 Southwark
Career: 14 contests, won 10, lost 4.

Matthew Hall

Middleton. *Born* Manchester, 5 July, 1984
L. Middleweight. Ht. 5'7³/₄"
Manager F. Warren/B. Hughes

28.09.02 Pedro Thompson W RSC 1 Manchester
14.12.02 Pedro Thompson W PTS 4 Newcastle
18.01.03 Clive Johnson W PTS 4 Preston
05.04.03 Brian Coleman W RSC 1 Manchester
08.05.03 Patrick Cito W PTS 4 Widnes
Career: 5 contests, won 5.

Matthew Hall   Les Clark

(Michael) Oscar Hall

Darlington. *Born* Darlington, 8 November,
1974
L. Welterweight. Northern Area
Welterweight Champion. Ht. 5'9"
Manager D. Ingle

09.05.98 Trevor Smith W PTS 4 Sheffield
27.02.99 Lee Molyneux W PTS 4 Oldham
15.05.99 Chris Price W PTS 4 Sheffield
29.05.99 Brian Gifford W RSC 1 Halifax
04.06.99 Arv Mittoo W PTS 6 Hull
27.09.99 Dave Gibson W PTS 6 Leeds
11.12.99 Brian Coleman W PTS 6 Liverpool
18.02.00 Jason Collins DREW 6 West Bromwich
02.03.00 Ernie Smith W PTS 6 Birkenhead
09.06.00 Dave Gibson W PTS 6 Hull
19.06.00 Paul Denton W PTS 4 Burton
13.08.00 Lee Molyneux W PTS 6 Nottingham
04.11.00 Ram Singh W PTS 6 Derby
24.11.00 Dean Nicholas W PTS 6 Darlington
11.12.00 Ram Singh W CO 4 Cleethorpes
16.06.01 David Kirk W PTS 6 Derby
18.08.01 David White W PTS 4 Dewsbury
22.09.01 Dean Nicholas W DIS 9 Newcastle
(Vacant Northern Area Welterweight Title)
17.11.01 Paul Lomax W PTS 4 Dewsbury
15.03.02 Stuart Rimmer W RSC 4 Spennymoor
19.04.02 Peter Dunn W PTS 6 Darlington
10.05.02 Arv Mittoo W PTS 4 Bethnal Green
28.01.03 Alan Bosworth W PTS 10 Nottingham
(Elim. British L. Welterweight Title)
Career: 23 contests, won 22, drew 1.

Gary Hamilton

Belfast. *Born* Belfast, 27 May, 1980
Lightweight. Ht. 5'8½"
Manager Self

20.10.00 Gyula Szabo W PTS 4 Belfast
10.12.00 Patrick Dominguez L RSC 3 Elgin, Illinois, USA
21.01.02 John Marshall L PTS 4 Glasgow
18.02.02 Tony McPake L PTS 4 Glasgow
24.04.02 Robert Murray L PTS 6 Dublin
05.04.03 Dafydd Carlin L PTS 10 Belfast
(Vacant Northern Ireland Lightweight Title)
Career: 6 contests, won 1, lost 5.

Anthony Hanna

Birmingham. *Born* Birmingham, 22 September, 1974
Featherweight. Former Undefeated Midlands Area Flyweight Champion. Ht. 5'6"
Manager Self

19.11.92 Nick Tooley L PTS 6 Evesham
10.12.92 Daren Fifield L RSC 6 Bethnal Green
11.05.93 Tiger Singh W PTS 6 Norwich
24.05.93 Lyndon Kershaw L PTS 6 Bradford
16.09.93 Chris Lyons W PTS 6 Southwark
06.10.93 Tiger Singh W PTS 6 Solihull
03.11.93 Mickey Cantwell L PTS 8 Bristol
25.01.94 Marty Chestnut W PTS 4 Picadilly
10.02.94 Allan Mooney W RTD 1 Glasgow
13.04.94 Allan Mooney L PTS 6 Glasgow
22.04.94 Jesper Jensen L PTS 6 Aalborg, Denmark
03.08.94 Paul Ingle L PTS 6 Bristol
01.10.94 Mark Hughes L PTS 4 Cardiff
30.11.94 Shaun Norman W PTS 10 Solihull
(Vacant Midlands Area Flyweight Title)
24.02.95 Darren Greaves W RSC 5 Weston super Mare
06.03.95 Mark Hughes L PTS 6 Mayfair

27.04.95 Mickey Cantwell L PTS 6 Bethnal Green
05.05.95 Mark Cokely W RSC 4 Swansea
04.06.95 Mark Reynolds L PTS 10 Bethnal Green
(Elim. British Flyweight Title)
02.07.95 Mickey Cantwell L PTS 6 Dublin
02.11.95 Shaun Norman DREW 10 Mayfair
(Midlands Area Flyweight Title Defence)
31.01.96 Marty Chestnut DREW 6 Stoke
20.03.96 Harry Woods L PTS 6 Cardiff
22.04.96 Neil Parry W PTS 6 Manchester
14.05.96 Dharmendra Singh Yadav L PTS 4 Dagenham
08.10.96 Marty Chestnut W PTS 6 Battersea
11.12.96 Mark Reynolds DREW 8 Southwark
28.01.97 Colin Moffett L PTS 4 Belfast
28.02.97 Paul Weir L PTS 8 Kilmarnock
14.03.97 Jesper Jensen L PTS 6 Odense, Denmark
30.04.97 Clinton Beeby DREW 6 Acton
10.05.97 Jason Booth L PTS 6 Nottingham
02.06.97 Keith Knox L PTS 6 Glasgow
14.10.97 Louis Veitch L PTS 6 Kilmarnock
27.10.97 Russell Laing W PTS 4 Musselburgh
13.11.97 Noel Wilders L PTS 6 Bradford
24.11.97 Shaun Anderson L PTS 8 Glasgow
20.12.97 Damaen Kelly L PTS 4 Belfast
31.01.98 Jason Booth L PTS 6 Edmonton
23.02.98 David Coldwell W PTS 6 Salford
19.03.98 Andy Roberts L PTS 6 Doncaster
18.05.98 Chris Emanuele W RSC 3 Cleethorpes
11.09.98 Nicky Booth DREW 6 Cleethorpes
18.09.98 Colin Moffett DREW 4 Belfast
29.10.98 Nick Tooley W RTD 6 Bayswater
25.11.98 Nicky Booth W PTS 6 Clydach
21.01.99 Ola Dali W PTS 6 Piccadilly
13.03.99 Damaen Kelly L PTS 12 Manchester
(Vacant British Flyweight Title. Commonwealth Flyweight Title Challenge)
24.04.99 Noel Wilders L PTS 6 Peterborough
07.06.99 Alston Buchanan W RSC 3 Glasgow
29.06.99 Tommy Waite L PTS 4 Bethnal Green
16.10.99 Stevie Quinn W PTS 4 Belfast
22.11.99 Frankie DeMilo L PTS 6 Piccadilly
04.12.99 Ady Lewis L PTS 6 Manchester
19.02.00 Ian Napa L PTS 6 Dagenham
13.03.00 Mzukisi Sikali L PTS 6 Bethnal Green
27.05.00 Nicky Cook L PTS 6 Mayfair
25.07.00 David Lowry L PTS 4 Southwark
19.08.00 Marc Callaghan L PTS 4 Brentwood
29.09.00 Rocky Dean L PTS 4 Bethnal Green
07.10.00 Oleg Kiryukhin L PTS 6 Doncaster
14.10.00 Danny Costello DREW 4 Wembley
31.10.00 Jason Booth L PTS 6 Hammersmith
10.02.01 Tony Mulholland L PTS 6 Widnes
19.02.01 Alex Moon L PTS 6 Glasgow
03.03.01 Marc Callaghan L PTS 6 Wembley
24.04.01 Silence Mabuza L PTS 6 Liverpool
06.05.01 Michael Hunter L PTS 4 Hartlepool
26.05.01 Mickey Bowden L PTS 4 Bethnal Green
04.06.01 Michael Hunter L PTS 4 Hartlepool
01.11.01 Nigel Senior L PTS 6 Hull
24.11.01 Martin Power L PTS 4 Bethnal Green
08.12.01 Faprakob Rakkiatgym L PTS 8 Dagenham
24.03.02 Mickey Coveney L PTS 4 Streatham
23.06.02 Johannes Maisa L PTS 4 Southwark
30.10.02 Mickey Bowden L PTS 4 Leicester Square
08.11.02 Sean Green L PTS 6 Doncaster
17.11.02 Shinny Bayaar L PTS 6 Shaw
14.12.02 Michael Hunter L PTS 8 Newcastle

15.02.03 Steve Gethin L PTS 6 Wolverhampton
24.02.03 Jackson Williams W PTS 6 Birmingham
08.06.03 Darryn Walton L PTS 6 Shaw
Career: 82 contests, won 19, drew 7, lost 56.

Martin Hardcastle

Leeds. *Born* Pontefract, 27 August, 1976
L. Welterweight. Ht. 5'6"
Manager T. O'Neill

02.03.02 Mick McPhilbin W RSC 4 Wakefield
28.05.02 Dave Curran W RSC 3 Leeds
05.10.02 Gwyn Wale L PTS 4 Huddersfield
12.11.02 Pete Buckley DREW 6 Leeds
20.12.02 Jon Honney L PTS 4 Bracknell
28.03.03 Silence Saheed L PTS 4 Millwall
17.04.03 Matt Teague W PTS 6 Hull
16.05.03 Colin Bain L PTS 6 Glasgow
24.05.03 Simon Chambers W RSC 2 Sheffield
15.06.03 Paul Rushton W RTD 2 Bradford
Career: 10 contests, won 5, drew 1, lost 4.

Martin Hardcastle   Les Clark

James Hare

Robertown. *Born* Dewsbury, 16 July, 1976
WBF Welterweight Champion. Former Undefeated Commonwealth & European Union Welterweight Champion. Ht. 5'6"
Manager T. Gilmour/C. Aston

20.01.96 Brian Coleman W PTS 6 Mansfield
25.06.96 Mike Watson W PTS 4 Mansfield
13.07.96 Dennis Griffin W RSC 4 Bethnal Green
14.09.96 Paul Salmon W RSC 4 Sheffield
14.12.96 Jon Harrison W PTS 4 Sheffield
25.02.97 Kid McAuley W PTS 4 Sheffield
12.04.97 Andy Peach W RSC 1 Sheffield
13.12.97 Costas Katsantonis W RSC 3 Sheffield
09.05.98 Peter Nightingale W PTS 4 Sheffield
18.07.98 Karl Taylor W PTS 4 Sheffield
28.11.98 Peter Nightingale W PTS 6 Sheffield
15.05.99 Lee Williamson W RSC 2 Sheffield

23.10.99 Mark Winters DREW 6 Telford
23.10.00 Dean Nicholas W RSC 1 Glasgow
23.01.01 Mark Ramsey W PTS 6 Crawley
26.02.01 Paul Denton W PTS 4 Nottingham
08.05.01 Jessy Moreaux W RSC 3 Barnsley
26.05.01 John Humphrey W RSC 7 Bethnal Green
(Elim. British Welterweight Title)
08.10.01 John Ameline W PTS 8 Barnsley
26.11.01 Paul Denton W RTD 4 Manchester
28.01.02 Monney Seka W PTS 10 Barnsley
(Vacant European Union Welterweight Title)
27.04.02 Julian Holland W RSC 6 Huddersfield
(Commonwealth Welterweight Title Challenge)
15.06.02 Abdel Mehidi W PTS 8 Leeds
05.10.02 Farai Musiiwa W RSC 8 Huddersfield
(Commonwealth Welterweight Title Defence)
30.11.02 Earl Foskin W RSC 1 Liverpool
(Commonwealth Welterweight Title Defence)

James Hare   Les Clark

22.02.03 Frans Hantindi W RSC 1 Huddersfield
(Commonwealth Welterweight Title Defence)
21.06.03 Roman Dzuman W PTS 12 Manchester
(Vacant WBF Welterweight Title)
Career: 27 contests, won 26, drew 1.

Mike Harrington
Torquay. *Born* Glasgow, 23 May, 1974
Lightweight. Ht. 5'8"
Manager G. Bousted

02.11.02 Kevin O'Hara L RSC 1 Belfast
15.05.03 Pete Buckley L PTS 4 Clevedon
Career: 2 contests, lost 2.

Audley Harrison
Wembley. *Born* Park Royal, 26 October, 1971
Heavyweight. Ht. 6'4³/₄"
Manager Self

19.05.01 Michael Middleton W RSC 1 Wembley
22.09.01 Derek McCafferty W PTS 6 Newcastle
20.10.01 Piotr Jurczyk W RSC 2 Glasgow
20.04.02 Julius Long W CO 2 Wembley
21.05.02 Mark Krence W RSC 6 Custom House
10.07.02 Dominic Negus W PTS 6 Wembley
05.10.02 Wade Lewis W RSC 2 Liverpool
23.11.02 Shawn Robinson W RSC 1 Atlantic City, New Jersey, USA
08.02.03 Rob Calloway W RSC 5 Brentford
29.03.03 Ratko Draskovic W PTS 8 Wembley
31.05.03 Matthew Ellis W RSC 2 Bethnal Green
Career: 11 contests, won 11.

Scott Harrison
Cambuslang. *Born* Bellshill, 19 August, 1977
WBO Featherweight Champion. Former Undefeated British, Commonwealth & IBO Inter-Continental Featherweight Champion. Ht. 5'7"
Manager F. Maloney

07.10.96 Eddie Sica W RSC 2 Lewisham
11.01.97 Pete Buckley W PTS 4 Bethnal Green
25.03.97 David Morris W PTS 4 Lewisham
04.10.97 Miguel Matthews L RSC 4 Muswell Hill
16.12.97 Stephane Fernandez DREW 6 Grand Synthe, France
31.01.98 Pete Buckley W PTS 4 Edmonton
09.06.98 Carl Allen W RSC 6 Hull
17.10.98 Rakhim Mingaleev W PTS 8 Manchester
06.03.99 John Matthews W RSC 4 Southwark
10.07.99 Smith Odoom W PTS 12 Southwark
(IBO Inter-Continental Featherweight Title Challenge)
24.01.00 Patrick Mullings W PTS 12 Glasgow
(Commonwealth Featherweight Title Challenge)
29.04.00 Tracy Harris Patterson W PTS 10 New York City, USA
15.07.00 Tom Johnson W PTS 12 Millwall
(IBO Inter-Continental Featherweight Title Defence)
11.11.00 Eric Odumasi W RSC 12 Belfast
(Commonwealth Featherweight Title Defence)
24.03.01 Richie Wenton W RSC 4 Sheffield
(Vacant British Featherweight Title. Commonwealth Featherweight Title Defence)
15.09.01 Gary Thornhill W RSC 5 Manchester
(British & Commonwealth Featherweight Title Defences)
17.11.01 Steve Robinson W RSC 3 Glasgow
(British & Commonwealth Featherweight Title Defences)
11.03.02 Tony Wehbee W RSC 3 Glasgow
(Commonwealth Featherweight Title Defence)
08.06.02 Victor Santiago W RSC 6 Renfrew
(Vacant WBO Interim Featherweight Title)
19.10.02 Julio Pablo Chacon W PTS 12 Renfrew
(WBO Featherweight Title Challenge)
22.03.03 Wayne McCullough W PTS 12 Renfrew
(WBO Featherweight Title Defence)
Career: 21 contests, won 19, drew 1, lost 1.

Lee Haskins

Bristol. *Born* Bristol, 29 November, 1983
Flyweight. Ht. 5'5"
Manager C. Sanigar

06.03.03 Ankar Miah W RSC 1 Bristol
13.06.03 Chris Edwards W PTS 6 Bristol
Career: 2 contests, won 2.

Mark Haslam

Manchester. *Born* Bury, 20 October, 1969
L. Welterweight. Ht. 5'8"
Manager Self

12.06.95 Steve Burton W PTS 6 Manchester
15.09.95 Thomas Bradley W CO 4 Mansfield
24.11.95 Anthony Campbell L PTS 4
        Manchester

13.01.96 Jon Harrison W PTS 6 Manchester
09.04.96 Pete Roberts W CO 2 Salford
25.10.96 Andy Robinson W RTD 4 Mere
09.11.96 Brian Coleman W PTS 6 Manchester
22.03.97 Mark Richards DREW 4 Wythenshawe
17.11.97 Tommy Peacock L DIS 5 Manchester
16.10.98 Arv Mittoo W PTS 6 Salford
20.12.98 Mark Harrison W RSC 3 Salford
13.03.99 Gary Hibbert L PTS 10 Manchester
        (Vacant Central Area Lightweight Title)
20.05.99 Colin Lynes L PTS 4 Barking
04.12.99 Wayne Rigby L CO 3 Manchester
11.06.00 Dave Tatton W PTS 4 Salford
10.02.01 Michael Jennings L RSC 2 Widnes
22.12.02 Tony Montana L PTS 6 Salford
08.02.03 Ricky Eccleston L PTS 6 Liverpool
Career: 18 contests, won 9, drew 1, lost 8.

Matthew Hatton

Manchester. *Born* Stockport, 15 May, 1981
Welterweight. Ht. 5'8½"
Manager F. Warren

23.09.00 David White W PTS 4 Bethnal Green
25.11.00 David White W PTS 4 Manchester
11.12.00 Danny Connelly W PTS 4 Widnes
15.01.01 Keith Jones W PTS 4 Manchester
10.02.01 Karl Taylor W PTS 4 Widnes
17.03.01 Assen Vassilev W RSC 5 Manchester
09.06.01 Brian Coleman W RTD 2 Bethnal Green
21.07.01 Ram Singh W RSC 2 Sheffield
15.09.01 Marcus Portman W RSC 3 Manchester
15.12.01 Dafydd Carlin W PTS 6 Wembley
09.02.02 Paul Denton W PTS 6 Manchester
04.05.02 Karl Taylor W RSC 3 Bethnal Green
20.07.02 Karl Taylor W RTD 2 Bethnal Green
28.09.02 David Kirk L PTS 6 Manchester
14.12.02 Paul Denton W PTS 6 Newcastle
15.02.03 David Keir L RSC 4 Wembley
08.05.03 Jay Mahoney W PTS 6 Widnes
Career: 17 contests, won 15, lost 2.

Ricky Hatton

Manchester. *Born* Stockport, 6 October, 1978
WBU L. Welterweight Champion. Former
Undefeated British, WBO Inter-Continental
& Central Area L. Welterweight Champion.
Ht. 5'7½"
Manager F. Warren

11.09.97 Kid McAuley W RTD 1 Widnes
19.12.97 Robert Alvarez W PTS 4 New York
        City, USA
17.01.98 David Thompson W RSC 1 Bristol
27.03.98 Paul Salmon W RSC 1 Telford
18.04.98 Karl Taylor W RSC 1 Manchester
30.05.98 Mark Ramsey W PTS 6 Bristol
18.07.98 Anthony Campbell W PTS 6 Sheffield
19.09.98 Pascal Montulet W CO 2 Oberhausen,
        Germany
31.10.98 Kevin Carter W RSC 1 Atlantic City,
        USA
19.12.98 Paul Denton W RSC 6 Liverpool
27.02.99 Tommy Peacock W RSC 2 Oldham
        (Vacant Central Area L. Welterweight
        Title)
03.04.99 Brian Coleman W CO 2 Kensington
29.05.99 Dillon Carew W RSC 5 Halifax
        (Vacant WBO Inter-Continental
        L. Welterweight Title)
17.07.99 Mark Ramsey W PTS 6 Doncaster
09.10.99 Bernard Paul W RTD 4 Manchester
        (WBO Inter-Continental
        L. Welterweight Title Defence)
11.12.99 Mark Winters W RSC 4 Liverpool
        (WBO Inter-Continental
        L. Welterweight Title Defence)
29.01.00 Leoncio Garces W RSC 3 Manchester
25.03.00 Pedro Teran W RSC 4 Liverpool
        (WBO Inter-Continental
        L. Welterweight Title Defence)
16.05.00 Ambioris Figuero W RSC 4 Warrington
        (WBO Inter-Continental
        L. Welterweight Title Defence)
10.06.00 Gilbert Quiros W CO 2 Detroit, USA
        (WBO Inter-Continental
        L. Welterweight Title Defence)
23.09.00 Giuseppe Lauri W RSC 5 Bethnal Green
        (WBO Inter-Continental
        L. Welterweight Title Defence. WBA
        Inter-Continental L. Welterweight Title
        Challenge)

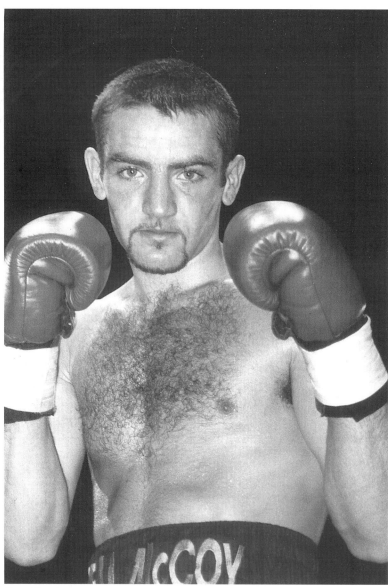

Scott Harrison   Les Clark

21.10.00   Jonathan Thaxton W PTS 12 Wembley
     (Vacant British L.Welterweight Title)
26.03.01   Tony Pep W CO 4 Wembley
     (Vacant WBU L. Welterweight Title)
07.07.01   Jason Rowland W CO 4 Manchester
     (WBU L.Welterweight Title Defence)
15.09.01   John Bailey W RSC 5 Manchester
     (WBU L.Welterweight Title Defence)
27.10.01   Fred Pendleton W CO 2 Manchester
     (WBU L.Welterweight Title Defence)
15.12.01   Justin Rowsell W RSC 2 Wembley
     (WBU L.Welterweight Title Defence)
09.02.02   Mikhail Krivolapov W RSC 9 Manchester
     (WBU L. Welterweight Title Defence)
01.06.02   Eamonn Magee W PTS 12 Manchester
     (WBU L. Welterweight Title Defence)
28.09.02   Stephen Smith W DIS 2 Manchester
     (WBU L.Welterweight Title Defence)
14.12.02   Joe Hutchinson W CO 4 Newcastle
     (WBU L. Welterweight Title Defence)
05.04.03   Vince Phillips W PTS 12 Manchester
     (WBU L.Welterweight Title Defence)

Career: 32 contests, won 32.

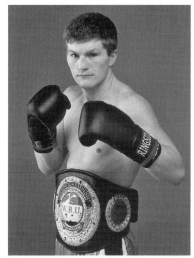

Ricky Hatton   Paul Speak

David Haye

Orpington. *Born* London, 13 October, 1980
Cruiserweight. Ht. 6'3"
Manager A. Booth

08.12.02   Tony Booth W RTD 2 Bethnal Green
24.01.03   Saber Zairi W RSC 4 Sheffield
04.03.03   Roger Bowden W RSC 2 Miami, Florida, USA
18.03.03   Phill Day W RSC 2 Reading

Career: 4 contests, won 4.

Peter Haymer

Enfield. *Born* London, 10 July, 1978
L. Heavyweight. Ht. 6'1¼"
Manager F. Maloney

25.11.00   Adam Cale W RSC 1 Manchester
27.01.01   Darren Ashton W PTS 4 Bethnal Green
10.03.01   Daniel Ivanov W CO 2 Bethnal Green
26.03.01   Radcliffe Green W PTS 4 Wembley
05.05.01   Terry Morrill W PTS 4 Edmonton
22.09.01   Tony Booth W PTS 4 Bethnal Green

24.11.01   Nathan King L PTS 4 Bethnal Green
12.02.02   Nathan King L PTS 4 Bethnal Green
09.05.02   Mark Snipe W PTS 4 Leicester Square
15.06.02   Paul Bonson W PTS 4 Tottenham
30.10.02   Jimmy Steel W PTS 4 Leicester Square
18.03.03   Mark Brookes W PTS 6 Reading

Career: 12 contests, won 10, lost 2.

Ciaran Healy

Belfast. *Born* Belfast, 25 December, 1974
Middleweight. Ht. 5'11"
Manager J. Rooney

05.04.03   Tomas da Silva W PTS 4 Belfast

Career: 1 contest, won 1.

Jamie Hearn

Colnbrook. *Born* Taplow, 4 June, 1982
L. Heavyweight. Ht. 5'11½"
Manager J. Evans

27.09.02   Jimmy Steel W PTS 4 Bracknell
03.12.02   Mark Phillips W PTS 4 Bethnal Green
20.12.02   Danny Norton W PTS 4 Bracknell
18.03.03   Darren Stubbs L RSC 3 Reading
13.06.03   Liam Lathbury W RSC 4 Bristol

Career: 5 contests, won 4, lost 1.

Jamie Hearn   Les Clark

(Donvill) Jimi Hendricks

Birmingham. *Born* Birmingham, 2 April, 1973
Middleweight. Ht. 5'10"
Manager J. Gill

21.02.03   Davey Jones L PTS 6 Doncaster
21.03.03   Kevin Phelan L RSC 6 Longford
09.05.03   Steve Scott W PTS 6 Doncaster
06.06.03   Steve Russell W PTS 6 Norwich

Career: 4 contests, won 2, lost 2.

Gary Hibbert

Oldham. *Born* Oldham, 5 February, 1975
Central Area Lightweight Champion. Ht. 5'8½"
Manager B. Hearn

02.06.96   John T. Kelly W PTS 6 Shaw
13.10.96   Sean Morrison W RSC 2 Shaw
16.03.97   David Kirk W PTS 6 Shaw
08.06.97   Bamana Dibateza W PTS 4 Shaw
18.09.98   Jimmy Phelan W PTS 6 Manchester
17.10.98   Dennis Griffin W RSC 4 Manchester
30.11.98   Carl Allen W PTS 4 Manchester
13.03.99   Mark Haslam W PTS 10 Manchester
     (Vacant Central Area Lightweight Title)
01.07.00   Marco Fattore W PTS 4 Manchester
09.09.00   Woody Greenaway W RSC 2 Manchester
03.02.01   Franck Benoni L PTS 6 Manchester
04.06.01   Alan Temple L PTS 6 Hartlepool
07.07.01   Gaeten Trovato W RSC 1 Amsterdam, Holland
06.10.01   Yannick Paget W RSC 2 Manchester
26.11.01   Rosalin Nasibulin W RSC 3 Manchester
09.03.02   Alan Temple W RSC 1 Manchester
23.03.02   Andrei Devyataykin L RSC 4 Southwark
07.09.02   David Burke L RSC 10 Liverpool
     (Vacant Commonwealth Lightweight Title)
08.02.03   Anthony Maynard DREW 6 Liverpool
19.04.03   Chris Barnett W RSC 7 Liverpool

Career: 20 contests, won 15, drew 1, lost 4.

Dean Hickman

West Bromwich. *Born* West Bromwich, 24 November, 1979
L. Welterweight. Ht. 5'7"
Manager D. Bradley

17.02.02   Wayne Wheeler DREW 6 Wolverhampton
13.04.02   Wayne Wheeler W PTS 6 Wolverhampton
13.07.02   Dai Bando W RSC 1 Wolverhampton
02.11.02   Darren Goode W RSC 2 Wolverhampton
15.02.03   Gareth Wiltshaw W PTS 6 Wolverhampton
21.03.03   David Vaughan W PTS 6 West Bromwich
30.06.03   Dave Hinds W RSC 4 Shrewsbury

Career: 7 contests, won 6, drew 1.

Herbie Hide

Norwich. *Born* Nigeria, 27 August, 1971
Heavyweight. Former WBO Heavyweight Champion. Former Undefeated British, WBC International & Penta-Continental Heavyweight Champion. Ht. 6'1½"
Manager R. McCracken

24.10.89   L. A. Williams W CO 2 Bethnal Green
05.11.89   Gary McCrory W RTD 1 Kensington
19.12.89   Steve Osborne W RSC 6 Bethnal Green
27.06.90   Alek Penarski W RSC 3 Kensington
05.09.90   Steve Lewsam W RSC 4 Brighton
26.09.90   Jonjo Greene W RSC 1 Manchester
17.10.90   Gus Mendes W RSC 2 Bethnal Green
18.11.90   Steve Lewsam W RSC 1 Birmingham
29.01.91   Lennie Howard W RSC 1 Wisbech
09.04.91   David Jules W RSC 1 Mayfair
14.05.91   John Westgarth W RTD 4 Dudley
03.07.91   Tucker Richards W RSC 3 Brentwood
15.10.91   Eddie Gonzalez W CO 2 Hamburg, Germany
29.10.91   Chris Jacobs W RSC 1 Cardiff

21.01.92 Conroy Nelson W RSC 2 Norwich
          (Vacant WBC International
          Heavyweight Title)
03.03.92 Percell Davis W CO 1 Amsterdam,
          Holland
08.09.92 Jean Chanet W RSC 7 Norwich
06.10.92 Craig Peterson W RSC 7 Antwerp,
          Belgium
          (WBC International Heavyweight Title
          Defence)
12.12.92 James Pritchard W RSC 2 Muswell Hill
30.01.93 Juan Antonio Diaz W RSC 3 Brentwood
          (Vacant Penta-Continental
          Heavyweight Title)
27.02.93 Michael Murray W RSC 5 Dagenham
          (Vacant British Heavyweight Title)
11.05.93 Jerry Halstead W RSC 4 Norwich
          (Penta-Continental Heavyweight Title
          Defence)
18.09.93 Everett Martin W PTS 10 Leicester
06.11.93 Mike Dixon W RSC 9 Bethnal Green
          (Penta-Continental Heavyweight Title
          Defence)
04.12.93 Jeff Lampkin W RSC 2 Sun City,
          South Africa
          (WBC International Heavyweight Title
          Defence)
19.03.94 Michael Bentt W CO 7 Millwall
          (WBO Heavyweight Title Challenge)
11.03.95 Riddick Bowe L CO 6 Las Vegas, USA
          (WBO Heavyweight Title Defence)
06.07.96 Michael Murray W RSC 6 Manchester
09.11.96 Frankie Swindell W CO 1 Manchester
28.06.97 Tony Tucker W RSC 2 Norwich
          (Vacant WBO Heavyweight Title)
18.04.98 Damon Reed W RSC 1 Manchester
          (WBO Heavyweight Title Defence)
26.09.98 Willi Fischer W RSC 2 Norwich
          (WBO Heavyweight Title Defence)
26.06.99 Vitali Klitschko L CO 2 Millwall
          (WBO Heavyweight Title Defence)
14.07.01 Alexei Osokin W RSC 3 Liverpool
22.09.01 Joseph Chingangu L RSC 2 Newcastle
16.04.03 Derek McCafferty W RSC 7
          Nottingham
27.05.03 Joseph Chingangu W CO 1 Dagenham
Career: 37 contests, won 34, lost 3.

Dave Hill

Hull. *Born* Hull, 14 May, 1974
Welterweight. Ht. 5'9¾"
Manager S. Pollard

17.04.03 Gary Cummings L CO 5 Hull
Career: 1 contest, lost 1.

Jamie Hill

Blackpool. *Born* Blackpool, 8 May, 1974
L. Welterweight. Ht. 5'6"
Manager L. Veitch

24.05.03 Lee Bedell L RSC 3 Sheffield
Career: 1 contest, lost 1.

Jon Hilton

Manchester. *Born* Pendleton, 25 March,
1982
L. Middleweight. Ht. 6'1"
Manager J. Gill

10.10.02 Ian Thomas L PTS 6 Stoke
25.10.02 Andy Halder L PTS 6 Cotgrave
02.12.02 Jimmy White W RSC 5 Leicester

09.12.02 Richard Swallow L PTS 6 Nottingham
17.02.03 Craig Dickson L RSC 2 Glasgow
13.04.03 Dave Wakefield L PTS 4 Streatham
Career: 6 contests, won 1, lost 5.

Dave Hinds

Birmingham. *Born* Leicester, 5 January, 1971
Lightweight. Ht. 5'5"
Manager Self

19.09.95 Martin Evans W RSC 5 Plymouth
08.11.95 Wayne Pardoe L CO 4 Walsall
04.04.96 Paul Salmon L RTD 5 Plymouth
06.10.97 Eddie Sica L RSC 1 Piccadilly
25.11.97 Graham McGrath W PTS 6
          Wolverhampton
06.12.97 Adam Spelling W RSC 1 Wembley
27.01.98 Malcolm Thomas L PTS 6 Piccadilly
06.03.98 Jon Dodsworth W RSC 1 Hull
12.03.98 Jamie McKeever L PTS 4 Liverpool
20.03.98 John O'Johnson L PTS 6 Ilkeston
23.04.98 Roy Rutherford L RSC 5 Edgbaston
26.05.98 David Kehoe L RSC 5 Mayfair
07.10.98 Steve Saville L PTS 6 Stoke
26.10.98 Eddie Nevins L PTS 6 Manchester
26.11.98 Steve Saville L PTS 6 Edgbaston
07.12.98 Danny Bell L PTS 6 Nottingham
13.02.99 Michael Gomez L PTS 6 Newcastle
23.04.99 Mark Ramsey L PTS 6 Clydach
17.05.99 Jesse James Daniel L PTS 6
          Cleethorpes
28.05.99 Jason Cook L RSC 1 Liverpool
17.07.99 Bradley Pryce L PTS 4 Doncaster
03.09.99 Young Muttley L RSC 4 West
          Bromwich
13.11.99 Humberto Soto L PTS 6 Hull
11.12.99 Gavin Rees L RSC 2 Liverpool
07.02.00 Liam Maltby L PTS 4 Peterborough
13.03.00 Danny Hunt L PTS 4 Bethnal Green
23.03.00 Marco Fattore L PTS 6 Bloomsbury
13.05.00 Alan Kershaw L PTS 4 Barnsley
22.05.00 Tony Conroy L PTS 4 Coventry
09.06.00 Elias Boswell W RSC 5 Blackpool
24.06.00 Brian Carr L PTS 4 Glasgow
01.07.00 Ricky Eccleston L PTS 4 Manchester
25.07.00 Kevin Lear L PTS 6 Southwark
09.09.00 Carl Greaves L PTS 6 Newark
16.09.00 Leo O'Reilly L RSC 2 Bethnal Green
27.11.00 Ricky Eccleston L PTS 4 Birmingham
04.12.00 Gavin Pearson L PTS 6 Bradford
11.12.00 Miguel Matthews W PTS 6
          Birmingham
11.02.01 James Rooney L PTS 6 Hartlepool
26.03.01 Kevin Lear L CO 1 Wembley
03.06.01 Dafydd Carlin L PTS 4 Southwark
16.06.01 Carl Greaves L PTS 6 Derby
29.09.01 Scott Lawton L RSC 2 Southwark
15.12.01 Danny Hunt L PTS 4 Wembley
26.01.02 Chris McDonagh L PTS 4 Bethnal
          Green
03.03.02 Mally McIver L PTS 6 Shaw
11.03.02 Willie Limond L PTS 6 Glasgow
11.05.02 Craig Spacie L PTS 6 Chesterfield
15.06.02 Dave Stewart L PTS 6 Tottenham
23.06.02 Peter McDonagh L PTS 6 Southwark
13.07.02 Tony McPake L RSC 3 Coventry
22.03.03 Baz Carey L PTS 6 Coventry
29.03.03 Martin Power L PTS 4 Portsmouth
13.04.03 Nadeem Siddique L PTS 4 Bradford
06.06.03 Paul Rushton W PTS 6 Hull
20.06.03 Steve Mullin L PTS 4 Liverpool
30.06.03 Dean Hickman L RSC 4 Shrewsbury
Career: 57 contests, won 7, lost 50.

Mark Hobson

Huddersfield. *Born* Workington, 7 May, 1976
Commonwealth Cruiserweight Champion.
Ht. 6'5"
Manager C. Aston/T. Gilmour

09.06.97 Michael Pinnock W PTS 6 Bradford
06.10.97 P. R. Mason W PTS 6 Bradford
13.11.97 P. R. Mason W PTS 6 Bradford
27.02.98 Colin Brown DREW 6 Irvine
21.05.98 Paul Bonson W PTS 6 Bradford
15.06.98 Martin Jolley W RSC 3 Bradford
25.10.98 Mark Snipe W RSC 3 Shaw
26.11.98 Danny Southam W RSC 5 Bradford
19.04.99 Mark Levy L PTS 8 Bradford
11.09.99 Paul Bonson W PTS 4 Sheffield
06.12.99 Brian Gascoigne W RSC 3 Bradford
11.03.00 Nikolai Ermenkov W RSC 3
          Kensington
27.03.00 Luke Simpkin W PTS 4 Barnsley
13.05.00 Paul Bonson W PTS 4 Barnsley
25.09.00 Mark Dawson W CO 1 Barnsley
26.02.01 Billy Bessey W PTS 4 Nottingham
24.04.01 Sebastiaan Rothmann L RTD 9
          Liverpool
          (WBU Cruiserweight Title Challenge)
08.10.01 Firat Arslan L RSC 7 Barnsley
10.12.01 Luke Simpkin W RTD 3 Liverpool
23.02.02 Valery Semishkur W PTS 6
          Nottingham
27.04.02 Lee Swaby W PTS 10 Huddersfield
          (Final Elim. British Cruiserweight
          Title)
05.10.02 Varuzhan Davtyan W RSC 3
          Huddersfield
25.01.03 Abdul Kaddu W RSC 4 Bridgend
          (Vacant Commonwealth Cruiserweight
          Title)
10.05.03 Muslim Biarslanov W RSC 2
          Huddersfield
Career: 24 contests, won 20, drew 1, lost 3.

Mark Hobson   Les Clark

Lee Hodgson

Hayes. *Born* Hammersmith, 28 June, 1973
Middleweight. Ht. 5'9½"
Manager D. Currivan

27.09.02 Kevin Phelan W RSC 1 Bracknell
03.12.02 Leigh Wicks W PTS 4 Bethnal Green
08.02.03 Dean Powell W PTS 4 Brentford
21.03.03 Elroy Edwards W RSC 3 Longford
29.03.03 Matthew Barr L RSC 1 Wembley
Career: 5 contests, won 4, lost 1.

Cristian Hodorogea

London. *Born* Romania, 17 August, 1978
Welterweight. Former Undefeated
Romanian S. Featherweight Champion
Ht. 5'7½"
Manager I. Akay

14.12.96 Adrian Ghiorgan W PTS 4 Iasi, Romania
28.06.97 Adrian Parlogea L PTS 6 Romania
25.10.97 El Omar Mouhammed L PTS 6 Italy
12.09.98 Zoltan Kalocsai NC 1 Szekszard, Hungary
12.12.98 Gheorghe Paraschiv W RSC 6 Romania
        (Romanian S.Featherweight Title Challenge)
28.03.99 Gheorghe Paraschiv W PTS 10 Romania
        (Romianian S.Featherweight Title Defence)
21.05.99 Laszlo Bognar L RSC 5 Montichiari, Italy
09.07.99 Manuel Calvo L RSC 5 Vigo, Spain
        (Trans-WBA Featherweight Title Challenge)
31.03.00 Paolo Pizzamiglio L CO 6 Piacenza, Italy
20.10.00 Marian Leondraliu L PTS 8 Bucharest, Romania
08.12.01 Darren Melville L PTS 4 Millwall
15.12.01 Matthew Macklin L CO 1 Wembley
03.12.02 Iain Eldridge W PTS 4 Bethnal Green
20.03.03 Ajose Olusegun L PTS 4 Queensway
26.04.03 Nathan Ward W RSC 1 Brentford
03.06.03 Elvis Mbwakongo L PTS 4 Bethnal Green
Career: 16 contests, won 5, lost 10, no contest 1.

Cristian Hodorogea   Les Clark

Gareth Hogg

Torquay. *Born* Newton Abbott, 21 October, 1977
L. Heavyweight. Ht. 6'2"
Manager C. Sanigar

13.02.98 Harry Butler W RSC 3 Weston super Mare
09.05.99 Matthew Barney L PTS 4 Bracknell
07.08.99 Clive Johnson W PTS 4 Dagenham
27.02.00 Darren Covill W RSC 3 Plymouth
29.03.00 Simon Andrews W RSC 5 Piccadilly
12.05.01 Oddy Papantoniou W RSC 2 Plymouth
10.07.01 Kevin Rainey W RSC 1 Montreal, Canada
23.06.02 Mark Phillips W PTS 4 Southwark
08.01.03 Darren Ashton W RSC 2 Aberdare
Career: 9 contests, won 8, lost 1.

Mike Holden

Manchester. *Born* Ashton under Lyme, 13 March, 1968
Heavyweight. Former Undefeated British
Heavyweight Champion. Ht. 6'4"
Manager Self

04.10.94 Gary Williams W RSC 4 Mayfair
20.12.94 Pat Passley L RTD 3 Bethnal Green
07.10.95 R. F. McKenzie W RSC 2 Belfast
14.11.95 Michael Murray L PTS 6 Bury
09.07.96 Julius Francis L PTS 10 Bethnal Green
28.09.96 Mikael Lindblad W PTS 6 Barking
26.06.97 Israel Ajose W RSC 1 Salford
02.09.97 Mika Kihlstrom W RSC 1 Southwark
12.12.98 Nigel Rafferty W RTD 2 Chester
08.05.99 Harry Senior L PTS 8 Bethnal Green
15.07.99 Derek McCafferty W RSC 1 Peterborough
13.03.00 Julius Francis W PTS 12 Bethnal Green
        (British Heavyweight Title Challenge)
03.04.01 Julius Francis L PTS 10 Bethnal Green
        (Final Elim. British Heavyweight Title)
13.09.01 Keith Long L PTS 10 Sheffield
        (Elim.British Heavyweight Title)
15.03.02 Luke Simpkin W PTS 6 Millwall
15.10.02 Antoine Palatis W PTS 6 Bethnal Green
24.01.03 Michael Sprott L RSC 4 Sheffield
12.04.03 Albert Sosnowski L PTS 6 Bethnal Green
Career: 18 contests, won 10, lost 8.

Martin Holgate

Walthamstow. *Born* Waltham Forest, 24 November, 1968
L. Welterweight. Ht. 5'6½"
Manager Self

02.06.95 Adam Baldwin W PTS 6 Bethnal Green
22.07.95 Mike Watson W PTS 6 Millwall
02.09.95 Trevor Smith W RSC 2 Wembley
21.10.95 John O. Johnson W PTS 4 Bethnal Green
09.12.95 Andrew Reed W RSC 1 Bethnal Green
13.02.96 Brian Coleman W PTS 4 Bethnal Green
13.07.96 John Smith W PTS 4 Bethnal Green
27.03.97 Danny Stevens W RSC 3 Norwich
29.05.97 Gary Hiscox W PTS 4 Mayfair
13.09.97 Jawaid Khaliq L RSC 6 Millwall
12.05.98 Steve Tuckett L PTS 6 Leeds
13.12.01 Liam Maltby W RSC 4 Leicester Square
09.05.02 Keith Jones W PTS 6 Leicester Square
30.10.02 Ajose Olusegun L RSC 7 Leicester Square
Career: 14 contests, won 11, lost 3.

Lee Holmes

Ellesmere Port. *Born* Chester, 18 April, 1975
S. Bantamweight. Ht. 5'6"
Manager M. Goodall

10.06.01 Paddy Folan W PTS 6 Ellesmere Port
26.08.01 Neil Read W PTS 6 Warrington
08.02.02 Sean Grant W CO 5 Preston
08.03.02 Dave Cotterill W PTS 6 Ellesmere Port
06.10.02 John Simpson W PTS 6 Rhyl
15.10.02 Malcolm Klaasen L RSC 4 Bethnal Green
Career: 6 contests, won 5, lost 1.

Jon Honney

Basingstoke. *Born* Basingstoke, 6 August, 1975
L. Welterweight. Ht. 5'7"
Manager Self

01.10.99 Peter Dunn W PTS 4 Bethnal Green
18.12.99 Marco Fattore W PTS 4 Southwark
21.02.00 Costas Katsantonis L RSC 1 Southwark
13.07.00 Mickey Yikealo L PTS 4 Bethnal Green
29.09.00 Manzo Smith L PTS 4 Bethnal Green
06.11.00 Jimmy Gould L PTS 6 Wolverhampton
16.03.01 Woody Greenaway W PTS 6 Portsmouth
07.09.01 Young Muttley L RSC 1 West Bromwich
20.10.01 Martin Watson L RSC 3 Glasgow
23.02.02 Darrell Grafton L RTD 1 Nottingham
28.11.02 Henry Jones W PTS 4 Finchley
20.12.02 Martin Hardcastle W PTS 4 Bracknell
05.03.03 Francis Barrett L PTS 10 Bethnal Green
        (Vacant Southern Area L.Welterweight Title)
27.05.03 Stephen Smith L PTS 8 Dagenham
Career: 14 contests, won 5, lost 9.

Chris Hooper

Scarborough. *Born* Barking, 28 September, 1977
Featherweight. Ht. 5'9"
Manager S. Pollard

01.11.01 Jason Nesbitt W RSC 6 Hull
28.01.02 Greg Edwards W RSC 2 Barnsley
27.07.02 John Mackay L PTS 4 Nottingham
26.09.02 Sid Razak W PTS 6 Hull
21.11.02 Baz Carey W RTD 3 Hull
03.04.03 Buster Dennis W RSC 1 Hull
Career: 6 contests, won 5, lost 1.

Petr Horacek

Maidenhead. *Born* Czechoslovakia, 11 January, 1974
Heavyweight. Ht. 6'4"
Manager J. Evans

29.01.00 Gary Williams W PTS 4 Manchester
08.09.00 Chris Woollas W PTS 4 Hammersmith
23.11.00 Neil Kirkwood W RSC 2 Bayswater
10.04.01 Shane Woollas DREW 4 Wembley
13.09.01 Mal Rice L RSC 1 Sheffield
22.11.01 Slick Miller W PTS 4 Paddington
09.02.02 Vladislav Druso W PTS 6 Prague, Czechoslovakia
15.02.02 Ervin Slonka W PTS 4 Brno, Czechoslovakia

03.08.02 Gifford Shillingford L RSC 4 Derby
13.12.02 Roman Kracik L PTS 6 Praha,
    Czechoslovakia
24.01.03 Mark Krence L RSC 4 Sheffield
11.02.03 Marek Gruszecki DREW 4 Praha,
    Czechoslovakia
10.06.03 Michael Sprott L CO 1 Sheffield
Career: 13 contests, won 6, drew 2, lost 5.

Shpetim Hoti

New Cross. *Born* Montenegro, 29
November, 1974
L. Heavyweight. Ht. 5'11½"
Manager Self

21.09.00 Elvis Michailenko L PTS 4
    Bloomsbury
30.11.00 Harry Butler L PTS 4 Bloomsbury
21.06.01 Harry Butler L PTS 4 Earls Court
31.01.02 Simeon Cover L PTS 6 Piccadilly
26.09.02 Mark Ellwood L PTS 6 Hull
17.11.02 Darren Stubbs L RTD 2 Shaw
20.06.03 David Louzan W RSC 5 Gatwick
Career: 7 contests, won 1, lost 6.

Ben Hudson

Cambridge. *Born* Cambridge, 29 March,
1973
L. Welterweight. Ht. 5'6"
Manager T. Sims

23.08.02 Pete Buckley DREW 4 Bethnal Green
06.09.02 Scott Lawton L PTS 4 Bethnal Green
26.09.02 Jas Malik W CO 3 Fulham
27.10.02 Peter McDonagh W PTS 6 Southwark
08.12.02 Daffyd Carlin W PTS 4 Bethnal Green
18.02.03 Brian Coleman W PTS 6 Bethnal
    Green
08.04.03 Peter McDonagh L PTS 4 Bethnal
    Green
26.04.03 Robert Lloyd-Taylor W PTS 4
    Brentford
27.05.03 Lenny Daws L RSC 2 Dagenham
Career: 9 contests, won 5, drew 1, lost 3.

Justin Hudson

Bexleyheath. *Born* Maidstone, 13 March,
1971
L. Middleweight. Ht. 5'9"
Manager E. Maloney

27.10.02 Elroy Edwards L RSC 3 Southwark
08.04.03 Arv Mittoo W PTS 4 Bethnal Green
03.06.03 Dave Wakefield W PTS 4 Bethnal
    Green
Career: 3 contests, won 2, lost 1.

Barry Hughes

Glasgow. *Born* Glasgow, 18 November,
1978
Lightweight. Ht. 5'8"
Manager Self

07.12.98 Woody Greenaway L PTS 6 Acton
18.02.99 Leon Dobbs W RSC 1 Glasgow
09.04.99 Gareth Dooley W PTS 6 Glasgow
26.06.99 Des Sowden W CO 1 Glasgow
04.10.99 Tony Smith W RSC 5 Glasgow
12.11.99 Brendan Ahearne W RSC 5 Glasgow
13.12.99 Jason Vlasman W RSC 2 Glasgow
24.02.00 No No Junior W RSC 1 Glasgow
18.03.00 Gary Flear W RSC 4 Glasgow
07.04.00 Billy Smith W PTS 6 Glasgow

12.08.00 Dave Travers W PTS 4 Wembley
15.03.02 Woody Greenaway W PTS 8 Glasgow
19.10.02 Arsen Vassilev W CO 3 Renfrew
08.12.02 Paul McIlwaine W RSC 2 Glasgow
16.05.03 Martin Watson L RTD 8 Glasgow
    (Vacant Scottish Lightweight Title)
Career: 15 contests, won 13, lost 2.

Sean Hughes

Pontefract. *Born* Pontefract, 5 June, 1982
S. Bantamweight. Ht. 5'9"
Manager M. Marsden

02.03.02 Paddy Folan W PTS 6 Wakefield
25.06.02 John Paul Ryan W PTS 6 Rugby
05.10.02 Paddy Folan W PTS 4 Huddersfield
10.02.03 Neil Read W PTS 6 Sheffield
24.05.03 John-Paul Ryan W PTS 6 Sheffield
Career: 5 contests, won 5.

John Humphrey

Newmarket. *Born* Kings Lynn, 24 July, 1980
L.Middleweight. Former Southern Area
L.Middleweight Champion. Former
Undefeated British Masters Welterweight
Champion. Ht. 6'2"
Manager Self

20.05.99 Arv Mittoo W PTS 6 Barking
13.09.99 Les Frost W CO 1 Bethnal Green
05.10.99 David Kehoe W PTS 4 Bloomsbury
06.11.99 Emmanuel Marcos W PTS 4 Bethnal
    Green
25.02.00 Matthew Barr L RSC 1 Newmarket
18.05.00 Lee Molyneux W PTS 6 Bethnal Green
29.09.00 Chris Henry W RSC 4 Bethnal Green
15.02.01 Kevin McIntyre W RSC 4 Glasgow
09.03.01 Harry Butler W RSC 1 Millwall
20.04.01 Mark Ramsey W PTS 10 Millwall
    *(Vacant British Masters Welterweight
    Title)*
26.05.01 James Hare L RSC 7 Bethnal Green
    (Elim. British Welterweight Title)
28.09.01 Clive Johnson W PTS 6 Millwall
23.11.01 Matthew Barr W RSC 2 Bethnal Green
16.03.02 Ojay Abrahams W PTS 10 Bethnal
    Green
    *(Vacant Southern Area L.Middleweight
    Title)*
19.10.02 Robert Burton W RSC 4 Norwich
08.02.03 Delroy Leslie W RSC 2 Norwich
    *(Southern Area L.Middleweight Title
    Defence)*
27.05.03 David Walker L CO 2 Dagenham
    *(Southern Area L.Middleweight Title
    Defence. Elim. British L. Middleweight
    Title)*
Career: 17 contests, won 14, lost 3.

Albi Hunt

Ealing. *Born* Hammersmith, 20 April, 1974
L. Welterweight. Ht. 5'9"
Manager E. Maloney

28.04.02 Jason Gonzales W PTS 6 Southwark
22.09.02 Daniel Thorpe W PTS 6 Southwark
Career: 2 contests, won 2.

Danny Hunt

Southend. *Born* Rochford, 1 May, 1981
Lightweight. Ht. 5'7"
Manager F. Maloney

29.11.99 Chris Lyons W PTS 4 Wembley
13.03.00 Dave Hinds W PTS 4 Bethnal Green
13.04.00 Steve Hanley W PTS 4 Holborn
13.07.00 Dave Travers W PTS 4 Bethnal Green
27.01.01 Lee Williamson L RSC 2 Bethnal
    Green
03.04.01 Lee Williamson W PTS 4 Bethnal
    Green
05.05.01 Pete Buckley W PTS 4 Edmonton
22.09.01 Dafydd Carlin W PTS 4 Bethnal Green
15.12.01 Dave Hinds W PTS 4 Wembley
02.03.02 Gary Flear W PTS 4 Bethnal Green
04.05.02 Jason Nesbitt W PTS 4 Bethnal Green
14.09.02 David Kehoe W RSC 3 Bethnal Green
15.02.03 Mark Bowen W RSC 1 Wembley
29.03.03 Daniel Thorpe W PTS 6 Portsmouth
Career: 14 contests, won 13, lost 1.

Michael Hunter

Hartlepool. *Born* Hartlepool, 5 May, 1978
WBF & Northern Area S. Bantamweight
Champion. Ht. 5'7½"
Manager D. Garside

23.07.00 Sean Grant W PTS 6 Hartlepool
01.10.00 Chris Emanuele W PTS 6 Hartlepool
24.11.00 Gary Groves W RSC 2 Darlington
09.12.00 Chris Jickells W PTS 4 Southwark
11.02.01 Paddy Folan W RSC 6 Hartlepool
06.05.01 Anthony Hanna W PTS 4 Hartlepool
04.06.01 Anthony Hanna W PTS 4 Hartlepool
09.09.01 John Barnes W RSC 8 Hartlepool
    *(Vacant Northern Area
    S.Bantamweight Title)*
29.11.01 Joel Viney W PTS 6 Hartlepool
26.01.02 Stevie Quinn W CO 2 Dagenham
18.03.02 Marc Callaghan DREW 6 Crawley
18.05.02 Mark Payne W PTS 8 Millwall
18.10.02 Frankie DeMilo W PTS 12 Hartlepool
    (Vacant WBF S. Bantamweight Title)
14.12.02 Anthony Hanna W PTS 8 Newcastle
07.06.03 Afrim Mustafa W RSC 5 Trieste, Italy
Career: 15 contests, won 14, drew 1.

Jamil Hussain

Bradford. *Born* Pakistan, 15 September,
1979
Bantamweight. Ht. 5'7"
Manager C. Aston/T. Gilmour

08.10.01 Andy Greenaway W RSC 3 Barnsley
28.01.02 Neil Read W CO 2 Barnsley
18.03.02 Darren Cleary DREW 4 Crawley
27.04.02 Darren Cleary DREW 4 Huddersfield
22.02.03 Danny Wallace L RSC 1 Huddersfield
Career: 5 contests, won 2, drew 2, lost 1.

Nasser Hussain

Bradford. *Born* Bradford, 26 October, 1974
Middleweight. Ht. 6'0"
Manager T. Miller

10.02.03 Ben Ogden L CO 2 Sheffield
Career: 1 contest, lost 1.

Wasim Hussain

Bradford. *Born* Bradford, 20 July, 1978
Welterweight. Ht. 5'10"
Manager C. Aston

26.02.03 Danny Gwilym L PTS 6 Bristol
13.04.03 Gary Cummings L RSC 2 Bradford
Career: 2 contests, lost 2.

Egbui Ikeagwo

Luton. *Born* Ibaden, Nigeria, 14 October, 1975
L. Heavyweight. Ht. 6'0½"
Manager J. Evans

12.05.03 Michael Matthewsian W PTS 6 Southampton
13.06.03 Leigh Alliss L PTS 6 Bristol
Career: 2 contests, won 1, lost 1.

David Ingleby

Morecambe. *Born* Lancaster, 14 June, 1980
Heavyweight. Ht. 6'3"
Manager B. Myers

09.06.03 Costi Marin L RSC 1 Bradford
Career: 1 contest, lost 1.

Richard Inquieti

Nottingham. *Born* Langley Mill, 19 October, 1968
Welterweight. Ht. 6'3¼"
Manager Self

30.09.96 Peter Varnavas L CO 2 Manchester
20.02.97 Paul Johnson W PTS 6 Mansfield
12.03.97 Tony Smith W RSC 2 Stoke
19.03.97 Andy Peach L RSC 1 Stoke
18.08.97 Jawaid Khaliq L RSC 5 Nottingham
18.09.97 Danny Bell L RSC 1 Alfreton
11.11.97 Trevor Smith L RSC 3 Edgbaston
08.12.97 Danny Bell L RSC 1 Nottingham
07.10.98 Sean O'Sullivan W PTS 6 Stoke
29.10.98 Dean Nicholas L RSC 1 Newcastle
02.12.98 Martyn Thomas L RSC 3 Stoke
25.03.99 Shane Junior L CO 2 Edgbaston
06.03.00 Martyn Bailey W RSC 5 Bradford
28.03.00 David Smales W PTS 6 Hartlepool
05.05.00 Martyn Bailey L PTS 6 Pentre Halkyn
20.11.00 Darren Spencer L RSC 1 Glasgow
04.02.01 Neil Bonner L PTS 6 Queensferry
23.02.01 Dean Nicholas L PTS 6 Irvine
08.03.01 Alan Campbell L PTS 6 Blackpool
01.04.01 Stuart Elwell L PTS 6 Wolverhampton
09.04.01 Gavin Wake L PTS 6 Bradford
20.04.01 Darren Williams L PTS 6 Dublin
03.06.01 Nicky Leech L PTS 6 Hanley
15.09.01 Andrei Ivanov DREW 6 Nottingham
23.09.01 Wayne Shepherd L PTS 6 Shaw
04.10.01 Danny Moir L PTS 6 Sunderland
15.10.01 Danny Parkinson L RSC 1 Bradford
13.11.01 Peter Dunn DREW 6 Leeds
24.11.01 Gavin Wake L PTS 6 Wakefield
06.12.01 John Jackson W RSC 3 Sunderland
08.02.02 Mark Paxford L PTS 6 Preston
18.03.02 Gavin Pearson L PTS 6 Glasgow
22.04.02 Ciaran Duffy L PTS 6 Glasgow
29.04.02 Gavin Pearson L PTS 6 Bradford
09.05.02 Lee Armstrong W RSC 5 Sunderland
03.06.02 Gary Porter L PTS 6 Glasgow
03.08.02 Dean Walker L PTS 6 Derby
28.09.02 Gavin Wake L PTS 6 Wakefield
10.10.02 Mark Paxford L PTS 6 Stoke
18.10.02 Franny Jones L PTS 6 Hartlepool
01.11.02 Michael Jennings L RSC 2 Preston
22.12.02 Danny Moir L RTD 3 Salford

20.01.03 Andy Gibson L RSC 5 Glasgow
14.04.03 Craig Dickson L PTS 4 Glasgow
02.06.03 Jamie Coyle L RSC 2 Glasgow
Career: 45 contests, won 7, drew 2, lost 36.

Andrei Ivanov

Nottingham. *Born* Rostov, Russia, 15 April, 1980
L. Middleweight. Ht. 6'0"
Manager J. Gill

15.09.01 Richard Inquieti DREW 6 Nottingham
10.10.01 Paddy Martin W RSC 2 Stoke
16.11.01 Peter Jackson L PTS 6 West Bromwich
12.12.01 Wayne Shepherd L PTS 6 Nottingham
17.12.01 Tony Montana DREW 6 Cleethorpes
07.02.02 Chris Steele W PTS 6 Stoke
08.03.02 Tony Byrne L PTS 6 Ellesmere Port
15.03.02 Paul Lomax L PTS 6 Spennymoor
02.06.02 Greg Hadwin W PTS 6 Shaw
05.10.02 Andy Halder L PTS 6 Coventry
17.04.03 Sonny Pollard L PTS 6 Hull
08.05.03 Paul Smith L RSC 2 Widnes
Career: 12 contests, won 3, drew 2, lost 7.

Peter Jackson

Halesowen. *Born* Wordsley, 27 January, 1976
S. Middleweight. Ht. 5'11"
Manager Self

28.01.01 Harry Butler W PTS 6 Wolverhampton
01.04.01 Jamie Logan W PTS 6 Wolverhampton
20.05.01 Jamie Logan W PTS 6 Wolverhampton
09.09.01 Neil Bonner W PTS 6 Hartlepool
16.11.01 Andrei Ivanov W PTS 6 West Bromwich
17.02.02 Alan Jones L PTS 6 Wolverhampton
13.04.02 Simon Andrews W PTS 4 Wolverhampton
03.08.02 Jimmy Steel W PTS 4 Blackpool
08.09.02 Mike Duffield W PTS 4 Wolverhampton
02.11.02 Mike Duffield L PTS 10 Wolverhampton
(Vacant Midlands Area S.Middleweight Title)
15.02.03 Simeon Cover L RSC 2 Wolverhampton
Career: 11 contests, won 8, lost 3.

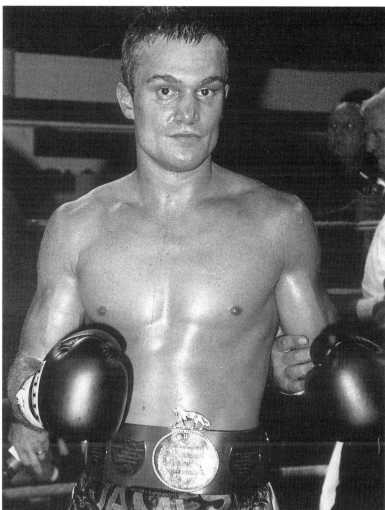

Brett James   Les Clark

Jacklord Jacobs

Kingston. *Born* Nigeria, 1 January, 1970
British Masters Heavyweight Champion.
Ht. 6'1"
Manager J. Evans

03.03.94	Cordwell Hylton W RSC 3 Ebbw Vale
30.07.94	Cordwell Hylton W RSC 4 Bethnal Green
01.11.94	Bobby Anderson DREW 4 Las Vegas, USA
14.11.95	John Pierre W PTS 6 Yarm
05.02.96	Tim Redman DREW 6 Bexleyheath
22.04.96	Chris Woollas DREW 4 Crystal Palace
27.08.96	Andrew Benson L CO 2 Windsor
22.01.00	Pele Reid W RSC 2 Birmingham
23.11.00	Gordon Minors W RSC 4 Bayswater
	(Vacant British Masters Heavyweight Title)
15.03.02	Rene Lillebuen L CO 4 Vilborg, Denmark
25.04.02	Omran Awaldi L RTD 2 Las Vegas, Nevada, USA
07.12.02	Albert Sosnowski L PTS 6 Brentwood
18.02.03	Matt Skelton L RSC 4 Bethnal Green

Career: 13 contests, won 5, drew 3, lost 5.

Hamid Jamali

Birmingham. *Born* Iran, 23 November, 1973
S. Middleweight. Ht. 5'9"
Manager P. Lynch

09.12.02	Dale Nixon W CO 1 Birmingham
24.02.03	Harry Butler W PTS 6 Birmingham

Career: 2 contests, won 2.

Brett James (Eleftheriou)

St Pancras. *Born* London, 3 November, 1975
Welterweight. Ht. 5'8"
Manager E. Maloney

20.01.00	Colin Vidler W PTS 6 Piccadilly
21.02.00	Julian Kacanolli W PTS 4 Southwark
04.07.00	Colin Vidler W PTS 4 Tooting
04.11.00	Matt Scriven W RTD 1 Bethnal Green
20.01.01	Jay Mahoney W PTS 4 Bethnal Green
07.04.01	Paul Denton W PTS 4 Wembley
16.06.01	Karl Taylor DREW 4 Wembley
14.07.01	Lee Williamson W PTS 6 Wembley
29.09.01	Ernie Smith W PTS 6 Southwark
12.02.02	Karl Taylor DREW 4 Bethnal Green
23.06.02	Lee Williamson W PTS 6 Southwark
23.08.02	Brian Coleman W PTS 6 Bethnal Green
25.10.02	David Walker L RSC 4 Bethnal Green
	(Southern Area Welterweight Title Challenge)
15.05.03	Keith Jones W PTS 4 Mayfair

Career: 14 contests, won 11, drew 2, lost 1.

Daniel James

Newmarket. *Born* Lincoln, 15 December, 1975
L. Welterweight. Former Undefeated Southern Area L. Welterweight Champion.
Ht. 5'9"
Manager Self

24.10.96	Shaba Edwards W PTS 6 Wembley
20.11.96	Costas Katsantonis W PTS 6 Wembley
11.02.97	Vince Burns W CO 2 Bethnal Green

03.04.97	Mark Allen W RSC 4 Wembley
09.09.97	Peter Nightingale W PTS 6 Bethnal Green
11.11.97	Marco Fattore W RSC 3 Bethnal Green
13.11.98	Woody Greenaway W PTS 4 Brighton
26.02.99	Tony Swift W PTS 6 Bethnal Green
20.05.99	Delroy Mellis W PTS 4 Barking
16.10.99	Steve Tuckett W RSC 1 Bethnal Green
25.02.00	John Paul Temple W PTS 10 Newmarket
	(Vacant Southern Area L. Welterweight Title)
06.10.00	Stephen Carr L RTD 5 Maidstone
28.09.01	Keith Jones W PTS 6 Millwall
23.11.01	Alan Bosworth L RSC 7 Bethnal Green
	(Elim. British L.Welterweight Title)
19.10.02	Gavin Down L RTD 5 Norwich

Career: 15 contests, won 12, lost 3.

Daniel James   Les Clark

Henry Janes

Cardiff. *Born* Cardiff, 24 May, 1983
S. Featherweight. Ht. 5'7"
Manager P. Boyce

24.05.03	Steve Foster L PTS 6 Bethnal Green
02.06.03	Matt Teague L PTS 6 Cleethorpes
20.06.03	Derry Matthews L RSC 1 Liverpool

Career: 3 contests, lost 3.

Michael Jennings

Chorley. *Born* Preston, 9 September, 1977
WBU Inter-Continental Welterweight Champion. Ht. 5'9½"
Manager F. Warren/B. Hughes

15.05.99	Tony Smith W RSC 1 Blackpool
11.12.99	Lee Molyneux W PTS 4 Liverpool
29.02.00	Lee Molyneux W PTS 6 Widnes
25.03.00	Brian Coleman W PTS 6 Liverpool
16.05.00	Brian Coleman W PTS 6 Warrington
29.05.00	William Webster W PTS 6 Manchester
08.07.00	Paul Denton W PTS 6 Widnes
04.09.00	Mark Ramsey W PTS 6 Manchester
25.11.00	Ernie Smith W PTS 4 Manchester

11.12.00	Paul Denton W PTS 4 Widnes
10.02.01	Mark Haslam W RSC 2 Widnes
07.07.01	David Kirk W PTS 6 Manchester
15.09.01	Gary Harrison W PTS 6 Manchester
09.02.02	James Paisley W RSC 3 Manchester
01.06.02	Lee Williamson W PTS 4 Manchester
28.09.02	Karl Taylor W RSC 4 Manchester
01.11.02	Richard Inquieti W RSC 2 Preston
18.01.03	Lee Williamson W RTD 4 Preston
08.05.03	Jimmy Gould W RTD 6 Widnes
	(Vacant WBU Inter-Continental Welterweight Title)

Career: 19 contests, won 19.

Michael Jennings   Les Clark

(Garnet) Chill John

Brighton. *Born* St Vincent, 11 August, 1977
Lightweight. Ht. 5'7"
Manager R. Davies

22.10.00	Paul Philpott W PTS 6 Streatham
03.02.01	Dave Travers W PTS 4 Brighton
25.02.01	Scott Hocking W RSC 4 Streatham
05.05.01	Woody Greenaway W PTS 6 Brighton
04.07.01	Steve Hanley W PTS 4 Bloomsbury
20.10.01	Mark Halstead W PTS 4 Portsmouth
01.12.01	Pete Buckley W PTS 4 Bethnal Green
13.04.02	Jonathan Thaxton L RSC 2 Norwich
12.07.02	Daniel Thorpe W PTS 4 Southampton
22.09.02	Jason Hall L PTS 6 Southwark
12.10.02	Graham Earl L PTS 10 Piccadilly
	(Southern Area Lightweight Title Challenge)
21.12.02	Lee Meager L RSC 5 Dagenham

Career: 12 contests, won 8, lost 4.

Clint Johnson

Leeds. *Born* Leeds, 13 April, 1974
Cruiserweight. Ht. 6'2"
Manager T. O'Neill

11.11.97	Jon Penn W RSC 2 Leeds
04.12.97	John O'Byrne L PTS 6 Sunderland
17.02.98	Rob Galloway W PTS 6 Leeds
20.09.98	Rob Galloway W PTS 6 Sheffield

29.10.98	Mike White L PTS 6 Newcastle
06.11.98	Gerard Zdiarski W PTS 4 Mayfair
07.12.98	Carl Nicholson W PTS 6 Bradford
16.02.99	Danny Southam L RSC 5 Leeds
15.09.99	Steve Loftus W PTS 6 Harrogate
28.03.00	Martin Jolley W PTS 6 Hartlepool
17.04.00	Alex Mason L PTS 6 Birmingham
20.05.00	Jason Barker L RSC 1 Rotherham
23.10.00	Joe Gillon L CO 4 Glasgow
17.05.01	Paul Bonson L PTS 6 Leeds
18.06.01	Mark Brookes L PTS 6 Bradford
13.09.01	Darren Littlewood W PTS 6 Sheffield
03.11.01	Joe Gillon W CO 3 Glasgow
03.12.01	Jimmy Steel DREW 6 Leeds
15.12.01	Mark Brookes L PTS 4 Sheffield
18.02.02	Billy McClung L PTS 6 Glasgow
01.03.02	Billy McClung L PTS 6 Irvine
16.03.02	Clinton Woods L RSC 3 Bethnal Green
08.10.02	Allan Foster L PTS 6 Glasgow
02.12.02	Greg Scott-Briggs W PTS 6 Leeds
08.02.03	Andrew Lowe L PTS 6 Brentford
05.04.03	Darren Corbett L RSC 4 Belfast

Career: 26 contests, won 10, drew 1, lost 15.

Clive Johnson

Basingstoke. *Born* Botswana, 18 October, 1977
L. Middleweight. Ht. 5'10"
Manager Self

18.02.99	Harry Butler W PTS 6 Barking
20.05.99	Joe Skeldon W PTS 6 Barking
07.08.99	Gareth Hogg L PTS 4 Dagenham
09.10.99	Jamie Moore L RSC 3 Manchester
07.04.00	Kevin Lang W RSC 1 Bristol
08.09.00	Chris Henry L PTS 4 Bristol
06.10.00	Colin Vidler L PTS 6 Maidstone
26.03.01	David Baptiste W PTS 6 Peterborough
28.09.01	John Humphrey L PTS 6 Millwall
09.02.02	Darren McInulty L PTS 8 Coventry
18.01.03	Matthew Hall L PTS 4 Preston

Career: 11 contests, won 4, lost 7.

Alan Jones

Aberystwyth. *Born* Aberystwyth, 6 October, 1976
S. Middleweight. Ht. 6'1"
Manager D. Davies

15.09.01	Martyn Woodward W CO 3 Swansea
21.10.01	Kenny Griffith W RSC 4 Pentre Halkyn
17.02.02	Peter Jackson W PTS 6 Wolverhampton
16.03.02	Allan Foster DREW 6 Northampton
07.10.02	Donovan Smillie W RSC 6 Birmingham
23.02.03	Leigh Wicks W PTS 8 Aberystwyth

Career: 6 contests, won 5, drew 1.

Davey Jones

Scunthorpe. *Born* Grimsby, 30 May, 1977
Middleweight. Ht. 5'11"
Manager J. Rushton

23.09.02	William Webster W PTS 6 Cleethorpes
08.11.02	William Webster W PTS 6 Doncaster
30.11.02	Matt Scriven W PTS 6 Newark
16.12.02	Gary Jones W PTS 6 Cleethorpes
21.02.03	Jimi Hendricks W PTS 6 Doncaster
09.05.03	Wayne Shepherd W PTS 6 Doncaster

Career: 6 contest, won 6.

Franny Jones

Darlington. *Born* Burnley, 7 February, 1981
L. Middleweight. Ht. 5'9½"
Manager M. Marsden

05.05.02	Surinder Sekhon W PTS 6 Hartlepool
28.09.02	Martin Scotland W PTS 6 Wakefield
18.10.02	Richard Inquieti W PTS 6 Hartlepool
27.02.03	Danny Moir DREW 6 Sunderland
17.03.03	Gary Porter W PTS 6 Glasgow

Career: 5 contests, won 4, drew 1.

Gary Jones

Birmingham. *Born* Birmingham, 26 October, 1976
Middleweight. Ht. 6'1"
Manager Self

15.07.00	Danny Smith L RSC 1 Norwich
16.09.00	Liam Lathbury L RSC 5 Bethnal Green
11.12.00	Andrew Facey L PTS 6 Cleethorpes
31.01.01	Paul Buchanan L RTD 1 Piccadilly
16.11.01	Tony Byrne L PTS 6 Preston
06.12.01	Danny Moir L PTS 6 Sunderland
26.09.02	Sonny Pollard L PTS 6 Hull
21.10.02	Dave Pearson W RSC 3 Cleethorpes
30.10.02	Mark Thornton L PTS 4 Leicester Square
29.11.02	Danny Grainger L PTS 6 Hull
16.12.02	Davey Jones L PTS 6 Cleethorpes
24.03.03	Ben Ogden L RSC 6 Barnsley
31.05.03	Dave Pearson W RSC 2 Barnsley
06.06.03	Amer Khan L PTS 6 Hull
13.06.03	Darren McDermott L RSC 1 Queensway

Career: 15 contests, won 2, lost 13.

Henry Jones

Pembroke. *Born* Haverfordwest, 23 December, 1975
L. Welterweight. Ht. 5'0"
Manager M. Goodall

17.06.95	Abdul Mannon W PTS 6 Cardiff
07.07.95	Harry Woods L PTS 4 Cardiff
07.10.95	Frankie Slane L PTS 4 Cardiff
28.11.95	Jason Thomas L PTS 4 Cardiff
20.12.95	Brendan Bryce W PTS 6 Usk
20.03.96	Danny Lawson W CO 1 Cardiff
29.05.96	Ian Turner L PTS 6 Ebbw Vale
02.10.96	Jason Thomas W PTS 4 Cardiff
26.10.96	Danny Costello L RSC 3 Liverpool
29.04.97	Tommy Waite L PTS 4 Belfast
19.05.97	Francky Leroy L RSC 1 Coudekerque, France
02.12.97	Ian Turner L RSC 8 Swansea *(Vacant Welsh Bantamweight Title)*
30.10.98	Tiger Singh W CO 4 Peterborough
05.05.00	Jason Edwards L PTS 6 Pentre Halkyn
28.11.02	Jon Honney L PTS 4 Finchley
23.02.03	David Vaughan L PTS 6 Aberystwyth
10.04.03	Daleboy Rees L PTS 4 Clydach
07.05.03	Jason Nesbitt W PTS 6 Ellesmere Port
15.06.03	Dean Lambert L RSC 4 Bradford

Career: 19 contests, won 6, lost 13.

Keith Jones

Cefn Hengoed. *Born* Bradwell, 4 December, 1968
Welterweight. Former Undefeated British Masters Lightweight Champion. Ht. 5'5¾"
Manager Self

17.05.94	Abdul Mannon L PTS 6 Kettering
13.06.94	G. G. Goddard L PTS 6 Liverpool
21.07.94	G. G. Goddard L RSC 1 Battersea
12.09.94	Marco Fattore L PTS 6 Mayfair
29.09.94	Marlon Ward L PTS 4 Bethnal Green
21.10.94	James Murray L CO 3 Glasgow
27.11.94	Daniel Lutaaya L CO 1 Southwark
03.09.96	Benny May W RSC 2 Bethnal Green
18.09.96	Kevin Sheil W PTS 4 Tylorstown
04.10.96	Andy Ross DREW 6 Pentre Halkyn
18.10.96	Wayne Jones DREW 6 Barnstaple
06.11.96	Robert Grubb W PTS 4 Tylorstown
22.11.96	Tony Mulholland L PTS 4 Liverpool
03.12.96	Alex Moon L RTD 5 Liverpool
21.01.97	Greg Upton DREW 6 Bristol
26.02.97	Greg Upton L PTS 4 Cardiff
07.03.97	Dean Murdoch L PTS 6 Weston super Mare
20.03.97	Kevin Sheil DREW 8 Solihull
04.04.97	Tony Mulholland L PTS 4 Liverpool
22.05.97	Darrell Easton L PTS 4 Southwark
02.10.98	Dean Pithie L PTS 8 Cheshunt
10.10.98	Steve Murray L RSC 4 Bethnal Green
21.11.98	Mat Zegan L PTS 4 Southwark
30.11.98	Eddie Nevins L PTS 4 Manchester
14.12.98	Roy Rutherford L PTS 6 Birmingham
12.01.99	Richard Evatt L PTS 4 Bethnal Green
23.02.99	Simon Chambers DREW 4 Cardiff
12.03.99	Maurycy Gojko L PTS 4 Bethnal Green
09.04.99	Brian Carr L PTS 8 Glasgow
23.04.99	Dewi Roberts W PTS 6 Clydach
01.05.99	Steve Murray L RSC 6 Crystal Palace
04.06.99	Luis Navarro L RSC 5 Malaga, Spain
02.07.99	Alan Bosworth L PTS 6 Bristol
15.07.99	Tomas Jansson L PTS 4 Peterborough
20.08.99	Jason Hall L PTS 6 Bloomsbury
02.10.99	Jason Dee L RSC 5 Cardiff
06.11.99	Isaac Sebaduka W PTS 4 Bethnal Green
14.11.99	Lee Armstrong L PTS 6 Bradford
04.12.99	Franny Hogg L PTS 4 Manchester
14.12.99	Roy Rutherford L PTS 4 Coventry
18.01.00	Carl Greaves L PTS 6 Mansfield
29.01.00	Steve Murray L PTS 4 Manchester
27.02.00	Mark McGowan W RSC 7 Plymouth *(British Masters Lightweight Title Challenge)*
25.03.00	Alex Moon L PTS 6 Liverpool
12.05.00	Jason Cook L PTS 10 Swansea *(Welsh L. Welterweight Title Challenge)*
01.07.00	Matty Leonard W RSC 4 Southwark
25.07.00	Koba Gogoladze L PTS 4 Southwark
19.08.00	Richard Evatt L PTS 6 Brentwood
16.09.00	David Walker L PTS 6 Bethnal Green
21.10.00	Francis Barrett L PTS 4 Wembley
16.11.00	Jimmy Phelan DREW 6 Hull
27.11.00	Kevin Bennett L PTS 4 Birmingham
11.12.00	Steve Saville L PTS 8 Birmingham
02.01.01	Mark Payne L PTS 6 Coventry
15.01.01	Matthew Hatton L PTS 4 Manchester
03.02.01	David Burke L PTS 4 Manchester
10.02.01	Nigel Wright L PTS 4 Widnes
23.02.01	Darren Melville L PTS 4 Barking
29.03.01	Ted Bami L PTS 4 Hammersmith
10.04.01	Dean Pithie L PTS 4 Wembley
22.04.01	Brian Gentry L PTS 8 Streatham
08.05.01	Kevin Bennett L PTS 6 Barnsley
20.05.01	Jimmy Gould L PTS 6 Wolverhampton
02.06.01	Mally McIver L PTS 6 Wakefield
23.06.01	Alan Bosworth L PTS 6 Peterborough
14.07.01	Wayne Rigby L CO 3 Wembley
18.08.01	Steve Conway L PTS 8 Dewsbury
28.09.01	Daniel James L PTS 6 Millwall

20.10.01	Ronnie Nailen L PTS 4 Glasgow	
10.11.01	Colin Lynes L PTS 6 Wembley	
17.11.01	Willie Limond L PTS 4 Glasgow	
24.11.01	Steve Murray L RSC 4 Bethnal Green	
13.04.02	Jimmy Gould L PTS 8 Wolverhampton	
27.04.02	Lee Armstrong L PTS 6 Huddersfield	
09.05.02	Martin Holgate L PTS 6 Leicester Square	
13.06.02	Ajose Olusegun L PTS 6 Leicester Square	
23.06.02	Ted Bami L RSC 4 Southwark	
15.09.02	Ross McCord W RSC 4 Swansea	
	(Vacant Welsh Welterweight Title)	
05.10.02	Tony Conroy W RSC 4 Coventry	

02.11.02	Gary Young L PTS 4 Belfast
16.11.02	Glenn McClarnon L PTS 6 Nottingham
09.12.02	Steve Saville L PTS 8 Birmingham
21.12.02	Francis Barrett L PTS 6 Dagenham
23.02.03	Jason Williams L PTS 10 Aberystwyth
	(Welsh Welterweight Title Defence)
08.03.03	Leo O'Reilly L PTS 6 Bethnal Green
21.03.03	Kevin Bennett L PTS 4 West Bromwich
05.04.03	Gary Greenwood DREW 8 Coventry
12.04.03	Barry Morrison L PTS 4 Bethnal Green
26.04.03	Ajose Olusegun L PTS 6 Brentford
15.05.03	Brett James L PTS 4 Mayfair

Career: 90 contests, won 9, drew 7, lost 74.

Michael Jones   Les Clark

120

Michael Jones

Liverpool. *Born* Liverpool, 14 November, 1974
L.Middleweight. Former Commonwealth L.Middleweight Champion. Ht. 6'0¼"
Manager J. Trickett

15.11.97	Harry Butler W PTS 4 Bristol
17.01.98	Martin Cavey W CO 1 Bristol
07.03.98	Darren McInulty W PTS 4 Reading
25.04.98	Koba Kulu W RSC 3 Cardiff
06.06.98	G. L. Booth W RSC 2 Liverpool
10.10.98	Takaloo W PTS 6 Bethnal Green
19.12.98	Ojay Abrahams W PTS 6 Liverpool
26.06.99	Paul King W PTS 6 Glasgow
11.03.00	Alan Gilbert W RTD 3 Kensington
02.06.00	Mohammed Boualleg W PTS 8 Ashford
03.02.01	Howard Clarke W PTS 4 Manchester
24.04.01	Judicael Bedel W PTS 6 Liverpool
06.10.01	Delroy Mellis W PTS 8 Manchester
10.12.01	Piotr Bartnicki W RSC 4 Liverpool
13.04.02	Mark Richards W RSC 1 Liverpool
28.05.02	Joshua Onyango W RSC 6 Liverpool
	(Commonwealth L. Middleweight Title Challenge)
08.02.03	Howard Clarke W PTS 6 Liverpool
19.04.03	Jamie Moore L PTS 12 Liverpool
	(Commonwealth L.Middleweight Title Defence. Vacant British L.Middleweight Title)

Career: 18 contests, won 17, lost 1.

(Lee) Taz Jones

Abercynon. *Born* Aberdare, 24 August, 1982
Welterweight. Ht. 5'11"
Manager P. Boyce

15.09.02	David White DREW 4 Swansea
02.11.02	Gerard McAuley DREW 4 Belfast
21.12.02	Luke Rudd W RTD 1 Millwall
08.01.03	Elroy Edwards W PTS 6 Aberdare

Career: 4 contests, won 2, drew 2.

(Nathaniel) Nate Joseph

Bradford. *Born* Bradford, 6 June, 1979
Cruiserweight. Ht. 5'10"
Manager C. Aston

20.11.02	Lee Mountford L PTS 6 Leeds
03.02.03	Gary Thompson W PTS 4 Bradford
13.04.03	Eamonn Glennon W PTS 6 Bradford
13.05.03	Lee Mountford W PTS 6 Leeds
31.05.03	Brian Gascoigne L RTD 1 Barnsley

Career: 5 contests, won 3, lost 2.

(Fation) No No Junior (Kacanolli)

Hayes. *Born* Kosovo, 20 October, 1977
Lightweight. Ht. 5'7"
Manager Self

18.11.99	Darren Woodley W RSC 1 Mayfair
19.12.99	Gary Reid W PTS 6 Salford
24.02.00	Barry Hughes L RSC 1 Glasgow
19.04.00	Woody Greenaway W PTS 4 Kensington
30.05.00	Phil Lashley W CO 2 Kensington
24.06.00	Steve Murray L RSC 4 Glasgow
10.03.01	Ivan Kirpa L RSC 1 Bethnal Green
04.10.01	Isaac Sebaduka W RSC 4 Finsbury
18.03.02	Jason Cook L RSC 1 Crawley
08.12.02	Ricky Burns L PTS 8 Glasgow

Career: 10 contests, won 5, lost 5.

Ryan Kasprzycki

Derby. *Born* Chesterfield, 28 April, 1983
S. Middleweight. Ht. 6'0"
Manager M. Shinfield

31.05.03 Patrick Cito L RSC 2 Barnsley
Career: 1 contest, lost 1.

Costas Katsantonis

St Pancras. *Born* London, 16 October, 1970
Welterweight. Former Undefeated Southern
Area L. Welterweight Champion. Ht. 5'8"
Manager Self

09.07.96 Gilbert Eastman L RSC 1 Bethnal
Green
28.09.96 Jason Campbell W PTS 6 Barking
24.10.96 Allan Gray L PTS 6 Mayfair
20.11.96 Daniel James L PTS 6 Wembley
19.02.97 Allan Gray L PTS 6 Acton
30.04.97 Kevin McCarthy W RSC 6 Acton
13.12.97 James Hare L RSC 3 Sheffield
21.02.98 Martin Renaghan L PTS 4 Belfast
21.02.00 Jon Honney W RSC 1 Southwark
13.07.00 Gary Harrison W PTS 4 Bethnal Green
18.11.00 Peter Richardson L PTS 4 Dagenham
17.02.01 Trevor Smith W RSC 3 Bethnal Green
10.04.01 Karl Taylor W PTS 4 Wembley
31.07.01 Woody Greenaway W RSC 4 Bethnal
Green
23.11.01 Iain Eldridge W RSC 1 Bethnal Green
*(Vacant Southern Area L.Welterweight
Title)*
10.05.02 Gary Harrison W PTS 10 Millwall
*(Southern Area L. Welterweight Title
Defence)*
15.10.02 David Keir L PTS 6 Bethnal Green
05.03.03 Paul Denton W PTS 6 Bethnal Green
Career: 18 contests, won 10, lost 8.

Marty Kayes

Downpatrick. *Born* Ashton under Lyne, 16
December, 1975
Bantamweight. Ht. 5'5¹/₂"
Manager Self

27.05.01 Darren Cleary L PTS 4 Manchester
07.07.01 Darren Cleary L PTS 4 Manchester
15.10.01 Darren Taylor L PTS 4 Southampton
26.01.02 Lee Georgiou L PTS 6 Bethnal Green
13.03.02 Sunkanmi Ogunbiyi L PTS 4 Mayfair
30.10.02 Sunkanmi Ogunbiyi L PTS 4 Leicester
Square
16.12.02 Andy Roberts L PTS 6 Cleethorpes
01.02.03 Stevie Quinn L PTS 4 Belfast
21.02.03 Andy Roberts L PTS 6 Doncaster
05.04.03 Stevie Quinn L RSC 5 Belfast
Career: 10 contests, lost 10.

David Kehoe

Northampton. *Born* Northampton, 24
December, 1972
Lightweight. Ht. 5'10¹/₂"
Manager Self

06.02.96 Simon Frailing W CO 1 Basildon
20.04.96 Paul Salmon W PTS 6 Brentwood

12.11.96 Peter Nightingale L PTS 6 Dudley
28.04.97 Craig Kelley L DIS 3 Enfield
18.11.97 Peter Nightingale DREW 4 Mansfield
27.01.98 Paul Miles L PTS 4 Bethnal Green
11.03.98 Trevor Tacy W RTD 1 Bethnal Green
28.03.98 David Thompson W PTS 6 Crystal
Palace
26.05.98 Dave Hinds W RSC 5 Mayfair
08.09.98 Marc Smith W PTS 6 Bethnal Green
12.01.99 Gary Flear L PTS 4 Bethnal Green
25.01.99 Roger Sampson L PTS 4 Glasgow
12.03.99 Jamie McKeever L RSC 2 Bethnal
Green
02.07.99 Mark McGowan L RSC 3 Bristol
*(Vacant British Masters Lightweight
Title)*
13.09.99 Stephen Smith L DIS 2 Bethnal Green

05.10.99 John Humphrey L PTS 4 Bloomsbury
24.10.99 Young Muttley L RTD 1
Wolverhampton
02.12.99 Liam Maltby L PTS 4 Peterborough
19.02.00 Dariusz Snarski DREW 6 Prestwick
10.03.00 Ted Bami L PTS 4 Bethnal Green
17.04.00 Mark Hawthorne L PTS 4 Birmingham
25.07.00 P.J.Gallagher L PTS 6 Southwark
08.09.00 Dariusz Snarski W PTS 4
Hammersmith
27.11.00 Anthony Maynard L RSC 5 Birmingham
16.03.02 Wayne Wheeler DREW 6 Northampton
28.05.02 Ricky Eccleston L RSC 4 Liverpool
14.09.02 Danny Hunt L RSC 3 Bethnal Green
16.11.02 Gwyn Wale L PTS 4 Nottingham
01.02.03 Mark Winters L RSC 2 Belfast
Career: 29 contests, won 7, drew 3, lost 19.

Damaen Kelly   Les Clark

121

David Keir

Liverpool. *Born* Liverpool, 23 September, 1977
Welterweight. Ht. 5'9½"
Manager T. Gilmour

10.12.01	Lee Williamson DREW 4 Liverpool	
11.02.02	Sammy Smith L PTS 6 Southampton	
13.04.02	Lee Williamson W PTS 4 Liverpool	
03.06.02	Paul McIlwaine W CO 2 Glasgow	
23.09.02	Gary Porter L PTS 8 Glasgow	
15.10.02	Costas Katsantonis W PTS 6 Bethnal Green	
15.02.03	Matthew Hatton W RSC 4 Wembley	
28.04.03	Darrell Grafton L DIS 5 Nottingham	
31.05.03	Robert Burton L RSC 9 Barnsley *(Central Area Welterweight Title Challenge)*	

Career: 9 contests, won 4, drew 1, lost 4.

Damaen Kelly

Belfast. *Born* Belfast, 3 April, 1973
WBF Flyweight Champion. Former Undefeated IBO Flyweight Champion. Former Undefeated European Flyweight Champion. Former Undefeated WBC International S. Flyweight Champion. Former British & Commonwealth Flyweight Champion. Ht. 5'5"
Manager Self

27.09.97	Chris Thomas W RSC 1 Belfast
22.11.97	Bojidar Ivanov W CO 1 Manchester
20.12.97	Anthony Hanna W PTS 4 Belfast
14.02.98	Hristo Lessov W RSC 2 Southwark
14.03.98	Mark Reynolds W RSC 4 Bethnal Green
02.05.98	Krasimir Tcholakov W RSC 3 Kensington
26.09.98	Mike Thomas W PTS 6 Uncasville, USA
12.12.98	Alfonso Zvenyika W PTS 12 Chester *(Commonwealth Flyweight Title Challenge)*
13.03.99	Anthony Hanna W PTS 12 Manchester *(Vacant British Flyweight Title. Commonwealth Flyweight Title Defence)*
22.05.99	Keith Knox L RTD 6 Belfast *(British & Commonwealth Flyweight Title Defences)*
16.10.99	Igor Gerasimov W RSC 4 Belfast *(Vacant WBC International S. Flyweight Title)*
12.02.00	Alexander Mahmutov W PTS 12 Sheffield *(European Flyweight Title Challenge)*
12.06.00	Jose Antonio Lopez Bueno W PTS 12 Belfast *(European Flyweight Title Defence)*
30.09.00	Zolile Mbitye W PTS 12 Peterborough *(IBO Flyweight Title Challenge)*
17.02.01	Paulino Villabos W PTS 12 Bethnal Green *(IBO Flyweight Title Defence)*
31.07.01	Sipho Mantyi W RSC 4 Bethnal Green
18.01.02	Simphewe Xabendini W RSC 1 Coventry
21.05.02	Celso Dangud W PTS 12 Custom House *(Vacant WBF Flyweight Title)*
05.10.02	Jovy Oracion W PTS 8 Liverpool

Career: 19 contests, won 18, lost 1.

Colin Kenna

Southampton. *Born* Dublin, 28 July, 1976
Heavyweight. Ht. 6'1"
Manager J. Bishop

25.02.01	Slick Miller W RSC 3 Streatham
22.04.01	Eamonn Glennon W PTS 4 Streatham
15.10.01	Tony Booth W PTS 6 Southampton
11.02.02	Dave Clarke W RSC 4 Southampton
08.04.02	James Gilbert W RSC 1 Southampton
12.07.02	Gary Williams W RSC 3 Southampton
01.11.02	Paul Buttery DREW 6 Preston
17.03.03	Derek McCafferty W PTS 6 Southampton
12.05.03	Paul Bonson W PTS 6 Southampton

Career: 9 contests, won 8, drew 1.

Ryan Kerr

Stirling. *Born* Falkirk, 19 March, 1982
Middleweight. Ht. 5'9"
Manager T. Conroy

17.09.01	Pedro Thompson W RSC 1 Glasgow
04.10.01	Colin McCash W PTS 6 Sunderland
03.11.01	Tomas da Silva W PTS 4 Glasgow
21.02.02	Wayne Shepherd W PTS 6 Sunderland
03.10.02	Steve Timms W RSC 1 Sunderland
05.12.02	Martin Thompson W RSC 4 Sunderland
27.02.03	Surinder Sekhon W PTS 6 Sunderland
17.03.03	Lee Molloy W PTS 8 Glasgow

Career: 8 contests, won 8.

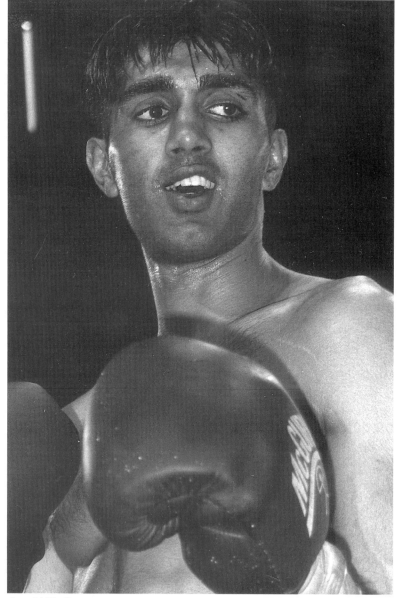

Jawaid Khaliq

Les Clark

Jawaid Khaliq (Akhtar)

Nottingham. *Born* Reading, 30 July, 1970
IBO Welterweight Champion. Former
Undefeated Commonwealth & Midlands
Area Welterweight Champion. Former
Undefeated Midlands Area & WBF
European L. Middleweight Champion.
Ht. 5'10^1/$_2$"
Manager T. Gilmour/C. Aston

18.08.97	Richard Inquieti W RSC 5 Nottingham
13.09.97	Martin Holgate W RSC 6 Millwall
13.12.97	Mark Ramsey DREW 4 Sheffield
07.02.98	Takaloo W RSC 4 Cheshunt
07.03.98	Koba Kulu W PTS 4 Reading
05.09.98	Harry Butler W PTS 4 Telford
03.12.98	Frederic Klose L PTS 8 Epernay, France
27.09.99	Lee Murtagh W RSC 5 Leeds
	(Vacant WBF European L. Middleweight Title)
14.12.99	Dirk Kaltenbach W CO 2 Telde, Gran Canaria
15.01.00	Lee Bird W RSC 4 Doncaster
27.02.00	Jason Collins W PTS 6 Leeds
21.05.00	Dennis Berry W RSC 6 Derby
	(Vacant Midlands Area L. Middleweight Title)
13.08.00	Ernie Smith W RSC 4 Nottingham
	(Vacant Midlands Area Welterweight Title)
28.10.00	Trevor Smith W RSC 1 Coventry
27.11.00	Sean Sullivan W PTS 12 Birmingham
	(Vacant Commonwealth Welterweight Title)
26.02.01	Howard Clarke W PTS 6 Nottingham
11.06.01	Willy Wise W PTS 12 Nottingham
	(IBO Welterweight Title Challenge)
15.09.01	Jacek Bielski W CO 5 Nottingham
	(IBO Welterweight Title Defence)
03.11.01	Luther Smith W RSC 3 Glasgow
23.02.02	Maxim Nesterenko W RSC 12 Nottingham
	(IBO Welterweight Title Defence)
27.07.02	Jose Rosa W PTS 12 Nottingham
	(IBO Welterweight Title Defence)
16.11.02	Roman Dzuman W PTS 12 Nottingham
	(IBO Welterweight Title Defence)
01.03.03	Jan Bergman W RSC 7 Carnival City, South Africa
	(IBO Welterweight Title Defence)

Career: 23 contests, won 21, drew 1, lost 1.

Amer Khan

Sheffield. *Born* Sheffield, 21 February, 1981
L. Heavyweight. Ht. 6'2"
Manager B. Ingle

06.06.03	Gary Jones W PTS 6 Hull

Career: 1 contest, won 1.

John Killian

Finchley. *Born* South Africa, 24 August, 1976
L. Heavyweight. Ht. 6'0"
Manager J. Oyebola

16.06.01	Calvin Stonestreet W PTS 4 Wembley
22.11.01	Dean Ashton W PTS 4 Mayfair
13.06.02	Darren Ashton W PTS 4 Leicester Square
30.10.02	Darren Ashton W PTS 4 Leicester Square

Career: 4 contests, won 4.

Nathan King

Mountain Ash. *Born* Aberdare, 19 March, 1981
L. Heavyweight. Ht. 6'3"
Manager F. Warren/E. Calzaghe

27.01.01	Tony Oakey L PTS 6 Bethnal Green
28.04.01	Pinky Burton W PTS 4 Cardiff
09.06.01	Michael Pinnock W PTS 4 Bethnal Green
09.10.01	Darren Ashton W PTS 6 Cardiff
24.11.01	Peter Haymer W PTS 4 Bethnal Green
12.02.02	Peter Haymer W PTS 4 Bethnal Green
20.04.02	Radcliffe Green W PTS 6 Cardiff
17.08.02	Valery Odin L PTS 6 Cardiff
14.12.02	Paul Bonson L PTS 4 Newcastle
10.04.03	Ovill McKenzie L PTS 4 Clydach
28.06.03	Varuzhan Davtyan W PTS 4 Cardiff

Career: 11 contests, won 7, lost 4.

David Kirk

Sutton in Ashfield. *Born* Mansfield, 5 October, 1974
Welterweight. Former Undefeated WBF
European Welterweight Champion. Ht. 5'8"
Manager Self

01.11.96	Arv Mittoo W PTS 6 Mansfield
04.12.96	Stuart Rimmer W PTS 6 Stoke
20.02.97	Chris Price W PTS 6 Mansfield
16.03.97	Gary Hibbert L PTS 6 Shaw
25.03.97	Miguel Matthews W PTS 6 Wolverhampton
28.04.97	Mark Breslin L PTS 8 Glasgow
06.10.97	Christian Brady L PTS 6 Birmingham
30.10.97	Trevor Tacy L PTS 6 Newark
08.12.97	Nick Hall L PTS 6 Nottingham
12.01.98	Juha Temonen DREW 6 Helsinki, Finland

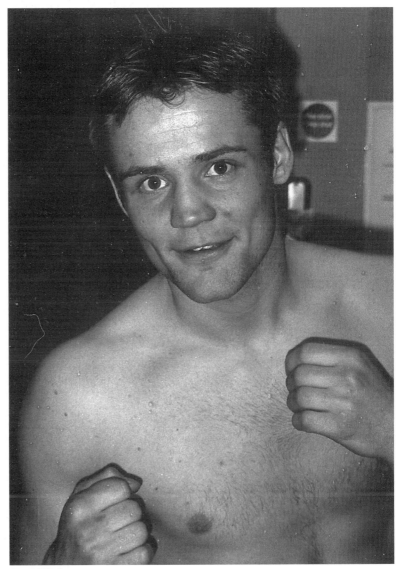

David Kirk   Les Clark

123

24.01.98 Jason Cook L RSC 3 Cardiff
24.02.98 Roy Rutherford L PTS 6 Edgbaston
11.03.98 Patrick Gallagher L PTS 6 Bethnal Green
27.04.98 Tommy Peacock L PTS 6 Manchester
08.05.98 Chris Barnett L PTS 6 Manchester
23.05.98 Graham Earl L PTS 4 Bethnal Green
04.06.98 Mark Richards L PTS 6 Dudley
21.09.98 Steve McLevy L PTS 8 Glasgow
12.10.98 Malcolm Melvin L PTS 10 Birmingham
          (Midlands Area L. Welterweight Title Challenge)
31.10.98 Bernard Paul L PTS 6 Southend
28.11.98 Glenn McClarnon L PTS 4 Belfast
11.12.98 Charlie Kane L PTS 8 Prestwick
20.02.99 Dennis Berry L PTS 10 Thornaby
          (Vacant Continental European Welterweight Title)
09.05.99 Sammy Smith L PTS 6 Bracknell
20.05.99 Steve Brumant W PTS 4 Kensington
05.06.99 Neil Sinclair L PTS 8 Cardiff
11.09.99 Glenn McClarnon L PTS 6 Sheffield
20.10.99 Dave Gibson W PTS 6 Stoke
18.11.99 Adrian Chase W PTS 10 Mayfair
          (Vacant WBF European Welterweight Title)
26.11.99 Gerard Murphy L RTD 3 Hull
25.03.00 Jacek Bielski L PTS 6 Liverpool
29.04.00 Eamonn Magee L RSC 8 Wembley
13.08.00 Ram Singh W PTS 6 Nottingham
09.09.00 Mally McIver L PTS 6 Newark
23.09.00 Steve Murray L PTS 4 Bethnal Green
09.10.00 Steve Saville W PTS 8 Birmingham
19.11.00 Gavin Down L PTS 10 Chesterfield
          (Vacant British Masters L.Welterweight Title)
01.12.00 Alan Bosworth DREW 8 Peterborough
04.02.01 Mark Winters L PTS 6 Queensferry
28.02.01 Ossie Duran L PTS 8 Kensington
          (Vacant WBF European Welterweight Title)
10.03.01 Junior Witter L RSC 2 Bethnal Green
10.04.01 Colin Lynes L PTS 6 Wembley
20.04.01 Mark Winters L PTS 6 Dublin
16.06.01 Oscar Hall L PTS 6 Derby
07.07.01 Michael Jennings L PTS 6 Manchester
28.07.01 Jonathan Thaxton L PTS 4 Wembley
13.09.01 David Walker DREW 8 Sheffield
17.11.01 Kevin McIntyre L PTS 6 Glasgow
24.11.01 Ivan Kirpa L PTS 4 Bethnal Green
08.12.01 Chris Saunders L CO 2 Chesterfield
26.01.02 Colin Lynes L PTS 6 Dagenham
09.02.02 David Barnes L RTD 1 Manchester
11.03.02 Matthew Macklin L PTS 4 Glasgow
25.05.02 Francis Barrett L PTS 6 Portsmouth
08.06.02 Kevin McIntyre L RTD 4 Renfrew
28.09.02 Matthew Hatton W PTS 6 Manchester
22.03.03 Kevin McIntyre L RSC 1 Renfrew
24.05.03 Nigel Wright L PTS 4 Bethnal Green
31.05.03 Sammy Smith L PTS 4 Bethnal Green
08.06.03 Adnan Amar L PTS 6 Nottingham
Career: 60 contests, won 10, drew 3, lost 47.

Neil Kirkwood

Barnsley. *Born* Barnsley, 30 November, 1969
Heavyweight. Former Undefeated Central
Area Heavyweight Champion. Ht. 6'4"
Manager Self

17.03.94 Gary Williams W RSC 1 Lincoln
16.05.94 Joey Paladino W RSC 2 Cleethorpes
26.08.94 Shane Woollas W RSC 6 Barnsley
11.03.95 Carl Gaffney W RSC 2 Barnsley
          (Vacant Central Area Heavyweight Title)

24.10.95 Julius Francis L RSC 7 Southwark
08.10.96 Nikolai Valouev L RSC 2 Battersea
11.04.97 Johnny Davison W RSC 3 Barnsley
23.10.98 Lennox Williams W RSC 2 Wakefield
27.05.00 Albert Sosnowski L RSC 1 Mayfair
21.10.00 Mark Krence L PTS 6 Sheffield
23.11.00 Petr Horacek L RSC 2 Bayswater
16.03.02 Mark Krence L RSC 4 Bethnal Green
28.04.02 Mark Potter L RSC 1 Southwark
08.12.02 Matt Skelton L RSC 1 Bethnal Green
Career: 14 contests, won 6, lost 8.

Eddie Knight

Ashford. *Born* Ashford, 4 October, 1966
Cruiserweight. Former Southern Area
L.Heavyweight Champion. Ht. 5'11"
Manager Self

05.10.92 Shaun McCrory L PTS 6 Bristol
29.10.92 Adrian Wright L PTS 6 Bayswater
25.11.92 Julian Johnson L RSC 2 Mayfair
15.09.93 Terry Duffus W PTS 6 Ashford
09.04.94 John Keeton L RTD 5 Mansfield
27.05.94 Lee Sara W CO 2 Ashford
09.07.94 Mark Delaney L CO 4 Earls Court
17.09.94 Mark Hale W PTS 6 Crawley
13.12.94 Tim Robinson W RTD 2 Potters Bar
09.05.95 Mark Delaney L RSC 2 Basildon
30.01.96 Graham Townsend W PTS 4 Barking
04.03.96 Marko Salminen W RSC 2 Helsinki, Finland
17.12.96 Monty Wright L RSC 5 Bethnal Green
          (Vacant Southern Area L. Heavyweight Title)
20.05.97 Martin Jolley W PTS 6 Gillingham
09.09.97 Graham Townsend W RSC 6 Bethnal Green
16.05.98 Paul Bowen L RSC 3 Bethnal Green
16.01.99 Monty Wright W RSC 2 Bethnal Green
          (Southern Area L. Heavyweight Title Challenge)
02.06.00 Martin Jolley W RSC 5 Ashford
14.10.00 Butch Lesley L RSC 6 Wembley
          (Southern Area L.Heavyweight Title Defence)
08.12.01 Dominic Negus L CO 2 Dagenham
          (Vacant WBU Inter-Continental S.Cruiserweight Title)
15.10.02 Spencer Wilding L RSC 2 Bethnal Green
Career: 21 contests, won 10, lost 11.

Paul Knights

Redhill. *Born* Redhill, 5 February, 1971
Welterweight. Former Undefeated Southern
Area Welterweight Champion. Ht. 5'10"
Manager Self

26.11.91 Steve Hearn W RSC 4 Bethnal Green
19.02.92 Seth Jones W RSC 5 Muswell Hill
16.06.92 Seth Jones W PTS 6 Dagenham
10.11.92 Alex Moffatt W CO 3 Dagenham
30.01.93 Dave Lovell W PTS 6 Brentwood
20.04.93 Mark Allen W PTS 6 Brentwood
26.06.93 Phil Found W PTS 4 Earls Court
28.09.93 Pat Delargy W RSC 3 Bethnal Green
11.01.94 Brian Coleman W RSC 4 Bethnal Green
09.02.94 Mark Allen W RSC 2 Brentwood
19.03.94 Alan Peacock W PTS 6 Millwall
11.06.94 John O. Johnson L PTS 6 Bethnal Green
17.09.94 Dewi Roberts W PTS 6 Crawley
17.02.95 Norman Dhalie W RTD 5 Crawley

16.03.95 Brian Coleman W RSC 2 Basildon
09.05.95 Alan Peacock W PTS 6 Basildon
28.10.95 Tony Swift W PTS 6 Kensington
23.01.96 Karl Taylor DREW 6 Bethnal Green
08.03.97 Dave Brazil L RSC 2 Brentwood
22.04.97 Peter Nightingale W PTS 6 Bethnal Green
11.07.97 Paul Miles W PTS 6 Brighton
27.01.98 Adrian Chase L RSC 1 Bethnal Green
20.05.99 Matthew Barr W RSC 1 Barking
29.06.99 Dean Nicholas W RSC 2 Bethnal Green
01.04.00 Delroy Mellis L RSC 3 Bethnal Green
23.01.01 Brian Coleman W PTS 6 Crawley
01.12.01 Paul Dyer W PTS 10 Bethnal Green
          (Southern Area Welterweight Title Challenge)
02.11.02 Neil Sinclair L RSC 2 Belfast
          (British Welterweight Title Challenge)
Career: 28 contests, won 22, drew 1, lost 5.

Paul Knights   Les Clark

Mark Krence

Chesterfield. *Born* Chesterfield, 24 August, 1976
Midlands Area Heavyweight Champion. Ht. 6'5"
Manager D. Hobson

09.04.00 Slick Miller W PTS 6 Alfreton
21.10.00 Neil Kirkwood W PTS 6 Sheffield
11.12.00 Tony Booth W PTS 6 Sheffield
20.01.01 Nigel Rafferty W PTS 4 Bethnal Green
24.03.01 Mark Williams W PTS 4 Sheffield
27.07.01 Shane Woollas W PTS 4 Sheffield
13.09.01 Luke Simpkin W PTS 4 Sheffield
25.09.01 Darren Chubbs W PTS 4 Liverpool
15.12.01 Eamonn Glennon W RSC 2 Sheffield
16.03.02 Neil Kirkwood W RSC 4 Bethnal Green
11.05.02 Gary Williams W PTS 6 Chesterfield
21.05.02 Audley Harrison L PTS 6 Custom House
03.08.02 Tony Booth W PTS 4 Derby
05.10.02 Gary Williams W RSC 4 Chesterfield
24.01.03 Petr Horacek W RSC 4 Sheffield
18.03.03 Paul Bonson W PTS 4 Reading
10.06.03 Luke Simpkin W RTD 8 Sheffield
          (Vacant Midlands Area Heavyweight Title)
Career: 17 contests, won 16, lost 1.

Jatinder Lal
Wednesfield. *Born* Walsall, 14 September, 1978
L. Welterweight. Ht. 5'8"
Manager D. Bradley

02.11.02 Dai Bando DREW 6 Wolverhampton
Career: 1 contest, drew 1.

Dean Lambert
Bradford. *Born* Bradford, 29 June, 1982
L. Welterweight. Ht. 5'8"
Manager M. Marsden

05.10.02 Arv Mittoo W PTS 4 Huddersfield
22.02.03 Pete Buckley W PTS 4 Huddersfield
15.06.03 Henry Jones W RSC 4 Bradford
Career: 3 contests, won 3.

Dean Lambert   Les Clark

Kenroy Lambert
Luton. *Born* Grenada, WI, 14 March, 1972
L. Middleweight. Ht. 5'9"
Manager Self

17.02.02 Mark Nilsen L PTS 6 Salford
27.03.02 Freddie Yemofio W PTS 6 Mayfair
17.09.02 Leigh Wicks W PTS 6 Bethnal Green
10.10.02 William Webster L PTS 6 Piccadilly
Career: 4 contests, won 2, lost 2.

Scott Lansdowne
Leicester. *Born* Leicester, 11 August, 1972
Midlands Area Cruiserweight Champion &
WBF European S.Cruiserweight Champion.
Ht. 5'10"
Manager Self

15.12.98 Gary Williams W PTS 6 Sheffield
11.09.99 Luke Simpkin W PTS 4 Sheffield
09.12.99 Geoff Hunter W PTS 6 Sheffield
20.05.00 Gary Williams W RSC 1 Leicester
          *(Vacant WBF European
          S. Cruiserweight Title)*
21.10.00 Adam Cale W RSC 5 Sheffield
29.01.01 Nigel Rafferty W PTS 4 Peterborough
28.04.02 Tony Booth L RSC 4 Southwark
23.06.02 Paul Bonson L PTS 4 Southwark
30.11.02 Tony Dowling W RSC 2 Newark
          *(Vacant Midlands Area Cruiserweight
          Title)*
16.03.03 Michael Pinnock W PTS 6 Nottingham
Career: 10 contests, won 8, lost 2.

Dean Larter
Brighton. *Born* Bromley, 4 February, 1975
L. Welterweight. Ht. 5'3½"
Manager L. Wicks

03.12.02 Nathan Ward L PTS 4 Bethnal Green
20.12.02 Robert Lloyd-Taylor L PTS 4
          Bracknell
23.02.03 Anthony Christopher W PTS 6
          Aberystwyth
22.03.03 Gary Young L RSC 2 Renfrew
Career: 4 contests, won 1, lost 3.

Dean Larter   Les Clark

Liam Lathbury
Chippenham. *Born* Bath, 10 February, 1981
S. Middleweight. Ht. 5'10"
Manager C. Sanigar

16.09.00 Gary Jones W RSC 5 Bethnal Green
09.12.00 Freddie Yemofio W PTS 4 Southwark
03.02.01 Rob Stevenson W PTS 6 Brighton
05.05.01 Harry Butler W PTS 6 Brighton
30.09.01 Leigh Wicks W PTS 4 Bristol
13.07.02 Danny Norton L PTS 4
          Wolverhampton
06.03.03 Dale Nixon W PTS 4 Bristol
13.06.03 Jamie Hearn L RSC 4 Bristol
Career: 8 contests, won 6, lost 2.

Scott Lawton
Stoke. *Born* Stoke, 23 September, 1976
Lightweight. Ht. 5'10"
Manager P. Dykes

29.09.01 Dave Hinds W RSC 2 Southwark
08.12.01 Ilias Miah W PTS 4 Dagenham
26.01.02 Pete Buckley W PTS 4 Bethnal Green
26.04.02 Pete Buckley W PTS 4 Coventry
06.09.02 Ben Hudson W PTS 4 Bethnal Green
30.01.03 Dave Stewart L PTS 6 Piccadilly
26.04.03 Chris McDonagh W RSC 2 Brentford
13.06.03 Jason Nesbitt W PTS 6 Queensway
Career: 8 contests, won 7, lost 1.

Kevin Lear
West Ham. *Born* Whitechapel, 3 May, 1977
WBU S. Featherweight Champion.
Ht. 5'7¼"
Manager F. Maloney

13.09.99 Demir Nanev W RSC 4 Bethnal Green
15.11.99 Steve Hanley W RSC 1 Bethnal Green
19.02.00 Lee Williamson W PTS 4 Dagenham
13.03.00 Marco Fattore W PTS 4 Bethnal Green
13.04.00 Rakhim Mingaleev W PTS 4 Holborn
25.07.00 Dave Hinds W PTS 6 Southwark
13.11.00 Pete Buckley W PTS 6 Bethnal Green
10.03.01 Joel Viney W RSC 2 Bethnal Green
26.03.01 Dave Hinds W CO 1 Wembley
03.04.01 Steve Hanley W PTS 6 Bethnal Green
28.07.01 Pete Buckley W PTS 4 Wembley
24.11.01 Gary Flear W PTS 4 Bethnal Green
01.06.02 Michael Gomez W RTD 8 Manchester
          (Vacant WBU S. Featherweight Title)
14.09.02 Kirkor Kirkorov W RTD 7 Bethnal
          Green
          (WBU S.Featherweight Title Defence)
Career: 14 contests, won 14.

Kevin Lear   Les Clark

James Lee (Birchall)
Portsmouth. *Born* Portsmouth, 29
December, 1974
L. Middleweight. Ht. 5'11"
Manager N. Christian

03.11.00 Neil Bonner W PTS 4 Ebbw Vale
11.12.00 Dean Walker W PTS 6 Sheffield
02.02.01 Robert Weston L PTS 6 Portsmouth
16.03.01 Jed Tytler W RSC 3 Portsmouth
15.10.01 Mark Sawyers L PTS 6 Southampton
12.12.01 Darren Williams L PTS 4 Clydach
11.02.02 Danny Gwilym W PTS 6 Southampton
08.04.02 Richie Murray L PTS 6 Southampton
29.09.02 Matt Scriven W RTD 4 Shrewsbury
Career: 9 contests, won 5, lost 4.

Marcus Lee (Marriott)

Bethnal Green. *Born* London, 13 April,
1972
Cruiserweight. Ht. 6'2"
Manager T. Sims

05.03.03 Paul Bonson L PTS 4 Bethnal Green
03.06.03 Scott Baker W RSC 3 Bethnal Green
Career: 2 contests, won 1, lost 1.

Nicky Leech

Nottingham. *Born* Nottingham, 6 June,
1981
Welterweight. Ht. 5'10"
Manager Self

03.06.01 Richard Inquieti W PTS 6 Hanley
06.12.01 Richie Caparelli W PTS 6 Stoke
04.03.02 Norman Dhalie W PTS 6 Birmingham
13.04.02 Tony Montana W PTS 6
Wolverhampton
11.05.03 Chris Steele W PTS 6 Newark
25.10.02 Robert Lloyd-Taylor W PTS 6
Cotgrave
09.12.02 Pete Buckley W PTS 6 Nottingham
Career: 7 contests, won 7.

Matt Legg

Milton Keynes. *Born* Northampton, 17
April, 1976
Heavyweight. Ht. 6'2"
Manager F. Maloney

28.07.01 Mal Rice W PTS 4 Wembley
24.11.01 Tony Booth W PTS 4 Bethnal Green
20.07.02 Dave Clarke W RSC 2 Bethnal Green
12.10.02 Slick Miller L RSC 2 Bethnal Green
Career: 4 contests, won 3, lost 1.

Delroy Leslie

Carshalton. *Born* Jamaica, 22 February,
1970
Middleweight. Former WBF Middleweight
Champion. Former Undefeated Southern
Area Middleweight Champion. Former
Undefeated Southern Area L. Middleweight
Champion. Ht. 5'11½"
Manager J. Harding/B. Baker

29.04.93 Phil Found W PTS 6 Mayfair
14.06.93 Jason Barker W RTD 3 Bayswater
16.09.93 Jamie Davidson W PTS 6 Southwark
06.03.95 Shaun Cogan W RSC 1 Mayfair
20.04.95 Clayton Hollingsworth W PTS 6
Mayfair
23.06.95 Jonathan Thaxton L PTS 6 Bethnal
Green
03.12.95 Adrian Chase W RSC 4 Southwark
02.04.96 Richie Edwards L RSC 3 Southwark
17.06.97 Ben Lockhart W CO 1 Nashville, USA
24.06.97 Julius Brown W CO 2 Nashville, USA
01.07.97 Booker T. Mulline W RSC 3 Nashville,
USA

08.07.97 Dexter Phillips W RSC 3 Nashville,
USA
24.07.97 Cassius Caldwell W CO 2 Cayce, USA
29.07.97 Mario Hereford W RSC 2 Nashville,
USA
05.08.97 Charles Brown W RSC 1 Nashville,
USA
12.08.97 William Lee W RSC 1 Nashville, USA
30.09.97 Don Greene W PTS 4 Nashville, USA
07.10.97 Reggie Strickland W PTS 4 Nashville,
USA
14.10.97 Reggie Strickland W PTS 6 Nashville,
USA
21.10.97 Tim Green W RSC 1 Nashville, USA
04.11.97 Jason Stewart W CO 1 Nashville, USA
25.11.97 Mario Hereford W RSC 3 Nashville,
USA
14.05.98 Matthew Tait L PTS 6 Acton
10.09.98 Ojay Abrahams W PTS 10 Acton
*(Vacant Southern Area
L. Middleweight Title)*
20.08.99 Ensley Bingham L RSC 9 Bloomsbury
*(British L. Middleweight Title
Challenge)*
05.10.99 Matthew Barney W PTS 10
Bloomsbury
*(Vacant Southern Area Middleweight
Title)*
10.03.00 Ruben Groenewald W PTS 12 Bethnal
Green
(Interim WBF Middleweight Title)
08.09.00 Lester Jacobs L RSC 8 Hammersmith
(WBF Middleweight Title Defence)
08.12.00 Darren Ashton W RTD 3 Crystal
Palace
19.05.01 Harry Butler W PTS 6 Wembley
09.09.01 Viktor Fesetchko W PTS 6 Southwark
12.02.02 Jason Collins W RSC 1 Bethnal Green
29.11.02 Scott Dann L RSC 1 Liverpool
*(Final Elim. British Middleweight
Title)*
08.02.03 John Humphrey L RSC 2 Norwich
*(Southern Area L. Middleweight Title
Challenge)*
Career: 34 contests, won 27, lost 7.

Lennox Lewis

Hadley Wood. *Born* London, 2 September,
1965
WBC & IBO Heavyweight Champion.
Former Undefeated WBA & IBF, British,
European & Commonwealth Heavyweight
Champion. Ht. 6'4¾"
Manager Self

27.06.89 Al Malcolm W CO 2 Kensington
21.07.89 Bruce Johnson W RSC 2 Atlantic City,
USA
25.09.89 Andrew Gerrard W RSC 4 Crystal
Palace
10.10.89 Steve Garber W CO 1 Hull
05.11.89 Melvin Epps W DIS 2 Kensington
18.12.89 Greg Gorrell W RSC 5 Kitchener,
Canada
31.01.90 Noel Quarless W RSC 2 Bethnal Green
22.03.90 Calvin Jones W CO 1 Gateshead
14.04.90 Mike Simwelu W CO 1 Kensington
09.05.90 Jorge Dascola W CO 1 Kensington
20.05.90 Dan Murphy W RSC 6 Sheffield
27.06.90 Ossie Ocasio W PTS 8 Kensington
11.07.90 Mike Acey W RSC 2 Mississauga,
Canada
31.10.90 Jean Chanet W RSC 6 Crystal Palace

(European Heavyweight Title Challenge)
06.03.91 Gary Mason W RSC 7 Wembley
*(British Heavyweight Title Challenge.
European Heavyweight Title Defence)*
12.07.91 Mike Weaver W CO 6 Lake Tahoe,
USA
30.09.91 Glenn McCrory W CO 2 Kensington
*(British & European Heavyweight Title
Defence)*
21.11.91 Tyrell Biggs W RSC 3 Atlanta, USA
01.02.92 Levi Billups W PTS 10 Las Vegas,
USA
30.04.92 Derek Williams W RSC 3 Kensington
*(British & European Heavyweight Title
Defence. Commonwealth Heavyweight
Title Challenge)*
11.08.92 Mike Dixon W RSC 4 Atlantic City,
USA
31.10.92 Razor Ruddock W RSC 2 Earls Court
*(Final Elim. WBC Heavyweight Title &
Commonwealth Heavyweight Title
Defence)*
08.05.93 Tony Tucker W PTS 12 Las Vegas,
USA
(WBC Heavyweight Title Defence)
01.10.93 Frank Bruno W RSC 7 Cardiff
(WBC Heavyweight Title Defence)
06.05.94 Phil Jackson W RSC 8 Atlantic City
(WBC Heavyweight Title Defence)
24.09.94 Oliver McCall L RSC 2 Wembley
(WBC Heavyweight Title Defence)
13.05.95 Lionel Butler W RSC 5 Sacramento,
USA
(Elim. WBC Heavyweight Title)
02.07.95 Justin Fortune W RSC 4 Dublin
07.10.95 Tommy Morrison W RSC 6 Atlantic
City, USA
10.05.96 Ray Mercer W PTS 10 New York City,
USA
07.02.97 Oliver McCall W RSC 5 Las Vegas,
USA
(Vacant WBC Heavyweight Title)
12.07.97 Henry Akinwande W DIS 5 Lake
Tahoe, USA
(WBC Heavyweight Title Defence)
04.10.97 Andrew Golota W RSC 1 Atlantic City,
USA
(WBC Heavyweight Title Defence)
28.03.98 Shannon Briggs W RSC 5 Atlantic
City, USA
(WBC Heavyweight Title Defence)
26.09.98 Zeljko Mavrovic W PTS 12 Uncasville,
USA
(WBC Heavyweight Title Defence)
13.03.99 Evander Holyfield DREW 12 New
York City, USA
*(WBC Heavyweight Title Defence.
WBA & IBF Heavyweight Title
Challenges)*
13.11.99 Evander Holyfield W PTS 12 Las
Vegas, USA
*(WBC Heavyweight Title Defence.
WBA & IBF Heavyweight Title
Challenges)*
29.04.00 Michael Grant W CO 2 New York
City, USA
*(WBC & IBF Heavyweight Title
Defences)*
15.07.00 Frans Botha W RSC 2 Millwall
*(WBC, IBF & IBO Heavyweight Title
Defences)*
11.11.00 David Tua W PTS 12 Las Vegas, USA
*(WBC, IBF & IBO Heavyweight Title
Defences)*

22.04.01 Hasim Rahman L CO 5 Brakpan, South
Africa
*(WBC, WBA & IBO Heavyweight Title
Defences)*
17.11.01 Hasim Rahman W CO 4 Las Vegas,
Nevada, USA
*(WBC, IBF & IBO Heavyweight Title
Challenges)*
08.06.02 Mike Tyson W CO 8 Memphis,
Tennessee, USA
*(WBC, IBF & IBO Heavyweight Title
Defences)*
21.06.03 Vitali Klitschko W RSC 6 Los
Angeles, California, USA
*(WBC & IBO Heavyweight Title
Defences)*
Career: 44 contests, won 41, drew 1, lost 2.

Lennox Lewis   Les Clark

Willie Limond

Glasgow. *Born* Glasgow, 2 February, 1979
S. Featherweight. Ht. 5'7"
Manager K. Morrison

12.11.99 Lennie Hodgkins W RTD 1 Glasgow
13.12.99 Steve Hanley W PTS 6 Glasgow
24.02.00 Nigel Senior W RSC 6 Glasgow
18.03.00 Phil Lashley W RSC 1 Glasgow
07.04.00 Jimmy Beech W RSC 2 Glasgow
26.05.00 Billy Smith W PTS 4 Glasgow
24.06.00 Haroon Din W PTS 4 Glasgow
10.11.00 Danny Connelly W PTS 6 Glasgow
17.12.00 Billy Smith W PTS 6 Glasgow
15.02.01 Marcus Portman W PTS 6 Glasgow
03.04.01 Trevor Smith W PTS 4 Bethnal Green
27.04.01 Choi Tseveenpurev W PTS 6 Glasgow
07.09.01 Gary Reid W PTS 8 Glasgow
03.11.01 Rakhim Mingaleev W PTS 6 Glasgow
17.11.01 Keith Jones W PTS 4 Glasgow
11.03.02 Dave Hinds W PTS 6 Glasgow
06.09.02 Assen Vassilev W RSC 3 Glasgow
22.03.03 Jimmy Beech W CO 4 Renfrew
Career: 18 contests, won 18.

Neil Linford

Leicester. *Born* Leicester, 29 September,
1977
L. Heavyweight. Ht. 5'10³/₄"
Manager K. Sanders

30.10.98 Israel Khumalo W RSC 2 Peterborough
30.11.98 David Baptiste W PTS 4 Peterborough
15.12.98 Johannes Ngiba W CO 2 Durban,
South Africa
16.01.99 Dean Powell W RSC 1 Bethnal Green
22.02.99 Leigh Wicks W PTS 4 Peterborough
24.04.99 Adrian Houldey W RSC 2 Peterborough
17.05.99 Jason Barker L RSC 3 Peterborough
15.07.99 Hussain Osman L RSC 5 Peterborough
07.02.00 Mark Dawson W PTS 4 Peterborough
04.03.00 Darren Ashton W PTS 6 Peterborough
25.05.00 Michael Pinnock W PTS 4 Peterborough
30.09.00 Matthew Barney W PTS 10
Peterborough
(Elim. British S. Middleweight Title)
30.11.00 Darren Ashton W PTS 4 Peterborough
29.01.01 Brian Magee L PTS 12 Peterborough
*(Vacant IBO Inter-Continental
S. Middleweight Title)*
23.06.01 Jon Penn W RSC 3 Peterborough
29.09.01 David Starie L RSC 6 Southwark
*(British & Commonwealth
S.Middleweight Title Challenges)*
26.01.02 Ali Forbes W PTS 6 Bethnal Green
23.06.02 Tony Booth W RSC 5 Southwark
22.09.02 Paul Bonson W PTS 6 Southwark
27.10.02 Radcliffe Green DREW 10 Southwark
*(Vacant British Masters L.Heavyweight
Title)*
29.03.03 Tony Oakey L PTS 12 Portsmouth
(WBU L. Heavyweight Title Challenge)
31.05.03 Andrew Lowe L PTS 10 Bethnal Green
(Elim. British L. Heavyweight Title)
Career: 22 contests, won 15, drew 1, lost 6.

Earl Ling

Ipswich. *Born* Kings Lynn, 9 March, 1972
L. Heavyweight. Ht. 5'10"
Manager Self

08.09.92 Eddie Collins W PTS 6 Norwich
11.05.93 Mark Hale L RSC 2 Norwich
12.12.94 Clinton Woods L RSC 5 Cleethorpes
04.12.95 Jeff Finlayson L PTS 6 Manchester
26.02.96 Peter Waudby L PTS 6 Hull
19.03.96 James Lowther L RSC 4 Leeds
16.05.98 Dean Ashton DREW 6 Chigwell
02.07.98 Dean Ashton L RSC 2 Ipswich
17.09.98 Jimmy Steel DREW 6 Brighton
19.01.99 Israel Khumalo L RSC 1 Ipswich
15.07.00 Mike Duffield W PTS 6 Norwich
04.11.00 Andrew Facey L PTS 6 Derby
16.06.01 Andrew Facey DREW 6 Derby
04.07.01 Calvin Stonestreet L PTS 4 Bloomsbury
13.04.02 Simeon Cover W CO 4 Norwich
25.04.02 Lee Whitehead W PTS 6 Hull
21.11.02 Michael Pinnock W PTS 6 Hull
12.04.03 Ryan Walls L RSC 4 Norwich
Career: 18 contests, won 5, drew 3, lost 10.

Wayne Llewelyn

Beckenham. *Born* Greenwich, 20 April, 1970
Heavyweight. Ht. 6'3½"
Manager Self

18.01.92 Chris Coughlan W RSC 3 Kensington
30.03.92 Steve Stewart W RSC 4 Eltham
23.04.92 Gary Charlton W RSC 6 Eltham

10.12.92 Gary McCrory W RSC 2 Glasgow
23.05.93 Cordwell Hylton W PTS 6 Brockley
01.12.93 Manny Burgo W PTS 6 Bethnal Green
14.04.94 Vance Idiens W RSC 1 Battersea
22.05.94 Cordwell Hylton W CO 2 Crystal
Palace
03.05.95 Mitch Rose W PTS 4 New York City,
USA
07.07.95 Vance Idiens W RSC 1 Cardiff
11.08.95 Carlos Monroe W RSC 3 Louisiana,
USA
26.04.96 Steve Garber W CO 1 Cardiff
08.06.96 Dermot Gascoyne W RSC 4 Newcastle
22.03.97 Mike Sedillo W CO 2 Wythenshawe
20.09.97 Michael Murray W RTD 4 Aachen,
Germany
21.03.98 Everton Davis W PTS 8 Bethnal Green
06.06.98 Pele Reid L CO 1 Liverpool
(Elim. British Heavyweight Title)
18.02.99 Derek Williams W RSC 3 Bossier City,
USA
03.06.99 Frankie Swindell L CO 2 Mount
Pleasant, USA
21.08.99 Terry Veners W RSC 3 Coachella, USA
28.11.99 Terry Veners W CO 2 Monterey, USA
10.03.00 William Barima W CO 1 Bethnal
Green
19.03.00 Augustin Corpus L PTS 8 Tunica, USA
14.10.00 Michael Sprott W RSC 3 Wembley
08.12.00 Alex Vasiliev L RSC 1 Crystal Palace
01.04.01 Luke Simpkin W PTS 6 Southwark
19.01.02 Andreas Simon W CO 1 Berlin,
Germany
22.03.02 Ladislav Husarik W PTS 6 Berlin,
Germany
07.09.02 Vladislav Druso W PTS 6 Munich,
Germany
Career: 29 contests, won 25, lost 4.

Robert Lloyd-Taylor (Lloyd)

Hayes. *Born* Perivale, 1 September, 1980
L. Welterweight. Ht. 5'11¼"
Manager G. Taylor

27.09.02 Wayne Wheeler W PTS 6 Bracknell
25.10.02 Nicky Leech L PTS 6 Cotgrave
20.12.02 Dean Larter W PTS 4 Bracknell
26.04.03 Ben Hudson L PTS 4 Brentford
31.05.03 Aidan Mooney W PTS 4 Bethnal
Green
Career: 5 contests, won 3, lost 2.

Robert Lloyd-Taylor   Les Clark

Gary Lockett

Cwmbran. *Born* Pontypool, 25 November, 1976
Middleweight. Former WBO Inter-Continental L. Middleweight Champion. Ht. 5'10"

Manager B. Hearn/B. Devine

06.09.96	Ernie Loveridge W PTS 4 Liverpool
26.10.96	Charlie Paine W RSC 4 Liverpool
24.10.98	Lee Bird W RSC 2 Liverpool
27.02.99	Carl Smith W RSC 2 Bethnal Green
15.05.99	Mike Whittaker W RSC 2 Blackpool
19.06.99	Kid Halls W CO 1 Dublin
09.03.00	Kevin Thompson W CO 2 Liverpool
04.11.00	David Baptiste W PTS 4 Bethnal Green
23.01.01	Abdul Mehdi W RSC 2 Crawley
03.03.01	Hussain Osman W CO 2 Wembley
07.04.01	Howard Clarke W RSC 2 Wembley
08.05.01	Mike Algoet W PTS 6 Barnsley
14.07.01	Howard Clarke W CO 1 Wembley
25.09.01	Denny Dalton W RSC 1 Liverpool
24.11.01	Chris Nembhard W RSC 2 Bethnal Green
09.02.02	Kevin Kelly W CO 4 Manchester
	(Vacant WBO Inter-Continental L.Middleweight Title)
20.04.02	Youri Tsarenko L PTS 12 Cardiff
	(WBO Inter-Continental L.Middleweight Title Defence)
23.11.02	Viktor Fesetchko W PTS 8 Derby
29.03.03	Jason Collins W CO 1 Portsmouth
08.05.03	Yuri Tsarenko W PTS 10 Widnes
28.06.03	Michael Monaghan W PTS 10 Cardiff

Career: 21 contests, won 20, lost 1.

Gary Lockett   Les Clark

Gary Logan

Croydon. *Born* Lambeth, 10 October, 1968
L. Middleweight. Former Southern Area Middleweight Champion. Former Undefeated Southern Area Welterweight Champion. Ht. 5'8¾"

Manager Self

05.10.88	Peppy Muire W RTD 3 Wembley
02.11.88	Tony Gibbs W PTS 6 Southwark
07.12.88	Pat Dunne W PTS 6 Piccadilly
12.01.89	Mike Russell W CO 1 Southwark
20.02.89	Dave Griffiths W RSC 5 Mayfair
29.03.89	Ronnie Campbell W PTS 6 Wembley
10.05.89	Tony Britland W CO 1 Kensington
07.06.89	Davey Hughes W CO 1 Wembley
24.08.89	Mike English W CO 2 Tampa, USA
04.10.89	Simon Eubank W PTS 6 Kensington
12.10.89	Jimmy Thornton W PTS 6 Southwark
08.11.89	Chris Blake L PTS 8 Wembley
10.01.90	Julian Eavis W PTS 8 Kensington
03.03.90	Anthony Joe Travis W CO 5 Wembley
09.05.90	Joseph Alexander W PTS 8 Wembley
13.09.90	Manuel Rojas W PTS 8 Watford
16.01.91	Julian Eavis W RSC 5 Kensington
18.02.91	Gordon Blair W CO 1 Mayfair
25.04.91	Trevor Ambrose W PTS 8 Mayfair
17.10.91	Des Robinson W PTS 8 Southwark
15.10.92	Mick Duncan W PTS 8 Lewisham
17.12.92	Roy Rowland W RSC 4 Wembley
	(Vacant Southern Area Welterweight Title)
23.05.93	Glyn Rhodes W CO 3 Brockley
25.06.93	Gordon Blair W RSC 6 Battersea
14.08.93	Paul King W CO 2 Hammersmith
28.11.93	Paul King W CO 4 Southwark
11.12.93	Horace Fleary W PTS 8 Dusseldorf, Germany
09.02.94	Graham Cheney L RSC 10 Bethnal Green
	(WBC International Welterweight Title Challenge)
29.09.94	Ojay Abrahams W PTS 10 Bethnal Green
	(Southern Area Welterweight Title Defence)
25.10.94	Nick Hall DREW 8 Southwark
02.06.95	Del Bryan L RSC 11 Bethnal Green
	(British Welterweight Title Challenge)
21.03.96	Paul Wesley W PTS 6 Southwark
13.04.96	Ensley Bingham L RSC 6 Wythenshawe
	(British L. Middleweight Title Challenge)
01.04.01	Adrian Kirkbride W RSC 1 Southwark
03.06.01	Spencer Fearon W RSC 2 Southwark
	(Vacant Southern Area Middleweight Title)
28.07.01	Ojay Abrahams W RSC 4 Wembley
28.10.01	Hussain Osman L PTS 10 Southwark
	(Southern Area Middleweight Title Defence)
04.05.02	Takaloo L RSC 10 Bethnal Green
	(WBU L.Middleweight Title Challenge)
20.07.02	Hussain Osman L PTS 12 Bethnal Green
	(Vacant WBO Inter-Continental Middleweight Title)
08.12.02	Wayne Asker W PTS 6 Bethnal Green
18.02.03	Matthew Tait W PTS 8 Bethnal Green

Career: 41 contests, won 33, drew 1, lost 7.

Paul Lomax

Sunderland. *Born* Sunderland, 11 May, 1974
Middleweight. Ht. 6'0½"
Manager T. Callighan

23.07.00	Reece McAllister L PTS 6 Hartlepool
10.06.01	Tony Byrne L PTS 6 Ellesmere Port
17.11.01	Oscar Hall L PTS 4 Dewsbury
09.12.01	Tony Byrne L PTS 6 Blackpool
15.03.02	Andrei Ivanov W PTS 6 Spennymoor
29.04.02	Martyn Bailey DREW 6 Bradford
28.05.02	James Davenport W CO 3 Liverpool
07.05.03	Martyn Bailey L RTD 3 Ellesmere Port
	(British Masters Middleweight Title Challenge)

Career: 8 contests, won 2, drew 1, lost 5.

Paul Lomax   Les Clark

Chris Long

Calne. *Born* Gloucester, 5 March, 1980
L. Welterweight. Ht. 5'9"
Manager T. Woodward

15.05.03 Darren Goode W RSC 1 Clevedon
Career: 1 contest, won 1.

Keith Long

Brixton. *Born* Greenwich, 30 July, 1968
Heavyweight. Ht. 5'11½"
Manager D. Williams/F. Warren

15.02.97	Steve Cranston W PTS 4 Tooting
04.02.99	Gordon Minors W PTS 6 Lewisham
24.04.99	Derek McCafferty L PTS 4 Peterborough
07.08.99	Israel Ajose DREW 6 Dagenham
29.11.99	Mark Potter W PTS 8 Wembley
13.04.00	Harry Senior W PTS 10 Holborn
18.11.00	Luke Simpkin W RSC 3 Dagenham
13.09.01	Mike Holden W PTS 10 Sheffield
	(Elim.British Heavyweight Title)
08.07.02	Alexei Varakin W RSC 4 Mayfair
17.09.02	Danny Williams L PTS 12 Bethnal Green
	(British & Commonwealth Heavyweight Title Challenges)
15.02.03	Slick Miller W RSC 1 Wembley

Career: 11 contests, won 8, drew 1, lost 2.

Keith Long   Les Clark

David Louzan

Guildford. *Born* Coruna, Spain, 3 June,1979
Cruiserweight. Ht. 5'10¾"
Manager J. Pyle

20.06.03 Shpetim Hoti L RSC 5 Gatwick
Career: 1 contest, lost 1.

Andrew Lowe

Hackney. *Born* Hackney, 23 June, 1974
Southern Area L. Heavyweight Champion.
Ht. 5'10"
Manager T. Sims

19.05.01	Rob Stevenson W PTS 4 Wembley
16.06.01	William Webster W RSC 2 Dagenham
20.10.01	Tom Cannon W PTS 4 Glasgow
24.11.01	Paul Wesley W PTS 4 Bethnal Green
15.12.01	Mark Snipe W PTS 4 Chigwell
12.02.02	Ali Forbes W PTS 4 Bethnal Green
04.05.02	Radcliffe Green W PTS 4 Bethnal Green
12.10.02	Paul Bonson W PTS 4 Bethnal Green
08.02.03	Clint Johnson W PTS 6 Brentford
29.03.03	Radcliffe Green W PTS 10 Wembley
	(Vacant Southern Area L.Heavyweight Title)
31.05.03	Neil Linford W PTS 10 Bethnal Green
	(Elim. British L. Heavyweight Title)

Career: 11 contests, won 11.

Craig Lynch

Edinburgh. *Born* Edinburgh, 22 July, 1974
Welterweight. Ht. 6'1"
Manager A. Bowers

13.05.95	James Clamp DREW 6 Glasgow
08.06.95	Gary Silvester W RSC 3 Glasgow
15.09.95	Adam Baldwin W PTS 6 Glasgow
25.11.95	Jim Rock L PTS 4 Dublin
02.03.96	Hughie Davey L PTS 4 Newcastle
08.06.96	Hughie Davey L PTS 4 Newcastle
24.10.96	Pat Wright L PTS 6 Wembley
21.02.02	Gary Firby W RSC 3 Sunderland

26.04.02	Kevin McIntyre L PTS 10 Glasgow
	(Vacant Scottish Welterweight Title)
25.10.02	Joel Ani W PTS 6 Millwall
23.11.02	Bradley Pryce L CO 4 Derby

Career: 11 contests, won 4, drew 1, lost 6.

Craig Lynch   Les Clark

Colin Lynes

Hornchurch. *Born* Whitechapel, 26 November, 1977
L. Welterweight. Former IBO Inter-Continental L. Welterweight Champion.
Ht. 5'7½"
Manager Self

04.06.98	Les Frost W CO 1 Barking
23.07.98	Ram Singh W CO 1 Barking
22.10.98	Brian Coleman W RSC 2 Barking
31.10.98	Marc Smith W PTS 4 Basingstoke
10.12.98	Trevor Smith W RSC 1 Barking
25.02.99	Dennis Griffin W PTS 6 Kentish Town
20.05.99	Mark Haslam W PTS 4 Barking
18.05.00	Jason Vlasman W RSC 2 Bethnal Green
16.09.00	Karl Taylor W PTS 6 Bethnal Green
14.10.00	Brian Coleman W PTS 6 Wembley
09.12.00	Jimmy Phelan W PTS 6 Southwark
17.02.01	Mark Ramsey W PTS 6 Bethnal Green
10.04.01	David Kirk W PTS 6 Wembley
10.11.01	Keith Jones W PTS 6 Wembley
01.12.01	Leonti Voronchuk W PTS 6 Bethnal Green
26.01.02	David Kirk W PTS 6 Dagenham
23.03.02	Peter Dunn W PTS 4 Southwark
18.05.02	Kevin Bennett W RSC 4 Millwall
29.06.02	Ian Smith W RSC 7 Brentwood
21.09.02	Abdelilah Touil W CO 7 Brentwood
07.12.02	Richard Kiley W RSC 9 Brentwood
	(Vacant IBO Inter-Continental L.Welterweight Title)
08.03.03	Samuel Malinga L RTD 8 Bethnal Green
	(IBO Inter-Continental L.Welterweight Title Defence)

Career: 22 contests, won 21, lost 1.

M

Lee McAllister

Aberdeen. *Born* Aberdeen, 5 October, 1982
L. Welterweight. Ht. 5'9"
Manager B. Ingle/F. Warren

19.10.02 Baz Carey W PTS 4 Renfrew
17.11.02 Arv Mittoo W PTS 6 Bradford
23.02.03 Lee Williamson W PTS 6 Shrewsbury
13.04.03 Ernie Smith W PTS 4 Bradford
12.05.03 Ernie Smith W PTS 6 Birmingham
15.06.03 Brian Coleman W PTS 6 Bradford
Career: 6 contests, won 6.

Gerard McAuley

Belfast. *Born* Belfast, 25 February, 1982
L. Middleweight. Ht. 5'9"
Manager M.Callahan/J.Breen/F.Warren
02.11.02 Taz Jones DREW 4 Belfast
Career: 1 contest, drew 1.

Kevin McBride

Clones. *Born* Monaghan, 10 May, 1973
All-Ireland Heavyweight Champion.
Ht. 6'5"
Manager Self

17.12.92 Gary Charlton DREW 6 Barking
13.02.93 Gary Williams W PTS 4 Manchester
15.09.93 Joey Paladino W CO 2 Bethnal Green
13.10.93 Chris Coughlan W PTS 4 Bethnal Green
01.12.93 John Harewood W RSC 3 Bethnal Green
06.05.94 Edgar Turpin W RSC 1 Atlantic City, USA
04.06.94 Roger Bryant W CO 1 Reno, USA
17.06.94 Stanley Wright W PTS 6 Atlantic City, USA
26.08.94 James Truesdale W RSC 3 Upper Marlboro, USA
24.09.94 Graham Arnold W RSC 2 Wembley
12.11.94 Dean Storey W RSC 3 Dublin
10.12.94 John Lamphrey W RSC 1 Portland, USA
07.02.95 Carl Gaffney W RSC 1 Ipswich
03.03.95 Carl McGrew W RSC 5 Boston, USA
22.04.95 Jimmy Harrison W RSC 1 Boston, USA
13.05.95 Atelea Kalhea W CO 1 Sacramento, USA
02.07.95 Steve Garber W RSC 7 Dublin
06.11.96 Shane Woollas W RSC 2 Hull
03.12.96 R.F. McKenzie W RSC 6 Liverpool
21.01.97 Tui Toia W RSC 2 Kansas City, USA
07.02.97 Louis Monaco L RSC 5 Las Vegas, USA
28.04.97 Stoyan Stoyanov W RSC 1 Hull
02.06.97 Paul Douglas W RSC 5 Belfast
 (Vacant All-Ireland Heavyweight Title)
30.08.97 Axel Schulz L RSC 9 Berlin, Germany
22.11.97 Yuri Yelistratov W RSC 1 Manchester
11.04.98 Michael Murray L RSC 3 Southwark
26.06.99 Domingo Monroe W CO 1 Boston, USA
11.08.01 Willie Phillips W PTS 10 Little Rock, Arkansas, USA
01.11.01 Rodney McSwain W PTS 10 Little Rock, Arkansas, USA
18.01.02 Davarryl Williamson L RSC 5 Las Vegas, Nevada, USA
27.05.02 Gary Winmon W RSC 2 Revere, Mass, USA
26.07.02 Reynaldo Minus W RSC 3 Boston, Mass, USA
26.10.02 Craig Tomlinson W RSC 3 Revere, Mass, USA
17.03.03 Najee Shaheed W RSC 7 Brockton, Mass, USA
Career: 34 contests, won 29, drew 1, lost 4.

Kevin McBride   Les Clark

Derek McCafferty

Kettering. *Born* Aberdeen, 10 November, 1968
Heavyweight. Ht. 6'3¹/₂"
Manager K. Sanders

22.02.99 Gary Williams W CO 1 Peterborough
24.04.99 Keith Long W PTS 4 Peterborough
15.07.99 Mike Holden L RSC 1 Peterborough
13.09.99 Mark Potter L PTS 6 Bethnal Green
18.12.99 Georgi Kandelaki L PTS 8 Southwark
22.09.01 Audley Harrison L PTS 6 Newcastle
13.12.01 Pele Reid L RSC 3 Leicester Square
26.01.02 Mark Potter L PTS 6 Bethnal Green
25.05.02 Georgie Kandelaki L RTD 5 Portsmouth
10.07.02 Mark Potter L RSC 6 Wembley
06.09.02 Pele Reid DREW 4 Bethnal Green
17.09.02 Michael Sprott L PTS 8 Bethnal Green
20.12.02 Roman Greenberg L PTS 4 Bracknell
15.02.03 John McDermott L PTS 4 Wembley
17.03.03 Colin Kenna L PTS 6 Southampton
29.03.03 Matthew Ellis L PTS 4 Wembley
16.04.03 Herbie Hide L RSC 7 Nottingham
21.06.03 Danny Venter L PTS 4 Manchester
Career: 18 contests, won 2, drew 1, lost 15.

Enzo Maccarinelli

Swansea. *Born* Swansea, 20 August, 1980
WBU Cruiserweight Champion. Ht. 6'4"
Manager F. Warren

02.10.99 Paul Bonson W PTS 4 Cardiff
11.12.99 Mark Williams W RSC 1 Merthyr
26.02.00 Nigel Rafferty W RSC 3 Swansea
12.05.00 Lee Swaby L CO 3 Swansea
11.12.00 Chris Woollas W PTS 4 Widnes
28.04.01 Darren Ashton W CO 1 Cardiff
09.10.01 Eamonn Glennon W RSC 2 Cardiff
15.12.01 Kevin Barrett W RSC 2 Wembley
12.02.02 James Gilbert W RSC 2 Bethnal Green
20.04.02 Tony Booth W PTS 4 Cardiff
17.08.02 Tony Booth W RTD 2 Cardiff
12.10.02 Dave Clarke W RSC 2 Bethnal Green
18.01.03 Paul Bonson W PTS 4 Preston
29.03.03 Valery Shemishkur W RSC 1 Portsmouth
28.06.03 Bruce Scott W RSC 4 Cardiff
 (Vacant WBU Cruiserweight Title)
Career: 15 contests, won 14, lost 1.

Glenn McClarnon

Lurgan. *Born* Carrickfergus, 1 July, 1974
Welterweight. Ht. 5'9"
Manager Self

20.12.97 Marc Smith W PTS 4 Belfast
21.02.98 Andrew Reed W CO 1 Belfast
28.04.98 Brian Robb W RSC 2 Belfast
18.09.98 Mark Ramsey W PTS 4 Belfast
28.11.98 David Kirk W PTS 4 Belfast
12.01.99 Ram Singh W RSC 1 Bethnal Green
25.01.99 Dean Nicholas W CO 1 Glasgow
12.03.99 Mark Ramsey W PTS 6 Bethnal Green
25.05.99 Steve Tuckett W PTS 6 Mayfair
11.09.99 David Kirk W PTS 6 Sheffield
27.11.99 Chris Barnett L PTS 12 Liverpool
 (Vacant IBO International L. Welterweight Title)
01.04.00 Bernard Paul W RTD 5 Bethnal Green
19.08.00 Brian Coleman W PTS 6 Brentwood
13.10.00 Allan Vester L PTS 12 Aarhus, Denmark
 (IBF Inter-Continental L.Welterweight Title Challenge)
02.12.00 John Ameline L PTS 4 Bethnal Green
03.03.01 Peter Dunn W PTS 4 Wembley
28.04.01 Jacek Bielski L PTS 12 Wroclaw, Poland
 (Vacant IBO Inter-Continental Welterweight Title)
25.09.01 Gary Ryder L PTS 8 Liverpool
10.11.01 Rosalin Nasibulin W PTS 6 Wembley
26.01.02 Kevin Bennett W PTS 8 Dagenham
16.11.02 Keith Jones W PTS 6 Nottingham
22.02.03 Ossie Duran L RSC 2 Huddersfield
Career: 22 contests, won 16, lost 6.

Ross McCord

Swansea. *Born* Swansea, 31 August, 1977
L. Welterweight. Ht. 5'10"
Manager Self

02.12.97 Harry Butler L RSC 3 Swansea
23.05.98 Sony Thind W RSC 1 Bethnal Green
25.11.98 Pedro Thompson W RSC 2 Clydach
07.12.98 Sammy Smith L RSC 5 Acton
20.02.99 Scott Garrett L RSC 2 Thornaby
23.04.99 Darren Underwood W RSC 1 Clydach
31.10.99 Arv Mittoo W PTS 6 Raynes Park
26.02.00 Woody Greenaway L PTS 4 Swansea
09.03.00 Karim Bouali L RSC 1 Bethnal Green
22.07.00 Iain Eldridge L RSC 2 Watford
12.12.00 Woody Greenaway L PTS 6 Clydach
15.09.01 Tony Smith W PTS 6 Swansea
12.12.01 Marcus Portman DREW 4 Clydach
24.04.02 Paul McIlwaine W PTS 4 Dublin
15.09.02 Keith Jones L RSC 4 Swansea
 (Vacant Welsh Welterweight Title)
Career: 15 contests, won 6, drew 1, lost 8.

Wayne McCullough

Belfast. *Born* Belfast, 7 July, 1970
Featherweight. Former WBC Bantamweight
Champion. Former Undefeated NABF
Bantamweight Champion. Ht. 5'7"
Manager Self

23.02.93 Alfonso Zamora W RSC 4 Reseda,
California, USA
18.03.93 Sergio Ramirez W CO 3 NYC, New
York, USA
26.03.93 Oscar Zamora W PTS 4 Reseda,
California, USA
16.04.93 Oscar Lopez W RTD 5 Boston, Mass,
USA
04.05.93 Manuel Ramirez W RSC 5 Denver,
Colorado, USA

01.06.93 Luis Rosario W RSC 6 Philadelphia,
Pennsylvania, USA
18.06.93 Conn McMullen W RSC 3 Belfast
24.09.93 Boualem Belkif W RSC 5 Dublin
16.11.93 Andres Gonzalez W CO 2 Fargo, North
Dakota, USA
30.11.93 Jerome Coffee W RTD 5 Pensacola,
Florida, USA
18.01.94 Javier Medina W RSC 7 Omaha,
Nebraska, USA
(Vacant NABF Bantamweight Title)
19.03.94 Mark Hargreaves W RSC 3 Millwall
17.06.94 Victor Rabanales W PTS 12 Atlantic
City, New Jersey, USA
(NABF Bantamweight Title Defence)
17.09.94 Andres Cazeres W CO 3 Las Vegas,
Nevada, USA

12.11.94 Fabrice Benichou W PTS 10 Dublin
14.03.95 Geronimo Cardoz W RSC 7 Kenner,
Louisiana, USA
30.07.95 Yasuei Yakushiji W PTS 12 Nagoya,
Japan
(WBC Bantamweight Title Challenge)
02.12.95 Johnny Bredahl W RSC 8 Belfast
(WBC Bantamweight Title Defence)
30.03.96 Jose Luis Bueno W PTS 12 Dublin
(WBC Bantamweight Title Defence)
13.07.96 Julio Cesar Cardona W PTS 10 Denver,
Colorado, USA
11.01.97 Daniel Zaragoza L PTS 12 Boston,
Mass, USA
(WBC Bantamweight Title Defence)
17.04.98 Antonio Salas W PTS 10 Uncasville,
Connecticut, USA
19.05.98 Juan Polo Perez W PTS 10 Corpus
Christie, Texas, USA
31.10.98 Prince Naseem Hamed L PTS 12
Atlantic City, New Jersey, USA
(WBO Featherweight Title Challenge)
30.08.99 Len Martinez W PTS 10 Las Vegas,
Nevada, USA
22.10.99 Erik Morales L PTS 12 Detroit,
Michigan, USA
*(WBC S. Bantamweight Title
Challenge)*
12.01.02 Alvin Brown W CO 2 Las Vegas,
Nevada, USA
14.09.02 Johannes Maisa W RSC 4 Bethnal
Green
02.11.02 Nikolai Eremeev W RTD 4 Belfast
22.03.03 Scott Harrison L PTS 12 Renfrew
(WBO Featherweight Title Challenge)
Career: 30 contests, won 26, lost 4.

Darren McDermott

Dudley. *Born* Dudley, 17 July, 1978
S. Middleweight. Ht. 6'1"
Manager D. Powell

26.04.03 Leigh Wicks W PTS 4 Brentford
13.06.03 Gary Jones W RSC 1 Queensway
Career: 2 contests, won 2.

John McDermott

Horndon. *Born* Basildon, 26 February, 1980
Heavyweight. Ht. 6'3"
Manager J. Branch

23.09.00 Slick Miller W RSC 1 Bethnal Green
21.10.00 Gary Williams W PTS 4 Wembley
13.11.00 Geoff Hunter W RSC 1 Bethnal Green
27.01.01 Eamonn Glennon W RSC 1 Bethnal
Green
24.02.01 Alexei Osokin W PTS 4 Bethnal Green
26.03.01 Mal Rice W RSC 2 Wembley
09.06.01 Luke Simpkin W PTS 6 Bethnal Green
22.09.01 Gary Williams W RSC 4 Bethnal
Green
24.11.01 Gordon Minors W RSC 3 Bethnal
Green
19.01.02 Tony Booth W RSC 1 Bethnal Green
04.05.02 Martin Roothman W RSC 1 Bethnal
Green
14.09.02 Alexander Mileiko W RSC 2 Bethnal
Green
12.10.02 Mindaugus Kulikauskas W PTS 6
Bethnal Green
14.12.02 Jason Brewster W RSC 1 Newcastle
15.02.03 Derek McCafferty W PTS 4 Wembley
08.05.03 Konstantin Prizyuk W PTS 8 Widnes
Career: 16 contests, won 16.

Wayne McCullough   Les Clark

Chris McDonagh

Maidenhead. *Born* Ascot, 9 July, 1978
Lightweight. Ht. 5'10"
Manager J. Evans

22.11.01	Jason Gonzales W PTS 6 Paddington
26.01.02	Dave Hinds W PTS 4 Bethnal Green
25.02.02	Baz Carey W PTS 6 Slough
19.03.02	Ray Wood W PTS 4 Slough
25.04.02	Vatche Wartanian L PTS 4 Las Vegas, Nevada, USA
21.05.02	Daniel Thorpe W PTS 6 Custom House
12.07.02	Tony Montana L PTS 4 Southampton
27.09.02	Gareth Wiltshaw L RSC 1 Bracknell
20.12.02	Jason Nesbitt W PTS 6 Bracknell
26.04.03	Scott Lawton L RSC 2 Brentford

Career: 10 contests, won 6, lost 4.

Peter McDonagh

Bermondsey. *Born* Galway, 21 December, 1977
L. Welterweight. Ht. 5'9"
Manager J. Rooney

28.04.02	Arv Mittoo W PTS 6 Southwark
23.06.02	Dave Hinds W PTS 6 Southwark
14.09.02	Pete Buckley W PTS 4 Bethnal Green
27.10.02	Ben Hudson L PTS 6 Southwark
18.02.03	Daffyd Carlin L PTS 4 Bethnal Green
08.04.03	Ben Hudson W PTS 4 Bethnal Green

Career: 6 contests, won 4, lost 2.

Peter McDonagh   Les Clark

Thomas McDonagh

Manchester. *Born* Manchester, 8 December, 1980
L. Middleweight. Ht. 6'0"
Manager F. Warren/B. Hughes

09.10.99	Lee Molyneux W PTS 4 Manchester
06.11.99	Lee Molyneux W PTS 4 Widnes
11.12.99	Arv Mittoo W RSC 2 Liverpool
29.01.00	Emmanuel Marcos W PTS 4 Manchester
29.02.00	William Webster W RTD 2 Widnes
25.03.00	Lee Molyneux W PTS 6 Liverpool

16.05.00	Richie Murray W PTS 4 Warrington
29.05.00	David Baptiste W PTS 6 Manchester
04.09.00	Colin Vidler W PTS 6 Manchester
11.12.00	Richie Murray W PTS 6 Widnes
15.01.01	Kid Halls W RSC 4 Manchester
10.02.01	Harry Butler W PTS 6 Widnes
17.03.01	David Baptiste W PTS 4 Manchester
07.07.01	Paul Denton W PTS 6 Manchester
15.09.01	Howard Clarke W PTS 6 Manchester
27.10.01	Mark Richards DREW 4 Manchester
09.02.02	Tomas da Silva DREW 4 Manchester
01.06.02	Delroy Mellis W PTS 4 Manchester
28.09.02	Brian Coleman W RSC 1 Manchester
18.01.03	Tomas da Silva W PTS 4 Preston
05.04.03	Paul Wesley W PTS 6 Manchester
08.05.03	Marcus Portman W PTS 6 Widnes

Career: 22 contests, won 20, drew 2.

Thomas McDonagh   Harry Goodwin

George McIlroy

Stevenston. *Born* Irvine, 12 March, 1984
Welterweight. Ht. 5'10"
Manager T. Gilmour

28.02.03	Paul McIlwaine W PTS 4 Irvine
14.04.03	Paul Rushton W RSC 1 Glasgow

Career: 2 contests, won 2.

Paul McIlwaine

Belfast. *Born* Belfast, 18 June, 1980
Welterweight. Ht. 5'5"
Manager P. McCausland

16.11.01	Robert Murray L RSC 6 Dublin
21.01.02	Tony McPake L RTD 1 Glasgow
11.03.02	Gary Young L CO 2 Glasgow
24.04.02	Ross McCord L PTS 4 Dublin
03.06.02	David Keir L CO 2 Glasgow
19.10.02	Luke Rudd L RTD 1 Norwich
08.12.02	Barry Hughes L RSC 2 Glasgow
28.02.03	George McIlroy L PTS 4 Irvine
05.04.03	Paul Rushton DREW 4 Belfast
12.04.03	Kevin Anderson L RSC 2 Bethnal Green
15.05.03	Gary Woolcombe L RSC 2 Mayfair
28.06.03	Tony Doherty L RSC 1 Cardiff

Career: 12 contests, drew 1, lost 11.

Paul McIlwaine   Les Clark

Conroy McIntosh

Wolverhampton. *Born* Wolverhampton, 5 December, 1973
Middleweight. Ht. 5'7"
Manager Self

31.01.01	Ross Murray W CO 1 Piccadilly
23.06.01	Francie Doherty L PTS 4 Peterborough
22.09.01	Tomas da Silva L PTS 4 Canning Town
11.02.02	Ty Browne DREW 4 Southampton
03.03.02	Wayne Shepherd DREW 6 Shaw
21.05.02	Ty Browne DREW 4 Custom House
13.07.02	Darren Covill W PTS 4 Wolverhampton
17.11.02	Gary Dixon W RSC 2 Shaw
30.11.02	Andy Halder L PTS 4 Coventry
22.02.03	George Robshaw L PTS 4 Huddersfield
08.03.03	Andy Halder L PTS 4 Coventry
20.06.03	Michael Thomas W CO 2 Gatwick

Career: 12 contests, won 4, drew 3, lost 5.

David McIntyre

Paisley. *Born* Paisley, 20 June, 1978
Featherweight. Ht. 5'5"
Manager K. Morrison

19.10.02	Andy Robinson W PTS 4 Renfrew
14.03.03	Stuart Sanderson L PTS 6 Glasgow
22.03.03	Steve Foster L PTS 4 Renfrew

Career: 3 contests, won 1, lost 2.

Kevin McIntyre

Paisley. *Born* Paisley, 5 May, 1978
Scottish Welterweight Champion.
Ht. 5'10½"
Manager N. Sweeney/A. Morrison

13.11.98	Ray Wood W RSC 4 Glasgow
18.02.99	Gareth Dooley W RSC 3 Glasgow
21.05.99	Mohamed Helel W PTS 6 Glasgow
26.06.99	Karim Bouali L RTD 1 Glasgow
18.03.00	Chris Hall W RSC 3 Glasgow
07.04.00	Dave Travers W RSC 4 Glasgow
26.05.00	Tommy Peacock W RSC 5 Glasgow
24.06.00	Lee Williamson W PTS 4 Glasgow
02.10.00	Paul Denton W PTS 6 Glasgow
10.11.00	Mark Ramsey W RSC 4 Glasgow

17.12.00	Ernie Smith W PTS 6 Glasgow
15.02.01	John Humphrey L RSC 4 Glasgow
27.04.01	Michael Smyth W PTS 6 Glasgow
17.11.01	David Kirk W PTS 4 Glasgow
16.12.01	Manzo Smith W PTS 6 Glasgow
11.03.02	Karl Taylor W PTS 4 Glasgow
26.04.02	Craig Lynch W PTS 10 Glasgow
	(Vacant Scottish Welterweight Title)
08.06.02	David Kirk W RTD 5 Renfrew
19.10.02	Nigel Wright W PTS 6 Renfrew
22.03.03	David Kirk W RSC 1 Renfrew

Career: 20 contests, won 18, lost 2.

Darren McInulty

Bedworth. *Born* Coventry, 10 November, 1970
L. Middleweight. Ht. 5'11"
Manager Self

20.05.91	Derek Binstead DREW 6 Leicester
01.10.91	Dean Carr W PTS 6 Bedworth
11.11.91	Rick North W PTS 6 Stratford upon Avon
20.01.92	Chris Mulcahy W PTS 6 Coventry
04.02.92	Richard O'Brien L PTS 4 Alfreton
11.03.92	Eddie King W RSC 1 Stoke
25.03.92	Robert Riley L PTS 6 Hinckley
28.04.92	Dean Bramhald W PTS 6 Wolverhampton
11.05.92	Dean Bramhald W PTS 6 Coventry
10.09.92	Hughie Davey L PTS 6 Sunderland
23.11.92	Mark Antony W PTS 6 Coventry
02.12.92	Dean Hiscox DREW 6 Bardon
27.02.93	Andreas Panayi L PTS 6 Ellesmere Port
24.03.93	Barry Thorogood L PTS 6 Cardiff
26.04.93	Ricky Mabbett L CO 3 Cleethorpes
17.06.93	Mark Antony L CO 2 Bedworth
25.11.97	Andy Peach W PTS 6 Wolverhampton
15.01.98	Ray Newby L PTS 6 Solihull
27.01.98	Darren Bruce L PTS 4 Bethnal Green
23.02.98	Derek Roche L PTS 6 Glasgow
07.03.98	Michael Jones L PTS 4 Reading
24.03.98	Nick Hall L PTS 6 Wolverhampton
23.04.98	Kevin Lang W PTS 6 Edgbaston
02.05.98	Georgie Smith L CO 2 Kensington
04.06.98	Darren Covill DREW 6 Barking
08.09.98	Darren Bruce L CO 1 Bethnal Green
26.10.98	Christian Brady L PTS 6 Manchester
30.01.99	Takaloo L RSC 5 Bethnal Green
17.11.01	Robbie Sivyer W RSC 1 Coventry
09.02.02	Clive Johnson W PTS 8 Coventry
26.04.02	Jimmy Vincent L CO 6 Coventry
	(British Masters L. Middleweight Title Challenge)
13.07.02	Pedro Thompson DREW 6 Coventry
26.10.02	Lee Blundell L RSC 1 Wigan
	(WBF Inter-Continental Middleweight Title Challenge)

Career: 33 contests, won 11, drew 4, lost 18.

(Malcolm) Mally McIver

Dewsbury. *Born* Dewsbury, 29 January, 1974
Lightweight. Ht. 5'9"
Manager T. Gilmour/C. Aston

12.02.00	Arv Mittoo W PTS 4 Sheffield
27.05.00	Paul Philpott W PTS 4 Southwark
09.09.00	David Kirk W PTS 6 Newark
05.02.01	Alan Kershaw W PTS 4 Hull
24.03.01	Steve Hanley W PTS 4 Sheffield
02.06.01	Keith Jones W PTS 6 Wakefield
18.08.01	Mark Bowen L RSC 1 Dewsbury

17.11.01	Daniel Thorpe W PTS 6 Dewsbury
03.03.02	Dave Hinds W PTS 6 Shaw
02.06.02	Gary Greenwood L RSC 1 Shaw
09.02.03	Jason Nesbitt W PTS 4 Bradford
31.05.03	Peter Allen W PTS 6 Barnsley
09.06.03	Chris Duggan W RSC 3 Bradford

Career: 13 contests, won 11, lost 2.

Jason McKay

County Down. *Born* Craigavon, NI, 11 October, 1977
S. Middleweight. Ht. 6'1"
Manager B. Hearn

18.02.02	Jimmy Steel W PTS 4 Glasgow
11.05.02	Harry Butler W PTS 4 Dagenham

27.07.02	Simon Andrews W RSC 3 Nottingham
08.10.02	Dean Cockburn W PTS 4 Glasgow
08.02.03	William Webster W RSC 1 Liverpool
12.04.03	Marcin Radola W RSC 1 Bethnal Green
17.05.03	Varuzhan Davtyan W PTS 6 Liverpool

Career: 7 contests, won 7.

John Mackay (Mukaya)

Canning Town. *Born* Uganda, 20 October, 1981
S. Bantamweight. Ht. 5'6"
Manager T. Bowers

15.06.01	Chris Emanuele L RSC 4 Millwall
22.09.01	Jason Nesbitt W PTS 4 Canning Town

Jamie McKeever   Les Clark

16.11.01 Willie Valentine W RSC 4 Dublin
28.11.01 Jamie Yelland W RSC 6 Bethnal Green
18.01.02 Stephen Chinnock L PTS 4 Coventry
20.04.02 Dazzo Williams W PTS 6 Wembley
02.06.02 Choi Tseveenpurev L RSC 5 Shaw
27.07.02 Chris Hooper W PTS 4 Nottingham
23.11.02 Henry Castle W RTD 8 Derby
22.03.03 Brian Carr W PTS 8 Renfrew

Career: 10 contests, won 7, lost 3.

Jamie McKeever

Birkenhead. *Born* Birkenhead, 7 July, 1979
Featherweight. Former British
Featherweight Champion. Former
Undefeated Central Area Featherweight
Champion. Ht. 5'6½"
Manager B. Hearn

12.03.98 Dave Hinds W PTS 4 Liverpool
08.04.98 Kid McAuley W RTD 1 Liverpool
06.06.98 Brian Coleman W PTS 4 Liverpool
21.07.98 Stuart Rimmer W PTS 4 Widnes
31.10.98 John T. Kelly L PTS 6 Southend
22.01.99 Garry Burrell W RSC 2 Carlisle
12.03.99 David Kehoe W RSC 2 Bethnal Green
28.05.99 Arv Mittoo W PTS 6 Liverpool
02.10.99 Lee Armstrong DREW 6 Cardiff
27.11.99 Nigel Leake W RSC 2 Liverpool
01.07.00 Gary Flear L PTS 4 Manchester
09.10.00 Marc Callaghan W PTS 6 Liverpool
20.03.01 Craig Docherty L RSC 3 Glasgow
25.09.01 Sebastian Hart W PTS 4 Liverpool
10.12.01 Andrew Ferrans W PTS 6 Liverpool
09.03.02 James Rooney W PTS 6 Manchester
13.04.02 Barry Hawthorne W PTS 6 Liverpool
07.09.02 Tony Mulholland W PTS 10 Liverpool
*(Vacant Central Area Featherweight
Title)*
08.02.03 Tony Mulholland W RSC 6 Liverpool
(Vacant British Featherweight Title)
17.05.03 Roy Rutherford L PTS 12 Liverpool
(British Featherweight Title Defence)

Career: 20 contests, won 15, drew 1, lost 4.

Dave McKenna

Port Glasgow. *Born* Greenock, 8 January,
1975
Heavyweight. Ht. 6'3"
Manager T. Gilmour

18.03.02 Leighton Morgan L DIS 3 Glasgow
14.04.03 Costi Marin L DIS 5 Glasgow

Career: 2 contests, lost 2.

Ovill McKenzie

Canning Town. *Born* Jamaica, 26
November, 1979
L. Heavyweight. Ht. 5'9"
Manager A. Bowers

06.03.03 Leigh Alliss W PTS 4 Bristol
10.04.03 Nathan King W PTS 4 Clydach
02.06.03 Pinky Burton L PTS 8 Glasgow

Career: 3 contests, won 2, lost 1.

Matthew Macklin

Birmingham. *Born* Birmingham, 14 May,
1982
L. Middleweight. Ht. 5'10"
Manager F. Maloney/F. Warren

17.11.01 Ram Singh W RSC 1 Glasgow

15.12.01 Christian Hodorogea W CO 1
Wembley
09.02.02 Dimitri Protkunas W RTD 3
Manchester
11.03.02 David Kirk W PTS 4 Glasgow
20.04.02 Illia Spassov W CO 3 Cardiff
01.06.02 Guy Alton W RSC 3 Manchester
28.09.02 Leonti Voronchuk W RSC 5
Manchester
15.02.03 Ruslan Yakupov W PTS 6 Wembley
24.05.03 Paul Denton W PTS 6 Bethnal Green

Career: 9 contests, won 9.

Tony McPake

Salsburgh. *Born* Bellshill, 3 December,
1979
Lightweight. Ht. 5'10"
Manager T. Gilmour

21.01.02 Paul McIlwaine W RTD 1 Glasgow
18.02.02 Gary Hamilton W PTS 4 Glasgow
15.03.02 Richie Caparelli W RSC 3 Glasgow
22.04.02 Leo Turner W RTD 4 Glasgow
28.05.02 Joel Viney W RSC 1 Liverpool
13.07.02 Dave Hinds W RSC 3 Coventry
21.10.02 Peter Allen W PTS 6 Glasgow
22.03.03 Nigel Senior W PTS 4 Renfrew
28.04.03 Jimmy Beech W PTS 6 Nottingham

Career: 9 contests, won 9.

Tony McPake   Les Clark

Brian Magee

Belfast. *Born* Lisburn, 9 June, 1975
IBO S. Middleweight Champion. Former
Undefeated IBO Inter-Continental
S. Middleweight Champion. Ht. 6'0"
Manager Self

13.03.99 Dean Ashton W RSC 2 Manchester
22.05.99 Richard Glaysher W RSC 1 Belfast
22.06.99 Chris Howarth W RSC 1 Ipswich
13.09.99 Dennis Doyley W RSC 3 Bethnal
Green
16.10.99 Michael Pinnock W RSC 3 Belfast
12.02.00 Terry Morrill W RTD 4 Sheffield
21.02.00 Rob Stevenson W RSC 5 Southwark
20.03.00 Darren Ashton W RTD 5 Mansfield

15.04.00 Pedro Carragher W CO 2 Bethnal
Green
12.06.00 Jason Barker W PTS 8 Belfast
11.11.00 Teimouraz Kikelidze W RSC 4 Belfast
29.01.01 Neil Linford W PTS 12 Peterborough
*(Vacant IBO Inter-Continental
S. Middleweight Title)*
31.07.01 Chris Nembhard W RSC 6 Bethnal
Green
10.12.01 Ramon Britez W CO 1 Liverpool
(IBO S. Middleweight Title Challenge)
18.03.02 Vage Kocharyan W PTS 8 Crawley
15.06.02 Mpush Makambi W RSC 7 Leeds
(IBO S. Middleweight Title Defence)
09.11.02 Jose Spearman W PTS 12 Altrincham
(IBO S. Middleweight Title Defence)
22.02.03 Miguel Jimenez W PTS 12
Huddersfield
(IBO S. Middleweight Title Defence)
21.06.03 Andre Thysse W RSC 10 Manchester
(IBO S.Middleweight Title Defence)

Career: 19 contests, won 19.

Eamonn Magee

Belfast. *Born* Belfast, 13 July, 1971
L.Welterweight. Former Undefeated
Commonwealth L.Welterweight Champion.
Ht. 5'9"
Manager Self

25.11.95 Pete Roberts W CO 4 Dublin
09.03.96 Steve McGovern W PTS 4 Millstreet
28.05.96 John Stovin W RSC 2 Belfast
03.09.96 Kevin McKillan W RTD 4 Belfast
05.11.96 Shaun Stokes W RSC 2 Belfast
28.01.97 Karl Taylor W PTS 6 Belfast
03.03.97 Troy Townsend W RSC 1 Austin, USA
28.03.97 Teddy Reid L PTS 6 Boston, USA
29.04.97 Peter Nightingale W RTD 2 Belfast
02.06.97 Kevin McKillan W RSC 3 Belfast
*(Elim. All-Ireland L. Welterweight
Title)*
14.02.98 Dennis Griffin W RSC 2 Southwark
26.09.98 Allan Hall W RSC 7 York
30.11.98 Paul Burke L PTS 12 Manchester
*(Vacant Commonwealth
L. Welterweight Title)*
22.05.99 Alan Temple W CO 3 Belfast
10.07.99 Karl Taylor W RTD 3 Southwark
13.09.99 Paul Burke W RSC 6 Bethnal Green
*(Commonwealth L. Welterweight Title
Challenge)*
16.10.99 Radoslav Gaidev W RSC 1 Belfast
04.03.00 Joseph Miyumo W RSC 1
Peterborough
*(Commonwealth L. Welterweight Title
Defence)*
29.04.00 David Kirk W RSC 8 Wembley
16.09.00 Pavel Melnikov W PTS 8 Bethnal
Green
11.11.00 Shea Neary W PTS 12 Belfast
*(Commonwealth L. Welterweight Title
Defence)*
13.03.01 Alan Bosworth W RSC 5 Plymouth
12.05.01 Harrison Methula W RSC 7 Plymouth
*(Commonwealth L. Welterweight Title
Defence)*
27.10.01 Matthews Zulu W PTS 12 Manchester
*(Commonwealth L.Welterweight Title
Defence)*
09.02.02 Jonathan Thaxton W RSC 6 Manchester
*(Commonwealth L. Welterweight Title
Defence)*

01.06.02 Ricky Hatton L PTS 12 Manchester
(*WBU L. Welterweight Title Challenge*)
28.09.02 Alan Bosworth W RSC 5 Manchester
14.06.03 Otkay Urkal L PTS 12 Magdeburg,
Germany
(*European L.Welterweight Title
Challenge*)
Career: 28 contests, won 24, lost 4.

(Jason) Jay Mahoney

Peterborough. *Born* Peterborough, 21
September, 1971
Welterweight. Ht 5'8"
Manager Self

05.12.94 Shaun O'Neill W PTS 6 Houghton le
Spring
20.02.95 David Thompson W RSC 4
Manchester
08.03.95 Peter Hickenbottom W PTS 6 Solihull
03.04.95 Blue Butterworth W PTS 6 Manchester
02.10.95 Anthony Maynard L PTS 8
Birmingham
17.12.96 Roger Hunte W RSC 5 Bethnal Green
24.02.97 Chris Barnett W PTS 6 Manchester
02.01.01 Andrzej Butowicz L PTS 4 Coventry
20.01.01 Brett James L PTS 4 Bethnal Green
25.02.01 Gavin Down L RSC 1 Derby

23.06.01 Gary Greenwood W PTS 4
Peterborough
29.03.03 Ross Minter L RSC 2 Portsmouth
08.05.03 Matthew Hatton L PTS 6 Widnes
24.05.03 Ross Minter L PTS 6 Bethnal Green
Career: 14 contests, won 7, lost 7.

(Jasim) Jas Malik

Wandsworth. *Born* Cardiff, 4 April, 1973
L. Welterweight. Ht. 5'11½"
Manager B. Baker

05.03.00 Steve Sharples W RSC 1 Shaw
04.07.00 Dave Travers W PTS 6 Tooting
30.11.00 Jimmy Phelan L RSC 4 Bloomsbury
29.03.01 Darren Melville L RSC 1
Hammersmith
26.09.02 Ben Hudson L CO 3 Fulham
Career: 5 contests, won 2, lost 3.

Abdul Mannon

Burnley. *Born* Bangladesh, India, 5 April,
1972
L. Welterweight. Ht. 5'3"
Manager Self

08.03.94 Brian Eccles W RSC 2 Kettering
17.05.94 Keith Jones W PTS 6 Kettering

27.10.94 Marty Chestnut L DIS 2 Millwall
24.01.95 Chris Lyons W PTS 6 Piccadilly
08.06.95 Brian Carr L PTS 6 Glasgow
17.06.95 Henry Jones L PTS 6 Cardiff
14.10.95 Stephen Smith L RSC 3 Munich,
Germany
22.11.95 Des Gargano L PTS 6 Mayfair
17.12.95 Brian Carr L PTS 8 Glasgow
05.02.96 Benny May L PTS 4 Bexleyheath
16.03.96 Mike Deveney L RSC 2 Glasgow
27.03.01 Dave Travers L PTS 6 Brierley Hill
05.10.02 Wayne Wheeler L RSC 2 Liverpool
Career: 13 contests, won 3, lost 10.

(Constantin) Costi Marin

Huddersfield. *Born* Romania, 11 May, 1970
Heavyweight. Ht. 6'1"
Manager C. Aston

20.11.02 Dave Clarke L RSC 2 Leeds
03.02.03 Steve Tuck W RSC 1 Bradford
26.02.03 Leighton Morgan W RSC 2 Bristol
17.03.03 Dave Clarke L PTS 6 Glasgow
14.04.03 Dave McKenna W DIS 5 Glasgow
28.04.03 Neil Cleaver W RSC 2 Nottingham
02.06.03 Brian Gascoigne L PTS 6 Glasgow
09.06.03 David Ingleby W RSC 1 Bradford
Career: 8 contests, won 5, lost 3.

John Marshall

Glossop. *Born* Australia, 28 May, 1975
L. Welterweight. Ht. 5'6"
Manager T. Gilmour

07.09.01 Dave Stewart L PTS 6 Glasgow
23.12.01 Arv Mittoo W RSC 1 Salford
21.01.02 Gary Hamilton W PTS 4 Glasgow
17.02.02 Joel Viney W RSC 6 Salford
31.05.02 Tony Montana W PTS 6 Hull
21.07.02 Daniel Thorpe W RSC 1 Salford
02.11.02 Mark Winters L RSC 5 Belfast
28.04.03 Young Muttley L RSC 5 Nottingham
Career: 8 contests, won 5, lost 3.

Jay Mahoney   Les Clark

John Marshall   Les Clark

Matthew Marshall

Torquay. *Born* Torquay, 6 February, 1979
Lightweight. Ht. 5'7"
Manager C. Sanigar

12.05.03 Baz Carey W PTS 6 Southampton
Career: 1 contest, won 1.

Derry Matthews

Liverpool. *Born* Liverpool, 23 September, 1983
S. Bantamweight. Ht. 5'8½"
Manager F. Warren/S. Vaughan

18.01.03 Sergei Tasimov W CO 1 Preston
05.04.03 Jus Wallie W PTS 4 Manchester
08.05.03 Steve Gethin W RSC 3 Widnes
20.06.03 Henry Janes W RSC 1 Liverpool
Career: 4 contests, won 4.

Michael Matthewsian

Southampton. *Born* Isle of Wight, 21 March, 1983
L. Heavyweight. Ht. 6'0"
Manager J. Bishop

17.03.03 Dale Nixon DREW 6 Southampton
12.05.03 Egbui Ikeagwo L PTS 6 Southampton
Career: 2 contests, drew 1, lost 1.

(Patrick) P.J. Maxwell (Drinkwater)

Manchester. *Born* USA, 20 March, 1979
Middleweight. Ht. 5'8"
Manager D. Hobson

17.03.98 Danny Thornton W PTS 6 Sheffield
12.08.00 Matthew Ashmole W RSC 3 Wembley
26.03.01 Jason Collins L PTS 4 Wembley
27.10.01 Prince Kasi Kaihau W CO 4 Manchester
09.02.02 Leigh Wicks W PTS 4 Manchester
09.03.03 Surinder Sekhon W RSC 1 Shaw
10.06.03 Andy Halder W RSC 1 Sheffield
Career: 7 contests, won 6, lost 1.

Anthony Maynard

Birmingham. *Born* Birmingham, 12 January, 1972
Midlands Area Lightweight Champion.
Ht. 5'8"
Manager Self

17.10.94 Malcolm Thomas W PTS 6 Birmingham
02.11.94 Dean Phillips W PTS 6 Birmingham
25.01.95 Neil Smith L PTS 6 Stoke
07.02.95 Anthony Campbell W PTS 8 Wolverhampton
08.03.95 Scott Walker W PTS 6 Solihull
28.03.95 Kid McAuley W PTS 8 Wolverhampton
11.05.95 Gary Hiscox W RSC 4 Dudley
06.06.95 Richard Swallow L RSC 2 Leicester
02.10.95 Jay Mahoney W PTS 8 Birmingham
26.10.95 Ray Newby W PTS 8 Birmingham
17.01.96 Tom Welsh W RSC 8 Solihull
06.03.96 G. G. Goddard W RSC 3 Solihull
20.03.97 Richard Swallow W PTS 6 Solihull
24.10.97 Brian Coleman W CO 1 Birmingham
27.03.98 Gary Flear W RSC 9 Telford
(*Vacant Midlands Area Lightweight Title*)
30.05.98 Michael Ayers W PTS 8 Bristol
21.11.98 Stephen Smith L PTS 10 Southwark

27.11.00 David Kehoe W RSC 5 Birmingham
07.04.01 Alfred Kotey L RTD 6 Wembley
(*Vacant WBF Inter-Continental Lightweight Title*)
11.06.01 Woody Greenaway W PTS 4 Nottingham
08.10.01 Bobby Vanzie L RSC 1 Barnsley
(*British Lightweight Title Challenge*)
09.03.02 David Burke L PTS 6 Manchester
09.11.02 Chris Barnett W PTS 6 Altrincham
08.02.03 Gary Hibbert DREW 6 Liverpool
Career: 24 contests, won 17, drew 1, lost 6.

Elvis Mbwakongo

Bermondsey. *Born* Zaire, 12 July, 1979
Welterweight. Ht. 5'10"
Manager E. Maloney

27.10.02 James Paisley W RSC 2 Southwark
08.12.02 Arv Mittoo W PTS 6 Bethnal Green
18.02.03 Neil Murray W RSC 1 Bethnal Green
08.04.03 Pedro Thompson W RSC 1 Bethnal Green
03.06.03 Cristian Hodorogea W PTS 4 Bethnal Green
Career: 5 contests, won 5.

Elvis Mbwakongo   Les Clark

Lee Meager

Salford. *Born* Salford, 18 January, 1978
Lightweight. Ht. 5'8"
Manager Self

16.09.00 Pete Buckley W PTS 4 Bethnal Green
14.10.00 Chris Jickells W PTS 4 Wembley
18.11.00 Billy Smith W RSC 1 Dagenham
09.12.00 Jason Nesbitt W RSC 2 Southwark
05.02.01 Carl Allen DREW 6 Hull
13.03.01 Lennie Hodgkins W RSC 3 Plymouth
12.05.01 Jason White W PTS 4 Plymouth
31.07.01 Steve Hanley W PTS 6 Bethnal Green
13.09.01 Arv Mittoo W PTS 6 Sheffield
16.03.02 Jason Nesbitt W PTS 6 Bethnal Green
10.05.02 Pete Buckley W PTS 6 Bethnal Green
25.10.02 Iain Eldridge W RSC 5 Bethnal Green
21.12.02 Chill John W RSC 5 Dagenham
28.01.03 Carl Allen W PTS 8 Nottingham
Career: 14 contests, won 13, drew 1.

Delroy Mellis

Brixton. *Born* Jamaica, 7 January, 1971
L. Middleweight. Former Undefeated Southern Area L. Middleweight Champion.
Ht. 5'8"
Manager B. Baker

27.02.98 Pat Larner L PTS 4 Brighton
16.04.98 Sonny Thind L RTD 5 Mayfair
09.06.98 Darren Christie L PTS 4 Hull
10.09.98 Paul Miles W RSC 3 Acton
03.10.98 Wayne Asker L PTS 6 Crawley
06.11.98 Darren Bruce L RTD 3 Mayfair
21.01.99 Darren Christie L PTS 6 Piccadilly
04.02.99 Sergei Dzindziruk L RSC 3 Lewisham
24.03.99 Martyn Thomas W RSC 3 Bayswater
20.05.99 Daniel James L PTS 4 Barking
02.07.99 Jason Williams L PTS 6 Bristol
30.09.99 Steve Brumant L PTS 6 Kensington
16.10.99 Jacek Bielski L PTS 4 Bethnal Green
18.11.99 Dennis Griffin W RSC 5 Mayfair
29.11.99 George Scott L PTS 6 Wembley
20.03.00 Lance Crosby L PTS 4 Mansfield
01.04.00 Paul Knights W RSC 3 Bethnal Green
15.05.00 Christian Brady W RSC 6 Birmingham
01.07.00 Cham Joof DREW 6 Southwark
22.07.00 Alan Gilbert W RSC 3 Watford
(*Vacant Southern Area L.Middleweight Title*)
22.10.00 Allan Gray W RSC 6 Streatham
(*Southern Area L.Middleweight Title Defence*)
23.01.01 Alan Gilbert W RSC 3 Crawley
(*Southern Area L. Middleweight Title Defence*)
20.04.01 Chris Nembhard W RSC 8 Millwall
(*Southern Area L. Middleweight Title Defence*)
07.09.01 Jason Collins L DIS 5 Bethnal Green
06.10.01 Michael Jones L PTS 8 Manchester
13.12.01 Ossie Duran L PTS 10 Leicester Square
(*WBF European Welterweight Title Challenge*)
01.06.02 Thomas McDonagh L PTS 4 Manchester
15.06.02 Chardan Ansoula L RTD 4 Tottenham
07.09.02 Jamie Moore L CO 6 Liverpool
Career: 29 contests, won 9, drew 1, lost 19.

Darren Melville

Canning Town. *Born* Tobago, 13 September, 1975
L. Welterweight. Ht. 5'8"
Manager T. Bowers

29.09.00 Lee Williamson W RSC 4 Bethnal Green
10.11.00 Jason McElligott W RSC 2 Mayfair
23.02.01 Keith Jones W PTS 4 Barking
09.03.01 Billy Smith W PTS 4 Millwall
29.03.01 Jas Malik W RSC 1 Hammersmith
20.04.01 Marcus Portman W RSC 3 Millwall
15.06.01 Isaac Sebaduka W PTS 6 Millwall
22.09.01 Steve Murray L PTS 8 Bethnal Green
08.12.01 Christian Hodorogea W PTS 4 Millwall
15.03.02 Mark Ramsey W PTS 6 Millwall
19.04.02 Jan Jensen DREW 6 Aarhus, Denmark
25.10.02 Sergei Starkov W PTS 6 Millwall
21.12.02 Alan Temple W PTS 8 Millwall
29.03.03 Nigel Wright L PTS 6 Portsmouth
Career: 14 contests, won 11, drew 1, lost 2.

Ankar Miah

Covent Garden. *Born* Bangladesh, India, 11 September, 1975
Flyweight. Ht. 5'0"
Manager A. Bowers

04.07.00 Delroy Spencer L RSC 3 Tooting
16.03.01 Gwyn Evans L PTS 6 Portsmouth
06.03.03 Lee Haskins L RSC 1 Bristol
Career: 3 contests, lost 3.

(Elviss) Elvis Michailenko

Canning Town. *Born* Jormala, Latvia, 13 September, 1976
WBA Inter-Continental & WBF European L. Heavyweight Champion. Ht. 5'11½"
Manager A. Bowers

18.05.00 Adam Cale W PTS 4 Bethnal Green
21.09.00 Shpetim Hoti W PTS 4 Bloomsbury
09.10.00 Tony Dodson DREW 6 Liverpool
02.11.00 Freddie Yemofio W PTS 6 Kensington
28.02.01 Tommy Matthews W PTS 4 Kensington
09.03.01 Tommy Matthews W PTS 4 Millwall
20.04.01 Dean Ashton W RSC 4 Millwall
16.06.01 Sven Hamer W RSC 6 Wembley
(Vacant WBF European L. Heavyweight Title)
28.09.01 Paul Bonson W PTS 6 Millwall
23.11.01 Paul Bonson W PTS 6 Bethnal Green
15.03.02 Hastings Rasani W RSC 5 Millwall
29.06.02 Varuzhan Davtyan W PTS 6 Brentwood
03.10.02 Alejandro Lakatus W PTS 12 Madrid, Spain
(Vacant WBA Inter-Continental L.Heavyweight Title)
24.05.03 Hastings Rasini W RSC 4 Bethnal Green
Career: 14 contests, won 13, drew 1.

(Alvin) Slick Miller

Doncaster. *Born* Doncaster, 12 May, 1968
Heavyweight. Ht. 6'2"
Manager J. Rushton

28.04.94 Declan Faherty L RSC 2 Hull
06.10.94 Kent Davis L PTS 6 Hull
17.11.94 Graham Wassell L RSC 1 Sheffield
29.09.95 Mark Richardson L PTS 6 Hartlepool
13.01.96 Geoff Hunter DREW 6 Halifax
13.02.96 Danny Williams L RSC 1 Bethnal Green
15.03.96 Tony Booth L PTS 6 Hull
22.03.96 Tony Dowling L RSC 4 Mansfield
26.09.96 Steve Pettit L PTS 6 Walsall
22.11.96 Tony Booth L RSC 5 Hull
17.03.97 Michael Sprott L CO 1 Mayfair
25.04.97 Pele Lawrence L PTS 6 Mere
16.05.97 Edwin Cleary DREW 6 Hull
20.10.97 Neil Simpson L RTD 1 Leicester
16.04.98 Kevin Mitchell L RSC 2 Mayfair
08.06.98 Stevie Pettit W CO 1 Birmingham
30.11.98 Neil Simpson L CO 3 Leicester
23.01.99 Faisal Mohammed L RSC 2 Cheshunt
25.03.99 Nigel Rafferty L PTS 8 Edgbaston
17.04.99 Ahmet Oner L RSC 1 Dublin
24.10.99 Nigel Rafferty W RSC 4 Wolverhampton
25.03.00 Brian Kilbride W RSC 1 Liverpool
09.04.00 Mark Krence L PTS 6 Alfreton
11.06.00 Glenn Williams L PTS 4 Salford
08.07.00 Tony Dowling L PTS 4 Widnes
23.09.00 John McDermott L RSC 1 Bethnal Green
03.02.01 Scott Baker W RSC 4 Brighton
18.02.01 Hughie Robertson W RSC 2 Southwark
25.02.01 Colin Kenna L RSC 3 Streatham
05.05.01 Danny Percival W CO 1 Edmonton
31.07.01 Neil Hosking L RSC 2 Bethnal Green
07.09.01 Jason Brewster L PTS 6 West Bromwich
22.09.01 Dennis Bakhtov L CO 1 Bethnal Green
22.11.01 Petr Horacek L PTS 4 Paddington
26.01.02 Fola Okesola L RSC 1 Dagenham
23.09.02 Tony Booth L PTS 6 Cleethorpes
12.10.02 Matt Legg W RSC 2 Bethnal Green
27.10.02 Matt Skelton L CO 1 Southwark
09.12.02 Paul Butlin L PTS 6 Nottingham
15.02.03 Keith Long L RSC 1 Wembley
Career: 40 contests, won 7, drew 2, lost 31.

Ross Minter

Crawley. *Born* Crawley, 10 November, 1978
Welterweight. Ht. 5'7¾"
Manager F. Warren/F. Maloney

26.03.01 Brian Coleman W PTS 4 Wembley
05.05.01 Trevor Smith W RTD 3 Edmonton
28.07.01 Lee Williamson W PTS 4 Wembley
24.11.01 Karl Taylor W PTS 4 Bethnal Green
15.12.01 Ernie Smith W RSC 2 Wembley
02.03.02 Paul Denton W PTS 6 Bethnal Green
25.05.02 Howard Clarke L RSC 2 Portsmouth
12.10.02 Dafydd Carlin W RSC 1 Bethnal Green
15.02.03 Karl Taylor W PTS 6 Wembley
29.03.03 Jay Mahoney W RSC 2 Portsmouth
24.05.03 Jay Mahoney W PTS 6 Bethnal Green
Career: 11 contests, won 10, lost 1.

Ross Minter　　　　Philip Sharkey

(Arvill) Arv Mittoo

Birmingham. *Born* Birmingham, 8 July, 1971
L. Middleweight. Ht. 5'8"
Manager Self

31.01.96 Alan Bosworth L PTS 6 Stoke
13.02.96 Tommy Janes L PTS 6 Cardiff
21.02.96 Danny Lutaaya L PTS 6 Piccadilly
20.05.96 Terry Whittaker L CO 5 Cleethorpes
29.06.96 Craig Stanley L PTS 4 Erith
23.09.96 Thomas Bradley DREW 6 Cleethorpes
03.10.96 John T. Kelly L PTS 6 Sunderland
01.11.96 David Kirk L PTS 6 Mansfield
14.11.96 Thomas Bradley L RSC 4 Sheffield
22.05.97 Craig Stanley W RSC 3 Southwark
02.09.97 Trevor Tacy L PTS 6 Manchester
22.09.97 Steve Conway L PTS 6 Cleethorpes
09.10.97 Steve Conway L PTS 6 Leeds
23.10.97 Marco Fattore W PTS 6 Mayfair
11.11.97 Kevin McCarthy L PTS 6 Bethnal Green
03.12.97 Marc Smith W PTS 6 Stoke
31.01.98 Harry Andrews L PTS 4 Edmonton
06.03.98 Gavin McGill W PTS 6 Hull
18.03.98 Marc Smith W PTS 6 Stoke
26.03.98 Danny Lutaaya DREW 6 Piccadilly
11.04.98 Charlie Rumbol L PTS 4 Southwark
21.04.98 Adam Spelling W PTS 4 Edmonton
02.10.98 Sammy Smith L PTS 4 Cheshunt
16.10.98 Mark Haslam L PTS 6 Salford
25.11.98 Brian Coleman L PTS 6 Clydach
27.01.99 Ernie Smith DREW 6 Stoke
26.02.99 Mark Payne L PTS 4 Coventry
17.03.99 Marc Smith L PTS 6 Stoke
20.05.99 John Humphrey L PTS 6 Barking
28.05.99 Jamie McKeever L PTS 6 Liverpool
04.06.99 Oscar Hall L PTS 6 Hull
02.07.99 Wahid Fats L PTS 6 Manchester
21.07.99 Brian Gentry L RSC 4 Bloomsbury
20.10.99 Steve Saville L PTS 8 Stoke
31.10.99 Ross McCord L PTS 6 Raynes Park
15.11.99 Lee Sharp L PTS 6 Glasgow
22.11.99 Mohamed Helel L PTS 6 Piccadilly
29.11.99 Peter Swinney L PTS 4 Wembley
11.12.99 Thomas McDonagh L RSC 2 Liverpool
12.02.00 Mally McIver L PTS 4 Sheffield
10.03.00 Jason Hall W RSC 3 Bethnal Green
08.04.00 Junior Witter L PTS 4 Bethnal Green
17.04.00 Gavin Pearson L PTS 6 Glasgow
13.05.00 Chris Steele W RSC 3 Barnsley
21.05.00 Gavin Down L PTS 6 Derby
06.06.00 Casey Brooke W PTS 6 Brierley Hill
15.07.00 Steve Conway L PTS 6 Norwich
30.09.00 Mark Florian L PTS 4 Peterborough
07.10.00 Jesse James Daniel L PTS 4 Doncaster
16.11.00 Lance Crosby L RSC 3 Hull
28.01.01 Stuart Elwell L PTS 6 Wolverhampton
19.02.01 Lee Sharp L PTS 6 Glasgow
26.02.01 Gavin Wake L PTS 6 Nottingham
24.03.01 Richard Holden L PTS 6 Newark
01.04.01 Babatunde Ajayi L PTS 6 Southwark
20.04.01 Manzo Smith L PTS 4 Millwall
08.05.01 Robert Burton L PTS 4 Barnsley
04.06.01 Gary Porter L PTS 6 Glasgow
16.06.01 Gavin Down L PTS 6 Derby
14.07.01 Lee Byrne L PTS 4 Wembley
13.09.01 Lee Meager L PTS 6 Sheffield
23.09.01 Anthony Christopher DREW 6 Shaw
28.10.01 Peter Swinney L PTS 4 Southwark
16.11.01 Terry Ham L PTS 6 Preston
10.12.01 Lee Armstrong L PTS 6 Bradford
23.12.01 John Marshall L RSC 1 Salford
15.04.02 Chris Duggan L PTS 6 Shrewsbury

28.04.02 Peter McDonagh L PTS 6 Southwark
10.05.02 Oscar Hall L PTS 4 Bethnal Green
15.06.02 Chris Saunders L PTS 6 Norwich
23.06.02 Mark Stupple L PTS 6 Southwark
17.09.02 Gwyn Wale L PTS 6 Bethnal Green
05.10.02 Dean Lambert L PTS 4 Huddersfield
17.11.02 Lee McAllister L PTS 6 Bradford
30.11.02 Richard Swallow L PTS 4 Coventry
08.12.02 Elvis Mbwakongo L PTS 6 Bethnal Green
20.12.02 Nathan Ward L PTS 6 Bracknell
23.02.03 Adnan Amar L PTS 6 Shrewsbury
16.03.03 Jonathan Woollins L PTS 4 Nottingham
08.04.03 Justin Hudson L PTS 4 Bethnal Green
28.04.03 Barry Morrison L RSC 3 Nottingham
03.06.03 Chas Simmonds L PTS 6 Bethnal Green
13.06.03 Gary Steadman L PTS 4 Queensway
Career: 83 contests, won 9, drew 4, lost 70.

(Qais) Mo (Ariya)
Sheffield. *Born* Kabul, Afghanistan, 15 February, 1979
Middleweight. Ht. 5'9"
Manager H. Rainey

12.07.02 Danny Gwilym L PTS 6 Southampton
27.09.02 Freddie Yemofio W PTS 4 Bracknell
09.05.03 Freddie Yemofio W PTS 4 Longford
Career: 3 contests, won 2, lost 1.

Colin Moffett
Belfast. *Born* Belfast, 15 April, 1975
Flyweight. Ht. 5'6"
Manager Self

05.11.96 Shane Mallon W RSC 2 Belfast
28.01.97 Anthony Hanna W PTS 4 Belfast
29.04.97 Gary Hickman W PTS 4 Belfast
02.06.97 Jason Thomas L RSC 3 Belfast
20.12.97 Graham McGrath DREW 4 Belfast
18.09.98 Anthony Hanna DREW 4 Belfast
28.11.98 Shaun Norman W PTS 4 Belfast
31.07.99 Waj Khan W CO 1 Carlisle
16.10.99 Delroy Spencer L PTS 4 Bethnal Green
05.06.00 Keith Knox L RSC 3 Glasgow
02.12.00 Dale Robinson L PTS 4 Bethnal Green
15.09.01 Chris Emanuele L RSC 4 Nottingham
27.04.02 Levi Pattison L RSC 2 Huddersfield
27.07.02 Jim Betts L RSC 3 Nottingham
Career: 14 contests, won 5, drew 2, lost 7.

Danny Moir
Gateshead. *Born* Gateshead, 21 January, 1972
L. Middleweight. Ht. 5'11"
Manager T. Conroy

04.10.01 Richard Inquieti W PTS 6 Sunderland
20.10.01 Lee Minter W RSC 1 Portsmouth
06.12.01 Gary Jones W PTS 6 Sunderland
08.02.02 Colin McCash W RSC 3 Preston
08.03.02 Martyn Bailey L PTS 6 Ellesmere Port
25.03.02 Gavin Pearson L PTS 6 Sunderland
03.10.02 Andy Gibson L RTD 4 Sunderland
22.12.02 Richard Inquieti W RTD 3 Salford
20.01.03 Gary Porter W PTS 6 Glasgow
27.02.03 Franny Jones DREW 6 Sunderland
17.03.03 Ciaran Duffy L PTS 6 Glasgow
29.05.03 Eusebio Montero L PTS 6 Sunderland
09.06.03 Danny Parkinson L PTS 6 Bradford
Career: 13 contests, won 6, drew 1, lost 6.

Lee Molloy
Liverpool. *Born* Liverpool, 20 July, 1974
Middleweight. Ht. 6'1¼"
Manager T. Gilmour

03.12.98 Wayne Shepherd W PTS 4 Mayfair
03.04.99 Adrian Kirkbride W PTS 4 Carlisle
28.05.99 Shaun O'Neill W PTS 4 Liverpool
27.11.99 Martyn Bailey W RSC 2 Liverpool
25.03.00 Danny Thornton L RSC 2 Liverpool
09.10.00 Martin Jolley W PTS 4 Liverpool
26.05.01 Hussain Osman L RSC 1 Bethnal Green
29.11.02 Freddie Yemofio W PTS 4 Liverpool
17.03.03 Ryan Kerr L PTS 8 Glasgow
Career: 9 contests, won 6, lost 3.

Michael Monaghan
Lincoln. *Born* Nottingham, 31 May, 1976
S. Middleweight. Ht. 5'10¾"
Manager Self

23.09.96 Lee Simpkin W PTS 6 Cleethorpes
24.10.96 Lee Bird W RSC 6 Lincoln
09.12.96 Lee Simpkin W PTS 6 Chesterfield
16.12.96 Carlton Williams W PTS 6 Cleethorpes
20.03.97 Paul Miles W PTS 6 Newark
26.04.97 Paul Ryan L RSC 2 Swadlincote
05.07.97 Ali Khattab W PTS 4 Glasgow
18.08.97 Trevor Meikle W PTS 6 Nottingham
12.09.97 Willie Quinn L PTS 6 Glasgow
19.09.97 Roy Chipperfield W PTS 6 Salford
30.09.97 George Richards L PTS 6 Edgbaston
10.03.98 Anthony van Niekirk L RTD 6 Hammanskraal, South Africa
23.04.98 Darren Sweeney L PTS 10 Edgbaston *(Midlands Area Middleweight Title Challenge)*
19.09.98 Jim Rock L PTS 12 Dublin *(Vacant WAA Inter-Continental S. Middleweight Title)*
27.11.98 Mark Dawson W PTS 6 Nottingham
07.12.98 Mike Whittaker L PTS 6 Manchester
14.09.02 Paul Billington W RSC 4 Newark
30.11.02 Gary Beardsley W PTS 6 Newark
24.02.03 Jason Collins W PTS 8 Birmingham
16.04.03 Carl Froch L RSC 3 Nottingham
28.06.03 Gary Lockett L PTS 10 Cardiff
Career: 21 contests, won 12, lost 9.

(Elton) Tony Montana (Gashi)
Sheffield. *Born* Yugoslavia, 5 August, 1982
L. Welterweight. Ht. 5'8"
Manager B. Ingle

24.11.00 Dave Gibson W PTS 6 Hull
03.12.00 Gary Greenwood DREW 6 Shaw
31.01.01 Pete Buckley W PTS 6 Piccadilly
13.02.01 Barrie Kelley L PTS 6 Brierley Hill
06.03.01 Chris Price W PTS 6 Yarm
18.03.01 Ray Wood DREW 6 Shaw
26.03.01 Francis Barrett L PTS 4 Wembley
24.05.01 Ajose Olusegun L RSC 1 Kensington
07.09.01 Mark Hawthorne L CO 3 Bethnal Green
16.11.01 Young Muttley L PTS 6 West Bromwich
30.11.01 Brian Gifford W PTS 6 Hull
17.12.01 Andrei Ivanov DREW 6 Cleethorpes
31.01.02 James Paisley W PTS 6 Piccadilly
11.02.02 Ernie Smith W PTS 6 Shrewsbury
13.04.02 Nicky Leech L PTS 6 Wolverhampton
11.05.02 Robbie Sivyer L PTS 6 Chesterfield
31.05.02 John Marshall L PTS 6 Hull
12.07.02 Chris McDonagh W PTS 4 Southampton
08.09.02 Jimmy Gould W PTS 8 Wolverhampton
21.09.02 Christophe de Busillet L PTS 6 Norwich
02.11.02 Young Muttley L PTS 4 Wolverhampton
22.12.02 Mark Haslam W PTS 6 Salford
28.01.03 Gavin Down L PTS 4 Nottingham
22.03.03 George Telfer W PTS 4 Renfrew
Career: 24 contests, won 10, drew 3, lost 11.

Alex Moon
Liverpool. *Born* Fazackerley, 17 November, 1971
S. Featherweight. Former Commonwealth S. Featherweight Champion. Former Undefeated WBU Inter-Continental Featherweight Champion. Ht. 5'7½"
Manager T. Gilmour

08.09.95 Marty Chestnut W RSC 3 Liverpool
24.11.95 G. G. Goddard L RTD 2 Chester
03.02.96 Chris Price W RSC 2 Liverpool
06.09.96 Jason Squire W PTS 4 Liverpool
26.10.96 Kelton McKenzie W RSC 3 Liverpool
03.12.96 Keith Jones W RTD 5 Liverpool
01.03.97 David Jeffrey W RSC 2 Liverpool
21.05.97 Miguel Matthews DREW 4 Liverpool
26.09.97 Bamana Dibateza W PTS 6 Liverpool
28.11.97 Elvis Parsley DREW 6 Bethnal Green
12.03.98 Deva Reymond W PTS 8 Liverpool
08.04.98 Stefy Bull W RSC 3 Liverpool
21.07.98 Georghe Parashiv W PTS 8 Widnes
24.10.98 Khayelethu Booi W PTS 12 Liverpool *(Vacant WBU Inter-Continental Featherweight Title)*
13.02.99 Jonjo Irwin L PTS 12 Newcastle *(British Featherweight Title Challenge)*
15.05.99 Jason Thomas W PTS 8 Blackpool
29.02.00 Craig Spacie L PTS 6 Widnes
25.03.00 Keith Jones W PTS 6 Liverpool
19.02.01 Anthony Hanna W PTS 6 Glasgow
20.03.01 Charles Shepherd W PTS 12 Glasgow *(Vacant Commonwealth S. Featherweight Title)*
24.04.01 Karim Nashar W PTS 12 Liverpool *(Commonwealth S. Featherweight Title Defence)*
06.10.01 Affif Djelti L RSC 6 Manchester *(IBO S.Featherweight Title Challenge)*
23.02.02 Pete Buckley W PTS 4 Nottingham
13.04.02 Mick O'Malley W RSC 8 Liverpool *(Commonwealth S. Featherweight Title Defence)*
13.07.02 Dean Pithie L PTS 12 Coventry *(Commonwealth S. Featherweight Title Defence)*
08.02.03 Vladimir Borov W PTS 6 Liverpool
26.04.03 Phillip Ndou L RSC 1 Brentford
Career: 27 contests, won 19, drew 2, lost 6.

Aidan Mooney
Risca. *Born* Newcastle, 7 July, 1980
Welterweight. Ht. 6'0"
Manager P. Boyce

08.01.03 Gareth Wiltshaw W PTS 4 Aberdare
31.05.03 Robert Lloyd-Taylor L PTS 4 Bethnal Green
Career: 2 contests, won 1, lost 1.

Jamie Moore

Salford. *Born* Salford, 4 November, 1978
British & Commonwealth L. Middleweight
Champion. Ht. 5'8"
Manager S. Wood

09.10.99	Clive Johnson W RSC 3 Manchester
13.11.99	Peter Nightingale W PTS 4 Hull
19.12.99	Paul King W PTS 6 Salford
29.02.00	David Baptiste W RSC 3 Manchester
20.03.00	Harry Butler W RSC 2 Mansfield
14.04.00	Jimmy Steel W PTS 6 Manchester
27.05.00	Koba Kulu W RTD 3 Southwark
07.10.00	Leigh Wicks W PTS 4 Doncaster
12.11.00	Prince Kasi Kaihau W RSC 2 Manchester
25.11.00	Wayne Shepherd W RSC 3 Manchester
17.03.01	Richie Murray W RSC 1 Manchester
27.05.01	Paul Denton W RSC 3 Manchester
07.07.01	Scott Dixon L CO 5 Manchester *(Vacant WBO Inter-Continental L.Middleweight Title)*
26.01.02	Harry Butler W RSC 3 Dagenham
09.03.02	Andrzej Butowicz W RSC 5 Manchester
07.09.02	Delroy Mellis W CO 6 Liverpool
08.02.03	Akhmed Oligov W PTS 6 Liverpool
19.04.03	Michael Jones W PTS 12 Liverpool *(Vacant British L. Middleweight Title. Commonwealth L. Middleweight Title Challenge)*

Career: 18 contests, won 17, lost 1.

(Jason) J.J. Moore

Mansfield. *Born* Nottingham, 28 February, 1972
S. Featherweight. Ht. 5'6"
Manager Self

25.02.01	Craig Spacie L PTS 4 Derby
06.03.01	Craig Spacie L PTS 6 Yarm
24.03.01	Wayne Wheeler W RSC 4 Newark
19.12.01	Baz Carey W PTS 4 Coventry
18.01.02	Baz Carey DREW 4 Coventry
14.09.02	Sid Razak W PTS 6 Newark
31.05.03	Jus Wallie L RSC 1 Bethnal Green

Career: 7 contests, won 3, drew 1, lost 3.

Tony Moran

Liverpool. *Born* Liverpool, 4 July, 1973
Cruiserweight. Ht. 6'6"
Manager T. Gilmour

26.04.01	Shaun Bowes L PTS 6 Gateshead
13.11.01	Paul Bonson L PTS 6 Leeds
19.03.02	Graham Nolan W PTS 6 Slough
10.05.02	Eamonn Glennon W RTD 1 Preston
03.06.02	Dave Clarke W PTS 6 Glasgow
07.09.02	Adam Cale W PTS 4 Liverpool
05.10.02	Jason Brewster W PTS 4 Liverpool
29.11.02	Adam Cale W RSC 1 Liverpool
08.02.03	Michael Pinnock W PTS 4 Liverpool
17.02.03	Brian Gascoigne W RSC 1 Glasgow
19.04.03	Paul Bonson W PTS 4 Liverpool
17.05.03	Tony Booth W PTS 6 Liverpool

Career: 12 contests, won 10, lost 2.

Leighton Morgan

Treharris. *Born* Caerphilly, 27 February, 1978
Heavyweight. Ht. 6'2"
Manager T. Woodward

16.06.01	Rasmus Ojemaye W RSC 3 Wembley
18.03.02	Dave McKenna W DIS 3 Glasgow
15.09.02	Scott Gammer L RSC 1 Swansea
30.10.02	Terry Dixon L RSC 1 Leicester Square
26.02.03	Costi Marin L RSC 2 Bristol

Career: 5 contests, won 2, lost 3.

Andy Morris   Les Clark

Andy Morris

Manchester. *Born* Manchester, 10 March, 1983
S. Featherweight. Ht. 5'6½"
Manager F. Warren/F. Maloney

18.01.03	Jason Nesbitt W PTS 4 Preston
05.04.03	Haroon Din W RSC 1 Manchester
08.05.03	Daniel Thorpe W PTS 4 Widnes

Career: 3 contests, won 3.

Barry Morrison   Les Clark

Barry Morrison

Motherwell. *Born* Bellshill, 8 May, 1980
Welterweight. Ht. 5'7"
Manager T. Gilmour

12.04.03	Keith Jones W PTS 4 Bethnal Green
28.04.03	Arv Mittoo W RSC 3 Nottingham

Career: 2 contests, won 2.

Lee Mountford

Pudsey. *Born* Leeds, 1 September, 1972
Cruiserweight. Ht. 6'2"
Manager T. O'Neill

19.04.02	Gary Thompson DREW 4 Darlington
24.06.02	Eamonn Glennon L PTS 6 Bradford
20.11.02	Nate Joseph W PTS 6 Leeds
03.02.03	Eamonn Glennon DREW 6 Bradford
28.02.03	Gary Thompson W PTS 6 Irvine
13.05.03	Nate Joseph L PTS 6 Leeds

Career: 6 contests, won 2, drew 2, lost 2.

Tony Mulholland

Liverpool. *Born* Liverpool, 24 November, 1972
Featherweight. Ht. 5'6¾"
Manager Self

16.08.96	Graham McGrath W RSC 3 Liverpool
22.11.96	Keith Jones W PTS 4 Liverpool
04.04.97	Keith Jones W PTS 4 Liverpool
11.09.97	Chris Williams W PTS 4 Widnes
18.04.98	Pete Buckley W PTS 4 Manchester
06.06.98	Pete Buckley W PTS 6 Liverpool
19.12.98	Chris Williams DREW 4 Liverpool
04.09.99	Dean Murdoch W PTS 4 Bethnal Green
06.11.99	Dean Murdoch W RSC 6 Widnes
11.12.99	Gary Flear W PTS 4 Liverpool
29.02.00	Pete Buckley W PTS 4 Widnes
25.03.00	Steve Hanley W PTS 6 Liverpool
08.07.00	Lee Williamson W PTS 8 Widnes
10.02.01	Anthony Hanna W PTS 4 Widnes
10.12.01	Gary Flear W PTS 4 Liverpool
09.03.02	Jimmy Beech W PTS 6 Manchester
13.04.02	Andrew Ferrans W PTS 4 Liverpool
28.05.02	Dariusz Snarski W PTS 6 Liverpool
07.09.02	Jamie McKeever L PTS 10 Liverpool *(Vacant Central Area Featherweight Title)*
08.02.03	Jamie McKeever L RSC 6 Liverpool *(Vacant British Featherweight Title)*

Career: 20 contests, won 17, drew 1, lost 2.

Steve Mullin

Liverpool. *Born* Liverpool, 7 July, 1983
Lightweight. Ht. 5'7"
Manager S. Vaughan

19.04.03	Daniel Thorpe L RSC 1 Liverpool
20.06.03	Dave Hinds W PTS 4 Liverpool

Career: 2 contests, won 1, lost 1.

Lawrence Murphy

Uddingston. *Born* Bellshill, 9 February, 1976
Middleweight. Ht. 6'1"
Manager A. Morrison

15.05.98	Mark Owens W RSC 2 Edinburgh
17.09.98	Lee Bird W RSC 3 Glasgow
13.11.98	Ian Toby W PTS 6 Glasgow

18.02.99 Mike Duffield W RSC 2 Glasgow
26.06.99 Harry Butler W RSC 1 Glasgow
17.12.00 Michael Alexander W PTS 6 Glasgow
07.09.01 Chris Nembhard DREW 6 Glasgow
17.11.01 Leigh Wicks W PTS 4 Glasgow
16.12.01 Kreshnik Qato W PTS 6 Glasgow
11.03.02 Rob Stevenson W RSC 1 Glasgow
22.03.03 Leigh Wicks W PTS 4 Renfrew

Career: 11 contests, won 10, drew 1.

Neil Murray

Glasgow. *Born* Glasgow, 9 August, 1980
Welterweight. Ht. 6'0"
Manager J. Murray

19.10.02 Ricky Burns L RSC 2 Renfrew
18.02.03 Elvis Mbwakongo L RSC 1 Bethnal
Green

Career: 2 contests, lost 2.

Neil Murray   Les Clark

Oneal Murray

Balham. *Born* Jamaica, 8 March, 1973
Cruiserweight. Ht. 6'0"
Manager M. Hill

29.03.01 Oddy Papantoniou L PTS 4
Hammersmith
04.10.01 Michael Pinnock W PTS 6 Finsbury
15.10.01 Joe Brame W RSC 2 Southampton
15.12.01 Steven Spartacus L RSC 4 Chigwell
27.01.02 Adam Cale W PTS 6 Streatham
23.02.03 Brodie Pearmaine L PTS 4 Streatham
13.04.03 Dave Clarke L PTS 4 Streatham

Career: 7 contests, won 3, lost 4.

Richie Murray

Liverpool. *Born* Liverpool, 1 April, 1970
Welterweight. Ht. 5'11"
Manager T. Gilmour

13.12.99 Ernie Smith W RSC 5 Cleethorpes
16.05.00 Thomas McDonagh L PTS 4
Warrington

13.11.00 Mickey Yikealo W RSC 3 Bethnal
Green
11.12.00 Thomas McDonagh L PTS 6 Widnes
17.03.01 Jamie Moore L RSC 1 Manchester
08.04.02 James Lee W PTS 6 Southampton
28.05.02 Piotr Bartnicki L RSC 2 Liverpool
02.12.02 Gavin Pearson L RTD 4 Bradford

Career: 8 contests, won 3, lost 5.

Steve Murray

Harlow. *Born* Harlow, 5 October, 1975
Lightweight. Former WBO Inter-
Continental Lightweight Champion.
Former Undefeated IBF Inter-Continental
Lightweight Champion. Ht. 5'6"
Manager F. Warren

10.10.98 Keith Jones W RSC 4 Bethnal Green
14.11.98 Dave Travers W RSC 2 Cheshunt
23.01.99 Marc Smith W RSC 1 Cheshunt
30.01.99 Dewi Roberts W RSC 1 Bethnal
Green
03.04.99 Woody Greenaway W CO 2
Kensington
01.05.99 Keith Jones W RSC 6 Crystal Palace
26.06.99 Brian Coleman W PTS 6 Millwall
07.08.99 Pete Buckley W PTS 6 Dagenham
15.11.99 Karl Taylor W RSC 1 Bethnal Green
29.01.00 Keith Jones W PTS 4 Manchester
19.02.00 Juan Carlos Zummaraga W RSC 1
Dagenham
*(Vacant IBF Inter-Continental
Lightweight Title)*
29.05.00 Wahid Fats W RSC 3 Manchester
24.06.00 Nono Junior W RSC 4 Glasgow
12.08.00 Alan Temple W RSC 2 Wembley
*(IBF Inter-Continental Lightweight
Title Defence. Elim. British
Lightweight Title)*
23.09.00 David Kirk W PTS 4 Bethnal Green
24.02.01 Serguei Starkov W PTS 8 Bethnal
Green
05.05.01 Bobby Vanzie L RSC 7 Edmonton
(British Lightweight Title Challenge)
22.09.01 Darren Melville W PTS 8 Bethnal
Green
24.11.01 Keith Jones W RSC 4 Bethnal Green
15.12.01 Jason Hall W RSC 4 Wembley
(Elim. British Lightweight Title)
02.03.02 Viktor Baranov W RSC 5 Bethnal
Green
*(Vacant WBO Inter-Continental
Lightweight Title)*
04.05.02 Rosalin Nasibulin W CO 5 Bethnal
Green
14.09.02 Yuri Romanov L RSC 10 Bethnal
Green
*(WBO Inter-Continental Lightweight
Title Defence)*
15.02.03 Graham Earl L RSC 2 Wembley
*(Southern Area Lightweight Title
Challenge. Final Elim. British
Lightweight Title)*

Career: 24 contests, won 21, lost 3.

Lee Murtagh

Leeds. *Born* Leeds, 30 September, 1973
Middleweight. Former British Masters
Middleweight Champion. Ht. 5'9¼"
Manager J. O'Neill/K. Walker

12.06.95 Dave Curtis W PTS 6 Bradford

25.09.95 Roy Gbasai W PTS 6 Bradford
30.10.95 Cam Raeside L PTS 6 Bradford
11.12.95 Donovan Davey W PTS 6 Bradford
13.01.96 Peter Varnavas W PTS 6 Halifax
05.02.96 Shamus Casey W PTS 6 Bradford
20.05.96 Shaun O'Neill W PTS 6 Bradford
24.06.96 Michael Alexander W PTS 6 Bradford
28.10.96 Jimmy Vincent L RSC 2 Bradford
14.04.97 Lee Simpkin W PTS 6 Bradford
09.10.97 Brian Dunn W PTS 6 Leeds
05.03.98 Wayne Shepherd W PTS 6 Leeds
08.08.98 Alan Gilbert W PTS 4 Scarborough
13.03.99 Keith Palmer DREW 6 Manchester
27.09.99 Jawaid Khaliq L RSC 5 Leeds
*(Vacant WBF European
L. Middleweight Title)*
27.02.00 Gareth Lovell W PTS 6 Leeds
24.09.00 Jon Foster W PTS 6 Shaw
03.12.00 Michael Alexander W PTS 6 Shaw
17.05.01 Ojay Abrahams L RSC 2 Leeds
*(Vacant British Masters
L. Middleweight Title)*
03.03.02 Howard Clarke NC 2 Shaw
19.04.02 Neil Bonner W PTS 6 Darlington
21.06.02 Wayne Shepherd W PTS 10 Leeds
*(Vacant British Masters Middleweight
Title)*
02.12.02 Martyn Bailey L RSC 6 Leeds
*(British Masters Middleweight Title
Defence)*
10.05.03 Darren Rhodes L PTS 6 Huddersfield

Career: 24 contests, won 16, drew 1, lost 6, no
contest 1.

(Nikos) Rocky Muscus (Agrapidis) Israel)

Chertsey. *Born* Athens, Greece, 5 August,
1983
Middleweight. Ht. 5'6½"
Manager J. Evans

12.05.03 Danny Cooper L PTS 6 Southampton

Career: 1 contest, lost 1.

(Lee) Young Muttley (Woodley)

West Bromwich. *Born* West Bromwich, 17
May, 1976
Midlands Area L. Welterweight Champion.
Ht. 5'8½"
Manager Self

03.09.99 Dave Hinds W RSC 4 West Bromwich
24.10.99 David Kehoe W RTD 1
Wolverhampton
22.01.00 Wahid Fats L PTS 4 Birmingham
18.02.00 Stuart Rimmer W RSC 1 West
Bromwich
27.11.00 Peter Dunn W RSC 3 Birmingham
07.09.01 Jon Honney W RSC 1 West Bromwich
16.11.01 Tony Montana W PTS 6 West
Bromwich
26.11.01 Lee Byrne W RSC 1 Manchester
23.02.02 Brian Coleman W PTS 4 Nottingham
23.03.02 Adam Zadworny W RSC 3 Southwark
02.11.02 Tony Montana W PTS 4
Wolverhampton
21.03.03 Gary Reid W RSC 7 West Bromwich
*(Vacant Midlands Area L.Welterweight
Title)*
28.04.03 John Marshall W RSC 5 Nottingham

Career: 13 contests, won 12, lost 1.

Dominic Negus

Havering. *Born* Bethnal Green, 28 July, 1970
Heavyweight. Former Undefeated WBU
Inter-Continental S. Cruiserweight
Champion. Former Southern Area
Cruiserweight Champion. Ht. 6'2"
Manager F. Maloney

03.09.96	Gareth Thomas W RSC 2 Bethnal Green
28.09.96	Patrick Lawrence W RSC 2 Barking
11.01.97	Naveed Anwar W RTD 2 Bethnal Green
04.03.97	Nigel Rafferty W PTS 4 Southwark
20.05.97	Nigel Rafferty W PTS 4 Edmonton
17.06.97	Chris Henry W RSC 10 Cheshunt *(Southern Area Cruiserweight Title Challenge)*
02.09.97	Trevor Small DREW 8 Southwark
11.11.97	Constantin Ochrej W CO 6 Bethnal Green
21.04.98	Bruce Scott L RSC 9 Edmonton *(Southern Area Cruiserweight Title Defence)*
22.10.98	Kevin Mitchell L RTD 5 Barking
18.02.99	Kevin Mitchell W PTS 10 Barking *(Vacant Southern Area Cruiserweight Title)*
13.09.99	Chris Woollas W PTS 10 Bethnal Green *(Elim. British Cruiserweight Title)*
08.09.00	Tony Booth L PTS 6 Bristol
06.10.00	Garry Delaney L PTS 10 Maidstone *(Southern Area Cruiserweight Title Defence)*
26.05.01	Paul Fiske W CO 1 Bethnal Green
29.09.01	Eamonn Glennon W PTS 6 Southwark
08.12.01	Eddie Knight W CO 2 Dagenham *(Vacant WBU Inter-Continental S.Cruiserweight Title)*
26.01.02	Paul Bonson W PTS 4 Bethnal Green
10.07.02	Audley Harrison L PTS 6 Wembley

Career: 19 contests, won 13, drew 1, lost 5.

Johnny Nelson

Sheffield. *Born* Sheffield, 4 January, 1967
WBO Cruiserweight Champion. Former
Undefeated British & European
Cruiserweight Champion. Former
Undefeated WBU Heavyweight Champion.
Former WBF Heavyweight Champion.
Former WBF Cruiserweight Champion.
Former Undefeated Central Area
Cruiserweight Champion. Ht. 6'2"
Manager Self

18.03.86	Peter Brown L PTS 6 Hull
15.05.86	Tommy Taylor L PTS 6 Dudley
03.10.86	Magne Havnaa L PTS 4 Copenhagen, Denmark
20.11.86	Chris Little W PTS 6 Bredbury
19.01.87	Gypsy Carman W PTS 6 Mayfair
02.03.87	Doug Young W PTS 6 Huddersfield
10.03.87	Sean Daly W RSC 1 Manchester
28.04.87	Brian Schumacher L PTS 8 Halifax
03.06.87	Byron Pullen W RSC 3 Southwark
14.12.87	Jon McBean W RSC 6 Edgbaston
01.02.88	Dennis Bailey L PTS 8 Northampton
24.02.88	Cordwell Hylton W RSC 1 Sheffield
25.04.88	Kenny Jones W CO 1 Liverpool
04.05.88	Crawford Ashley W PTS 8 Solihull
06.06.88	Lennie Howard W CO 2 Mayfair
31.08.88	Andrew Gerrard W PTS 8 Stoke
26.10.88	Danny Lawford W RSC 2 Sheffield *(Vacant Central Area Cruiserweight Title)*
04.04.89	Steve Mormino W RSC 2 Sheffield
21.05.89	Andy Straughn W CO 8 Finsbury Park *(British Cruiserweight Title Challenge)*
02.10.89	Ian Bulloch W CO 2 Hanley *(British Cruiserweight Title Defence)*
27.01.90	Carlos de Leon DREW 12 Sheffield *(WBC Cruiserweight Title Challenge)*
14.02.90	Dino Homsey W RSC 7 Brentwood
28.03.90	Lou Gent W CO 4 Bethnal Green *(British Cruiserweight Title Defence)*
27.06.90	Arthur Weathers W RSC 2 Kensington
05.09.90	Andre Smith W PTS 8 Brighton
14.12.90	Markus Bott W RSC 12 Karlsruhe, Germany *(Vacant European Cruiserweight Title)*
12.03.91	Yves Monsieur W RTD 8 Mansfield *(European Cruiserweight Title Defence)*
16.05.92	James Warring L PTS 12 Fredericksburg, USA *(IBF Cruiserweight Title Challenge)*
15.08.92	Norbert Ekassi L RSC 3 Ajaccio, France
29.10.92	Corrie Sanders L PTS 10 Morula, South Africa
30.04.93	Dave Russell W RSC 11 Melbourne, Australia *(WBF Cruiserweight Title Challenge)*
11.08.93	Tom Collins W RSC 1 Mansfield *(WBF Cruiserweight Title Defence)*
01.10.93	Francis Wanyama L DIS 10 Waregem, Belgium *(WBF Cruiserweight Title Defence)*
20.11.93	Jimmy Thunder W PTS 12 Auckland, New Zealand *(WBF Heavyweight Title Challenge)*
05.04.94	Henry Akinwande L PTS 10 Bethnal Green
05.11.94	Nikolai Kulpin W PTS 12 Bangkok, Thailand *(WBF Heavyweight Title Defence)*
22.08.95	Adilson Rodrigues L PTS 12 Sao Paulo, Brazil *(WBF Heavyweight Title Defence)*
03.12.95	Adilson Rodrigues L PTS 12 Sao Paulo, Brazil *(WBF Heavyweight Title Challenge)*
20.01.96	Tony Booth W RSC 2 Mansfield
14.12.96	Dennis Andries W RSC 7 Sheffield *(Vacant British Cruiserweight Title)*
22.02.97	Patrice Aouissi W RSC 7 Berck sur Mer, France *(Vacant European Cruiserweight Title)*
19.07.97	Michael Murray W PTS 4 Wembley
11.10.97	Dirk Wallyn W RSC 1 Sheffield *(European Cruiserweight Title Defence)*
18.07.98	Peter Oboh W RTD 6 Sheffield
27.03.99	Carl Thompson W RSC 5 Derby *(WBO Cruiserweight Title Challenge)*
15.05.99	Bruce Scott W PTS 12 Sheffield *(WBO Cruiserweight Title Defence)*
07.08.99	Willard Lewis W RTD 4 Dagenham *(WBO Cruiserweight Title Defence)*
18.09.99	Sione Asipeli W PTS 12 Las Vegas, USA *(WBO Cruiserweight Title Defence)*
06.11.99	Christophe Girard W CO 4 Widnes *(WBO Cruiserweight Title Defence)*
08.04.00	Pietro Aurino W RTD 7 Bethnal Green *(WBO Cruiserweight Title Defence)*
07.10.00	Adam Watt W RSC 5 Doncaster *(WBO Cruiserweight Title Defence)*
27.01.01	George Arias W PTS 12 Bethnal Green *(WBO Cruiserweight Title Defence)*
21.07.01	Marcelo Dominguez W PTS 12 Sheffield *(WBO Cruiserweight Title Defence)*
24.11.01	Alex Vasiliev W PTS 12 Bethnal Green *(Vacant WBU Heavyweight Title)*
06.04.02	Ezra Sellers W CO 8 Copenhagen, Denmark *(WBO Cruiserweight Title Defence)*
23.11.02	Guillermo Jones DREW 12 Derby *(WBO Cruiserweight Title Defence)*

Career: 56 contests, won 42, drew 2, lost 12.

Johnny Nelson   Les Clark

Chris Nembhard

Leytonstone. *Born* Jamaica, 26 December, 1976
Middleweight. Ht. 6'1"
Manager T. Bowers

29.09.00	Gary Ojuederie W RSC 1 Bethnal Green
02.11.00	Koba Kulu W PTS 6 Kensington
10.11.00	William Webster W RSC 1 Mayfair
15.02.01	Keith Ellwood W RSC 2 Glasgow
23.02.01	David Baptiste W PTS 8 Barking
09.03.01	Rob Stevenson W RSC 2 Millwall
20.04.01	Delroy Mellis L RSC 8 Millwall *(Southern Area L. Middleweight Title Challenge)*
31.07.01	Brian Magee L RSC 6 Bethnal Green
07.09.01	Lawrence Murphy DREW 6 Glasgow
24.11.01	Gary Lockett L RSC 2 Bethnal Green
13.09.02	Mark Graversen W RTD 2 Aarhus, Denmark
20.10.02	Matthew Barney L PTS 10 Southwark *(Southern Area S. Middleweight Title Challenge)*

Career: 12 contests, won 7, drew 1, lost 4.

Jason Nesbitt

Birmingham. *Born* Birmingham, 15
December, 1973
Lightweight. Ht. 5'9"
Manager Self

06.11.00	Stephen Chinnock L PTS 6 Wolverhampton
09.12.00	Lee Meager L RSC 2 Southwark
29.01.01	Henry Castle L CO 6 Peterborough
27.03.01	Billy Smith W PTS 6 Brierley Hill
21.05.01	Sid Razak L PTS 6 Birmingham
04.06.01	Andrew Ferrans L RSC 2 Glasgow
07.07.01	Colin Toohey L PTS 4 Manchester
15.09.01	Colin Toohey L PTS 4 Manchester
22.09.01	John Mackay L PTS 4 Canning Town
01.11.01	Chris Hooper L RSC 6 Hull
16.03.02	Lee Meager L PTS 6 Bethnal Green
27.03.02	Greg Edwards W RSC 5 Mayfair
20.04.02	Henry Castle L PTS 4 Cardiff
04.05.02	Danny Hunt L PTS 4 Bethnal Green
15.06.02	Jesse James Daniel L PTS 4 Leeds
27.07.02	Craig Spacie L PTS 4 Nottingham
23.08.02	Billy Corcoran L PTS 4 Bethnal Green
25.10.02	Billy Corcoran L RSC 2 Bethnal Green
03.12.02	Mark Bowen L PTS 6 Shrewsbury
11.12.02	Matt Teague L PTS 6 Hull
20.12.02	Chris McDonagh L PTS 6 Bracknell
18.01.03	Andy Morris L PTS 4 Preston
09.02.03	Mally McIver L PTS 6 Bradford
09.03.03	Choi Tseveenpurev L PTS 8 Shaw
29.03.03	Kevin O'Hara L RSC 3 Portsmouth
07.05.03	Henry Jones L PTS 6 Ellesmere Port
02.06.03	Stefy Bull L PTS 6 Cleethorpes
13.06.03	Scott Lawton L PTS 6 Queensway

Career: 28 contests, won 2, lost 26.

Eddie Nevins

Manchester. *Born* Manchester, 17 April,
1975
Central Area S. Featherweight Champion.
Ht. 5'6"
Manager S. Foster/S. Wood

17.10.98	Simon Chambers W RSC 4 Manchester
26.10.98	Dave Hinds W PTS 6 Manchester
30.11.98	Keith Jones W PTS 4 Manchester
13.03.99	Gary Jenkinson W PTS 4 Manchester
02.07.99	Ram Singh W CO 1 Manchester
06.11.99	Bradley Pryce L RSC 2 Widnes
21.05.00	Lennie Hodgkins W RSC 1 Shaw
12.08.00	Paul Halpin L PTS 6 Wembley
12.11.00	Mohamed Helel W PTS 4 Manchester
15.01.01	Pete Buckley W PTS 4 Manchester
10.02.01	Alex Arthur L RSC 1 Widnes
26.03.01	Henry Castle L RSC 2 Peterborough
21.07.02	Carl Allen W PTS 4 Salford
09.11.02	Gareth Wiltshaw W PTS 4 Altrincham
16.02.03	Daniel Thorpe W RSC 8 Salford
	(Vacant Central Area S. Featherweight Title)

Career: 15 contests, won 11, lost 4.

Dale Nixon

Taunton. *Born* Exeter, 11 May, 1970
L. Heavyweight. Ht. 6'2"
Manager N. Christian

09.03.93	Ian Vokes W RSC 2 Bristol
27.05.93	Chris Nurse W RSC 2 Bristol
26.06.93	Tim Robinson W RSC 2 Keynsham
03.11.93	Jason McNeill W RSC 1 Bristol
10.03.94	Jerry Mortimer DREW 4 Bristol

31.03.94	Steve Thomas DREW 4 Bristol
25.06.94	Robert Peel W PTS 6 Cullompton
07.10.94	Robert Peel W RSC 7 Taunton
06.05.95	Darren Ashton L RSC 4 Shepton Mallet
09.12.02	Hamid Jamali L CO 1 Birmingham
06.03.03	Liam Lathbury L PTS 4 Bristol
17.03.03	Michael Matthewsian DREW 6 Southampton
05.04.03	Mark Phillips W PTS 6 Coventry
13.06.03	Darren Dorrington L RSC 5 Bristol

Career: 14 contest, won 7, drew 3, lost 4.

Danny Norton

Stourbridge. *Born* Wordsley, 8 November,
1969
S. Middleweight. Ht. 6'0"
Manager D. Bradley

07.10.01	Mark Phillips W PTS 6 Wolverhampton
19.04.02	Andy Vickers W CO 2 Darlington
13.07.02	Liam Lathbury W PTS 4 Wolverhampton
20.12.02	Jamie Hearn L PTS 4 Bracknell

Career: 4 contests, won 3, lost 1.

Danny Norton   Les Clark

Laura Norton

London. *Born* Glasgow, 18 August, 1976
Bantamweight. Ht. 5'5¹⁄₂"
Manager J. Feld

12.12.02	Krampe Reva W PTS 4 Leicester Square

Career: 1 contest, won 1.

Robert Norton

Stourbridge. *Born* Dudley, 20 January,
1972
Cruiserweight. Former WBU Cruiserweight
Champion.
Ht. 6'2"
Manager Self

30.09.93	Stuart Fleet W CO 2 Walsall
27.10.93	Kent Davis W PTS 6 West Bromwich

02.12.93	Eddie Pyatt W RSC 2 Walsall
26.01.94	Lennie Howard W PTS 6 Birmingham
17.05.94	Steve Osborne W PTS 6 Kettering
05.10.94	Chris Woollas DREW 6 Wolverhampton
30.11.94	L. A. Williams W RSC 2 Wolverhampton
10.02.95	Newby Stevens W RSC 3 Birmingham
22.02.95	Steve Osborne W PTS 6 Telford
21.04.95	Cordwell Hylton W PTS 6 Dudley
25.10.95	Nigel Rafferty W RSC 6 Telford
31.01.96	Gary Williams W RSC 2 Birmingham
25.04.96	Steve Osborne W RSC 5 Mayfair
01.10.96	Andrew Benson W RSC 6 Birmingham
12.11.96	Nigel Rafferty W PTS 8 Dudley
11.02.97	Touami Benhamed W RSC 5 Bethnal Green
16.04.97	Tony Booth W RSC 4 Bethnal Green
20.12.97	Darren Corbett L PTS 12 Belfast *(Commonwealth Cruiserweight Title Challenge)*
03.04.98	Adrian Nicolai W RSC 2 West Bromwich
03.10.98	Tim Brown W CO 3 West Bromwich
01.04.99	Jacob Mofokeng W PTS 12 Birmingham *(WBU Cruiserweight Title Challenge)*
24.09.99	Sebastiaan Rothmann L RSC 8 Merthyr *(WBU Cruiserweight Title Defence)*
30.09.00	Tony Booth W RSC 3 Peterborough
18.11.00	Darron Griffiths W PTS 10 Dagenham *(Elim. British Cruiserweight Title)*
05.02.01	Lee Swaby W PTS 8 Hull
30.11.02	Paul Bonson W PTS 6 Coventry

Career: 26 contests, won 23, drew 1, lost 2.

Robert Norton   Les Clark

(Paulus) Ali Nuumbembe

Glossop. *Born* Oshakati, Namibia, 24 June,
1978
Welterweight. Ht. 5'8¹⁄₂"
Manager B. Ingle

16.04.03	Dai Bando W PTS 4 Nottingham
15.06.03	Ernie Smith W PTS 4 Bradford

Career: 2 contests, won 2.

Tony Oakey

Portsmouth. *Born* Portsmouth, 2 January, 1976
WBU L. Heavyweight Champion. Former Undefeated Commonwealth & Southern Area L. Heavyweight Champion. Ht. 5'8"
Manager F. Maloney

12.09.98	Smokey Enison W RSC 2 Bethnal Green	
21.11.98	Zak Chelli W RSC 1 Southwark	
16.01.99	Jimmy Steel W PTS 4 Bethnal Green	
06.03.99	Mark Dawson W PTS 4 Southwark	
10.07.99	Jimmy Steel W PTS 4 Southwark	
01.10.99	Michael Pinnock W PTS 4 Bethnal Green	
21.02.00	Darren Ashton W PTS 4 Southwark	

13.03.00	Martin Jolley W PTS 6 Bethnal Green	
21.10.00	Darren Ashton W PTS 4 Wembley	
27.01.01	Nathan King W PTS 6 Bethnal Green	
26.03.01	Butch Lesley W PTS 10 Wembley	
	(Southern Area L. Heavyweight Title Challenge)	
08.05.01	Hastings Rasani W RSC 10 Barnsley	
	(Vacant Commonwealth L. Heavyweight Title)	
09.09.01	Konstantin Ochrej W RSC 4 Southwark	
20.10.01	Chris Davies W PTS 12 Portsmouth	
	(Commonwealth L.Heavyweight Title Defence)	
02.03.02	Konstantin Shvets W PTS 12 Bethnal Green	
	(Vacant WBU L. Heavyweight Title)	
25.05.02	Neil Simpson W PTS 12 Portsmouth	
	(WBU L. Heavyweight Title Defence)	
12.10.02	Andrei Kaersten W PTS 12 Bethnal Green	
	(WBU L. Heavyweight Title Defence)	
29.03.03	Neil Linford W PTS 12 Portsmouth	
	(WBU L. Heavyweight Title Defence)	

Career: 18 contests, won 18.

Peter Oboh

Brockley. *Born* Nigeria, 6 September, 1968
British & Commonwealth L. Heavyweight Champion. Ht. 6'2"
Manager D. Powell

12.05.93	Antonio Russo W RSC 5 Cassino, Italy	
14.01.94	Ridha Soussi W PTS 6 Tagliacozzo, Italy	
13.05.94	Antonio Pasqualino W RSC 2 Avellino, Italy	
16.10.95	Tim Redman W RTD 2 Mayfair	
09.07.96	Yuri Yelistratov W PTS 6 Bethnal Green	
27.08.96	Joe Siluvangi L RSC 6 Windsor	
03.12.96	Andy Lambert W CO 1 Liverpool	
04.03.97	Garry Delaney L DIS 8 Southwark	
01.11.97	Scott Welch L PTS 6 Glasgow	
18.07.98	Johnny Nelson L RTD 6 Sheffield	
26.09.98	Ole Klemetsen W CO 1 York	
21.11.98	Terry Dunstan L PTS 8 Southwark	
18.06.99	Thomas Hansvoll W RSC 2 Vejle, Denmark	
21.07.99	Ray Kane W RSC 2 Bloomsbury	
29.01.01	Chris Davies W RSC 8 Peterborough	
	(Elim. Commonwealth L. Heavyweight Title)	
06.09.02	George Adipo W CO 1 Bethnal Green	
	(Vacant Commonwealth L.Heavyweight Title)	
08.03.03	Neil Simpson W RSC 11 Coventry	
	(Commonwealth L.Heavyweight Title Defence. Vacant British L.Heavyweight Title)	

Career: 17 contests, won 12, lost 5.

Peter Oboh   Les Clark

Valery Odin

Canning Town. *Born* Guadeloupe, 23 December, 1974
L. Heavyweight. Ht. 6'2½"
Manager B. Lawrence

15.06.01	Tom Cannon W PTS 4 Millwall	
22.09.01	Mark Brookes W PTS 4 Canning Town	
09.10.01	Wayne Ellcock L PTS 4 Cardiff	

Tony Oakey   Les Clark

10.11.01 Tony Dodson L RSC 4 Wembley
13.12.01 Calvin Stonestreet W RSC 2 Leicester Square
10.02.02 Radcliffe Green W PTS 6 Southwark
20.04.02 Toks Owoh W PTS 8 Wembley
21.05.01 Mark Smallwood L RSC 4 Custom House
17.08.02 Nathan King W PTS 6 Cardiff
17.09.02 Charden Ansoula L PTS 6 Bethnal Green
26.10.02 Chris Davies L PTS 6 Maesteg
28.01.03 Carl Froch L RSC 6 Nottingham
Career: 12 contests, won 6, lost 6.

Ben Ogden

Ripley. *Born* Nottingham, 2 December, 1977
Middleweight. Ht. 5'11"
Manager M. Shinfield

10.02.03 Nasser Hussain W CO 2 Sheffield
24.03.03 Gary Jones W RSC 6 Barnsley
28.04.03 Alan Gilbert W RSC 1 Nottingham
Career: 3 contests, won 3.

Ben Ogden   Les Clark

Sunkanmi Ogunbiyi

London. *Born* Nigeria, 5 May, 1977
Flyweight. Ht. 5'5"
Manager J. Oyebola

24.05.01 Sergei Tasimov W PTS 4 Kensington
16.06.01 Delroy Spencer W PTS 4 Wembley
09.09.01 Frank Amissi W PTS 6 Lagos, Nigeria
13.12.01 Naji Hassan L PTS 6 Leicester Square
13.03.02 Marty Kayes W PTS 4 Mayfair
13.06.02 Lee Georgiou W CO 1 Leicester Square
30.10.02 Marty Kayes W PTS 4 Leicester Square
20.03.03 Shinny Bayaar W PTS 4 Queensway
Career: 8 contests, won 7, lost 1.

Kevin O'Hara

Belfast. *Born* Belfast, 21 September, 1981
Featherweight. Ht. 5'6"
Manager M.Callahan/J.Breen/F.Warren

02.11.02 Mike Harrington W RSC 1 Belfast
01.02.03 Jus Wallie W RSC 2 Belfast
29.03.03 Jason Nesbitt W RSC 3 Portsmouth
14.06.03 Piotr Niesporek W PTS 4 Magdeburg, Germany
Career: 4 contests, won 4.

Ajose Olusegun

London. *Born* Nigeria, 6 December, 1979
L. Welterweight. Ht. 5'9"
Manager J. Oyebola

24.05.01 Tony Montana W RSC 1 Kensington
21.06.01 Woody Greenaway W RSC 1 Earls Court
09.09.01 Sunni Ajayi W PTS 6 Lagos, Nigeria
04.10.01 Stuart Rimmer W RTD 2 Finsbury
13.03.02 Gary Flear W PTS 4 Mayfair
13.06.02 Keith Jones W PTS 6 Leicester Square
30.10.02 Martin Holgate W RSC 7 Leicester Square
27.11.02 Vladimir Kortovski W RSC 1 Tel Aviv, Israel
15.12.02 Adewale Adegbusi W RSC 6 Lagos, Nigeria
20.03.03 Cristian Hodorogea W PTS 4 Queensway
26.04.03 Keith Jones W PTS 6 Brentford
Career: 11 contests, won 11.

Leo O'Reilly

Bexleyheath. *Born* Gravesend, 4 October, 1979
Welterweight. Ht. 5'6"
Manager T. Gilmour/A. Phillips

16.09.00 Dave Hinds W RSC 2 Bethnal Green
30.09.00 Stuart Rimmer W RSC 2 Peterborough
14.10.00 Marco Fattore W PTS 4 Wembley
18.11.00 Dave Travers W RSC 3 Dagenham
09.12.00 Pete Buckley W PTS 4 Southwark
05.02.01 Woody Greenaway W CO 1 Hull
13.03.01 Barrie Kelley W RSC 5 Plymouth
12.05.01 David White W PTS 4 Plymouth
13.09.01 Ernie Smith W PTS 6 Sheffield
16.03.02 Lance Crosby W PTS 8 Bethnal Green
10.05.02 Paul Denton W PTS 6 Bethnal Green
26.10.02 Alan Temple L RSC 4 Maesteg
08.03.03 Keith Jones W PTS 6 Bethnal Green
Career: 13 contests, won 12, lost 1.

Hussain Osman

Paddington. *Born* Syria, 25 July, 1973
Middleweight. Former IBO Inter-Continental & Southern Area S. Middleweight Champion. Former Undefeated WBO Inter-Continental Southern Area Middleweight Champion. Ht. 5'9½"
Manager Self

09.05.99 Wayne Asker W PTS 4 Bracknell
20.05.99 Karim Bouali W PTS 4 Barking
15.07.99 Neil Linford W RSC 5 Peterborough
05.10.99 Ojay Abrahams W PTS 4 Bloomsbury
05.02.00 Joey Ainscough W PTS 4 Bethnal Green
01.04.00 George Foreman W PTS 4 Bethnal Green
22.05.00 Steve Timms W RSC 2 Coventry
25.09.00 James Lowther L PTS 8 Barnsley
03.03.01 Gary Lockett L CO 2 Wembley

26.05.01 Lee Molloy W RSC 1 Bethnal Green
04.06.01 Richard Williams L PTS 10 Hartlepool
28.10.01 Gary Logan W PTS 10 Southwark
(Southern Area Middleweight Title Challenge)
26.01.02 Matthew Barney W RTD 9 Dagenham
(Vacant IBO Inter-Continental S.Middleweight Title. Southern Area S.Middleweight Title Challenge)
08.04.02 Matthew Barney L PTS 12 Southampton
(IBO Inter-Continental & Southern Area S. Middleweight Title Defences)
21.05.02 Darren Rhodes W PTS 10 Custom House
20.07.02 Gary Logan W PTS 12 Bethnal Green
(Vacant WBO Inter-Continental Middleweight Title)
21.12.02 Howard Eastman L RTD 4 Dagenham
31.05.03 Gary Beardsley W RSC 5 Bethnal Green
Career: 18 contests, won 13, lost 5.

Paul Owen

Sheffield. *Born* Sheffield, 3 October, 1975
S. Middleweight. Ht. 5'10½"
Manager D. Hobson

05.05.00 Shane Thomas DREW 6 Pentre Halkyn
08.07.00 Chris Crook W RSC 1 Rotherham
05.10.00 Andy Vickers L PTS 6 Sunderland
24.11.00 Reece McAllister L PTS 6 Darlington
07.12.00 Ian Toby L RTD 5 Sunderland
05.02.01 Steve Timms L RSC 1 Bradford
10.05.01 Gary Dixon W RSC 3 Sunderland
21.06.01 Reece McAllister DREW 6 Sheffield
13.09.01 Reece McAllister W RSC 1 Sheffield
08.02.02 Lee Woodruff W RSC 2 Preston
22.09.02 Matthew Barney L CO 7 Southwark
(Vacant British Masters S.Middleweight Title)
02.12.02 Jimmy Steel W PTS 6 Bradford
14.03.03 Barry Connell L PTS 6 Glasgow
Career: 13 contests, won 5, drew 2, lost 6.

Paul Owen   Les Clark

Alan Page (Paige)
Hattersley. *Born* Manchester, 17 April, 1976
L. Heavyweight. Ht. 6'0"
Manager F. Maloney/S. Foster/S. Wood

01.07.00	William Webster W PTS 4 Manchester
09.09.00	Piotr Bartnicki W PTS 4 Manchester
12.11.00	Dean Ashton W RSC 2 Manchester
22.12.02	Harry Butler W RSC 1 Salford
16.02.03	Darren Ashton W PTS 4 Salford
08.06.03	Patrick Cito W RSC 3 Shaw
21.06.03	Marcin Radola W RSC 2 Manchester

Career: 7 contests, won 7.

Alan Page   Les Clark

James Paisley
Larne. *Born* Ballymena, 4 January 1980
L. Welterweight. Ht. 5'8"
Manager A. Wilton

09.09.01	Babatunde Ajayi L PTS 4 Southwark
28.10.01	Carl Walton W PTS 4 Southwark
15.12.01	David Barnes L RTD 2 Wembley
31.01.02	Tony Montana L PTS 6 Piccadilly
09.02.02	Michael Jennings L RSC 3 Manchester
11.03.02	Nigel Wright L PTS 4 Glasgow
23.06.02	Jason Gonzales W PTS 6 Southwark
17.09.02	Dave Stewart L RSC 5 Bethnal Green
20.10.02	Pete Buckley W PTS 4 Southwark
27.10.02	Elvis Mbwakongo L RSC 2 Southwark
22.02.03	Gwyn Wale L RSC 1 Huddersfield

Career: 11 contests, won 3, lost 8.

Danny Parkinson
Bradford. *Born* Bradford, 6 August, 1980
Welterweight. Ht. 5'11"
Manager C. Aston

12.06.00	Ram Singh W RSC 3 Bradford
04.12.00	Ram Singh W PTS 6 Bradford
05.02.01	Dean Nicholas W PTS 6 Bradford
19.03.01	Lee Sharp L PTS 6 Glasgow
15.10.01	Richard Inquieti W RSC 1 Bradford
04.03.02	Matt Scriven W PTS 6 Bradford
09.06.03	Danny Moir W PTS 6 Bradford

Career: 7 contests, won 6, lost 1.

Justin Parsons
Ystradgynlais. *Born* Swansea, 18 October, 1981
L. Welterweight. Ht. 5'11"
Manager A. Gower

26.10.02	Wayne Wheeler L CO 2 Maesteg

Career: 1 contest, lost 1.

Levi Pattison
Leeds. *Born* Kings Lynn, 10 September, 1975
Flyweight. Ht. 5'5½"
Manager M. Marsden

17.07.99	Graham McGrath W PTS 4 Doncaster
15.01.00	Sean Green L PTS 4 Doncaster
25.06.00	Paddy Folan W PTS 6 Wakefield
27.11.00	Chris Edwards L PTS 4 Birmingham
08.05.01	Delroy Spencer W PTS 4 Barnsley
17.05.01	Gary Ford W RSC 5 Leeds
08.10.01	Chris Edwards W PTS 4 Barnsley
24.11.01	Andy Greenaway W PTS 6 Wakefield
28.01.02	Delroy Spencer W RSC 5 Barnsley
27.04.02	Colin Moffett W RSC 2 Huddersfield
16.11.02	Alain Bonnel W RSC 6 Nottingham

Career: 11 contests, won 9, lost 2.

Mark Paxford
Wigan. *Born* Leigh, 18 February, 1979
Welterweight. Ht. 5'9¼"
Manager Self

22.09.00	Colin McCash DREW 6 Wrexham
03.12.00	Paddy Martin W RSC 3 Shaw
04.02.01	Matt Scriven W PTS 6 Queensferry
10.12.01	Pedro Thompson W PTS 6 Bradford
08.02.02	Richard Inquieti W PTS 6 Preston
09.05.02	Gavin Pearson L PTS 6 Sunderland
10.10.02	Richard Inquieti W PTS 6 Stoke
26.10.02	Wayne Shepherd W PTS 6 Wigan

Career: 8 contests, won 6, drew 1, lost 1.

Gareth Payne
Coventry. *Born* Coventry, 14 April, 1973
British Masters Bantamweight Champion.
Midlands Area S.Bantamweight Champion.
Ht. 5'3"
Manager A. Phillips

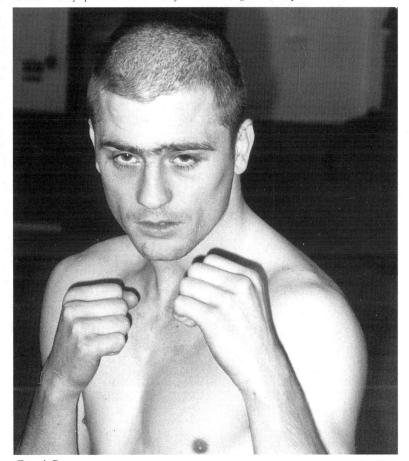

Gareth Payne   Les Clark

12.07.99	Lennie Hodgkins W PTS 4 Coventry
22.10.99	Danny Mulligan W RSC 2 Coventry
14.12.99	Paul Quarmby W PTS 4 Coventry
22.01.00	Sean Grant W RSC 1 Birmingham
22.05.00	Nicky Booth L PTS 4 Coventry
28.10.00	Chris Emanuele W CO 1 Coventry
02.01.01	Danny Lawson W RSC 1 Coventry
19.12.01	Delroy Spencer W PTS 4 Coventry
18.01.02	Delroy Spencer L PTS 4 Coventry
25.02.02	Jamie Yelland L RSC 3 Slough
26.04.02	Chris Emanuele W RSC 3 Coventry
	(British Masters Bantamweight Title Challenge)
18.05.02	Jim Betts L PTS 6 Millwall
10.10.02	Jamie Yelland L PTS 10 Stoke
22.03.03	John-Paul Ryan W PTS 4 Coventry
07.06.03	Neil Read W RSC 5 Coventry
	(Vacant Midlands Area S.Bantamweight Title)

Career: 15 contests, won 10, lost 5.

Mark Payne　　　　　　Les Clark

Mark Payne

Coventry. *Born* Coventry, 29 March, 1976
S. Bantamweight. Ht. 5'6"
Manager Self

11.05.98	Dave Travers W RTD 3 Leicester
24.09.98	David Jeffrey W RSC 2 Edgbaston
30.11.98	Danny Lawson W RSC 1 Leicester
11.12.98	Stevie Quinn W RSC 2 Cheshunt
26.02.99	Arv Mittoo W PTS 4 Coventry
12.07.99	John Barnes W PTS 4 Coventry
05.10.99	Isaac Sebaduka L PTS 6 Bloomsbury
14.12.99	Harry Woods W PTS 4 Coventry
10.03.00	Vlado Varhegyi W PTS 6 Bethnal Green
08.09.00	Vladimir Borov W PTS 6 Hammersmith
28.10.00	Rakhim Mingaleev W PTS 6 Coventry
02.01.01	Keith Jones W PTS 6 Coventry
19.05.01	Dazzo Williams L PTS 8 Wembley
22.09.01	Rakhim Mingaleev W PTS 6 Newcastle
19.12.01	Stevie Quinn W RTD 2 Coventry

18.05.02	Michael Hunter L PTS 8 Millwall
16.04.03	Billy Corcoran DREW 4 Nottingham

Career: 17 contests, won 14, drew 1, lost 2.

Brodie Pearmaine

Lewes. *Born* London, 3 April, 1967
Cruiserweight. Ht. 6'0"
Manager R. Davies

24.02.00	Paul Fiske L PTS 6 Sunderland
11.02.02	Mark Gladwell W RSC 3 Southampton
08.04.02	Joe Brame W RSC 1 Southampton
23.06.02	Tommy Eastwood L PTS 4 Southwark
21.12.02	James Zikic L PTS 4 Millwall
23.02.03	Oneal Murray W PTS 4 Streatham

Career: 6 contests, won 3, lost 3.

Dave Pearson

Middlesbrough. *Born* Middlesbrough, 1
April, 1974
Middleweight. Ht. 6'2¾"
Manager M. Shinfield

15.04.02	Ian Thomas L CO 3 Shrewsbury
03.10.02	Gary Firby W CO 3 Sunderland
21.10.02	Gary Jones L RSC 3 Cleethorpes
05.12.02	Chris Steele W PTS 6 Sunderland
24.03.03	Reagan Denton L PTS 6 Barnsley
31.05.03	Gary Jones L RSC 2 Barnsley

Career: 6 contests, won 2, lost 4.

Gavin Pearson　　　　　　Les Clark

Gavin Pearson

Bradford. *Born* Bradford, 10 March, 1977
Welterweight. Ht. 5'10"
Manager Self

26.11.98	Bobby Lyndon W PTS 6 Bradford
07.12.98	Dale Lowe L PTS 6 Cleethorpes
21.02.99	Les Frost W PTS 6 Bradford
12.03.99	Piotr Banicki DREW 4 Bethnal Green
03.04.99	Piotr Banicki DREW 4 Carlisle
06.05.99	Paul Swindles W PTS 6 Sunderland
29.05.99	Craig Smith L RSC 1 South Shields

12.09.99	Mike Watson W PTS 6 Nottingham
14.11.99	Chris Steele W PTS 6 Bradford
26.11.99	Peter Dunn DREW 6 Wakefield
09.12.99	John Marsden W PTS 6 Sunderland
06.03.00	John Marsden W PTS 6 Bradford
20.03.00	Joe Miller L PTS 6 Glasgow
17.04.00	Arv Mittoo W PTS 6 Glasgow
15.05.00	John Marsden W CO 5 Bradford
25.06.00	Robbie Sivyer L PTS 6 Wakefield
04.12.00	Dave Hinds W PTS 6 Bradford
05.02.01	Robert Burton L RSC 3 Bradford
17.05.01	Peter Dunn W PTS 6 Leeds
08.10.01	Robert Burton L RSC 2 Barnsley
18.03.02	Richard Inquieti W PTS 6 Glasgow
25.03.02	Danny Moir W PTS 6 Sunderland
29.04.02	Richard Inquieti W PTS 6 Bradford
09.05.02	Mark Paxford W PTS 6 Sunderland
20.11.02	Ciaran Duffy DREW 6 Leeds
02.12.02	Richie Murray W RTD 4 Bradford

Career: 26 contests, won 16, drew 4, lost 6.

Kevin Phelan

Slough. *Born* Slough, 11 June, 1977
Middleweight. Ht. 6'1"
Manager J. Evans

27.09.02	Lee Hodgson L RSC 1 Bracknell
21.03.03	Jimi Hendricks W RSC 6 Longford
12.04.03	Steve Russell W PTS 4 Norwich
26.04.03	Dave Wakefield W PTS 4 Brentford
09.05.03	Leigh Wicks W PTS 6 Longford

Career: 5 contests, won 4, lost 1.

Mark Phillips　　　　　　Les Clark

Mark Phillips

St Clare's. *Born* Carmarthen, 28 April,
1975
L. Heavyweight. Ht. 6'0"
Manager N. Christian

26.10.00	Shayne Webb W PTS 6 Clydach
12.12.00	Tommy Matthews W PTS 6 Clydach
13.03.01	William Webster W RTD 1 Plymouth
07.10.01	Danny Norton L PTS 6 Wolverhampton
12.12.01	Simon Andrews W PTS 6 Clydach

25.04.02   Mark Ellwood L PTS 6 Hull
10.05.02   Scott Dann L PTS 6 Bethnal Green
23.06.02   Gareth Hogg L PTS 4 Southwark
10.07.02   Scott Dann L PTS 4 Wembley
03.12.02   Jamie Hearn L PTS 4 Bethnal Green
20.12.02   Ryan Walls L PTS 4 Bracknell
06.03.03   Darren Dorrington L PTS 8 Bristol
21.03.03   Steve Timms L PTS 6 West Bromwich
05.04.03   Dale Nixon L PTS 6 Coventry
13.04.03   Donovan Smillie L PTS 6 Bradford
12.05.03   Leigh Alliss L PTS 6 Southampton
27.05.03   Steven Spartacus L RSC 2 Dagenham
30.06.03   Roddy Doran L PTS 6 Shrewsbury

Career: 18 contests, won 4, lost 14.

Esham Pickering

Newark. *Born* Newark, 7 August, 1976
Commonwealth S. Bantamweight
Champion. Former Undefeated British
Masters Bantamweight Champion. Ht. 5'5"
Manager B. Ingle/F. Warren

23.09.96   Brendan Bryce W RSC 5 Cleethorpes
24.10.96   Kevin Sheil W PTS 6 Lincoln
22.11.96   Amjid Mahmood W RSC 2 Hull
09.12.96   Des Gargano W RTD 2 Chesterfield
16.12.96   Graham McGrath W PTS 6
            Cleethorpes
20.03.97   Robert Braddock W RSC 6 Newark
12.04.97   Graham McGrath W PTS 4 Sheffield
26.04.97   Mike Deveney W PTS 4 Swadlincote
16.05.97   Chris Price W PTS 6 Hull
26.06.97   Graham McGrath W PTS 6 Salford
01.11.97   Mike Deveney W RSC 8 Glasgow
            (Elim. British Featherweight Title)
09.05.98   Jonjo Irwin L PTS 12 Sheffield
            (Vacant British Featherweight Title)
11.09.98   Louis Veitch W PTS 6 Newark
15.08.99   Chris Lyons W RSC 2 Derby
23.10.99   Ian Turner W PTS 6 Telford
20.11.99   Marc Smith W PTS 6 Grantham
19.02.00   Kevin Gerowski W PTS 10 Newark
            (Vacant British Masters Bantamweight
            Title. Elim. British Bantamweight Title)
13.08.00   Lee Williamson W PTS 6 Nottingham
16.12.00   Mauricio Martinez L RSC 1 Sheffield
            (WBO Bantamweight Title Challenge)
15.09.01   Carl Allen W PTS 6 Derby
08.12.01   Carl Allen W PTS 8 Chesterfield
20.04.02   Carl Allen W PTS 6 Derby
24.09.02   Alejandro Monzon L PTS 12 Gran
            Canaria, Spain
            (Vacant WBA Inter-Continental
            S.Featherweight Title)
02.12.02   Carl Allen W PTS 6 Leicester
08.02.03   Duncan Karanja W CO 5 Brentford
            (Vacant Commonwealth
            S.Bantamweight Title)

Career: 25 contests, won 22, lost 3.

Wayne Pinder

Manchester. *Born* Manchester, 15 April,
1978
Middleweight. Former WBF Middleweight
Champion. Ht. 6'0"
Manager S. Wood/T. Gilmour

27.04.98   C. J. Jackson W PTS 6 Manchester
01.06.98   Carlton Williams W PTS 6 Manchester
26.10.98   Mark Owens DREW 6 Manchester
28.02.99   Lee Bird W RSC 4 Shaw
13.03.99   Paul O'Rourke W RSC 3 Manchester
02.05.99   Carl Smith W RSC 5 Shaw

02.07.99   Donovan Davey W PTS 6 Manchester
19.09.99   Paul King W PTS 6 Shaw
11.06.00   Colin Vidler W PTS 6 Salford
01.07.00   Gary Beardsley W PTS 4 Manchester
09.09.00   Ian Toby W PTS 4 Manchester
12.11.00   James Donoghue W PTS 6 Manchester
17.03.01   Leigh Wicks W PTS 4 Manchester
27.05.01   Dean Ashton W PTS 6 Manchester
07.07.01   Ian Toby W RTD 5 Manchester
26.11.01   Howard Clarke W PTS 6 Manchester
09.03.02   Jimmy Steel W PTS 4 Manchester
21.07.02   Darren Covill W CO 2 Salford
09.11.02   Darren Rhodes W RSC 4 Altrincham
28.01.03   Damon Hague W RSC 7 Nottingham
            (Vacant WBF Middleweight Title)
16.04.03   Damon Hague L RSC 2 Nottingham
            (WBF Middleweight Title Defence)
21.06.03   Howard Clarke W PTS 4 Manchester

Career: 22 contests, won 20, drew 1, lost 1.

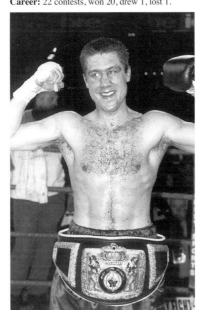

Wayne Pinder   Les Clark

Michael Pinnock

Birmingham. *Born* Birmingham, 6 June,
1965
Cruiserweight. Ht. 6'0"
Manager Self

19.05.95   David Flowers L PTS 6 Leeds
13.06.95   Mark Snipe L PTS 6 Basildon
20.06.95   Darren Sweeney L PTS 8 Birmingham
06.09.95   Steve Loftus L PTS 6 Stoke
21.09.95   Luan Morena L PTS 4 Battersea
24.10.95   Graham Townsend L PTS 4 Southwark
17.11.95   Graham Townsend L PTS 4 Bethnal
            Green
03.12.95   Neville Smith L RSC 5 Southwark
23.01.96   Butch Lesley L PTS 4 Bethnal Green
05.03.96   Panayiotis Panayiotiou L PTS 4
            Bethnal Green
16.03.96   Mark Hickey L PTS 6 Barnstaple
25.03.96   Lee Simpkin W PTS 6 Birmingham
03.04.96   Jason Hart L PTS 6 Bethnal Green
24.04.96   Gordon Behan L PTS 6 Solihull
03.05.96   David Larkin DREW 6 Sheffield

14.05.96   Mervyn Penniston L RSC 2 Dagenham
19.07.96   Chris Davies L PTS 6 Ystrad
29.07.96   Stuart Fleet L RSC 3 Skegness
04.10.96   Paul Bonson L PTS 6 Wakefield
28.10.96   Zak Goldman DREW 6 Leicester
14.11.96   Paul Bonson DREW 6 Sheffield
21.11.96   Darren Sweeney W RSC 5 Solihull
26.11.96   Mark Smallwood L PTS 6
            Wolverhampton
03.02.97   Neil Simpson L PTS 6 Leicester
09.06.97   Mark Hobson L PTS 6 Bradford
05.07.97   Paschal Collins L PTS 6 Glasgow
02.09.97   Mike Gormley L PTS 6 Manchester
18.09.97   Martin Jolley DREW 6 Alfreton
04.10.97   Zoltan Sarossy L PTS 4 Muswell Hill
27.10.97   Johnny Hooks DREW 6 Nottingham
11.11.97   Graham Townsend L PTS 8 Bethnal
            Green
25.11.97   Barry Thorogood L PTS 8
            Wolverhampton
15.12.97   Greg Scott-Briggs L PTS 6 Nottingham
02.02.98   Glenn Williams L CO 5 Manchester
30.04.98   Bobby Banghar L PTS 6 Purfleet
18.05.98   Jon O'Brien L PTS 6 Cleethorpes
22.10.98   Paul Carr L PTS 6 Barking
29.10.98   Paul Carr DREW 6 Bayswater
05.12.98   Dave Stenner W RSC 3 Bristol
03.04.99   Robert Zlotkowski L PTS 4 Carlisle
15.05.99   Damon Hague L PTS 4 Sheffield
05.06.99   Leif Keiski L PTS 6 Cardiff
02.07.99   Mike Gormley L RSC 6 Manchester
01.10.99   Tony Oakey L PTS 4 Bethnal Green
16.10.99   Brian Magee L RSC 3 Belfast
17.04.00   Gordon Behan L PTS 6 Birmingham
15.05.00   Tony Booth L PTS 6 Cleethorpes
25.05.00   Neil Linford L PTS 4 Peterborough
08.09.00   Steven Spartacus L PTS 4
            Hammersmith
10.11.00   Tony Griffiths L PTS 4 Mayfair
01.12.00   Allan Foster L PTS 4 Peterborough
29.01.01   Ivan Botton W PTS 4 Peterborough
20.03.01   Joe Gillon L PTS 6 Glasgow
28.03.01   Darren Ashton DREW 6 Piccadilly
09.06.01   Nathan King L PTS 4 Bethnal Green
21.06.01   Paul Bonson L PTS 6 Sheffield
27.07.01   Mark Brookes L PTS 4 Sheffield
15.09.01   Tony Dowling L PTS 6 Derby
04.10.01   Oneal Murray L PTS 6 Finsbury
21.10.01   Peter Merrall DREW 6 Pentre Halkyn
28.10.01   Radcliffe Green L PTS 4 Southwark
24.11.01   Steven Spartacus L PTS 4 Bethnal
            Green
09.12.01   Andrew Facey L PTS 6 Shaw
16.12.01   Sam Price L PTS 4 Southwark
16.03.02   Carl Froch L RSC 4 Bethnal Green
21.11.02   Earl Ling L PTS 6 Hull
16.12.02   Eamonn Glennon DREW 6
            Cleethorpes
08.02.03   Tony Moran L PTS 4 Liverpool
23.02.03   Ryan Walls L PTS 6 Streatham
16.03.03   Scott Lansdowne L PTS 6 Nottingham
24.03.03   Pinky Burton L PTS 4 Barnsley
10.06.03   Mark Brookes L PTS 4 Sheffield

Career: 72 contests, won 4, drew 9, lost 59.

Dean Pithie

Coventry. *Born* Coventry, 18 January 1974
S. Featherweight. Former Undefeated WBC
International S. Featherweight Champion.
Former Commonwealth & WBO Inter-
Continental S. Featherweight Champion.
Ht. 5'5"
Manager Self

17.02.95 Kid McAuley W RSC 3 Cumbernauld
13.04.95 Kid McAuley W RSC 1 Bloomsbury
01.07.95 Pete Buckley W PTS 4 Kensington
22.07.95 G. G. Goddard W PTS 4 Millwall
21.10.95 Anthony Campbell W PTS 4 Bethnal Green
10.11.95 Kelton McKenzie DREW 6 Derby
26.04.96 Kelton McKenzie W PTS 6 Cardiff
25.06.96 Lewis Reynolds W RSC 2 Mansfield
14.09.96 Miguel Matthews W PTS 4 Sheffield
14.12.96 Marty Chestnut W RSC 3 Sheffield
18.01.97 Harry Escott W RSC 4 Swadlincote
25.02.97 Pete Buckley W PTS 4 Sheffield
26.04.97 David Morris W PTS 8 Swadlincote
11.10.97 Stefy Bull W RSC 11 Sheffield
(Vacant WBO Inter-Continental S. Featherweight Title)
27.03.98 Paul Griffin W RSC 9 Telford
(WBO Inter-Continental S. Featherweight Title Defence)
06.06.98 Gary Thornhill L CO 8 Liverpool
(WBO Inter-Continental S. Featherweight Title Defence)
02.10.98 Keith Jones W PTS 8 Cheshunt
11.12.98 Kelton McKenzie W RSC 7 Cheshunt
(Elim. British S. Featherweight Title)
26.02.99 Andrew Matabola L RSC 8 Coventry
(Vacant WBC International S. Featherweight Title)
12.07.99 Andrew Matebola W RSC 2 Coventry
(WBC International S. Featherweight Title Challenge)
22.10.99 Frank Kiwanuka W RSC 2 Coventry
(WBC International S. Featherweight Title Defence)
14.12.99 Mzonke Fana W PTS 12 Coventry
(WBC International S. Featherweight Title Defence)
29.02.00 Michael Gomez L PTS 12 Widnes
(British S. Featherweight Title Challenge)
22.05.00 Wiseman Jim DREW 12 Coventry
(Vacant WBF Inter-Continental S. Featherweight Title)
28.10.00 Affif Djelti L CO 6 Coventry
(IBO S.Featherweight Title Challenge)
10.04.01 Keith Jones W PTS 4 Wembley
14.07.01 Jason White W PTS 4 Liverpool
17.11.01 Woody Greenaway W PTS 6 Coventry
09.02.02 Isaac Sebaduka W PTS 8 Coventry
26.04.02 Nigel Senior W PTS 6 Coventry
13.07.02 Alex Moon W PTS 12 Coventry
(Commonwealth S.Featherweight Title Challenge)
12.04.03 Craig Docherty L CO 8 Bethnal Green
(Commonwealth S. Featherweight Title Defence)
Career: 32 contests, won 25, drew 2, lost 5.

(Stephen) Sonny Pollard

Hull. *Born* Hull, 3 November, 1976
L. Middleweight. Ht. 5'9¼"
Manager S. Pollard

09.06.98 Shamus Casey W PTS 4 Hull
08.08.98 Harry Butler L RSC 4 Scarborough
04.03.00 Wayne Elcock L RSC 3 Peterborough
26.09.02 Gary Jones W PTS 6 Hull
11.12.02 Martin Scotland W RSC 2 Hull
03.04.03 Wayne Shepherd W PTS 6 Hull
17.04.03 Andrei Ivanov W PTS 6 Hull
Career: 7 contests, won 5, lost 2.

Gary Porter

Glasgow. *Born* Glasgow, 12 September, 1978
L. Middleweight. Ht. 5'9"
Manager B. Watt

04.06.01 Arv Mittoo W PTS 6 Glasgow
17.09.01 Carl Walton W PTS 6 Glasgow
03.11.01 Sam Mottram W PTS 4 Glasgow
22.04.02 Matt Scriven W PTS 6 Glasgow
03.06.02 Richard Inquieti W PTS 6 Glasgow
23.09.02 David Keir W PTS 8 Glasgow
20.01.03 Danny Moir L PTS 6 Glasgow
17.03.03 Franny Jones L PTS 6 Glasgow
Career: 8 contests, won 6, lost 2.

Keith Porter

Belfast. *Born* Belfast, 18 March, 1981
Lightweight. Ht. 5'8"
Manager A. Wilton

28.11.02 Dai Bando W PTS 4 Finchley
Career: 1 contest, won 1.

Marcus Portman

West Bromwich. *Born* West Bromwich, 26 September, 1980
Welterweight. Ht. 6'0"
Manager Self

18.02.00 Ray Wood W PTS 6 West Bromwich
28.03.00 Billy Smith W PTS 6 Wolverhampton
10.09.00 Alan Kershaw W RSC 2 Walsall
15.02.01 Willie Limond L PTS 6 Glasgow
01.04.01 Tony Smith W PTS 6 Wolverhampton
20.04.01 Darren Melville L RSC 3 Millwall
07.09.01 Tony Smith W PTS 6 West Bromwich
15.09.01 Matthew Hatton L RSC 3 Manchester
12.12.01 Ross McCord DREW 4 Clydach
18.01.02 Andy Egan W PTS 4 Coventry
25.02.02 Sammy Smith W PTS 6 Slough
27.04.02 Gavin Wake W PTS 4 Huddersfield
08.05.03 Thomas McDonagh L PTS 6 Widnes
17.05.03 Scott Dixon W PTS 6 Liverpool
30.06.03 Wayne Wheeler W RSC 3 Shrewsbury
Career: 15 contests, won 10, drew 1, lost 4.

Mark Potter

Walthamstow. *Born* Rush Green, 27 February, 1975
Heavyweight. Former Southern Area Heavyweight Champion. Ht. 6'1"
Manager Self

19.07.97 J. A. Bugner W PTS 6 Wembley
02.09.97 Rob Albon W RSC 1 Southwark
06.12.97 Johnny Davison W CO 1 Wembley
27.02.98 Lennox Williams W CO 1 Brighton
21.04.98 Geoff Hunter W RSC 1 Edmonton
23.05.98 Shane Woollas W PTS 4 Bethnal Green
12.09.98 Abdelrani Berbachi W RTD 4 Bethnal Green
22.09.98 Antoine Palatis L PTS 8 Pont Audemir, France
21.11.98 Ladislav Husarik W RSC 6 Southwark
08.05.99 Piotr Jurczyk W RSC 1 Bethnal Green
10.07.99 Stanislav Tomcatchov W RSC 3 Southwark
13.09.99 Derek McCafferty W PTS 6 Bethnal Green
29.11.99 Keith Long L PTS 8 Wembley

13.03.00 Danny Watts W RSC 6 Bethnal Green
(Vacant Southern Area Heavyweight Title)
27.05.00 Mal Rice W CO 1 Southwark
23.09.00 Luke Simpkin W PTS 6 Bethnal Green
21.10.00 Danny Williams L RSC 6 Wembley
(Commonwealth & WBO Inter-Continental Heavyweight Title Challenges. Vacant British Heavyweight Title)
05.05.01 Michael Murray W PTS 8 Edmonton
28.07.01 Alex Vasiliev L RSC 7 Wembley
(Vacant WBU Inter-Continental Heavyweight Title)
08.12.01 Gary Williams W RSC 3 Dagenham
26.01.02 Derek McCafferty W PTS 6 Bethnal Green
28.04.02 Neil Kirkwood W RSC 1 Southwark
10.07.02 Derek McCafferty W RSC 6 Wembley
23.08.02 Luke Simpkin W PTS 6 Bethnal Green
03.12.02 Osborne Mashimane W CO 3 Bethnal Green
18.03.03 Michael Sprott L RSC 3 Reading
(Southern Area Heavyweight Title Defence. Elim. British Heavyweight Title)
Career: 26 contests, won 21, lost 5.

Dean Powell

Peckham. *Born* Salisbury, 4 June, 1970
Middleweight. Ht. 5'9"
Manager J. Evans

17.12.96 Matthew Tait L PTS 6 Bethnal Green
11.02.97 Matthew Tait L RSC 4 Bethnal Green
26.09.98 Brian Knudsen L PTS 4 York
12.12.98 Jeff Mills W RSC 3 Southwark
16.01.99 Neil Linford L RSC 1 Bethnal Green
22.11.01 Darren Covill W PTS 4 Mayfair
15.10.02 Alan Gilbert L PTS 4 Bethnal Green
03.12.02 Tomas da Silva W PTS 4 Bethnal Green
08.02.03 Lee Hodgson L PTS 4 Brentford
13.04.03 Michael Thomas L RSC 1 Streatham
20.06.03 Mark Thornton L PTS 6 Gatwick
Career: 11 contests, won 3, lost 8.

Martin Power   Les Clark

Martin Power

St Pancras. *Born* London, 14 February, 1980
Bantamweight. Ht. 5'6"
Manager Self

09.06.01	Sean Grant W PTS 4 Bethnal Green	
28.07.01	Andrew Greenaway W RSC 3 Wembley	
22.09.01	Stevie Quinn W RSC 2 Bethnal Green	
24.11.01	Anthony Hanna W PTS 4 Bethnal Green	
19.01.02	Gareth Wiltshaw W PTS 4 Bethnal Green	
08.07.02	Darren Cleary W PTS 4 Mayfair	
12.10.02	Stevie Quinn W RSC 4 Bethnal Green	
15.02.03	Stevie Quinn W RTD 1 Wembley	
29.03.03	Dave Hinds W PTS 4 Portsmouth	

Career: 9 contests, won 9.

Sam Price

Reading. *Born* Hillingdon, 6 July, 1981
L. Heavyweight. Ht. 6'0½"
Manager E. Maloney/F. Maloney

16.12.01	Michael Pinnock W PTS 4 Southwark
10.02.02	Calvin Stonestreet W PTS 4 Southwark
19.03.02	Jimmy Steel W PTS 4 Slough
21.03.03	Harry Butler W PTS 4 Longford

Career: 4 contests, won 4.

Bradley Pryce (Price)

Newbridge. *Born* Newport, 15 March, 1981
Welterweight. Former Undefeated IBF
Inter-Continental L.Welterweight
Champion. Former Undefeated WBO Inter-
Continental Lightweight Champion.
Ht. 5'11"
Manager E. Calzaghe/F. Warren

17.07.99	Dave Hinds W PTS 4 Doncaster
23.10.99	David Jeffrey W RSC 3 Telford
06.11.99	Eddie Nevins W RSC 2 Widnes
29.01.00	Pete Buckley W PTS 4 Manchester
29.02.00	Carl Allen W PTS 4 Widnes
16.05.00	Carl Allen W RSC 3 Warrington
15.07.00	Gary Flear W RSC 1 Millwall
07.10.00	Gary Reid W RSC 5 Doncaster
27.01.01	Joel Viney W RSC 3 Bethnal Green
17.03.01	Brian Coleman W PTS 4 Manchester
28.04.01	Jason Hall W PTS 12 Cardiff
	(Vacant WBO Inter-Continental Lightweight Title)
21.07.01	Stuart Patterson W RSC 5 Sheffield
09.10.01	Lucky Sambo W PTS 12 Cardiff
	(WBO Inter-Continental Lightweight Title Defence)
12.02.02	Gavin Down W RSC 9 Bethnal Green
	(Vacant IBF Inter-Continental L.Welterweight Title)
20.04.02	Dafydd Carlin W RSC 8 Cardiff
08.06.02	Pete Buckley W RSC 1 Renfrew
17.08.02	Ted Bami L RSC 6 Cardiff
23.11.02	Craig Lynch W CO 4 Derby
01.02.03	Neil Sinclair L RSC 8 Belfast
	(British Welterweight Title Challenge)
08.05.03	Ivan Kirpa W PTS 10 Widnes

Career: 20 contests, won 18, lost 2.

Kreshnik Qato

Wembley. *Born* Albania, 13 August, 1978
Middleweight. Ht. 5'9½"
Manager F. Warren

28.09.01	Erik Teymour L PTS 6 Millwall
16.12.01	Lawrence Murphy L PTS 6 Glasgow
08.04.02	Ty Browne W PTS 4 Southampton
10.05.02	Paul Jones L PTS 6 Millwall
20.03.03	Jason Collins W PTS 4 Queensway
13.04.03	Mark Thornton W RSC 3 Streatham
13.05.03	Danny Thornton W PTS 6 Leeds

Career: 7 contests, won 4, lost 3.

Mickey Quinn (McAllister)

Belfast. *Born* Belfast, 7 January, 1979
Middleweight. Ht. 5'10¼"
Manager J. Breen/M. Callahan

01.06.02	Harry Butler W PTS 4 Manchester
28.09.02	Lee Williamson W RSC 2 Manchester
01.02.03	Joel Ani W PTS 4 Belfast
14.06.03	Vedran Akrap L PTS 4 Magdeburg, Germany

Career: 4 contests, won 3, lost 1.

Stevie Quinn

Newtownards. *Born* Newtonards, 14
November, 1969
Bantamweight. Ht. 5'7"

Manager Self

07.02.98	Stephen Oates L PTS 4 Cheshunt
28.04.98	Tommy Waite L RSC 3 Belfast
11.12.98	Mark Payne L RSC 2 Cheshunt
17.04.99	Chris Edwards W RSC 4 Dublin
22.05.99	Ross Cassidy W PTS 4 Belfast
16.10.99	Anthony Hanna L PTS 4 Belfast
19.02.00	Barry Hawthorne W RSC 5 Prestwick
12.06.00	Mickey Coveney L PTS 4 Belfast
20.10.00	Sean Grant W RSC 2 Belfast
11.11.00	Paul Weir W PTS 4 Belfast
27.01.01	Hussein Hussein L RTD 2 Bethnal Green
01.04.01	Richmond Asante W PTS 4 Southwark
28.04.01	Noel Wilders L RTD 6 Cardiff
22.09.01	Martin Power L RSC 2 Bethnal Green
19.12.01	Mark Payne L RTD 2 Coventry
26.01.02	Michael Hunter L CO 2 Dagenham
12.10.02	Martin Power L RSC 4 Bethnal Green
07.12.02	Marc Callaghan W PTS 4 Brentwood
01.02.03	Marty Kayes W PTS 4 Belfast
15.02.03	Martin Power L RTD 1 Wembley
05.04.03	Marty Kayes W RSC 5 Belfast

Career: 21 contests, won 9, lost 12.

Stevie Quinn Les Clark

(Shahid) Sid Razak

Birmingham. *Born* Birmingham, 9 March, 1973
S. Featherweight. Ht. 5'7"
Manager D. Poston

13.02.01 Neil Read W PTS 6 Brierley Hill
27.03.01 Tommy Thomas W RSC 2 Brierley Hill
21.05.01 Jason Nesbitt W PTS 6 Birmingham
08.10.01 Gareth Wiltshaw L PTS 6 Birmingham
14.09.02 J.J.Moore L PTS 6 Newark
26.09.02 Chris Hooper L PTS 6 Hull
Career: 6 contests, won 3, lost 3.

Neil Read

Bilston. *Born* Wolverhampton, 9 February, 1972
Bantamweight. Ht. 5'4"
Manager Self

08.02.00 Gary Groves W PTS 6 Wolverhampton
10.09.00 Stephen Chinnock L RSC 5 Walsall
30.11.00 Paddy Folan L PTS 6 Blackpool
13.02.01 Sid Razak L PTS 6 Brierley Hill
08.03.01 John-Paul Ryan W PTS 6 Stoke
26.08.01 Lee Holmes L PTS 6 Warrington
06.12.01 Chris Edwards L PTS 8 Stoke
28.01.02 Jamil Hussain L CO 2 Barnsley
13.04.02 Stephen Chinnock L CO 3 Wolverhampton
(Midlands Area Featherweight Title Challenge)
29.06.02 Jamie Yelland L PTS 6 Brentwood
03.08.02 Isaac Ward L RSC 1 Blackpool
23.09.02 Andy Roberts L PTS 6 Cleethorpes
10.10.02 Chris Edwards L PTS 6 Stoke
08.11.02 Andy Roberts L PTS 6 Doncaster
02.12.02 Steve Gethin L RTD 3 Leicester
10.02.03 Sean Hughes L PTS 6 Sheffield
17.03.03 Junior Anderson W CO 2 Southampton
07.06.03 Gareth Payne L RSC 5 Coventry
(Vacant Midlands Area S.Bantamweight Title)
Career: 18 contests, won 3, lost 15.

(Dale) Daleboy Rees

Swansea. *Born* Swansea, 7 July, 1979
Lightweight. Ht. 5'7"
Manager P. Boyce

15.09.02 Greg Edwards W PTS 4 Swansea
08.01.03 Joel Viney W RSC 5 Aberdare
25.01.03 Pavel Potipko W PTS 4 Bridgend
10.04.03 Henry Jones W PTS 4 Clydach
Career: 4 contests, won 4.

Gavin Rees

Newbridge. *Born* Newport, 10 May, 1980
S. Featherweight. WBO Inter-Continental
Featherweight Champion. Ht. 5'7"
Manager F. Warren/E. Calzaghe

05.09.98 John Farrell W PTS 4 Telford
05.12.98 Ernie Smith W PTS 4 Bristol
27.03.99 Graham McGrath W RSC 2 Derby
05.06.99 Wayne Jones W RSC 2 Cardiff

11.12.99 Dave Hinds W RSC 2 Liverpool
19.02.00 Pete Buckley W PTS 4 Dagenham
29.05.00 Willie Valentine W RSC 3 Manchester
23.09.00 Pete Buckley W PTS 4 Bethnal Green
13.11.00 Steve Hanley W RSC 1 Bethnal Green
15.01.01 Chris Jickells W RSC 2 Manchester
28.04.01 Vladimir Borov W RSC 4 Cardiff
(Vacant WBO Inter-Continental Featherweight Title)
21.07.01 Nigel Senior W RSC 2 Sheffield
09.10.01 Nikolai Eremeev W PTS 12 Cardiff
(WBO Inter-Continental Featherweight Title Defence)
12.02.02 Rakhim Mingaleev W PTS 6 Bethnal Green
20.04.02 Gary Flear W RTD 4 Cardiff
08.07.02 Ernie Smith W RSC 5 Mayfair
17.08.02 Sergei Andreychikov W RTD 1 Cardiff
14.12.02 Jimmy Beech W PTS 4 Newcastle
15.02.03 Andrei Devyataykin W PTS 6 Wembley
28.06.03 Daniel Thorpe W RSC 1 Cardiff
Career: 20 contests, won 20.

Gary Reid

Telford. *Born* Jamaica, 20 November, 1972
Lightweight. Ht. 5'5½"
Manager A. Phillips/T. Gilmour

09.12.98 Carl Tilley W CO 1 Stoke
11.02.99 Ted Bami L RSC 2 Dudley
23.03.99 Lee Williamson W PTS 6 Wolverhampton
07.10.99 Stuart Rimmer W RSC 2 Mere
19.12.99 No No Junior L PTS 6 Salford
14.04.00 Lee Molyneux W PTS 6 Manchester
18.05.00 Sammy Smith W RSC 1 Bethnal Green
23.07.00 Kevin Bennett L RSC 4 Hartlepool
21.09.00 Karim Bouali L PTS 4 Bloomsbury
07.10.00 Bradley Pryce L RSC 5 Doncaster
07.09.01 Willie Limond L PTS 8 Glasgow
22.09.01 Francis Barrett L PTS 4 Bethnal Green
17.02.02 Richie Caparelli W PTS 6 Salford
02.03.02 Paul Halpin L RSC 3 Bethnal Green
26.04.02 Martin Watson L PTS 6 Glasgow
28.05.02 Gareth Jordan DREW 6 Liverpool
13.07.02 Gary Greenwood L RSC 5 Coventry
05.10.02 Joel Viney W CO 2 Coventry
18.11.02 Martin Watson L RSC 4 Glasgow
21.03.03 Young Muttley L RSC 7 West Bromwich
(Vacant Midlands Area L.Welterweight Title)
Career: 20 contests, won 7, drew 1, lost 12.

Pele Reid

Birmingham. *Born* Birmingham, 11 January, 1973
Heavyweight. Former Undefeated WBO
Inter-Continental Heavyweight Champion.
Ht. 6'3"
Manager Self

24.11.95 Gary Williams W RSC 1 Manchester
20.01.96 Joey Paladino W RSC 1 Mansfield
26.01.96 Vance Idiens W RSC 1 Brighton
11.05.96 Keith Fletcher W CO 1 Bethnal Green
25.06.96 Andy Lambert W CO 1 Mansfield
12.10.96 Eduardo Carranza W CO 2 Milan, Italy
02.11.96 Ricky Sullivan W RSC 2 Garmisch, Germany
25.02.97 Michael Murray W RSC 1 Sheffield
28.06.97 Ricardo Kennedy W RSC 1 Norwich
(Vacant WBO Inter-Continental Heavyweight Title)

11.10.97 Eli Dixon W CO 9 Sheffield
(WBO Inter-Continental Heavyweight Title Defence)
15.11.97 Albert Call W RSC 2 Bristol
06.06.98 Wayne Llewelyn W CO 1 Liverpool
(Elim. British Heavyweight Title)
19.09.98 Biko Botowamungo W RTD 3 Oberhausen, Germany
30.01.99 Julius Francis L RSC 3 Bethnal Green
(British & Commonwealth Heavyweight Title Challenges)
26.06.99 Orlin Norris L RSC 1 Millwall
22.01.00 Jacklord Jacobs L RSC 2 Birmingham
04.10.01 Mal Rice W PTS 4 Finsbury
13.12.01 Derek McCafferty W RSC 3 Leicester Square
27.01.02 Luke Simpkin DREW 4 Streatham
09.05.02 Michael Sprott L RSC 7 Leicester Square
(Vacant WBF European Heavyweight Title)
06.09.02 Derek McCafferty DREW 4 Bethnal Green
15.10.02 Joseph Chingangu W RSC 3 Bethnal Green
Career: 22 contests, won 16, drew 2, lost 4.

Robin Reid

Runcorn. Liverpool, 19 February, 1971
WBF S. Middleweight Champion. Former
WBC S. Middleweight Champion. Ht. 5'9"
Manager Self

27.02.93 Mark Dawson W RSC 1 Dagenham
06.03.93 Julian Eavis W RSC 2 Glasgow
10.04.93 Andrew Furlong W PTS 6 Swansea
10.09.93 Juan Garcia W PTS 6 San Antonio, USA
09.10.93 Ernie Loveridge W PTS 4 Manchester
18.12.93 Danny Juma DREW 6 Manchester
09.04.94 Kesem Clayton W RSC 1 Mansfield
04.06.94 Andrew Furlong W RSC 2 Cardiff
17.09.94 Andrew Jervis W RSC 2 Sheffield
19.11.94 Chris Richards W RSC 3 Cardiff
04.02.95 Bruno Westenberghs W RSC 1 Cardiff
04.03.95 Marvin O'Brien W RSC 6 Livingston
06.05.95 Steve Goodwin W CO 1 Shepton Mallet
10.06.95 Martin Jolley W CO 1 Manchester
22.07.95 John Duckworth W PTS 8 Millwall
15.09.95 Trevor Ambrose W CO 5 Mansfield
10.11.95 Danny Juma W PTS 8 Derby
26.01.96 Stinger Mason W RSC 2 Brighton
16.03.96 Andrew Flute W RSC 7 Glasgow
26.04.96 Hunter Clay W RSC 1 Cardiff
08.06.96 Mark Dawson W RSC 5 Newcastle
31.08.96 Don Pendleton W RTD 4 Dublin
12.10.96 Vincenzo Nardiello W CO 7 Milan, Italy
(WBC S. Middleweight Title Challenge)
08.02.97 Giovanni Pretorius W RSC 7 Millwall
(WBC S. Middleweight Title Defence)
03.05.97 Henry Wharton W PTS 12 Manchester
(WBC S. Middleweight Title Defence)
11.09.97 Hassine Cherifi W PTS 12 Widnes
(WBC S. Middleweight Title Defence)
19.12.97 Thulani Malinga L PTS 12 Millwall
(WBC S. Middleweight Title Defence)
18.04.98 Graham Townsend W RSC 6 Manchester
13.02.99 Joe Calzaghe L PTS 12 Newcastle
(WBO S. Middleweight Title Challenge)
24.06.00 Silvio Branco L PTS 12 Glasgow
(WBU S. Middleweight Title Challenge)

08.12.00 Mike Gormley W RSC 1 Crystal
Palace
(Vacant WBF S. Middleweight Title)
19.05.01 Roman Babaev W RSC 3 Wembley
(WBF S. Middleweight Title Defence)
14.07.01 Soon Botes W RSC 4 Liverpool
(WBF S.Middleweight TitleDefence)
20.10.01 Jorge Sclarandi W CO 3 Glasgow
(WBF S. Middleweight Title Defence)
19.12.01 Julio Cesar Chavez W PTS 12
Coventry
(WBF S. Middleweight Title Defence)
10.07.02 Francisco Mora W PTS 12 Wembley
(WBF S. Middleweight Title Defence)
29.11.02 Mondili Mbonambi W RSC 2
Liverpool
05.04.03 Enrique Carlos Campos W RSC 8
Leipzig, Germany
Career: 38 contests, won 34, drew 1, lost 3.

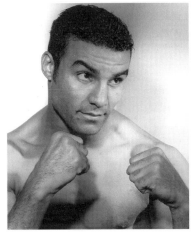

Robin Reid   Harry Goodwin

Darren Rhodes

Leeds. *Born* Leeds, 16 September, 1975
Middleweight. Ht. 5'11"
Manager Self

18.07.98 Andy Kemp W RSC 1 Sheffield
10.10.98 Perry Ayres W CO 2 Bethnal Green
27.02.99 Gareth Lovell W PTS 4 Oldham
01.05.99 Carlton Williams W RSC 4 Crystal
Palace
29.05.99 Sean Pritchard DREW 4 Halifax
09.10.99 Leigh Wicks W PTS 4 Manchester
11.12.99 Leigh Wicks W PTS 4 Liverpool
25.03.00 Leigh Wicks W PTS 4 Liverpool
29.05.00 Dean Ashton W RSC 3 Manchester
08.07.00 Jason Collins DREW 4 Widnes
04.09.00 Jason Collins L PTS 4 Manchester
11.12.00 Paul Wesley W PTS 4 Widnes
17.03.01 Andrew Facey W PTS 4 Manchester
07.07.01 Wayne Elcock L PTS 4 Manchester
24.11.01 Simeon Cover W RSC 5 Wakefield
02.03.02 Andrew Facey L RSC 6 Wakefield
*(Vacant Central Area Middleweight
Title)*
21.05.02 Hussain Osman L PTS 10 Custom House
15.06.02 Harry Butler W PTS 4 Leeds
28.09.02 Martin Thompson W PTS 8 Wakefield
09.11.02 Wayne Pinder L RSC 4 Altrincham
12.04.03 Mihaly Kotai L PTS 10 Bethnal Green
10.05.03 Lee Murtagh W PTS 6 Huddersfield
Career: 22 contests, won 14, drew 2, lost 6.

Darren Rhodes   Les Clark

Ryan Rhodes

Sheffield. *Born* Sheffield, 20 November,
1976
Middleweight. Former Undefeated WBO
Inter-Continental Middleweight Champion.
Former Undefeated British & IBF Inter-
Continental L. Middleweight Champion.
Ht. 5'8½"
Manager B. Ingle/F. Warren

04.02.95 Lee Crocker W RSC 2 Cardiff
04.03.95 Shamus Casey W CO 1 Livingston
06.05.95 Chris Richards W PTS 6 Shepton
Mallet
15.09.95 John Rice W RSC 2 Mansfield
10.11.95 Mark Dawson W PTS 6 Derby
20.01.96 John Duckworth W RSC 2 Mansfield
26.01.96 Martin Jolley W CO 3 Brighton
11.05.96 Martin Jolley W RSC 2 Bethnal Green
25.06.96 Roy Chipperfield W RSC 1 Mansfield
14.09.96 Del Bryan W PTS 6 Sheffield
14.12.96 Paul Jones W RSC 8 Sheffield
(Vacant British L. Middleweight Title)
25.02.97 Peter Waudby W CO 1 Sheffield
(British L. Middleweight Title Defence)
14.03.97 Del Bryan W RSC 7 Reading
(British L. Middleweight Title Defence)
12.04.97 Lindon Scarlett W RSC 1 Sheffield
*(Vacant IBF Inter-Continental
L. Middleweight Title)*
02.08.97 Ed Griffin W RSC 2 Barnsley
*(IBF Inter-Continental L. Middleweight
Title Defence. Vacant WBO
L. Middleweight Title)*
11.10.97 Yuri Epifantsev W RSC 2 Sheffield
(Final Elim. WBO Middleweight Title)
13.12.97 Otis Grant L PTS 12 Sheffield
(Vacant WBO Middleweight Title)
18.07.98 Lorant Szabo W RSC 8 Sheffield
*(WBO Inter-Continental Middleweight
Title Challenge)*
28.11.98 Fidel Avendano W RSC 1 Sheffield
*(WBO Inter-Continental Middleweight
Title Defence)*
27.03.99 Peter Mason W RSC 1 Derby
17.07.99 Jason Matthews L CO 2 Doncaster
(Vacant WBO Middleweight Title)

15.01.00 Eddie Haley W RSC 5 Doncaster
16.05.00 Ojay Abrahams W PTS 6 Warrington
21.10.00 Michael Alexander W PTS 6 Wembley
16.12.00 Howard Clarke W PTS 6 Sheffield
21.07.01 Youri Tsarenko W PTS 6 Sheffield
27.10.01 Jason Collins W PTS 4 Manchester
16.03.02 Lee Blundell L RSC 3 Bethnal Green
*(Vacant WBF Inter-Continental
Middleweight Title)*
16.04.03 Paul Wesley W CO 3 Nottingham
Career: 29 contests, won 26, lost 3.

Mal Rice

Flint. *Born* Mancot, 19 July, 1975
Heavyweight. Ht. 6'2"
Manager Self

26.11.97 Gary Cavey W CO 2 Stoke
29.01.98 Lennox Williams W PTS 6 Pentre
Halkyn
30.03.98 Bruno Foster L PTS 6 Bradford
30.04.98 Lennox Williams W PTS 6 Pentre
Halkyn
21.06.98 Shane Woollas L PTS 6 Liverpool
18.02.00 Gary Williams L PTS 6 Pentre Halkyn
13.03.00 Patrick Halberg W RSC 2 Bethnal
Green
05.05.00 Gary Williams L PTS 4 Pentre Halkyn
27.05.00 Mark Potter L CO 1 Southwark
26.03.01 John McDermott L RSC 2 Wembley
28.07.01 Matt Legg L PTS 4 Wembley
13.09.01 Petr Horacek W RSC 1 Sheffield
04.10.01 Pele Reid L PTS 4 Finsbury
16.12.01 Greg Wedlake L RSC 3 Bristol
18.05.02 Danny Watts L RTD 3 Millwall
29.03.03 Terry Dixon L PTS 4 Wembley
Career: 16 contests, won 5, lost 11.

Paul Richardson

Blackpool. *Born* Oxford, 17 October, 1972
Cruiserweight. Ht. 5'10½"
Manager L. Veitch

09.06.00 Jason Brewster W PTS 6 Blackpool
30.11.00 Dave Faulkner W PTS 6 Blackpool
22.01.01 Paul Fiske W PTS 6 Glasgow
08.03.01 Dave Faulkner W RSC 2 Blackpool
01.04.01 Jason Brewster W RSC 4
Wolverhampton
15.10.01 Huggy Osman L PTS 6 Bradford
16.11.01 Huggy Osman W PTS 6 Preston
26.10.02 Gary Thompson DREW 6 Wigan
Career: 8 contests, won 6, drew 1, lost 1.

Wayne Rigby

Manchester. *Born* Manchester, 19 July,
1973
L.Welterweight. Former WBF
L.Welterweight Champion. Former
Undefeated IBO Inter-Continental
Lightweight Champion. Former British
Lightweight Champion. Former Undefeated
Central Area Lightweight Champion.
Ht. 5'6"
Manager J. Trickett

27.02.92 Lee Fox L PTS 6 Liverpool
08.06.92 Leo Turner W PTS 6 Bradford
02.07.92 Leo Turner W CO 5 Middleton
05.10.92 Colin Innes W PTS 6 Manchester
01.12.92 John T. Kelly L PTS 6 Hartlepool
02.06.94 Kid McAuley W PTS 6 Middleton
13.06.94 Chris Clarkson W PTS 6 Liverpool

22.09.94 Mark Hargreaves W PTS 6 Bury
06.03.95 Kelton McKenzie L PTS 8 Leicester
18.05.95 John T. Kelly W PTS 6 Middleton
05.06.95 Hugh Collins W RSC 4 Glasgow
17.01.96 Kid McAuley W PTS 6 Solihull
24.03.96 Steve Tuckett W PTS 6 Shaw
27.09.96 Jimmy Phelan W PTS 10 Hull
  (Central Area Lightweight Title Challenge)
07.03.97 Alan Bosworth W RSC 5 Northampton
10.01.98 Tanveer Ahmed W PTS 12 Bethnal Green
  (Vacant British Lightweight Title)
11.04.98 Matt Brown W RTD 3 Southwark
  (British Lightweight Title Defence)
17.10.98 Bobby Vanzie L RSC 10 Manchester
  (British Lightweight Title Defence)
31.07.99 Mark McGowan W RSC 4 Carlisle
11.09.99 Alan Temple L PTS 8 Sheffield
04.12.99 Mark Haslam W CO 3 Peterborough
27.05.00 Dariusz Snarski W RSC 8 Mayfair
  (Vacant IBO Inter-Continental Lightweight Title)
01.07.00 Michael Ayers L RSC 10 Manchester
  (IBO Lightweight Title Challenge)
03.03.01 Michael Ayers L PTS 12 Wembley
  (IBO Lightweight Title Challenge)
14.07.01 Keith Jones W CO 3 Wembley
26.11.01 Antonio Ramirez W PTS 12 Manchester
  (Vacant WBF L.Welterweight Title)
09.03.02 Sedat Puskulla W CO 1 Manchester
  (Vacant WBF L. Welterweight Title)
18.05.02 Colin Dunne L RTD 10 Millwall
  (WBU Lightweight Title Challenge. Vacant WBF Lightweight Title)
09.11.02 Gary Ryder L PTS 12 Altrincham
  (WBF L. Welterweight Title Defence)
Career: 29 contests, won 20, lost 9.

Stuart Rimmer

St Helens. *Born* St Helens, 22 April, 1971
L. Welterweight. Ht. 5'6"
Manager Self

13.02.90 Dave Croft W PTS 6 Wolverhampton
07.03.90 Mark Antony L RSC 1 Doncaster
23.04.90 Dave Croft W CO 2 Birmingham
01.05.90 Neil Foran L RSC 2 Oldham
04.06.90 Frankie Foster L PTS 6 Glasgow
27.06.90 Bernard McComiskey L PTS 6 Kensington
12.09.90 Steve Griffith W RSC 2 Bethnal Green
27.09.90 Andrew Morgan W PTS 6 Birmingham
09.10.90 Jim Lawler W CO 2 Wolverhampton
29.10.90 Tony Feliciello L RSC 5 Birmingham
27.11.90 Alan Peacock L RSC 4 Glasgow
12.02.91 Andrew Morgan L PTS 8 Wolverhampton
24.04.91 Steve Winstanley L PTS 6 Preston
04.06.91 Michael Ayers L CO 1 Bethnal Green
10.09.91 Shaun Cooper L RSC 2 Wolverhampton
27.03.96 Wayne Pardoe L RSC 3 Stoke
02.10.96 Vic Broomhead W CO 5 Stoke
29.11.96 Rocky Ferrari W RSC 5 Glasgow
04.12.96 David Kirk L PTS 6 Stoke
23.10.97 Bobby Vanzie L RTD 8 Mayfair
  (Vacant Central Area Lightweight Title)
28.11.97 Gerard Murphy L PTS 6 Hull
06.05.98 Brian Coleman W PTS 6 Blackpool
05.06.98 Terry Roberts L PTS 4 Southend
21.07.98 Jamie McKeever L PTS 4 Widnes
01.12.98 Andy Green L RTD 5 Yarm
15.05.99 Gary Ryder L RSC 1 Blackpool

07.10.99 Gary Reid L RSC 2 Mere
18.02.00 Young Muttley L RSC 1 West Bromwich
27.05.00 David Walker L RSC 2 Southwark
30.09.00 Leo O'Reilly L RSC 2 Peterborough
04.10.01 Ajose Olusegun L RTD 2 Finsbury
06.12.01 Drea Dread W PTS 6 Stoke
15.03.02 Oscar Hall L RSC 4 Spennymoor
10.10.02 Gary Greenwood L RSC 1 Stoke
Career: 34 contests, won 9, lost 25.

Andy Roberts

Doncaster. *Born* Doncaster, 4 March, 1976
Bantamweight. Former Undefeated Central
Area Bantamweight Champion. Former
Central Area Flyweight Champion. Ht. 5'3"
Manager J. Rushton

20.10.94 Robert Grubb DREW 6 Walsall
12.12.94 Jason Morris W PTS 6 Doncaster
09.02.95 Robert Grubb DREW 6 Doncaster
22.03.95 Michael Edwards L PTS 6 Stoke
06.04.95 Steve Williams L PTS 6 Sheffield
05.05.95 Jason Morris W PTS 6 Doncaster
22.06.95 Paul Quarmby L PTS 6 Houghton le Spring
30.06.95 Stefy Bull L PTS 4 Doncaster
17.10.95 Robert Grubb L PTS 6 Wolverhampton
08.11.95 Graham McGrath W PTS 6 Scunthorpe
28.11.95 Graham McGrath L PTS 6 Wolverhampton
26.01.96 Darren Greaves W RSC 5 Doncaster
29.03.96 Graham McGrath L PTS 6 Doncaster
20.05.96 Neil Parry L PTS 6 Bradford
24.06.96 Neil Parry W PTS 6 Bradford
12.09.96 Steve Williams L PTS 6 Doncaster
23.09.96 Willie Smith W RSC 4 Bradford
03.10.96 Chip O'Neill W PTS 6 Sunderland
17.12.96 Neil Parry DREW 6 Doncaster
20.03.97 Marcus Duncan W PTS 10 Doncaster
  (Central Area Bantamweight Title Challenge)
10.07.97 David Coldwell W RSC 3 Doncaster
  (Vacant Central Area Flyweight Title)
12.11.97 Louis Veitch L PTS 10 Blackpool
  (Central Area Flyweight Title Defence)
04.12.97 David Coldwell L PTS 6 Doncaster
19.03.98 Anthony Hanna W PTS 6 Doncaster
13.05.98 Graham McGrath DREW 6 Scunthorpe
18.09.98 Barry Waite L RSC 1 Belfast
18.03.99 Terry Gaskin L RSC 8 Doncaster
17.07.99 Chris Emanuele L PTS 4 Doncaster
15.01.00 Terry Gaskin L RSC 8 Doncaster
  (Vacant Central Area Flyweight Title)
21.05.00 Gary Ford DREW 6 Shaw
23.07.00 Mbwana Matumla L RSC 2 Dar es Salaam, Tanzania
  (WBA Inter-Continental S.Flyweight Title Challenge)
07.10.00 Chris Edwards L PTS 4 Doncaster
23.09.02 Neil Read W PTS 6 Cleethorpes
08.11.02 Neil Read W PTS 6 Doncaster
30.11.02 Steve Williams L PTS 6 Newark
16.12.02 Marty Kayes W PTS 6 Cleethorpes
21.02.03 Marty Kayes W PTS 6 Doncaster
Career: 37 contests, won 13, drew 5, lost 19.

Steve Roberts

West Ham. *Born* Newham, 3 December, 1972
L.Middleweight. Former WBF
L.Middleweight Champion. Former
Undefeated WBF S.Middleweight

Champion. Former Undefeated Southern
Area L.Middleweight Champion. Ht. 5'11"
Manager B. Hearn

16.03.95 Julian Eavis W PTS 6 Basildon
23.05.95 Andy Peach W RSC 3 Potters Bar
13.06.95 Robbie Dunn W RSC 3 Basildon
20.09.95 Jason Hart W RSC 5 Potters Bar
30.09.95 Dick Hanns-Kat W CO 1 Basildon
25.11.95 Ernie Loveridge W PTS 4 Dagenham
23.01.96 Andrew Jervis W PTS 6 Bethnal Green
20.04.96 Peter Vosper W PTS 6 Brentwood
04.05.96 George Richards W PTS 6 Dagenham
27.09.96 Rob Stevenson W PTS 6 Stevenage
27.11.96 Lindon Scarlett W PTS 6 Bethnal Green
08.03.97 Adan Lugo W CO 4 Brentwood
08.04.97 Gilbert Jackson W PTS 10 Bethnal Green
  (Vacant Southern Area L. Middleweight Title)
30.08.97 Peter Mitchell W PTS 6 Cheshunt
08.10.97 Darren Covill W PTS 6 Poplar
05.06.98 Danny Quacoe W RTD 4 Southend
20.12.99 Mike Whittaker W PTS 6 Bethnal Green
05.02.00 Danny Thornton W PTS 6 Bethnal Green
01.04.00 Chris Crook W RSC 3 Bethnal Green
16.06.00 Mike Algoet W PTS 12 Bloomsbury
  (Vacant WBF S. Middleweight Title)
19.08.00 Scott Dixon W RSC 9 Brentwood
  (Vacant WBF L.Middleweight Title)
02.12.00 Mohammed Hissani W RSC 7 Bethnal Green
  (WBF L. Middleweight Title Defence)
03.03.01 Sergio Acuna W RSC 1 Wembley
  (WBF L. Middleweight Title Defence)
07.04.01 Keith Mullings W RSC 2 Wembley
  (WBF L. Middleweight Title Defence)
26.05.01 William Gare W RSC 9 Bethnal Green
  (WBF L. Middleweight Title Defence)
15.09.01 Andrzej Butowicz W RTD 7 Nottingham
  (WBF L. Middleweight Title)
10.11.01 Ron Weaver W PTS 12 Wembley
  (WBF L. Middleweight Title Defence)
28.01.02 Troy Lowry W RSC 4 Barnsley
  (WBF L. Middleweight Title Defence)
23.03.02 Kirino Garcia W PTS 12 Southwark
  (WBF L. Middleweight Title Defence)
27.07.02 Andre Pestriaev L PTS 12 Nottingham
  (WBF L. Middleweight Title Defence)
Career: 30 contests, won 29, lost 1.

Andy Robinson

Wolverhampton. *Born* Birmingham, 6
November, 1965
S. Featherweight. Ht. 5'6"
Manager D. Poston

14.06.88 Darryl Pettit DREW 6 Birmingham
29.09.88 Darryl Pettit W PTS 6 Stafford
17.10.88 Sean Hogg L PTS 6 Birmingham
01.12.88 Mark Antony L PTS 6 Stafford
12.12.88 Peter Bowen L CO 4 Birmingham
15.03.89 Phil Lashley W PTS 6 Stoke
10.10.89 Jamie Morris W PTS 6 Wolverhampton
07.03.90 Dean Bramhald W PTS 6 Doncaster
19.03.90 Peter Judson L PTS 6 Cleethorpes
11.04.90 Tony Silkstone L PTS 6 Dewsbury
26.04.90 Tony Silkstone L PTS 6 Halifax

30.05.90 Kruga Hydes L PTS 6 Stoke
21.06.90 Mark Antony L PTS 6 Alfreton
10.07.90 Bradley Stone L PTS 6 Canvey Island
27.09.90 Elvis Parsley L RTD 3 Birmingham
24.10.90 Richard Woolgar L RSC 3 Dudley
26.11.90 Sugar Free Somerville W PTS 6 Bethnal Green
15.04.91 Finn McCool DREW 6 Leicester
13.05.91 Dean Bramhald W RTD 1 Birmingham
16.05.91 Craig Dermody L PTS 6 Liverpool
29.04.92 Lee Fox L PTS 6 Stoke
04.12.95 Graham McGrath W PTS 6 Birmingham
17.01.96 Carl Allen W PTS 6 Solihull
30.01.96 Chris Francis L PTS 6 Barking
21.02.96 Thomas Padgett W PTS 6 Batley
25.10.96 Mark Haslam L RTD 4 Mere
02.12.96 Norman Dhalie L PTS 6 Birmingham
17.12.96 Richard Evatt L RSC 2 Doncaster
20.05.97 Tontcho Tontchev L RSC 2 Edmonton
14.10.98 Carl Greaves L PTS 6 Stoke
21.09.02 Matthew Burke L PTS 4 Brentwood
19.10.02 David McIntyre L PTS 4 Renfrew
21.11.02 Matt Teague L RTD 3 Hull

Career: 33 contests, won 9, drew 2, lost 22.

Dale Robinson   Les Clark

Dale Robinson

Huddersfield. *Born* Huddersfield, 9 April, 1980
Commonwealth Flyweight Champion. Former Undefeated Central Area Flyweight Champion. Ht. 5'4"
Manager T. Gilmour/C. Aston

25.09.00 John Barnes W PTS 4 Barnsley
28.10.00 Delroy Spencer W RSC 4 Coventry
02.12.00 Colin Moffett W PTS 4 Bethnal Green
26.02.01 Christophe Rodrigues W PTS 6 Nottingham
07.04.01 Andrei Kostin W PTS 6 Wembley
08.05.01 Terry Gaskin W RTD 3 Barnsley
(Central Area Flyweight Title Challenge)
27.04.02 Jason Thomas W RSC 4 Huddersfield
18.05.02 Sergei Tasimov W RSC 3 Millwall

15.06.02 Kakhar Sabitov W PTS 6 Leeds
05.10.02 Alain Bonnel W PTS 8 Huddersfield
30.11.02 Marc Dummett W RSC 3 Liverpool
22.02.03 Spencer Matsangura W PTS 12 Huddersfield
(Vacant Commonwealth Flyweight Title)
10.05.03 Zolile Mbityi W PTS 12 Huddersfield
(Commonwealth Flyweight Title Defence)

Career: 13 contests, won 13.

George Robshaw

Leeds. *Born* Hull, 14 March, 1976
Middleweight. Ht. 6'0"
Manager F. Maloney

07.10.00 William Webster W PTS 4 Doncaster
16.12.01 Dean Ashton W RTD 2 Southwark
09.11.02 Piotr Bartnicki W PTS 4 Altrincham
22.02.03 Conroy McIntosh W PTS 4 Huddersfield
10.05.03 Dean Cockburn W PTS 6 Huddersfield

Career: 5 contests, won 5.

Reggie Robshaw

Leeds. *Born* Wakefield, 10 June, 1977
L. Middleweight. Ht. 5'10"
Manager Self

01.04.01 Jason McElligott W PTS 4 Southwark
24.03.02 Pedro Thompson W PTS 6 Streatham
09.11.02 Martin Scotland W RSC 1 Altrincham
22.02.03 Elroy Edwards W PTS 4 Huddersfield
10.05.03 Michael Thomas L RSC 5 Huddersfield

Career: 5 contests, won 4, lost 1.

Derek Roche

Leeds. *Born* Bedford, 19 July 1972
Welterweight. Former British Welterweight Champion. Former Undefeated Central Area Welterweight Champion. Ht. 5'9"
Manager T. Gilmour

26.09.94 Michael Alexander W RSC 6 Bradford
05.12.94 Shamus Casey W PTS 6 Bradford
30.01.95 Carl Smith W RSC 3 Bradford
23.02.95 Charlie Paine W CO 1 Hull
25.03.95 Rob Stevenson W PTS 6 Rothwell
12.06.95 Paul King W PTS 6 Bradford
25.09.95 Hughie Davey W PTS 6 Bradford
11.11.95 Rick North W RSC 2 Halifax
11.12.95 Kevin McKenzie W RSC 3 Bradford
13.01.96 Shamus Casey W PTS 6 Halifax
07.03.96 Wayne Shepherd W RSC 3 Bradford
23.09.96 Trevor Meikle W PTS 10 Bradford
(Central Area Welterweight Title Challenge)
23.10.96 Paul Miles W RSC 2 Halifax
09.12.96 Gary Beardsley W RSC 2 Bradford
17.02.97 Michael Alexander W DIS 4 Bradford
09.06.97 Chris Saunders W RSC 4 Bradford
(Central Area Welterweight Title Defence. Elim. British Welterweight Title)
13.11.97 Hughie Davey W RSC 3 Bradford
23.02.98 Darren McInulty W PTS 6 Glasgow
06.11.98 Del Bryan W RSC 10 Mayfair
(Vacant IBO Inter-Continental L. Middleweight Title)
10.04.99 Charlie Kane W RSC 7 Manchester
(Vacant British Welterweight Title)
31.07.99 Georgie Smith W PTS 12 Carlisle
(British Welterweight Title Defence)

22.10.99 Scott Dixon W PTS 12 Coventry
(British Welterweight Title Defence)
27.03.00 Harry Dhami L PTS 12 Barnsley
(British Welterweight Title Defence)
25.09.00 Brian Coleman W PTS 6 Barnsley
11.11.00 Adrian Stone L RSC 2 Belfast
(IBO L.Middleweight Title Challenge)
08.05.01 Paul Denton W PTS 6 Barnsley
07.07.01 Zoltan Szili W RSC 4 Amsterdam, Holland
08.10.01 Adam Zadworny W RSC 4 Barnsley
26.01.02 Jan Bergman L PTS 12 Bethnal Green
(WBU Welterweight Title Challenge)
15.06.02 Neil Sinclair L CO 1 Leeds
(British Welterweight Title Challenge)
21.09.02 Darren Bruce W PTS 8 Brentwood
10.05.03 Jason Williams W RSC 2 Huddersfield
07.06.03 Silvio Rojas W PTS 6 Trieste, Italy

Career: 33 contests, won 29, lost 4.

Jim Rock

Dublin. *Born* Dublin, 12 March, 1972
L. Middleweight. All-Ireland S. Middleweight & L. Middleweight Champion. Former Undefeated WAA Inter-Continental S. Middleweight Champion. WBF European L. Middleweight Champion. Ht. 5'11"
Manager M. O'Callaghan

25.11.95 Craig Lynch W PTS 4 Dublin
09.03.96 Peter Mitchell W PTS 6 Millstreet
03.09.96 Rob Stevenson W PTS 6 Belfast
05.11.96 Danny Quacoe W RSC 4 Belfast
28.01.97 Roy Chipperfield W RTD 2 Belfast
12.04.97 George Richards W PTS 6 Sheffield
13.09.97 Robert Njie W CO 3 Millwall
18.04.98 Ensley Bingham L RSC 7 Manchester
19.09.98 Michael Monaghan W PTS 12 Dublin
(Vacant WAA Inter-Continental S. Middleweight Title)
14.12.98 Perry Ayres W RTD 3 Cleethorpes
22.01.99 Jimmy Vincent W PTS 10 Dublin
20.02.99 Pedro Carragher W RSC 3 Thornaby
(Vacant WBF European L. Middleweight Title)
17.04.99 Michael Alexander W RSC 1 Dublin
(Vacant All-Ireland S. Middleweight Title)
19.06.99 Kevin Thompson W PTS 4 Dublin
15.04.00 Allan Gray W PTS 10 Bethnal Green
(Vacant All-Ireland L. Middleweight Title)
12.06.00 Alan Gilbert W PTS 6 Belfast
20.10.00 Brooke Welby W RSC 3 Belfast
11.11.00 David Baptiste W PTS 4 Belfast
08.12.00 Tommy Attardo W PTS 8 Worcester, Mass, USA
24.03.01 Hollister Elliott W CO 6 Worcester, Mass, USA
20.04.01 Jason Collins W PTS 6 Dublin
01.12.01 Ian Cooper L PTS 6 Bethnal Green
24.04.02 Harry Butler W PTS 6 Dublin
01.02.03 Takaloo L RSC 9 Belfast
(Vacant WBU L. Middleweight Title)

Career: 24 contests, won 21, lost 3.

Jason Rowland

West Ham. *Born* London, 6 August, 1970
Welterweight. Former Undefeated WBU & British L.Welterweight Champion. Ht. 5'9¾"
Manager F. Warren

19.09.89	Terry Smith W RSC 1 Millwall
15.11.89	Mike Morrison W PTS 6 Reading
14.02.90	Eamonn Payne W PTS 6 Millwall
17.04.90	Dave Jenkins W CO 1 Millwall
22.05.90	Mike Morrison W PTS 6 St Albans
12.02.91	Vaughan Carnegie W PTS 6 Basildon
07.03.91	Vaughan Carnegie W CO 2 Basildon
11.12.91	Brian Cullen W RSC 4 Basildon
30.04.92	Steve Pollard W RSC 2 Kensington
17.12.92	Jimmy Vincent W PTS 6 Wembley
10.02.93	Seth Jones W RSC 2 Lewisham
18.03.93	John Smith W PTS 6 Lewisham
04.03.94	Dewi Roberts W RSC 1 Bethnal Green
26.04.94	Ray Hood W CO 1 Bethnal Green
12.09.94	Steve Burton W RSC 1 Mayfair
11.10.94	Phil Found W RSC 4 Bethnal Green
09.11.94	Floyd Churchill W RSC 2 Millwall
09.12.94	Richard Swallow W RSC 2 Bethnal Green
03.03.95	Nigel Bradley W RSC 3 Bethnal Green
29.11.95	Bernard Paul L CO 1 Bethnal Green
	(Southern Area L. Welterweight Title Challenge. Elim. British L. Welterweight Title)
27.03.97	Kevin McKillan W PTS 8 Norwich
13.09.97	Brian Coleman W PTS 8 Millwall
16.05.98	Mark Winters W PTS 8 Bethnal Green
	(British L. Welterweight Title Challenge)
01.05.99	Alan Temple W PTS 6 Crystal Palace
15.11.99	Jonathan Thaxton W RSC 5 Bethnal Green
	(British L. Welterweight Title Defence)
21.10.00	Victor Baranov W PTS 12 Wembley
	(Vacant WBU L.Welterweight Title)
07.07.01	Ricky Hatton L CO 4 Manchester
	(WBU L.Welterweight Title Challenge)
08.04.03	Paul Denton W PTS 6 Bethnal Green
Career: 28 contests, won 26, lost 2.

Luke Rudd

Kings Lynn. *Born* Kings Lynn, 17 June, 1982
Welterweight. Ht. 6'0"
Manager A. Bowers

19.10.02	Paul McIlwaine W RTD 1 Norwich
21.12.02	Taz Jones L RTD 1 Millwall
08.02.03	Wayne Wheeler W RSC 2 Norwich
Career: 3 contests, won 2, lost 1.

Jason Rushton

Doncaster. *Born* Doncaster, 15 February, 1983
L. Middleweight. Ht. 5'10"
Manager J. Rushton/F. Warren

27.10.01	Ram Singh W PTS 6 Manchester
09.02.02	Brian Gifford W RSC 1 Manchester
01.06.02	Tony Smith W PTS 4 Manchester
08.11.02	Gary Hadwin W CO 4 Doncaster
21.02.03	Wayne Shepherd W PTS 6 Doncaster
Career: 5 contests, won 5.

Paul Rushton

Barnsley. *Born* Barnsley, 28 February, 1973
L. Welterweight. Ht. 5'9"
Manager T. Schofield

21.10.02	Craig Dickson L RSC 2 Glasgow
10.02.03	Lee Bedell L RSC 3 Sheffield
05.04.03	Paul McIlwaine DREW 4 Belfast

14.04.03	George McIlroy L RSC 1 Glasgow
06.06.03	Dave Hinds L PTS 6 Hull
15.06.03	Martin Hardcastle L RTD 2 Bradford
Career: 6 contests, drew 1, lost 5.

Steve Russell

Norwich. *Born* Norwich, 1 September, 1979
Middleweight. Ht. 5'10"
Manager J. Ingle

12.04.03	Kevin Phelan L PTS 4 Norwich
06.06.03	Jimi Hendricks L PTS 6 Norwich
20.06.03	Carl Wall L PTS 4 Liverpool
Career: 3 contests, lost 3.

Roy Rutherford

Coventry. *Born* Coventry, 4 August, 1973
British Featherweight Champion. Ht. 5'6"
Manager P. Lynch

24.02.98	David Kirk W PTS 6 Edgbaston
26.03.98	Vic Broomhead W PTS 6 Solihull
23.04.98	Dave Hinds W RSC 5 Edgbaston
21.05.98	Carl Allen W PTS 6 Solihull
24.09.98	Dean Murdoch W RSC 3 Edgbaston
14.12.98	Keith Jones W PTS 6 Birmingham
08.03.99	Marc Smith W PTS 6 Birmingham
19.06.99	Marc Smith W RTD 2 Dublin
22.10.99	Woody Greenaway W PTS 4 Coventry
14.12.99	Keith Jones W PTS 4 Coventry
22.01.00	Chris Williams W PTS 8 Birmingham
22.05.00	Alexander Tiranov W PTS 6 Coventry
28.10.00	Richard Evatt L PTS 10 Coventry
07.04.01	Nikolai Eremeev DREW 4 Wembley
26.05.01	Marc Callaghan W RSC 3 Bethnal Green
10.12.01	Frederic Bonifai W RSC 4 Liverpool
12.04.03	Dariusz Snarski W RSC 4 Bethnal Green
17.05.03	Jamie McKeever W PTS 12 Liverpool
	(British Featherweight Title Challenge)
Career: 18 contests, won 16, drew 1, lost 1.

Roy Rutherford　　　　　　　Les Clark

John-Paul Ryan

Northampton. *Born* Enfield, 1 April, 1971
Featherweight. Ht. 5'5"
Manager J. Cox

07.12.00	Paddy Folan W PTS 6 Stoke
08.03.01	Neil Read L PTS 6 Stoke
28.05.02	Paddy Folan W PTS 6 Leeds
25.06.02	Sean Hughes L PTS 6 Rugby
18.10.02	Isaac Ward L PTS 6 Hartlepool
20.01.03	John Simpson L PTS 6 Glasgow
16.02.03	Simon Chambers L RSC 2 Salford
22.03.03	Gareth Payne L PTS 4 Coventry
24.05.03	Sean Hughes L PTS 6 Sheffield
Career: 9 contests, won 2, lost 7.

Gary Ryder

Liverpool. *Born* Fazackerley, 17 December, 1971
L.Welterweight. Former WBF L.Welterweight Champion. Ht. 5'7"
Manager T. Gilmour

03.02.96	Andy Davidson W RSC 1 Liverpool
05.03.99	Trevor Tacy W PTS 4 Liverpool
15.05.99	Stuart Rimmer W RSC 1 Blackpool
09.03.00	Benny Jones W PTS 4 Liverpool
19.02.01	Mohamed Helel W RSC 1 Glasgow
04.06.01	Kevin Bennett W RSC 6 Hartlepool
25.09.01	Glenn McClarnon W PTS 8 Liverpool
09.03.02	David Smales W RSC 1 Manchester
05.10.02	David White W PTS 6 Liverpool
09.11.02	Wayne Rigby W PTS 12 Altrincham
	(WBF L. Welterweight Title Challenge)
08.03.03	Pablo Sarmiento L RSC 8 Bethnal Green
	(WBF L.Welterweight Title Defence. IBO L.Welterweight Title Challenge)
Career: 11 contests, won 10, lost 1.

Gary Ryder　　　　　　　Les Clark

(Saheed) Silence Saheed (Salawu)

Canning Town. *Born* Ibadan, Nigeria, 1 January, 1978
Lightweight. Ht. 5'6"
Manager A. Bowers

28.03.03 Martin Hardcastle W PTS 4 Millwall
10.04.03 Ceri Hall DREW 4 Clydach
27.05.03 Francis Barrett W RSC 1 Dagenham
Career: 3 contests, won 2, drew 1.

Silence Saheed   Les Clark

Jason Samuels

Cardiff. *Born* Newport, 11 December, 1973
Middleweight. Ht. 6'0"
Manager Self

02.07.99 Luke Clayfield W RSC 1 Bristol
10.10.00 Steve Brumant W PTS 6 Brierley Hill
23.09.02 Andy Gibson L PTS 4 Glasgow
25.01.03 Paul Astley W CO 1 Bridgend
17.05.03 Geard Ajetovic L PTS 4 Liverpool
Career: 5 contests, won 3, lost 2.

Paul Samuels

Newport. *Born* Newport, 23 March, 1973
L.Middleweight. Former Undefeated IBF
Inter-Continental & Welsh L.Middleweight
Champion. Ht. 6'0"
Manager Self

11.11.95 Wayne Windle W RSC 2 Halifax
13.02.96 Jon Harrison W CO 1 Cardiff
05.03.96 Tom Welsh W RSC 3 Bethnal Green
13.03.96 Brian Coleman W PTS 6 Wembley
15.05.96 Gary Hiscox W RSC 3 Cardiff
12.11.96 Mark Ramsey W RSC 4 Dudley
21.06.97 Howard Clarke W PTS 8 Caridff

15.11.97 Justin Simmons W CO 1 Bristol
24.01.98 Prince Kasi Kaihau W CO 3 Cardiff
25.04.98 Del Bryan W PTS 8 Cardiff
05.09.98 Spencer McCracken W PTS 8 Telford
05.12.98 Craig Winter W CO 2 Bristol
          (Vacant Welsh L. Middleweight Title)
27.03.99 Pedro Carragher W RSC 2 Derby
05.06.99 Eric Holland W RSC 9 Cardiff
          *(Vacant IBF Inter-Continental
          L. Middleweight Title)*
23.10.99 Ojay Abrahams W PTS 8 Telford
19.02.00 Wayne Alexander L RSC 3 Dagenham
          (Vacant British L. Middleweight Title)
23.01.01 Rob Dellapenna DREW 4 Crawley
27.01.02 Howard Clarke W PTS 6 Streatham
29.06.02 Richard Williams T DRAW 3
          Brentwood
          (IBO L. Middleweight Title Challenge)
07.12.02 Richard Williams L RSC 10
          Brentwood
          (IBO L. Middleweight Title Challenge)
25.01.03 Howard Clarke W PTS 6 Bridgend
Career: 21 contests, won 17, drew 2, lost 2.

Stuart Sanderson

Coatbridge. *Born* Bellshill, 21 November, 1981
Featherweight. Ht. 5'9"
Manager R. Bannon

24.05.01 Jason Thomas DREW 6 Glasgow
14.03.03 David McIntyre W PTS 6 Glasgow
Career: 2 contests, won 1, drew 1.

Chris Saunders

Barnsley. *Born* Barnsley, 15 August, 1969
Former British Welterweight Champion.
Ht. 5'8"
Manager D. Ingle

22.02.90 Malcolm Melvin W PTS 4 Hull
10.04.90 Mike Morrison W PTS 6 Doncaster
20.05.90 Justin Graham W RSC 3 Sheffield
29.11.90 Ross Hale L PTS 6 Bayswater
05.03.91 Rocky Ferrari L PTS 4 Glasgow
19.03.91 Richard Woolgar W RSC 3 Leicester
26.03.91 Felix Kelly L PTS 6 Bethnal Green
17.04.91 Billy Schwer L RSC 1 Kensington
16.05.91 Richard Burton L PTS 6 Liverpool
06.06.91 Mark Tibbs W RSC 6 Barking
30.06.91 Billy Schwer L PTS 3 Southwark
01.08.91 James Jiora W PTS 6 Dewsbury
03.10.91 Gary Flear L PTS 6 Burton
24.10.91 Ron Shinkwin W PTS 6 Dunstable
21.11.91 J. P. Matthews L RSC 4 Burton
30.01.92 John O. Johnson L PTS 6 Southampton
11.02.92 Eddie King W RSC 4 Wolverhampton
27.02.92 Richard Burton L PTS 10 Liverpool
          *(Vacant Central Area L. Welterweight
          Title)*
09.09.92 John O. Johnson DREW 6 Stoke
01.10.92 Mark McCreath L RSC 4 Telford
01.12.92 Shea Neary L PTS 6 Liverpool
22.02.93 Cham Joof L PTS 4 Eltham
16.03.93 Mark Elliot L PTS 6 Wolverhampton
26.04.93 Dean Hollington W RSC 5 Lewisham
23.10.93 Michael Smyth L PTS 6 Cardiff
02.12.93 Rob Stewart L PTS 4 Sheffield
03.03.94 Kevin Lueshing W RSC 4 Ebbw Vale
04.06.94 Jose Varela W CO 2 Dortmund,
          Germany
26.08.94 Julian Eavis W PTS 6 Barnsley
26.09.94 Julian Eavis W PTS 6 Cleethorpes

26.10.94 Lindon Scarlett W PTS 8 Leeds
17.12.94 Roberto Welin W RSC 7 Cagliari, Italy
15.09.95 Del Bryan W PTS 12 Mansfield
          (British Welterweight Title Challenge)
13.02.96 Kevin Lueshing L RSC 3 Bethnal
          Green
          (British Welterweight Title Defence)
25.06.96 Michael Carruth L RSC 10 Mansfield
09.06.97 Derek Roche L RSC 4 Bradford
          *(Central Area Welterweight Title
          Challenge. Elim. British Welterweight
          Title)*
27.02.98 Scott Dixon L PTS 10 Glasgow
          (Elim. British Welterweight Title)
17.04.99 Michael Carruth L RSC 5 Dublin
08.12.01 David Kirk W CO 2 Chesterfield
15.06.02 Arv Mittoo W PTS 6 Norwich
24.09.02 Robert Pacuraru W RTD 4 Gran
          Canaria, Spain
09.02.03 Richard Swallow W PTS 4 Bradford
Career: 42 contests, won 20, drew 1, lost 21.

Steve Saville

Wolverhampton. *Born* Wolverhampton, 29 September, 1976
L. Welterweight. Ht. 5'4"
Manager Self

08.06.98 Simon Chambers W RSC 2
          Birmingham
07.10.98 Dave Hinds W PTS 6 Stoke
26.11.98 Dave Hinds W PTS 6 Edgbaston
14.12.98 Woody Greenaway L PTS 6
          Birmingham
27.01.99 Darren Woodley W PTS 6 Stoke
23.03.99 Benny Jones W PTS 6 Wolverhampton
14.06.99 Trevor Tacy L PTS 8 Birmingham
12.10.99 Gary Flear W RSC 6 Wolverhampton
20.10.99 Arv Mittoo W PTS 8 Stoke
08.02.00 Marc Smith W PTS 6 Wolverhampton
13.03.00 Dave Gibson W RSC 6 Birmingham
09.10.00 David Kirk L PTS 8 Birmingham
06.11.00 Woody Greenaway W CO 5
          Wolverhampton
28.11.00 Danny Connelly W PTS 8 Brierley Hill
11.12.00 Keith Jones W PTS 8 Birmingham
01.04.01 Gavin Down L RSC 3 Alfreton
          *(Vacant Midlands Area L. Welterweight
          Title)*
13.07.02 Wayne Wheeler W RSC 2
          Wolverhampton
07.10.02 Gareth Wiltshaw W RSC 3
          Birmingham
09.12.02 Keith Jones W PTS 8 Birmingham
Career: 19 contests, won 15, lost 4.

Martin Scotland

West Bromwich. *Born* Birmingham, 8 October, 1975
Middleweight. Ht. 5'10½"
Manager Self

24.02.00 Pedro Thompson L RSC 4 Edgbaston
20.05.00 Paddy Martin W RSC 5 Leicester
09.03.02 James Davenport L RSC 1 Manchester
13.05.02 Ernie Smith L RTD 2 Birmingham
13.07.02 Andy Halder L PTS 4 Coventry
28.09.02 Franny Jones L PTS 6 Wakefield
05.10.02 Dean Walker L PTS 6 Chesterfield
09.11.02 Reggie Robshaw L RSC 1 Altrincham
11.12.02 Sonny Pollard L RSC 2 Hull
Career: 9 contests, won 1, lost 8.

Martin Scotland Les Clark

Bruce Scott

Hackney. *Born* Jamaica, 16 August, 1969
Cruiserweight. Former Undefeated British,
Commonwealth & WBU Inter-Continental
Cruiserweight Champion. Former
Undefeated Southern Area Cruiserweight
Champion. Ht. 5'9½"
Manager F. Warren

25.04.91	Mark Bowen L PTS 6 Mayfair
16.09.91	Randy B. Powell W RSC 5 Mayfair
21.11.91	Steve Osborne W PTS 6 Burton
27.04.92	John Kaighin W CO 4 Mayfair
07.09.92	Lee Prudden W PTS 6 Bethnal Green
03.12.92	Mark Pain W RSC 5 Lewisham
15.02.93	Paul McCarthy W PTS 6 Mayfair
22.04.93	Sean O'Phoenix W RSC 3 Mayfair
14.06.93	John Oxenham W RSC 1 Bayswater
04.10.93	Simon McDougall W PTS 6 Mayfair
16.12.93	Bobby Mack W RSC 4 Newport
05.04.94	Steve Osborne W RSC 5 Bethnal Green
17.10.94	Bobbi Joe Edwards W PTS 8 Mayfair
09.12.94	John Keeton W CO 2 Bethnal Green
19.04.95	Nigel Rafferty W RSC 2 Bethnal Green
19.05.95	Cordwell Hylton W RSC 1 Southwark
11.11.95	Tony Booth W RSC 3 Halifax
05.03.96	Nick Manners W RSC 5 Bethnal Green
13.07.96	Tony Booth W PTS 8 Bethnal Green
30.11.96	Nicky Piper L RSC 7 Tylorstown *(Commonwealth L. Heavyweight Title Challenge)*
15.05.97	Grant Briggs W RSC 2 Reading
04.10.97	Tony Booth L PTS 8 Muswell Hill
21.04.98	Dominic Negus W RSC 9 Edmonton *(Southern Area Cruiserweight Title Challenge)*
28.11.98	Darren Corbett W RSC 10 Belfast *(Commonwealth Cruiserweight Title Challenge. Vacant British Cruiserweight Title)*
15.05.99	Johnny Nelson L PTS 12 Sheffield *(WBO Cruiserweight Title Challenge)*
17.07.99	Juan Carlos Gomez L RSC 6 Dusseldorf, Germany *(WBC Cruiserweight Title Challenge)*
08.04.00	Chris Woollas W RSC 2 Bethnal Green
24.06.00	Adam Watt L RSC 4 Glasgow *(Vacant Commonwealth Cruiserweight Title)*
16.12.00	John Keeton W CO 6 Sheffield *(Vacant British Cruiserweight Title)*
10.03.01	Garry Delaney W RTD 3 Bethnal Green *(British Cruiserweight Title Defence. Vacant Commonwealth Cruiserweight Title)*
28.07.01	Rene Janvier W PTS 12 Wembley *(Vacant WBU Inter-Continental Cruiserweight Title)*
28.06.03	Enzo Maccarinelli L RSC 4 Cardiff *(Vacant WBU Cruiserweight Title)*

Career: 32 contests, won 25, lost 7.

Dean Scott

Nottingham. *Born* Kettering, 28 January,
1981
Lightweight. Ht. 5'8"
Manager M. Shinfield

11.05.02	Daniel Thorpe L RSC 1 Chesterfield
10.10.02	Baz Carey L RSC 2 Stoke

Career: 2 contests, lost 2.

Steve Scott

Doncaster. *Born* Doncaster, 22 October,
1970
L. Heavyweight. Ht. 5'11"
Manager J. Rushton

21.02.03	Martin Thompson DREW 6 Doncaster
09.05.03	Jimi Hendricks L PTS 6 Doncaster
02.06.03	Ben Coward DREW 6 Cleethorpes

Career: 3 contests, drew 2, lost 1.

Greg Scott-Briggs

Chesterfield. *Born* Swaziland, 6 February,
1966
Cruiserweight. Ht. 6'1"
Manager M. Shinfield

04.02.92	Mark McBiane W PTS 6 Alfreton
03.03.92	Tony Colclough W RSC 2 Cradley Heath
30.03.92	Carl Smallwood L PTS 6 Coventry
27.04.92	Richard Atkinson L PTS 6 Bradford
28.05.92	Steve Walton W RSC 2 Gosforth
04.06.92	Joe Frater L PTS 6 Cleethorpes
30.09.92	Carl Smallwood L PTS 6 Solihull
17.03.93	Carl Smallwood L PTS 6 Stoke
26.04.93	Tony Colclough W RSC 4 Glasgow
08.06.93	Peter Flint W RSC 1 Derby
07.09.93	Steve Loftus W RSC 2 Stoke
22.09.93	Paul Hanlon W PTS 6 Chesterfield
04.11.93	Lee Archer L PTS 8 Stafford
24.11.93	Tony Colclough W PTS 6 Solihull
08.12.93	Lee Archer W RTD 6 Stoke
08.02.94	Nigel Rafferty L PTS 6 Wolverhampton
17.02.94	Lee Archer L PTS 8 Walsall
11.03.94	Monty Wright L CO 1 Bethnal Green
26.09.94	Dave Battey W RSC 4 Cleethorpes
11.10.94	Mark Smallwood L PTS 8 Wolverhampton
29.10.94	Mark Smallwood L PTS 6 Cannock
12.11.94	Thomas Hansvoll L PTS 4 Randers, Denmark
30.11.94	Monty Wright L PTS 6 Wolverhampton
06.03.95	Neil Simpson L RTD 5 Leicester
15.09.95	David Flowers L PTS 6 Darlington
29.11.95	Neil Simpson L DIS 7 Solihull *(Vacant Midlands Area L. Heavyweight Title)*
20.03.96	Stinger Mason W PTS 6 Stoke
26.10.96	Danny Peters L PTS 6 Liverpool
13.06.97	Jamie Warters L RSC 5 Leeds
15.12.97	Michael Pinnock W PTS 6 Nottingham
11.05.98	Neil Simpson L PTS 6 Leicester
25.11.98	Sven Hamer L CO 2 Streatham
13.03.99	Ole Klemetsen L CO 4 Manchester
24.04.99	Monty Wright W RSC 3 Peterborough
20.05.99	Sven Hamer W RSC 5 Kensington
03.10.99	Carl Smallwood W PTS 6 Chesterfield
09.04.00	Tony Booth L PTS 10 Alfreton *(Vacant British Masters L. Heavyweight Title)*
15.07.00	Clinton Woods L RSC 3 Millwall
03.08.02	Lee Swaby L RSC 4 Derby
21.10.02	Chris Woollas L PTS 6 Cleethorpes
02.12.02	Clint Johnson L PTS 6 Leeds

Career: 41 contests, won 15, lost 26.

Matt Scriven

Nottingham. *Born* Nottingham, 1
September, 1973
British Masters & Midlands Area
L.Middleweight Champion. Ht. 5'10"
Manager Self

26.11.97	Shamus Casey W PTS 6 Stoke
08.12.97	Shane Thomas W PTS 6 Bradford
20.03.98	C. J. Jackson L PTS 6 Ilkeston
15.05.98	Lee Bird W RSC 5 Nottingham
08.10.98	Stevie McCready L RTD 3 Sunderland
01.04.99	Adrian Houldey W PTS 6 Birmingham
25.04.99	Danny Thornton L RSC 4 Leeds
27.06.99	Shane Junior L RSC 2 Alfreton
11.09.99	David Arundel L RTD 1 Sheffield
20.03.00	James Docherty L PTS 8 Glasgow
27.03.00	Matt Mowatt L PTS 4 Barnsley
09.04.00	David Matthews W PTS 6 Alfreton
06.06.00	Jackie Townsley L RSC 3 Motherwell
04.11.00	Brett James L RTD 1 Bethnal Green
04.02.01	Mark Paxford L PTS 6 Queensferry
26.02.01	Pedro Thompson W RTD 1 Nottingham
12.03.01	Ernie Smith W PTS 6 Birmingham
20.03.01	James Docherty L RSC 1 Glasgow
21.05.01	Christian Brady L RSC 5 Birmingham *(Vacant Midlands Area Welterweight Title)*
21.10.01	Neil Bonner NC 1 Glasgow
04.03.02	Danny Parkinson L PTS 6 Bradford
22.04.02	Gary Porter L PTS 6 Glasgow
28.05.02	Peter Dunn W PTS 8 Leeds
14.09.02	Ernie Smith W PTS 6 Newark
29.09.02	James Lee L RTD 4 Shrewsbury
30.11.02	Davey Jones L PTS 6 Newark
16.03.03	Lee Williamson W PTS 10 Nottingham *(Vacant Midlands Area & British Masters L. Middleweight Titles)*
08.06.03	Wayne Shepherd W PTS 10 Nottingham *(British Masters L.Middleweight Title Defence)*

Career: 27 contests, won 11, lost 15, no contest 1.

Surinder Sekhon

Barnsley. *Born* Birmingham, 4 October, 1979
Middleweight. Ht. 5'9"
Manager T. Schofield

05.05.02	Franny Jones L PTS 6 Hartlepool
28.09.02	Peter Dunn W PTS 6 Wakefield
27.02.03	Ryan Kerr L PTS 6 Sunderland
09.03.03	P.J.Maxwell L RSC 1 Shaw

Career: 4 contests, won 1, lost 3.

Nigel Senior

Nottingham. *Born* Wallsend, 19 November, 1962
Lightweight. Former British Masters Lightweight Champion. Ht. 5'5"
Manager J. Gill

03.10.85 Mark Needham W RSC 4 Nottingham
14.10.85 Anthony Brown L PTS 6 Leicester
21.10.85 Peter Bowen DREW 6 Nottingham
11.11.85 Sugar Gibiliru L RSC 5 Liverpool
24.03.86 Joe Donohoe L PTS 6 Mayfair
07.04.86 Billy Joe Dee W PTS 6 Nottingham
15.04.86 Ricky Andrews W PTS 6 Merton
23.04.86 Nigel Haddock L PTS 6 Stoke
19.05.86 Nigel Haddock DREW 6 Nottingham
09.06.86 Nigel Crook W PTS 6 Manchester
23.08.86 Tony Graham DREW 6 Manchester
04.09.86 Gary King W PTS 6 Merton
23.09.86 Carl Cleasby W PTS 6 Batley
20.10.86 Gary Maxwell L PTS 6 Nottingham
29.10.86 Nigel Haddock L PTS 6 Ebbw Vale
11.11.86 Darren Connellan L PTS 6 Batley
28.11.86 Ian Honeywood W RSC 5 Peterborough
16.12.86 Paul Timmons L PTS 6 Alfreton
27.01.87 Russell Davison DREW 8 Manchester
09.02.87 Joe Duffy W CO 3 Glasgow
16.02.87 Dean Bramhald W PTS 8 Glasgow
14.03.87 Floyd Havard L RSC 5 Southwark
13.04.87 John Bennie L PTS 6 Glasgow
01.05.87 Gary de Roux L PTS 8 Peterborough
04.06.87 John Feeney L PTS 8 Sunderland
28.09.87 George Jones L PTS 8 Birmingham
09.11.87 Rocky Lawlor L RSC 5 Birmingham
27.01.88 Ronnie Green L PTS 8 Stoke
24.02.88 John Bennie L PTS 6 Glasgow
08.03.88 Billy Joe Dee W PTS 6 Batley
23.03.88 Glyn Rhodes L PTS 8 Sheffield
30.03.88 Paul Gadney L PTS 6 Bethnal Green
17.04.88 Dave Kettlewell W PTS 6 Peterborough
25.04.88 Dean Bramhald L PTS 8 Nottingham
10.09.88 Herve Jacob L PTS 8 Grande-Synthe, France
07.10.88 Daniel Londas L PTS 8 Bordeaux, France
25.01.89 Henry Armstrong L PTS 8 Stoke
14.02.89 John Davison L RSC 8 Sunderland
20.03.89 Wayne Weekes L PTS 6 Nottingham
24.04.89 Ian Honeywood L PTS 4 Nottingham
10.05.89 Nigel Wenton L RSC 2 Kensington
19.04.90 Les Walsh L PTS 8 Oldham
30.04.90 Kruga Hydes W PTS 6 Nottingham
21.05.90 Peter Konyegwachie L RSC 7 Mayfair
07.09.90 Jimmy Owens L PTS 6 Liverpool
18.10.90 Frankie Foster L CO 2 Hartlepool
(Vacant Northern Area S. Featherweight Title)
03.12.90 Mark Antony L PTS 8 Cleethorpes
10.12.90 Noel Carroll W PTS 6 Nottingham

06.03.91 Richard Joyce L PTS 8 Croydon
01.12.99 Chris Jickells L RSC 2 Stoke
24.02.00 Willie Limond L RSC 6 Glasgow
26.03.00 Steve Brook L PTS 6 Nottingham
17.04.00 Steve Brook L PTS 6 Bradford
11.05.00 John Barnes L PTS 6 Sunderland
20.05.00 Gary Wilson L PTS 6 Rotherham
06.06.00 Barry Hawthorne L PTS 6 Motherwell
10.09.00 Steve Gethin DREW 6 Walsall
22.09.00 Jason Edwards W PTS 6 Wrexham
01.10.00 James Rooney L PTS 6 Hartlepool
09.10.00 Ricky Eccleston L PTS 4 Liverpool
26.10.00 Nigel Leake W PTS 6 Stoke
04.11.00 Marc Callaghan L RSC 4 Bethnal Green
07.12.00 Alex Stewart W PTS 8 Stoke
22.01.01 Craig Docherty L RSC 4 Glasgow
08.03.01 Jason White L PTS 8 Stoke
24.03.01 Carl Greaves L CO 6 Newark
(Vacant Midlands Area S. Featherweight Title)
18.06.01 Dave Cotterill L PTS 6 Bradford
21.07.01 Gavin Rees L RSC 2 Sheffield
15.09.01 Inderpaul Sandhu L PTS 4 Nottingham
24.09.01 Haroon Din L PTS 6 Cleethorpes
07.10.01 Pete Buckley W PTS 6 Wolverhampton
01.11.01 Anthony Hanna W PTS 6 Hull
17.11.01 Gary Greenwood L PTS 6 Coventry
01.12.01 Marc Callaghan W CO 1 Bethnal Green
09.12.01 Pete Buckley L PTS 6 Shaw
17.12.01 Haroon Din L PTS 6 Cleethorpes
25.02.02 Brian Gentry W RSC 8 Slough
(British Masters Lightweight Title Challenge)
26.04.02 Dean Pithie L PTS 6 Coventry
28.05.02 Colin Toohey L PTS 4 Liverpool
08.09.02 Stephen Chinnock L PTS 6 Wolverhampton
17.11.02 Charles Shepherd L PTS 6 Shaw
30.11.02 Gary Greenwood L PTS 4 Coventry
22.03.03 Tony McPake L PTS 4 Renfrew
26.04.03 Dave Stewart L RSC 2 Brentford
(British Masters Lightweight Title Defence)
06.06.03 Jackson Williams L PTS 8 Norwich
15.06.03 Nadeem Siddique L PTS 6 Bradford
Career: 86 contests, won 20, drew 5, lost 61.

Charles Shepherd

Carlisle. *Born* Burnley, 28 June, 1970
S.Featherweight. Former IBO S.Featherweight Champion. Former Undefeated British, Commonwealth & IBO Inter-Continental S.Featherweight Champion. Ht. 5'4"
Manager J. Doughty

28.10.91 Chris Aston W PTS 6 Leicester
31.01.92 Alan McDowall L RSC 3 Glasgow
18.05.92 Mark Legg W PTS 6 Marton
25.09.92 George Naylor W RSC 4 Liverpool
22.10.92 Didier Hughes L PTS 4 Bethnal Green
13.02.93 Nigel Wenton W PTS 8 Manchester
23.05.93 Cham Joof W PTS 4 Brockley
21.10.93 Karl Taylor W RTD 5 Bayswater
09.02.94 Justin Juuko L PTS 8 Bethnal Green
21.04.94 Tony Foster L PTS 10 Hull
(Vacant Central Area Lightweight Title)
29.09.94 Frankie Foster W RSC 3 Tynemouth
08.03.95 Bamana Dibateza W PTS 8 Solihull
26.04.95 Kelton McKenzie W RSC 7 Solihull

23.05.95 Michael Ayers L RSC 3 Potters Bar
(British Lightweight Title Challenge)
14.11.95 John Stovin W RSC 4 Bury
22.04.96 Marc Smith W RSC 2 Crystal Palace
29.06.96 P. J. Gallagher L PTS 12 Erith
(British S. Featherweight Title Challenge)
28.10.96 Harry Escott W PTS 8 Glasgow
22.09.97 Dave McHale W RSC 10 Glasgow
(Vacant British S. Featherweight Title)
08.11.97 Matt Brown W PTS 12 Southwark
(British S. Featherweight Title Defence)
02.05.98 Peter Judson W PTS 12 Kensington
(British S. Featherweight Title Defence)
22.01.99 Trust Ndlovu W CO 6 Carlisle
(Vacant Commonwealth S. Featherweight Title)
03.04.99 Smith Odoom W PTS 12 Carlisle
(Commonwealth S. Featherweight Title Defence)
31.07.99 Tom Johnson W PTS 12 Carlisle
(Vacant IBO S. Featherweight Title)
26.02.00 Affif Djelti L RSC 6 Carlisle
(IBO S. Featherweight Title Defence)
05.06.00 Rakhim Mingaleev W PTS 12 Glasgow
(Vacant IBO Inter-Continental S. Featherweight Title)
18.09.00 James Armah L RTD 9 Glasgow
(Vacant Commonwealth S. Featherweight Title)
11.11.00 Tontcho Tontchev L PTS 12 Belfast
(WBA International S. Featherweight Title Challenge)
20.03.01 Alex Moon L PTS 12 Glasgow
(Vacant Commonwealth S. Featherweight Title)
14.07.01 Isaac Sebaduka L RSC 5 Wembley
17.11.02 Nigel Senior W PTS 6 Shaw
Career: 31 contests, won 20, lost 11.

Wayne Shepherd

Carlisle. *Born* Whiston, 3 June, 1959
L. Middleweight. Ht. 5'6"
Manager Self

07.10.91 Benji Joseph W PTS 6 Bradford
28.10.91 Noel Henry W PTS 6 Leicester
16.12.91 Dave Maj DREW 6 Manchester
03.02.92 Dave Maj L PTS 6 Manchester
30.03.92 Hughie Davey L PTS 6 Bradford
18.05.92 Dave Whittle W PTS 6 Marton
14.10.92 Richard Swallow L PTS 8 Stoke
31.10.92 George Scott L RSC 6 Earls Court
13.02.93 Delroy Waul L RSC 5 Manchester
31.03.93 Derek Grainger L RSC 4 Barking
11.06.93 Hughie Davey L PTS 6 Gateshead
06.09.93 Shea Neary L RTD 2 Liverpool
26.01.94 James McGee W PTS 6 Stoke
28.02.94 Craig Winter L PTS 6 Manchester
02.03.95 Denny Johnson L PTS 6 Cramlington
06.04.95 Shaun Stokes L PTS 6 Sheffield
22.05.95 Peter Varnavas W PTS 6 Morecambe
01.06.95 Tommy Quinn L PTS 6 Musselburgh
29.07.95 Shaun O'Neill L PTS 4 Whitley Bay
07.10.95 Neil Sinclair L PTS 6 Belfast
30.10.95 John Stronach L PTS 6 Bradford
11.12.95 Shamus Casey L PTS 6 Morecambe
07.03.96 Derek Roche L RSC 3 Bradford
22.04.96 Gilbert Eastman L PTS 4 Crystal Palace
25.06.96 Geoff McCreesh L PTS 4 Stevenage
26.09.96 John Docherty L PTS 6 Glasgow

10.11.96	John Docherty L PTS 6 Glasgow
22.12.96	Chris Barnett L PTS 6 Salford
16.03.97	C. J. Jackson L PTS 6 Shaw
14.10.97	Joe Townsley L PTS 8 Kilmarnock
22.11.97	G. L. Booth L PTS 4 Manchester
05.03.98	Lee Murtagh L PTS 6 Leeds
20.03.98	Wayne Burchell L PTS 6 Leeds
28.04.98	Danny Ryan L DIS 4 Belfast
14.06.98	Matt Mowatt DREW 6 Shaw
20.09.98	Matt Mowatt W PTS 6 Sheffield
12.10.98	Danny Thornton L PTS 6 Bradford
03.12.98	Lee Molloy L PTS 4 Mayfair
22.01.99	Lee Bird W PTS 6 Carlisle
16.02.99	Paul O'Rourke L PTS 6 Leeds
07.08.99	Alan Gilbert DREW 8 Dagenham
	(Vacant British Masters
	L. Middleweight Title)
28.10.99	Matt Mowatt W PTS 6 Burnley
15.11.99	James Docherty L PTS 8 Glasgow
14.12.99	Joe Townsley L PTS 6 Coventry
26.02.00	Martin Thompson W PTS 4 Carlisle
05.03.00	Jason Collins L PTS 6 Shaw
21.05.00	Andy Vickers L PTS 6 Shaw
23.10.00	Jackie Townsley L PTS 4 Glasgow
25.11.00	Jamie Moore L RSC 3 Manchester
22.01.01	Joe Townsley L PTS 6 Glasgow
20.03.01	Scott Dixon L PTS 6 Glasgow
28.03.01	Andrew Buchanan L RSC 2 Piccadilly
23.09.01	Richard Inquieti W PTS 6 Shaw
21.10.01	Martyn Bailey L PTS 6 Pentre Halkyn
03.11.01	Ciaran Duffy L PTS 6 Glasgow
10.12.01	Andrei Ivanov W PTS 6 Nottingham
09.02.02	Brendan Halford L PTS 6 Coventry
21.02.02	Ryan Kerr L PTS 6 Sunderland
03.03.02	Conroy McIntosh DREW 6 Shaw
02.06.02	Dean Walker L PTS 6 Shaw
21.06.02	Lee Murtagh L PTS 10 Leeds
	(Vacant British Masters Middleweight
	Title)
06.10.02	Neil Bonner L PTS 6 Rhyl
26.10.02	Mark Paxford L PTS 6 Wigan
17.11.02	Sam Gorman W PTS 6 Shaw
21.02.03	Jason Rushton L PTS 6 Doncaster
09.03.03	Brian Coleman W PTS 6 Shaw
03.04.03	Sonny Pollard L PTS 6 Hull
09.05.03	Davey Jones L PTS 6 Doncaster
08.06.03	Matt Scriven L PTS 10 Nottingham
	(British Masters L.Middleweight Title
	Challenge)

Career: 69 contests, won 13, drew 4, lost 52.

Gifford Shillingford

Sheffield. *Born* Sheffield, 2 April, 1965
Heavyweight. Ht. 6'2"
Manager Self

26.09.88	Steve Garber L RSC 4 Bradford
25.01.89	Michael Howells W CO 1 Stoke
21.06.02	Steve Tuck W RSC 1 Leeds
03.08.02	Petr Horacek W RSC 4 Derby
22.09.02	Matt Skelton L RSC 2 Southwark

Career: 5 contests, won 3, lost 2.

Nadeem Siddique

Bradford. *Born* Bradford, 28 October, 1977
Lightweight. Ht. 5'8"
Manager J. Ingle

17.11.02	Daniel Thorpe W PTS 4 Bradford
09.02.03	Norman Dhalie W PTS 4 Bradford
13.04.03	Dave Hinds W PTS 4 Bradford
15.06.03	Nigel Senior W PTS 6 Bradford

Career: 4 contests, won 4.

Chas Simmonds

Croydon. *Born* Croydon, 8 July, 1982
L. Welterweight. Ht. 5'6"
Manager E. Maloney

18.02.03	Darren Goode W RSC 2 Bethnal Green
08.04.03	Lee Bedell W PTS 4 Bethnal Green
03.06.03	Arv Mittoo W PTS 6 Bethnal Green

Career: 3 contests, won 3.

Chas Simmonds   Les Clark

Luke Simpkin

Swadlincote. *Born* Derby, 5 May, 1979
Heavyweight. Ht. 6'2"
Manager N. Nobbs

24.09.98	Simon Taylor W CO 3 Edgbaston
16.10.98	Chris P. Bacon L PTS 6 Salford
10.12.98	Jason Flisher W RSC 5 Barking
04.02.99	Danny Watts L CO 3 Lewisham
28.05.99	Tommy Bannister W RSC 4 Liverpool
07.08.99	Owen Beck L PTS 4 Dagenham
11.09.99	Scott Lansdowne L PTS 4 Sheffield
11.03.00	Albert Sosnowski L PTS 4 Kensington
27.03.00	Mark Hobson L PTS 4 Barnsley
29.04.00	Johan Thorbjoernsson L PTS 4 Wembley
23.09.00	Mark Potter L PTS 6 Bethnal Green
30.09.00	Gordon Minors DREW 4 Peterborough
18.11.00	Keith Long L RSC 3 Dagenham
03.02.01	Paul Buttery W RSC 1 Manchester
01.04.01	Wayne Llewelyn L PTS 6 Southwark
24.04.01	Darren Chubbs L PTS 4 Liverpool
06.05.01	Billy Bessey L PTS 6 Hartlepool
09.06.01	John McDermott L PTS 6 Bethnal Green
13.09.01	Mark Krence L PTS 4 Sheffield
10.12.01	Mark Hobson L RTD 3 Liverpool
27,.01.02	Pele Reid DREW 4 Streatham
15.03.02	Mike Holden L PTS 6 Millwall
13.04.02	Fola Okesola W PTS 4 Liverpool
10.05.02	Julius Francis DREW 6 Millwall
23.08.02	Mark Potter L PTS 6 Bethnal Green

10.06.03	Mark Krence L RTD 8 Sheffield
	(Vacant Midlands Area Heavyweight
	Title)

Career: 26 contests, won 5, drew 3, lost 18.

John Simpson

Greenock. *Born* Greenock, 26 July, 1983
Featherweight. Ht. 5'7"
Manager T. Gilmour

23.09.02	Simon Chambers W RSC 1 Glasgow
06.10.02	Lee Holmes L PTS 6 Rhyl
07.12.02	Matthew Burke W PTS 4 Brentwood
20.01.03	John-Paul Ryan W PTS 6 Glasgow
17.02.03	Joel Viney W RTD 1 Glasgow
14.04.03	Simon Chambers W PTS 6 Glasgow

Career: 6 contests, won 5, lost 1.

Neil Simpson

Coventry. *Born* London, 5 July, 1970
L.Heavyweight. Former Undefeated British
& Commonwealth L.Heavyweight
Champion. Former Midlands Area
L.Heavyweight Champion. Ht. 6'2"
Manager A. Phillips

04.10.94	Kenny Nevers W PTS 4 Mayfair
20.10.94	Johnny Hooks W RSC 2 Walsall
05.12.94	Chris Woollas L PTS 6 Cleethorpes
15.12.94	Paul Murray W PTS 6 Walsall
06.03.95	Greg Scott-Briggs W RTD 5 Leicester
17.03.95	Thomas Hansvold L PTS 4 Copenhagen, Denmark
26.04.95	Craig Joseph L PTS 6 Solihull
11.05.95	Andy McVeigh L CO 2 Dudley
24.06.95	Dave Owens W RSC 1 Cleethorpes
25.09.95	Tony Booth L PTS 8 Cleethorpes
11.10.95	Darren Ashton W RSC 3 Solihull
29.11.95	Greg Scott-Briggs W DIS 7 Solihull
	(Vacant Midlands Area L. Heavyweight
	Title)
19.02.96	Stephen Wilson L PTS 6 Glasgow
27.03.96	Tony Booth W PTS 6 Whitwick
26.04.96	Dean Francis L RSC 3 Cardiff
02.10.96	Chris Davies W PTS 4 Cardiff
28.10.96	Nigel Rafferty W PTS 8 Leicester
03.12.96	Danny Peters L PTS 6 Liverpool
03.02.97	Michael Pinnock W PTS 6 Leicester
25.04.97	Stuart Fleet L PTS 10 Cleethorpes
	(Midlands Area L. Heavyweight Title
	Defence)
20.10.97	Slick Miller W RTD 1 Leicester
15.12.97	Chris Woollas L PTS 6 Cleethorpes
11.05.98	Greg Scott-Briggs W PTS 6 Leicester
30.11.98	Slick Miller W CO 3 Leicester
26.02.99	Adam Cale W RSC 3 Coventry
12.07.99	Tony Booth W PTS 10 Coventry
	(Elim. British L. Heavyweight Title)
14.12.99	Darren Corbett L PTS 12 Coventry
	(Vacant IBO Inter-Continental
	L. Heavyweight Title)
22.05.00	Mark Baker W PTS 12 Coventry
	(Vacant British & Commonwealth
	L. Heavyweight Titles)
18.11.00	Mark Delaney W RSC 1 Dagenham
	(British L. Heavyweight Title Defence)
02.01.01	Hastings Rasani W CO 4 Coventry
	(Vacant Commonwealth
	L. Heavyweight Title)
06.04.01	Yawe Davis L RSC 3 Grosseto, Italy
	(Vacant European L. Heavyweight
	Title)

25.05.02 Tony Oakey L PTS 12 Portsmouth
   (WBU L. Heavyweight Title Challenge)
08.03.03 Peter Oboh L RSC 11 Coventry
   (Commonwealth L.Heavyweight Title
   Challenge. Vacant British
   L.Heavyweight Title)
Career: 33 contests, won 19, lost 14.

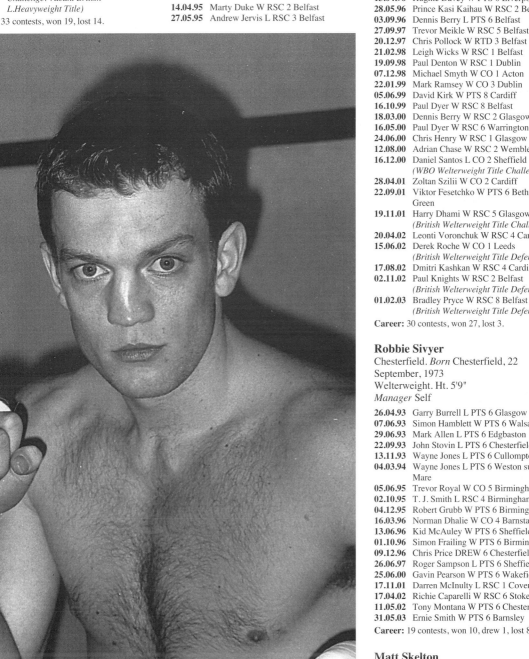

Neil Sinclair   Les Clark

Neil Sinclair

Belfast. *Born* Belfast, 23 February, 1974
British Welterweight Champion. Ht. 5'10½"
Manager J. Breen

14.04.95 Marty Duke W RSC 2 Belfast
27.05.95 Andrew Jervis L RSC 3 Belfast
17.07.95 Andy Peach W RSC 1 Mayfair
26.08.95 George Wilson W PTS 4 Belfast
07.10.95 Wayne Shepherd W PTS 6 Belfast
02.12.95 Brian Coleman W RTD 1 Belfast
13.04.96 Hughie Davey W PTS 6 Liverpool
28.05.96 Prince Kasi Kaihau W RSC 2 Belfast
03.09.96 Dennis Berry L PTS 6 Belfast
27.09.97 Trevor Meikle W RSC 5 Belfast
20.12.97 Chris Pollock W RTD 3 Belfast
21.02.98 Leigh Wicks W RSC 1 Belfast
19.09.98 Paul Denton W RSC 1 Dublin
07.12.98 Michael Smyth W CO 1 Acton
22.01.99 Mark Ramsey W CO 3 Dublin
05.06.99 David Kirk W PTS 8 Cardiff
16.10.99 Paul Dyer W RSC 8 Belfast
18.03.00 Dennis Berry W RSC 2 Glasgow
16.05.00 Paul Dyer W RSC 6 Warrington
24.06.00 Chris Henry W RSC 1 Glasgow
12.08.00 Adrian Chase W RSC 2 Wembley
16.12.00 Daniel Santos L CO 2 Sheffield
   (WBO Welterweight Title Challenge)
28.04.01 Zoltan Szilii W CO 2 Cardiff
22.09.01 Viktor Fesetchko W PTS 6 Bethnal
   Green
19.11.01 Harry Dhami W RSC 5 Glasgow
   (British Welterweight Title Challenge)
20.04.02 Leonti Voronchuk W RSC 4 Cardiff
15.06.02 Derek Roche W CO 1 Leeds
   (British Welterweight Title Defence)
17.08.02 Dmitri Kashkan W RSC 4 Cardiff
02.11.02 Paul Knights W RSC 2 Belfast
   (British Welterweight Title Defence)
01.02.03 Bradley Pryce W RSC 8 Belfast
   (British Welterweight Title Defence)
Career: 30 contests, won 27, lost 3.

Robbie Sivyer

Chesterfield. *Born* Chesterfield, 22
September, 1973
Welterweight. Ht. 5'9"
Manager Self

26.04.93 Garry Burrell L PTS 6 Glasgow
07.06.93 Simon Hamblett W PTS 6 Walsall
29.06.93 Mark Allen L PTS 6 Edgbaston
22.09.93 John Stovin L PTS 6 Chesterfield
13.11.93 Wayne Jones L PTS 6 Cullompton
04.03.94 Wayne Jones L PTS 6 Weston super
   Mare
05.06.95 Trevor Royal W CO 5 Birmingham
02.10.95 T. J. Smith L RSC 4 Birmingham
04.12.95 Robert Grubb W PTS 6 Birmingham
16.03.96 Norman Dhalie W CO 4 Barnstaple
13.06.96 Kid McAuley W PTS 6 Sheffield
01.10.96 Simon Frailing W PTS 6 Birmingham
09.12.96 Chris Price DREW 6 Chesterfield
26.06.97 Roger Sampson L PTS 6 Sheffield
25.06.00 Gavin Pearson W PTS 6 Wakefield
17.11.01 Darren McInulty L RSC 1 Coventry
17.04.02 Richie Caparelli W RSC 6 Stoke
11.05.02 Tony Montana W PTS 6 Chesterfield
31.05.03 Ernie Smith W PTS 6 Barnsley
Career: 19 contests, won 10, drew 1, lost 8.

Matt Skelton

Bedford. *Born* Bedford, 23 January, 1968
Heavyweight. Ht. 6'3"
Manager K. Sanders

22.09.02 Gifford Shillingford W RSC 2
   Southwark
27.10.02 Slick Miller W CO 1 Southwark

08.12.02 Neil Kirkwood W RSC 1 Bethnal Green
18.02.03 Jacklord Jacobs W RSC 4 Bethnal Green
08.04.03 Alexei Varakin W CO 2 Bethnal Green
15.05.03 Dave Clarke W RSC 1 Mayfair
Career: 6 contests, won 6.

Matt Skelton   Les Clark

Mark Smallwood

Atherstone. *Born* Nuneaton, 30 January, 1975
Cruiserweight. Ht. 6'2"
Manager J. Weaver

22.02.93 John Dempsey W CO 1 Bedworth
17.03.93 Sean Smith W RSC 1 Stoke
10.05.93 Tim Robinson W RSC 4 Cleethorpes
17.06.93 Phil Ball W RSC 1 Bedworth
24.11.93 Darren Littlewood W PTS 8 Solihull
24.02.94 Jerry Mortimer W PTS 6 Walsall
18.04.94 Gil Lewis W RSC 5 Walsall
23.05.94 Dean Ashton W RTD 3 Walsall
11.10.94 Greg Scott-Briggs W PTS 8 Wolverhampton
29.10.94 Greg Scott-Briggs W PTS 6 Cannock
29.11.94 Paul Murray W PTS 8 Wolverhampton
18.01.95 Marvin O'Brien W PTS 6 Solihull
26.11.96 Michael Pinnock W PTS 6 Wolverhampton
16.01.97 Chris Woollas W PTS 8 Solihull
09.05.98 Sven Hamer W PTS 8 Sheffield
30.11.98 Clinton Woods L RSC 7 Manchester
15.06.99 Juan Perez Nelongo L RSC 6 Tenerife, Spain
  (Vacant WBA Continental Euro-African L. Heavyweight Title)
22.03.02 Paul Bonson W PTS 6 Coventry
26.04.02 Jon Penn W PTS 6 Coventry
21.05.02 Valery Odin W RSC 4 Custom House
13.07.02 Ganny Dovidovas W RSC 3 Coventry
Career: 21 contests, won 19, lost 2.

Donovan Smillie

Bradford. *Born* Bradford, 9 August, 1975
British Masters S.Middleweight Champion.
Ht. 5'10½"
Manager J. Ingle

10.04.99 Sean Pritchard W RSC 1 Manchester
02.05.99 Mark Dawson W PTS 6 Shaw
04.12.99 Mark Dawson W PTS 4 Manchester
14.04.00 Dennis Doyley W PTS 4 Manchester
25.11.00 Ojay Abrahams L RSC 2 Manchester
30.11.01 Rob Stevenson W PTS 6 Hull
17.12.01 Mark Chesters W PTS 6 Cleethorpes
17.02.02 William Webster W PTS 6 Salford
20.04.02 Mike Duffield L PTS 4 Derby
15.06.02 Wayne Asker DREW 6 Norwich
07.10.02 Alan Jones L RSC 6 Birmingham
17.11.02 William Webster W PTS 6 Bradford
09.02.03 Robert Burton W PTS 6 Bradford
13.04.03 Mark Phillips W PTS 6 Bradford
15.06.03 Mike Duffield W RSC 3 Bradford
  (Vacant British Masters S.Middleweight Title)
Career: 15 contests, won 11, drew 1, lost 3.

Danny Smith

Lowestoft. *Born* Great Yarmouth, 6 October, 1979
Middleweight. Ht. 6'0"
Manager S. Pollard

15.07.00 Gary Jones W RSC 1 Norwich
04.11.00 Rob Stevenson DREW 6 Derby
28.03.01 Simeon Cover W PTS 6 Piccadilly
08.06.01 Rob Stevenson W PTS 6 Hull
13.04.02 Freddie Yemofio W PTS 6 Norwich
15.06.02 William Webster W PTS 6 Norwich
21.09.02 Mike Duffield W PTS 6 Norwich
12.04.03 Simeon Cover W CO 5 Norwich
06.06.03 Gary Cummings W PTS 6 Norwich
Career: 9 contests, won 8, drew 1.

Ernie Smith

Stourport. *Born* Kidderminster, 10 June, 1978
Welterweight. Ht. 5'8"
Manager Self

24.11.98 Woody Greenaway L PTS 6 Wolverhampton
05.12.98 Gavin Rees L PTS 4 Bristol
27.01.99 Arv Mittoo DREW 6 Stoke
11.02.99 Tony Smith W PTS 6 Dudley
22.02.99 Liam Maltby W PTS 4 Peterborough
08.03.99 Wayne Jones W PTS 6 Birmingham
18.03.99 Carl Greaves L PTS 6 Doncaster
25.03.99 Brian Coleman L PTS 6 Edgbaston
27.05.99 Brian Coleman W PTS 6 Edgbaston
14.06.99 Dave Gibson W PTS 6 Birmingham
22.06.99 Koba Gogoladze L RSC 1 Ipswich
03.10.99 Gavin Down L RSC 1 Chesterfield
30.11.99 Brian Coleman L PTS 8 Wolverhampton
13.12.99 Richie Murray L RSC 5 Cleethorpes
24.02.00 Brian Coleman L PTS 6 Edgbaston
02.03.00 Oscar Hall L PTS 6 Birkenhead
10.03.00 John Tiftik L PTS 4 Chigwell
18.03.00 Biagio Falcone L PTS 4 Glasgow
07.04.00 Barry Connell L PTS 6 Glasgow
14.04.00 Jose Luis Castro L PTS 6 Madrid, Spain
06.05.00 Matthew Barr L PTS 4 Southwark
15.05.00 Harry Butler L PTS 6 Birmingham

26.05.00 Biagio Falcone L PTS 4 Glasgow
06.06.00 Chris Henry L PTS 8 Brierley Hill
08.07.00 Takaloo L RSC 4 Widnes
13.08.00 Jawaid Khaliq L RSC 4 Nottingham
  (Vacant Midlands Area Welterweight Title)
24.09.00 Shaun Horsfall L PTS 6 Shaw
09.10.00 Dave Gibson W PTS 6 Birmingham
22.10.00 Matthew Barr L PTS 4 Streatham
06.11.00 Stuart Elwell L PTS 6 Wolverhampton
25.11.00 Michael Jennings L PTS 4 Manchester
03.12.00 Shaun Horsfall L PTS 6 Shaw
17.12.00 Kevin McIntyre L PTS 6 Glasgow
20.01.01 David Walker L RTD 1 Bethnal Green
12.03.01 Matt Scriven L PTS 6 Birmingham
24.03.01 Bobby Banghar L PTS 4 Chigwell
12.05.01 Jon Harrison L PTS 4 Plymouth
21.05.01 Brian Coleman W PTS 6 Birmingham
03.06.01 Babatunde Ajayi L PTS 4 Southwark
16.06.01 Bobby Banghar L PTS 4 Dagenham
26.07.01 Andy Abrol L PTS 6 Blackpool
13.09.01 Leo O'Reilly L PTS 6 Sheffield
29.09.01 Brett James L PTS 6 Southwark
01.11.01 Lance Crosby L PTS 6 Hull
17.11.01 Nigel Wright L PTS 4 Glasgow
15.12.01 Ross Minter L RSC 2 Wembley
11.02.02 Tony Montana L PTS 6 Shrewsbury
13.05.02 Martin Scotland W RTD 2 Birmingham
15.06.02 Gavin Wake L PTS 4 Leeds
08.07.02 Gavin Rees L RSC 5 Mayfair
06.09.02 Ricky Burns L PTS 6 Glasgow
14.09.02 Matt Scriven L PTS 6 Newark
29.09.02 Anthony Christopher L PTS 6 Shrewsbury
18.11.02 Craig Dickson L PTS 6 Glasgow
03.12.02 Anthony Christopher W PTS 6 Shrewsbury
23.02.03 Gary Greenwood L PTS 4 Shrewsbury
24.03.03 Darrell Grafton L PTS 6 Barnsley
13.04.03 Lee McAllister L PTS 4 Bradford
28.04.03 Adnan Amar L PTS 6 Cleethorpes
12.05.03 Lee McAllister L PTS 6 Birmingham
31.05.03 Robbie Sivyer L PTS 6 Barnsley
08.06.03 Jonathan Woollins W PTS 4 Nottingham
15.06.03 Ali Nuumembe L PTS 4 Bradford
Career: 63 contests, won 10, drew 1, lost 52.

Paul Smith   Les Clark

Paul Smith

Liverpool. *Born* Liverpool, 6 October, 1982
Middleweight. Ht. 5'11"
Manager F. Warren

05.04.03	Howard Clarke W PTS 4 Manchester
08.05.03	Andrei Ivanov W RSC 2 Widnes
20.06.03	Elroy Edwards W RSC 2 Liverpool

Career: 3 contests, won 3.

Sammy Smith

Bracknell. *Born* Chichester, 12 May, 1978
Welterweight. Ht. 5'6"
Manager J. Evans

26.03.98	Shaba Edwards W PTS 6 Acton
28.04.98	Les Frost W CO 2 Brentford
02.10.98	Arv Mittoo W PTS 4 Cheshunt
27.10.98	Rudy Valentino W PTS 6 Brentford
07.12.98	Ross McCord W RSC 5 Acton
25.02.99	Trevor Smith W RSC 2 Kentish Town
08.03.99	Brian Coleman L PTS 8 Birmingham
09.05.99	David Kirk W PTS 6 Bracknell
09.04.00	Gavin Down L PTS 6 Alfreton
18.05.00	Gary Reid L RSC 1 Bethnal Green
11.02.02	David Keir W PTS 6 Southampton
25.02.02	Marcus Portman L PTS 6 Slough
09.05.03	Brian Coleman W PTS 6 Longford
31.05.03	David Kirk W PTS 4 Bethnal Green

Career: 14 contests, won 10, lost 4.

Stephen Smith

Kentish Town. *Born* Hammersmith, 18
July, 1973
L.Welterweight. Former Undefeated IBC
L.Welterweight Champion. Former
Undefeated IBF Inter-Continental
Lightweight Champion. Former Undefeated
German International S.Featherweight
Champion. Ht. 5'8"
Manager A. Booth

17.09.94	Marty Chestnut W RSC 5 Leverkusen, Germany
08.10.94	Jason Lepre W RSC 1 Halle, Germany
11.02.95	Fred Reeve W CO 1 Frankfurt, Germany
25.03.95	Pascal Ragaut W PTS 6 Dusseldorf, Germany
27.05.95	Vladimir Komarov W RSC 5 Dortmund, Germany
09.09.95	Juan Leiva W RSC 6 Bielfield, Germany
14.10.95	Abdul Mannon W RSC 3 Munich, Germany
17.02.96	Kid McAuley W RSC 4 Dortmund, Germany
20.04.96	Senturk Ozdemir W PTS 10 Dusseldorf, Germany *(German International S. Featherweight Title Challenge)*
25.05.96	Chris Jickells W RSC 3 Leipzig, Germany
22.06.96	Brian Robb W RSC 4 Dortmund, Germany
31.08.96	Angel Vasilev W PTS 8 Palma de Mallorca
23.11.96	Manny Santiago W PTS 8 Munich, Germany
15.02.97	Ullises Chong W RSC 2 Vienna, Austria
13.04.97	Peter Feher W CO 1 Cologne, Germany
01.06.97	Emmanuel Burton W DIS 3 Riesa, Germany
05.10.97	Bruno Rabanales W RSC 7 Gera, Germany
08.11.97	Rudy Valentino W PTS 8 Southwark
11.04.98	Ervine Blake W RTD 4 Southwark
30.05.98	Ferenc Szakallas W RSC 3 Riesa, Germany
21.11.98	Anthony Maynard W PTS 10 Southwark
06.03.99	Gary Flear W RTD 7 Southwark *(Vacant IBF Inter-Continental Lightweight Title)*
08.05.99	Ivo Golakov W RSC 3 Bethnal Green *(IBF Inter-Continental Lightweight Title Defence)*
13.09.99	David Kehoe W DIS 2 Bethnal Green
21.02.00	Bobby Vanzie L RSC 9 Southwark *(British & Commonwealth Lightweight Title Challenges)*
27.05.00	Michael Davies W PTS 10 Southwark
13.07.00	Assen Vassilev W RSC 1 Bethnal Green
18.11.00	Leonti Voronchuk W PTS 6 Dagenham
10.04.01	Zoltan Kalocsai W PTS 12 Wembley *(Vacant IBC L. Welterweight Title)*
22.09.01	Melikhaya August W CO 4 Newcastle *(IBC L. Welterweight Title Defence)*
28.11.01	Victor Hugo Paz W PTS 12 Bethnal Green *(IBC L. Welterweight Title Defence)*
20.04.02	Rocky Martinez W PTS 12 Wembley *(IBC L. Welterweight Title Defence)*
28.09.02	Ricky Hatton L DIS 2 Manchester *(WBU L.Welterweight Challenge)*
27.05.03	Jon Honney W PTS 8 Dagenham

Career: 34 contests, won 32, lost 2.

Craig Spacie   Les Clark

Craig Spacie

Chesterfield. *Born* Chesterfield, 13 March,
1976
S. Featherweight. Ht. 5'5½"
Manager M. Shinfield

18.09.97	Robert Braddock W RSC 6 Alfreton
03.12.97	Dave Travers W RSC 3 Stoke
16.05.98	Michael Gomez L RSC 3 Bethnal Green
14.10.98	Chris Williams W PTS 6 Stoke
02.12.98	David Morris DREW 6 Stoke
17.03.99	Carl Allen L PTS 8 Stoke
03.10.99	Dean Murdoch W RSC 5 Chesterfield
28.11.99	Andy Green W PTS 6 Chesterfield
18.01.00	Marco Fattore W RTD 1 Mansfield
29.02.00	Alex Moon W PTS 6 Widnes
20.03.00	Chris Williams L PTS 6 Mansfield
11.05.00	Pete Buckley W PTS 4 Newark
25.02.01	J.J.Moore W PTS 4 Derby
06.03.01	J.J.Moore W PTS 6 Yarm
17.04.02	Mark Bowen L PTS 8 Stoke
11.05.02	Dave Hinds W PTS 6 Chesterfield
27.07.02	Jason Nesbitt W PTS 4 Nottingham
16.11.02	Richard Evatt W RSC 2 Nottingham
28.04.03	Andrew Ferrans W PTS 6 Nottingham

Career: 19 contests, won 14, drew 1, lost 4.

Steven Spartacus   Les Clark

Steven Spartacus (Smith)

Ipswich. *Born* Bury St Edmunds, 3
November, 1976
Cruiserweight. Ht. 5'10½"
Manager T. Sims

08.09.00	Michael Pinnock W PTS 4 Hammersmith
30.09.00	Martin Jolley W PTS 6 Chigwell
24.03.01	Calvin Stonestreet W PTS 4 Chigwell
16.06.01	Kevin Burton W RSC 1 Dagenham
07.09.01	Rob Stevenson W RSC 4 Bethnal Green
27.10.01	Darren Ashton W PTS 4 Manchester

24.11.01 Michael Pinnock W PTS 4 Bethnal Green
15.12.01 Oneal Murray W RSC 4 Chigwell
19.01.02 Darren Ashton W PTS 4 Bethnal Green
14.09.02 Calvin Stonestreet W RSC 3 Bethnal Green
08.02.03 Paul Bonson W PTS 6 Norwich
27.05.03 Mark Phillips W RSC 2 Dagenham
Career: 12 contests, won 12.

Michael Sprott   Les Clark

Michael Sprott

Reading. *Born* Reading, 16 January, 1975
WBF European Heavyweight Champion.
Ht. 6'0³/₄"
Manager D. Powell

20.11.96 Geoff Hunter W RSC 1 Wembley
19.02.97 Johnny Davison W CO 2 Acton
17.03.97 Slick Miller W CO 1 Mayfair
16.04.97 Tim Redman W CO 2 Bethnal Green
20.05.97 Waldeck Fransas W PTS 6 Edmonton
02.09.97 Gary Williams W PTS 6 Southwark
08.11.97 Darren Fearn W PTS 6 Southwark
06.12.97 Nick Howard W RSC 1 Wembley
10.01.98 Johnny Davison W RSC 2 Bethnal Green
14.02.98 Ray Kane W RTD 1 Southwark
14.03.98 Michael Murray W PTS 6 Bethnal Green
12.09.98 Harry Senior L RSC 6 Bethnal Green
(Vacant Southern Area Heavyweight Title)
16.01.99 Gary Williams W PTS 6 Bethnal Green
10.07.99 Chris Woollas W RTD 4 Southwark
18.01.00 Tony Booth W PTS 6 Mansfield
14.10.00 Wayne Llewelyn L RSC 3 Wembley
17.02.01 Timo Hoffmann W PTS 8 Bethnal Green
24.03.01 Timo Hoffmann L PTS 8 Magdeburg, Germany
03.11.01 Corrie Sanders L RSC 1 Brakpan, South Africa
20.12.01 Jermell Lamar Barnes W PTS 8 Rotterdam, Holland
12.02.02 Danny Williams L RTD 8 Bethnal Green
(British & Commonwealth Heavyweight Title Challenges)
09.05.02 Pele Reid W RSC 7 Leicester Square
(Vacant WBF European Heavyweight Title)
10.07.02 Garing Lane W PTS 6 Wembley
17.09.02 Derek McCafferty W PTS 8 Bethnal Green
12.12.02 Tamas Feheri W RSC 2 Leicester Square
24.01.03 Mike Holden W RSC 4 Sheffield
18.03.03 Mark Potter W RSC 3 Reading
(Southern Area Heavyweight Title Challenge. Elim. British Heavyweight Title)
10.06.03 Petr Horacek W CO 1 Sheffield
Career: 28 contests, won 23, lost 5.

David Starie

Bury St Edmunds. *Born* Bury St Edmunds, 11 June, 1974
S.Middleweight. Former Undefeated British & IBO Inter-Continental S.Middleweight Champion. Former Commonwealth S.Middleweight Champion. Ht. 6'0"
Manager Self

24.09.94 Paul Murray W RSC 2 Wembley
25.10.94 Dave Owens W PTS 6 Southwark
07.02.95 Marvin O'Brien W PTS 6 Ipswich
30.03.95 Mark Dawson W RSC 1 Bethnal Green
17.05.95 Marvin O'Brien W RSC 5 Ipswich
14.09.95 John Duckworth W PTS 6 Battersea
20.10.95 Hunter Clay W PTS 8 Ipswich
15.12.95 Carlos Christie W CO 4 Bethnal Green
21.03.96 Paul Murray W RSC 1 Southwark
14.05.96 Phil Ball W RSC 1 Dagenham
09.07.96 John Duckworth W RSC 1 Bethnal Green
03.09.96 Pascal Mercier W RSC 3 Bethnal Green
26.11.96 Ray Webb W RSC 6 Bethnal Green

08.04.97 Sammy Storey W RSC 7 Bethnal
Green
(Vacant British S. Middleweight Title)
19.07.97 Dean Francis L RSC 6 Wembley
(British S. Middleweight Title Defence)
14.02.98 Enzo Giordano W RSC 4 Southwark
28.03.98 Clinton Woods W PTS 12 Hull
*(Commonwealth S. Middleweight Title
Challenge)*
02.07.98 Danny Juma W RSC 1 Ipswich
21.11.98 Ali Forbes W CO 11 Southwark
*(Commonwealth S. Middleweight Title
Defence. Vacant British
S. Middleweight Title)*
19.01.99 Willie Quinn W RSC 3 Ipswich
*(British & Commonwealth
S. Middleweight Title Defences)*
24.04.99 Zaourbek Hetagourov W RSC 1
Peterborough
22.06.99 Mark Baker W PTS 12 Ipswich
*(British & Commonwealth
S. Middleweight Title Defences)*
19.10.99 Teimouraz Kikelidze W PTS 12
Bethnal Green
*(Vacant IBO Inter-Continental
S. Middleweight Title)*
29.01.00 Joe Calzaghe L PTS 12 Manchester
*(WBO S. Middleweight Title
Challenge)*
18.11.00 Guy Waters W RSC 6 Dagenham
*(Commonwealth S. Middleweight Title
Defence)*
09.12.00 Alex Mason W CO 3 Southwark
(British S. Middleweight Title Defence)
24.03.01 Andrew Flute W RTD 3 Sheffield
25.07.01 Bruno Godoy W RSC 3 Brakpan,
South Africa
29.09.01 Neil Linford W RSC 6 Southwark
*(British & Commonwealth
S.Middleweight Title Defences)*
08.12.01 Paul Wesley W CO 1 Dagenham
02.03.02 Marc Bargero W CO 1 Brakpan, South
Africa
*(Commonwealth S. Middleweight Title
Defence)*
08.06.02 Ron Martinez W RSC 1 Memphis,
Tennessee, USA
17.09.02 Ojay Abrahams W RSC 4 Bethnal
Green
01.03.03 Andre Thysse L PTS 12 Carnival City,
South Africa
*(Commonwealth S. Middleweight Title
Defence)*
14.06.03 Sven Ottke L PTS 12 Magdeburg,
Germany
*(WBA & IBF S.Middleweight Title
Challenges)*
Career: 35 contests, won 31, lost 4.

Gary Steadman

West Ham. *Born* London, 31 December,
1978
Lightweight Ht. 5'9$^{1/2}$"
Manager Self

10.12.98 Chris Lyons W PTS 6 Barking
18.02.99 Dave Travers W PTS 6 Barking
27.04.99 Gary Groves W RSC 2 Bethnal Green
19.10.99 Pete Buckley W PTS 4 Bethnal Green
15.11.99 Chris Lyons W PTS 4 Bethnal Green
13.03.00 Marc Smith NC 3 Bethnal Green
13.06.03 Arv Mittoo W PTS 4 Queensway
Career: 7 contests, won 6, no contest 1.

Jimmy Steel

Stoke. *Born* Stoke, 22 June, 1970
Cruiserweight. Ht. 5'7"
Manager Self

25.04.96 Andy Gray W PTS 6 Mayfair
13.10.96 Johnny Whiteside L RSC 2 Shaw
11.01.97 Enzo Giordano L PTS 4 Bethnal
Green
04.04.97 Michael Thomas L PTS 6 Brighton
19.09.97 Jason Ratcliff L PTS 6 Southend
11.11.97 Enzo Giordano L RSC 1 Bethnal
Green
21.12.97 Mike Gormley L PTS 6 Salford
06.02.98 Pedro Carragher L PTS 6 Wakefield
17.02.98 Gary Savage W PTS 6 Leeds
17.03.98 Jason Barker L PTS 6 Sheffield
05.04.98 Jon Penn L RSC 5 Shaw
01.06.98 Jeff Finlayson DREW 6 Manchester
09.06.98 Zoltan Sarossy L RSC 1 Hull
17.09.98 Earl Ling DREW 6 Brighton
14.10.98 Jeff Finlayson DREW 6 Blackpool
13.11.98 Tony Griffiths L PTS 4 Brighton
27.11.98 Damon Hague DREW 6 Nottingham
16.01.99 Tony Oakey L PTS 4 Bethnal Green
26.02.99 Ganny Dovidovas L PTS 6 Bethnal
Green
06.05.99 Dave Johnson L PTS 6 Sunderland
28.05.99 Robert Zlotkowski L PTS 6 Liverpool
10.07.99 Tony Oakey L PTS 4 Southwark
07.10.99 Mike White L PTS 6 Mere
30.10.99 Mike White L PTS 4 Peterlee
14.12.99 Jim Twite L PTS 4 Coventry
12.02.00 Jon Penn L PTS 6 Sheffield
29.02.00 Mike Gormley L RSC 3 Manchester
14.04.00 Jamie Moore L PTS 6 Manchester
13.05.00 Andy Manning L PTS 4 Barnsley
27.05.00 Dean Doyle L PTS 4 Mayfair
19.08.00 Tony Dodson L RSC 3 Brentwood
11.12.00 Mark Brookes L PTS 6 Sheffield
03.12.01 Clint Johnson DREW 6 Leeds
16.12.01 Scott Baker L PTS 4 Southwark
18.02.02 Jason McKay L PTS 4 Glasgow
25.02.02 Tony Strong DREW 4 Slough
09.03.02 Wayne Pinder L PTS 4 Manchester
19.03.02 Sam Price L PTS 4 Slough
20.04.02 Damon Hague L PTS 6 Derby
03.08.02 Peter Jackson L PTS 4 Blackpool
27.09.02 Jamie Hearn L PTS 4 Bracknell
30.10.02 Peter Haymer L PTS 4 Leicester
Square
16.11.02 Carl Wright L PTS 6 Coventry
02.12.02 Paul Owen L PTS 6 Bradford
21.03.03 Ryan Walls L PTS 6 Longford
Career: 45 contests, won 2, drew 6, lost 37.

Chris Steele

Dodworth. *Born* Barnsley, 28 March, 1980
Middleweight. Ht. 6'0"
Manager Self

14.11.99 Gavin Pearson L PTS 6 Bradford
02.03.00 Elias Boswell W RSC 4 Blackpool
13.05.00 Arv Mittoo L RSC 3 Barnsley
05.12.00 Colin McCash L RSC 4 Nottingham
08.03.01 Andy Abrol L RSC 6 Blackpool
08.04.01 David Smales L PTS 6 Wrexham
26.04.01 Sam Mottram L PTS 6 Gateshead
10.05.01 Sam Mottram L PTS 6 Sunderland
11.06.01 Darrell Grafton L RSC 1 Nottingham
07.02.02 Andrei Ivanov L PTS 6 Stoke
17.02.02 James Davenport L PTS 6 Salford
22.04.02 Scott Millar L PTS 6 Glasgow

11.05.02 Nicky Leech L PTS 6 Newark
05.12.02 Dave Pearson L PTS 6 Sunderland
08.01.03 Paul Astley L PTS 4 Aberdare
24.01.03 Andy Halder L PTS 4 Sheffield
Career: 16 contests, won 1, lost 15.

Chris Steele   Les Clark

Dave Stewart

Ayr. *Born* Irvine, 5 September, 1975
British Masters Lightweight Champion.
Ht. 6'0$^{1/4}$"
Manager A. Sims

15.02.01 Danny Connelly W PTS 6 Glasgow
27.04.01 Woody Greenaway W PTS 6 Glasgow
07.09.01 John Marshall W PTS 6 Glasgow
15.06.02 Dave Hinds W PTS 6 Tottenham
06.09.02 Pete Buckley W PTS 6 Bethnal Green
17.09.02 James Paisley W RSC 5 Bethnal
Green
30.01.03 Scott Lawton W PTS 6 Piccadilly
26.04.03 Nigel Senior W RSC 2 Brentford
*(British Masters Lightweight Title
Challenge)*
27.05.03 Pete Buckley W PTS 4 Dagenham
Career: 9 contests, won 9.

Adrian Stone

Bristol. *Born* Bristol, 19 July, 1971
Welterweight. Former Undefeated IBO
L.Middleweight Champion. Former
Undefeated IBO Inter-Continental
Welterweight Champion. Ht. 5'7"
Manager C. Sanigar

06.02.93 Sean Daughtry W PTS 6 New York
City, USA
16.04.93 James Crosby T. DRAW 2 Hamilton,
USA
08.05.93 Rey Robinson W PTS 4 East Mahanoy,
USA
28.05.93 Nate Reynolds W RSC 4 Hamilton,
USA
10.07.93 George Mitchell W RSC 2 Bushill, USA

163

10.11.93	Ernest Stroman W PTS 4 Atlantic City, USA	
23.01.94	Sylvie Furlong W CO 1 Boston, USA	
20.02.94	Robert West W CO 2 Biloxi, USA	
21.04.94	Victor Perez W PTS 8 Ledyard, USA	
22.07.94	John Jester W CO 3 Robinsonville, USA	
18.08.94	Wayne Richards W CO 5 Melville, USA	
19.10.94	Curtis Peoples W RSC 7 Catskill, USA	
14.12.94	Israel Figueroa W RSC 2 Boston, USA	
17.02.95	Ross Thompson W DIS 7 Atlantic City, USA	
07.04.95	James Hughes L RSC 10 Salem, USA	
	(USBA Welterweight Title Challenge)	
21.07.95	John Duplessis W RSC 5 New Orleans, USA	
10.11.95	Roger Turner W RSC 9 Atlantic City, USA	
03.02.96	Darryl Lattimore W RSC 1 Liverpool	
01.04.96	Mroslav Gregoriev W CO 1 Den Bosch, Holland	
14.05.96	Skipper Kelp L PTS 10 Ledyard, USA	
18.10.96	Gilberto Flores T. DRAW 5 New York City, USA	
15.11.96	Otilio Villareal W PTS 10 Somerset, USA	
12.12.96	Johar Lashlin W CO 2 Vancouver, Canada	
	(Vacant IBO Inter-Continental Welterweight Title)	
27.03.97	John-John Pacquing W RSC 6 Edmonton, Canada	
29.07.97	Greg Johnson W RSC 4 New York City, USA	
12.12.97	Bobby Butters W RSC 2 Mason City, USA	
25.04.98	Desi Ford W CO 4 Biloxi, USA	
18.08.98	Vernon Forrest L RSC 11 Tunica, USA	
	(Vacant NABF Welterweight Title)	
18.02.99	Darren Covill W RSC 2 Barking	
28.08.99	Benji Singleton W RSC 3 Hamilton, USA	
14.01.00	Michael Corleone W RSC 3 Long Island, USA	
15.04.00	Michael Carruth W RTD 5 Bethnal Green	
	(Vacant IBO L. Middleweight Title)	
15.07.00	Geoff McCreesh W RSC 6 Millwall	
	(IBO L.Middleweight Title Defence)	
11.11.00	Derek Roche W RSC 2 Belfast	
	(IBO L. Middleweight Title Defence)	
13.03.01	Joe Townsley W PTS 12 Plymouth	
	(IBO L. Middleweight Title Defence)	
21.07.01	Shane Mosley L RSC 3 Las Vegas, USA	
	(WBC Welterweight Title Challenge)	
08.02.03	Sultan Dondon W RSC 4 Brentford	
29.03.03	Carlito Brozas W RSC 2 Wembley	

Career: 38 contests, won 32, drew 2, lost 4.

Calvin Stonestreet

Tunbridge Wells. *Born* Pembury, 8 June, 1974
L. Heavyweight. Ht. 5'11¹/₂"
Manager M. O'Callaghan

23.01.01	Paul Bonson L PTS 4 Crawley	
24.03.01	Steven Spartacus L PTS 4 Chigwell	
26.04.01	Oddy Papantoniou W PTS 6 Kensington	
16.06.01	John Killian L PTS 4 Wembley	
04.07.01	Earl Ling W PTS 4 Bloomsbury	
13.12.01	Valery Odin L RSC 2 Leicester Square	

10.02.02	Sam Price L PTS 4 Southwark	
24.03.02	Alex Gething DREW 4 Streatham	
20.04.02	Gabrill Thorli W PTS 4 Wembley	
14.09.02	Steven Spartacus L RSC 3 Bethnal Green	

Career: 10 contests, won 3, drew 1, lost 6.

Darren Stubbs

Oldham. *Born* Manchester, 16 October, 1971
S. Middleweight. Ht. 5'10"
Manager J. Doughty

02.06.02	Adam Cale W RSC 6 Shaw	
21.06.02	Dean Cockburn L RSC 1 Leeds	
17.11.02	Shpetim Hoti W RTD 2 Shaw	
29.11.02	Jamie Wilson W PTS 6 Hull	
09.03.03	Martin Thompson W RSC 3 Shaw	
18.03.03	Jamie Hearn W RSC 3 Reading	
08.06.03	Danny Grainger L RSC 2 Shaw	

Career: 7 contests, won 5, lost 2.

Lee Swaby   Les Clark

Lee Swaby

Lincoln. *Born* Lincoln, 14 May, 1976
Cruiserweight. Former Undefeated British Masters Cruiserweight Champion. Ht. 6'2"
Manager D. Hobson

29.04.97	Naveed Anwar W PTS 6 Manchester	
19.06.97	Liam Richardson W RSC 4 Scunthorpe	
30.10.97	Phil Ball W RSC 3 Newark	
17.11.97	L. A. Williams W PTS 6 Manchester	
02.02.98	Tim Redman L PTS 6 Manchester	
27.02.98	John Wilson W CO 3 Glasgow	
07.03.98	Phill Day L PTS 4 Reading	
08.05.98	Chris P. Bacon L RSC 3 Manchester	
17.07.98	Chris P. Bacon L PTS 6 Mere	
19.09.98	Cathal O'Grady L RSC 1 Dublin	
20.12.98	Mark Levy L RTD 5 Salford	
23.06.99	Lee Archer W RSC 6 West Bromwich	
04.09.99	Garry Delaney L PTS 8 Bethnal Green	
03.10.99	Brian Gascoigne DREW 6 Chesterfield	

11.12.99	Owen Beck L PTS 4 Liverpool	
05.03.00	Kelly Oliver L PTS 10 Peterborough	
	(Vacant British Masters Cruiserweight Title)	
15.04.00	Mark Levy W PTS 4 Bethnal Green	
12.05.00	Enzo Maccarinelli W CO 3 Swansea	
26.05.00	Steffen Nielsen L PTS 4 Holbaek, Denmark	
09.09.00	Tony Dowling W RSC 9 Newark	
	(Vacant British Masters Cruiserweight Title)	
05.02.01	Robert Norton L PTS 8 Hull	
24.03.01	Crawford Ashley L PTS 8 Sheffield	
30.04.01	Eamonn Glennon W PTS 6 Glasgow	
02.06.01	Denzil Browne DREW 8 Wakefield	
31.07.01	Stephane Allouane W PTS 4 Bethnal Green	
13.09.01	Kevin Barrett W PTS 4 Sheffield	
15.12.01	Chris Woollas W RSC 4 Sheffield	
27.04.02	Mark Hobson L PTS 10 Huddersfield	
	(Final Elim. British Cruiserweight Title)	
03.08.02	Greg Scott-Briggs W RSC 4 Derby	
05.12.02	Eamonn Glennon W PTS 4 Sheffield	
24.01.03	Tommy Eastwood W PTS 6 Sheffield	
10.06.03	Paul Bonson W PTS 4 Sheffield	

Career: 32 contests, won 17, drew 2, lost 13.

Richard Swallow

Northampton. *Born* Northampton, 10 February, 1970
Welterweight. Ht. 5'8"
Manager Self

15.10.90	Richard O'Brien L RTD 1 Kettering	
14.02.91	Dave Fallon W RSC 4 Southampton	
06.03.91	Carl Brasier W PTS 6 Croydon	
02.05.91	Mike Morrison W PTS 6 Northampton	
24.03.92	Dean Bramhald W PTS 8 Wolverhampton	
06.04.92	Dean Bramhald W PTS 6 Northampton	
29.04.92	Chris Aston W RSC 3 Solihull	
14.10.92	Wayne Shepherd W PTS 8 Stoke	
24.11.92	Chris Mulcahy W PTS 6 Wolverhampton	
20.01.93	Ray Newby W PTS 8 Solihull	
03.03.93	Ray Newby L PTS 8 Solihull	
11.06.93	Soren Sondergaard L RTD 3 Randers, Denmark	
08.02.94	Billy McDougall W PTS 6 Wolverhampton	
30.09.94	Bernard Paul W PTS 8 Bethnal Green	
31.10.94	Carl Wright L PTS 6 Liverpool	
09.12.94	Jason Rowland L RSC 2 Bethnal Green	
14.02.95	Jason Beard L PTS 6 Bethnal Green	
17.03.95	Frank Olsen L RSC 1 Copenhagen, Denmark	
06.06.95	Anthony Maynard W RSC 2 Leicester	
23.10.95	Shaun Stokes L PTS 6 Leicester	
22.11.95	Gary Beardsley DREW 6 Sheffield	
17.01.96	Shaun Stokes W PTS 6 Solihull	
12.02.96	Nicky Bardle W RSC 4 Heathrow	
28.10.96	Bobby Vanzie L PTS 6 Bradford	
20.03.97	Anthony Maynard L PTS 6 Solihull	
12.05.97	Nigel Bradley W PTS 6 Leicester	
16.11.02	Lee Williamson W PTS 4 Coventry	
30.11.02	Arv Mittoo W PTS 4 Coventry	
09.12.02	Jon Hilton W PTS 6 Nottingham	
09.02.03	Chris Saunders L PTS 4 Bradford	
07.06.03	Tony Conroy L RSC 5 Coventry	
	(Vacant Midlands Area Welterweight Title)	

Career: 31 contests, won 18, drew 1, lost 12.

T

Matthew Tait

Harrow. *Born* Hillingdon, 15 April, 1973
L. Middleweight. Ht. 5'10½"
Manager Self

17.12.96	Dean Powell W PTS 6 Bethnal Green
29.01.97	Paul Webb W RTD 1 Bethnal Green
11.02.97	Dean Powell W PTS 6 Bethnal Green
12.07.97	Lee Bird W PTS 6 Earls Court
09.09.97	Chris Pollock W RSC 5 Bethnal Green
28.11.97	Mark Sawyers W PTS 6 Bethnal Green
11.03.98	Vince Rose W PTS 6 Bethnal Green
28.04.98	Freddie Yemofio W PTS 6 Brentford
14.05.98	Delroy Leslie W PTS 6 Acton
17.02.01	William Webster W PTS 4 Bethnal Green
24.03.01	Andrew Facey L PTS 4 Chigwell
27.10.02	Tomas da Silva W PTS 6 Southwark
08.12.02	Howard Clarke W PTS 6 Bethnal Green
18.02.03	Gary Logan L PTS 8 Bethnal Green
03.06.03	Wayne Asker W RSC 7 Bethnal Green

Career: 15 contests, won 13, lost 2.

(Mehrdud) Takaloo (Takalobigashi)

Margate. *Born* Iran, 23 September, 1975
WBU L.Middleweight Champion. Former
Undefeated IBF Inter-Continental
L.Middleweight Champion. Ht. 5'9"
Manager F. Warren

19.07.97	Harry Butler W RSC 1 Wembley
13.09.97	Michael Alexander W PTS 4 Millwall
15.11.97	Koba Kulu W RSC 3 Bristol
19.12.97	Mark Sawyers W PTS 4 Millwall
07.02.98	Jawaid Khaliq L RSC 4 Cheshunt
16.05.98	Anas Oweida W RSC 1 Bethnal Green
10.10.98	Michael Jones L PTS 6 Bethnal Green
30.01.99	Darren McInulty W RSC 5 Bethnal Green
03.04.99	Gareth Lovell W RSC 6 Kensington
26.06.99	Leigh Wicks W CO 3 Millwall
04.09.99	Carlton Williams W RSC 4 Bethnal Green
23.10.99	Prince Kasi Kaihau W RSC 3 Telford
29.01.00	Paul King W RSC 2 Manchester
08.04.00	Biagio Falcone W RTD 4 Bethnal Green
08.07.00	Ernie Smith W RSC 4 Widnes
12.08.00	Howard Clarke W PTS 12 Wembley
	(Vacant IBF Inter-Continental L.Middleweight Title)
13.11.00	Jason Collins W RSC 2 Bethnal Green
24.02.01	James Lowther W PTS 12 Bethnal Green
	(IBF Inter-Continental L.Middleweight Title Defence)
07.07.01	Anthony Farnell W RSC 1 Manchester
	(Vacant WBU L.Middleweight Title)
22.09.01	Scott Dixon W CO 1 Bethnal Green
	(WBU L. Middleweight Title Defence)
04.05.02	Gary Logan W RSC 10 Bethnal Green
	(WBU L. Middleweight Title Defence)
17.08.02	Daniel Santos L PTS 12 Cardiff
	(WBO L.Middleweight Title Challenge. WBU L.Middleweight Title Defence)
01.02.03	Jim Rock W RSC 9 Belfast
	(Vacant WBU L. Middleweight Title)
24.05.03	Jose Rosa W PTS 12 Bethnal Green
	(WBU L.Middleweight Title Defence)

Career: 24 contests, won 21, lost 3.

Karl Taylor

Birmingham. *Born* Birmingham, 5 January, 1966
Welterweight. Former Undefeated Midlands
Area Lightweight Champion. Ht. 5'5"
Manager Self

18.03.87	Steve Brown W PTS 6 Stoke
06.04.87	Paul Taylor L PTS 6 Southampton
12.06.87	Mark Begley W RSC 1 Leamington
18.11.87	Colin Lynch W RSC 4 Solihull
29.02.88	Peter Bradley L PTS 8 Birmingham
04.10.89	Mark Antony W CO 2 Stafford
30.10.89	Tony Feliciello L PTS 8 Birmingham
06.12.89	John Davison L PTS 8 Leicester
23.12.89	Regilio Tuur L RTD 1 Hoogvliet, Holland
22.02.90	Mark Ramsey L RSC 4 Hull
29.10.90	Steve Walker DREW 6 Birmingham
10.12.90	Elvis Parsley L PTS 6 Birmingham
16.01.91	Wayne Windle W PTS 8 Stoke
02.05.91	Billy Schwer L RSC 2 Northampton
25.07.91	Peter Till L RSC 4 Dudley
	(Midlands Area Lightweight Title Challenge)
24.02.92	Charlie Kane L PTS 8 Glasgow
28.04.92	Richard Woolgar W PTS 6 Wolverhampton
29.05.92	Alan McDowall L PTS 6 Glasgow
25.07.92	Michael Armstrong L RSC 3 Manchester
02.11.92	Hugh Forde L PTS 6 Wolverhampton
23.11.92	Dave McHale L PTS 8 Glasgow
22.12.92	Patrick Gallagher L RSC 3 Mayfair
13.02.93	Craig Dermody L RSC 5 Manchester
31.03.93	Craig Dermody W PTS 6 Barking
07.06.93	Mark Geraghty W PTS 8 Glasgow
13.08.93	Giorgio Campanella L CO 6 Arezzo, Italy
05.10.93	Paul Harvey W PTS 6 Mayfair
21.10.93	Charles Shepherd L RTD 5 Bayswater
21.12.93	Patrick Gallagher L PTS 6 Mayfair
09.02.94	Alan Levene W RSC 2 Brentwood
01.03.94	Shaun Cogan L PTS 6 Dudley
15.03.94	Patrick Gallagher L PTS 6 Mayfair
18.04.94	Peter Till W PTS 10 Walsall
	(Midlands Area Lightweight Title Challenge)

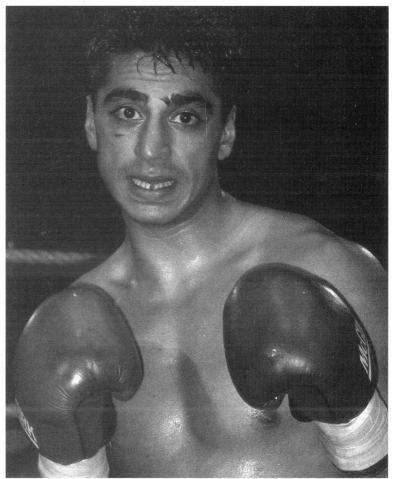

Takaloo   Les Clark

24.05.94	Michael Ayers DREW 8 Sunderland
12.11.94	P. J. Gallagher L PTS 6 Dublin
29.11.94	Dingaan Thobela W PTS 8 Cannock
31.03.95	Michael Ayers L RSC 8 Crystal Palace
	(British Lightweight Title Challenge)
06.05.95	Cham Joof W PTS 8 Shepton Mallet
23.06.95	Poli Diaz L PTS 8 Madrid, Spain
02.09.95	Paul Ryan L RSC 3 Wembley
04.11.95	Carl Wright L PTS 6 Liverpool
15.12.95	Peter Richardson L PTS 8 Bethnal Green
23.01.96	Paul Knights DREW 6 Bethnal Green
05.03.96	Andy Holligan L PTS 6 Barrow
20.03.96	Mervyn Bennett W PTS 8 Cardiff
21.05.96	Malcolm Melvin L PTS 10 Edgbaston
	(Midlands Area L. Welterweight Title Challenge)
07.10.96	Joshua Clottey L RSC 2 Lewisham
20.12.96	Anatoly Alexandrov L RSC 7 Bilbao, Spain
28.01.97	Eamonn Magee L PTS 6 Belfast
28.02.97	Mark Breslin L RSC 6 Kilmarnock
30.08.97	Gilbert Eastman L PTS 4 Cheshunt
25.10.97	Tontcho Tontchev L PTS 4 Queensferry
22.11.97	Bobby Vanzie L PTS 6 Manchester
18.04.98	Ricky Hatton L RSC 1 Manchester
18.07.98	James Hare L PTS 4 Sheffield
26.09.98	Oktay Urkal L PTS 8 Norwich
28.11.98	Junior Witter L PTS 4 Sheffield
06.03.99	George Scott L RSC 4 Southwark
15.05.99	Jon Thaxton L PTS 6 Sheffield
10.07.99	Eamonn Magee L RTD 3 Southwark
06.11.99	Alan Sebire W PTS 6 Widnes
15.11.99	Steve Murray L RSC 1 Bethnal Green
19.08.00	Iain Eldridge L PTS 4 Brentwood
04.09.00	Tomas Jansson L PTS 6 Manchester
16.09.00	Colin Lynes L PTS 6 Bethnal Green
09.12.00	David Walker L PTS 6 Southwark
10.02.01	Matthew Hatton L PTS 4 Widnes
10.03.01	Francis Barrett L RSC 3 Bethnal Green
10.04.01	Costas Katsantonis L PTS 4 Wembley
16.06.01	Brett James DREW 4 Wembley
15.09.01	David Barnes L PTS 4 Manchester
28.10.01	Babatunde Ajayi L PTS 4 Southwark
24.11.01	Ross Minter L PTS 4 Bethnal Green
15.12.01	Alexandra Vetoux L PTS 4 Wembley
12.02.02	Brett James DREW 4 Bethnal Green
11.03.02	Kevin McIntyre L PTS 4 Glasgow
04.05.02	Matthew Hatton L RSC 3 Bethnal Green
25.06.02	Rimell Taylor DREW 6 Rugby
20.07.02	Matthew Hatton L RTD 2 Bethnal Green
28.09.02	Michael Jennings L RSC 4 Manchester
16.11.02	Gavin Wake L PTS 4 Nottingham
30.11.02	Tony Conroy L PTS 4 Coventry
14.12.02	Alexander Vetoux L RTD 3 Newcastle
15.02.03	Ross Minter L PTS 6 Wembley
29.03.03	Alexander Vetoux L RSC 1 Portsmouth
08.05.03	Tony Doherty L PTS 4 Widnes

Career: 86 contests, won 15, drew 6, lost 65.

Rimell Taylor

Hinckley. *Born* Nuneaton, 28 February, 1981
L. Middleweight. Ht. 5'11"
Manager J. Weaver

25.06.02	Karl Taylor DREW 6 Rugby
07.06.03	Pete Buckley DREW 6 Coventry

Career: 2 contests, drew 2.

Matt Teague

Grimsby. *Born* Grimsby, 14 July, 1980
Featherweight. Ht. 5'9"
Manager S. Fleet/S. Pollard

21.11.02	Andy Robinson W RTD 3 Hull
11.12.02	Jason Nesbitt W PTS 6 Hull
17.04.03	Martin Hardcastle L PTS 6 Hull
02.06.03	Henry Janes W PTS 6 Cleethorpes

Career: 4 contests, won 3, lost 1.

George Telfer

Hawick. *Born* Hawick, 26 May, 1979
L. Welterweight. Ht. 5'7"
Manager K. Morrison

14.03.03	Vince Baldassara W PTS 4 Glasgow
22.03.03	Tony Montana L PTS 4 Renfrew

Career: 2 contests, won 1, lost 1.

Alan Temple

Hartlepool. *Born* Hartlepool, 21 October, 1972
Lightweight. Ht. 5'8"
Manager Self

29.09.94	Stevie Bolt W CO 2 Bethnal Green
22.11.94	Phil Found W PTS 4 Bristol
07.02.95	Brian Coleman W PTS 6 Ipswich
27.04.95	Everald Williams L PTS 6 Bethnal Green
29.09.95	Kevin McKillan W PTS 6 Hartlepool
23.11.95	Rudy Valentino L RSC 3 Marton
02.03.96	Tony Foster W PTS 6 Newcastle
08.06.96	Micky Hall W RSC 2 Newcastle
20.09.96	Scott Dixon L PTS 4 Glasgow
24.10.96	Billy Schwer L PTS 8 Wembley
04.12.96	Harry Escott W PTS 8 Hartlepool
12.02.97	Tanveer Ahmed L RSC 8 Glasgow
	(Elim. British Lightweight Title)
13.02.98	Bobby Vanzie L CO 3 Seaham
	(Elim. British Lightweight Title)
21.03.98	Michael Ayers L RSC 2 Bethnal Green
31.10.98	Alan Bosworth W PTS 6 Basingstoke
20.02.99	Ivan Walker W PTS 4 Thornaby
05.03.99	David Burke L PTS 8 Liverpool
01.05.99	Jason Rowland L PTS 6 Crystal Palace
22.05.99	Eamonn Magee L CO 3 Belfast
26.06.99	Steve McLevy W RSC 6 Glasgow
11.09.99	Wayne Rigby W PTS 8 Sheffield
02.11.99	Souleymane M'Baye L RTD 7 Ciudad Real, Spain
12.08.00	Steve Murray L RSC 2 Wembley
	(IBF Inter-Continental Lightweight Title Challenge. Elim. British Lightweight Title)
26.03.01	Jonathan Thaxton L PTS 4 Wembley
04.06.01	Gary Hibbert W PTS 6 Hartlepool
21.07.01	Junior Witter L CO 5 Sheffield
10.11.01	Colin Dunne L RSC 7 Wembley
09.03.02	Gary Hibbert L RSC 1 Manchester
26.10.02	Leo O'Reilly W RSC 4 Maesteg
21.12.02	Darren Melville L PTS 8 Millwall

Career: 30 contests, won 13, lost 17.

(Eranos) Erik Teymour (Teymurazov)

Canning Town. *Born* Moscow, Russia, 1 March, 1979
S. Middleweight. Ht. 5'8½"
Manager A. Bowers

14.07.01	Dean Ashton W RSC 2 Liverpool

31.07.01	Leigh Wicks W RSC 1 Bethnal Green
28.09.01	Kreshnik Qato W PTS 6 Millwall
23.11.01	Harry Butler W RSC 2 Bethnal Green
16.12.01	Howard Clarke W PTS 6 Southwark
15.03.02	Darren Littlewood W RSC 1 Millwall
26.04.02	Sam Soliman L PTS 8 Glasgow
21.05.02	Toks Owoh W PTS 6 Custom House
25.10.02	Donatas Bondarevas W RSC 3 Millwall
30.11.02	Varuzhan Davtyan W PTS 6 Liverpool
08.02.03	Radcliffe Green W RTD 1 Norwich
28.03.03	Paul Bonson W PTS 6 Millwall
24.05.03	Varuzhan Davtyan W PTS 4 Bethnal Green

Career: 13 contests, won 12, lost 1.

Jonathan Thaxton

Norwich. *Born* Norwich, 10 September, 1974
Lightweight. Former Southern Area, IBF & WBO Inter-Continental L. Welterweight Champion. Ht. 5'6"
Manager B. Ingle/F. Warren

09.12.92	Scott Smith W PTS 6 Stoke
03.03.93	Dean Hiscox W PTS 6 Solihull
17.03.93	John O. Johnson W PTS 6 Stoke
23.06.93	Brian Coleman W PTS 8 Gorleston
22.09.93	John Smith W PTS 6 Wembley
07.12.93	Dean Hollington W RSC 3 Bethnal Green
10.03.94	B. F. Williams W RSC 4 Watford
	(Vacant Southern Area L. Welterweight Title)
18.11.94	Keith Marner L PTS 10 Bracknell
	(Southern Area L. Welterweight Title Defence)
26.05.95	David Thompson W RSC 6 Norwich
23.06.95	Delroy Leslie W PTS 6 Bethnal Green
12.08.95	Rene Prins L PTS 8 Zaandam, Holland
08.12.95	Colin Dunne L RSC 5 Bethnal Green
	(Vacant Southern Area Lightweight Title)
20.01.96	John O. Johnson W RSC 4 Mansfield
13.02.96	Paul Ryan W RSC 1 Bethnal Green
25.06.96	Mark Elliot W CO 5 Mansfield
	(Vacant IBF Inter-Continental L. Welterweight Title)
14.09.96	Bernard Paul W PTS 12 Sheffield
	(Vacant WBO Inter-Continental L. Welterweight Title)
27.03.97	Paul Burke W RSC 9 Norwich
	(IBF & WBO Inter-Continental L. Welterweight Title Defences)
28.06.97	Gagik Chachatrian W RSC 2 Norwich
	(IBF & WBO Inter-Continental L. Welterweight Title Defences)
29.11.97	Rimvidas Billius W PTS 12 Norwich
	(IBF & WBO Inter-Continental L. Welterweight Title Defences)
26.09.98	Emanuel Burton L RSC 7 Norwich
	(IBF & WBO Inter-Continental L. Welterweight Title Defences)
15.05.99	Karl Taylor W PTS 6 Sheffield
07.08.99	Brian Coleman W PTS 6 Dagenham
15.11.99	Jason Rowland L RSC 5 Bethnal Green
	(British L. Welterweight Title Challenge)
15.07.00	Kimoun Kouassi W RSC 3 Norwich
21.10.00	Ricky Hatton L PTS 12 Wembley
	(Vacant British L.Welterweight Title)
26.03.01	Alan Temple W PTS 4 Wembley
28.07.01	David Kirk W PTS 4 Wembley
09.02.02	Eamonn Magee L RSC 6 Manchester
	(Commonwealth L.Welterweight Title Challenge)

13.04.02 Chill John W RSC 2 Norwich
15.06.02 Marc Waelkens W RSC 7 Norwich
21.09.02 Victor Baranov W RSC 1 Norwich
Career: 31 contests, won 24, lost 7.

Ashley Theophane
London. *Born* London, 20 August, 1980
Welterweight. Ht. 5'7"
Manager I. Akay

03.06.03 Lee Bedell W RSC 4 Bethnal Green
Career: 1 contest, won 1.

Matthew Thirlwall
Bermondsey. *Born* Middlesbrough, 28
November, 1980
Middleweight. Ht. 5'9½"
Manager R. McCracken

16.03.02 William Webster W RSC 1 Bethnal Green
10.05.02 Leigh Wicks W PTS 4 Bethnal Green
23.08.02 Harry Butler W RSC 3 Bethnal Green
25.10.02 Jason Collins W RSC 5 Bethnal Green
21.12.02 Howard Clarke W PTS 6 Dagenham
28.01.03 Gary Beardsley L PTS 6 Nottingham
16.04.03 Gary Beardsley W PTS 6 Nottingham
27.05.03 Leigh Wicks W PTS 6 Dagenham
Career: 8 contests, won 7, lost 1.

Ian Thomas
Stoke. *Born* Stoke, 18 March, 1970
Middleweight. Ht. 5'11¼"
Manager P. Dykes

15.04.02 Dave Pearson W CO 3 Shrewsbury
09.05.02 Gary Firby DREW 6 Sunderland
10.10.02 Jon Hilton W PTS 6 Stoke
Career: 3 contests, won 2, drew 1.

Jason Thomas
Merthyr Tydfill. *Born* Pontypridd, 7
October, 1976
Bantamweight. Ht. 5'6"
Manager Self

28.11.95 Henry Jones W PTS 4 Cardiff
08.12.95 John Sillo L PTS 6 Liverpool
13.01.96 Paul Griffin L RSC 2 Manchester
02.10.96 Henry Jones L PTS 4 Cardiff
23.10.96 Noel Wilders L PTS 6 Halifax
27.11.96 Jason Booth L PTS 4 Swansea
02.06.97 Colin Moffett W RSC 3 Belfast
02.08.97 Peter Culshaw L PTS 8 Barnsley
14.10.97 Graham McGrath W PTS 6
Wolverhampton
25.10.97 Keith Knox W PTS 8 Queensferry
04.12.97 Sean Green DREW 4 Doncaster
13.02.98 Nick Tooley W PTS 6 Weston super
Mare
18.04.98 Hector Orozco DREW 4 Manchester
14.05.98 John Matthews L PTS 6 Acton
03.10.98 Michael Alldis L PTS 6 Crawley
06.02.99 Noel Wilders L PTS 10 Halifax
(Elim. British Bantamweight Title)
15.05.99 Alex Moon L PTS 8 Blackpool
24.09.99 Frankie DeMilo W RSC 2 Merthyr
15.11.99 Stephen Oates L PTS 6 Bethnal Green
19.02.00 Stephen Oates L PTS 6 Dagenham
29.03.00 Frankie DeMilo L RSC 8 Piccadilly
*(Vacant British Masters
S. Bantamweight Title)*
06.10.00 Takalani Ndlovu L RSC 2 Maidstone
05.12.00 Kevin Gerowski L PTS 8 Nottingham

24.05.01 Stuart Sanderson DREW 6 Glasgow
08.06.01 Karim Quibir L CO 4 Orense, Spain
17.11.01 Chris Emanuele L RSC 1 Coventry
23.02.02 Jason Booth L PTS 6 Nottingham
27.04.02 Dale Robinson L RSC 4 Huddersfield
05.10.02 Gary Davis L RSC 5 Liverpool
24.03.03 Chris Emanuele W PTS 4 Barnsley
Career: 30 contests, won 7, drew 3, lost 20.

Jeff Thomas
St Annes. *Born* Holland, 30 October, 1981
Lightweight. Ht. 5'10"
Manager L. Veitch

09.12.01 Peter Allen W PTS 6 Blackpool
20.07.02 Pete Buckley W PTS 4 Bethnal Green
03.08.02 Gareth Wiltshaw W DIS 2 Blackpool
26.10.02 Dave Curran W RSC 6 Wigan
28.04.03 Daniel Thorpe W PTS 6 Cleethorpes
09.05.03 Carl Allen DREW 6 Doncaster
08.06.03 Norman Dhalie W PTS 6 Shaw
Career: 7 contests, won 6, drew 1.

Michael Thomas
Brighton. *Born* Nigeria, 14 September,
1971
Middleweight. Ht. 6'1"
Manager J. Pyle

04.04.97 Jimmy Steel W PTS 6 Brighton
23.02.03 Joel Ani L DIS 1 Streatham
13.04.03 Dean Powell W RSC 1 Streatham
10.05.03 Reggie Robshaw W RSC 5
Huddersfield
20.06.03 Conroy McIntosh L CO 2 Gatwick
Career: 5 contests, won 3, lost 2.

(Adrian) Carl Thompson
Manchester. *Born* Manchester, 26 May,
1964
Cruiserweight. Former IBO & WBO
Cruiserweight Champion. Former
Undefeated European, British & WBC
International Cruiserweight Champion.
Ht. 6'0"
Manager D. Hobson

06.06.88 Darren McKenna W RSC 2 Manchester
11.10.88 Paul Sheldon W PTS 6
Wolverhampton
13.02.89 Steve Osborne W PTS 6 Manchester
07.03.89 Sean O'Phoenix W RSC 4 Manchester
04.04.89 Keith Halliwell W RSC 1 Manchester
04.05.89 Tenko Ernie W CO 4 Mayfair
12.06.89 Steve Osborne W PTS 8 Manchester
11.07.89 Peter Brown W RSC 5 Batley
31.10.89 Crawford Ashley L RSC 6 Manchester
*(Vacant Central Area L. Heavyweight
Title)*
21.04.90 Francis Wanyama L PTS 6 St
Amandsberg, Belgium
07.03.91 Terry Dixon W PTS 8 Basildon
01.04.91 Yawe Davis L RSC 2 Monaco, Monte
Carlo
04.09.91 Nicky Piper W RSC 3 Bethnal Green
04.06.92 Steve Lewsam W RSC 8 Cleethorpes
(Vacant British Cruiserweight Title)
17.02.93 Arthur Weathers W CO 2 Bethnal
Green
*(Vacant WBC International
Cruiserweight Title)*
31.03.93 Steve Harvey W CO 1 Bethnal Green
25.07.93 Willie Jake W CO 3 Oldham

02.02.94 Massimiliano Duran W CO 8 Ferrara,
Italy
*(European Cruiserweight Title
Challenge)*
14.06.94 Akim Tafer W RSC 6 Epernay, France
*(European Cruiserweight Title
Defence)*
10.09.94 Dionisio Lazario W RSC 1
Birmingham
13.10.94 Tim Knight W RSC 5 Paris, France
10.06.95 Ralf Rocchigiani L RSC 11
Manchester
(Vacant WBO Cruiserweight Title)
13.04.96 Albert Call W RTD 4 Wythenshawe
09.11.96 Jason Nicholson W PTS 8 Manchester
26.04.97 Keith McMurray W RSC 4 Zurich,
Switzerland
04.10.97 Ralf Rocchigiani W PTS 12 Hannover,
Germany
(WBO Cruiserweight Title Challenge)
18.04.98 Chris Eubank W PTS 12 Manchester
(WBO Cruiserweight Title Defence)
18.07.98 Chris Eubank W RSC 9 Sheffield
(WBO Cruiserweight Title Defence)
27.03.99 Johnny Nelson L RSC 5 Derby
(WBO Cruiserweight Title Defence)
03.12.99 Terry Dunstan W CO 12 Peterborough
(Vacant British Cruiserweight Title)
13.05.00 Alain Simon W RSC 6 Barnsley
*(Vacant European Cruiserweight
Title)*
25.09.00 Alexei Illiin W RSC 2 Barnsley
*(European Cruiserweight Title
Defence)*
03.02.01 Uriah Grant W RSC 5 Manchester
(IBO Cruiserweight Title Challenge)
26.11.01 Ezra Sellers L RSC 4 Manchester
(IBO Cruiserweight Title Defence)
10.06.03 Phill Day W CO 4 Sheffield
Career: 35 contests, won 29, lost 6.

Gary Thompson
Lancaster. *Born* Darwen, 22 June, 1981
Cruiserweight. Ht. 5'9"
Manager B. Myers

22.09.01 Michael Thompson L RSC 3 Newcastle
16.11.01 Adam Cale W PTS 6 Preston
10.12.01 Rob Galloway W PTS 6 Bradford
23.12.01 Lee Whitehead L PTS 4 Salford
08.02.02 Shane White DREW 6 Preston
17.02.02 Lee Whitehead DREW 6 Salford
19.04.02 Lee Mountford DREW 4 Darlington
11.05.02 Tony Dowling L RSC 3 Newark
18.10.02 Michael Thompson L PTS 4 Hartlepool
26.10.02 Paul Richardson DREW 6 Wigan
02.12.02 Danny Thornton L PTS 6 Leeds
03.02.03 Nate Joseph L PTS 4 Bradford
28.02.03 Lee Mountford L PTS 6 Irvine
07.06.03 Carl Wright L RTD 2 Coventry
Career: 14 contests, won 2, drew 4, lost 8.

Martin Thompson
Barnsley. *Born* Barnsley, 6 July, 1967
S. Middleweight. Ht. 5'11"
Manager Self

03.12.98 Matthew Pepper W CO 4 Hull
16.02.99 Wayne Burchell L PTS 6 Leeds
14.06.99 Danny Thornton L PTS 6 Bradford
09.12.99 Andy Vickers L PTS 6 Sheffield
26.02.00 Wayne Shepherd L PTS 4 Carlisle
28.09.02 Darren Rhodes L PTS 8 Wakefield
21.10.02 Andy Vickers L PTS 6 Glasgow

21.11.02	Mark Ellwood L PTS 6 Hull	
05.12.02	Ryan Kerr L RSC 4 Sunderland	
21.02.03	Steve Scott DREW 6 Doncaster	
09.03.03	Darren Stubbs L RSC 3 Shaw	
07.05.03	Karl Wheeler L PTS 6 Ellesmere Port	
16.05.03	Barry Connell DREW 4 Glasgow	

Career: 13 contests, won 1, drew 2, lost 10.

Michael Thompson

Spennymoor. *Born* Bishop Auckland, 2
March, 1971
Cruiserweight. Ht. 6'3"
Manager Self

13.11.99	Anthony Wright W PTS 4 Hull
20.03.00	Mark Williams W PTS 4 Mansfield
22.09.01	Gary Thompson W RSC 3 Newcastle
15.03.02	Paul Bonson W PTS 6 Spennymoor
19.04.02	Paul Bonson W PTS 6 Darlington
18.10.02	Gary Thompson W PTS 4 Hartlepool
14.12.02	Darren Ashton W PTS 4 Newcastle

Career: 7 contests, won 7.

(Patrick) Pedro Thompson

Birmingham. *Born* Birmingham, 27 July,
1962
L. Middleweight. Ht. 5'9½"
Manager Self

03.10.98	Joe Skeldon W RSC 5 West Bromwich
25.11.98	Ross McCord L RSC 2 Clydach
22.04.99	Craig Clayton W PTS 6 Dudley
15.05.99	Reagan Denton L PTS 4 Sheffield
20.09.99	Sergei Dziniruk L RTD 2 Peterborough
02.12.99	Julian Kacanolli W PTS 6 Peterborough
12.12.99	Darren Boys L PTS 6 Chigwell
24.02.00	Martin Scotland W RSC 4 Edgbaston
23.03.00	Ojay Abrahams DREW 6 Bloomsbury
25.05.00	Brendan Rollinson L RSC 2 Hull
02.10.00	Keith Ellwood L RSC 3 Glasgow
28.11.00	Simon Sherrington L RSC 5 Brierley Hill
04.02.01	Martyn Bailey L PTS 6 Queensferry
26.02.01	Matt Scriven L RTD 1 Nottingham
17.09.01	Ryan Kerr L RSC 1 Glasgow
03.12.01	Ciaran Duffy L PTS 6 Leeds
10.12.01	Mark Paxford L PTS 6 Bradford
04.03.02	Lee Williamson L PTS 6 Bradford
24.03.02	Reggie Robshaw L PTS 6 Streatham
28.04.02	Mark Stupple W RSC 4 Southwark
10.05.02	David Walker L RSC 3 Bethnal Green
25.06.02	Sam Gorman L PTS 6 Rugby
13.07.02	Darren McInulty DREW 6 Coventry
28.09.02	Matthew Hall L RSC 1 Manchester
14.12.02	Matthew Hall L PTS 4 Newcastle
21.12.02	Gilbert Eastman L RSC 2 Dagenham
22.03.03	Tony Conroy L PTS 6 Coventry
08.04.03	Elvis Mbwakongo L RSC 1 Bethnal Green
12.05.03	Adnan Amar L RSC 4 Birmingham

Career: 29 contests, won 5, drew 2, lost 22.

Gary Thornhill

Liverpool. *Born* Liverpool, 11 February, 1968
Featherweight. Former Undefeated British
Featherweight Champion. Former
Undefeated WBO Inter-Continental &
Central Area S. Featherweight Champion.
Ht. 5'6½"
Manager Self

27.02.93	Brian Hickey W CO 4 Ellesmere Port
02.07.93	Dougie Fox W CO 1 Liverpool
30.10.93	Miguel Matthews W PTS 6 Chester
01.12.93	Wayne Windle W PTS 6 Stoke
25.02.94	Edward Lloyd DREW 6 Chester
06.05.94	Derek Amory W RSC 1 Liverpool
25.03.95	Craig Kelley W PTS 6 Chester
20.04.95	Michael Hermon W RSC 6 Liverpool
30.06.95	Chip O'Neill W RTD 3 Liverpool
04.11.95	Kid McAuley W PTS 6 Liverpool
08.12.95	Des Gargano W RTD 2 Liverpool
	(Vacant Central Area S. Featherweight Title)
13.04.96	Dominic McGuigan W RSC 3 Liverpool
25.06.96	Chris Jickells W PTS 6 Stevenage
11.12.96	Justin Juuko L RSC 8 Southwark
	(Commonwealth S. Featherweight Title Challenge)
13.12.97	Pete Buckley W PTS 6 Sheffield
06.06.98	Dean Pithie W CO 8 Liverpool
	(WBO Inter-Continental S. Featherweight Title Challenge)
19.12.98	Steve Conway W RSC 9 Liverpool
	(WBO Inter-Continental S. Featherweight Title Defence)
07.08.99	Chris Jickells W RSC 4 Dagenham
04.09.99	Michael Gomez L RSC 2 Bethnal Green
	(Vacant British S. Featherweight Title)
06.11.99	Marc Smith W PTS 6 Widnes
11.12.99	Pete Buckley W PTS 6 Liverpool
29.02.00	Benny Jones W PTS 6 Widnes
16.05.00	Richie Wenton W RTD 8 Warrington
	(Vacant British Featherweight Title)
09.06.01	Pete Buckley W PTS 4 Bethnal Green
15.09.01	Scott Harrison L RSC 5 Manchester
	(British & Commonwealth Featherweight Title Challenges)
06.09.02	Rakhim Mingaleev W PTS 6 Glasgow
05.10.02	Nicky Cook L RSC 7 Liverpool
	(WBF Inter-Continental S.Featherweight Title Challenge)

Career: 27 contests, won 22, drew 1, lost 4.

Gary Thornhill   Les Clark

Danny Thornton

Leeds. *Born* Leeds, 20 July, 1978
Central Area Middleweight Champion.
Ht. 5'10"
Manager Self

06.10.97	Pedro Carragher L PTS 6 Bradford
13.11.97	Shaun O'Neill DREW 6 Bradford
08.12.97	Shaun O'Neill DREW 6 Bradford
09.02.98	Roy Chipperfield W RSC 4 Bradford
17.03.98	P. J. Maxwell L PTS 6 Sheffield
30.03.98	Mark Owens W PTS 6 Bradford
15.05.98	Danny Bell W PTS 6 Nottingham
15.06.98	Jimmy Hawk W PTS 6 Bradford
12.10.98	Wayne Shepherd W PTS 6 Bradford
21.02.99	Shaun O'Neill W RSC 5 Bradford
25.04.99	Matt Scriven W RSC 4 Leeds
14.06.99	Martin Thompson W PTS 6 Bradford
18.10.99	Paul Henry W PTS 4 Bradford
14.11.99	Dean Ashton W PTS 4 Bradford
06.12.99	Lee Blundell L PTS 6 Bradford
05.02.00	Steve Roberts L PTS 6 Bethnal Green
25.03.00	Lee Molloy W RSC 2 Liverpool
06.06.00	Joe Townsley L RSC 7 Motherwell
	(IBO Inter-Continental L. Middleweight Title Challenge)
30.11.00	Lee Blundell L RSC 8 Blackpool
	(Vacant Central Area L. Middleweight Title)
20.03.01	Ian Toby W PTS 8 Leeds
13.11.01	Matt Galer L RSC 4 Leeds
02.12.02	Gary Thompson W PTS 6 Leeds
13.05.03	Kreshnik Qato L PTS 6 Leeds
06.06.03	Jason Collins W PTS 10 Hull
	(Vacant Central Area Middleweight Title)

Career: 24 contests, won 14, drew 2, lost 8.

Danny Thornton   Les Clark

Mark Thornton

Horsham. *Born* Crawley, 22 March, 1977
Middleweight. Ht. 6'0¾"
Manager J. Feld

30.10.02	Gary Jones W PTS 4 Leicester Square
12.12.02	Dave Wakefield W PTS 4 Leicester Square
23.02.03	Freddie Yemofio W RSC 1 Streatham
13.04.03	Kreshnik Qato L RSC 3 Streatham
20.06.03	Dean Powell W PTS 6 Gatwick

Career: 5 contests, won 4, lost 1.

Barry Thorogood

Cardiff. *Born* Cardiff, 1 December, 1972
L.Middleweight. Former Undefeated Welsh
Middleweight Champion. Ht. 6'0"
Manager P. Boyce

28.10.92	Robert Peel W PTS 6 Cardiff	
14.12.92	James Campbell W RSC 4 Cardiff	
27.01.93	Russell Washer W PTS 6 Cardiff	
24.03.93	Darren McInulty W PTS 6 Cardiff	
28.04.93	Stuart Dunn L RSC 2 Solihull	
13.09.93	Glenn Catley L PTS 4 Bristol	
23.10.93	Mark Atkins W PTS 4 Cardiff	
10.11.93	Robert Peel W PTS 6 Ystrad	
29.01.94	Darren Dorrington DREW 6 Cardiff	
02.03.94	Darren Pilling W PTS 6 Solihull	
12.03.94	Geoff McCreesh L PTS 6 Cardiff	
27.04.94	Dave Johnson DREW 8 Solihull	
20.05.94	Andrew Furlong L RSC 4 Acton	
17.10.94	Howard Eastman L RSC 6 Mayfair	
29.11.94	Robert Peel W PTS 10 Cardiff	
	(Vacant Welsh Middleweight Title)	
08.03.95	Paul Matthews W PTS 4 Cardiff	
12.04.95	Robert Peel W RSC 8 Llanelli	
	(Welsh Middleweight Title Defence)	
07.07.95	Cornelius Carr L RSC 6 Cardiff	
28.11.95	Paul Busby L PTS 8 Cardiff	
25.11.97	Michael Pinnock W PTS 8 Wolverhampton	
21.01.98	Michael Alexander W PTS 8 Stoke	
10.02.98	Phil Epton L PTS 8 Wolverhampton	
26.03.98	Peter Waudby W PTS 8 Solihull	
14.12.98	Kevin Burton W PTS 8 Birmingham	
27.01.99	Phil Epton W PTS 8 Stoke	
17.03.03	Dean Cockburn L PTS 4 Southampton	

Career: 26 contests, won 15, drew 2, lost 9.

Daniel Thorpe

Sheffield. *Born* Sheffield, 24 September, 1977
Lightweight. Ht. 5'7½"
Manager J. Ingle

07.09.01	Brian Gifford DREW 4 Bethnal Green	
24.09.01	Ram Singh W RSC 4 Cleethorpes	
17.11.01	Mally McIver L PTS 6 Dewsbury	
10.12.01	Jason Gonzales W RSC 2 Birmingham	
17.12.01	Joel Viney L RSC 2 Cleethorpes	
11.02.02	Gareth Wiltshaw L PTS 6 Shrewsbury	
04.03.02	Dave Travers W PTS 6 Birmingham	
13.04.02	Jackson Williams L PTS 6 Norwich	
11.05.02	Dean Scott W RSC 1 Chesterfield	
21.05.02	Chris McDonagh L PTS 6 Custom House	
08.06.02	Gary Young L RSC 1 Renfrew	
12.07.02	Chill John L PTS 4 Southampton	
21.07.02	John Marshall L RSC 1 Salford	
22.09.02	Albi Hunt L PTS 6 Southwark	
05.10.02	Gavin Down L RSC 2 Chesterfield	
17.11.02	Nadeem Siddique L PTS 4 Bradford	
29.11.02	Pete Buckley W PTS 6 Hull	
21.12.02	Billy Corcoran L CO 2 Dagenham	
16.02.03	Eddie Nevins L RSC 8 Salford	
	(Vacant Central Area S.Featherweight Title)	
22.03.03	Jamie Arthur L PTS 4 Renfrew	
29.03.03	Danny Hunt L PTS 6 Portsmouth	
12.04.03	Jackson Williams L PTS 6 Norwich	
19.04.03	Steve Mullin W RSC 1 Liverpool	
28.04.03	Jeff Thomas L PTS 6 Cleethorpes	
08.05.03	Andy Morris L PTS 4 Widnes	
08.06.03	Choi Tseveenpurev L PTS 8 Shaw	
20.06.03	Colin Toohey L PTS 6 Liverpool	
28.06.03	Gavin Rees L RSC 1 Cardiff	

Career: 28 contests, won 6, drew 1, lost 21.

Steve Timms

West Bromwich. *Born* West Bromwich, 10 December, 1974
Middleweight. Ht. 5'11"
Manager Self

30.04.99	Matthew Pepper W RSC 3 Scunthorpe	
02.07.99	Paul O'Rourke W RSC 2 Manchester	
03.09.99	William Webster W RSC 4 West Bromwich	
03.12.99	Allan Foster L RSC 4 Peterborough	
22.01.00	Pedro Carragher DREW 4 Birmingham	
02.03.00	Pedro Carragher W PTS 6 Blackpool	
28.03.00	Andy Vickers W RSC 4 Hartlepool	
22.05.00	Hussain Osman L RSC 2 Coventry	
05.02.01	Paul Owen W RSC 1 Bradford	
26.04.01	Andrew Buchanan L RSC 4 Gateshead	
03.10.02	Ryan Kerr L RSC 1 Sunderland	
21.03.03	Mark Phillips W PTS 6 West Bromwich	

Career: 12 contests, won 7, drew 1, lost 4.

Steve Timms   Les Clark

Colin Toohey

Liverpool. *Born* Liverpool, 19 October, 1975
Lightweight. Ht. 5'7½"
Manager S. Vaughan

07.07.01	Jason Nesbitt W PTS 4 Manchester	
15.09.01	Jason Nesbitt W PTS 4 Manchester	
28.05.02	Nigel Senior W PTS 4 Liverpool	
07.09.02	Carl Allen DREW 6 Liverpool	
30.11.02	Andrew Ferrans W PTS 6 Liverpool	
08.02.03	Pete Buckley W PTS 6 Liverpool	
20.06.03	Daniel Thorpe W PTS 6 Liverpool	

Career: 7 contests, won 6, drew 1.

Choi Tseveenpurev

Oldham. *Born* Mongolia, 6 October, 1971
British Masters Featherweight Champion.
Ht. 5'5¾"
Manager J. Doughty

22.11.96	Jeun-Tae Kim W CO 8 Seoul, South Korea	
01.05.99	Bugiarso L PTS 12 Kalimanton, Indonesia	
12.08.99	Hasabayar W RSC 4 Ulan-Bator, Mongolia	
22.08.99	Con Roksa W CO 3 Seinyeng, China	
21.05.00	David Jeffrey W RSC 2 Shaw	
24.09.00	Billy Smith W RTD 2 Shaw	
03.12.00	Chris Williams W PTS 4 Shaw	
27.04.01	Willie Limond L PTS 6 Glasgow	
23.09.01	Steve Hanley W PTS 6 Shaw	
06.10.01	Livinson Ruiz W PTS 4 Manchester	
09.12.01	Kevin Gerowski W RSC 5 Shaw	
	(Vacant British Masters Featherweight Title)	
22.03.02	Chris Emanuele W PTS 4 Coventry	
02.06.02	John Mackay W RSC 5 Shaw	
17.11.02	Peter Allen W RSC 4 Shaw	
09.03.03	Jason Nesbitt W PTS 8 Shaw	
08.06.03	Daniel Thorpe W PTS 8 Shaw	

Career: 16 contests, won 14, lost 2.

Steve Tuck

Halifax. *Born* Halifax, 20 June, 1971
Heavyweight. Ht. 6'1½"
Manager K. Walker/T. O'Neill

21.06.02	Gifford Shillingford L RSC 1 Leeds	
03.02.03	Costi Marin L RSC 1 Bradford	

Career: 2 contests, lost 2.

Ian Turner

Tredegar. *Born* Abergavenny, 6 November, 1975
Bantamweight. Former Undefeated Welsh
Bantamweight Champion. Ht. 5'8"
Manager D. Gardiner

29.05.96	Henry Jones W PTS 6 Ebbw Vale	
19.07.96	Marty Chestnut W PTS 6 Ystrad	
02.10.96	Kevin Sheil W PTS 6 Cardiff	
14.10.97	Dave Travers DREW 6 Wolverhampton	
02.12.97	Henry Jones W RSC 8 Swansea	
	(Vacant Welsh Bantamweight Title)	
03.04.98	Matthew Harris W PTS 8 Ebbw Vale	
25.10.98	Ady Lewis DREW 8 Shaw	
23.02.99	David Morris L PTS 10 Cardiff	
	(Vacant Welsh Featherweight Title)	
23.10.99	Esham Pickering L PTS 6 Telford	
03.12.99	Frankie DeMilo L PTS 6 Peterborough	
12.05.00	David Jeffrey W PTS 6 Swansea	
26.05.00	Brian Carr L PTS 6 Glasgow	
03.11.00	Frankie DeMilo L PTS 10 Ebbw Vale	
	(British Masters S. Bantamweight Title Challenge)	
08.06.01	German Guartos L PTS 6 Orense, Spain	
30.09.01	Simon Stowell W PTS 4 Bristol	
01.12.01	John Armour L PTS 8 Bethnal Green	
18.03.02	Jim Betts L RTD 4 Crawley	
08.07.02	Steve Foster L RSC 1 Mayfair	
12.04.03	Danny Wallace L RSC 4 Bethnal Green	

Career: 19 contests, won 7, drew 2, lost 10.

Martin Turner

Poole. *Born* Poole, 3 December, 1981
Lightweight. Ht. 5'6"
Manager N. Christian

15.09.02	Ceri Hall L RSC 1 Swansea	
12.12.02	Ryan Barrett L RSC 1 Leicester Square	

Career: 2 contests, lost 2.

UV

Bobby Vanzie

Bradford. *Born* Bradford, 11 January, 1974
British Lightweight Champion. Former Commonwealth Lightweight Champion. Former Undefeated Central Area Lightweight Champion. Ht. 5'5"
Manager J. Doughty

22.05.95	Alan Peacock W RSC 1 Morecambe
29.10.95	Steve Tuckett W RSC 2 Shaw
14.11.95	John Smith W PTS 6 Bury
07.03.96	John Smith W PTS 6 Bradford
02.06.96	Anthony Campbell W PTS 6 Shaw
28.10.96	Richard Swallow W PTS 6 Bradford
24.02.97	Mark Ramsey DREW 8 Glasgow
08.06.97	C. J. Jackson W RSC 3 Shaw
23.10.97	Stuart Rimmer W RTD 8 Mayfair
	(Vacant Central Area Lightweight Title)
22.11.97	Karl Taylor W PTS 6 Manchester
13.02.98	Alan Temple W CO 3 Seaham
	(Elim. British Lightweight Title)
01.06.98	Gary Flear W PTS 6 Manchester
17.10.98	Wayne Rigby W RSC 10 Manchester
	(British Lightweight Title Challenge)
01.04.99	Anthony Campbell W PTS 12 Birmingham
	(British Lightweight Title Defence)
28.05.99	Athanus Nzau W RSC 10 Liverpool
	(Vacant Commonwealth Lightweight Title)
13.09.99	Brian Coleman W PTS 6 Bethnal Green
04.12.99	Vincent Howard W PTS 12 Manchester
	(Commonwealth Lightweight Title Defence)
21.02.00	Stephen Smith W RSC 9 Southwark
	(British & Commonwealth Lightweight Title Defences)
17.04.00	Paul Kaoma W RSC 2 Birmingham
	(Commonwealth Lightweight Title Defence)
09.09.00	Joseph Charles W RSC 6 Manchester
	(Commonwealth Lightweight Title Defence)
09.10.00	Laatekwei Hammond W RSC 8 Liverpool
	(Commonwealth Lightweight Title Defence)
03.02.01	James Armah L PTS 12 Manchester
	(Commonwealth Lightweight Title Defence)
05.05.01	Steve Murray W RSC 7 Edmonton
	(British Lightweight Title Defence)
08.10.01	Anthony Maynard W RSC 1 Barnsley
	(British Lightweight Title Defence)
01.06.02	Viktor Baranov W PTS 8 Manchester
12.10.02	Andrei Devyataykin W PTS 8 Bethnal Green
18.01.03	Yuri Romanov L RSC 8 Preston
	(WBO Inter-Continental Lightweight Title Challenge)

Career: 27 contests, won 24, drew 1, lost 2.

David Vaughan

Blackwood. *Born* Caerphilly, 12 April, 1978
L. Welterweight. Ht. 5'8"
Manager D. Gardiner

23.02.03	Henry Jones W PTS 6 Aberystwyth
08.03.03	Ryan Barrett DREW 4 Bethnal Green
21.03.03	Dean Hickman L PTS 6 West Bromwich
10.05.03	Gwyn Wale DREW 4 Huddersfield

Career: 4 contests, won 1, drew 2, lost 1.

Bobby Vanzie   Les Clark

David Vaughan   Les Clark

Andy Vickers

Darlington. *Born* Darlington, 18 June, 1976
Middleweight. Ht. 5'10¾"
Manager T. O'Neill

25.04.99 Matt Mowatt W PTS 6 Leeds
11.10.99 Peter McCormack W PTS 6
           Birmingham
30.10.99 Rob Galloway W PTS 6 Peterlee
09.12.99 Martin Thompson W PTS 6 Sheffield
24.02.00 Chris Crook L PTS 6 Sunderland
28.03.00 Steve Timms L RSC 4 Hartlepool
21.05.00 Wayne Shepherd W PTS 6 Shaw
05.10.00 Paul Owen W PTS 6 Sunderland
24.11.00 Keith Palmer W RSC 3 Darlington
11.02.01 Ian Toby W PTS 6 Hartlepool
17.05.01 Reece McAllister L RSC 1 Leeds
03.12.01 Dean Ashton W PTS 6 Leeds
19.04.02 Danny Norton L CO 2 Darlington
21.10.02 Martin Thompson W PTS 6 Glasgow
Career: 14 contests, won 10, lost 4.

Jimmy Vincent

Birmingham. *Born* Barnet, 5 June, 1969
Welterweight. Former Undefeated British
Masters L Middleweight Champion.
Ht. 5'8"
Manager Self

19.10.87 Roy Williams W PTS 6 Birmingham
11.11.87 Mick Greenwood W PTS 6 Stafford
19.11.87 Darryl Pettit W RSC 6 Ilkeston
24.11.87 Roy Williams W PTS 6
           Wolverhampton
14.02.88 Niel Leggett L PTS 6 Peterborough
29.02.88 Billy Cawley W CO 1 Birmingham
13.04.88 Dave Croft W PTS 6 Wolverhampton
16.05.88 Barry North W PTS 6 Wolverhampton
14.06.88 Dean Dickinson W PTS 6 Birmingham
20.09.88 Henry Armstrong L PTS 6 Stoke
10.10.88 Henry Armstrong L PTS 6 Manchester
17.10.88 Dean Dickinson W PTS 6 Birmingham
14.11.88 Peter Gabbitus L PTS 6 Stratford upon
           Avon
22.11.88 Barry North W RSC 4 Wolverhampton

12.12.88 Tony Feliciello L PTS 8 Birmingham
09.09.92 Mark Dawson L PTS 6 Stoke
23.09.92 Mark Epton W RSC 6 Leeds
17.12.92 Jason Rowland L PTS 6 Wembley
06.03.93 Mark Tibbs W PTS 6 Glasgow
27.08.96 Geoff McCreesh L RSC 1 Windsor
26.09.96 David Bain W RSC 3 Walsall
28.10.96 Lee Murtagh W RSC 2 Bradford
18.01.97 Tommy Quinn W RSC 1 Swadlincote
25.02.97 Kevin Adamson W PTS 6 Sheffield
25.03.97 Gary Jacobs L RSC 1 Lewisham
25.10.97 Ahmed Dottuev L PTS 6 Queensferry
29.01.98 Craig Winter L PTS 6 Pentre Halkyn
28.03.98 Zoltan Sarossy DREW 6 Hull
18.09.98 Danny Ryan L PTS 12 Belfast
           *(Vacant IBO Inter-Continental
           S. Middleweight Title)*
24.10.98 Darren Dorrington DREW 6 Bristol
25.11.98 Cornelius Carr L PTS 6 Streatham
05.12.98 Wayne Alexander L RSC 3 Bristol
22.01.99 Jim Rock L PTS 10 Dublin
29.04.99 Anthony McFadden L PTS 6 Bethnal
           Green
11.12.00 Harry Butler W PTS 6 Birmingham
31.10.01 Jason Williams W PTS 10
           Birmingham
           *(Vacant British Masters
           L.Middleweight Title)*
10.12.01 Ojay Abrahams W PTS 10 Birmingham
           *(British Masters L.Middleweight Title
           Defence)*
26.04.02 Darren McInulty W CO 6 Coventry
           *(British Masters L. Middleweight Title
           Defence)*
21.12.02 David Walker W RSC 8 Dagenham
           *(Final Elim. British Welterweight
           Title)*
Career: 39 contests, won 21, drew 2, lost 16.

Joel Viney

Blackpool. *Born* Manchester, 25
September, 1973
Lightweight. Ht. 5'7¾"
Manager Self

02.03.00 Duncan Armstrong W PTS 6 Blackpool
09.06.00 Gareth Wiltshaw W PTS 6 Blackpool
30.11.00 Dave Cotterill L RSC 1 Blackpool
27.01.01 Bradley Pryce L RSC 3 Bethnal Green
10.03.01 Kevin Lear L RSC 2 Bethnal Green
04.06.01 Barry Hawthorne L PTS 8 Glasgow
11.06.01 Inderpaul Sandhu L PTS 4 Nottingham
26.07.01 Mark Winters L RSC 4 Blackpool
15.10.01 Tasawar Khan L PTS 6 Bradford
29.11.01 Michael Hunter L PTS 6 Hartlepool
09.12.01 Paddy Folan W PTS 6 Blackpool
17.12.01 Daniel Thorpe W RSC 2 Cleethorpes
21.01.02 Andrew Ferrans L PTS 8 Glasgow
17.02.02 John Marshall L RSC 6 Salford
18.03.02 Craig Docherty L CO 1 Glasgow
05.05.02 Andy McLean L PTS 6 Hartlepool
28.05.02 Tony McPake L RSC 1 Liverpool
29.06.02 Matthew Burke L PTS 4 Brentwood
17.08.02 Henry Castle L RSC 1 Cardiff
23.09.02 Sean Green L PTS 6 Cleethorpes
05.10.02 Gary Reid L CO 2 Coventry
09.11.02 Darryn Walton L PTS 6 Altrincham
18.11.02 Andrew Ferrans L PTS 6 Glasgow
02.12.02 Gareth Wiltshaw W PTS 6 Bradford
16.12.02 Pete Buckley W PTS 6 Cleethorpes
08.01.03 Daleboy Rees L RSC 5 Aberdare
08.02.03 Jackson Williams L PTS 4 Norwich
17.02.03 John Simpson L RTD 1 Glasgow
22.03.03 Martin Watson L RSC 2 Renfrew
09.05.03 Stefy Bull L RTD 3 Doncaster
07.06.03 Baz Carey L PTS 6 Coventry
Career: 31 contests, won 6, lost 25.

Jimmy Vincent (left)   Les Clark

WXYZ

Gavin Wake

Leeds. *Born* Leeds, 25 June, 1979
L. Middleweight. Ht. 5'11"
Manager M. Marsden

26.02.01 Arv Mittoo W PTS 4 Nottingham
09.04.01 Richard Inquieti W PTS 6 Bradford
08.05.01 Brian Coleman W PTS 4 Barnsley
21.06.01 Lee Williamson W PTS 6 Sheffield
22.10.01 Darren Spencer W RSC 3 Glasgow
24.11.01 Richard Inquieti W PTS 6 Wakefield
27.04.02 Marcus Portman L PTS 4 Huddersfield
15.06.02 Ernie Smith W PTS 4 Leeds
28.09.02 Richard Inquieti W PTS 6 Wakefield
16.11.02 Karl Taylor W PTS 4 Nottingham
22.02.03 Lee Armstrong L PTS 10 Huddersfield
(Vacant Central Area L.Middleweight Title)

Career: 11 contests, won 9, lost 2.

Dave Wakefield

Tooting. *Born* London, 8 January, 1979
Middleweight. Ht. 5'11"
Manager D. Powell

12.12.02 Mark Thornton L PTS 4 Leicester Square
13.04.03 Jon Hilton W PTS 4 Streatham
26.04.03 Kevin Phelan L PTS 4 Brentford
03.06.03 Justin Hudson L PTS 4 Bethnal Green
13.06.03 William Webster DREW 6 Queensway
Career: 5 contests, won 1, drew 1, lost 3.

Gwyn Wale

Barnsley. *Born* Barnsley, 24 August, 1984
L. Welterweight. Ht. 5'8"
Manager T. Gilmour/C. Aston

17.09.02 Arv Mittoo W PTS 6 Bethnal Green
05.10.02 Martin Hardcastle W PTS 4 Huddersfield
16.11.02 David Kehoe W PTS 4 Nottingham
22.02.03 James Paisley W RSC 1 Huddersfield
10.05.03 David Vaughan DREW 4 Huddersfield
Career: 5 contests, won 4, drew 1.

David Walker

Bermondsey. *Born* Bromley, 17 June, 1976
Southern Area L.Middleweight Champion.
Former Undefeated Southern Area
Welterweight Champion. Ht. 5'10"
Manager Self

29.04.00 Dave Fallon W RSC 1 Wembley
27.05.00 Stuart Rimmer W RSC 2 Southwark
15.07.00 Billy Smith W RTD 2 Millwall
16.09.00 Keith Jones W PTS 6 Bethnal Green
14.10.00 Jason Vlasman W RSC 1 Wembley
18.11.00 Gary Flear W PTS 4 Dagenham
09.12.00 Karl Taylor W PTS 6 Southwark
20.01.01 Ernie Smith W RTD 1 Bethnal Green
17.02.01 Paul Denton W PTS 4 Bethnal Green
19.05.01 Mark Ramsey W PTS 4 Wembley
14.07.01 David White W PTS 4 Liverpool
13.09.01 David Kirk DREW 8 Sheffield
16.03.02 Paul Dyer W RSC 6 Bethnal Green
(Vacant Southern Area Welterweight Title)

10.05.02 Pedro Thompson W RSC 3 Bethnal Green
23.08.02 Robert Burton W RSC 2 Bethnal Green
25.10.02 Brett James W RSC 4 Bethnal Green
(Southern Area Welterweight Title Defence)
21.12.02 Jimmy Vincent L RSC 8 Dagenham
(Final Elim. British Welterweight Title)
05.03.03 Ojay Abrahams W PTS 6 Bethnal Green
16.04.03 Leigh Wicks W PTS 6 Nottingham
27.05.03 John Humphrey W CO 2 Dagenham
(Southern Area L.Middleweight Title Challenge. Elim. British L.Middleweight Title)

Career: 20 contests, won 18, drew 1, lost 1.

Dean Walker

Sheffield. *Born* Sheffield, 25 April, 1979
L. Middleweight. Ht. 5'11"
Manager D. Hobson

21.10.00 Colin McCash DREW 6 Sheffield
11.12.00 James Lee L PTS 6 Sheffield
27.07.01 Chris Duggan W RSC 4 Sheffield
15.12.01 William Webster W PTS 6 Sheffield
03.03.02 Shaun Horsfall W PTS 6 Shaw
02.06.02 Wayne Shepherd W PTS 6 Shaw
03.08.02 Richard Inquieti W PTS 6 Derby
05.10.02 Martin Scotland W PTS 6 Chesterfield
24.05.03 Neil Bonner W PTS 6 Sheffield

Career: 9 contests, won 7, drew 1, lost 1.

David Walker Les Clark

Carl Wall

Liverpool. *Born* Liverpool, 29 July, 1976
Middleweight. Ht. 5'10¾"
Manager S. Vaughan

11.12.00	Rob Stevenson W PTS 4 Widnes
10.02.01	Brian Coleman W RSC 1 Widnes
20.06.03	Steve Russell W PTS 4 Liverpool

Career: 3 contest, won 3.

Carl Wall   Les Clark

Danny Wallace   Les Clark

Danny Wallace

Leeds. *Born* Leeds, 12 July, 1980
Bantamweight. Ht. 5'7"
Manager M. Marsden

24.08.01	Roger Glover W PTS 4 Atlantic City, USA
12.04.02	Michael Weaver DREW 4 Philadelphia, USA
22.02.03	Jamil Hussain W RSC 1 Huddersfield
12.04.03	Ian Turner W RSC 4 Bethnal Green
10.05.03	Marcel Kasimov L RSC 3 Huddersfield

Career: 5 contests, won 3, drew 1, lost 1.

(Walisundra) Jus Wallie (Mudiyanselage)

Balham. *Born* Sri Lanka, 14 May, 1976
S. Featherweight. Ht. 5'5"
Manager E. Maloney

01.02.03	Kevin O'Hara L RSC 2 Belfast
29.03.03	Henry Castle W RSC 2 Portsmouth
05.04.03	Derry Matthews L PTS 4 Manchester
08.05.03	Steve Bell DREW 4 Widnes
31.05.03	J.J.Moore W RSC 1 Bethnal Green

Career: 5 contests, won 2, drew 1, lost 2.

Ryan Walls

Slough. *Born* Reading, 29 January, 1979
L. Heavyweight. Ht. 6'0½"
Manager G. Carmen

20.12.02	Mark Phillips W PTS 4 Bracknell
23.02.03	Michael Pinnock W PTS 6 Streatham
21.03.03	Jimmy Steel W PTS 6 Longford
12.04.03	Earl Ling W RSC 4 Norwich
09.05.03	Darren Ashton W PTS 6 Longford

Career: 5 contests, won 5.

Darryn Walton

Sale. *Born* Manchester, 30 June, 1973
Lightweight. Ht. 5'7"
Manager S. Wood/T. Gilmour

09.11.02	Joel Viney W PTS 6 Altrincham
16.02.03	Peter Allen W PTS 6 Salford
08.06.03	Anthony Hanna W PTS 6 Shaw

Career: 3 contest, won 3.

Darryn Walton   Les Clark

Isaac Ward

Darlington. *Born* Darlington, 7 April, 1977
Bantamweight. Ht. 5'5"
Manager M. Marsden

03.08.02	Neil Read W RSC 1 Blackpool
18.10.02	John-Paul Ryan W PTS 6 Hartlepool
14.12.02	Steve Gethin W PTS 4 Newcastle

Career: 3 contests, won 3.

Nathan Ward

Reading. *Born* Reading, 19 July, 1979
L. Welterweight. Ht. 5'10"
Manager J. Evans

27.09.02	Darren Goode W RSC 1 Bracknell
03.12.02	Dean Larter W PTS 4 Bethnal Green
20.12.02	Arv Mittoo W PTS 6 Bracknell
18.03.03	Pete Buckley W PTS 4 Reading
26.04.03	Cristian Hodorogea L RSC 1 Brentford

Career: 5 contests, won 4, lost 1.

Nathan Ward   Les Clark

Jamie Warters

Leeds. *Born* York, 16 December, 1973
Cruiserweight. Ht. 6'1"
Manager Self

15.09.95	Phil Reid W RSC 5 Darlington
07.12.95	Scott Beasley W PTS 6 Hull
19.03.96	Declan Faherty W PTS 6 Leeds
13.06.97	Greg Scott-Briggs W RSC 5 Leeds
11.11.97	Danny Southam W PTS 6 Leeds
17.02.98	P. R. Mason W CO 2 Leeds
12.05.98	Warren Stowe W PTS 6 Leeds
26.09.98	Tim Brown L RSC 4 York
15.07.99	Kevin Mitchell W CO 1 Peterborough
13.11.99	Terry Morrill W PTS 8 Hull
21.10.00	Jason Barker W PTS 4 Sheffield
21.11.02	Tony Booth L PTS 8 Hull
03.04.03	Darren Ashton W PTS 6 Hull
17.04.03	Phill Day DREW 6 Hull

Career: 14 contests, won 11, drew 1, lost 2.

Martin Watson

Coatbridge. *Born* Bellshill, 12 May, 1981
Scottish Lightweight Champion. Ht. 5'8"
Manager R. Bannon/K. Morrison

24.05.01	Shaune Danskin W RSC 3 Glasgow	
20.10.01	Jon Honney W RSC 3 Glasgow	
16.12.01	Richie Caparelli W PTS 6 Glasgow	
11.03.02	Pete Buckley W PTS 4 Glasgow	
26.04.02	Gary Reid W PTS 6 Glasgow	
08.06.02	Scott Miller W RSC 2 Renfrew	
18.11.02	Gary Reid W RSC 4 Glasgow	
22.03.03	Joel Viney W RSC 2 Renfrew	
16.05.03	Barry Hughes W RTD 8 Glasgow	
	(Vacant Scottish Lightweight Title)	

Career: 9 contests, won 9.

Danny Watts

Peckham. *Born* London, 5 April, 1973
Heavyweight. Ht. 6'7"
Manager F. King

02.09.97	Johnny Davison W CO 2 Southwark
10.01.98	Steve Cranston W RSC 4 Bethnal Green
11.04.98	Gavin McGhin W PTS 4 Southwark
12.09.98	Ladislav Husarik W PTS 4 Bethnal Green
04.02.99	Luke Simpkin W CO 3 Lewisham
06.03.99	Piotr Jurczyk W PTS 4 Southwark
22.05.99	Gordon Minors L CO 1 Belfast
18.12.99	Adey Cook W RSC 1 Southwark
13.03.00	Mark Potter L RSC 6 Bethnal Green
	(Vacant Southern Area Heavyweight Title)
23.03.02	Valery Semishkur W RSC 1 Southwark
18.05.02	Mal Rice W RTD 3 Millwall
07.12.02	Mindaugas Kulikauskas W RSC 5 Brentwood

Career: 12 contests, won 10, lost 2.

William Webster

Birmingham. *Born* Birmingham, 14 March, 1970
S. Middleweight. Ht. 6'0"
Manager Self

05.06.99	Brian Knudsen L RSC 4 Cardiff
15.08.99	Edwin Cleary L PTS 6 Derby
03.09.99	Steve Timms L RSC 4 West Bromwich
12.11.99	Biagio Falcone L PTS 6 Glasgow
20.11.99	Gary Beardsley L PTS 6 Grantham
02.12.99	Wayne Elcock L PTS 6 Peterborough
13.12.99	Biagio Falcone L RSC 1 Glasgow
21.02.00	Scott Millar L PTS 6 Glasgow
29.02.00	Thomas McDonagh L RTD 2 Widnes
28.03.00	Peter McCormack L PTS 6 Wolverhampton
13.04.00	Steve Ryan L PTS 4 Holborn
15.05.00	Mike Duffield W PTS 6 Birmingham
29.05.00	Michael Jennings L PTS 6 Manchester
19.06.00	Damon Hague L PTS 4 Burton
01.07.00	Alan Page L PTS 4 Manchester
25.09.00	Reagan Denton L PTS 4 Barnsley
07.10.00	George Robshaw L PTS 4 Doncaster
10.11.00	Chris Nembhard L RSC 1 Mayfair
28.01.01	Peter Nightingale L PTS 6 Wolverhampton
17.02.01	Matthew Tait L PTS 4 Bethnal Green
25.02.01	Gary Beardsley L PTS 6 Derby
13.03.01	Mark Phillips L RTD 1 Plymouth
16.06.01	Andrew Lowe L RSC 2 Dagenham
15.12.01	Dean Walker L PTS 6 Sheffield
23.12.01	James Davenport L RSC 5 Salford

17.02.02	Donovan Smillie L PTS 6 Salford
03.03.02	Gary Dixon L PTS 6 Shaw
16.03.02	Matthew Thirlwall L RSC 1 Bethnal Green
15.04.02	Roddy Doran L PTS 8 Shrewsbury
15.06.02	Danny Smith L PTS 6 Norwich
23.09.02	Davey Jones L PTS 6 Cleethorpes
10.10.02	Kenroy Lambert W PTS 6 Piccadilly
25.10.02	Andrew Facey L PTS 4 Cotgrave
08.11.02	Davey Jones L PTS 6 Doncaster
17.11.02	Donovan Smillie L PTS 6 Bradford
11.12.02	Mark Ellwood L PTS 6 Hull
21.12.02	Darren Covill W PTS 4 Dagenham
08.02.03	Jason McKay L RSC 1 Liverpool
13.06.03	Dave Wakefield DREW 6 Queensway

Career: 39 contests, won 3, drew 1, lost 35.

Paul Wesley

Birmingham. *Born* Birmingham, 2 May, 1962
S. Middleweight. Ht. 5'9"
Manager Self

20.02.87	B. K. Bennett L PTS 6 Maidenhead
18.03.87	Darryl Ritchie DREW 4 Stoke
08.04.87	Dean Murray W PTS 6 Evesham
29.04.87	John Wright W PTS 6 Loughborough
12.06.87	Leon Thomas W RSC 2 Leamington
16.11.87	Steve McCarthy L CO 8 Southampton
25.01.88	Paul Murray W PTS 8 Birmingham
29.02.88	Paul Murray DREW 8 Birmingham
15.03.88	Johnny Williamson W CO 2 Bournemouth
09.04.88	Joe McKenzie W RSC 6 Bristol
10.05.88	Tony Meszaros W PTS 8 Edgbaston
21.03.89	Carlton Warren L CO 2 Wandsworth
10.05.89	Rod Douglas L CO 1 Kensington
24.10.89	Nigel Rafferty L PTS 6 Wolverhampton
22.11.89	Nigel Rafferty L PTS 8 Stafford
28.11.89	Nigel Rafferty L PTS 6 Wolverhampton
05.12.89	Ian Strudwick L PTS 6 Catford
24.01.90	Rocky Feliciello W PTS 6 Solihull
19.02.90	Nigel Rafferty L PTS 8 Birmingham
22.03.90	John Ashton L PTS 10 Wolverhampton
	(Midlands Area Middleweight Title Challenge)
17.04.90	Winston May DREW 8 Millwall
09.05.90	Alan Richards W PTS 8 Solihull
04.06.90	Julian Eavis W PTS 8 Birmingham
18.09.90	Shaun Cummins L RSC 1 Wolverhampton
17.10.90	Julian Eavis W PTS 6 Stoke
23.01.91	Wally Swift Jnr L PTS 10 Solihull
	(Midlands Area L. Middleweight Title Challenge)
20.03.91	Horace Fleary L RSC 5 Solihull
16.05.91	Delroy Waul L RSC 7 Liverpool
04.07.91	Neville Brown W RSC 1 Alfreton
31.07.91	Francesco dell'Aquila L PTS 8 Casella, Italy
03.10.91	Neville Brown L PTS 8 Burton
29.10.91	Tony Collins DREW 8 Kensington
03.03.92	Antonio Fernandez L PTS 10 Cradley Heath
	(Vacant Midlands Area Middleweight Title)
10.04.92	Jean-Charles Meuret L PTS 8 Geneva, Switzerland
03.06.92	Sumbu Kalambay L PTS 10 Salice Terme, Italy
29.10.92	Ian Strudwick W RSC 1 Bayswater
14.11.92	Paul Busby L PTS 8 Cardiff

24.11.92	Paul Jones W RSC 2 Doncaster
16.03.93	Chris Pyatt L PTS 10 Mayfair
04.06.93	Jacques le Blanc L PTS 10 Moncton, Canada
28.07.93	Antonio Fernandez L RSC 3 Brixton
	(Midlands Area Middleweight Title Challenge)
09.10.93	Warren Stowe W PTS 10 Manchester
	(Elim. British L. Middleweight Title)
09.02.94	Steve Collins L PTS 8 Brentwood
10.02.95	Robert McCracken L PTS 12 Birmingham
	(British L. Middleweight Title Challenge)
24.02.95	Scott Doyle W PTS 8 Weston super Mare
18.03.95	Crisanto Espana L PTS 6 Millstreet
21.04.95	Gilbert Jackson L RSC 6 Dudley
	(Elim. British L. Middleweight Title)
31.01.96	Howard Eastman L RSC 1 Birmingham
21.03.96	Gary Logan L PTS 6 Southwark
13.04.96	Harry Simon L RTD 4 Wythenshawe
26.09.96	Nigel Rafferty DREW 6 Walsall
19.10.96	Glenn Catley L RSC 7 Bristol
25.03.97	Chris Johnson L CO 2 Lewisham
07.02.98	Paul Carr L PTS 6 Cheshunt
07.03.98	Omar Sheika L RTD 4 Reading
23.09.98	Lester Jacobs L CO 4 Bloomsbury
13.02.99	Geoff McCreesh L PTS 8 Newcastle
03.04.99	Toks Owoh L CO 5 Kensington
23.03.00	Lester Jacobs L PTS 6 Bloomsbury
13.04.00	Sam Soliman L PTS 6 Holborn
19.08.00	Adrian Dodson L PTS 4 Brentwood
18.11.00	Paul Bowen L PTS 4 Dagenham
11.12.00	Darren Rhodes L PTS 4 Widnes
08.03.01	Lee Blundell L RSC 3 Blackpool
25.09.01	Tony Dodson L PTS 6 Liverpool
17.11.01	Dean Cockburn L PTS 4 Glasgow
24.11.01	Andrew Lowe L PTS 4 Bethnal Green
08.12.01	David Starie L CO 1 Dagenham
05.04.03	Thomas McDonagh L PTS 6 Manchester
16.04.03	Ryan Rhodes L CO 3 Nottingham

Career: 70 contests, won 16, drew 5, lost 49.

Karl Wheeler

Peterborough. *Born* Peterborough, 30 May, 1982
L. Heavyweight. Ht. 6'3"
Manager M. Goodall

07.05.03	Martin Thompson W PTS 6 Ellesmere Port
29.05.03	Paul Billington W PTS 6 Sunderland

Career: 2 contests, won 2.

Wayne Wheeler

Plymouth. *Born* Plymouth, 24 February, 1970
L. Welterweight. Ht. 5'8"
Manager N. Christian

24.03.01	J.J. Moore L RSC 4 Newark
12.05.01	Byron Pryce L RSC 2 Plymouth
16.12.01	Danny Gwilym W RSC 2 Bristol
17.02.02	Dean Hickman DREW 6 Wolverhampton
16.03.02	David Kehoe DREW 6 Northampton
13.04.02	Dean Hickman L PTS 6 Wolverhampton
11.05.02	Carl Greaves L RSC 1 Newark
13.07.02	Steve Saville L RSC 2 Wolverhampton
27.09.02	Robert Lloyd-Taylor L PTS 6 Bracknell

05.10.02 Abdul Mannon W RSC 2 Liverpool
15.10.02 Iain Eldridge DREW 4 Bethnal Green
26.10.02 Justin Parsons W CO 2 Maesteg
30.11.02 Andy Egan L RSC 1 Coventry
08.02.03 Luke Rudd L RSC 2 Norwich
13.06.03 Nathan Wyatt W PTS 6 Bristol
30.06.03 Marcus Portman L RSC 3 Shrewsbury
Career: 16 contests, won 4, drew 3, lost 9.

David White
Cardiff. *Born* Cardiff, 18 April, 1975
Welterweight. Ht. 5'9"
Manager D. Gardiner

23.09.00 Matthew Hatton L PTS 4 Bethnal
Green
25.11.00 Matthew Hatton L PTS 4 Manchester
28.01.01 Jimmy Gould L PTS 6 Wolverhampton
05.02.01 Lance Crosby DREW 4 Hull
24.02.01 Francis Barrett L PTS 4 Bethnal Green
28.04.01 Ahmet Kaddour L PTS 4 Cardiff
12.05.01 Leo O'Reilly L PTS 4 Manchester
24.05.01 Ronnie Nailen L PTS 6 Glasgow
14.07.01 David Walker L PTS 4 Liverpool
18.08.01 Oscar Hall L PTS 6 Dewsbury
15.09.02 Taz Jones DREW 4 Swansea
05.10.02 Gary Ryder L PTS 6 Liverpool
Career: 12 contests, drew 2, lost 10.

Jason White
Cardiff. *Born* Cardiff, 18 November, 1978
S. Featherweight. Ht. 5'6"
Manager D. Gardiner

27.11.00 Stephen Chinnock L PTS 4
Birmingham
16.12.00 Scott Miller L PTS 4 Sheffield
08.03.01 Nigel Senior W PTS 8 Stoke
12.05.01 Lee Meager L PTS 4 Plymouth
14.07.01 Dean Pithie L PTS 4 Liverpool
18.08.01 Jesse James Daniel L PTS 6 Dewsbury
28.09.02 Steve Foster L RSC 3 Manchester
Career: 7 contests, won 1, lost 6.

Jimmy White
Cardiff. *Born* Cardiff, 29 March, 1983
L. Middleweight. Ht. 5'9"
Manager D. Gardiner

02.12.02 Jon Hilton L RSC 5 Leicester
Career: 1 contest, lost 1.

Lee Whitehead
Manchester. *Born* Barton, 16 July, 1965
Cruiserweight. Ht. 5'10¾"
Manager Self

09.10.95 Roy Chipperfield W RSC 2 Manchester
04.12.95 Phil Ball W PTS 6 Manchester
13.01.96 Elwen Brooks W PTS 6 Manchester
26.02.96 Kevin Burton W PTS 6 Manchester
13.04.96 Mark Snipe L PTS 4 Wythenshawe
02.06.96 Andy Fletcher W RSC 2 Shaw
22.08.96 Peter Mason W PTS 4 Manchester
19.09.96 Brian Galloway W PTS 4 Manchester
22.12.96 Martin Jolley DREW 6 Salford
18.01.97 Mark Dawson W PTS 6 Manchester
26.06.97 Martin Jolley W PTS 6 Salford
19.09.97 Carl Nicholson L PTS 6 Salford
22.11.97 Kevin Burton DREW 4 Manchester
21.12.97 Mark Dawson L RSC 4 Salford
23.02.98 Peter Federenko L PTS 6 Salford
27.05.01 Darren Ashton L RSC 2 Manchester
23.12.01 Gary Thompson W PTS 4 Salford

17.02.02 Gary Thompson DREW 6 Salford
25.04.02 Earl Ling L PTS 6 Hull
21.07.02 Eamonn Glennon W PTS 6 Salford
03.08.02 Eamonn Glennon L PTS 6 Blackpool
Career: 21 contests, won 11, drew 3, lost 7.

Leigh Wicks
Brighton. *Born* Worthing, 29 July, 1965
S. Middleweight. Ht. 5'6¼"
Manager Self

29.04.87 Fidel Castro W PTS 6 Hastings
26.09.87 Jason Rowe W PTS 6 Hastings
18.11.87 Lou Ayres W PTS 6 Holborn
26.01.88 Theo Marius L PTS 8 Hove
15.02.88 Shamus Casey W PTS 6 Copthorne
26.04.88 Franki Moro DREW 8 Hove
04.05.88 Tony Britton W PTS 8 Wembley
18.05.88 Mark Howell W RSC 8 Portsmouth
25.05.88 Newton Barnett DREW 8 Hastings
22.11.88 Roy Callaghan L PTS 8 Basildon
16.03.89 Tony Britland W PTS 8 Southwark
12.10.89 Tony Gibbs W CO 2 Southwark
08.02.90 Ernie Noble W PTS 8 Southwark
26.04.90 Julian Eavis DREW 8 Mayfair
06.11.90 Gordon Blair W PTS 8 Mayfair
10.01.91 Barry Messam W PTS 6 Wandsworth
14.02.91 Kevin Thompson W PTS 8
Southampton
21.10.91 Tony Britland W RSC 3 Mayfair
20.02.92 Mick Duncan L PTS 8 Glasgow
30.04.92 Darren Morris DREW 6 Mayfair
19.10.92 Bozon Haule W PTS 8 Mayfair
20.01.93 Robert McCracken L PTS 8
Wolverhampton
17.02.93 Kevin Lueshing L PTS 6 Bethnal Green
22.04.93 Warren Stowe L PTS 6 Bury
27.10.95 Danny Quacoe W RSC 4 Brighton
18.11.95 Gary Jacobs L RTD 3 Glasgow
26.01.96 Wayne Appleton L PTS 6 Brighton
05.03.96 Kevin Thompson L PTS 6 Bethnal
Green
24.03.97 Ross Hale L PTS 6 Bristol
08.04.97 Ahmet Dottuev L RSC 1 Bethnal Green
29.05.97 Nicky Thurbin L PTS 8 Mayfair
11.07.97 Darren Covill L RSC 2 Brighton
27.11.97 Lester Jacobs L PTS 6 Bloomsbury
06.12.97 Rhoshi Wells L PTS 4 Wembley
21.02.98 Neil Sinclair L RSC 1 Belfast
24.03.98 Ojay Abrahams L PTS 6 Bethnal Green
05.06.98 Darren Bruce L PTS 6 Southend
25.11.98 Darren Covill L PTS 4 Streatham
22.02.99 Neil Linford L PTS 4 Peterborough
26.06.99 Takaloo L CO 3 Millwall
09.10.99 Darren Rhodes L PTS 4 Manchester
27.11.99 Geoff McCreesh L PTS 6 Lubeck,
Germany
11.12.99 Darren Rhodes L PTS 4 Liverpool
21.02.00 Sergei Dzinziruk L RSC 2 Southwark
25.03.00 Darren Rhodes L PTS 4 Glasgow
08.04.00 Spencer Fearon L PTS 4 Bethnal Green
02.06.00 Allan Foster L PTS 4 Ashford
24.06.00 Scott Dixon L PTS 4 Glasgow
01.07.00 Karim Hussine L PTS 6 Southwark
30.09.00 Bobby Banghar L PTS 4 Peterborough
07.10.00 Jamie Moore L PTS 4 Doncaster
11.11.00 Brian Knudsen L RSC 5 Belfast
17.03.01 Wayne Pinder L PTS 4 Manchester
29.03.01 Lester Jacobs L PTS 6 Hammersmith
05.05.01 Ty Browne L PTS 6 Brighton
08.06.01 Jason Collins L PTS 4 Hull
21.07.01 Damon Hague L PTS 4 Sheffield
31.07.01 Erik Teymour L RSC 1 Bethnal Green
30.09.01 Liam Lathbury L PTS 4 Bristol

09.10.01 Ruben Groenewald L PTS 6 Cardiff
28.10.01 Allan Gray L PTS 4 Southwark
17.11.01 Lawrence Murphy L PTS 4 Glasgow
08.12.01 Wayne Asker L PTS 4 Dagenham
16.12.01 Allan Gray L PTS 4 Southwark
31.01.02 Freddie Yemofio W PTS 6 Piccadilly
09.02.02 P.J. Maxwell L PTS 4 Manchester
13.04.02 Andrew Facey L PTS 6 Norwich
10.05.02 Matthew Thirlwall L PTS 4 Bethnal
Green
17.09.02 Kenroy Lambert L PTS 6 Bethnal
Green
23.11.02 Damon Hague L PTS 6 Derby
03.12.02 Lee Hodgson L PTS 4 Bethnal Green
08.02.03 Spencer Fearon L PTS 6 Brentford
23.02.03 Alan Jones L PTS 8 Aberystwyth
22.03.03 Lawrence Murphy L PTS 4 Renfrew
16.04.03 David Walker L PTS 6 Nottingham
26.04.03 Darren McDermott L PTS 4 Brentford
09.05.03 Kevin Phelan L PTS 6 Longford
27.05.03 Matthew Thirlwall L PTS 6 Dagenham
20.06.03 Alan Gilbert L PTS 4 Gatwick
Career: 79 contests, won 17, drew 4, lost 58.

Noel Wilders
Castleford. *Born* Castleford, 4 January,
1975
Bantamweight. Former European
Bantamweight Champion. Former
Undefeated IBO, British & Central Area
Bantamweight Champion. Ht. 5'5"
Manager T. Callighan

16.03.96 Neil Parry W RTD 4 Sheffield
04.06.96 Graham McGrath W PTS 6 York
04.10.96 Tiger Singh W PTS 4 Wakefield
23.10.96 Jason Thomas W PTS 6 Halifax
12.03.97 John Matthews W PTS 6 Stoke
20.04.97 Shaun Anderson W PTS 6 Leeds
13.11.97 Anthony Hanna W PTS 6 Bradford
06.02.98 Marcus Duncan W RSC 6 Wakefield
*(Vacant Central Area Bantamweight
Title)*
21.05.98 Matthew Harris W PTS 6 Bradford
18.07.98 Sean Grant W RSC 4 Sheffield
23.10.98 Fondil Madani W DIS 7 Wakefield
28.11.98 Ross Cassidy W PTS 8 Sheffield
06.02.99 Jason Thomas W PTS 10 Halifax
(Elim. British Bantamweight Title)
24.04.99 Anthony Hanna W PTS 6 Peterborough
22.06.99 Ady Lewis W RSC 6 Ipswich
(Final Elim. British Bantamweight Title)
30.10.99 Francis Ampofo W PTS 12 Peterlee
(Vacant British Bantamweight Title)
18.01.00 Steve Williams W RTD 11 Mansfield
(British Bantamweight Title Defence)
20.03.00 Kamel Guerfi W PTS 12 Mansfield
(Vacant IBO Bantamweight Title)
15.07.00 Paul Lloyd W PTS 12 Millwall
(IBO Bantamweight Title Defence)
28.04.01 Stevie Quinn W RTD 6 Cardiff
21.07.01 Chris Emanuele W PTS 6 Sheffield
15.06.02 Sean Grant W RSC 3 Leeds
28.01.03 Fabien Guillerme W PTS 12 Nice,
France
(Vacant European Bantamweight Title)
18.03.03 Frederic Patrac DREW 4 Reading
*(European Bantamweight Title
Defence)*
10.06.03 David Guerault L RSC 7 Sheffield
*(European Bantamweight Title
Defence)*
Career: 25 contests, won 23, drew 1, lost 1.

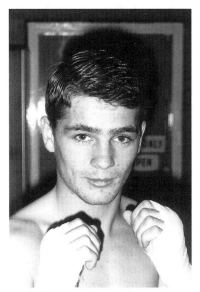

Noel Wilders   Les Clark

Spencer Wilding

Rhyl. *Born* St Asaph, 26 July, 1972
Cruiserweight. Ht. 6'7"
Manager M. Goodall

08.03.02   Adam Cale W PTS 6 Ellesmere Port
10.05.02   Jon Penn W RTD 1 Preston
15.10.02   Eddie Knight W RSC 2 Bethnal Green
01.11.02   Chris Woollas DREW 6 Preston
Career: 4 contests, won 3, drew 1.

Danny Williams

Brixton. *Born* London, 13 July, 1973
British & Commonwealth Heavyweight
Champion. Former Undefeated WBO Inter-
Continental Heavyweight Champion. Ht. 6'3"
Manager F. Warren

21.10.95   Vance Idiens W CO 2 Bethnal Green
09.12.95   Joey Paladino W RSC 1 Bethnal Green
13.02.96   Slick Miller W RSC 1 Bethnal Green
09.03.96   James Wilder W PTS 4 Millstreet
13.07.96   John Pierre W PTS 4 Bethnal Green
31.08.96   Andy Lambert W RSC 2 Dublin
09.11.96   Michael Murray W CO 1 Manchester
08.02.97   Shane Woollas W RSC 2 Millwall
03.05.97   Albert Call W RSC 4 Manchester
19.07.97   R. F. McKenzie W RSC 2 Wembley
15.11.97   Bruce Douglas W RSC 2 Bristol
19.12.97   Derek Amos W RSC 4 New York City,
     USA
21.02.98   Shane Woollas W RSC 2 Belfast
16.05.98   Antonio Diaz W CO 3 Bethnal Green
10.10.98   Antoine Palatis W PTS 12 Bethnal
     Green
     (Vacant WBO Inter-Continental
     Heavyweight Title)
03.04.99   Julius Francis L PTS 12 Kensington
     (British & Commonwealth
     Heavyweight Title Challenges)
02.10.99   Ferenc Deak W RTD 1 Namur, Belgium
18.12.99   Harry Senior W PTS 12 Southwark
     (Vacant Commonwealth Heavyweight
     Title)

19.02.00   Anton Nel W CO 5 Dagenham
06.05.00   Michael Murray W RSC 6 Frankfurt,
     Germany
24.06.00   Craig Bowen-Price W CO 1 Glasgow
23.09.00   Quinn Navarre W RSC 6 Bethnal
     Green
21.10.00   Mark Potter W RSC 6 Wembley
     (Commonwealth & WBO Inter-
     Continental Heavyweight Title
     Defences. Vacant British Heavyweight
     Title)
09.06.01   Kali Meehan W RSC 1 Bethnal Green
     (Commonwealth Heavyweight Title
     Defence)
28.07.01   Julius Francis W CO 4 Wembley
     (British & Commonwealth
     Heavyweight Title Defences)
15.12.01   Shawn Robinson W RSC 2
     Mashantucket Connecticut, USA
12.02.02   Michael Sprott W RTD 7 Bethnal
     Green
     (British & Commonwealth
     Heavyweight Title Defences)
17.09.02   Keith Long W PTS 12 Bethnal Green
     (British & Commonwealth
     Heavyweight Title Defences)
08.02.03   Sinan Samil Sam L RSC 6 Berlin,
     Germany
     (European Heavyweight Title
     Challenge)
26.04.03   Bob Mirovic W RSC 4 Brentford
     (Commonwealth Heavyweight Title
     Defence)
Career: 30 contests, won 28, lost 2.

(Darren) Dazzo Williams

Hereford. *Born* Lambeth, 19 March, 1974
S. Bantamweight. Ht. 5'8"
Manager T. Gilmour

24.02.01   Mickey Coveney W CO 1 Bethnal
     Green
19.05.01   Mark Payne W PTS 8 Wembley
14.07.01   Dimitri Gorodetsky W RSC 3
     Liverpool
19.12.01   Mark Alexander W PTS 6 Coventry

18.01.02   Zolani Msolo W RSC 2 Coventry
20.04.02   John Mackay L PTS 6 Wembley
26.10.02   Carl Allen L RSC 2 Maesteg
25.01.03   Vladimir Borov W PTS 6 Bridgend
08.03.03   Marc Callaghan W PTS 8 Bethnal
     Green
17.05.03   Stephen Chinnock W PTS 10 Liverpool
     (Elim. British Featherweight Title)
Career: 10 contests, won 8, lost 2.

Gary Williams

Nottingham. *Born* Nottingham, 25
September, 1965
Heavyweight, Ht. 5'11½"
Manager Self

27.04.92   Damien Caesar L RSC 4 Mayfair
07.09.92   J. A. Bugner L PTS 4 Bethnal Green
06.10.92   Scott Welch L PTS 4 Antwerp,
     Belgium
01.12.92   Kenny Sandison W PTS 6 Liverpool
27.01.93   Kenny Sandison DREW 6 Stoke
13.02.93   Kevin McBride L PTS 4 Manchester
01.03.93   Ashley Naylor DREW 6 Bradford
29.03.93   Kevin Cullinane W RSC 2 Liverpool
26.04.93   Ashley Naylor W PTS 6 Bradford
10.08.93   Peter Smith L RSC 4 Marula, South
     Africa
08.12.93   Graham Arnold L PTS 6 Hull
02.02.94   Vincenzo Cantatore L CO 2 Ferrara,
     Italy
17.03.94   Neil Kirkwood L RSC 1 Lincoln
10.09.94   Clayton Brown L PTS 4 Birmingham
04.10.94   Mike Holden L RSC 4 Mayfair
13.12.94   Damien Caesar L RSC 2 Ilford
18.03.95   Darren Corbett DREW 4 Millstreet
06.05.95   Clayton Brown L PTS 4 Shepton Mallet
10.06.95   Joey Paladino L PTS 6 Manchester
15.09.95   Adrian Kneeshaw W RSC 6 Mansfield
11.10.95   Shane Woollas L PTS 6 Solihull
03.11.95   Tony Henry W PTS 6 Dudley
24.11.95   Pele Reid L RSC 1 Manchester
12.01.96   John Pettersson DREW 4 Copenhagen,
     Denmark
31.01.96   Robert Norton L RSC 2 Birmingham
21.03.96   Mika Kihlstrom L PTS 4 Southwark

Danny Williams   Les Clark

02.04.96 Doug Liggion L PTS 4 Southwark
22.04.96 Shane Woollas L PTS 10 Cleethorpes
(Vacant Midlands Area Heavyweight Title)
27.05.96 Jukka Jarvinen L PTS 6 Helsinki, Finland
09.07.96 Sugar Raj Kumar Sangwan L PTS 4 Bethnal Green
08.10.96 Owen Bartley L PTS 4 Battersea
26.11.96 Israel Ajose L CO 2 Bethnal Green
18.01.97 Craig Bowen-Price L CO 1 Manchester
28.04.97 Jarrod Corrigan W RSC 4 Hull
02.09.97 Michael Sprott L PTS 6 Southwark
06.10.97 Johnny Davison L PTS 8 Piccadilly
15.12.97 Shane Woollas L RSC 8 Cleethorpes
(Midlands Area Heavyweight Title Challenge)
15.12.98 Scott Lansdowne L PTS 6 Sheffield
16.01.99 Michael Sprott L PTS 6 Bethnal Green
04.02.99 Rimas Priczmantas L PTS 4 Lewisham
22.02.99 Derek McCafferty L CO 1 Peterborough
27.04.99 Tommy Bannister L PTS 4 Bethnal Green
28.05.99 Albert Sosnowski L RSC 4 Liverpool
26.06.99 Patrick Halberg L PTS 4 Millwall
17.07.99 Roman Bugaj L RSC 4 Gdansk, Poland
07.10.99 Paul Fiske L PTS 6 Sunderland
27.11.99 Tommy Bannister W PTS 4 Liverpool
09.12.99 Paul Fiske W PTS 6 Sunderland
29.01.00 Petr Horacek L PTS 4 Manchester
18.02.00 Mal Rice L PTS 6 Pentre Halkyn
05.05.00 Mal Rice W PTS 4 Pentre Halkyn
20.05.00 Scott Lansdowne L RSC 1 Leicester
(Vacant WBF European S. Cruiserweight Title)
21.10.00 John McDermott L PTS 4 Wembley
13.11.00 Danny Percival L PTS 4 Bethnal Green
04.06.01 Billy Bessey L PTS 4 Hartlepool
22.09.01 John McDermott L RSC 4 Bethnal Green
08.12.01 Mark Potter L RSC 3 Dagenham
11.05.02 Mark Krence L PTS 6 Chesterfield
12.07.02 Colin Kenna L RSC 3 Southampton
05.10.02 Mark Krence L RSC 4 Chesterfield
16.11.02 Paul Butlin L RSC 1 Coventry
08.03.03 Carl Wright L PTS 6 Coventry
18.03.03 Roman Greenberg L RSC 1 Reading
Career: 63 contests, won 12, drew 4, lost 47.

Jackson Williams

Norwich. *Born* Norwich, 19 June, 1981
Lightweight. Ht. 5'6½"
Manager J. Ingle

13.04.02 Daniel Thorpe W PTS 6 Norwich
15.06.02 Jason Gonzales W PTS 6 Norwich
21.09.02 Baz Carey W PTS 6 Norwich
10.10.02 Jason Gonzales W PTS 4 Piccadilly
08.02.03 Joel Viney W PTS 4 Norwich
24.02.03 Anthony Hanna L PTS 6 Birmingham
12.04.03 Daniel Thorpe W PTS 6 Norwich
06.06.03 Nigel Senior W PTS 8 Norwich
Career: 8 contests, won 7, lost 1.

(Leon) Jason Williams

Swansea. *Born* Swansea, 11 July, 1974
Welsh Welterweight Champion. Ht. 5'11"
Manager D. H. Davies

19.04.97 Jon Harrison L PTS 6 Plymouth
21.06.97 Dewi Roberts W RSC 1 Cardiff
26.09.97 Darren Covill W PTS 6 Port Talbot
15.11.97 Peter Federenko W PTS 4 Bristol
24.01.98 Danny Quacoe W PTS 4 Cardiff
23.02.98 Adrian Chase W PTS 6 Windsor
30.03.98 Rob Pitters W RSC 3 Tenerife
30.05.98 Prince Kasi Kaihau W CO 2 Bristol
14.07.98 Jon Harrison W RTD 2 Reading
05.12.98 Mark Ramsey W PTS 6 Bristol
23.04.99 Harry Butler W RSC 7 Clydach
05.06.99 Paul Miles W RSC 2 Cardiff
02.07.99 Delroy Mellis W PTS 6 Bristol
24.09.99 Michael Smyth L RSC 3 Merthyr
(Vacant Welsh Welterweight Title)
07.04.00 David Baptiste W PTS 6 Bristol
08.09.00 Karim Bouali L RSC 5 Bristol
03.11.00 Mark Ramsey L CO 6 Ebbw Vale
15.09.01 Mark Richards W PTS 6 Swansea
31.10.01 Jimmy Vincent L PTS 10 Birmingham
(Vacant British Masters L.Middleweight Title)
16.03.02 Charden Ansoula L RSC 5 Northampton
23.02.03 Keith Jones W PTS 10 Aberystwyth
(Welsh Welterweight Title Challenge)
10.05.03 Derek Roche L RSC 2 Huddersfield
Career: 22 contests, won 15, lost 7.

Richard Williams

Stockwell. *Born* London, 9 May, 1971
L.Middleweight. Former IBO
L.Middleweight Champion. Former
Undefeated Commonwealth & WBF
L.Middleweight Champion. Ht. 5'9½"
Manager B. Hearn

08.03.97 Marty Duke W RSC 3 Brentwood
30.06.97 Danny Quacoe W PTS 4 Bethnal Green
02.09.97 Michael Alexander L PTS 4 Southwark
16.10.99 Pedro Carragher W RSC 2 Bethnal Green
06.11.99 Lee Bird W RSC 4 Bethnal Green
20.12.99 Harry Butler W RSC 1 Bethnal Green
17.04.00 Kevin Thompson W CO 1 Birmingham
16.06.00 Piotr Bartnicki W RSC 3 Bloomsbury
08.09.00 Dean Ashton W RSC 1 Hammersmith
04.11.00 Howard Clarke W CO 4 Bethnal Green
02.12.00 Aziz Daari W RSC 2 Bethnal Green
23.01.01 Tony Badea W RSC 3 Crawley
(Commonwealth L. Middleweight Title Challenge)
04.06.01 Hussain Osman W PTS 10 Hartlepool
25.09.01 Andrew Murray W RSC 3 Liverpool
(Commonwealth L. Middleweight Title Defence)
20.10.01 Viktor Fesetchko W RSC 6 Portsmouth
01.12.01 Shannan Taylor W RSC 4 Bethnal Green
(Commonwealth L. Middleweight Title Defence. Vacant IBO L. Middleweight Title)
29.06.02 Paul Samuels T DRAW 3 Brentwood
(IBO L. Middleweight Title Defence)
07.12.02 Paul Samuels W RSC 10 Brentwood
(IBO L. Middleweight Title Defence)
08.03.03 Andrei Pestriaev W PTS 12 Bethnal Green
(IBO L. Middleweight Title Defence. WBF L. Middleweight Title Challenge)
21.06.03 Sergio Martinez L PTS 12 Manchester
(IBO L.Middleweight Title Defence)
Career: 20 contests, won 17, drew 1, lost 2.

Steve Williams

Mansfield. *Born* Worksop, 11 October, 1968
S.Bantamweight. Former Undefeated
Midlands Area Bantamweight Champion.
Ht. 5'7"
Manager Self

06.03.95 Shaun Hall DREW 6 Bradford
06.04.95 Andy Roberts W PTS 6 Sheffield
20.10.95 Terry Gaskin W PTS 6 Mansfield
22.11.95 Neil Parry W PTS 6 Sheffield
22.03.96 Darren Noble W PTS 6 Mansfield
12.09.96 Andy Roberts W PTS 6 Doncaster
01.11.96 Tiger Singh W PTS 6 Mansfield
20.02.97 Neil Parry W PTS 8 Mansfield
08.05.97 Mark Reynolds L RTD 6 Mansfield
(Elim. British Flyweight Title)
19.03.98 Sean Green W PTS 6 Doncaster
14.10.98 Ross Cassidy W PTS 6 Stoke
18.03.99 Ross Cassidy W PTS 6 Doncaster
27.06.99 Shaun Norman W PTS 10 Alfreton
(Vacant Midlands Area Bantamweight Title)
18.01.00 Noel Wilders L RTD 11 Mansfield
(British Bantamweight Title Challenge)
11.05.02 Tasawar Khan W PTS 6 Newark
30.11.02 Andy Roberts W PTS 6 Newark
Career: 16 contests, won 13, drew 1, lost 2.

Jackson Williams   Les Clark   *Jason Williams*   Les Clark

Lee Williamson

Worcester. *Born* Worcester, 3 February, 1974
L. Middleweight. Ht. 5'9"
Manager Self

26.10.98	Trevor Tacy L PTS 6 Manchester
26.11.98	David Smales W PTS 6 Bradford
16.01.99	Graham Earl L RSC 4 Bethnal Green
23.03.99	Gary Reid L PTS 6 Wolverhampton
22.04.99	Brian Gifford W PTS 6 Dudley
15.05.99	James Hare L RSC 2 Sheffield
11.10.99	Carl Allen W PTS 6 Birmingham
28.10.99	Mark Hargreaves L PTS 6 Burnley
30.11.99	Marc Smith W PTS 6 Wolverhampton
11.12.99	Brian Carr DREW 6 Liverpool
24.01.00	Craig Docherty L PTS 6 Glasgow
08.02.00	Carl Allen L PTS 8 Wolverhampton
19.02.00	Kevin Lear L PTS 4 Dagenham
04.03.00	Liam Maltby L PTS 6 Peterborough
28.03.00	Carl Allen L PTS 8 Wolverhampton
06.06.00	Dave Travers W PTS 6 Brierley Hill
24.06.00	Kevin McIntyre L PTS 4 Glasgow
08.07.00	Tony Mulholland L PTS 8 Widnes
13.08.00	Esham Pickering L PTS 6 Nottingham
29.09.00	Darren Melville L RSC 4 Bethnal Green
21.10.00	Graham Earl L RSC 3 Wembley
24.11.00	Pete Buckley W PTS 6 Hull
09.12.00	Terry Butwell L PTS 4 Southwark
27.01.01	Danny Hunt W RSC 2 Bethnal Green
10.02.01	Geir Inge Jorgensen L RSC 3 Widnes
20.03.01	James Rooney L PTS 4 Glasgow
26.03.01	Liam Maltby L PTS 6 Peterborough
03.04.01	Danny Hunt L PTS 4 Bethnal Green
06.05.01	James Rooney L PTS 6 Hartlepool
21.06.01	Gavin Wake L PTS 6 Sheffield
14.07.01	Brett James L PTS 6 Wembley
28.07.01	Ross Minter L PTS 4 Wembley
15.09.01	Gavin Down L PTS 6 Derby
10.12.01	David Keir DREW 4 Liverpool
04.03.02	Pedro Thompson W PTS 6 Bradford
13.04.02	David Keir L PTS 4 Liverpool
13.05.02	Chris Duggan W RSC 3 Birmingham
01.06.02	Michael Jennings L PTS 4 Manchester
23.06.02	Brett James L PTS 6 Southwark
28.09.02	Mickey Quinn L RSC 2 Manchester
16.11.02	Richard Swallow L PTS 4 Coventry
30.11.02	Mark Dillon W PTS 4 Liverpool
18.01.03	Michael Jennings L RTD 4 Preston
23.02.03	Lee McAllister L PTS 6 Shrewsbury
16.03.03	Matt Scriven L PTS 10 Nottingham
	(Vacant Midlands Area & British Masters L. Middleweight Titles)
07.06.03	Andy Egan L PTS 6 Coventry

Career: 46 contests, won 10, drew 2, lost 34.

Jamie Wilson

Hull. *Born* North Ferriby, 28 May, 1978
L. Heavyweight. Ht. 6'4"
Manager M. Toomey

30.11.01	Matthew Pepper W RSC 3 Hull
31.05.02	Mike Duffield L PTS 6 Hull
05.10.02	Danny Grainger L PTS 6 Chesterfield
21.10.02	Danny Grainger L PTS 6 Cleethorpes
29.11.02	Darren Stubbs L PTS 6 Hull

Career: 5 contests, won 1, lost 4.

Gareth Wiltshaw

Stoke. *Born* Stoke, 22 August, 1980
L. Welterweight. Ht. 5'7"
Manager W. Swift

17.04.00	John Meade W PTS 6 Bradford
09.06.00	Joel Viney L PTS 6 Blackpool
08.07.00	Kevin England DREW 6 Rotherham
20.11.00	Al Garrett L PTS 6 Glasgow
30.11.00	Mickey Coveney L PTS 4 Peterborough
18.02.01	Richmond Asante L PTS 4 Southwark
08.04.01	Jason Edwards L PTS 6 Wrexham
20.05.01	Stephen Chinnock L PTS 6 Wolverhampton
03.06.01	Mickey Coveney L PTS 4 Southwark
08.10.01	Sid Razak W PTS 6 Birmingham
27.10.01	Steve Foster L PTS 4 Manchester
19.01.02	Martin Power L PTS 4 Bethnal Green
11.02.02	Daniel Thorpe W PTS 6 Shrewsbury
02.03.02	Jesse James Daniel L RSC 3 Wakefield
20.04.02	Haroon Din L PTS 6 Derby
04.05.02	Steve Foster L PTS 4 Bethnal Green
13.06.02	Ryan Barrett L PTS 4 Leicester Square
03.08.02	Jeff Thomas L DIS 2 Blackpool
27.09.02	Chris McDonagh W RSC 1 Bracknell
07.10.02	Steve Saville L RSC 3 Birmingham
09.11.02	Eddie Nevins L PTS 4 Altrincham
17.11.02	Haroon Din L PTS 6 Bradford
02.12.02	Joel Viney L PTS 6 Bradford
08.01.03	Aidan Mooney L PTS 4 Aberdare
15.02.03	Dean Hickman L PTS 6 Wolverhampton
16.03.03	Adnan Amar L PTS 6 Nottingham

Career: 26 contests, won 4, drew 1, lost 21.

Craig Winter

Rhyl. *Born* Aylesbury, 10 September, 1971
S. Middleweight. Ht. 5'10"
Manager Self

19.12.93	Allan Logan W PTS 6 Glasgow
28.02.94	Wayne Shepherd W PTS 6 Manchester
18.04.94	John Duckworth W RSC 5 Manchester
26.09.94	Dave Whittle W PTS 6 Liverpool
10.12.94	Hughie Davey W PTS 6 Manchester
25.03.95	David Maw W RSC 3 Rothwell
20.04.95	Paul King W RSC 4 Liverpool
16.06.95	Ernie Loveridge W PTS 6 Liverpool
08.09.95	Ernie Loveridge W PTS 6 Liverpool
14.02.96	Mark Cichocki W PTS 6 Sunderland
09.05.96	Peter Waudby L RSC 5 Hull
	(Elim. British L. Middleweight Title)
04.10.96	Robert Harper W RSC 5 Pentre Halkyn
31.01.97	Martin Jolley W RSC 3 Pentre Halkyn
25.10.97	George Richards W RSC 2 Queensferry
29.01.98	Jimmy Vincent W PTS 6 Pentre Halkyn
30.04.98	Jason Barker W PTS 6 Pentre Halkyn
31.10.98	Peter Mason W RSC 4 Basingstoke
05.12.98	Paul Samuels L CO 2 Bristol
	(Vacant Welsh L. Middleweight Title)
06.10.02	Harry Butler W PTS 6 Rhyl

Career: 19 contests, won 17, lost 2.

Juliette Winter

Derby. *Born* Whitehaven, 21 February, 1973
Bantamweight. Ht. 5'6"
Manager C. Mitchell

16.06.01	Sara Hall L RTD 4 Derby
20.09.01	Claire Cooper L RSC 4 Blackfriars
20.03.03	Cathy Brown W PTS 4 Queensway

Career: 3 contests, won 1, lost 2.

Mark Winters

Antrim. *Born* Antrim, 29 December, 1971
Lightweight. Former British
L. Welterweight Champion. Ht. 5'8"
Manager Self

04.03.95	Trevor Smith W PTS 6 Livingston
10.06.95	Mark McGowan W PTS 6 Manchester
09.09.95	Anthony Campbell W PTS 4 Cork
25.11.95	John O. Johnson W RSC 2 Dublin
13.01.96	Rick North W PTS 4 Manchester
09.03.96	Danny Quacoe W RSC 2 Millstreet
08.06.96	Brian Coleman W PTS 4 Newcastle
31.08.96	John Smith W PTS 4 Dublin
30.11.96	Paul Dyer W PTS 6 Tylorstown
14.03.97	Paul Denton W PTS 8 Reading
03.05.97	Jimmy Phelan W PTS 4 Manchester
11.10.97	Carl Wright W PTS 12 Sheffield
	(Vacant British L. Welterweight Title)
21.02.98	Bernard Paul W PTS 12 Belfast
	(British L. Welterweight Title Defence)
16.05.98	Jason Rowland L PTS 12 Bethnal Green
	(British L. Welterweight Title Defence)
05.09.98	Junior Witter L PTS 8 Telford
23.10.99	James Hare DREW 6 Telford
11.12.99	Ricky Hatton L RSC 4 Liverpool
	(WBO Inter-Continental L. Welterweight Title Challenge)
04.02.01	David Kirk W PTS 6 Queensferry
20.04.01	David Kirk W PTS 6 Dublin
26.07.01	Joel Viney W RSC 4 Blackpool
15.12.01	Graham Earl L PTS 10 Wembley
	(Elim. British Lightweight Title)
02.11.02	John Marshall W RSC 5 Belfast
01.02.03	David Kehoe W RSC 2 Belfast

Career: 23 contests, won 18, drew 1, lost 4.

Junior Witter

Bradford. *Born* Bradford, 10 March, 1974
British, Commonwealth, European Union & WBU Inter-Continental L.Welterweight Champion. Former Undefeated WBF L.Welterweight Champion. Ht. 5'7"
Manager D. Ingle

18.01.97	Cam Raeside DREW 6 Swadlincote
04.03.97	John Green W PTS 6 Yarm
20.03.97	Lee Molyneux W RSC 6 Salford
25.04.97	Trevor Meikle W PTS 6 Mere
15.05.97	Andreas Panayi W RSC 5 Reading
02.08.97	Brian Coleman W PTS 4 Barnsley
04.10.97	Michael Alexander W PTS 4 Hannover, Germany
07.02.98	Mark Ramsey DREW 6 Cheshunt
05.03.98	Brian Coleman W PTS 6 Leeds
18.04.98	Jan Bergman W PTS 6 Manchester
05.09.98	Mark Winters W PTS 8 Telford
28.11.98	Karl Taylor W PTS 4 Sheffield
13.02.99	Malcolm Melvin W RSC 2 Newcastle
	(Vacant WBF L. Welterweight Title)
17.07.99	Isaac Cruz W PTS 8 Doncaster
06.11.99	Harry Butler W PTS 6 Widnes
21.03.00	Mrhai Iourgh W RSC 1 Telde, Gran Canaria
08.04.00	Arv Mittoo W PTS 4 Bethnal Green
24.06.00	Zab Judah L PTS 12 Glasgow
	(IBF L. Welterweight Title Challenge)
20.10.00	Steve Conway W RTD 4 Belfast
25.11.00	Chris Henry W RSC 3 Manchester
10.03.01	David Kirk W RSC 2 Bethnal Green
22.05.01	Fabrice Faradji W RSC 1 Telde, Gran Canaria

21.07.01	Alan Temple W CO 5 Sheffield	
27.10.01	Colin Mayisela W RSC 2 Manchester	
	(Vacant WBU Inter-Continental	
	L.Welterweight Title)	
16.03.02	Alan Bosworth W RSC 3 Northampton	
	(Vacant British L.Welterweight Title)	
08.07.02	Laatekwi Hammond W RSC 2 Mayfair	
	(Vacant Commonwealth	
	L.Welterweight Title)	
19.10.02	Lucky Samba W RSC 2 Renfrew	
23.11.02	Giuseppe Lauri W RSC 2 Derby	
	(Final Elim. WBO L. Welterweight	
	Title)	
05.04.03	Jurgen Haeck W RTD 4 Manchester	
	(Vacant European Union	
	L.Welterweight Title)	

Career: 29 contests, won 26, drew 2, lost 1.

Junior Witter   Les Clark

Clinton Woods

Sheffield. *Born* Sheffield, 1 May, 1972
L.Heavyweight. Former Undefeated British,
European, WBC International &
Commonwealth L.Heavyweight Champion.
Former Commonwealth S.Middleweight
Champion. Former Undefeated Central
Area S.Middleweight Champion. Ht. 6'2"
Manager Self

17.11.94	Dave Proctor W PTS 6 Sheffield
12.12.94	Earl Ling W RSC 5 Cleethorpes
23.02.95	Paul Clarkson W RSC 1 Hull
06.04.95	Japhet Hans W RSC 3 Sheffield
16.05.95	Kevin Burton W PTS 6 Cleethorpes
14.06.95	Kevin Burton W RSC 6 Batley
21.09.95	Paul Murray W PTS 6 Sheffield
20.10.95	Phil Ball W RSC 4 Mansfield
22.11.95	Andy Ewen W RSC 3 Sheffield
05.02.96	Chris Walker W RSC 6 Bradford
16.03.96	John Duckworth W PTS 8 Sheffield
13.06.96	Ernie Loveridge W PTS 6 Sheffield
14.11.96	Craig Joseph W PTS 10 Sheffield
	(Vacant Central Area S. Middleweight Title)
20.02.97	Rocky Shelly W RSC 2 Mansfield
10.04.97	Darren Littlewood W RSC 6 Sheffield
	(Central Area S.Middleweight Title Defence)
26.06.97	Darren Ashton W PTS 6 Sheffield
25.10.97	Danny Juma W PTS 8 Queensferry
26.11.97	Jeff Finlayson W PTS 8 Sheffield
06.12.97	Mark Baker W PTS 12 Wembley
	(Vacant Commonwealth S.Middleweight Title)
28.03.98	David Starie L PTS 12 Hull
	(Commonwealth S. Middleweight Title Defence)
18.06.98	Peter Mason W RTD 4 Sheffield
30.11.98	Mark Smallwood W RSC 7 Manchester
13.03.99	Crawford Ashley W RSC 8 Manchester
	(British, Commonwealth & European L. Heavyweight Title Challenges)
10.07.99	Sam Leuii W RSC 6 Southwark
	(Commonwealth L. Heavyweight Title Defence)
11.09.99	Lenox Lewis W RSC 10 Sheffield
	(Commonwealth L. Heavyweight Title Defence)
10.12.99	Terry Ford W RTD 4 Warsaw, Poland
12.02.00	Juan Perez Nelongo W PTS 12 Sheffield
	(European L. Heavyweight Title Defence)
29.04.00	Ole Klemetsen W RSC 9 Wembley
	(European L. Heavyweight Title Defence)
15.07.00	Greg Scott-Briggs W RSC 3 Millwall
24.03.01	Ali Forbes W RTD 10 Sheffield
	(Vacant WBC International L. Heavyweight Title)
27.07.01	Paul Bonson W PTS 6 Sheffield
13.09.01	Yawe Davis W PTS 12 Sheffield
	(Final Elim.WBC L.Heavyweight Title)
16.03.02	Clint Johnson W RSC 3 Bethnal Green
07.09.02	Roy Jones L RSC 6 Portland, Oregon, USA
	(WBC, WBA & IBF L.Heavyweight Title Challenges)
24.01.03	Sergio Martin Beaz W RSC 3 Sheffield
18.03.03	Arturo Rivera W RSC 2 Reading
10.06.03	Demetrius Jenkins W RSC 7 Sheffield

Career: 37 contests, won 35, lost 2.

Gary Woolcombe

Welling. *Born* London, 4 August, 1982
Welterweight. Ht. 5'10³/₄"
Manager E. Maloney

15.05.03	Paul McIlwaine W RSC 2 Mayfair

Career: 1 contest, won 1.

Chris Woollas

Epworth. *Born* Scunthorpe, 22 November, 1973
Heavyweight. Former Undefeated Midlands Area Cruiserweight Champion. Ht. 5'11"
Manager Self

17.08.94	Darren Littlewood W RSC 4 Sheffield
05.10.94	Robert Norton DREW 6 Wolverhampton

05.12.94	Neil Simpson W PTS 6 Cleethorpes
10.02.95	Monty Wright L RSC 4 Birmingham
30.06.95	Kenny Nevers L RSC 2 Doncaster
25.09.95	Cliff Elden DREW 6 Cleethorpes
08.11.95	Stevie Pettit W PTS 6 Walsall
17.11.95	Markku Salminen L PTS 6 Helsinki, Finland
11.12.95	Cliff Elden DREW 6 Cleethorpes
15.02.96	Pele Lawrence W RSC 6 Sheffield
29.02.96	John Pierre DREW 6 Scunthorpe
16.03.96	David Jules W PTS 6 Sheffield
22.04.96	Jacklord Jacobs DREW 4 Crystal Palace
30.05.96	Martin Langtry L RSC 6 Lincoln
	(Midlands Area Cruiserweight Title Challenge)
03.09.96	Darren Corbett L RSC 7 Belfast
02.10.96	Rocky Shelly W RSC 6 Stoke
09.10.96	Nigel Rafferty W PTS 6 Stoke
28.10.96	Colin Brown L PTS 8 Glasgow
10.11.96	Michael Gale DREW 6 Glasgow
25.11.96	Albert Call L PTS 6 Cleethorpes
17.12.96	Darren Corbett L RSC 1 Doncaster
16.01.97	Mark Smallwood L PTS 8 Solihull
31.01.97	Tim Redman L PTS 6 Pentre Halkyn
14.03.97	Kelly Oliver L PTS 6 Reading
24.03.97	Mikael Lindblad L RSC 7 Helsinki, Finland
19.06.97	Ian Henry W PTS 6 Scunthorpe
02.08.97	Kelly Oliver L RSC 3 Barnsley
15.12.97	Neil Simpson W PTS 6 Cleethorpes
26.01.98	Colin Brown W PTS 6 Glasgow
26.03.98	Cliff Elden L PTS 4 Scunthorpe
06.05.98	Simon McDougall W PTS 6 Blackpool
21.07.98	Matthew Ellis L RSC 5 Widnes
11.09.98	Lennox Williams W PTS 6 Cleethorpes
12.03.99	Albert Sosnowski L PTS 4 Bethnal Green
27.05.99	Nigel Rafferty W PTS 10 Edgbaston
	(Midlands Area Cruiserweight Title Challenge)
10.07.99	Michael Sprott L RTD 4 Southwark
13.09.99	Dominic Negus L PTS 10 Bethnal Green
	(Elim. British Cruiserweight Title)
09.10.99	Chris P. Bacon L PTS 4 Manchester
30.10.99	Terry Dunstan L RSC 1 Southwark
08.04.00	Bruce Scott L RSC 2 Bethnal Green
13.07.00	Firat Aslan L RSC 2 Bethnal Green
08.09.00	Petr Horacek L PTS 4 Hammersmith
21.10.00	Danny Percival L PTS 4 Wembley
18.11.00	Matthew Ellis L PTS 4 Dagenham
11.12.00	Enzo Maccarinelli L PTS 4 Widnes
15.12.01	Lee Swaby L RSC 4 Sheffield
21.10.02	Greg Scott-Briggs W PTS 6 Cleethorpes
01.11.02	Spencer Wilding DREW 6 Preston
28.04.03	Eamonn Glennon W PTS 6 Cleethorpes

Career: 49 contests, won 15, drew 7, lost 27.

Shane Woollas

Epworth. *Born* Scunthorpe, 28 July, 1972
Heavyweight. Former Undefeated Midlands Area Heavyweight Champion. Ht. 6'2"
Manager M. Shinfield

26.08.94	Neil Kirkwood L RSC 6 Barnsley
28.07.95	Rob Albon W RTD 4 Epworth
11.10.95	Gary Williams W PTS 6 Solihull
08.11.95	David Jules W PTS 6 Scunthorpe
26.01.96	Nigel Williams W RSC 2 Doncaster
31.01.96	David Jules L PTS 6 Stoke
22.04.96	Gary Williams W PTS 10 Cleethorpes
	(Vacant Midlands Area Heavyweight Title)

29.07.96	David Jules L PTS 6 Skegness
31.08.96	Willi Fischer L CO 2 Palma de Mallorca
08.10.96	Mika Kihlstrom L PTS 4 Battersea
06.11.96	Kevin McBride L RSC 2 Hull
08.02.97	Danny Williams L RSC 2 Millwall
19.06.97	Lennox Williams W PTS 6 Scunthorpe
15.12.97	Gary Williams W RSC 8 Cleethorpes
	(Midlands Area Heavyweight Title Defence)
11.01.98	Fred Westgeest L PTS 6 Riesa, Germany
21.02.98	Danny Williams L RSC 2 Belfast
23.05.98	Mark Potter L PTS 4 Bethnal Green
21.06.98	Mal Rice W PTS 6 Liverpool
02.07.98	Georgi Kandelaki L RSC 4 Ipswich
11.09.98	Bruno Foster W PTS 6 Cleethorpes
26.09.98	Luan Krasniqi L RSC 3 York
30.11.98	Craig Bowen-Price L RSC 2 Manchester
30.04.99	Brian Gascoigne DREW 6 Scunthorpe
30.10.99	Gavin McGhin L CO 4 Peterlee
12.02.00	Patrick Halberg L PTS 6 Sheffield
05.02.01	Crawford Ashley L RSC 4 Hull
10.04.01	Petr Horacek DREW 4 Wembley
16.06.01	Eric Butterbean Esch L RSC 1 Wembley
27.07.01	Mark Krence L PTS 4 Sheffield
28.04.03	Dave Clarke W PTS 6 Cleethorpes

Career: 30 contests, won 10, drew 2, lost 18.

Jonathan Woollins

Sheffield. *Born* Mansfield, 14 May, 1983
L. Middleweight. Ht. 6'1"
Manager J. Ingle

16.03.03	Arv Mittoo W PTS 4 Nottingham
08.06.03	Ernie Smith L PTS 4 Nottingham

Career: 2 contests, won 1, lost 1.

Carl Wright

Rugby. *Born* Rugby, 26 April, 1978
Cruiserweight. Ht. 6'1¼"
Manager J. Weaver

25.06.02	Dave Clarke W PTS 6 Rugby
05.10.02	Adam Cale W PTS 6 Coventry
16.11.02	Jimmy Steel W PTS 6 Coventry
08.03.03	Gary Williams W PTS 6 Coventry
16.03.03	Darren Ashton DREW 6 Nottingham
07.06.03	Gary Thompson W RTD 2 Coventry

Career: 6 contests, won 5, drew 1.

Nigel Wright

Hartlepool. *Born* Bishop Auckland, 22 June, 1979
L. Welterweight. Ht. 5'9"
Manager G. Robinson

10.02.01	Keith Jones W PTS 4 Widnes
15.09.01	Tommy Peacock W RSC 1 Manchester
17.11.01	Ernie Smith W PTS 4 Glasgow
19.01.02	Woody Greenaway W CO 2 Bethnal Green
11.03.02	James Paisley W PTS 4 Glasgow
19.10.02	Kevin McIntyre L PTS 6 Renfrew
29.03.03	Darren Melville W PTS 6 Portsmouth
24.05.03	David Kirk W PTS 4 Bethnal Green

Career: 8 contests, won 7, lost 1.

Nathan Wyatt

Gloucester. *Born* Gloucester, 4 May, 1979
L. Middleweight. Ht. 5'8"

Manager C. Sanigar

13.06.03	Wayne Wheeler L PTS 6 Bristol

Career: 1 contest, lost 1.

Jamie Yelland

Finchley. *Born* London, 5 March, 1975
Bantamweight. Ht. 5'5"
Manager P. Rees

11.03.00	Chris Emanuele W PTS 4 Kensington
22.07.00	Daniel Ring W PTS 4 Watford
06.10.00	Simon Stowell DREW 4 Maidstone
31.10.00	John Barnes W PTS 6 Hammersmith
07.04.01	John Barnes W PTS 4 Wembley
31.07.01	Paddy Folan W RSC 5 Bethnal Green
28.11.01	John Mackay L RSC 6 Bethnal Green
25.02.02	Gareth Payne W RSC 3 Slough
29.06.02	Neil Read W PTS 6 Brentwood
10.10.02	Gareth Payne W PTS 10 Stoke
28.04.03	Nicky Booth L PTS 12 Nottingham
	(British Bantamweight Title Challenge)

Career: 11 contests, won 8, drew 1, lost 2.

Freddie Yemofio

Hayes. *Born* London, 15 July, 1969
S. Middleweight. Ht. 5'10"
Manager D. Currivan

31.08.93	Lee Sara L PTS 6 Croydon
30.09.93	Martin Rosamond L PTS 6 Hayes
20.05.94	Lee Blundell L RSC 6 Acton
30.09.94	Jason Hart L PTS 6 Bethnal Green
26.05.95	Robert Harper W PTS 6 Norwich
28.04.98	Matthew Tait L PTS 6 Brentford
14.05.98	Matt Galer L RSC 4 Acton
07.12.98	Matthew Barney L PTS 4 Acton
12.08.00	Spencer Fearon L RSC 2 Wembley
02.11.00	Elvis Michailenko L PTS 6 Kensington
09.12.00	Liam Lathbury L PTS 4 Southwark
29.01.01	Francie Doherty L RSC 4 Peterborough
05.05.01	Danny Wray L PTS 6 Brighton
12.05.01	Simon Andrews L PTS 4 Plymouth
31.01.02	Leigh Wicks L PTS 6 Piccadilly
11.02.02	Roddy Doran L PTS 8 Shrewsbury
27.03.02	Kenroy Lambert L PTS 6 Mayfair
13.04.02	Danny Smith L PTS 6 Norwich
27.09.02	Mo L PTS 4 Bracknell
10.10.02	Darren Covill W PTS 4 Piccadilly
29.11.02	Lee Molloy L PTS 4 Liverpool
23.02.03	Mark Thornton L RSC 1 Streatham
09.05.03	Mo L PTS 4 Longford

Career: 23 contests, won 2, lost 21.

Gary Young

Edinburgh. *Born* Edinburgh, 23 May, 1983
L. Welterweight. Ht. 5'7"
Manager F. Maloney

11.03.02	Paul McIlwaine W CO 2 Glasgow
08.06.02	Daniel Thorpe W RSC 1 Renfrew
02.11.02	Keith Jones W PTS 4 Belfast
22.03.03	Dean Larter W RSC 2 Renfrew

Career: 4 contests, won 4.

James Zikic

Watford. *Born* Harrow, 31 March, 1977
Cruiserweight. Ht. 6'2"
Manager A. Bowers

19.10.02	Tony Booth W PTS 4 Norwich
21.12.02	Brodie Pearmaine W PTS 4 Millwall

Career: 2 contests, won 2.

British Area Title Bouts During 2002-2003

Central Area

Titleholders at 30 June 2003
Fly: *vacant*. **Bantam:** *vacant*. **S.Bantam:** *vacant*. **Feather:** *vacant*. **S.Feather:** Eddie Nevins. **Light:** Gary Hibbert. **L.Welter:** *vacant*. **Welter:** Robert Burton. **L.Middle:** Lee Armstrong. **Middle:** Danny Thornton. **S.Middle:** Tony Dodson. **L.Heavy:** *vacant*. **Cruiser:** Denzil Browne. **Heavy:** *vacant*.

7 September	Jamie McKeever W PTS 10 Tony Mulholland, Liverpool (Vacant Featherweight Title)
16 February	Eddie Nevins W RSC 8 Daniel Thorpe, Salford (Vacant S.Featherweight Title)
22 February	Lee Armstrong W PTS 10 Gavin Wake, Huddersfield (Vacant L.Middleweight Title)
31 May	Robert Burton W RSC 9 David Keir, Barnsley (Welterweight Title Defence)
6 June	Danny Thornton W PTS 10 Jason Collins, Hull (Vacant Middleweight Title)

Between 1 July 2002 and 30 June 2003, Dale Robinson (Fly), Jamie McKeever (Feather) and Andrew Facey (Middle) relinquished their titles, while Neil Kirkwood (Heavy) forfeited his on being restricted to contests of two-minute rounds.

Midlands Area

Titleholders at 30 June 2003
Fly: *vacant*. **Bantam:** *vacant*. **S.Bantam:** Gareth Payne. **Feather:** Stephen Chinnock. **S.Feather:** *vacant*. **Light:** Anthony Maynard. **L.Welter:** Young Muttley. **Welter:** Tony Conroy. **L.Middle:** Matt

Lee Armstrong (left) seen here winning the vacant Central Area title when outpointing Gavin Wake at Huddersfield

Les Clark

Scriven. **Middle:** vacant. **S.Middle:** Mike Duffield. **L.Heavy:** vacant. **Cruiser:** Scott Lansdowne. **Heavy:** Mark Krence.

2 November	Mike Duffield W PTS 10 Peter Jackson, Wolverhampton (Vacant S.Middleweight Title)
30 November	Scott Lansdowne W RSC 2 Tony Dowling, Newark (Vacant Cruiserweight Title)
16 March	Matt Scriven W PTS 10 Lee Williamson, Nottingham (Vacant L.Middleweight Title)
21 March	Young Muttley W RSC 7 Gary Reid, West Bromwich (Vacant L.Welterweight Title)
7 June	Tony Conroy W RSC 5 Richard Swallow, Coventry (Vacant Welterweight Title)
7 June	Gareth Payne W RSC 5 Neil Read, Coventry (Vacant Bantamweight Title)
10 June	Mark Krence W RTD 8 Luke Simpkin, Sheffield (Vacant Heavyweight Title)

Between 1 July 2002 and 30 June 2003, Anthony Hanna (Fly), Carl Allen (S.Bantam), Gavin Down (L.Welter), Gordon Behan (Middle), Damon Hague (S.Middle) and Darren Ashton (L.Heavy) relinquished their titles, while Christian Brady (Welter) retired and Chris Woollas (Cruiser) and Shane Woollas (Heavy) forfeited their titles, the former being restricted to contests of two-minute rounds.

Northern Area

Titleholders at 30 June 2003

Fly: vacant. **Bantam:** vacant. **S.Bantam:** Michael Hunter. **Feather:** vacant. **S.Feather:** vacant. **Light:** vacant. **L.Welter:** vacant. **Welter:** Oscar Hall. **L.Middle:** vacant. **Middle:** Eddie Haley. **S.Middle:** vacant. **L.Heavy:** vacant. **Cruiser:** vacant. **Heavy:** vacant.

Between 1 July 2002 and 30 June 2003, Ian Cooper (S.Middle) forfeited his title due to his unavailability to defend.

Northern Ireland Area

Titleholders at 30 June 2003

Fly: vacant. **Bantam:** vacant. **S.Bantam:** vacant. **Feather:** vacant. **S.Feather:** vacant. **Light:** Dafydd Carlin. **L.Welter:** vacant. **Welter:** vacant. **L.Middle:** vacant. **Middle:** vacant. **S.Middle:** vacant. **L.Heavy:** vacant. **Cruiser:** vacant. **Heavy:** vacant.

| 5 April | Dafydd Carlin W PTS 10 Gary Hamilton, Belfast (Vacant Lightweight Title) |

Scottish Area

Titleholders at 30 June 2003

Fly: vacant. **Bantam:** vacant. **S.Bantam:** vacant. **Feather:** Brian Carr. **S.Feather:** vacant. **Light:** Martin Watson. **L.Welter:** vacant. **Welter:** Kevin McIntyre. **L.Middle:** vacant. **Middle:** vacant. **S.Middle:** vacant. **L.Heavy:** vacant. **Cruiser:** vacant. **Heavy:** vacant.

| 16 May | Martin Watson W RTD 8 Barry Hughes, Glasgow (Vacant Lightweight Title) |

Between 1 July 2002 and 30 June 2003, Shaun Anderson

(S.Bantam), John Docherty (Middle) and Jason Barker (S.Middle) had their titles vacated due to inactivity.

Southern Area

Titleholders at 30 June 2003

Fly: Ian Napa. **Bantam:** vacant. **S.Bantam:** vacant. **Feather:** vacant. **S.Feather:** vacant. **Light:** Graham Earl. **L.Welter:** Francis Barrett. **Welter:** vacant. **L.Middle:** David Walker. **Middle:** Allan Gray. **S.Middle:** vacant. **L.Heavy:** Andrew Lowe. **Cruiser:** Garry Delaney. **Heavy:** Michael Sprott.

12 October	Graham Earl W PTS 10 Chill John, Bethnal Green (Lightweight Title Defence)
20 October	Matthew Barney W PTS 10 Chris Nembhard, Southwark (S.Middleweight Title Defence)
25 October	David Walker W RSC 4 Brett James, Bethnal Green (Welterweight Title Defence)
12 December	Allan Gray W PTS 10 Ojay Abrahams, Leicester Square (Middleweight Title Defence)
8 February	John Humphrey W RSC 2 Delroy Leslie, Norwich (L.Middleweight Title Defence)
15 February	Graham Earl W RSC 2 Steve Murray, Wembley (Lightweight Title Defence)
5 March	Francis Barrett W PTS 10 Jon Honney, Bethnal Green (Vacant L.Welterweight Title)
18 March	Mark Potter L RSC 3 Michael Sprott, Reading (Heavyweight Title Defence
29 March	Andrew Lowe W PTS 10 Radcliffe Green, Wembley (Vacant L.Heavyweight Title)
27 May	John Humphrey L CO 2 David Walker, Dagenham (L.Middleweight Title Defence)

Between 1 July 2002 and 30 June 2003, Costas Katsantonis (L.Welter), David Walker (Welter) and Matthew Barney (S.Middle) relinquished their titles.

Welsh Area

Titleholders at 30 June 2003

Fly: vacant. **Bantam:** vacant. **S.Bantam:** vacant. **Feather:** vacant. **S.Feather:** vacant. **Light:** vacant. **L.Welter:** Jason Cook. **Welter:** Jason Williams. **L.Middle:** vacant. **Middle:** vacant. **S.Middle:** vacant. **L.Heavy:** vacant. **Cruiser:** vacant. **Heavy:** vacant.

| 15 September | Keith Jones W RSC 4 Ross McCord, Swansea (Vacant Welterweight Title) |
| 23 February | Keith Jones L PTS 10 Jason Williams, Aberystwyth (Welterweight Title Defence) |

Between 1 July 2002 and 30 June 2003, Darron Griffiths (Cruiser) retired.

Western Area

Titleholders at 30 June 2003

Fly: vacant. **Bantam:** vacant. **S.Bantam:** Frankie DeMilo. **Feather:** vacant. **S.Feather:** vacant. **Light:** vacant. **L.Welter:** vacant. **Welter:** vacant. **L.Middle:** vacant. **Middle:** vacant. **S.Middle:** Darren Dorrington. **L.Heavy:** vacant. **Cruiser:** vacant. **Heavy:** vacant.

British Title Bouts During 2002-2003

All of last season's title bouts are shown in date order within their weight divisions and give the contestants respective weights, along with the scorecard if going to a decision. Every contest is summarised briefly and all referees are named.

Flyweight

Jason Booth (England) failed to defend during the period.

Bantamweight

28 April 2003   Nicky Booth 8.5¼ (England) W PTS 12 Jamie Yelland 8.6 (England), The Harvey Hadden Leisure Centre, Nottingham. Referee: Mickey Vann 118-114. In a tough fight in which the challenger showed a positive attitude, Booth came back strongly in the final stages to make sure of the decision after being given a stern test. Despite finishing exhausted, Yelland, who showed a good left hand, had surpassed himself and will be a much better fighter for the experience.

S. Bantamweight

Michael Alldis (England) retired in December 2002 following a car accident.

Featherweight

8 February 2003   Jamie McKeever 9.0 (England) W RSC 6 Tony Mulholland 8.13½ (England), Everton Park Sports Centre, Liverpool. Billed for the vacant title after Scott Harrison (Scotland) relinquished on becoming the WBO champion on 19 October 2002, McKeever showed himself to be a much improved fighter as he dominated proceedings from the opening bell. The pair had met earlier in a battle for the Central Area title and McKeever had won a controversial decision, but this time round there was only one winner. Mulholland was beaten to the punch too often and following a body attack which floored him the referee, Richie Davies, called a halt to the action at 2.55 of the sixth round.

17 May 2003   Jamie McKeever 8.13¼ (England) L PTS 12 Roy Rutherford 8.12½ (England), Everton Park Sports Centre, Liverpool. Referee: Dave Parris 112-117. Despite taking the fight at 16 days notice, Rutherford took the opportunity with both hands and was well worth his victory. Both men were cut over their right eyes, but it was the challenger who produced the most impressive work, dropping McKeever in the third with a body punch, and generally having the better of it. McKeever finished with a damaged left hand, but will come again.

S. Featherweight

19 October 2002   Alex Arthur 9.4 (Scotland) W CO 4 Steve Conway 9.4 (England), Braehead Arena, Renfrew. With Michael Gomez (England) relinquishing the title in April 2002 to concentrate on getting a world title shot, this

pairing came together to contest the vacancy after Willie Limond, Arthur's original opponent, pulled out injured. The southpaw Conway gave it his best shot despite being weight drained, but always looked vulnerable against a man who appeared to be merely biding his time. The inevitable happened when he was counted out by Dave Parris after 19 seconds of the fourth round had elapsed, a left hook that thudded against his jaw doing the damage.

14 December 2002   Alex Arthur 9.3¼ (Scotland) W RSC 6 Carl Greaves 9.3¾ (England), The Telewest Arena, Newcastle. Making his first defence of the Lonsdale Belt, Arthur proved too strong for his game challenger, who was cut over the left eye in the fifth round and under the cosh when the referee, Larry O'Connell, stopped it in the sixth. It was a well-timed intervention and saved Greaves, who had done well, from a possible battering, while the

Nicky Booth (left) made a fifth successful defence of his British bantamweight title when outscoring Jamie Yelland, who made a determined effort   Les Clark

champion looks likely to run out of home opposition before too long.

Lightweight

Bobby Vanzie (England) failed to defend during the period.

L. Welterweight

Junior Witter (England) failed to defend during the period.

Welterweight

2 November 2002   Neil Sinclair 10.7 (Ireland) W RSC 2 Paul Knights 10.6$^1/_2$ (England), Maysfield Leisure Centre, Belfast. Given less than a week's notice, Knights gave it his best but was simply outgunned. Having been cut over the left eye following a clash of heads after just 40 seconds, Sinclair got to work quickly and put the challenger down early in the second round. Although the corner threw the towel in, it was initially ignored by the referee, Terry O'Connor, who then stopped it after 1.07 of the round had elapsed, with Knights unable to defend himself.

1 February 2003   Neil Sinclair 10.6$^1/_4$ (Ireland) W RSC 8 Bradley Pryce 10.6$^1/_2$ (Wales), The Odyssey Arena, Belfast. Up until the fifth, Pryce was in the fight, but then the champion's extra power began to tell, the challenger somehow surviving a relentless barrage in that round to keep going for the next couple of sessions. Strangely, at that time, Mark Green, the referee, had Pryce ahead, but that was made irrelevant when Pryce was put down for six by a heavy left hook in the eighth. After enduring a solid battering, on getting up, the towel came in for the second time and the action was stopped at 1.54. Having won the Lonsdale Belt outright, Sinclair relinquished the title in April 2003 to concentrate on getting a world championship opportunity.

L. Middleweight

19 April 2003   Jamie Moore 10.13$^3/_4$ (England) W PTS 12 Michael Jones 10.13$^3/_4$ (England), Everton Park Sports Centre, Liverpool. With Wayne Alexander (England) handing back the belt in January 2003 to move up a weight, Moore was matched against the Commonwealth champion, Jones, to contest the vacant British title after Paul Samuels had pulled out with flu. Surprising the majority, Moore overcame a disparate reach advantage to clearly dictate matters, flooring Jones with a short right hook in the third and maintaining his workrate to clearly deserve the 118-111 decision rendered by John Coyle. In losing his Commonwealth crown, Jones finished well-marked up, having lost his gumshield a record nine times as he struggled with a suspected broken nose.

Middleweight

16 April 2003   Howard Eastman 11.5 (England) W RSC 3 Scott Dann 11.5$^1/_2$ (England), The Ice Rink, Nottingham. With Eastman's British, European and Commonwealth titles on the line, the challenger gave it his best try but was ultimately found wanting. However, he made a good start, always looking for the southpaw right-hand counter, and had some success until undone in the third as Eastman decided to walk through the punches to land his own. A right over the top felled Dann for a nine count and on rising he was subjected to an assault which only ended when the referee, Larry O'Connell, called a halt to proceedings at 2.52.

S. Middleweight

29 March 2003   Matthew Barney 11.13 (England) W PTS 12 Dean Francis 11.13 (England), The Conference Centre, Wembley. Billed for the vacant title after David Starie (England) decided to give up the belt in December 2002 in order to concentrate on getting a crack at one of the world titles on offer, Barney surprised the form book. Boxing on the back foot and showing a good jab all night, he took Terry O'Connor's 115-112 decision despite being floored in the ninth from a left to the body. However, the truth of the matter was that Francis, back after a long spell out of the ring due to right shoulder problems, was unable to use his right effectively and was generally outboxed. Both men finished with cut eyes due to a head clash.

L. Heavyweight

8 March 2003   Peter Oboh 12.6 (England) W RSC 11 Neil Simpson 12.6 (England), The AT7 Centre, Coventry. Simpson had relinquished the title in April 2002 to concentrate on a fight against Tony Oakey for the WBU championship, but having lost he came back to meet Oboh, whose Commonwealth title was also on the line, in an effort to regain his former laurels. Although level at the half-way stage, Simpson, who was floored in the eighth and finished the session with his right eye virtually closed, continued in vain only to be rescued by Ian John-Lewis after 1.05 of the 11th round had elapsed, having risen from a count of nine. It had been a messy affair with the Nigerian-born Oboh's added strength winning the day.

Cruiserweight

Bruce Scott (England) forfeited the title in April 2003 after failing to defend within the expected period.

Heavyweight

17 September 2002   Danny Williams 17.10 (England) W PTS 12 Keith Long 15.8$^1/_2$ (England), York Hall, Bethnal Green, London. While winning the Lonsdale Belt outright and, at the same time, successfully defending the Commonwealth crown, Williams was well worth John Keane's 117-113 decision in what was a highly entertaining fight. However, Long, who did his best work on the inside, proved extremely tough and durable, never once wilting even under sustained pressure, and could be proud of his performance in a contest where not many expected him to last the course.

Lord Lonsdale Challenge Belts: Outright Winners

Outright Winners of the National Sporting Club's Challenge Belt, 1909-1935 (21)

Under pressure from other promoters with bigger venues, and in an effort to sustain their monopoly – having controlled championship fights in Britain up until that point in time – the National Sporting Club launched the belt in 1909. They did so on the proviso that there should be eight weight divisions – fly, bantam, feather, light, welter, middle, light-heavy, and heavy – and that to win a belt outright a champion must score three title-match victories at the same weight, but not necessarily consecutively. Worth a substantial amount of money, and carrying a £1 a week pension from the age of 50, the President of the NSC, Lord Lonsdale, donated the first of 22 belts struck. Known as the Lonsdale Belt, despite the inscription reading: 'The National Sporting Club's Challenge Belt', the first man to put a notch on a belt was Freddie Welsh, who outpointed Johnny Summers for the lightweight title on 8 November 1909, while Jim Driscoll became the first man to win one outright. The record time for winning the belt is held by Jim Higgins (279 days).

FLYWEIGHT	Jimmy Wilde; Jackie Brown
BANTAMWEIGHT	Digger Stanley; Joe Fox; Jim Higgins; Johnny Brown; Dick Corbett; Johnny King
FEATHERWEIGHT	Jim Driscoll; Tancy Lee; Johnny Cuthbert; Nel Tarleton
LIGHTWEIGHT	Freddie Welsh
WELTERWEIGHT	Johnny Basham; Jack Hood
MIDDLEWEIGHT	Pat O'Keefe; Len Harvey; Jock McAvoy
L. HEAVYWEIGHT	Dick Smith
HEAVYWEIGHT	Bombardier Billy Wells; Jack Petersen

Note: Both Dick Corbett and Johnny King – with one notch apiece on the 'special' British Empire Lonsdale Belt that was struck in 1933 and later presented to the winner of the Tommy Farr v Joe Louis fight – were allowed to keep their Lonsdale Belts with just two notches secured; Freddie Welsh, also with two notches, was awarded a belt due to his inability to defend because of the First World War; the first bantam belt came back into circulation and was awarded to Johnny Brown; Al Foreman, with just one notch on the second lightweight belt, took it back to Canada with him without the consent of the BBBoC; while the second light-heavy belt was awarded to Jack Smith of Worcester for winning a novices heavyweight competition. Having emigrated to New Zealand, Smith later presented the visiting Her Majesty The Queen with the belt and it now hangs in the BBBoC's offices.

Outright Winners of the BBBoC Lord Lonsdale Challenge Belt, 1936-2003 (110)

Re-introduced by the British Boxing Board of Control as the Lord Lonsdale Challenge Belt, but of less intrinsic value – Benny Lynch's eight-round win over Pat Palmer (16 September 1936 at Shawfield Park, Glasgow) got the new version underway – Eric Boon became the first man to win one outright, in 1939, following victories over Dave Crowley (2) and Arthur Danahar. Since those early days, six further weight divisions have been added and, following on from Henry Cooper's feat of winning three Lonsdale Belts outright, on 10 June 1981 the BBBoC's rules and regulations were amended to read that no boxer shall receive more than one belt as his own property, in any one weight division. From 1 September 1999, any boxer putting a notch on a Lonsdale Belt for the first time will require three more notches at the same weight before he can call the belt his own. However, men who already have a notch on the Lonsdale Belt prior to 1 September 1999 can contest it under the former ruling of three winning championship contests at the same weight. Incidentally, the fastest of the modern belt winners is Ryan Rhodes (90 days), while Chris and Kevin Finnegan are the only brothers to have each won a belt outright.

FLYWEIGHT	Jackie Paterson; Terry Allen; Walter McGowan; John McCluskey; Hugh Russell; Charlie Magri; Pat Clinton; Robbie Regan; Francis Ampofo; Ady Lewis
BANTAMWEIGHT	Johnny King; Peter Keenan (2); Freddie Gilroy; Alan Rudkin; Johnny Owen; Billy Hardy; Drew Docherty; Nicky Booth
S. BANTAMWEIGHT	Richie Wenton; Michael Brodie; Michael Alldis
FEATHERWEIGHT	Nel Tarleton; Ronnie Clayton (2); Charlie Hill; Howard Winstone (2); Evan Armstrong; Pat Cowdell; Robert Dickie; Paul Hodkinson; Colin McMillan; Sean Murphy; Jonjo Irwin

S. FEATHERWEIGHT	Jimmy Anderson; John Doherty; Floyd Havard; Charles Shepherd; Michael Gomez
LIGHTWEIGHT	Eric Boon; Billy Thompson; Joe Lucy; Dave Charnley; Maurice Cullen; Ken Buchanan; Jim Watt; George Feeney; Tony Willis; Carl Crook; Billy Schwer; Michael Ayers; Bobby Vanzie
L. WELTERWEIGHT	Joey Singleton; Colin Power; Clinton McKenzie; Lloyd Christie; Andy Holligan; Ross Hale
WELTERWEIGHT	Ernie Roderick; Wally Thom; Brian Curvis (2); Ralph Charles; Colin Jones; Lloyd Honeyghan; Kirkland Laing; Del Bryan; Geoff McCreesh; Derek Roche; Neil Sinclair
L. MIDDLEWEIGHT	Maurice Hope; Jimmy Batten; Pat Thomas; Prince Rodney; Andy Till; Robert McCracken; Ryan Rhodes; Ensley Bingham
MIDDLEWEIGHT	Pat McAteer; Terry Downes; Johnny Pritchett; Bunny Sterling; Alan Minter; Kevin Finnegan; Roy Gumbs; Tony Sibson; Herol Graham; Neville Brown; Howard Eastman
S. MIDDLEWEIGHT	Sammy Storey; David Starie
L. HEAVYWEIGHT	Randy Turpin; Chic Calderwood; Chris Finnegan; Bunny Johnson; Tom Collins; Dennis Andries; Tony Wilson; Crawford Ashley
CRUISERWEIGHT	Johnny Nelson; Terry Dunstan; Bruce Scott
HEAVYWEIGHT	Henry Cooper (3); Horace Notice; Lennox Lewis; Julius Francis; Danny Williams

Note: Walter McGowan and Charlie Magri, with one notch apiece, kept their belts under the three years/no available challengers' ruling, while Johnny King, with two notches, was awarded the belt on the grounds that the Second World War stopped him from making further defences. Incidentally, King and Nel Tarleton are the only men to have won both the NSC and BBBoC belts outright.

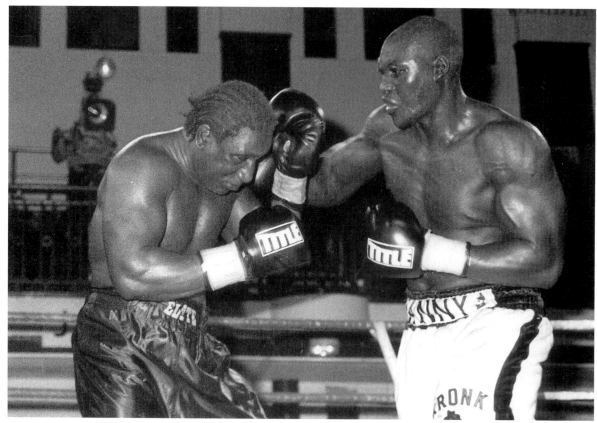

Danny Williams (right) secured the Lonsdale Belt following his points win over Keith Long　　　　Les Clark

British Champions Since Gloves, 1878-2003

The listings below show the tenure of all British champions at each weight since gloves (two ounces or more) were introduced to British rings under Queensberry Rules. Although Charley Davis (147 lbs) had beaten Ted Napper (140 lbs) with gloves in 1873, we start with Denny Harrington, who defeated George Rooke for both the English and world middleweight titles in London on 12 March 1878. We also make a point of ignoring competition winners, apart from Anthony Diamond who beat Dido Plumb for the middles title over 12 rounds, basically because full championship conditions or finish fights of three-minute rounds were not applied. Another point worth bearing in mind, is that prior to the 1880s there were only five weights – heavy, middle, light, feather and bantam. Anything above 154 lbs, the middleweight limit, was classified a heavyweight contest, whereas lightweight, feather and bantamweight poundages were much looser. Therefore, to put things into current perspective, in many cases we have had to ascertain the actual poundage of fighters concerned and relate them to the modern weight classes. Another point worth remembering is that men born outside Britain who won international titles in this country, are not recorded for fear of added confusion and, although many of the champions or claimants listed before 1909 were no more than English titleholders, having fought for the 'championship of England', for our purposes they carry the 'British' label.

Prior to 1909, the year that the Lord Lonsdale Challenge Belt was introduced and weight classes subsequently standardised, poundages within divisions could vary quite substantially, thus enabling men fighting at different weights to claim the same 'title' at the same time. A brief history of the weight fluctuations between 1891 and 1909, shows:

Bantamweight   With the coming of gloves, the division did not really take off until Nunc Wallace established himself at 112 lbs on beating (small) Bill Goode after nine rounds in London on 12 March 1889. Later, with Wallace fighting above the weight, Billy Plimmer was generally recognised as the country's leading eight stoner, following victories over Charles Mansford and Jem Stevens, and became accepted as world champion when George Dixon, the number one in America's eyes, gradually increased his weight. In 1895, Pedlar Palmer took the British title at 112 lbs, but by 1900 he had developed into a 114 pounder. Between 1902 and 1904, Joe Bowker defended regularly at 116 lbs and in 1909 the NSC standardised the weight at 118 lbs, even though the USA continued for a short while to accept only 116 lbs.

Featherweight   Between 1886 and 1895, one of the most prestigious championship belts in this country was fought for at 126 lbs and, although George Dixon was recognised in the USA as world featherweight champion – gradually moving from 114 to 122 lbs – no major international contests took place in Britain during the above period at his weight. It was only in 1895, when Fred Johnson took the British title at 120 lbs, losing it to Ben Jordan two years later, that we came into line with the USA. Ben Jordan became an outstanding champion who, between 1898 and 1899, was seen by the NSC as world champion at 120 lbs. However, first Harry Greenfield, then Jabez White and Will Curley, continued to claim the 126 lbs version of the British title and it was only in 1900, when Jack Roberts beat Curley, that the weight limit was finally standardised at nine stone.

Lightweight   Outstanding champions often carried their weights as they grew in size. A perfect example of this was Dick Burge, the British lightweight champion from 1891-1901, who gradually increased from 134 to 144 lbs, while still maintaining his right to the title. It was not until 1902 that Jabez White brought the division into line with the USA. Later, both White, and then Goldswain, carried their weight up to 140 lbs and it was left to Johnny Summers to set the current limit of 135 lbs.

Welterweight   The presence of Dick Burge fighting from 134 to 144 lbs plus up until 1900, explains quite adequately why the welterweight division, although very popular in the USA, did not take off in this country until 1902. The championship was contested between 142 and 146 lbs in those days and was not really supported by the NSC, but by 1909 with their backing it finally became established at 147 lbs.

On 8 September 1970, Bunny Sterling became the first immigrant to win a British title under the ten-year residential ruling, while earlier, on 28 June 1948, Dick Turpin won the British middleweight title and, in doing so, became the first coloured fighter to win the title, thus breaking down the so-called 'colour bar'.

Note that the Lonsdale Belt notches (title bout wins) relate to NSC, 1909-1935, and BBBoC, 1936-2003.

Champions in **bold** are accorded national recognition.

*Undefeated champions (Does not include men who forfeited titles).

Title Holder	Lonsdale Belt Notches	Tenure	Title Holder	Lonsdale Belt Notches	Tenure	Title Holder	Lonsdale Belt Notches	Tenure
Flyweight (112 lbs)			**Percy Jones**	1	1914	**Joe Symonds**	1	1915-1916
Sid Smith		1911	Joe Symonds		1914	**Jimmy Wilde***	3	1916-1923
Sid Smith	1	1911-1913	**Tancy Lee**	1	1914-1915	**Elky Clark***	2	1924-1927
Bill Ladbury		1913-1914	Jimmy Wilde		1914-1915	**Johnny Hill***	1	1927-1929

187

Title Holder	Lonsdale Belt Notches	Tenure
Jackie Brown		1929-1930
Bert Kirby	1	1930-1931
Jackie Brown	3	1931-1935
Benny Lynch*	2	1935-1938
Jackie Paterson	4	1939-1948
Rinty Monaghan*	1	1948-1950
Terry Allen	1	1951-1952
Teddy Gardner*	1	1952
Terry Allen*	2	1952-1954
Dai Dower*	1	1955-1957
Frankie Jones	2	1957-1960
Johnny Caldwell*	1	1960-1961
Jackie Brown	1	1962-1963
Walter McGowan*	1	1963-1966
John McCluskey*	3	1967-1977
Charlie Magri*	1	1977-1981
Kelvin Smart	1	1982-1984
Hugh Russell*	3	1984-1985
Duke McKenzie*	2	1985-1986
Dave Boy McAuley*	1	1986-1988
Pat Clinton*	3	1988-1991
Robbie Regan	1	1991
Francis Ampofo	1	1991
Robbie Regan*	2	1991-1992
Francis Ampofo	3	1992-1996
Mickey Cantwell*	1	1996-1997
Ady Lewis*	3	1997-1998
Damaen Kelly	1	1999
Keith Knox	1	1999
Jason Booth	2	1999-

Bantamweight (118 lbs)

Title Holder	Lonsdale Belt Notches	Tenure
Nunc Wallace*		1889-1891
Billy Plimmer		1891-1895
Tom Gardner		1892
Willie Smith		1892-1896
Nunc Wallace		1893-1895
George Corfield		1893-1896
Pedlar Palmer		1895-1900
Billy Plimmer		1896-1898
Harry Ware		1899-1900
Harry Ware		1900-1902
Andrew Tokell		1901-1902
Jim Williams		1902
Andrew Tokell		1902
Harry Ware		1902
Joe Bowker		1902-1910
Owen Moran		1905-1907
Digger Stanley		1906-1910
Digger Stanley	2	1910-1913
Bill Beynon	1	1913
Digger Stanley	1	1913-1914
Curley Walker*	1	1914-1915
Joe Fox*	3	1915-1917
Tommy Noble	1	1918-1919
Walter Ross*	1	1919-1920
Jim Higgins	3	1920-1922
Tommy Harrison		1922-1923
Bugler Harry Lake	1	1923
Johnny Brown	3	1923-1928
Alf Pattenden	2	1928-1929
Johnny Brown		1928
Teddy Baldock		1928-1929
Teddy Baldock*	1	1929-1931
Dick Corbett	1	1931-1932
Johnny King	1	1932-1934
Dick Corbett*	1	1934

Title Holder	Lonsdale Belt Notches	Tenure
Johnny King	1+2	1935-1947
Jackie Paterson	2	1947-1949
Stan Rowan*	1	1949
Danny O'Sullivan	1	1949-1951
Peter Keenan	3	1951-1953
John Kelly	1	1953-1954
Peter Keenan	3	1954-1959
Freddie Gilroy*	4	1959-1963
Johnny Caldwell	1	1964-1965
Alan Rudkin	1	1965-1966
Walter McGowan	1	1966-1968
Alan Rudkin*	4	1968-1972
Johnny Clark*	1	1973-1974
Dave Needham	1	1974-1975
Paddy Maguire	1	1975-1977
Johnny Owen*	4	1977-1980
John Feeney	1	1981-1983
Hugh Russell	1	1983
Davy Larmour	1	1983
John Feeney	1	1983-1985
Ray Gilbody	2	1985-1987
Billy Hardy*	5	1987-1991
Joe Kelly	1	1992
Drew Docherty	4	1992-1997
Paul Lloyd	2	1997-1999
Noel Wilders*	2	1999-2000
Ady Lewis	1	2000
Tommy Waite	1	2000
Nicky Booth	5	2000-

S. Bantamweight (122 lbs)

Title Holder	Lonsdale Belt Notches	Tenure
Richie Wenton*	3	1994-1996
Michael Brodie*	3	1997-1999
Patrick Mullings	1	1999
Drew Docherty*	1	1999
Michael Alldis	3	1999-2001
Patrick Mullings	1	2001
Michael Alldis*	1	2002

Featherweight (126 lbs)

Title Holder	Lonsdale Belt Notches	Tenure
Bill Baxter		1884-1891
Harry Overton		1890-1891
Billy Reader		1891-1892
Fred Johnson		1891-1895
Harry Spurden		1892-1895
Jack Fitzpatrick		1895-1897
Fred Johnson		1895-1897
Harry Greenfield		1896-1899
Ben Jordan*		1897-1900
Jabez White		1899-1900
Will Curley		1900-1901
Jack Roberts		1901-1902
Will Curley		1902-1903
Ben Jordan*		1902-1905
Joe Bowker		1905
Johnny Summers		1906
Joe Bowker		1905-1906
Jim Driscoll		1906-1907
Spike Robson		1906-1907
Jim Driscoll*	3	1907-1910
Spike Robson		1907-1910
Ted Kid Lewis*	1	1913-1914
Llew Edwards*	1	1915-1917
Charlie Hardcastle	1	1917
Tancy Lee*	3	1917-1919
Mike Honeyman	2	1920-1921
Joe Fox*	1	1921-1922

Title Holder	Lonsdale Belt Notches	Tenure
George McKenzie	2	1924-1925
Johnny Curley	2	1925-1927
Johnny Cuthbert	1	1927-1928
Harry Corbett	1	1928-1929
Johnny Cuthbert	2	1929-1931
Nel Tarleton	1	1931-1932
Seaman Tommy Watson	2	1932-1934
Nel Tarleton	2	1934-1936
Johnny McGrory	1	1936-1938
Jim Spider Kelly	1	1938-1939
Johnny Cusick	1	1939-1940
Nel Tarleton*	3	1940-1947
Ronnie Clayton	6	1947-1954
Sammy McCarthy	1	1954-1955
Billy Spider Kelly	1	1955-1956
Charlie Hill	3	1956-1959
Bobby Neill	1	1959-1960
Terry Spinks	2	1960-1961
Howard Winstone*	7	1961-1969
Jimmy Revie	2	1969-1971
Evan Armstrong	2	1971-1972
Tommy Glencross	1	1972-1973
Evan Armstrong	2	1973-1975
Vernon Sollas	1	1975-1977
Alan Richardson	2	1977-1978
Dave Needham	2	1978-1979
Pat Cowdell*	3	1979-1982
Steve Sims*	1	1982-1983
Barry McGuigan*	2	1983-1986
Robert Dickie	3	1986-1988
Peter Harris	1	1988
Paul Hodkinson*	3	1988-1990
Sean Murphy	2	1990-1991
Gary de Roux	1	1991
Colin McMillan*	3	1991-1992
John Davison*	1	1992-1993
Sean Murphy	1	1993
Duke McKenzie*	1	1993-1994
Billy Hardy*	1	1994
Michael Deveney	1	1995
Jonjo Irwin	2	1995-1996
Colin McMillan	1	1996-1997
Paul Ingle*	3	1997-1998
Jonjo Irwin*	2	1998-1999
Gary Thornhill	1	2000
Scott Harrison*	3	2001-2002
Jamie McKeever	1	2003
Roy Rutherford	1	2003-

S. Featherweight (130 lbs)

Title Holder	Lonsdale Belt Notches	Tenure
Jimmy Anderson*	3	1968-1970
John Doherty	1	1986
Pat Cowdell	1	1986
Najib Daho	1	1986-1987
Pat Cowdell	1	1987-1988
Floyd Havard	1	1988-1989
John Doherty	1	1989-1990
Joey Jacobs	1	1990
Hugh Forde	1	1990
Kevin Pritchard	1	1990-1991
Robert Dickie	1	1991
Sugar Gibiliru	1	1991
John Doherty	1	1991-1992
Michael Armstrong	1	1992
Neil Haddock	2	1992-1994
Floyd Havard*	3	1994-1995
P. J. Gallagher	2	1996-1997

Title Holder	Lonsdale Belt Notches	Tenure
Charles Shepherd	3	1997-1999
Michael Gomez*	5	1999-2002
Alex Arthur	2	2002-

Lightweight (135 lbs)

Title Holder	Lonsdale Belt Notches	Tenure
Dick Burge		1891-1897
Harry Nickless		1891-1894
Tom Causer		1894-1897
Tom Causer		1897
Dick Burge*		1897-1901
Jabez White		1902-1906
Jack Goldswain		1906-1908
Johnny Summers		1908-1909
Freddie Welsh	1	1909-1911
Matt Wells	1	1911-1912
Freddie Welsh*	1	1912-1919
Bob Marriott*	1	1919-1920
Ernie Rice	1	1921-1922
Seaman Nobby Hall		1922-1923
Harry Mason		1923-1924
Ernie Izzard	2	1924-1925
Harry Allum		1924-1925
Harry Mason*	1	1925-1928
Sam Steward		1928-1929
Fred Webster		1929-1930
Al Foreman	1	1930-1932
Johnny Cuthbert		1932-1934
Harry Mizler		1934
Jackie Kid Berg		1934-1936
Jimmy Walsh	1	1936-1938
Dave Crowley	1	1938
Eric Boon	3	1938-1944
Ronnie James*	1	1944-1947
Billy Thompson	3	1947-1951
Tommy McGovern	1	1951-1952
Frank Johnson	1	1952-1953
Joe Lucy	1	1953-1955
Frank Johnson	1	1955-1956
Joe Lucy	2	1956-1957
Dave Charnley*	3	1957-1965
Maurice Cullen	4	1965-1968
Ken Buchanan*	2	1968-1971
Willie Reilly*	1	1972
Jim Watt	1	1972-1973
Ken Buchanan*	1	1973-1974
Jim Watt*	2	1975-1977
Charlie Nash*	1	1978-1979
Ray Cattouse	2	1980-1982
George Feeney*	3	1982-1985
Tony Willis	3	1985-1987
Alex Dickson	1	1987-1988
Steve Boyle	2	1988-1990
Carl Crook	5	1990-1992
Billy Schwer	1	1992-1993
Paul Burke	1	1993
Billy Schwer*	2	1993-1995
Michael Ayers*	5	1995-1997
Wayne Rigby	2	1998
Bobby Vanzie	5	1998-

L. Welterweight (140 lbs)

Title Holder	Lonsdale Belt Notches	Tenure
Des Rea	1	1968-1969
Vic Andreetti*	2	1969-1970
Des Morrison	1	1973-1974
Pat McCormack	1	1974
Joey Singleton	3	1974-1976
Dave Boy Green*	1	1976-1977

Title Holder	Lonsdale Belt Notches	Tenure
Colin Power*	2	1977-1978
Clinton McKenzie	1	1978-1979
Colin Power	1	1979
Clinton McKenzie	5	1979-1984
Terry Marsh*	1	1984-1986
Tony Laing*	1	1986
Tony McKenzie	2	1986-1987
Lloyd Christie	3	1987-1989
Clinton McKenzie*	1	1989
Pat Barrett*	2	1989-1990
Tony Ekubia	1	1990-1991
Andy Holligan	3	1991-1994
Ross Hale	4	1994-1995
Paul Ryan	1	1995-1996
Andy Holligan*	1	1996-1997
Mark Winters	2	1997-1998
Jason Rowland*	2	1998-2000
Ricky Hatton*	1	2000-2001
Junior Witter	1	2002-

Welterweight (147 lbs)

Title Holder	Lonsdale Belt Notches	Tenure
Charlie Allum		1903-1904
Charlie Knock		1904-1906
Curly Watson		1906-1910
Young Joseph		1908-1910
Young Joseph	1	1910-1911
Arthur Evernden		1911-1912
Johnny Summers		1912
Johnny Summers	2	1912-1914
Tom McCormick		1914
Matt Wells		1914
Johnny Basham	3	1914-1920
Matt Wells		1914-1919
Ted Kid Lewis		1920-1924
Tommy Milligan*		1924-1925

John H. Stracey, the British welterweight champion, 1973-1975

Harry Goodwin

Title Holder	Lonsdale Belt Notches	Tenure
Hamilton Johnny Brown		1925
Harry Mason		1925-1926
Jack Hood*	3	1926-1934
Harry Mason		1934
Pat Butler*		1934-1936
Dave McCleave		1936
Jake Kilrain	1	1936-1939
Ernie Roderick	5	1939-1948
Henry Hall	1	1948-1949
Eddie Thomas	2	1949-1951
Wally Thom	1	1951-1952
Cliff Curvis*	1	1952-1953
Wally Thom	2	1953-1956
Peter Waterman*	2	1956-1958
Tommy Molloy	2	1958-1960
Wally Swift	1	1960
Brian Curvis*	7	1960-1966
Johnny Cooke	2	1967-1968
Ralph Charles*	3	1968-1972
Bobby Arthur	1	1972-1973
John H. Stracey*	1	1973-1975
Pat Thomas	2	1975-1976
Henry Rhiney	2	1976-1979
Kirkland Laing	1	1979-1980
Colin Jones*	3	1980-1982
Lloyd Honeyghan*	2	1983-1985
Kostas Petrou	1	1985
Sylvester Mittee	1	1985
Lloyd Honeyghan*	1	1985-1986
Kirkland Laing	4	1987-1991
Del Bryan	2	1991-1992
Gary Jacobs*	2	1992-1993
Del Bryan	4	1993-1995
Chris Saunders	1	1995-1996
Kevin Lueshing	1	1996-1997
Geoff McCreesh*	4	1997-1999
Derek Roche	3	1999-2000
Harry Dhami	3	2000-2001
Neil Sinclair*	4	2001-2003

L. Middleweight (154 lbs)

Title Holder	Lonsdale Belt Notches	Tenure
Larry Paul	2	1973-1974
Maurice Hope*	3	1974-1977
Jimmy Batten	3	1977-1979
Pat Thomas	3	1979-1981
Herol Graham*	2	1981-1983
Prince Rodney*	1	1983-1984
Jimmy Cable	2	1984-1985
Prince Rodney	2	1985-1986
Chris Pyatt*	1	1986
Lloyd Hibbert*	1	1987
Gary Cooper	1	1988
Gary Stretch	2	1988-1990
Wally Swift Jnr	2	1991-1992
Andy Till	3	1992-1994
Robert McCracken*	3	1994-1995
Ensley Bingham*	2	1996
Ryan Rhodes*	3	1996-1997
Ensley Bingham	3	1997-1999
Wayne Alexander*	2	2000-2003
Jamie Moore	1	2003-

Middleweight (160 lbs)

Title Holder	Lonsdale Belt Notches	Tenure
Denny Harrington		1878-1880
William Sheriff*		1880-1883
Bill Goode		1887-1890
Toff Wall*		1890

Title Holder	Lonsdale Belt Notches	Tenure
Ted Pritchard		1890-1895
Ted White		1893-1895
Ted White*		1895-1896
Anthony Diamond*		1898
Dick Burge*		1898-1900
Jack Palmer		1902-1903
Charlie Allum		1905-1906
Pat O'Keefe		1906
Tom Thomas	1	1906-1910
Jim Sullivan*	1	1910-1912
Jack Harrison*	1	1912-1913
Pat O'Keefe	2	1914-1916
Bandsman Jack Blake	1	1916-1918
Pat O'Keefe*	1	1918-1919
Ted Kid Lewis		1920-1921
Tom Gummer	1	1920-1921
Gus Platts		1921
Johnny Basham		1921
Ted Kid Lewis	2	1921-1923
Johnny Basham		1921
Roland Todd		1923-1925
Roland Todd		1925-1927
Tommy Milligan	1	1926-1928
Frank Moody		1927-1928
Alex Ireland		1928-1929
Len Harvey	5	1929-1933
Jock McAvoy	3+2	1933-1944
Ernie Roderick	1	1945-1946
Vince Hawkins	1	1946-1948
Dick Turpin	2	1948-1950
Albert Finch	1	1950
Randy Turpin*	1	1950-1954
Johnny Sullivan	1	1954-1955
Pat McAteer*	3	1955-1958
Terry Downes	1	1958-1959
John Cowboy McCormack	1	1959
Terry Downes	2	1959-1962
George Aldridge	1	1962-1963
Mick Leahy	1	1963-1964
Wally Swift	1	1964-1965
Johnny Pritchett*	4	1965-1969
Les McAteer	1	1969-1970
Mark Rowe	1	1970
Bunny Sterling	4	1970-1974
Kevin Finnegan*	1	1974
Bunny Sterling*	1	1975
Alan Minter	3	1975-1977
Kevin Finnegan	1	1977
Alan Minter*	1	1977-1978
Tony Sibson	1	1979
Kevin Finnegan*	1	1979-1980
Roy Gumbs	3	1981-1983
Mark Kaylor	1	1983-1984
Tony Sibson*	1	1984
Herol Graham*	1	1985-1986
Brian Anderson	1	1986-1987
Tony Sibson*	1	1987-1988
Herol Graham	4	1988-1992
Frank Grant	2	1992-1993
Neville Brown	6	1993-1998
Glenn Catley*	1	1998
Howard Eastman	4	1998-

S. Middleweight (168 lbs)

Title Holder	Lonsdale Belt Notches	Tenure
Sammy Storey	2	1989-1990
James Cook*	1	1990-1991
Fidel Castro	2	1991-1992
Henry Wharton*	1	1992-1993
James Cook	1	1993-1994
Cornelius Carr*	1	1994
Ali Forbes	1	1995
Sammy Storey*	1	1995
Joe Calzaghe*	2	1995-1997
David Starie	1	1997
Dean Francis*	2	1997-1998
David Starie*	5	1998-2003
Matthew Barney	1	2003-

L. Heavyweight (175lbs)

Title Holder	Lonsdale Belt Notches	Tenure
Dennis Haugh		1913-1914
Dick Smith	2	1914-1916
Harry Reeve*	1	1916-1917
Dick Smith*	1	1918-1919
Boy McCormick*	1	1919-1921
Jack Bloomfield*	1	1922-1924
Tom Berry	1	1925-1927
Gipsy Daniels*	1	1927
Frank Moody	1	1927-1929
Harry Crossley	1	1929-1932
Jack Petersen	1	1932
Len Harvey*	1	1933-1934
Eddie Phillips		1935-1937
Jock McAvoy	1	1937-1938
Len Harvey	2	1938-1942
Freddie Mills*	1	1942-1950
Don Cockell	2	1950-1952
Randy Turpin*	1	1952
Dennis Powell	1	1953
Alex Buxton	2	1953-1955
Randy Turpin*	1	1955
Ron Barton*	1	1956
Randy Turpin*	2	1956-1958
Chic Calderwood	3	1960-1963
Chic Calderwood*	1	1964-1966
Young John McCormack	2	1967-1969
Eddie Avoth	2	1969-1971
Chris Finnegan	2	1971-1973
John Conteh*	2	1973-1974
Johnny Frankham	1	1975
Chris Finnegan*	1	1975-1976
Tim Wood	1	1976-1977
Bunny Johnson*	3	1977-1981
Tom Collins	3	1982-1984
Dennis Andries*	5	1984-1986
Tom Collins*	1	1987
Tony Wilson	3	1987-1989
Tom Collins	1	1989-1990
Steve McCarthy	1	1990-1991
Crawford Ashley*	3	1991-1992
Maurice Core*	2	1992-1994
Crawford Ashley	3	1994-1999
Clinton Woods*	1	1999-2000
Neil Simpson*	2	2000-2002
Peter Oboh	1	2003-

Cruiserweight (190 lbs)

Title Holder	Lonsdale Belt Notches	Tenure
Sam Reeson*	1	1985-1986
Andy Straughn	1	1986-1987
Roy Smith	1	1987
Tee Jay	1	1987-1988
Glenn McCrory*	2	1988
Andy Straughn	1	1988-1989
Johnny Nelson*	3	1989-1991
Derek Angol*	2	1991-1992
Carl Thompson*	1	1992-1994
Dennis Andries	1	1995
Terry Dunstan*	3	1995-1996
Johnny Nelson*	1	1996-1998
Bruce Scott	1	1998-1999
Carl Thompson*	1	1999-2000
Bruce Scott	2	2000-2003

Heavyweight (190 lbs +)

Title Holder	Lonsdale Belt Notches	Tenure
Tom Allen*		1878-1882
Charlie Mitchell*		1882-1894
Jem Smith		1889-1891
Ted Pritchard		1891-1895
Jem Smith		1895-1896
George Chrisp		1901
Jack Scales		1901-1902
Jack Palmer		1903-1906
Gunner Moir		1906-1909
Iron Hague		1909-1910
P.O. Curran		1910-1911
Iron Hague		1910-1911
Bombardier Billy Wells	3	1911-1919
Joe Beckett		1919
Frank Goddard	1	1919
Joe Beckett*	1	1919-1923
Frank Goddard		1923-1926
Phil Scott*		1926-1931
Reggie Meen		1931-1932
Jack Petersen	3	1932-1933
Len Harvey		1933-1934
Jack Petersen		1934-1936
Ben Foord		1936-1937
Tommy Farr*	1	1937-1938
Len Harvey*	1	1938-1942
Jack London	1	1944-1945
Bruce Woodcock	2	1945-1950
Jack Gardner	1	1950-1952
Johnny Williams	1	1952-1953
Don Cockell*	1	1953-1956
Joe Erskine	2	1956-1958
Brian London	1	1958-1959
Henry Cooper*	9	1959-1969
Jack Bodell	1	1969-1970
Henry Cooper	1	1970-1971
Joe Bugner	1	1971
Jack Bodell	1	1971-1972
Danny McAlinden	1	1972-1975
Bunny Johnson	1	1975
Richard Dunn	2	1975-1976
Joe Bugner*	1	1976-1977
John L. Gardner*	2	1978-1980
Gordon Ferris	1	1981
Neville Meade	1	1981-1983
David Pearce*	1	1983-1985
Hughroy Currie	1	1985-1986
Horace Notice*	4	1986-1988
Gary Mason	2	1989-1991
Lennox Lewis*	3	1991-1993
Herbie Hide*	1	1993-1994
James Oyebola	1	1994-1995
Scott Welch*	1	1995-1996
Julius Francis	4	1997-2000
Mike Holden*	1	2000
Danny Williams	4	2000-

Retired or Inactive Post-War British Champions: Career Summary

Includes all British champions, along with British boxers who have won major international titles since 1945, who had retired by July 2002 or have been inactive since that date. The section does not include champions still active (for their records see under Active British-Based Boxers), while undefeated champions are those who relinquished their titles, not forfeited them.

George Aldridge British Middleweight Champion, 1962-1963. *Born* 01.02.36. *From* Market Harborough. *Pro Career* 1956-1963 (52 contests, won 36, drew 2, lost 14).

Michael Alldis British S. Bantamweight Champion, 1999-2001. Undefeated British and Commonwealth S. Bantamweight Champion, 2002. *Born* 25.05.68. *From* Crawley. *Pro Career* 1992-2002 (21 contests, won 24, lost 8).

Terry Allen British Flyweight Champion, 1951-1952. Undefeated British Flyweight Champion, 1952-1954. European and World Flyweight Champion, 1950. *Born* 18.06.24. *From* Islington. *Birthname* Edward Govier. *Deceased* 1987. *Pro Career* 1942-1954 (74 contests, won 60, drew 1, lost 13).

Brian Anderson British Middleweight Champion, 1986-1987. *Born* 09.07.61. *From* Sheffield. *Pro Career* 1980-1987 (39 contests, won 27, drew 3, lost 9).

Jimmy Anderson Undefeated British S. Featherweight Champion, 1968-1970. *Born* 01.10.42. *From* Waltham Cross. *Pro Career* 1964-1971 (37 contests, won 27, drew 1, lost 9).

Vic Andreetti Undefeated British L. Welterweight Champion, 1969-1970. *Born* 29.01.42. *From* Hoxton. *Pro Career* 1961-1969 (67 contests, won 51, drew 3, lost 13).

Dennis Andries Undefeated British L. Heavyweight Champion, 1984-86. World L. Heavyweight Champion (WBC version), 1986-1987, 1989, and 1990-1991. British Cruiserweight Champion, 1995. *Born* Guyana 05.11.53. *From* Hackney. *Pro Career* 1978-1996 (65 contests, won 49, drew 2, lost 14).

Derek Angol Undefeated British Cruiserweight Champion, 1991-1992. Undefeated Commonwealth Cruiserweight Champion, 1989-1993. *Born* 28.11.64. *From* Camberwell. *Pro Career* 1986-1996 (31 contests, won 28, lost 3).

Evan Armstrong British Featherweight Champion, 1971-1972. Undefeated British Featherweight Champion, 1973-1975. Commonwealth Featherweight Champion, 1974. *Born* 15.02.43. *From* Ayr. *Pro Career* 1963-1974 (54 contests, won 39, drew 1, lost 14).

Michael Armstrong British S. Featherweight Champion, 1992. *Born* 18.12.68. *From* Moston. *Birthname* Morris. *Pro Career* 1987-1994 (26 contests, won 18, drew 1, lost 7).

Bobby Arthur British Welterweight Champion, 1972-1973. *Born* 25.07.47. *From* Coventry. *Pro Career* 1967-1976 (41 contests, won 26, lost 15).

Crawford Ashley Undefeated British L. Heavyweight Champion, 1991-1992. British L. Heavyweight Champion, 1994-1999. European L. Heavyweight Champion, 1997 and 1998-1999. Commonwealth L. Heavyweight Champion, 1998-1999. *Born* 20.05.64. *From* Leeds. *Birthname* Gary Crawford. *Pro Career* 1987-2001 (44 contests, won 33, drew 1, lost 10).

Eddie Avoth British L. Heavyweight Champion, 1969-1971. Commonwealth L. Heavyweight Champion, 1970-1971. *Born* 02.05.45. *From* Cardiff. *Pro Career* 1963-1972 (53 contests, won 44, lost 9).

Michael Ayers Undefeated British Lightweight Champion, 1995-1997. *Born* 26.01.65. *From* Tooting. *Pro Career* 1989-2001 (36 contests, won 31, drew 1, lost 4).

Pat Barrett Undefeated British L. Welterweight Champion, 1989-1990. European L. Welterweight Champion, 1990-1992. *Born* 22.07.67. *From* Manchester. *Pro Career* 1987-1994 (42 contests, won 37, drew 1, lost 4).

Ron Barton Undefeated British L. Heavyweight Champion, 1956. *Born* 25.02.33. *From* West Ham. *Pro Career* 1954-1961 (31 contests, won 26, lost 5).

Jimmy Batten British L. Middleweight Champion, 1977-1979. *Born* 07.11.55. *From* Millwall. *Pro Career* 1974-1983 (49 contests, won 40, lost 9).

Nigel Benn Commonwealth Middleweight Champion, 1988-1989. World Middleweight Champion (WBO version), 1990. World S. Middleweight Champion (WBC version), 1992-1996. *Born* 22.01.64. *From* Ilford. *Pro Career* 1987-1996 (48 contests, won 42, drew 1, lost 5).

Ensley Bingham Undefeated British L. Middleweight Champion, 1996. British L. Middleweight Champion, 1997-1999. *Born* 27.05.63. *From* Manchester. *Pro Career* 1986-1999 (28 contests, won 20, lost 8).

Jack Bodell British Heavyweight Champion, 1969-1970 and 1971-1972. Commonwealth Heavyweight Champion, 1971-1972. European Heavyweight Champion, 1971. *Born* 11.08.40. *From* Swadlincote. *Pro Career* 1962-1972 (71 contests, won 58, lost 13).

Steve Boyle British Lightweight Champion, 1988-1990. *Born* 28.11.62. *From* Glasgow. *Pro Career* 1983-1993 (33 contests, won 25, drew 2, lost 6).

Cornelius Boza-Edwards Undefeated European S. Featherweight Champion, 1982. World S. Featherweight Champion, 1981 (WBC version). *Born* Uganda, 27.05.56. *From* London. *Pro Career* 1976-1987 (53 contests, won 45, drew 1, lost 7).

Jim Brady British Empire Bantamweight Championship Claimant, 1941-1945. *From* Dundee. *Deceased* 1980. *Pro Career* 1932-1947 (169 contests, won 104, drew 15, lost 50).

Jackie Brown British and British Empire Flyweight Champion, 1962-1963. *Born* 02.03.35. *From* Edinburgh. *Pro Career* 1958-1966 (44 contests, won 32, drew 1, lost 10, no contest 1).

Neville Brown British Middleweight Champion, 1993-1998. *Born* 26.02.66. *From* Burton. *Pro Career* 1989-2000 (40 contests, won 32, lost 8).

Frank Bruno Undefeated European Heavyweight Champion, 1985-1986. World Heavyweight Champion (WBC version), 1995-96. *Born* 16.11.61. *From* Wandsworth. *Pro Career* 1982-1996 (45 contests, won 40, lost 5).

Del Bryan British Welterweight Champion, 1991-1992 and 1993-1995. *Born* 16.04.1967. *From* Birmingham. *Pro Career* 1986-1998 (52 contests, won 32, drew 1, lost 19).

Ken Buchanan Undefeated British Lightweight Champion, 1968-1971, and 1973-1974. Undefeated European Lightweight Champion, 1974-1975. World Lightweight Champion, 1970-1971. World Lightweight Champion, (WBA version), 1971-1972. *Born* 28.06.45. *From* Edinburgh. *Pro Career* 1965-1982 (69 contests, won 61, lost 8).

Joe Bugner British, Commonwealth and European Heavyweight Champion, 1971. Undefeated European Heavyweight Champion, 1972-1975. European Heavyweight Champion, 1976-1977. Undefeated British and Commonwealth Heavyweight Champion, 1976-1977. *Born* Hungary, 13.03.50. *From* Bedford. *Pro Career* 1967-1999 (83 contests, won 69, drew 1, lost 13).

Paul Burke British and Commonwealth Lightweight Champion, 1993. Commonwealth L. Welterweight Champion, 1997 and 1998-1999. *Born* 25.07.66. *From* Preston. *Pro Career* 1987-1999 (43 contests, won 28, drew 2, lost 13).

Alex Buxton British L. Heavyweight Champion, 1953-1955. *Born* 10.05.25. *From* Watford. *Pro Career* 1942-1963 (125 contests, won 78, drew 4, lost 43).

Jimmy Cable British L. Middleweight Champion, 1984-1985. European L. Middleweight Champion, 1984. *Born* 07.09.57. *From* Crawley. *Pro Career* 1980-1988 (41 contests, won 30, drew 2, lost 9).

Chic Calderwood British and British Empire L. Heavyweight Champion,

1960-1963. Undefeated British L. Heavyweight Champion, 1964-1966. *Born* 09.01.37. *From* Craigneuk. *Birthname* Charles Calderwood. *Deceased* 1966. *Pro Career* 1957-1966 (55 contests, won 44, drew 1, lost 9, no contest 1).

Johnny Caldwell Undefeated British Flyweight Champion, 1960-1961. British and British Empire Bantamweight Champion, 1964-1965. World Bantamweight Champion (EBU version), 1961-1962. *Born* 07.05.38. *From* Belfast. *Pro Career* 1958-1965 (35 contests, won 29, drew 1, lost 5).

Mickey Cantwell Undefeated British Flyweight Champion, 1996-1997. *Born* 23.11.64. *From* Eltham. *Pro Career* 1991-2001 (22 contests, won 14, drew 1, lost 7).

Cornelius Carr Undefeated British S. Middleweight Champion, 1994. *Born* 09.04.69. *From* Middlesbrough. *Pro Career* 1987-2001 (38 contests, won 34, lost 4).

Fidel Castro British S. Middleweight Champion, 1991-1992. *Born* 17.04.63. *From* Nottingham. *Birthname* Smith. *Pro Career* 1987-1995 (30 contests, won 22, lost 8).

Ray Cattouse British Lightweight Champion, 1980-1982. *Born* 24.07.52. *From* Balham. *Pro Career* 1975-1983 (31 contests, won 26, drew 3, lost 2).

Ralph Charles Undefeated British and British Empire/Commonwealth Welterweight Champion, 1968-1972. European Welterweight Champion, 1970-1971. *Born* 05.02.43. *From* West Ham. *Pro Career* 1963-1972 (43 contests, won 39, lost 4).

Dave Charnley Undefeated British Lightweight Champion, 1957-1965. British Empire Lightweight Champion, 1959-1962. European Lightweight Champion, 1960-1963. *Born* 10.10.35. *From* Dartford. *Pro Career* 1954-1964 (61 contests, won 48, drew 1, lost 12).

Lloyd Christie British L. Welterweight Champion, 1987-1989. *Born* 28.02.62. *From* Wolverhampton. *Pro Career* 1981-1989 (46 contests, won 24, drew 1, lost 21).

Johnny Clark Undefeated British and European Bantamweight Champion, 1973-1974. *Born* 10.09.47. *From* Walworth. *Pro Career* 1966-1974 (43 contests, won 39, drew 1, lost 3).

Ronnie Clayton British Featherweight Champion, 1947-1954. British Empire Featherweight Championship Claimant, 1947-1951. European Featherweight Champion, 1947-1948. *Born* 09.02.23. *From* Blackpool. *Deceased* 1999. *Pro Career* 1941-1954 (113 contests, won 79, drew 8, lost 26).

Pat Clinton Undefeated British Flyweight Champion, 1988-1991. Undefeated European Flyweight Champion, 1990-1991. World Flyweight Champion (WBO version), 1992-1993. *Born* 04.04.64. *From* Croy. *Pro Career* 1985-1991 (23 contests, won 20, lost 3).

Ray Close Undefeated European S. Middleweight Champion, 1993. *Born* 20.01.69. *From* Belfast. *Pro Career* 1988-1997 (29 contests, won 25, drew 1, lost 3).

Don Cockell British L. Heavyweight Champion, 1950-1952. Undefeated European L. Heavyweight Champion, 1951-1952. Undefeated British Heavyweight Champion, 1953-1956. British Empire Heavyweight Championship Claimant, 1953-1954. Undefeated British Empire Heavyweight Champion, 1954-1956. *Born* 22.09.28. *From* Battersea. *Deceased* 1983. *Pro Career* 1946-1956 (80 contests, won 65, drew 1, lost 14).

Steve Collins Undefeated World Middleweight Champion (WBO version), 1994-1995. Undefeated World S. Middleweight Champion (WBO version), 1995-1997. *Born* 21.07.64. *From* Dublin. *Pro Career* 1986-1997 (39 contests, won 36, lost 3).

Tom Collins British L. Heavyweight Champion, 1982-1984. Undefeated British L. Heavyweight Champion, 1987 and 1989-1990. European L. Heavyweight Champion, 1987-1988 and 1990-1991. *Born* Curacao, 01.07.55. *From* Leeds. *Pro Career* 1977-1993 (50 contests, won 26, drew 2, lost 22).

John Conteh Undefeated British, Commonwealth and European L. Heavyweight Champion, 1973-1974. World L. Heavyweight Champion (WBC version), 1974-1977. *Born* 27.05.51. *From* Liverpool. *Pro Career* 1971-1980 (39 contests, won 34, drew 1, lost 4).

James Cook Undefeated British S. Middleweight Champion, 1990-1991. British S. Middleweight Champion, 1993-1994. European S. Middleweight Champion, 1991-1992. *Born* Jamaica, 17.05.59. *From* Peckham. *Pro Career* 1982-1994 (35 contests, won 25, lost 10).

Johnny Cooke British and British Empire Welterweight Champion, 1967-1968. *Born* 17.12.34. *From* Bootle. *Pro Career* 1960-1971 (93 contests, won 52, drew 7, lost 34).

Gary Cooper British L. Middleweight Champion, 1988. *Born* 31.05.57. *From* Lymington. *Pro Career* 1978-1989 (27 contests, won 16, drew 2, lost 9).

Henry Cooper Undefeated British Heavyweight Champion, 1959-1969. British Heavyweight Champion, 1970-1971. British Empire/Commonwealth Heavyweight Champion, 1959-1971. Undefeated European Heavyweight Champion, 1964 and 1968-1969. European Heavyweight Champion, 1970-1971. *Born* 03.05.34. *From* Bellingham. *Pro Career* 1954-1971 (55 contests, won 40, drew 1, lost 14).

Maurice Core Undefeated British L. Heavyweight Champion, 1992-1994. *Born* 22.06.65. *From* Manchester. *Birthname* Maurice Coore. *Pro Career* 1990-1996 (18 contests, won 15, drew 1, lost 2).

Pat Cowdell Undefeated British Featherweight Champion, 1979-1982. Undefeated European Featherweight Champion, 1982-1983. British S. Featherweight Champion, 1986 and 1987-1988. European S. Featherweight Champion, 1984-1985. *Born* 18.08.53. *From* Warley. *Pro Career* 1977-1988 (42 contests, won 36, lost 6).

Carl Crook British and Commonwealth Lightweight Champion, 1990-1992. *Born* 10.11.63. *From* Chorley. *Pro Career* 1985-1993 (31 contests, won 26, drew 1, lost 4).

Maurice Cullen British Lightweight Champion, 1965-1968. *Born* 30.12.37. *From* Shotton. *Deceased* 2001. *Pro Career* 1959-1970 (55 contests, won 45, drew 2, lost 8).

Hughroy Currie British Heavyweight Champion, 1985-1986. *Born* Jamaica, 09.02.59. *From* Catford. *Pro Career* 1981-1989 (29 contests, won 17, drew 1, lost 11).

Brian Curvis Undefeated British and British Empire Welterweight Champion, 1960-1966. *Born* 14.08.37. *From* Swansea. *Birthname* Brian Nancurvis. *Pro Career* 1959-1966 (41 contests, won 37, lost 4).

Cliff Curvis Undefeated British Welterweight Champion, 1952-1953. British Empire Welterweight Championship Claimant, 1952. *Born* 02.11.27. *From* Swansea. *Birthname* Cliff Nancurvis. *Pro Career* 1944-1953 (55 contests, won 42, drew 1, lost 12).

Najib Daho British S. Featherweight Champion, 1986-1987. Commonwealth Lightweight Champion, 1989-1990. *Born* Morocco, 13.01.59. *From* Manchester. *Deceased* 1993. *Pro Career* 1977-1991 (60 contests, won 34, drew 1, lost 25).

John Davison Undefeated British Featherweight Champion, 1992-1993. *Born* 30.09.58. *From* Newcastle. *Pro Career* 1988-1993 (20 contests, won 15, lost 5).

Garry Delaney Commonwealth L. Heavyweight Champion, 1994-1995. *Born* 12.08.70. *From* West Ham. *Pro Career* 1991-2002 (37 contests, won 30, drew 1, lost 6).

Gary DeRoux British Featherweight Champion, 1991. *Born* 04.11.62. *From* Peterborough. *Pro Career* 1986-1993 (22 contests, won 13, drew 1, lost 8).

Mike Deveney British Featherweight Champion, 1995. *Born* 14.12.65. *From* Paisley. *Pro Career* 1991-1998 (42 contests, won 22, drew 1, lost 19).

Harry Dhami British Welterweight Champion, 2000-2001. *Born* 17.04.72. *From* Gravesend. *Pro Career* 1992-2001 (22 contests, won 16, drew 1, lost 5).

Robert Dickie British Featherweight Champion, 1986-1988. British S. Featherweight Champion, 1991. *Born* 23.06.64. *From* Swansea. *Pro Career* 1983-1993 (28 contests, won 22, drew 2, lost 4).

Alex Dickson British Lightweight Champion, 1987-1988. *Born* 01.10.62. *From* Larkhall. *Pro Career* 1985-1989 (22 contests, won 18, drew 1, lost 3).

Drew Docherty Undefeated British S. Bantamweight Champion, 1999.

British Bantamweight Champion, 1992-1997. *Born* 29.11.65. *From* Condorrat. *Pro Career* 1989-2000 (24 contests, won 16, drew 1, lost 7).

John Doherty British S. Featherweight Champion, 1986, 1989-1990, and 1991-1992. *Born* 17.07.62. *From* Bradford. *Pro Career* 1982-1992 (39 contests, won 28, drew 3, lost 8).

Pat Doherty Commonwealth Lightweight Champion, 1989. *Born* 12.04.62. *From* Croydon. *Pro Career* 1981-1989 (32 contests, won 18, drew 3, lost 11).

Dai Dower Undefeated British Flyweight Champion, 1955-1957. Undefeated British Empire Flyweight Champion, 1954-1957. European Flyweight Champion, 1955. *Born* 26.06.33. *From* Abercynon. *Pro Career* 1953-1958 (37 contests, won 34, lost 3).

Terry Downes British Middleweight Champion, 1958-1959 and 1959-1962. World Middleweight Champion (NY/EBU version), 1961-1962. *Born* 09.05.36. *From* Paddington. *Pro Career* 1957-1964 (44 contests, won 35, lost 9).

Richard Dunn British and Commonwealth Heavyweight Champion, 1975-1976. European Heavyweight Champion, 1976. *Born* 19.01.45. *From* Bradford. *Pro Career* 1969-1977 (45 contests, won 33, lost 12).

Terry Dunstan Undefeated British Cruiserweight Champion, 1995-1996. Undefeated European Cruiserweight Champion, 1998. *Born* 21.10.68. *From* Vauxhall. *Pro Career* 1992-1999 (21 contests, won 19, lost 2).

Tony Ekubia British L. Welterweight Champion, 1990-1991. Commonwealth L. Welterweight Champion, 1989-1991. *Born* Nigeria, 06.03.60. *From* Manchester. *Pro Career* 1986-1993 (25 contests, won 21, lost 4).

Joe Erskine British Heavyweight Champion, 1956-1958. British Empire Heavyweight Champion, 1957-1958. *Born* 26.01.34. *From* Cardiff. *Deceased* 1990. *Pro Career* 1954-1964 (54 contests, won 45, drew 1, lost 8).

Chris Eubank Undefeated WBO Middleweight Champion, 1990-1991. WBO S. Middleweight Title, 1991-1995. *Born* 08.08.1966. *From* Brighton. *Pro Career* 1985-1998 (52 contests, won 45, drew 2, lost 5).

George Feeney Undefeated British Lightweight Champion, 1982-1985. *Born* 09.02.57. *From* West Hartlepool. *Pro Career* 1977-1984 (29 contests, won 19, lost 10).

John Feeney British Bantamweight Champion, 1981-1983 and 1983-1985. *Born* 15.05.58. *From* West Hartlepool. *Pro Career* 1977-1987 (48 contests, won 35, lost 13).

Gordon Ferris British Heavyweight Champion, 1981. *Born* 21.11.52. *From* Enniskillen. *Pro Career* 1977-1982 (26 contests, won 20, lost 6).

Darren Fifield Commonwealth Flyweight Champion, 1993-1994. *Born* 09.10.69. *From* Henley. *Pro Career* 1992-1996 (13 contests, won 7, drew 2, lost 4).

Albert Finch British Middleweight Champion, 1950. *Born* 16.05.26. *From* Croydon. *Pro Career* 1945-1958 (103 contests, won 72, drew 9, lost 21, no contest 1).

Chris Finnegan British L. Heavyweight Champion, 1971-1973. Undefeated British L. Heavyweight Champion, 1975-1976. Commonwealth L. Heavyweight Champion, 1971-1973. European L. Heavyweight Champion, 1972. *Born* 05.06.44. *From* Iver. *Pro Career* 1968-1975 (37 contests, won 29, drew 1, lost 7).

Kevin Finnegan British Middleweight Champion, 1977. Undefeated British Middleweight Champion, 1974 and 1979-1980. European Middleweight Champion, 1974-1975 and 1980. *Born* 18.04.48. *From* Iver. *Pro Career* 1970-1980 (47 contests, won 35, drew 1, lost 11).

Ali Forbes British S. Middleweight Champion, 1995. *Born* 07.03.61. *From* Sydenham. *Pro Career* 1989-2002 (25 contests, won 14, drew 1, lost 10).

Hugh Forde British S. Featherweight Champion, 1990. Commonwealth S. Featherweight Champion, 1991. *Born* 07.05.64. *From* Birmingham. *Pro Career* 1986-1995 (31 contests, won 24, lost 7).

Steve Foster Commonwealth L. Middleweight Champion, 1996-1997. *Born* 28.12.60. *From* Salford. *Pro Career* 1981-1999 (39 contests, won 20, drew 2, lost 17).

Johnny Frankham British L. Heavyweight Champion, 1975. *Born* 06.06.48. *From* Reading. *Pro Career* 1970-1976 (40 contests, won 28, drew 1, lost 11).

P.J. Gallagher British S. Featherweight Champion, 1996-1997. *Born* 14.02.73. *From* Wood Green. *Pro Career* 1993-2000 (20 contests, won 19, lost 1).

Jack Gardner British Heavyweight Champion, 1950-1952. British Empire Heavyweight Championship Claimant, 1950-1952. European Heavyweight Champion, 1951. *Born* 06.11.26. *From* Market Harborough. *Deceased* 1978. *Pro Career* 1948-1956 (34 contests, won 28, lost 6).

John L. Gardner Undefeated British Heavyweight Champion, 1978-1980. Undefeated Commonwealth Heavyweight Champion, 1978-1981. Undefeated European Heavyweight Champion, 1980-1981. *Born* 19.03.53. *From* Hackney. *Pro Career* 1973-1983 (39 contests, won 35, lost 4).

Teddy Gardner Undefeated British and European Flyweight Champion, 1952. British Empire Flyweight Championship Claimant, 1952. *Born* 27.01.22. *From* West Hartlepool. *Deceased* 1977. *Pro Career* 1938-1952 (66 contests, won 55, drew 3, lost 8).

Sugar Gibiliru British S. Featherweight Champion, 1991. *Born* 13.07.66. *From* Liverpool. *Pro Career* 1984-1995 (55 contests, won 16, drew 7, lost 32).

Ray Gilbody British Bantamweight Champion, 1985-1987. *Born* 21.03.60. *From* Warrington. *Pro Career* 1983-1987 (16 contests, won 11, drew 1, lost 4).

Freddie Gilroy Undefeated British and British Empire Bantamweight Champion, 1959-1963. European Bantamweight Champion, 1959-1960. *Born* 07.03.36. *From* Belfast. *Pro Career* 1957-1962 (31 contests, won 28, lost 3).

Tommy Glencross British Featherweight Champion, 1972-1973. *Born* 31.07.47. *From* Glasgow. *Pro Career* 1967-1978 (48 contests, won 31, drew 1, lost 16).

Herol Graham Undefeated British L. Middleweight Champion, 1981-1983. Undefeated Commonwealth L. Middleweight Champion, 1981-1984. Undefeated European L. Middleweight Champion, 1983-1984. Undefeated British Middleweight Champion, 1985-1986. British Middleweight Champion, 1988-1992. European Middleweight Champion, 1986-1987. *Born* 13.09.59. *From* Sheffield. *Pro Career* 1978-1998 (54 contests, won 48, lost 6).

Frank Grant British Middleweight Champion, 1992-1993. *Born* 22.05.65. *From* Bradford. *Pro Career* 1986-1993 (26 contests, won 22, lost 4).

Dave Boy Green Undefeated British and European L. Welterweight Champion, 1976-1977. European Welterweight Champion, 1979. *Born* 02.06.53. *From* Chatteris. *Pro Career* 1974-1981 (41 contests, won 37, lost 4).

Roy Gumbs British Middleweight Champion, 1981-1983. Commonwealth Middleweight Champion, 1983. *Born* St Kitts, 05.09.54. *From* Tottenham. *Pro Career* 1976-1985 (40 contests, won 26, drew 3, lost 11).

Neil Haddock British S. Featherweight Champion, 1992-1994. *Born* 22.06.64. *From* Llanelli. *Pro Career* 1987-1994 (26 contests, won 14, drew 1, lost 11).

Ross Hale British and Commonwealth L. Welterweight Champion, 1994-1995. *Born* 28.02.1967. *From* Bristol. *Pro Career* 1989-1998 (33 contests, won 29, lost 4).

Henry Hall British Welterweight Champion, 1948-1949. *Born* 06.09.22. *From* Sheffield. *Deceased* 1979. *Pro Career* 1945-1952 (66 contests, won 43, drew 3, lost 20).

Prince Naseem Hamed Undefeated European Bantamweight Champion, 1994-1995. Undefeated WBO Featherweight Champion, 1997-2000. Undefeated IBF Featherweight Champion, 1997. WBC Featherweight Champion, 1999-2000. *Born* 12.02.74. *From* Sheffield. *Pro Career* 1992-2002 (37 contests, won 36, lost 1).

Billy Hardy Undefeated British Bantamweight Champion, 1987-1991. Undefeated British Featherweight Champion, 1994. Undefeated Commonwealth Featherweight Champion, 1992-1996. European

Featherweight Champion, 1995-1998. *Born* 05.09.1964. *From* Sunderland. *Pro Career* 1983-1998 (48 contests, won 37, drew 2, lost 9).

Paul Harvey Commonwealth S. Featherweight Champion, 1991-1992. *Born* 10.11.64. *From* Ilford. *Pro Career* 1989-1994 (22 contests, won 16, drew 1, lost 5).

Floyd Havard British S. Featherweight Champion, 1988-1989. Undefeated British S. Featherweight Champion, 1994-1995. *Born* 16.10.65. *From* Swansea. *Pro Career* 1985-1996 (36 contests, won 34, lost 2).

Vince Hawkins British Middleweight Champion, 1946-1948. *Born* 15.04.23. *From* Eastleigh. *Pro Career* 1940-1950 (86 contests, won 75, drew 1, lost 10).

Lloyd Hibbert Undefeated British L. Middleweight Champion, 1987. Commonwealth L. Middleweight Champion, 1987. *Born* 29.06.59. *From* Birmingham. *Pro Career* 1979-1987 (23 contests, won 19, lost 4).

Herbie Hide Undefeated British Heavyweight Champion, 1993-1994. WBO Heavyweight Champion, 1997-1999. *Born* 27.08.1971. *From* Norwich. *Pro Career* 1989-1999 (33 contests, won 31, lost 2).

Charlie Hill British Featherweight Champion, 1956-1959. *Born* 20.06.30. *From* Cambuslang. *Pro Career* 1953-1959 (36 contests, won 31, lost 5).

Paul Hodkinson Undefeated British Featherweight Champion, 1988-1990. Undefeated European Featherweight Champion, 1989-1991. World Featherweight Champion, 1991-1993 (WBC version). *Born* 14.09.65. *From* Liverpool. *Pro Career* 1986-1994 (26 contests, won 22, drew 1, lost 3).

Andy Holligan British and Commonwealth L. Welterweight Champion, 1991-1994 and 1996-1997. *Born* 06.06.67. *From* Liverpool. *Pro Career* 1987-1998 (30 contests, won 27, lost 3).

Lloyd Honeyghan Undefeated British Welterweight Champion, 1983-1985 and 1985-1986. Undefeated Commonwealth & European Champion, 1985-1986. World Welterweight Champion, 1986. World Welterweight Champion (WBC version), 1986-1987 and 1988-1989. World Welterweight Champion (IBF version), 1988. Commonwealth L. Middleweight Champion, 1993-1994. *Born* 22.04.60, Jamaica. *From* Bermondsey. *Pro Career* 1980-1995 (48 contests, won 43, lost 5).

Maurice Hope Undefeated British L. Middleweight Champion, 1974-1977. Undefeated Commonwealth L. Middleweight Champion, 1976-1979. Undefeated European L. Middleweight Champion, 1976-1978. World L. Middleweight Champion (WBC version), 1979-1981. *Born* Antigua, 06.12.51. *From* Hackney. *Pro Career* 1973-1982 (35 contests, won 30, drew 1, lost 4).

Mickey Hughes Commonwealth L. Middleweight Champion, 1992-1993. *Born* 13.06.62. *From* St Pancras. *Pro Career* 1985-1993 (31 contests, won 24, lost 7).

Mo Hussein Commonwealth Lightweight Champion, 1987-1989. *Born* 17.11.62. *From* West Ham. *Pro Career* 1982-1989 (27 contests, won 23, lost 4).

Paul Ingle World Featherweight Champion (IBF Version), 1999-2000. Undefeated British Featherweight Champion, 1997-1998. Undefeated Commonwealth and European Champion, 1997-1999. *Born* 22.06.72. *From* Scarborough. *Pro Career* (25 contests, won 23, lost 2).

Jonjo Irwin British Featherweight Champion, 1995-1996. Undefeated British Featherweight Champion, 1998-1999. Commonwealth Featherweight Champion, 1996-1997. *Born* 31.05.69. *From* Doncaster. *Pro Career* 1992-1999 (24 contests, won 19, lost 5).

Gary Jacobs Undefeated British Welterweight Champion, 1992-1993. Commonwealth Welterweight Champion, 1988-1989. European Welterweight Champion, 1993-1994. *Born* 10.12.65. *From* Glasgow. *Pro Career* 1985-1997 (53 contests, won 45, lost 8).

Joey Jacobs British S. Featherweight Champion, 1990. *Born* 01.10.60. *From* Manchester. *Pro Career* 1986-1991 (15 contests, won 10, lost 5).

Ronnie James Undefeated British Lightweight Champion, 1944-1947. *Born* 08.10.17. *From* Swansea. *Deceased* 1977. *Pro Career* 1933-1947 (119 contests, won 98, drew 5, lost 16).

Tee Jay British Cruiserweight Champion, 1987-1988. *Born* Ghana,

21.01.62. *Birthname* Taju Akay. *From* Notting Hill. *Pro Career* 1985-1991 (19 contests, won 14, drew 1, lost 4).

Bunny Johnson British and Commonwealth Heavyweight Champion, 1975. Undefeated British L. Heavyweight Champion, 1977-1981. *Born* Jamaica, 10.05.47. *From* Birmingham. *Birthname* Fitzroy Johnson. *Pro Career* 1968-1981 (73 contests, won 55, drew 1, lost 17).

Frank Johnson British Lightweight Champion, 1952-1953 and 1955-1956. British Empire Lightweight Championship Claimant, 1953. *Born* 27.11.28. *From* Manchester. *Birthname* Frank Williamson. *Deceased* 1970. *Pro Career* 1946-1957 (58 contests, won 47, lost 11).

Barry Jones Undefeated WBO S. Featherweight Champion, 1997-1998. *Born* 03.05.74. *From* Cardiff. *Pro Career* 1992-2000 (20 contests, won 18, drew 1, lost 1).

Colin Jones Undefeated British Welterweight Champion, 1980-1982. Undefeated Commonwealth Welterweight Champion, 1981-1984. Undefeated European Welterweight Champion, 1982-1983. *Born* 21.03.59. *From* Gorseinon. *Pro Career* 1977-1985 (30 contests, won 26, drew 1, lost 3).

Frankie Jones British Flyweight Champion, 1957-1960. British Empire Flyweight Champion, 1957. *Born* 12.02.33. *From* Plean. *Deceased* 1991. *Pro Career* 1955-1960 (25 contests, won 17, lost 8).

Paul Jones Commonwealth Middleweight Champion, 1998-1999. *Born* 19.11.66. *From* Sheffield. *Pro Career* 1986-2002 (44 contests, won 31, drew 1, lost 12).

Peter Kane Undefeated World Flyweight Champion, 1938-1939. European Bantamweight Champion, 1947-1948. *Born* 28.04.18. *From* Golborne. *Birthname* Peter Cain. *Deceased* 1991. *Pro Career* 1934-1948 (102 contests, won 92, drew 2, lost 7, no contest 1).

Mark Kaylor British and Commonwealth Middleweight Champion, 1983-1984. *Born* 11.05.61. *From* West Ham. *Pro Career* 1980-1991 (48 contests, won 40, drew 1, lost 7).

Peter Keenan British Bantamweight Champion, 1951-1953 and 1954-1959. British Empire Bantamweight Champion, 1955-1959. European Bantamweight Champion, 1951-1952 and 1953. *Born* 08.08.28. *From* Glasgow. *Deceased* 2000. *Pro Career* 1948-1959 (66 contests, won 54, drew 1, lost 11).

Billy Spider Kelly British Featherweight Champion, 1955-1956. British Empire Featherweight Championship Claimant, 1954. British Empire Featherweight Champion, 1954-1955. *Born* 21.04.32. *From* Londonderry. *Pro Career* 1950-1962 (83 contests, won 56, drew 4, lost 23).

Joe Kelly British Bantamweight Champion, 1992. *Born* 18.05.64. *From* Glasgow. *Pro Career* 1985-1992 (27 contests, won 18, drew 2, lost 7).

John Kelly British and European Bantamweight Champion, 1953-1954. *Born* 17.01.32. *From* Belfast. *Pro Career* 1951-1957 (28 contests, won 24, lost 4).

Johnny King British Bantamweight Champion, 1932-1934 and 1935-1947. British Empire Bantamweight Championship Claimant, 1932-1934. *Born* 08.01.12. *From* Manchester. *Deceased* 1963. *Pro Career* 1926-1947 (222 contests, won 158, drew 15, lost 48, no contest 1).

Keith Knox British and Commonwealth Flyweight Champion, 1999. *Born* 20.06.67. *From* Bonnyrigg. *Pro Career* 1994-2001 (23 contests, won 13, drew 2, lost 8).

Kirkland Laing British Welterweight Champion, 1987-1991. European Welterweight Champion, 1990. *Born* 20.06.54, Jamaica. *From* Nottingham. *Pro Career* 1975-1994 (56 contests, won 43, drew 1, lost 12).

Tony Laing Undefeated British L. Welterweight Champion, 1986. Commonwealth L. Welterweight Champion, 1987-1988. *Born* 22.09.57. *From* Nottingham. *Pro Career* 1977-1988 (18 contests, won 13, drew 1, lost 4).

Davy Larmour British Bantamweight Champion, 1983. *Born* 02.04.52. *From* Belfast. *Pro Career* 1977-1983 (18 contests, won 11, lost 7).

Mick Leahy British Middleweight Champion, 1963-1964. *Born* Cork, 12.03.35. *From* Coventry. *Pro Career* 1956-1965 (72 contests, won 46, drew 7, lost 19).

Ady Lewis Undefeated British and Commonwealth Flyweight Champion, 1997-1998. British and Commonwealth Bantamweight Champion, 2000. *Born* 31.05.75. *From* Bury. *Pro Career* 1994-2001 (25 contests, won 19, drew 1, lost 5).

Stewart Lithgo Commonwealth Cruiserweight Champion, 1984. *Born* 02.06.57. *From* West Hartlepool. *Pro Career* 1977-1987 (30 contests, won 16, drew 2, lost 12).

Paul Lloyd British Bantamweight Champion, 1997-1999. Undefeated Commonwealth Bantamweight Champion, 1996-2000. Undefeated European Bantamweight Champion, 1998-1999. *Born* 07.12.68. *From* Ellesmere Port. *Pro Career* 1992-2000 (27 contests, won 20, lost 7).

Brian London British and British Empire Heavyweight Champion, 1958-1959. *Born* 19.06.34. *From* Blackpool. *Birthname* Brian Harper. *Pro Career* 1955-1970 (58 contests, won 37, drew 1, lost 20).

Jack London British Heavyweight Champion, 1944-1945. British Empire Heavyweight Championship Claimant, 1944-1945. *Born* 23.06.13. *From* West Hartlepool. *Birthname* Jack Harper. *Deceased* 1964. *Pro Career* 1931-1949 (141 contests, won 95, drew 5, lost 39, no contests 2).

Eamonn Loughran Undefeated Commonwealth Welterweight Champion, 1992-1993. WBO Welterweight Champion, 1993-1996. *Born* 05.06.70. *Fron* Ballymena. *Pro Career* 1987-1996 (30 contests, won 26, drew 1, lost 2, no contest 1).

Joe Lucy British Lightweight Champion, 1953-1955 and 1956-1957. *Born* 09.02.30. *From* Mile End. *Deceased* 1991. *Pro Career* 1950-1957 (37 contests, won 27, lost 10).

Kevin Lueshing British Welterweight Champion, 1996-1997. *Born* 17.04.1968. *From* Beckenham. *Pro Career* 1991-1999 (25 contests, won 21, lost 4).

Danny McAlinden British and Commonwealth Heavyweight Champion, 1972-1975. *Born* Newry, 01.06.47. *From* Coventry. *Pro Career* 1969-1981 (45 contests, won 31, drew 2, lost 12).

Les McAteer British and British Empire Middleweight Champion, 1969-1970. *Born* 19.08.45. *From* Birkenhead. *Pro Career* 1965-1979 (39 contests, won 27, drew 2, lost 10).

Pat McAteer Undefeated British Middleweight Champion, 1955-1958. British Empire Middleweight Champion, 1955-1958. *Born* 17.03.32. *From* Birkenhead. *Pro Career* 1952-1958 (57 contests, won 49, drew 2, lost 6).

Dave McAuley Undefeated British Flyweight Champion, 1986-1988. World Flyweight Champion (IBF version), 1989-1992. *Born* 15.06.61. *From* Larne. *Pro Career* 1983-1992 (23 contests, won 18, drew 2, lost 3).

Sammy McCarthy British Featherweight Champion, 1954-1955. *Born* 05.11.31. *From* Stepney. *Pro Career* 1951-1957 (53 contests, won 44, drew 1, lost 8).

Steve McCarthy British L. Heavyweight Champion, 1990-1991. *Born* 30.07.62. *From* Southampton. *Pro Career* 1987-1994 (17 contests, won 12, drew 1, lost 4).

John McCluskey Undefeated British Flyweight Champion, 1967-1977. Commonwealth Flyweight Champion, 1970-1971. *Born* 23.01.44. *From* Hamilton. *Pro Career* 1965-1975 (38 contests, won 23, lost 15).

John Cowboy McCormack British Middleweight Champion, 1959. European Middleweight Champion, 1961-1962. *Born* 09.01.35. *From* Maryhill. *Pro Career* 1957-1966 (45 contests, won 38, lost 7).

Young John McCormack British L. Heavyweight Champion, 1967-1969. *Born* Dublin, 11.12.44. *From* Brixton. *Pro Career* 1963-1970 (42 contests, won 33, drew 1, lost 8).

Pat McCormack British L. Welterweight Champion, 1974. *Born* Dublin, 28.04.46. *From* Brixton. *Pro Career* 1968-1975 (49 contests, won 30, drew 1, lost 18).

Robert McCracken Undefeated British L. Middleweight Champion, 1994-1995. Commonwealth Middleweight Champion, 1995-1997. *Born* 31.05.68. *From* Birmingham. *Pro Career* 1991-2001 (35 contests, won 33, lost 2).

Geoff McCreesh Undefeated British Welterweight Champion, 1997-1999. *Born* 12.06.70. *From* Bracknell. *Pro Career* 1994-2001 (30 contests, won 23, lost 7).

Glenn McCrory Undefeated British Cruiserweight Champion, 1988. Undefeated Commonwealth Cruiserweight Champion, 1987-1989. World Cruiserweight Champion (IBF version), 1989-1990. *Born* 23.09.64. *From* Annfield Plain. *Pro Career* 1984-1993 (39 contests, won 30, drew 1, lost 8).

Jim McDonnell Undefeated European Featherweight Champion, 1985-1987. *Born* 12.09.60. *From* Camden Town. *Pro Career* 1983-1998 (30 contests, won 26, lost 4).

Tommy McGovern British Lightweight Champion, 1951-1952. *Born* 05.02.24. *From* Bermondsey. *Deceased* 1989. *Pro Career* 1947-1953 (66 contests, won 45, drew 4, lost 17).

Walter McGowan Undefeated British Flyweight Champion, 1963-1966. Undefeated British Empire Flyweight Champion, 1963-1969. World Flyweight Champion (WBC version), 1966. British and British Empire Bantamweight Champion, 1966-1968. *Born* 13.10.42. *From* Hamilton. *Pro Career* 1961-1969 (40 contests, won 32, drew 1, lost 7).

Barry McGuigan Undefeated British Featherweight Champion, 1983-1986. Undefeated European Featherweight Champion, 1983-1985. World Featherweight Champion (WBA version), 1985-1986. *Born* 28.02.61. *From* Clones. *Pro Career* 1981-1989 (35 contests, won 32, lost 3).

Clinton McKenzie British L. Welterweight Champion, 1978-1979 and 1979-1984. Undefeated British L. Welterweight Champion, 1989. European L. Welterweight Champion, 1981-1982. *Born* 15.09.55. *From* Croydon. *Pro Career* 1976-1989 (50 contests, won 36, lost 14).

Duke McKenzie Undefeated British Flyweight Champion, 1985-1986. Undefeated European Flyweight Champion, 1986-1988. World Flyweight Champion (IBF version), 1988-1989. World Bantamweight Champion (WBO version), 1991-1992. World S. Bantamweight Champion (WBO version), 1992-1993. Undefeated British Featherweight Champion, 1993-1994. *Born* 05.05.63. *From* Croydon. *Pro Career* 1982-1998 (46 contests, won 39, lost 7).

Tony McKenzie British L. Welterweight Champion, 1986-1987. *Born* 04.03.63. *From* Leicester. *Pro Career* 1983-1993 (34 contests, won 26, drew 1, lost 7).

Ian McLeod Undefeated Commonwealth S. Featherweight Champion, 2000. *Born* 11.06.69. *From* Kilmarnock. *Pro Career* 1992-2000 (14 contests, won 11, drew 1, lost 2).

Colin McMillan Undefeated British Featherweight Champion, 1991-1992. British Featherweight Champion, 1996-1997. Undefeated Commonwealth Featherweight Champion, 1992. World Featherweight Champion (WBO version), 1992. *Born* 12.02.66. *From* Barking. *Pro Career* 1988-1997 (35 contests, won 31, lost 4).

Noel Magee Commonwealth L. Heavyweight Champion, 1995. *Born* 16.12.65. *From* Belfast. *Pro Career* 1985-1997 (37 contests, won 27, drew 2, lost 8).

Charlie Magri Undefeated British Flyweight Champion, 1977-1981. Undefeated European Flyweight Champion, 1979-1983 and 1984-1985. European Flyweight Champion, 1985-1986. World Flyweight Champion (WBC version), 1983. *Born* Tunisia, 20.07.56. *From* Stepney. *Pro Career* 1977-1986 (35 contests, won 30, lost 5).

Paddy Maguire British Bantamweight Champion, 1975-1977. *Born* 26.09.48. *From* Belfast. *Pro Career* 1969-1977 (35 contests, won 26, drew 1, lost 8).

Terry Marsh Undefeated British L. Welterweight Champion, 1984-1986. European L. Welterweight Champion, 1985-1986. Undefeated World L. Welterweight Champion (IBF version), 1987. *Born* 07.02.58. *From* Basildon. *Pro Career* 1981-1987 (27 contests, won 26, drew 1).

Gary Mason British Heavyweight Champion, 1989-1991. *Born* Jamaica, 15.12.62. *From* Wandsworth. *Pro Career* 1984-1991 (36 contests, won 35, lost 1).

Jason Matthews Undefeated Commonwealth Middleweight Champion, 1999. WBO Middleweight Champion, 1999. *Born* 20.07.70. *From* Hackney. *Pro Career* 1995-1999 (23 contests, won 21, lost 2).

Neville Meade British Heavyweight Champion, 1981-1983. *Born* Jamaica, 12.09.48. *From* Swansea. *Pro Career* 1974-1983 (34 contests, won 20, drew 1, lost 13).

Freddie Mills Undefeated British L. Heavyweight Champion, 1942-1950. British Empire L. Heavyweight Championship Claimant, 1942-1950. Undefeated European L. Heavyweight Champion, 1947-1950. World L. Heavyweight Champion (GB version), 1942-1946. World L. Heavyweight Champion, 1948-1950. *Born* 26.06.19. *From* Bournemouth. *Deceased* 1965. *Pro Career* 1936-1950 (101 contests, won 77, drew 6, lost 18).

Alan Minter British Middleweight Champion, 1975-1977. Undefeated British Middleweight Champion, 1977-1978. European Middleweight Champion, 1977. Undefeated European Middleweight Champion, 1978-1979. World Middleweight Champion, 1980. *Born* 17.08.51. *From* Crawley. *Pro Career* 1972-1981 (49 contests, won 39, lost 9, no contest 1).

Sylvester Mittee British Welterweight Champion, 1985. Commonwealth Welterweight Champion, 1984-1985. *Born* St Lucia, 29.10.56. *From* Bethnal Green. *Pro Career* 1977-1988 (33 contests, won 28, lost 5).

Tommy Molloy British Welterweight Champion, 1958-1960. *Born* 02.02.34. *From* Birkenhead. *Pro Career* 1955-1963 (43 contests, won 34, drew 2, lost 6, no contest 1).

Rinty Monaghan Undefeated British and World Flyweight Champion, 1948-1950. British Empire Flyweight Championship Claimant, 1948-1950. Undefeated European Flyweight Champion, 1949-1950. World Flyweight Champion (NBA version), 1947-1948. *Born* 21.08.20. *From* Belfast. *Birthname* John Monaghan. *Deceased* 1984. *Pro Career* 1934-1949 (66 contests, won 51, drew 6, lost 9).

Des Morrison British L. Welterweight Champion, 1973-1974. *Born* Jamaica, 01.02.50. *From* Bedford. *Pro Career* 1970-1982 (50 contests, won 36, drew 2, lost 12).

Patrick Mullings British S. Bantamweight Champion, 1999 and 2001. Commonwealth Featherweight Champion, 1999-2000. *Born* 19.10.70. *From* Harlesden. *Pro Career* 1994-2001 (30 contests, won 24, lost 6).

Sean Murphy British Featherweight Champion, 1990-1991 and 1993. *Born* 01.12.64. *From* St Albans. *Pro Career* 1986-1994 (27 contests, won 22, lost 5).

Charlie Nash Undefeated British Lightweight Champion, 1978-1979. Undefeated European Lightweight Champion, 1979-1980. European Lightweight Champion, 1980-1981. *Born* 10.05.51. *From* Derry. *Pro Career* 1975-1983 (30 contests, won 25, lost 5).

Dave Needham British Bantamweight Champion, 1974-1975. British Featherweight Champion, 1978-1979. *Born* 15.08.51. *From* Nottingham. *Pro Career* 1971-1980 (39 contests, won 30, drew 1, lost 8).

Bobby Neill British Featherweight Champion, 1959-1960. *Born* 10.10.33. *From* Edinburgh. *Pro Career* 1955-1960 (35 contests, won 28, lost 7).

Horace Notice Undefeated British and Commonwealth Heavyweight Champion, 1986-1988. *Born* 07.08.57. *From* Birmingham. *Pro Career* 1983-1988 (16 contests, won 16).

John O'Brien British Empire Featherweight Champion, 1967. *Born* 20.02.37. *From* Glasgow. *Deceased* 1979. *Pro Career* 1956-1971 (47 contests, won 30, lost 17).

Chris Okoh Commonwealth Cruiserweight Champion, 1995-1997. *Born* 18.04.69. *From* Croydon. *Pro Career* 1993-1999 (16 contests, won 14, lost 2).

Spencer Oliver European S. Bantamweight Champion, 1997-1998. *Born* 27.03.75. *From* Barnet. *Pro Career* 1995-1998 (15 contests, won 14, lost 1).

Danny O'Sullivan British Bantamweight Champion, 1949-1951. *Born* 06.01.23. *From* Finsbury Park. *Deceased* 1990. *Pro Career* 1947-1951 (43 contests, won 33, drew 1, lost 9).

Johnny Owen Undefeated British Bantamweight Champion, 1977-1980. Undefeated Commonwealth Bantamweight Champion, 1978-1980. Undefeated European Bantamweight Champion, 1980. *Born* 07.01.56. *From* Merthyr. *Deceased* 1980. *Pro Career* 1976-1980 (28 contests, won 25, drew 1, lost 2).

James Oyebola British Heavyweight Champion, 1994-1995. *Born* Nigeria 10.06.61. *From* Paddington. *Pro Career* 1987-1996 (23 contests, won 18, drew 1, lost 4).

Jackie Paterson British Flyweight Champion, 1939-1948. British Empire

Flyweight Championship Claimant, 1940-1948. World Flyweight Champion, 1943-1947. World Flyweight Champion (GB/NY version), 1947-1948. British Bantamweight Champion, 1947-1949. British Empire Bantamweight Championship Claimant, 1945-1949. European Bantamweight Champion, 1946. *Born* 05.09.20. *From* Springfield. *Deceased* 1966. *Pro Career* 1938-1950 (92 contests, won 64, drew 3, lost 25).

Bernard Paul Commonwealth L. Welterweight Champion, 1997-1999. *Born* 22.20.65. *From* Tottenham. *Pro Career* 1991-2000 (35 contests, won 21, drew 4, lost 10).

Larry Paul British L. Middleweight Champion, 1973-1974. *Born* 19.04.52. *From* Wolverhampton. *Pro Career* 1973-1978 (40 contests, won 30, drew 1, lost 9).

David Pearce Undefeated British Heavyweight Champion, 1983-1985. *Born* 08.05.59. *From* Newport. *Deceased* 2000. *Pro Career* 1978-1984 (21 contests, won 17, drew 1, lost 3).

Kostas Petrou British Welterweight Champion, 1985. *Born* 17.04.59. *From* Birmingham. *Pro Career* 1981-1988 (37 contests, won 30, lost 7).

Tiger Al Phillips European Featherweight Champion, 1947. British Empire Featherweight Championship Claimant, 1947. *Born* 25.01.20. *From* Aldgate. *Deceased* 1999. *Pro Career* 1938-1951 (89 contests, won 72, drew 3, lost 14).

Nicky Piper Undefeated Commonwealth L. Heavyweight Champion, 1995-1997. *Born* 05.05.66. *From* Cardiff. *Pro Career* 1989-1997 (33 contests, won 26, drew 2, lost 5).

Dennis Powell British L. Heavyweight Champion, 1953. *Born* 12.12.24. *From* Four Crosses. *Deceased* 1993. *Pro Career* 1947-1954 (68 contests, won 42, drew 4, lost 22).

Colin Power Undefeated British L. Welterweight Champion, 1977-1978. British L. Welterweight Champion, 1979. European L. Welterweight Champion, 1978. *Born* 02.02.56. *From* Paddington. *Pro Career* 1975-1983 (34 contests, won 28, drew 1, lost 5).

Kevin Pritchard British S. Featherweight Champion, 1990-1991. *Born* 26.09.61. *From* Liverpool. *Pro Career* 1981-1991 (48 contests, won 23, drew 3, lost 22).

Johnny Pritchett Undefeated British Middleweight Champion, 1965-1969. Undefeated British Empire Middleweight Champion, 1967-1969. *Born* 15.02.43. *From* Bingham. *Pro Career* 1963-1969 (34 contests, won 32, drew 1, lost 1).

Chris Pyatt Undefeated British L. Middleweight Champion, 1986. European L. Middleweight Champion, 1986-1987. Undefeated Commonwealth L. Middleweight Champion, 1991-1992. Commonwealth L. Middleweight Champion, 1995-1996. World Middleweight Champion (WBO version), 1993-1994. *Born* 03.07.63. *From* Leicester. *Pro Career* 1983-1997 (51 contests, won 46, lost 5).

Des Rea British L. Welterweight Champion, 1968-1969. *Born* 09.01.44. *From* Belfast. *Pro Career* 1964-1974 (69 contests, won 28, drew 5, lost 36).

Mark Reefer Undefeated Commonwealth S. Featherweight Champion, 1989-1990. *Born* 16.03.64. *Birthname* Mark Thompson. *From* Dagenham. *Pro Career* 1983-1992 (32 contests, won 23, drew 1, lost 8).

Sam Reeson Undefeated British Cruiserweight Champion, 1985-1986. Undefeated European Cruiserweight Champion, 1987-1988. *Born* 05.01.63. *From* Battersea. *Pro Career* 1983-1989 (26 contests, won 24, lost 2).

Robbie Regan Undefeated World Bantamweight Champion (WBO version), 1996-1997. British Flyweight Champion, 1991. Undefeated British Flyweight Champion, 1991-1992. Undefeated European Flyweight Champion, 1992-1993 and 1994-1995. *Born* 30.08.68. *From* Cefn Forest. *Pro Career* 1989-1996 (22 contests, won 17, drew 3, lost 2).

Willie Reilly Undefeated British Lightweight Champion, 1972. *Born* 25.03.47. *From* Glasgow. *Pro Career* 1968-1972 (23 contests, won 13, drew 3, lost 7).

Jimmy Revie British Featherweight Champion, 1969-1971. *Born* 08.07.47. *From* Stockwell. *Pro Career* 1966-1976 (48 contests, won 38, drew 1, lost 9).

Henry Rhiney British Welterweight Champion, 1976-1979. European Welterweight Champion, 1978-1979. *Born* Jamaica, 28.11.51. *From* Luton. *Pro Career* 1973-1980 (57 contests, won 32, drew 6, lost 19).

Alan Richardson British Featherweight Champion, 1977-1978. *Born* 04.11.48. *From* Fitzwilliam. *Pro Career* 1971-1978 (27 contests, won 17, drew 1, lost 9).

Dick Richardson European Heavyweight Champion, 1960-1962. *Born* 01.06.34. *From* Newport. *Deceased* 1999. *Pro Career* 1954-1963 (47 contests, won 31, drew 2, lost 14).

Steve Robinson European Featherweight Champion, 1999-2000. WBO Featherweight Champion, 1993-1995. *Born* 13.12.68. *From* Cardiff. *Pro Career* 1989-2002 (51 contests, won 32, drew 2, lost 17).

Ernie Roderick British Welterweight Champion, 1939-1948. European Welterweight Champion, 1946-1947. British Middleweight Champion, 1945-1946. *Born* 25.01.14. *From* Liverpool. *Deceased* 1986. *Pro Career* 1931-1950 (142 contests, won 114, drew 4, lost 24).

Prince Rodney Undefeated British L. Middleweight Champion, 1983-1984. British L. Middleweight Champion, 1985-1986. *Born* 31.10.58. *From* Huddersfield. *Pro Career* 1977-1990 (41 contests, won 31, drew 1, lost 9).

Stan Rowan Undefeated British Bantamweight Champion, 1949. British Empire Bantamweight Championship Claimant, 1949. *Born* 06.09.24. *From* Liverpool. *Deceased* 1997. *Pro Career* 1942-1953 (67 contests, won 46, drew 5, lost 16).

Mark Rowe British and Commonwealth Middleweight Champion, 1970. *Born* 12.07.47. *Born* 12.07.47. *From* Camberwell. *Pro Career* 1966-1973 (47 contests, won 38, drew 1, lost 8).

Alan Rudkin British Bantamweight Champion, 1965-1966. Undefeated British Bantamweight Champion, 1968-1972. British Empire Bantamweight Champion, 1965-1966 and 1968-1969. European Bantamweight Champion, 1971. Undefeated Commonwealth Bantamweight Champion, 1970-1972. *Born* 18.11.41. *From* Liverpool. *Pro Career* 1962-1972 (50 contests, won 42, lost 8).

Hugh Russell Undefeated British Flyweight Champion, 1984-1985. British Bantamweight Champion, 1983. *Born* 15.12.59. *From* Belfast. *Pro Career* 1981-1985 (19 contests, won 17, lost 2).

Paul Ryan British and Commonwealth L. Welterweight Champion, 1995-1996. *Born* 02.02.65. *From* Hackney. *Pro Career* 1991-1997 (28 contests, won 25, lost 3).

Billy Schwer British Lightweight Champion, 1992-1993. Undefeated British Lightweight Champion, 1993-1995. Commonwealth Lightweight Champion, 1992-1993 and 1993-1995. Undefeated European Lightweight Champion, 1997-1999. *Born* 12.04.69. *From* Luton. *Pro Career* 1990-2001 (45 contests, won 39, lost 6).

Tony Sibson British Middleweight Champion, 1979. Undefeated British Middleweight Champion, 1984 and 1987-1988. Undefeated Commonwealth Middleweight Champion, 1980-1983 and 1984-1988. Undefeated European Middleweight Champion, 1980-1982. European Middleweight Champion, 1984-1985. *Born* 09.04.58. *From* Leicester. *Pro Career* 1976-1988 (63 contests, won 55, drew 1, lost 7).

Steve Sims Undefeated British Featherweight Champion, 1982-1983. *Born* 10.10.58. *From* Newport. *Pro Career* 1977-1987 (29 contests, won 14, drew 1, lost 14).

Joey Singleton British L. Welterweight Champion, 1974-1976. *Born* 06.06.51. *From* Kirkby. *Pro Career* 1973-1982 (40 contests, won 27, drew 2, lost 11).

Kelvin Smart British Flyweight Champion, 1982-1984. *Born* 18.12.60. *From* Caerphilly. *Pro Career* 1979-1987 (29 contests, won 17, drew 2, lost 10).

Roy Smith British Cruiserweight Champion, 1987. *Born* 31.08.61. *From* Nottingham. *Pro Career* 1985-1991 (26 contests, won 18, lost 8).

Vernon Sollas British Featherweight Champion, 1975-1977. *Born* 14.08.54. *From* Edinburgh. *Pro Career* 1973-1977 (33 contests, won 25, drew 1, lost 7).

Terry Spinks British Featherweight Champion, 1960-1961. *Born* 28.02.38. *From* Canning Town. *Pro Career* 1957-1962 (49 contests, won 41, drew 1, lost 7).

Bunny Sterling British Middleweight Champion, 1970-1974. Undefeated British Middleweight Champion, 1975. Commonwealth Middleweight Champion, 1970-1972. European Middleweight Champion, 1976. *Born* Jamaica, 04.04.48. *From* Finsbury Park. *Pro Career* 1966-1977 (57 contests, won 35, drew 4, lost 18).

John H. Stracey Undefeated British Welterweight Champion, 1973-1975. Undefeated European Welterweight Champion, 1974-1975. World Welterweight Champion (WBC version), 1975-1976. *Born* 22.09.50. *From* Bethnal Green. *Pro Career* 1969-1978 (51 contests, won 45, drew 1, lost 5).

Andy Straughn British Cruiserweight Champion, 1986-1987 and 1988-1989. *Born* Barbados, 25.12.59. *From* Hitchin. *Pro Career* 1982-1990 (27 contests, won 18, drew 2, lost 7).

Gary Stretch British L. Middleweight Champion, 1988-1990. *Born* 04.11.65. *From* St Helens. *Pro Career* 1985-1993 (25 contests, won 23, lost 2).

Johnny Sullivan British Empire Middleweight Championship Claimant, 1954. British and British Empire Middleweight Champion, 1954-1955. *Born* 19.12.32. *From* Preston. *Birthname* John Hallmark. *Pro Career* 1948-1960 (97 contests, won 68, drew 3, lost 26).

Wally Swift British Welterweight Champion, 1960. British Middleweight Champion, 1964-1965. *Born* 10.08.36. *From* Nottingham. *Pro Career* 1957-1969 (88 contests, won 68, drew 3, lost 17).

Wally Swift Jnr British L. Middleweight Champion, 1991-1992. *Born* 17.02.66. *From* Birmingham. *Pro Career* 1985-1994 (38 contests, won 26, drew 1, lost 11).

Nel Tarleton British Featherweight Champion, 1931-1932 and 1934-1936. Undefeated British Featherweight Champion, 1940-1947. Undefeated British Empire Featherweight Championship Claimant, 1940-1947. *Born* 14.01.06. *From* Liverpool. *Deceased* 1956. *Pro Career* 1926-1945 (144 contests, won 116, drew 8, lost 20).

Wally Thom British Welterweight Champion, 1951-1952 and 1953-1956. British Empire Welterweight Championship Claimant, 1951-1952. European Welterweight Champion, 1954-1955. *Born* 14.06.26. *From* Birkenhead. *Deceased* 1980. *Pro Career* 1949-1956 (54 contests, won 42, drew 1, lost 11).

Eddie Thomas British Welterweight Champion, 1949-1951. European Welterweight Champion, 1951. British Empire Welterweight Championship Claimant, 1951. *Born* 27.07.26. *From* Merthyr. *Deceased* 1997. *Pro Career* 1946-1954 (48 contests, won 40, drew 2, lost 6).

Pat Thomas British Welterweight Champion, 1975-1976. British L. Middleweight Champion, 1979-1981. *Born* St Kitts, 05.05.50. *From* Cardiff. *Pro Career* 1970-1984 (57 contests, won 35, drew 3, lost 18, no contest 1).

Billy Thompson British Lightweight Champion, 1947-1951. European Lightweight Champion, 1948-1949. *Born* 20.12.25. *From* Hickleton Main. *Pro Career* 1945-1953 (63 contests, won 46, drew 4, lost 13).

Andy Till British L. Middleweight Champion, 1992-1994. *Born* 22.08.63. *From* Northolt. *Pro Career* 1986-1995 (24 contests, won 19, lost 5).

Dick Turpin British Middleweight Champion, 1948-1950. British Empire Middleweight Championship Claimant, 1948-1949. *Born* 26.11.20. *From* Leamington Spa. *Deceased* 1990. *Pro Career* 1937-1950 (103 contests, won 76, drew 6, lost 20, no contest 1).

Randy Turpin Undefeated British Middleweight Champion, 1950-1954. British Empire Middleweight Championship Claimant, 1952-1954. European Middleweight Champion, 1951-1954. World Middleweight Champion, 1951. World Middleweight Champion (EBU version), 1953. Undefeated British L. Heavyweight Champion, 1952, 1955, and 1956-1958. British Empire L. Heavyweight Championship Claimant, 1952-1954. Undefeated British Empire L. Heavyweight Champion, 1954-1955. *Born* 07.06.28. *From* Leamington Spa. *Deceased* 1966. *Pro Career* 1946-1958 (73 contests, won 64, drew 1, lost 8).

Keith Wallace Undefeated Commonwealth Flyweight Champion, 1983-1984. *Born* 29.03.61. *From* Liverpool. *Deceased* 2000. *Pro Career* 1982-1990 (25 contests, won 20, lost 5).

Peter Waterman Undefeated British Welterweight Champion, 1956-1958.

197

Undefeated European Welterweight Champion, 1958. *Born* 08.12.34. *From* Clapham. *Deceased* 1986. *Pro Career* 1952-1958 (46 contests, won 41, drew 2, lost 3).

Michael Watson Undefeated Commonwealth Middleweight Champion, 1989-1991. *Born* 15.03.65. *From* Islington. *Pro Career* 1984-1991 (30 contests, won 25, drew 1, lost 4).

Jim Watt British Lightweight Champion, 1972-1973. Undefeated British Lightweight Champion, 1975-1977. Undefeated European Lightweight Champion, 1977-1979. World Lightweight Champion (WBC version), 1979-1981. *Born* 18.07.48. *From* Glasgow. *Pro Career* 1968-1981 (46 contests, won 38, lost 8).

Paul Weir Undefeated WBO M. Flyweight Champion, 1993-1994. WBO L. Flyweight Champion, 1994-1995. *Born* 16.09.67. *From* Irvine. *Pro Career* 1992-2000 (20 contests, won 14, lost 6).

Scott Welch Undefeated British Heavyweight Champion, 1995-1996. Commonwealth Heavyweight Champion, 1995-1997. *Born* 21.04.1968. *From* Shoreham. *Pro Career* 1992-1999 (26 contests, won 22, lost 4).

Richie Wenton Undefeated British S. Bantamweight Champion, 1994-1996. *Born* 28.10.67. *From* Liverpool. *Pro Career* 1988-2001 (30 contests, won 24, lost 6).

Henry Wharton Undefeated British S. Middleweight Champion, 1992-1993. Undefeated Commonwealth Champion, 1991-1997. Undefeated European S. Middleweight Champion, 1995-1996. *Born* 23.11.1967. *From* York. *Pro Career* 1989-1998 (31 contests, won 27, drew 1, lost 3).

Derek Williams Commonwealth Heavyweight Champion, 1988-1992. European Heavyweight Champion, 1989-1992. *Born* 11.03.65. *From* Peckham. *Pro Career* 1984-1999 (35 contests, won 22, lost 13).

Johnny Williams British Heavyweight Champion, 1952-1953. British Empire Heavyweight Championship Claimant, 1952-1953. *Born* 25.12.26. *From* Rugby. *Pro Career* 1946-1956 (75 contests, won 60, drew 4, lost 11).

Tony Willis British Lightweight Champion, 1985-1987. *Born* 17.06.60. *From* Liverpool. *Pro Career* 1981-1989 (29 contests, won 25, lost 4).

Nick Wilshire Commonwealth L. Middleweight Champion, 1985-1987. *Born* 03.11.61. *From* Bristol. *Pro Career* 1981-1987 (40 contests, won 36, lost 4).

Tony Wilson British L. Heavyweight Champion, 1987-1989. *Born* 25.04.64. *From* Wolverhampton. *Pro Career* 1985-1993 (29 contests, won 20, drew 1, lost 8).

Howard Winstone Undefeated British Featherweight Champion, 1961-1969. European Featherweight Champion, 1963-1967. World Featherweight Champion (WBC version), 1968. *Born* 15.04.39. *From* Merthyr. *Deceased* 2000. *Pro Career* 1959-1968 (67 contests, won 61, lost 6).

Tim Wood British L. Heavyweight Champion, 1976-1977. *Born* 10.08.51. *From* Leicester. *Pro Career* 1972-1979 (31 contests, won 19, drew 1, lost 11).

Bruce Woodcock British Heavyweight Champion, 1945-1950. British Empire Heavyweight Championship Claimant, 1945-1950. European Heavyweight Champion, 1946-1949. *Born* 18.01.21. *From* Doncaster. *Deceased* 1997. *Pro Career* 1942-1950 (39 contests, won 35, lost 4).

Richie Woodhall WBC S. Middleweight Champion, 1998-1999. Commonwealth Middleweight Champion, 1992-1995. Undefeated European Middleweight Champion, 1995-1996. *Born* 17.04.68. *From* Telford. *Pro Career* 1990-2000 (29 contests, won 26, lost 3).

Len Harvey, seen on one knee, regained the British heavyweight title when Eddie Phillips was disqualified in round four of their contest at Harringay Arena on 1 December 1938

Commonwealth Title Bouts During 2002-2003

All of last season's title bouts are shown in date order within their weight divisions and give the contestants respective weights, along with the scorecard if going to a decision. Every contest involving a British fighter is summarised briefly and all British officials are named.

Flyweight

22 February 2003   Dale Robinson 7.12¾ (England) W PTS 12 Spencer Matsangura 7.13¼ (Zimbabwe), The Leisure Centre, Huddersfield. Referee: Paul Thomas 118-111. When Jason Booth (England) relinquished the title in February 2003 in order to prepare for an IBO championship fight mooted for April, Robinson got his chance to land a title, but had to go the full route. The extremely competitive Matsangura proved a tough customer, surviving two knockdowns, but despite marking Robinson up was well behind at the finish.

10 May 2003   Dale Robinson 8.0 (England) W PTS 12 Zolile Mbitye 7.13¾ (South Africa), The Leisure Centre, Huddersfield. Referee: Howard Foster 115-113. This was Robinson's toughest test thus far, a messy affair in which the experienced South African brawled and mauled his way through the fight and generally upset the champion's rhythm. However, getting his act together over the last third, Robinson took control with straighter punches and just about justified the decision over Mbitye, who had a point deducted for holding in round four.

Bantamweight

27 July 2002   Nicky Booth 8.5 (England) W CO 5 Moses Kinyua 8.4½ (Kenya), The Harvey Hadden Leisure Centre, Nottingham. Referee: Marcus McDonnell. Scorning his defence, Booth quickly realised that the tiny Kenyan couldn't hurt him and stalked his man continuously, throwing punches from both hands. Kinyua, who was a neat little boxer but lacked power, finally succumbed from a burst of combination punches in the fifth round and was counted out with 2.34 on the clock

21 September 2002   Nicky Booth 8.4½ (England) L PTS 12 Steve Molitor 8.5½ (Canada), The International Centre, Brentwood. Referee: Larry O'Connell 112-116. Booth, put down in the first, certainly met his match in the Canadian, who generally outboxed him throughout and was well worth the decision, despite the scorecard appearing to make it closer that it actually was. Cut under the left eye in the fifth, the champion, who never gave up trying, survived the fight mainly due to Molitor's lack of power.

S. Bantamweight

8 February 2003   Esham Pickering 8.9½ (England) W CO 5 Duncan Karanja 8.9½ (Kenya), The Fountain Leisure Centre, Brentford, London. Referee: Dave Parris. In a match made for the vacant title, Michael Alldis (England) retiring in December 2002, the ungainly Kenyan was no match for Pickering, who won as he pleased. Knocked down in the third, it seemed that it would be only a matter of time before Karanja was put out of his misery, despite Pickering being a non puncher, and he was counted out at 0.40 of the fifth, having been put down by a cracking right hand.

Featherweight

8 February 2003   Nicky Cook 9.0 (England) W RSC 12 Mishek Kondwani 8.12¼ (Zimbabwe), The Fountain Leisure Centre, Brentford, London.   Following the announcement that Scott Harrison (Scotland) had relinquished the title after becoming the WBO champion on 19 October 2002, Cook, who seemed very big for a featherweight, was matched against Kondwani and came through his toughest test to date successfully. Cut under the left eye in the 10th, Cook started to look for an inside-the-distance win in earnest and was punching the Zimbabwean without reply when the referee, Mickey Vann, called a halt at 1.24 of the 12th and final round.

31 May 2003   Nicky Cook 9.0 (England) W CO 2 David Kiilu 9.0 (Kenya), York Hall, Bethnal Green, London. Making his first defence, it appeared that Cook was in for a difficult night when he was cut under the right eye and generally outboxed by the smart Kenyan in the opening session. However, the champion made the body his target in the second, a decision that proved to be the right one, and a cluster of punches downstairs put Kiilu on the deck, where he was counted out by Mark Green on the 1.35 mark.

S. Featherweight

13 July 2002   Alex Moon 9.3¾ (England) L PTS 12 Dean Pithie 9.4 (England), The Skydome, Coventry. Referee: Larry O'Connell 114-116. Getting off to good start, Pithie answered some of the doubters as he took advantage of a one-paced Moon to dictate matters and put points in the bag. There was never much between them though, Moon starting to make up some leeway in the last quarter when working the challenger's body, but he had left it too late and the local man was good value for the win.

12 April 2003   Dean Pithie 9.4 (England) L CO 8 Craig Docherty 9.3½ (Scotland), York Hall, Bethnal Green, London. Although Pithie won most of the early rounds due to his better boxing, once Docherty had targeted the midsection towards the end of the sixth he began to have more success. Despite that, it was a surprise to most when Pithie, having taken a series of body shots, climaxed with a short left to the pit of the stomach, went down on one knee and was counted out by Richie Davies at 1.47 of round eight.

Lightweight

7 September 2002   David Burke 9.8 (England) W RSC 10 Gary Hibbert 9.8¼ (England), Everton Park Sports Centre, Liverpool. Burke was matched against Michael Muya (Kenya) for the vacant title after James Armah (Ghana), who was suffering from a stomach and kidney complaint, relinquished the belt a matter of days before meeting Burke on the understanding that he would be given a crack at the winner when fit again. Unfortunately, Muya couldn't get

visa clearance in time and Hibbert, who had been Burke's sparring partner in the days leading up to the Armah match, stepped into the breach. It wasn't a great arrangement, but Hibbert, who took two counts and was systematically outboxed, gave it his best shot before being rescued by the referee, Terry O'Connor, in the 10th when he was not hitting back following a knockdown. Burke automatically relinquished the title on becoming the WBU champion on 7 December 2002.

29 March 2003 Michael Muya 9.8$\frac{1}{2}$ (Kenya) w pts 12 Chaurembo Palasa 9.8$\frac{1}{2}$ (Tanzania), Nairobi, Kenya. Scorecards: 117-111, 116-112, 116-113.

L. Welterweight

8 July 2002 Junior Witter 9.13$\frac{3}{4}$ (England) W RSC 2 Laatekwei Hammond 10.0 (Ghana), Grosvenor House Hotel, Mayfair. Witter seemed a natural choice to contest the vacant title after Eamonn Magee (Ireland) had handed back the belt at the end of May 2002 to concentrate on a WBU challenge against Richard Hatton, and was matched against Hammond, who had given Bobby Vanzie all kinds of problems in a lightweight title bout in 2000. This time round, the Ghanaian was no match for the speedy Witter and was floored three times before being rescued by Richie Davies at 1.56 of the second round.

Welterweight

5 October 2002 James Hare 10.6$\frac{3}{4}$ (England) W RSC 8 Farai Musiiwa 10.6$\frac{1}{4}$ (Zimbabwe), The Leisure Centre, Huddersfield. Preferring to box his way in without taking risks, Hare was much too good for his challenger, whose greatest asset was his ungainliness. Knocked down in the fourth, despite being called a slip, Musiiwa came apart in the eighth and was put down twice and rescued by John Keane on the two-minute mark.

30 November 2002 James Hare 10.6 (England) W RSC 1 Earl Foskin 10.5$\frac{3}{4}$ (Jamaica), Everton Park Sports Centre, Liverpool. At the age of 35, Foskin was clearly not up to the job and quickly crumbled, being put down twice, once from a jab, and was rescued by the referee, Mickey Vann, with just 1.27 worth of activity on the clock.

22 February 2003 James Hare 10.6$\frac{1}{2}$ (England) W RSC 1 Frans Hantindi 10.6$\frac{3}{4}$ (Namibia), The Leisure Centre, Huddersfield. In yet another first-round finish for Hare in a Commonwealth title defence, the Namibian was on the floor three times before Marcus McDonnell stopped the bout at the 1.14 mark. The challenger towered over Hare, but was sluggish and easy to hit, lacked any kind of movement, and simply folded under the pressure. Hare relinquished the title on 21 June, having become the WBF champion on that date.

L. Middleweight

19 April 2003 Michael Jones 10.13$\frac{1}{2}$ (England) L PTS 12 Jamie Moore 10.13$\frac{1}{2}$ (England), Everton Park Sports Centre, Liverpool. For a summary, see under British Title Bouts During 2002-2003.

Middleweight

16 April 2003 Howard Eastman 11.5 (England) W RSC 3 Scott Dann 11.5$\frac{1}{2}$ (England), The Ice Rink, Nottingham. For a summary, see under British Title Bouts During 2002-2003.

S. Middleweight

1 March 2003 David Starie 11.12 (England) L PTS 12 Andre Thysse 11.13 (South Africa), Carnival City, South Africa. Scorecards: 112-116, 112-116, 110-112. In what was an extremely untidy affair, Starie struggled to overcome the height and reach disadvantages and clutching tactics of the ungainly Thysse and was badly cut prior to being floored twice in the ninth round. It was only his supreme courage that kept him going as he was on the verge of being knocked out several times before the final bell came to his rescue. Thysse automatically forfeited the title on losing an IBO title challenge to the Irishman, Brian Magee, on 21 June 2003.

L. Heavyweight

6 September 2002 Peter Oboh 12.4 (England) W CO 1 George Adipo 12.7 (Kenya), York Hall, Bethnal Green, London. When Tony Oakey (England) relinquished the title on becoming the WBU champion on 2 March 2002, Oboh, a London-based Nigerian, took the opportunity of fighting for the vacancy with both hands, despite having prepared to meet Neil Simpson, who pulled out with a damaged shoulder days earlier. The Kenyan had only been in the country for three days prior to the opening bell and although he tried to make a fight of it, Oboh's body shots quickly had an effect, Adipo being counted out by Mickey Vann on the 2.17 mark, his right eye bleeding and swollen.

8 March 2003 Peter Oboh 12.6 (England) W RSC 11 Neil Simpson 12.6 (England), The AT7 Centre, Coventry. For a summary, see under British Title Bouts During 2002-2003.

Cruiserweight

25 January 2003 Mark Hobson 13.8 (England) W RSC 4 Abdul Kaddu 13.7$\frac{1}{2}$ (Uganda), The Recreation Centre, Bridgend. Unable to get fit enough for a defence, Bruce Scott (England), who was still recovering from Achilles tendon surgery, relinquished the title in January 2003. Although Hobson v Kaddu was approved as a title match, the 41-year-old Ugandan was dwarfed by the Englishman and could never get into the fight, being all over the place at times, and was dropped twice before the referee, Ian John-Lewis, called it off after 1.48 of the fourth had elapsed. Despite showing braveness under fire, Kaddu simply wasn't up to the task.

Heavyweight

17 September 2002 Danny Williams 17.10 (England) W PTS 12 Keith Long 15.8$\frac{1}{2}$ (England), York Hall, Bethnal Green, London. For a summary, see under British Title Bouts During 2002-2003.

26 April 2003 Danny Williams 17.7 (England) W RSC 4 Bob Mirovic 18.12 (Australia), The Fountain Leisure Centre, Brentford, London. Referee: John Keane. Having been destroyed in a European title challenge in his previous contest, it was still a surprise that it took Williams three rounds to find his way back and being hurt in the process. However, the fourth round saw Williams pick up the pace before putting Mirovic down with a low blow, which earned him a lengthy rest. From then on it was just a matter of time as Williams punched away incessantly to force a stoppage on the 2.33 mark.

Commonwealth Champions, 1887-2003

Since the 1997 edition, Harold Alderman's magnificent research into Imperial British Empire title fights has introduced many more claimants/champions than were shown previously. Prior to 12 October 1954, the date that the British Commonwealth and Empire Boxing Championships Committee was formed, there was no official body as such and the Australian and British promoters virtually ran the show, with other members of the British Empire mainly out in the cold. We have also listed Canadian representatives, despite championship boxing in that country being contested over ten or 12 rounds at most, but they are not accorded the same kind of recognition that their British and Australian counterparts are. On 8 September 1970, Bunny Sterling became the first immigrant to win a British title under the ten-year residential ruling and from that date on champions are recorded by domicile rather than by birthplace. Reconstituted as the British Commonwealth Boxing Championships Committee on 22 November 1972, and with a current membership that includes Australia, Bahama, Ghana, Guyana, Jamaica, Kenya, New Zealand, Nigeria, South Africa, Tanzania, Trinidad and Tobago, Zambia, and Zimbabwe, in 1989 the 'British' tag was dropped.

COMMONWEALTH COUNTRY CODE
A = Australia; BAH = Bahamas; BAR = Barbados; BER = Bermuda; C = Canada; E = England; F = Fiji; GH = Ghana; GU = Guyana; I = Ireland; J = Jamaica; K = Kenya; N = Nigeria; NZ = New Zealand; NI = Northern Ireland; PNG = Papua New Guinea; SA = South Africa; SAM = Samoa; S = Scotland; T = Tonga; TR = Trinidad; U = Uganda; W = Wales; ZA = Zambia; ZI = Zimbabwe.

Champions in **bold** denote those recognised by the British Commonwealth and Empire Boxing Championships Committee (1954 to date) and, prior to that, those with the best claims

*Undefeated champions (Does not include men who forfeited titles)

Title Holder	Birthplace/ Domicile	Tenure	Title Holder	Birthplace/ Domicile	Tenure	Title Holder	Birthplace/ Domicile	Tenure
Flyweight (112 lbs)			**Bantamweight (118 lbs)**			**Paul Ferreri**	A	1981-1986
Elky Clark*	S	1924-1927	**Digger Stanley**	E	1904-1905	**Ray Minus***	BAH	1986-1991
Harry Hill	E	1929	**Owen Moran**	E	1905	**John Armour***	E	1992-1996
Frenchy Belanger	C	1929	**Ted Green**	A	1905-1911	**Paul Lloyd***	E	1996-2000
Vic White	A	1929-1930	**Charlie Simpson***	A	1911-1912	**Ady Lewis**	E	2000
Teddy Green	A	1930-1931	**Jim Higgins**	S	1920-1922	**Tommy Waite**	NI	2000
Jackie Paterson	S	1940-1948	**Tommy Harrison**	E	1922-1923	**Nicky Booth**	E	2000-2002
Rinty Monaghan*	NI	1948-1950	**Bugler Harry Lake**	E	1923	**Steve Molitor**	C	2002-
Teddy Gardner	E	1952	**Johnny Brown**	E	1923-1928			
Jake Tuli	SA	1952-1954	Billy McAllister	A	1928-1930	**S. Bantamweight (122 lbs)**		
Dai Dower*	W	1954-1957	**Teddy Baldock***	E	1928-1930	**Neil Swain**	W	1995
Frankie Jones	S	1957	Johnny Peters	E	1930	**Neil Swain**	W	1996-1997
Dennis Adams*	SA	1957-1962	**Dick Corbett**	E	1930-1932	**Michael Brodie**	E	1997-1999
Jackie Brown	S	1962-1963	**Johnny King**	E	1932-1934	**Nedal Hussein***	A	2000-2001
Walter McGowan*	S	1963-1969	**Dick Corbett**	E	1934	**Brian Carr**	S	2001-2002
John McCluskey	S	1970-1971	Frankie Martin	C	1935-1937	**Michael Alldis**	E	2002
Henry Nissen	A	1971-1974	Baby Yack	C	1937	**Esham Pickering**	E	2003-
Big Jim West*	A	1974-1975	Johnny Gaudes	C	1937-1939			
Patrick Mambwe	ZA	1976-1979	Lefty Gwynn	C	1939	**Featherweight (126 lbs)**		
Ray Amoo	N	1980	Baby Yack	C	1939-1940	**Jim Driscoll***	W	1908-1913
Steve Muchoki	K	1980-1983	**Jim Brady**	S	1941-1945	**Llew Edwards**	W	1915-1916
Keith Wallace*	E	1983-1984	**Jackie Paterson**	S	1945-1949	**Charlie Simpson***	A	1916
Richard Clarke	J	1986-1987	**Stan Rowan**	E	1949	Tommy Noble	E	1919-1921
Nana Yaw Konadu*	GH	1987-1989	**Vic Toweel**	SA	1949-1952	**Bert Spargo**	A	1921-1922
Alfred Kotey*	GH	1989-1993	**Jimmy Carruthers***	A	1952-1954	**Bert McCarthy**	A	1922
Francis Ampofo*	E	1993	**Peter Keenan**	S	1955-1959	**Bert Spargo**	A	1922-1923
Daren Fifield	E	1993-1994	**Freddie Gilroy***	NI	1959-1963	**Billy Grime**	A	1923
Francis Ampofo	E	1994-1995	**Johnny Caldwell**	NI	1964-1965	**Ernie Baxter**	A	1923
Danny Ward	SA	1995-1996	**Alan Rudkin**	E	1965-1966	Leo Kid Roy	C	1923
Peter Culshaw	E	1996-1997	**Walter McGowan**	S	1966-1968	**Bert Ristuccia**	A	1923-1924
Ady Lewis*	E	1997-1998	**Alan Rudkin**	E	1968-1969	Barney Wilshur	C	1923
Alfonso Zvenyika	ZI	1998	**Lionel Rose***	A	1969	Benny Gould	C	1923-1924
Damaen Kelly	NI	1998-1999	**Alan Rudkin***	E	1970-1972	**Billy Grime**	A	1924
Keith Knox	S	1999	**Paul Ferreri**	A	1972-1977	Leo Kid Roy	C	1924-1932
Jason Booth*	E	1999-2003	**Sulley Shittu**	GH	1977-1978	**Johnny McGrory**	S	1936-1938
Dale Robinson	E	2003-	**Johnny Owen***	W	1978-1980	**Jim Spider Kelly**	NI	1938-1939

Steve Molitor, Canada's Commonwealth bantamweight champion

Les Clark

Title Holder	Birthplace/ Domicile	Tenure
Johnny Cusick	E	1939-1940
Nel Tarleton	E	1940-1947
Tiger Al Phillips	E	1947
Ronnie Clayton	E	1947-1951
Roy Ankrah	GH	1951-1954
Billy Spider Kelly	NI	1954-1955
Hogan Kid Bassey*	N	1955-1957
Percy Lewis	TR	1957-1960
Floyd Robertson	GH	1960-1967
John O'Brien	S	1967
Johnny Famechon*	A	1967-1969
Toro George	NZ	1970-1972
Bobby Dunne	A	1972-1974
Evan Armstrong	S	1974
David Kotey*	GH	1974-1975
Eddie Ndukwu	N	1977-1980
Pat Ford*	GU	1980-1981
Azumah Nelson*	GH	1981-1985
Tyrone Downes	BAR	1986-1988
Thunder Aryeh	GH	1988-1989
Oblitey Commey	GH	1989-1990
Modest Napunyi	K	1990-1991
Barrington Francis*	C	1991
Colin McMillan*	E	1992
Billy Hardy*	E	1992-1996
Jonjo Irwin	E	1996-1997
Paul Ingle*	E	1997-1999
Patrick Mullings	E	1999-2000
Scott Harrison*	S	2000-2002
Nicky Cook	E	2003-

S. Featherweight (130 lbs)

Title Holder	Birthplace/ Domicile	Tenure
Billy Moeller	A	1975-1977
Johnny Aba*	PNG	1977-1982
Langton Tinago	ZI	1983-1984
John Sichula	ZA	1984
Lester Ellis*	A	1984-1985
John Sichula	ZA	1985-1986
Sam Akromah	GH	1986-1987
John Sichula	ZA	1987-1989
Mark Reefer*	E	1989-1990
Thunder Aryeh	GH	1990-1991
Hugh Forde	E	1991
Paul Harvey	E	1991-1992
Tony Pep	C	1992-1995
Justin Juuko	U	1995-1998
Charles Shepherd*	E	1999
Mick O'Malley	A	1999-2000
Ian McLeod*	S	2000
James Armah*	GH	2000-2001
Alex Moon	E	2001-2002
Dean Pithie	E	2002-2003
Craig Docherty	S	2003-

Lightweight (135 lbs)

Title Holder	Birthplace/ Domicile	Tenure
Jim Burge	A	1890
George Dawson*	A	1890
Harry Nickless	E	1892-1894
Arthur Valentine	E	1894-1895
Dick Burge*	E	1894-1895
Jim Murphy*	NZ	1894-1897
Eddie Connolly*	C	1896-1897
Jack Goldswain	E	1906-1908
Jack McGowan	A	1909
Hughie Mehegan	A	1909-1910
Johnny Summers*	E	1910
Hughie Mehegan	A	1911
Freddie Welsh*	W	1912-1914
Ernie Izzard	E	1928
Tommy Fairhall	A	1928-1930
Al Foreman	E	1930-1933
Jimmy Kelso	A	1933
Al Foreman*	E	1933-1934
Laurie Stevens*	SA	1936-1937
Dave Crowley	E	1938
Eric Boon	E	1938-1944
Ronnie James	W	1944-1947
Arthur King	C	1948-1951
Frank Johnson	E	1953
Pat Ford	A	1953-1954
Ivor Germain	BAR	1954
Pat Ford	A	1954-1955
Johnny van Rensburg	SA	1955-1956
Willie Toweel	SA	1956-1959
Dave Charnley	E	1959-1962
Bunny Grant	J	1962-1967
Manny Santos*	NZ	1967
Love Allotey	GH	1967-1968
Percy Hayles	J	1968-1975
Jonathan Dele	N	1975-1977
Lennox Blackmore	GU	1977-1978
Hogan Jimoh	N	1978-1980
Langton Tinago	ZI	1980-1981
Barry Michael	A	1981-1982
Claude Noel	T	1982-1984
Graeme Brooke	A	1984-1985
Barry Michael*	A	1985-1986
Langton Tinago	ZI	1986-1987
Mo Hussein	E	1987-1989
Pat Doherty	E	1989
Najib Daho	E	1989-1990
Carl Crook	E	1990-1992
Billy Schwer	E	1992-1993
Paul Burke	E	1993
Billy Schwer	E	1993-1995
David Tetteh	GH	1995-1997
Billy Irwin	C	1997
David Tetteh	GH	1997-1999
Bobby Vanzie	E	1999-2001
James Armah*	GH	2001-2002
David Burke*	E	2002
Michael Muya	K	2003-

L. Welterweight (140 lbs)

Title Holder	Birthplace/ Domicile	Tenure
Joe Tetteh	GH	1972-1973
Hector Thompson	A	1973-1977
Baby Cassius Austin	A	1977-1978
Jeff Malcolm	A	1978-1979
Obisia Nwankpa	N	1979-1983
Billy Famous	N	1983-1986
Tony Laing	E	1987-1988
Lester Ellis	A	1988-1989
Steve Larrimore	BAH	1989
Tony Ekubia	E	1989-1991
Andy Holligan	E	1991-1994
Ross Hale	E	1994-1995
Paul Ryan	E	1995-1996
Andy Holligan	E	1996-1997
Bernard Paul	E	1997-1999
Eamonn Magee	NI	1999-
Paul Burke	E	1997
Felix Bwalya*	ZA	1997
Paul Burke	E	1998-1999
Eamonn Magee*	NI	1999-2002
Junior Witter	E	2002-

Welterweight (147 lbs)

Title Holder	Birthplace/ Domicile	Tenure
Tom Williams	A	1892-1895
Dick Burge	E	1895-1897
Eddie Connelly*	C	1903-1905
Joe White*	C	1907-1909
Johnny Summers	E	1912-1914
Tom McCormick	I	1914
Matt Wells	E	1914-1919
Fred Kay	A	1915
Tommy Uren	A	1915-1916
Fritz Holland	A	1916
Tommy Uren	A	1916-1919
Fred Kay	A	1919-1920
Johnny Basham	W	1919-1920
Bermondsey Billy Wells	E	1922
Ted Kid Lewis	E	1920-1924
Tommy Milligan*	S	1924-1925
Jack Carroll	A	1928
Charlie Purdie	A	1928-1929
Wally Hancock	A	1929-1930
Tommy Fairhall*	A	1930
Jack Carroll	A	1934-1938
Eddie Thomas	W	1951
Wally Thom	E	1951-1952
Cliff Curvis	W	1952
Gerald Dreyer	SA	1952-1954
Barry Brown	NZ	1954
George Barnes	A	1954-1956
Darby Brown	A	1956
George Barnes	A	1956-1958
Johnny van Rensburg	SA	1958
George Barnes	A	1958-1960
Brian Curvis*	W	1960-1966
Johnny Cooke	E	1967-1968
Ralph Charles*	E	1968-1972
Clyde Gray	C	1973-1979
Chris Clarke	C	1979
Clyde Gray*	C	1979-1980
Colin Jones*	W	1981-1984
Sylvester Mittee	E	1984-1985
Lloyd Honeyghan*	E	1985-1986
Brian Janssen	A	1987
Wilf Gentzen	A	1987-1988
Gary Jacobs	S	1988-1989
Donovan Boucher	C	1989-1992
Eamonn Loughran*	NI	1992-1993
Andrew Murray*	GU	1993-1997
Kofi Jantuah*	GH	1997-2000
Scott Dixon*	S	2000
Jawaid Khaliq*	E	2000-2001
Julian Holland	A	2001-2002
James Hare*	E	2002-2003

L. Middleweight (154 lbs)

Title Holder	Birthplace/ Domicile	Tenure
Charkey Ramon*	A	1972-1975
Maurice Hope*	E	1976-1979

Title Holder	Birthplace/ Domicile	Tenure
Kenny Bristol	GU	1979-1981
Herol Graham*	E	1981-1984
Ken Salisbury	A	1984-1985
Nick Wilshire	E	1985-1987
Lloyd Hibbert	E	1987
Troy Waters*	A	1987-1991
Chris Pyatt*	E	1991-1992
Mickey Hughes	E	1992-1993
Lloyd Honeyghan	E	1993-1994
Leo Young	A	1994-1995
Kevin Kelly	A	1995
Chris Pyatt	E	1995-1996
Steve Foster	E	1996-1997
Kevin Kelly	A	1997-1999
Tony Badea	C	1999-2001
Richard Williams*	E	2001
Joshua Onyango	K	2002
Michael Jones	E	2002-2003
Jamie Moore	E	2003-

Middleweight (160 lbs)

Title Holder	Birthplace/ Domicile	Tenure
Chesterfield Goode	E	1887-1890
Toff Wall	E	1890-1891
Jim Hall	A	1892-1893
Bill Heffernan	NZ	1894-1896
Bill Doherty	A	1896-1897
Billy Edwards	A	1897-1898
Dido Plumb*	E	1898-1901
Tom Duggan	A	1901-1903
Jack Palmer*	E	1902-1904
Jewey Cooke	E	1903-1904
Tom Dingey	C	1904-1905
Jack Lalor	SA	1905
Ted Nelson	A	1905
Tom Dingey	C	1905
Sam Langford*	C	1907-1911
Ed Williams	A	1908-1910
Arthur Cripps	A	1910
Dave Smith	A	1910-1911
Jerry Jerome	A	1913
Arthur Evernden	E	1913-1914
Mick King	A	1914-1915
Les Darcy*	A	1915-1917
Ted Kid Lewis	E	1922-1923
Roland Todd	E	1923-1926
Len Johnson	E	1926-1928
Tommy Milligan	S	1926-1928
Alex Ireland	S	1928-1929
Len Harvey	E	1929-1933
Del Fontaine	C	1931
Ted Moore	E	1931
Jock McAvoy	E	1933-1939
Ron Richards*	A	1940
Ron Richards*	A	1941-1942
Bos Murphy	NZ	1948
Dick Turpin	E	1948-1949
Dave Sands*	A	1949-1952
Randy Turpin	E	1952-1954
Al Bourke	A	1952-1954
Johnny Sullivan	E	1954-1955
Pat McAteer	E	1955-1958
Dick Tiger	N	1958-1960
Wilf Greaves	C	1960
Dick Tiger*	N	1960-1962

Title Holder	Birthplace/ Domicile	Tenure
Gomeo Brennan	BAH	1963-1964
Tuna Scanlon*	NZ	1964
Gomeo Brennan	BAH	1964-1966
Blair Richardson*	C	1966-1967
Milo Calhoun	J	1967
Johnny Pritchett*	E	1967-1969
Les McAteer	E	1969-1970
Mark Rowe	E	1970
Bunny Sterling	E	1970-1972
Tony Mundine*	A	1972-1975
Monty Betham	NZ	1975-1978
Al Korovou	A	1978
Ayub Kalule	U	1978-1980
Tony Sibson*	E	1980-1983
Roy Gumbs	E	1983
Mark Kaylor	E	1983-1984
Tony Sibson*	E	1984-1988
Nigel Benn	E	1988-1989
Michael Watson*	E	1989-1991
Richie Woodhall	E	1992-1995
Robert McCracken	E	1995-1997
Johnson Tshuma	SA	1997-1998
Paul Jones	E	1998-1999
Jason Matthews*	E	1999
Alain Bonnamie*	C	1999-2000
Sam Soliman	A	2000
Howard Eastman	GU	2000-

S. Middleweight (168 lbs)

Title Holder	Birthplace/ Domicile	Tenure
Rod Carr	A	1989-1990
Lou Cafaro	A	1990-1991
Henry Wharton*	E	1991-1997
Clinton Woods	E	1997-1998
David Starie	E	1998-2003
Andre Thysse	SA	2003

L. Heavyweight (175 lbs)

Title Holder	Birthplace/ Domicile	Tenure
Dave Smith*	A	1911-1915
Jack Bloomfield*	E	1923-1924
Tom Berry	E	1927
Gipsy Daniels*	W	1927
Len Harvey	E	1939-1942
Freddie Mills*	E	1942-1950
Randy Turpin*	E	1952-1955
Gordon Wallace	C	1956-1957
Yvon Durelle*	C	1957-1959
Chic Calderwood	S	1960-1963
Bob Dunlop*	A	1968-1970
Eddie Avoth	W	1970-1971
Chris Finnegan	E	1971-1973
John Conteh*	E	1973-1974
Steve Aczel	A	1975
Tony Mundine	A	1975-1978
Gary Summerhays	C	1978-1979
Lottie Mwale	ZA	1979-1985
Leslie Stewart*	TR	1985-1987
Willie Featherstone	C	1987-1989
Guy Waters*	A	1989-1993
Brent Kosolofski	C	1993-1994
Garry Delaney	E	1994-1995
Noel Magee	I	1995
Nicky Piper*	W	1995-1997
Crawford Ashley	E	1998-1999
Clinton Woods*	E	1999-2000

Title Holder	Birthplace/ Domicile	Tenure
Neil Simpson	E	2001
Tony Oakey*	E	2001-2002
Peter Oboh	E	2002-

Cruiserweight (190 lbs)

Title Holder	Birthplace/ Domicile	Tenure
Stewart Lithgo	E	1984
Chisanda Mutti	ZA	1984-1987
Glenn McCrory*	E	1987-1989
Apollo Sweet	A	1989
Derek Angol*	E	1989-1993
Francis Wanyama	U	1994-1995
Chris Okoh	E	1995-1997
Darren Corbett	NI	1997-1998
Bruce Scott	E	1998-1999
Adam Watt*	A	2000-2001
Bruce Scott*	E	2001-2003
Mark Hobson	E	2003-

Heavyweight (190 lbs +)

Title Holder	Birthplace/ Domicile	Tenure
Peter Jackson*	A	1889-1901
Dan Creedon	NZ	1896-1903
Billy McColl	A	1902-1905
Tim Murphy	A	1905-1906
Bill Squires	A	1906-1909
Bill Lang	A	1909-1910
Tommy Burns*	C	1910-1911
P.O. Curran	I	1911
Dan Flynn	I	1911
Bombardier Billy Wells	E	1911-1919
Bill Lang	A	1911-1913
Dave Smith	A	1913-1917
Joe Beckett*	E	1919-1923
Phil Scott	E	1926-1931
Larry Gains	C	1931-1934
Len Harvey	E	1934
Jack Petersen	W	1934-1936
Ben Foord	SA	1936-1937
Tommy Farr	W	1937
Len Harvey*	E	1939-1942
Jack London	E	1944-1945
Bruce Woodcock	E	1945-1950
Jack Gardner	E	1950-1952
Johnny Williams	W	1952-1953
Don Cockell	E	1953-1956
Joe Bygraves	J	1956-1957
Joe Erskine	W	1957-1958
Brian London	E	1958-1959
Henry Cooper	E	1959-1971
Joe Bugner	E	1971
Jack Bodell	E	1971-1972
Danny McAlinden	NI	1972-1975
Bunny Johnson	E	1975
Richard Dunn	E	1975-1976
Joe Bugner*	E	1976-1977
John L. Gardner*	E	1978-1981
Trevor Berbick	C	1981-1986
Horace Notice*	E	1986-1988
Derek Williams	E	1988-1992
Lennox Lewis*	E	1992-1993
Henry Akinwande	E	1993-1995
Scott Welch	E	1995-1997
Julius Francis*	E	1997-1999
Danny Williams	E	1999-

European Title Bouts During 2002-2003

All of last season's title bouts are shown in date order within their weight divisions and give the boxers respective weights, along with the scorecard if going to a decision. There is also a short summary of any bout that involved a British contestant and British officials are listed where applicable.

Flyweight
19 May 2003   Mimoun Chent 7.13$^1/_4$ (France) L RSC 8 Alexander Mahmutov 7.13$^1/_2$ (Russia), Levallois Perret, France. Referee: Mickey Vann.

Bantamweight
28 January 2003   Noel Wilders 8.5 (England) W PTS 12 Fabien Guillerme 8.5 (France), Nice, France. Scorecards: 116-112, 115-113, 115-113. After Spend Abazi (Sweden), who had already won the WBA International featherweight belt, decided that he could no longer make 118lbs and handed his championship belt back at the end of August 2002, Wilders was selected to meet Guillerme to contest the vacant title on away territory. Despite the closeness of the official verdict this was not a close one, southpaw Wilders taking control from the opening bell and appearing to win in a canter. Both men were cut over their right eyes, due to head clashes, but the Englishman remained unfazed as he romped to victory.

18 March 2003   Noel Wilders 8.6 (England) T Draw 4 Frederic Patrac 8.5$^1/_2$ (France), The Rivermead Leisure Centre, Reading. Making his first defence, Wilders was a disappointment, being put down in the second and given no room to work by a tenacious opponent. However, it was bad cuts on the left eye and nose caused by clashing heads that forced Wilders out of the contest and, because four rounds had not been completed, he remained the champion. Under EBU championship rules, when an accidental injury forces a man to be pulled out before four rounds have been completed the result doesn't hinge on the scorecards and the champion retained his title on that basis.

10 June 2003   Noel Wilders 8.5 (England) L RSC 7 David Guerault 8.6 (France), Ponds Forge International Centre, Sheffield. In a battle of southpaws, the light-hitting Wilders suffered at the hands of the taller Guerault, who simply walked though the champion's defence to get his punches off. Knocked down three times and badly cut on both eyes, Wilders looked a mess and it was no surprise after he was put down heavily in the seventh that the referee finally put him out of his misery with 2.15 of the round gone.

S. Bantamweight
13 July 2002   Mahyar Monshipour 8.7$^1/_2$ (France) W RSC 6 Tuncan Kaya 8.9$^1/_4$ (France), Palavas, France. Billed for the vacant title after Salim Medjkoune (France) handed in his belt in June 2002 to concentrate on a crack at the WBA crown.

5 December 2002   Mahyar Monshipour 8.8$^1/_4$ (France) W RSC 6 Mustapha Hame 8.9$^1/_4$ (France), Levallois Perret, France.

4 April 2003   Mahyar Monshipour 8.9 (France) W RSC 3 German Guartos 8.9$^3/_4$ (Spain), Clermont Ferrand, France.

Featherweight
21 December 2002   Cyril Thomas 8.13$^1/_4$ (France) W RSC 6 Alessandro di Mecco 8.13$^1/_2$ (Italy), Brolo, Italy. Following a second-round technical draw in Gubbio, Italy on 15 June 2002, the pair met yet again to find a new champion, Manuel Calvo having abdicated in January 2002 to concentrate on an IBO title opportunity.

7 March 2003   Cyril Thomas 8.13$^1/_2$ (France) W PTS 12 Oscar Sanchez 9.0 (Spain), Saint Quentin, France. Scorecards: 119-109, 118-110, 118-110.

20 June 2003   Cyril Thomas 8.13$^3/_4$ (France) W TD 9 Manuel Calvo 9.0 (Spain), Saint Quentin, France. Scorecards: 90-81, 90-82, 89-83.

S. Featherweight
6 July 2002   Pedro Oscar Miranda 9.2$^1/_2$ (Spain) L PTS 12 Affif Djelti 9.1$^1/_2$ (France), Telde, Gran Canaria, Spain. Scorecards: 115-113, 114-115, 113-115.

2 November 2002   Affif Djelti 9.2$^1/_2$ (France) W PTS 12 Bouziane Oudji 9.2 (France), Elbeuf, France. Scorecards: 118-111, 116-113, 116-114.

15 April 2003   Affif Djelti 9.2 (France) W RSC 8 Youssouf Djibaba 9.2 (France), Piacenza, Italy.

Lightweight
3 August 2002   Jason Cook 9.8$^1/_2$ (Wales) W RSC 3 Sandro Casamonica 9.8 (Italy), San Mango D'Aquino, Italy. In a match made for the vacant title after Stefano Zoff (Italy) handed in his belt in February 2002 to mount a challenge for the IBF crown, Cook, who took the fight at just nine days notice, came through with the best punch he has ever thrown to become the new champion. Despite boxing well in the proceeding rounds, the Welshman was put down early in the third but suddenly found a peach of a left hook and that was it, the referee quickly dispensing with the count so that Casamonica could be attended to.

26 October 2002   Jason Cook 9.8$^3/_4$ (Wales) W RSC 5 Nasser Lakrib 9.8$^3/_4$ (France), The Sports Centre, Maesteg. While the action lasted, the Frenchman put up stubborn resistance but was gradually outgunned to the point where he was not fighting back and was rescued by the referee after 40 seconds of the fifth round had elapsed. It was a timely decision, despite there had being no knockdowns, as Lakrib was cut on the right eye and on the point of folding, having soaked up a real battering.

25 January 2003   Jason Cook 9.10$^1/_2$ (Wales) W PTS 12 Stefano Zoff 9.8$^1/_4$ (Italy), The Recreation Centre, Bridgend. Disastrously for Cook he failed to make the championship weight so the title was declared vacant, but, despite this, the contest went ahead on the grounds that if Zoff won he would be declared champion. Forcing the fight from the off, Cook set a tough pace and ran out of gas towards the end when the experienced and tricky Italian came more and more into the fight. Despite it being painfully close it was not enough for Zoff, the scorecards reading 115-114, 115-114, 113-115. Following the result, Zoff was matched to fight England's David Burke for the vacant title.

7 June 2003   Stefano Zoff 9.6$^1/_4$ (Italy) W PTS 12 David

Burke 9.8$^{1}/_{4}$ (England), Trieste, Italy. Scorecards: 116-112, 115-114, 115-114. Unfortunately for Burke he just couldn't get going, the stifling heat having an adverse effect on him. Boxing behind the southpaw lead, the Liverpudlian, who was cut by the right eye early on, appeared rigid and too often stood back, while the wily old campaigner, Zoff, enjoyed himself without being put under pressure by the younger man. Although he tried to put in a storming finish it was too little and too late for Burke and the closeness of the scorecards failed to paint an accurate picture.

L. Welterweight

28 September 2002   Oktay Urkal 10.0 (Germany) W PTS 12 Gabriel Mapouka 9.13$^{1}/_{4}$ (France), Zwickau, Germany. Following Gianluca Branco's decision to relinquish the title in early July after falling foul of the law outside the ring, an Urkal v Mapouka match was made to decide a new champion.
1 February 2003   Oktay Urkal 9.13$^{1}/_{2}$ (Germany) W PTS 12 Salvatore Battaglia 9.13 (Italy), Chemnitz, Germany. Scorecards: 116-112, 116-112, 113-115.
14 June 2003   Oktay Urkal 9.13$^{3}/_{4}$ (Germany) W PTS 12 Eamonn Magee 9.13$^{3}/_{4}$ (Ireland), Magdeburg, Germany. Scorecards: 116-112, 116-112, 115-112.

Welterweight

17 August 2002   Michel Trabant 10.6$^{1}/_{2}$ (Germany) W RSC 5 Joszef Matolcsi 10.6$^{1}/_{4}$ (Hungary), Berlin, Germany.
18 January 2003   Michel Trabant 10.5$^{1}/_{2}$ (Germany) W PTS 12 Frederic Klose 10.5$^{1}/_{2}$ (France), Essen, Germany. Scorecards: 117-113, 116-114, 115-115. Referee: John Coyle. Trabant relinquished the title in April 2003 to prepare for a proposed WBA title fight against Denmark's Thomas Damgaard, which ultimately never came off.
19 June 2003   Frederic Klose 10.5$^{1}/_{2}$ (France) W PTS 12 Alexander Vetoux 10.5 (Ukraine), Levallois, France. Scorecards: 117-112, 115-112, 114-113.

L. Middleweight

7 February 2003   Roman Karmazin 10.13$^{1}/_{2}$ (Russia) W CO 5 Jorge Araujo 10.12$^{3}/_{4}$ (Spain), Madrid, Spain. Karmazin was matched against Araujo to contest the vacant title after the champion, Wayne Alexander (England), handed his belt in on 14 October 2002 to campaign at a higher weight.
13 June 2003   Roman Karmazin 10.13 1/2 (Russia) W RSC 2 Michael Rask 11.0 (Denmark), Aalborg, Denmark.

Middleweight

28 January 2003   Howard Eastman 11.5$^{1}/_{2}$ (England) W RTD 4 Christophe Tendil 11.5$^{1}/_{4}$ (France), The Ice Rink, Nottingham. Morrade Hakkar (France), who was due to defend against Tendil, relinquished the title on 29 October 2002 to prepare for a world title shot against Bernard Hopkins, leaving Eastman and Tendil to battle for the championship. Despite the Frenchman being a tough nut to crack, once Eastman had got going it was just a matter of time and so it proved. At the end of the fourth, with cuts on both eyes and a damaged jaw to contend with, the challenge was over, Tendil retiring on his stool.
16 April 2003   Howard Eastman 11.5 (England) W RSC 3 Scott Dann 11.5$^{1}/_{2}$ (England), The Ice Rink, Nottingham. For a summary, see under British Title Bouts During 2002-2003.

S. Middleweight

28 September 2002   Danilo Haeussler 11.13$^{1}/_{4}$ (Germany) W PTS 12 Juan Perez Nelongo 11.1$^{1}/_{2}$ (Spain), Zwickau, Germany. Scorecards: 118-110, 117-111, 116-113.
1 February 2003   Danilo Haeussler 11.13$^{1}/_{4}$ (Germany) W TD 5 Glenn Catley 11.12$^{1}/_{2}$ (England), Chemnitz, Germany. Scorecards: 49-44, 48-45, 48-46. Cut on the left eye in the opening session but allowed to box on, Haeussler dropped Catley with a great right hand at the end of the round. From then on the Englishman was struggling, having a point deducted for dangerous headwork in the third before the referee decided that the German's eye was too bad for him to continue and reverted to the scorecards after ruling that the cut had been caused by an accidental head butt.
31 May 2003   Danilo Haeussler 11.13$^{1}/_{4}$ (Germany) W PTS 12 Rachid Kanfouah 11.13 (France), Frankfurt-Oder, Germany. Scorecards: 115-113, 115-113, 115-114.

L. Heavyweight

12 October 2002   Yawe Davis 12.6$^{1}/_{2}$ (Italy) L CO 2 Thomas Ulrich 12.7 (Germany), Schwerin, Germany. Ulrich was sick hours before defending against Silvio Branco and relinquished the title to allow Stipe Drews to be drafted in to decide the championship, on the grounds that he would challenge the winner.
8 February 2003   Stipe Drews 12.7 (Croatia) W PTS 12 Silvio Branco 12.7 (Italy), Berlin, Germany. Scorecards: 117-111, 116-112, 115-114.

Cruiserweight

5 November 2002   Pietro Aurino 13.7$^{1}/_{2}$ (Italy) W RSC 5 Turan Bagci 13.8 (France), Cernobbio, Italy. Alexander Gurov (Ukraine) relinquished his hold on the championship in March 2002 in order to pursue a world title opportunity and Aurino v Bagci were matched to decide the vacant title.
22 February 2003   Pietro Aurino 13.8 (Italy) W RSC 10 Vincenzo Rossitto 13.3$^{1}/_{4}$ (Italy), Teramo, Italy.
31 May 2003   Pietro Aurino 13.8 (Italy) W PTS 12 Jesper Kristiansen 13.5$^{1}/_{2}$ (Denmark), Aversa, Italy. Scorecards: 118-110, 119-110, 119-111.

Heavyweight

20 July 2002   Luan Krasniqi 16.1 (Germany) L RSC 9 Przemyslaw Saleta 15.13 (Poland), Dortmund, Germany.
12 October 2002   Przemyslaw Saleta 16.2$^{3}/_{4}$ (Poland) L RSC 7 Sinan Samil Sam 17.0$^{1}/_{4}$ (Turkey), Schwerin, Germany.
8 February 2003   Sinan Samil Sam 17.0$^{1}/_{2}$ (Turkey) W RSC 6 Danny Williams 18.6 (England), Berlin, Germany. Showing a good chin and good offensive work, Sam lived up to his world amateur title status as he broke down Williams' defences, putting him down twice in the fourth before going for the finish in round six. Having taken time out after being hit low, Sam got in with a right counter that had Williams all over the place and as the towel came in the referee jumped in to the rescue with 2.56 on the clock.
26 April 2003   Sinan Samil Sam 16.13 (Turkey) W RSC 7 Julius Francis 18.1$^{1}/_{2}$ (England), Schwerin, Germany. After six competitive rounds, Sam finally got to Francis, having been in his face for three minutes of every session and always looking for a finisher. Hurt by a body punch early in the seventh, Francis went down in some pain and on getting up he was soon put down by another marked assault to the body, which downed him again and led to the referee calling a halt to the action on the 1.37 mark.

European Champions, 1909-2003

Prior to 1946, the championship was contested under the auspices of the International Boxing Union, re-named that year as the European Boxing Union (EBU). The IBU had come into being when Victor Breyer, a Paris-based journalist and boxing referee who later edited the Annuaire du Ring (first edition in 1910), warmed to the idea of an organisation that controlled boxing right across Europe, regarding rules and championship fights between the champions of the respective countries. He first came to London at the end of 1909 to discuss the subject with the NSC, but went away disappointed. However, at a meeting between officials from Switzerland and France in March 1912, the IBU was initially formed and, by June of that year, had published their first ratings. By April 1914, Belgium had also joined the organisation, although it would not be until the war was over that the IBU really took off. Many of the early champions shown on the listings were the result of promoters, especially the NSC, billing their own championship fights. Although the (French dominated) IBU recognised certain champions, prior to being re-formed in May 1920, they did not find their administrative 'feet' fully until other countries such as Italy (1922), Holland (1923), and Spain (1924), produced challengers for titles. Later in the 1920s, Germany (1926), Denmark (1928), Portugal (1929) and Romania (1929) also joined the fold. Unfortunately, for Britain, its representatives (Although the BBBoC, as we know it today, was formed in 1929, an earlier attempt to form a Board of Control had been initiated in April 1918 by the NSC and it was that body who were involved here) failed to reach agreement on the three judges' ruling, following several meetings with the IBU early in 1920 and, apart from Elky Clark (fly), Ernie Rice and Alf Howard (light), and Jack Hood (welter), who conformed to that stipulation, fighters from these shores would not be officially recognised as champions until the EBU was formed in 1946. This led to British fighters claiming the title after beating IBU titleholders, or their successors, under championship conditions in this country. The only men who did not come into this category were Kid Nicholson (bantam), and Ted Kid Lewis and Tommy Milligan (welter), who defeated men not recognised by the IBU. For the record, the first men recognised and authorised, respectively, as being champions of their weight classes by the IBU were: Sid Smith and Michel Montreuil (fly), Charles Ledoux (bantam), Jim Driscoll and Louis de Ponthieu (feather), Freddie Welsh and Georges Papin (light), Georges Carpentier and Albert Badoud (welter), Georges Carpentier and Ercole Balzac (middle), Georges Carpentier and Battling Siki (light-heavy and heavy).

EUROPEAN COUNTRY CODE

AU = Austria; BEL = Belgium; BUL = Bulgaria; CRO = Croatia; CZ = Czechoslovakia; DEN = Denmark; E = England; FIN = Finland; FR = France; GER = Germany; GRE = Greece; HOL = Holland; HUN = Hungary; ITA = Italy; KAZ = Kazakhstan; LUX = Luxembourg; NI = Northern Ireland; NOR = Norway; POL = Poland; POR = Portugal; ROM = Romania; RUS = Russia; S = Scotland; SP = Spain; SWE = Sweden; SWI = Switzerland; TU = Turkey; UK = Ukraine; W = Wales; YUG = Yugoslavia.

Champions in **bold** denote those recognised by the IBU/EBU

*Undefeated champions (Does not include men who may have forfeited titles)

Title Holder	Birthplace/ Domicile	Tenure	Title Holder	Birthplace/ Domicile	Tenure	Title Holder	Birthplace/ Domicile	Tenure
Flyweight (112 lbs)			Nazzareno Giannelli	ITA	1954-1955	**Bantamweight (118 lbs)**		
Sid Smith	E	1913	**Dai Dower**	W	1955	Joe Bowker	E	1910
Bill Ladbury	E	1913-1914	**Young Martin**	SP	1955-1959	Digger Stanley	E	1910-1912
Percy Jones	W	1914	**Risto Luukkonen**	FIN	1959-1961	**Charles Ledoux**	FR	1912-1921
Joe Symonds	E	1914	**Salvatore Burruni***	ITA	1961-1965	Bill Beynon	W	1913
Tancy Lee	S	1914-1916	**Rene Libeer**	FR	1965-1966	Tommy Harrison	E	1921-1922
Jimmy Wilde	W	1914-1915	**Fernando Atzori**	ITA	1967-1972	**Charles Ledoux**	FR	1922-1923
Jimmy Wilde*	W	1916-1923	**Fritz Chervet**	SWI	1972-1973	Bugler Harry Lake	E	1923
Michel Montreuil	BEL	1923-1925	**Fernando Atzori**	ITA	1973	Johnny Brown	E	1923-1928
Elky Clark*	S	1925-1927	**Fritz Chervet***	SWI	1973-1974	**Henry Scillie***	BEL	1925-1928
Victor Ferrand	SP	1927	**Franco Udella**	ITA	1974-1979	Kid Nicholson	E	1928
Emile Pladner	FR	1928-1929	**Charlie Magri***	E	1979-1983	Teddy Baldock	E	1928-1931
Johnny Hill	S	1928-1929	**Antoine Montero**	FR	1983-1984	**Domenico Bernasconi**	ITA	1929
Eugene Huat	FR	1929	**Charlie Magri***	E	1984-1985	**Carlos Flix**	SP	1929-1931
Emile Degand	BEL	1929-1930	**Franco Cherchi**	ITA	1985	**Lucien Popescu**	ROM	1931-1932
Kid Oliva	FR	1930	**Charlie Magri**	E	1985-1986	**Domenico Bernasconi**	ITA	1932
Lucien Popescu	ROM	1930-1931	**Duke McKenzie***	E	1986-1988	**Nicholas Biquet**	BEL	1932-1935
Jackie Brown	E	1931-1935	**Eyup Can***	TU	1989-1990	**Maurice Dubois**	SWI	1935-1936
Praxile Gyde	FR	1932-1935	**Pat Clinton***	S	1990-1991	**Joseph Decico**	FR	1936
Benny Lynch	S	1935-1938	**Salvatore Fanni**	ITA	1991-1992	**Aurel Toma**	ROM	1936-1937
Kid David*	BEL	1935-1936	**Robbie Regan***	W	1992-1993	**Nicholas Biquet**	BEL	1937-1938
Ernst Weiss	AU	1936	**Luigi Camputaro**	ITA	1993-1994	**Aurel Toma**	ROM	1938-1939
Valentin Angelmann*	FR	1936-1938	**Robbie Regan***	W	1994-1995	**Ernst Weiss**	AU	1939
Enrico Urbinati*	ITA	1938-1943	**Luigi Camputaro***	ITA	1995-1996	**Gino Cattaneo**	ITA	1939-1941
Raoul Degryse	BEL	1946-1947	**Jesper Jensen**	DEN	1996-1997	**Gino Bondavilli***	ITA	1941-1943
Maurice Sandeyron	FR	1947-1949	**David Guerault***	FR	1997-1999	**Jackie Paterson**	S	1946
Rinty Monaghan*	NI	1949-1950	**Alexander Mahmutov**	RUS	1999-2000	**Theo Medina**	FR	1946-1947
Terry Allen	E	1950	**Damaen Kelly***	NI	2000	**Peter Kane**	E	1947-1948
Jean Sneyers*	BEL	1950-1951	**Alexander Mahmutov**	RUS	2000-2002	**Guido Ferracin**	ITA	1948-1949
Teddy Gardner*	E	1952	**Mimoun Chent**	FR	2002-2003	**Luis Romero**	SP	1949-1951
Louis Skena*	FR	1953-1954	**Alexander Mahmutov**	RUS	2003-	**Peter Keenan**	S	1951-1952

Title Holder	Birthplace/Domicile	Tenure
Jean Sneyers*	BEL	1952-1953
Peter Keenan	S	1953
John Kelly	NI	1953-1954
Robert Cohen*	FR	1954-1955
Mario D'Agata	ITA	1955-1958
Piero Rollo	ITA	1958-1959
Freddie Gilroy	NI	1959-1960
Pierre Cossemyns	BEL	1961-1962
Piero Rollo	ITA	1962
Alphonse Halimi	FR	1962
Piero Rollo	ITA	1962-1963
Mimoun Ben Ali	SP	1963
Risto Luukkonen	FIN	1963-1964
Mimoun Ben Ali	SP	1965
Tommaso Galli	ITA	1965-1966
Mimoun Ben Ali	SP	1966-1968
Salvatore Burruni*	ITA	1968-1969
Franco Zurlo	ITA	1969-1971
Alan Rudkin	E	1971
Agustin Senin*	SP	1971-1973
Johnny Clark*	E	1973-1974
Bob Allotey	SP	1974-1975
Daniel Trioulaire	FR	1975-1976
Salvatore Fabrizio	ITA	1976-1977
Franco Zurlo	ITA	1977-1978
Juan Francisco Rodriguez	SP	1978-1980
Johnny Owen*	W	1980
Valerio Nati	ITA	1980-1982
Giuseppe Fossati	ITA	1982-1983
Walter Giorgetti	ITA	1983-1984
Ciro de Leva	ITA	1984-1986
Antoine Montero	FR	1986-1987
Louis Gomis*	FR	1987-1988
Fabrice Benichou	FR	1988
Vincenzo Belcastro*	ITA	1988-1990
Thierry Jacob*	FR	1990-1992
Johnny Bredahl*	DEN	1992
Vincenzo Belcastro	ITA	1993-1994
Prince Naseem Hamed*	E	1994-1995
John Armour*	E	1995-1996
Johnny Bredahl	DEN	1996-1998
Paul Lloyd*	E	1998-1999
Johnny Bredahl*	DEN	1999-2000
Luigi Castiglione	ITA	2000-2001
Fabien Guillerme	FR	2001
Alex Yagupov	RUS	2001
Spend Abazi	SWE	2001-2002
Noel Wilders	E	2003
David Guerault	FR	2003-

S. Bantamweight (122 lbs)

Title Holder	Birthplace/Domicile	Tenure
Vincenzo Belcastro	ITA	1995-1996
Salim Medjkoune	FR	1996
Martin Krastev	BUL	1996-1997
Spencer Oliver	E	1997-1998
Sergei Devakov	UK	1998-1999
Michael Brodie*	E	1999-2000
Vladislav Antonov	RUS	2000-2001
Salim Medjkoune*	FR	2001-2002
Mahyar Monshipour	FR	2002-

Featherweight (126 lbs)

Title Holder	Birthplace/Domicile	Tenure
Young Joey Smith	E	1911
Jean Poesy	FR	1911-1912
Jim Driscoll*	W	1912-1913
Ted Kid Lewis*	E	1913-1914
Louis de Ponthieu*	FR	1919-1920
Arthur Wyns	BEL	1920-1922
Billy Matthews	E	1922
Eugene Criqui*	FR	1922-1923
Edouard Mascart	FR	1923-1924
Charles Ledoux	FR	1924
Henri Hebrans	BEL	1924-1925
Antonio Ruiz	SP	1925-1928
Luigi Quadrini	ITA	1928-1929
Knud Larsen	DEN	1929
Jose Girones	SP	1929-1934
Maurice Holtzer*	FR	1935-1938
Phil Dolhem	BEL	1938-1939
Lucien Popescu	ROM	1939-1941
Ernst Weiss	AU	1941
Gino Bondavilli	ITA	1941-1945
Ermanno Bonetti*	ITA	1945-1946
Tiger Al Phillips	E	1947
Ronnie Clayton	E	1947-1948
Ray Famechon	FR	1948-1953
Jean Sneyers	BEL	1953-1954
Ray Famechon	FR	1954-1955
Fred Galiana*	SP	1955-1956
Cherif Hamia	FR	1957-1958
Sergio Caprari	ITA	1958-1959
Gracieux Lamperti	FR	1959-1962
Alberto Serti	ITA	1962-1963
Howard Winstone	W	1963-1967
Jose Legra*	SP	1967-1968
Manuel Calvo	SP	1968-1969
Tommaso Galli	ITA	1969-1970
Jose Legra*	SP	1970-1972
Gitano Jimenez	SP	1973-1975
Elio Cotena	ITA	1975-1976
Nino Jimenez	SP	1976-1977
Manuel Masso	SP	1977
Roberto Castanon*	SP	1977-1981
Salvatore Melluzzo	ITA	1981-1982
Pat Cowdell*	E	1982-1983
Loris Stecca*	ITA	1983
Barry McGuigan*	NI	1983-1985
Jim McDonnell*	E	1985-1987
Valerio Nati*	ITA	1987
Jean-Marc Renard*	BEL	1988-1989
Paul Hodkinson*	E	1989-1991
Fabrice Benichou	FR	1991-1992
Maurizio Stecca	ITA	1992-1993
Herve Jacob	FR	1993
Maurizio Stecca	ITA	1993
Stephane Haccoun	FR	1993-1994
Stefano Zoff	ITA	1994
Medhi Labdouni	FR	1994-1995
Billy Hardy	E	1995-1998
Paul Ingle*	E	1998-1999
Steve Robinson	W	1999-2000
Istvan Kovacs*	HUN	2000-2001
Manuel Calvo*	SP	2001-2002
Cyril Thomas	FR	2002-

S. Featherweight (130 lbs)

Title Holder	Birthplace/Domicile	Tenure
Tommaso Galli	ITA	1971-1972
Domenico Chiloiro	ITA	1972
Lothar Abend	GER	1972-1974
Sven-Erik Paulsen*	NOR	1974-1976
Roland Cazeaux	FR	1976
Natale Vezzoli	ITA	1976-1979
Carlos Hernandez	SP	1979
Rodolfo Sanchez	SP	1979
Carlos Hernandez	SP	1979-1982
Cornelius Boza-Edwards*	E	1982
Roberto Castanon	SP	1982-1983
Alfredo Raininger	ITA	1983-1984
Jean-Marc Renard	BEL	1984
Pat Cowdell	E	1984-1985
Jean-Marc Renard*	BEL	1986-1987
Salvatore Curcetti	ITA	1987-1988
Piero Morello	ITA	1988
Lars Lund Jensen	DEN	1988
Racheed Lawal	DEN	1988-1989
Daniel Londas*	FR	1989-1991
Jimmy Bredahl*	DEN	1992
Regilio Tuur	HOL	1992-1993
Jacobin Yoma	FR	1993-1995
Anatoly Alexandrov*	KAZ	1995-1996
Julian Lorcy*	FR	1996
Djamel Lifa	FR	1997-1998
Anatoly Alexandrov*	RUS	1998
Dennis Holbaek Pedersen	DEN	1999-2000
Boris Sinitsin	RUS	2000
Dennis Holbaek Pedersen*	DEN	2000
Tontcho Tontchev*	BUL	2001
Boris Sinitsin	RUS	2001-2002
Pedro Oscar Miranda	SP	2002
Affif Djelti	FR	2002-

Lightweight (135 lbs)

Title Holder	Birthplace/Domicile	Tenure
Freddie Welsh	W	1909-1911
Matt Wells	E	1911-1912
Freddie Welsh*	W	1912-1914
Georges Papin	FR	1920-1921
Ernie Rice	E	1921-1922
Seaman Nobby Hall	E	1922-1923
Harry Mason	E	1923-1926
Fred Bretonnel	FR	1924
Lucien Vinez	FR	1924-1927
Luis Rayo*	SP	1927-1928
Aime Raphael	FR	1928-1929
Francois Sybille	BEL	1929-1930
Alf Howard	E	1930
Harry Corbett	E	1930-1931
Francois Sybille	BEL	1930-1931
Bep van Klaveren	HOL	1931-1932
Cleto Locatelli	ITA	1932
Francois Sybille	BEL	1932-1933
Cleto Locatelli*	ITA	1933
Francois Sybille	BEL	1934
Carlo Orlandi*	ITA	1934-1935
Enrico Venturi*	ITA	1935-1936
Vittorio Tamagnini	ITA	1936-1937
Maurice Arnault	FR	1937
Gustave Humery	FR	1937-1938
Aldo Spoldi*	ITA	1938-1939
Karl Blaho	AU	1940-1941
Bruno Bisterzo	ITA	1941
Ascenzo Botta	ITA	1941
Bruno Bisterzo	ITA	1941-1942
Ascenzo Botta	ITA	1942
Roberto Proietti	ITA	1942-1943
Bruno Bisterzo	ITA	1943-1946
Roberto Proietti*	ITA	1946
Emile Dicristo	FR	1946-1947
Kid Dussart	BEL	1947
Roberto Proietti	ITA	1947-1948
Billy Thompson	E	1948-1949
Kid Dussart	BEL	1949
Roberto Proietti*	ITA	1949-1950
Pierre Montane	FR	1951
Elis Ask	FIN	1951-1952
Jorgen Johansen	DEN	1952-1954
Duilio Loi*	ITA	1954-1959
Mario Vecchiatto	ITA	1959-1960
Dave Charnley	E	1960-1963
Conny Rudhof*	GER	1963-1964
Willi Quatuor*	GER	1964-1965
Franco Brondi	ITA	1965
Maurice Tavant	FR	1965-1966
Borge Krogh	DEN	1966-1967
Pedro Carrasco*	SP	1967-1969
Miguel Velazquez	SP	1970-1971
Antonio Puddu	ITA	1971-1974
Ken Buchanan*	S	1974-1975

Title Holder	Birthplace/ Domicile	Tenure
Fernand Roelandts	BEL	1976
Perico Fernandez*	SP	1976-1977
Jim Watt*	S	1977-1979
Charlie Nash*	NI	1979-1980
Francisco Leon	SP	1980
Charlie Nash	NI	1980-1981
Joey Gibilisco	ITA	1981-1983
Lucio Cusma	ITA	1983-1984
Rene Weller	GER	1984-1986
Gert Bo Jacobsen	DEN	1986-1988
Rene Weller*	GER	1988
Policarpo Diaz*	SP	1988-1990
Antonio Renzo	ITA	1991-1992
Jean-Baptiste Mendy*	FR	1992-1994
Racheed Lawal	DEN	1994
Jean-Baptiste Mendy*	FR	1994-1995
Angel Mona	FR	1995-1997
Manuel Carlos Fernandes	FR	1997
Oscar Garcia Cano	SP	1997
Billy Schwer*	E	1997-1999
Oscar Garcia Cano	SP	1999-2000
Lucien Lorcy*	FR	2000-2001
Stefano Zoff*	ITA	2001-2002
Jason Cook	W	2002-2003
Stefano Zoff	ITA	2003-

L. Welterweight (140 lbs)

Title Holder	Birthplace/ Domicile	Tenure
Olli Maki	FIN	1964-1965
Juan Sombrita-Albornoz	SP	1965
Willi Quatuor*	GER	1965-1966
Conny Rudhof	GER	1967
Johann Orsolics	AU	1967-1968
Bruno Arcari*	ITA	1968-1970
Rene Roque	FR	1970-1971
Pedro Carrasco*	SP	1971-1972
Roger Zami	FR	1972
Cemal Kamaci	TU	1972-1973
Toni Ortiz	SP	1973-1974
Perico Fernandez*	SP	1974
Jose Ramon Gomez-Fouz	SP	1975
Cemal Kamaci*	TU	1975-1976
Dave Boy Green*	E	1976-1977
Primo Bandini	ITA	1977
Jean-Baptiste Piedvache	FR	1977-1978
Colin Power	E	1978
Fernando Sanchez	SP	1978-1979
Jose Luis Heredia	SP	1979
Jo Kimpuani	FR	1979-1980
Giuseppe Martinese	ITA	1980
Antonio Guinaldo	SP	1980-1981
Clinton McKenzie	E	1981-1982
Robert Gambini	FR	1982-1983
Patrizio Oliva*	ITA	1983-1985
Terry Marsh	E	1985-1986
Tusikoleta Nkalankete	FR	1987-1989
Efren Calamati	ITA	1989-1990
Pat Barrett	E	1990-1992
Valery Kayumba	ITA	1992-1993
Christian Merle	FR	1993-1994
Valery Kayumba	FR	1994
Khalid Rahilou*	FR	1994-1996
Soren Sondergaard*	DEN	1996-1998
Thomas Damgaard*	DEN	1998-2000
Oktay Urkal*	GER	2000-2001
Gianluca Branco*	ITA	2001-2002
Oktay Urkal	GER	2002-

Welterweight (147 lbs)

Title Holder	Birthplace/ Domicile	Tenure
Young Joseph	E	1910-1911
Georges Carpentier*	FR	1911-1912
Albert Badoud*	SWI	1915-1921
Johnny Basham	W	1919-1920
Ted Kid Lewis	E	1920-1924
Piet Hobin	BEL	1921-1925
Billy Mack	E	1923
Tommy Milligan	S	1924-1925
Mario Bosisio*	ITA	1925-1928
Leo Darton	BEL	1928
Alf Genon	BEL	1928-1929
Gustave Roth	BEL	1929-1932
Adrien Aneet	BEL	1932-1933
Jack Hood*	E	1933
Gustav Eder	GER	1934-1936
Felix Wouters	BEL	1936-1938
Saverio Turiello	ITA	1938-1939
Marcel Cerdan*	FR	1939-1942
Ernie Roderick	E	1946-1947
Robert Villemain*	FR	1947-1948
Livio Minelli	ITA	1949-1950
Michele Palermo	ITA	1950-1951
Eddie Thomas	W	1951
Charles Humez*	FR	1951-1952
Gilbert Lavoine	FR	1953-1954
Wally Thom	E	1954-1955
Idrissa Dione	FR	1955-1956
Emilio Marconi	ITA	1956-1958
Peter Waterman*	E	1958
Emilio Marconi	ITA	1958-1959
Duilio Loi*	ITA	1959-1963
Fortunato Manca*	ITA	1964-1965
Jean Josselin	FR	1966-1967
Carmelo Bossi	ITA	1967-1968
Fighting Mack	HOL	1968-1969
Silvano Bertini	ITA	1969
Jean Josselin	FR	1969
Johann Orsolics	AU	1969-1970
Ralph Charles	E	1970-1971
Roger Menetrey	FR	1971-1974
John H. Stracey*	E	1974-1975
Marco Scano	ITA	1976-1977
Jorgen Hansen	DEN	1977
Jorg Eipel	GER	1977
Alain Marion	FR	1977-1978
Jorgen Hansen	DEN	1978
Josef Pachler	AU	1978
Henry Rhiney	E	1978-1979
Dave Boy Green	E	1979
Jorgen Hansen	DEN	1979-1981
Hans-Henrik Palm	DEN	1982
Colin Jones*	W	1982-1983
Gilles Elbilia	FR	1983-1984
Gianfranco Rosi	ITA	1984-1985
Lloyd Honeyghan*	E	1985-1986
Jose Varela	GER	1986-1987
Alfonso Redondo	SP	1987
Mauro Martelli*	SWI	1987-1988
Nino la Rocca	ITA	1989
Antoine Fernandez	FR	1989-1990
Kirkland Laing	E	1990
Patrizio Oliva*	ITA	1990-1992
Ludovic Proto	FR	1992-1993
Gary Jacobs*	S	1993-1994
Jose Luis Navarro	SP	1994-1995
Valery Kayumba	FR	1995
Patrick Charpentier*	FR	1995-1996
Andrei Pestriaev*	RUS	1997
Michele Piccirillo*	ITA	1997-1998
Maxim Nesterenko	RUS	1998-1999
Alessandro Duran	ITA	1999
Andrei Pestriaev	RUS	1999-2000
Alessandro Duran	ITA	2000
Thomas Damgaard	DEN	2000-2001
Alessandro Duran	ITA	2001-2002
Christian Bladt	DEN	2002
Michel Trabant*	GER	2002-2003
Frederic Klose	FR	2003-

L. Middleweight (154 lbs)

Title Holder	Birthplace/ Domicile	Tenure
Bruno Visintin	ITA	1964-1966
Bo Hogberg	SWE	1966
Yolande Leveque	FR	1966
Sandro Mazzinghi*	ITA	1966-1968
Remo Golfarini	ITA	1968-1969
Gerhard Piaskowy	GER	1969-1970
Jose Hernandez	SP	1970-1972
Juan Carlos Duran	ITA	1972-1973
Jacques Kechichian	FR	1973-1974
Jose Duran	SP	1974-1975
Eckhard Dagge	GER	1975-1976
Vito Antuofermo	ITA	1976
Maurice Hope*	E	1976-1978
Gilbert Cohen	FR	1978-1979
Marijan Benes	YUG	1979-1981
Louis Acaries	FR	1981
Luigi Minchillo*	ITA	1981-1983
Herol Graham*	E	1983-1984
Jimmy Cable	E	1984
Georg Steinherr	GER	1984-1985
Said Skouma*	FR	1985-1986
Chris Pyatt	E	1986-1987
Gianfranco Rosi*	ITA	1987
Rene Jacquot*	FR	1988-1989
Edip Secovic	AU	1989
Giuseppe Leto	ITA	1989
Gilbert Dele*	FR	1989-1990
Said Skouma	FR	1991
Mourad Louati	HOL	1991
Jean-Claude Fontana	FR	1991-1992
Laurent Boudouani	FR	1992-1993
Bernard Razzano	FR	1993-1994
Javier Castillejos	SP	1994-1995
Laurent Boudouani*	FR	1995-1996
Faouzi Hattab	FR	1996
Davide Ciarlante*	ITA	1996-1997
Javier Castillejo*	SP	1998
Mamadou Thiam*	FR	1998-2000
Roman Karmazin*	RUS	2000
Mamadou Thiam*	FR	2001
Wayne Alexander*	E	2002
Roman Karmazin	RUS	2003-

Middleweight (160 lbs)

Title Holder	Birthplace/ Domicile	Tenure
Georges Carpentier*	FR	1912-1918
Ercole Balzac	FR	1920-1921
Gus Platts	E	1921
Willem Westbroek	HOL	1921
Johnny Basham	W	1921
Ted Kid Lewis	E	1921-1923
Roland Todd	E	1923-1924
Ted Kid Lewis	E	1924-1925
Bruno Frattini	ITA	1924-1925
Tommy Milligan	S	1925-1928
Rene Devos	BEL	1926-1927
Barthelemy Molina	FR	1928
Alex Ireland	S	1928-1929
Mario Bosisio	ITA	1928
Leone Jacovacci	ITA	1928-1929
Len Johnson	E	1928-1929
Marcel Thil	FR	1929-1930
Mario Bosisio	ITA	1930-1931
Poldi Steinbach	AU	1931
Hein Domgoergen	GER	1931-1932
Ignacio Ara	SP	1932-1933
Gustave Roth	BEL	1933-1934
Marcel Thil*	FR	1934-1938
Edouard Tenet	FR	1938
Bep van Klaveren	HOL	1938
Anton Christoforidis	GRE	1938-1939
Edouard Tenet	FR	1939
Josef Besselmann*	GER	1942-1943

Title Holder	Birthplace/ Domicile	Tenure
Marcel Cerdan	FR	1947-1948
Cyrille Delannoit	BEL	1948
Marcel Cerdan*	FR	1948
Cyrille Delannoit	BEL	1948-1949
Tiberio Mitri*	ITA	1949-1950
Randy Turpin	E	1951-1954
Tiberio Mitri	ITA	1954
Charles Humez	FR	1954-1958
Gustav Scholz*	GER	1958-1961
John Cowboy McCormack	S	1961-1962
Chris Christensen	DEN	1962
Laszlo Papp*	HUN	1962-1965
Nino Benvenuti*	ITA	1965-1967
Juan Carlos Duran	ITA	1967-1969
Tom Bogs	DEN	1969-1970
Juan Carlos Duran	ITA	1970-1971
Jean-Claude Bouttier	FR	1971-1972
Tom Bogs*	DEN	1973
Elio Calcabrini	ITA	1973-1974
Jean-Claude Bouttier	FR	1974
Kevin Finnegan	E	1974-1975
Gratien Tonna*	FR	1975
Bunny Sterling	E	1976
Angelo Jacopucci	ITA	1976
Germano Valsecchi	ITA	1976-1977
Alan Minter	E	1977
Gratien Tonna	FR	1977-1978
Alan Minter*	E	1978-1979
Kevin Finnegan	E	1980
Matteo Salvemini	ITA	1980
Tony Sibson*	E	1980-1982
Louis Acaries	FR	1982-1984
Tony Sibson	E	1984-1985
Ayub Kalule	DEN	1985-1986
Herol Graham	E	1986-1987
Sumbu Kalambay*	ITA	1987
Pierre Joly	FR	1987-1988
Christophe Tiozzo*	FR	1988-1989
Francesco dell' Aquila	ITA	1989-1990
Sumbu Kalambay	ITA	1990-1993
Agostino Cardamone*	ITA	1993-1994
Richie Woodhall*	E	1995-1996
Alexandre Zaitsev	RUS	1996
Hassine Cherifi*	FR	1996-1998
Agostino Cardamone*	ITA	1998
Erland Betare*	FR	1999-2000
Howard Eastman*	E	2001
Christian Sanavia	ITA	2001-2002
Morrade Hakkar*	FR	2002
Howard Eastman	E	2003-

S. Middleweight (168 lbs)

Title Holder	Birthplace/ Domicile	Tenure
Mauro Galvano*	ITA	1990-1991
James Cook	E	1991-1992
Franck Nicotra*	FR	1992
Vincenzo Nardiello	ITA	1992-1993
Ray Close*	NI	1993
Vinzenzo Nardiello	ITA	1993-1994
Frederic Seillier*	FR	1994-1995
Henry Wharton*	E	1995-1996
Frederic Seillier*	FR	1996
Andrei Shkalikov*	RUS	1997
Dean Francis*	E	1997-1998
Bruno Girard*	FR	1999
Andrei Shkalikov	RUS	2000-2001
Danilo Haeussler	GER	2001-

L. Heavyweight (175 lbs)

Title Holder	Birthplace/ Domicile	Tenure
Georges Carpentier	FR	1913-1922
Battling Siki	FR	1922-1923
Emile Morelle	FR	1923
Raymond Bonnel	FR	1923-1924
Louis Clement	SWI	1924-1926
Herman van T'Hof	HOL	1926
Fernand Delarge	BEL	1926-1927
Max Schmeling*	GER	1927-1928
Michele Bonaglia*	ITA	1929-1930
Ernst Pistulla*	GER	1931-1932
Adolf Heuser	GER	1932
John Andersson	SWE	1933
Martinez de Alfara	SP	1934
Marcel Thil	FR	1934-1935
Merlo Preciso	ITA	1935
Hein Lazek	AU	1935-1936
Gustave Roth	BEL	1936-1938
Adolf Heuser*	GER	1938-1939
Luigi Musina*	ITA	1942-1943
Freddie Mills*	E	1947-1950
Albert Yvel	FR	1950-1951
Don Cockell*	E	1951-1952
Conny Rux*	GER	1952
Jacques Hairabedian	FR	1953-1954
Gerhard Hecht	GER	1954-1955
Willi Hoepner	GER	1955
Gerhard Hecht	GER	1955-1957
Artemio Calzavara	ITA	1957-1958
Willi Hoepner	GER	1958
Erich Schoeppner	GER	1958-1962
Giulio Rinaldi	ITA	1962-1964
Gustav Scholz*	GER	1964-1965
Giulio Rinaldi	ITA	1965-1966
Piero del Papa	ITA	1966-1967
Lothar Stengel	GER	1967-1968
Tom Bogs*	DEN	1968-1969
Yvan Prebeg	YUG	1969-1970
Piero del Papa	ITA	1970-1971
Conny Velensek	GER	1971-1972
Chris Finnegan	E	1972
Rudiger Schmidtke	GER	1972-1973
John Conteh*	E	1973-1974
Domenico Adinolfi	ITA	1974-1976
Mate Parlov*	YUG	1976-1977
Aldo Traversaro	ITA	1977-1979
Rudi Koopmans	HOL	1979-1984
Richard Caramonolis	FR	1984
Alex Blanchard	HOL	1984-1987
Tom Collins	E	1987-1988
Pedro van Raamsdonk	HOL	1988
Jan Lefeber	HOL	1988-1989
Eric Nicoletta	FR	1989-1990
Tom Collins	E	1990-1991
Graciano Rocchigiani*	GER	1991-1992
Eddie Smulders	HOL	1993-1994
Fabrice Tiozzo*	FR	1994-1995
Eddy Smulders	HOL	1995-1996
Crawford Ashley	E	1997
Ole Klemetsen*	NOR	1997-1998
Crawford Ashley	E	1998-1999
Clinton Woods*	E	1999-2000
Yawe Davis	ITA	2001-2002
Thomas Ulrich*	GER	2002-2003
Stipe Drews	CRO	2003-

Cruiserweight (190 lbs)

Title Holder	Birthplace/ Domicile	Tenure
Sam Reeson*	E	1987-1988
Angelo Rottoli	ITA	1989
Anaclet Wamba*	FR	1989-1990
Johnny Nelson*	E	1990-1992
Akim Tafer*	FR	1992-1993
Massimiliano Duran	ITA	1993-1994
Carl Thompson	E	1994
Alexander Gurov	UK	1995
Patrice Aouissi	FR	1995
Alexander Gurov*	UK	1995-1996
Akim Tafer*	FR	1996-1997
Johnny Nelson	E	1997-1998
Terry Dunstan*	E	1998
Alexei Iliin	RUS	1999
Torsten May*	GER	1999-2000
Carl Thompson*	E	2000-2001
Alexander Gurov*	UK	2001-2002
Pietro Aurino	ITA	2002-

Heavyweight (190 lbs +)

Title Holder	Birthplace/ Domicile	Tenure
Georges Carpentier	FR	1913-1922
Battling Siki	FR	1922-1923
Erminio Spalla	ITA	1923-1926
Paolino Uzcudun	SP	1926-1928
Harry Persson	SWE	1926
Phil Scott	E	1927
Pierre Charles	BEL	1929-1931
Hein Muller	GER	1931-1932
Pierre Charles	BEL	1932-1933
Paolino Uzcudun	SP	1933
Primo Carnera	ITA	1933-1935
Pierre Charles	BEL	1935-1937
Arno Kolblin	GER	1937-1938
Hein Lazek	AU	1938-1939
Adolf Heuser	GER	1939
Max Schmeling*	GER	1939-1941
Olle Tandberg	SWE	1943
Karel Sys*	BEL	1943-1946
Bruce Woodcock	E	1946-1949
Joe Weidin	AU	1950-1951
Jack Gardner	E	1951
Hein Ten Hoff	GER	1951-1952
Karel Sys	BEL	1952
Heinz Neuhaus	GER	1952-1955
Franco Cavicchi	ITA	1955-1956
Ingemar Johansson*	SWE	1956-1959
Dick Richardson	W	1960-1962
Ingemar Johansson*	SWE	1962-1963
Henry Cooper*	E	1964
Karl Mildenberger	GER	1964-1968
Henry Cooper*	E	1968-1969
Peter Weiland	GER	1969-1970
Jose Urtain	SP	1970
Henry Cooper	E	1970-1971
Joe Bugner	E	1971
Jack Bodell	E	1971
Jose Urtain	SP	1971-1972
Jurgen Blin	GER	1972
Joe Bugner*	E	1972-1975
Richard Dunn	E	1976
Joe Bugner	E	1976-1977
Jean-Pierre Coopman	BEL	1977
Lucien Rodriguez	FR	1977
Alfredo Evangelista	SP	1977-1979
Lorenzo Zanon	SP	1979-1980
John L. Gardner*	E	1980-1981
Lucien Rodriguez	FR	1981-1984
Steffen Tangstad	NOR	1984-1985
Anders Eklund	SWE	1985
Frank Bruno*	E	1985-1986
Steffen Tangstad	NOR	1986
Alfredo Evangelista	SP	1987
Anders Eklund	SWE	1987
Francesco Damiani	ITA	1987-1989
Derek Williams	E	1989-1990
Jean Chanet	FR	1990
Lennox Lewis*	E	1990-1992
Henry Akinwande*	E	1993-1995
Zeljko Mavrovic*	CRO	1995-1998
Vitali Klitschko*	UK	1998-1999
Vladimir Klitschko*	UK	1999-2000
Vitali Klitschko*	UK	2000-2001
Luan Krasniqi	GER	2002
Przemyslaw Saleta	POL	2002
Sinan Samil Sam	TU	2002-

A-Z of Current World Champions

by Eric Armit

Shows the record since 1 July 2002, plus career summary and pen portrait, of all men holding IBF, WBA, WBC and WBO titles as at 30 June 2003. The author has also produced the same data for those who first won titles between 1 July 2002 and 30 June 2003, but were no longer champions at the end of the period in question. Incidentally, the place name given is the respective boxer's domicile and may not necessarily be his birthplace, while all nicknames are shown where applicable in brackets. Not included are British fighters, Lennox Lewis (WBC and IBF heavyweight champion), Joe Calzaghe (WBO super-middleweight champion), Johnny Nelson (WBO cruiserweight champion) and Scott Harrison (WBO featherweight champion). Their full records can be found among the Active British-Based Boxers: Career Records' section.

Jose Antonio (Jaguar) Aguirre

Cardenas, Mexico. *Born* 5 July, 1975
WBC M. Flyweight Champion

Major Amateur Honours: His amateur record shows 15 wins in 18 fights and he was the Mexican Golden Gloves Champion in 1995
Turned Pro: February 1995
Significant Results: Cruz Zamora L PTS 10, Paulino Villalobos W PTS 10, Gustavo Andrade W CO 1, Rafael Orozco W CO 2, Wandee Singwangcha W PTS 12, Jose Luis Zepeda W CO 5, Manny Melchor W PTS 12, Wolf Tokimitsu W RSC 3
Type/Style: A switch hitter and a good, if upright, technician with a strong body attack and a solid chin
Points of Interest: 5'4" tall. Is the first world champion from Tabasco State and originally studied to be a Doctor. Won the WBC title in February 2000 and, due to a serious shoulder injury and a car crash, he would have made more than just seven defences. Unbeaten in his last 18 fights, he has 19 wins inside the distance

19.10.02	Juan Palacios W PTS 12 Villahermosa *(WBC M.Flyweight Title Defence)*
22.02.03	Juan Alfonso Keb W RTD 7 Mexico City *(WBC M.Flyweight Title Defence)*
23.06.03	Keitaro Hoshino W RSC 12 Yokohama *(WBC M.Flyweight Title Defence)*
Career: 32 contests, won 30, lost 1, drew 1.	

Rosendo (Buffalo) Alvarez

Managua, Nicaragua. *Born* 6 May, 1970
WBA L.Flyweight Champion. Former WBA M.Flyweight Champion

Major Amateur Honours: Competed in the 1991 Pan-American Games and claims 66 wins in 78 fights
Turned Pro: December 1992
Significant Results: José Bonilla W PTS 12 and W CO 11, Chana Porpaoin W PTS 12, Kermin Guardia W CO 3, Eric Chavez W PTS 12, Songkram Porpaoin W RSC 11, Ricardo Lopez T Draw 7 and L PTS 12, Beibis Mendoza L DIS 7 and W PTS 12, Pitchitnoi Chor Siriwat W RSC 12
Type/Style: A fine boxer, who is both skilful and fast, he is also a good in-fighter with a fair punch. However, he has poor discipline
Points of Interest: 5'5" tall. Has 21 wins inside the distance under his belt and has beaten both of the Porpaoin twins. Made five defences of his WBA mini-flyweight title before losing it when he failed to make the weight for his second fight with Ricardo Lopez. Lost for the vacant title to Beibis Mendoza in August 2000, but outpointed him in March 2001 to become champion again and has made two defences. Has had problems with drink and drugs

31.03.03	Beibis Mendoza W PTS 12 Little Rock *(WBA L.Flyweight Title Defence)*
Career: 35 contests, won 32, drew 1, lost 2.	

Rosendo Alvarez

Noel Arambulet

Churuguara, Venezuela. *Born* 18 May, 1974

WBA M.Flyweight Champion

Major Amateur Honours: A former Venezuelan national champion, he claims 128 wins in 144 fights
Turned Pro: November 1996
Significant Results: Jose Garcia L PTS 12 and W PTS 12, Jomo Gamboa W PTS 12 and L PTS 12
Type/Style: Busy and clever, he is a hit-and-run type
Points of Interest: First won the WBA title in October 1999 by beating Jomo Gamboa, before losing it to the same man in his second defence, he is not a puncher and has only 10 wins inside the distance. Is married and has two children

29.07.02	Keitaro Hoshino W PTS 12 Yokohama *(WBA M.Flyweight Title Challenge)*
20.12.02	Keitaro Hoshino W PTS 12 Osaka *(WBA M.Flyweight Title Defence)*
Career: 23 contests, won 19, drew 1, lost 2, no contest 1.	

Jorge (Travieso) Arce

Los Mochis, Mexico. *Born* 27 July, 1979

WBC L.Flyweight Champion. Former WBO L.Flyweight Champion

Major Amateur Honours: None known, but claims 37 wins in 40 bouts
Turned Pro: January 1996
Significant Results: Jose Victor Burgos L PTS 12, Miguel Martinez W CO 2, Juan Domingo Cordoba W PTS 12, Salvatore Fanni W RSC 6, Michael Carbajal L RSC 11, Juanito Rubillar W PTS 12
Type/Style: Tall and slim, he is a stylish fighter with good speed and power and seems to be growing in stature
Points of Interest: 5'7" tall. A stablemate to the Morales brothers, Erik and Diego, he has 24 wins by stoppage or kayo

06.07.02	Yo-Sam Choi W RSC 6 Seoul *(WBC L.Flyweight Title Challenge)*
16.11.02	Agustin Luna W RSC 3 Las Vegas *(WBC L.Flyweight Title Defence)*
22.02.03	Ernesto Castro W CO 1 Mexico City *(WBC L.Flyweight Title Defence)*
03.05.03	Melchor Cob Castro W TD 7 Las Vegas *(WBC L.Flyweight Title Defence)*
Career: 38 contest, won 34, drew 1, lost 3.	

Miguel Barrera

Puerto Escondido, Colombia. *Born* 5 November, 1978

IBF M. Flyweight Champion

Major Amateur Honours: None known
Turned Pro: March 1999
Significant Results: Ilson Diaz W CO 2, Jhon Molina W PTS 10, Roberto Leyva T Draw 3
Type/Style: Strong, rough, aggressive and a good body puncher
Points of Interest: 5'0" tall. With 12 wins inside the distance, he fought a technical draw with Roberto Leyva in September 2001 in his first title challenge. Having won the title, he was hospitalised with brain damage after losing to Edgar Cardenas, but has thankfully recovered

09.08.02	Roberto Leyva W PTS 12 Las Vegas *(IBF M.Flyweight Title Challenge)*
22.03.03	Roberto Leyva W CO 3 Las Vegas *(IBF M. Flyweight Title Defence)*
31.05.03	Edgar Cardenas L CO 10 Tijuana *(IBF M. Flyweight Title Defence)*
Career: 23 contests, won 20, drew 2, lost 1.	

Markus Beyer

Eriabrunn, Germany. *Born* 28 April, 1971

WBC S. Middleweight Champion. Former Undefeated German S.Middleweight Champion

Major Amateur Honours: Won a gold medal in the 1988 European Junior Championships, competed in the 1992 and 1996 Olympics, was a bronze medallist in the 1995 World Championships and won a silver medal in the 1996 European Championships
Turned Pro: November 1996
Significant Results: Juan Carlos Viloria W PTS 12, Richie Woodhall W PTS 10, Leif Keiski W CO 7, Glenn Catley L RSC 12
Type/Style: A smart-boxing southpaw who is a real tactician, but not a puncher
Points of Interest: Won his European Junior gold medal at flyweight. He is in his second reign as WBC champion, having beaten Richie Woodhall for the title in October 1999 and lost it to Glenn Catley in his second defence in May 2000. Has only 11 wins inside the distance

24.08.02	Ron Martinez W RSC 4 Leipzig
05.04.03	Eric Lucas w pts 12 Leipzig *(WBC S. Middleweight Title Challenge)*
Career: 28 contests, won 27, lost 1.	

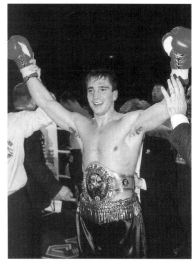

Markus Beyer Les Clark

Wayne (Big Truck) Braithwaite

Plaisience, Guyana. *Born* 9 August, 1975

WBC Cruiserweight Champion. Former Undefeated Guyanan L.Heavyweight Champion

Major Amateur Honours: A four-time Guyanan champion, he competed in the 1996 South American Olympic trials and claims 57 wins in 60 amateur fights
Turned Pro: February 1997
Significant Results: Wayne Harris W CO 7, Adam Watt W RSC 1, Dale Brown W RSC 8, Louis Azile W RSC 12
Type/Style: Is a pressure fighter and big-punching southpaw who often switches guards
Points of Interest: 6'4" tall. Now based in New York, he has won his last 14 contests inside the distance

11.10.02	Vincenzo Cantatore W RSC 10 Campione d'Italia *(Vacant WBC Cruiserweight Title)*
21.02.03	Ravea Springs W RSC 4 Miami *(WBC Cruiserweight Title Defence)*
Career: 19 contests, won 19.	

Johnny Bredahl

Copenhagen, Denmark. *Born* 27 August, 1968
WBA Bantamweight Champion. Former WBO S.Flyweight Champion. Former Undefeated European Bantamweight Champion

Major Amateur Honours: A bronze medallist in the 1986 European Youth Championships and 1987 Senior Championships and a Scandinavian and Danish champion, he competed in the 1988 Olympics
Turned Pro: December 1988
Significant Results: Jose Quirino W PTS 12, Rafael Caban W PTS 12, Wayne McCullough L RSC 8, Efrain Pintor W RSC 2, Alex Yagupov W PTS 12 (twice), Paul Lloyd W RSC 1, Paulie Ayala L PTS 12, Eidy Moya W CO 9
Type/Style: Is a stylish, upright boxer with an excellent jab. He is also a sharp puncher and has good stamina
Points of Interest: 5'8" tall. Failed in bids to win WBC and WBA titles before finding success against Eidy Moya in April 2002 and has made one defence. Was unbeaten in eight European title fights. With 26 wins by stoppage or knockout, he is now trained by Freddie Roach

08.11.02	Leo Gamez W PTS 12 Copenhagen *(WBA Bantamweight Title Defence)*

Career: 55 contests, won 53, lost 2.

Jose Victor Burgos

Puebla, Mexico. *Born* 10 April, 1974
IBF L. Flyweight Champion. Former Mexican L. Flyweight Champion

Major Amateur Honours: None known
Turned Pro: February 1993
Significant Results: Edgar Cardenas W PTS 12, Alex Sanchez L PTS 12 and DREW 12, Jorge Arce W PTS 12, Jacob Matlala L TD 8, Eric Morel L PTS 12, Jesper Jensen L PTS 12, Roberto Leyva L RSC 8, Juan Keb-Baas W PTS 10
Type/Style: Is flashy and has a good jab with fast hands
Points of Interest: 5'2" tall. Although winning the WBO title in his second try after losing to Alex Sanchez in a previous effort in 1997, for a long time he was considered to be only a journeyman, but has lost only one of his last 14 fights. His record shows 21 wins inside the distance, but he has been stopped four times

15.02.03	Alex Sanchez W RSC 12 Las Vegas *(Vacant IBF L. Flyweight Title)*

Career: 51 contests, won 36, drew 2, lost 13.

Chris (Rapid Fire) Byrd

Flint, Michigan, USA. *Born* 15 August, 1970
IBF Heavyweight Champion. Former WBO Heavyweight Champion

Major Amateur Honours: A United States Champion in 1989 at 156lbs and in 1991 and 1992 at 165 lbs, he won a silver medal in 1992 Olympic Games
Turned Pro: January 1993
Significant Results: Arthur Williams W PTS 10, Phil Jackson W PTS 12, Lionel Butler W RSC 8, Uriah Grant W PTS 10, Ike Ibeabuchi L RSC 5, Vitali Klitschko W RTD 9, Vladimir Klitschko L PTS 12, David Tua W PTS 12
Type/Style: Is a slick, fast moving southpaw
Points of Interest: Comes from a family of boxers, his father having been the head coach for the United States amateur team, while other members of his family, including a sister, have also fought as professionals. Won the WBO title by beating Vitali Klitschko in April 2000, but lost in his first defence six months later to Vladimir Klitschko

14.12.02	Evander Holyfield W PTS 12 Atlantic City *(Vacant IBF Heavyweight Title)*

Career: 38 contests, won 36, lost 2.

Chris Byrd   Les Clark

Ivan (Iron Boy) Calderon

Bayamon, Puerto Rico. *Born* 27 January, 1975
WBO M.Flyweight Champion

Major Amateur Honours: Claiming 110 wins in 130 contests, he won a bronze medal in the 1999 Pan-American Games, a silver medal in the 1999 Central American Games and competed in the 1999 World Championships and the 2000 Olympic Games
Turned Pro: February 2001
Significant Results: Jorge Romero W RTD 4
Type/Style: Southpaw. Is a good counter puncher, but lacks power
Points of Interest: 5'0" tall. Voted "Newcomer of the Year" in Puerto Rico in 2002, he is an extrovert who is tremendously popular in Puerto Rico. Has only four wins by stoppage or kayo

30.07.02	Alejandro Moreno W PTS 10 Concho
06.09.02	Roberto Gomez W PTS 10 Victoria
22.11.02	Lee Sandoval W PTS 12 Caguas
20.12.02	Valentin Leon W PTS 10 Aibonito
07.03.03	Juan Carlos Perez W PTS 10 San Juan
03.05.03	Eduardo Marquez W TD 9 Las Vegas *(WBO M. Flyweight Title Challenge)*

Career: 16 contests, won 16.

Cruz (Costenito) Carbajal

Vera Cruz, Mexico. *Born* 3 May, 1974
WBO Bantamweight Champion. Former Undefeated Mexican Bantamweight Champion

Major Amateur Honours: A five-times State Champion, he claims only one loss in 39 fights
Turned Pro: May 1992
Significant Results: Jose Luis Bueno W CO 2, Lehlohonolo Ledwaba L PTS 12, Samson Toyota L CO 5, Genaro Garcia W RSC 8, Hugo Dianzo L PTS 10 and W PTS 12, Johnny Bredahl L PTS 8, Fernando Montiel L RSC 4, Alejandro Estrada W RSC 6, Mauricio Martinez W RSC 9
Type/Style: Although a strong and aggressive, brutal body puncher, he is fairly limited and has a poor defence
Points of Interest: Started boxing at 12 after being inspired by the achievements of Salvador Sanchez. Having worked as a butcher before turning

pro, at one stage he had a spell of eight losses in ten fights. Having almost had the WBO title taken off him due to a dispute over the sanction fee, he has made just the one defence. Has 19 wins inside the distance to his credit

27.09.02	Danny Romero W RTD 4 Albuquerque (WBO Bantamweight Title Defence)
12.04.03	Steve Dotse W RTD 2 Las Vegas
Career:	35 contests, won 23, drew 1, lost 11.

Edgar (Tun Tun) Cardenas

Mexico City, Mexico. *Born* 16 September, 1974
IBF M. Flyweight Champion. Former Undefeated Mexican M. Flyweight Champion

Major Amateur Honours: None known
Turned Pro: October 1991
Significant Results: Jesus Chong L PTS 12 and W DIS 9, Jose Victor Burgos L PTS 12, Alex Sanchez W PTS 10, Juan Keb-Baas W PTS 12, Alejandro Montiel L RSC 10, Jesper Jensen L PTS 12
Type/Style: Is tough and aggressive, but not a hard puncher
Points of Interest: 5'0" tall. Started boxing at the age of 10 and was a member of the same team as Erik Morales. Retired in 2001 before being talked into trying again by Morales, he has 16 wins inside the distance and his victory over previously unbeaten Miguel Barrera was a big upset

12.07.02	Lupe Arce W RSC 2 Tijuana
01.11.02	Marino Montiel W PTS 12 Tijuana (Vacant Mexican M.Flyweight Title)
31.05.03	Miguel Barrera W CO 10 Tijuana (IBF M.Flyweight Title Challenge)
Career:	41 contests, won 29, drew 2, lost 10.

DeMarcus (Chop Chop) Corley

Washington, USA. *Born* 3 June, 1974
WBO L. Welterweight Champion

Major Amateur Honours: Was the national Golden Gloves champion in 1995 before losing to Fernando Vargas in the Olympic trials the following year
Turned Pro: May 1996
Significant Results: Dillon Carew T Draw 3, Daniel Lujan L PTS 10, Ener Julio W PTS 12 (twice), Felix Flores W RSC 1

Type/Style: Is a flashy, quick-punching southpaw
Points of Interest: Starting boxing at the age of 10, he gave it up for a while and worked as a lifeguard. Only received the chance to win the WBO title when the champion, and former victim, Ener Julio, was shown to have cataracts in both eyes five days before a title defence in June 2001, Corley stepping in as a late substitute to stop Felix Flores to win the title. Extremely colourful, he designs his own ring outfits and has been known to wear red tights and yellow boots into the ring. Outside the ring, he suffered two gun shot wounds a few years back when being robbed. Has 16 wins inside the distance

| 04.01.03 | Randall Bailey W PTS 12 Washington DC (WBO L.Welterweight Title Defence) |
| **Career:** | 30 contests, won 28, drew 1, lost 1. |

Oscar (Golden Boy) De La Hoya

Montebello, USA. *Born* 4 February, 1973
WBC & WBA L. Middleweight Champion. Former WBC Welterweight Champion. Former Undefeated WBC L.Welterweight Champion. Former Undefeated IBF & WBO Lightweight Champion. Former Undefeated WBO S.Featherweight Champion

Major Amateur Honours: The United States champion in 1990/91, he won gold at the 1992 Olympics. Was also the national Golden Gloves champion in 1989
Turned Pro: November 1992
Significant Results: Genaro Hernandez W RSC 6, James Leija W RSC 2, Julio Cesar Chavez W RSC 4 and W RTD 8, Miguel Gonzalez W PTS 12, Pernell Whitaker W PTS 12, Hector Camacho W PTS 12, Ike Quartey W PTS 12, Oba Carr W RSC 11, Felix Trinidad L PTS 12, Derrell Coley W RSC 7, Shane Mosley L PTS 12, Arturo Gatti W RSC 5, Javier Castillejo W RSC 12
Type/Style: Is recognised as a smooth, classy boxer and a fast and accurate puncher
Points of Interest: 5'11" tall. Has beaten 14 world or former world champions,

has won six versions of world titles in five divisions and has been boxing since the age of six. Lost the WBC welterweight title to Felix Trinidad, but defeated Derrell Coley in an eliminator and was declared WBC champion again when Trinidad moved up, only to lose the title again to Shane Mosley in June 2000. Moved up to light-middleweight and won the title by beating Javier Castillejo in June 2001

14.09.02	Fernando Vargas W RSC 11 Las Vegas (WBC L.Middleweight Title Defence. WBA L.Middleweight Title Challenge)
03.05.03	Luis Campas W RSC 7 Las Vegas (WBC & WBA L. Middleweight Title Defences)
Career:	38 contests, won 36, lost 2.

Oscar de la Hoya

Nelson Dieppa

Vieques, Puerto Rico. *Born* 25 February, 1971
WBO L. Flyweight Champion

Major Amateur Honours: Won a bronze medal in the 1991 World Championships and a bronze medal in the 1991 Pan-American Games. Also competed in the 1992 Olympic Games
Turned Pro: February 1993

Significant Results: Pablo Tiznado W CO 6, Carlos Murillo L PTS 10, Ramon Hurtado W CO 3, Will Grigsby L PTS 12, Julio Coronel W PTS 10, Andy Tabanas W RSC 11, Fahlan Sakkririn W PTS 12

Type/Style: Is a clever, slick boxing, right-hand puncher

Points of Interest: Trained by Felix Trinidad (senior), he has 11 wins inside the distance. His first crack at the title saw the winner, Will Grigsby, fail a drugs test before being stripped. Won the vacant title when beating Andy Tabanas in April 2001 and has made two defences

24.08.02	John Molina T DRAW 2 Carolina
	(WBO L. Flyweight Title Defence)
Career: 23 contests, won 19, drew 2, lost 2.	

Leonardo (Leo the Lion) Dorin

Montreal, Canada. *Born* Costana, Romania 10 April, 1970
WBA Lightweight Champion

Major Amateur Honours: Won a bronze medal in the 1992 Olympics, a bronze medal in the 1993 European Championships, a gold medal in the 1995 World Championships, a gold medal in the European championships in 1995, a bronze medal in the 1996 Olympics and competed in the 1997 World Championships. Claims only 15 losses in 254 fights

Leonardo Dorin

Turned Pro: May 1998

Significant Results: Gustavo Cuello W PTS 10, Gary St Clair W PTS 10, Martin O'Malley W RSC 9, Raul Balbi W PTS 12 (twice)

Type/Style: Although being a rough, tough, strong and aggressive pressure fighter, he is not a big puncher

Points of Interest: 5'4" tall with a 64" reach. Born Leonard Doroftei, he is based in Canada and won the WBA title by beating Raul Balbi in January 2002. Was inactive for 10 months before the Paul Spadafora bout after suffering a broken arm. Has only seven wins inside the distance

17.05.03	Paul Spadafora DREW 12 Pittsburg
	(WBA Lightweight Title Defence.
	IBF Lightweight Title Challenge)
Career: 22 contests, won 21, drew 1.	

Acelino (Popo) Freitas

Salvador de Bahia, Brazil. *Born* 21 September, 1975
WBO & WBA S.Featherweight Champion. Former Undefeated Brazilian Lightweight Champion

Major Amateur Honours: Won a silver medal in the 1995 Pan-American Games and claims 72 wins in 74 fights

Turned Pro: July 1995

Significant Results: Anatoly Alexandrov W CO 1, Claudio Martinet W CO 3, Barry Jones W RSC 8, Javier Jauregui W RSC 1, Lemuel Nelson W RSC 2,Carlos Rios W RSC 9, Orlando Soto W RSC 4, Alfred Kotey W PTS 10, Joel Casamayor W PTS 12

Type/Style: Strong and aggressive, he has fast hands, is a quick starter, and is a crushing puncher with his right hand, but can get careless

Points of Interest: 5'7" tall. Brother Luiz Carlos is also a pro and a double Brazilian champion. Won his first 29 fights inside the distance, 22 within the first three rounds, and has 12 first-round finishes. Has made seven defences of his WBO title, including the double title victory over Joel Casamayor, and two defences of his combined title

03.08.02	Daniel Attah W PTS 12 Phoenix
	(WBO & WBA S.Featherweight
	Title Defences)
15.03.03	Juan Carlos Ramirez W RSC 4 Chicago
	(WBO & WBA S.Featherweight
	Title Defences)
Career: 33 contests, won 33.	

Acelino Freitas   Les Clark

Derrick (Smoke) Gainer

Pensacola, USA. *Born* 22 August, 1972
WBA Featherweight Champion

Major Amateur Honours: None, but had around 30 bouts

Turned Pro: July 1990

Significant Results: Harold Warren W

215

PTS 12 (twice), Kevin Kelley L CO 8, Donovan Carey W RSC 6, Diego Corrales L RSC 3

Type/Style: Is a good but cautious, upright southpaw with not too sound a chin

Points of Interest: 5'9" tall with a 72" reach. Earlier managed by Roy Jones, he was initially a flyweight when he turned pro. Having lost in challenge for the IBF title to Diego Corrales, his fight with Freddie Norwood in September 2000 was for the vacant WBA title after Norwood had been stripped for failing to make the weight. Has made just three defences in almost three years

24.08.02	Daniel Seda T Draw 2 Carolina
	(WBA Featherweight Title Defence)
12.04.03	Oscar Leon W PTS 12 Las Vegas
	(WBA Featherweight Title Defence)
Career: 45 contests, won 39, drew 1, lost 5.	

Artur (Atuiz) Grigorian

Tashkent, Uzbekistan. *Born* 20 October,1967
WBO Lightweight Champion

Major Amateur Honours: Won a gold medal in the 1990 Goodwill Games, a silver medal in 1991 World Championships, a gold medal in the 1994 Chemical Cup and competed in the 1992 Olympics and the 1993 World Championships. Claims 361 wins in 384 fights
Turned Pro: April 1994
Significant Results: Antonio Rivera W CO 12, David Armstrong W PTS 12, Marco Rudolph W RSC 6, Oscar Garcia Cano W PTS 12, Michael Clark W CO 5, Wilson Galli W RSC 10, Sandro Casamonica W RSC 9, Antonio Pitalua W PTS 12, Aldo Rios W PTS 12
Type/Style: Is a stylish box-fighting southpaw
Points of Interest: 5'9" tall with a 69" reach. A former WBO interim champion who was awarded the full title without fighting for it, he beat Shane Mosley as an amateur. Has been the WBO champion since 1996 and has made 17 title defences

14.09.02	Stefano Zoff W PTS 12 Braunschweig
	(WBO Lightweight Title Defence)
18.01.03	Matt Zegan W PTS 12 Essen
	(WBO Lightweight Title Defence)
Career: 36 contests, won 36.	

Joan (Little Tyson) Guzman

Santo Domingo, Dominican Republic.
Born 1 May, 1976
WBO S.Bantamweight Champion.
Former Undefeated Dominican Featherweight Champion. Former Undefeated Dominican S.Bantamweight Champion

Major Amateur Honours: A three-time Central American champion, he competed in the 1995 Pan-American games and the 1996 Olympics
Turned Pro: September 1997
Significant Results: Francisco DeLeon W CO 11, Hector Avila W CO 2, Edgar Ruiz W PTS 12
Type/Style: Is a compact, powerful, short-armed fighter and a strong body puncher
Points of Interest: 5'7" tall. Has had only had one fight in the past 16 months. Known for his punching power only four of his opponents have managed to go the distance

17.08.02	Fabio Oliva W CO 3 Cardiff
	(Vacant WBO S.Bantamweight Title)
Career: 18 contests, won 18.	

Carlos (Famoso) Hernandez

Bellflower, California, USA. *Born* 23 January, 1971
IBF S.Featherweight Champion

Major Amateur Honours: None, but claims 21 wins in 25 fights
Turned Pro: January 1992
Significant Results: Gregorio Vargas W PTS 10, Genaro Hernandez L PTS 12, Floyd Mayweather L PTS 12, Justin Juuko W PTS 10, Mark Burse W PTS 10
Type/Style: Very strong, he is bullish, aggressive and has a good left hook and a good chin
Points of Interest: Although his parents are from El Salvador, Carlos was born in California and counts scuba diving and rock climbing among his hobbies. With 24 stoppage wins to his name, he is a good example of trying again, having failed against Genaro Hernandez in 1997 and Floyd Mayweather in 2001 in previous attempts to win a version of the title

01.02.03	David Santos W TD 8 Las Vegas
	(Vacant IBF S. Featherweight Title)
30.05.03	Moises Pedroza W CO 2 Eagle Pass
Career: 43 contests, won 39, drew 1, lost 3.	

Bernard Hopkins

Bernard (The Executioner) Hopkins

Philadelphia, USA. *Born* 15 January, 1965
WBC, WBA and IBF Middleweight Champion

Major Amateur Honours: None, but claims 95 wins in 99 fights
Turned Pro: October 1988
Significant Results: Roy Jones L PTS 12, Lupe Aquino W PTS 12, Segundo Mercado DREW 12 and W PTS 12, Robert Allen NC 4 and W RSC 7, Antwun Echols W PTS 12 and W RSC 10, Syd Vanderpool W PTS 12, Keith Holmes W PTS 12, Felix Trinidad W RSC 12, Carl Daniels W RTD 10
Type/Style: A strong if mechanical boxer, he is a powerful puncher with fast hands
Points of Interest: 6'0" tall with a 71" reach. A nephew of the former pro, Art McCloud, he spent five years in jail. Entering the ring wearing an executioners mask and a cape is his trademark and despite losing his first paid fight, he can now boast of 28 wins inside the distance. Lost to Roy Jones in his first attempt to win the IBF title and drew with Segundo Mercado for the vacant title before beating Mercado in a return in April 1995. Has made 13 defences of his IBF title and carried off the WBC title by outpointing Keith Holmes in April 2001 and then the WBA title when halting Felix Trinidad in September 2001. Injured his ankle against Robert Allen when he was pushed out of the ring and the bout was declared a no-contest. Has 31 wins inside the distance

29.03.03	Morrade Hakkar W RTD 8 Philadelphia (IBF, WBA & WBC Middleweight Title Defences)

Career: 46 contests, won 42, drew 1, lost 2, no contests 1.

Roy Jones

Roy Jones

Pensacola, USA. *Born* 16 January, 1969
WBA Heavyweight Champion.
Former Undefeated WBC,WBA & IBF L.Heavyweight Champion. Former Undefeated IBF S.Middleweight Champion

Major Amateur Honours: A silver medallist in the 1988 Olympics, he was also a National Golden Gloves champion in 1986 and 1987
Turned Pro: May 1989
Significant Results: Bernard Hopkins W PTS 12, James Toney W PTS 12, Mike McCallum W PTS 12, Montell Griffin L DIS 9 and W RSC 1, Virgil Hill W CO 4, Louis Del Valle W PTS 12, Reggie Johnson W PTS 12, David Telesco W PTS 12, Richard Hall W RSC 11, Eric Harding W RTD 10, Julio Gonzalez W PTS 12, Glen Kelly W CO 7
Type/Style: A brilliant boxer who is fast, skilful, has lightning reflexes and a kayo punch in either hand
Points of Interest: 5'11" tall. Originally trained and managed by his father Roy, he also plays basketball to a high standard and has appeared in films. Only a welterweight when he won the Golden Gloves, he made eight defences of his IBF super-middleweight title, lost his WBC light-heavyweight title title to Montell Griffin in March 1997

before winning it back just four months later. He also became the first former world middleweight champion to win a version of the heavyweight title when he beat John Ruiz. Has 38 wins inside the distance

07.09.02	Clinton Woods W RSC 6 Portland (WBC, WBA & IBF L.Heavyweight Title Defences)
01.03.03	John Ruiz W PTS 12 Las Vegas (WBA Heavyweight Title Challenge)

Career: 49 contests, won 48, lost 1.

Oscar (Chololo) Larios

Guadalajara, Mexico. *Born* 1 November, 1976
WBC S.Bantamweight Champion.
Former Undefeated Mexican S.Bantamweight Champion

Major Amateur Honours: None known, but claims 48 wins in 50 fights
Turned Pro: January 1994
Significant Results: Agapito Sanchez L RSC 5, Cesar Soto W PTS 12, Willie Jorrin L PTS 12, John Lowey W PTS 10, Angel Chacon W PTS 12, Israel Vazquez L RSC 1 and W CO 12
Type/ Style: Is a fast jab-and-move fighter
Points of Interest: A former stonemason, he was trained at one time by former WBC featherweight champion, Marcos Villasana, and made seven defences of his Mexican title before moving into world class. Was the WBC interim champion from May 2002 until beating Willie Jorrin for the full title in November 2002 and, despite retaining it in his first defence, against Shigeru Nakazato, suffered a broken jaw. Has 33 wins inside the distance

24.08.02	Manabu Fukushima W RSC 8 Tokyo
01.11.02	Willie Jorrin W RSC 1 Sacramento (WBC S.Bantamweight Title Challenge)
16.01.03	Marcos Licona W PTS 10 Los Angeles
26.04.03	Shigeru Nakazato W PTS 12 Tokyo (WBC S.Bantamweight Title Defence)

Career: 52 contests, won 48, drew 1, lost 3.

Antonio Margarito

Tijuana, Mexico. *Born* 18 March, 1978
WBO Welterweight Champion

Major Amateur Honours: None known

Turned Pro: January 1994
Significant Results: Larry Dixon L PTS 10, Rodney Jones L PTS 10, Alfred Ankamah W CO 4, Danny Perez W PTS 8, David Kamau W CO 2, Frankie Randall W RSC 4, Daniel Santos NC 1, Antonio Diaz W RSC 10
Type/Style: Is a tall, strong, aggressive banger, although a bit one paced, but has a good jab and a strong chin
Points of Interest: 6'0" tall. Turned pro at the age of 15 and suffered three early defeats, but is unbeaten in his last 20 bouts. His fight with Daniel Santos for the WBO title was stopped and declared a no-contest when he suffered a bad cut, prior to him winning the vacant title by beating Antonio Diaz in March 2002. Has made two defences and has 19 wins inside the distance

12.10.02	Danny Perez W PTS 12 Anaheim (WBO Welterweight Title Defence)
08.02.03	Andrew Lewis W RSC 2 Las Vegas (WBO Welterweight Title Defence)

Career: 32 contests, won 28, lost 3, no contest 1.

Eduardo Marquez

Managua, Nicaragua. *Born* 5 February, 1976
Former WBO M.Flyweight Champion

Major Amateur Honours: None known
Turned Pro: March 1996
Significant Results: Lee Sandoval L PTS 12 and L RSC 10, Juan Centeno L PTS 12, Oscar Murillo W PTS 10
Type/Style: Has a walk-in, crude style
Points of Interest: Prior to winning the WBO title, after coming in as late substitute, he had won only one of his five previous contests and turned out to be one the poorest champions ever, losing the title just 36 days later. Has seven stoppage wins

26.07.02	Jose Martinez W PTS 10 Managua
19.10.02	Lee Sandoval DREW 10 San Salvador
28.03.03	Jorge Mata W RSC 11 Madrid (WBO M.Flyweight Title Challenge)
03.05.03	Ivan Calderon L TD 9 Las Vegas (WBO M.Flyweight Title Defence)

Career: 20 contests, won 11, drew 2, lost 6, no decision 1.

Juan Manuel Marquez

Mexico City, Mexico. *Born* 23 August, 1973
IBF Featherweight Champion

Major Amateur Honours: None known, but claims 32 wins in 33 bouts
Turned Pro: May 1993
Significant Results: Julian Wheeler W RSC 10, Julio Gervacio W CO 10, Agapito Sanchez W PTS 12, Alfred Kotey W PTS 12, Freddy Norwood L PTS 12, Daniel Jimenez W RTD 7, Julio Gamboa W RTD 6, Robbie Peden W RSC 10
Type/Style: A solid, compact stylist who is a hard puncher with either hand
Points of Interest: 5'7" tall. A brother of the IBF bantamweight champion, Rafael Martinez, he started boxing at the age of 12. Lost his first pro fight on a disqualification and was outpointed by Freddy Norwood in a challenge for the WBA title in September 1999 prior to beating Manuel Medina. Has 32 wins inside the distance

01.02.03	Manuel Medina W RSC 7 Las Vegas *(Vacant IBF Featherweight Title)*
Career: 42 contests, won 40, lost 2.	

Rafael Marquez

Mexico City, Mexico. *Born* 25 March, 1975
IBF Bantamweight Champion

Major Amateur Honours: None known
Turned Pro: September 1995
Significant Results: Victor Rabanales L CO 8, Francisco Mateos L RSC 3, Tomas Rivera W CO 2, Genaro Garcia L RSC 2, Aquiles Guzman W RSC 7, Gerardo Espinoza W RSC 4, Mark Johnson W PTS 10 and W RSC 8
Type/Style: Is a compact and solid fighter with a big right-hand punch, but has not too sound a defence
Points of Interest: 5'5" tall. Following his father, Rafael, who was a pro in the 1950s, he won the IBF title just two weeks after his brother, Juan Manuel Marquez, had lifted the IBF featherweight title. Has 27 wins inside the distance and all of his losses have come inside the distance

12.07.02	Jorge Otero W RSC 6 McAllen
15.02.03	Tim Austin W RSC 8 Las Vegas *(IBF Bantamweight Title Challenge)*
Career: 32 contests, won 29, lost 3.	

Jorge Mata

Leon, Spain. Born 26 April, 1970
Former WBO M.Flyweight Champion

Major Amateur Honours: Was the Spanish amateur champion in 1998
Turned Pro: November 1998
Significant Results: Dunoy Pena W PTS 12, Christophe Rodrigues DREW 6, Reynaldo Frutos W CO 9
Type/Style: Is fleet footed with a good jab, but is not a puncher
Points of Interest: His win over Reynaldo Frutos in June 2002 was only to be for the interim title, but was later recognised as being a full title fight when Kermin Guardia decided he could no longer make the weight. Has six wins inside the distance

22.11.02	Jairo Arango W PTS 12 Leon *(WBO M.Flyweight Title Defence)*
28.03.03	Eduardo Marquez L RSC 11 Madrid *(WBO M.Flyweight Title Defence)*
Career: 13 contests, won 10, drew 2, lost 1.	

Ricardo (El Matador) Mayorga

Costa Rica. Born Granada, Nicaragua, 3 October, 1973
WBA & WBC Welterweight Champion. Former Undefeated Nicaraguan L.Welterweight Champion

Major Amateur Honours: None known
Turned Pro: August 1993
Significant Results: Roger Flores L PTS 10, Henry Castillo L PTS 10 and W RSC 7, Diosbelys Hurtado T Draw 2, Elio Ortiz W CO 10, Andrew Lewis NC 2 and W RSC 5
Type/Style: Although a bit wild and unconventional, he is very strong and a hard puncher
Points of Interest: Born in Nicaragua, but now a Costa Rican citizen, he lost his first professional fight on a stoppage, but is now undefeated in his last 17. Has 23 wins by kayo or stoppage

25.01.03	Vernon Forrest W RSC 3 Temecula *(WBA Welterweight Title Defence. WBC Welterweight Title Challenge)*
Career: 29 contests, won 24, drew 1, lost 3, no contest 1.	

Floyd (Little Stone) Mayweather

Grand Rapids, USA. *Born* 24 February, 1977

WBC Lightweight Champion. Former Undefeated WBC S. Featherweight Champion

Major Amateur Honours: A national Golden Gloves champion in 1993, 1994 and 1996, his first national title was at 106lbs. As the United States champion in 1995, he competed in the 1995 World Championships and won an Olympic bronze medal in 1996. Won 84 of 90 fights
Turned Pro: October 1996
Significant Results: Genaro Hernandez W RTD 8, Angel Manfredy W RSC 2, Carlos Rios W PTS 12, Justin Juuko W RSC 9, Carlos Gerena W RTD 7, Gregorio Vargas W PTS 12, Diego Corrales W RSC 10, Carlos Hernandez W PTS 12, Jesus Chavez W RTD 9, Jose Luis Castillo W PTS 12
Type/Style: Is a talented, flashy fighter with fast hands, great reflexes and a hard punch
Points of Interest: 5'8" tall. His father, Floyd, was a good professional and uncle, Roger, was WBA super-featherweight and WBC light-welterweight champion. Has made eight defences of his super-featherweight title and has 20 wins inside the distance

07.12.02	Jose Luis Castillo W PTS 12 Las Vegas *(WBC Lightweight Title Defence)*
19.04.03	Victoriano Sosa w pts 12 Fresno *(WBC Lightweight Title Defence)*
Career: 30 contests, won 30.	

Salim Medjkoune

Aubiere, France. *Born* 4 January, 1972
WBA S.Bantamweight Champion. Former Undefeated European S.Bantamweight Champion. Former Undefeated French S.Bantamweight Champion

Major Amateur Honours: French amateur champion in 1992
Turned Pro: November 1992
Significant Results: Akim Ouchen W PTS 10, Vincenzo Belcastro W RSC 8, Martin Krastev L CO 1 and W RSC 2, Michael Brodie L RSC 9 (twice), Vladislav Antonov W TD 7
Type/Style: A busy southpaw, he can box on the inside or at distance
Points of Interest: 5'6" tall. Managed by Michael Acaries, he has held the

European title twice. With 21 wins by stoppage or kayo, and all of his losses being inside the distance, he has yet to travel the full route

10.08.02	Dimitar Alipiev W CO 1 Marseilles	
09.10.02	Osamu Sato W PTS 12 Tokyo *(WBA S. Bantamweight Title Challenge)*	
04.04.03	Vincenzo Gigliotti W PTS 12 Clermont Ferrand *(WBA S. Bantamweight Title Defence)*	
Career: 45 contests, won 41, drew 1, lost 3.		

Dariusz Michalczewski

Hamburg, Germany. *Born* Gdansk, Poland, 5 May, 1968
WBO L. Heavyweight Champion. Former Undefeated WBA and IBF L. Heavyweight Champion. Former Undefeated WBO Cruiserweight Champion

Major Amateur Honours: A bronze medal winner in the 1986 European Junior Championships, as a senior he went on to win a silver medal in the 1989 European Championships and a Gold medal in the 1991 European Championships
Turned Pro: September 1991
Significant Results: Leonzer Barber W PTS 12, Nestor Giovanni W CO 10, Graciano Rocchigiani W DIS 7 and W RTD 9, Virgil Hill W PTS 12, Nicky Piper W RTD 7, Mark Prince W RSC 8, Drake Thadzi W RSC 9, Montell Griffin W RSC 4, Richard Hall W RSC 11
Type/Style: Is a strong, hard-punching and aggressive pressure fighter with a solid jab. However, his defence is not too sound
Points of Interest: Won championships in both Poland and Germany as an amateur. As a pro he won the WBA and IBF titles by beating Virgil Hill in June 1997, but relinquished both titles in the same month that he won them. Has made 23 defences of his WBO title and beaten his last 14 challengers inside the distance. Only 10 opponents have lasted the distance with him

14.09.02	Richard Hall W RSC 10 Braunschweig *(WBO L.Heavyweight Title Defence)*	
29.03.03	Derrick Harmon W CO 9 Hamburg *(WBO L.Heavyweight Title Defence)*	
Career: 48 contests, won 48.		

Fernando (Cochulito) Montiel

Los Mochis, Mexico. *Born* 1 March, 1979
WBO S.Flyweight Champion. Former Undefeated WBO Flyweight Champion

Major Amateur Honours: A local Golden Gloves champion, he claims 33 wins in 36 fights
Turned Pro: December 1996
Significant Results: Paulino Villalobos DREW 10 and W PTS 10, Sergio Milan W PTS 10, Cruz Carbajal W RSC 4, Isidro Garcia W RSC 7, Zoltan Lunka W RSC 7, Juan Domingo Cordoba W CO 1, Jose Lopez W PTS 12, Pedro Alcazar W RSC 6
Type/Style: Is a clever, stylish boxer with a good uppercut
Points of Interest: 5'4" tall. As the youngest of a fighting family, his father and four brothers were all boxers, he won his first 11 bouts inside the distance and is jointly trained by his father, Manuel, and a Japanese trainer based in Mexico. Won the WBO title when stopping Isidro Garcia in December 2000 and made three defences before moving up to win the super-flyweight title, beating Pedro Alcazar in June 2002. Sadly, Alcazar collapsed and died after the fight

18.01.03	Roy Doliguez W CO 2 Los Mochis *(WBO S.Flyweight Title Defence)*	
09.05.03	Ruben Sanchez Leon W RSC 2 San Diego	
Career: 27 contests, won 26, drew 1.		

Erik (The Terrible) Morales

Tijuana, Mexico. *Born* 1 September,1976
WBC Featherweight Champion. Former Undefeated WBC S.Bantamweight Champion. Former Undefeated WBO S.Bantamweight Champion. Former Undefeated Mexican S.Bantamweight Champion

Major Amateur Honours: None, but claims 108 wins in 114 fights
Turned Pro: March 1993
Significant Results: Daniel Zaragoza W CO 11, Jose Luis Bueno W CO 2, Hector Acero Sanchez W PTS 12, Junior Jones W RSC 4, Angel Chacon W RSC 2, Juan Carlos Ramirez W RSC 9, Reynante Jamili W RSC 6, Wayne McCullough W PTS 12, Marco Antonio Barrera W PTS 12 and L PTS 12, Guty Espadas W PTS 12, In-Jin Chi W PTS 12
Type/Style: Is a cool, upright, pressure fighter who can bang hard with both hands
Points of Interest: 5'8" tall. From a fighting family, his dad fought Orlando Canizales as a pro and brother, Diego, is a former WBO super-flyweight champion, he turned pro at the age of 16. Made nine defences of his WBC super-bantamweight title before relinquishing it last year and, after he beat Marco Antonio Barrera for the WBO title on a hotly-disputed decision, he also gave that up. Won the WBC title by decisioning Guty Espadas in February 2001, then lost it to Barrera in June 2002, before regaining it by outpointing Paulie Ayala. Has taken part in 16 WBC title fights and has 33 wins inside the distance

16.11.02	Paulie Ayala W PTS 12 Las Vegas *(Vacant WBC Featherweight Title)*	
22.02.03	Eddie Croft W RSC 3 Mexico City *(WBC Featherweight Title Defence)*	
03.05.03	Fernando Velardez W RSC 5 Las *(WBC Featherweight Title Defence)*	
Career: 45 contests, won 44, lost 1.		

Erik Morales

219

Eric (Little Hands of Stone) Morel

Madison, Wisconsin, USA. *Born* Puerto Rico, 1 October, 1975
WBA Flyweight Champion

Major Amateur Honours: Won a silver medal in the 1992 World Junior Championships for Puerto Rico, a silver medal in the 1993 national Golden Gloves, was the USA junior champion in 1993, won a gold medal in the 1994 National Golden Gloves, a silver medal in the 1994 and 1996 United States Championships and competed in the 1995 Pan-American Games and 1996 Olympic Games
Turned Pro: October 1996
Significant Results: Rodolfo Blanco W PTS 12, Ysaias Zamudio W RSC 7, Miguel Granados W PTS 12, Sornpichai Kratingdaeng W PTS 12, Gilberto Keb-Baas W PTS 12, Jose De Jesus W RTD 8, Alex Baba W PTS 10
Type/ Style: Is a string-bean, slick, upright southpaw with a sharp jab
Points of Interest: 5'3" tall. Started boxing at the age of eight in Puerto Rico. Moved down from super-fly-weight to win the WBA flyweight title, outpointing Sornpichai Kratingdaeng in August 2000, and has made five defences, but only two since June 2001. Has 18 wins inside the distance

12.10.02	Denkaosaen Kaowichit W RSC 11 Anaheim
	(WBA Flyweight Title Defence)
28.06.03	Isidro Garcia W PTS 12 Bayamon
	(WBA Flyweight Title Defence)
Career: 33 contests, won 33.	

Jean-Marc Mormeck

Pointe-A-Pitre, Guadeloupe. *Born* 3 June, 1972
WBA Cruiserweight Champion.
Former Undefeated French L. Heavyweight Champion

Major Amateur Honours: None, but claims 13 wins in 15 fights
Turned Pro: March 1995
Significant Results: Lee Manuel Osie L PTS 4, Alain Simon W PTS 10, Pascual Warusfel W PTS 10, Valery Vikhor W RSC 3, Virgil Hill W RTD 8
Type/Style: Although a strong, stocky, aggressive pressure fighter with a hard, clubbing right hand, he is not a devasta-ting puncher

Points of Interest: Only took up boxing after being injured at football when 15 and later worked as a security guard at McDonalds. Won the WBA title by beating Virgil Hill in February 2002 and has made two defences. Although suffering from injuries, having three operations on his right hand, he has 21 wins by stoppage or kayo. Now based in the USA with Don King as his promoter

10.08.02	Dale Brown W RSC 8 Marseilles
	(WBA Cruiserweight Title Defence)
01.03.03	Alexander Gurov W RSC 8 Las Vegas
	(WBA Cruiserweight Title Defence)
Career: 31 contests, won 29, lost 2.	

Alexander (Explosivo) Munoz

Miranda, Venezuela. *Born* 8 February, 1979
WBA S. Flyweight Champion

Major Amateur Honours: An out-standing amateur who claims 129 wins in 158 fights, he competed in the World Junior Championships in 1997 and won a silver medal in the Americas Championships the same year
Turned Pro: March 1998
Significant Results: Ramon Games W RSC 10, Sornpichai Kratchingdaeng W RSC 5, Shoji Kobayashi W RSC 8
Type/Style: With an all-out aggressive style and a punch to match, he is deadly with the left hook
Points of Interest: Holds the record for the most consecutive inside-the-distance wins by a Venezuelan fighter, having won all of his 23 fights by kayo or stoppage, and had Shoji Kobayashi on the floor five times when winning the WBA title in March 2002. Injured in a street mugging, he has since been inactive

31.07.02	Eiji Kojima W CO 2 Osaka
	(WBA S.Flyweight Title Defence)
Career: 23 contests, won 23.	

Omar (Huracan) Narvaez

Chubut, Argentina. *Born* 7 October, 1975
WBO Flyweight Champion

Major Amateur Honours: Won a bronze medal in 1997 World Championships,

a silver medal in the 1999 World Championships, a gold medal in the 1999 Pan-American Games and competed in the 1996 and 2000 Olympics
Turned Pro: December 2000
Significant Results: Carlos Montiveros DREW 4, Wellington Vicente W PTS 10, Marcos Obregon W PTS 10
Type/Style: A stocky, aggressive southpaw with fast hands
Points of Interest: The first of the 2000 Olympians to win a version of a world title, he beat the current WBO super-bantamweight champion, Joan Guzman, in the 1996 Olympics. Trained by the Cuban, Sarbelio Fuentes, he won the WBO title in only his 12th fight

13.07.02	Adonis Rivas W PTS 12 Buenos Aires
	(WBO Flyweight Title Defence)
13.09.02	Luis Lazarte W DIS 10 Santa Cruz
	(WBO Flyweight Title Defence)
14.12.02	Andrea Sarritzu W PTS 12 Cagliari
	(WBO Flyweight Title Defence)
07.06.03	Everardo Morales W RSC 5 Buenos Aires
	(WBO Flyweight Title Defence)
Career: 15 contests, won 14, drew 1.	

Sven Ottke

Berlin, Germany. *Born* 3 June, 1967
IBF S. Middleweight Champion.
Former Undefeated German L.Heavyweight Champion

Major Amateur Honours: A quarter-finalist in the 1988 Olympic Games, he won a bronze medal in the 1989 World Championships, gold medals in the 1991 and 1996 European Championships, a bronze medal in the 1993 Championships, a silver medal in the 1994 World Cup and competed in the 1992 and 1996 Olympics
Turned Pro: March 1997
Significant Results: Charles Brewer W PTS 12 (twice), Giovanni Nardiello W CO 3, Thomas Tate W TD 11 and W PTS 12, Glencoffe Johnson W PTS 12, Lloyd Bryan W PTS 12, Silvio Branco W PTS 12, Tony Mundine W CO 10
Type/Style: A good tactician, he is a clever southpaw with an awkward style, but starts slowly and is not a hard puncher
Points of Interest: 5'11" tall. Did not turn professional until he was 29,

having beaten Chris Byrd, Juan Carlos Gomez and Michael Moorer in the amateur ranks. Has only stopped or knocked out five opponents, but has defended his IBF title 18 times since winning it from Charles Brewer in October 1998

24.08.02	Joe Gatti W CO 9 Leipzig
	(IBF S.Middleweight Title Defence)
16.11.02	Rudy Markussen W PTS 12 Nuremburg
	(IBF S.Middleweight Title Defence)
15.03.03	Byron Mitchell W PTS 12 Berlin
	(IBF S. Middleweight Title Defence. WBA S.Middleweight Title Challenge)
14.06.03	David Starie W PTS 12 Magdeburg
	(IBF & WBA S. Middleweight Title Defences)
Career: 31 contests, won 31.	

Irene (Mambaco) Pacheco

San Juan de Uraba, Colombia. *Born* 26 March, 1971
IBF Flyweight Champion

Major Amateur Honours: None known
Turned Pro: November 1993
Significant Results: Luis Cox W RSC 9, Ferid Ben Jeddu W RSC 4, Pedro Pena W CO 11, Hawk Makepula W PTS 12, Mike Trejo W RSC 4
Type/Style: A clever boxer, and an awkward, spidery southpaw who can switch, he is also a good body puncher
Points of Interest: 5'6" tall. Never fought for any other major title before becoming IBF champion, when stopping Luis Cox in April 1999, and has since made five defences. Has stopped or knocked out 20 of his opponents and has only been taken the distance seven times, but suffers from a brittle right hand and has made only one defence since November 2001

29.11.02	Alejandro Montiel W PTS 12 El Paso
	(IBF Flyweight Title Defence)
Career: 27 contests, won 27.	

Manny Pacquiao

Bukidnon, Philippines. *Born* 17 December, 1976
IBF S. Bantamweight Champion.
Former WBC Flyweight Champion

Major Amateur Honours: None, but started at 13 and won 60 of 64 fights
Turned Pro: January 1995

Significant Results: Chockchai Chokwiwat W CO 5, Melvin Magramo W PTS 10, Chatchai Sasakul W CO 8, Gabriel Mira W CO 4, Medgoen Singsurat L CO 3, Reynante Jamili W RSC 2, Arnulfo Barotillo W CO 4, Agapito Sanchez T DRAW 6, Jorge Julio W RSC 2
Type/Style: Is a stocky, aggressive and hard-punching southpaw whose defence is not too hot
Points of Interest: His brother is the Philippines super-featherweight champion and he turned pro at the age of 18. Won the WBC flyweight title by knocking out Chatchai Sasakul in December 1998 and made one defence before losing his crown to Medgoen Singsurat in September 1999. Promptly moved straight up to super-bantamweight, winning the IBF title in June 2001 with an upset stoppage victory over Lehlonolo Ledwaba, after coming in as a substitute at two weeks notice. Has 27 wins inside the distance and is trained by Freddie Roach

26.10.02	Fahprakob Rakkiatgym w RSC 1 Davao City
	(IBF S.Bantamweight Title Defence)
15.03.03	Serikzhan Yeshmangbetov W RSF 5 Manila
Career: 39 contests, won 36, drew 1, lost 2.	

Luis Alberto (Dinamita) Perez

Managua, Nicaragua. *Born* 6 April, 1978
IBF S.Flyweight Champion

Major Amateur Honours: None known
Turned Pro: November 1996
Significant Results: Leon Salazar W RSC 4, Justo Zuniga W CO 1, Vernie Torres L PTS 12, Moises Castro W PTS 10, Edicson Torres W PTS 12 (twice)
Type/Style: Is a skinny, skilful southpaw with a strong jab, but is not a big puncher
Points of Interest: Had only five days notice of the fight with Felix Machado. Managed by Anna Alvarez, the wife of the WBA light-flyweight champion, Rosendo Alvarez, he has 14 wins inside the distance

06.07.02	Roberto Bonilla W CO 1 Washington
04.01.03	Felix Machado W PTS 12 Washington DC
	(IBF S.Flyweight Title Challenge)
Career: 22 contests, won 21, lost 1.	

Veeraphol (Death Mask) Sahaprom

Nakhon Ratchaseema, Thailand. *Born* 16 November, 1968
WBC Bantamweight Champion.
Former WBA Bantamweight Champion

Major Amateur Honours: None
Turned Pro: December 1994
Significant Results: Daourang Chuwatana W PTS 12, Nana Yaw Konadu L RSC 2, Rolando Pascua W PTS 10, Joichiro Tatsuyoshi W CO 6, Adan Vargas W PTS 12, Toshiaki Nishioka W PTS 12 and DREW 12, Oscar Arciniega W RSC 5, Julio Coronel W PTS 12
Type/Style: Is a flat-footed stalker with a high, tight guard and a big right-hand punch
Points of Interest: 5'4" tall. Came out of kickboxing to professional boxing, winning the WBC International title in his first fight and the WBA title in his fourth. His real name is Veeraphol Sumranklang, but he now fights as Veeraphol Sahaprom and gets his nickname from his stony expression when in the ring. Although he held the WBA title for only four months, he has made 10 defences of his WBC title and his fight with Julio Coronel was the first world title fight to be held on a bridge. Has won 29 bouts inside the distance

24.08 02	Dawin Bermudez w CO 3 Bangkok
25.10.02	Alex Escaner W RSF 6 Nonthaburi
13.01.03	Nathan Barcelona W RSC 6 Bangkok
01.05.03	Hugo Dianzo W PTS 12 Bangkok
	(WBC Bantamweight Title Defence)
Career: 44 contests, won 42, drew 1, lost 1.	

Mehedi (Kounet) Sahnoune

Marseilles, France. *Born* 25 May, 1976
WBA L. Heavyweight Champion.
Former Undefeated French S.Middleweight Champion

Major Amateur Honours: None known
Turned Pro: December 1997
Significant Results: Claude Dutard W CO 2, Youssef Temsoury W PTS 8 and W CO 2, Andrei Shkalikov W PTS 12, Joe Siluvangi W PTS 8
Type/Style: Is a strong, fit, pressure

fighter with plenty of stamina and heavy hands

Points of Interest: Managed and promoted by the Acaries brothers, he has 21 wins inside the distance and received full recognition as the WBA champion when Roy Jones relinquished his WBA super title in April

13.07.02	Ivica Cukusic W RSC 5 Palavas
10.08.02	Joe Siluvangi W PTS 8 Marseilles
29.11.02	Geoffroy Gordian W RTD 7 Les Pennes
08.03.03	Bruno Girard W RSC 7 Marseilles *(WBA Interim L.Heavyweight Title Challenge)*
Career: 24 contests, won 24.	

Corrie Sanders

Britz, South Africa. *Born* 7 January, 1966
WBO Heavyweight Champion.
Former Undefeated South African Heavyweight Champion

Major Amateur Honours: Was a seven-times South African champion
Turned Pro: April 1989
Significant Results: Johnny Du Plooy W CO 1, Johnny Nelson W PTS 10, Bert Cooper W RTD 3, Nate Tubbs L CO 2, Carlos De Leon W RSC 1, Ross Puritty W PTS 12, Bobby Czyz W RSC 2, Al Cole W RSC 1, Hasim Rahman L RSC 7, Michael Sprott W RSC 1
Type/Style: Although a fleshy south-paw, he is mobile with fast hands and a big punch
Points of Interest: A former police-man, who is trained by Harold Volbrecht, he has 29 wins inside the distance. Had only two fights in two years before beating Vladimir Klitschko

09.11.02	Otis Tisdale W RSC 2 Oklahoma City
08.03.03	Vladimir Klitschko w rsf 2 Hanover *(WBO Heavyweight Title Challenge)*
Career: 41 contests, won 39, lost 2.	

Daniel Santos

San Juan, Puerto Rico. *Born* 10 October, 1975
WBO L. Middleweight Champion.
Former Undefeated WBO Welterweight Champion

Major Amateur Honours: Won a bronze medal in the 1992 World Junior Championships, competed in the 1993 World Championship and the 1994 Goodwill Games, won a silver medal in the 1995 Pan-American Games, competed in the 1995 World Championships and won bronze in the 1996 Olympic Games
Turned Pro: September 1996
Significant Results: Luis Verdugo T DRAW 1, William Ruiz W RSC 3, Ray Lovato W RSC 2, Kofi Jantuah L RSC 5, Ahmed Katajev L PTS 12 and W CO 5, Giovanni Parisi W RSC 4, Neil Sinclair W CO 2, Antonio Margarito NC 1, Luis Campas W RSC 11
Type/Style: Is a fast, clever, flashy southpaw and a heavy left-hand puncher, but his chin is questionable and so is his stamina
Points of Interest: 6'0" tall. Lost to David Reid in the Pan-American Games. Unbeaten in his first 21 fights, he lost a disputed decision to Ahmed Katajev in first challenge for the WBO welterweight title, a decision followed by the WBO ordering a rematch which he won in May 2000. Made three defences of his welterweight title

before winning the light-middleweight title when beating Luis Campas in March 2002. Has 20 wins inside the distance

17.08.02	Mehrdud Takaloo W PTS 12 Cardiff *(WBO L.Middleweight Title Defence)*
28.06.03	Fulgencio Zuniga W PTS 12 Bayamon *(WBO L.Middleweight Title Defence)*
Career: 31 contests, won 27, drew 1, lost 2, no contest 1.	

Harry (Exterminator) Simon

Walvis Bay, Namibia. *Born* 21 October, 1972
WBO Middleweight Champion.
Former Undefeated WBO L.Middleweight Champion

Major Amateur Honours: Competed in the 1992 Olympic Games but lost in the first series. An African Champion and three times South African Champion, he claims just two losses in 273 fights
Turned Pro: January 1994
Significant Results: Del Bryan W RSC 6, Ronald Wright W PTS 12, Kevin Lueshing W RSC 3, Rodney Jones W PTS 12, Wayne Alexander W RSC 5

Harry Simon (left) in action against England's Wayne Alexander   Les Clark

Type/Style: Strong and powerful, and a charismatic boxer with a sound defence, he has a good chin and plenty of stamina

Points of Interest: Real name Harry Saayman. Having started boxing in 1980 before working in a diamond mine, Harry is the first ever world boxing champion from Namibia. Trained by the former WBA champion, Brian Mitchell, he has 17 wins inside the distance, but made only four defences of his WBO light-middleweight title in three years. Won the WBO middleweight title by beating Hacine Cherifi, only to have the bout later declared as being for the interim title

INACTIVE DURING 2002-03	
Career: 23 Contests, won 23.	

Sirimongkol Singmanassak

Bangkok,Thailand.*Born* 2 March, 1977
WBC S.Featherweight Champion. Former WBC Bantamweight Champion

Major Amateur Honours: None
Turned Pro: May 1994
Significant Results: Thalernsak Sitbaobey W RSC 3, Jose Luis Bueno W CO 6
Type/Style: Is a strong, stand-up boxer who is not a big puncher
Points of Interest: 5'7" tall. Won the WBC bantamweight title in his 14th fight, having previously been the interim champion, and made three defences. Has 23 wins inside the distance

24.08.02	Kengo Nagashima W CO 2 Tokyo *(Vacant WBC S.Featherweight Title)*
25.10.02	Richard Carillo W KO 2 Nonthaburi
13.01.03	Yong-Soo Choi W PTS 12 Tokyo *(WBC S.Featherweight Title Defence)*
01.05.03	Anthony Tshela W RSC 6 Bangkok
Career: 41 contests, won 40, lost 1.	

Cory Spinks

St Louis, Missouri, USA. *Born* 20 February, 1978
IBF Welterweight Champion

Major Amateur Honours: Won a gold medal in the 1997 Police Athletic League Championships and claims 78 wins in 81 contests
Turned Pro: November 1997
Significant Results: Antonio Diaz L PTS 12, Jorge Vaca W RSC 7, Edgar Ruiz W PTS 10, Larry Marks W PTS 12, Michele Piccirillo L PTS 12
Type/Style: Is a tall, upright southpaw with good speed, who is also a fine combination puncher
Points of Interest: 5'10" tall. The son of the former world heavyweight champion, Leon Spinks, his loss to Michele Piccirillo for the vacant IBF title in April 2002 was so controversial that it led to a return fight which saw him become champion. Has only 11 wins by stoppage or kayo

23.08.02	Rafael Pineda W TD 7 Miami
22.03.03	Michele Piccirillo W PTS 12 Campione d'Italia *(IBF Welterweight Title Challenge)*
Career: 33 contests, won 31, lost 2.	

Cory Spinks

Antonio (The Magic Man) Tarver

Orlando, Florida, USA. *Born* 21 November, 1968
WBC & IBF L.Heavyweight Champion

Major Amateur Honours: Was the United States champion 1993 and 1995 and the Golden Gloves champion in 1994. He also won gold medals in both the 1995 Pan-American Games and the 1995 World Championships and a bronze medal in the 1996 Olympic Games
Turned Pro: February 1997
Significant Results: Mohamed Ben Guesima W RSC 9, Ernest Mateen W RSC 1, Eric Harding L PTS 12, Chris Johnson W RSC 10, Reggie Johnson W PTS 12
Type/Style: Is a tall, skinny southpaw with a good jab and a fair punch
Points of Interest: 6'2" tall. Trained by Buddy McGirt, he has been known to wear a top hat and cape into the ring. Before turning to the paid ranks, he was awarded the keys to the City of Orlando for his exploits as an amateur. Has 17 wins inside the distance

20.07.02	Eric Harding W RSC 5 Indianapolis
26.04.03	Montell Griffin W PTS 12 Mashantucket *(Vacant WBC & IBF L.Heavyweight Titles)*
Career: 22 contests, won 21, lost 1.	

Masamori Tokuyama

North Korea. *Born* Tokyo, Japan, 17 September, 1974
WBC S. Flyweight Champion

Major Amateur Honours: None. Strangely, he recorded only 12 wins in 17 fights
Turned Pro: September 1994
Significant Results: Manny Melchor L PTS 10, Nolito Cabato DREW 10 and L TD 7, Hiroki Ioka W RSC 5, Pone Saengmorakot W PTS 12, In-Joo Cho W PTS 12 and W CO 5, Akihiko Nago W PTS 12, Gerry Penalosa W PTS 12
Type/Style: Is a tall, upright boxer with a sharp jab and fast hand speed, but has no punch to talk of
Points of Interest: 5'8" tall. Masamori, whose father was a karate teacher and whose real name is Chang-Soo Hong, became the first North Korean to win a world title when he beat In-Joo Cho in August 2000 and his title defence against Cho in May 2001 was the first time that a North Korean and a South Korean have fought each other for a world title in Korea. Has only eight wins inside the distance on his record, but has defended his title seven times

26.08.02	Erik Lopez W RTD 6 Saitama
	(WBC S.Flyweight Title Defence)
20.12.02	Gerry Penalosa W PTS 12 Osaka
	(WBC S.Flyweight Title Defence)
23.06.03	Katsushigi Kawashima W PTS 12
	Yokohama
	(WBC S.Flyweight Title Defence)

Career: 32 contests, won 29, drew 1, lost 2.

James (Lights Out) Toney

Grand Rapids, Michigan, USA. *Born* 24 August, 1968
IBF Cruiserweight Champion. Former Undefeated IBF Middleweight champion. Former IBF S. Middleweight Champion

Major Amateur Honours: None known
Turned Pro: October 1988
Significant Results: Michael Nunn W RSC 11, Reggie Johnson W PTS 12, Mike McCallum DREW 12 and W PTS 12, Iran Barkley W RSC 9, Roy Jones L PTS 12, Montell Griffin L PTS 12, Ramon Garbey W PTS 10
Type/Style: A lazy, laid-back fighter who often does just enough to win, he has an excellent defence and a great chin. He is also a good puncher with either hand
Points of Interest: He first won the IBF middleweight title in 1991, beating Michael Nunn, and went on to make six defences before winning the IBF super-middleweight title in 1993 when stopping Iran Barkley, a feat that was followed by four defences. From a fighting family, his dad was a pro in the 1940s, he has weighed as high as 16 stones for a fight. Has 42 wins inside the distance and has never been stopped

18.08.02	Jason Robinson W CO 7 Temecula
26.04.03	Vassily Jirov W PTS 12
	Mashantucket
	(IBF Cruiserweight Title Challenge)

Career: 72 contests, won 66, drew 2, lost 4.

Kostya Tszyu

Australia. *Born* Serov, Russia, 19 September, 1969
WBC, WBA and IBF L.Welterweight Champion.

Major Amateur Honours: Won a gold medal in the European Junior Championships in 1986, a silver medal in the World Junior Championships in 1987,

a gold medal in the European Championships in 1989 and 1991, a bronze medal in the 1989 World Championships and a gold medal in the 1991 World Championships
Turned Pro: March 1992
Significant Results: Jake Rodriguez W RSC 6, Roger Mayweather W PTS 12, Hugo Pineda W RSC 11, Jan Bergman W CO 6, Vince Phillips L RSC 10, Rafael Ruelas W RSC 8, Diosbelys Hurtado W RSC 5, Miguel Gonzalez W RSC 10, Julio Cesar Chavez W RSC 6, Sharmba Mitchell W RTD 7, Oktay Urkal W PTS 12, Zab Judah W RSC 2, Ben Tackie W PTS 12
Type/Style: Is an aggressive, two-fisted fighter and a dangerous puncher with both hands
Points of Interest: 5'7" tall. Born in Russia, but now based in Australia, he made six defences of the IBF title before being stopped by Vince Phillips in May 1997. He then won the vacant WBC title by halting Miguel Gonzalez in August 1999, the WBA title by retiring Sharmba Mitchell in February 2001, and became a triple champion following his win over Zab Judah in November 2001. Has 24 wins inside the distance

19.01.03	James Leija W RTD 6 Melbourne
	(WBC, WBA & IBF L.Welterweight Title Defences)

Career: 32 contests, won 30, drew 1, lost 1.

Pongsaklek Wonjongkam

Nakhornatchaseema, Thailand. *Born* 11 August, 1977
WBC Flyweight Champion

Major Amateur Honours: None
Turned Pro: December 1994
Significant Results: Randy Mangubat W CO 3, Mzukisi Sikali W RSC 1, Juanito Rubillar W PTS 10, Malcolm Tunacao W RSC 1, Daisuke Naito W CO 1
Type/Style: Is a tough, aggressive pressure-fighting southpaw with a wicked right hook
Points of Interest: 5'1" tall. With a real name of Dongskorn Wonjongkan and having has also boxed under the names of Nakornthong Parkview and Sithkanongsak, his last loss was in December 1995 and he is unbeaten in

his last 37 bouts. Won the WBC title by halting Malcolm Tunacao in March 2001 and has made seven defences. Has 25 wins by stoppage or kayo

06.09.02	Jesus Martinez W PTS 12 Rangsit
	(WBC Flyweight Title Defence)
26.11.02	Hidenobu Honda W PTS 12 Osaka
	(WBC Flyweight Title Defence)
06.06.03	Randy Mangubat W PTS 12
	Songkla
	(WBC Flyweight Title Defence)

Career: 49 contests, won 47, lost 2.

Ronald (Winkie) Wright

St Petersburg, USA. *Born* 26 November, 1971
IBF L. Middleweight Champion. Former WBO L. Middleweight Champion

Major Amateur Honours: He was a gold medallist in the Olympic Festival of 1990, a quarter-finalist in the 1989 Golden Gloves and an amateur international at the age of 18
Turned Pro: October 1990
Significant Results: Julio Cesar Vasquez L PTS 12, Tony Marshall W PTS 12, Bronco McKart W PTS 12 (twice), Ensley Bingham W PTS 12, Steve Foster W RSC 6, Adrian Dodson W RSC 6, Harry Simon L PTS 12, Fernando Vargas L PTS 12, Keith Mullings W PTS 12, Robert Frazier W PTS 12, Jason Papillion W RSC 5
Type/Style: Well recognised as a slick, clever southpaw
Points of Interest: 5'10" tall. Although floored six times by Julio Cesar Vasquez in an unsuccessful challenge for the WBA title in 1994, he went on to beat Bronco McKart for the WBO title in May 1996, before losing it to Harry Simon in August 1998. Next lost to Fernando Vargas in a challenge for the IBF title in December 1999, but then won the vacant IBF title by beating Robert Frazier in October 2001 and has made three defences. Has 25 wins by stoppage or knockout

07.09.02	Bronco McKart W DIS 8 Portland
	(IBF L.Middleweight Title Defence)
01.03.03	Juan Candelo W PTS 12 Las Vegas
	(IBF L.Middleweight Title defence)

Career: 48 contests, won 45, lost 3.

World Title Bouts During 2002-2003

by Bob Yalen

All of last season's title bouts for the IBF, WBA, WBC and WBO are shown in date order within their weight division and give the boxers' respective weights, along with the scorecard if going to a decision. There is also a short summary of every bout that involved a British contestant, and British officials, where applicable, are listed. Yet again there were no WORLD TITLE FIGHTS as such – even if you allow for Kostya Tszyu (L. Welter) and Bernard Hopkins (Middle), who hold three of the four major titles – just a proliferation of champions recognised by the above four commissions and spread over 17 weight divisions. Below the premier league, come other commissions such as the WBU, IBO, IBC and WBF, etc, etc, which would devalue the world championships even further if one recognised their champions as being the best in the world. Right now, the WBA have decided to continue recognising their champions who move on to claim other commissions' titles as super champions – despite vacating the title and creating a new champion, who, for our purposes, will be classified as a secondary champion – which if taken up in general could eventually lead to the best man at his weight being recognised universally as a world champion if the fights can be made.

M. Flyweight

IBF

9 August 2002   Roberto Levya 7.6$^{1}/_{2}$ (Mexico) L PTS 12 Miguel Barrera 7.6$^{1}/_{2}$ (Columbia), Las Vegas, Nevada, USA. Scorecards: 113-115, 113-115, 112-116.

22 March 2003   Miguel Barrera 7.6$^{1}/_{2}$ (Colombia) W CO 3 Roberto Levya 7.5 (Mexico), Las Vegas, Nevada, USA.

31 May 2003   Miguel Barrera 7.5$^{3}/_{4}$ (Colombia) L CO 10 Edgar Cardenas 7.5 (Mexico), Tijuana, Mexico.

WBA

29 July 2002   Keitaro Hoshino 7.7 (Japan) L PTS 12 Noel Arambulet 7.7 (Venezuela), Yokohama, Japan. Scorecards: 112-109, 111-107, 114-114.

20 December 2002   Noel Arambulet 7.6$^{3}/_{4}$ (Venezuela) W PTS 12 Keitaro Hoshino 7.6$^{1}/_{4}$ (Japan), Osaka, Japan. Scorecards: 115-113, 115-113, 115-115.

WBC

19 October 2002   Jose Antonio Aguirre 7.5$^{1}/_{2}$ (Mexico) W PTS 12 Juan Palacios 7.7 (Nicaragua), Villahermosa, Mexico. Scorecards: 115-112, 115-112, 112-115.

22 February 2003   Jose Antonio Aguirre 7.7 (Mexico) W RTD 7 Juan Alfonso Keb 7.6 (Mexico), Mexico City, Mexico.

23 June 2003   Jose Antonio Aguirre 7.7 (Mexico) W RSC 12 Keitaro Hoshino 7.7 (Japan), Yokohama, Japan.

WBO

22 November 2002   Jorge Mata 7.7 (Spain) W PTS 12 Jairo Arango 7.7 (Panama), Leon, Spain. Scorecards: 116-111, 117-110, 117-111. Earlier, with Kermin Guardia (Colombia) inactive and unlikely to fight at the weight again, Mata was recognised as being the champion following his ninth-round interim title fight stoppage win over Reynaldo Frutos (Panama) in Palma de Mallorca, Spain on 29 June 2002.

28 March 2003   Jorge Mata 7.6$^{1}/_{2}$ (Spain) L RSC 11 Eduardo Marquez 7.6$^{1}/_{2}$ (Nicaragua), Madrid Spain. Judge: Roy Francis.

3 May 2003   Eduardo Marquez 7.7 (Nicaragua) L TD 9 Ivan Calderon 7.6 (Puerto Rico), Las Vegas, Nevada, USA. Scorecards: 81-89, 80-90, 80-90.

L. Flyweight

IBF

15 February 2003   Jose Victor Burgos 7.9 (Mexico) W RSC 12 Alex Sanchez 7.9 (Puerto Rico), Las Vegas, Nevada, USA. For the vacant title after Ricardo Lopez (Mexico) announced his retirement from boxing in December 2002.

WBA

31 March 2003   Rosendo Alvarez 7.10 (Nicaragua) W PTS 12 Beibis Mendoza 7.9$^{1}/_{2}$ (Colombia), Little Rock, Arkansas, USA. Scorecards: 116-112, 116-112, 114-114.

WBC

6 July 2002   Yo-Sam Choi 7.10 (South Korea) L RSC 6 Jorge Arce 7.9$^{1}/_{2}$ (Mexico), Seoul, South Korea. Referee: Larry O'Connell.

16 November 2002   Jorge Arce 7.10 (Mexico) W RSC 3 Agustin Luna 7.9 (Mexico), Las Vegas, Nevada, USA.

22 February 2003   Jorge Arce 7.9$^{3}/_{4}$ (Mexico) W CO 1 Ernesto Castro 7.9$^{3}/_{4}$ (Nicaragua), Mexico City, Mexico.

3 May 2003   Jorge Arce 7.9 (Mexico) W TD 7 Melchor Cob Castro 7.10 (Mexico), Las Vegas, Nevada, USA. Scorecards: 59-55, 58-56, 59-55.

WBO

24 August 2002   Nelson Dieppa 7.10 (Puerto Rico) T DRAW 2 Jhon Molina 7.10 (Colombia), Carolina, Puerto Rico. Scorecards: 10-9, 10-9, 10-9.

Flyweight

IBF

29 November 2002   Irene Pacheco 7.13 (Colombia) W PTS 12 Alejandro Montiel 8.0 (Mexico), El Paso, Texas, USA. Scorecards: 115-112, 118-109, 117-110.

WBA

12 October 2002   Eric Morel 8.0 (USA) W RSC 11 Denkaosaen Kaowichit 7.13$^{1}/_{2}$ (Thailand), Anaheim, California, USA.

28 June 2003   Eric Morel 8.0 (USA) W PTS 12 Isidro Garcia 7.13 (USA), Bayamon, Puerto Rico. Scorecards: 116-110, 115-111, 115-111.

WBC

6 September 2002   Pongsaklek Wonjongkam 8.0

(Thailand) W PTS 12 Jesus Martinez 8.0 (Mexico), Rangsit, Thailand. Scorecards: 120-107, 119-109, 120-106.

26 November 2002   Pongsaklek Wonjongkam 7.13^1/$_2$ (Thailand) W PTS 12 Hidenobu Honda 7.13^3/$_4$ (Japan), Osaka, Japan. Scorecards: 119-109, 115-113, 116-112.

6 June 2003   Pongsaklek Wonjongkam 8.0 (Thailand) W PTS 12 Randy Mangubat 8.0 (Philippines), Songkla, Thailand. Scorecards: 118-109, 118-109, 119-110.

WBO

13 July 2002   Adonis Rivas 7.13^1/$_2$ (Nicaragua) L PTS 12 Omar Narvaez 7.13^3/$_4$ (Argentina), Buenos Aires, Argentina. Scorecards: 109-117, 109-117, 107-119. Rivas had been named champion after Fernando Montiel had moved up a division on 22 June 2002.

13 September 2002   Omar Narvaez 8.0 (Argentina) W DIS 10 Luis Lazarte 7.11^1/$_2$ (Argentina), Santa Cruz, Argentina.

14 December 2002   Omar Narvaez 7.13^1/$_4$ (Argentina) W PTS 12 Andrea Sarritzu 7.13^3/$_4$ (Italy), Cagliari, Italy. Scorecards: 112-116, 116-113, 116-112.

7 June 2003   Omar Narvaez 8.0 (Argentina) W RSC 5 Everardo Morales 7.13^1/$_2$ (Mexico), Buenos Aires, Argentina.

S. Flyweight
IBF

4 January 2003   Felix Machado 8.2 (Venezuela) L PTS 12 Luis Perez 8.2 (Nicaragua), Washington DC, USA. Scorecards: 112-115, 117-110, 113-114.

WBA

31 July 2002   Alexander Munoz 8.2^3/$_4$ (Venezuela) W CO 2 Eiji Kojima 8.3 (Japan), Osaka, Japan.

WBC

26 August 2002   Masamori Tokuyama 8.2^3/$_4$ (Japan) W RTD 6 Erik Lopez 8.3 (Mexico), Saitama, Japan.

20 December 2002   Masamori Tokuyama 8.3 (Japan) W PTS 12 Gerry Penalosa 8.2^3/$_4$ (Philippines), Osaka, Japan. Scorecards: Richie Davies 116-111, 114-113, 113-114.

23 June 2003   Masamori Tokuyama 8.3 (Japan) W PTS 12 Katsushigi Kawashima 8.3 (Japan), Yokohama, Japan. Scorecards: 116-114, 116-112, 116-112.

WBO

18 January 2003   Fernando Montiel 8.3 (Mexico) W CO 2 Roy Doliguez 8.2^1/$_2$ (Philippines), Los Mochis, Mexico.

Bantamweight
IBF

27 July 2002   Tim Austin 8.6 (USA) W RSC 10 Adan Vargas 8.5 (Mexico), Las Vegas, Nevada, USA.

15 February 2003   Tim Austin 8.6 (USA) L RSC 8 Rafael Marquez 8.6 (Mexico), Las Vegas, Nevada, USA.

WBA

8 November 2002   Johnny Bredahl 8.5 (Denmark) W PTS 12 Leo Gamez 8.4^1/$_4$ (Venezuela), Copenhagen, Denmark. Scorecards: 115-114, 117-112, 117-113.

WBC

1 May 2003   Veeraphol Sahaprom 8.6 (Thailand) W PTS 12 Hugo Dianzo 8.6 (Mexico), Bangkok, Thailand. Scorecards: 118-110, 118-110, 117-111.

WBO

27 September 2002   Cruz Carbajal 8.5^3/$_4$ (Mexico) W RTD 4 Danny Romero 8.6 (USA), Albuquerque, New Mexico, USA.

S. Bantamweight
IBF

26 October 2002   Manny Pacquiao 8.10 (Philippines) W RSC 1 Fahprakob Rakkiatgym 8.9 (Thailand), Davao City, Philippines.

WBA

9 October 2002   Osamu Sato 8.10 (Japan) L PTS 12 Salim Medjkoune 8.10 (France), Tokyo, Japan. Scorecards: 112-116, 111-117, 110-119.

4 April 2003   Salim Medjkoune 8.10 (France) W PTS 12 Vincenzo Gigliotti 8.10 (Italy), Clermont Ferrand, France. Scorecards: 115-113, 117-112, 116-111.

WBC

1 November 2002   Willie Jorrin 8.10 (USA) L RSC 1 Oscar Larios 8.10 (Mexico), Sacramento, California, USA. Earlier, on 24 August, in Tokyo, Japan, Larios had retained the interim title on stopping Manabu Fukushima (Japan) inside eight rounds.

26 April 2003   Oscar Larios 8.10 (Mexico) W PTS 12 Shigeru Nakazato 8.10 (Japan), Tokyo, Japan. Scorecards: 114-111, 116-110, 116-110.

WBO

17 August 2002   Joan Guzman 8.10 (Dominican Republic) W CO 3 Fabio Oliva 8.10 (Argentina), Cardiff Castle, Cardiff, Wales. Judges: Mickey Vann, John Coyle.

Agapito Sanchez (Dominican Republic) had been due to defend against Guzman but was forced to vacate after it was discovered that he had cataract problems and Oliva was rushed in to take his place in a fight that carried the vacant title.

Featherweight
IBF

1 February 2003   Juan Manuel Marquez 8.13^1/$_2$ (Mexico) W RSC 7 Manuel Medina 8.13 (Mexico), Las Vegas, Nevada, USA. Contested for the vacant title after Johnny Tapia (USA) had been stripped in October 2002 for agreeing to take on Marco Antonio Barrera (Mexico) in a 12-round non-title fight at the weight and refusing to hand over a sanctioning fee. For the record, Barrera won on points in Las Vegas on 2 November and would continue to be recognised as the best man in the division despite not being interested in holding a commission title.

WBA

24 August 2002   Derrick Gainer 9.0 (USA) T DRAW 2 Daniel Seda 9.0 (Puerto Rico), Carolina, Puerto Rico. Scorecards: 10-8, 10-8, 10-8.

12 April 2003   Derrick Gainer 9.0 (USA) W PTS 12 Oscar Leon 9.0 (Colombia), Las Vegas, Nevada, USA. Scorecards: 112-114, 114-112, 117-110.

WBC

16 November 2002   Erik Morales 9.0 (Mexico) W PTS 12 Paulie Ayala 9.0 (USA), Las Vegas, Nevada, USA. Scorecards: John Keane 117-111, 117-111, 116-112. Billed for the vacant title following Marco Antonio Barrera's decision to move on immediately after becoming champion on beating Morales on 22 June 2002.

22 February 2003   Erik Morales 9.0 (Mexico) W RSC 3 Eddie Croft 9.0 (USA), Mexico City, Mexico, USA.

3 May 2003   Erik Morales 9.0 (Mexico) W RSC 5 Fernando Velardez 9.0 (USA), Las Vegas, Nevada, USA.

WBO

19 October 2002   Julio Pablo Chacon 8.13¾ (Argentina) L PTS 12 Scott Harrison 9.0 (Scotland), Braehead Arena, Renfrew, Scotland. Scorecards: Dave Parris 112-117, 111-117, 111-117. It was a tough fight to score, but Harrison's constant aggression eventually overcame the counter-punching Chacon, who failed to dictate and ultimately didn't get on top at any given stage of the contest. However, it was close and fought in such a sportsmanlike manner that it did boxing proud and certainly raised the Scot's stock to new heights.

22 March 2003   Scott Harrison 8.13¾ (Scotland) W PTS 12 Wayne McCullough 8.13 (Ireland), Braehead Arena, Renfrew, Scotland. Scorecards: Mickey Vann 119-108, 120-108, 119-109. Referee: John Coyle. On top throughout, Harrison once again proved what a strong man at the weight he is as he forced the former Olympic silver medallist to give ground continuously, systematically cutting the ring down and punching well with both hands. By the eighth round many felt that it had become too one-sided and should have been called off, but McCullough bravely stayed the distance, despite never looking likely to win, and once again showed his ability to take a good punch.

S. Featherweight
IBF

1 February 2003   Carlos Hernandez 9.3½ (USA) W TD 8 David Santos 9.2½ ((USA), Las Vegas, Nevada, USA. Scorecards: 77-74, 78-73, 77-74. Earlier, on 18 August 2002, in Temecula, California, USA, the USA's Steve Forbes (9.6¾) had come in over the weight for a defence against Santos and although the fight went ahead, Forbes winning on points over 12 rounds, the title was declared vacant.

WBA

3 August 2002   Acelino Freitas 9.4 (Brazil) W PTS 12 Daniel Attah 9.4 (Nigeria), Phoenix, Arizona, USA. Scorecards: 117-110, 117-110, 117-110. With Freitas recognised by the WBA as their super champion, Yodsanan Nanthachai (Thailand) stopped Lamont Pearson (USA) in the ninth round in Bangkok, Thailand on 5 December to retain the secondary title.

15 March 2003   Acelino Freitas 9.4 (Brazil) W RSC 4 Juan Carlos Ramirez 9.4 (Mexico), Chicago, Illinois, USA.

WBC

24 August 2002   Sirimongkol Singmanassak 9.4 (Thailand) W CO 2 Kengo Nagashima 9.4 (Japan), Tokyo, Japan. This one was billed for the vacant title after Floyd Mayweather (USA) had relinquished his belt on winning the WBC championship on 20 April 2002.

13 January 2003   Sirimongkol Singmanassak 9.4 (Thailand) W PTS 12 Yong-Soo Choi 9.4 (South Korea), Tokyo, Japan. Scorecards: 119-109, 119-109, 118-110.

WBO

3 August 2002   Acelino Freitas 9.4 (Brazil) W PTS 12 Daniel Attah 9.4 (Nigeria), Phoenix, Arizona, USA. Scorecards: 117-110, 117-110, 117-110.

15 March 2003   Acelino Freitas 9.4 (Brazil) W RSC 4 Juan Carlos Ramirez 9.4 (Mexico), Chicago, Illinois, USA.

Lightweight
IBF

9 November 2002   Paul Spadafora 9.9 (USA) W PTS 12 Dennis Holbaek 9.8½ (Denmark), Chester, West Virginia, USA. Scorecards: 117-111, 117-111, 118-110.

17 May 2003   Paul Spadafora 9.8½ (USA) DREW 12 Leonardo Dorin 9.9 (Romania), Pittsburgh, Pennsylvania, USA. Scorecards: 114-114, 113-115, 115-114. Towards the end of June, Spadafora relinquished the title in order to fight in a higher weight division.

WBA

17 May 2003   Leonardo Dorin 9.9 (Romania) DREW 12 Paul Spadafora 9.8½ (USA), Pittsburgh, Pennsylvania, USA. Scorecards: 114-114, 115-113, 114-115.

WBC

7 December 2002   Floyd Mayweather 9.8 (USA) W PTS 12 Jose Luis Castillo 9.9 (Mexico), Las Vegas, Nevada, USA. Scorecards: Larry O'Connell 116-113, 115-113, 115-113.

19 April 2003   Floyd Mayweather 9.8 (USA) W PTS 12 Victoriano Sosa 9.8 (Dominican Republic), Fresno, California, USA. Scorecards: 118-110, 119-109, 118-110.

WBO

14 September 2002   Artur Grigorian 9.9 (Uzbekistan) W PTS 12 Stefano Zoff 9.8¼ (Italy), Braunschweig, Germany. Scorecards: 115-113, 115-113, 118-110.

18 January 2003   Artur Grigorian 9.9 (Uzbekistan) W PTS 12 Matt Zegan 9.8½ (Poland), Essen, Germany. Scorecards: 114-114, 116-112, 115-113.

L. Welterweight
IBF

19 January 2003   Kostya Tszyu 9.13¾ (Russia) W RTD 6 James Leija 9.13 (USA), Melbourne, Australia.

WBA

19 January 2003   Kostya Tszyu 9.13¾ (Russia) W RTD 6 James Leija 9.13 (USA), Melbourne, Australia. With Tszyu considered to be the WBA super champion,

Diosbelys Hurtado (Cuba) lost the secondary title to Guyana's Vivian Harris when he was stopped in the second round of their contest in Houston, Texas, USA on 19 October 2002.

WBC

19 January 2003   Kostya Tszyu 9.13^3/$_4$ (Russia) W RTD 6 James Leija 9.13 (USA), Melbourne, Australia.

WBO

4 January 2003   DeMarcus Corley 10.0 (USA) W PTS 12 Randall Bailey 9.13 (USA), Washington DC, USA. Scorecards: 117-111, 116-112, 117-111.

Welterweight

IBF

22 March 2003   Michele Piccirillo 10.6^1/$_2$ (Italy) L PTS 12 Cory Spinks 10.6^1/$_4$ (USA), Campione d'Italia, Italy. Scorecards: 112-117, 111-117, 113-115.

WBA

25 January 2003   Ricardo Mayorga 10.6 (Nicaragua) W RSC 3 Vernon Forrest 10.6^1/$_2$ (USA), Temecula, California, USA. Judge: John Keane.

WBC

20 July 2002   Vernon Forrest 10.7 (USA) W PTS 12 Shane Mosley 10.7 (USA), Indianapolis, Indiana, USA. Scorecards: 115-113, 116-112, 117-111.

25 January 2003   Vernon Forrest 10.6^1/$_2$ (USA) L RSC 3 Ricardo Mayorga 10.6 (Nicaragua), Temecula, California, USA. Judge: John Keane.

WBO

12 October 2002   Antonio Margarito 10.6^1/$_2$ (Mexico) W PTS 12 Danny Perez 10.5^1/$_2$ (USA), Anaheim, California, USA. Scorecards: 120-108, 118-110, 120-108.

8 February 2003   Antonio Margarito 10.6^1/$_2$ (Mexico) W RSC 2 Andrew Lewis 10.7 (Guyana), Las Vegas, Nevada, USA.

L. Middleweight

IBF

7 September 2002   Ronald Wright 10.13^3/$_4$ (USA) W DIS 8 Bronco McKart 10.13^1/$_2$ (USA), Portland, Oregon, USA.

1 March 2003   Ronald Wright 10.13^1/$_2$ (USA) W PTS 12 Juan Candelo 10.13 (USA), Las Vegas, Nevada, USA. Scorecards: 118-110, 117-111, 117-111.

WBA

14 September 2002   Fernando Vargas 11.0 (USA) L RSC 11 Oscar de la Hoya 11.0 (USA), Las Vegas, Nevada, USA. Earlier, on 10 August, in Marseilles, France, Santiago Samaniego (Panama) stopped Mamadou Thiam (France) in the 12th round to land the vacant interim title. With de la Hoya recognised by the WBA as their super champion, Samaniego next won the vacant secondary title when stopping Alejandro Garcia (Mexico) in the third round at Las Vegas on 1 March 2003.

3 May 2003   Oscar de la Hoya 11.0 (USA) W RSC 7 Luis Campas 10.13^1/$_2$ (Mexico), Las Vegas, Nevada, USA.

WBC

14 September 2002   Oscar de la Hoya 11.0 (USA), W

RSC 11 Fernando Vargas 11.0 (USA), Las Vegas, Nevada, USA. Earlier, on 13 July, in Paria, Spain, Javier Castillejo (Spain) won the vacant interim title when outpointing Russia's Roman Karmazin over 12 rounds.

3 May 2002   Oscar de la Hoya 11.0 (USA) W RSC 7 Luis Campas 10.13^1/$_2$ (Mexico), Las Vegas, USA. On 9 May in Leganes, Spain, Javier Castillejo (Spain) successfully defended the interim title when stopping Diego Castillo (Colombia) in the first round.

WBO

17 August 2002   Daniel Santos 11.0 (Puerto Rico) W PTS 12 Mehrdud Takaloo 11.0 (England), Cardiff Castle, Cardiff, Wales. Scorecards: Mickey Vann 116-112, 117-110, 116-111.

28 June 2003   Daniel Santos 11.0 (Puerto Rico) W PTS 12 Fulgencio Zuniga 10.13 (Colombia), Bayamon, Puerto Rico. Scorecards: 118-110, 118-110, 118-110. Cut over the right eye as early as the opening round, Takaloo bravely stuck to the task, but never looked likely to upset the smooth-moving southpaw champion. It was a solid performance from Santos, his accurate punching and excellent movement keeping him in control, and although the English-based Iranian did his best he was up against a man who was always one move ahead.

Middleweight

IBF

29 March 2003   Bernard Hopkins 11.4^1/$_2$ (USA) W RTD 8 Morrade Hakkar 11.5 (France), Philadelphia, Pennsylvania, USA.

WBA

29 March 2003   Bernard Hopkins 11.4^1/$_2$ (USA) W RTD 8 Morrade Hakkar 11.5 (France), Philadelphia, Pennsylvania, USA. Earlier, on 10 October, William Joppy (USA) retained the secondary title when stopping Naotaka Hozumi (Japan) inside 10 rounds in Tokyo, Japan.

WBC

29 March 2003   Bernard Hopkins 11.4^1/$_2$ (USA) W RTD 8 Morrade Hakkar 11.5 (France), Philadelphia, Pennsylvania, USA.

WBO

With Harry Simon (Namibia) failing to make a defence due to receiving injuries during a car crasn, Hector Javier Velazco (Argentina) forced Andras Galfo (Hungary) to retire at the end of the seventh round to win the interim title in Buenos Aires, Argentina on 10 May 2003.

S. Middleweight

IBF

24 August 2002   Sven Ottke 11.13^1/$_2$ (Germany) W CO 9 Joe Gatti 12.0 (Canada), Leipzig, Germany.

16 November 2002   Sven Ottke 11.13^1/$_2$ (Germany) W PTS 12 Rudy Markussen 11.12 (Denmark), Nuremburg, Germany. Scorecards: 116-112, 116-112, 116-112.

15 March 2003   Sven Ottke 11.13 (Germany) W PTS 12 Byron Mitchell 11.13^1/$_4$ (USA), Berlin, Germany. Scorecards: 115-113, 112-116, 116-114.

14 June 2003   Sven Ottke 11.13^1/$_2$ (Germany) W PTS 12 David Starie 12.0 (England), Magdeburg, Germany. Scorecards: 116-112, 116-113, 115-113. Although Starie threw far more punches than the German, who conserved his energy throughout, it was the champion who landed more and ultimately just about deserved the decision. It had appeared closer than the scorecards, but this was Germany and to wrench the title away from the 36-year-old Ottke the Englishman possibly would have been better served taking more risks.

WBA

27 July 2002   Byron Mitchell 11.13^1/$_2$ (USA) W RSC 4 Julio Cesar Green 12.0 (USA), Las Vegas, Nevada, USA.

15 March 2003   Byron Mitchell 11.13^1/$_4$ (USA) L PTS 12 Sven Ottke 11.13 (Germany), Berlin, Germany. Scorecards: 113-115, 116-112, 114-116.

14 June 2003   Sven Ottke 11.13^1/$_2$ (Germany) W PTS 12 David Starie 12.0 (England), Magdeburg, Germany. Scorecards: 116-112, 116-113, 115-113. For a summary see under IBF title bouts.

WBC

6 September 2002   Eric Lucas 11.12^3/$_4$ (Canada) W PTS 12 Omar Sheika 11.13 (USA), Montreal, Canada, USA. Scorecards: 117-111, 117-111, 119-109.

5 April 2003   Eric Lucas 11.12^1/$_4$ (Canada) L PTS 12 Markus Beyer 11.13^1/$_4$ (Germany), Leipzig, Germany. Scorecards: John Keane 115-114, 113-116, 113-116.

WBO

17 August 2002   Joe Calzaghe 11.13^3/$_4$ (Wales) W PTS 12 Miguel Jimenez 12.0 (Puerto Rico), Cardiff Castle, Cardiff, Wales. Scorecards: John Coyle 120-107, 120-107, 120-107. Referee: Dave Parris. In damaging his left hand and with an opponent intent on survival, Calzaghe ultimately had to settle for a lopsided points win despite being far the better man. It was unfortunate, but at the end of the day Calzaghe had successfully defended his belt for the 11th time and proved he was the man to beat in a lacklustre division.

14 December 2002   Joe Calzaghe 11.13^1/$_4$ (Wales) W RSC 2 Tocker Pudwill 11.13^1/$_2$ (USA), Telewest Arena, Newcastle, England. Referee: Dave Parris. Judge: Mickey Vann. Despite the American, who came in at short notice, lasting 12 rounds with the IBF champion, Sven Ottke, this was a mismatch. Dumped three times in the opener and his right eye a mess, Pudwill came out for the second round, only to be stopped with 39 seconds on the clock when he was rescued by the referee, having been floored with a body punch.

28 June 2003   Joe Calzaghe 11.13 (Wales) W RSC 2 Byron Mitchell 12.0 (USA), The International Arena, Cardiff, Wales. Referee: Dave Parris. Judge: John Coyle. Knocked down for the first time in his career, when nailed by a short right hook in the second, Calzaghe got up at eight and came back swiftly to belt Mitchell to the canvas with big left. Having also taken an eight count, the challenger got up but was immediately set about and driven to the ropes where the referee rescued him after 2.36 of the

round had elapsed. This was a good win for the Welshman against a top man and augurs well for the future.

L. Heavyweight
IBF

7 September 2002   Roy Jones 12.6^3/$_4$ (USA) W RSC 6 Clinton Woods 12.6 (England), Portland, Oregon, USA. Up against the man many rate as the best pound-for-pound fighter around, Woods did not let anyone down before succumbing in the sixth, having given of his best to no effect. Despite battling bravely, Woods soon became a target for Jones' brilliant array of punches and by the fourth round it seemed to be only a matter of time. However, although there had been no knockdowns the challenger was being sickened by blows to both head and body and the fight was stopped at 1.29 of round six to save Woods from further punishment. Jones forfeited the title in November 2002, having decided to take on John Ruiz for the WBA heavyweight title on 1 March 2003.

26 April 2003   Antonio Tarver 12.7 (USA) W PTS 12 Montell Griffin 12.7 (USA), Mashantucket, Connecticut, USA. Scorecards: 120-106, 120-106, 120-106.

WBA

7 September 2002   Roy Jones 12.6^3/$_4$ (USA) W RSC 6 Clinton Woods 12.6 (England), Portland, Oregon, USA. For a summary see under IBF title bouts. Earlier, on 13 July, Bruno Girard (France) outpointed Lou del Valle (USA) over 12 rounds in Palavas les Flots, France to retain the secondary title, prior to losing it when stopped by his fellow countryman, Mehdi Sahnoune, in the seventh on 8 March in Marseilles, France. Following the announcement that Jones would be relinquishing the super title in early April 2003, having won the WBA heavyweight crown on 1 March, Sahnoune automatically took over full recognition as the WBA champion.

WBC

7 September 2002   Roy Jones 12.6^3/$_4$ (USA) W RSC 6 Clinton Woods 12.6 (England), Portland, Oregon, USA. For a summary see under IBF title bouts. Jones relinquished the title in early April, having beaten John Ruiz for the WBA heavyweight championship on 1 March 2003.

26 April 2003   Antonio Tarver 12.7 (USA) W PTS 12 Montell Griffin 12.7 (USA), Mashantucket, Connecticut, USA. Scorecards: 120-106, 120-106, 120-106.

WBO

14 September 2002   Dariusz Michalczewski 12.7 (Poland) W RSC 10 Richard Hall 12.7 (Jamaica), Braunschweig, Germany.

29 March 2003   Dariusz Michaczewski 12.6^1/$_2$ (Poland) W CO 9 Derrick Harmon 12.7 (USA), Hamburg, Germany.

Cruiserweight
IBF

26 April 2003   Vassily Jirov 13.6 (Kazakhstan) L PTS 12 James Toney 13.8 (USA), Mashantucket, Connecticut, USA. Scorecards: 110-116, 109-117, 109-117.

WBA

10 August 2002   Jean-Marc Mormeck 13.6 (France) W RSC 8 Dale Brown 13.7$^{1}/_{2}$ (Canada), Marseilles, France.

1 March 2003   Jean-Marc Mormeck 13.5$^{1}/_{2}$ (France) W RSC 8 Alexander Gurov 13.6$^{1}/_{2}$ (Ukraine), Las Vegas, Nevada, USA.

WBC

11 October 2002   Wayne Braithwaite 13.4 (Guyana) W RSC 10 Vincenzo Cantatore 13.8 (Italy), Campione d'Italia, Italy. Judge: Mark Green. With Juan Carlos Gomez (Cuba) having moved up to fight at heavyweight in March 2002, this one was billed for the vacant title.

21 February 2003   Wayne Braithwaite 13.4 (Guyana) W RSC 4 Ravea Springs 13.2$^{1}/_{2}$ (USA), Miami, Florida, USA.

WBO

23 November 2002   Johnny Nelson 13.7 (England) DREW 12 Guillermo Jones 13.7 (Panama), The Storm Arena, Derby, England. Scorecards: 116-113, 113-115, 114-114. Referee: Paul Thomas. Lucky to escape with his title intact, Nelson somehow held on to it due to some surprising scoring to say the least. Whatever fighting there was came from Jones, but it was an untidy affair, with much cuffing and slapping, and fell far below championship standard.

Heavyweight

IBF

14 December 2002   Chris Byrd 15.4 (USA) W PTS 12 Evander Holyfield 15.10 (USA), Atlantic City, New Jersey, USA. Scorecards: 116-112, 117-111, 117-111. Billed for the vacant title after Lennox Lewis gave up the belt on 5 September 2002, rather than defend against Byrd.

WBA

27 July 2002   John Ruiz 16.9 (USA) W DIS 10 Kirk Johnson 17.0 (Canada), Las Vegas, Nevada, USA.

1 March 2003   John Ruiz 16.2 (USA) L PTS 12 Roy Jones 13.11 (USA), Las Vegas, Nevada, USA. Scorecards: 111-117, 112-116, 110-118.

WBC

21 June 2003   Lennox Lewis 18.4 (England) W RSC 6 Vitali Klitschko 17.10 (Ukraine), Los Angeles, California, USA. Looking overweight and sluggish, Lewis turned in one of his worst championship performances and would surely have lost had it not been for Klitschko suffering from an horrendous cut around his left eye from the third round, an injury which eventually necessitated 60 stitches. At the end of the sixth the doctor failed to let the challenger continue and the fight was called off, not going to the scorecards because the initial punch that did the damage was deemed to be legal.

WBO

7 December 2002   Vladimir Klitschko 17.2 (Ukraine) W RTD 10 Jamie McCline 18.11 (USA), Las Vegas, Nevada, USA.

8 March 2003   Vladimir Klitschko 17.4 (Ukraine) L RSC 2 Corrie Sanders 16.1 (South Africa), Hanover, Germany.

Johnny Nelson (left) evades Guillermo Jones' right jab   Les Clark

World Champions Since Gloves, 1889-2003

Since I began to carry out extensive research into world championship boxing from the very beginnings of gloved action, I discovered much that needed to be amended regarding the historical listings as we know them, especially prior to the 1920s. Although yet to finalise my researches, despite making considerable changes, the listings are the most comprehensive ever published. Bearing all that in mind, and using a wide range of American newspapers, the aim has been to discover just who had claims, valid or otherwise. Studying the records of all the recognised champions, supplied by Professor Luckett Davis and his team, fights against all opposition have been analysed to produce the ultimate data. Because there were no boxing commissions as such in America prior to the 1920s, the yardstick used to determine valid claims were victories over the leading fighters of the day and recognition given within the newspapers. Only where that criteria has been met have I adjusted previous information.

Championship Status Code:

AU = Austria; AUST = Australia; CALIF = California; CAN = Canada; CLE = Cleveland Boxing Commission; EBU = European Boxing Union; FL = Florida; FR = France; GB = Great Britain; GEO = Georgia; H = Hawaii; IBF = International Boxing Federation; IBU = International Boxing Union; ILL = Illinois; LOUIS = Louisiana; MARY = Maryland; MASS = Massachusetts; MICH = Michigan; NBA = National Boxing Association; NC = North Carolina; NY = New York; PEN = Pennsylvania; SA = South Africa; TBC = Territorial Boxing Commission; USA = United States; WBA = World Boxing Association; WBC = World Boxing Council; WBO = World Boxing Organisation.

Champions in **bold** are accorded universal recognition.

*Undefeated champions (Only relates to universally recognised champions prior to 1962 and thereafter WBA/WBC/IBF/WBO champions. Does not include men who forfeited titles).

Title Holder	Birthplace	Tenure	Status	Title Holder	Birthplace	Tenure	Status
				Eduardo Marquez	Nicaragua	2003	WBO
M. Flyweight (105 lbs)				Ivan Calderon	Puerto Rico	2003-	WBO
Kyung-Yung Lee*	S Korea	1987	IBF	Edgar Cardenas	Mexico	2003-	IBF
Hiroki Ioka	Japan	1987-1988	WBC				
Silvio Gamez*	Venezuela	1988-1989	WBA	**L. Flyweight (108 lbs)**			
Samuth Sithnaruepol	Thailand	1988-1989	IBF	Franco Udella	Italy	1975	WBC
Napa Kiatwanchai	Thailand	1988-1989	WBC	Jaime Rios	Panama	1975-1976	WBA
Bong-Jun Kim	S Korea	1989-1991	WBA	Luis Estaba	Venezuela	1975-1978	WBC
Nico Thomas	Indonesia	1989	IBF	Juan Guzman	Dom Republic	1976	WBA
Rafael Torres	Dom Republic	1989-1992	WBO	Yoko Gushiken	Japan	1976-1981	WBA
Eric Chavez	Philippines	1989-1990	IBF	Freddie Castillo	Mexico	1978	WBC
Jum-Hwan Choi	S Korea	1989-1990	WBC	Sor Vorasingh	Thailand	1978	WBC
Hideyuki Ohashi	Japan	1990	WBC	Sun-Jun Kim	S Korea	1978-1980	WBC
Fahlan Lukmingkwan	Thailand	1990-1992	IBF	Shigeo Nakajima	Japan	1980	WBC
Ricardo Lopez*	Mexico	1990-1997	WBC	Hilario Zapata	Panama	1980-1982	WBC
Hi-Yon Choi	S Korea	1991-1992	WBA	Pedro Flores	Mexico	1981	WBA
Manny Melchor	Philippines	1992	IBF	Hwan-Jin Kim	S Korea	1981	WBA
Hideyuki Ohashi	Japan	1992-1993	WBA	Katsuo Tokashiki	Japan	1981-1983	WBA
Ratanapol Sowvoraphin	Thailand	1992-1996	IBF	Amado Ursua	Mexico	1982	WBC
Chana Porpaoin	Thailand	1993-1995	WBA	Tadashi Tomori	Japan	1982	WBC
Paul Weir*	Scotland	1993-1994	WBO	Hilario Zapata	Panama	1982-1983	WBC
Alex Sanchez	Puerto Rico	1993-1997	WBO	Jung-Koo Chang*	S Korea	1983-1988	WBC
Rosendo Alvarez	Nicaragua	1995-1998	WBA	Lupe Madera	Mexico	1983-1984	WBA
Ratanapol Sowvoraphin	Thailand	1996-1997	IBF	Dodie Penalosa	Philippines	1983-1986	IBF
Ricardo Lopez*	Mexico	1997-1998	WBC/WBO	Francisco Quiroz	Dom Republic	1984-1985	WBA
Zolani Petelo*	S Africa	1997-2000	IBF	Joey Olivo	USA	1985	WBA
Ricardo Lopez*	Mexico	1998	WBC	Myung-Woo Yuh	S Korea	1985-1991	WBA
Eric Jamili	Philippines	1998	WBO	Jum-Hwan Choi	S Korea	1986-1988	IBF
Kermin Guardia*	Colombia	1998-2002	WBO	Tacy Macalos	Philippines	1988-1989	IBF
Ricardo Lopez*	Mexico	1998-1999	WBA/WBC	German Torres	Mexico	1988-1989	WBC
Wandee Chor Chareon	Thailand	1999-2000	WBC	Yul-Woo Lee	S Korea	1989	WBC
Noel Arambulet	Venezuela	1999-2000	WBA	Muangchai Kitikasem	Thailand	1989-1990	IBF
Jose Antonio Aguirre	Mexico	2000-	WBC	Jose de Jesus	Puerto Rico	1989-1992	WBO
Jomo Gamboa	Philippines	2000	WBA	Humberto Gonzalez	Mexico	1989-1990	WBC
Keitaro Hoshino	Japan	2000-2001	WBA	Michael Carbajal*	USA	1990-1993	IBF
Chana Porpaoin	Thailand	2001	WBA	Rolando Pascua	Philippines	1990-1991	WBC
Roberto Levya	Mexico	2001-2003	IBF	Melchor Cob Castro	Mexico	1991	WBC
Yutaka Niida*	Japan	2001	WBA	Humberto Gonzalez	Mexico	1991-1993	WBC
Keitaro Hoshino	Japan	2002	WBA	Hiroki Ioka	Japan	1991-1992	WBA
Jorge Mata	Spain	2002-2003	WBO	Josue Camacho	Puerto Rico	1992-1994	WBO
Noel Arambulet	Venezuela	2002-	WBA	Myung-Woo Yuh*	S Korea	1992-1993	WBA
Miguel Barrera	Colombia	2002-2003	IBF				

Title Holder	Birthplace	Tenure	Status	Title Holder	Birthplace	Tenure	Status
Michael Carbajal	USA	1993-1994	IBF/WBC	**Pone Kingpetch**	Thailand	1963	
Silvio Gamez	Venezuela	1993-1995	WBA	**Hiroyuki Ebihara**	Japan	1963-1964	
Humberto Gonzalez	Mexico	1994-1995	WBC/IBF	**Pone Kingpetch**	Thailand	1964-1965	
Michael Carbajal*	USA	1994	WBO	**Salvatore Burruni**	Italy	1965	
Paul Weir	Scotland	1994-1995	WBO	Salvatore Burruni	Italy	1965-1966	WBC
Hi-Yong Choi	S Korea	1995-1996	WBA	Horacio Accavallo*	Argentina	1966-1968	WBA
Saman Sorjaturong*	Thailand	1995	WBC/IBF	Walter McGowan	Scotland	1966	WBC
Jacob Matlala*	South Africa	1995-1997	WBO	Chartchai Chionoi	Thailand	1966-1969	WBC
Saman Sorjaturong	Thailand	1995-1999	WBC	Efren Torres	Mexico	1969-1970	WBC
Carlos Murillo	Panama	1996	WBA	Hiroyuki Ebihara	Japan	1969	WBA
Michael Carbajal	USA	1996-1997	IBF	Bernabe Villacampo	Philippines	1969-1970	WBA
Keiji Yamaguchi	Japan	1996	WBA	Chartchai Chionoi	Thailand	1970	WBC
Pichitnoi Chor Siriwat	Thailand	1996-2000	WBA	Berkrerk Chartvanchai	Thailand	1970	WBA
Mauricio Pastrana	Colombia	1997-1998	IBF	Masao Ohba*	Japan	1970-1973	WBA
Jesus Chong	Mexico	1997	WBO	Erbito Salavarria	Philippines	1970-1971	WBC
Melchor Cob Castro	Mexico	1997-1998	WBO	Betulio Gonzalez	Venezuela	1971-1972	WBC
Mauricio Pastrana	Colombia	1997-1998	IBF	Venice Borkorsor*	Thailand	1972-1973	WBC
Juan Domingo Cordoba	Argentina	1998	WBO	Chartchai Chionoi	Thailand	1973-1974	WBA
Jorge Arce	Mexico	1998-1999	WBO	Betulio Gonzalez	Venezuela	1973-1974	WBC
Will Grigsby	USA	1998-1999	IBF	Shoji Oguma	Japan	1974-1975	WBC
Michael Carbajal*	USA	1999-2000	WBO	Susumu Hanagata	Japan	1974-1975	WBA
Ricardo Lopez*	Mexico	1999-2002	IBF	Miguel Canto	Mexico	1975-1979	WBC
Yo-Sam Choi	S Korea	1999-2002	WBC	Erbito Salavarria	Philippines	1975-1976	WBA
Masibuleke Makepula*	S Africa	2000	WBO	Alfonso Lopez	Panama	1976	WBA
Will Grigsby	USA	2000	WBO	Guty Espadas	Mexico	1976-1978	WBA
Beibis Mendoza	Colombia	2000-2001	WBA	Betulio Gonzalez	Venezuela	1978-1979	WBA
Rosendo Alvarez	Nicaragua	2001-	WBA	Chan-Hee Park	S Korea	1979-1980	WBC
Nelson Dieppa	Puerto Rico	2001-	WBO	Luis Ibarra	Panama	1979-1980	WBA
Jorge Arce	Mexico	2002-	WBC	Tae-Shik Kim	S Korea	1980	WBA
Jose Victor Burgos	Mexico	2003-	IBF	Shoji Oguma	Japan	1980-1981	WBC
				Peter Mathebula	S Africa	1980-1981	WBA
Flyweight (112 lbs)				Santos Laciar	Argentina	1981	WBA
Johnny Coulon	Canada	1910	USA	Antonio Avelar	Mexico	1981-1982	WBC
Sid Smith	England	1911-1913	GB	Luis Ibarra	Panama	1981	WBA
Sid Smith	England	1913	GB/IBU	Juan Herrera	Mexico	1981-1982	WBA
Bill Ladbury	England	1913-1914	GB/IBU	Prudencio Cardona	Colombia	1982	WBC
Percy Jones	Wales	1914	GB/IBU	Santos Laciar*	Argentina	1982-1985	WBA
Tancy Lee	Scotland	1915	GB/IBU	Freddie Castillo	Mexico	1982	WBC
Joe Symonds	England	1915-1916	GB/IBU	Eleonicio Mercedes	Dom Republic	1982-1983	WBC
Jimmy Wilde	Wales	1916	GB/IBU	Charlie Magri	Tunisia	1983	WBC
Jimmy Wilde	Wales	1916-1923		Frank Cedeno	Philippines	1983-1984	WBC
Pancho Villa*	Philippines	1923-1925		Soon-Chun Kwon	S Korea	1983-1985	IBF
Fidel la Barba	USA	1925-1927	NBA/CALIF	Koji Kobayashi	Japan	1984	WBC
Fidel la Barba*	USA	1927		Gabriel Bernal	Mexico	1984	WBC
Johnny McCoy	USA	1927-1928	CALIF	Sot Chitalada	Thailand	1984-1988	WBC
Izzy Schwartz	USA	1927-1929	NY	Hilario Zapata	Panama	1985-1987	WBA
Frenchy Belanger	Canada	1927-1928	NBA	Chong-Kwan Chung	S Korea	1985-1986	IBF
Newsboy Brown	Russia	1928	CALIF	Bi-Won Chung	S Korea	1986	IBF
Frankie Genaro	USA	1928-1929	NBA	Hi-Sup Shin	S Korea	1986-1987	IBF
Emile Pladner	France	1929	NBA/IBU	Fidel Bassa	Colombia	1987-1989	WBA
Frankie Genaro	USA	1929-1931	NBA/IBU	Dodie Penalosa	Philippines	1987	IBF
Midget Wolgast	USA	1930-1935	NY	Chang-Ho Choi	S Korea	1987-1988	IBF
Young Perez	Tunisia	1931-1932	NBA/IBU	Rolando Bohol	Philippines	1988	IBF
Jackie Brown	England	1932-1935	NBA/IBU	Yong-Kang Kim	S Korea	1988-1989	WBC
Jackie Brown	England	1935	GB/NBA	Duke McKenzie	England	1988-1989	IBF
Benny Lynch	Scotland	1935-1937	GB/NBA	Elvis Alvarez*	Colombia	1989	WBO
Small Montana	Philippines	1935-1937	NY/CALIF	Sot Chitalada	Thailand	1989-1991	WBC
Valentin Angelmann	France	1936-1938	IBU	Dave McAuley	Ireland	1989-1992	IBF
Peter Kane*	England	1938-1939	NBA/NY/GB/IBU	Jesus Rojas	Venezuela	1989-1900	WBA
Little Dado	Philippines	1938-1939	CALIF	Yukihito Tamakuma	Japan	1990-1991	WBA
Little Dado	Philippines	1939-1943	NBA/CALIF	Isidro Perez	Mexico	1990-1992	WBO
Jackie Paterson	Scotland	1943-1947		Yul-Woo Lee	S Korea	1990	WBA
Jackie Paterson	Scotland	1947-1948	GB/NY	Muangchai Kitikasem	Thailand	1991-1992	WBC
Rinty Monaghan	Ireland	1947-1948	NBA	Elvis Alvarez	Colombia	1991	WBA
Rinty Monaghan*	Ireland	1948-1950		Yong-Kang Kim	S Korea	1991-1992	WBA
Terry Allen	England	1950		Pat Clinton	Scotland	1992-1993	WBO
Dado Marino	Hawaii	1950-1952		Rodolfo Blanco	Colombia	1992	IBF
Yoshio Shirai	Japan	1952-1954		Yuri Arbachakov	Russia	1992-1997	WBC
Pascual Perez	Argentina	1954-1960		Aquiles Guzman	Venezuela	1992	WBA
Pone Kingpetch	Thailand	1960-1962		Pichit Sitbangprachan*	Thailand	1992-1994	IBF
Fighting Harada	Japan	1962-1963		David Griman	Venezuela	1992-1994	WBA

Title Holder	Birthplace	Tenure	Status
Jacob Matlala	S Africa	1993-1995	WBO
Saen Sorploenchit	Thailand	1994-1996	WBA
Alberto Jimenez	Mexico	1995-1996	WBO
Francisco Tejedor	Colombia	1995	IBF
Danny Romero*	USA	1995-1996	IBF
Mark Johnson*	USA	1996-1998	IBF
Jose Bonilla	Venezuela	1996-1998	WBA
Carlos Salazar	Argentina	1996-1998	WBO
Chatchai Sasakul	Thailand	1997-1998	WBC
Hugo Soto	Argentina	1998-1999	WBA
Ruben Sanchez	Mexico	1998-1999	WBO
Manny Pacquiao	Philippines	1998-1999	WBC
Silvio Gamez	Venezuela	1999	WBA
Irene Pacheco	Colombia	1999-	IBF
Jose Antonio Lopez	Spain	1999	WBO
Sornpichai Pisanurachan	Thailand	1999-2000	WBA
Medgoen Singsurat	Thailand	1999-2000	WBC
Isidro Garcia	Mexico	1999-2000	WBO
Malcolm Tunacao	Philippines	2000-2001	WBC
Eric Morel	USA	2000-	WBA
Fernando Montiel*	Mexico	2000-2002	WBO
Pongsaklek Wonjongkam	Thailand	2001-	WBC
Adonis Rivas	Nicaragua	2002	WBO
Omar Narvaez	Argentina	2002-	WBO

S. Flyweight (115 lbs)

Title Holder	Birthplace	Tenure	Status
Rafael Orono	Venezuela	1980-1981	WBC
Chul-Ho Kim	S Korea	1981-1982	WBC
Gustavo Ballas	Argentina	1981	WBA
Rafael Pedroza	Panama	1981-1982	WBA
Jiro Watanabe	Japan	1982-1984	WBA
Rafael Orono	Venezuela	1982-1983	WBC
Payao Poontarat	Thailand	1983-1984	WBC
Joo-Do Chun	S Korea	1983-1985	IBF
Jiro Watanabe	Japan	1984-1986	WBC
Kaosai Galaxy*	Thailand	1984-1992	WBA
Elly Pical	Indonesia	1985-1986	IBF
Cesar Polanco	Dom Republic	1986	IBF
Gilberto Roman	Mexico	1986-1987	WBC
Elly Pical	Indonesia	1986-1987	IBF
Santos Laciar	Argentina	1987	WBC
Tae-Il Chang	S Korea	1987	IBF
Jesus Rojas	Colombia	1987-1988	WBC
Elly Pical	Indonesia	1987-1989	IBF
Gilberto Roman	Mexico	1988-1989	WBC
Jose Ruiz	Puerto Rico	1989-1992	WBO
Juan Polo Perez	Colombia	1989-1990	IBF
Nana Yaw Konadu	Ghana	1989-1990	WBC
Sung-Il Moon	S Korea	1990-1993	WBC
Robert Quiroga	USA	1990-1993	IBF
Jose Quirino	Mexico	1992	WBO
Katsuya Onizuka	Japan	1992-1994	WBA
Johnny Bredahl	Denmark	1992-1994	WBO
Julio Cesar Borboa	Mexico	1993-1994	IBF
Jose Luis Bueno	Mexico	1993-1994	WBC
Hiroshi Kawashima	Japan	1994-1997	WBC
Harold Grey	Colombia	1994-1995	IBF
Hyung-Chul Lee	S Korea	1994-1995	WBA
Johnny Tapia*	USA	1994-1997	WBO
Alimi Goitia	Venezuela	1995-1996	WBA
Carlos Salazar	Argentina	1995-1996	IBF
Harold Grey	Colombia	1996	IBF
Yokthai Sith-Oar	Thailand	1996-1997	WBA
Danny Romero	USA	1996-1997	IBF
Gerry Penalosa	Philippines	1997-1998	WBC
Johnny Tapia*	USA	1997-1998	IBF/WBO
Satoshi Iida	Japan	1997-1998	WBA
In-Joo Cho	S Korea	1998-2000	WBC
Victor Godoi	Argentina	1998-1999	WBO
Jesus Rojas	Venezuela	1998-1999	WBA
Mark Johnson	USA	1999-2000	IBF

Title Holder	Birthplace	Tenure	Status
Diego Morales	Mexico	1999	WBO
Hideki Todaka	Japan	1999-2000	WBA
Adonis Rivas	Nicaragua	1999-2001	WBO
Felix Machado	Venezuela	2000-2003	IBF
Masamori Tokuyama	Japan	2000-	WBC
Silvio Gamez	Venezuela	2000-2001	WBA
Celes Kobayashi	Japan	2001-2002	WBA
Pedro Alcazar	Panama	2001-2002	WBO
Alexander Munoz	Venezuela	2002-	WBA
Fernando Montiel	Mexico	2002-	WBO
Luis Perez	Nicaragua	2003-	IBF

Bantamweight (118 lbs)

Title Holder	Birthplace	Tenure	Status
Tommy Kelly	USA	1889	
George Dixon	Canada	1889-1890	
Chappie Moran	England	1889-1890	
Tommy Kelly	USA	1890-1892	
Billy Plimmer	England	1892-1895	
Pedlar Palmer	England	1895-1899	
Terry McGovern	USA	1899	USA
Pedlar Palmer	England	1899-1900	GB
Terry McGovern*	USA	1899-1900	
Clarence Forbes	USA	1900	
Johnny Reagan	USA	1900-1902	
Harry Ware	England	1900-1902	GB
Harry Harris	USA	1901	
Harry Forbes	USA	1901-1902	
Kid McFadden	USA	1901	
Dan Dougherty	USA	1901	
Andrew Tokell	England	1902	GB
Harry Ware	England	1902	GB
Harry Forbes	USA	1902-1903	USA
Joe Bowker	England	1902-1904	GB
Frankie Neil	USA	1903-1904	USA
Joe Bowker*	England	1904-1905	
Frankie Neil	USA	1905	USA
Digger Stanley	England	1905-1907	
Owen Moran	England	1905-1907	
Jimmy Walsh	USA	1905-1908	USA
Owen Moran	England	1907	GB
Monte Attell	USA	1908-1910	
Jimmy Walsh	USA	1908-1911	
Digger Stanley	England	1909-1912	GB
Frankie Conley	Italy	1910-1911	
Johnny Coulon	Canada	1910-1911	
Monte Attell	USA	1910-1911	
Johnny Coulon	Canada	1911-1913	USA
Charles Ledoux	France	1912-1913	GB/IBU
Eddie Campi	USA	1913-1914	
Johnny Coulon	Canada	1913-1914	
Kid Williams	Denmark	1913-1914	
Kid Williams	Denmark	1914-1915	
Kid Williams	Denmark	1915-1917	
Johnny Ertle	USA	1915-1918	
Pete Herman	USA	1917-1919	
Pal Moore	USA	1918-1919	
Pete Herman	USA	1919-1920	
Joe Lynch	USA	1920-1921	
Pete Herman	USA	1921	
Johnny Buff	USA	1921-1922	
Joe Lynch	USA	1922-1923	
Joe Lynch	USA	1923-1924	NBA
Joe Burman	England	1923	NY
Abe Goldstein	USA	1923-1924	NY
Joe Lynch	USA	1924	
Abe Goldstein	USA	1924	
Eddie Martin	USA	1924-1925	
Charley Rosenberg	USA	1925-1926	
Charley Rosenberg	USA	1926-1927	NY
Bud Taylor*	USA	1926-1928	NBA
Bushy Graham*	Italy	1928-1929	NY

Title Holder	Birthplace	Tenure	Status
Al Brown	Panama	1929-1931	
Al Brown	Panama	1931	NY/IBU
Pete Sanstol	Norway	1931	CAN
Al Brown	Panama	1931-1933	
Al Brown	Panama	1933-1934	NY/NBA/IBU
Speedy Dado	Philippines	1933	CALIF
Baby Casanova	Mexico	1933-1934	CALIF
Sixto Escobar	Puerto Rico	1934	CAN
Sixto Escobar	Puerto Rico	1934-1935	NBA
Al Brown	Panama	1934-1935	NY/IBU
Lou Salica	USA	1935	CALIF
Baltazar Sangchilli	Spain	1935-1938	IBU
Lou Salica	USA	1935	NBA/NY
Sixto Escobar	Puerto Rico	1935-1937	NBA/NY
Harry Jeffra	USA	1937-1938	NY/NBA
Sixto Escobar	Puerto Rico	1938-1939	NY/NBA
Al Brown	Panama	1938	IBU
Sixto Escobar	Puerto Rico	1939	
George Pace	USA	1939-1940	NBA
Lou Salica	USA	1939	CALIF
Tony Olivera	USA	1939-1940	CALIF
Little Dado	Philippines	1940	CALIF
Lou Salica	USA	1940-1941	
Kenny Lindsay	Canada	1941	CAN
Lou Salica	USA	1942	NY
David Kui Kong Young	Hawaii	1941-1943	TBC
Lou Salica	USA	1941-1942	NY/NBA
Manuel Ortiz	USA	1942-1943	NBA
Manuel Ortiz	USA	1943-1945	NY/NBA
David Kui Kong Young	Hawaii	1943	TBC
Rush Dalma	Philippines	1943-1945	TBC
Manuel Ortiz	USA	1945-1947	
Harold Dade	USA	1947	
Manuel Ortiz	USA	1947-1950	
Vic Toweel	S Africa	1950-1952	
Jimmy Carruthers*	Australia	1952-1954	
Robert Cohen	Algeria	1954	
Robert Cohen	Algeria	1954-1956	NY/EBU
Raton Macias	Mexico	1955-1957	NBA
Mario D'Agata	Italy	1956-1957	NY/EBU
Alphonse Halimi	Algeria	1957	NY/EBU
Alphonse Halimi	Algeria	1957-1959	
Joe Becerra*	Mexico	1959-1960	
Alphonse Halimi	Algeria	1960-1961	EBU
Eder Jofre	Brazil	1960-1962	NBA
Johnny Caldwell	Ireland	1961-1962	EBU
Eder Jofre	Brazil	1962-1965	
Fighting Harada	Japan	1965-1968	
Lionel Rose	Australia	1968-1969	
Ruben Olivares	Mexico	1969-1970	
Chuchu Castillo	Mexico	1970-1971	
Ruben Olivares	Mexico	1971-1972	
Rafael Herrera	Mexico	1972	
Enrique Pinder	Panama	1972	
Enrique Pinder	Panama	1972-1973	WBC
Romeo Anaya	Mexico	1973	WBA
Rafael Herrera	Mexico	1973-1974	WBC
Arnold Taylor	S Africa	1973-1974	WBA
Soo-Hwan Hong	S Korea	1974-1975	WBA
Rodolfo Martinez	Mexico	1974-1976	WBC
Alfonso Zamora	Mexico	1975-1977	WBA
Carlos Zarate	Mexico	1976-1979	WBC
Jorge Lujan	Panama	1977-1980	WBA
Lupe Pintor*	Mexico	1979-1983	WBC
Julian Solis	Puerto Rico	1980	WBA
Jeff Chandler	USA	1980-1984	WBA
Albert Davila	USA	1983-1985	WBC
Richard Sandoval	USA	1984-1986	WBA
Satoshi Shingaki	Japan	1984-1985	IBF
Jeff Fenech*	Australia	1985-1987	IBF
Daniel Zaragoza	Mexico	1985	WBC

Title Holder	Birthplace	Tenure	Status
Miguel Lora	Colombia	1985-1988	WBC
Gaby Canizales	USA	1986	WBA
Bernardo Pinango*	Venezuela	1986-1987	WBA
Takuya Muguruma	Japan	1987	WBA
Kelvin Seabrooks	USA	1987-1988	IBF
Chang-Yung Park	S Korea	1987	WBA
Wilfredo Vasquez	Puerto Rico	1987-1988	WBA
Kaokor Galaxy	Thailand	1988	WBA
Orlando Canizales*	USA	1988-1994	IBF
Sung-Il Moon	S Korea	1988-1989	WBA
Raul Perez	Mexico	1988-1991	WBC
Israel Contrerras*	Venezuela	1989-1991	WBO
Kaokor Galaxy	Thailand	1989	WBA
Luisito Espinosa	Philippines	1989-1991	WBA
Greg Richardson	USA	1991	WBC
Gaby Canizales	USA	1991	WBO
Duke McKenzie	England	1991-1992	WBO
Joichiro Tatsuyushi*	Japan	1991-1992	WBC
Israel Contrerras	Venezuela	1991-1992	WBA
Eddie Cook	USA	1992	WBA
Victor Rabanales	Mexico	1992-1993	WBC
Rafael del Valle	Puerto Rico	1992-1994	WBO
Jorge Elicier Julio	Colombia	1992-1993	WBA
Il-Jung Byun	S Korea	1993	WBC
Junior Jones	USA	1993-1994	WBA
Yasuei Yakushiji	Japan	1993-1995	WBC
John Michael Johnson	USA	1994	WBA
Daorung Chuwatana	Thailand	1994-1995	WBA
Alfred Kotey	Ghana	1994-1995	WBO
Harold Mestre	Colombia	1995	IBF
Mbulelo Botile	S Africa	1995-1997	IBF
Wayne McCullough	Ireland	1995-1997	WBC
Veeraphol Sahaprom	Thailand	1995-1996	WBA
Daniel Jimenez	Puerto Rico	1995-1996	WBO
Nana Yaw Konadu	Ghana	1996	WBA
Robbie Regan*	Wales	1996-1998	WBO
Daorung Chuwatana	Thailand	1996-1997	WBA
Sirimongkol Singmanassak	Thailand	1997	WBC
Nana Yaw Konadu	Ghana	1997-1998	WBA
Tim Austin	USA	1997-2003	IBF
Joichiro Tatsuyoshi	Japan	1997-1998	WBC
Jorge Elicier Julio	Colombia	1998-2000	WBO
Johnny Tapia	USA	1998-1999	WBA
Veeraphol Sahaprom	Thailand	1998-	WBC
Paulie Ayala	USA	1999-2001	WBA
Johnny Tapia*	USA	2000	WBO
Mauricio Martinez	Panama	2000-2002	WBO
Eidy Moya	Venezuela	2001-2002	WBA
Cruz Carbajal	Mexico	2002-	WBO
Johnny Bredahl	Denmark	2002-	WBA
Rafael Marquez	Mexico	2003-	IBF

S. Bantamweight (122 lbs)

Title Holder	Birthplace	Tenure	Status
Rigoberto Riasco	Panama	1976	WBC
Royal Kobayashi	Japan	1976	WBC
Dong-Kyun Yum	S Korea	1976-1977	WBC
Wilfredo Gomez*	Puerto Rico	1977-1983	WBC
Soo-Hwan Hong	S Korea	1977-1978	WBA
Ricardo Cardona	Colombia	1978-1980	WBA
Leo Randolph	USA	1980	WBA
Sergio Palma	Argentina	1980-1982	WBA
Leonardo Cruz	Dom Republic	1982-1984	WBA
Jaime Garza	USA	1983-1984	WBC
Bobby Berna	Philippines	1983-1984	IBF
Loris Stecca	Italy	1984	WBA
Seung-In Suh	S Korea	1984-1985	IBF
Victor Callejas	Puerto Rico	1984-1986	WBA
Juan Meza	Mexico	1984-1985	WBC
Ji-Won Kim*	S Korea	1985-1986	IBF
Lupe Pintor	Mexico	1985-1986	WBC
Samart Payakarun	Thailand	1986-1987	WBC

Title Holder	Birthplace	Tenure	Status
Louie Espinosa	USA	1987	WBA
Seung-Hoon Lee*	S Korea	1987-1988	IBF
Jeff Fenech*	Australia	1987-1988	WBC
Julio Gervacio	Dom Republic	1987-1988	WBA
Bernardo Pinango	Venezuela	1988	WBA
Daniel Zaragoza	Mexico	1988-1990	WBC
Jose Sanabria	Venezuela	1988-1989	IBF
Juan J. Estrada	Mexico	1988-1989	WBA
Fabrice Benichou	Spain	1989-1990	IBF
Kenny Mitchell	USA	1989	WBO
Valerio Nati	Italy	1989-1990	WBO
Jesus Salud	USA	1989-1990	WBA
Welcome Ncita	S Africa	1990-1992	IBF
Paul Banke	USA	1990	WBC
Orlando Fernandez	Puerto Rico	1990-1991	WBO
Luis Mendoza	Colombia	1990-1991	WBA
Pedro Decima	Argentina	1990-1991	WBC
Kiyoshi Hatanaka	Japan	1991	WBC
Jesse Benavides	USA	1991-1992	WBO
Daniel Zaragoza	Mexico	1991-1992	WBC
Raul Perez	Mexico	1991-1992	WBA
Thierry Jacob	France	1992	WBC
Wilfredo Vasquez	Puerto Rico	1992-1995	WBA
Tracy Harris Patterson	USA	1992-1994	WBC
Duke McKenzie	England	1992-1993	WBO
Kennedy McKinney	USA	1992-1994	IBF
Daniel Jimenez	Puerto Rico	1993-1995	WBO
Vuyani Bungu *	S Africa	1994-1999	IBF
Hector Acero-Sanchez	Dom Republic	1994-1995	WBC
Marco Antonio Barrera	Mexico	1995-1996	WBO
Antonio Cermeno *	Venezuela	1995-1997	WBA
Daniel Zaragoza	Mexico	1995-1997	WBC
Junior Jones	USA	1996-1997	WBO
Erik Morales*	Mexico	1997-2000	WBC
Kennedy McKinney*	USA	1997-1998	WBO
Enrique Sanchez	Mexico	1998	WBA
Marco Antonio Barrera	Mexico	1998-2000	WBO
Nestor Garza	Mexico	1998-2000	WBA
Lehlohonola Ledwaba	S Africa	1999-2001	IBF
Erik Morales	Mexico	2000	WBC/WBO
Erik Morales*	Mexico	2000	WBC
Marco Antonio Barrera*	Mexico	2000-2001	WBO
Clarence Adams	USA	2000-2001	WBA
Willie Jorrin	USA	2000-2002	WBC
Manny Pacquiao	Philippines	2001-	IBF
Agapito Sanchez*	Dom Republic	2001-2002	WBO
Yober Ortega	Venezuela	2001-2002	WBA
Yoddamrong Sithyodthong	Thailand	2002	WBA
Osamu Sato	Japan	2002	WBA
Joan Guzman	Dom Republic	2002-	WBO
Salim Medjkoune	France	2002-	WBA
Oscar Larios	Mexico	2002-	WBC

Featherweight (126 lbs)

Title Holder	Birthplace	Tenure	Status
Ike Weir	Ireland	1889-1890	
Billy Murphy	New Zealand	1890-1893	
George Dixon	Canada	1890-1893	
Young Griffo	Australia	1890-1893	
Johnny Griffin	USA	1891-1893	
Solly Smith	USA	1893	
George Dixon	Canada	1893-1896	
Solly Smith	USA	1896-1898	
Frank Erne	USA	1896-1897	
George Dixon	Canada	1896-1900	
Harry Greenfield	England	1897-1899	
Ben Jordan	England	1897-1899	
Will Curley	England	1897-1899	
Dave Sullivan	Ireland	1898	
Ben Jordan	England	1899-1905	GB
Eddie Santry	USA	1899-1900	
Terry McGovern	USA	1900	

Title Holder	Birthplace	Tenure	Status
Terry McGovern	USA	1900-1901	USA
Young Corbett II	USA	1901-1903	USA
Eddie Hanlon	USA	1903	
Young Corbett II	USA	1903-1904	
Abe Attell	USA	1903-1904	
Abe Attell	USA	1904-1911	USA
Joe Bowker	England	1905-1907	GB
Jim Driscoll	Wales	1907-1912	GB
Abe Attell	USA	1911-1912	
Joe Coster	USA	1911	
Joe Rivers	Mexico	1911	
Johnny Kilbane	USA	1911-1912	
Jim Driscoll*	Wales	1912-1913	GB/IBU
Johnny Kilbane	USA	1912-1922	USA
Johnny Kilbane	USA	1922-1923	NBA
Johnny Dundee	Italy	1922-1923	NY
Eugene Criqui	France	1923	
Johnny Dundee*	Italy	1923-1924	
Kid Kaplan	Russia	1925	NY
Kid Kaplan*	Russia	1925-1926	
Honeyboy Finnegan	USA	1926-1927	MASS
Benny Bass	Russia	1927-1928	NBA
Tony Canzoneri	USA	1928	
Andre Routis	France	1928-1929	
Bat Battalino	USA	1929-1932	
Bat Battalino	USA	1932	NBA
Tommy Paul	USA	1932-1933	NBA
Kid Chocolate*	Cuba	1932-1934	NY
Baby Arizmendi	Mexico	1932-1933	CALIF
Freddie Miller	USA	1933-1936	NBA
Baby Arizmendi	Mexico	1934-1935	NY
Baby Arizmendi	Mexico	1935-1936	NY/MEX
Baby Arizmendi	Mexico	1936	MEX
Petey Sarron	USA	1936-1937	NBA
Henry Armstrong	USA	1936-1937	CALIF/MEX
Mike Belloise	USA	1936	NY
Maurice Holtzer	France	1937-1938	IBU

Petey Sarron, the NBA featherweight champion, 1936-1937

Title Holder	Birthplace	Tenure	Status
Henry Armstrong*	USA	1937-1938	NBA/NY
Leo Rodak	USA	1938	MARY
Joey Archibald	USA	1938-1939	NY
Leo Rodak	USA	1938-1939	NBA
Joey Archibald	USA	1939-1940	
Joey Archibald	USA	1940	NY
Petey Scalzo	USA	1940-1941	NBA
Jimmy Perrin	USA	1940	LOUIS
Harry Jeffra	USA	1940-1941	NY/MARY
Joey Archibald	USA	1941	NY/MARY
Richie Lemos	USA	1941	NBA
Chalky Wright	Mexico	1941-1942	NY/MARY
Jackie Wilson	USA	1941-1943	NBA
Willie Pep	USA	1942-1946	NY
Jackie Callura	Canada	1943	NBA
Phil Terranova	USA	1943-1944	NBA
Sal Bartolo	USA	1944-1946	NBA
Willie Pep	USA	1946-1948	
Sandy Saddler	USA	1948-1949	
Willie Pep	USA	1949-1950	
Sandy Saddler*	USA	1950-1957	
Hogan Kid Bassey	Nigeria	1957-1959	
Davey Moore	USA	1959-1963	
Sugar Ramos	Cuba	1963-1964	
Vicente Saldivar*	Mexico	1964-1967	
Raul Rojas	USA	1967	CALIF
Howard Winstone	Wales	1968	WBC
Raul Rojas	USA	1968	WBA
Johnny Famechon	France	1968-1969	AUST
Jose Legra	Cuba	1968-1969	WBC
Shozo Saijyo	Japan	1968-1971	WBA
Johnny Famechon	France	1969-1970	WBC
Vicente Saldivar	Mexico	1970	WBC
Kuniaki Shibata	Japan	1970-1972	WBC
Antonio Gomez	Venezuela	1971-1972	WBA
Clemente Sanchez	Mexico	1972	WBC
Ernesto Marcel*	Panama	1972-1974	WBA
Jose Legra	Cuba	1972-1973	WBC
Eder Jofre	Brazil	1973-1974	WBC
Ruben Olivares	Mexico	1974	WBA
Bobby Chacon	USA	1974-1975	WBC
Alexis Arguello*	Nicaragua	1974-1977	WBA
Ruben Olivares	Mexico	1975	WBC
David Kotey	Ghana	1975-1976	WBC
Danny Lopez	USA	1976-1980	WBC
Rafael Ortega	Panama	1977	WBA
Cecilio Lastra	Spain	1977-1978	WBA
Eusebio Pedroza	Panama	1978-1985	WBA
Salvador Sanchez*	Mexico	1980-1982	WBC
Juan Laporte	Puerto Rico	1982-1984	WBC
Min-Keun Oh	S Korea	1984-1985	IBF
Wilfredo Gomez	Puerto Rico	1984	WBC
Azumah Nelson*	Ghana	1984-1988	WBC
Barry McGuigan	Ireland	1985-1986	WBA
Ki-Yung Chung	S Korea	1985-1986	IBF
Steve Cruz	USA	1986-1987	WBA
Antonio Rivera	Puerto Rico	1986-1988	IBF
Antonio Esparragoza	Venezuela	1987-1991	WBA
Calvin Grove	USA	1988	IBF
Jeff Fenech*	Australia	1988-1989	WBC
Jorge Paez*	Mexico	1988-1990	IBF
Maurizio Stecca	Italy	1989	WBO
Louie Espinosa	USA	1989-1990	WBO
Jorge Paez*	Mexico	1990-1991	IBF/WBO
Marcos Villasana	Mexico	1990-1991	WBC
Kyun-Yung Park	S Korea	1991-1993	WBA
Troy Dorsey	USA	1991	IBF
Maurizio Stecca	Italy	1991-1992	WBO
Manuel Medina	Mexico	1991-1993	IBF
Paul Hodkinson	England	1991-1993	WBC
Colin McMillan	England	1992	WBO

Title Holder	Birthplace	Tenure	Status
Ruben Palacio	Colombia	1992-1993	WBO
Tom Johnson	USA	1993-1997	IBF
Steve Robinson	Wales	1993-1995	WBO
Gregorio Vargas	Mexico	1993	WBC
Kevin Kelley	USA	1993-1995	WBC
Eloy Rojas	Venezuela	1993-1996	WBA
Alejandro Gonzalez	Mexico	1995	WBC
Manuel Medina	Mexico	1995	WBC
Prince Naseem Hamed*	England	1995-1997	WBO
Luisito Espinosa	Philippines	1995-1999	WBC
Wilfredo Vasquez	Puerto Rico	1996-1998	WBA
Prince Naseem Hamed *	England	1997	WBO/IBF
Prince Naseem Hamed*	England	1997-1999	WBO
Hector Lizarraga	Mexico	1997-1998	IBF
Freddie Norwood	USA	1998	WBA
Manuel Medina	Mexico	1998-1999	IBF
Antonio Cermeno	Venezuela	1998-1999	WBA
Cesar Soto	Mexico	1999	WBC
Freddie Norwood	USA	1999-2000	WBA
Prince Naseem Hamed	England	1999-2000	WBC/WBO
Paul Ingle	England	1999-2000	IBF
Prince Naseem Hamed*	England	2000	WBO
Gustavo Espadas	Mexico	2000-2001	WBC
Derrick Gainer	USA	2000-	WBA
Mbulelo Botile	S Africa	2000-2001	IBF
Istvan Kovacs	Hungary	2001	WBO
Erik Morales	Mexico	2001-2002	WBC
Frankie Toledo	USA	2001	IBF
Julio Pablo Chacon	Argentina	2001-2002	WBO
Manuel Medina	Mexico	2001-2002	IBF
Johnny Tapia	USA	2002	IBF
Marco Antonio Barrera*	Mexico	2002	WBC
Scott Harrison	Scotland	2002-	WBO
Erik Morales	Mexico	2002-	WBC
Juan Manuel Marquez	Mexico	2003-	IBF

S. Featherweight (130 lbs)

Title Holder	Birthplace	Tenure	Status
Johnny Dundee	Italy	1921-1923	NY
Jack Bernstein	USA	1923	NY
Jack Bernstein	USA	1923	NBA/NY
Johnny Dundee	Italy	1923-1924	NBA/NY
Kid Sullivan	USA	1924-1925	NBA/NY
Mike Ballerino	USA	1925	NBA/NY
Tod Morgan	USA	1925-1929	NBA/NY
Benny Bass	Russia	1929-1930	NBA/NY
Benny Bass	Russia	1930-1931	NBA
Kid Chocolate	Cuba	1931-1933	NBA
Frankie Klick	USA	1933-1934	NBA
Sandy Saddler	USA	1949-1950	NBA
Sandy Saddler	USA	1950-1951	CLE
Harold Gomes	USA	1959-1960	NBA
Flash Elorde	Philippines	1960-1962	NBA
Flash Elorde	Philippines	1962-1967	WBA
Raul Rojas	USA	1967	CALIF
Yoshiaki Numata	Japan	1967	WBA
Hiroshi Kobayashi	Japan	1967-1971	WBA
Rene Barrientos	Philippines	1969-1970	WBC
Yoshiaki Numata	Japan	1970-1971	WBC
Alfredo Marcano	Venezuela	1971-1972	WBA
Ricardo Arredondo	Mexico	1971-1974	WBC
Ben Villaflor	Philippines	1972-1973	WBA
Kuniaki Shibata	Japan	1973	WBA
Ben Villaflor	Philippines	1973-1976	WBA
Kuniaki Shibata	Japan	1974-1975	WBC
Alfredo Escalera	Puerto Rico	1975-1978	WBC
Sam Serrano	Puerto Rico	1976-1980	WBA
Alexis Arguello*	Nicaragua	1978-1980	WBC
Yasutsune Uehara	Japan	1980-1981	WBA
Rafael Limon	Mexico	1980-1981	WBC
Cornelius Boza-Edwards	Uganda	1981	WBC
Sam Serrano	Puerto Rico	1981-1983	WBA

Title Holder	Birthplace	Tenure	Status
Rolando Navarrete	Philippines	1981-1982	WBC
Rafael Limon	Mexico	1982	WBC
Bobby Chacon	USA	1982-1983	WBC
Roger Mayweather	USA	1983-1984	WBA
Hector Camacho*	Puerto Rico	1983-1984	WBC
Rocky Lockridge	USA	1984-1985	WBA
Hwan-Kil Yuh	S Korea	1984-1985	IBF
Julio Cesar Chavez*	Mexico	1984-1987	WBC
Lester Ellis	England	1985	IBF
Wilfredo Gomez	Puerto Rico	1985-1986	WBA
Barry Michael	England	1985-1987	IBF
Alfredo Layne	Panama	1986	WBA
Brian Mitchell*	S Africa	1986-1991	WBA
Rocky Lockridge	USA	1987-1988	IBF
Azumah Nelson	Ghana	1988-1994	WBC
Tony Lopez	USA	1988-1989	IBF
Juan Molina*	Puerto Rico	1989	WBO
Juan Molina	Puerto Rico	1989-1990	IBF
Kamel Bou Ali	Tunisia	1989-1992	WBO
Tony Lopez	USA	1990-1991	IBF
Joey Gamache*	USA	1991	WBA
Brian Mitchell*	S Africa	1991-1992	IBF
Genaro Hernandez	USA	1991-1995	WBA
Juan Molina*	Puerto Rico	1992-1995	IBF
Daniel Londas	France	1992	WBO
Jimmy Bredahl	Denmark	1992-1994	WBO
Oscar de la Hoya*	USA	1994	WBO
James Leija	USA	1994	WBC
Gabriel Ruelas	USA	1994-1995	WBC
Regilio Tuur*	Surinam	1994-1997	WBO
Eddie Hopson	USA	1995	IBF
Tracy Harris Patterson	USA	1995	IBF
Yong-Soo Choi	S Korea	1995-1998	WBA
Arturo Gatti*	Canada	1995-1997	IBF
Azumah Nelson	Ghana	1996-1997	WBC
Genaro Hernandez	USA	1997-1998	WBC
Barry Jones*	Wales	1997-1998	WBO
Roberto Garcia	USA	1998-1999	IBF
Anatoly Alexandrov	Kazakhstan	1998-1999	WBO
Takenori Hatakeyama	Japan	1998-1999	WBA
Floyd Mayweather*	USA	1998-2002	WBC
Lakva Sim	Mongolia	1999	WBA
Acelino Freitas*	Brazil	1999-2002	WBO
Diego Corrales*	USA	1999-2000	IBF
Jong-Kwon Baek	S Korea	1999-2000	WBA
Joel Casamayor	Cuba	2000-2002	WBA
Steve Forbes	USA	2000-2002	IBF
Acelino Freitas	Brazil	2002-	WBO/WBA
Sirimongkol Singmanassak	Thailand	2002-	WBC
Carlos Hernandez	USA	2003-	IBF

Lightweight (135 lbs)

Title Holder	Birthplace	Tenure	Status
Jack McAuliffe	Ireland	1889-1894	USA
Jem Carney	England	1889-1891	
Jimmy Carroll	England	1889-1891	
Dick Burge	England	1891-1896	GB
George Lavigne	USA	1894-1896	USA
George Lavigne	USA	1896	
George Lavigne	USA	1896-1897	
Eddie Connolly	Canada	1896-1897	
George Lavigne	USA	1897-1899	
Frank Erne	Switzerland	1899-1902	
Joe Gans	USA	1902	
Joe Gans	USA	1902-1906	
Jabez White	England	1902-1905	GB
Jimmy Britt	USA	1902-1905	
Battling Nelson	Denmark	1905-1907	
Joe Gans	USA	1906-1908	
Battling Nelson	Denmark	1908-1910	
Ad Wolgast	USA	1910-1912	
Willie Ritchie	USA	1912	

Title Holder	Birthplace	Tenure	Status
Freddie Welsh	Wales	1912-1914	GB
Willie Ritchie	USA	1912-1914	USA
Freddie Welsh	Wales	1914-1917	
Benny Leonard*	USA	1917-1925	
Jimmy Goodrich	USA	1925	NY
Rocky Kansas	USA	1925-1926	
Sammy Mandell	USA	1926-1930	
Al Singer	USA	1930	
Tony Canzoneri	USA	1930-1933	
Barney Ross*	USA	1933-1935	
Tony Canzoneri	USA	1935-1936	
Lou Ambers	USA	1936-1938	
Henry Armstrong	USA	1938-1939	
Lou Ambers	USA	1939-1940	
Sammy Angott	USA	1940-1941	NBA
Lew Jenkins	USA	1940-1941	NY
Sammy Angott*	USA	1941-1942	
Beau Jack	USA	1942-1943	NY
Slugger White	USA	1943	MARY
Bob Montgomery	USA	1943	NY
Sammy Angott	USA	1943-1944	NBA
Beau Jack	USA	1943-1944	NY
Bob Montgomery	USA	1944-1947	NY
Juan Zurita	Mexico	1944-1945	NBA
Ike Williams	USA	1945-1947	NBA
Ike Williams	USA	1947-1951	
Jimmy Carter	USA	1951-1952	
Lauro Salas	Mexico	1952	
Jimmy Carter	USA	1952-1954	
Paddy de Marco	USA	1954	
Jimmy Carter	USA	1954-1955	
Wallace Bud Smith	USA	1955-1956	
Joe Brown	USA	1956-1962	
Carlos Ortiz	Puerto Rico	1962-1963	
Carlos Ortiz*	Puerto Rico	1963-1964	WBA/WBC
Kenny Lane	USA	1963-1964	MICH
Carlos Ortiz	Puerto Rico	1964-1965	
Ismael Laguna	Panama	1965	
Carlos Ortiz	Puerto Rico	1965-1966	
Carlos Ortiz*	Puerto Rico	1966-1967	WBA
Carlos Ortiz	Puerto Rico	1967-1968	
Carlos Teo Cruz	Dom Republic	1968-1969	
Mando Ramos	USA	1969-1970	
Ismael Laguna	Panama	1970	
Ismael Laguna	Panama	1970	WBA
Ken Buchanan*	Scotland	1970-1971	WBA
Ken Buchanan	Scotland	1971	
Ken Buchanan	Scotland	1971-1972	WBA
Pedro Carrasco	Spain	1971-1972	WBC
Mando Ramos	USA	1972	WBC
Roberto Duran*	Panama	1972-1978	WBA
Chango Carmona	Mexico	1972	WBC
Rodolfo Gonzalez	Mexico	1972-1974	WBC
Guts Ishimatsu	Japan	1974-1976	WBC
Esteban de Jesus	Puerto Rico	1976-1978	WBC
Roberto Duran*	Panama	1978-1979	
Jim Watt	Scotland	1979-1981	WBC
Ernesto Espana	Venezuela	1979-1980	WBA
Hilmer Kenty	USA	1980-1981	WBA
Sean O'Grady	USA	1981	WBA
Alexis Arguello*	Nicaragua	1981-1983	WBC
Claude Noel	Trinidad	1981	WBA
Arturo Frias	USA	1981-1982	WBA
Ray Mancini	USA	1982-1984	WBA
Edwin Rosario	Puerto Rico	1983-1984	WBC
Charlie Choo Choo Brown	USA	1984	IBF
Harry Arroyo	USA	1984-1985	IBF
Livingstone Bramble	USA	1984-1986	WBA
Jose Luis Ramirez	Mexico	1984-1985	WBC
Jimmy Paul	USA	1985-1986	IBF
Hector Camacho*	Puerto Rico	1985-1987	WBC

237

Title Holder	Birthplace	Tenure	Status	Title Holder	Birthplace	Tenure	Status
Edwin Rosario	Puerto Rico	1986-1987	WBA	Bruno Arcari*	Italy	1970-1974	WBC
Greg Haugen	USA	1986-1987	IBF	Alfonso Frazer	Panama	1972	WBA
Vinny Pazienza	USA	1987-1988	IBF	Antonio Cervantes	Colombia	1972-1976	WBA
Jose Luis Ramirez	Mexico	1987-1988	WBC	Perico Fernandez	Spain	1974-1975	WBC
Julio Cesar Chavez*	Mexico	1987-1988	WBA	Saensak Muangsurin	Thailand	1975-1976	WBC
Greg Haugen	USA	1988-1989	IBF	Wilfred Benitez	USA	1976	WBA
Julio Cesar Chavez*	Mexico	1988-1989	WBA/WBC	Miguel Velasquez	Spain	1976	WBC
Mauricio Aceves	Mexico	1989-1990	WBO	Saensak Muangsurin	Thailand	1976-1978	WBC
Pernell Whitaker*	USA	1989	IBF	Antonio Cervantes	Colombia	1977-1980	WBA
Edwin Rosario	Puerto Rico	1989-1990	WBA	Wilfred Benitez*	USA	1977-1978	NY
Pernell Whitaker*	USA	1989-1990	IBF/WBC	Sang-Hyun Kim	S Korea	1978-1980	WBC
Juan Nazario	Puerto Rico	1990	WBA	Saoul Mamby	USA	1980-1982	WBC
Pernell Whitaker*	USA	1990-1992	IBF/WBC/WBA	Aaron Pryor*	USA	1980-1984	WBA
Dingaan Thobela*	S Africa	1990-1992	WBO	Leroy Haley	USA	1982-1983	WBC
Joey Gamache	USA	1992	WBA	Bruce Curry	USA	1983-1984	WBC
Miguel Gonzalez*	Mexico	1992-1996	WBC	Johnny Bumphus	USA	1984	WBA
Giovanni Parisi*	Italy	1992-1994	WBO	Bill Costello	USA	1984-1985	WBC
Tony Lopez	USA	1992-1993	WBA	Gene Hatcher	USA	1984-1985	WBA
Fred Pendleton	USA	1993-1994	IBF	Aaron Pryor	USA	1984-1985	IBF
Dingaan Thobela	S Africa	1993	WBA	Ubaldo Sacco	Argentina	1985-1986	WBA
Orzubek Nazarov	Kyrghyzstan	1993-1998	WBA	Lonnie Smith	USA	1985-1986	WBC
Rafael Ruelas	USA	1994-1995	IBF	Patrizio Oliva	Italy	1986-1987	WBA
Oscar de la Hoya*	USA	1994-1995	WBO	Gary Hinton	USA	1986	IBF
Oscar de la Hoya*	USA	1995	WBO/IBF	Rene Arredondo	Mexico	1986	WBC
Oscar de la Hoya*	USA	1995-1996	WBO	Tsuyoshi Hamada	Japan	1986-1987	WBC
Phillip Holiday	S Africa	1995-1997	IBF	Joe Manley	USA	1986-1987	IBF
Jean-Baptiste Mendy	France	1996-1997	WBC	Terry Marsh*	England	1987	IBF
Artur Grigorian	Uzbekistan	1996-	WBO	Juan M. Coggi	Argentina	1987-1990	WBA
Steve Johnston	USA	1997-1998	WBC	Rene Arredondo	Mexico	1987	WBC
Shane Mosley*	USA	1997-1999	IBF	Roger Mayweather	USA	1987-1989	WBC
Jean-Baptiste Mendy	France	1998-1999	WBA	James McGirt	USA	1988	IBF
Cesar Bazan	Mexico	1998-1999	WBC	Meldrick Taylor	USA	1988-1990	IBF
Steve Johnston	USA	1999-2000	WBC	Hector Camacho	Puerto Rico	1989-1991	WBO
Julien Lorcy	France	1999	WBA	Julio Cesar Chavez*	Mexico	1989-1990	WBC
Stefano Zoff	Italy	1999	WBA	Julio Cesar Chavez*	Mexico	1990-1991	IBF/WBC
Paul Spadafora*	USA	1999-2003	IBF	Loreto Garza	USA	1990-1991	WBA
Gilberto Serrano	Venezuela	1999-2000	WBA	Greg Haugen	USA	1991	WBO
Takanori Hatakeyama	Japan	2000-2001	WBA	Hector Camacho	Puerto Rico	1991-1992	WBO
Jose Luis Castillo	Mexico	2000-2002	WBC	Edwin Rosario	Puerto Rico	1991-1992	WBA
Julien Lorcy	France	2001	WBA	Julio Cesar Chavez	Mexico	1991-1994	WBC
Raul Balbi	Argentina	2001-2002	WBA	Rafael Pineda	Colombia	1991-1992	IBF
Leonardo Dorin	Romania	2002-	WBA	Akinobu Hiranaka	Japan	1992	WBA
Floyd Mayweather	USA	2002-	WBC	Carlos Gonzalez	Mexico	1992-1993	WBO
				Pernell Whitaker*	USA	1992-1993	IBF

L. Welterweight (140 lbs)

Title Holder	Birthplace	Tenure	Status	Title Holder	Birthplace	Tenure	Status
Pinkey Mitchell	USA	1922-1926	NBA	Morris East	Philippines	1992-1993	WBA
Mushy Callahan	USA	1926-1927	NBA	Juan M. Coggi	Argentina	1993-1994	WBA
Mushy Callahan	USA	1927-1930	NBA/NY	Charles Murray	USA	1993-1994	IBF
Mushy Callahan	USA	1930	NBA	Zack Padilla*	USA	1993-1994	WBO
Jackie Kid Berg	England	1930-1931	NBA	Frankie Randall	USA	1994	WBC
Tony Canzoneri	USA	1931-1932	NBA	Jake Rodriguez	USA	1994-1995	IBF
Johnny Jadick	USA	1932	NBA	Julio Cesar Chavez	Mexico	1994-1996	WBC
Johnny Jadick	USA	1932-1933	PEN	Frankie Randall	USA	1994-1996	WBA
Battling Shaw	Mexico	1933	LOUIS	Konstantin Tszyu	Russia	1995-1997	IBF
Tony Canzoneri	USA	1933	LOUIS	Sammy Fuentes	Puerto Rico	1995-1996	WBO
Barney Ross*	USA	1933-1935	ILL	Juan M. Coggi	Argentina	1996	WBA
Maxie Berger	Canada	1939	CAN	Giovanni Parisi	Italy	1996-1998	WBO
Harry Weekly	USA	1941-1942	LOUIS	Oscar de la Hoya*	USA	1996-1997	WBC
Tippy Larkin	USA	1946-1947	NY/NBA	Frankie Randall	USA	1996-1997	WBA
Carlos Ortiz	Puerto Rico	1959-1960	NBA	Khalid Rahilou	France	1997-1998	WBA
Duilio Loi	Italy	1960-1962	NBA	Vince Phillips	USA	1997-1999	IBF
Duilio Loi	Italy	1962	WBA	Carlos Gonzalez	Mexico	1998-1999	WBO
Eddie Perkins	USA	1962	WBA	Sharmba Mitchell	USA	1998-2001	WBA
Duilio Loi*	Italy	1962-1963	WBA	Terron Millett	USA	1999	IBF
Roberto Cruz	Philippines	1963	WBA	Randall Bailey	USA	1999-2000	WBO
Eddie Perkins	USA	1963-1965	WBA	Kostya Tszyu*	Russia	1999-2001	WBC
Carlos Hernandez	Venezuela	1965-1966	WBA	Zab Judah	USA	2000-2001	IBF
Sandro Lopopolo	Italy	1966-1967	WBA	Ener Julio	Colombia	2000-2001	WBA
Paul Fujii	Hawaii	1967-1968	WBA	Kostya Tszyu*	Russia	2001	WBA/WBC
Nicolino Loche	Argentina	1968-1972	WBA	DeMarcus Corley	USA	2001-	WBO
Pedro Adigue	Philippines	1968-1970	WBC	Kostya Tszyu	Russia	2001-	WBA/WBC/IBF

Title Holder	Birthplace	Tenure	Status		Title Holder	Birthplace	Tenure	Status
Welterweight (147 lbs)					Dixie Kid	USA	1904-1905	
Paddy Duffy	USA	1889-1890			Buddy Ryan	USA	1904-1905	
Tommy Ryan	USA	1891-1894			Sam Langford	Canada	1904-1905	
Mysterious Billy Smith	USA	1892-1894			George Petersen	USA	1905	
Tommy Ryan	USA	1894-1897	USA		Jimmy Gardner	USA	1905	
Tommy Ryan	USA	1897-1899			Mike Twin Sullivan	USA	1905-1906	
Dick Burge	GB	1897			Joe Gans	USA	1906	
George Green	USA	1897			Joe Walcott	Barbados	1906	USA
Tom Causer	GB	1897			Honey Mellody	USA	1906	USA
Joe Walcott	Barbados	1897			Honey Mellody	USA	1906-1907	
George Lavigne	USA	1897-1899			Joe Thomas	USA	1906-1907	
Dick Burge	GB	1897-1898			Mike Twin Sullivan	USA	1907-1911	
Mysterious Billy Smith	USA	1898-1900			Jimmy Gardner	USA	1907-1908	
Bobby Dobbs	USA	1898-1902			Frank Mantell	USA	1907-1908	
Rube Ferns	USA	1900			Harry Lewis	USA	1908-1910	
Matty Matthews	USA	1900			Jack Blackburn	USA	1908	
Eddie Connolly	Canada	1900			Jimmy Gardner	USA	1908-1909	
Matty Matthews	USA	1900-1901			Willie Lewis	USA	1909-1910	
Rube Ferns	USA	1901			Harry Lewis	USA	1910-1911	GB/FR
Joe Walcott	Barbados	1901-1906			Jimmy Clabby	USA	1910-1911	
Eddie Connolly	Canada	1902-1903	GB		Dixie Kid	USA	1911-1912	GB/FR
Matty Matthews	USA	1902-1903			Ray Bronson	USA	1911-1914	
Rube Ferns	USA	1903			Marcel Thomas	France	1912-1913	FR
Martin Duffy	USA	1903-1904			Wildcat Ferns	USA	1912-1913	
Honey Mellody	USA	1904			Spike Kelly	USA	1913-1914	
Jack Clancy	USA	1904-1905	GB		Mike Glover	USA	1913-1915	

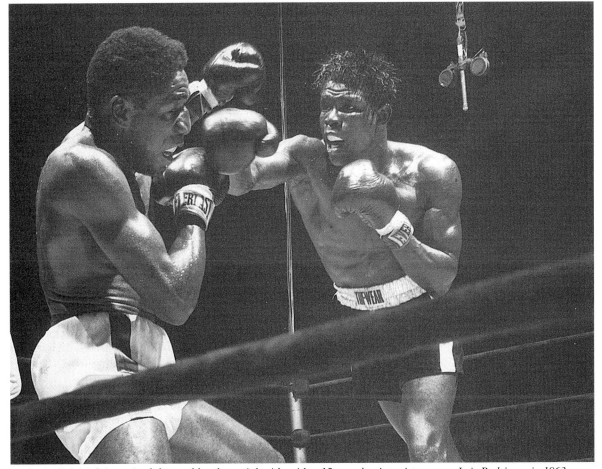

Emile Griffith (right) regained the world welterweight title with a 15-round points victory over Luis Rodriguez in 1963

Title Holder	Birthplace	Tenure	Status
Mike Gibbons	USA	1913-1914	
Waldemar Holberg	Denmark	1914	
Tom McCormick	Ireland	1914	
Matt Wells	England	1914-1915	AUSTR
Kid Graves	USA	1914-1917	
Jack Britton	USA	1915	
Ted Kid Lewis	England	1915-1916	
Jack Britton	USA	1916-1917	
Ted Kid Lewis	England	1917	
Ted Kid Lewis	England	1917-1919	
Jack Britton	USA	1919-1922	
Mickey Walker	USA	1922-1923	
Mickey Walker	USA	1923-1924	NBA
Dave Shade	USA	1923	NY
Jimmy Jones	USA	1923	NY/MASS
Mickey Walker	USA	1924-1926	
Pete Latzo	USA	1926-1927	
Joe Dundee	Italy	1927-1928	
Joe Dundee	Italy	1928-1929	NY
Jackie Fields	USA	1929	NBA
Jackie Fields	USA	1929-1930	
Young Jack Thompson	USA	1930	
Tommy Freeman	USA	1930-1931	
Young Jack Thompson	USA	1930	
Lou Brouillard	Canada	1931-1932	
Jackie Fields	USA	1932-1933	
Young Corbett III	Italy	1933	
Jimmy McLarnin	Ireland	1933-1934	
Barney Ross	USA	1934	
Jimmy McLarnin	Ireland	1934-1935	
Barney Ross	USA	1935-1938	
Barney Ross	USA	1938	NY/NBA
Felix Wouters	Belgium	1938	IBU
Henry Armstrong	USA	1938-1940	
Fritzie Zivic	USA	1940	
Fritzie Zivic	USA	1940-1941	NY/NBA
Izzy Jannazzo	USA	1940-1942	MARY
Red Cochrane	USA	1941-1942	NY/NBA
Red Cochrane	USA	1942-1946	
Marty Servo	USA	1946	
Sugar Ray Robinson*	USA	1946-1951	
Johnny Bratton	USA	1951	NBA
Kid Gavilan	Cuba	1951-1952	NBA/NY
Kid Gavilan	Cuba	1952-1954	
Johnny Saxton	USA	1954-1955	
Tony de Marco	USA	1955	
Carmen Basilio	USA	1955-1956	
Johnny Saxton	USA	1956	
Carmen Basilio*	USA	1956-1957	
Virgil Akins	USA	1957-1958	MASS
Virgil Akins	USA	1958	
Don Jordan	Dom Republic	1958-1960	
Benny Kid Paret	Cuba	1960-1961	
Emile Griffith	Virgin Islands	1961	
Benny Kid Paret	Cuba	1961-1962	
Emile Griffith	Virgin Islands	1962-1963	
Luis Rodriguez	Cuba	1963	
Emile Griffith*	Virgin Islands	1963-1966	
Willie Ludick	S Africa	1966-1968	SA
Curtis Cokes*	USA	1966	WBA
Curtis Cokes*	USA	1966-1967	WBA/WBC
Charley Shipes	USA	1966-1967	CALIF
Curtis Cokes	USA	1968-1969	
Jose Napoles	Cuba	1969-1970	
Billy Backus	USA	1970-1971	
Jose Napoles	Cuba	1971-1972	
Jose Napoles*	Cuba	1972-1974	WBA/WBC
Hedgemon Lewis	USA	1972-1974	NY
Jose Napoles	Cuba	1974-1975	
Jose Napoles	Cuba	1975	WBC
Angel Espada	Puerto Rico	1975-1976	WBA

Title Holder	Birthplace	Tenure	Status
John H. Stracey	England	1975-1976	WBC
Carlos Palomino	Mexico	1976-1979	WBC
Pipino Cuevas	Mexico	1976-1980	WBA
Wilfred Benitez	USA	1979	WBC
Sugar Ray Leonard	USA	1979-1980	WBC
Roberto Duran	Panama	1980	WBC
Thomas Hearns	USA	1980-1981	WBA
Sugar Ray Leonard	USA	1980-1981	WBC
Sugar Ray Leonard*	USA	1981-1982	
Don Curry*	USA	1983-1984	WBA
Milton McCrory	USA	1983-1985	WBC
Don Curry*	USA	1984-1985	WBA/IBF
Don Curry	USA	1985-1986	
Lloyd Honeyghan	Jamaica	1986	
Lloyd Honeyghan	Jamaica	1986-1987	WBC/IBF
Mark Breland	USA	1987	WBA
Marlon Starling	USA	1987-1988	WBA
Jorge Vaca	Mexico	1987-1988	WBC
Lloyd Honeyghan	Jamaica	1988-1989	WBC
Simon Brown*	Jamaica	1988-1991	IBF
Tomas Molinares	Colombia	1988-1989	WBA
Mark Breland	USA	1989-1990	WBA
Marlon Starling	USA	1989-1990	WBC
Genaro Leon*	Mexico	1989	WBO
Manning Galloway	USA	1989-1993	WBO
Aaron Davis	USA	1990-1991	WBA
Maurice Blocker	USA	1990-1991	WBC
Meldrick Taylor	USA	1991-1992	WBA
Simon Brown*	Jamaica	1991	WBC/IBF
Simon Brown	Jamaica	1991	WBC
Maurice Blocker	USA	1991-1993	IBF
James McGirt	USA	1991-1993	WBC
Crisanto Espana	Venezuela	1992-1994	WBA
Gert Bo Jacobsen*	Denmark	1993	WBO
Pernell Whitaker	USA	1993-1997	WBC
Felix Trinidad*	Puerto Rico	1993-2000	IBF
Eamonn Loughran	Ireland	1993-1996	WBO
Ike Quartey	Ghana	1994-1998	WBA
Jose Luis Lopez	Mexico	1996-1997	WBO
Michael Loewe*	Romania	1997-1998	WBO
Oscar de la Hoya	USA	1997-1999	WBC
Ahmed Kotiev	Russia	1998-2000	WBO
James Page	USA	1998-2000	WBA
Oscar de la Hoya	USA	2000	WBC
Daniel Santos*	Puerto Rico	2000-2002	WBO
Shane Mosley	USA	2000-2002	WBC
Andrew Lewis	Guyana	2001-2002	WBA
Vernon Forrest	USA	2001	IBF
Vernon Forrest	USA	2002-2003	WBC
Antonio Margarito	Mexico	2002-	WBO
Ricardo Mayorga*	Nicaragua	2002-2003	WBA
Michele Piccirillo	Italy	2002-2003	IBF
Ricardo Mayorga	Nicaragua	2003-	WBA/WBC
Cory Spinks	USA	2003-	IBF

L. Middleweight (154 lbs)

Title Holder	Birthplace	Tenure	Status
Emile Griffith*	USA	1962-1963	AU
Denny Moyer	USA	1962-1963	WBA
Ralph Dupas	USA	1963	WBA
Sandro Mazzinghi	Italy	1963-1965	WBA
Nino Benvenuti	Italy	1965-1966	WBA
Ki-Soo Kim	S Korea	1966-1968	WBA
Sandro Mazzinghi	Italy	1968-1969	WBA
Freddie Little	USA	1969-1970	WBA
Carmelo Bossi	Italy	1970-1971	WBA
Koichi Wajima	Japan	1971-1974	WBA
Oscar Albarado	USA	1974-1975	WBA
Koichi Wajima	Japan	1975	WBA
Miguel de Oliveira	Brazil	1975	WBC
Jae-Do Yuh	S Korea	1975-1976	WBA
Elisha Obed	Bahamas	1975-1976	WBC

Title Holder	Birthplace	Tenure	Status	Title Holder	Birthplace	Tenure	Status
Koichi Wajima	Japan	1976	WBA	Jim Hall	Australia	1892-1893	GB
Jose Duran	Spain	1976	WBA	**Bob Fitzsimmons**	England	1893-1894	
Eckhard Dagge	Germany	1976-1977	WBC	Bob Fitzsimmons	England	1894-1899	
Miguel Castellini	Argentina	1976-1977	WBA	Frank Craig	USA	1894-1895	GB
Eddie Gazo	Nicaragua	1977-1978	WBA	Dan Creedon	New Zealand	1895-1897	GB
Rocky Mattioli	Italy	1977-1979	WBC	Tommy Ryan	USA	1895-1896	
Masashi Kudo	Japan	1978-1979	WBA	Kid McCoy	USA	1896-1898	
Maurice Hope	Antigua	1979-1981	WBC	Tommy Ryan	USA	1898-1905	
Ayub Kalule	Uganda	1979-1981	WBA	Charley McKeever	USA	1900-1902	
Wilfred Benitez	USA	1981-1982	WBC	George Gardner	USA	1901-1902	
Sugar Ray Leonard*	USA	1981	WBA	Jack O'Brien	USA	1901-1905	
Tadashi Mihara	Japan	1981-1982	WBA	George Green	USA	1901-1902	
Davey Moore	USA	1982-1983	WBA	Jack Palmer	England	1902-1903	GB
Thomas Hearns*	USA	1982-1986	WBC	Hugo Kelly	USA	1905-1908	
Roberto Duran*	Panama	1983-1984	WBA	Jack Twin Sullivan	USA	1905-1908	
Mark Medal	USA	1984	IBF	Sam Langford	Canada	1907-1911	
Mike McCallum*	Jamaica	1984-1987	WBA	Billy Papke	USA	1908	
Carlos Santos	Puerto Rico	1984-1986	IBF	Stanley Ketchel	USA	1908	
Buster Drayton	USA	1986-1987	IBF	Billy Papke	USA	1908	
Duane Thomas	USA	1986-1987	WBC	Stanley Ketchel	USA	1908-1910	
Matthew Hilton	Canada	1987-1988	IBF	Billy Papke	USA	1910-1913	
Lupe Aquino	Mexico	1987	WBC	Stanley Ketchel*	USA	1910	
Gianfranco Rosi	Italy	1987-1988	WBC	Hugo Kelly	USA	1910-1912	
Julian Jackson*	Virgin Islands	1987-1990	WBA	Cyclone Johnny Thompson	USA	1911-1912	
Don Curry	USA	1988-1989	WBC	Harry Lewis	USA	1911	
Robert Hines	USA	1988-1989	IBF	Leo Houck	USA	1911-1912	
John David Jackson*	USA	1988-1993	WBO	Georges Carpentier	France	1911-1912	
Darrin van Horn	USA	1989	IBF	Jack Dillon	USA	1912	
Rene Jacqot	France	1989	WBC	Frank Mantell	USA	1912-1913	
John Mugabi	Uganda	1989-1990	WBC	Frank Klaus	USA	1912-1913	
Gianfranco Rosi	Italy	1989-1994	IBF	Georges Carpentier	France	1912	IBU
Terry Norris	USA	1990-1993	WBC	Jack Dillon	USA	1912-1915	
Gilbert Dele	France	1991	WBA	Eddie McGoorty	USA	1912-1913	
Vinny Pazienza*	USA	1991-1992	WBA	Frank Klaus	USA	1913	IBU
Julio Cesar Vasquez	Argentina	1992-1995	WBA	Jimmy Clabby	USA	1913-1914	
Verno Phillips	USA	1993-1995	WBO	George Chip	USA	1913-1914	
Simon Brown	USA	1993-1994	WBC	Joe Borrell	USA	1913-1914	
Terry Norris	USA	1994	WBC	Jeff Smith	USA	1913-1914	
Vince Pettway	USA	1994-1995	IBF	Eddie McGoorty	USA	1914	AUSTR
Luis Santana	Dom Republic	1994-1995	WBC	Jeff Smith	USA	1914	AUSTR
Pernell Whitaker*	USA	1995	WBA	Al McCoy	USA	1914-1917	
Gianfranco Rosi	Italy	1995	WBO	Jimmy Clabby	USA	1914-1915	
Carl Daniels	USA	1995	WBA	Mick King	Australia	1914	AUSTR
Verno Phillips	USA	1995	WBO	Jeff Smith	USA	1914-1915	AUSTR
Paul Vaden	USA	1995	IBF	Young Ahearn	England	1915-1916	
Terry Norris*	USA	1995	WBC	Les Darcy*	Australia	1915-1917	AUSTR
Paul Jones	England	1995-1996	WBO	Mike Gibbons	USA	1916-1917	
Terry Norris	USA	1995-1997	IBF/WBC	**Mike O'Dowd**	USA	1917-1920	
Julio Cesar Vasquez	Argentina	1995-1996	WBA	**Johnny Wilson**	USA	1920-1921	
Bronco McKart	USA	1996	WBO	Johnny Wilson	USA	1921-1922	NBA/NY
Ronald Wright	USA	1996-1998	WBO	Bryan Downey	USA	1921-1922	OHIO
Laurent Boudouani	France	1996-1999	WBA	Johnny Wilson	USA	1922-1923	NBA
Terry Norris	USA	1997	WBC	Dave Rosenberg	USA	1922	NY
Raul Marquez	USA	1997	IBF	Jock Malone	USA	1922-1923	OHIO
Luis Campas	Mexico	1997-1998	IBF	Mike O'Dowd	USA	1922-1923	NY
Keith Mullings	USA	1997-1999	WBC	**Johnny Wilson**	USA	1923	
Harry Simon*	Namibia	1998-2001	WBO	**Harry Greb**	USA	1923-1926	
Fernando Vargas	USA	1998-2000	IBF	**Tiger Flowers**	USA	1926	
Javier Castillejo	Spain	1999-2001	WBC	**Mickey Walker**	USA	1926-1931	
David Reid	USA	1999-2000	WBA	Gorilla Jones	USA	1932	NBA
Felix Trinidad*	Puerto Rico	2000	WBA	Marcel Thil	France	1932-1933	NBA/IBU
Felix Trinidad*	Puerto Rico	2000-2001	IBF/WBA	Marcel Thil	France	1933-1937	IBU
Oscar de la Hoya*	USA	2001-2002	WBC	Ben Jeby	USA	1933	NY
Fernando Vargas	USA	2001-2002	WBA	Lou Brouillard	Canada	1933	NY
Ronald Wright	USA	2001-	IBF	Lou Brouillard	Canada	1933	NY/NBA
Daniel Santos	Puerto Rico	2002-	WBO	Vearl Whitehead	USA	1933	CALIF
Oscar de la Hoya	USA	2002-	WBA/WBC	Teddy Yarosz	USA	1933-1934	PEN
				Vince Dundee	USA	1933-1934	NY/NBA

Middleweight (160 lbs)

Title Holder	Birthplace	Tenure	Status	Title Holder	Birthplace	Tenure	Status
Nonpareil Jack Dempsey	Ireland	1889-1891	USA	Teddy Yarosz	USA	1934-1935	NY/NBA
Bob Fitzsimmons	England	1891-1893	USA	Babe Risko	USA	1935-1936	NY/NBA
				Freddie Steele	USA	1936-1938	NY/NBA

Title Holder	Birthplace	Tenure	Status
Fred Apostoli	USA	1937-1938	IBU
Edouard Tenet	France	1938	IBU
Young Corbett III	Italy	1938	CALIF
Freddie Steele	USA	1938	NBA
Al Hostak	USA	1938	NBA
Solly Krieger	USA	1938-1939	NBA
Fred Apostoli	USA	1938-1939	NY
Al Hostak	USA	1939-1940	NBA
Ceferino Garcia	Philippines	1939-1940	NY
Ken Overlin	USA	1940-1941	NY
Tony Zale	USA	1940-1941	NBA
Billy Soose	USA	1941	NY
Tony Zale	USA	1941-1947	
Rocky Graziano	USA	1947-1948	
Tony Zale	USA	1948	
Marcel Cerdan	Algeria	1948-1949	
Jake la Motta	USA	1949-1950	
Jake la Motta	USA	1950-1951	NY/NBA
Sugar Ray Robinson	USA	1950-1951	PEN
Sugar Ray Robinson	USA	1951	
Randy Turpin	England	1951	
Sugar Ray Robinson*	USA	1951-1952	
Randy Turpin	England	1953	GB/EBU
Carl Bobo Olson	Hawaii	1953-1955	
Sugar Ray Robinson	USA	1955-1957	
Gene Fullmer	USA	1957	
Sugar Ray Robinson	USA	1957	
Carmen Basilio	USA	1957-1958	
Sugar Ray Robinson	USA	1958-1959	
Sugar Ray Robinson	USA	1959-1960	NY/EBU
Gene Fullmer	USA	1959-1962	NBA
Paul Pender	USA	1960-1961	NY/EBU
Terry Downes	England	1961-1962	NY/EBU
Paul Pender	USA	1962	NY/EBU
Dick Tiger	Nigeria	1962-1963	NBA
Dick Tiger	Nigeria	1963	
Joey Giardello	USA	1963-1965	
Dick Tiger	Nigeria	1965-1966	
Emile Griffith	Virgin Islands	1966-1967	
Nino Benvenuti	Italy	1967	
Emile Griffith	Virgin Islands	1967-1968	
Nino Benvenuti	Italy	1968-1970	
Carlos Monzon	Argentina	1970-1974	
Carlos Monzon*	Argentina	1974-1976	WBA
Rodrigo Valdez	Colombia	1974-1976	WBC
Carlos Monzon*	Argentina	1976-1977	
Rodrigo Valdez	Colombia	1977-1978	
Hugo Corro	Argentina	1978-1979	
Vito Antuofermo	Italy	1979-1980	
Alan Minter	England	1980	
Marvin Hagler	USA	1980-1987	
Marvin Hagler	USA	1987	WBC/IBF
Sugar Ray Leonard	USA	1987	WBC
Frank Tate	USA	1987-1988	IBF
Sumbu Kalambay	Zaire	1987-1989	WBA
Thomas Hearns	USA	1987-1988	WBC
Iran Barkley	USA	1988-1989	WBC
Michael Nunn	USA	1988-1991	IBF
Roberto Duran	Panama	1989-1990	WBC
Doug de Witt	USA	1989-1990	WBO
Mike McCallum	Jamaica	1989-1991	WBA
Nigel Benn	England	1990	WBO
Chris Eubank*	England	1990-1991	WBO
Julian Jackson	Virgin Islands	1990-1993	WBC
James Toney*	USA	1991-1993	IBF
Gerald McClellan*	USA	1991-1993	WBO
Reggie Johnson	USA	1992-1993	WBA
Gerald McClellan*	USA	1993-1995	WBC
Chris Pyatt	England	1993-1994	WBO
Roy Jones*	USA	1993-1994	IBF
John David Jackson	USA	1993-1994	WBA

Title Holder	Birthplace	Tenure	Status
Steve Collins*	Ireland	1994-1995	WBO
Jorge Castro	Argentina	1994	WBA
Julian Jackson	Virgin Islands	1995	WBC
Bernard Hopkins*	USA	1995-2001	IBF
Lonnie Bradley*	USA	1995-1998	WBO
Quincy Taylor	USA	1995-1996	WBC
Shinji Takehara	Japan	1995-1996	WBA
Keith Holmes	USA	1996-1998	WBC
William Joppy	USA	1996-1997	WBA
Julio Cesar Green	Dom Republic	1997-1998	WBA
William Joppy	USA	1998-2001	WBA
Hassine Cherifi	France	1998-1999	WBC
Otis Grant*	Canada	1998	WBO
Bert Schenk	Germany	1999	WBO
Keith Holmes	USA	1999-2001	WBC
Jason Matthews	England	1999	WBO
Armand Krajnc	Slovenia	1999-2002	WBO
Bernard Hopkins*	USA	2001	WBC/IBF
Felix Trinidad	Puerto Rico	2001	WBA
Bernard Hopkins	USA	2001-	WBC/WBA/IBF
Harry Simon	Namibia	2002-	WBO

S. Middleweight (168 lbs)

Title Holder	Birthplace	Tenure	Status
Murray Sutherland	Scotland	1984	IBF
Chong-Pal Park*	S Korea	1984-1987	IBF
Chong-Pal Park	S Korea	1987-1988	WBA
Graciano Rocchigiani*	Germany	1988-1989	IBF
Fully Obelmejias	Venezuela	1988-1989	WBA
Sugar Ray Leonard*	USA	1988-1990	WBC
Thomas Hearns*	USA	1988-1991	WBO
In-Chul Baek	S Korea	1989-1990	WBA
Lindell Holmes	USA	1990-1991	IBF
Christophe Tiozzo	France	1990-1991	WBA
Mauro Galvano	Italy	1990-1992	WBC
Victor Cordoba	Panama	1991-1992	WBA
Darrin van Horn	USA	1991-1992	IBF
Chris Eubank	England	1991-1995	WBO
Iran Barkley	USA	1992-1993	IBF
Michael Nunn	USA	1992-1994	WBA
Nigel Benn	England	1992-1996	WBC
James Toney	USA	1993-1994	IBF
Steve Little	USA	1994	WBA
Frank Liles	USA	1994-1999	WBA
Roy Jones*	USA	1994-1997	IBF
Steve Collins*	Ireland	1995-1997	WBO
Thulani Malinga	S Africa	1996	WBC
Vincenzo Nardiello	Italy	1996	WBC
Robin Reid	England	1996-1997	WBC
Charles Brewer	USA	1997-1998	IBF
Joe Calzaghe	Wales	1997-	WBO
Thulani Malinga	S Africa	1997-1998	WBC
Richie Woodhall	England	1998-1999	WBC
Sven Ottke*	Germany	1998-2003	IBF
Byron Mitchell	USA	1999-2000	WBA
Markus Beyer	Germany	1999-2000	WBC
Bruno Girard	France	2000-2001	WBA
Glenn Catley	England	2000	WBC
Dingaan Thobela	S Africa	2000	WBC
Dave Hilton	Canada	2000-2001	WBC
Byron Mitchell	USA	2001-2003	WBA
Eric Lucas	Canada	2001-2003	WBC
Sven Ottke	Germany	2003-	IBF/WBA
Markus Beyer	Germany	2003-	WBC

L. Heavyweight (175 lbs)

Title Holder	Birthplace	Tenure	Status
Jack Root	Austria	1903	
George Gardner	Ireland	1903	
George Gardner	Ireland	1903	USA
Bob Fitzsimmons	England	1903-1905	USA
Jack O'Brien	USA	1905-1911	
Sam Langford	Canada	1911-1913	

Title Holder	Birthplace	Tenure	Status
Georges Carpentier	France	1913-1920	IBU
Jack Dillon	USA	1914-1916	USA
Battling Levinsky	USA	1916-1920	USA
Georges Carpentier	France	1920-1922	
Battling Siki	Senegal	1922-1923	
Mike McTigue	Ireland	1923-1925	
Paul Berlenbach	USA	1925-1926	
Jack Delaney*	Canada	1926-1927	
Jimmy Slattery	USA	1927	NBA
Tommy Loughran	USA	1927	NY
Tommy Loughran*	USA	1927-1929	
Jimmy Slattery	USA	1930	NY
Maxie Rosenbloom	USA	1930-1931	
Maxie Rosenbloom	USA	1931-1933	NY
George Nichols	USA	1932	NBA
Bob Godwin	USA	1933	NBA
Maxie Rosenbloom	USA	1933-1934	
Maxie Rosenbloom	USA	1934	NY
Joe Knight	USA	1934-1935	FL/NC/GEO
Bob Olin	USA	1934-1935	NY
Al McCoy	Canada	1935	CAN
Bob Olin	USA	1935	NY/NBA
John Henry Lewis	USA	1935-1938	NY/NBA
Gustav Roth	Belgium	1936-1938	IBU
Ad Heuser	Germany	1938	IBU
John Henry Lewis	USA	1938	
John Henry Lewis	USA	1938-1939	NBA
Melio Bettina	USA	1939	NY
Len Harvey	England	1939-1942	GB
Billy Conn	USA	1939-1940	NY/NBA
Anton Christoforidis	Greece	1941	NBA
Gus Lesnevich	USA	1941	NBA
Gus Lesnevich	USA	1941-1946	NY/NBA
Freddie Mills	England	1942-1946	GB
Gus Lesnevich	USA	1946-1948	
Freddie Mills	England	1948-1950	
Joey Maxim	USA	1950-1952	
Archie Moore	USA	1952-1960	
Archie Moore	USA	1960-1962	NY/EBU
Harold Johnson	USA	1961-1962	NBA
Harold Johnson	USA	1962-1963	
Willie Pastrano	USA	1963	
Willie Pastrano*	USA	1963-1964	WBA/WBC
Eddie Cotton	USA	1963-1964	MICH
Willie Pastrano	USA	1964-1965	
Jose Torres	Puerto Rico	1965-1966	
Dick Tiger	Nigeria	1966-1968	
Bob Foster	USA	1968-1970	
Bob Foster*	USA	1970-1972	WBC
Vicente Rondon	Venezuela	1971-1972	WBA
Bob Foster*	USA	1972-1974	
John Conteh	England	1974-1977	WBC
Victor Galindez	Argentina	1974-1978	WBA
Miguel Cuello	Argentina	1977-1978	WBC
Mate Parlov	Yugoslavia	1978	WBC
Mike Rossman	USA	1978-1979	WBA
Marvin Johnson	USA	1978-1979	WBC
Victor Galindez	Argentina	1979	WBA
Matt Saad Muhammad	USA	1979-1981	WBC
Marvin Johnson	USA	1979-1980	WBA
Mustafa Muhammad	USA	1980-1981	WBA
Michael Spinks*	USA	1981-1983	WBA
Dwight Muhammad Qawi	USA	1981-1983	WBC
Michael Spinks*	USA	1983-1985	
J. B. Williamson	USA	1985-1986	WBC
Slobodan Kacar	Yugoslavia	1985-1986	IBF
Marvin Johnson	USA	1986-1987	WBA
Dennis Andries	Guyana	1986-1987	WBC
Bobby Czyz	USA	1986-1987	IBF
Thomas Hearns*	USA	1987	WBC
Leslie Stewart	Trinidad	1987	WBA

Title Holder	Birthplace	Tenure	Status
Virgil Hill	USA	1987-1991	WBA
Charles Williams	USA	1987-1993	IBF
Don Lalonde	Canada	1987-1988	WBC
Sugar Ray Leonard*	USA	1988	WBC
Michael Moorer*	USA	1988-1991	WBO
Dennis Andries	Guyana	1989	WBC
Jeff Harding	Australia	1989-1990	WBC
Dennis Andries	Guyana	1990-1991	WBC
Leonzer Barber	USA	1991-1994	WBO
Thomas Hearns	USA	1991-1992	WBA
Jeff Harding	Australia	1991-1994	WBC
Iran Barkley*	USA	1992	WBA
Virgil Hill*	USA	1992-1996	WBA
Henry Maske	Germany	1993-1996	IBF
Mike McCallum	Jamaica	1994-1995	WBC
Dariusz Michalczewski*	Poland	1994-1997	WBO
Fabrice Tiozzo	France	1995-1997	WBC
Virgil Hill	USA	1996-1997	IBF/WBA
Roy Jones	USA	1997	WBC
Montell Griffin	USA	1997	WBC
Dariusz Michalczewski*	Poland	1997	WBO/IBF/WBA
Dariusz Michalczewski	Poland	1997-	WBO
William Guthrie	USA	1997-1998	IBF
Roy Jones*	USA	1997-1998	WBC
Lou del Valle	USA	1997-1998	WBA
Reggie Johnson	USA	1998-1999	IBF
Roy Jones*	USA	1998-1999	WBC/WBA
Roy Jones*	USA	1999-2002	WBC/WBA/IBF
Roy Jones*	USA	2002-2003	WBA/WBC
Mehdi Sahnoune	France	2003-	WBA
Antoine Tarver	USA	2003-	IBF/WBC

Cruiserweight (190 lbs)

Title Holder	Birthplace	Tenure	Status
Marvin Camel	USA	1979-1980	WBC
Carlos de Leon	Puerto Rico	1980-1982	WBC
Ossie Ocasio	Puerto Rico	1982-1984	WBA
S. T. Gordon	USA	1982-1983	WBC
Marvin Camel	USA	1983-1984	IBF
Carlos de Leon	Puerto Rico	1983-1985	WBC
Lee Roy Murphy	USA	1984-1986	IBF
Piet Crous	S Africa	1984-1985	WBA
Alfonso Ratliff	USA	1985	WBC
Dwight Muhammad Qawi	USA	1985-1986	WBA
Bernard Benton	USA	1985-1986	WBC
Carlos de Leon	Puerto Rico	1986-1988	WBC
Evander Holyfield*	USA	1986-1987	WBA
Rickey Parkey	USA	1986-1987	IBF
Evander Holyfield*	USA	1987-1988	WBA/IBF
Evander Holyfield*	USA	1988	
Taoufik Belbouli*	France	1989	WBA
Carlos de Leon	Puerto Rico	1989-1990	WBC
Glenn McCrory	England	1989-1990	IBF
Robert Daniels	USA	1989-1991	WBA
Boone Pultz	USA	1989-1990	WBO
Jeff Lampkin*	USA	1990-1991	IBF
Magne Havnaa*	Norway	1990-1992	WBO
Masimilliano Duran	Italy	1990-1991	WBC
Bobby Czyz	USA	1991-1993	WBA
Anaclet Wamba	Congo	1991-1995	WBC
James Warring	USA	1991-1992	IBF
Tyrone Booze	USA	1992-1993	WBO
Al Cole*	USA	1992-1996	IBF
Marcus Bott	Germany	1993	WBO
Nestor Giovannini	Argentina	1993-1994	WBO
Orlin Norris	USA	1993-1995	WBA
Dariusz Michalczewski*	Poland	1994-1995	WBO
Ralf Rocchigiani	Germany	1995-1997	WBO
Nate Miller	USA	1995-1997	WBA
Marcelo Dominguez	Argentina	1995-1998	WBC
Adolpho Washington	USA	1996-1997	IBF
Uriah Grant	USA	1997	IBF

243

Carl Thompson	England	1997-1999	WBO
Imamu Mayfield	USA	1997-1998	IBF
Fabrice Tiozzo	France	1997-2000	WBA
Juan Carlos Gomez*	Cuba	1998-2002	WBC
Arthur Williams	USA	1998-1999	IBF
Johnny Nelson	England	1999-	WBO
Vassily Jirov	Kazakhstan	1999-2003	IBF
Virgil Hill	USA	2000-2002	WBA
Jean-Marc Mormeck	Guadeloupe	2002-	WBA
Wayne Braithwaite	Guyana	2002-	WBC
James Toney	USA	2003-	IBF

Heavyweight (190 lbs+)

John L. Sullivan	USA	1889-1892	USA
Peter Jackson	Australia	1889-1892	
Frank Slavin	Australia	1890-1892	GB/AUST
Peter Jackson	Australia	1892-1893	GB/AUST
James J. Corbett	USA	1892-1894	USA
James J. Corbett	USA	1894-1895	
James J. Corbett	USA	1895-1897	
Peter Maher	Ireland	1895-1896	
Bob Fitzsimmons	England	1896-1897	
Bob Fitzsimmons	England	1897-1899	
James J. Jeffries	USA	1899-1902	
James J. Jeffries	USA	1902-1905	
Denver Ed Martin	USA	1902-1903	
Jack Johnson	USA	1902-1908	
Bob Fitzsimmons	England	1905	
Marvin Hart	USA	1905-1906	
Jack O'Brien	USA	1905-1906	
Tommy Burns	Canada	1906-1908	
Jack Johnson	USA	1908-1909	
Jack Johnson	USA	1909-1915	
Sam Langford	USA	1909-1911	
Sam McVey	USA	1911-1912	
Sam Langford	USA	1912-1914	
Luther McCarty	USA	1913	
Arthur Pelkey	Canada	1913-1914	
Gunboat Smith	USA	1914	
Harry Wills	USA	1914	
Georges Carpentier	France	1914	
Sam Langford	USA	1914-1915	
Jess Willard	USA	1915-1919	
Joe Jeannette	USA	1915	
Sam McVey	USA	1915	
Harry Wills	USA	1915-1916	
Sam Langford	USA	1916-1917	
Bill Tate	USA	1917	
Sam Langford	USA	1917-1918	
Harry Wills	USA	1918-1926	
Jack Dempsey	USA	1919-1926	
Gene Tunney*	USA	1926-1928	
Max Schmeling	Germany	1930-1932	
Jack Sharkey	USA	1932-1933	
Primo Carnera	Italy	1933-1934	
Max Baer	USA	1934-1935	
James J. Braddock	USA	1935	
James J. Braddock	USA	1935-1936	NY/NBA
George Godfrey	USA	1935-1936	IBU
James J. Braddock	USA	1936-1937	
Joe Louis*	USA	1937-1949	
Ezzard Charles	USA	1949-1950	NBA
Lee Savold	USA	1950-1951	GB/EBU
Ezzard Charles	USA	1950-1951	NY/NBA
Joe Louis	USA	1951	GB/EBU
Jersey Joe Walcott	USA	1951	NY/NBA
Jersey Joe Walcott	USA	1951-1952	
Rocky Marciano*	USA	1952-1956	
Floyd Patterson	USA	1956-1959	
Ingemar Johansson	Sweden	1959-1960	
Floyd Patterson	USA	1960-1962	
Sonny Liston	USA	1962-1964	
Muhammad Ali	USA	1964	

Muhammad Ali*	USA	1964-1967	WBC
Ernie Terrell	USA	1965-1967	WBA
Muhammad Ali	USA	1967	
Muhammad Ali	USA	1967-1968	WBC
Joe Frazier*	USA	1968-1970	NY/MASS
Jimmy Ellis	USA	1968-1970	WBA
Joe Frazier	USA	1970-1973	
George Foreman	USA	1973-1974	
Muhammad Ali	USA	1974-1978	
Leon Spinks	USA	1978	
Leon Spinks	USA	1978	WBA
Larry Holmes*	USA	1978-1983	WBC
Muhammad Ali*	USA	1978-1979	WBA
John Tate	USA	1979-1980	WBA
Mike Weaver	USA	1980-1982	WBA
Michael Dokes	USA	1982-1983	WBA
Gerrie Coetzee	S Africa	1983-1984	WBA
Larry Holmes	USA	1983-1985	IBF
Tim Witherspoon	USA	1984	WBC
Pinklon Thomas	USA	1984-1986	WBC
Greg Page	USA	1984-1985	WBA
Tony Tubbs	USA	1985-1986	WBA
Michael Spinks	USA	1985-1987	IBF
Tim Witherspoon	USA	1986	WBA
Trevor Berbick	Jamaica	1986	WBC
Mike Tyson*	USA	1986-1987	WBC
James Smith	USA	1986-1987	WBA
Mike Tyson*	USA	1987	WBA/WBC
Tony Tucker	USA	1987	IBF
Mike Tyson	USA	1987-1989	
Mike Tyson	USA	1989-1990	IBF/WBA/WBC
Francesco Damiani	Italy	1989-1991	WBO
James Douglas	USA	1990	IBF/WBA/WBC
Evander Holyfield	USA	1990-1992	IBF/WBA/WBC
Ray Mercer	USA	1991-1992	WBO
Michael Moorer*	USA	1992-1993	WBO
Riddick Bowe	USA	1992	IBF/WBA/WBC
Riddick Bowe	USA	1992-1993	IBF/WBA
Lennox Lewis	England	1992-1994	WBC
Tommy Morrison	USA	1993	WBO
Michael Bentt	England	1993-1994	WBO
Evander Holyfield	USA	1993-1994	WBA/IBF
Herbie Hide	England	1994-1995	WBO
Michael Moorer	USA	1994	WBA/IBF
Oliver McCall	USA	1994-1995	WBC
George Foreman	USA	1994-1995	WBA/IBF
Riddick Bowe*	USA	1995-1996	WBO
George Foreman*	USA	1995	IBF
Bruce Seldon	USA	1995-1996	WBA
Frank Bruno	England	1995-1996	WBC
Frans Botha	S Africa	1995-1996	IBF
Mike Tyson	USA	1996	WBC
Michael Moorer	USA	1996-1997	IBF
Henry Akinwande*	England	1996-1997	WBO
Mike Tyson	USA	1996	WBA
Evander Holyfield*	USA	1996-1997	WBA
Lennox Lewis*	England	1997-1999	WBC
Herbie Hide	England	1997-1999	WBO
Evander Holyfield	USA	1997-1999	IBF/WBA
Vitali Klitschko	Ukraine	1999-2000	WBO
Lennox Lewis*	England	1999-2000	IBF/WBA/WBC
Chris Byrd	USA	2000	WBO
Lennox Lewis	England	2000-2001	IBF/WBC
Evander Holyfield	USA	2000-2001	WBA
Vladimir Klitschko	Ukraine	2000-2003	WBO
John Ruiz	USA	2001-2003	WBA
Hasim Rahman	USA	2001	WBC/IBF
Lennox Lewis*	England	2001-2002	WBC/IBF
Lennox Lewis	England	2002-	WBC
Chris Byrd	USA	2002-	IBF
Roy Jones	USA	2003-	WBA
Corrie Sanders	S Africa	2003-	WBO

Early Gloved Championship Boxing: The True Facts (Part 5)

by Harold Alderman

Following on from our previous exploration of how the weight classes came into being in the early days of gloved boxing, this time round we examine 138 to 152lbs. Recognising that many fights listed by weight division prior to the advent of the named weight divisions and weight limits announced by the National Sporting Club on 11 February 1909 did not add up, I started my research in the early 1960s. Using world-wide newspaper reports, which included a thorough examination of the *Sporting Life*, *Bells Life*, *Mirror of Life*, *Sportsman*, and *Police Gazette*, etc, it did not take long to discover that the vast majority of fights, certainly in this country, were made at every two pounds, plus or minus two pounds. This is how it was as boxing transferred from the bare-knuckle days to gloves, passing through phases of driving gloves, kid gloves, and two-ounce gloves to what we have today. This section also includes much of Barry Hugman's research within the American newspaper libraries and takes us through to 1909.

138lbs to 140lbs (9st 12lbs to 10st)

1872

10 February   Tom McKelvey, in *Bells Life*, stated that he would put up a 140lbs silver championship cup (value £50). The winner of same must then defend it, if challenged, every month for six months. If successful on each occasion, the cup would become the winner's own property. Each winner to get £5 and half of the gate money to go towards the Jerry Noon monument. Noon's real name was John Calvan.

22 March   Bat Mullins w pts 3 J.Warden, The Royal Victoria Palace Theatre, London. The final of a 140lbs competition for a £50 silver cup, only two of the entries turned up. Absent were Ted Napper, Charley Davis, Abe Daultry and Denny Harrington. Mullins' real first name was Bartholomew, while his opponent's surname was given at a later date as being Wharton.

1875

12 January   'Lumpy' Hughes w pts 3 Tom Hooker, St Luke's, The Hall of Science, Old Street, London. The final of a 140lbs lightweight competition. Refereed by Mr J.Vardy, plus two judges, Hughes looked a good winner, but Hooker threw his gloves down on the result and some of his supporters, strongly protesting the decision, took possession of the stage before being induced to leave by several prominent boxers. In previous rounds of the competition, held on 26 and 28 December 1874, Hughes had beaten H.Moss and Tom Symonds, while Hooker beat H.King and drew the bye.

26 July   'Young' Bill Charlton walked over 'Lumpy' Hughes, who had to withdraw when unwell at the Running Grounds, Hackney Wick, London, leaving Charlton to spar against Tom Symonds. In the previous round, Charlton had beaten 'Young' Bibby, while Hughes beat E.Seekree.

1876

18 March   Bob Habbijam (Birmingham) w pts 3 Jim Laxton (St Luke's), The Royal Agricultural Hall, Islington, London. The final of a 140lbs world championship competition, in previous rounds (competition had started on 13 March) Habbijam had drawn a bye then beaten Tom Sterck and 'Lumpy' Hughes, while Laxton had beaten W.Fletcher and Tom Hooker before drawing the bye.

27 March   Jim Laxton (St Luke's) w pts 3 P.Habbijam (Birmingham), St Helena Gardens Concert Rooms, Rotherhithe, London. The final of a 140lbs lightweight silver cup competition, there were only two entries, P.Habbijam, brother to Bob, who boxed in another competition on the same bill, and Laxton. Also, William 'Soldier' Robinson outpointed Alf Patten in the final of a 140lbs middleweight silver cup competition over three rounds. In previous rounds, Robinson beat Bob Habbijam and 'Lumpy' Hughes, while Patten drew byes in both rounds. There was some confusion, with both competitions at a later date stated to have been at 140lbs.

6 May   Bob Habbijam offered to take the place of George Dove and box Jerry Hawkes for the 116lbs lightweight 'Bow Cup', a drop of nearly two stone.

20 October   Bob Habbijam forfeited to 'Young' Bill Charlton – *Bells Life*.

21 October   'Young' Bill Charlton, surprised at Habbijam forfeiting to him, will still meet the latter, if he pleases, to spar for endurance at 120lbs with gloves – *Bells Life*. Note: 6 May and 21 October bouts put in this list to show how various boxers, of whom Bob Habbijam was one, seemed to slide up and down the weight scales due to the scarcity of men over 126lbs among the professionals.

1877

3 March   Bob Habbijam (Birmingham) to William 'Soldier' Robinson for a handicap catchweight bout, with Habbijam confined to 120lbs and Robinson to 126, MoQ Rules, with gloves over five rounds. Robinson, in accepting on 10 March, asked for an ordinary catchweight bout with no restrictions – *Bells Life*.

12 March   Bob Habbijam (Birmingham) w pts 3 Jim Laxton (St Luke's), McDonalds Music Hall, High Street, Hoxton, London. Refereed by Jim Goode, this was the final of a 140lbs competition (three entries). In the first series on 12 February, Habbijam sparred the bye, while Jim Laxton beat Bob Puryess, also given as Peryes and Peryess.

30 March   William 'Soldier' Robinson w pts 3 Jim Laxton (St Luke's), Saddlers Wells Theatre, Clerkenwell, London. The final of an all-England 140lbs silver cup and £5 competition, in previous rounds of the competition, which had started on 24 March, Robinson had beaten Tom Hooker and 'Young' Ward, then sparred a bye, while Laxton had beaten 'Young' Donnelly, Bill Green and Bill Kennedy.

18 June   At The Ship Tavern, Millbank, London, a proposed 140lbs competition for Charlie Fletcher's silver cup on this date was cancelled when only one, Bob Habbijam, of the four entries, turned up, 'Young' Bill Kennedy, William 'Soldier' Robinson and 'Young' Johnny Walker (real surname Badman) all failing to make it.

18 August   William 'Soldier' Robinson accepts the challenge of Bill Kennedy at 140lbs, MoQ with gloves – *Bells Life*.

1 September   'Young' Johnny Walker, the son of the old London prize ring rules (bare knuckles) champion of same name, accepted the challenge of Jim Laxton (St Luke's) to a bout with gloves, MoQ Rules, for a £20 cup, each to subscribe £10 – *Bells Life*.

27 November   William 'Soldier' Robinson w co 7 Tom Stockley, Islington Green Hall, London. Referee Mr J.Jenn. Made for a finish, with gloves, at catchweights, for £10, it was originally advertised as being for a £50 silver cup, which wasn't forthcoming. Was the pro debut of Stockley, a long-time amateur, who also promoted the show.

1878

21 January   W.Dowdell w pts 3 C.Arundell, East London Gym, Number One Arch, Station Place, Shadwell, London. Refereed by Mr J.Jenn, this was the final of a 140lbs competition. In previous rounds, Dowdell beat C.Brooks and E.Jamp, with Arundell beating B.Chatterway, then sparring a bye against R.Bryan.

20 March   Joe Collins (Leicester), alias 'Tug Wilson', to world at 136lbs to 140lbs, at £25 or £50 a side – *Sporting Life*.

29 June   Tom Brown (Northwich), alias 'Red Bob', challenges any 140lbs man in England, Pat Perry (Birmingham) or Jimmy Ireland/Highland preferred – *Sporting Life*. MoQ Rules, gloves, £50 or £100 a side.

1879

15 April   Tom Jenkins w pts 3 Bob Puryer, Royal Agricultural Hall, Islington, London. The second and final day of a 140lbs professional competition, in previous rounds Jenkins beat W.Dowdell and W.Crane, while Puryer beat 'Young' Dutchy and Tom Symonds.

23 April   Joe Collins, alias 'Tug Wilson', to all at 140lbs for a £50 cup – *Sporting Life*.

29 November   William Sherriff (Leicester), alias 'The Prussian', to all England at 140lbs, or Pat Perry to a restricted weights bout, Sherriff to be 139lbs, Perry 132lbs – *Bells Life*. In the 18 November *Bell's Life*, Perry, primarily a bare-knuckle fighter, had challenged all England at 132lbs.

24 December   Dan Crutchley (Birmingham) w disq12 Jack Weston, Signer Durlings Theatre. Under MoQ Rules, gloves, for £30 cup, with no title billing, Crutchley scaled 140lbs.

1880

22 January   W.Messinger w pts 3 H.Patow, The Cherry Tree, Kingsland Road, Shoreditch, London. Referee Mr H.Pearce. In a 140lbs competition, only three turned up, Messinger beating Tom Hoover, while Patow sparred the bye.

17 May   Andrew McLaren (Glasgow) w rtd 4 Billy Steel (Irongate), The Wallace Gym, Irongate, Glasgow. At 140lbs for the Scottish 140lbs title and championship belt, which McLaren had won by beating A Laird, year, date and venue unknown. Bout was with gloves, MoQ Rules, and also for £20.

29 November   Andrew McLaren (Glasgow) w co 7 Tom Donnelly (Liverpool), Mr Wallace's Gym, Irongate, Glasgow. Made at catchweights for £30, McLaren (136lbs) remained unbeaten after beating Donnelly (126lbs).

1881

3 September   Pat Perry (Birmingham), self-styled world 134lbs champion, challenges the world, 134lbs up to 140lbs, £50 or £100 a side – *Sporting Life*. Am certain this pertains mainly to bare knuckles.

17 October   George Nottace w rtd 3 Tom Jevins (two minutes, 20 seconds), The Blue Coat Boy, Dorset Street, Spitalfields. The final of a 140lbs competition.

5 December   Jim Steadman w pts 3 Harry Mead (Clerkenwell), The Five Inkhorns, New Nichol Street, Shoreditch, London. The final of a 140lbs lightweight competition for Pat Perry and Jack Gorman's Cup, in later years Steadman was called an ex-140lbs lightweight champion

1882

23 January   Arthur Cooper w pts 3 George Roberts, The Goldsmiths Arms, Little Sutton Street, Clerkenwell. The final of Mr Ward's 140lbs competition, despite the advert calling it a 146lbs competition. It was also called an amateur competition in one report.

1 March   Bob Habbijam called the world 140lbs lightweight champion – repeated in the 19 August *Sporting Life*. R.A.Habbijam had retired from boxing, having the final bout of his career in 1877, so no way could the above claim be taken seriously. It was most likely a misprint with ex left out.

11 March   The Scottish 140lbs lightweight championship belt has never been won outright – *Sporting Life*.

20 August   Charlie Roberts w pts 3 G Kingston (Mile End), The Spread Eagle, Kingsland Road, Shoreditch, London. The final of a 140lbs competition.

25 September   George Say (Haggerston) w pts 4 Dick Roberts (Clerkenwell), The West End School of Arms, 74 Newman Street, off Oxford Street, London. Reported as the final of a 140lbs professional competition for a £10 cup, under ABA Rules.

2 October   Dick Roberts (Clerkenwell) w pts 3 Arthur Cooper (St Luke's), West End School of Arms, 74 Newman Street, off Oxford Street, London. The final of Wilson and Habbijam's 140lbs professional competition for £10.

1883

19 January   Owen Hannan w pts 3 Bill Goode, Old Mile End Gate Tavern, Whitechapel, London. Referee Mr H Woodstock. Hannan scaled 126lbs to Goode's 140lbs in this, the final of an open 140lbs competition for a silver cup.

27 January   Dick Roberts (Clerkenwell) is the winner of Watson and Habbijam's 140lbs competition for £10 – *Sporting Life*.

4 March   James Weedon (Pittsburgh, Pennsylvania, USA, born Kendal, Yorkshire), who was called the 140lbs lightweight champion of America, having gone to the USA in 1879, is sailing from New York on 3 May 1883 for Liverpool on the Nevada Guionline – *Sporting Life*.

1884

19 February   As Connie Collins aspires to the English 140lbs middleweight championship, Moss Kirby (Bermondsey) will box him any style at the weight, £10 or £25 a side – *Sporting Life*.

5 March   Noble w pts 6 Conners (three extra rounds fought), Lambeth Baths Gym, London. Referee Mr Bob Watson. The final of a 140lbs competition, prior to the bout the referee cautioned both men to box only for points and to avoid fighting, but they ignored him and engaged in a fight, which had the large crowd roaring. Feeling let down, after two minutes, 30 seconds of the first round had elapsed Watson left the building in disgust. Another referee took over and three rounds were fought on the same lines, pure fighting, plus two more. The *Sporting Life* made the comment that this sort of fight would bring boxing the wrong kind of support and it would fall foul of the law. This bout preceded that of 16 April of the same year, 1884, when Johnny Robinson (South Shields) used this type of 'all-out fighting to win' style throughout in winning a 144 to 146lbs competition at the Horse Shoes, Clerkenwell Close, Clerkenwell. This was the start of modern boxing as it is known today.

24 April   In Boston, Mass, USA, Charlie Norton (Newark, N.J., USA, born Birmingham, England), is called the world 140lbs lightweight champion. Norton, who had boxed from 132lbs up to 140lbs, but now boxed mainly in exhibitions, had left England in 1880 – *Sporting Life*.

7 May   Johnny Robinson (South Shields) to Bill 'Chesterfield' Goode at 136 to 140lbs with gloves or bare knuckles – *Sporting Life*.

12 July   'Nonpareil' Jack Dempsey (real name John Kelly and born Co. Kildare, Ireland) w rtd 21 George Fulljames (Winnipeg, Canada, born London, England) Staten Island, USA. Lasting 35 minutes, 22 rounds and 41 minutes, 37 seconds also reported elsewhere. Referee Ned Mallahan. Contested at catchweights with 'kid' gloves and under London Prize Ring Rules to a finish, which, in effect, rules it out as a genuine glove bout, kid gloves being more deadly than bare knuckles. Weights given for this bout vary from 137lbs, 140lbs and 145lbs for Dempsey and 124lbs, 128lbs, 136lbs and 156lbs (certain misprint for this one) for Fulljames. The only solid fact is that it was a genuine catchweight bout involving no titles.

1885

8 January   Dan Callaghan, the Irish 140lbs champion challenges any 140lbs man in England, £100 a side. It was reported that Callaghan is now in UK, but due to go to USA – *Sporting Life*.

26 February   Jim Berry (Marylebone) to the world at 140lbs, £50 or £100 a side, with the stipulation that a deposit must be put down – *Sporting Life*.

31 March   'Brewery' Edwards (Holloway) stated he didn't send out a challenge on 27 March – *Sporting Life*.

23 April   Jim Berry (Marylebone) is the English 140lbs limit champion – *Sporting Life*.

30 April   Johnny Robinson (South Shields) to any man in England, 136lbs up to 142lbs, £50 or £100 a side, with or without gloves, Jim Berry (Marylebone, London) preferred – *Sporting Life*.

20 May   Jim Berry (Marylebone, London) to any man in England, Johnny Robinson (South Shields) preferred – *Sporting Life*. Berry is about to go to USA where he hopes to get a bout with either John L.Sullivan (Boston, Mass.) or Charlie Mitchell (Birmingham, England).

12 October   Jim Kendrick (Lambeth) w pts 3 Sam Baxter (Shoreditch), The Blue Anchor, Church Lane, Shoreditch. The final of Tom Symonds' 140lbs English championship competition, in previous rounds, Kendrick, who was born in Clounleham, Co. Limerick and whose surname was really Enwright, beat Patsy Griffiths and Bill Cheese, while Baxter beat Mark Dooley and Harry Bartlett.

1886

6 January   Jim Kendrick (Lambeth) is the English 140lbs champion and challenges all England at 140lbs – *Sporting Life*. This is repeated in 26 June and 21 August editions of the *Sporting Life*.

28 April   Jim Hayes (Marylebone) challenges any 140lbs man in the world, £100 a side, winner of the Bill Goode versus Jim Kendrick bout preferred – *Sporting Life*. This was repeated on 12 and 22 May, with Hayes saying he was surprised not to have got a reply to his challenge from Johnny Robinson

6 May (South Shields). It was also repeated in the paper on 22 June, with Robinson preferred. Robinson accepted on 3 July.

6 May The death of Jim Berry/Barry (Marylebone), aged 25, in St Mary's Hospital, Praed Street, Paddington, London is announced. A year previous, Berry had been claiming the English 140lbs championship. His last bout had been with bare knuckles some years earlier against Jim Hayes (Marylebone) at Six Mile Bottom, Newmarket, which was drawn when police called a halt.

8 September Johnny Robinson (South Shields) challenges Jim Kendrick (Lambeth), the claimant to the English 140lbs limit lightweight title. Kendrick accepted on 11 September in the *Sporting Life*, if it can be arranged within one month as he is going to the USA.

15 November Bill Natty drew 12 Pat Condon (Haggerston), The School of Arms, Lambeth Walk, Paradise Street, Lambeth, London. At the 140lbs limit for Harry Clarke's and J.Nanson's English championship belt plus £10, no result was given, but they had met recently in a 140lbs competition, Condon winning according to the *Sporting Life*. However, this was not mentioned in the *Sportsman* and not traced.

21 December England's boxing talent is comparable to any in the world and undoubtedly has the world champion at 140lbs, at 130lbs and at 154lbs, while heavyweight is a moot point – *Sporting Life*.

1887

14 January Jim Kendrick (Lambeth) drew 12 Jack Hickey (Birmingham), Lambeth School of Arms, Lambeth Walk, Paradise Street, Lambeth, London. At catchweights, Hickey, 149lbs, born in Eunis, County Clare, Ireland, who put Kendrick, 143lbs, the English 140lbs champion, down in the eighth had refused a £10 bet on the result immediately prior to the fight.

15 February Jim Hayes (Marylebone) is the English 140lbs champion, while Johnny Robinson (South Shields) is the North of England 140lbs champion. Hayes challenges the world at the weight, £100 a side – *Sporting Life*.

12 April 'Young' Mitchell (San Francisco) drew 47 Jack Hall (Melbourne, late of London), Sydney, Australia. In a finish fight, which was billed as being for the world 140lbs lightweight title, with no individual weights given, Hall was reported to be the Australian 140lbs champion. Mitchell's real name was John L.Herget.

25 April Ben Seth (Lambeth) w pts 12 Bill Cheese (Hoxton), Lambeth School of Arms, Paradise Street, Lambeth, London. Judges J.T.Hulls, E.Sampson and G. T.Dunning. No actual title billing, but the win over Cheese (140lbs) gave Seth (138lbs) the basis for later title claims.

21 July Bill Natty challenged all England at 140lbs, Alec Roberts preferred – *Sporting Life*. It was a certain misprint as, on 15 November 1886, Natty had drawn in a bout for the English 148lbs championship belt, while Roberts had won an English 148lbs championship competition on 18 January 1887.

3 September 'Young' Mitchell (San Francisco) drew 40 Peter Boland (Melbourne, Australia), outside of Albury, Victoria, Australia. Reported to be a finish fight made at 140lbs, with no weights given and no title billing.

1888

21 April Peter Boland (Melbourne) w pts 12 Patrick Carroll (South Australia), near Dandenong, Australia. Contested with gloves and billed as being for the Australian 140lbs lightweight title, the attendance was restricted to just 50 people. No weights were given.

23 April Frank Howson (Sheffield) w disq 2 Dick Burge (Newcastle on Tyne), The Grand Cross, Sheffield. Referee J.J.Hulls. Contested under MoQ Rules, with gloves, for a £50 cup, there was no actual title billing and no weight given for Howson. It was stated to be a blatant fix, as Burge (137lbs) had been the 3-1 on favourite prior to bout before the odds changed to 6-4 on Howson by fight time. Burge, who deliberately hit Howson twice when he was down, had been warned the first time, but ignored Hulls and hit a second time, thus being disqualified.

11 July Felix Scott (Liverpool) w pts 4 Lachie Thompson (Glasgow), The Lyceum Theatre, Pembroke Place, Liverpool. Refereed by Teddy Carney (York), it was the final of a world 140lbs championship belt (made by Elringtons) competition and saw an extra round boxed. In previous rounds, Scott beat Tom Longer and 'Young' Williams, while Thompson, billed as the Scottish 140lbs champion, drew a bye before defeating 'Young' Higham. Scott, billed as the 'coloured' 140lbs champion of England, was arrested after the final on the

charge of assaulting a policeman some time previous and, on 1 August, got 18 months in prison.

4 September Jim Kendrick (Lambeth, born Ireland), now in New York, challenges the world at 140lbs. In a 1924 article in Boxing, Kendrick was called England's best-ever 140lbs man.

26 November Alec Roberts is the English 140lbs champion – *Sportsman*. This was a misprint for being the 148lbs champion, a problem that was to occur throughout Roberts' career.

26 December Jack McAuliffe (Brooklyn, born Co Cork) w co 9 'Young' Jacob Hyams (London, England), The Palace Rink, Brooklyn, New York, USA. Refereed by Dave Holland, it was a catchweight bout with no title billing, but Hyams (139lbs), who started boxing as 'Young Jacob', always insisted it was a finish fight for the world 140lbs lightweight title with six-ounce gloves, which replaced the proposed two-ounce gloves, and was contested under MoQ Rules. McAuliffe weighed 139lbs.

Jack McAuliffe

1889

9 March Jim Kendrick (Lambeth), the English 140lbs limit champion, challenges all England at the weight for a purse of not less than £100 plus side stake – *Sporting Life*. Kendrick had, at this time, been boxing at 144lbs or more and there was some doubt that he could get to 140lbs.

7 April Dick Burge (Newcastle on Tyne) w pts 3 Alf Kilbride (Bradford), The Floral Hall, Leicester. The final of an all-England 140lbs competition for £20.

27 April Bill Cheese (Hoxton) w pts 3 Arthur Gutteridge (Islington), Royal Agricultural Hall, Islington, London. The final round of Ben Hyams' English 140lbs championship competition spread over six days, in previous rounds Cheese beat Bill Gunn and Dick Leary, while Gutteridge beat Alf Suffolk and Dave Burke.

21 May Dave Galvin w co 4 Andy Cannon (St Luke's), The Pelican Club, Denman Street, Soho, London. The final of another all-England 140lbs limit competition, in previous rounds Galvin beat J.Collins and J.Leach, while Cannon beat Jim Hayes/Haines (Marylebone) and Nat Bell.

7 December Bill Cheese (Hoxton) w pts 4 Alf Suffolk (Vauxhall), The Royal Aquarium Theatre, Westminster, London. The final of Frank Hinde's English 140lbs six-day championship competition, in previous rounds Cheese beat Lachie Thompson and Ching Ghook and Suffolk beat Tom Jefford and Bill Whatley.

19 December George Sullivan (Shoreditch) w pts 3 George Baxter (Shoreditch), The Albany Club, Holloway, London. The final of a 140lbs competition, in previous rounds Sullivan had a bye and beat Tom Meadows (Australia), while Baxter beat Jim Verrall, then drew the bye.

1890

8 February Felix Scott (Liverpool), 'The Black', now out of prison, challenged any of the so-called 140lbs limit champions of Great Britain, with Harry Stevens (Notting Hill) preferred – *Sporting Life*.

11 February Lachie Thompson (Glasgow), the Scottish 140lbs champion, accepted Scott's challenge – *Sporting Life*.

11 February The *Sporting Life* stated that on Monday, 24 February, Harry Houldsworth was to meet Terry Callan (Wood Green) for the 140lbs title. However, there was no further mention of this.

2 April Bill Hatcher (Islington) to all England at 140lbs – *Sportsman*.

17 April Alf Suffolk (Vauxhall) is the English 140lbs limit champion – *Sportsman*.

18 April Jim Verrall (Peckham) w co 5 George Sullivan (Shoreditch), The Exchange Club, Queen Street, Cheapside, London. Made at 140lbs, with no weights given and no title billing.

28 April 'Ironbark' Jim Burge drew 50 George Dawson, Sydney, Australia. Billed as a world, Australian and Commonwealth 140lbs limit title fight, Burge weighed 130lbs to Dawson's 138.

6 May Sam Powell (Holloway) challenges all England at 140lbs – *Sporting Life*.

31 May Arthur Gutteridge (Islington) w pts 3 Andy Cannon (St Luke's), Royal Agricultural Hall, Islington, London. This was the final of an all-England 140lbs competition that was spread over five nights and put on by the National Physical Recreation Society, with the Prince of Wales attending the final night. In previous rounds, Gutteridge beat Alf Suffolk and William Robinson, alias 'Cock Robin', while Cannon beat Nat Bell and Dan Doherty.

22 July William Robinson w co 3 Nat Bell, John Fleming's private show in a saloon in a southern suburb of London. Refereed by Bob Watson and made at 140lbs, which both men came in at, there was no title billing.

12 August George Dawson w co 18 Billy 'Shadow' Maber, Sydney, Australia. Billed for the Australian 140lbs limit title and *Sydney Referee* championship belt to a finish, Maber came in as a substitute for 'Ironbark' Jim Burge, who refused to box for a purse of less than £200. No weights were given.

8 September Joe Wilson (Leicester) w co 16 Frank Howson (local), The Drill Hall, Edmund Road, Sheffield. Refereed by J.J.Hulls, this was a catchweight bout with Wilson (138lbs) restricted to 140lbs at an 8 pm weigh-in and Howson (146lbs) to be any weight.

13 September Bill Moore (Chelsea) to any of the self-styled 140lbs English champions, the former ABA champion, Andrew J.Newton, preferred – *Sporting Life*.

5 October Tommy Ryan (New York) w co 28 Charles 'Con' Doyle (Chicago), Selby, Indiana, USA. Billed for the American 140lbs limit title to a finish, no weights were given. Ryan, whose real name was Joseph Youngs, had an English mother and a French father.

15 November William Robinson w pts 3 Arthur Gutteridge (Islington), The Pelican Club, Gerrard Street, Shaftsbury Avenue, Soho, London. The final of the Pelican Club all-England 140lbs limit competition, in previous rounds Robinson beat J.Harland and Bill Cheese, while Gutteridge beat A.McDonald and C.Davis.

24 November George Dawson w rsc 31 'Ironbark' Jim Burge, Sydney, Australia. Billed as a world, Australian and Commonwealth 140lbs limit title fight to a finish, no weights were given. Also reported as ending in both the 32nd and 33rd round.

1891

12 January 'Doc' O'Connell (Boston, Mass) w co 6 Eddie Conley (Boston), New Orleans, USA. Billed for the American 140lbs limit title, no weights were given.

16 February Tommy Ryan (New York) w co 76 Danny Needham (St Paul, Minnesota), Minneapolis, USA. Reported as an American and world 140lbs title fight to a finish with four-ounce gloves, but not given overall title billing in reports, Ryan weighed 139lbs to Needham's 137½lbs. It was called the greatest glove bout ever seen in America up to that time.

4 April J.Harland (ex amateur) w pts 6 J.Ashman, Her Majesty's Theatre, Westminster, London. The final of Frank Hinde's English 140lbs limit championship competition. A week-long show, in previous rounds Harland beat 'Con' Griffiths and A.McDonald and Ashman beat Harry Houldsworth/Holdsworth and George Baxter.

20 April Alf Suffolk (Vauxhall) w rtd 2 H.Smith (Islington), NSC, Covent Garden, London. The final of an NSC all-England 140lbs competition, in previous rounds Suffolk beat Nat Bell and George Baxter, while Smith sparred a bye and then beat Felix Scott.

28 April George Dawson w rtd 17 Harry 'Dummy' Mace, The Gymnastic Club, Sydney, Australia. Billed as an Australian 140lbs limit title fight.

1 May Bill Cheese (Hoxton), 'The Bit of Gorganzola', challenges the world at the 140lbs limit – *Sporting Life*.

31 August Tom Williams (Melbourne) w co 2 Ben Seth (late Lambeth, London), The Melbourne Athletic Club, Melbourne, Australia. Made at 140lbs, there was no title billing and no weights given.

25 September William Robinson, alias 'Cock Robin', to all England at 140lbs – *Sportsman*.

31 October Tom Williams (Melbourne) w co 4 George Dawson, Melbourne, Australia. An Australian 140lbs limit title bout, with both men inside 136lbs to 138lbs class.

30 November Harry Nickless (The Borough) w co 9 Bill Hatcher (Islington), The Bolingbroke Club, Clapham Junction, London. Billed as being for the English 140lbs to 142lbs title and made at 140lbs, 'give or take two pounds', with Hatcher (140lbs) and Nickless weighing 139¾lbs, the latter laid claim to the English 138lbs to 140lbs limit title, besides the English 142 to 144lbs title he already held.

5 December Harry Nickless is the English 140lbs champion – *Sporting Life*.

22 December Billy Myer/Mayer/Meyer (Chicago) w co 3 Jimmy Carroll (born London), New Orleans, USA. An American/world 140lbs limit title fight billed for a finish, no weights were given.

1892

14 January Harry Nickless (The Borough, born Kew), the English 140lbs limit champion, to the world at 138lbs to 140lbs. Also the holder of the 142 to 144lbs limit English title. Repeated throughout the year – *Sporting Life*.

9 February George Dawson, the Australian 140lbs limit champion, arrived in San Francisco seeking bout for the world title at the weight – *Sporting Life*.

10 February Alf Suffolk (Vauxhall) is the true English 138lbs to 140lbs limit champion – *Sporting Life*.

16 February 'Mysterious' Billy Smith (Eastport, USA) w co 7 Frank Kelly, San Francisco, USA. Seen as an American/world 140lbs title fight, no weights were given. Smith, whose real name was Amos Smith, was not born in Birmingham, England as sometimes claimed.

21 March 'Mysterious' Billy Smith (Eastport, USA) w co 13 Billy Armstrong, San Francisco, USA. Reportedly an American/world 140lbs limit title fight, no weights were given though.

18 April George Dawson (Australia) w co 42 Billy Gallagher, San Francisco, USA. Made at 140lbs, no weights were given and there was no title billing as such.

26 July George Dawson (Australia) w co 29 Danny Needham (St Paul, Minnesota). Billed as a finish fight for the world 140lbs limit welterweight title.

21 September 'Mysterious' Billy Smith w co 26 Billy 'Shadow' Maber (Australia), Portland, USA. Given world 140lbs title billing, with three-ounce gloves to a finish, no weights given.

24 October Harry Nickless (The Borough), the English 140lbs limit champion, withdrew the £100 deposit he had laying at the *Sporting Life* office to bind a match with Dick Burge or anyone else in the world at the weight and, surprised that none of the aspirants to his 140lbs limit title had taken up his challenge, said that Joe Wilson (Leicester) can have a bout at 138 to 140lbs if he wishes. Nickless was now claiming the world 140lbs title, as no one had covered his challenge – *Sporting Life*.

1 November Efforts are being made to match Harry Nickless and Austin Gibbons (Paterson, New Jersey, born Liverpool) for the world 138 to 140lbs title, £200 a side and best purse – *Sporting Life*.

3 November Tom Williams (Melbourne, Australia) stated that he did accept Harry Nickless' challenge to the world at the 140lbs limit and was surprised when Nickless ignored it. Although Williams had to forfeit to Nickless previously, due to illness, he would now box him for £300, up to £390 a side, at the 140lbs limit, for an NSC purse – *Sporting Life*.

3 November George Dawson (Australia), now in USA, is the world 140lbs limit champion – *Sporting Life*.

5 November Tom Tracey w disq 3 Harry 'Dummy' Mace. Billed for the vacant Australian 140lbs lightweight title, 7 November was also given.

22 November Harry Nickless (The Borough) is the world 140lbs limit champion – *Sporting Life*.

30 November Tom Williams (Melbourne) still claims to be Australian 140lbs limit champion, despite forfeiting when running out on a return bout with Dawson and leaving Australia – *Sportsman*.

8 December   George Dawson (Australia) w co 20 'Doc' O'Conner (Boston), San Francisco, USA. Advertised as being to a finish for the world 140lbs title, Dawson weighed 140lbs to O'Connor's 139.

1893

24 January   Dick Burge, having just returned from the USA, challenges all England at 138 to 140lbs.

3 March   A proposed USA bout between Tommy Ryan and George Dawson for the world 140lbs limit title fell through on this day when Dawson announced his retirement from boxing.

6 April   Harry Nickless (The Borough), the English and world 140lbs limit champion, is also the English 142 to 144lbs limit champion – *Sporting Life*. Repeated throughout the year, there were also constant comments passed as to how a wild swinging, 'hit-or-be-hit' type like Nickless, with no boxing science whatsoever, ever reached championship level.

17 April   'Mysterious' Billy Smith w co 2 Tom Williams (Melbourne, Australia), Coney Island, Brooklyn, New York, USA. Refereed by Johnny Eckhardt, it was billed as being for the world 140lbs limit lightweight title. The term welterweight was also given. Smith was expected to move up into the 142lbs limit class soon, but, on 25 April, in the *Sporting Life*, he challenged Dick Burge at 140lbs.

'Mysterious' Billy Smith

29 April   Tom Williams (Melbourne, Australia) challenges all England at the 140lbs limit, £100 up to £320 a side, for an NSC purse. This was repeated throughout May – *Sportsman*.

5 July   In the USA, Fred Morris, a negro known as 'Muldoon's Cyclone', challenged any 140lbs man in the world to box either in the USA or the UK – *Sporting Life*.

12 September   Andrew J.Newton (St Pancras), the ABA lightweight champion of 1888, and now a professional, challenges any man breathing in the world at the 140lbs limit – *Sporting Life*. This was repeated on 13 September and was accepted by George Baxter (Shoreditch) in the same issue, although Baxter, in the 12 September issue, had challenged the world at 140 to 142lbs – *Sporting Life*.

2 October   Harry Neumier (Stepney) challenges Harry Nickless to a bout for the world 140lbs limit title – *Sporting Life*.

3 October   Harry Nickless' backer, Jim Burrows, stated that Harry Neumier (Stepney) could have a bout for the world 140lbs limit title and all he had to was put down a deposit as part of the £200 a side to bind the match – *Sporting Life*.

1894

17 January   Harry Nickless is the 140lbs champion – *Sporting Life*.

19 April   Joe Walcott (New York, born Barbados) w rsc 16 Tom Tracey (Australia), Boston, Mass, USA. Although no weights were given or stipulated and there was no title billing, it was later rumoured as having 140lbs world title billing, which Tracey (the half-brother to Dan Creedon), as the Australian 140lbs champion, had part claim to anyway.

4 May   Dick Burge (Newcastle on Tyne) w co 28 Harry Nickless (Battersea, late The Borough, born Kew), The Bolingbroke Club, North Cote Road, Clapham Junction, London. Refereed by Bob Watson, who acted inside the ring throughout all the fights he officiated at, it was billed for the world and English 140lbs limit titles, £200 a side, plus a £200 purse (total £600) and a ringside weigh-in. Immediately following this win, Burge announced his retirement, which lasted about as long as it took him to say it, but was, in fact, Nickless' final bout (apart from exhibitions), although he continued to issue challenges.

8 May   Tom Williams (Melbourne, Australia) challenges the world at 140lbs, Dick Burge preferred – *Sporting Life*. On 9 May, Burge accepted if for £500 a side and at the Bolingbroke Club only.

12 May   Johnny Boyle (Glasgow) to Tom Williams (Australia) and Harry Nickless (London), £100 a side, an NSC purse and 140lbs ringside – *Sporting Life*.

22 May   Harry Overton (Birmingham) will come out of retirement to box Johnny Boyle (Glasgow) at the 140lbs limit. On 25 May, Boyle accepted the challenge – *Sporting Life*.

4 August   Dick Burge again formally announces his retirement from boxing – *Mirror of Life*.

27 August   Jack McAuliffe (Brooklyn, born Ireland) w pts 10 'Young' Griffo (NY, late Australia), Coney Island, New York, USA. The *New Orleans Daily Picayune* gave it world 140lbs title billing, but no individual weights were given and it was not over a recognised title distance, 12 rounds being considered the lowest number of rounds allowed for a major title bout. Also, on this day, a proposed September meet between Joe Walcott and Harry Nickless for the world 140lbs title bout fell through.

18 September   Dick Burge is calling himself the world 140lbs champion once again. Tom Williams was also claiming to be the world 140lbs limit champion and on 30 November, in the *Sporting Life*, Burge was to challenge Williams to a bout for that title, in spite of the fact that throughout November 1894 he was calling himself the world 144lbs limit champion and challenging the world at that weight for £1,000 a side.

1 October   Harry Overton (Birmingham) w pts 12 Tom Woolley (Walsall), The Curzon Hall, Suffolk Street, Birmingham. Refereed by George Dunning, Overton, making a comeback, weighed 139½lbs to Woolley's 137. Made at the 140lbs limit, with five-ounce gloves, £25 a side and a £70 purse (total £120), it was not given major title billing and was later stated to have involved the Midland's 140lbs title, which seems much more likely.

11 October   George Glover, the 140lbs limit champion of Canada now in the UK, challenges all England at the weight, William Robinson, alias 'Cock Robin', preferred – *Sporting Life*. This was accepted by 'Cock Robin' on 13 October – *Sporting Life*.

15 October   Joe Walcott (New York) w co 4 Austin Gibbons (Patterson, N.J., born Liverpool), The Old Sea Beach Palace, Coney

Island, New York, USA. Refereed by Johnny Eckhardt, no weights were given or stipulated and there was no title billing.

20 October Tom Williams (Melbourne, Australia) w co 2 Johnny Boyle, NSC, Covent Garden, London. Refereed by Mr B.J.Angle and made at the 140lbs limit, the weight Williams (138lbs) was making unfounded world title claims at. Both men were in the 136lbs to 138lbs class at the weigh-in. Articled at £100 a side and a £100 purse (total £300), there was no title billing and Boyle (137lbs) was stated to be an unknown who sent out lots of challenges but didn't appear to box at all.

10 November Dick Burge again claims to be the world 140lbs limit champion – *Sporting Life*.

15 November Harry Nickless is the ex-world and English 140lbs champion – *Sporting Life*.

22 December Tom Kelly (Mount Clemens, Michigan, USA) challenges Harry Nickless (The Borough), the 140lbs limit champion, to a bout at the weight, £200 a side and a £200 purse. The Bollingbroke Club had agreed to put up a £200 purse – *Sporting Life*.

1895

21 January Dick Burge (Newcastle on Tyne) w co 4 Tom Williams (Australia), NSC Covent Garden, London. Refereed by B.J.Angle and billed for the world 138 to 140lbs limit title, which both men claimed, other conditions included £300 a side, a £200 purse (total £800) and a 2pm weigh-in. Also given Imperial Empire and English title billing, Williams was born in Australia and was thus not eligible to contest an English title. Also, at least one report gave it as being for the 140 to 142lbs limit title. The fight ended when Williams (139½lbs), who was put down and his head hit the boards with a resounding thud, was counted out. Burge weighed 138lbs.

4 February A subscription fund is to be started to buy a world 140lbs lightweight championship belt for Dick Burge – *Sporting Life*.

2 March Arthur Valentine (Lambeth) w disq 5 Jim Perry (Cardiff), The Central Hall, Holborn, London. Referee T.J.McNeil. Made at the 140lbs limit, £50 a side and £70 purse (total £170), there was no title billing. Valentine (140lbs) was billed as the 134lbs limit champion, while Perry (137½lbs) claimed an outstanding two-year American record.

5 March Dick Burge's subscription world 140lbs lightweight championship belt is made of solid gold and inscribed 'To Dick Burge, 140lbs Champion of the World'. Burge, a natural 140lbs man, would be foolish to try to box below that weight ever again – *Sporting Life*.

14 September Andy Cannon (St Luke's) to all England at 140lbs – *Sporting Life*.

18 December Dick Burge's subscription world 140lbs championship belt was put on display at Morris Abrahams' pub, The Black Horse, Haymarket until 23 December – *Sporting Life*.

28 December The *Mirror of Life* stated that during 1894, Dick Burge had received a 140lbs championship belt from the National Sporting Club, Covent Garden. This was almost certainly a mix up by the newspaper with Burge's subscription belt of 1895.

1896

11 January Dick Burge to the world at 140lbs, which was repeated on 15 February – *Mirror of Life*.

21 January Harry Nickless (The Borough), the ex-world and English 140lbs champion, announced his retirement from boxing due to an injury to his left eye and by August 1896 he was stated to be blind in that eye – *Sporting Life*.

8 February 'Mysterious' Billy Smith (USA) called the world 140lbs limit welterweight champion in the *Mirror of Life*, which was repeated in the 28 February issue, but, on 29 June, in the *Sporting Life*, Smith issued a statement that he was not the 140lbs limit champion, but the 138lbs class champion.

10 February Arthur Valentine (Lambeth) w disq 2 Tom Lynch (Ireland), NSC, Covent Garden, London. Valentine (139lbs), recently back from USA and billed as the 132 to 134lbs English champion, had suffered ill health in the USA and seemed a broken man, being cautioned for holding in the first round after slipping down. At the end of the round, Lynch (138lbs) was the odds-on favourite, but in the second session he was twice warned for holding before being disqualified, giving Valentine the win. There was no title billing.

30 March Owen Sweeney (Fulham) w co 2 George King (Wandsworth), NSC, Covent Garden, London. Made at 140lbs, no weights were given and there was no title billing.

On the same show, Tom Tracey (Australia, born New Zealand) knocked out Tom Williams (Aldershot, late Melbourne, Australia) in 35 seconds. Made at 138lbs to 140lbs, no title billing was mentioned and no weights were given, but it was later stated to have been for the world 138lbs to 140lbs title. Australian 138lbs to 140lbs title billing was also given.

16 May On this day it was reported in the *Mirror of Life* that Tom Tracey, the world and Australian 138lbs to 140lbs limit champion, was presented with a gold medal set in diamonds and rubies as emblematic of the world 140lbs championship. In the centre of the medal was a South African 'pond' piece, of the size and value of a British sovereign dated 1896, bearing the medallion of president Kruger and surrounded by a large, heavy gold frame in which jewels had been tastefully imbedded. On the reverse side was the inscription, "Presented to Tom Tracey, 10 Stone Champion of the World, by His Friend and Well-Wisher, Charles S.Fleet – April 28 1896". Note: Mr Fleet was a wealthy Australian Mine owner.

7 September Owen Sweeney (Fulham) to all England at 140lbs for up to £100 a side – *Sporting Life*.

29 October Matty Matthews (New York) w co 7 Stanton Abbott (Providence, NJ, late London, England), Buffalo, New York, USA. No weights were given or stipulated and there was no title billing.

1897

15 February Pat Daly/Daley (Westminster, late New York, born Ireland) challenges the world at the 140lbs limit. This was repeated on 11 August, Joe Walcott or Jack McAuliffe preferred – *Sporting Life*.

2 June Alf Bannister (Camden Town) to all at 138lbs to 140lbs, 'Jewey' Cook, Arthur Callan, Harry Webster and Pat Daly/Daley preferred – *Sporting Life*.

2 October Chris Jacoby, 'The California Kid', is now in Britain and challenges all England at 140lbs – *Sporting Life*.

1898

1 January Arthur Lock (Camberwell, born Merthyr, South Wales) to all England at the 140lbs limit – *Sporting Life*.

17 February In Chicago, USA, the death of Charles 'Con' Doyle (Chicago), in his 28th year, was reported. His last bout was on 8 January 1898, when he lost on a two-round police stoppage to Billy Sturt in Chicago.

16 April Dick Burge, the 140lbs champion, was also claiming to be the 144lbs limit champion – *Sporting Life*.

21 September Pat Daly/Daley challenges the world at 138 to 144lbs – *Sporting Life*.

21 October Jim Curran (Rotherham), now in the USA, to the world at 136 to 140lbs – *Sporting Life*.

26 October Sam Lewis (Australia) to all England at 140lbs. Lewis was accepted on 5 November by 'Wag' Dowd (Islington) – *Sporting Life*.

November Jim Curran (Rotherham) w disq 5 Jack Fox, The Pelican Club, Chicago, USA. No weights given or stipulated.

15 November George Kerwin (Chicago) w pts 6 Jim Curran (England), Chicago, USA. No weights given or stipulated, Kerwin was known as 'The Mystery'.

6 December A.J.Francis (Bath) challenges 'Jewey' Cooke, Owen Sweeney or Arthur Callan at 138 to 140lbs, up to £100 a side and a purse offered by the New Olympic Club, Birmingham – *Sporting Life*.

20 December It was reported in the *Sporting Life* that Jim Holloway (Pretoria, South Africa), the South African 140lbs lightweight champion, challenges all England at 140lbs. Holloway was a true South African champion, having been born and bred there. Normally, in South Africa, anyone who stepped off a boat and won a contest claimed the national title.

20 December Bobby Dobbs (Kentucky, USA), who was a negro, challenges the world at 136lbs up to 140lbs – *Sporting Life*.

24 December Jim Curran (Rotherham), now back from the USA, to the world from 135lbs to 140lbs, £100 up to £500 a side and over 20 rounds, Bobby Dobbs, Tom Causer or Johnny Hughes preferred – *Sporting Life*.

1899

21 January Pat Daly/Daley challenges Jim Curran (Rotherham) at 140lbs, £100 a side – *Sporting Life*.

21 January Dick Burge is the world 140lbs champion – *Sporting Life*.

23 January Jim Curran (Rotherham) to all England at 140lbs – *Sporting Life*.

30 January Jim Holloway (Pretoria, South Africa) w pts 'Jewey' Cooke

(Bloomsbury), NSC, Covent Garden, London. Made at 140lbs, with both men scaling 139lbs, there was no title billing and two-minute rounds were called for at the NSC after a new ruling, which didn't last long, was passed following a recent death there.

13 March	Jim Holloway (Pretoria, South Africa) w disq 13 Jim Curran (Rotherham), NSC, Covent Garden, London. Referee B.J. Angle. Holloway weighed 139lbs in a match made at 140lbs with no title billing.
12 April	Jim Curran (Rotherham) announced his retirement from boxing and is now a publican – *Mirror of Life*.
12 July	Pat Daly/Daley challenges the world at 140lbs, £100 a side, Frank Erne (USA, born Zurich) preferred – *Mirror of Life*.
11 October	Johnny Hughes (Canning Town) to Pat Daly/Daley at 140lbs, £200 up to £300 a side and an NSC purse. Also challenged on the same terms was Alf Bannister at 136lbs, or the world at 138lbs – *Mirror of Life*.

1900

23 January	Maurice Greenfield (Birmingham), the son of the late Alf Greenfield, the ex-English heavyweight champion, challenges all England at 140lbs. He then challenged the world at 140lbs, £100 a side, two days later and was accepted on 7 February by 'Pedlar' McMahon (Swansea and Sunderland), before that fell through – *Sporting Life*.
21 March	Jack Grace (New York) to all England at 136 to 140lbs – *Mirror of Life*.
21 March	On this day, Bill Whatley (Walworth) was called the ex-English 140lbs limit champion – *Sporting Life*.
4 May	Matty Matthews (New York) drew 10 William 'Kid' Parker (Denver, born Boston), Denver, Colorado, USA. Billed as an American/world 140lbs limit title fight, despite it not being over a recognised distance. No weights given.
5 June	Eddie Connolly (New Brunswick, Canada) w pts 25 Matty Matthews (New York), Brooklyn, New York, USA. Billed for the world 140lbs limit title, no weights were given.
13 August	Jim 'The Rube' Ferns (Pittsburg) w rtd 15 Eddie Connolly (New Brunswick), Buffalo, New York, USA. Billed as an American/world 140lbs limit title bout, Ferns was also known as 'The Kansas Rube'.

Jim 'The Rube' Ferns

23 August	Johnny Hughes (Canning Town) should be recognised as the English 140lbs champion – *Sporting Life*.
31 August	Jack Everhardt (New Orleans) is the American 140lbs lightweight champion – *Sporting Life*. There was nothing in his record to support this.
3 September	Jack Everhardt (New Orleans) w disq 10 Tom Ireland (Mile End), Wonderland, Whitechapel Road, London. Originally billed as for the world, not English, 140lbs limit title, which the American was not eligible for, Everhardt (141lbs) was one pound overweight and, with the contest only being over two-minute rounds, it carried little credence. It was also stated to be 'a known fix', with Ireland (137lbs) deliberately

getting himself disqualified through his second entering the ring.

14 September	Billy Gordon (Boston, USA), a negro, challenges Jack Everhardt (New Orleans, USA) at 140lbs over 15 or 20 rounds – *Sporting Life*.
16 October	Matty Matthews (New York, USA) w pts 15 Jim 'The Rube' Ferns (Pittsburg, USA), Detroit, USA. Billed for the American 140lbs title, no weights were given.
26 December	Dick Burge, still claiming to be the official English 140lbs lightweight champion, was thought to have refused to meet Tom Woodley (Fulham) for this title when the latter refused to 'dive' – *Mirror of Life*.

1901

30 January	Ted Cain (Birmingham) to any 140lbs man in England, Tom Woodley (Fulham) preferred – *Sporting Life*.
11 February	Dick Burge, who had weighed 144lbs for the final bout of his career on 28 January 1901, stated that the forthcoming Pat Daly/Daley v Johnny Hughes bout couldn't be for the English 140lbs limit title as he was still champion at that weight. There was no mention of his many retirements from boxing, or the fact that he had long been unable to get down to 140lbs – *Sporting Life*.
12 February	Pat Daly/Daley challenges the world at 138 to 140lbs for the world title, £200 up to £500 a side. This was repeated throughout the year – *Sporting Life*.
5 March	Pat Daly/Daley is now the official English 140lbs limit lightweight champion – *Sporting Life*.
11 March	Pat Daly/Daley (Co Cork) w co 12 Johnny Hughes (Canning Town), NSC, Covent Garden, London. Refereed by Mr J.H.Douglas, it was billed for the English 140lbs limit lightweight title, £100 a side and an NSC purse. Douglas, who was unsighted and didn't see anything, refused a claim of foul by the Hughes' corner, it being stated that in a mix up on the ropes Daly (139½lbs) had accidently caught Hughes (138lbs) in the groin with his knee, which was supported by a doctor's examination after the bout. It was also stated that prior to the above, the men had met in private at the Royal Agricultural Hall, Isleworth during the six-weeks stay there of Hughes' father, Harry Hughes, whose booth was there over the Christmas period, and Hughes had stopped Daly inside the distance. However, the story was never confirmed and it seems highly unlikely, giving Daly's untrusting nature and the fact that Hughes never fully recovered from a badly broken leg during 1899. Added to which, the Daly versus Hughes match had been signed and sealed on 29 November 1900, so such an impromptu match seems highly unlikely.
6 April	Tom Ireland (Mile End) w pts 6 Bill Nolan (Drury Lane), Wonderland, Whitechapel Road, London. Refereed by Harry Cooper, it was the final of Joe Smith's 140lbs limit £100 English championship belt competition, which had started on 4 April. In previous rounds, Ireland beat Peter Brown and 'Cush' Darvie, while Nolan beat Charlie Tilley and Jack Fairclough.
19 April	It was reported that strong efforts were being made to make a Pat Daly/Daley versus William 'Spike' Sullivan match for the world 140lbs limit title – *Sporting Life*.
25 April	Jack Fairclough (St Helen's) w rsc 2 Sam Harper (St James, London), RN Gym, Burnaby Road, Portsmouth. Refereed by Mr Godtschack (London), it was the final of an all-England 140lbs limit competition which had started the previous day. In previous rounds, Fairclough beat Harry Fowler and J.Winters, while Harper beat Fred Duffett and Alf Bannister. There was a real mix up in the details of this competition, the *Mirror of Life* giving the result as Fairclough w rsc 1, while the *Sporting Life*, *Sportsman* and *Hampshire Telegraph* all gave w rsc 2, plus reports that support that. It was also reported in the first series that Winters beat Sam Harper, while Jim Harper beat Duffett, but in the semi-final it was Sam Harper who beat Alf Bannister before losing to Fairclough in the final.
29 April	Matty Matthews (New York, USA) w pts 20 Tom Couhig (New York, USA), Detroit (Louisville also given), USA. Reported to be an American/world 140lbs limit title fight, no weights were given.
20 May	Tom Ireland (Mile End) to all England at the 140lbs limit – *Sporting Life*.
22 May	Charlie Knock (Stratford) accepts the challenge of Tom Ireland (Mile End) to all England at 140lbs and if Ireland won't accept the fight he will box anyone else in England at the weight, Jack Goldswain preferred. This was repeated on 19 October – *Sporting Life*.

30 October Bill Chester (Mile End) challenges all England 134lbs to 140lbs, up to £200 a side – *Sporting Life*.

5 November Jim Roberts (South Africa, born Brynmawr, South Wales) w rtd 12 Alf Bannister (St Luke's, London), The New Adelphi Club, Maiden Lane, London. Referee Ed Plummer. Made at 138lbs, there was no title billing (see note to 18 December bout).

12 December George 'Kid' Lavigne (Saginaw, USA) w co 4 Jim Hegerty (Australia), The Alma Club, California, USA. There was no title billing and no weights given or stipulated, despite Hegerty being billed as the Australian champion.

17 December Jack Taper won a 140lbs competition – *Sporting Life*.

18 December Jim Maloney (Hackney) w rtd 8 Jim Roberts (South Africa), The Atheneum Theatre, Tottenham Court Road, London. Referee Ed Plummer. Made at 138lbs to 140lbs with a 2pm weigh-in, £25 a side and £15 purse (total £65), there was no title billing given. Note that the *South African Review* of 22 January 1902, which had previously stated that Jim Roberts (137lbs) was unknown in South Africa, named a photo of Roberts as being that of Bob James of Cape Colony, South Africa, who was also far removed from championship class. Maloney scaled 138³/₄lbs.

31 December Pat Daly/Daley, the official English 140lbs limit lightweight champion, challenges Frank Erne (Buffalo, born Zurich) for the world 140lbs limit lightweight title – *Sporting Life*.

1902

3 February Tom Ireland (Mile End) w rtd 2 Harry Webster (Kings Cross, late Kentish Town), NSC, Covent Garden, London. The final of a world 140lbs competition (all-England also given), in previous rounds Ireland had beaten Sam Cavil (Australia), a coloured fighter, and Jack Woods, while Webster had defeated Charlie Tilley and Harry Greenfield.

22 February Dick Burge, the ex-140lbs champion, got 10 years for his part in the Liverpool bank frauds, even though he and his wife, Bella, were the only ones to pay most, if not all, of their share back. During the trial, Burge stated that the 140lbs world championship belt he was presented with had gone, three years earlier, to a Manchester publican whom he owed £200.

6 March Pat Daly/Daley, the English 140lbs limit champion, to the world at 140lbs. This was repeated throughout the year – *Sporting Life*.

26 March Joe Scott challenges all England at 138lbs, just to secure who is the rightful English 138lbs champion, Jack Goldswain, Ernie Veitch, Tom Ireland or Jim Maloney preferred – *Sporting Life*.

23 May Jim Maloney to Eddie Connolly (USA and Canada) at 140lbs – *Sporting Life*.

23 June George Penny (Kentish Town) w pts 10 Peter Brown (Woolwich), The New Adelphi Club, Maiden Lane, The Strand, London. Refereed by Harry Cooper, this was a bout for the English 140lbs lightweight Coronation Championship Belt. Penny, a substitute for Jim Maloney (Hackney), was presented with the belt on 24 July 1902 by Mr Terry Wilson. In later years this belt was called both the 140lbs and 144lbs championship belt, but 140lbs is correct.

3 July Andrew Jeptha (Cape Town, South Africa) is the 'coloured' 140lbs champion of South Africa – *Mirror of Life*.

8 July Pat Daly/Daley challenges Charlie Knock (Stratford) at 140lbs, £100 up to £200 a side and a 2pm weigh-in – *Sporting Life*.

22 July The veteran American negro, Bobby Dobbs (Kentucky), aged 42, challenges all England at 138lbs up to 142 lbs, £100 a side. This was accepted on 23 July by Jim Maloney (Hackney) – *Sporting Life*.

23 August Pat Daly/Daley, the English 140lbs limit champion, challenges the world at 140lbs, Bobby Dobbs (Kentucky) preferred. Dobbs accepted on 29 August – *Sporting Life*.

26 August Jim Maloney (Hackney) to Pat Daly/Daley at the 140lbs limit and £100 a side – *Sporting Life*.

3 November Jack Goldswain (Bermondsey) w co 6 Charley Evans (Deptford), NSC, Covent Garden, London. Made at 138 to 140lbs, with no title billing and not over a championship distance, Goldswain scaled 136³/₄lbs to Evans' 139.

20 November Jim Maloney (Hackney) w pts 20 Bobby Dobbs (Kentucky), The National Athletic Club, Marylebone Road, London. Billed for the world 138 to 140lbs title, £100 a side and purse, with Dobbs called the holder.

1903

9 February William 'Spike' Sullivan (Boston, born Co Cork) w co 1 Jim Maloney (Hackney), NSC, Covent Garden, London. Billed

for the world 138 to 140lbs limit title, both were inside but no actual weights were given. Sullivan stated to already hold the world 136lbs limit title.

4 March Pat Daly/Daley, the recognised English 140lbs limit champion, having received forfeit from Jim Clark (Australia and America), challenges any 140lbs man in the world to a bout for the world title at the weight, black or white, no one barred – *Sporting Life*.

16 May Pat O'Keefe (Canning Town) to all England at 140lbs – *Sporting Life*.

8 June Jack Bayley (Birmingham) to all England at 140lbs, £50 or £100 a side, Jim Maloney (Hackney) preferred – *Sporting Life*.

15 June William 'Spike' Sullivan (USA, born Co. Cork) drew 20 Jack Nelson (local), Ginnett's Circus, Newcastle on Tyne. Referee J.R.Smoult. Made at 140lbs for the world title, £100 a side and a £150 purse (total £350), Sullivan weighed 140lbs to Nelson's 138.

21 October Peter Brown (Woolwich) to all England at 140lbs, Jim Clarke or Charlie Knock preferred – *Mirror of Life*.

12 December Jim Hook (Bethnal Green) w co 13 Jack Nelson (local), Ginnett's Circus, Newcastle on Tyne. Referee Billy Bell. Made at 138lbs to 140lbs, for a £50 purse, while Hook weighed in at 139lbs, Nelson (145lbs) was well over the prescribed weight. There was no title billing.

31 December Jack Goldswain (Bermondsey) w pts 3 Tom Edmunds (Birmingham), Olympia, Kensington, London. Refereed by Tom Scott, this was the final of an English 140lbs championship competition, which was misprinted as 126lbs elsewhere. In previous rounds, Goldswain beat Alf Garrett and Jim Maloney, while Edmunds beat Arthur Warner and George Brooks. Although the *Sporting Life* reported that the bout went the distance, with Goldswain a points winner, the latter always stated that he stopped Edmunds in the third round, as he had in their previous bout on 9 November 1903, which was never disputed by Edmunds. To confuse matters even further, the *Birmingham Sports Argus* gave the result as Goldswain w co 1.

1904

23 January Jack Nelson (local) w co 6 Jim Hook (Bethnal Green), Ginnett's Circus, Newcastle on Tyne. Made at the 140lbs limit, with no title billing and for a £60 purse, Nelson weighed 139lbs to Hook's 138. Hook was the son of the old-timer, Bill 'Tricky' Hook.

15 February Bill Chester (Mile End) w pts 12 Jim Hook (Billingsgate and Bethnal Green), Wonderland, Whitechapel Road, London. Referee J.T.Hulls. Made at catchweights, no weights were given and there was no title billing.

20 February Jack Nelson (local) drew 20 Jack Bayley (Birmingham), Ginnett's Circus, Newcastle on Tyne. Made at catchweights, this was a substitute bout on 10 days notice for Frank 'Spike' Robson (North Shields) versus George Dixon (USA), the negro.

25 March Joe Gans (Baltimore, USA) w pts 15 Jack Blackburn (Philadelphia, USA), Baltimore, USA. Reportedly an American/world 140lbs limit title bout, both men came in on the weight.

2 April Jack Nelson (local) w disq 6 Bobby Dobbs (Kentucky), Ginnett's Circus, Newcastle on Tyne. In a match made at 140lbs, with no weights given and no title billing, for £100 purse, both men agreed to meet again on the following Monday over 20 rounds.

4 April Bobby Dobbs (Kentucky) w co 8 Jack Nelson (local), Ginnett's Circus, Newcastle on Tyne. At catchweights for £25 a side, although no weights were given both were about 140lbs There was no title billing.

18 June Bobby Dobbs (Kentucky) w pts 20 Peter Brown (Woolwich), Ginnett's Circus, Newcastle on Tyne. Referee Billy Bell. Billed as for the world 140lbs limit title, with 140 to 142lbs also given, £50 a side and a £100 purse, Brown, thought to be about 146lbs, was stated to be out of condition and no weights were reported in what was almost certainly a catchweight contest.

23 July Bobby Dobbs (Kentucky) w co 2 Bill Chester (Mile End), Ginnett's Circus, Newcastle on Tyne. Originally billed as being for the world 140lbs limit title, Dobbs (144lbs) was over the weight, so the bout went on at catchweights, for a £100 purse, only £50 a side and the side stakes being dropped. Chester's weight, which was announced as 139lbs, was also misprinted as being 129lbs.

25 July Jim Courtney (Barry, born London) drew 15 Harry 'Fatty'

Mansfield (Bristol), Welsh NSC, Queen Street, Cardiff. Billed as an English, Welsh and West of England 140lbs limit title, it was disqualified from major title billing as of only two-minute rounds. Also given as a catchweight bout with no weights reported in any of the papers, that could well be correct.

2 November Jack Goldswain (Bermondsey) challenges all England at the 140lbs limit, £25 or £50 a side – *Sporting Life*.

7 November Harry 'Fatty' Mansfield (Bristol) w co 15 Jim Courtney (Barry, born London), The Queen Street Hall, Cardiff. Note that this was identical to their 25 July bout in every detail, even down to being called a catchweight bout. Courtney was knocked out with just 15 seconds remaining.

3 December Jack Nelson (local) w pts 20 Harry Greenfield (Camden Town), Ginnett's Circus, Newcastle on Tyne. Billed for the English 136 to 138lbs limit title, although no weights were given, but as Nelson seemed to go up and down the scales both men were put in as being 140lbs for a £100 purse.

1905

7 January Jack Goldswain (Bermondsey) challenges the world at 140lbs and, on 17 January, challenged any one in England for the English 140lbs limit title – *Sporting Life*.

19 January Jim Hook (Bethnal Green and Billingsgate) will meet Jack Goldswain over 15 three-minute rounds, 8pm weigh-in, for the English 140lbs limit title – *Sporting Life*.

10 February Bob (misprinted as Bert) Russell (Limehouse), seeing that Jack Goldswain now claims the English 140lbs limit title, challenges him for £50 a side and an NSC purse – *Sporting Life*.

6 March Jack Nelson (local) w co 13 Jim Harper (St James, London), Ginnett's Circus, Newcastle on Tyne. Made at 140lbs, for a £100 purse, no weights were given and there was no title billing.

7 March Bill Wood (Clapton), seeing that there are so many English 140lbs champions, challenges any of them for that title – *Sporting Life*.

20 March Harry Greenfield (Kentish Town, later Camden Town) w rtd 7 Morty Murphy (Ireland), The North London Baths. At 140lbs, with no title billing, for £25 a side and a £25 purse (total £75), the 32-year-old Greenfield (139lbs) topped the bill and promoted the show. Murphy also weighed 139lbs.

18 April Pat Daly/Daley challenges Harry Greenfield over 15 or 20 rounds of three minutes duration for the 140lbs limit title he had won on 11 February 1901 by beating Johnny Hughes, as he had never lost this title. Note that Daly was, at this time, also claiming the English 144lbs limit title and seeing that on 5 March 1900 he had won an English heavyweight championship belt competition, a belt he never lost, he could certainly claim a unique record in regards to English championship title claims – *Sporting Life*. On 6 May, in the *Sporting Life*, Daly repeated his challenge to Harry Greenfield to a bout at the 140lbs limit for the English title.

9 May In list of champions, Jack Goldswain is shown as being the English 140lbs limit champion. This was repeated again on 2 December – *Sporting Life*.

28 October Tom Edmunds (Birmingham) to all England at 140lbs – *Sporting Life*.

1 November Jack Goldswain to the world at 140lbs – *Sporting Life*.

4 November Bill Wood (Clapton) challenges Jack Goldswain at the 140lbs limit – *Sporting Life*.

1906

3 January Frank Lowry to all England at 140lbs over 15 or 20 rounds – *Sporting Life*.

17 January Jack Goldswain (Bermondsey) is the English 138lbs to 140lbs class lightweight champion – *Sporting Life*.

17 January Pat Daly/Daley again claims that he is still the English 140lbs limit champion and would defend same against the English 134 to 136lbs champion, Jabez White (Birmingham). Note: Daly, in fact, after 11 February 1901 never fought at less than 144lbs again, so any claims that he still held the 138lbs to 140lbs English title had long gone – *Mirror of Life*.

19 January Jack Goldswain (Bermondsey) w co 13 Fred Buckland (Barnsbury, born Peterborough, late South Africa), NSC, Covent Garden, London. Referee J.H.Douglas. Billed for the English 138lbs to 140lbs limit title and also given Imperial Empire billing, Buckland (138½lbs) was claiming to be the 140lbs South African champion. Goldswain scaled 139lbs.

8 February Jack Goldswain, the English 140lbs limit champion, offers to defend this against anyone in England, Jabez White preferred. This was repeated on 15 February, again in the *Sporting Life*.

23 April Jack Goldswain (Bermondsey) w pts 20 Jabez White (Birmingham), NSC, Covent Garden, London. Referee Tom Scott. Billed for the 138 to 140lbs limit lightweight title, White (140lbs) was the English 134 to 136lbs limit lightweight champion. Goldswain weighed 138½lbs.

28 June Bill Ward (Clapton) challenges all England from 134 to 140lbs. This was repeated in the 5 July *Sporting Life*, but at the 140lbs limit, with Jabez White or Jack Goldswain preferred.

7 July Fred Buckland w co 4 Gus Oliver, Assembly Hall, Boksburg, South Africa. Referee Mr H.S.Thompson. Reported as being for the South African lightweight title at 140lbs, no weights were given.

29 August Pat Daly/Daley challenges Jack Goldswain to a bout for the English 140lbs limit lightweight title over 15 or 20 three-minute rounds and £100 a side, which was repeated on 19 September – *Sporting Life*.

6 September Pat Daly/Daley challenges the world at the 140lbs limit, £200 up to £500 a side, Joe Gans, the Baltimore negro, preferred, for the world 140lbs title over 20 rounds or to a finish – *Sporting Life*.

11 September Jim Maloney (Hackney) to the world at the 140lbs limit, Jack Goldswain, Pat Daly/Daley, Jabez White and Bobby Dobbs preferred – *Sporting Life*.

3 October Bob Russell (Limehouse) is the English 140lbs limit champion – *Sporting Life*.

4 October If Jack Goldswain's 140lbs English title defence against Jabez White is not made within one week, Goldswain will defend same against either Joe Fletcher or Pat Daly/Daley. This was repeated on 6 October and 1 November in the *Sporting Life*. In the latter it stated: 'It's a known fact that Daly can't get below 144lbs, let alone make 140lbs'.

1907

4 January Jabez White (Birmingham) to Jack Goldswain or Pat Daly/Daley at the 140lbs limit, £200 a side – *Sporting Life*.

26 January Jack Goldswain is the English 140lbs limit champion – *Mirror of Life*.

28 January The Jack Goldswain versus Pat Daly/Daley 140lbs limit English title bout is postponed until 11 February, due to a training accident to Daly.

11 February Jack Goldswain (Bermondsey) w co 5 Pat Daly/Daley (London, born Ireland), NSC, Covent Garden, London. Referee J.H.Douglas. Originally billed as being for the English 140lbs limit title, but Daly (148lbs) was well over the weight, for which he paid forfeit. In one of the worst bouts ever seen, for which no blame could be put on Goldswain (139lbs), Daly, who was pitiful, had not boxed at 140lbs since 1901 but had insisted he could make the weight.

18 April Freddie Welsh (Pontypridd), real surname Thomas, who challenged Jack Goldswain at the 140lbs limit, was stated to have put down a £20 deposit – *Sporting Life*.

26 April Jack Goldswain stated that if Welsh covered the £20 deposit he had put down a bout could be made. However, Welsh claimed he had put down the £20 deposit, which the *Sporting Life* of 18 April confirmed.

13 May Jabez White is too busy to box Freddie Welsh now, but will do so next season – *Sporting Life*.

30 May Freddie Welsh (Pontypridd) reminded Jack Goldswain, the English 140lbs champion, that he too has had a £25 deposit held by the *Sporting Life* for some time and as he had challenged both Goldswain and Jabez White at the 140lbs limit, ringside weigh-in, £200 a side, with no takers, if Goldswain really wanted to defend his English 140lbs limit title, he would meet him on 3 June at the *Sporting Life* office to make the match – *Sporting Life*.

31 May Jack Goldswain challenges the world at the 140lbs limit with a 2pm weigh-in. In a reply to Freddie Welsh, Goldswain stated that when he had put a deposit down Welsh had failed to cover it and the Welshman would now have to wait until next season for a match. In the same issue of the *Sporting Life*, 'Young' Joseph (Aldgate) challenged Goldswain, £200 up to £500 a side, 20 rounds, 3pm weigh-in, in a catchweight bout with Goldswain restricted to 140lbs and Joseph to 134lbs.

1908

18 January Joe Fletcher (Camberwell), the English 136lbs limit champion, challenges the winner of the 'Young' Joseph versus Jack Goldswain bout for £100 a side – *Sporting Life*. In the same issue, Fred Buckland (South Africa, born England) challenged all England at 140lbs.

20 January 'Young' Joseph (Aldgate) w pts 20 Jack Goldswain, Wonderland, Whitechapel Road, London. Referee J.T.Hulls. Made at 142 to 144lbs, according to the *Sporting Life*, and 140lbs to 142lbs in the *Mirror of Life*, £200 a side and a £165 purse (total £565), Joseph (142lbs) tried to claim the English title with this win over Goldswain (141½lbs), but had no grounds for doing so as the bout was made above the 140lbs limit and was also contested over two-minute rounds. It was later pointed out that the bout was contested at the 140 to 142lbs limit, not at the 144lbs limit, but then the promoter, Harry Jacobs, said bout was made at 144lbs.

29 January Sam Harris (Boston, Mass, born England) challenges Jack Goldswain to a bout for the English 140lbs limit title. Later, on 4 March, contracts were signed for them to meet for the title, but the bout fell through when no purse offers were made due to the fact that Harris was stated to be unknown – *Sporting Life*.

24 June Bill Wood (Clapton) to all England at the 140lbs limit, Jack Goldswain preferred – *Sporting Life*.

13 July Jack Goldswain to Jimmy Britt (San Francisco, USA) at the 140lbs limit – *Sporting Life*.

14 July 'Young' Joseph (Aldgate) challenges Jimmy Britt (San Francisco, USA) at the 140lbs limit, 10, 15 or 20 rounds – *Sporting Life*.

26 October Joe Fletcher (Camberwell) to Jack Goldswain for the English 140lbs limit title – *Sporting Life*.

23 November Johnny Summers (Canning Town) w rsc 14 Jack Goldswain (Bermondsey), NSC, Covent Garden, London. Referee Eugene Corri. Made at catchweights, Goldswain (144lbs) coming in as a substitute for Roufe O'Brien (USA), who was to have met Summers at 134lbs but was taken ill. Goldswain weighed 160lbs the week prior to the bout when agreeing to substitute for O'Brien, who suffered from concussion in training and was advised to rest for at least 12 months by the NSC doctor. Summers (134lbs), real surname Sommers, versus Goldswain was for a total of £225. On 11 February, the NSC introduced eight-named weight divisions, which effectively ended the every two-pound classes, and although the 140lbs limit continued within the welterweight division before dying out in the early 1920s it was quickly re-introduced as the light-welterweight division.

140lbs to 142lbs (10st to 10st 2lbs)

1873
22 February W.Cook (The Commercial Road) to Dan Tracey with gloves, same conditions as for 'Bow Cups', at 140lbs up to 142lbs, £10 or £15 a side and a £1 deposit put down – *Bells Life*.

1879
23 April Joe Collins (Leicester), alias 'Tug Wilson', challenges all England at 140lbs for a £50 cup. Also in 138lbs to 140lbs class – *Sporting Life*.

1880
20 January Jim Goodwin (Birmingham) drew 41 Joe Thorley, The Argyll Rooms, Lower Loveday Street, Birmingham. No title billing. Made at the 142lbs limit for £50, MoQ Rules, with gloves and to a finish, Goodwin weighed 140½lbs and Joe Thorley 142lbs. Attendance 1000. Thorley sprained his right hand early on, but fought on with the injury.

1884
19 April Bill Goode to Johnny Robinson (South Shields) – *Sporting Life*.

1 May Johnny Robinson accepted above, but bout to be at the 142lbs limit – *Sporting Life*.

1885
7 April Bill Goode accepted challenge of Johnny Robinson (South Shields) at the 142lbs limit, but only with gloves, not bare knuckles as Robinson's challenge stipulated. Bout to be for endurance, an 'off-hand' bout, involve a trophy and Goode will stake £50 to Robinson's £40 – *Sporting Life*.

30 April Johnny Robinson (South Shields) to any man in England, 138lbs up to 142lbs with or without gloves, £50 or £100 a side, Jim Berry (Marylebone, London) preferred – *Sporting Life*. This was repeated on 23 May.

1888
14 April Ben Seth (Lambeth) w pts 4 Dick Leary (Deptford), Royal Agricultural Hall, High Street, Islington, London. The final of Ben Hyams' 142lbs English championship competition, Seth weighed 138lbs to Leary's 141. In previous rounds, Seth beat Jim Mallett and George Wilson (Leicester), while Leary eliminated Jack Donovan and Ching Ghook.

29 August Ching Ghook (Shoreditch) is the 142lbs limit 'coloured' champion of England – *Sporting Life*.

4 September Jim Kendrick (Lambeth, born Ireland), real surname Enwright, has been fighting at 144lbs in the USA but is now in New York and challenges the world at 140lbs – The *Sportsman*.

30 October 'Paddy' Duffy (Boston, Mass) w co 17 Billy McMillan (billed from England), Fort Erie, Canada. Given billing for the world 142lbs limit title, it was later stated to have been for the 144lbs limit title. Reported variously as both lightweight and middleweight, the term welterweight also used, no individual weights were given.

December Ted Pritchard (Lambeth) w pts 4 'Veteran' Dave Burke (Bethnal Green), The Aquarium Theatre, Westminster, London. The final of an English 142lbs limit championship competition, in previous rounds Pritchard beat Dave Galvin and Dick Leary and Burke beat Ching Ghook and Alf Suffolk.

15 December Ted Pritchard challenges all England and the world at 144lbs over 12 rounds, £50 or £100 a side, or for endurance, and put down a £10 deposit. This challenge showed that Pritchard had moved into the 144lbs to 146lbs class and was unable to get down to the 140 to 142lbs limit class – *Sporting Life*.

1889
29 March 'Paddy' Duffy (Boston) w disq 45 Tom Meadows (Sydney, Australia), The California AC, San Francisco, USA. To a finish, Duffy weighed 139lbs, while Tom Meadows, stated to have been born in Liverpool, England, weighed 141½lbs. Advertised as being for the world 142lbs limit title, but not given world title billing in all reports, both the *Sportsman* and *San Francisco Chronicle* failing to report it as a title bout. Contested with small lace-up gloves, it was stated to be Meadows' first recorded loss and the final bout of Duffy's career.

12 June Lachie Thompson (Glasgow), real name Lachlan McTavish, to all England at 140 to 142lbs, Anthony Diamond (Birmingham) preferred, for a £50 purse and for endurance at The Pelican Club, London – *Sporting Life*.

5 December Mike Daly (Bangor, Maine) drew Jack McAuliffe (New York), Boston, Mass, USA. A catchweight affair with Daly weighing 138lbs and McAuliffe 141lbs, the latter having the best of it, McAuliffe had agreed to the bout being called a draw if he failed to stop Daly. Some reports give it American/world 141lbs title billing, without any basis.

1890
21 May George Baxter (Shoreditch) to the world, 140 up to 144lbs, Harry Nickless (The Borough) preferred – *Sporting Life*.

19 July The death is announced of 'Paddy' Duffy (Boston, Mass), the world 142lbs limit champion, aged 25, having passed away on 10 July.

1891
11 March Harry Nickless (The Borough) w rtd 6 Johnny Robinson (South Shields), The Ormonde Club, Walworth Road, Walworth, London. Although billed as an English 144lbs limit title for £100, both men came in under 142lbs. Nickless, who weighed 141lbs, also had a valid claim to the 140 to 142lbs limit title and later dropped down to win 138 to 140lbs limit title claims, both English and world. Robinson, also weighing 141lbs, was forced to retire with an injury, fracturing two small bones in his ankle.

24 April Charlie Kemmick (New York) w co 3 James Scully (Woon Socket, Rhode Island), Minneapolis, USA. Billed for the American 140 to 142lbs limit title, Kemmick weighed 141½lbs to Scully's 142lbs.

30 May Joe Wilson (Leicester) w co 4 Jack Ashman (Forest Hill), Her Majesty's Theatre, The Haymarket, Westminster, London. The final of a 142lbs limit English championship competition, in previous rounds Wilson beat Fred Callan and Alex Young, while Ashman defeated Fred Dorking and 'Barney' Lambert.

22 September William Robinson, alias 'Cock Robin', to all England at the 140lbs, give or take two pounds, to 142lbs limit – *Sporting Life*.

30 November Harry Nickless (The Borough) w co 9 Bill Hatcher (Islington), Bolingbroke Club, Clapham Junction, London. Although billed for the English 140 to 142lbs title, with both men under 140lbs, Nickless 137½lbs and Hatcher 140lbs, the former laid claim to the 138 to 140lbs limit title, which, in effect, made him champion at three weights - 138 to 140lbs, 140 to 142lbs and 142 to 144lbs. Regardless, he was given little credit by the critics, being just a 'hit or be hit' type of fighter with no boxing science at all.

1892

5 January A subscription 142 to 144lbs championship belt will be presented to Harry Nickless – *Sporting Life*.

11 February William Robinson (Homerton) w co 6 Frank Callan (Wood Green), The Goodwin Gym, Kingsland Road, Shoreditch, London. Refereed by Mr B.J.Angle, it was seen by some as being for the English 140 to 142lbs limit title, but not given as such in all reports in the sporting press, with no weights given. Articled for £25 a side and a £50 purse, a total of £100, and four-ounce gloves.

17 February William Robinson, 'Cock Robin', the English 142lbs limit champion, won the title when beating Frank Callan. This was repeated on 19 February, 3 April and 14 April – *Sporting Life*.

1 March Danny Needham (St Paul) w co 10 'Texas' Jack Burke, New Orleans, USA. Burke (136lbs) was a substitute for Tommy Ryan (New York) who was ill, the original bout, Needham (142lbs) versus Ryan, being billed for the American/world 142lbs limit title. Despite Burke, real name George Campbell, being drafted in, some reports still gave it title billing.

30 July Tommy Ryan (New York) w co 17 Jack Wilkes, Omaha, USA. Reported as being for the American/world 142lbs limit title, no weights were given, although both were reported as being 'just inside'.

26 September William Robinson (Hackney) w rtd 8 Alf Suffolk (Vauxhall), NSC, Covent Garden, London. Billed for the English 142 to 144lbs title, held by Robinson, with both men weighing 142lbs (2pm weigh in), £100 a side plus £100 purse (total £300) that belt was also at stake.

26 November 'Cock Robin' will defend his English 140 to 142lbs limit title against Dick Burge for £200, up to £500 a side, and an NSC purse – *Sporting Life*.

29 November Austin Gibbons (Patterson, NJ, born Liverpool) challenges 'Cock Robin', £100 a side and best purse, at the 142lbs limit, with a ringside weigh-in – *Sporting Life*.

1893

21 June J. Doran (USA) better known as 'Bart' Doran, the 142lbs welterweight champion of the west, killed his 10-month old son with morphine, then committed suicide by throwing himself in front of a moving train in Rochester, New York.

12 July Charlie Kemmick (St Paul), now battling consumption, is the former American 142lbs champion – *Sporting Life*.

24 July Jack Dempsey (Oregon, USA) to the world at the 140 to 142lbs limit, Dick Burge (England), Tom Williams (Australia), Tommy Ryan (Chicago) or 'Mysterious' Billy Smith (Oregon) preferred, $5,000 a side and best purse – *Sporting Life*. This was accepted by Dick Burge on 25 July, £1,000 a side and best purse – *Sporting Life*.

16 August Harry Neumier (Syracuse, New York, late of Bethnal Green, London) to Tom Williams (Australia), Harry Nickless (Battersea) or William Robinson (Hackney), the 'Cock Robin', 140 to 142lbs and £200 a side – *Sporting Life*.

22 August Dick Burge's backer stated, seeing that Jack Dempsey, real name John Kelly, had forfeited to Dick Burge, his man would meet 'Mysterious' Billy Smith instead with the same terms applying – *Sporting Life*.

12 September George Baxter (Shoreditch) to the world, 140 to 142lbs. In the same issue, the 1888 ABA lightweight champion, Andrew J. Newton (St Pancras), challenged the world at 140lbs and Baxter accepted this challenge on 13 September – *Sporting Life*.

5 October William Robinson (Hackney), the 'Cock Robin', accepted the challenge of Harry Neumier (Syracuse, New York, late of Bethnal Green) to a bout at 140 to 142lbs, £200 a side – *Sporting Life*.

1894

26 July Tommy Ryan (New York) w pts 20 'Mysterious' Billy Smith, Minneapolis, USA. Billed for the American/world 142lbs limit title, no weights were given.

11 October George Glover, 140lbs champion of Canada, challenges all England at 140lbs, William Robinson, the 'Cock Robin', preferred – *Sporting Life*. 'Cock Robin' accepted on 14 October at 140 to 142lbs – *Sporting Life*.

1895

21 January Dick Burge (Newcastle) w co 4 Tom Williams (Australia), NSC, Covent Garden, London. Refereed by Mr B.J.Angle and billed for the world 140 to 142lbs limit title (English title also carried in some reports, but Williams not eligible for same, only Imperial Empire/Commonwealth title), with both

men under 140lbs, which was also given as being the limit, Burge weighing 138lbs to Williams' 139¹/₂lbs, the 138 to 140lbs title could also have been at stake.

23 January Dick Burge challenges any man in the world at 140 to 142lbs, £100 or £200 a side, Tommy Ryan (USA) or Joe Walcott (USA, born Barbados) preferred – *Sporting Life*.

28 March Dick Burge, the world 140lbs champion, is now matched with Tommy Ryan (USA) for the world 140 to 142lbs title, for an NSC purse, on 25 November. Hopefully, the date is suitable to Ryan. This bout had come about with Ryan's 26 March challenge to Burge, with which Ryan had put down $500 deposit, but on the same date Joe Walcott, 'The Barbados Demon', had also put down a $500 deposit for bout with Burge on the same terms. Now it's up to Burge to which challenge he accepts – *Sporting Life*.

6 May Arthur Valentine (Lambeth) w pts 10 Charley Johnson (St Paul, Minnesota), The Central Hall, Holborn, London. Referee Jack Jones (Lambeth). Although it was contested at the 142lbs limit it was just a normal international bout, not being over a recognised title distance, with no weights given and no title billing. Johnson, real surname Palmer, in his English debut had boxed at 146lbs.

7 May Tommy Ryan (Syracuse) nc 18 'Mysterious' Billy Smith, Brooklyn, New York, USA. Stopped by the police, having been billed for the American/world 142lbs limit title, no weights were given. Earlier, the police had entered the ring in the 11th round, but let the contest continue.

23 August Charlie Kemmic (St Paul, Minnesota, USA), an ex-American 142lbs champion, died of consumption, aged 25.

1896

11 January The *Mirror of Life* publishes a list of the Australian champions, with Tom Tracey listed as the Australian 142lbs lightweight champion. Later, it was stated that this list was all wrong as it listed men who had long since departed Australia – Tracey, for instance, had left Australia in 1892 just after winning the title and never returned.

16 March Joe Walcott (New York) w co 7 'Bright Eyes' (Dallas, Texas), New York, USA. Billed as being for the American/ world 142lbs limit welterweight title, with both being negros it was also given 'coloured' title billing. No weights were given. 'Bright Eyes'' real name was Scott Collins.

14 October Joe Walcott (New York), the American negro, challenges Dick Burge at the 142lbs limit – *Sporting Life*.

16 October Pat Daly/Daley, the English 134lbs champion, to 'Ginger' Stewart (Battersea) at 142lbs. Stewart had challenged all at 144lbs – *Sporting Life*.

1 November The top class in the English lightweight division is the 140 to 142lbs class, while Dick Burge is champion of the 142 to 144lbs class which belongs to the bottom of the middleweight division – *Mirror of Life*. Note: In America this weight class was now called welterweight in most quarters.

11 December Joe Walcott (New York) drew 19 Tommy West (New York, born Cardiff), Marlborough AC, The Bicycle Academy, 53rd Street and Broadway, New York, USA. Refereed by Charlie White, this was a catchweight bout with no weights given, West coming in as a substitute after both Dick O'Brien and 'Mysterious' Billy Smith had refused to meet Walcott. The latter was twice 'saved by the bell', before the timekeeper got muddled up and the bout ended one round short, leaving the referee to call it a draw.

1897

8 March Bill Whatley (Camberwell, late Walworth) w co 4 Tom Williams (Aldershot, late Melbourne, Australia), NSC, Covent Garden, London. Referee B.J. Angle. Made at 142lbs, £50 a side and purse, with Whatley weighing 140lbs to Williams' 142lbs, there was no title billing as it was not over a championship course, being scheduled for just 10 rounds, and Whatley based his claim to the English 142lbs limit title on this win.

5 May Tom Williams (Aldershot, late Australia) to any man in the world at 142lbs – *Mirror of Life*.

31 May Tom Causer (Bermondsey) w disq 7 Dick Burge (Newcastle on Tyne), NSC, Covent Garden, London. Referee B.J.Angle. Billed as an English 142 to 144lbs limit lightweight title fight, £200 a side and £400 purse (total £800), Causer weighed 138lbs, but with Burge at 142lbs it must also be seen as involving any claim to the 140 to 142lbs limit title he had. Stated to be a fix on the part of Burge, in order to 'make a killing' on a proposed return bout, Causer was stated to have jumped up in order to make the punch go low. Causer

was billed as the English 132 to 134lbs limit lightweight champion.

2 October Pat Daly/Daley, the English 140lbs limit champion, to Tom Causer at the 142lbs limit, £200 a side and an NSC purse – *Sporting Life*.

29 October George 'Kid' Lavigne (Saginaw) w rtd 12 Joe Walcott (New York), San Francisco, USA. Walcott (140lbs) injured his leg early on, but carried on until the 12th round of a fight billed as being for the world/American 142lbs limit welterweight title. However, with neither men over 140lbs, Lavigne scaling 136lbs, it should also belong to the 138 to 140lbs list.

1898

12 August Jim Curran (Rotherham, England) w pts 20 Fred Casey (Brooklyn), New York, USA. No weights were given or stipulated and there was no title billing as such.

25 August 'Mysterious' Billy Smith w pts 25 Matty Matthews (New York City), The Lennox AC, New York City, USA. Referee Charley White. Made at the 142lbs limit and reported in some quarters as being for the American/world title, no weights were given, although it was announced that both men were just inside. Just nine days later, Smith boxed in a billed 145lbs limit title bout, while George 'Kid' Lavigne was recorded as being the American/world 142lbs limit champion.

21 September Pat Daly/Daley (Westminster, born Ireland) to the world at 136lbs up to 144lbs – *Sporting Life*.

3 October 'Mysterious' Billy Smith w co 20 Jim Judge, Scranton, Pennsylvania, USA. Reported as an American/world 145lbs limit title fight, 3pm weigh-in, no weights were given and both were announced as being inside.

7 October 'Mysterious' Billy Smith w pts 25 Charley McKeever (Philadelphia), New York City, USA. Made at the 142lbs limit although no weights were announced, there was no title billing given in the majority of reports, but the *Mirror of Life* gave it as being for the world 142lbs welterweight title. The paper went on to say that George 'Kid' Lavigne should be recognised as the 142lbs limit holder, with Smith holding down the 145lbs limit title. It seems possible that some of Smith's reported 142lbs bouts were misprints for 145lbs.

25 November George 'Kid' Lavigne (Saginaw) w pts 20 Tom Tracey (Australia), San Francisco, California, USA. Refereed by Jim McDonald, an umpire in the national baseball league, it was billed for the world 142lbs limit welterweight title, claimed by both Lavigne and Tracey. No weights were given.

1899

10 March 'Mysterious' Billy Smith w rsc 14 George 'Kid' Lavigne, San Francisco, USA. Billed for the world/American 142lbs limit welterweight title, Smith weighed 142lbs to Lavigne's 139.

30 June 'Mysterious' Billy Smith drew 20 Charley McKeever (Philadelphia), The Broadway AC, New York, USA. Refereed by John White and made at catchweights with no weights given or stipulated and no title billing, the *Sporting Life* reported that both men claimed to have weighed-in at 142lbs. However, both were undoubtedly heavier according to the American reports, so was it a 142lbs limit title bout, a 145lbs limit bout or, as largely claimed, a non-title catchweight bout?

28 October Charley Esmond to Pat Daly/Daley at 142lbs – *Sporting Life*.

1900

3 February Pat Daly/Daley to all England at 142lbs – *Sporting Life*.

13 February Harry Greenfield (Camden Town) to George Penny at 142lbs, £50 or £100 a side and best purse – *Sporting Life*.

17 April Matty Matthews (New York City) w co 19 'Mysterious' Billy Smith, New York City, USA. Billed for the American/world 142lbs limit title, no weights were given.

24 May Jim 'The Rube' Ferns w co 1 Jack Bennett (Billed as of Great Britain), Toronto, Canada. Billed as being an American/world 142lbs limit title fight.

17 August Owen Sweeney (Fulham) to Jack Everhardt (USA) or Pat Daly/Daley at 140lbs up to 144lbs and an NSC purse – *Sporting Life*.

30 August Jim 'The Rube' Ferns w pts 15 Matty Matthews (New York), Detroit, USA. Billed for the American/world 142lbs limit title, no weights were given.

20 November Pat Daly/Daley to Johnny Hughes (Canning Town) at 142lbs, 15 or 20 rounds, £100 up to £500 a side and an NSC purse, in defence of Daly's English 142lbs limit title. Daly went on to say, on 23 November, that he would box any man in the world at the 142lbs limit – *Sporting Life*.

1901

24 May Jim 'The Rube' Ferns w co 10 Matty Matthews (New York), Toronto, Canada. Billed for the American/world 142lbs limit title.

10 July Jack Grace (New York City) to all England at 140 to 142lbs, £100 a side – *Sporting Life*. This was accepted on 13 July by Pat Daly/Daley for the world 140 to 142lbs limit title. However, Grace returned to the USA on 20 July and the bout did not happen.

23 September Jim 'The Rube' Ferns w co 9 Frank Erne, Fort Erie, Canada. Advertised as being for the American/world 142lbs limit title, no weights were given and the *Sporting Life* report called Ferns the world 145lbs limit champion.

30 October 'Jewey' Cook (Hammersmith) to all England at 140 to 142lbs, £100 a side, 15 or 20 three minute rounds, Pat Daly/Daley preferred – *Sporting Life*. Daly accepted on 3 December – *Sporting Life*.

George 'Kid' Lavigne

31 October Pat Daly/Daley to all England, 138lbs up to 144lbs, £100 or £200 a side – *Sporting Life*. Later, on 8 November, the *Sporting Life* reported that Daly, the English 140lbs limit champion, challenged all England at 140 to 142lbs.

12 November Owen Sweeney (Fulham) to Pat Daly/Daley, 'Jewey' Cook and 'Philadelphia' Dave Barry, 140lbs up to 144lbs – *Sporting Life*.

23 November Harry Ward (Stepney) to all England at 142lbs – *Sporting Life*.

10 December Charlie Knock (Stratford) to all England, 140 to 144lbs, Pat Daly/Daley preferred – *Sporting Life*. This was repeated on 20 December.

18 December Joe Walcott (New York) w rsc 5 Jim 'The Rube' Ferns, Fort Erie, Canada. Reported as an American/world 142lbs limit title with no weights given.

1902

16 January In a list of world champions given by weight, not named divisions, the 142lbs limit champion was given as Joe Walcott (Boston), the Barbados-born negro.

17 May Eddie Connolly (Canada) to Pat Daly/Daley, 140lbs up to 146lbs – *Sporting Life*. This was accepted by Daly but when they fought it was at 144 to 146lbs.

22 July Veteran Bobby Dobbs (Kentucky), a negro, to all England from 136lbs up to 142lbs – *Sporting Life*.

1903

7 January Jim Maloney (Hackney) to Charlie Knock (Stratford) at the 142lbs limit – *Sporting Life*.

28 February Jack Nelson (local) w pts 20 Tom Ireland (Mile End), Ginnett's Circus, Newcastle on Tyne. Refereed by J.B.Emoult, Nelson scaled 141lbs to Ireland's 142$^{1}/_2$ in a contest at the 142lbs limit. Ireland was half a pound overweight and, as the custom of the day, had to pay forfeit, there being no time allowed to 'get to weight' as the time spent in training was considered to be all that was needed. There was no title billing and the purse was given as being £50.

1 April Joe Walcott (New York) drew 20 Billy Woods, Los Angeles, California, USA. Although reported in some papers as involving the world/American and 'coloured' 142lbs limit title, no weights were given, leaving some doubt as to the validity of those reports.

28 April Pat Daly/Daley to all England at 142lbs over 15 or 20 rounds, £100 a side and the best purse, Charlie Knock (Stratford) preferred – *Sporting Life*. This was repeated throughout year with variations.

28 May Martin Duffy (Chicago) w co 13 Jim 'The Rube' Ferns, Louisville, USA. Made at the 142lbs limit, despite a lack of weights it almost certainly involved the American/world 'white' title.

3 July Joe Walcott w co 3 Mose La Fontise, Butte, Montana, USA. Reported for the American/world 142lbs limit title, although no weights were given La Fontise was said to have made the weight.

31 August Martin Duffy (Chicago) drew 10 Gus Gardner (Philadelphia), Fort Huron, USA. Made at catchweights and over a non-title distance, while no weights given Duffy was reported to be over 14lbs heavier than Gardner.

1904

2 January Jack Blackburn (Philadelphia) w pts 12 Jimmy Gardner (Boston, born Ireland), Boston, Mass, USA. Billed as an American 142lbs limit title fight.

13 January Billy 'Honey' Mellody w pts 12 Matty Matthews (New York), Boston, Mass, USA. Billed as being for the 'white' world/American 142lbs limit title.

31 March Jack Clancy (San Francisco) challenges the world at 140lbs up to the 146lbs limit – *Sporting Life*.

22 April Billy 'Honey' Mellody w co 4 Martin Duffy, Chicago, USA. Mellody scaled 142lbs to Duffy's 147$^{1}/_2$lbs and although it was just a six-round catchweight contest, Duffy's claim at 142lbs evaporated on the result.

13 June Billy 'Honey' Mellody (Boston, Mass) drew 20 Jack O'Keefe, Butte, Montana, USA. Billed for the American/world 'white' 142lbs limit title, both men were inside but no actual weights were given.

18 June Bobby Dobbs (Kentucky) w pts 20 Peter Brown (Woolwich), Ginnett's Circus, Newcastle on Tyne. Referee Billy Bell. Although billed for the world 142lbs limit title, 1pm weigh-in, £50 a side and £100 purse (total £200), no weights were given and Brown was stated to be out of condition. It was also stated to have been at 142lbs, give or take two pounds,

to 144lbs, which seems more likely, Dobbs having claimed the title in both classes.

5 September Joe Walcott (New York) drew 15 Sam Langford (Boston, born Canada), Manchester, USA. Although stated to be for the American/world 'coloured' 142lbs limit title, no weights were given.

30 September Joe Walcott (New York) drew 20 Joe Gans (Baltimore), San Francisco, USA. Billed for the world/American 'coloured' 142lbs limit title, Walcott scaled 141lbs to Gans' 137.

October Joe Walcott accidentally shot himself through the right hand, killing his fellow boxer, Nelson Hall, and in November he announced his retirement due to this accident.

24 October Billy 'Honey' Mellody (Boston) w pts 10 Jack O'Keefe, Chicago, USA. Although advertised as being an American/world 'white' 142lbs limit title, it was not over a championship distance and no weights were given.

14 November William 'Buddy' Ryan (Chicago) w co 1 Billy 'Honey' Mellody, Chicago, USA. Although given American/world 142lbs limit 'white' title billing, it was not over a title distance and Ryan, who claimed the title on the result, was reported as being both 142 and 148lbs, depending on what papers you read.

8 December The veteran, Bobby Dobbs (Kentucky), challenges the world at 142lbs, £100 a side, with any one of the other so-called world 142lbs limit champions preferred, just to settle who is the true world 142lbs limit champion – *Sporting Life*.

Joe Walcott

9 December   Sam Langford (Boston, born Canada) drew 15 Jack Blackburn, Marlboro, USA. Reported as an American/world 'coloured' 142lbs limit title fight, while no weights were given both men were said to be inside and both preferred it to be called a draw if it went the distance.

1905

7 February   Jack Bayley (Birmingham) to all England at 140 to 142lbs, £100 or £200 a side, Jim Courtney (Barry) preferred – *Sporting Life*. This was accepted by Joe Smith (Canning Town, London) on 10 February.

13 February   Peter Brown (Woolwich) to all England at 142lbs and an NSC purse, Jack Goldswain preferred – *Sporting Life*.

13 February   Sam Langford (Boston, born Canada) drew 15 Dave Holly, Salem, Mass, USA. Billed for the world 'coloured' 142lbs limit title, Langford forfeited his title claim when coming in a pound overweight, thus giving Holly a claim to the title.

25 August   Jimmy Gardner w rtd 15 William 'Buddy' Ryan (Chicago), San Francisco, USA. Billed for the world/American 'white' 142lbs limit title, although no weights were given it was stated that both men were inside. On 4 July, Ryan had won a bout billed for the 144lbs limit title and on 19 July he had won a bout billed as being for the 145lbs limit title.

20 September   Sam Langford (Boston) drew 10 Jack Blackburn (Philadelphia), Allentown, Pennsylvania, USA. Advertised for the world 142lbs 'coloured' title, although not over a championship distance, both were stated to be inside the weight limit but no weights were given and there were doubts as to Langford's weight (limit also given as 138lbs, but was a certain misprint). Blackburn laid claim to the world 'coloured' 142lbs limit title after the result, as it was stated that Langford could no longer make 142lbs.

24 November   Mike 'Twin' Sullivan w pts 20 Jimmy Gardner, San Francisco, USA. Billed as an American/world 'white' 142lbs limit title fight, both were said to be inside, but no actual weights given. Also called a catchweights bout.

1906

19 January   Joe Gans (Baltimore) w co 15 Mike 'Twin' Sullivan, San Francisco, USA. Billed for the American/world 142lbs limit title, no weights were given.

17 March   Joe Gans w co 5 Mike 'Twin' Sullivan, Los Angeles, USA. Originally billed for the world 142lbs limit, but Sullivan was six pounds overweight.

19 July   Joe Walcott (New York) w co 8 Jack Dougherty, Chelsea, Mass, USA. Billed for the American/world 142lbs limit title.

26 September   Joe Walcott (New York) drew 20 Billy Rhodes, Kansas City, USA. Billed for the American/world 142lbs limit title, no weights were given.

29 November   Billy 'Honey' Mellody w rsc 12 Joe Walcott (New York), Chelsea, Mass, USA. Billed for the American/world 142lbs title, no weights were given.

1907

21 May   Jimmy Gardner w pts 10 Harry Lewis (New York), Denver, USA. Made at 142lbs, despite a lack of title billing and no weights being given, Gardner challenged the world at 142lbs and claimed the world/American 142lbs limit title.

23 October   'Young' Joseph (Aldgate) to all England at 140lbs, give or take two pounds – *Sporting Life*. Again reported on 30 October and deposit put down with *Sporting Life*. Repeated throughout the rest of the year.

1 November   Mike 'Twin' Sullivan (Cambridge, Mass) w pts 20 Frank Fields, Goldfield, Nevada, USA. No weights were given or stipulated and there was no title billing, but thought to involve the championship.

27 November   Mike 'Twin' Sullivan w co 13 'Kid' Farmer, Los Angeles, USA. Billed as an American/world 142lbs limit title fight, but also stated to be at catchweights, no weights were given.

1908

7 January   Jimmy Gardner (Boston, Mass) w pts 12 Joe Walcott (New York), Boston, Mass, USA. Originally billed for the world 142lbs limit title, but Walcott was overweight so it went on at catchweights, with no actual weights given. Gardner was billed as the 142lbs champion.

20 January   'Young' Joseph (Aldgate) w pts 20 Jack Goldswain (Bermondsey), Wonderland, Whitechapel Road, London. Refereed by J.T.Hulls, Goldswain (141½lbs) seemed over trained, with Joseph (142lbs) winning nearly every round. Reported to be at the 140 to 142lbs limit in the *Mirror of Life* and at 142 to 144lbs in the *Sporting Life*, £200 a side and £165 purse (total £565). Following this win, Joseph tried to claim the 138 to 140lbs limit title, but the *Mirror of Life* pointed out that the bout was not at the 138 to 140lbs limit,

which was the title held by Jack Goldswain, but at the 142lbs limit and also stated that it was over two-minute rounds instead of the three minutes required in a major title bout. Film of the bout was taken by the Warwick Trading Company and shown at Holborn Empire the following night. Wonderland was packed solid, with over 4,000 in attendance and more than 1,500 turned away.

23 January   Harry Lewis (New York) w co 3 Frank Mantell, New Haven, USA. Billed for the 142lbs limit world/American title, with both men stated to be inside the limit despite a lack of weight details, doubts were raised that Lewis, whose real name was Henry Besterman, could, in fact, ever make 142lbs.

23 April   Mike 'Twin' Sullivan (Cambridge, Mass) w pts 25 Jimmy Gardner (Boston), Los Angeles, USA. Reported to be for the American/world 142lbs title, Gardner scaled 141½lbs to Sullivan's 142. It was to be the last time Sullivan ever made this weight and he quickly went up to the 145lbs limit class.

27 April   Harry Lewis (New York) w co 3 Larry Conley, Augusta, USA. Made at 142lbs, it was just a normal no-decision bout over a non-title course, involving no titles.

11 May   Joe Fletcher (Camberwell) nc 17 Sam Harris (USA, born London), NSC, Covent Garden, London. Referee J.H. Douglas. Declared a no contest because neither man was trying, although Harris at least attempted to make a fight of it early on, Fletcher weighed 137½lbs, while Harris, 139½lbs, claimed to be unbeaten. Made at 140 to 142lbs, with both 'inside' 140 and Fletcher billed as the 138lbs champion of England, £100 a side and £75 purse (total £265), there was no actual title billing.

20 May   'Young' Joseph (Aldgate) is claiming to be the English 140 to 142lbs limit champion – *Sporting Life*.

19 October   'Young' Joseph (Aldgate) w pts 15 'Lance Corporal' A.Baker (Royal West Kent, Maidstone), NSC, Covent Garden, London. Refereed by Mr J.H.Douglas, the contest was made at 142lbs, Joseph weighing 140¾lbs and Baker 140lbs. The majority of the sporting press did not give it as a title bout, but it does get mentioned in certain papers and some old record books as being for the English 142lbs limit title.

7 November   Jimmy Gardner (Boston) w pts 15 Jimmy Clabby (Norwalk, Conn), New Orleans, USA. Made at 142lbs, Gardner weighing 142lbs and Clabby 138lbs, it was billed as being for the vacant American/world 142lbs limit title.

26 November   Jimmy Gardner (Boston) drew 20 Jimmy Clabby (Norwalk, Conn), New Orleans, USA. Made for the 142lbs American/world title with no weights given, Gardner gave up his claim to the 142lbs title when it was stated he was no longer able to get down to the weight, although the following year, 1909, he was again claiming the title.

1909

3 February   'Young' Joseph (Aldgate) offers to defend his English 140 to 142lbs limit title against Jack Goldswain (Bermondsey), the English 138 to 140lbs champion – *Sporting Life*. Although the Americans recognised the 142lbs weight class as being the welterweight limit and contested it as such right up to 1920, in Britain the weight class was included within the new 147lbs welterweight division following the announcement of named-weight divisions by the NSC on 11 February 1909. There was to be, however, one last major contest at the weight in Britain when, on 9 November 1911, the 'Dixie Kid' knocked out Johnny Summers (Canning Town, born Middlesbrough) inside two rounds at Liverpool Stadium in a contest billed for the world 142lbs title.

142lbs to 144lbs (10st 2lbs to 10st 4lbs)

1872

13 May   Charley Davis (Stepney) w pts 3 Denny Harrington (Shoreditch, born Co Cork, Ireland), Jemmy Shaw's, London. The final of a £10 silver English championship competition at 144lbs, this was reported as a 137lbs competition, but 144lbs is correct. Davis' first name was Michael, but he boxed as Charley.

1873

10 March   Charley Davis (Stepney and Mile End) is the 144lbs limit middleweight champion – *Sportsman*.

1880

December   Bat Mullins (134lbs) to the world at the 144lbs limit, £500 a side upwards and £250 to be posted to make sure of a match – *Sporting Life*.

1882

23 December   Charlie Mitchell (Birmingham) w pts 3 Dick Roberts (Clerkenwell), St George's Hall, Opposite Langham Hotel,

Regent Street, London. This was the final of Billy Madden's English heavyweight championship competition for a £40 trophy, with the two who reached the final being the two lightest men in this competition, both being under 144lbs, Mitchell scaling 143lbs to Roberts 142lbs. These two were put on the list after only 21 out of 32 entrants turned up, of which just three were genuine heavyweights and were little more than novice third-raters, with the ex amateur heavyweight champion, George Fyer (Northampton), being the best. The only true first-class men in this competition were all under 11 stone, the two above plus Jim Goode and Bill Springhall, being the genuine first class men and a few veterans thrown in for good measure. Starting on 21 December at Chelsea baths, in previous rounds Mitchell beat George Cox (21 December), Bill Springhall (22 December), J.Stubbins and W.Heal, alias 'Curly' (23 December), while Roberts, who sparred a bye (21 December), beat W.Shaw (22 December) and Pat Condon and Jim Goode (23 December), appeared to have beaten Mitchell in the final, but the latter was given the decision on the referee's 'casting vote'.

1883

23 January Bill Natty w pts 3 John Donogue, Bob Habbijam's West-End School of Arms, Newman Street, off Oxford Street, London. The final of an all-England 144lbs limit, £10 competition, in previous rounds Natty beat J.Handley and Jim Gleason, while Donogue eliminated Jack Natty and Bill Brazier.

29 May George Wilson (Leicester) w pts 3 Ching Ghook (Shoreditch), The Alexandra Rink, Nottingham. The final of an all-England 144lbs limit competition, the second and final day results of the first series were not given, just the names of the winners in the semi-finals held on 29 May. Wilson beat Will Atkins (Northampton), aged 43, while Ching Ghook beat Walter Pickard (Bradford).

26 November Jim Picton w pts 3 Ching Ghook (Shoreditch), The Blue Anchor, Church Lane, Shoreditch, London. The final of an all-England 144lbs limit, £10 championship competition, in previous rounds Picton beat Alec Roberts and J.McFarlane, while Ghook beat Arthur Cooper and Pat Condon.

1884

15 February Charlie 'Toff' Wall (Hackney) w pts 3 Tom Picton, The Blue Anchor, Church Lane, Shoreditch, London. The final of an all-England 144lbs limit, £10 championship competition, in previous rounds Wall beat Jack Donogue and Arthur Cooper and Picton, the brother of Jim, beat Alec Roberts and Ching Ghook.

29 February Arthur Cooper w pts 3 J.McFarlane, Bob Habbijam's West-End School of Arms, Newman Street, off Oxford Street, London. The final of an all-England 144lbs limit competition, in previous rounds Cooper beat Alec Roberts and Jack Donogue, while McFarlane defeated Jim Gleason and Tom Picton.

27 March Both Charlie 'Toff' Wall and Jim Picton have won English 144lbs limit championship competitions at The Blue Anchor, Church Lane, Shoreditch (stated to really be in Bethnal Green), London, staged by ex boxer, Tom Symonds – *Sporting Life*.

7 December Arthur Cooper w pts 3 Jim Picton, The Blue Anchor, Church Lane, Shoreditch, London. The final of an all-England 144lbs limit championship competition for £10, in previous rounds Cooper beat Jack Donogue and Ching Ghook, while Picton beat Bill Cheese and J.McFarlane.

1885

26 February Charlie 'Toff' Wall (Hackney) is the English 144lbs limit champion – *Sporting Life*.

23 May Johnny Robinson (South Shields) to Jim Barry (Marylebone, London) at 140lbs up to 144lbs, £50 or £100 a side. All Barry has to do is to put down a deposit – *Sporting Life*.

1886

21 January Charlie 'Toff' Wall (Hackney) w pts 3 Ted Burchell, The Blue Anchor, Church Lane, Shoreditch, London. The final of an all-England 144lbs limit championship competition, in previous rounds Wall beat 'Baby Jack' Partridge and Jack Donogue, while Burchell had a bye before beating Jim Picton.

6 May The death of Jim Barry (Marylebone), aged 25, is announced.

16 December Sam Baxter (Bethnal Green) w pts 3 Ted Burchell, The Blue Anchor, Church Lane, Shoreditch, London. The final of an all-England 144lbs limit championship competition for a £5 gold medal, in previous rounds Baxter (126lbs) had beaten Bill Hatcher and Jim Picton, while Burchell beat his brother, Jim Burchell, and Bill Cheese.

1887

19 January Sam Baxter (Shoreditch) w pts 3 Jim Burchell, The Blue Anchor, Church Lane, Shoreditch, London. The final of an all-England 144lbs limit middleweight competition, in previous rounds Baxter, the world 130lbs limit champion, beat Ching Ghook and Bill Cheese, while Burchell eliminated Harry Avis and Alf Kilbride (Leicester and Bradford).

31 March Anthony Diamond (Birmingham) w pts 10 Sam Baxter (Shoreditch), Mayfair, London. Postponed from 25 February, Diamond being injured in training, this was a catchweights bout with Diamond, the ex ABA champion at both lightweight and middleweight, being 14lbs heavier than Baxter, but with no actual weight being given. Billed for the English and world 144lbs limit championship it was the professional debut of the winner.

5 April Anthony Diamond (Birmingham) is the English 144lbs lightweight champion – *Sportsman*.

20 April 'Paddy' Duffy w rsc 7 Jack McGinley (New York), The Athenian Club, Boston, Mass, USA. Jack McGinley's surname believed to be McGinty. No weights or title billing was given in the *Sporting Life* report, which called it the greatest fight ever seen.

1 June Johnny Reagan (New York City) w co 44 John Files, near New York City, USA. Reagan weighed 146lbs according to the *New York Herald* and 144lbs according to the *New York World*, with Files at 144lbs. Billed as being an American/world 144lbs limit title fight, it was contested with skin-tight gloves under M of Q Rules.

21 July Arthur Bobbett (Fulham) w pts 12 Jim Kendrick (Chelsea, late Lambeth), School of Arms, Lambeth Walk, Paradise Street, Lambeth, London. Made at the 144lbs limit, although there was no actual title billing given in any reports seen, Bobbett (140lbs) laid claim to the English 144lbs limit title with this win over Kendrick (143lbs).

26 July Denny Kelliher w co 1 Jack McGee (Boston, born Londonderry, Ireland), Boston, Mass, USA. McGee was the only man to beat 'Paddy' Duffy (Boston). There were no weights given or stipulated and no title billing reported.

8 August Johnny Reagan (New York City) drew 39 Tom Henry (England). Contested five miles up the Hudson River, above New York City, USA, Reagan scaled 142lbs to Henry's 145lbs in a bout billed for the world 144 to 146lbs title under MoQ Rules, using hard gloves. It was also wrongly given as being for the 142 to 144lbs title, so has been put in both lists.

15 August Arthur Bobbett (Fulham) drew 13 Sam Baxter (Shoreditch), School of Arms, Lambeth Walk, Paradise Street, Lambeth, London. This was a 12-round bout at catchweights, with an extra round fought by mistake and Bobbett called the English 144lbs champion, but no weights given or stipulated and no title billing. However, his title claim could have been at stake if he was 144lbs or less.

26 November George Wilson (Leicester) w pts 3 Anthony Diamond (Birmingham), The Grand Circus, Peter Street, Manchester. The *Manchester Sporting Chronicle* stated this to be an English 144lbs limit championship competition with 15 guineas to the winner. In the final, Diamond looked to have won and the decision did not meet with full approval. In previous rounds, Wilson had a bye then beat Bill Cheese in the semi-final, while Diamond beat H.Daultry and drew a bye in the semi-final. Only four took part out of 10 who entered, Jim Kendrick (Lambeth) being overweight and the other five, M.Carnelly, Joe Firden and Joe Keaton (Manchester) and Ching Ghook and Alec Roberts (London) were all absent.

19 December Jim Kendrick (Lambeth, born Ireland), real surname Enwright, is the English 144lbs limit champion – *Sporting Life*.

1888

9 February 'Paddy' Duffy (Boston, Mass) w co 9 Jack McGinty, Boston, Mass, USA. No weights were given or stipulated and there was no title billing, but Duffy was claiming to be the American 144lbs limit champion.

2 May Jim Kendrick (Lambeth, born Ireland), the claimant of the English 144lbs limit title, left for the USA. Although stated to be a wreck of a man at this time, due to booze and other excesses, he was a well-educated, intelligent and nice man and a stonemason by trade.

11 July In a no-decision trial bout over four rounds, Jim Kendrick (England), making his USA debut, took on 'Paddy' Duffy (Boston), the American 144lbs champion, in Boston, Mass, USA. Kendrick, who was called the English 144lbs limit champion, had all the best of it.

27 July Jim Kendrick (England) drew 15 Jack McGee (Boston), Boston, Mass, USA. No weights were given or stipulated and there was no title billing in a contest using two-ounce gloves for a $500 purse. After 15 rounds both men agreed to carry on, but their offer was turned down. McGee, also given as McMagee, was the only man to have beaten 'Paddy' Duffy (19 December 1884) officially and had only lost once, while Kendrick had all the best of it in a no-decision four-round bout with Duffy.

1 August In the USA efforts are being made to match Jim Kendrick with Johnny Reagan, the American claimant to the world 144lbs limit title – *Sportsman*.

24 August Tom Meadows is the Australian 144lbs limit lightweight champion – *Sportsman*.

26 August Johnny Reagan (New York City) took on 'Paddy' Duffy (Boston, Mass) in a three-round exhibition contest in Brooklyn, New York, USA. Reagan was billed as the American 146lbs limit champion and Duffy as the 144lbs limit American champion.

4 September Jim Kendrick (Lambeth), now in New York, challenges the world at the 144lbs limit – *Sportsman*. Also misprinted as 140lbs.

October Jim Kendrick returned to England and taking into account that prior to his trip to the USA he was stated to be a wreck of a man, his performances there in two traced American bouts against two of the best men at their weight in America, was remarkable. It just shows what he could have achieved had he looked after himself and was the reason that an article in *Boxing* in 1924 called him best 140lbs man ever seen in Britain.

30 October 'Paddy' Duffy (Boston, Mass) w co 17 Billy McMillan, Fort Virginia, USA. Billed as of England, McMillan was from Liverpool and had set sail on 5 November 1887 when unable to get a match in his hometown. Given world 144lbs billing, 142lbs limit was also given, no weights reported.

15 December Ted Pritchard (Lambeth), born in South Wales but taken to Lambeth while still a youth, won a 142lbs limit championship competition on 8 December. In consequence, Pritchard challenges all England and the world at 144lbs limit (as no longer able to make 142lbs) over 12 rounds or for endurance, £50 or £100 a side.

1889

23 February Ted White (Clerkenwell) w pts 4 Andy Cannon (St Luke's), The Royal Aquarium Theatre, Westminster, London. The final of Frank Hinde's 144lbs limit world championship competition, the show had started six days previously, in previous rounds White beat J.Cashley ('Yorkey') of Leeds and Arthur Gutteridge, while Cannon beat Jim Adds and Bill Cheese.

9 March Johnny Robinson (South Shields), the English 144lbs limit champion and the holder of the English 144lbs championship belt which he won some five years ago, wants to know by what right Ted Pritchard or any one else has in claiming the title without first beating him for it – *Sporting Life*. Repeated on 18 March, the *Sporting Life* on 18 and 19 March called Pritchard the 145lbs limit English champion who challenges anyone breathing at the 147lbs limit. The championship belt competition Robinson had won on 16 April 1884 was for the 144lbs to 146lbs limit English championship, not the 144lbs limit title. However, Robinson was to write in this vein for over two years, never mentioning that his belt was at 144lbs to 146lbs.

16 March Sam Baxter (Shoreditch) w pts 4 Ted White (Clerkenwell), The Royal Agricultural Hall, Islington, London. The final of a 144lbs limit English championship competition, in previous rounds Baxter had beaten W.Gunn and Arthur Gutteridge, while White eliminated Bill Hatcher and Ching Ghook.

19 August Harry Nickless (The Borough, born Kew) w co 15 Alf Suffolk (Vauxhall), The South London School of Arms, Mountford Place, Kennington Road, London. A catchweight bout with no title billing saw Nickless scale 148lbs to Suffolk's 138. The *Sportsman* report stated that this was only the third bout of Nickless' career, but with this win he started claiming the English 144lbs limit title with no basis at all, unless his given weight of 148lbs was a misprint and was really 144.

26 September Harry Nickless (The Borough) is called the English 144lbs limit champion – *Sporting Life*.

31 October Harry Nickless (Lambeth and local) w rtd 15 Jim Townsend (St Luke's), The Hop and Malt Exchange, Kingshead Yard,

The High Street, The Borough, London. Refereed by Mr W.McNeff and advertised as being for the English 144lbs limit title, a £50 purse, four-ounce gloves and to a finish, Townsend was stated to be 'but a novice'.

30 November Anthony Diamond (Birmingham) challenges the world at 144lbs, £50 or £100 a side with any size gloves. If no one accepts, a sportsman will put up a £50 purse for a bout with Lachie Thompson (Glasgow) – *Sporting Life*.

14 December Harry Nickless (The Borough) is the English 144lbs limit champion – *Sporting Life*.

14 December Alf Suffolk (Vauxhall) w pts 4 Bill Cheese (Hoxton), Saddlers Wells Theatre, St John Street, Clerkenwell (also stated to be Islington), London. The final bout of a six-night show and the final of an English 144lbs limit championship competition, in previous rounds Suffolk beat Jim Sullivan and Lachie Thompson, while Cheese, 'The Bit of Gorgonzola', defeated Andy Cannon and Ned McGrath.

20 December Anthony Diamond (Birmingham) is the English 144lbs champion – *Sportsman*.

1890

20 January Harry Nickless (The Borough) w co 13 Alf Suffolk (Lambeth, late Vauxhall), The South London AC, Kennington Green, London. Referee A.J.McNeil. Scheduled to a finish, with Nickless scaling 144lbs and Suffolk 143lbs, and billed for the English 144lbs limit title. Because it was also given as being for the 145lbs limit title (almost certainly a misprint), I have also included the contest in the 144 to 146lbs list.

1 February Harry Nickless is the English 144lbs champion – *Sportsman*. This was repeated throughout the year.

12 March Harry Neumier (Bethnal Green) to Harry Nickless for the English 144lbs limit title – *Sporting Life*.

22 March Harry Nickless, the English 144lbs limit champion, to the world at the 144lbs limit for the world title at this weight – *Sporting Life*.

25 March Ching Ghook and Felix Scott (Liverpool) to meet for the English 'coloured' 144lbs middleweight title – *Sporting Life*. In the same issue, it is stated that Tom Meadows is the Australian 144lbs limit lightweight champion.

28 March Ted Pleydell (Cardiff) challenges Harry Nickless for the 144lbs limit English title – *Sporting Life*.

29 March The *Sporting Life* calls Harry Nickless the self-styled English 144lbs limit champion.

7 April Jim Kendrick (Lambeth) challenges all at 144lbs and is accepted on 8 April by William Robinson (Hackney), alias 'Cock Robin', at 144lbs – *Sporting Life*. Robinson also challenged any man at 144lbs and is accepted on 10 April by Alf Suffolk (Lambeth and Vauxhall).

19 May Frank Howson (Sheffield) w co 2 'Young' Crookes (Sheffield), The Circus, Tudor Street, Sheffield. No weights were given or stipulated and no title billing was reported.

21 May George Baxter (Shoreditch) to anyone between 140 to 144lbs, Harry Nickless preferred – *Sporting Life*.

30 May Lachie Thompson (Glasgow) w rsc 2 Alf Hanlon (local), The Grand Circus, Peter Street, Manchester. Made at 144lbs, with both men weighing 144lbs, £25 a side and £50 purse, there was no title billing, although Thompson at later dates was making claims on the title on strength of this win. The police stepped in and stopped the bout in the second round as it was getting too rough and referee awarded bout to Thompson, who had all the best of it up to the intervention.

9 June Harry Nickless, the English 144lbs limit champion, to the world at 144lbs, Tom Meadows, the Australian 144lbs champion, preferred – *Sporting Life*. World title challenges were repeated throughout the year.

17 June Jim Adds (Balls Pond Road) challenges Harry Nickless at the 144lbs limit, for endurance and English title at the weight and is accepted a day later – *Sporting Life*.

2 July Alec Roberts, called the English 144lbs champion, challenges the world at 144lbs no one barred – *Sporting Life*. Roberts reportedly put money down with the *Sporting Life*, but the challenge was never taken up. This is one of several misprints in regards to Roberts, who never won any championship belts or competitions under 147, but kept getting in his challenges, normally made at 148lbs, but sometimes at either 140 or 144lbs, even after he had retired. Was also often referred to as being either the ex-140lbs or ex-144lbs champion, instead of an ex-147 or 148lbs champion, which he was.

4 July Jim Kendrick (Lambeth, born Ireland), who has put down a deposit, challenges the world at 142 to 144lbs, no one barred – *Sporting Life*.

23 July   Jim Adds (Balls Pond Road) challenges the world at the 144lbs limit and is accepted by Harry Nickless – *Sporting Life*. Five days later, Adds failed to turn up at the *Sporting Life* office to sign for the 144lbs title match with Harry Nickless, but the latter left a £10 deposit for Adds to cover if he still wanted the match.

30 July   Tom Mallett (Holloway) accepts the challenge of Jim Adds to the world at 144lbs, £50 a side, any style – *Sporting Life*.

5 September   Jim Connelly (Bethnal Green) to all England at 144lbs – *Sportsman*.

9 September   William Robinson (Hackney and Homerton), alias 'Cock Robin', accepts the challenge of Harry Nickless to all at 144lbs – *Sporting Life*.

13 September Harry Neumier (Bethnal Green) to any man at 144lbs, George Baxter (Shoreditch) preferred – *Sporting Life*.

19 September Felix Scott (Liverpool), a negro, to all England at 144lbs, Jim Haines, also coloured and not to be confused with Jim Haynes/Haines of Marylebone, and A.Whiteman preferred – *Sporting Life*.

20 September Anthony Diamond (Birmingham) is the 144lbs champion of England, while Harry Nickless is only the 144lbs champion of London – *Sporting Life*.

17 October   Dick Burge (Newcastle on Tyne) to Anthony Diamond for the English 144lbs title – *Sporting Life*.

7 November   Jim Townsend (St Luke's) accepts another one of the repeated challenges of Harry Nickless to the world at 144lbs – *Sporting Life*.

13 November Anthony Diamond is the world 144lbs champion. – *Sporting Life*. On 25 November, the *Sporting Life* was to say he was the world 150lbs champion and in their 24 November edition it mentions that he was to challenge Dick Burge at 146lbs.

18 November The *Sporting Life* carried a false challenge purporting to come from Dick Burge, which Burge strongly denied in the 21 November edition of the *Sporting Life*.

21 November Lachie Thompson (Glasgow) challenges anybody in London at 144lbs, Harry Nickless preferred, and puts a £10 deposit down. He is accepted on 22 November by Johnny Robinson (South Shields) – *Sporting Life*.

24 November Lachie Thompson and Johnny Robinson are now matched for the English 144lbs title – *Sporting Life*.

5 December   Harry Nickless, the 144lbs champion, has now gained a second victory over Jack Bennett (Warwick) – *Sporting Life*. However, no bouts versus Jack Bennett (Warwick) have yet been traced for Harry Nickless.

1891

11 March   Harry Nickless (The Borough) w rtd 6 Johnny Robinson (South Shields), The Ormonde Club, Walworth Road, London. Billed as being for the English 144lbs limit title, which Robinson claimed to have won on 16 April 1884 (despite it being a 144 to 146lbs championship bout competition he had won), Nickless weighed 141lbs. No weight was given for Robinson, who was forced to retire due to an injury, having broken two small bones in his ankle.

11 April   Harry Nickless is the 144lbs limit champion. This is repeated on 23 June and 2 July, but soon after he was to drop down to 140 to 142lbs, then to 138 to 140lbs, thus foresaking the 142 to 144lbs class – *Sporting Life*.

9 August   Tommy Ryan (Syracuse) w co 3 Billy McMillan, Richardson, Illinois, USA. With no weights given it was billed for the world/American 144lbs limit title, with McMillan billed as of the USA, late England.

3 December   Lachie Thompson (Glasgow) accepts the challenge of Dick Burge to bout at 144lbs, two-ounce gloves and £200 up to £500 a side – *Sporting Life*.

13 December Tommy Ryan (Syracuse) w co 14 Frank Howson (Sheffield, England), near Chicago (in the morning), USA. Refereed by George Siler and billed as being for the world 144lbs limit title, $1,000 a side, Ryan was unmarked while Howson was badly marked up with one eye closed and his cheek cut open. The bout took place in the early hours of the morning and was reported in *New York Herald* of the same day.

1892

16 February Harry Nickless is still the English 144lbs limit champion. This was repeated on 27 February and 23 March, but after that Nickless seems to have dropped his 144lbs limit English title in favour of a 140lbs limit world and English title claim – *Sporting Life*.

30 April   Alf Suffolk (Vauxhall) to William Robinson, the 'Cock Robin', the 140 to 142lbs champion, at the 144lbs limit, four-ounce gloves and £500 or £100 a side. – *Sporting Life*.

2 May   Tom Williams (Australia) w co 1 Bill Hatcher (Islington), NSC, Covent Garden, London. Refereed by Mr T.Anderson and made at 143 to 144lbs (occasionally reported as being at 143 give or take a pound), both men weighed 142lbs. There was no actual title billing, but it had a bearing on the Commonwealth-Imperial Empire 144lbs limit title claim of Williams following his victory, despite the 32-year-old Hatcher not being the English champion. With neither being over 142lbs, the contest has also been put in the 140 to 142lbs class.

7 May   William Robinson, the 'Cock Robin', to anyone at 142 to 144lbs – *Sporting Life*. In the same issue, Andy Cannon (St Luke's) challenged all England from 136 to 144lbs.

27 June   Dick Burge (Newcastle on Tyne) w co 2 Lachie Thompson (Glasgow), The Kensington Social Club, London. Open to club members only, there was an attendance of 200. Referee George Vize. Not actually billed for the English 144 to 146lbs title, being made at 144 give or take two pounds, but Burge later claimed it on account of the above win. The *Sporting Life* gave the weights as Burge 137lbs and Thompson 144lbs, the *Sportsman* gave Burge 138lbs and Thompson 145lbs, while the *Licensed Victuallers Gazette* reported Burge to be 138lbs to Thompson's 144lbs, as did the *Newcastle Daily Chronicle*. On the following day, 28 June, Thompson challenged Burge to a return at 146lbs limit. This was also given as being at the 144lbs limit, so which is correct is anyone's choice.

26 September William Robinson (Hackney) w rtd 8 Alf Suffolk (Vauxhall), NSC, Covent Garden, London. Recognised as being for the English 142 to 144lbs title, made at 142, give or take two pounds, with both men weighing 142lbs it could also have involved the 140 to 142lbs limit title, which 'Cock Robin' was stated to hold.

27 September Tom Burrows (Australia), the world champion sculler and trainer to Tom Phillips, challenges 'Cock Robin' at the 144lbs limit, £100 a side – *Sporting Life*.

3 November George Dawson, the Australian 144lbs limit champion, is now in the USA – *Sporting Life*.

5 December   William Robinson (Homerton) w co 3 Tom Burrows (Australia), NSC, Covent Garden, London. With both men weighing 143lbs, it was Burrows' ring debut. Made at the 144lbs limit, £100 a side and £50 purse (total £250), there was no title billing and the bout was heavily criticised. The *Sporting Life* reported that a championship claimant against a raw novice should never have been allowed to happen, especially at, of all places, the NSC. Following this bout, on the next day, 'Cock Robin' was challenged by Tom Williams (Melbourne, Australia), who Burrows trained, for £50 with a £100 bet that Williams would stop his man inside eight rounds of a bout to be held in private on Saturday 10 December. On same day, 6 December, 'Cock Robin' was also challenged by Dick Burge, who stated that he would postpone his 10 December departure to USA in order to meet 'Cock Robin', who was due to get married over the Christmas period, but the bout had to be at catchweights. 'Cock Robin', who in his private life had a reputation as a 'bully boy', had certainly done himself no favours by his decisive beating of the very popular Tom Burrows who, although a world champion in his own sport, had never appeared in a boxing ring before, outside of exhibitions and sparring sessions. The NSC was also blamed for allowing Robinson versus Burrows to take place.

14 December 'Mysterious' Billy Smith w co 14 Danny Needham, San Francisco, USA. With Smith scaling 142lbs to Needham's 143, the fight was given some credence as being for the world/American 144lbs limit title, although not in the majority of reports.

1893

4 January   William Robinson (Homerton), the 'Cock Robin', is the English 144lbs limit champion – *Sporting Life*. This was repeated in the 22 August issue of the *Sporting Life*, before the 30 August issue claimed it to be the 146lbs limit title that was in question.

11 January The 'Cock Robin' has now taken over the gym attached to The Jolly Anglers' pub at Lea Bridge, London, where he will run public and private boxing from 14 January onwards – *Sporting Life*.

8 February   Alf James to all England at 144lbs – *Sporting Life*.

12 February Lachie Thompson (Glasgow) to 'Cock Robin' at 144lbs, £200 a side – *Sporting Life*.

20 February William Robinson w rsc 10 Jim Townsend (St Luke's), NSC,

Covent Garden, London. Refereed by Mr B.J.Angle, the bout was made at 144lbs and originally billed as being for the English 144lbs limit title. However, Townsend came in six pounds overweight, claiming to have been unwell over the last three days of his training, and 'Cock Robin' (143lbs) raised no objections to the bout going on at catchweights. The fight went ahead and, after eight rounds of just light sparring, the referee warned both men that if they did not try harder a no-contest would be declared. In the ninth, Townsend was put down twice and saved by the bell and in the 10th Robinson slipped down before Townsend went down three times 'very suspiciously' and the referee, Mr Angle, stopped the bout. It was doubtful if Townsend would ever be allowed to box at the NSC again as his display had disgusted everyone.

23 February Bill Cheese (Hoxton) to 'Cock Robin' at the 144lbs limit, £50 or £100 a side. This was repeated on 28 February – *Sporting Life*.

28 February Lachie Thompson (Glasgow) to the three claimants of the English 144lbs limit title, Dick Burge, 'Cock Robin' and Harry Nickless, or anyone else in England at 144lbs – *Sporting Life*. In the same issue, 'Cock Robin' challenged Dick Burge at the 144lbs limit, £200 a side.

6 March Articles have been signed for a 25 April bout at the NSC between Harry Nickless and Lachie Thompson at the 144lbs limit. However, on 17 April, Thompson forfeited the £200 deposit already put down to Nickless.

3 May Harry Nickless is again claiming to be the English 144lbs limit champion – *Sporting Life*.

17 May Tom Williams (Australia) to William Robinson, the 'Cock Robin', at the 144lbs limit for an NSC purse – *Sporting Life*.

9 September Anthony Diamond (Birmingham) to William Robinson, the 'Cock Robin', £100 a side – *Sporting Life*.

20 September Tom Williams (Australia) to William Robinson, the 'Cock Robin', at 144lbs – *Sporting Life*.

11 December William Robinson (Hackney) drew 20 Tom Williams (Australia), NSC, Covent Garden, London. Refereed by Mr B.J.Angle and made at 144 to 146lbs, as the men came in at 144lbs this contest is included in both lists. There was no title billing given. Articled for £100 a side and a £100 purse (total £300), Williams fractured his left arm in the fourth round but continued.

1894

7 March William Robinson, the 'Cock Robin', is the English 144lbs champion – *Sporting Life*.

20 October 'Ginger' Stewart (Battersea) walked over Charlie Rowles (Wood Green), who had to withdraw with a sprained ankle from the final of Frank Hinde's English 144lbs championship competition at the Central Hall, Holborn, London. Referee J.T. Hulls. Spread over seven days, in previous rounds Stewart beat Jack Fitzgibbons and had a bye, while Rowles beat Bill Dorton and George Baxter.

Dick Burge pictured in British Army uniform at a later date

14 November Dick Burge, the world 144lbs limit champion, challenges the world at 142 to 144lbs, £100 a side – *Sporting Life*. This was repeated on 28 November in the *Sporting Life*, but on 30 November, just two days later, in the same paper, Burge was calling himself world 140lbs limit champion and challenging Tom Williams (Australia) at that weight (unless a misprint).

17 November Jack Fitzgibbons (St George's) w pts 4 Harry Harrison (Tottenham), Central Hall, Holborn, London. This was the final day of a seven-day show and the final of Frank Hinde's 144lbs limit English championship competition. In previous rounds, Fitzgibbons had a bye then beat Owen Sweeney, while Harrison eliminated Walter Gunn and Ted Dorkings.

26 December Harry Neumier (New York, late of Stepney and Bethnal Green) to all England at the 144lbs limit – *Sporting Life*.

1895

16 January Harry Neumier (New York late London, England) is the 144lbs limit champion – *Sporting Life*.

18 January Tommy Ryan (Syracuse) w rsc 3 'Nonpareil' Jack Dempsey (New York), Coney Island, Brooklyn, New York, USA. With Ryan weighing 144lbs to Dempsey's 142lbs, this one was given billing as an American/world 144lbs limit title. However, Dempsey was a very sick man and should not have been allowed to box.

24 January Tommy Ryan (USA) to Dick Burge at 142lbs, give or take two pounds, for the 144lbs limit world welterweight title. Ryan repeated the challenge, this time to Harry Nickless, on 29 January – *Sporting Life*. Nickless accepted in the 4 February issue of the *Sporting Life* but had, in fact, fought the final bout of his career in May 1894.

1 February 'Ginger' Stewart (Battersea) w co 4 George Haskell, Central Hall, Holborn, London. The sixth and final night of a Frank Hinde's 144lbs English championship competition, in previous rounds Stewart beat George Baxter and Harry Harrison, while Haskell beat Alf Jackson and Jack Philo.

11 February It has been reported that 'Nonpareil' Jack Dempsey (USA), who is seriously ill and has been pronounced insane, will be put into an insane asylum. Dempsey had fought Tommy Ryan on 18 January – *Sporting Life*.

29 March Lachie Thompson to the world at 144lbs – *Sporting Life*.

6 April William Robinson, the 'Cock Robin', is the English 144lbs champion – *Sporting Life*. Strangely, in the same issue, he is called the ex-English 144lbs champion.

6 April 'Ginger' Stewart (Battersea) w rtd 2 Harry Collins (Billingsgate), The Central Hall, Holborn, London. Refereed by Mr E.Weeks and Mr Wallis, this was the sixth and final night of a Frank Hinde's English 144lbs limit championship competition. In previous rounds, Stewart had beaten Jim Richardson and George Haskell, while Collins had eliminated Bill Gray and Fred Greenbank.

29 April William Robinson (Hackney), the 'Cock Robin', is still the English 144lbs limit champion – *Sporting Life*.

27 May Tommy Ryan drew 18 'Mysterious' Billy Smith, The Seaside AC, Coney Island, New York, USA. Refereed by Mr Hurst, a no-contest result was also given due to it being stopped by the police and was stated to be the greatest bout ever seen. Given billing as a world 142 to 144lbs title bout, 140 to 142lbs was also given, and the *Mirror of Life* insisted it was at catchweights.

21 September Bill Cheese (Hoxton) to all England at 142 to 144lbs – *Sporting Life*.

2 November In the USA, the death of 'Nonpareil' Jack Dempsey, real name John Kelly, from tuberculosis, in Portland, Oregon, aged 32, is announced.

1896

24 January Harry Nickless (The Borough and Battersea), the ex-English 144lbs champion, announced his retirement from boxing due to an injury to the left eye – *Sporting Life*. Nickless had not fought since 4 May 1894, when losing to Dick Burge. On 15 August, the *Sporting Life* stated him to now be blind in his left eye, with his sight impaired in the right eye.

29 February Andrew J.Newton, the ex-ABA lightweight champion, challenges all England at 144lbs – *Sporting Life*.

24 July Alf Suffolk (Vauxhall) is the ex-English 144lbs champion – *Sporting Life*.

17 August 'Ginger' Stewart (Battersea) to any 144lb man in England or America – *Sporting Life*.

7 October Dick Burge is the world 144lbs limit champion – *Sporting Life*. This was repeated on 7 November and in the 4 December issue of the *Sporting Life* he challenged the world at 144lbs, £500 up to £1,000 a side.

1897

28 January   Dick Burge (Newcastle on Tyne) drew 10 Eddie Connolly (Canada), The Olympic Club, Berwick Street, Birmingham. Refereed by George T.Dunning, of the *Sportsman*, and made at catchweights, despite it being billed as for the world 144lbs limit title for £100, the terms of the articles stated that if Burge paid a £100 forfeit he could come in at any weight over 146lbs. The fight saw Burge (144lbs) well on top, having had Connolly (137lbs) down several times. Connolly was saved by the bell in the sixth, although several people, Burge included, claimed that the Canadian was counted out in the 10th round, before the bout was stopped by Dunning on the orders of the Olympic Club management, the Barnes brothers, both late of the USA, and a draw declared.

17 February   Pat Daly/Daley (Westminster, born Ireland) to the world at 142 to 144lbs for the world title, £200 up to £500 a side, Dick Burge or Eddie Connolly preferred – *Sporting Life*.

8 March   'Kid' McPartland (New York City) w rsc 13 Sam Tonkins (New York), The American SC, New York, USA. Made at 144lbs, but with a lack of weights and no title billing. McPartland's real name was William Lawrence.

10 March   Dick Burge is the 144lbs champion – *Sporting Life*.

17 March   Tom Causer (Bermondsey) challenges Dick Burge at 144lbs, £200 up to £500 a side and an NSC purse, with Causer's backer putting down a £100 deposit – *Sporting Life*.

31 May   Tom Causer (Bermondsey) w disq 7 Dick Burge (Newcastle on Tyne), NSC, Covent Garden, London. Billed as being for the English 144lbs limit title, £200 a side and a £400 purse (total £800), Causer (138lbs) was reported as the 134lbs English champion, with Burge (142lbs) shown as the holder of the title contested (English 144lbs limit). Interestingly, with neither over 142lbs a case could have been made for the 140 to 142lbs limit title being involved, but it wasn't. The bout itself was stated to have been a blatant fix on the part of Burge in order to make a killing on a return bout, Causer stated to have jumped up, causing the blow to go low.

4 June   Pat Daly/Daley (Westminster, born Co. Cork) to Tom Causer at 144lbs, £200 a side and an NSC purse. – *Sporting Life*. In the same issue, Patsy McCoy challenged any one of the many 144lbs champions of England.

21 June   Tommy Ryan (Syracuse) w co 2 Tom Williams (Australia), The Empire AC, Syracuse, New York, USA. Billed as a world 144lbs limit title fight, but no weights were given.

23 July   Jim Styles (Marylebone) to all at 144lbs – *Sporting Life*.

8 October   Dick Burge (Newcastle on Tyne) w co 1 Tom Causer (Bermondsey), The Bolingbrooke Club, Walworth, London. With the referee, Bob Watson, inside the ring as always, the bout was won in 61 seconds. Given English and world 144lbs limit title billing, but no weights were given.

25 October   Pat 'Paddy' Purtell (USA) stated he could not make 144lbs – *Sporting Life*.

1898

5 January   According to the *Mirror of Life*, Dick Burge once again announced his retirement from boxing, yet in the 10 and 14 March issues of the *Sporting Life* Burge was called the world 144lbs limit lightweight champion. This was repeated on 6 April in the *Mirror of Life*.

21 September   Pat Daly/Daley (Westminster, born Ireland) to the world at 136 up to 144lbs – *Mirror of Life*.

1 October   Patsy Donovan (South Africa) to all England at 144lbs – *Sporting Life*.

12 December   Bobby Dobbs (Kentucky, USA) w rtd 8 Dick Burge (local), The Peoples Palace, Newcastle on Tyne. Referee George T.Dunning of the *Sportsman*. Billed as involving the world 144lbs limit lightweight title and £850, Burge, aged 32, had fixed the fight for him to win on a foul. However, when he went down claiming a foul and that he couldn't go on, Dunning, an honest man, awarded the bout to Dobbs, a negro aged 39, on the retirement of Burge, who was billed as the title holder.

1899

2 January   Matty Matthews (New York) drew 20 Owen Zeigler, The Greenwood AC, Brooklyn, New York, USA. No weights were given or stipulated and no title billing was reported.

24 January   The *Sporting Life* called Dick Burge the world 144lbs limit champion and did so throughout the year, but, of course, he wasn't, having lost his claim on 12 December 1898.

25 January   Jim Holloway (Pretoria, South Africa), the South African 144lbs limit lightweight champion, came to England in order to get a bout with either Dick Burge or Bobby Dobbs for the world 144lbs limit title, but finding no chance of getting a bout with either he settled for one against 'Jewey' Cooke (Hammersmith and Bloomsbury), who was a trifle removed from the top class – *Sporting Life*.

22 February   Bobby Dobbs (Kentucky) no contest 1 Joe McDonald (Glasgow), The Wellington Palace, Glasgow. Billed as being a world 144lbs title fight, which was a bit ludicrous seeing that McDonald was a novice having only his second bout. In any case, McDonald should have been disqualified earlier on when knocked out of the ring and being helped back in again, before the police then entered the ring to stop the bout as it was too fierce, arresting both men on charge of assault. A drawn verdict was later given as agreed on. No weights were announced.

1 March   Bobby Dobbs (Kentucky) w co 2 Joe McDonald (Glasgow), The Standard Theatre, Gateshead. Referee George T.Dunning of the *Sportsman*. Billed as for the world 144lbs limit title claimed by Dobbs, aged 40. With no weights given, any credence Dobbs' title claims may have had were not improved with bouts against the likes of the novice, McDonald, who could state that he had fought twice for the world title in one week, having had only three bouts!

18 March   Bobby Dobbs (Kentucky) is the world 144lbs limit lightweight champion – *Sporting Life*. This was reported throughout the year.

10 July   Pat Daly/Daley (London, born Ireland) to the world at 144lbs, £100 a side, Bobby Dobbs preferred – *Sporting Life*. Although this was reported at regular intervals, Daly stated in the 15 September issue of the *Sporting Life* that he couldn't get under 144lbs.

14 September   Matty Matthews (New York) w disq 25 Bobby Dobbs (Kentucky), Coney Island AC, New York, USA. No weights given or stipulated and no title billing, but if at 144lbs or under it would obviously have involved Dobbs' title claim, but if over 144lbs then Dobbs would still have a title claim.

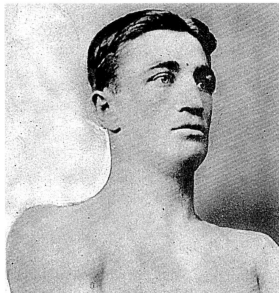

Matty Matthews

6 October   Jim 'The Rube' Ferns (Pittsburg) w pts 20 Bobby Dobbs (Kentucky), The Hawthorne AC, Buffalo, New York, USA. No weights given or stipulated and no title billing, but both men thought to be inside 144lbs.

7 November   Harry Webster (Kentish Town) to all England at 144lbs, Pat Daly/Daley preferred – *Sporting Life*.

14 November   Dick Burge, surprised at Pat Daly/Daley not turning up to make a match but instead taking on an easier task in Harry Webster, is still willing to box Daly, £500 a side upwards – *Sporting Life*.

17 November   Pat Daly/Daley to all England at 144lbs, £200 up to £500 a side – *Sporting Life*. This was again reported on 22 November.

20 November Bobby Dobbs (Kentucky) w disq 18 Ed (Jim also given) Darrell (Australia), The Hercules AC, Brooklyn, New York, USA. Both men were thought to be inside 144lbs, but no weights were given or stipulated and there was no title billing. Dobbs was down in 17th and seemed very lucky to win, after Darrell, a substitute for Jim Ferris who didn't turn up, was disqualified when his seconds entered the ring.

5 December Joe Walcott (New York, born Barbados) w co 6 Bobby Dobbs (Kentucky), Broadway AC, New York, USA. No weights were given or stipulated and there was no title billing reported in an all-negro battle that was thought to involve a 144lbs claim.

6 December Pat Daly/Daley challenges Dick Burge for the English 144lbs limit championship, £200 a side and an NSC purse, and looks to meet the latter on 7 December at the NSC to make the bout – *Sporting Life*.

1900

13 July Jack Everhardt (New Orleans), who is in the UK, challenges all England at 144lbs, £200 a side and an NSC purse, Dick Burge preferred – *Sporting Life*. The challenge was accepted on 17 July in the *Sporting Life* by Pat Daly/Daley.

11 August Pat Daly/Daley challenges all England at 144lbs, £100 a side, and offers Jack Everhardt (New Orleans) the same terms, but Daly had already arranged to be at the *Sporting Life* office on this same day (11 August) to sign for a bout with Everhardt, for the world 144lbs limit title, to take place in October. However, although Everhardt turned up, Daly didn't – *Sporting Life*.

17 August Owen Sweeney (Fulham) to Jack Everhardt (USA) or Pat Daly/Daley at 140 to 144lbs and an NSC purse. In the same issue, Billy Morgan (Swansea), the Welsh 144lbs champion, challenged all England at 144lbs limit, £50 up to £100 a side – *Sporting Life*.

24 August Tom Woodley (Fulham) to Pat Daly/Daley, Billy Morgan (Swansea) and Maurice Greenfield (Birmingham) at 144lbs for 20 rounds of two minutes only and an NSC purse. However, because Woodley had no backer he couldn't wager £100 or £200 a side. The challenge was also unusual in so much that a top-class man was asking for two-minute rounds.

29 August Dick Burge formally announced his retirement from boxing yet again and in the 18 September *Sporting Life* a letter appeared from Burge, dated 17 September, confirming his retirement, while the 19 September *Mirror of Life* stated that Burge had now retired for good.

24 September At the *Sporting Life* office, Dick Burge and Jack Everhardt met to sign for a bout at the 144lbs limit, £200 a side, but Everhardt's backer, 'Jolly Jumbo' Ecclestone, refused to sign.

4 October Pat Daly/Daley challenges all England at 144lbs now that Dick Burge has retired, 20 rounds, £200 a side upwards and best purse – *Sporting Life*.

19 November Felix Scott (Liverpool), 'The Veteran', to all at 144lbs over 20 rounds – *Sporting Life*.

1901

29 January Tom Woodley (Fulham) to Jim Styles (Marylebone) at 150lbs, up to £100 a side – *Sporting Life*.

12 August George Bell of America having claimed to be the 144lbs champion of America, and matched with 'Jewey' Cooke (Hammersmith and Bloomsbury), was exposed as a complete novice by Dave Barry (late of Philadelphia). Following the discovery, the bout with Cooke was cancelled. The *Sporting Life* reported that Bell was most likely to be a seaman who had either jumped ship or was on shore leave pretending to be some sort of American champion. It was also said that many of the so-called coloured Americans were either from the Caribbean or the Africas and had never seen America. This practice, in fact, went on for many years and was common in every country where boxing was held, as was the practice of men from other lands pretending to be champions of their native land when visiting a foreign country.

5 September Tom Woodley (Fulham) to all England from 144lbs up to 150lbs, 15 or 20 rounds, Jack Palmer (Benwell, Newcastle) or Harry Neumier preferred. However, on the 23 October in the *Sporting Life* Woodley was challenging at 144 to 148lbs, but by December he was giving notice that he could no longer make 144lbs and was looking for contests at 146 to 148lbs.

4 October Harry Slater (Birmingham), who is just back from San Francisco after 12 years where he claimed nearly 100 bouts, challenges all England at 144lbs – *Sporting Daily*. Accepted on 5 October by Pat Daly/Daley, Slater failed to show up at a

meeting arranged for 7 October at the *Sporting Life* office and in the 8 October issue of the *Sporting Life* he challenged all England at 146 to 148lbs, admitting he couldn't make 144lbs.

8 October Pat Daly/Daley to the world at 144lbs, £100 or £200 a side – *Sporting Life*. This was repeated for the rest of the year.

12 November Owen Sweeney (Fulham) to Pat Daly/Daley, 'Jewey' Cooke or 'Philadelphia' Dave Barry at 140 to 144lbs – *Sporting Life*.

7 December Jim Styles (Marylebone) is called the ex-English 144lbs champion – *Sporting Life*. However, it was the 144 to 146lbs limit championship he claimed after a 4 February 1897 NSC competition win.

10 December Charlie Knock (Stratford) to all England at 140 up to 144lbs, Pat Daly/Daley preferred – *Sporting Life*. Again reported on 20 December in the *Sporting Life*, with Joe White (Liverpool, late Canada) added.

1902

11 January 'Jewey' Cook (Hammersmith) w pts 7 Dave Barry (London, late Philadelphia, USA), Wonderland, Whitechapel Road, London. Refereed by Mr R.Joseph, this was the final of a world 144lbs limit championship competition, six rounds cut from eight and with extra round. In previous rounds, Cooke, real name Abraham Cohen, beat Tom Ireland and Charlie Knock, while Barry defeated the negro, Jack Camperdown (New York), and George Penny. Originally billed for the English 144lbs championship, with neither Barry or Camperdown eligible for an English championship, the word English was simply replaced by world.

22 January Pat Daly/Daley to Tom Woodley (Fulham) at 144lbs, 15 or 20 rounds, £50 or £100 a side – *Sporting Life*. In the 23 January issue of the *Sporting Life*, Woodley accepted but only if at 146lbs. Then, in the 26 January issue of the *Sporting Life*, he stated that he would meet Daly at the 144lbs limit, £100 a side.

29 April Pat Daly/Daley (Westminster, born Ireland) is the English 144lbs limit champion – *Sporting Life*.

14 May Charlie Knock (Stratford) challenges all England at 144lbs, £100 or £200 a side, Peter Brown (Woolwich) or Pat Daly/Daley preferred – *Sporting Life*. This was repeated on 9 October and 3 November.

21 June Eddie Connolly (born Canada) w pts 15 Pat Daly/Daley (Westminster, born Ireland), NSC, Covent Garden, London. Referee Tom Scott. Billed as for the world 144 to 146lbs lightweight championship, with both men weighing 144lbs, according to reports and given weights, and by Daly himself, it was also advertised as being at the 138 to 140lbs limit, as well as the 140 to 142lbs limit and the 142 to 144lbs limit. 144lbs was the weight at which Daly claimed the world title at and prior to the bout, Connolly had, on 17 May, in the *Sporting Life*, challenged Daly at 140lbs up to 146. At that time, Daly was training for a proposed bout with the ex-world 133lbs champion, Frank Erne, which fell through because of a dispute over weight, Erne wanting 137lbs and Daly 140, so the bout with Connolly was then made. Connolly was also stated to have been 144½lbs for the above fight and in November of the same year was boxing at 150lbs.

23 June George Penny (Kentish Town) w pts 10 Peter Brown (Woolwich), The New Adelphi Club, Maiden Lane, The Strand, London. Refereed by Harry Cooper, the rounds were cut from 15 to 10 and the contest billed for the English lightweight Coronation championship with no actual weight given, 140 to 144lbs being the weights the men were thought to be about. Penny, a substitute for Jim Maloney (Hackney), was presented with his championship belt on 24 July by Mr Teddy Wilson and, on 28 August 1903, the *Mirror of Life* carried a photo of Penny wearing his 140lbs lightweight championship belt, while the 7 October 1905 issue of the *Sporting Life* called Penny the winner of the 144lbs Coronation championship cup. Note: Both the above statements are typical of the confusion that was caused by varying reports carried by the different sporting papers as to actual weights bouts were fought at.

1 August Charlie Knock (Manchester, late of Stratford) challenges Andrew Jeptha (Cape Town, South Africa), a negro, at 144lbs – *Sporting Life*.

15 September Tom Woodley (Fulham) w pts 11 Eddie Connolly (Canada), Wonderland, Whitechapel Road, London. Billed for the world 144lbs limit title, £150 a side and £100 purse (total £400), £200 a side and purse was also given. Also given English and Imperial Empire title billing, apart from the fact

that Connolly wasn't eligible to contest an English title bout, it was disqualified from major title recognition as it was only over two-minute rounds and not over a championship distance. With the bout being even after 10 rounds the referee, not named, incorrectly ordered an extra round

29 December Jim Clarke w pts 15 Eddie Connolly (Canada), The Coronation Gym, Formerly The Adelphi Theatre, Liverpool. Refereed by Bob Watson, for a £50 purse, no weights or title billing was given or stipulated. Interestingly, Clarke was billed as the Australian lightweight champion, although later stated to come from California, USA, and eventually thought to be Tom Dingley of Canada, but not proved.

1903

21 January Eddie Connolly is the 144lbs champion of America – *Sporting Life*.

31 January The *Rand Daily Mail*, Johannesburg called 'Jewey' Cooke (Hammersmith) the English 144lbs limit champion and holder of the 144lbs championship belt. This was repeated at odd times during Cooke's South African stay.

4 February Tom Ireland (Mile End) is the winner of an English 144lbs championship belt competition – *Sporting Life*. Ireland won a 140lbs limit championship belt competition on 6 April 1901, not a 144lbs one.

5 March Bobby Dobbs (Kentucky) w rtd 6 Harry Lewis (Cardiff), Corporation Gym, Dale Street, Liverpool. Made at catchweights, £25 a side and a £50 purse (total £100), Lewis claimed a foul, which, when disallowed, saw him retire. No weights were given and there was no title billing.

12 March Bobby Dobbs (Kentucky) w co 4 Fred Higgins (Birmingham, late of London), Corporation Gym, Dale Street, Liverpool. Made at catchweights, no weights were given and there was no title billing.

25 April Jim Lloyd (South Shields) w rtd 6 Tom Ireland (Mile End), Ginnett's Circus, Newcastle on Tyne. Made at catchweights, £50 a side and purse, although no weights were given and there was no title billing, both looked to be about 144lbs.

25 April Charlie Knock (Stratford) w co 4 Tom Woodley (Fulham), Wonderland, Whitechapel Road, London. Although at catchweights, with four-ounce gloves, no weights being given, no title billing, not over a recognised title distance and only two-minute rounds in play, Knock tried to claim the English 144lbs limit title on the strength of this win.

2 July Charlie Knock (Stratford) claims to be the English 144lbs limit champion and will defend same against anyone, no one barred, for up to £200 a side. This also applied to the world, no one barred, any colour or creed, but Pat Daly/Daley preferred – *Sporting Life*. Was repeated throughout the rest of the year.

11 July Tom Woodley (Fulham) stated that he was the English 144lbs limit champion and holder of English 144lbs limit championship belt, which is now on display at The Builders Arms, Kings Road, Chelsea, London. Woodley went on to say that Charlie Knock is not the champion, as when he lost to Knock it was in a catchweight bout over a non-title course with only two-minute rounds in play and not at 144lbs. It was also stated that Knock had no claim on title whatsoever, while Woodley would defend the English 144lbs limit title against Knock or anyone else, £200 a side.

16 July Charlie Knock (Stratford) offers Woodley a chance to regain his lost laurels – *Sporting Life*.

18 July William 'Spike' Sullivan (Boston, born Ireland) w pts 20 Bobby Dobbs (Kentucky), Ginnett's Circus, Newcastle on Tyne. Refereed by J.R.Smoult, it was made at 144lbs for a £70 purse, with no weights given and no title billing.

16 September Tom Woodley to Charlie Knock at 148lbs – *Sporting Life*. This gave the impression Woodley was no longer able to get to 144lbs.

17 September Charlie Knock again stated he was a 144lbs man, not a 148lbs man, but he would box Tom Woodley at 146lbs – *Sporting Life*.

19 September Pat Daly/Daley stated that he was the true English 144lbs limit champion and would defend against anyone over 20 three-minute rounds, £50 or £100 a side and an NSC purse, Charlie Knock preferred – *Sporting Life*. This was repeated on 24 September and 5 October.

6 October On this date at *Sporting Life* office, Charlie Knock failed to show up to sign for an English 144lbs title bout with Pat Daly/Daley, thus forfeiting any claim he had to the said title to Daly.

18 November Charlie Allum's 144lbs English championship cup is now on display at The Kings Arms, Walmer Road, Notting Hill. Allum's cup was at the 144 to 146lbs limit not at the 144lbs limit.

2 December Bobby Dobbs, the 44-year-old negro, is the 144lbs 'coloured' champion – *Sporting Life*.

21 December On this date, Jack Clancy (San Francisco) failed to turn up at the *Sporting Life* office to sign for a bout with Pat Daly/Daley at the 144lbs limit for the world title and in the 24 December issue of the *Sporting Life* Daly challenged the world at 144lbs, Clancy preferred.

1904

20 January Charlie Allum (Notting Hill) is the English 144lbs champion – *Sporting Life*. However, this was a mistake as it was the 144 to 146lbs limit title that Allum had a claim to. Was to be repeated in the *Sporting Life* on 20 March.

4 February Charlie Knock (Stratford) is the English 144lbs limit lightweight champion – *Sporting Life*.

20 February Jack Nelson (local) drew 20 Jack Bayley (Birmingham), Ginnett's Circus, Newcastle on Tyne. Made at catchweights, with Nelson scaling 141lbs and Bayley 144, no weights were given, there was no title billing and it was a substitute bout on 10 days notice for Frank 'Spike' Robson (North Shields) versus George Dixon (USA), the great negro, but was a truly great bout.

21 February Peter Brown (Woolwich), the present English 148lbs limit champion, to all England at the 144lbs limit, 20 rounds of three minutes each, or Bobby Dobbs (Kentucky) the same terms – *Sporting Life*. This was repeated on 15 December – *Sporting Life*.

31 March Jack Clancy (San Francisco) challenges the world at 140 to 146lbs – *Sporting Life*. In the 19 April and 16 May issues of the *Sporting Life*, Clancy was being called the world 146lbs limit champion.

2 May Jack Clancy (San Francisco) w pts 10 Peter Brown (Woolwich), Wonderland, Whitechapel Road, London. Refereed by Victor Mansill, this was the final of a world 144lbs limit gold and silver championship belt competition contested over three-minute rounds and not as in the 1996 *Yearbook*, plus £250 in prize money. The belt, once owned by the late Ted Pritchard (Lambeth, born Wales), was also called an international championship belt and also an English championship belt, but Clancy was not eligible to contest an English championship competition. In previous rounds of the competition, which had started on 18 April, Clancy beat Maurice Greenfield and Charlie Knock, while Brown had a bye and beat Charlie Allum in the semi-final.

14 May Jack Clancy (San Francisco) w pts 20 Bobby Dobbs (Kentucky), Ginnett's Circus, Newcastle on Tyne. Billed as a world 142 to 144lbs title fight, with Clancy as the holder, and a £100 purse, Clancy was two pounds overweight at 146lbs. Although his weight was also given as being 144lbs, 146lbs is believed to be correct in this case and Dobbs (140lbs) laid claim to the title by forfeit.

18 June Bobby Dobbs (Kentucky) w pts 20 Peter Brown (Woolwich), Ginnett's Circus, Newcastle on Tyne. Referee Bill Bell. Stated to be for the world 142lbs limit title, 142lbs, give or take two pounds, also given, taking it to 144lbs. This would appear the more likely as Dobbs had just laid claim to the 142 to 144lbs by right of forfeit, but no weights given and Brown was stated to be out of condition in a contest for £50 a side and a £100 purse (total £200).

10 September Jack Clancy (San Francisco) drew 20 Bobby Dobbs (Kentucky), Ginnett's Circus, Newcastle on Tyne. Referee Billy Bell. With Clancy scaling 142lbs and Dobbs 143lbs, it was reported and advertised in the *Newcastle Daily Chronicle* as being for the world 142 to 144lbs limit title, although Clancy seemed weak at the weight.

1905

11 January Tom Woodley (Fulham) to Charlie Knock (Stratford) to decide the English 144lbs limit title over 15 three-minute rounds – *Sporting Life*.

20 February Tom Woodley (Fulham) w disq 5 Charlie Knock (Stratford), Wonderland, Whitechapel Road, London. Referee G.H.Holloway. Billed as for the English 144lbs limit lightweight title, plus £325, with four-ounce gloves, no weights were given and the *Mirror of Life* report stated that neither man was within a street of championship class. Also, no sign of a weigh-in was seen and it was felt that there was no way that Knock could make 144lbs, while the referee was a complete novice, having seen his first bout only six months ago. The *Mirror of Life* also stated that the bout was only

over two-minute rounds (which was normal practice at this venue), whereas articles and reports in both the *Sportsman* and *Sporting Life* all state three-minute rounds. Called one of the worse bouts ever seen by the *Sporting Life*, both men continuously holding and hitting for which they were repeatedly cautioned, with Knock also hitting low, which he did once too often and was disqualified.

12 April The *Mirror of Life* publishes a photo of Peter Brown (Woolwich) with the English 144lbs championship belt he won on 4 January 1904. This was in fact a 148lbs competition belt.

4 July William 'Buddy' Ryan (Chicago) w co 11 George Herberts, Butte, Montana, USA. With Ryan weighing 142lbs to Herberts' 143 1/2lbs, the American 'white' 144lbs title was on the line.

19 August Peter Brown (Woolwich) to all England at 144lbs – *Sporting Life*.

21 October Jack Goldswain (Bermondsey) to Jack Bayley (Birmingham) at 144lbs over 15 or 20 rounds – *Sporting Life*.

15 November Bobby Dobbs (Kentucky) w co 2 Bill Chester (Mile End), The Queens Hall, Cardiff, South Wales. Referee Harry Wheeler (Cardiff). Dobbs, who was reported to be 46 years old, won this catchweight contest for a £50 purse. No weights were given and there was no title billing attached.

1906

2 January Jack Meekins (Battersea, late Army) to all England at 144lbs – *Sporting Life*.

10 March Peter Brown (Woolwich) to all England at 144lbs – *Sporting Life*.

30 April Bobby Dobbs (Kentucky) is the world 144lbs limit champion – *Mirror of Life*.

27 September Bobby Dobbs (Kentucky) w disq 9 Charlie Knock, Liverpool Gym Club, Christian Street, Liverpool. Referee J.T.Hulls. A catchweight contest with no weights given and no title billing, £50 a side and £65 purse (total £165), it would have been disqualified as a title bout in any case as it was only over two-minute rounds.

3 December Peter Brown (Woolwich) w rsc 14 Jim Courtney (Barry), The Badminton Club, St Mary's Street, Cardiff. Referee W.Lucas. Made at catchweights, with no weights given and no title billing, Brown looked to be about 156lbs. Regardless of weights, it would have not not qualified as a title bout as it was contested over two-minute rounds. In August, Brown had challenged all England at 146lbs, Courtney preferred.

1907

14 January Bobby Dobbs (Kentucky) to all England at 142 to 144lbs, £50 a side – *Sporting Life*. Dobbs is now in Hamburg, Germany, but will shortly be returning to the UK. This was repeated in the 9 February issue of the *Sporting Life*.

11 February Robert 'Curly' Watson (RN Chatham, born Barrow) w pts 20 Andrew Jeptha (Cape Town, South Africa), Wonderland, Whitechapel Road, London. Referee Mr B.A.Humphreys. Watson scaled 141lbs, while Jeptha, who was coloured, was given as being 142 1/2lbs. There was no mention of any title involvement in adverts, previews or articles, but in certain fight reports it was given as being for the English 142 to 144lbs limit title, with Watson called the Army and Navy middleweight champion of 1905-1906 and Jeptha called the South African lightweight champion, which he wasn't. Jeptha, who had just won Charles 'Kid' McCoy's open competition in Cape Town, was also wrongly called the Scottish champion. As a South African he was ineligible to contest either the Scottish or English (British) title, while the bout with Watson was also disqualified as a title bout as it was only over two-minute rounds. Also, Watson also had no claim on English 144lbs limit title.

25 March Andrew Jeptha (Cape Town) w co 4 Robert 'Curly' Watson (Bow, late RN Chatham, born Barrow In Furness), Wonderland, Whitechapel Road, London. Referee Mr E.A.Humphreys. Made at the 142 to 144lbs limit for £200 a side and a £150 purse (total £350), Watson (142lbs) and Jeptha (141lbs) were ineligible to contest an English title, and even the Imperial British Empire title, as this was contested over two-minute rounds. No title billing was mentioned in any adverts or preview reports in any of the sporting press and it was only later that Jeptha tried to claim he had won the English 144lbs limit title with this win, which he hadn't. However, this was common with winners of international bouts, no matter what country they took place in.

30 May Bobby Dobbs (Kentucky) to Andrew Jeptha (Cape Town) at

144lbs over 20 three-minute rounds, £100 a side with four-ounce gloves – *Mirror of Life*.

8 August Joe White (Cardiff, born Canada) w pts 15 Andrew Jeptha (Cape Town), The National AC, Castle Street, Merthyr, South Wales. Referee Harry Wheeler (Cardiff). An opening show, no weights were given despite the fight being announced as being at the 142 to 144lbs limit. Articled for £150 a side and purse, it was given English and Welsh 144lbs limit title billing, but neither man was eligible to box for same and even a claim to the Imperial Empire title would have been disqualified as a title bout as it was only contested over two-minute rounds.

5 October Robert 'Curly' Watson (Bow, late RN Chatham) is called the English 144lbs limit champion in the *Mirror of Life* and, on 26 October, in the *Sporting Life* he challenged the world at 144lbs, Andrew Jeptha or Charlie Knock preferred. If there were no acceptors, Watson would leave with his trainer for the USA to try and get bouts.

21 October 'Young' Joseph (Aldgate) w pts 20 Jack Goldswain (Bermondsey), Wonderland, Whitechapel Road, London. Referee Eugene Corri. Stated to have been made at the 144lbs limit for £100 a side and a £125 purse (total £325), no weights were given and both men were said to be over 144lbs, thus making it a catchweight bout. This, plus two-minute rounds, disqualified it as a title bout, although the contest had originally been given as being over three-minute rounds, which was later corrected. Joseph did start trying to claim the English 140lbs limit title with this win over Goldswain, who was recognised as the English 138 to 140lbs limit champion, but without any foundation. It was the same with his attempts to claim the English 142lbs limit and 144lbs limit titles.

26 October Andrew Jeptha (Cape Town) to 'Young' Joseph (Aldgate) at 142 to 144lbs over 20 three-minute rounds, £200 up to £1,000 a side – *Mirror of Life*.

1908

1 January Andrew Jeptha (Cape Town) to all England at the 144lbs limit, £200 a side – *Sporting Life*. This was repeated in the 18 January issue of the *Sporting Life*.

20 January 'Young' Joseph (Aldgate) w pts 20 Jack Goldswain (Bermondsey), Wonderland, Whitechapel Road, London. Referee J.T.Hulls. Articled for £200 a side and a £165 purse (total £565), it was reported to be at 140 to 142lbs in the *Mirror of Life* and 142 to 144lbs in the *Sporting Life*. Goldswain (141 1/2lbs) was the English 138 to 140lbs limit champion, a title that Joseph (142lbs), who won nearly every round, tried to claim afterwards. However, the *Mirror of Life* pointed out that the bout wasn't at the 138 to 140lbs limit, but at the 144lbs limit. Strangely, they also reported the fight in the 142lbs limit list also.

11 April Andrew Jeptha (Cape Town) is called the welterweight champion of both South Africa and England by the *Sporting Life* when, in fact, he had never fought for the South African title and wasn't eligible to contest an English title. At one time he had even been called the Scottish welterweight champion, another title he wasn't eligible for.

20 May Arthur Warner (Bethnal Green), the ABA featherweight champion in 1901 and 1902, was now claiming the English 144lbs limit title – *Sporting Life*.

12 December 'Bombardier' Davis (local) w co 8 Joe Smith (Canning Town, London), Jimmy Lowes' Sports Club, Newcastle on Tyne. Made at 144lbs, no weights were given and there was no title billing as such, but that didn't stop the veteran, Bobby Dobbs (USA), reportedly in his 50th year, challenging the winner, £25 a side. On 11 February 1909, the NSC introduced the eight-named weight divisions and in Britain the 144lbs class quickly became part of the 147lbs welterweight division, while in America it was only when Jack Britton was deposed in 1922 that 147lbs was fully adopted internationally.

144lbs to 146lbs (10st 4lbs to 10st 6lbs)

1880

3 May The White Bear, Long Walk, Bermondsey Square, London. The landlord, Mr J.Glaney, in the *Sporting Life*, Glancy in the *Sportsman*, put up a silver cup for a 146lbs competition – First Series: T. Bundle (Walworth) 'walked over' Butcher, absent. Dick Marshall (local) w disq 2 (shouldering his man) John Bates (local). M. Graham (local) w pts 3 A.Ripley (local). Moss Kirby (local) w pts 3 Alf Smith, alias 'Drum', (local). The semi-finals and final were due to take place on

Monday, 10 May and Tuesday, 11 May, but the whole show was cancelled when the authorities prevented it from continuing. They also stopped a proposed show by Mick Welsh (late Birmingham) at his newly acquired rooms at 23 Star Corner, Bermondsey, London. There was no record of this 146lbs limit competition ever being finished.

1881

20 October Johnny Walker w pts 3 George Say (Haggerston), The Griffin, High Street, Shoreditch, London. The final of a 146lbs limit competition for a silver cup. Walker, whose real surname was Badman and was the son of a famous old-time bare-knuckle boxer, Johnny Walker, beat Bob Feathers in a previous round, while Say, a well-known walker, beat Jack Watts (Clerkenwell). The referee for the competition was Mr H.Green.

1882

23 January Arthur Cooper (St Luke's) w pts 3 George Roberts (Clerkenwell), The Goldsmiths Arms, Little Sutton Street, Clerkenwell, London. The final of a 146lbs limit competition, in some reports it was advertised as a 140lbs limit competition and, on 28 June, the *Sporting Life* called Cooper the winner of Mr Ward's 140lbs competition, which qualified it for the 138 to 140lbs list.

1883

19 November Bill 'Chesterfield' Goode drew 9 Dick Roberts (Clerkenwell). Contested in the Hackney Road, London, it was a private show in a 12-foot ring, being attended by just 100 people. Refereed by Tommy Trew, under MoQ Rules, with gloves, endurance and £50, it was stated to be at catchweights with no title billing. Goode (146lbs), who was well on top, floored Roberts in the eighth, before the cry of 'police' saw the gas lights put out and the men carrying on with just tapers and fighting in utter darkness. However, after the ninth round started, it was stopped and, at a meeting the next day, the bout was ordered to be continued at a future date.

27 November Bill 'Chesterfield' Goode w rtd 21 Dick Roberts (Clerkenwell), The Rodney Arms (over the skittle alley), Walworth, London. Attendance restricted to 40. The continuation of the 19 November bout, it was one of the finest glove bouts ever seen.

31 December Bill 'Chesterfield' Goode to Pat Perry (London, late of Birmingham) for £100 a side – *Sporting Life*.

1884

16 April Johnny Robinson (South Shields) w rsc 2 Arthur Cooper, The Horse Shoe, Clerkenwell Close, Clerkenwell, London. The final of W.Holmes' 144 to 146lbs limit silver championship belt competition, which, in later years, was often wrongly called the 144lbs championship belt. With the preliminary bouts being held at the Islington Green Hall, in previous rounds Robinson had beaten J.Handley, w rtd 1, after Handley had walked out of the ring in protest at Robinson's style of 'fighting to win' instead of 'boxing for points'. He then stopped Harry Mead, while Cooper beat W.Preston and J.Walker, both on points. Reports didn't actually give Robinson as the winner, just stating that the bout was stopped by the referee as the crowd was creating such an uproar because Cooper was getting such a beating. Robinson's style astounded everyone, being more or less unheard of, and because of this his first-round opponent retired. There had been one previous case, just over a month before, in the final of a 140lbs competition, that saw Noble and Connors just standing and fighting, but that was in a final only. In the above competition, Robinson had fought that way throughout. This was, in fact, the start of boxing as it is known today, as others followed Robinson's example, but it took time to get completely accepted by the law, which, in many cases, still wanted the exhibition style of boxing for points as practised by the amateurs and the only type of boxing allowed up to that time. In the case of Connors and Noble, it was because they had a grudge against one another, but that wasn't so with Johnny Robinson and his fighting style was what started amateur and professional boxing to drift apart. Yet Robinson's place in boxing's history is largely forgotten, his name being unknown today, instead of being in the *Old Timers (Pioneers) Section of The Boxing Hall of Fame* in Canastota, New York, where it belongs.

19 April Johnny Robinson challenged Cooper to a return, or anyone else who was in the 16 April English 146lbs lightweight championship belt competition – *Sporting Life*. The challenge was for the belt and £50, but not in London this time. This was repeated in the 29th April issue of the

Sporting Life, in which Robinson himself was challenged by Bill 'Chesterfield' Goode.

1 May Johnny Robinson accepted the challenge of 'Chesterfield' Goode if at 142lbs. This from a man claiming to be the English 146lbs limit champion, so it may have been a misprint – *Sporting Life*.

16 June Alec Roberts (Clerkenwell) w pts 3 Arthur Cooper (St Luke's), Bob Habbijam's West-End School of Arms, Newman Street, off Oxford Street, London. The final of an all-England 146lbs limit competition, in previous rounds Roberts beat Harry Bartlett and Ching Ghook, while Cooper eliminated 'Young' Jacob Hyams and Tom Sterck (also given as Stirk).

1885

7 March Bill 'Chesterfield' Goode (Shadwell) to the world at 146lbs – *Sporting Life*. This was repeated on 21 May.

1886

4 January In the USA, Arthur Chambers (Philadelphia, late of Salford, England), on behalf of Jack Fogarty (Philadelphia), challenged George LaBlanche (born Canada) and 'Nonpareil' Jack Dempsey (New York, born Ireland) at 145lbs, or at catchweights, $1,000 a side, MoQ or London Prize Ring Rules, small gloves, to a finish – *Bells Life*.

15 January 'Nonpareil' Jack Dempsey (New York, born Ireland), whose real name was John Kelly, is the world 146lbs middleweight champion – *Bells Life*.

2 February 'Nonpareil' Jack Dempsey (New York) w rtd 27 Jack Fogarty (Philadelphia), The Clarendon Hall, New York, USA. A private show with the attendance restricted to 10 persons from each side, it was stated to be at catchweights with no weights stipulated and no title billing given, but was later given credit as being for the American/world 146lbs middleweight title. But the given weights were also not above suspicion, as Dempsey was stated to look at least 155lbs. The reporter from the *New York World*, who claimed to be the only reporter at the bout, stated that the match was made at 150lbs and under London Prize Ring Rules, although gloves were worn.

1887

1 June Johnny Reagan (New York City) w co 44 John Files, near New York City, USA. Billed as for the world/American 146lbs title (144lbs also given), other reports stated that the bout was made at 144lbs, give or take two pounds, and that both men weighed 144lbs, as well as giving Reagan at 146lbs. It was contested under MoQ Rules in skin-tight gloves.

8 August Johnny Reagan (New York City) drew 39 Tom Henry. In a fight that was contested 70 miles up the Hudson River, above New York City, Reagan came in at 142lbs, while Henry, billed from England, made 145lbs. Given American/world 146lbs title billing, and under MoQ Rules with hard gloves, it was stated that Jim Kendrick (London, England, born Ireland) was now in the USA trying to get a match with Reagan, which both men want, but bare knuckles preferred.

1888

14 January Bill 'Chesterfield' Goode is the English 146lbs limit champion – *Sporting Life*.

16 April Alf Suffolk (Kennington) w disq 11 Ted Barrett (Wandsworth), Lambeth School Of Arms, Lambeth Walk, Paradise Street, London. Made at catchweights with no title billing, the winner, Alf Suffolk (135lbs), who was making his professional debut, was awarded a silver belt presented by Harry Clarke (Lambeth) after Barrett (145lbs) had been disqualified for back heeling by the referee, George T.Dunning, of the *Sportsman*.

26 August Johnny Reagan (New York City) versus 'Paddy' Duffy (Boston, Mass.), Brooklyn, New York, USA was just an exhibition three-round bout, Reagan being the 146lbs limit champion and Duffy, the 144lbs limit champion.

15 December Alec Burns (Lambeth) w pts 4 Ted White (Westminster), Her Majesty's Theatre, The Haymarket, London. The final of Mr Ernest Wells and John Fleming's Pelican Club world and English 146lbs championship competition spread over six nights, in previous rounds Burns had beaten J.Cashley ('Yorkey') of Leeds and Jim Gleeson, while White, the 1887 ABA heavyweight champion, beat Jim Kendrick before getting a bye.

1889

19 February Ted Pritchard (Lambeth) w disq 4 Jim 'Darby' Hayes (Marylebone), Lambeth School of Arms, Lambeth Walk, Paradise Street, London. Referee Bernard J.Angle. Billed as

an English 144 to 145lbs title fight as per the *Sporting Life* and made at 144 give or take a pound, £100 a side, it was not given title billing in the *Sportsman*. The contest, which came about as a result of Pritchard's challenge to the world at 144lbs, saw Hayes (144lbs), not to be confused with the coloured man of same name and weight, outclassed. Put down in the fourth, Hayes seemed to have failed to beat the count, but got up only to be put down again, whereupon his seconds rushed into the ring, picked him up and took him to his corner. Following an organised interruption with 30 seconds still to go, and with everyone under the impression that Pritchard had won, Angle, all in a dither, announced that he was adjourning the fight and would give his decision at 1am the following day. On 20 February, Angle found in favour of Pritchard by disqualification, due to Hayes' seconds entering the ring, but Hayes' backer, Bob Habbijam, refused to pay over the stakes when failing to accept the referee's decision. Habbijam stated that he, Mr Angle, couldn't give two decisions and the adjournment of the bout meant that it had to be fought for again. Habbijam also denied that it was him who had organised Hayes' seconds going into the ring and picking Hayes up. The above decision resulted in several letters to the papers on weak, pompous and self-important referees who should be weeded out.

4 March   Bill Husband w pts 3 J.Bird, The Pelican Club, London. The final of the Pelican Club all-England 146lbs limit competition, in previous rounds Husband beat F.Coine and Simon Soloman, while Bird defeated H.Collins and J.Flynn. There was not a true first-class man amongst them.

9 March   Johnny Robinson (South Shields), the 144lbs champion and holder of the 144lbs lightweight championship belt he won some five years ago in 1894, on seeing that Ted Pritchard claims to be the English 145lbs limit champion, will give him the one pound, and box him for that title, small gloves - but would prefer bare knuckles - £100 a side and a £10 deposit – *Sporting Life*. It was a 146lbs championship belt that Robinson had won on 16 April 1894, being at the 144 to 146lbs limit.

9 March   Ted Pritchard is the English 144 to 146lbs limit champion – *Sporting Life*. This was repeated on 14 March.

22 March   A proposed Pritchard versus Robinson bout fell through when the former admitted that he couldn't get down to 146lbs – The *Sportsman*.

29 June   Tom Meadows, the 146lbs lightweight champion of Australia and California, challenges the world at the 146lbs limit – *Sporting Life*.

2 July   Lachie Thompson (Glasgow) accepted Tom Meadows' challenge – *Sporting Life*.

10 July   Bill Hatcher (Islington) also accepted the challenge made by Tom Meadows – *Sporting Life*.

1890

20 January   Harry Nickless (The Borough) w co 13 Alf Suffolk (Lambeth), The South London School of Arms, Kennington Green, London. Refereed by T.J.McNeil, Nickless scaled 144lbs to Suffolk's 143½. Contested in four-ounce gloves at 145lbs, although no title billing was given it was reported as being for the English 144lbs limit title.

26 March   Tom Meadows, the 146lbs lightweight champion of Australia and California, to both Anthony Diamond (Birmingham) and Harry Nickless (London) for the world 146lbs limit title – *Sporting Life*.

28 March   Lachie Thompson (Glasgow) w co 11 Alf Hanlon (local), The Lyceum, Liverpool. No weights were given or stipulated and there appears to have been no title billing. Hanlon, who was well on top when he walked on to a kayo punch, was stated to have suffered his first loss, while Thompson finished badly marked up. There was also some confusion as to which of the Hanlon brothers this was, Alf or George, but am certain it was Alf. A return was arranged at £100 a side.

28 May   Once again a misprint was made when Alec Roberts was called the English 146lbs champion. Roberts, whose final bout of his career had been on 25 September 1888 and who had claimed the English 148lbs limit title, had never been below 147lbs in his entire recorded career – *Sporting Life*.

30 May   Tom Shawcross (Manchester), who has won, lost and drawn with the negro, Felix Scott (Liverpool), to Tom Meadows (Australia) at 144 or 146lbs with small gloves and a £25 purse – *Sporting Life*.

30 May   Lachie Thompson (Glasgow) w rsc 2 Alf Hanlon, The Grand Circus, Peter Street, Manchester. Refereed by Andrew Marsden and made at the 146lbs limit, £25 a side and £50

purse (total £100), Thompson's weight was given as 145lbs by the *Sporting Life* and 144lbs by the *Sportsman*, with Hanlon weighing 144lbs. Hanlon, on being floored by a right to the jaw, got up badly dazed but as Thompson went in to finish the fight, the chief of police jumped into the ring and stopped it, whereupon the referee awarded the bout to Thompson.

26 July   Bill Husband accepts a challenge to all by Jim Adds, but at 146lbs. Adds had challenged all at 144lbs – *Sporting Life*.

13 September   Jim Burchell to any 146lbs man for a £50 purse – *Sporting Life*.

18 October   William Robinson (Shoreditch, London) w pts 4 James Lowes (local), Ginnett's Circus, Bath Road, Newcastle on Tyne. The final of Mr Shelley's 146lbs all-England competition for £20 first prize, although being scheduled for three rounds an extra round was thrown in for good measure. A competition spread over six nights, having started on Monday 13 October, in previous rounds 'Cock Robin' beat J.Forest and had a bye, while Lowes had a bye and then a no-decision bout with Arthur Gutteridge (Islington, London). With the referee, Jimmy Hulls, refusing to give a decision, Gutteridge withdrew and Lowes went in to the final.

24 November   Anthony Diamond challenges Dick Burge for the 146lbs limit title – *Sporting Life*.

27 November   Felix Scott (Liverpool), a coloured man, challenges any of the many 144 or 146lbs champions, or any man in the UK – *Sporting Life*.

1891

12 February   Jim Burchell is the 146lbs champion – *Sporting Life*.

1892

13 January   Ted Bryant (Chelsea) to the world at 144 to 146lbs, Harry Nickless (The Borough) preferred – *Sporting Life*.

15 January   Ted Bryant's challenge is accepted by Harry Neumier (Bethnal Green and Stepney) at 146lbs – *Sporting Life*.

4 June   Ted Dorkings (Cambridge) w pts 4 Felix Scott (Seaford), The Central Hall, Holborn, London. The final of Frank Hinde's 146lbs limit competition, which started on Monday 30 May, in previous rounds Dorkings beat Ted Jupp and Bill Cheese, while the coloured man, Scott, defeated Alex Young and George Baxter.

25 June   Paddy Gorman (Australia), now in the UK, challenges the world at 146lbs, £100 a side and best purse, with 'Cock Robin' and Ted White preferred. He then put a £100 deposit down to bind a match at *Sporting Life* office – *Sporting Life*. This was repeated on 29 June and 24 October.

27 June   Dick Burge (Newcastle on Tyne) w co 2 Lachie Thompson (Glasgow), The Kensington Social Club, London. Referee George Vize. With 200 in attendance, Burge weighed 144lbs, while Thompson's weight was given as 142lbs according to the *Sporting Life*, although it was shown as being 145lbs in the *Sportsman*. Not actually billed as an English 144 to 146lbs title, being made at 144lbs, give or take two pounds, £200 a side and £150 purse (total £550), winner takes all, Thompson, who took a count of nine prior to the kayo, challenged Burge the next day to a return at 146lbs, £200 up to £500 a side. This was also stated to be at 144lbs, which seems doubtful.

24 December   Lachie Thompson (Glasgow) to all England at 144 to 146lbs, £100 to £200 a side – *Sporting Life*.

1893

30 August   William Robinson (Homerton), alias 'Cock Robin', is the English 146lbs limit champion – *Sporting Life*. Repeated on 23 September and 26 December, previously, Robinson had called himself the English 142 to 144lbs limit champion.

17 October   'Cock Robin' to Tom Williams (Australia) at 146lbs, £100 a side and an NSC purse – *Sporting Life*.

18 October   Phillip Murphy (North Woolwich) to all England at 144 to 146lbs, 20 rounds or endurance, as he shortly leaves for the USA – *Sporting Life*.

25 October   Phillip Murphy's challenge is accepted by Dave Falkerall.

11 December   Tom Williams (Australia) drew 20 William Robinson (Hackney and Homerton), NSC, Covent Garden, London. Refereed by Bernard J.Angle, both men weighed 144lbs for a contest articled at £100 a side and a £100 purse (total £300) and made at 144 to 146lbs. Although there was no title billing, there was possible Imperial Empire (Commonwealth) involvement.

1894

13 September   Tommy Ryan (New York) w co 4 Billy Layton (USA). Contested on a sandbank in the Missouri River, near St Louis, Missouri, USA, having been banned from taking place

in St Joseph, it was billed as an American/world 146lbs title fight and both men weighed 146lbs.

1895

18 January   Tommy Ryan (Syracuse) w rsc 3 'Nonpareil' Jack Dempsey, Brooklyn, New York, USA. Billed as an American/world 145lbs title fight, Ryan weighed 145lbs and Dempsey 142.

11 February   Charley Johnson (St Paul, Minnesota) w disq 10 William Robinson (Hackney), The Central Hall, Holborn, London. Johnson, real surname Palmer, weighed 145lbs, while the 'Cock Robin' came in at 145³/₄lbs for a fight made at the 146lbs limit. There was no title billing, it being Johnson's UK debut, and the 'Cock Robin' looked fat and out of condition and far above his given weight in what was a terrible bout, all hugging and holding.

18 July   Charley Johnson (St Paul, Minnesota) w rtd 7 Dick Ambrose (Swansea), The Strand, Swansea. A catchweight bout with no weights given or stipulated, £25 a side and gate and winner take all, it poured with rain throughout.

20 July   Billy McCoy (Brooklyn, New York) to all England at 146lbs, £100 or £200 a side – *Mirror of Life*.

7 August   Charley Johnson (St Paul, Minnesota) is called the English 146lbs champion – *Sporting Life*. This was pure publicity, as an American-born citizen couldn't contest an English (British) title.

1896

10 April   Patsy Donovan (South Africa) w co 4 'Dutchy' Walton (Australia), Johannesburg, South Africa. Thought to have been contested prior to 10 April, it was made at 146lbs for a £100 purse and no weights were given.

9 November   William Robinson (Hackney), alias 'Cock Robin', challenges all England at 146lbs, 20 rounds, £50 or £100 a side and best purse – *Sporting Life*. This was repeated on 16 November and 4 December.

13 November   Harry Neumier (Stepney) challenges all England at 146lbs – *Sporting Life*. This was repeated on 16 November and 4 December.

16 November   Harry Neumier's challenge was accepted by William Robinson, the 'Cock Robin' – *Sporting Life*.

17 November   Bill Husband challenges 'Cock Robin' and all England at 146lbs – *Sporting Life*.

25 November   Tommy Ryan (Syracuse) w disq 9 'Mysterious' Billy Smith, New York City, USA. Made at 145lbs for the world/American titles in some reports (*New York World*, etc), but no weights were given. Other newspapers, such as the *Mirror of Life*, reported it at catchweights.

23 December   Tommy Ryan (Syracuse) w co 4 Billy Payne (Philadelphia), Syracuse, USA. At catchweights, Ryan weighed 145lbs, while no weight was given for Payne and no title billing was reported.

1897

4 February   Jim Styles (Marylebone) w pts 8 William Robinson (Walthamstow, late Hackney), NSC, Covent Garden, London. The final of a 146lbs limit competition with only four entries, in the semi-final leg Styles beat 'Driver' Pinchin and 'Cock Robin', on a comeback, beat Tom Williams (Australia).

24 February   Tommy Ryan (New York) w co 9 Tom Tracey (Australia), Syracuse, New York, USA. A catchweight bout with Ryan (144lbs) restricted to 145lbs and Tracey (139lbs), called the world 140lbs limit champion, allowed to be any weight. Some reports gave it as being for the world 145lbs title.

17 March   George Green (San Francisco) w co 12 'Mysterious' Billy Smith, Carson City, USA. Made at 145lbs, American/world title billing was given in some quarters and Green, the original 'Young Corbett', laid claim to this on his win, but no weights were given.

26 May   George Green w co 15 Charley McKeever (Philadelphia), San Francisco, USA. No weights were given or stipulated and despite a lack of title billing it was thought to involve Green's claim.

21 June   Tommy Ryan (local) w co 2 Tom Williams (Australia), Syracuse, USA. Billed as being for the world 145lbs title, no weights were given for either man.

26 August   Joe Walcott (New York, born Barbados) w co 18 George Green (San Francisco), Woodwards Pavillion, San Francisco, USA. Made at 145lbs with both inside, no actual weights were given. Some reports gave it world/American title billing, but not in general.

8 November   Tom Woodley (Fulham) w pts 20 Jim Styles (Marylebone), NSC, Covent Garden, London. Referee Bernard J.Angle.

This most certainly involved the English 146lbs limit middleweight title which Styles had won on 4 February at this venue, but it was not given title billing generally. Both men weighed 146lbs.

10 November   George Green (local) w co 1 Owen Zeigler, San Francisco, USA. No weights given or stipulated and no title billing reported, but 146lbs was a weight that both men could make.

1898

19 January   Tom Woodley (Fulham) to all England at 146lbs, £50 a side. This was accepted the following day, 20 January, by Jim Styles (Marylebone) – *Sporting Life*.

8 February   Owen Sweeney (Fulham) challenged Jim Styles (Marylebone), the self-styled English 146lbs limit champion, to a bout for this title, £50 a side and an NSC purse, 2pm weigh-in – *Sporting Life*.

5 March   Jim Styles (Marylebone) to all England at 144 to 146lbs – *Sporting Life*.

10 June   The death of the ex-English 146lbs lightweight championship belt winner, Johnny Robinson (South Shields), aged 36, is announced in South Shields.

29 July   'Mysterious' Billy Smith w pts 25 George Green (San Francisco), New York City, USA. Although it was reported from ringside that both men weighed 146lbs and it was stated to be for the 145 to 146lbs American/world title, it was also rumoured to be a catchweight bout and, in some quarters, Smith's weight also given as 147lbs. There were even some doubts to the correctness of the two different weights given for Smith and, depending on what papers were read, three different weights also persisted for the bout. Strong rumours also persisted that Green was paid $1,500 to lose.

8 August   Andy Walsh (Brooklyn) w pts 20 Charley Johnson (Philadelphia), The Greenwood Club, Brooklyn, New York, USA. Contested at catchweights with no weights given or stipulated and no title billing, both men were believed to be way above 145lbs, at about 150.

23 August   The death was announced of Jim Kendrick, real name Enright, sometimes given as Enwright (Lambeth, born Clounleham, Co Limerick, Ireland), aged 34, from consumption, at Eversleigh Road, Battersea. He was buried on 27 August at St Martin's Catholic Cemetery, Kensal Green, London. Kendrick was a one-time claimant to the English 144lbs title and was considered one of the greatest men at this weight, in spite of him burning the candle, not only at both ends, but also in the middle.

5 September   William Robinson, the 'Cock Robin', who, after being bitten by a dog, had the middle finger of his right hand amputated as a precaution to save the rest of his hand, is expected to retire from boxing.

5 September   'Mysterious' Billy Smith drew 25 Andy Walsh (Brooklyn), The Coney Island AC, New York, USA. Refereed by Alex Brown and billed as an American/world 145lbs limit welterweight title, the report stated that Smith was fighting too often.

3 October   'Mysterious' Billy Smith w co 20 Jim Judge, USA. Made at catchweights, Smith seemed much heavier, but no weights were given.

25 October   Tom Woodley (Fulham) challenges all England, 144 up to 150lbs, £50 a side – *Sporting Life*.

2 December   Tom Woodley (Fulham) to Jim Styles (Marylebone) at 146lbs (10.6), misprinted as 11.6, and an NSC purse – *Sporting Life*.

3 December   Styles accepted Woodley's challenge at 146lbs – *Sporting Life*.

5 December   'Mysterious' Billy Smith w pts 20 Joe Walcott (New York, born Barbados), The Lennox AC, New York City, USA. Billed as being for the American/world 145lbs limit title, no weights were given. Was refereed by Charley White.

1899

22 April   Jim Styles (Marylebone) is the English 146lbs champion – *Sporting Life*. This was repeated on 4 November.

15 May   Pat Gorman (USA), who is now in the UK, challenges all England at 146lbs – *Sporting Life*.

3 June   'Mysterious' Billy Smith drew 20 Charley McKeever (Philadelphia), New York City, USA. According to the *New York Times*, Smith v McKeever was made at catchweights, while the *New York Herald* doesn't mention weights or titles. Despite no weights being given or stipulated and no title billing, both men were thought to be around 145lbs, a weight that Smith claimed the world title at.

8 June   Tom Woodley (Fulham), the claimant to the English 146lbs

269

(10.6) title, is called the 11 stone English champion – *Sporting Life*. This is almost certain to have been a misprint.

6 November Pat Daly/Daley (Westminster) w pts 15 Tom Woodley (Fulham), NSC, Covent Garden, London. Refereed by B.J.Angle, Woodley scaled 146lbs to Daly's 145 in a contest made at the 146lbs limit, £50 a side and purse. Regardless of the lack of title billing, the win gave Daly a claim to the English 146lbs limit title if he cared to press it.

8 November 'Mysterious' Billy Smith w pts 20 Charley McKeever (Philadelphia), New York City, USA. Smith weighed 145lbs and McKeever 144 in a catchweight bout, which was also given as being at 145lbs for the American/world titles by some papers. The *New York Herald* gives no report of any title involvement, which was in keeping with the 'hit or miss' reporting attitude the New York papers seemed to show towards boxing at the time, being either 'all for it' or 'couldn't care less', you get what you are given.

15 November Billy Morgan (Swansea), the Welsh champion, to Pat Daly/Daley over 15 or 20 rounds at 146lbs – *Sporting Life*.

13 December Tom Woodley (Fulham) w pts 15 'Jewey' Cooke (Hammersmith), The Goodwin Club, Kingsland Road, Shoreditch, London. Made at catchweights, with no title billing and no weights given.

1900

15 January Jim 'The Rube' Ferns w disq 21 'Mysterious' Billy Smith, Buffalo, New York, USA. Billed as being for the American/world 145lbs limit title, which Smith held, Ferns was down 15 times about the bout. It was also stated that Smith was still the 142lbs limit champion. No weights were given for the bout.

17 February Tom Woodley (Fulham) to all England at 146lbs – *Sporting Life*.

22 February Jim 'The Rube' Ferns w pts 20 Mike Donovan, Buffalo, New York, USA. Billed for the American/world 145lbs title, but no weights were given.

12 March 'Mysterious' Billy Smith drew 25 'Young' John Mahoney (Philadelphia), Brooklyn, New York, USA. Billed as an American/world 145lbs limit welterweight title fight, no weights were given. Somehow, Smith's loss of this title claim to Jim Ferns on 15 January seems to have been overlooked.

26 April The proposed bout between the Welsh champion, Billy Morgan (Swansea), and 'Dido' Plumb, to be held on 5 May at the NSC, and stipulated for 15 three-minute rounds, £200 a side, has been called off, as Plumb is unable to get down to 146lbs – *Sporting Life*.

12 June 'Young' Peter Jackson (Baltimore), real name Sim Thompkins, challenges all England at 145 to 148lbs, Dick Burge preferred – *Sporting Life*. Burge accepted on 14 June on condition that there was a sidestake of either £200 or £500 a side.

10 July Charley McKeever (Philadelphia) to Pat Daly/Daley at 144lbs, or all England at 145lbs, 'Dido' Plumb preferred – *Sporting Life*.

29 September Jack Everhardt (New Orleans) to all England, 144 up to 148lbs, Billy Morgan (Swansea), Jim Curran (Rotherham), Walter Eyles (Islington), Dave Peters (Cardiff), Pat Daly/Daley (London), Tom Woodley (Fulham), Jack (misprinted as Joe) Palmer (Benwell, Newcastle on Tyne), Maurice Greenfield (Birmingham) and George Penny (Islington) preferred, or will box Owen Sweeney (Fulham) or Harry Webster (Kentish Town) at catchweights – *Sporting Life*.

28 November Tom Woodley (Fulham) to Morris/Maurice Greenfield (Birmingham) or Harry Webster (Kentish Town) at 144 to 146lbs, up to £100 a side – *Sporting Life*.

26 December Dick Burge is stated to have refused to box Tom Woodley (Fulham) as the latter refused to take a 'dive' – *Mirror of Life*.

1901

5 September Tom Woodley (Fulham) to all England, 144 up to 150lbs, Jack Palmer (Benwell, Newcastle on Tyne) or Harry Neumier (Stepney) preferred – *Sporting Life*. In the 23 October issue of the *Sporting Life* it was 144 to 148lbs and on 7 December it was 146 to 148lbs, £500 a side. On 25 September, in the *Sporting Life*, Woodley challenged 'Philadelphia' Jack O'Brien, Jack Scales and Jack Palmer (Benwell) at catchweights. All three men were known as 'arrangement fighters', so Woodley, with his known refusal to take part in a fake fight had no chance of a match with any of those named.

14 November Pat Daly/Daley to Charley McKeever (Philadelphia) for world 145lbs limit welterweight title, 15 or 20 three-minute rounds, £100 or £200 a side, or failing that he would box 'Jewey' Cooke, Willie Holt or Owen Sweeney – *Sporting Life*. In response, McKeever stated that he couldn't make 145lbs and could only box Daly/Daley at 148 up to 152lbs – *Sporting Life*.

22 November Tom Woodley (Fulham) to all England at 146lbs, Pat Daly/Daley preferred – *Sporting Life*. In the same issue, Woodley challenged Dave Peters at 150lbs or catchweights.

22 November Jim 'The Rube' Ferns w pts 15 Charley 'Dutch' Thurston, Detroit, USA. Billed as an American/world 145lbs limit welterweight title, no weights were given.

7 December Jim Styles (Marylebone) is the ex-English 144lbs champion – *Sporting Life*. However, it was the 144 to 146lbs title he claimed with his 4 February 1897 NSC competition win.

1902

20 January Tom Woodley (Fulham) w co 14 Jim Styles (Marylebone), Ginnett's Circus, Newcastle on Tyne. Refereed by Ed Plummer of the *Sporting Life* and billed as an English 146lbs limit title fight, 2pm weigh-in, £50 a side and £90 purse (total £190), winner 75%, loser 25%, and using four-ounce gloves, it was said to be one of the best, if not the best, bouts ever seen in Newcastle on Tyne.

23 January Tom Woodley stated that he would box Pat Daly/Daley at the 146lbs limit for the English title and on 29 January the two men signed contracts to meet for the English 146lbs limit title. However, it was with the stipulation that if no purse was offered there would be no match as they wouldn't box for side stakes only – *Sporting Life*.

19 March Tom Woodley to all England at 144 to 146lbs, £100 a side. Woodley is still willing to defend the English 144 to 146lbs limit title he won on 20 January against Pat Daly/Daley – *Sporting Life*. This was repeated on 26 March – *Mirror of Life*.

26 March Charlie Knock (Stratford) to all England, Pat Daly/Daley, Jabez White or 'Jewey' Cooke preferred, but no weight stipulated – *Sporting Life*.

12 April Tom Woodley (Fulham) to all England at 144 to 146lbs, £100 a side, and as Pat Daly/Daley had failed to meet him for the English 146lbs limit title, which Woodley had already won in a bout on 20 January, Woodley now formally claimed it – *Sporting Life*. In 15 April issue of the *Sporting Life*, Daly stated that he didn't see how Woodley could claim this title as he beat him for it on 6 November 1899 and had never never lost it.

23 May Joe White (Boston, Mass, born Canada), real name Jack Robertson, who had recently arrived in the UK, challenges all England at 146lbs – *Sporting Life*. This was repeated on 14 June, but extended to the world. It was the same in the 2 July issue of the *Sporting Life*, but misprinted as 11.4 to 11.6 instead of 10.4 to 10.6.

29 May Jim 'The Rube' Ferns w co 3 Owen Zeigler, Joplin, Missouri, USA. Some reports give this as an American/world 145lbs limit title fight, but no weights were given or stipulated in the majority of reports.

21 June Eddie Connolly (Canada) w pts 15 Pat Daly/Daley (London, born Co Cork), NSC, Covent Garden, London. Referee Tom Scott. Although billed in most papers as being for the world 144 to 146lbs limit title following the challenge of Connolly (144½lbs) to Daly (144lbs) on 17 May, at 140lbs up to 146, the *Sporting Life* gave it as being for the 140lbs limit title, which was almost certainly a misprint, with 142 to 144lbs also given. Daly had been in training for a bout against Frank Erne, which was called off in a dispute over weight, Erne wanting 133lbs and Daly 140.

23 June Joe Walcott (New York, born Barbados) w pts 15 Tommy West (Chicago, born Cardiff, South Wales), NSC, Covent Garden, London. Referee Tom Scott. Made at catchweights, with no weights announced, although advertised and billed as being for the 146lbs limit welterweight title, West was a 152 to 158lbs man and there was no way that he was able to get down to that weight. The Monday 21 June bout between Connolly and Daly/Daley bears out the fact that Walcott versus West was a catchweight bout with no title involvement, otherwise it meant that two bouts, involving four different men, one of whom couldn't get below 152lbs, fighting for same title inside three days. It was just a big mix up by the press in their reporting of the Walcott versus West bout.

28 August Tom Woodley to all England 144 up to 150lbs – *Sporting Life*. This was repeated on 3 October, but at 144 to 148lbs,

with Pat Daly/Daley preferred, while the 10 October issue gave 144 to 146lbs. The advert continued to be shown right to the end of the year with variations.

8 October Charlie Knock (Stratford) is the English 146lbs champion – *Mirror of Life*.

22 December Matty Matthews (New York) w pts 10 Jim 'The Rube' Ferns, Pittsburgh, USA. Made at 145lbs, but with no title billing, no weights given and not over a recognised championship distance, Matthews still claimed the 'white' 145lbs world title with this win.

23 December Tom Woodley, besides challenging any 146lbs man in the UK, challenges Jack Palmer (Benwell), 'Dido' Plumb (Balls Pond Road) and Charlie Wilson (Notting Hill) to catchweight bouts, with the three named limited to 156lbs and Woodley to 146lbs.

1903

26 January Eddie Connolly (Canada) w pts 15 Tom Woodley (Fulham), NSC, Covent Garden, London. Originally billed as being for the world 146lbs limit title, £50 a side and purse, that was negated when Woodley came in two pounds over the weight at 148lbs, while Connolly weighed in at 144lbs. The bout still went ahead and was given credence in some quarters as involving the world 148lbs limit title.

23 February Matty Matthews (New York) w pts 10 Tom Couhig, Pittsburg, USA. Billed as involving the American/world 'white' 145lbs limit title, no weights were given and it was not over a recognised title distance.

26 March Bobby Dobbs (Kentucky) w pts 20 Joe White (Cardiff, born Canada), The Corporation Gym, Liverpool. Made at catchweights, £50 a side and a £100 purse, no weights were given and there was no title billing. White's real name was Jack Robertson.

13 April Eddie Connolly (born Canada) w pts 20 Pat Daly/Daley (Grafton Park, born Co Cork), The Warwickshire Horse Repository, Birmingham. An Easter Monday match, refereed by George T.Dunning of the *Sportsman*, it went on at catchweights with Daly at least 14lbs heavier. Claiming to be a three-day substitute for Tom Woodley (Fulham), who had signed to meet Connolly at 146lbs limit on this date, Daly's claim doesn't stand up as The *Birmingham Sports Argus* had advertised Connolly versus Daly from their 20 March issue onwards and had confirmed the bout in their 4 April issue. Connolly, down in 18th, took 'nine' and was saved by the bell, while Daly took 'five' in the 20th, before flooring Connolly for 'seven'. However, the verdict was just, as Connolly won on his condition, while Daly was untrained. At the pay-out the following day, Daly claimed to have floored Connolly with a single punch following an insult at the bar overnight.

25 April Charlie Knock (Stratford) w co 4 Tom Woodley (Fulham), Wonderland, Whitechapel Road, London. Referee Joe Wyman. Although a catchweight contest for a £25 purse, using four-ounce gloves, stipulating two-minute rounds, with no weights given, no title billing and not over a recognised title distance, Knock tried to claim the 144lbs title on his win (144 to 146lbs was also given).

27 April Jim 'The Rube' Ferns w rsc 19 Matty Matthews (New York), Fort Erie, Canada. Billed as an American/world 'white' 145lbs title fight, no weights were given.

18 June Joe Walcott drew 20 'Young' Peter Jackson (Baltimore), The Pastime AC, Portland, Oregon, USA. Billed as a world 145lbs limit title fight and also given 'coloured' title billing, no weights were announced.

23 July Charlie Allum (Notting Hill) to all England at 146lbs – *Sporting Life*.

25 August Martin Duffy w pts 10 Matty Matthews, Fort Huron, USA. Billed as an American/world 'white' 145lbs title fight, no weights were given and it was not over a recognised title distance.

31 August Martin Duffy drew 10 Gus Gardner, Fort Huron, USA. Given as an American/world 'white' 145lbs limit title, in truth, it was merely a catchweight bout with Duffy stated to be 15lbs heavier.

17 September Charlie Knock (Stratford) stated that although he was a 144lbs man he would give Tom Woodley, who had challenged him at 144lbs, a return at 146lbs – *Sporting Life*.

3 October Dick Bailey to all England at 144 to 146lbs – *Sporting Life*.

16 November Charlie Allum (Notting Hill) w co 9 Charlie Knock (Stratford), Wonderland, Whitechapel Road, London. Referee Tom Craze. Allum scaled 146lbs to Knock's 144 in a fight that the *Mirror of Life* report called an English 144 to 146lbs limit

title fight, give or take two pounds. However, the 10 November issue of the *Sporting Life* stated that the bout was articled at catchweights for £50 a side and a £60 purse (total £160), plus a silver cup. The *Mirror of Life* was to state on 21 September 1904, that Charlie Allum won the English 144lbs title in a scheduled 12 rounder, give or take two pounds, in this fight with a four-round kayo win over Charlie Knock (Stratford), which was a certain misprint for nine, while *Sporting Life* report misprinted the weights as Allum 8st 6lbs and Knock 6st 4lbs.

16 December Jack Clancy (San Francisco) to the world at 144 to 148lbs, £25 up to £100 a side, with Pat Daly/Daley, Jim Hook, Charlie Allum or Tom Woodley preferred – *Sporting Life*.

18 December Tom Woodley challenges all England at 144 to 148lbs – *Sporting Life*.

1904

15 February Jack Clancy (San Francisco) w pts 15 Pat Daly/Daley (London, born Ireland), NSC, Covent Garden, London. Referee Mr J.H.Douglas. Billed for the world 146lbs limit title, no weights being given, using four-ounce gloves, it was a really poor bout, all holding, with Clancy cautioned in the ninth for holding and both cautioned in the 14th for foul play.

31 March Jack Clancy (San Francisco) to the world at 140 up to 146lbs – *Sporting Life*. However, the 9 April and 16 May issues of the *Sporting Life* called Clancy the world 146lbs champion.

13 April Edwin Hanby w co 12 'Cape Town Joe', The Savannah AC, Savannah, USA. Billed as being for the 'coloured' welterweight title, with no weights given or stipulated, Joe ended up with a broken jaw. 'Cape Town Joe's' real name not known.

29 April 'Dixie Kid' w disq 20 Joe Walcott (New York, born Barbados), San Francisco, USA. Made at catchweights, 'Dixie Kid' (139lbs), a negro whose real name was Aaron Brown, was getting well beaten when Walcott (144½lbs), also a negro and a claimant of the world 142lbs limit title, was suddenly disqualified for no reason at all. It later came out that the referee, not named, had a bet on the 'Kid' to win and the result was more or less disregarded. Although a catchweight bout with no title billing, it was stated that the 'Kid' laid claim to the title, but just what did he claim? Walcott was nearly three pounds over the weight limit of the title he claimed and half a pound over the next class up, 142 to 144lbs, while the 'Kid' himself was at the top end of the 136 to 138lbs class, or at the bottom end of the 138 to 140lbs class. However, from March 1905 to August 1908, he was inactive due to serving a prison sentence.

4 June Jack Clancy (San Francisco) w co 3 Charlie Allum (Notting Hill), Ginnett's Circus, Newcastle on Tyne. Referee Billy Bell. Billed for the world 146lbs limit title and £100, in the *Sporting Life* 20 rounds were reported, while in the *Mirror of Life* it was 15 rounds. There were no weights given.

12 September Jack Clancy (San Francisco) drew 20 Bobby Dobbs (Kentucky), Ginnett's Circus, Newcastle on Tyne. Billed for the world 144 to 146lbs limit title, no weights were given.

25 October Tom Woodley (Fulham), the English 144 to 146lbs limit champion, to all England at 144 to 146lbs, £50 a side – *Sporting Life*.

21 November Bobby Dobbs (Kentucky) w rsc 8 Pat Daly/Daley (London, born Ireland), Ginnett's Circus, Newcastle on Tyne. Refereed by Billy Bell, Dobbs, a negro, weighed 142½lbs to Daly's 145 (146 also given). Billed as a world 146lbs limit lightweight title fight, £50 a side and a £100 purse (total £200), the *Newcastle Daily Chronicle* and the *Sporting Man* both reported Daly to be behind when he was floored in the eighth and the bout was stopped by the referee in favour of Dobbs. But Daly himself claimed that he was winning easily when he tried his favourite trick of pretending to be hurt in order to lure Dobbs in, but Dobbs stood back and the referee, Billy Bell, said to be one of promoter Jimmy Lowes' contract boxers, as was Dobbs, stopped the bout in Dobbs' favour. Daly also alleged that he was boxing for 25% of the gate, plus two weeks training expenses and Lowes, said to be a real crook, 'rooked' him over the sell-out gate. One must ask why Daly, an experienced pro aged 29, knowing Lowes and Bell to be part of same syndicate as he claimed was Dobbs, would try to pull such a well-known trick on a clever old pro like Dobbs and, of course, at the same time play into the hands of Lowe and Bell. This doesn't hold water somehow, as Daly doesn't seem to have been that stupid.

2 December Charlie Knock to Tom Woodley at 146lbs, £100 or £200 a side – *Sporting Life*.

7 December	The caption with the front cover photo of Peter Brown (Woolwich), the ex-English 148lbs limit champion, states that he challenges anyone at 144lbs. Give or take two pounds was later given – *Mirror of Life*.
26 December	'Dixie Kid' drew 15 'Young' Peter Jackson, Baltimore, USA. No title billing and no weights given or stipulated.

1905

20 January	Pat O'Keefe (Canning Town) to all England at 146lbs – *Sporting Life*.
17 June	George Petersen (Colma) w pts 20 Jack Clancy (San Francisco), San Francisco, USA. Billed for the world 145lbs limit title, with Clancy recognised as the holder, no weights were given.
19 July	William 'Buddy' Ryan (Chicago) w rtd 19 George Petersen (Colma), San Francisco, USA. Billed for the world/American 145lbs title, no weights were given and two weeks previous, on 4 July, Ryan won a bout reported to be for the world 144lbs limit title.
25 August	Jimmy Gardner w rtd 15 William 'Buddy' Ryan (Chicago), San Francisco, USA. Billed as a world 142lbs title bout, with both inside, but no actual weights given.
13 October	Joe Bayley (London), who is just back from Canada, challenges all England at 146lbs – *Sporting Life*.

1906

27 January	Charlie Knock (Stratford) is the English 144 to 146lbs champion – *Sporting Life*. In the 5 June 1905 issue of the *Sporting Life*, Knock had been called the English 148lbs limit champion, but, in truth, it is hard to see where Knock had any basis for his English title claims, as all of his bouts seemed to be either at catchweight or over two-minute rounds, or both.
10 February	Charlie Duncan (Meat Market) is the 146lbs champion – *Sporting Life*. For certain, this means Duncan is the 146lbs champion of the meat market and not the English 146lbs champion.
9 May	Charlie Knock (Stratford) is the English 144 to 146lbs limit champion – *Sporting Life*.
21 May	Charlie Knock (Stratford) w rtd 17 'Seaman' Robert 'Curly' Watson (RN Chatham), Wonderland, Whitechapel Road, London. Referee J.T.Hulls. Billed as for the English 144 to 146lbs title, but made at 144, give or take two pounds, it was disqualified as a title bout as it was only over two minute-rounds. Also, no weights were given, with both men stated to be inside. At end of the 16th round, Watson went to his corner where his second, Bill Natty, accidentally spilt smelling salts into Watson's eyes and with Watson stating he couldn't see the referee stepped into the ring and stopped the bout in Knock's favour, with Watson in front up to the unfortunate ending. Accusations of 'a fix' by promoter, Harry Jacobs, in order to pull off a betting coup on Knock winning, in which Natty was involved, were made, but strongly denied by promoter Jacobs, not known as the most honest of men. The accusation was refuted by both Natty and Watson in letters to the *Mirror of Life*. The *Mirror of Life* editor, Frank J.Bradley, also stated that Bill Natty was a truly honest man and, if he said it was by accident that he spilt the smelling salts into Watson's eyes, then an accident it was, as Natty, in 25 years involvement with boxing, had an unblemished record. Watson stated that the smelling salts were 'a bit sharp' and he went to push them away, causing some to splash into his eyes and on to his bruised and tender face.
25 May	Charlie Knock, the English 144 to 146lbs limit lightweight champion, offers Watson a return at 144lbs, give or take two pounds – *Sporting Life*. On 4 August, Knock lost in a billed English 148 to 150lbs title bout, giving the impression that the 21 May bout truly was at 144 to 146lbs, as he seemed to be moving up in weight almost bout by bout.
16 August	Jack Hayes to all England at 146lbs, £100 a side, Charlie Allum preferred – *Sporting Life*.
17 August	Peter Brown (Woolwich) to all England at 146lbs, £25 or £50 a side, over 15 or 20 rounds, Jim Courtney (Barry, born London) preferred – *Sporting Life*.
3 September	Joe Thomas w co 11 Billy 'Honey' Mellody, Chelsea, Mass, USA. Made at 145lbs, despite a lack of title billing and no weights given following this win Thomas started claiming the American/world 145lbs limit title.
27 September	Bobby Dobbs (Kentucky) w disq 9 Charlie Knock (Stratford), Gymnastic Club, Christian Street, Liverpool. Referee Mr J.T.Hulls. Made at catchweight with no weights given or stipulated and with no title billing, it should have

	been disqualified from title consideration in any case as it was contested over two-minute rounds, for £50 a side and a £65 purse (total £165). Knock was disqualified for throwing his man, Dobbs, a negro, aged 47.
16 October	Billy 'Honey' Mellody w pts 15 Joe Walcott (New York), Chelsea, Mass, USA. Billed as an American/world 145lbs limit title, with no weights given. Mellody ignored Joe Thomas' claim as it was considered doubtful whether he could ever get down to 145lbs again.
3 December	Peter Brown (Woolwich) w rsc 14 Jim Courtney (Barry, born London), The Badminton Club, St Mary's Street, Cardiff. Referee W.Lucas. Made at catchweights, no weights were given but Brown looked to be about 156lbs, although he had, in August, challenged Courtney at 146. Regardless, the fight would have been disqualified as a major title bout in any case as it was contested over two-minute rounds.

1907

8 January	Billy 'Honey' Mellody w pts 15 Terry Martin, Augusta, USA. Reported to be an American/world 145lbs limit title, no weights were given.
23 April	Mike 'Twin' Sullivan w pts 20 Billy 'Honey' Mellody, Los Angeles, USA. Billed for the American/world 145lbs limit title, no weights were given and Mellody claimed that Sullivan was nearer 150lbs than 145, which would have made it a catchweight bout.
4 June	Peter Brown (Woolwich) challenges Robert 'Curly' Watson (Chatham) over 15 or 20 rounds, £50 up to £100 a side and the best purse at 144 to 146lbs – *Sporting Life*.
6 September	Robert 'Curly' Watson challenged all England at 144lbs, £100 a side – *Sporting Life*. In the same issue, Watson was challenged at 150lbs by Charlie Allum (Notting Hill).
9 September	Andrew Jeptha (Cape Town, South Africa), a coloured man, challenges the world at 144lbs – *Sporting Life*.
20 September	Robert 'Curly' Watson (Chatham) is the English 144 to 145lbs limit champion – *Sporting Life*. This was repeated at odd times for the rest of the year.
1 November	Mike 'Twin' Sullivan w pts 20 Frank Field, Goldfield, Nevada, USA. No weights were given or stipulated, and there was no title billing, but Sullivan was challenged by Billy 'Honey' Mellody at 145lbs immediately afterwards.
1 November	Frank Mantell w co 15 Billy 'Honey' Mellody, Dayton, Ohio, USA. Reported to be an American/world 145lbs limit title fight, no weights were given or stipulated.
18 November	Robert 'Curly' Watson (Chatham) w pts 15 Andrew Jeptha (Cape Town, South Africa), NSC, Covent Garden, London. Referee J.H.Douglas. Watson weighed 144lbs and Jeptha 144½ in an international bout made at 144 to 146lbs for £50 a side and a £60 purse (total £160). Although given in some record books as being for the English 144 to 146lbs title, it wasn't, as Jeptha was not eligible for same, being a coloured South African. Jeptha, who seemed like many Americans of the time, prone to claim the championship of any country he passed through, in fact, never won any titles, including those of his native South Africa. The only title Jeptha could have boxed Watson for was that of the Imperial Empire (Commonwealth).

1908

1 February	Jim Connelly, the ex-146lbs champion of England, is now seriously ill in Whipps Cross Infirmary, Leytonstone, London – *Sporting Life*.
11 May	Bobby Dobbs, the Kentucky negro, aged 49, challenges Joe White (Cardiff, born Canada) over 20 three-minute rounds and £25 a side at 144 to 146lbs – *Sporting Life*.
23 June	Harry Lewis (New York) w pts 12 Larry Temple, Boston, Mass, USA. Advertised and billed as for the American/world 145lbs limit title, no weights were given, just the statement that the coloured man, Temple, was inside 145lbs, while Lewis was over the weight, which meant Temple could have claimed title by forfeit, although there is no trace of him having done so.
3 October	Joe White (Cardiff, born Canada) is called the English welterweight champion, as he had been for some time, but no actual weight was given – *Sporting Life*.
12 December	Harry Lewis (New York) drew 12 Willie Lewis (New York City), New Haven, Connecticut, USA. Made at catchweights, with no weights given and no title billing, at least one paper, the *Boston Post*, previewed it as being for the world/American 145lbs limit title. On 11 February 1909, the NSC introduced the eight-named weight divisions and, in Britain, the weight class became part of the 147lbs welterweight division very quickly, while, in America, as in the 140 to

142lbs and 142 to 144lbs weight classes, 144 to 146lbs would only be fully integrated into the welter division once Jack Britton had been deposed in 1922. However, in the meantime, there were many title bouts that took place at the weight in America and, although not listed here due to lack of space, they have been noted.

146lbs to 148lbs (10st 6lbs to 10st 8lbs)

1873

21 April Charley Davis (Mile End and Stepney) w rtd 25 Ted Napper, The Grafton Hall, Grafton Street, Soho, London. Considered in some quarters as involving the English 148lbs limit title, by others as a catchweight bout, with Davis weighing 147lbs and Napper 140, it was billed as being a defence of the English 154lbs championship and 'Bow Cup', held by Davis. However, Davis was said to have forfeited his claim at 154lbs when six pounds over the weight for a 7 January defence of this title and the 'Bow Cup'. Nevertheless, following the above win, Davis was presented with the 11 stone middleweight 'Bow Cup' on 28 April, so in the light of that this bout must also go in the 154lbs list, despite both men being so much below the 11-stone mark.

1875

30 August Bill Kennedy w pts 3 Tim Harrington, Running Grounds, Hackney Wick, London. Refereed by Mr J.Jane and the final of a 148lbs limit silver cup competition (only three entered), in the previous round Kennedy outscored William 'Soldier' Robinson, while Tim (not Tom as also given) Harrington, the brother of Denny Harrington, drew a bye. Robinson claimed that during their first-round bout he twice had Kennedy down, both times for over 30 seconds, and that, on the second occasion, Kennedy's seconds assisted him up, for which he should have been disqualified. The verdict in Kennedy's favour caused much comment. On 11 September, in *Bells Life*, Mr J.Jane stated that Kennedy was only down once in the Robinson bout and then only for 'five', while on the so-called second occasion Robinson had pushed Kennedy through the ropes and Kennedy had to hang on to the bottom rope to avoid a six-foot fall from the stage. He was then assisted by others, not his one and only second, Ted Napper, to get back on to the platform and actually resumed boxing within 14 seconds of being ejected from the ring.

1877

1 February Hugh Burns drew 35 Jim Goode, McDonalds Music Hall, High Street, Hoxton, London. Refereed by Joe Vesey and articled to a finish under MoQ Rules, using gloves, for a £50 silver cup, there was no title billing and no weights given or stipulated. The bout lasted two hours and the *Sportsman* misprinted Goode as Gold.

1878

5 April William C. McClellan (New York, born England) w disq 14 Mike Donovan (Chicago), San Francisco, USA. Billed as an American 148lbs middleweight title fight, to a finish, MoQ Rules, ordinary gloves, the *New York Herald* gave it as a 16th round disqualification win for McClellan. The bout lasted 55 minutes and no weights were given.

18 May Mike Donovan w disq 8 William C.McClellan, New York City, USA. Billed as an American 148lbs limit middleweight title fight to a finish, eight rounds and seven also given, it was under MoQ Rules with hard gloves. The bout was given as lasting 14 minutes, although the *New York Herald* gives 18 minutes. Following the fight, Donovan challenged the world at 140lbs. If this was not a misprint, McClellan could have had a return at any weight.

1879

18 August Mike Donovan drew 94 William C.McClellan, Platts Hall, San Francisco, USA. With both men weighing 147lbs in a fight billed for the American 148lbs limit title, under MoQ Rules and using hard gloves, the bout lasted three hours and 48 minutes for $1,000.

1880

28 July William Sherriff (Leicester), alias 'The Prussian', to the world at 148lbs – *Sporting Life*.

1881

22 January Joe Collins (Leicester), alias 'Tug Wilson', to Bat Mullins at 148lbs and £100 up to £500 a side – *Sporting Life*.

1882

3 April Charlie Mitchell (Birmingham) w pts 4 Bill Harnetty (Fulham), Kings Road Baths Gym, Chelsea, London. The final of a professional 147lbs limit competition, which was organised by the ABA, it had started on 27 March with just four entries. In the earlier rounds, Mitchell beat Pat Condon, while Harnetty eliminated Jim Daley. On 21 March, Harnetty had weighed 133lbs when losing a bare-knuckle bout to Peter Brislin.

2 December Bill Springhall (Battersea), the 154lbs champion, to George Roberts at 148lbs, £100 a side or more – *Sporting Life*.

16 December Bat Mullins, aged 32, is the 148lbs middleweight champion – *Sporting Life*.

1884

30 April Bill 'Chesterfield' Goode, the younger brother of Jim Goode, is challenged by William Halford (Nottingham) at 148lbs for a trophy, not exceeding £25 a side – *Sporting Life*.

1 September Bill Springhall (Battersea), the English 11 stone limit champion, challenges any man in the world at 148lbs – *Sporting Life*.

5 September Bill Springhall's challenge is accepted by Bill 'Chesterfield' Goode at 148lbs – *Sporting Life*. On 18 September, the *Sporting Life* stated that there had been an attempt to make this match but it fell through. Although Springhall was willing to weigh in the same day, he wouldn't accept Goode's other terms.

1885

13 April Alec Roberts w pts 3 George Cashley (Forest Gate), Waites Rooms, 19 Brewer Street, off Regent Street, Piccadilly Circus, London. The final of Ned Donnelly's 147lbs limit competition, £15 to the winner, in previous rounds Roberts beat Jim Hook and Bill Cheese, while Cashley beat Tom Smith and Josh Alexander.

Mike Donovan

1886

13 March   Charlie 'Toff' Wall (Hackney) to all England at 148lbs, £200 a side and a £50 purse – *Sporting Life*. This was repeated on 19 and 29 March when Wall was called the English 148lbs middleweight champion.

20 March   Wall's challenge is accepted by Bill 'Chesterfield' Goode at 148lbs – *Sporting Life*.

6 May   Jim Kendrick (Lambeth, born Ireland) drew 20 Bill 'Chesterfield' Goode (Shadwell), Lambeth School of Arms, Lambeth Walk, Paradise Street, London. Stopped by the police in round 20, Kendrick, who weighed 145lbs, had the best of it up until then against Goode (147lbs). Stated to be a catchweight bout, although the 148lbs English title was hinted at, there was no actual title billing. It was contested under MoQ Rules in a 14-foot ring, despite MoQ Rules calling for a 24-foot ring. Following the stoppage, the backers of both men met on Wednesday 12 May and a draw was agreed to. On 19 May, both men were arrested and charged at Lambeth Police Court and, after two adjournments, the case was heard at the Surrey Sessions on 9 June before Sir William Hardman. The jury, after being out for 45 minutes, found both men 'not guilty' and soft glove boxing of limited rounds legal. In later years, it was always recognised that the result of this case had legalised gloved boxing of limited rounds in England, although occasional court cases still arose over this point from time to time.

1887

19 January   Alec Roberts (Clerkenwell) w pts 3 Jack Donogue (Clerkenwell), Bob Habbijam's West-End School of Arms, Newman Street, Oxford Street, London. The final of Bob Habbijam's English 148lbs championship belt competition, in previous rounds Roberts beat J.Passfield and J.Alexander, while Donogue defeated Jim Kendrick and Arthur Bobbett. This was the first time this belt had been contested for.

26 March   Jack Hickey (Birmingham, born Ireland) to the world at 147 or 148lbs, £100 up to £200 a side – *Midland Sporting News*. In the 4 June issue of the *Sportsman*, Hickey was called the 150lbs limit champion and had gone to the USA.

15 June   Alec Roberts (Clerkenwell) is the English 148lbs limit champion – *Sportsman*. This was repeated on 27 September.

20 September Bill 'Chesterfield' Goode (Shadwell) to the world, 146 up to 150lbs and £100 up to £500 a side – *Sporting Life*.

17 October   Alec Roberts (Clerkenwell) drew 13 Alec Burns (Battersea), Lambeth School of Arms, Lambeth Walk, Paradise Street, London. A 12-round contest, with an extra round boxed, although Roberts was the holder of the English 148lbs championship belt given by Bob Habbijam, no weights given or stipulated and there was no title billing. Strangely, the referee left the building and the judges' decision was not given, but was believed to be for Roberts. However, it was later stated that the official decision of the judges was a draw.

16 December Alec Roberts is the English 148lbs champion – *Sportsman*.

1888

25 January   Alec Roberts (Clerkenwell) w pts 3 Arthur Cooper (Billingsgate), Bob Habbijam's West-End School of Arms, Newman Street, Oxford Street, London. The final of Bob Habbijam's English 148lbs limit championship belt competition, with both men weighing 147lbs, the winner also got £10. Following the fight, the belt became Roberts' own property on his winning it for a second time. In previous rounds, Roberts drew the bye then beat the ex-amateur, Jack Edmunds (Birmingham), who was making his pro debut, while Cooper beat W.Bullion and Jack Donogue.

17 March   Bill 'Chesterfield' Goode (Shadwell) is the English 148lbs champion – *Midland Sporting News*.

25 September Alec Roberts (Westminster) drew 33 Arthur Bobbett (Fulham), Bob Kirby's Lambeth School of Arms, Lambeth Walk, Paradise Street, London. Referee Mr B.J.Angle. Made at catchweights, with Roberts scaling 147½lbs to Bobbett's 152, £200 a side, no weights stipulated and no title billing, in some quarters it was later given as an English 148lbs title bout, lasting three hours, 30 minutes and 45 seconds.

26 November Alec Roberts is the English 148lbs champion – *Sporting Life*. Also misprinted as being the 10-stone champion, it was repeated in the 12 and 21 December *Sporting Life*.

1889

15 January   Alec Roberts is the 148lbs champion – *Sporting Life*. It was once again misprinted that Roberts was the 10-stone champion, a weight he had never boxed at in his life. This was repeated on 12 November.

18 March   Ted Pritchard, the English 145lbs champion, to the world, 145 up to 150lbs, and any man breathing at 147lbs – *Sporting Life*. This was accepted by Alec Roberts for £500 a side and Roberts was called, by his backer, Bob Habbijam, the rightful 145lbs champion. Roberts, in fact, had won his title claims at the 147lbs limit and 148lbs limit and had the final bout of his career on 25 September 1888.

6 June   Ted Pritchard (Lambeth, born South Wales) w co 2 Alec Burns (Battersea), Lambeth School of Arms, Lambeth, London. Referee B.J.Angle. Billed for the English 146 to 148lbs limit middleweight title, Pritchard weighed 146lbs to Burns' 147.

16 July   Ted Pritchard (Lambeth) is the English 148lbs champion – *Sportsman*.

4 August   Johnny Robinson (South Shields) to any 148lbs middleweight, Bill 'Chesterfield' Goode preferred – *Sporting Life*.

28 October   Ted White (Walthamstow) w disq 8 Tom Meadows (Australia), South London Gym Club, Mountford Place, Kennington Green, London. Referee Mr R.Wilson. Reported at 148lbs in the *Sportsman*, and at catchweights in the *Sporting Life*, with no weights given at all and no title billing, Meadows was disqualified for holding the ropes while hitting his man. The *Sportsman* gave Meadows as being born in Sydney, Australia, while the *Sporting Life* stated that he was born in Liverpool, England.

12 November Jim Hayes stated he would box Johnny Robinson (South Shields) at 148lbs, £50 a side, using two or four-ounce gloves, in London – *Sporting Life*.

7 December   Jim Burchell (Shoreditch) w pts 4 Bill Husband (Knightsbridge), Royal Aquarium Theatre, Westminster, London. The final of Frank Hinde's 148lbs championship competition and the final night of a six-night show, in previous rounds Burchell beat Jim Kendrick and Bill Hatcher, while Husband beat Tom Meadows and J.Ellis.

1890

6 February   Ted Pritchard (Lambeth, born Wales) is the English 147lbs champion – *Sporting Life*.

8 February   Jim Verrall (Walworth) w co 18 Jack Ashman (Forest Hill), Gravesend, Kent. A Con Donovan private show, with a restricted attendance, it was contested at catchweights with no title billing, no weights given or stipulated and to a finish. Ashman was over 14lbs heavier.

19 May   Jim Verrall (Peckham and Walworth) w rsc 18 Jim 'Ginger' Elmer, The Exchange, Queen Street, Cheapside, London. Made at catchweights, no weights were given or stipulated and there was no title billing.

16 October   Jim Verrall (Peckham) w co 6 Alf Suffolk (Lambeth), Lambeth School of Arms, Paradise Street, Lambeth, London. Made at 146 to 148lbs, with four-ounce gloves, £50 a side and no title billing, Verrall scaled 147lbs to Suffolk's 148.

25 October   Alec Roberts is the retired English 148lbs champion – *Sporting Life*. However, this was once again misprinted as him being the 144lbs champion.

7 November   Lachie Thompson (Glasgow) w co 3 Harry Downie (Australia, born Edinburgh). Held at a private show with a restricted attendance in London and billed as being for the 149lbs English title, in view that the weight for each man was 148lbs it seems more likely that it was made at 148lbs, with 149 being a misprint as, on 3 November, Anthony Diamond had won a 148lbs title bout.

25 November Ted Bryant (Chelsea) w co 1 John O'Brien (Roath, Cardiff), Bob Habbijam's West-End School of Arms, Newman Street, off Oxford Street, London. Made at catchweights, with O'Brien 14lbs heavier and considered a dead cert to win being kayoed in 37 seconds, including the count. That was what the *Sportsman* reported, but the *Sporting Life* gave it as 47 seconds, including the count. There was no title billing as it was a catchweight bout, but Bryant, with this upset win over one of the top 158lbs men in the country, started claiming the English 148lbs limit title. On 28 November, in the *Sporting Life*, an offer of a return was made to O'Brien, if at the 148lbs limit, a weight he could never make.

1891

4 March   Felix Scott (Liverpool), the 'coloured' champion of England, to any one in the world, 146 up to 150lbs, either in England or the USA – *Sportsman*.

22 June   Alf Suffolk (Lambeth) w co 1 William Robinson (Hackney), NSC, Covent Garden, London. The final of an NSC all-England 148lbs limit competition, with Suffolk the winner in two minutes, 45 seconds. In previous rounds, Suffolk beat George Ingram and Fred Greenbank, while Robinson, the

31 October   'Cock Robin', defeated R.Treacher and Bill Cheese. Suffolk's win over the highly regarded 'Cock Robin' was a real shock.
Ted Bryant (Chelsea) to all England at 146 to 148lbs. Bryant, who seldom fought, was not too highly regarded, despite his shock kayo win over John O'Brien, which, although considered a fluke, had thrown him into the spotlight and gave some weight to his claim to the 148lbs limit title. However, in truth, Bryant's challenge was little more than a publicity stunt, as he always seemed reluctant to fight anyone, being content to rest on his laurels.

30 November   Lachie Thompson (Glasgow) w co 6 Arthur Akers (Leicester), The Pelican Club, Gerrard Street, Soho, London. Billed as being for the 148lbs limit English title, £200 a side and purse, both men weighed 148lbs.

5 December   William Robinson (Hackney) w pts 7 Walter Gunn (Plumsted), The Goodwin Club, Kingsland Road, Shoreditch, London. The final of Ben Hyams' all-England 148lbs competition scheduled for seven rounds, and the final night of a six-night show, in previous rounds Robinson, the 'Cock Robin', beat Frank Callas and Bill Cheese, while Gunn eliminated 'Barney' Lambert and T.Hicks.

1892

30 Janaury   Lachie Thompson (Glasgow) is the English 148lbs limit champion – *Sporting Life*.

1893

20 September Alf Bowman, the ABA heavyweight champion in 1889, is the English 148lbs champion – *Sporting Life*

1894

15 December Alf Suffolk (Vauxhall) w co 1 George Haskell (Fulham), The Central Hall, Holborn, London. Referee Bob Watson. The final of Frank Hinde's 148lbs English championship competition, and the final night of a seven-night show, in previous rounds Suffolk beat Jack Osbourne and Andy Cannon, while Haskell beat Walter Gunn and Jim Kendrick. The final lasted just 60 seconds.

1897

15 February Alf Suffolk (Bradford, late London) w disq 9 Harry Brady (Huddersfield), The Canal Theatre, Canal Road, Bradford, Yorkshire. Referee Ed Plummer. Made at 148lbs for a £50 purse, no weights were given and no title billing was attached.

17 March   William 'Bill' Robinson (Hackney), alias 'Cock Robin', to Lachie Thompson (Glasgow) at 146 to 148lbs – *Sporting Life*.

25 October   Pat 'Paddy' Purtell (USA) can't make 144lbs but will box Dick Burge and Arthur Akers at 148lbs – *Sporting Life*.

20 November Bill Husband to all England at 148lbs up to £100 a side – *Sporting Life*.

1898

21 January   Harry Neumier (Stepney) to all England at 148 – *Sporting Life*.

19 February Ted Heymes (Haymes also given) to all England at 148lbs – *Sporting Life*.

10 October   'Wilmington' Jack Daly w pts 25 Owen Ziegler, The Coney Island AC, New York, USA. No weights were given or stipulated and there was no title billing, but just eight days later Daly boxed in a catchweight bout weighing 147lbs.

25 October   Tom Woodley (Fulham) to all England, 144 up to 150lbs, £50 a side – *Sporting Life*.

1899

24 January   'Mysterious' Billy Smith w co 14 'Australian' Billy Edwards, New York City, USA. Made at the 147lbs limit, catchweights also given, no weights were announced and no title billing was attached. There was some doubt that Edwards could get under 150lbs.

13 March   Tom Woodley (Fulham) to Pat Daly/Daley (born Ireland) at 148lbs, 20 rounds and £100 a side upwards – *Sporting Life*.

15 March   Tom Pearman to Tom Woodley (Fulham) at 148lbs, 20 rounds, four-ounce gloves and £100 a side upwards – *Sporting Life*.

20 March   Harry Neumier (Stepney) to all England at 148lbs – *Sporting Life*.

20 March   'Young' Sharkey (San Francisco, California) to all England at 148lbs, Jim Styles (Marylebone) or Tom Woodley (Fulham) preferred – *Sporting Life*.

5 October   The death has occured of the ex-148lbs champion (144lbs also given), Alec Roberts, aged 39, of acute pneumonia. Roberts was one of five brothers, four of whom boxed. His death was reported in the *Sporting Life* on 6 October and the *Mirror of Life* on 11 October. It was also announced in the *Sportsman* of 6 October and various other newspapers.

1900

24 January   Jim Styles (Marylebone) to all England at 146 to 148lbs – *Sporting Life*.

26 January   'Mysterious' Billy Smith w co 22 Frank McConnell (San Francisco), The Broadway AC, New York City, USA. Reported in the *Sporting Life* as taking place on 27 January, it was billed as being for the American/world 148lbs welterweight title with both men weighing 148lbs, despite Smith looking at least 10 pounds heavier than his given weight. The finish came when McConnell's head hit the floor with a terrific thud and he was out for over five minutes. For the first time in a New York ring, two judges, Samuel C.Austin and John Boden, were used as well as the referee, who was only to vote if the judges disagreed, the same as in the UK.

12 June   'Young' Peter Jackson (USA), a negro whose real name was Sim Thompkins, the 145lbs champion of the Pacific Coast, challenges all England at 145 to 148lbs, Dick Burge preferred. Burge accepted on 14 June for side stakes of either £200 or £500 a side – *Sporting Life*.

18 July   'Titch' Morgan (South Africa, but stated also to be an Australian) to all England at 147 to 149lbs, £200 a side – *Sporting Life*. This was repeated on 25 October and extended to the world at 147 to 149lbs, £200 up to £500 a side. On 26 October, Morgan's challenge was accepted by 'Barney' Maloney (South Africa), who lost to Morgan in Australia at 148lbs, £200 up to £500 a side.

1901

22 May   Harry Neumier (St George's and Stepney) to 'Jewey' Cooke at 148lbs, over 15 or 20 rounds and £50 or £100 a side – *Sporting Life*.

5 September Tom Woodley to all England at 144 up to 150lbs, Jack Palmer (Benwell) or Harry Neumier preferred – *Sporting Life*. This was repeated throughout the rest of the year.

25 October   Harry Slater (Birmingham), back after 12 years in San Francisco where he claimed nearly 100 bouts, challenges Pat Daly/Daley at 148lbs ringside – *Sporting Life*.

1902

10 July   Tom Woodley (Fulham) to all England at 146 to 148lbs, over 15 or 20 rounds, three minutes each round – *Sporting Life*. This was repeated through the rest of the year, with weights varying from 144 to 150lbs and 144 to 148lbs. The 3 October issue of the *Sporting Life* stated that Pat Daly/Daley was preferred and the 10 December issue of the *Sporting Life* stated that the winner of Bobby Dobbs (Kentucky) versus Joe White (Canada) was preferred, £50 or £100 a side.

1903

26 January   Eddie Connolly (New Brunswick, Canada) w pts 15 Tom Woodley (Fulham), NSC, Covent Garden, London. Billed as being for the world 144 to 146lbs limit title, £50 a side and purse, Woodley (148lbs) was two pounds over the weight, while Connolly came in at 144lbs.

15 August   Charlie Allum (Notting Hill) to all England at 148lbs – *Sporting Life*.

16 September Tom Woodley to all England at 148lbs, £100 a side, Charlie Knock preferred – *Sporting Life*. In the 17 September issue of the *Sporting Life*, Knock stated that he was a 144lbs man, but would box Woodley at 146 for £100 a side and an NSC purse.

28 October   A photo of George Penny (Kentish Town), who is now a 148lbs man, shows him wearing his English 10-stone Coronation championship belt – *Mirror of Life*.

16 December Jack Clancy (San Francisco) to the world at 144 to 148lbs, over 20 rounds for a £100 purse, Pat Daly/Daley, Jim Hook, Charlie Allum or Tom Woodley preferred – *Sporting Life*.

18 December Tom Woodley (Fulham) challenges all England at 144 to 148lbs and also accepts the challenge of Jack Clancy at 148lbs – *Sporting Life*.

1904

4 January   Peter Brown (Woolwich) w pts 6 Jack Kingsland (Paddington), The International AC (formerly The National AC), 241 Marylebone Road, London. The final of an English 146 to 148lbs limit championship belt competition, in previous rounds Brown beat Pat O'Keefe and Jack Goldswain, while Kingsland drew a bye, then defeated Ernie Veitch. On 10 February, the front cover of the *Mirror of Life* had a photo of Brown with his belt.

26 February   Martin Duffy (Chicago) w pts 20 Jim 'The Rube' Ferns, Hot Springs, Arkansas, USA. Billed as an American/world 148lbs 'white' title fight, no weights were given.

275

28 February Peter Brown (Woolwich), the present English 148lbs limit champion, challenges all England at 144lbs – *Sporting Life*. This is a possible misprint, as in the 9 April issue of the *Sporting Life* his challenge is to all England at 146 to 148lbs.

22 April Billy 'Honey' Mellody w co 4 Martin Duffy, Chicago, USA. Mellody scaled 142lbs to Duffy's 147¹/₂ in what was a catchweight non-title bout with no championship conditions applied.

10 June 'Young' Peter Jackson (local) w co 4 Joe Walcott. Baltimore, USA. There is some confusion here as, although it is stated to have been for the world 148lbs limit title, no weight is given for Walcott. It was also stated to have been a catchweight bout, with Jackson (148lbs) heavier than Walcott, the 142lbs limit champion.

26 August 'Young' Peter Jackson, a negro whose real name is Sim Thompkins, is the world 148lbs limit champion, having beaten Joe Walcott to win this title. Jackson is also the holder of the world middleweight title, which he won by beating the holder, Charley McKeever, in five rounds – *Sporting Life*. Jackson had beaten McKeever on a foul inside six rounds (not five) on 21 April 1902 in a six-round no-decision bout in Philadelphia. McKeever had won a billed world 152lbs middleweight title bout in England on 15 October 1900, but the 1902 no-decision bout could have no title involvement and was just Philadelphia's way of keeping in the boxing headlines, which they did throughout the no-decision era.

26 September 'Young' Peter Jackson w co 3 Charlie Knock (Stratford), Wonderland, Whitechapel Road, London. Referee James T.Hulls. Billed for the world 148lbs limit title, with Jackson as holder, it was disqualified from full title recognition as it was contested over two-minute rounds only. Although it also got billed as being over 20 rounds of three minutes each, the impression given in the reports is that it was cut to 15 rounds of two minutes each, although the *Sporting Life* reports give it as 20 rounds of two minutes each, while the *Mirror of Life* says 15 rounds of two minutes each.

15 October Bobby Dobbs (Kentucky) w pts 20 Jack Kingsland (Kensington, London), Ginnett's Circus, Newcastle on Tyne. In a bout originally made at the 147lbs limit, Dobbs came in at 142lbs but, with Kingsland weighing 149lbs, two pounds over the weight, it eventually went on at catchweights.

25 October Tom Woodley (Fulham), the English 144 to 146lbs champion, to 'Young' Peter Jackson at 148lbs – *Sporting Life*.

7 December The caption on a front cover photo of Peter Brown (Woolwich), the ex English 148lbs limit lightweight champion, states that he will meet all at 144lbs – *Mirror of Life*.

26 December 'Young' Peter Jackson drew 15 'Dixie Kid', Baltimore, USA. Although no weights were given or stipulated and there was no title billing, one would have thought it would get American/world or, at least, 'coloured' world title billing. So, more than likely, it was a catchweight bout. The 'Dixie Kid's' real name was Aaron Brown.

1905

13 January Charlie Knock (Stratford) to the world at 148lbs, Charlie Allum (Notting Hill) preferred, £100 a side – *Sporting Life*.

17 February Jack Bayley (Birmingham) to all England at 147lbs, £100 or £200 a side – *Sporting Life*.

10 April Peter Brown (Woolwich) is the English 148lbs champion – *Sporting Life*.

4 June Charlie Knock (Stratford) is the English 148lbs lightweight champion – *Sporting Life*.

7 August Charlie Knock to Pat O'Keefe (Canning Town) at 148lbs – *Sporting Life*.

19 August Pat O'Keefe (Canning Town) to all England at 148lbs and an NSC purse, Charlie Knock preferred – *Sporting Life*.

1906

17 March Pat Daly/Daley (London, born Ireland) is the English 148lbs welterweight champion, a title he won when beating Mike Crawley on 26 February 1906 (see 148 to 150lbs list), and would defend this against Charlie Knock (Stratford) – *Sporting Life*. In the 21 April issue of the *Sporting Life*, Daly stated that 148lbs was his best weight, then challenged all at 11 stone.

3 December Peter Brown (Woolwich) w co 14 Jim Courtney (Barry, born London), The Badminton Club, St Mary's Street, Cardiff. Made at catchweights, while Courtney scaled 142lbs no weight was given for Brown, who looked to be about 156lbs. Contested over two-minute rounds, there was no title billing.

1907

11 February Jack Goldswain (Bermondsey) w co 5 Pat Daly/Daley (London, born Cork), NSC, Covent Garden, London. In a contest articled for the English 140lbs limit lightweight title, Goldswain scaling 139¹/₂lbs, unfortunately, Daly came in at 148lbs, being eight pounds over the weight, for which he paid forfeit. However, the loss to Goldswain could be said to effect all the other titles he laid claim to, one of which was the English 146 to 148lbs title, although this was really safeguarded as Goldswain was far below 146lbs. One of worst bouts ever seen, but no blame could be laid on Goldswain, Daly was pitiful. In reality, it was only a catchweight bout involving no titles.

11 February Billy 'Honey' Mellody w rsc 4 Willie Lewis (New York), Valley Falls, New York, USA. Thought to be for the American/world 147lbs limit title, some adverts gave it as being at 142lbs, which was surely a misprint.

14 August Bobby Dobbs (Kentucky) challenges all England at 147lbs, over 20 three-minute rounds, Joe White (Cardiff, late Canada) preferred – *Sporting Life*.

7 September Arthur Harman (Lambeth) to all England at 146lbs, give or take two pounds – *Sporting Life*.

9 September Mike Crawley (Limehouse) w rsc 11 Arthur Harman (Lambeth), Norfolk Road Drill Hall, Sheffield. With no weights given or stipulated and no title billing, it was almost certainly contested over two-minute rounds, but not actually stated.

23 September Bobby Dobbs (now of Kilmarnock, Scotland), a negro, late of Kentucky, USA and now almost 50, announces his retirement from boxing, due to failing eye sight.

1 November Mike 'Twin' Sullivan (Cambridge, Mass) w pts 20 Frank Fields, Goldfield, Nevada, USA. Believed to be at catchweights, but not sure. Despite being recorded in the *Ring Record Book* as a title fight, no weights were given or stipulated and there was no title billing.

27 November Mike 'Twin' Sullivan w co 13 'Kid' Farmer, Los Angeles, USA. Stated to be at catchweights by the *Sportsman*, *Sporting Life* and *San Francisco Chronicle*, the *Los Angeles Times* called it a title bout but gave no weights.

1908

26 March Harry Lewis (New York City) w pts 15 Terry Martin, Baltimore, USA. No weights given or stipulated and there was no title billing.

18 April Robert 'Curly' Watson (Chatham) w pts 10 Charlie Knock (Stratford), Wonderland, Whitechapel Road, London. Referee Ed Humphries. The final of a £100 English 148lbs limit championship belt competition, in the first series and semi-finals on 30 March Watson had beaten Billy Edwards and 'Seaman' Willis, while Knock, who still had his arm bandaged up, having not fully recovered from breaking it in March in Paris, had beaten 'Gunner' Gorman and Sid Doyle.

20 April Harry Lewis (New York) w co 4 Billy 'Honey' Mellody, Boston, Mass, USA. Made at 147lbs, with both men weighing 147, there was no actual title billing and a stipulated number of rounds were not given.

18 May Joe White (Cardiff, born New Brunswick, Canada) to Willie Lewis (New York), £100 up to £200 a side at 148lbs – *Sporting Life*.

21 May Joe White (Cardiff, born Canada) w pts 20 Robert 'Curly' Watson (Chatham, born Stockport. Barrow in Furness also given), The Gymnastic Club, Christian Street, Liverpool. Made at catchweights, no weights being given or stipulated and no title billing, for £50 a side and a £70 purse (total £170), it was possibly contested over two-minute rounds but not stated. If so, it would automatically disqualify it from title recognition. Often put in the record books as being an English 148lbs title bout, White, born in Canada, was not eligible. However, a Canadian could well contest an Imperial Commonwealth title if it had been billed as such, but in any case it was made at catchweights.

14 November Jack Kingsland (Kensington) is the English 148lbs limit welterweight champion – *Sporting Life*.

21 December 'Peggy' Bettinson stated that the NSC was in the process of standardising weights in a bid to stop champions at every two pounds, one pound in some cases, and would be introducing a welterweight division with a limit of 148lbs. And, of course, only British-born persons of British parents would be able to contest an English title, thus remaining the same as it always has been, and English titles would become British titles.

22 December Jim Sullivan (Bermondsey) is called the English 148lbs welterweight champion – *Sportsman*.

1909

1 February Jack Kingsland (Kensington) is the English 148lbs welterweight champion – *Sportsman*. On 11 February, the NSC introduced the eight-named weight divisions and, in Britain, the 146 to 148lbs class was immediately integrated into the new 147lbs welterweight division, the final major contest at the weight taking place on 26 May 1909 at the Villiers Street Arms, Charing Cross, London between Willie Lewis (USA) and Andrew Jeptha (South Africa). Billed for the world 148lbs title, Lewis won via a third-round kayo and effectively closed the book on title fights at that weight in Britain.

148lb to 150lbs (10st 8 to 10st 10)

1877

6 January Denny Harrington is the 148lbs middleweight champion – *Bells Life*.

14 April Denny Harrington to all at the 148 to 150lbs limit with gloves, £50 or £100 a side – *Sporting Life*.

5 May J. Guppy (Pall Mall, London) challenges E. Whenman (could be Whyman) of Kings Cross, with gloves for a silver cup valued at not less than £25, under MoQ Rules with gloves – *Bells Life*.

3 November George Rooke (born Dundalk, Ireland), the American champion, to Denny Harrington (London, born Cork, Ireland) at 150lbs, £100 a side, with gloves – *Bells Life*.

1878

21 May Pat Condon w pts 3 Andy Elms, The Peacock Tavern, Cambridge Heath Road, Bethnal Green, London. The final of a middleweight competition for a silver cup, the exact weight was not given. There were four entries, Elms eliminating J.Poole and Condon beating W.Ames in the first series, but in the following weeks the *Sportsman* stated that Condon won this competition by beating Andy Elines (misprint for Elms) and Bob Peryer in the final.

7 September 'Florey' Barnett, in reply to Alf Greenfield (Birmingham), stated that he couldn't box at 148lbs but would box him at 152lbs, £50 a side – *Sporting Life*.

1879

11 September Thomas Morgan (London, late Bristol) to the world at 150lbs, £25 or £50 a side – *Sporting Life*.

1886

2 February 'Nonpareil' Jack Dempsey (born Ireland) w co 27 Jack Fogarty, The Clarendon Hall, New York City, USA. A private show which billed the above as being for the American/world 150lbs limit title, no weights were given and it was also stated to have been at catchweights, thus making title involvement doubtful. Contested in skin-tight gloves or bare knuckles, it was made under London prize ring rules, but MoQ Rules were stated to have been used instead.

1887

14 January Jim Kendrick (Lambeth, born Ireland) drew 12 Jack Hickey (Birmingham, born Ireland), Lambeth School of Arms, Lambeth Walk, Paradise Street, Lambeth, London. Made at catchweights, £50 a side, with no title billing, the winner was to have got a diamond pin from Bob Habbijam. This was the pro debut of the ex-amateur, Hickey, who weighed 149lbs to Kendrick's 143.

22 February W.Brown (Birmingham) w pts Bill Cheese (Hoxton), The Imperial Theatre Aquarium, Westminster, London. The final of the *Sportsman*'s all-England 150lbs limit competition for £25, with Brown, the 1884 ABA middleweight champion, scaling 149lbs and Cheese coming in at 150lbs. In previous rounds, Brown beat Bill Hatcher and Ching Ghook, while Cheese defeated J.Glover before drawing a bye.

26 March Jack Hickey (Birmingham, born Ireland) challenges the world at 148lbs, give or take two pounds, £100 or £200 a side – *Midland Sporting News*.

26 April Jack Hickey (Birmingham, born Ireland) is the English 150lbs champion – *Sportsman*. This was to be repeated throughout the year.

30 April Harry Downie, the champion of California who was born in Edinburgh, challenges any man in England at 150lbs, nobody barred, but Johnny Robinson (South Shields) preferred, £100 a side – *Sporting Life*.

4 June Jack Hickey, the English 150lbs champion, has now gone to the USA looking for a match against 'Nonpareil' Jack Dempsey (also born in Ireland), the American 150lbs champion, in order to decide the world 150lbs championship – *Sportsman*. Interestingly, Hickey had only one traced pro bout, the 14 January bout versus Jim Kendrick.

26 July Jack Hickey, the English 150lbs champion, is now back from the USA as he was unable to get a bout there and challenges the world at 150lbs, £100 or £200 a side – *Sportsman*.

10 September Hickey repeats the above challenge and claims forfeit from Arthur Bobbett, who failed to turn up to sign for a match – *Sportsman*.

1888

2 January Jack Hickey (Birmingham, born Ireland) is the English 150lbs limit champion – *Sportsman*. This was repeated on 15 February.

18 February Alec Roberts (Clerkenwell) w pts 12 Alec Burns (Battersea), Lambeth School of Arms, Lambeth Walk, Paradise Street, Lambeth, London. Reported as a catchweight bout with no title billing, Roberts weighed 146lbs to Burns' 149lbs.

1889

14 January Ted White (Walthamstow) w pts 4 Bill Husband, The Pelican Club, Denham Street, off Shaftsbury Avenue and Piccadilly Circus, Soho, London. The final of an all-England 150lbs limit competition for £15, in previous rounds White, the ABA heavyweight champion of 1887, beat George Burgin and J.Bird, while Husband eliminated Alf Suffolk and Charlie Bartlett, 'The Meat Market Black'.

19 January Bill 'Chesterfield' Goode (Shadwell) to the world at 150lbs – *Sporting Life*.

27 February Ted Pritchard (Lambeth, born Wales) challenges the world at 150lbs, 'Nonpareil' Jack Dempsey (USA, born Ireland) or Bill 'Chesterfield' Goode preferred, for a world 150lbs limit middleweight title bout, but no one barred and the colour bar will not be drawn – *Sporting Life*. This was repeated in the 8 June issues of the *Sporting Life* and 9 July *Sportsman*.

2 March Bill 'Chesterfield' Goode (Shadwell) accepts the challenge of Ted Pritchard for a bout to be for the English 150lbs limit title, the winner to meet 'Nonpareil' Jack Dempsey, the American champion, for the world 150lbs limit middleweight title – *Sporting Life*. However, Goode was already due to go to the USA to meet Dempsey for that purpose. In the same issue, Dempsey also accepted Ted Pritchard's challenge, or that of any other 150lbs limit middleweight, for £1,000 and to toss for choice, England or USA, and £100 to be allowed for expenses, Charlie Mitchell (Birmingham) preferred.

'Nonpareil' Jack Dempsey

1890

10 May 'Young' Mitchell (San Francisco), whose real name was J.L.Herget, challenges all England at 146 to 150lbs – *Sporting Life*.

19 July Wal Haxell to any 148 to 152lbs middleweight, £50 a side and best purse, winner take all – *Sporting Life*.

16 August Arthur Bobbett (Fulham) to the world at 150lbs – *Sporting Life*.

4 October   Ted White (Walthamstow) stated that he was only a 150lbs man – *Sporting Life*.

15 October   'Young' Mitchell (San Francisco) to all England at 150 to 154lbs, Ted Pritchard or Charlie 'Toff' Wall preferred – *Sporting Life*.

3 November   Anthony Diamond (Birmingham) w co 10 Arthur Bobbett (Fulham), Bill Reader's School of Arms, Fulham, London. Although billed for the English 148 to 150lbs limit middleweight title and £100 a side, there were some disputes as to the weights between the various sporting papers. The *Sportsman* gave Diamond as being 147³/₄lbs to Bobbett's 148, but the *Sporting Life* gave Diamond as being 148¹/₄lbs and Bobbett as 153lbs, three pounds overweight. However, all other reports gave Bobbett as 148, so one can only assume that the 153lbs reported in the 4 November issue of the *Sporting Life* was a misprint.

7 November   Lachie Thompson (Glasgow) w co 3 Harry Downie (late of Australia and California, born Edinburgh). Contested at a private show in London, with both men weighing 148lbs, it was billed as being for the English 149lbs limit middleweight title in some quarters, but not given much recognition because of the 3 November bout between Anthony Diamond and Arthur Bobbett, covering 148 to 150lbs, and the odd weight poundage not really being considered in the UK. Although there were several attempts to make it like the USA with just 'give or take a pound', give or take two pounds seemed more genuine in the UK. Downie was sometimes reported as Downe.

25 November   Anthony Diamond (Birmingham) is called the world 150lbs limit middleweight champion – *Sportsman*. This was repeated on 3 December.

6 December   William Robinson (Hackney) w pts 3 Felix Scott (Liverpool), The Pelican Club, New Headquarters in Gerrard Street, Soho, London. The final of the Pelican Club's all-England 150lbs limit competition, in previous rounds Robinson, known as the 'Cock Robin', beat 'Barney' Lambert and Ted Bryant (Chelsea), while Scott, a negro, eliminated Alf Bowman and H.Smith, who was making his pro debut in this competition, which was also Scott's 'comeback'.

1891
4 April   Bill Husband (Knightsbridge) w pts 6 Alf Suffolk (Lambeth), Her Majesty's Theatre, Westminster, London. The final day of a seven-day show and the final of Frank Hinde's all-England 150lbs limit competition, in previous rounds Husband beat Frank Young and Bill Cheese, while Suffolk defeated Jim Adds and drew the bye.

1892
4 May   Fred Greenbank (Cranford) to all England at 148lbs, give or take two pounds, over 12 rounds, using four-ounce gloves, £25 a side and best purse – *Sporting Life*.

24 October   Ted Rich (Walworth) to any of the claimants of the English 150lbs limit title for same – *Sporting Life*.

1893
10 January   Fred Greenbank (Cranford, Essex) to all England at 148 to 150lbs – *Sporting Life*.

13 September   Ted White (Walthamstow) to the world at 148 to 150lbs, Anthony Diamond (Birmingham) preferred – *Sporting Life*. This was repeated on 19 September.

1894
16 May   Ted White (Walthamstow) is the English 150lbs limit champion – *Sporting Life*. This was repeated on 10 December.

7 December   'Dido' Plumb (Balls Pond Road), whose real name was Charles Plumb, to all at 148 to 150lbs – *Sporting Life*.

1895
2 November   Ted White (Walthamstow), due to make a comeback, challenges all England at 150lbs over 20 three-minute rounds – *Sporting Life*.

1896
1 February   'Dido' Plumb (Balls Pond Road) to the world at 150lbs – *Mirror of Life*.

1897
14 April   Harry Neumier (Stepney) to all England at 150lbs, George Chrisp (Newcastle on Tyne) preferred – *Sporting Life*. This was repeated on 19 April, but with Chrisp, who stated he couldn't get under 156lbs, dropped from the challenge.

20 April   Jim Brady (Canning Town) accepts Neumier's challenge, stating that they could now meet for the 150lbs limit title – *Sporting Life*.

20 August   Pat 'Paddy' Purtell (Kansas City) w rsc 6 Lachie Thompson (Glasgow), The Olympic Club, Berwick Street, Birmingham. Referee John Barnes. Billed as for the world 148 to 150lbs title, at the first weigh-in Thompson came in at 149lbs, but Purtell was overweight at 150¹/₂. However, Thompson waived the forfeit, prior to the scales being found to be faulty. With new scales in use, Thompson scaled 148lbs to Purtell's 149¹/₂. For this bout, Purtell had been kept off the booze and trained really well, with the result that he gave one of his best-ever performances. Note: In those days there were no second bites of the cherry, if one failed to make the weight at the first attempt that was it, training being considered as weight-making time.

13 September   Arthur Akers (Leicester) w co 1 Bill Shingleton (Dudley), The Olympic Club, Berwick Street, Birmingham. Referee John Barnes. When the match was made in July, it was articled as being for the English 150lbs limit heavyweight title, but the reports place much more emphasis on it being for the Midlands title, other than English. Although it was for £350, which well qualified it money-wise as an English title bout, and although the 31-year-old Akers was a top-class man, the 44-year-old Shingleton could hardly be classed as such. No weights were given and the bout lasted one minute and 57 seconds.

20 December   Tommy Ryan (New York) w co 3 Bill Heffernan (South Africa, late New Zealand, born Scotland), Buffalo, New York. Billed for the world 150lbs limit middleweight title.

1898
17 January   Jerry Driscoll (Pimlico, late RN) w pts 20 Tom Woodley (Fulham), NSC, Covent Garden, London. Referee Mr B.J.Angle. Made at the 150lbs limit, £50 a side and a £100 purse (total £200), Driscoll scaled 149¹/₂lbs to Woodley's 146. Given no title billing in reports of the major sporting papers, it was regarded by many as involving the English 150lbs limit title, although Driscoll, the most unassuming of men, never really pushed his claim.

9 February   Harry Neumier (Stepney) to Aubury Clifford (Tasmania) at 150lbs, £50 up to £100 a side – *Sporting Life*.

13 June   Tommy West (New York, born Cardiff) is the American/world 150lbs champion – *Sporting Life*.

14 September   Aubury Clifford (Tasmania) to the world at 147 to 149lbs, £100 a side – *Mirror of Life*.

25 October   Tom Woodley (Fulham) to all England at 144 up to 150lbs, £50 a side, 10 or 25 rounds, which could be a misprint for 15 or 20 rounds – *Sporting Life*.

30 December   Harry Neumier (Stepney) to all at 148 up to 154lbs – *Sporting Life*.

1899
1 March   Tommy Ryan (Syracuse) w co 8 Charley Johnson (USA), Hot Springs, Arkansas, USA. Billed as a world/American 150lbs limit title fight, weights were not given. Ryan not only claimed the above title but also the 158lbs title, which was not at stake, in the above match as he was eight pounds below that weight.

13 March   Jerry Driscoll (Pimlico, late RN) to all England at 150lbs – *Sporting Life*. The challenge was accepted two days later by Harry Neumier (Stepney), who also challenged all England at 148 to 154lbs.

20 March   'Young' Sharkey (San Francisco) to Jerry Driscoll at 150lbs and an NSC purse – *Sporting Life*.

28 March   'Australian' Billy Edwards to all England at 148 up to 152lbs, 'Dido' Plumb preferred – *Sporting Life*.

4 August   'Mysterious' Billy Smith drew 25 Andy Walsh, Brooklyn, New York, USA. Made at the 150lbs limit, no weights were given and there was no title billing attached.

15 August   Dick Burge (Newcastle on Tyne, born Cheltenham) to 'Dido' Plumb at 148 to 150lbs, £300 or £500 a side – *Sporting Life*. This was repeated on 17 August.

31 August   Tommy Ryan w pts 20 Jack Moffatt (USA), Dubuque, USA. Although given world/American 150lbs limit title billing, with both men weighing 152lbs, two pounds over the weight, it couldn't have been. However, the *Chicago Tribune* shows it as being at the 152lbs limit, which seems more likely.

22 September   Harry Neumier (Stepney) to all England at 150lbs – *Sporting Life*. In the same issue, Tom Woodley (Fulham) challenged all England at 148 to 150lbs for an NSC purse – *Sporting Life*.

1900
29 November   Owen Ziegler w co 2 Eddie Connolly (New Brunswick, Canada), Hartford, Connecticut, USA. Made at catchweights, Connolly, a last-minute substitute, weighed 150lbs, but

Ziegler, having accepted the bout at catchweights, gave no weight. There was no title billing given.

27 December 'Mysterious' Billy Smith no contest 11 'Young' John Mahoney (Philadelphia), The Passiac County AC, Patterson, New Jersey, USA. Referee Edward Doughtery. Made at the 150lbs limit, with no weights given and no title billing, the men were thrown out for not trying.

1901

21 June The death of Patrick 'Paddy' Purtell (Saginaw, Michigan) at his saloon in Cripple Creek, Colorado (Leadville, Colorado also given as place of death) of heart failure, aged about 29, is announced – *Sporting Life*.

5 September Tom Woodley (Fulham) to all England at 144 up to 150lbs, over 15 or 20 rounds, Jack Palmer (Benwell) or Harry Neumier (Stepney) preferred – *Sporting Life*.

15 November Charley McKeever (Philadelphia) will box Pat Daly/Daley (London, born Cork) at 148lbs up to 152lbs for £500 a side – *Sporting Life*.

22 November Tom Woodley (Fulham) to Dave Peters (Treorchy) at 150lbs or at catchweights – *Sporting Life*.

29 November Harry Neumier (Stepney) to all England at 148 up to 150lbs, Tom Woodley (Fulham) or 'Jewey' Cooke (Bloomsbury and Hammersmith) preferred – *Sporting Life*.

1902

1 June Larry Temple (USA), a negro, to all England at 148 to 150lbs – *Sporting Life*. This was repeated in the 25 June issue of the *Mirror of Life*.

24 June Tom Woodley (Fulham) w pts 10 Jim Styles (Marylebone), The New Adelphi Club, The Strand, London. Referee Harry Cooper. After a contest that was cut from 15 rounds down to 10 for the English Coronation 150lbs limit middleweight championship belt, Woodley was presented with the belt on 24 July by Mr Jack Nanson. At first just called the middleweight championship belt, some time later it was stated that it was contested at the 150lbs limit.

29 August Tom Woodley (Fulham) to all England at 144 to 150lbs – *Sporting Life*.

1903

8 April 'Jewey' Cooke (Hammersmith, London) w pts 20 Tom Duggan (Australia), The Pavilion, Johannesburg, South Africa. Given South African 150lbs middleweight title billing, the Imperial Empire title was also given and, although an unofficial title, it was more realistic than the South African title tag. Unfortunately, the papers had the habit of reporting all international bouts in South Africa as being for the national title, something that really caused confusion as well as cheapening the South African titles themselves. Duggan weighed 147lbs.

18 June Joe Walcott (New York, born Barbados) drew 20 'Young' Peter Jackson, (Baltimore), Portland, USA. Billed as an American/world 150lbs limit title bout, no weights were given. Jackson's real name was Sim Thompkins.

3 October Jack Clancy (San Francisco) w rsc 5 Jim Lloyd, Ginnett's Circus, Newcastle on Tyne. Made at 148 to 150lbs with no title billing, Clancy scaled 146lbs.

1904

15 March Jim Styles (Marylebone), owing to a severely injured right knee, forfeited to Jack Kingsland (Paddington and Kensington), whom he should have met over 15 three-minute rounds for the English 150lbs limit title at the International AC, 24 Marylebone Road, off Edgware Road, London.

9 April Jack Kingsland (Kensington and Paddington) is the English 150lbs limit champion – *Sporting Life*.

16 November Charlie Allum (Notting Hill) is the English 150lbs limit champion – *Sporting Life*.

21 November 'Young' Peter Jackson (Baltimore) w co 6 Charlie Allum (Notting Hill), Wonderland, Whitechapel Road, London. An international match at catchweights, with Jackson restricted to 150lbs and Allum, billed as the English 150lbs champion, being at any weight he wanted it to be, it was for £100 a side and a £100 purse (total £300). In some quarters it was reported as being for the world 150lbs limit title, as Jackson was restricted to that weight, but nothing is known of Allum's weight.

23 December 'Young' Peter Jackson (local) drew 15 'Dixie Kid', The Eureka Club, Baltimore, USA. No weights were given and there was no title billing, but both negros were believed to be at catchweights.

1905

11 January Jack Kingsland (Paddington, late Army) to Charlie Allum

(Notting Hill) for the English 150lbs limit title, £50 or £100 a side, an NSC purse and over15 or 20 rounds of three minutes each – *Sporting Life*.

22 February 'Young' Peter Jackson (Baltimore), is the world 146 to 148lbs limit champion, winning the title from Joe Walcott on 10 June 1904 and defending it on 26 September 1904 against Charlie Knock (w co 3). He is also the 148 to 150lbs limit world champion after winning a bout billed for that title on 21 November 1904. However, both the Knock and Allum bouts were disqualified as title bouts as they were contested over two-minute rounds – *Mirror of Life*.

27 February Charlie Allum (Notting Hill) w rsc 10 Jack Kingsland (Paddington), With both men weighing 149lbs, it was billed as an English 150lbs limit middleweight title fight, £50 a side and a £100 purse (total £200).

6 November Charlie Allum to all England at the 150lbs limit – *Sporting Life*. Accepted on 7 November by Jack Kingsland, if Allum didn't agree to the fight Kingsland would box anyone in England at 150lbs – *Sporting Life*.

15 November 'Young' Peter Jackson, the Baltimore negro, is the world 150lbs limit champion – *Mirror of Life*.

16 December Jack Kingsland (Paddington) to Charlie Allum for the English 150lbs limit title, £100 a side and over 15 or 20 three-minute rounds – *Sporting Life*.

1906

26 February Pat Daly/Daley (London, born Ireland) w co 5 Mike Crawley (Lime House), Wonderland, Whitechapel Road, London. Referee Ted Humphreys. Billed for the English 148 to 150lbs limit title, plus a £100 purse, it was disqualified as a recognised title bout as only two-minute rounds were applied, which was both advertised and reported as such. Although Daly stated it was over three-minute rounds at his insistence, he also stated that there were several doctors sat ringside and on him scoring the kayo with series of body blows, his second, Joe Filkins, insisted that one of the doctors enter the ring to examine Crawley, which he did. The doctor then agreed that the kayo was perfectly fair in order to protect Daly against a gang of ringside gamblers who had put their money on Crawley, a 3-1 favourite. Crawley was also backed by the promoter, Harry Jacobs, who Daly claimed was a 'real crook'.

10 March Charlie Allum to all England at 150lbs for the English 150lbs limit title – *Sporting Life*. This was repeated on 29 June.

10 March 'Bombardier' Davis w disq 9 Jack Kingsland (Birmingham, late London), Newcastle on Tyne. Referee Billy Bell. Made at catchweights with no weights given and no title billing, despite both being 150lbs men with Davis said to be unbeaten, it was for £25 a side and a percentage of the gate. Kingsland was eventually ruled out for hitting and holding.

13 March Charlie Allum challenges Jack Kingsland, the claimant of the English 150lbs limit title, to a match to decide the title – *Sporting Life*. Kingsland accepted on 15 March if Allum agreed to put down a deposit, although it seems strange as Allum had beaten Kingsland for this self same title on 27 February 1905 and there was no record of either Allum losing this title or Kingsland winning it prior to the above. Kingsland's claim most likely stemmed from his six-round kayo win over the 10 pounds heavier and unbeaten Tom Lancaster of Spennymoor, in a catchweight bout on 24 February 1906 at Newcastle on Tyne.

17 May Mike Crawley (Limehouse) to all England at 148 up to 154lbs – *Sporting Life*.

17 July Charlie Allum (Notting Hill) to the world at 150lbs, or the winner of the Charlie Knock versus Pat Daly/Daley contest, for the English 150lbs limit title – *Sporting Life*. This was repeated on 4 August, the day of the Knock versus Daly bout.

4 August Pat Daly/Daley (London, born Ireland) w co 9 Charlie Knock (Stratford), Wonderland, Whitechapel Road, London. Referee James T.Hulls. Billed and reported as being for the English 148 to 150lbs limit welterweight title for £100 a side and a £150 purse (total £350). Daly scaled 150lbs to Knock's 148½. Although reported as being contested over two-minute rounds, as per normal at this venue and a stipulation that would disqualify it from full title recognition, Daly himself claimed that the bout was over three-minute rounds, again at his insistence, and for £100 a side plus 35% of the gate. Unfortunately for Knock, his ankle went during the bout, which was called the greatest welterweight contest ever seen. When the bout was first mooted, it was stated that it was to be for the English 152lbs limit welterweight title held by Daly.

6 August — Mike Crawley to Pat Daly/Daley for the English 150lbs limit title – *Sporting Life*.

8 August — Charlie Allum to Pat Daly/Daley for the English 150lbs limit title – *Sporting Life*.

5 October — Jack Kingsland is the 150lbs English champion – *Sporting Life*.

1907

1 January — Jack Kingsland to all England at 150lbs and over 20 three-minute rounds – *Sporting Life*.

11 February — Jack Goldswain (Bermondsey) w co 5 Pat Daly/Daley (London, born Ireland), NSC, Covent Garden, London. Referee Mr J.H.Douglas. Articled to be for the English 140lbs limit lightweight title, Daly came in at 148lbs, some eight pounds overweight for which he paid forfeit. However, the bout could still be seen as involving several titles claimed by Daly, especially at 146 to 148lbs, which he had no real claim to, or his 148 to 150lbs title claim. The fact of the matter was that, with Goldswain (139lbs) far below the stipulated weight, the bout was, in reality, just a catchweight contest involving no titles.

14 February — Charlie Knock (Stratford) to all England at 150lbs ringside, £100 a side – *Sporting Life*.

21 March — Charlie Allum, the English 150lbs champion, to the world at 150lbs – *Mirror of Life*. This was repeated throughout the year and in the 26 April issue of the *Sporting Life* Allum challenged Sam Langford (USA) at 150lbs.

15 April — Sam Langford (Boston, Mass, born in Canada), now in the UK and training at The Coach & Horses, Stonebridge Park, London, now weighs 150lbs. The 3 June issue of the *Sporting Life* called Langford an American.

4 July — Joe Thomas drew 20 Stanley Ketchel (Michigan), Marysville, USA. With Thomas scaling 150lbs to Ketchel's 147, the American/world 150lbs limit title was up for grabs.

3 August — Arthur Daley (Poplar, London), no relation to Pat Daly/Daley, challenges all England at 148 up to 154lbs – *Mirror of Life*. This was repeated on 7 December.

2 September — Stanley Ketchel w co 32 Joe Thomas, Colma Arena, San Francisco, USA. Made at 150lbs, this fight was given American/world title billing in some papers, but there was no mention of titles in the *San Francisco Chronicle* and no weights given. The *Sporting Life*, in their report, called Thomas the Californian state welterweight champion, but also gave no weights or title billing.

19 September — Charlie Knock (Stratford) to all England at 150lbs, 2pm weigh-in, over 20 rounds and £100 a side, Robert 'Curly' Watson preferred – *Sporting Life*.

16 November — Charlie Knock (Stratford) w pts 10 Charlie Allum (Notting Hill), Wonderland, Whitechapel Road, London. With no title billing and not over a championship distance, and only two-minute rounds being contested, it was advertised as for the Monday 18 November show, but in the 23 November issue of the *Sporting Life* it was given as an addition to the Saturday 16 November show, which had been left out of the report. Allum, just two days previous, had lost to James 'Tiger' Smith (co 1) at the NSC.

4 December — Charlie Knock (Stratford) w co 11 Peter Brown (Woolwich), Salle Wagram, Paris, France. Referee Francis Richel. Made at catchweights, with no weights given or stipulated and no title billing, the show was put back from the previous week. Brown, a substitute for Charlie Allum (Notting Hill) who had met with an accident, was put down, got up, but fell back down to be counted out.

1908

9 January — Jack Palmer (Plumstead, Kent) w pts 20 Bobby Dobbs (Kentucky), Christian Street Gym Club, Liverpool. Articled at catchweights, £50 a side, with no weights given and no title billing, it was almost certainly contested over two-minute rounds. Incidentally, 'Plumstead' Jack Palmer was a different man to Jack Palmer (Benwell, Newcastle on Tyne), whose real surname was Liddell and an English title claimant.

4 April — Charlie Allum (Notting Hill) is the English 150lbs champion – *Sporting Life*. This was supported in the 10 April issue of the *Sporting Life*, in which Allum was listed as the 150lbs champion in a list of English champions.

2 May — Willie Lewis (New York) w co 5 Walter Stanton (California), Cirque de Paris, Paris, France. Referee Tommy Burns. With Lewis weighing 148½lbs, it was billed as being for the world 150lbs welterweight title and carried an £800 purse.

26 May — Joe White (Cardiff, born Canada) to all at 146 to 150lbs,

£100 up to £500 a side. Accepted by Jim Sullivan (Bermondsey) on 30 May at 150lbs, £50 a side, Sullivan said he would also box Tom Lancaster (Spennymoor) on the same terms – *Sporting Life*.

4 June — Bart Connolly (Maine, USA) w rsc 13 'Plumstead' Jack Palmer, Christian Street Gym Club, Liverpool. Made at catchweights for £145, but no weights given and no title billing, it was almost certainly contested over two-minute rounds in keeping with the venue. Joe White (Cardiff, born Canada) challenged the winner at 148lbs, give or take two pounds, over 20 rounds at £50 or £100 a side.

13 June — Charlie Allum (Notting Hill) to all England at 150lbs, £100 a side, 'Bombardier' Davis, Sid Doyle or Robert 'Curly' Watson preferred – *Sporting Life*. This was repeated on 19 June, to Joe White (Cardiff, born Canada) only.

16 June — Joe White (Cardiff, born Canada) to all England at 148lbs, give or take two pounds, £100 or £200 a side. In the same issue, Jim Sullivan (Bermondsey) challenged Joe White or Bart Connolly at 150lbs, £50 a side and best purse – *Sporting Life*.

9 November — Tom Stokes (Mexborough) w co 3 Jerry Thompson (Grimsby), Rifle Barracks, Londeaborough Street, Hull. Made at 150lbs for a £80 purse, plus £47 and 10 shillings (£47.50p) side stakes (total £127.50p), Stokes weighed 149½lbs with no weight given for Thompson, 'The Fighting Fisherman', and there was no title billing, being due to two-minute rounds being in place. Stokes was the 'The English Pitmens' 150lbs champion.

28 November — Andrew Jeptha (late South Africa), the coloured fighter, challenges all England at 150lbs, Joe White (Cardiff, late Canada) preferred – *Mirror of Life*.

30 November — Alf Hewitt (Bermondsey) w co 12 Charlie Knock (Stratford), Wonderland, Whitechapel Road, London. Made at 148 to 150lbs, no weights were given and no title billing was applied, with two-minute rounds being in place. Much was made of the fact that Hewitt was a well-known wrestler and the referee, Eugene Corri, entered the ring in the third round and stayed there.

21 December — Jim Sullivan (Bermondsey) is the English 150lbs welterweight champion – *Sporting Life*. On 11 February 1909, the NSC launched their eight-named weight divisions to end the every two-pound era and 148 to 150lbs became part of the new middleweight division.

150lbs to 152lbs (10st 10lbs to 10st 12lbs)
1877

3 November — George Rooke (born Ireland), the American champion, to Denny Harrington (London, born Ireland) at 150lbs, £100 a side, with gloves – *Bells Life*.

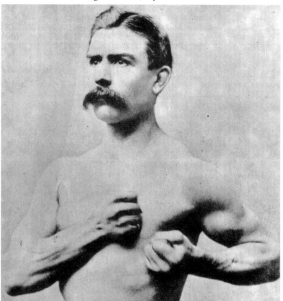

George Rooke

17 November George Rooke to the world at 152lbs, MoQ Rules, for a cup valued at £50 or £100 and the middleweight championship – *Sporting Life*.

1878
2 March Denny Harrington (London, born Ireland) w co 6 George Rooke (USA, born Dundalk, Ireland), The Royal Surrey Gardens, Walworth, London. Billed for the world 154lbs title, to a finish, under MoQ Rules, with gloves and a £105 championship cup, Harrington, known as the 'Cherub', weighed 152lbs and Rooke 151½lbs according to the *Sporting Life*, although *Bells Life* gave Harrington at 153½lbs and Rooke as being 150½. They also reported the fight being held in Camberwell. If the *Sporting Life* is correct then the fight could also be considered as involving the 152lbs title, which was the weight Rooke challenged at. The referee was Mr Conquest.

7 September 'Florey' Barnett, in reply to Alf Greenfield (Birmingham), said that he would box him at 152lbs for £50 a side – *Sporting Life*.

1879
20 August Alf Greenfield (Birmingham) to any man breathing at 148 to 150 or 152lbs for £50 up to £500 a side – *Sporting Life*.

11 September Thomas Morgan (London, late Bristol) to the world at 150lbs for £25 or £50 a side – *Sporting Life*.

1880
17 December William Sherriff (Leicester) won 11 Denny Harrington (London, born Cork, Ireland), Birmingham District of Lapworth, near Kingswood in a meadow near The Boot Inn public house. Refereed by Charles Bedford with an 8.45am start, it was contested in a 24-foot ring, pitched on high ground, under MoQ Rules with ordinary gloves. It was given as involving the world and English middleweight titles with no actual title billing and no announced weights, although 152lbs, 154lbs and even 157lbs were given as the stipulated weights at various times over the years. If at the latter limit, it seems really strange that both men would weigh so much below it, Sherriff, alias 'The Prussian', making 152lbs to Harrington's 149lbs, when it was normal practice to get either 'dead on' the stipulated weight or one or two pounds below it. When the police stopped the bout, in which Sherriff had had all the best of, an attempt was made to continue at Marston Green, about 10 and a half miles away, but the police confiscated the ropes and stakes. At a meeting that evening at The Red Lion, Hampton Street, Birmingham, Sherriff was offered £25 to agree to a draw, which was the decision *Bells Life* of 18 December gave, but Sherriff refused, stating that it was the verdict he wanted not the money, whereon Harrington's party agreed for Sherriff to be returned as the winner. He also got the £25. The *Sporting Life* stated that the referee had named Sherriff as the winner on Harrington's refusal to continue the bout, which had lasted 44 minutes. Harrington, who the *Sporting Life* stated was in really poor condition, had not looked after himself in training, was so badly used up he wouldn't have been able to continue and wasn't able to attend the meeting that evening at The Red Lion to come to a decision, his backers having to speak for him. Other reports had him both overtrained and ill and, whatever the case, he never fought again outside of exhibitions.

1887
15 December Ted Burchell (Hackney) w co 12 Arthur Bobbett (Fulham). Held at a private show in the west-end of London and made at 152lbs, with both men on the mark, like the majority of bouts outside of competitions at this time there was no actual title billing given, but the win gave Burchell a sound claim to the title.

1888
14 April Jim Kendrick (Lambeth, born Ireland) w pts 4 Bill Corcoran (St Luke's), Royal Agricultural Hall, Islington, London. The final of Ben Hyams' United Kingdom (English) championship competition, which had been spread over six days, it was the debut of this kind of week-long show. In previous rounds, Kendrick, whose real name was Enright/Enwright, had beaten Jack Gleeson and Ted White, while Corcoran beat 'Con' Griffiths and J.Cashley ('Yorkey') of Leeds.

11 July Albert Peace (Newcastle on Tyne) challenged Felix Scott (Liverpool) to a finish bout, £50 a side, for the English 152lbs limit 'coloured' championship. On this day, Scott won the final of a 140lbs championship belt competition before being arrested for the assault of a policeman some

time previous. On 1 August, Scott got 18 months in prison – *Liverpool Daily Post*.

25 September Alec Roberts drew 53 Arthur Bobbett (Fulham), Lambeth School of Arms, Lambeth Walk, Paradise Street, Lambeth, London. Reported as being at 152lbs, but corrected by Bobbett in the *Sportsman* of 10 October, Roberts weighed 147½lbs and Bobbett 151. Articled at catchweights, with no title billing, although £100 and £200 a side, it was to be the final bout of Alex Roberts' career.

23 November Bill 'Chesterfield' Goode (Shadwell) w pts 12 Arthur Bobbett (Fulham), The Grand Circus, Peter Street, Manchester. Billed for the English 152lbs limit middleweight title, Goode weighing 150lbs and Bobbett 152lbs, when the bout was first reported as having been made, in the 23 July issue of the *Sporting Life*, it was articled as being for the 154lbs limit title, with Goode staking £250 to Bobbett's £200. It was later amended to be for the 152lbs limit title, although the bout was actually articled as at catchweights.

1891
14 January Bob Fitzsimmons (citizen of USA, late New Zealand, born Helston, Cornwall) w co 13 'Nonpareil' Jack Dempsey (New York, born Ireland), New Orleans, USA. Billed as an American/world 154lbs limit middleweight title fight with, in some cases, 152lbs stated to be the limit, Fitzsimmons announced as being 150½lbs and Dempsey, whose real name was John Kelly, 147½lbs.

3 February Arthur Akers (Leicester) to the world at 152lbs – *Sporting Life*.

7 to 12 March A proposed 152lbs English championship competition scheduled to take place during this week on Ben Hyams' six-day show at the Goodwin Gym, Kingsland Road, Shoreditch, was cancelled, as was a 10st 2lbs competition, due to a lack of entries. Two 8st 10lbs competitions took place instead.

30 May Ted White (Walthamstow) w pts 4 Bill Husband (Knightsbridge), Her Majesty's Theatre, The Haymarket, Westminster, London. The final of Frank Hinde's 152lbs English championship competition spread over seven days, in previous rounds White beat Bill Bullions and then had a bye, while Husband beat George Baxter and A.Ames.

14 October Arthur Bobbett (Fulham) to all England at 150 to 152lbs – *Sporting Life*.

1894
15 January Ted White (Walthamstow) w pts 20 Anthony Diamond (Birmingham), NSC, Covent Garden, London. Referee B.J.Angle. Made at the 152lbs limit, give or take two pounds, both men weighed 151lbs. Although not reported as a title bout in the *Sporting Life* it was regarded by all as being for the English 152lbs title.

1895
10 September 'Dido' Plumb (Kingsland Road, Shoreditch) to all England at either 150 or 154lbs – *Sporting Life*.

25 November Ted White (Walthamstow) w pts 10 Charles 'Kid' McCoy (USA), NSC, Covent Garden, London. Made at the 152lbs limit, with no weights given and no title billing, although a good win for White it was not over a recognised title distance, 12 rounds being the least accepted number of rounds for a major championship bout at this time. McCoy's real name was Norman Selby.

1896
11 January 'Dido' Plumb (Balls Pond Road) to the world at 150 to 152lbs – *Mirror of Life*.

22 June Tommy Ryan (Syracuse) w co 9 Billy 'Shadow' Maber (Australia), Lyceum Theatre, Boston, Mass, USA. Although no weights were stipulated and no title billing given, the *Sportsman* gave Ryan as being 147lbs and Maber 152lbs.

28 September 'Young' Bill England (Hackney) to all England at 150 up to 154lbs – *Sporting Life*. England was the son of the old-time brick carrier and heavyweight boxer of the same name.

4 October Pat Daly/Daley, the English 140lbs limit champion, to 'Dido' Plumb (Balls Pond Road), the world/English 154lbs limit champion, at 152lbs, over 20 rounds, £100 or £200 a side – *Sporting Life*.

1898
17 June Tommy Ryan (New York) w rsc 14 Tommy West (New York, born Cardiff), The Lennox Club, New York, USA. Made at catchweights, but also given American/world 152lbs limit title billing, Ryan (146lbs) was billed as the 150lbs limit champion and was seemingly on his way to becoming a multiple champion by picking up titles at every two pounds. West weighed 152lbs.

17 October 'Wilmington' Jack Daly w pts 20 Jim Curran (Rotherham, England), Alhambra Theatre, Syracuse, USA. Referee 'Yank' Sullivan. Made at catchweights, with no title billing, Daly scaled 147lbs to Curran's 151. 18 October was also given as the date.

30 December Harry Neumier (Stepney) to all England at 148lbs up to 154 – *Sporting Life*.

1899

28 March 'Australian' Billy Edwards to all England at 148 to 152lbs, 'Dido' Plumb preferred – *Sporting Life*.

31 August Tommy Ryan (New York) w pts 20 Jack Moffatt. Dubuque, Iowa, USA. With both men weighing 152lbs, it was given American/world 152lbs welterweight (middleweight also reported) title billing and was also given as a championship match at the 150lbs limit, which was possibly a misprint unless the bout had been made at 150lbs, give or take two pounds.

20 December 'Dido' Plumb, the 154lbs champion, to Bobby Dobbs, the Kentucky negro, at 152lbs with a 3pm weigh-in – *Sporting Life*.

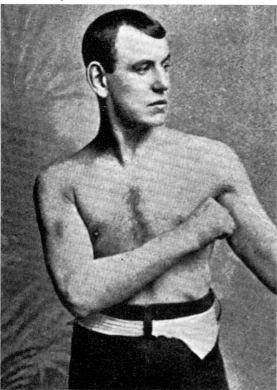

'Dido' Plumb

1900

18 August Charley McKeever (Philadelphia) is the American 152lbs limit welterweight champion – *Sporting Life*. On 30 August, he signed to meet 'Dido' Plumb, the English 152lbs limit champion, for the world title at the weight.

15 October Charley McKeever (Philadelphia) w pts 15 'Dido' Plumb, NSC, Covent Garden, London. Referee Jack Douglas. Billed as a world 152lbs limit welterweight title fight for £200 a side, with McKeever scaling 150lbs to Plumb's 152, it was also normal for an international match in the UK to be given English title billing, for which McKeever wasn't eligible.

17 October Charley McKeever, the world 152lbs limit champion, to all England at the weight for £500 a side – *Sporting Life*. On 31 October, McKeever returned to the USA.

10 November Tommy Ryan (New York) w co 3 Geoff Thorne (Greenwich, England), Chicago, USA. Given as both a catchweights bout and one at the 152lbs limit, there was no title billing and it wasn't over a championship distance. Back home, some

amazement was shown as to how Thorne, real name Geoff Townsend, and a novice pro despite being a former ABA middleweight champion in 1895 and at heavyweight in 1897 and 1898, kept getting thrown in with all the top pros in the USA, all of whom stopped him in short order.

24 November 'Dido' Plumb accepts the challenge of Pat Daly/Daley, if at 152lbs, £100 a side and a 2pm weigh-in – *Sporting Life*.

1901

15 November Charley McKeever (Philadelphia) would accept the challenge of Pat Daly/Daley if at 148 to 152lbs and £500 a side – *Sporting Life*.

29 November Harry Neumier (Stepney) to all England at 148 up to 154lbs, Tom Woodley (Fulham) or 'Jewey' Cooke (Hammersmith) preferred – *Sporting Life*.

1902

21 April 'Young' Peter Jackson (Baltimore) w disq 6 Charley McKeever (local), Philadelphia, USA. Although only a six-round no-decision contest, Jackson, in later years, supported by the *Sporting Life* on 26 August 1904, amazingly claimed that he won the world 152lbs limit middleweight title held by McKeever with this win.

1903

8 April 'Jewey' Cooke (London, England) w pts 20 Tom Duggan (Australia), The Pavilion, Johannesburg, South Africa. Cooke weighed 150½lbs and Duggan 147. Billed as being for the South African 152lbs middleweight title, this billing caused angry letters, stating that only men born in a country should be allowed to compete for its title. Other complainants stated that although a new, sparsely populated country could impose a residential qualification, in South Africa every boxer from another country seemed to make his debut in a South African title bout, which was farcical. The newspapers made it worse by going along with it, but it wasn't fair on those boxers who were South African-born and therefore genuine South African champions and only those should have been chronicled as South African champions. During and after the Boer war, every British serviceman and visitor who engaged in a winning bout in a South African ring seemed to claim that they had won a South African championship.

27 August Joe Platford (Tottenham) to all England at 152lbs – *Sporting Life*.

29 August Three men, namely Charlie Allum (Notting Hill), Jack Kingsland (Kensington and Paddington) and Dick Bailey accept Joe Platford's challenge – *Sporting Life*.

1905

8 April Charlie Allum (Notting Hill) to all England at 150 to 154lbs for £50 or £100 a side – *Sporting Life*.

1906

3 February Charlie Allum is now running a boxing school in Stockholm, Sweden – *Sporting Life*. On 21 April, the paper reported that Allum boxes frequently on the continent and invariably wins. However, apart from one French bout, which he won, no other continental bouts have ever been traced for him, although the writer has made several attempts to check certain European papers without any success.

2 May Charlie Allum (Notting Hill) to all England at 150 to 154lbs – *Sporting Life*. Four days later he is accepted by Joe Platford (Tottenham).

6 November Allum again challenges all England, but this time for £200 up to £500 a side and the English middleweight title. A day later, the challenge was accepted by Harry Neumier (Stepney), just back from USA – *Sporting Life*.

1907

3 August Arthur Daley (Poplar) to all England at 148 up to 154lbs – *Mirror of Life*. This was repeated on 7 December.

16 September Charlie Allum (Notting Hill) challenges 'Seaman' Robert 'Curly' Watson (late RN, Chatham, born Barrow in Furness) at 152lbs for £100 or £200 a side. Watson had been brought out of the Navy in January.

1908

2 March Peter Brown (Woolwich) w rtd 4 Charlie Knock (Stratford), The Salle Wagram, Paris, France. At catchweights, with no weights given or stipulated and no title billing, Knock, who had been floored in the second round, broke his right arm just below the elbow and was forced to retire in the fourth. At the end of the bout, Walter Stanton (California) challenged Brown. On 11 February 1909, the 150 to 152lbs title became part of the new 160lbs middleweight class when the NSC introduced their eight-named weight divisions.

Highlights from the 2002-2003 Amateur Season

by Chris Kempson

A very successful season opened with the Commonwealth Games in Manchester and continued with excellent results at home and abroad in international and multi-national events. On the domestic front there were pleasing performances not only at senior level, but among our schoolboys, juniors and cadets, the bedrock hopefully of our sport for some years to come. Let us take a closer look at some of those who made the headlines over the past year.

JULY

On the international front the new season started with the European Senior Championships in Perm, Russia from 12-21 July and it turned out to be a dismal time with David Mulholland (Salisbury, Liverpool) at featherweight, the only boxer from Britain or Ireland to win a bout before losing out to a Georgian in the quarter-finals.

However, there had been better news from overseas earlier in the month when England's 10 cadets all won a medal in the annual Junior Olympic International tournament at Northern Michigan University in Marquette from 28 June to 7 July. The medal breakdown was three gold, two silver and five bronze against opponents from America (who fielded two teams), Puerto Rico, the Bahamas and Quebec.

Further English success was achieved in the Four Nations Cadets (15-16 years), which were held at the Everton Park Sports Centre in Liverpool on 5-6 July. England notched up 19 medals in all, eight gold, six silver and five bronze. Ireland took seven gold, nine silver and five bronze, Scotland came third on six-two-10 with Wales in fourth place on one-five-seven.

Continuing on home soil, in Manchester to be precise, all eyes were focused on the Commonwealth Games from 26 July-3 August, which produced some excellent boxing from the English, Scottish and Welsh contestants, with only Northern Ireland finishing medal less.

Golds for England were secured by Repton's very promising Darren Barker at light-welterweight, and triple ABA heavyweight champion, David Dolan (Plains Farm), who won at super-heavyweight. Silvers for England were won by Darran Langley at light-flyweight, Paul Smith at light-middleweight and Steven Birch at middleweight. Our two bronzes went to Mark Moran at bantamweight and Andrew Morris at lightweight.

Wales earned their first Commonwealth gold for 44 years via the trusty fists of Jamie Arthur at lightweight, while their bronze was bagged by Kevin Evans at super-heavyweight. The Scots two bronzes were won by Craig McEwan at light-middleweight and Andrew Young at heavyweight. On the gold standard, Australia came out top with three medals.

The month ended on a successful note for England at the Brandenburg Cup under-19 multi-nations tournament in Frankfurt-Oder in Germany, from 31 July to 4 August. Tony Quigley (Tower Hill) won gold at light-welterweight, while there were bronzes for Don Broadhurst (Birmingham Irish) at flyweight, Nathan Brough (Salisbury, Liverpool) at featherweight and Stephen Jennings (Tower Hill) at lightweight. It was England's first time at this tournament, in its sixth edition.

AUGUST

Ireland's bantamweight, Dean Murphy (St Saviour's), secured a fine bronze medal at the seventh European Cadet (under-17) Championships which were staged at Lvov, Ukraine from 3-12 August. Ireland shared their two match series with the United States, winning the opening match by three bouts to two in Denver, while their American hosts came out on top with a four to three scoreline in Scranton. The matches were held on 16 August and 23 August, respectively.

SEPTEMBER

Ireland performed very well in the World Military Championships held at the Curragh army camp in Kildare, with Dundalk's Michael Kelly striking gold at light-welterweight, while Mayo light-middleweight, Henry Coyle, and Kildare light-heavyweight, Tommy Sheahan, each took silver.

The World Junior Championships took place in Santiago De Cuba from 15-22 September and resulted in a bronze for England and a silver medal for Ireland. At featherweight, Nathan Brough (Salisbury, Liverpool) won three times for his bronze, while the Irish southpaw, London-born Andy Lee, boxed successfully on four occasions for his fine silver medal at light-middleweight.

On the junior international front, Ireland twice triumphed over Queensland, winning seven bouts to four in Dublin on 25 September and then by five bouts to four in Enniscorthy three nights later.

Ireland netted both gold and bronze medals at the Nations Cup Tournament in Wiener-Neustadt in Austria from 26-27 September, with gold for Desmond Toman (St Patrick's, Newry) at lightweight and a bronze for Aodh Carlyle (Golden Cobra,Dublin) at light-welterweight.

England won two bronze medals at the fourth Karl Leman Cup in Tallinn, Estonia from 27-29 September. The two successful contestants were the Middlesbrough lightweight, Savdhul Zaman, and Kirkdale's middleweight, Neil Perkins. At light-welterweight, Michael Kelly (Dealgan) also won a bronze medal for Ireland.

OCTOBER

Ireland found life rather tough against Hungary in their senior international in Dublin on 4 October, the visitors taming their Irish hosts by eight bouts to three. The Hungarians were again successful two days later in

Templemore, County Tipperary, winning by six bouts to three.

The southpaw flyweight, Stewart Langley (Hollington), won a fine silver medal at the prestigious annual Feliks Stamm multi-nations tournament held in the Polish capital, Warsaw from 10-12 October.

England stamped their mark at the annual Tammer tournament in Tampere, Finland from 17-19 October. Bromley and Downham light-middleweight, Sam Webb, took silver, while the Army flyweight, Duncan Barriball, landed bronze.

NOVEMBER

England secured two gold medals and the Irish one at the Junior multi-nations tournament in Salonika, Greece from 7-11 November. Joe Smyth (middleweight) and Sam Sexton at heavyweight were the English winners, while Darren O'Neill, Ireland's light-heavyweight, triumphed for gold. There were also four bronze for England, plus one silver and two bronze for the Irish.

Ireland beat Italy by six bouts to three in Dublin on 8 November, in an international consisting of juniors and cadets. While at the Park Lane Hotel in London's Mayfair, on 11 November, England lost by three bouts to four to the United States, the away side chalking up their first victory since 1999 in this annual fixture. Two nights later (13 November) at the famous St George's Hall in Liverpool, England's first international against the United States outside London for 20 years ended with honours even, with four bouts apiece being the final score between the two countries. Over the two matches the visitors triumphed by eight bouts to seven over their English hosts.

Wales found themselves a new hero in Cwmavon Hornets tall southpaw, Darren Edwards, who struck gold at featherweight in the Copenhagen Box Cup in Denmark from 28 November –1 December. He boxed four times for his golden triumph. The principality also gained two bronzes through Peter Ashton at lightweight and welterweight, Jamie Way. England, too, annexed a fine medal haul with a silver for Craig Lyon at light-flyweight, and bronzes for Femi Fehintola at lightweight, the London southpaw, Lee Beavis, at light-welterweight, Ricardo Samms at middleweight, Tony Marsden at light-heavyweight and David Price at super-heavyweight.

DECEMBER

International action this month saw Young England thump Young Ireland by six bouts to two in Dublin on 13 December, while a rather weakened England went down by seven bouts to one against France in Bordeaux on 20 December. At domestic championship level, the NACYP Class A finals were staged at the Peter Paine Sports Centre, Boston, Lincolnshire; the NACYP Class B finals were boxed off at the Middleton Civic Centre in Manchester on 13 December; while the senior NACYP Class C finals took place at the Royal Lancaster Hotel in London on 9 December. The National Novices finals were held in their now familiar setting of Knottingley Leisure Centre in Yorkshire on 14 December. The Irish

Intermediate Championship finals took place in Dublin on 6 December.

JANUARY

The new weights came in to being on New Year's Day, light-welterweight increasing from 63.5 kgs to 64, welterweight moving from 67 to 69 and light-middleweight (71) disappearing. Cruiserweight (86kgs), which has never existed outside England and, more recently, Scotland, was removed from the ABA title race.

Ireland 'bested' Germany/Belgium by eight bouts to three in Dublin on 10 January, although the German/Belgium selection won the second international by a similar score in Drogheda, County Louth, two nights later. Wales won two medals at the Norway Box Cup in Oslo from 24-26 January, James Whitfield achieving a silver at light-heavyweight, with Vivian Bryan securing bronze in the light-welterweight division. The Ulster Senior Championships culminated with finals night at the Ulster Hall in Belfast on 30 January.

FEBRUARY

England's 17-year-old youngsters boxed very well in their junior international against Germany to win by five bouts to two at the Royal Lancaster Hotel in London's Bayswater on 3 February. The Irish Senior Championships finals took place in Dublin on 21 February and the star of the show was Limerick's brilliant teenager, Andy Lee (St Francis), who triumphed at middleweight, thus adding to his silver medal in the World Junior Championships in Cuba last September.

England's four-man team won two golds, plus a silver and a bronze at the YMCA International Championships in New Delhi, India from 3-9 February. The golds went to Stephen Smith (Rotunda) at bantamweight and Tony Jeffries (Sunderland Boxing Academy) at middleweight, while silver went to John O'Donnell (Dale Youth) at lightweight, with Finchley's Grant Skehill taking bronze at light-welterweight.

MARCH

England's Commonwealth Games super-heavyweight champion, David Dolan (Plains Farm), came back down to heavyweight and lifted a fine bronze medal at the Grand Prix multi-nations in Usti nad Labem, Czech Republic from 4-10 March.

Young England won the final bout of the evening to edge to victory over Young Ireland by five bouts to four at the Sports Centre in Basingstoke on 7 March. The Irish seniors lost their two international matches in the United States, going down by six bouts to one in Cleveland, Ohio on 12 March and then by seven bouts to three in Harvey, Illinois three days later. The Welsh held their ABA Championship finals at the Afan Lido, Port Talbot on 14 March

The National Schoolboy finals took place at the Metrodome in Barnsley on 29 and 30 March, with Cheshunt's Tom Saunders (Class 4 71kgs), the star of the show, joining the exclusive club of youngsters to have won

four successive national schoolboy titles. Ireland got back to winning ways at international level when they defeated Wales by six bouts to four in Dublin on 28 March.

Ireland came away with the 'Best Team' award after their quartet of boxers won three golds and a bronze in the inaugural 'Six Nations Cup' tournament staged in Bari, Italy on 29-30 March. Gold medals went to Eric Donovan of St Michael's, Athy at bantamweight, Moate's Eamonn Tuohey in the featherweight division and Dungloe's Cathal McAuley at welterweight, while Pearce Brolly from Errigal won a bronze at light-welterweight.

APRIL

Further Irish success came via the Dublin light-heavyweight, Kenneth Egan, who won a gold medal in the finals of the GeeBee multi-nations event in Helsinki, Finland from 3-7 April. Four other Irish boxers claimed silver, namely: Cavan's Andrew Murray at lightweight, Derry's Paul McCloskey (St Canice's) at light-welterweight, that man again from Limerick, Andy Lee (St Francis), at middleweight and the Sligo heavyweight, Alan Reynolds (St Joseph's).

The Scottish Senior finals were staged at the Time Capsule, Monklands in Coatbridge on 4 April and the same evening the English ABA finals were taking place at the famous York Hall, Bethnal Green, in east London. The return to the capital after an 11-year absence was a considerable 'coup' for the London ABA and not least its hardworking and very well respected Honorary Secretary, Keith Walters. Four teenagers won titles and there were two more first-time champions for good measure. Star on the night, and of the championships throughout, was West Ham's 18-year-old big-punching featherweight sensation, Kevin Mitchell. Sadly, Mitchell is now a fledgling professional and his services are lost to the amateur code.

David Dolan, the Plains Farm heavyweight, continued his magnificent season with a silver medal, which might easily have been gold but for injury in the prestigious annual Feliks Stamm multi-nations event in Warsaw, Poland from 9-12 April. Hematoma to the muscle fibre in both arms, but mainly the left, prevented David boxing Victor Zuev of Belarus in the final.

In Cardiff on 16 and 17 April, Ireland came out on top of the Four Nations tournament, winning five of the 11 titles up for grabs. Host nation Wales and England took three, with Scotland finishing with none. The event was held at Welsh Institute of Sport.

The Irish Boys Championships were held in Dublin from 22-26 April.

England's three representatives in the President's Cup under-19 multi-nations event in Wloclawek, Poland from 28 April-2 May, each returned home to these shores with a bronze medal. They were Repton's young light-welterweight prospect, Daniel Herdman, the Wombwell

West Ham's pride and joy, Kevin Mitchell (left), won the ABA featherweight title when outscoring Gareth Couch (Thame)

Les Clark

welterweight, Thomas Coward, and Sam Sexton, a super-heavyweight from Norwich Lads.

MAY

Ireland came out on top of the Four Nations Boys Championships, held in County Meath, Ireland on 8 and 9 May, with no fewer than eight golds, two silvers and five bronze in this annual event. England gained second place with six golds, five silvers and two bronze; Wales finished with one gold, three silver and eight bronze; with Scotland last after collecting four silvers and five bronze.

The ABA Junior Finals took place at what was for them a new venue at Bridlington Spa Royal Hall on the Yorkshire coast on 24 May. The only downside was that there were some disgraceful crowd scenes after the 18-17 victory of Rotunda's Joe Selkirk over John Fewkes in the Class 6 64kgs.

England gained one silver and three bronze medals at the fifth Arena Cup in Pula, Croatia from 14-17 May. Hollington's flyweight, Stewart Langley, got the silver, West Ham's bantamweight, Lloyd Otte, making his international debut, gained a bronze, while bronze also went to Miguel's super-heavyweight prospect, Ian Lewison.

Ireland trounced Denmark twice with scores of eight nil and six nil in Give and Hadsund on 9 and 11 May, respectively, the two matches being of the mixed junior/senior variety.

Young England scooped three golds and one silver as a result of their endeavours in the Six Nations Italia Cup in the open air in Rome from 17-18 May. Frankie Gavin (Hall Green) at featherweight, Tony Quigley (Tower Hill) at welterweight and super-heavyweight, Barry Smith (Ferry Street), each hit the gold standard, while Tony Jeffries (Sunderland Boxing Academy) collected a silver medal at middleweight.

Scotland hit a high note at the BoxAm multi-nations tournament in Seville, Spain from 19-25 May, bagging no fewer than six medals in total. Kenneth Anderson at light-heavyweight won gold, Craig McEwan at welterweight took silver, while the four bronzes went to David Ellis at flyweight, Scott Flynn at bantamweight, James Ancliffe in the featherweight division and Andrew Young at super-heavyweight.

The Irish Junior Championships were boxed off in Dublin on 23 and 24 May, with the finals taking place on 30 May.

Hollington light-flyweight, Darran Langley, gained a brilliant gold medal at the Acropolis Cup in Athens from 29 May-1 June, while Stephen Burke (Salisbury, Liverpool) struck silver and Tony Davies (Army) came home with a bronze.

Scotland hosted the Four Nations Cadets tournament, with three venues - Edinburgh, Newtongrange and Musselburgh - in use on 30 May and 1 June. England just came out on top with 23 medals in total; 10 gold, six silver and seven bronze, next came Ireland (22), eight, five and nine; then Scotland (18), four, three and 11; with the Welsh (23) in last spot with two, 10 and 11.

JUNE

Scotland gained an impressive six bouts to three triumph over Ireland in a marquee erected in the grounds of Craigengillan Mansion House, Dalmellington on 7 June.

An England under-19 squad lost by five bouts to three against the French at Rochefort-sur-Mer on 7 June.

The inaugural European Union Championships took place in the suburbs of Strasbourg from 10-14 June and proved to be a successful tournament for both Ireland and England, Wales not winning a medal. The Irish heroes were the light-welterweight, Paul McCloskey, and light-heavyweight, Kenneth Egan, who won silvers, with bronzes going to Brian Gillen at bantamweight, Andrew Murray at lightweight and Alan Reynolds up at heavyweight. The English successes came via David Mulholland, with a silver, and bronzes for Don Broadhurst at flyweight and Ricardo Samms at middleweight.

Repton's Ryan Pickard won a tremendous silver medal at 70kgs in the World Cadet (under-17) Championships in Bucharest, Romania from 22-29 June, while Ireland's Keith Boyle won a bronze at 63 kgs.

England squeezed home by nine bouts to eight against Ireland in a schoolboy international match at the Anderstown Leisure Centre in Belfast on 27 June.

In the Four Nations Junior tournament, which was held at Everton Park Sports Centre in Liverpool on 27 and 28 June, England came out on top. Their record haul of 12 golds, four silver and five bronze gave a fair reflection of their overall superiority, Ireland finishing with five golds and Scotland and Wales with two apiece.

Our sport seldom receives the accolades it often deserves and the capital's amateur scene, and indeed far beyond too for that matter, was delighted to learn on 14 June of the award of an MBE in the Queen's Birthday Honours to Fitzroy Lodge supremo, Mick Carney.

At international level, Scotland felt badly aggrieved when they lost by three bouts to two against Italy in Salerno on 14 June. Sparta's David Appleby was adjudged to have lost against Luca Mellis, but the Italian squad manager was so disgusted with the decision that he presented the Scot with the winner's medal in his dressing room. Bad decisions continue to bedevil the sport, but this is nothing new.

Winding up the season's action, Young England acquired two silver medals at the Balaton Cup multi-nations event in Siofok, Hungary from 25-29 June, Tom Coward (Wombwell) at welterweight and Frankie Gavin (Hall Green) at featherweight, being our successful pair.

As we look forward to the new season all eyes will be fixed firmly on the various Olympic qualifying tournaments ahead of the Athens Games in 2004. Never an easy task to qualify, nevertheless, we look forward with hope and anticipation that someone from these islands will pick up the torch so magnificently kindled by one Audley Harrison, MBE in Sydney in 2000. Only time will tell whether this dream will become a reality once more, or be simply an Olympic wish that remains unfulfilled. We shall see.

ABA National Championships, 2002-2003

Note: Only men who actually fought are included, with those who were accorded divisional title status without having to win a contest not included.

Combined Services v Home Counties/Eastern Counties

Combined Services   **Nelson Barracks, Portsmouth – 30 January**
L.Fly: no entries. **Fly:** *final:* D.Barriball (Army) wo. **Bantam:** *final:* P.Murray (Army) wo. **Feather:** *final:* J.Elfidh (Army) wo. **Light:** *final:* N.Robinson (Army) wo. **L.Welter:** *final:* S.Patterson (Army) w pts M.Hardy (RAF). **Welter:** *final:* S.Briggs (Army) w pts S.Elwell (RN). **Middle:** *final:* S.McDonald (RN) w pts D.Frost (Army). **L.Heavy:** *final:* T.Davies (Army) wo. **Heavy:** M.O'Connell (RN) w pts N.Okoth (Army). **S.Heavy:** *final:* N.Suko (RN) wo.

Home Counties   **Football Ground, Thame – 15 February**
L. Fly: no entries. **Fly:** *final:* D. Culling (Stevenage) w rsc 1 D. Ward (Thames Valley). **Bantam:** *final:* L. Lewis (Wolvercote) wo. **Feather:** *final:* G. Couch (Thame) wo. **Light:** *final:* A. Lever (Bedford) w pts D. Phillips (Luton Shamrock). **L. Welter:** *semi-finals:* P. Steadman (Wolvercote) wo, D. Khan (Haileybury) w pts M. Douglas (Bulmershe); *final:* D. Khan w pts P. Steadman. **Welter:** *semi-finals:* J. Nevin (Thame) wo, P. Mullins (Wolvercote) w pts J. Grant (Berinsfield); *final:* J. Nevin w pts P. Mullins. **Middle:** *final:* B. Dempsey (Lewsey Centre) w pts C. Woods (Wolvercote). **L. Heavy:** *semi-finals:* C. Marshall (Hitchin) wo, D. Edwards (Thame) w pts F. Flanagan (Milton Keynes Royals): *final:* D. Edwards w pts C. Marshall. **Heavy:** *final:* C. Goldhawk (Cheshunt) w pts P. Reading (Hitchin). **S. Heavy:** *final:* L. Howkins (Pinewood Starr) w pts R. James-Bowen (Milton Keynes Royals).

Eastern Counties
Essex Division   **The Toot, Tilbury – 24 January**
L.Fly: no entries. **Fly:** no entries. **Bantam:** no entries. **Feather:** no entries. **Light:** no entries. **L.Welter:** *final:* J.Martin (Canvey) w pts N.Wicks (Chelmsford). **Welter:** no entries. **Middle:** *final:* J.Cullinane (Southend) wo. **L.Heavy:** *final:* H.Seaman (Castle) wo. **Heavy:** *final:* S.St John (Berry Boys) w pts H.Moldavian (Southend). **S.Heavy:** no entries.

Mid-Anglia Division
L.Fly: no entries. **Fly:** no entries. **Bantam:** no entries. **Feather:** no entries. **Light:** no entries. **L.Welter:** no entries. **Welter:** no entries. **Middle:** no entries. **L.Heavy:** no entries. **Heavy:** *final:* S.Whitwell (Cambridge Police) wo. **S.Heavy:** no entries.

Norfolk Division   **The Ocean Rooms, Gorleston – 22 January**
L.Fly: no entries. **Fly:** no entries. **Bantam:** no entries. **Feather:** *final:* C.Weston (Norwich Lads) wo. **Light:** no entries. **L.Welter:** no entries. **Welter:** *semi-finals:* S.Rice (Dereham) wo, S.Crompton (Kingfisher) w pts M.Cooper (Aylsham); *final:* S.Compton w pts S.Rice. **Middle:** no entries. **L.Heavy:** *final:* M.Redhead (Kingfisher) w pts D.McIntosh (Norwich Lads). **Heavy:** no entries. **S.Heavy:** no entries.

Suffolk Division   **The Ocean Rooms, Gorleston – 22 January**
L.Fly: no entries. **Fly:** no entries. **Bantam:** no entries. **Feather:** no entries. **Light:** no entries. **L.Welter:** *final:* K.Jackson (Haverhill) wo. **Welter:** no entries. **Middle:** *final:* W.Bayliss (Bury St Edmunds) w rsc 1 S.Mallett (Eastgate). **L.Heavy:** *final:* P.Davies (Lowestoft) wo. **Heavy:** no entries. **S.Heavy:** no entries.

Eastern Counties Semi-Finals & Finals   **Civic Hall, Grays – 31 January**
L.Fly: no entries. **Fly:** no entries. **Bantam:** no entries. **Feather:** *final:* C.Weston (Norwich Lads) wo. **Light:** no entries. **L.Welter:** *final:* J.Martin (Canvey) w pts K.Jackson (Haverhill). **Welter:** *final:* S.Crompton (Kingfisher) wo. **Middle:** *final:* W.Bayliss (Bury St Edmunds) w pts J.Cullinane (Southend). **L.Heavy:** *semi-finals:* H.Seaman (Castle) wo, M.Redhead (Kingfisher) w pts P.Davies (Lowestoft); *final:* M.Redhead w pts H.Seaman. **Heavy:** *final:* S.St John (Berry Boys) wo S.Whitwell (Cambridge Police). **S.Heavy:** no entries.

Home Counties v Eastern Counties   **RAF Naphill, High Wycombe – 22 February**
L.Fly: no entries. **Fly:** D.Culling (Stevenage) wo. **Bantam:** L.Lewis (Wolvercote) wo. **Feather:** G.Couch (Thame) w pts C.Weston (Norwich Lads). **Light:** A.Lever (Bedford) wo. **L.Welter:** J.Martin (Canvey) w pts D.Khan (Haileybury). **Welter:** J.Nevin (Thame) w pts S.Crompton (Kingfisher). **Middle:** B.Dempsey (Lewsey Centre) w rsc 3 W.Bayliss (Bury St Edmunds). **L.Heavy:** M.Redhead (Kingfisher) w pts D.Edwards (Thame). **Heavy:** C.Goldhawk (Cheshunt) w pts S.Whitwell (Cambridge Police) – replaced S.St John (Berry Boys). **S.Heavy:** L.Howkins (Pinewood Starr) wo.

Combined Services v Home Counties/Eastern Counties
L.Fly: no entries. **Fly:** D.Barriball (Army) w pts D.Culling (Stevenage). **Bantam:** L.Lewis (Wolvercote) w rsc 2 P.Murray (Army). **Feather:** G.Couch (Thame) w rtd 3 J.Elfidh (Army). **Light:** N.Robinson (Army) w pts A.Lever (Bedford). **L.Welter:** J.Martin (Canvey) w pts S.Patterson (Army). **Welter:** S.Briggs (Army) w rtd 4 J.Nevin (Thame). **Middle:** S.McDonald (RN) w pts B.Dempsey (Lewsey). **L.Heavy:** T.Davies (Army) w pts M.Redhead (Kingfisher). **Heavy:** M.O'Connell (RN) w pts C.Goldhawk (Cheshunt). **S.Heavy:** N.Suko (RN) w pts L.Howkins (Pinewood Starr).

London v North-West Counties

London
North-East Division   **York Hall, Bethnal Green – 6 February**
L.Fly: no entries. **Fly:** M.Marsh (West Ham) wo. **Bantam:** L.Otte (West Ham) wo. **Feather:** *semi-finals:* M.Gadaffi (Repton) wo, K.Mitchell (West Ham) w rsc 3 R.Barabash (Repton); *final:* K.Mitchell w rsc 2 M.Gadaffi. **Light:** *semi-finals:* R.Hewitt (West Ham) wo, L.Ballard (Repton) w pts J.Shotter (West Ham); *final:* L.Ballard w pts R.Hewitt. **L.Welter:** *semi-finals:* D.Sinyo (Lion) wo, D.Herdman (Repton) w pts J.Eley (Peacock); *final:* D.Herdman w rsc 2 D.Sinyo. **Welter:** *semi-finals:* D.Happe (Repton) w pts J.Benn (Peacock), T.Cesay (Repton) w pts G.Wild (West Ham); *final:* D.Happe w rsc 1 T.Cesay. **Middle:** *final:* D.Barker (Repton) w rsc 4 P.Masterson (Peacock). **L.Heavy:**

semi-finals: D.Cadman (Repton) w pts S.Lee (West Ham), A.Southwick (Dagenham Police) w pts A.Boyd (Peacock); *final:* D.Cadman w co 3 A.Southwick. **Heavy:** no entries. **S.Heavy:** *semi-finals:* J.Young (Repton) wo, D.Campbell (Repton) w rtd 2 T.Foy (Dagenham Police); *final:* J.Young wo D.Campbell.

North-West Division   Brent Community Centre, Wembley – 10 February
L.Fly: no entries. **Fly:** no entries. **Bantam:** no entries. **Feather:** *final:* P.Liggins (Trojan) w pts M.Tesanovic (All Stars). **Light:** *semi-finals:* P.Corcoran (Stowe) w pts B.Moyo (All Stars), M.Grant (Haringey Police) w pts M.Sazish (Hanwell); *final:* M.Grant w pts P.Corcoran. **L.Welter:** *final:* L.Beavis (Dale Youth) w pts Jamal Morrison (All Stars). **Welter:** *semi-finals:* Jamie Morrison (All Stars) wo, G.Hillyard (St Pancras) w pts D.Barrett (Trojan); *final:* Jamie Morrison w pts G.Hillyard. **Middle:** *semi-finals:* T.Simao (All Stars) wo, C.Campbell (Trojan) w pts A.Haliti (St Pancras); *final:* C.Campbell w rsc 1 T.Simao. **L.Heavy:** *semi-finals:* N.Mirza (Haringey Police) wo, D.Mohseni (All Stars) w pts J.Barrett (Trojan); *final:* D.Mohseni w pts N.Mirza. **Heavy:** *semi-finals:* C.Barrett (Trojan) w pts S.Goodwin (St Pancras), D.Cunnage (Northolt) w pts A.Alsady (All Stars); *final:* C.Barrett w pts D.Cunnage. **S.Heavy:** *final:* P.Pierson (Trojan) wo.

South-East Division   National Sports Centre, Crystal Palace – 13 February & York Hall, Bethnal Green – 14 February
L.Fly: *final:* Scott McDonald (Fitzroy Lodge) w pts D.Langley (Hollington). **Fly:** *final:* S.Langley (Hollington) w rsc 3 C.Brahmbhatt (Danson Youth). **Bantam:** *final:* A.Bhatia (Eltham) w pts S.Gregory (Samuel Montagu). **Feather:** *final:* D.Easton (New Addington) wo. **Light:** *final:* A.Ideh (Honor Oak) w pts D.Pereira (Fitzroy Lodge). **L.Welter:** *quarter-finals:* D.Gregory (Fitzroy Lodge) wo, D.Byrnes (Fisher) wo, M.Olwale (Honor Oak) wo, G.Woolcombe (Fisher) w pts N.Weise (Eltham); *semi-finals:* D.Byrnes w pts M.Olwale, G.Woolcombe w pts D.Gregory; *final:* D.Byrnes wp G.Woolcombe. **Welter:** *quarter-finals:* A.Small (Fitzroy Lodge) wo, M.Reigate (Fitzroy Lodge) wo, S.Webb (Bromley & Downham) w rsc 1 C.Talbot (Honor Oak), F.Smythe (Fisher) w pts M.Barber (Fisher); *semi-finals:* A.Small w pts M.Reigate, S.Webb w co 1 F.Smythe; *final:* S.Webb w pts A.Small. **Middle:** *semi-finals:* M.Talbot (Honor Oak) w pts B.Aird (Fisher), Mark Thirlwall (Fisher) w pts C.Imaga (Lynn); *final:* Mark Thirlwall w rsc 1 M.Talbot. **L.Heavy:** *final:* D.Kubyak (Lynn) w rsc 1 J.Weekes (Nemesis). **Heavy:** *final:* Stephen McDonald (Honor Oak) wo. **S.Heavy:** *final:* I.Lewison (Miguel's) wo.

South-East Division   Earlsfield ABC, Wandsworth – 7 February
L.Fly: no entries. **Fly:** no entries. **Bantam:** no entries. **Feather:** no entries. **Light:** no entries. **L.Welter:** *final:* G.Lowndes (Kingston) w rsc 2 A.Feeman (Kingston). **Welter:** *final:* S.Barr (Kingston) wo. **Middle:** *final:* E.Matthews (Balham) w pts H.Chick (Kingston). **L.Heavy:** *final:* J.Philip St John (Kingston) w rsc 3 S.Hutchinson (Balham). **Heavy:** *final:* A.Stables (Earlsfield) wo. **S.Heavy:** no entries.

London Semi-Finals & Finals   York Hall, Bethnal Green – 20 & 27 February
L.Fly: *final:* Scott McDonald (Fitzroy Lodge) wo. **Fly:** *final:* M.Marsh (West Ham) w dis 3 S.Langley (Hollington). **Bantam:** *final:* L.Otte (West Ham) w pts A.Bhatia (Eltham). **Feather:** *semi-finals:* P.Liggins (Trojan) wo, K.Mitchell (West Ham) w rtd 4 D.Easton (New Addington); *final:* K.Mitchell w rtd 2 P.Liggins. **Light:** L.Ballard (Repton) withdrew. *final:* M.Grant (Haringey Police) w pts A.Ideh (Honor Oak). **L.Welter:** *semi-finals:* L.Beavis (Dale Youth) w pts D.Herdman (Repton), D.Byrnes

(Fisher) w pts G.Lowndes (Kingston); *final:* L.Beavis w pts D.Byrnes. **Welter:** *semi-finals:* Jamie Morrison (All Stars) w pts S.Barr (Kingston), D.Happe (Repton) w pts S.Webb (Bromley & Downham); *final:* D.Happe w pts Jamie Morrison. **Middle:** *semi-finals:* C.Campbell (Trojan) wo D.Barker (Repton), E.Matthews (Balham) w rsc 3 Mark Thirlwall (Fisher); *final:* C.Campbell wo E.Matthews. **L.Heavy:** *semi-finals:* J.Philip St John (Kingston) wo D.Cadman (Repton), D.Kubyak (Lynn) w rsc 2 D.Mohseni (All Stars); *final:* D.Kubyak w rsc 3 J.Philip St John. **Heavy:** *semi-finals:* A.Stables (Earlsfield) wo, C.Barrett (Trojan) w pts Stephen McDonald (Honor Oak); *final:* C.Barrett w rsc 1 A.Stables. **S.Heavy:** *semi-finals:* J.Young (Repton) wo, I.Lewison (Miguel's) w pts P.Pierson (Trojan); *final:* I.Lewison w pts J.Young.

North-West Counties
East Lancs & Cheshire Division   New Larches Social Club, Preston – 7 February
L.Fly: no entries. **Fly:** *final:* D.Brewster (Ashton Albion) wo. **Bantam:** no entries. **Feather:** *final:* J.Kays (Nichols Police) w pts S.McFadden (Sandygate). **Light:** *semi-finals:* J.Murray (Northside) wo, J.Gaskill (Nichols Police) w pts C.White (Lancaster Lads); *final:* J.Murray w rtd 4 J.Gaskill. **L.Welter:** *semi-finals:* L.Graves (Chorley) w rsc 2 D.Boone (Tyldesley Centurians), G.O'Connor (Northside) w pts R.McGroty (Droylsden); *final:* L.Graves w pts G.O'Connor. **Welter:** *semi-finals:* T.Loco (Shannon) wo, J.Hussey (Hulton Police) w pts C.O'Brien (Sandygate); *final:* J.Hussey w co 2 T.Loco. **Middle:** no entries. **L.Heavy:** no entries. **Heavy:** no entries. **S.Heavy:** no entries.

West Lancs & Cheshire Division   Everton Park Sports Centre, Liverpool – 14 & 21 February
L.Fly: *final:* C.Lyon (Wigan) wo. **Fly:** *semi-finals:* J.Donnelly (Croxteth) wo, D.Swanson (Tower Hill) w pts M.Sedgewick (Wigan); *final:* D.Swanson w pts J.Donnelly. **Bantam:** *final:* N.McDonald (Vauxhall Motors) wo. **Feather:** *final:* D.Mulholland (Salisbury) wo. **Light:** *semi-finals:* S.Burke (Salisbury) wo, S.Mullin (Golden Gloves) w pts L.Jennings (Tower Hill); *final:* S.Burke w pts S.Mullin. **L.Welter:** *semi-finals:* J.Watson (Higherside Police) w pts A.Davies (Tower Hill), D.Angus (Salisbury) w pts E.Roberts (Golden Gloves); *final:* J.Watson w rtd 2 D.Angus. **Welter:** *semi-finals:* P.Jones (Stockbridge) w pts L.Kempster (Halewood), T.Quigley (Tower Hill) w pts L.Siner (Salisbury); *final:* T.Quigley w rsc 4 P.Jones. **Middle:** *final:* N.Perkins (Kirkdale) w pts G.Cummings (Higherside Police). **L.Heavy:** *final:* J.Ainscough (Kirkdale) w pts P.Keir (Rotunda). **Heavy:** *final:* M.Stafford (Kirkby) w pts M.Carroll (Kirkdale). **S.Heavy:** *final:* D.Price (Salisbury) wo.

North-West Counties Finals   Everton Park Sports Centre, Liverpool – 28 February
L.Fly: C.Lyon (Wigan) wo. **Fly:** D.Swanson (Tower Hill) w rsc 3 D.Brewster (Ashton Albion). **Bantam:** N.McDonald (Vauxhall Motors) wo. **Feather:** D.Mulholland (Salisbury) w pts J.Kays (Nichols Police). **Light:** S.Burke (Salisbury) w pts J.Murray (Northside). **L.Welter:** J.Watson (Higherside Police) w pts L.Graves (Chorley). **Welter:** T.Quigley (Tower Hill) w pts J.Hussey (Hulton Police). **Middle:** N.Perkins (Kirkdale) wo. **L.Heavy:** J.Ainscough (Kirkdale) wo. **Heavy:** M.Stafford (Kirkby) wo. **S.Heavy:** D.Price (Salisbury) wo.

London v North-West Counties   National Sports Centre, Crystal Palace – 8 March
L.Fly: C.Lyon (Wigan) w pts Scott McDonald (Fitzroy Lodge). **Fly:** M.Marsh (West Ham) w pts D.Swanson (Tower Hill).

Bantam: N.McDonald (Vauxhall Motors) w pts L.Otte (West Ham). **Feather:** K.Mitchell (West Ham) w pts D.Mulholland (Salisbury). **Light:** S.Burke (Salisbury) w pts M.Grant (Haringey Police). **L.Welter:** L.Beavis (Dale Youth) w pts J.Watson (Higherside Police). **Welter:** D.Happe (Repton) w pts T.Quigley (Tower Hill). **Middle:** N.Perkins (Kirkdale) wo C.Campbell (Trojan). **L.Heavy:** D.Kubyak (Lynn) w rsc 3 J.Ainscough (Kirkdale). **Heavy:** M.Stafford (Kirkby) w pts C.Barrett (Trojan). **S.Heavy:** D.Price (Salisbury) w pys I.Lewison (Miguel's).

North-East Counties v Midland Counties

North-East Counties
Tyne, Tees & Wear   Borough Hall, Hartlepool – 12 & 20 February
L.Fly: no entries. **Fly:** no entries. **Bantam:** *final:* J.Watson (Grainger Park) wo. **Feather:** *final:* R.Boyle (Birtley Police) w pts S.Hall (Albert Hill). **Light:** *final:* S.Zaman (Middlesbrough) w rtd 2 S.Murray (Newbiggin). **L.Welter:** *semi-finals:* P.Boyle (Middlesbrough) wo, G.Gallone (Spennymoor) w pts J.Donkin (Lambton Street); *final:* G.Gallone w pts P.Boyle. **Welter:** *quarter-finals:* J.McCrory (Forrest Hall) wo, I.Greenwell (Sunderland) wo, G.Wharton (Shildon) w pts A.Oliver (Spennymoor), L.Marsden (Harry Marsden's) w pts M.Marshall (Plains Farm); *semi-finals:* G.Wharton w pts J.McCrory, I.Greenwell w pts L.Marsden; *final:* I.Greenwell w co 3 G.Wharton. **Middle:** *semi-finals:* M.Denton (Headland) w rsc 2 L.Creighton (Albert Hill), G.Barr (Birtley Police) w pts S.McCrone (Spennymoor); *final:* G.Barr w pts M.Denton. **L.Heavy:** *semi-finals:* C.Wake (Shildon) wo, D.Pendleton (Louisa) w co 3 W.Mullen (Sunderland); *final:* D.Pendleton w pts C.Wake. **Heavy:** *final:* C.Clift (Lambton Street) wo. **S.Heavy:** *semi-finals:* D.Ferguson (Birtley Police) wo, C.Burton (Headland) w pts B.Robinson (South Durham); *final:* D.Ferguson w pts C.Burton.

Yorkshire & Humberside   Kerrisforth Hall, Barnsley – 7 February & Mexborough – 20 February
L.Fly: no entries. **Fly:** *final:* H.Nasser (Unity) wo. **Bantam:** *final:* S.Doherty (Bradford Police) wo. **Feather:** *final:* G.Sykes (Cleckheaton) w rsc 3 Jamie Dyer (Burmantofts). **Light:** *final:* F.Fehintola (Karmand Centre) w pts John Dyer (Burmantofts). **L.Welter:** *semi-finals:* A.MacIver (Cleckheaton) w pts G.Smith (Karmand Centre), C.Sebine (Burmantofts) w rsc 3 P.Clarke (Harrogate); *final:* C.Sebine w pts A.MacIver. **Welter:** *final:* J.Fletcher (Karmand Centre) w pts D.Reynolds (Sharkey's). **Middle:** *semi-finals:* D.Teasdale (Rotherham) w rsc 4 A.Ainger (Handsworth Police), S.Manocher (Unity) w co 1 K.Connolly (Bateson's); *final:* S.Manocher w pts D.Teasdale. **L.Heavy:** *final:* A.Khan (Unity) w pts J.Ibbotson (Sheffield). **Heavy:** *final:* N.McGarry (Doncaster Plant) w co 1 O.Bouryo (Unity). **S.Heavy:** *final:* C.Baker (Unity) w co 1 W.Crummack (Temple).

North-East Counties Finals   The Manor Social Club, Sheffield – 27 February
L.Fly: no entries. **Fly:** H.Nasser (Unity) wo. **Bantam:** J.Watson (Grainger Park) w pts S.Doherty (Bradford Police). **Feather:** G.Sykes (Cleckheaton) w rsc 4 R.Boyle (Birtley Police). **Light:** F.Fehintola (Karmand) w pts S.Zaman (Middlesbrough). **L.Welter:** C.Sebine (Burmantofts) w rsc 3 G.Gallone (Spennymoor). **Welter:** J.Fletcher (Karmand) w pts I.Greenwell (Sunderland). **Middle:** G.Barr (Birtley Police) w pts S.Manocher (Unity). **L.Heavy:** A.Khan (Unity) w pts D.Pendleton (Louisa). **Heavy:** C.Clift

(Lambton Street) w rsc 3 N.McGarry (Doncaster Plant). **S.Heavy:** C.Baker (Unity) w dis 3 D.Ferguson (Birtley Police).

Midland Counties
West Mercia, Staffs & Birmingham   Yew Tree Labour Club, Walsall – 7 February, The Irish Club, Digbeth 16 February, British Legion, Oldbury – 10 February, Drayton Manor Park, Tamworth – 19 February & The Tile Hill Social Club, Coventry – 1 March
L.Fly: no entries. **Fly:** final D.Broadhurst (Birmingham Irish) w pts A.Odud (Birmingham City Police). **Bantam:** no entries. **Feather:** *final:* S.Walton (Donnington Ex-Servicemen) wo. **Light:** semi-finals M.Gethin (Wednesbury) w pts C.Trueman (Aston), D.Harrison (Wolverhampton) w pts R.Wyatt (Lye); *final:* D.Harrison w pts M.Gethin. **L.Welter:** *semi-finals:* T.Walker (Tamworth) w pts D.English (Birmingham Irish), S.Myatt (Donnington Ex-Servicemen) w pts G.Coombes (Birmingham Irish); *final:* T.Walker w rsc 2 S.Myatt. **Welter:** *quarter-finals:* J.Scanlon (Birmingham City) w pts J.Cox (Heath Town), T.Adams (Birmingham Irish) w rsc 4 M.Greening (Droitwich), J.McDermott (Priory Park) w pts A.Hussain (Burton), G.Harris (Ironworks) w pts D.Johnson (Queensberry); *semi-finals:* T.Adams w pts J.Scanlon, G.Harris w pts J.McDermott; *final:* T.Adams w pts G.Harris. **Middle:** *quarter-finals:* D.McDermott (Priory Park) wo, M.Hough (Pleck) wo, M.Fowles (Birmingham City) wo, K.Smith (Heath Town) w pts M.Curley (Hobs Moat); *semi-finals:* D.McDermott w rsc 2 M.Hough, M.Fowles w pts K.Smith; *final:* D.McDermott w pts M.Fowles. **L.Heavy:** *final:* J.Boyd (Donnington Ex-Servicemen) wo. **Heavy:** *final:* P.Scope (Burton) wo. **S.Heavy:** no entries.

Warwicks, Derbys, Notts & Lincs   Pennine Hotel, Derby – 4 February, Byron House, Nottingham – 17 February & Jungle Club, Leicester – 20 February
L.Fly: *final:* U.Ahmed (Merlin) wo. **Fly:** no entries. **Bantam:** no entries. **Feather:** *semi-finals:* A.Hayes (Braunstone) wo, R.Cartlidge (St George's) w rsc 1 R.Highton (Coventry); *final:* R.Cartlidge w pts A.Hayes. **Light:** *final:* C.Johnson (Chesterfield) w pts R.Monroe (Old Robin Hood). **L.Welter:** *final:* J.Flinn (Triumph) w rsc 3 A.Hall (South Normanton). **Welter:** *quarter-finals:* M.Concepcion (Belgrave) wo, C.Smith (Kettering) wo, D.McClellan (Chesterfield) wo, J.Elliott (South Normanton) w pts N.Asghar (One Nation); *semi-finals:* M.Concepcion w pts J.Elliott, C.Smith w pts D.McClellan; *final:* M.Concepcion w pts C.Smith. **Middle:** *semi-finals:* A.Farrell (Triumph) wo, R.Samms (Phoenix) w rsc 2 C.Broomhead (Buxton); *final:* R.Samms w pts A.Farrell. **L.Heavy:** no entries. **Heavy:** *final:* J.Neil (Triumph) wo. **S.Heavy:** *final:* S.Wilson (Triumph) w pts M.Williams (Ruddington).

Midland Counties Finals   Tile Hill Social Club, Coventry – 1 March
L.Fly: U.Ahmed (Merlin) wo. **Fly:** D.Broadhurst (Birmingham Irish) wo. **Bantam:** no entries. **Feather:** S.Walton (Donnington Ex-Servicemen) w pts R.Cartlidge (St George's). **Light:** D.Harrison (Wolverhampton) w dis 3 C.Johnson (Chesterfield). **L.Welter:** J.Flinn (Triumph) w pts T.Walker (Tamworth). **Welter:** M.Concepcion (Belgrave) w co 2 T.Adams (Birmingham Irish). **Middle:** R.Samms (Phoenix) w pts D.McDermott (Priory Park). **L.Heavy:** J.Boyd (Donnington Ex-Servicemen) wo. **Heavy:** J.Neil (Triumph) w rsc 3 P.Scope (Burton). **S.Heavy:** S.Wilson (Triumph) wo.

North-East Counties v Midland Counties   The Manor Social Club, Sheffield – 6 March
L.Fly: U.Ahmed (Merlin) wo. **Fly:** D.Broadhurst (Birmingham Irish) w co 1 H.Nasser (Unity). **Bantam:** J.Watson (Grainger Park) wo. **Feather:** G.Sykes (Cleckheaton) w pts S.Walton (Donnington Ex-Servicemen). **Light:** F.Fehintola (Karmand Centre) w pts D.Harrison (Wolvehampton). **L.Welter:** C.Sebine (Burmantofts) w pts T.Walker (Tamworth) – replaced J.Flinn (Triumph). **Welter:** J.Fletcher (Karmand Centre) w pts M.Concepcion (Belgrave). **Middle:** G.Barr (Birtley Police) w pts R.Samms (Phoenix). **L.Heavy:** J.Boyd (Donnington Ex-Servicemen) w pts A.Khan (Unity). **Heavy:** C.Clift (Lambton Street) w rsc 3 J.Neil (Triumph). **S.Heavy:** C.Baker (Unity) w pts S.Wilson (Triumph).

Western Counties v Southern Counties

Western Counties
Southern Division   The Labour Club, Poole – 1 February
L.Fly: no entries. **Fly:** no entries. **Bantam:** *final:* J.Saygi (Paignton) w co 2 R.Bailey (Devonport). **Feather:** *final:* D.O'Connor (Devonport) w pts P.Wiffen (Weymouth). **Light:** *final:* B.Burns (Devonport) w pts J.Leando (Pisces). **L.Welter:** *final:* S.Yates (Torbay) wo. **Welter:** *final:* C.Drake (Mayflower) wo. **Middle:** *final:* W.Ambrose (Bournemouth) wo. **L.Heavy:** *final:* L.Wayne (Apollo) wo. **Heavy:** no entries. **S.Heavy:** *semi-finals:* M.Elkins (Barnstaple) wo, D.Lund (Leonis) w pts N.Kendal (Apollo); *final:* D.Lund w pts M.Elkins.

Northern Division   The BAWA Centre, Bristol – 1 February & Jurys Hotel, Bristol – 10 February
L.Fly: no entries. **Fly:** no entries. **Bantam:** no entries. **Feather:** *final:* S.Hussain (Walcot Boys) wo. **Light:** semi-finals J.Nicholas (National Smelting) wo, R.Scutt (Sydenham) w co 1 S.Mourant (Frome); *final:* J.Nicholas w pts R.Scutt. **L.Welter:** *final:* D.Entwhistle (Watchet) w pts J.Hicks (Yeovil/Reckleford). **Welter:** *semi-finals:* A.Cummings (National Smelting) wo, A.Woodward (Watchet) w pts J.Turley (Penhill RBL); *final:* A.Woodward w pts A.Cummings. **Middle:** *final:* D.Guthrie (Yeovil/Reckleford) w pts S.Mullins (Yeovil/Reckleford). **L.Heavy:** *final:* P.Smyth (Synwell) wo. **Heavy:** *final:* G.Lee (Synwell) wo. **S.Heavy:** *final:* D.Poulson (Taunton) w pts B.Harding (Penhill RBL).

Western Counties Finals   The Badger Hill Pub, Frome – 22 February
L.Fly: no entries. **Fly:** no entries. **Bantam:** J.Saygi (Paignton) wo. **Feather:** S.Hussain (Walcot Boys) w pts D.O'Connor (Devonport). **Light:** J.Nicholas (National Smelting) w pts B.Burns (Devonport). **L.Welter:** S.Yates (Torbay) w pts D.Entwhistle (Watchet). **Welter:** A.Woodward (Watchet) w pts C.Drake (Mayflower). **Middle:** D.Guthrie (Yeovil/Reckleford) w rsc 2 W.Ambrose (Bournemouth). **L.Heavy:** P.Smyth (Synwell) w pts L.Wayne (Apollo). **Heavy:** G.Lee (Synwell) wo. **S.Heavy:** D.Lund (Leonis) w pts D.Poulson (Taunton).

Southern Counties   The Athletic Club, Bexhill – 15 & 22 February
L.Fly: no entries. **Fly:** *final:* S.Brazil (Aldershot & Farnham) wo. **Bantam:** *final:* J.Bousquet (St Mary's) wo. **Feather:** *final:* A.Goff (St Mary's) w rsc 3 G.Mitchell (Basingstoke). **Light:** *quarter-finals:* B.Jones (Crawley) wo, B.Buchanan (West Hill) wo, M.Tew (Southampton) w pts W.Dunkley (Swanley), L.Cook (Foley) w pts S.Tobias (Woking); *semi-finals:* B.Jones w pts B.Buchanan,

M.Tew w pts L.Cook; *final:* M.Tew w pts B.Jones. **L.Welter:** *quarter-finals:* N.Wray (Southwick) wo, J.Berry (Sandwich) wo, F.Jones (Woking) w pts A.Martin (Foley), A.Tew (Southampton) w pts S.Watson (Lawrence); *semi-finals:* A.Tew w pts A.Berry, N.Wray w co 1 F.Jones; *final:* N.Wray w co 2 A.Tew. **Welter:** *quarter-finals:* S.Woolford (The Grange) wo, A.Young (Crawley) wo, M.Welsh (Swanley) wo, I.Hudson (Faversham) w pts J.Morris (Newport, IoW); *semi-finals:* S.Woolford w pts A.Young, M.Welsh w co 3 I.Hudson; *final:* S.Woolford w pts M.Welsh. **Middle:** *final:* S.Ede (Southampton) w dis 2 D.Goode (Lawrence). **L.Heavy:** *semi-finals:* G.Kelly (Stacey) wo, D.Taylor (Southampton) w rsc 3 D.Orwell (Shepway); *final:* D.Taylor w rsc 2 G.Kelly. **Heavy:** *final:* S.Reed (White Hawk) w rsc 3 F.Booker (Hove). **S.Heavy:** M.Thomas (Woking) w rsc 3 G.Potter (The Grange).

Western Counties v Southern Counties   Butlins Holiday Camp, Minehead – 8 March
L.Fly: no entries. **Fly:** S.Brazil (Aldershot & Farnham) wo. **Bantam:** J.Saygi (Paignton) w pts J.Bousquet (St Mary's). **Feather:** S.Hussain (Walcot Boys) w rsc 1 A.Goff (St Mary's). **Light:** J.Nicholas (National Smelting) w rsc 2 M.Tew (Southampton). **L.Welter:** N.Wray (Southwick) w pts S.Yates (Torbay). **Welter:** A.Woodward (Watchet) w pts S.Woolford (The Grange). **Middle:** D.Guthrie (Yeovil/Reckleford) w rsc 1 S.Ede (Southampton). **L.Heavy:** D.Taylor (Southampton) w co 3 P.Smyth (Synwell). **Heavy:** G.Lee (Synwell) w pts S.Reed (White Hawk). **S.Heavy:** M.Thomas (Woking) w rsc 3 D.Lund (Leonis).

English ABA Semi-Finals & Finals

McEwan's Centre, Houghton le Spring – 21 March, The Leisure Centre, Crawley – 22 March & York Hall, Bethnal Green – 4 April
L.Fly: *semi-finals:* C.Lyon (Wigan) wo, J.Fowl (Haileybury) w pts U.Ahmed (Merlin); *final:* C.Lyon w pts J.Fowl. **Fly:** *semi-finals:* D.Broadhurst (Birmingham Irish) w co 1 S.Brazil (Aldershot & Farnham), M.Marsh (West Ham) w pts D.Barriball (Army); *final:* D.Broadhurst w pts M.Marsh. **Bantam:** *semi-finals:* L.Lewis (Wolvercote) w pts J.Saygi (Paignton), N.McDonald (Vauxhall Motors) w pts J.Watson (Grainger Park); *final:* N.McDonald w rsc 4 L.Lewis. **Feather:** *semi-finals:* G.Couch (Thame) w rsc 3 S.Hussain (Walcot Boys), K.Mitchell (West Ham) w pts S.Walton (Donnington Ex-Servicemen) – replaced G.Sykes (Cleckheaton); *final:* K.Mitchell w pts G.Couch. **Light:** *semi-finals:* S.Burke (Salisbury) w pts N.Robinson (Army), F.Fehintola (Karmand Centre) w rsc 3 J.Nicholas (National Smelting); *final:* S.Burke w pts F.Fehintola. **L.Welter:** *semi-finals:* L.Beavis (Dale Youth) w dis 1 N.Wray (Southwick), C.Sebine (Burmantofts) w pts J.Martin (Canvey); *final:* L.Beavis w pts C.Sebine. **Welter:** *semi-finals:* D.Happe (Repton) w pts S.Briggs (Army), J.Fletcher (Karmand Centre) w pts S.Woolford (The Grange) – replaced A.Woodward (Watchet); *final:* D.Happe w pts J.Fletcher. **Middle:** *semi-finals:* N.Perkins (Kirkdale) w rsc 4 D.Guthrie (Yeovil/Reckleford), G.Barr (Birtley Police) w pts S.McDonald (RN); *final:* N.Perkins w rsc 4 G.Barr. **L.Heavy:** *semi-finals:* T.Davies (Army) w co 3 D.Taylor (Southampton), J.Boyd (Donnington Ex-Servicemen) w pts D.Kubyak (Lynn); *final:* J.Boyd w pts T.Davies. **Heavy:** *semi-finals:* M.Stafford (Kirkby) w rsc 1 G.Lee (Synwell), M.O'Connell (RN) w pts C.Clift (Lambton Street); *final:* M.O'Connell w pts M.Stafford. **S.Heavy:** *semi-finals:* D.Price (Salisbury) w pts M.Thomas (Woking), N.Suku (RN) w pts C.Baker (Unity); *final:* D.Price w pts N.Suku.

Irish Championships, 2002-2003

Senior Tournament

The National Stadium, Dublin – 7, 8, 14, 15 & 21 February
L. Fly: *semi-finals:* P. Baker (Immaculata, Belfast) w rsc 2 J. Moore (St. Francis, Limerick), J.P. Kinsella (Ballybrack, Dublin) w pts C. Ahern (Baldoyle, Dublin); *final:* P. Baker w pts J.P. Kinsella. **Fly:** *semi-finals:* T. Lee (Oughterard, Galway) wo, Paul Hyland (Golden Cobra, Dublin) w pts D. McArdle (Dealgan, Louth); *final:* Paul Hyland w pts T. Lee. **Bantam:** *quarter-finals:* M. Lindsay (Immaculata, Belfast) wo, D. Lawlor (Muine Beag, Carlow) wo, D. McKenna (Holy Family, Belfast) wo, B. Gillen (Holy Trinity, Belfast) w pts E. Donovan (St. Michael's, Athy); *semi-finals:* M. Lindsay w pts D. Lawlor, B. Gillen w pts D. McKenna; *final:* B. Gillen w pts M. Lindsay. **Feather:** *quarter-finals:* S. Ormond (Quarryvale, Dublin) wo, H. Cunningham (Saints, Belfast) wo, R. Kane (Bishop Kelly, Tyrone) w pts S. McAnee (Ring. Derry), E. Touhey (Moate, Westmeath) w pts Patrick Hyland (Golden Cobra, Dublin); *semi-finals:* S. Ormonde w pts R. Kane, E. Touhey wo (H. Cunningham withdrew); *final:* S. Ormond w pts E. Touhey. **Light:** *quarter-finals:* A. Murray (Cavan) w pts T. Carlyle (Crumlin, Dublin), J.P. Campbell (South Meath) w pts E. Hyland (Golden Cobra, Dublin), N. Monteith (Dockers, Belfast) w pts P. Simpson (Saviour's/Crystal, Waterford), G. Dunne (Neilstown, Dublin) w pts J. McDonagh (Brosna, Offaly); *semi-finals:* A. Murray w pts J.P. Campbell, G. Dunne w pts N. Monteith; *final:* A. Murray w pts G. Dunne. **L. Welter:** *quarter-finals:* P. McCloskey (St. Canice's, Derry) w pts J. Dowling (Paulstown, Kilkenny), F. Turner (St. Ibar's, Wexford) w pts D. Hamill (All Saints, Ballymena), M. Kelly (Dealgan, Louth) w pts A. Carlyle (Golden Cobra, Dublin), R. Sheahan (St. Michael's, Athy) w pts T. O'Neill (Mount Tallant, Dublin); *semi-finals:* P. McCloskey w pts F. Turner, M. Kelly w pts R. Sheahan; *final:* P. McCloskey w pts M. Kelly. **Welter:** *prelims:* J. Moore (Arklow, Wicklow) wo, C. Curtis (Dealgan, Louth) wo, H. Coyle (Geesala, Mayo) wo, J. Harkin (Dunfanaghy, Donegal) wo, T. Blaney (Westside, Dublin) wo, E. Colgan (Avona, Dublin) wo, B. Kerr (Holy Trinity, Belfast) w pts P. Jennings (Quarryvale, Dublin), H. Joyce (St. Michael's, Athy) w pts T. Hamill (All Saints, Ballymena); *quarter-finals:* J. Moore w rsc 4 C. Curtis, H. Coyle w pts J. Harkin, T. Blaney w pts E. Colgan, H. Joyce w pts B. Kerr; *semi-finals:* J. Moore w pts H. Coyle, T. Blaney w pts H. Joyce; *final:* J. Moore w rsc 3 T. Blaney. **Middle:** *prelims:* T. Moran (St. Anne's, Westport) wo, E. O'Kane (St. Canice's, Derry) wo, E. Healy (Portlaoise, Laois) wo, S. O'Meara (Holy Trinity, Belfast) w pts K. Whelan (Saviour's/Crystal, Waterford), L. Senior (Crumlin, Dublin) w pts P. Murray (St. Matthew's, Dublin), P. Whelan (Enniscorthy, Wexford) w pts R. Fox (Phibsboro, Dublin), D. Sutherland (St. Saviour's, Dublin) w pts J. Waldron (Castlebar, Mayo), A. Lee (St. Francis, Limerick) w pts F. O'Brien (Crumlin, Dublin): *quarter-finals:* E. O'Kane w pts E. Healy, T. Moran w pts S. O'Meara, L. Senior w pts P. Whelan, A. Lee w pts D. Sutherland; *semi-finals:* E. O'Kane w pts T. Moran, A. Lee w pts L. Senior; *final:* A. Lee w pts E. O'Kane. **L. Heavy:** *prelims:* I. Timms (Quarryvale, Dublin) wo, M. Lee (Oughterard, Galway) wo, C. Carmichael (Holy Trinity, Belfast) wo, S. O'Grady (St. Saviour's, Dublin) wo, K. Egan (Neilstown, Dublin) wo, D.

Cutriss (St. Colman's, Cork) wo, M. McDonagh (Brosna, Offaly) wo, P. Smyth (Keady, Armagh) w rsc 4 S. O'Sullivan (St. Colman's, Cork); *quarter-finals:* I. Timms w pts M. Lee, C. Carmichael w pts S. O'Grady, K. Egan w rsc 2 D. Cutriss, M. McDonagh w pts P. Smyth; *semi-finals:* C., Carmichael w pts I. Timms, K. Egan w pts M. McDonagh; *final:* K. Egan w pts C. Carmichael. **Heavy:** *quarter-finals:* A. Reynolds (St. Joseph's, Sligo) wo, P. Byrne (Swinford, Mayo) wo, J. Upton (Crumlin, Dublin) wo, T. Donnelly (Mark Heagney, Tyrone) w rsc 3 J. McKeogh (Brosna, Offaly); *semi-finals:* A. Reynolds w rsc 3 P. Byrne, T. Donnelly w pts J. Upton; *final:* A. Reynolds w pts T. Donnelly. **S. Heavy:** *semi-finals:* M. Rogan (Immaculata, Belfast) w rsc 1 G. Dargan (CIE, Dublin), T. Crampton (St. Broughan's, Offaly) w rsc 3 B. Sherry (Mark Heagney, Tyrone); *final:* T. Crampton w pts M. Rogan.

Intermediate Finals

The National Stadium, Dublin – 6 December
L. Fly: C. Ahern (Baldoyle, Dublin) w pts D. McArdle (Dealgan, Louth). **Fly:** B. McCafferty (St. John Bosco, Belfast) wo. **Bantam:** D. Murphy (St. Saviour's, Dublin) w pts B. Harkin (Twin Towns, Donegal). **Feather:** E. Touhey (Moate, Westmeath) w rsc 2 W. Casey (Southside, Limerick). **Light:** D. McFadden (St. Joseph's, Derry) w pts J. Connor (Dockers, Belfast). **L.Welter:** T. O'Neill (Mount Tallant, Dublin) w pts C. O'Conaire (St. Saviour's, Dublin). **Welter:** J. Dowling (Paulstown, Kilkenny) w pts O. Kelly (Galway). L. **Middle:** E. Colgan (Avona, Dublin) w pts P. Moffett (Abbey, Down). **Middle:** P. Murray (St. Matthew's, Dublin) w pts E. Healy (Portlaoise, Laois). **L. Heavy:** S. O'Sullivan (St. Colman's, Cork) w pts J. Sweeney (Dungloe, Donegal). **Heavy:** P. Byrne (Swinford, Mayo) w pts G. Smith (Cabra Panthers, Dublin). **S. Heavy:** M. Rogan (Immaculata, Belfast) w pts S. Tuthill (Crumlin, Dublin).

Junior Finals

The National Stadium, Dublin – 30 May
L. Fly: R. Hickey (Grangecon, Kildare) w pts D. Thorpe (St. Aidan's, Wexford). **Fly:** T.J. Doheny (Portlaoise, Laois) w pts B. McCafferty (St. John Bosco, Belfast). **Bantam:** E. Donovan (St. Michael's, Athy) wo, D. Joyce (St. Michael's, Athy) withdrew. **Feather:** D. Murphy (St. Saviour's, Dublin) w pts E. Touhey (Moate, Westmeath). **Light:** J. Quinn (St. Saviour's, Dublin) w pts T. Dwyer (St. Aidan's, Wexford). **L. Welter:** J. McDonagh (Brosna, Offaly) w pts D. Toman (Newry, Down). **Welter:** M. Gallagher (Dunfanaghy, Donegal) w pts C. Moran (St. Saviour's, Dublin). **Middle:** P. Lee (Oughterard, Galway) w pts B. Fitzpatrick (Ballina, Mayo). **L. Heavy:** D. O'Neill (Paulstown, Kilkenny) w rsc 2 J. Cummins (Loughglynn, Roscommon). **Heavy:** P. Kearns (St. Brigid's, Dublin) w ret 4 M. Kelly (Glin, Dublin). **S. Heavy:** S. Belshaw (Lisburn, Antrim) w pts G. Barrett (Olympic, Galway).

Scottish and Welsh Senior Championships, 2002-2003

Scotland ABA

The Time Capsule, Coatbridge – 22 March & 4 April, Pettycur Bay Arena, Kinghorn – 28 March & The Tree Tops Hotel, Aberdeen – 29 March

L. Fly: *quarter-finals:* I.McCabe (Lesmahagow) wo, S.Moles (Denny) wo, U.Hussain (Kinross) wo, G.Jones (Gryffe) w pts J.McPherson (Cleland); *semi-finals:* U.Hussain wo G.Jones, I.McCabe w pts S.Moles; *final:* I.McCabe w pts U.Hussain. **Fly:** *final:* L.Munro (Dennistoun) w pts D.Ellis (Barn). **Bantam:** *final:* S.Flynn (Gilmerton) w pts M.Crossan (Dennistoun). **Feather:** *quarter-finals:* F.Rafiq (Dennistoun) wo, J.Ancliffe (Granite City) wo, M.Chalmers (Glenrothes) wo, J.Bothwell (Dennistoun) w pts R.Park (Blantyre); *semi-finals:* F.Rafiq w pts J.Ancliffe, J.Bothwell w pts M.Chalmers; *final:* F.Rafiq w pts J.Bothwell. **Light:** *prelims:* D.Johnstone (Blantyre) wo, G.Clarke (Gilmerton) wo, M.Hastie (Forgewood) wo, N.Iqbal (Glenrothes) wo, M.Prince (Broadwood) wo, S.Carroll (Granite City) wo, J.Gilhaney (Blantyre) w pts E.Doyle (Glenboig), K.Green (Cardenden) w rsc 3 D.Ross (Kincorth); *quarter-finals:* D.Johnstone w pts G.Clarke, M.Hastie w pts N.Iqbal, M.Prince w pts S.Carroll, K.Green w pts J.Gilhaney; *semi-finals:* M.Prince w rsc 3 D.Johnstone, M.Hastie w pts K.Green; *final:* M.Hastie w pts M.Prince. **L.Welter:** *quarter-finals:* S.Green (Glenrothes) w rsc 3 R.Scott (Springhill), J.Murphy (Barn) w pts J.Cusick (Cardenden), J.Price (Peterhead) w pts P.Pollock (Lanark), P.Burns (Forgewood) w pts J.McLevy (Clydeview); *semi-finals:* J.Murphy w pts S.Green, P.Burns w pts J.Price; *final:* J.Murphy w pts P.Burns. **Welter:** *prelims:* S.Shedden (Springhill) wo, S.Fitzsimmons (Gilmerton) wo, B.Lee (Arbroath) wo, D.Campbell (Denbeath) wo, C.McEwen (Clovenstone) w rsc 1 B.McLaughlin (Newarthill), A.Montgomery (Forgewood) w pts L.Burnett (Kincorth), D.Ross (Inverness) w pts F.Mahura (Sparta), G.Mathieson (Aberdeen) w pts R.Cunningham (Madison); *quarter-finals:* S.Shedden w pts S.Fitzsimmons, B.Lee w pts D.Campbell, C.McEwen w pts A.Montgomery, D.Ross w pts G.Mathieson; *semi-finals:* B.Lee w rsc 3 S.Shedden, C.McEwen w pts D.Ross; *final:* C.McEwen w rsc 3 B.Lee. **Middle:** *quarter-finals:* C.Black (Barn) w pts A.Will (Sparta), K.Bruce (Kingdom) w rsc 4 W.Blackwood (Garnock Valley), B.Moore (Perth Railways) w pts P.Warner (Springhill), S.McGuire (Glenrothes) w pts I.Donnelly (Four Isles); *semi-finals:* K.Bruce w pts C.Black, S.McGuire w pts B.Moore; *final:* K.Bruce w pts S.McGuire. **L.Heavy:** *semi-finals:* K.Anderson (Elston Cadell) w pts M.Warner (Springhill), M.Ross (Larkfield) w pts K.Reynolds (Barn); *final:* K.Anderson w rsc 3 M.Ross. **Heavy:** *semi-finals:* A.Young (Inverness) w rsc 4 B.Graham (Newarthill), S.Robb (Lochside) w pts D.McConnell (Larkfield); *final:* A.Young w rsc 3 S.Robb. **S.Heavy:** *semi-finals:* I.Millarvie (Fauldhouse) w rsc 1 J.Perry (Larkhall), A.Martin (Hawick) w pts A.Boyle (Bannockburn); *final:* I.Millarvie w pts A.Martin.

Wales ABA

The Sports Centre, Neath – 15 & 16 February & Afan Lido, Port Talbot – 14 March

L. Fly: *final:* N.Morrisey (Colcot Sports) w pts J.Beasley (Aberystwyth). **Fly:** *final:* M.Edmonds (St Joseph's) wo. **Bantam:** *semi-finals:* F.Janes (Highfields) w pts D.Jones (Gelligaer), N.Probert (Pembroke) w pts J.Mwasigallah (Splott Adventure); *final:* N.Probert w pts F.Janes. **Feather:** *semi-finals:* D.Edwards (Cwmavon Hornets) wo, D.Davies (Merthyr) w rsc 3 M.Roberts (Wrexham); *final:* D.Edwards w pts D.Davies. **Light:** *semi-finals:* P.Ashton (St Joseph's) w pts J.Crees (Prince of Wales), J.Evans (Army) w pts J.Rawlinson (Colcot Sports); *final:* J.Evans w pts P.Ashton. **L.Welter:** *prelims:* T.Davies (Kyber Colts) wo, P.Hayhurst (Carmarthen) wo, G.Perkins (Premier) wo, N.Burchett (Army) wo, R.James (Merthyr Ex-Servicemen) wo, G.Tate (Carmarthen) wo, V.Bryan (Splott Adventure) w rtd 3 L.Davies (Caerau Dragons), T.Mohamed (Colcot Sports) w rsc 4 N.James (Neath); *quarter-finals:* V.Bryan w pts T.Mohamed, T.Davies w rsc 3 P.Hayhurst, G.Perkins w pts N.Burchett, R.James w rsc 1 G.Tate; *semi-finals:* R.James w pts V.Bryan, G.Perkins w pts T.Davies; *final:* G.Perkins w pts T.Davies. **Welter:** *prelims:* A.Doherty (Pontypool & Panteg) wo, M.Rees (Penyrheol) wo, A.Thomas (Clwyd) wo, W.Jones (Buckley) wo, G.Harvey (Kyber Colts) wo, C.Brophy (Premier) wo, B.Holland (Army) wo, J.Way (Cwmcarn) w pts J.Clarke (Duffryn); *quarter-finals:* A.Doherty w rsc 2 M.Rees, A.Thomas w rsc 3 W.Jones, G.Harvey w pts C.Brophy, J.Way w pts B.Holland; *semi-finals:* A.Doherty w pts A.Thomas, J.Way w pts G.Harvey; *final:* A.Doherty w pts J.Way. **Middle:** *prelims:* T.Jones (Cwmgorse) wo, J.Deforges (Gilfach Goch) w rsc 3 C.Evans (Llanelli Welsh), D.Tang (RN) w pts P.Killian (Cwmgorse), K.Thomas (Prince of Wales) w rsc 3 J.Collier (Coed Eva), M.Allen (Palace) w pts L.Trott (Towy), F.Borg (Prince of Wales) w pts N.Addis (Kyber Colts), J.Whitfield (Army) w pts M.Rourke (Merthyr), S.Hughes (Red Dragon) w pts G.Evans (Colcot Sports); *quarter-finals:* D.Tang w dis 4 T.Jones, M.Allen w rsc 3 K.Thomas, F.Borg w pts J.Whitfield, S.Hughes w pts J.Deforges; *semi-finals:* M.Allen w pts D.Tang, F.Borg w pts S.Hughes; *final:* F.Borg w pts M.Allen. **L.Heavy:** *prelims:* J.Jones (Army) wo, J.Jones (Newport Sports) wo, R.Allen (Palace) wo, G.Harvey (Crindau Harlequins) wo, J.Walters (Prince of Wales) wo, G.Evans (Pontypool & Panteg) wo, B.Hayward (Heads of the Valleys) wo, R.Boyd (Carmarthen) w pts A.Matthews (Gilfach Goch); *quarter-finals:* J.Jones w rsc 3 J.Hughes, R.Allen w pts G.Harvey, J.Walters w pts G.Edwards, B.Hayward w pts R.Boyd; *semi-finals:* B.Hayward w rtd 2 J.Walters, J.Jones w rsc 1 R.Allen; *final:* J.Jones w co 2 B.Hayward. **Heavy:** *quarter-finals:* S.Frith (Army) wo, A.Holloway (Fhoose) wo, M.Davies (Penyrheol) wo, D.Mais (Splott Adventure) w pts G.Paders (Crindau Harlequins); *semi-finals:* S.Frith w rsc 3 A.Holloway, M.Davies w pts D.Mais; *final:* M.Davies w rsc 3 S.Frith. **S.Heavy:** *semi-finals:* L.Milsjen (Coed Eva) w pts A.Thomas (Merthyr Ex-Servicemen), K.Evans (Carmarthen) w pts D.Morgan (Bonymaen); *final:* K.Evans w rsc 2 L.Milsjen.

Four Nations Tournament, 2003

The Welsh Institute of Sport, Cardiff   16 & 17 April
L. Fly: *semi-finals:* I.McCabe (S) w pts N.Morrissey (W), C.Lyon (E) w pts C.Ahern (I); *final:* C.Lyon w pts I.McCabe. *3rd place:* C.Ahern w rtd 2 N.Morrissey. **Fly:** *semi-finals:* M.Edmonds (W) w pts P.Hyland (I), D.Broadhurst (E) w co 1 L.Munro (S); *final:* M.Edmonds w pts D.Broadhurst. *3rd place:* P.Hyland wo L.Munro. **Bantam:** *semi-finals:* E.Donovan (I) w pts S.Flynn (S), N.McDonald (E) w pts N.Probert; *final:* E.Donovan w pts N.McDonald. *3rd place:* S.Flynn w pts N.Probert. **Feather:** *semi-finals:* D.Edwards (W) w pts F.Rafiq (S), S.Ormond (I) wo K.Mitchell (E); *final:* D.Edwards w pts S.Ormond. *3rd place:* F.Rafiq wo K.Mitchell. **Light:** *semi-finals:* S.Burke (E) w pts A.Murray (I), M.Hastie (S) w pts J.Evans (W); *final:* S.Burke w pts M.Hastie. *3rd place:* A.Murray wo J.Evans. **L.Welter:** *semi-finals:* P.McCloskey (I) w pts R.James (W), L.Beavis (E) w pts P.Burns (S); *final:* P.McCloskey w pts L.Beavis. *3rd place:*
R.James w pts P.Burns. **Welter:** J.Moore (I) w rsc 3 J.Way (W), C.McEwan (S) w pts J.Fletcher (E); *final:* J.Moore w pts C.McEwan. *3rd place:* J.Fletcher w pts J.Way. **Middle:** A.Lee (I) w rsc 3 F.Borg (W), N.Perkins (E) wo S.McGuire (S); *final:* A.Lee w pts N.Perkins. *3rd place:* F.Borg wo S.McGuire. **L.Heavy:** K.Egan (I) w pts K.Anderson (S), T.Davies (E) w pts J.Jones (W); *final:* T.Davies w pts K.Egan. *3rd place:* K.Anderson w pts J.Jones. **Heavy:** A.Reynolds (I) w rtd 2 M.O'Connell (E), A.Young (S) w pts M.Davies (W); *final:* A.Reynolds w rsc 2 A.Young. *3rd place:* M.Davies wo M.O'Connell. **S.Heavy:** D.Price (E) w pts T.Crampton (I), K.Evans (W) w pts I.Millarvie (S); *final:* K.Evans w pts D.Price. *3rd place:* I.Millarvie wo T.Crampton.

Code: E = England, I = Ireland, S = Scotland, W = Wales

England's middleweight candidate from Kirkdale, Neil Perkins (right), is seen in action defeating Birtley Police's Gary Barr in the 2003 ABA final

Les Clark

British and Irish International Matches, 2002-2003

Does not include Multi-nation or championship tournaments, despite them being recognised as international appearances, merely because space will not allow. British and Irish interest in the major tournaments can be found within the pages of Chris Kempson's Highlights from the 2002-2003 Amateur Season, elsewhere in the book. We apologise if any international matches have been missed, but we have covered all of those we have been made aware of.

Ireland (3) v USA (2)   Denver, Colorado – 16 August
(Irish names first): **Bantam:** M. Lindsay w pts T. Daniels. **Feather:** G. Brown (Crumlin, Dublin) l rsc 3 A. Welch. **Light:** N. Monteith l pts V. Escobedo. **Welter:** D. Conlon w pts R. Biggs. **L. Middle:** H. Joyce w pts E. Joseph.

Ireland (3) v USA (4)   Scranton, Pennsylvania – 23 August
(Irish names first): **Fly:** T. Lee w pts D. McFadden. **Bantam:** M. Lindsay w pts R. Jefferson, D. Lawlor l pts T. Daniels. **Light:** N. Monteith l pts D. Jimenez. **Welter:** D. Conlon l pts T. Bradley. **L. Middle:** H. Joyce l pts J. Hernandez. **L. Heavy:** P. Smyth w ret 4 C. Stevens.

Ireland (3) v Hungary (8)   National Stadium, Dublin – 4 October
(Irish names first): **L. Fly:** J.P. Kinsella l pts P. Bedak. **Fly:** D. Campbell l pts O. Musci. **Bantam:** D. Lawlor l pts Z. Bedak. **Feather:** S. Ormond w pts G. Farkas. **Light:** T. Carlyle w pts H. Kertesz. **L. Welter:** R. Sheahan w pts G. Kate. **Welter:** J. Moore w pts V. Balog. **L. Middle:** H. Coyle l rsc 3 J. Nagy. **Middle:** K. Egan w rsc 2 K. Balzsay. **L. Heavy:** I. Timms l rsc 1 I. Szucs. **Heavy:** A. Reynolds l pts E. Garai.

Ireland (3) v Hungary (6)   Templemore, Co. Tipperary – 6 October
(Irish names first): **L. Fly:** P. Baker l pts P. Bedak. **Fly:** T. Lee w pts O. Musci. **Bantam:** D. Lawlor w pts D. Oltvanyi. **Feather:** J. Phillips w pts G. Farkas. **Light:** G. Dunne l pts H. Kertesz. **L. Welter:** T. Carlyle l pts G. Kate. **Welter:** T. Blaney l pts J. Meszaros. **L. Middle:** D. Conlon l pts J. Nagy. **L. Heavy:** M. McDonagh l pts I. Szello.

Young Ireland (6) v Young Italy (3)   National Stadium, Dublin – 8 November
(Irish names first): **L. Fly:** D. Joyce w rsc 2 Mario De Mita. **Bantam:** T. Dwyer w pts L. Melis, D. Murphy w pts A. Di Savino. **Feather:** E. Donovan w pts D. Valentino. **Light:** G. McBride l pts F. Allegretta, D. Toman w pts C. Tommasone. **L. Welter:** T. O'Neill w rsc 1 L. Marasco. **Welter:** W. McLaughlin l pts S. Grieco. **L. Heavy:** J. Quinn l pts F. M. Gallo.

England (3) v USA (4)   Park Lane Hilton Hotel, Mayfair, London – 11 November
(English names first): **L. Fly:** D. Langley l pts A. Juarez. **Bantam:** M. Moran w pts R. Jefferson. **Light:** M. Grant l pts V. Escobedo. **Welter:**

Stephen Burke (right), the 2003 ABA lightweight champion, was a winner for England against the USA during the season

Les Clark

D. Barker l pts T. Bradley. **L. Middle:** S. Webb l pts A. Dirrell. **Middle:** S. Birch w pts M. Martinez. **Heavy:** D. Dolan w pts D. Vargas.

England (4) v USA (4)   St George's Hall, Liverpool – 13 November
(English names first): **L. Fly:** C. Lyon l pts A. Juarez. **Feather:** D. Mulholland w pts J. Edwards. **Light:** S. Burke w pts V. Escobedo. **L. Welter:** S. Matthews l pts L. Peterson. **L. Middle:** P. Smith l pts A. Dirrell. **Middle:** N. Perkins w pts M. Martinez. **L. Heavy:** C. Fry w pts J. Garretson. **Heavy:** M. Stafford l pts D. Vargas.

Young Ireland (2) v Young England (6)   National Stadium, Dublin – 13 December
(Irish names first): **L. Fly:** C. Ahern w pts J. Fowl. **Fly:** Paul Hyland l pts D. Swanson. **Bantam:** D. Murphy l pts N. McDonald. **Light:** D. Toman l pts N. Brough, T. Ward l ret 2 S. Jennings. **L. Welter:** J. McDonagh w pts T. Coward. **Middle:** B. Fitzpatrick l pts T. Jeffries, B. Barrett l pts J. Smyth.

England (1) v France (7)   Bordeaux, France – 20 December
(English names first): **Fly:** D. Barriball l pts J. Thomas; S. Langley w pts K. El-Khallouki. **Feather:** D. Mulholland l pts A. Hallab. **Light:** S. Burke l pts G. Salingue. **Welter:** S. Briggs l rtd 1 X. Noel. **Middle:** R. Samms l pts D. Bertu; D. Frost l pts J. T. Borges. **Heavy:** P. Souter l rtd 1 O. Bellouati.

Ireland (8) v Germany/Belgium combined (3)   National Stadium, Dublin – 10 January
(Irish names first): **L. Fly:** E. Wansboro l pts D. Sovokin (G). **Fly:** P. Duncliffe w pts D. Britsch (G). **Bantam:** D. Murphy w pts B. Fuchs (G). **Feather:** R. Traynor l rsc 2 A. Miller (G), P. Roche w pts D. Siegmann (G). **L. Welter:** T. O'Neill w pts V. Wolf (G). **Welter:** F. Turner w pts H. Firens (B). **L. Middle:** T. Blaney w pts B. Balcaen (B), A. Lee w pts J. Shanab (G). **Middle:** D. Sutherland w pts M. Henrotin (B), J. Monaghan l pts 2 G. Weiss (G). Note: Wansboro, Duncliffe, Traynor and Monaghan represented Ireland at boys level, and Murphy, Roche, O'Neill and Lee at junior level.

Ireland (3) v Germany/Belgium combined (8)   Europa Hotel, Drogheda, Co. Louth – 12 January
(Irish names first): **L. Fly:** S. Kilroy l rsc 3 D. Sovokin (G). **Fly:** D. Joyce w rsc 3 D. Britsch (G). **Bantam:** C. Fleming l pts B. Fuchs (G), C. Maguire l rsc 2 D. Siegmann (G). **Feather:** J. Joyce l ret 2 A. Miller (G). **L. Welter:** J. Quinn l pts V. Wolf (G). **Welter:** C. Curtis w pts H. Firens (B). **L. Middle:** H. Joyce w rsc 1 B. Balcaen (B), P. Moffat l pts J. Shanab (G). **Middle:** P. Murray l pts M. Henrotin (B). **L. Heavy:** J. Sweeney l pts B. Schmidt (G). Note: Kilroy, D. Joyce and J. Joyce represented Ireland at boys level, and Fleming, Maguire, Quinn, Moffat and Sweeney at junior level.

Young England (5) v Young Germany (2)   Royal Lancaster Hotel, Bayswater, London – 3 February
(English names first): **Bantam:** F. Gavin w pts M. Abramowski. **Feather:** E. Corcoran w pts D. Doehl. **Light:** S. Joplong l pts I. Sperling; S. Kennedy w pts S. Alms. **L. Welter:** B. Rose w pts E. Hoeschele. **Welter:** N. Gittus l pts T. May. **L. Heavy:** D. Price w pts R. Krause.

Young England (5) v Young Ireland (4)   The Sports Centre, Basingstoke – 7 March
(English names first): **L. Fly:** P. Dixon l pts R. Hickey. **Bantam:** P. Truscott w pts A. Hopkins; B. Ward w rtd 2 D. Joyce. **Feather:** E. Corcoran l pts E. Touhy. **Light:** S. Jennings w rsc 3 T. Ward, N.

Brough l pts G. Dunne. **L. Welter:** D. Herdman w pts P. Brolly. **Welter:** R. Ashworth l pts C. McAuley. **Middle:** S. O'Donnell w rtd 2 H. Moyna.

Ireland (1) v USA (6)   Cleveland, Ohio – 12 March
(Irish names first): **Feather:** Patrick Hyland l pts M. Bey. **Light:** E. Hyland l rsc 3 V. Kimbrough. **L. Welter:** M. Kelly w pts L. Reynolds. **Welter:** H. Coyle l ret 3 A. Berto, T. Blaney l ret 1 J. McPherson. **Middle:** E. O'Kane l pts J. Gonzales. **L. Heavy:** C. Carmichael l pts A. Ward.

Ireland (3) v USA (6)   Harvey, Illinois – 15 March
(Irish names first): **Fly:** T. Lee l pts R. Benitez. **Bantam:** B. Gillen w pts T. Daniels. **Light:** E. Hyland l pts K. Dargan. **L. Welter:** M. Kelly l pts R. Allen, R. Sheahan w pts C. Aquino. **Welter:** T. Blaney l rsc 3 A. Berto, H. Coyle l pts Anthony Dirrell. **Middle:** E. O'Kane l pts Andre Dirrell. **L. Heavy:** C. Carmichael w pts C. Stevens.

Ireland (6) v Wales (4)   National Stadium, Dublin – 28 March
(Irish names first): **Fly:** T. Lee w pts M. Edmonds. **Bantam:** S. McAnee l pts N. Probert. **Feather:** Patrick Hyland l pts D. Davies. **Light:** G. Dunne w pts J. Evans. **L. Welter:** M. Kelly w pts R. James. **Welter:** T. Blaney w pts J. Way, H. Coyle w pts A. Thomas. **Middle:** E. O'Kane l pts F. Borg. **L. Heavy:** C. Carmichael w pts D. Tang. **Heavy:** T. Donnelly l pts M. Davies.

Ireland (8) v Denmark (0)   Give, Denmark – 9 May
(Irish names first): **Fly:** E. Donovan w pts N. Yiman. **Feather:** S. Ormond w pts E. Masha, D. Murphy w pts T. Keller. **Light:** A. Murray w pts L. Kristjansen. **L. Welter:** P. McCloskey w pts C. Christensen, R. Sheahan w rsc 2 J. Hansen. **Middle:** A. Lee w pts B. Brantley. **Heavy:** A. Reynolds w pts J. Andersen. Note: Murphy and Sheahan represented Ireland at junior level.

Ireland (6) v Denmark (0)   Hadsund, Denmark – 11 May
(Irish names first): **Feather:** D. Murphy w pts M. Tabaje. **Light:** A. Murray w pts F. Abdulla. **L. Welter:** P. McCloskey w pts C. Christensen, R. Sheahan w pts T. Povlsen. **Middle:** A. Lee w pts D. Sorensen. **Heavy:** A. Reynolds w pts B. Ali-Sen. Note: Murphy and Sheahan represented Ireland at junior level.

Ireland (3) v Scotland (6)   Craigenillan Mansion House, Dalmellington – 7 June
(Scottish names first): **Bantam:** C. Breen w pts T. Lee. **Feather:** F. Rafiq l pts P. Hyland. **Light:** M. Prince w pts G. Dunne. **L. Welter:** J. Cusick w pts A. Carlyle; J. Carlin w pts T. O'Neill. **Welter:** C. McEwan w rsc 1 B. Kerr. **Middle:** C. Black l pts E. O'Kane. **L. Heavy:** D. Stewart w pts S. O'Hagen. **S. Heavy:** A. Martin l rtd 2 J. Upton.

Young France (5) v Young England (3)   Rochefort-sur-Mer, France – 7 June
(English names first): **Bantam:** S. Smith l pts J. Outin. **Feather:** M. Graydon l pts A. Vastine. **Light:** J. O'Donnell w pts M. Souli. **L. Welter:** D. Herdman w pts S. Rachidi; J. Selkirk l pts K. Abdessalem. **Welter:** T. Coward l pts A. Bouneb; B. Rose l pts A. Belhachemi. **L. Heavy:** D. Price w pts G. Tornu.

Scotland (2) v Italy (3)   Salerno, Italy – 14 June
(Scottish names first): **Fly:** D. Ellis l pts M. Damita. **Bantam:** D. Appleby l pts L. Mellis. **Light:** R. Brolly w pts G. Russo. **L. Welter:** W. Billans w rsc 3 V. Spampinato. **L. Heavy:** M. Warner l pts C. Ambrosoli.

British Junior Championship Finals, 2002-2003

National Association of Clubs for Young People (NACYP)

Peter Paine Sports Centre, Boston – 7 December

Class A: 42 kg: D.Hyland (Salisbury, Liverpool) w pts J.Cole (Dagenham). 45 kg: V.Mitchell (West Ham) w pts L.Campbell (St Paul's, Hull). 48 kg: J.Allen (Mr Smart's) w pts C.Duffield (West Ham). 51 kg: A.Sexton (Finchley) w pts M.Connors (Larne). 54 kg: G.Barker (Repton) w pts A.Anwar (Bateson's). 57 kg: D.McAdam (Glasgow Noble Art) w pts B.Skeete (Earlsfield). 60 kg: J.Creamer (Portsmouth) w pts J.Hillerby (Sandy Row, NI). 63.5 kg: T.Jacobs (Harwich) w pts D.Simms (St Helens). 67 kg: T.McDonagh (South Norwood & Victory) w pts T.Carthy (Sunderland). 71 kg: T.Saunders (Cheshunt) w pts D.Wigby (Trinity).

The Civic Centre, Middleton – 13 December

Class B: 45 kg: L.Fort (Jim Driscoll's) w pts P.Dixon (Birtley Police). 48 kg: M.Nasir (St Joseph's East) w pts A.Silk (Northside). 51 kg: J.McElvaney (South Bank) w pts T.Mills (St Mary's, Chatham). 54 kg: B.Ward (Dagenham) w pts P.Truscott (South Bank). 57 kg: A.Khan (Chorley) w rsc 1 M.Poston (Harwich). 60 kg: R.Brawley (Springside) w pts B.Gladman (Finchley). 63.5 kg: W.Bilan (Denbeath) w pts R.Saunders (Victoria Park). 67 kg: J.Spence (Forgewood) w pts R.Pickard (Repton). 71 kg: T.Crewe (Plains Farm) w pts T.Hill (Golden Ring, Hants). 75 kg: J.Weston (Eastleigh) w pts S.Kehoe (Gemini).

Royal Lancaster Hotel, Lancaster Gate – 9 December

Class C: 48 kg: I.McCabe (Lesmahagow) wo A.Bibby (Finchley). 51 kg: D.Ellis (Barn) w rsc 1 D.Pryce (Cwmcarn). 54 kg: S.Smith (Rotunda) w rsc 1 J.Anthony (Dagenham). 57 kg: G.Sykes (Cleckheaton) w rsc 3 J.Richardson (Golden Ring, Hants). 60 kg: J.Selkirk (Rotunda) w rsc 4 M.C.McDonagh (Hollington). 63.5 kg: B.Jones (Ferndale) w pts J.Spence (Kingsthorpe). 67 kg: L.Morris (Phoenix, Notts) w pts W.Hibbert (Newham). 71 kg: M.O.McDonagh (Hollington) w pts S.Rao (Dennistoun). 75 kg: Z.Marks (Greenock) w pts D.Ojuederie (St Pancras). 81 kg: D.Price (West Way) w rsc 2 R.Newland (Repton).

Schools

The Metrodome, Barnsley – 29 & 30 March

Class 1: 32 kg: J.Quigley (Tower Hill) w pts S.Sutherland (Stevenage). 34 kg: D.Arnold (Wednesbury) w pts M.McCarthy (Dagenham). 36 kg: C.Jacobs (Harwich) w pts M.Channing (Kettering). 39 kg: M.Tallon (Salisbury, Liverpool) w pts S.Cairns (St Mary's, Chatham). 42 kg: S.Varley (Karmand Centre) w pts S.Wortham (St Mary's, Chatham). 45 kg: R.Rose (Medway Golden Gloves) w pts J.Rodgers (Parsons Cross). 48 kg: W.Claydon (Onslow Lions) w pts N.Hill (Trinity). 51 kg: S.Osmond (The Grange) w pts S.Cardle (Kirkham). 54 kg: N.Sladen (Red Triangle) w pts N.Garvey (Earlsfield). 57 kg: M.Nugent (West Ham) w pts V.Graham (Grainger Park). 60 kg: D.Londers (Hornchurch & Elm Park) wo.

Class 2: 36 kg: M.Hadfield (Headland) w pts J.Brooker (West Hill). 39 kg: K.D'eath (Northside) w pts J.Blower-Saeed (Eltham). 42 kg: M.McGuire (Kettering) w pts J.O'Donnell (Dale Youth). 45 kg: P.Jones (Bracebridge) w pts C.Poxton (Lowestoft). 48 kg: B.J.Saunders (Cheshunt) w pts G.Watson (Hartlepool Catholic). 51 kg: M.McDonagh (South Norwood & Victory) w pts T.Costello (Small Heath). 54 kg: M.Pealing (Transport) w pts R.Garvey Earlsfield). 57 kg: J.Carroll (Eltham) w pts J.Springer (Karmand Centre). 60 kg: A.Agogo (Triple A) w pts L.Holland (Altrincham). 63 kg: L.Ripley (Eltham) w pts R.Smith (Darlington). 66 kg: S.Griffiths (Donnington) w pts B.Eastwood (Sporting Ring). 69 kg: P.O'Connor (Northwood) w pts M.Burnett (St Paul's, Hull).

Class 3: 39 kg: M.Ward (Birtley Police) w pts L.Langley (Repton). 42 kg: A.Dainty (Canvey) w dis 2 G.Cullen (Stockbridge). 45 kg: J.Perry (Stevenage) w pts U.Malik (Merlin). 48 kg: L.Turner (Repton) w pts D.Watson (Shildon). 51 kg: R.Simmonds (St Mary's, Chatham) w pts A.Mytton (Droitwich). 54 kg: L.Powell (Meanwood) w pts B.Saunders (Repton). 57 kg: C.Riley (Wellington) w pts B.Skeete (Earlsfield). 60 kg: T.Dickenson (Birtley Police) w pts J.Gillingwater (Canvey). 63 kg: T.Jacobs (Harwich) w pts A.Fletcher (Shildon). 66 kg: M.Shinkwin (Bushey) w pts C.Chiverton (Mansfield). 69 kg: C.McClennan (Chesterfield) w pts J.Bowers (Peacock). 72 kg: G.Groves (Dale Youth) w rsc 1 S.Brookes (Wombwell).

Class 4: 42 kg: J.Murray (Northside) w pts J.Cole (Dagenham). 45 kg: V.Mitchell (West Ham) w rsc 2 R.Smart (Corby). 48 kg: P.Edwards (Salisbury, Liverpool) w pts J.Upton (Dagenham). 51 kg: D.Fieldhouse (Northside) w pts R.O'Grady (Golden Ring, Hants). 54 kg: G.Barker (Repton) w pts J.McElvaney (South Bank). 57 kg: M.Murnane (Chalvedon) w pts R.Lee (Pleck). 60 kg: A.Khan (Bury) w rtd 1 S.McDonagh (Stowe). 63.5 kg: A.Bowker (Northside) w rsc 2 J.Begley (Canvey). 67 kg: T.McDonagh (South Norwood & Victory) w pts D.Booth (Pool of Life). 71 kg: T.Saunders (Cheshunt) w pts P.Ward (Birtley Police). 75 kg: M.Stanton (Kirkby) w rsc 3 J.Mitchell (Pinewood Starr). 81 kg: J.Loveday (Birmingham Irish) wo M.Henderson (Hornchurch & Elm Park).

ABA Youth

The Spa Royal Hall, Bridlington – 24 May

Class 5 (born 1986): 48 kg: J.McDonnell (Wombwell) w pts A.Silk (Northside). 51 kg: R.Walsh (Kingfisher) w dis 3 J.Mason (Hinckley). 54 kg: R.Ward (Repton) w pts L.Walsh (Kingfisher). 57 kg: B.Saunders South Durham) w rsc 2 M.Poston (Harwich). 60 kg: A.Khan (Bury) w pts N.Smedley (Steel City). 64 kg: E.Brook (Unity) w pts C.Bunn (Northside). 69 kg: T.Crewe (Plains Farm) w pts R.Pickard (Repton). 75 kg: T.Hill (Golden Ring) w pts S.O'Donnell (Dale Youth). 81 kg: J.Dickenson (Birtley Police) w pts J.Degale (Dale Youth).

Class 6 (born 1985): 48 kg: P.Jamieson (Transport) w pts M.Gallett (Pleck). 51 kg: J.Chidgey (Herne Bay) w pts S.Leonard (Darlington). 54 kg: S.Smith (Rotunda) wo A.Brennan (Triumph). 57 kg: M.Graydon (Broad Plain) w pts D.Smith (Dagenham). 60 kg: J.O'Donnell (Dale Youth) w pts L.Shinkwin (Bushey). 64 kg: J.Selkirk (Rotunda) w pts J.Fewkes (Sheffield BC). 69 kg: B.Rose (Blackpool & Fylde) w pts C.Johnson (Terry Allen Unique). 75 kg: M.Boylan (Radford) w pts B.Tansley (Ferry Street). 81 kg: D.Price (West Way) w rsc 4 D.Sadler (Barking). 91 kg: T.Dallas (St Mary's, Chatham) w rsc 2 W.Baister (Marley Potts). 91+ kg: B.Smith (Ferry Street) w pts J.Lewis (Middlesbrough).

ABA Champions, 1881-2003

L. Flyweight
1971 M. Abrams
1972 M. Abrams
1973 M. Abrams
1974 C. Magri
1975 M. Lawless
1976 P. Fletcher
1977 P. Fletcher
1978 J. Dawson
1979 J. Dawson
1980 T. Barker
1981 J. Lyon
1982 J. Lyon
1983 J. Lyon
1984 J. Lyon
1985 M. Epton
1986 M. Epton
1987 M. Epton
1988 M. Cantwell
1989 M. Cantwell
1990 N. Tooley
1991 P. Culshaw
1992 D. Fifield
1993 M. Hughes
1994 G. Jones
1995 D. Fox
1996 R. Mercer
1997 I. Napa
1998 J. Evans
1999 G. Jones
2000 J. Mulherne
2001 C. Lyon
2002 D. Langley
2003 C. Lyon

Flyweight
1920 H. Groves
1921 W. Cuthbertson
1922 E. Warwick
1923 L. Tarrant
1924 E. Warwick
1925 E. Warwick
1926 J. Hill
1927 J. Roland
1928 C. Taylor
1929 T. Pardoe
1930 T. Pardoe
1931 T. Pardoe
1932 T. Pardoe
1933 T. Pardoe
1934 P. Palmer
1935 G. Fayaud
1936 G. Fayaud
1937 P. O'Donaghue
1938 A. Russell
1939 D. McKay
1944 J. Clinton
1945 J. Bryce
1946 R. Gallacher
1947 J. Clinton
1948 H. Carpenter
1949 H. Riley
1950 A. Jones
1951 G. John
1952 D. Dower
1953 R. Currie
1954 R. Currie
1955 D. Lloyd

1956 T. Spinks
1957 R. Davies
1958 J. Brown
1959 M. Gushlow
1960 D. Lee
1961 W. McGowan
1962 M. Pye
1963 M. Laud
1964 J. McCluskey
1965 J. McCluskey
1966 P. Maguire
1967 S. Curtis
1968 J. McGonigle
1969 D. Needham
1970 D. Needham
1971 P. Wakefield
1972 M. O'Sullivan
1973 R. Hilton
1974 M. O'Sullivan
1975 C. Magri
1976 C. Magri
1977 C. Magri
1978 G. Nickels
1979 R. Gilbody
1980 K. Wallace
1981 K. Wallace
1982 J. Kelly
1983 S. Nolan
1984 P. Clinton
1985 P. Clinton
1986 J. Lyon
1987 J. Lyon
1988 J. Lyon
1989 J. Lyon
1990 J. Armour
1991 P. Ingle
1992 K. Knox
1993 P. Ingle
1994 D. Costello
1995 D. Costello
1996 D. Costello
1997 M. Hunter
1998 J. Hegney
1999 D. Robinson
2000 D. Robinson
2001 M. Marsh
2002 D. Barriball
2003 D. Broadhurst

Bantamweight
1884 A. Woodward
1885 A. Woodward
1886 T. Isley
1887 T. Isley
1888 H. Oakman
1889 H. Brown
1890 J. Rowe
1891 E. Moore
1892 F. Godbold
1893 E. Watson
1894 P. Jones
1895 P. Jones
1896 P. Jones
1897 C. Lamb
1898 F. Herring
1899 A. Avent
1900 J. Freeman
1901 W. Morgan

1902 A. Miner
1903 H. Perry
1904 H. Perry
1905 W. Webb
1906 T. Ringer
1907 E. Adams
1908 H. Thomas
1909 J. Condon
1910 W. Webb
1911 W. Allen
1912 W. Allen
1913 A. Wye
1914 W. Allen
1919 W. Allen
1920 G. McKenzie
1921 L. Tarrant
1922 W. Boulding
1923 A. Smith
1924 L. Tarrant
1925 A. Goom
1926 F. Webster
1927 E. Warwick
1928 J. Garland
1929 F. Bennett
1930 H. Mizler
1931 F. Bennett
1932 J. Treadaway
1933 G. Johnston
1934 A. Barnes
1935 L. Case
1936 A. Barnes
1937 A. Barnes
1938 J. Pottinger
1939 R. Watson
1944 R. Bissell
1945 P. Brander
1946 C. Squire
1947 D. O'Sullivan
1948 T. Proffitt
1949 T. Miller
1950 K. Lawrence
1951 T. Nicholls
1952 T. Nicholls
1953 J. Smillie
1954 J. Smillie
1955 G. Dormer
1956 O. Reilly
1957 J. Morrissey
1958 H. Winstone
1959 D. Weller
1960 F. Taylor
1961 P. Benneyworth
1962 P. Benneyworth
1963 B. Packer
1964 B. Packer
1965 R. Mallon
1966 J. Clark
1967 M. Carter
1968 M. Carter
1969 M. Piner
1970 A. Oxley
1971 G. Turpin
1972 G. Turpin
1973 P. Cowdell
1974 S. Ogilvie
1975 S. Ogilvie
1976 J. Bambrick
1977 J. Turner

1978 J. Turner
1979 R. Ashton
1980 R. Gilbody
1981 P. Jones
1982 R. Gilbody
1983 J. Hyland
1984 J. Hyland
1985 S. Murphy
1986 S. Murphy
1987 J. Sillitoe
1988 K. Howlett
1989 K. Howlett
1990 P. Lloyd
1991 D. Hardie
1992 P. Mullings
1993 R. Evatt
1994 S. Oliver
1995 N. Wilders
1996 L. Eedle
1997 S. Oates
1998 L. Pattison
1999 M. Hunter
2000 S. Foster
2001 S. Foster
2002 D. Matthews
2003 N. McDonald

Featherweight
1881 T. Hill
1882 T. Hill
1883 T. Hill
1884 E. Hutchings
1885 J. Pennell
1886 T. McNeil
1887 J. Pennell
1888 J. Taylor
1889 G. Belsey
1890 G. Belsey
1891 F. Curtis
1892 F. Curtis
1893 T. Davidson
1894 R. Gunn
1895 R. Gunn
1896 R. Gunn
1897 N. Smith
1898 P. Lunn
1899 J. Scholes
1900 R. Lee
1901 C. Clarke
1902 C. Clarke
1903 J. Godfrey
1904 C. Morris
1905 H. Holmes
1906 A. Miner
1907 C. Morris
1908 T. Ringer
1909 A. Lambert
1910 C. Houghton
1911 H. Bowers
1912 G. Baker
1913 G. Baker
1914 G. Baker
1919 G. Baker
1920 J. Fleming
1921 G. Baker
1922 E. Swash
1923 E. Swash
1924 A. Beavis

1925 A. Beavis
1926 R. Minshull
1927 F. Webster
1928 F. Meachem
1929 F. Meachem
1930 J. Duffield
1931 B. Caplan
1932 H. Mizler
1933 J. Walters
1934 J. Treadaway
1935 E. Ryan
1936 J. Treadaway
1937 A. Harper
1938 C. Gallie
1939 C. Gallie
1944 D. Sullivan
1945 J. Carter
1946 P. Brander
1947 S. Evans
1948 P. Brander
1949 H. Gilliland
1950 P. Brander
1951 J. Travers
1952 P. Lewis
1953 P. Lewis
1954 D. Charnley
1955 T. Nicholls
1956 T. Nicholls
1957 M. Collins
1958 M. Collins
1959 G. Judge
1960 P. Lundgren
1961 P. Cheevers
1962 B. Wilson
1963 A. Riley
1964 R. Smith
1965 K. Buchanan
1966 H. Baxter
1967 K. Cooper
1968 J. Cheshire
1969 A. Richardson
1970 D. Polak
1971 T. Wright
1972 K. Laing
1973 J. Lynch
1974 G. Gilbody
1975 R. Beaumont
1976 P. Cowdell
1977 P. Cowdell
1978 M. O'Brien
1979 P. Hanlon
1980 M. Hanif
1981 P. Hanlon
1982 H. Henry
1983 P. Bradley
1984 K. Taylor
1985 F. Havard
1986 P. Hodkinson
1987 P. English
1988 D. Anderson
1989 P. Richardson
1990 B. Carr
1991 J. Irwin
1992 A. Temple
1993 J. Cook
1994 D. Pithie
1995 D. Burrows
1996 T. Mulholland

1997 S. Bell	1903 H. Fergus	1938 T. McGrath	1973 T. Dunn	**L. Welterweight**
1998 D. Williams	1904 M. Wells	1939 H. Groves	1974 J. Lynch	1951 W. Connor
1999 S. Miller	1905 M. Wells	1944 W. Thompson	1975 P. Cowdell	1952 P. Waterman
2000 H. Castle	1906 M. Wells	1945 J. Williamson	1976 S. Mittee	1953 D. Hughes
2001 S. Bell	1907 M. Wells	1946 E. Thomas	1977 G. Gilbody	1954 G. Martin
2002 D. Mulholland	1908 H. Holmes	1947 C. Morrissey	1978 T. Marsh	1955 F. McQuillan
2003 K. Mitchell	1909 F. Grace	1948 R. Cooper	1979 G. Gilbody	1956 D. Stone
	1910 T. Tees	1949 A. Smith	1980 G. Gilbody	1957 D. Stone
Lightweight	1911 A. Spenceley	1950 R. Latham	1981 G. Gilbody	1958 R. Kane
1881 F. Hobday	1912 R. Marriott	1951 R. Hinson	1982 J. McDonnell	1959 R. Kane
1882 A. Bettinson	1913 R. Grace	1952 F. Reardon	1983 K. Willis	1960 R. Day
1883 A. Diamond	1914 R. Marriott	1953 D. Hinson	1984 A. Dickson	1961 B. Brazier
1884 A. Diamond	1919 F. Grace	1954 G. Whelan	1985 E. McAuley	1962 B. Brazier
1885 A. Diamond	1920 F. Grace	1955 S. Coffey	1986 J. Jacobs	1963 R. McTaggart
1886 G. Roberts	1921 G. Shorter	1956 R. McTaggart	1987 M. Ayers	1964 R. Taylor
1887 J. Hair	1922 G. Renouf	1957 J. Kidd	1988 C. Kane	1965 R. McTaggart
1888 A. Newton	1923 G. Shorter	1958 R. McTaggart	1989 M. Ramsey	1966 W. Hiatt
1889 W. Neale	1924 W. White	1959 P. Warwick	1990 P. Gallagher	1967 B. Hudspeth
1890 A. Newton	1925 E. Viney	1960 R. McTaggart	1991 P. Ramsey	1968 E. Cole
1891 E. Dettmer	1926 T. Slater	1961 P. Warwick	1992 D. Amory	1969 J. Stracey
1892 E. Dettmer	1927 W. Hunt	1962 B. Whelan	1993 B. Welsh	1970 D. Davies
1893 W. Campbell	1928 F. Webster	1963 B. O'Sullivan	1994 A. Green	1971 M. Kingwell
1894 W. Campbell	1929 W. Hunt	1964 J. Dunne	1995 R. Rutherford	1972 T. Waller
1895 A. Randall	1930 J. Waples	1965 A. White	1996 K. Wing	1973 N. Cole
1896 A. Vanderhout	1931 D. McCleave	1966 J. Head	1997 M. Hawthorne	1974 P. Kelly
1897 A. Vanderhout	1932 F. Meachem	1967 T. Waller	1998 A. McLean	1975 J. Zeraschi
1898 H. Marks	1933 H. Mizler	1968 J. Watt	1999 S. Burke	1976 C. McKenzie
1899 H. Brewer	1934 J. Rolland	1969 H. Hayes	2000 A. McLean	1977 J. Douglas
1900 G. Humphries	1935 F. Frost	1970 N. Cole	2001 S. Burke	1978 D. Williams
1901 A. Warner	1936 F. Simpson	1971 J. Singleton	2002 A. Morris	1979 E. Copeland
1902 A. Warner	1937 A. Danahar	1972 N. Cole	2003 S. Burke	1980 A. Willis

Dale Youth's Lee Beavis (right) outpointed Burmantoft's Chris Sebine to win the ABA light-welter title   Les Clark

1981 A. Willis
1982 A. Adams
1983 D. Dent
1984 D. Griffiths
1985 I. Mustafa
1986 J. Alsop
1987 A. Holligan
1988 A. Hall
1989 A. Hall
1990 J. Pender
1991 J. Matthews
1992 D. McCarrick
1993 P. Richardson
1994 A. Temple
1995 A. Vaughan
1996 C. Wall
1997 R. Hatton
1998 N. Wright
1999 D. Happe
2000 N. Wright
2001 G. Smith
2002 L. Daws
2003 L. Beavis

Welterweight
1920 F. Whitbread
1921 A. Ireland
1922 E. White
1923 P. Green
1924 P. O'Hanrahan
1925 P. O'Hanrahan
1926 B. Marshall
1927 H. Dunn
1928 H. Bone
1929 T. Wigmore
1930 F. Brooman
1931 J. Barry
1932 D. McCleave
1933 P. Peters
1934 D. McCleave
1935 D. Lynch
1936 W. Pack
1937 D. Lynch
1938 C. Webster
1939 R. Thomas
1944 H. Hall
1945 R. Turpin
1946 J. Ryan
1947 J. Ryan
1948 M. Shacklady
1949 A. Buxton
1950 T. Ratcliffe
1951 J. Maloney
1952 J. Maloney
1953 L. Morgan
1954 N. Gargano
1955 N. Gargano
1956 N. Gargano
1957 R. Warnes
1958 B. Nancurvis
1959 J. McGrail
1960 C. Humphries
1961 A. Lewis
1962 J. Pritchett
1963 J. Pritchett
1964 M. Varley
1965 P. Henderson
1966 P. Cragg
1967 D. Cranswick
1968 A. Tottoh
1969 T. Henderson

1970 T. Waller
1971 D. Davies
1972 T. Francis
1973 T. Waller
1974 T. Waller
1975 W. Bennett
1976 C. Jones
1977 C. Jones
1978 E. Byrne
1979 J. Frost
1980 T. Marsh
1981 T. Marsh
1982 C. Pyatt
1983 R. McKenley
1984 M. Hughes
1985 E. McDonald
1986 D. Dyer
1987 M. Elliot
1988 M. McCreath
1989 M. Elliot
1990 A. Carew
1991 J. Calzaghe
1992 M. Santini
1993 C. Bessey
1994 K. Short
1995 M. Hall
1996 J. Khaliq
1997 F. Barrett
1998 D. Walker
1999 A. Cesay
2000 F. Doherty
2001 M. Macklin
2002 M. Lomax
2003 D. Happe

L. Middleweight
1951 A. Lay
1952 B. Foster
1953 B. Wells
1954 B. Wells
1955 B. Foster
1956 J. McCormack
1957 J. Cunningham
1958 S. Pearson
1959 S. Pearson
1960 W. Fisher
1961 J. Gamble
1962 J. Lloyd
1963 A. Wyper
1964 W. Robinson
1965 P. Dwyer
1966 T. Imrie
1967 A. Edwards
1968 E. Blake
1969 T. Imrie
1970 D. Simmonds
1971 A. Edwards
1972 L. Paul
1973 R. Maxwell
1974 R. Maxwell
1975 A. Harrison
1976 W. Lauder
1977 C. Malarkey
1978 E. Henderson
1979 D. Brewster
1980 J. Price
1981 E. Christie
1982 D. Milligan
1983 R. Douglas
1984 R. Douglas
1985 R. Douglas

1986 T. Velinor
1987 N. Brown
1988 W. Ellis
1989 N. Brown
1990 T. Taylor
1991 T. Taylor
1992 J. Calzaghe
1993 D. Starie
1994 W. Alexander
1995 C. Bessey
1996 S. Dann
1997 C. Bessey
1998 C. Bessey
1999 C. Bessey
2000 C. Bessey
2001 M. Thirwall
2002 P. Smith

Middleweight
1881 T. Bellhouse
1882 A. H. Curnick
1883 A. J. Curnick
1884 W. Brown
1885 M. Salmon
1886 W. King
1887 R. Hair
1888 R. Hair
1889 G. Sykes
1890 J. Hoare
1891 J. Steers
1892 J. Steers
1893 J. Steers
1894 W. Sykes
1895 G. Townsend
1896 W. Ross
1897 W. Dees
1898 G. Townsend
1899 R. Warnes
1900 E. Mann
1901 R. Warnes
1902 E. Mann
1903 R. Warnes
1904 E. Mann
1905 J. Douglas
1906 A. Murdock
1907 R. Warnes
1908 W. Child
1909 W. Child
1910 R. Warnes
1911 W. Child
1912 E. Chandler
1913 W. Bradley
1914 H. Brown
1919 H. Mallin
1920 H. Mallin
1921 H. Mallin
1922 H. Mallin
1923 H. Mallin
1924 J. Elliot
1925 J. Elliot
1926 F. P. Crawley
1927 F. P. Crawley
1928 F. Mallin
1929 F. Mallin
1930 F. Mallin
1931 F. Mallin
1932 F. Mallin
1933 A. Shawyer
1934 J. Magill
1935 J. Magill
1936 A. Harrington

1937 M. Dennis
1938 H. Tiller
1939 H. Davies
1944 J. Hockley
1945 R. Parker
1946 R. Turpin
1947 R. Agland
1948 J. Wright
1949 S. Lewis
1950 P. Longo
1951 E. Ludlam
1952 T. Gooding
1953 R. Barton
1954 K. Phillips
1955 F. Hope
1956 R. Redrup
1957 P. Burke
1958 P. Hill
1959 F. Elderfield
1960 R. Addison
1961 J. Caiger
1962 A. Matthews
1963 A. Matthews
1964 W. Stack
1965 W. Robinson
1966 C. Finnegan
1967 A. Ball
1968 P. McCann
1969 D. Wallington
1970 J. Conteh
1971 A. Minter
1972 F. Lucas
1973 F. Lucas
1974 D. Odwell
1975 D. Odwell
1976 E. Burke
1977 R. Davies
1978 H. Graham
1979 N. Wilshire
1980 M. Kaylor
1981 B. Schumacher
1982 J. Price
1983 T. Forbes
1984 B. Schumacher
1985 D. Cronin
1986 N. Benn
1987 R. Douglas
1988 M. Edwards
1989 S. Johnson
1990 S. Wilson
1991 M. Edwards
1992 L. Woolcock
1993 J. Calzaghe
1994 D. Starie
1995 J. Matthews
1996 J. Pearce
1997 I. Cooper
1998 J. Pearce
1999 C. Froch
2000 S. Swales
2001 C. Froch
2002 N. Perkins
2003 N. Perkins

L. Heavyweight
1920 H. Franks
1921 L. Collett
1922 H. Mitchell
1923 H. Mitchell
1924 H. Mitchell
1925 H. Mitchell

1926 D. McCorkindale
1927 A. Jackson
1928 A. Jackson
1929 J. Goyder
1930 J. Murphy
1931 J. Petersen
1932 J. Goyder
1933 G. Brennan
1934 G. Brennan
1935 R. Hearns
1936 J. Magill
1937 J. Wilby
1938 A. S. Brown
1939 B. Woodcock
1944 E. Shackleton
1945 A. Watson
1946 J. Taylor
1947 A. Watson
1948 D. Scott
1949 *Declared no contest*
1950 P. Messervy
1951 G. Walker
1952 H. Cooper
1953 H. Cooper
1954 A. Madigan
1955 D. Rent
1956 D. Mooney
1957 T. Green
1958 J. Leeming
1959 J. Ould
1960 J. Ould
1961 J. Bodell
1962 J. Hendrickson
1963 P. Murphy
1964 J. Fisher
1965 E. Whistler
1966 R. Tighe
1967 M. Smith
1968 R. Brittle
1969 J. Frankham
1970 J. Rafferty
1971 J. Conteh
1972 W. Knight
1973 W. Knight
1974 W. Knight
1975 M. Heath
1976 G. Evans
1977 C. Lawson
1978 V. Smith
1979 A. Straughn
1980 A. Straughn
1981 A. Straughn
1982 G. Crawford
1983 A. Wilson
1984 A. Wilson
1985 J. Beckles
1986 J. Moran
1987 J. Beckles
1988 H. Lawson
1989 N. Piper
1990 J. McCluskey
1991 A. Todd
1992 K. Oliver
1993 K. Oliver
1994 K. Oliver
1995 K. Oliver
1996 C. Fry
1997 P. Rogers
1998 C. Fry
1999 J. Ainscough
2000 P. Haymer

2001 C. Fry
2002 T. Marsden
2003 J. Boyd

Cruiserweight
1998 T. Oakey
1999 M. Krence
2000 J. Dolan
2001 J. Dolan
2002 J. Dolan

Heavyweight
1881 R. Frost-Smith
1882 H. Dearsley
1883 H. Dearsley
1884 H. Dearsley
1885 W. West
1886 A. Diamond
1887 E. White
1888 W. King
1889 A. Bowman
1890 J. Steers
1891 V. Barker
1892 J. Steers
1893 J. Steers
1894 H. King
1895 W. E. Johnstone
1896 W. E. Johnstone
1897 G. Townsend
1898 G. Townsend

1899 F. Parks
1900 W. Dees
1901 F. Parks
1902 F. Parks
1903 F. Dickson
1904 A. Horner
1905 F. Parks
1906 F. Parks
1907 H. Brewer
1908 S. Evans
1909 C. Brown
1910 F. Storbeck
1911 W. Hazell
1912 R. Smith
1913 R. Smith
1914 E. Chandler
1919 H. Brown
1920 R. Rawson
1921 R. Rawson
1922 T. Evans
1923 E. Eagan
1924 A. Clifton
1925 D. Lister
1926 T. Petersen
1927 C. Capper
1928 J. L. Driscoll
1929 P. Floyd
1930 V. Stuart
1931 M. Flanagan
1932 V. Stuart

1933 C. O'Grady
1934 P. Floyd
1935 P. Floyd
1936 V. Stuart
1937 V. Stuart
1938 G. Preston
1939 A. Porter
1944 M. Hart
1945 D. Scott
1946 P. Floyd
1947 G. Scriven
1948 J. Gardner
1949 A. Worrall
1950 P. Toch
1951 A. Halsey
1952 E. Hearn
1953 J. Erskine
1954 B. Harper
1955 D. Rowe
1956 D. Rent
1957 D. Thomas
1958 D. Thomas
1959 D. Thomas
1960 L. Hobbs
1961 W. Walker
1962 R. Dryden
1963 R. Sanders
1964 C. Woodhouse
1965 W. Wells
1966 A. Brogan

1967 P. Boddington
1968 W. Wells
1969 A. Burton
1970 J. Gilmour
1971 L. Stevens
1972 T. Wood
1973 G. McEwan
1974 N. Meade
1975 G. McEwan
1976 J. Rafferty
1977 G. Adair
1978 J. Awome
1979 A. Palmer
1980 F. Bruno
1981 A. Elliott
1982 H. Hylton
1983 H. Notice
1984 D. Young
1985 H. Hylton
1986 E. Cardouza
1987 J. Moran
1988 H. Akinwande
1989 H. Akinwande
1990 K. Inglis
1991 P. Lawson
1992 S. Welch
1993 P. Lawson
1994 S. Burford
1995 M. Ellis
1996 T. Oakey

1997 B. Stevens
1998 N. Hosking
1999 S. St John
2000 D. Dolan
2001 D. Dolan
2002 D. Dolan
2003 M. O'Connell

S. Heavyweight
1982 A. Elliott
1983 K. Ferdinand
1984 R. Wells
1985 G. Williamson
1986 J. Oyebola
1987 J. Oyebola
1988 K. McCormack
1989 P. Passley
1990 K. McCormack
1991 K. McCormack
1992 M. Hopper
1993 M. McKenzie
1994 D. Watts
1995 R. Allen
1996 D. Watts
1997 A. Harrison
1998 A. Harrison
1999 W. Bessey
2000 J. McDermott
2001 M. Grainger
2002 M. Grainger
2003 D. Price

The Royal Navy's Mick O'Connell (left) created a surprise when outscoring Michael Stafford (Kirkby) to land the 2003 ABA heavyweight title

Les Clark

International Amateur Champions, 1904-2003

Shows all Olympic, World, European & Commonwealth champions since 1904. British silver and bronze medal winners are shown throughout, where applicable.

Country Code

ALG = Algeria; ARG = Argentina; ARM = Armenia; AUS = Australia; AUT = Austria; AZE = Azerbaijan; BE = Belarus; BEL = Belgium; BUL = Bulgaria; CAN = Canada; CEY = Ceylon (now Sri Lanka); CI = Channel Islands; CUB = Cuba; DEN = Denmark; DOM = Dominican Republic; ENG = England; ESP = Spain; EST = Estonia; FIJ = Fiji Islands; FIN = Finland; FRA = France; GBR = United Kingdom; GDR = German Democratic Republic; GEO = Georgia; GER = Germany (but West Germany only from 1968-1990); GHA = Ghana; GUY = Guyana; HOL = Netherlands; HUN = Hungary; IND = India; IRL = Ireland; ITA = Italy; JAM = Jamaica; JPN = Japan; KAZ = Kazakhstan; KEN = Kenya; LIT = Lithuania; MAS = Malaysia; MEX = Mexico; MRI = Mauritius; NKO = North Korea; NIG = Nigeria; NIR = Northern Ireland; NOR = Norway; NZL = New Zealand; PAK = Pakistan; POL = Poland; PUR = Puerto Rico; ROM = Romania; RUS = Russia; SAF = South Africa; SCO = Scotland; SKO = South Korea; SR = Southern Rhodesia; STV = St Vincent; SWE = Sweden; TCH = Czechoslovakia; THA = Thailand; TUR = Turkey; UGA = Uganda; UKR = Ukraine; URS = USSR; USA = United States of America; UZB = Uzbekistan; VEN = Venezuela; WAL = Wales; YUG = Yugoslavia; ZAM = Zambia.

Olympic Champions, 1904-2000

St Louis, USA - 1904
Fly: G. Finnegan (USA). **Bantam:** O. Kirk (USA). **Feather:** O. Kirk (USA). **Light:** H. Spangler (USA). **Welter:** A. Young (USA). **Middle:** C. May (USA). **Heavy:** S. Berger (USA).

London, England - 1908
Bantam: H. Thomas (GBR). **Feather:** R. Gunn (GBR). **Light:** F. Grace (GBR). **Middle:** J.W.H.T. Douglas (GBR). **Heavy:** A. Oldman (GBR). **Silver medals:** J. Condon (GBR), C. Morris (GBR), F. Spiller (GBR), S. Evans (GBR).
Bronze medals: W. Webb (GBR), H. Rodding (GBR), T. Ringer (GBR), H. Johnson (GBR), R. Warnes (GBR), W. Philo (GBR), F. Parks (GBR).

Antwerp, Belgium - 1920
Fly: F. Genaro (USA). **Bantam:** C. Walker (SAF). **Feather:** R. Fritsch (FRA). **Light:** S. Mossberg (USA). **Welter:** T. Schneider (CAN). **Middle:** H. Mallin (GBR). **L. Heavy:** E. Eagan (USA). **Heavy:** R. Rawson (GBR).
Silver medal: A. Ireland (GBR).
Bronze medals: W. Cuthbertson (GBR), G. McKenzie (GBR), H. Franks (GBR).

Paris, France - 1924
Fly: F. la Barba (USA). **Bantam:** W. Smith (SAF). **Feather:** J. Fields (USA). **Light:** H. Nielson (DEN). **Welter:** J. Delarge (BEL). **Middle:** H. Mallin (GBR). **L. Heavy:** H. Mitchell (GBR). **Heavy:** O. von Porat (NOR).
Silver medals: J. McKenzie (GBR), J. Elliot (GBR).

Amsterdam, Holland - 1928
Fly: A. Kocsis (HUN). **Bantam:** V. Tamagnini (ITA). **Feather:** B. van Klaveren (HOL). **Light:** C. Orlando (ITA). **Welter:** E. Morgan (NZL). **Middle:** P. Toscani (ITA). **L. Heavy:** V. Avendano (ARG). **Heavy:** A. Rodriguez Jurado (ARG).

Los Angeles, USA - 1932
Fly: I. Enekes (HUN). **Bantam:** H. Gwynne (CAN). **Feather:** C. Robledo (ARG). **Light:** L. Stevens (SAF). **Welter:** E. Flynn (USA). **Middle:** C. Barth (USA). **L. Heavy:** D. Carstens (SAF). **Heavy:** A. Lovell (ARG).

Berlin, West Germany - 1936
Fly: W. Kaiser (GER). **Bantam:** U. Sergo (ITA). **Feather:** O. Casanova (ARG). **Light:** I. Harangi (HUN). **Welter:** S. Suvio (FIN). **Middle:** J. Despeaux (FRA). **L. Heavy:** R. Michelot (FRA). **Heavy:** H. Runge (GER).

London, England - 1948
Fly: P. Perez (ARG). **Bantam:** T. Csik (HUN). **Feather:** E. Formenti (ITA). **Light:** G. Dreyer (SAF). **Welter:** J. Torma (TCH). **Middle:** L. Papp (HUN). **L. Heavy:** G. Hunter (SAF). **Heavy:** R. Iglesas (ARG).
Silver medals: J. Wright (GBR), D. Scott (GBR).

Helsinki, Finland - 1952
Fly: N. Brooks (USA). **Bantam:** P. Hamalainen (FIN). **Feather:** J. Zachara (TCH). **Light:** A. Bolognesi (ITA). **L. Welter:** C. Adkins (USA). **Welter:** Z. Chychla (POL). **L. Middle:** L. Papp (HUN). **Middle:** F. Patterson (USA). **L. Heavy:** N. Lee (USA). **Heavy:** E. Sanders (USA).
Silver medal: J. McNally (IRL).

Melbourne, Australia - 1956
Fly: T. Spinks (GBR). **Bantam:** W. Behrendt (GER). **Feather:** V. Safronov (URS). **Light:** R. McTaggart (GBR). **L. Welter:** V. Jengibarian (URS). **Welter:** N. Linca (ROM). **L. Middle:** L. Papp (HUN). **Middle:** G. Schatkov (URS). **L. Heavy:** J. Boyd (USA). **Heavy:** P. Rademacher (USA).
Silver medals: T. Nicholls (GBR), F. Tiedt (IRL).
Bronze medals: J. Caldwell (IRL), F. Gilroy (IRL), A. Bryne (IRL), N. Gargano (GBR), J. McCormack (GBR).

Rome, Italy - 1960
Fly: G. Torok (HUN). **Bantam:** O. Grigoryev (URS). **Feather:** F. Musso (ITA). **Light:** K. Pazdzior (POL). **L. Welter:** B. Nemecek (TCH). **Welter:** N. Benvenuti (ITA). **L. Middle:** W. McClure (USA). **Middle:** E. Crook (USA). **L. Heavy:** C. Clay (USA). **Heavy:** F. de Piccoli (ITA).
Bronze medals: R. McTaggart (GBR), J. Lloyd (GBR), W. Fisher (GBR).

Tokyo, Japan - 1964
Fly: F. Atzori (ITA). **Bantam:** T. Sakurai (JPN). **Feather:** S. Stepashkin (URS). **Light:** J. Grudzien (POL). **L. Welter:** J. Kulej (POL). **Welter:** M. Kasprzyk (POL). **L. Middle:** B. Lagutin (URS). **Middle:** V. Popenchenko (URS). **L. Heavy:** C. Pinto (ITA). **Heavy:** J. Frazier (USA).
Bronze medal: J. McCourt (IRL).

Mexico City, Mexico - 1968
L. Fly: F. Rodriguez (VEN). **Fly:** R. Delgado (MEX). **Bantam:** V. Sokolov (URS). **Feather:** A. Roldan (MEX). **Light:** R. Harris (USA). **L. Welter:** J. Kulej (POL). **Welter:** M. Wolke (GDR). **L. Middle:** B. Lagutin (URS). **Middle:** C. Finnegan (GBR). **L. Heavy:** D. Poznyak (URS). **Heavy:** G. Foreman (USA).

Munich, West Germany - 1972
L. Fly: G. Gedo (HUN). **Fly:** G. Kostadinov (BUL). **Bantam:** O. Martinez (CUB). **Feather:** B. Kusnetsov (URS). **Light:** J. Szczepanski (POL). **L. Welter:** R. Seales (USA). **Welter:** E. Correa (CUB). **L. Middle:** D. Kottysch (GER). **Middle:** V. Lemeschev (URS). **L. Heavy:** M. Parlov (YUG). **Heavy:** T. Stevenson (CUB).
Bronze medals: R. Evans (GBR), G. Turpin (GBR), A. Minter (GBR).

Montreal, Canada - 1976
L. Fly: J. Hernandez (CUB). **Fly:** L. Randolph (USA). **Bantam:** Y-J. Gu (NKO). **Feather:** A. Herrera (CUB). **Light:** H. Davis (USA). **L. Welter:** R. Leonard (USA). **Welter:** J. Bachfield (GDR). **L. Middle:** J. Rybicki (POL). **Middle:** M. Spinks (USA). **L. Heavy:** L. Spinks (USA). **Heavy:** T. Stevenson (CUB).
Bronze medal: P. Cowdell (GBR).

Moscow, USSR - 1980
L. Fly: S. Sabirov (URS). **Fly:** P. Lessov (BUL). **Bantam:** J. Hernandez (CUB). **Feather:** R. Fink (GDR). **Light:** A. Herrera (CUB). **L. Welter:** P. Oliva (ITA). **Welter:** A. Aldama (CUB). **L. Middle:** A. Martinez (CUB). **Middle:** J. Gomez (CUB). **L. Heavy:** S. Kacar (YUG). **Heavy:** T. Stevenson (CUB).
Bronze medals: H. Russell (IRL), A. Willis (GBR).

Los Angeles, USA - 1984
L. Fly: P. Gonzalez (USA). **Fly:** S. McCrory (USA). **Bantam:** M. Stecca (ITA). **Feather:** M. Taylor (USA). **Light:** P. Whitaker (USA). **L. Welter:** J. Page (USA). **Welter:** M. Breland (USA). **L. Middle:** F. Tate (USA). **Middle:** J-S. Shin (SKO). **L. Heavy:** A. Josipovic (YUG). **Heavy:** H. Tillman (USA). **S. Heavy:** T. Biggs (USA).
Bronze medal: B. Wells (GBR).

Seoul, South Korea - 1988

L. Fly: I. Mustafov (BUL). **Fly:** H-S. Kim (SKO). **Bantam:** K. McKinney (USA). **Feather:** G. Parisi (ITA). **Light:** A. Zuelow (GDR). **L. Welter:** V. Yanovsky (URS). **Welter:** R. Wangila (KEN). **L. Middle:** S-H. Park (SKO). **Middle:** H. Maske (GDR). **L. Heavy:** A. Maynard (USA). **Heavy:** R. Mercer (USA). **S. Heavy:** L. Lewis (CAN).
Bronze medal: R. Woodhall (GBR).

Barcelona, Spain - 1992

L. Fly: R. Marcelo (CUB). **Fly:** C-C. Su (NKO). **Bantam:** J. Casamayor (CUB). **Feather:** A. Tews (GER). **Light:** O. de la Hoya (USA). **L. Welter:** H. Vinent (CUB). **Welter:** M. Carruth (IRL). **L. Middle:** J. Lemus (CUB). **Middle:** A. Hernandez (CUB). **L. Heavy:** T. May (GER). **Heavy:** F. Savon (CUB). **S. Heavy:** R. Balado (CUB).
Silver medal: W. McCullough (IRL).
Bronze medal: R. Reid (GBR).

Atlanta, USA - 1996

L. Fly: D. Petrov (BUL). **Fly:** M. Romero (CUB). **Bantam:** I. Kovaks (HUN). **Feather:** S. Kamsing (THA). **Light:** H. Soltani (ALG). **L. Welter:** H. Vinent (CUB). **Welter:** O. Saitov (RUS). **L. Middle:** D. Reid (USA). **Middle:** A. Hernandez (CUB). **L. Heavy:** V. Jirov (KAZ). **Heavy:** F. Savon (CUB). **S. Heavy:** Vladimir Klitschko (UKR).

Sydney, Australia - 2000

L. Fly: B. Aslom (FRA). **Fly:** W. Ponlid (THA). **Bantam:** G. Rigondeaux Ortiz (CUB). **Feather:** B. Sattarkhanov (KAZ). **Light:** M. Kindelan (CUB). **L. Welter:** M. Abdullaev (UZB). **Welter:** O. Saitov (RUS). **L. Middle:** Y. Ibraimov (KAZ). **Middle:** J. Gutierrez Espinosa (CUB). **L. Heavy:** A. Lebziak (RUS). **Heavy:** F. Savon (CUB). **S. Heavy:** A. Harrison (ENG).

World Champions, 1974-2003

Havana, Cuba - 1974

L. Fly: J. Hernandez (CUB). **Fly:** D. Rodriguez (CUB). **Bantam:** W. Gomez (PUR). **Feather:** H. Davis (USA). **Light:** V. Solomin (URS). **L. Welter:** A. Kalule (UGA). **Welter:** E. Correa (CUB). **L. Middle:** R. Garbey (CUB). **Middle:** R. Riskiev (URS). **L. Heavy:** M. Parlov (YUG). **Heavy:** T. Stevenson (CUB).

Belgrade, Yugoslavia - 1978

L. Fly: S. Muchoki (KEN). **Fly:** H. Strednicki (POL). **Bantam:** A. Horta (CUB). **Feather:** A. Herrera (CUB). **Light:** D. Andeh (NIG). **L. Welter:** V. Lvov (URS). **Welter:** V. Rachkov (URS). **L. Middle:** V. Savchenko (URS). **Middle:** J. Gomez (CUB). **L. Heavy:** S. Soria (CUB). **Heavy:** T. Stevenson (CUB).

Munich, West Germany - 1982

L. Fly: I. Mustafov (BUL). **Fly:** Y. Alexandrov (URS). **Bantam:** F. Favors (USA). **Feather:** A. Horta (CUB). **Light:** A. Herrera (CUB). **L. Welter:** C. Garcia (CUB). **Welter:** M. Breland (USA). **L. Middle:** A. Koshkin (URS). **Middle:** B. Comas (CUB). **L. Heavy:** P. Romero (CUB). **Heavy:** A. Jagubkin (URS). **S. Heavy:** T. Biggs (USA).
Bronze medal: T. Corr (IRL).

Reno, USA - 1986

L. Fly: J. Odelin (CUB). **Fly:** P. Reyes (CUB). **Bantam:** S-I. Moon (SKO). **Feather:** K. Banks (USA). **Light:** A. Horta (CUB). **L. Welter:** V. Shishov (URS). **Welter:** K. Gould (USA). **L. Middle:** A. Espinosa (CUB). **Middle:** D. Allen (USA). **L. Heavy:** P. Romero (CUB). **Heavy:** F. Savon (CUB). **S. Heavy:** T. Stevenson (CUB).

Moscow, USSR - 1989

L. Fly: E. Griffin (USA). **Fly:** Y. Arbachakov (URS). **Bantam:** E. Carrion (CUB). **Feather:** A. Khamatov (URS). **Light:** J. Gonzalez (CUB). **L. Welter:** I. Ruzinkov (URS). **Welter:** F. Vastag (Rom). **L. Middle:** I. Akopokhian (URS). **Middle:** A. Kurniavka (URS). **L. Heavy:** H. Maske (GDR). **Heavy:** F. Savon (CUB). **S. Heavy:** R. Balado (CUB).
Bronze medal: M. Carruth (IRL).

Sydney, Australia - 1991

L. Fly: E. Griffin (USA). **Fly:** I. Kovacs (HUN). **Bantam:** S. Todorov (BUL). **Feather:** K. Kirkorov (BUL). **Light:** M. Rudolph (GER). **L. Welter:** K. Tsziu (URS). **Welter:** J. Hernandez (CUB). **L. Middle:** J. Lemus (CUB). **Middle:** T. Russo (ITA). **L. Heavy:** T. May (GER). **Heavy:** F. Savon (CUB). **S. Heavy:** R. Balado (CUB).

Tampere, Finland - 1993

L. Fly: N. Munchian (ARM). **Fly:** W. Font (CUB). **Bantam:** A. Christov (BUL). **Feather:** S. Todorov (BUL). **Light:** D. Austin (CUB). **L. Welter:**

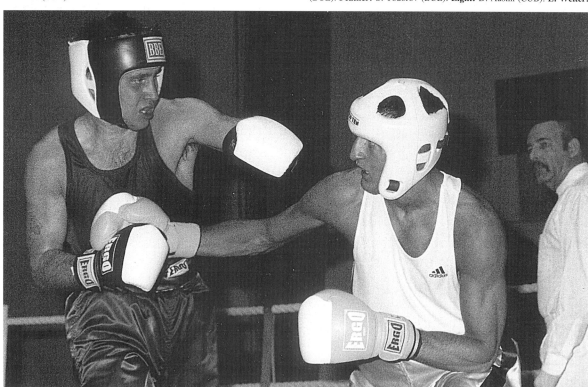

Carl Froch (right), currently a promising pro, was a bronze medallist at the 2001 World Championships   Les Clark

H. Vinent (CUB). **Welter:** J. Hernandez (CUB). **L. Middle:** F. Vastag (ROM). **Middle:** A. Hernandez (CUB). **L. Heavy:** R. Garbey (CUB). **Heavy:** F. Savon (CUB). **S. Heavy:** R. Balado (CUB).
Bronze medal: D. Kelly (IRL).

Berlin, Germany - 1995
L. Fly: D. Petrov (BUL). **Fly:** Z. Lunka (GER). **Bantam:** R. Malachbekov (RUS). **Feather:** S. Todorov (BUL). **Light:** L. Doroftel (ROM). **L. Welter:** H. Vinent (CUB). **Welter:** J. Hernandez (CUB). **L. Middle:** F. Vastag (ROM). **Middle:** A. Hernandez (CUB). **L. Heavy:** A. Tarver (USA). **Heavy:** F. Savon (CUB). **S. Heavy:** A. Lezin (RUS).

Budapest, Hungary - 1997
L. Fly: M. Romero (CUB). **Fly:** M. Mantilla (CUB). **Bantam:** R Malakhbekov (RUS). **Feather:** I. Kovacs (HUN). **Light:** A. Maletin (RUS). **L. Welter:** D. Simion (ROM). **Welter:** O. Saitov (RUS). **L. Middle:** A. Duvergel (CUB). **Middle:** Z. Erdei (HUN). **L. Heavy:** A. Lebsiak (RUS). **Heavy:** F. Savon (CUB). **S. Heavy:** G. Kandelaki (GEO).
Bronze medal: S. Kirk (IRL).

Houston, USA - 1999
L. Fly: B. Viloria (USA). **Fly:** B. Jumadilov (KAZ). **Bantam:** R. Crinu (ROM). **Feather:** R. Juarez (USA). **Light:** M. Kindelan (CUB). **L. Welter:** M. Abdullaev (UZB). **Welter:** J. Hernandez (CUB). **L. Middle:** M. Simion (ROM). **Middle:** U. Haydarov (UZB). **L. Heavy:** M. Simms (USA). **Heavy:** M. Bennett (USA). **S. Heavy:** S. Samilsan (TUR).
Bronze medal: K. Evans (WAL).

Belfast, Northern Ireland - 2001
L. Fly: Y. Bartelemi Varela (CUB). **Fly:** J. Thomas (FRA). **Bantam:** G. Rigondeaux Ortiz (CUB). **Feather:** R. Palyani (TUR). **Light:** M. Kindelan (CUB). **L. Welter:** Q. Luna Martinez (CUB). **Welter:** L. Aragon (CUB). **L. Middle:** D. Austin Echemendia (CUB). **Middle:** A. Gogolev (RUS). **L. Heavy:** Y. Makarenko (RUS). **Heavy:** O. Solis (CUB). **S. Heavy:** R. Chagaev (UZB).
Silver medal: D. Haye (ENG).
Bronze medals: J. Moore (IRL), C. Froch (ENG).

Bangkok, Thailand - 2003
L. Fly: S. Karazov (RUS). **Fly:** S. Jongjohor (THA). **Bantam:** A. Mamedov (AZE). **Feather:** G. Jafarov (KAZ). **Light:** M. Kindelan (CUB). **L. Welter:** W. Blain (FRA). **Welter:** L. Aragon (CUB). **Middle:** G. Golovkin (KAZ). **L. Heavy:** Y. Makarenko (RUS). **Heavy:** O. Solis (CUB). **S. Heavy:** A. Povetkin (RUS).

World Junior Champions, 1979-2002

Yokohama, Japan - 1979
L. Fly: R. Shannon (USA). **Fly:** P. Lessov (BUL). **Bantam:** P-K. Choi (SKO). **Feather:** Y. Gladychev (URS). **Light:** R. Blake (USA). **L. Welter:** I. Akopokhian (URS). **Welter:** M. McCrory (USA). **L. Middle:** A. Mayes (USA). **Middle:** A. Milov (URS). **L. Heavy:** A. Lebedev (URS). **Heavy:** M. Frazier (USA).
Silver medals: N. Wilshire (ENG), D. Cross (ENG).
Bronze medal: I. Scott (SCO).

Santa Domingo, Dominican Republic - 1983
L. Fly: M. Herrera (DOM). **Fly:** J. Gonzalez (CUB). **Bantam:** J. Molina (PUR). **Feather:** A. Miesses (DOM). **Light:** A. Beltre (DOM). **L. Welter:** A. Espinoza (CUB). **Welter:** M. Watkins (USA). **L. Middle:** U. Castillo (CUB). **Middle:** R. Batista (CUB). **L. Heavy:** O. Pought (USA). **Heavy:** A. Williams (USA). **S. Heavy:** L. Lewis (CAN).

Bucharest, Romania - 1985
L. Fly: R-S. Hwang (SKO). **Fly:** T. Marcelica (ROM). **Bantam:** R. Diaz (CUB). **Feather:** D. Maeran (ROM). **Light:** J. Teiche (GDR). **L. Welter:** W. Saeger (GDR). **Welter:** A. Stoianov (BUL). **L. Middle:** M. Franek (TCH). **Middle:** O. Zahalotskih (URS). **L. Heavy:** B. Riddick (USA). **Heavy:** F. Savon (CUB). **S. Heavy:** A. Prianichnikov (URS).

Havana, Cuba - 1987
L. Fly: E. Paisan (CUB). **Fly:** C. Daniels (USA). **Bantam:** A. Moya (CUB). **Feather:** G. Iliyasov (URS). **Light:** J. Hernandez (CUB). **L. Welter:** L. Mihai (ROM). **Welter:** F. Vastag (ROM). **L. Middle:** A. Lobsyak (URS). **Middle:** W. Martinez (CUB). **L. Heavy:** D. Yeliseyev (URS). **Heavy:** R. Balado (CUB). **S. Heavy:** L. Martinez (CUB).
Silver medal: E. Loughran (IRL).
Bronze medal: D. Galvin (IRL).

San Juan, Puerto Rico - 1989
L. Fly: D. Petrov (BUL). **Fly:** N. Monchai (FRA). **Bantam:** J. Casamayor (CUB). **Feather:** C. Febres (PUR). **Light:** A. Acevedo (PUR). **L. Welter:**

E. Berger (GDR). **Welter:** A. Hernandez (CUB). **L. Middle:** L. Bedey (CUB). **Middle:** R. Garbey (CUB). **L. Heavy:** R. Alvarez (CUB). **Heavy:** K. Johnson (CAN). **S. Heavy:** A. Burdiantz (URS).
Silver medals: E. Magee (IRL), R. Reid (ENG), S. Wilson (SCO).

Lima, Peru - 1990
L. Fly: D. Alicea (PUR). **Fly:** K. Pielert (GDR). **Bantam:** K. Baravi (URS). **Feather:** A. Vaughan (ENG). **Light:** J. Mendez (CUB). **L. Welter:** H. Vinent (CUB). **Welter:** A. Hernandez (CUB). **L. Middle:** A. Kakauridze (URS). **Middle:** J. Gomez (CUB). **L. Heavy:** B. Torsten (GDR). **Heavy:** I. Andreev (URS). **S. Heavy:** J. Quesada (CUB).
Bronze medal: P. Ingle (ENG).

Montreal, Canada - 1992
L. Fly: W. Font (CUB). **Fly:** J. Oragon (CUB). **Bantam:** N. Machado (CUB). **Feather:** M. Stewart (CAN). **Light:** D. Austin (CUB). **L. Welter:** O. Saitov (RUS). **Welter:** L. Brors (GER). **L. Middle:** J. Acosta (CUB). **Middle:** I. Arsangaliev (RUS). **L. Heavy:** S. Samilsan (TUR). **Heavy:** G. Kandeliaki (GEO). **S. Heavy:** M. Porchnev (RUS).
Bronze medal: N. Sinclair (IRL).

Istanbul, Turkey - 1994
L. Fly: J. Turunen (FIN). **Fly:** A. Jimenez (CUB). **Bantam:** J. Despaigne (CUB). **Feather:** D. Simion (ROM). **Light:** L. Diogenes (CUB). **L. Welter:** V. Romero (CUB). **Welter:** E. Aslan (TUR). **L. Middle:** G. Ledsvanys (CUB). **Middle:** M. Genc (TUR). **L. Heavy:** P. Aurino (ITA). **Heavy:** M. Lopez (CUB). **S. Heavy:** P. Carrion (CUB).

Havana, Cuba - 1996
L. Fly: L. Hernandez (CUB). **Fly:** L. Cabrera (CUB). **Bantam:** P. Miradal (CUB). **Feather:** E. Rodriguez (CUB). **Light:** R. Vaillan (CUB). **L. Welter:** T. Mergadze (RUS). **Welter:** J. Brahmer (GER). **L. Middle:** L. Mezquia (CUB). **Middle:** V. Pletniov (RUS). **L. Heavy:** O. Simon (CUB). **Heavy:** A. Yatsenko (UKR). **S. Heavy:** S. Fabre (CUB).
Bronze medal: R. Hatton (ENG).

Buenos Aires, Argentina - 1998
L. Fly: S. Tanasie (ROM). **Fly:** S. Yeledov (KAZ). **Bantam:** S. Suleymanov (UKR). **Feather:** I. Perez (ARG). **Light:** A. Solopov (RUS). **L. Welter:** Y. Tomashov (UKR). **Welter:** K. Oustarkhanov (RUS). **L. Middle:** S. Kostenko (UKR). **Middle:** M. Kempe (GER). **L. Heavy:** H. Yohanson Martinez (CUB). **Heavy:** O. Solis Fonte (CUB). **S. Heavy:** B. Ohanyan (ARM).
Silver medal: H. Cunningham (IRL).
Bronze medal: D. Campbell (IRL).

Budapest, Hungary - 2000
L. Fly: Y. Leon Alarcon (CUB). **Fly:** O. Franco Vaszquez (CUB). **Bantam:** V. Tajbert (GER). **Feather:** G. Kate (HUN). **Light:** F. Adzsanalov (AZE). **L. Welter:** G. Galovkin (KAZ). **Welter:** S. Ustunel (TUR). **L. Middle:** D. Chernysh (RUS). **Middle:** F. Sullivan Barrera (CUB). **L. Heavy:** A. Shekmourov (RUS). **Heavy:** D. Medzhydov (UKR). **S. Heavy:** A. Dmitrienko (RUS).
Bronze medal: C. Barrett (IRL).

Santiago, Cuba - 2002
L. Fly: D. Acripitian (RUS). **Fly:** Y. Fabregas (CUB). **Bantam:** S. Bahodirijan (UZB). **Feather:** A. Tishinko (RUS). **Light:** S. Mendez (CUB). **L. Welter:** K. Iliyasov (KAZ). **Welter:** J. McPherson (USA). **L. Middle:** V. Diaz (CUB). **Middle:** A. Duarte (CUB). **L. Heavy:** R. Zavalnyuyk (UKR). **Heavy:** Y. P. Hernandez (CUB). **S. Heavy:** P. Portal (CUB).
Silver medal: A. Lee (IRL).
Bronze medal: N. Brough (ENG).

European Champions, 1924-2002

Paris, France - 1924
Fly: J. McKenzie (GBR). **Bantam:** J. Ces (FRA). **Feather:** R. de Vergnie (BEL). **Light:** N. Nielsen (DEN). **Welter:** J. Delarge (BEL). **Middle:** H. Mallin (GBR). **L. Heavy:** H. Mitchell (GBR). **Heavy:** O. von Porat (NOR).

Stockholm, Sweden - 1925
Fly: E. Pladner (FRA). **Bantam:** A. Rule (GBR). **Feather:** P. Andren (SWE). **Light:** S. Johanssen (SWE). **Welter:** H. Nielsen (DEN). **Middle:** F. Crawley (GBR). **L. Heavy:** T. Petersen (DEN). **Heavy:** B. Persson (SWE).
Silver medals: J. James (GBR), E. Viney (GBR), D. Lister (GBR).

Berlin, Germany - 1927
Fly: L. Boman (SWE). **Bantam:** K. Dalchow (GER). **Feather:** F. Dubbers (GER). **Light:** H. Domgoergen (GER). **Welter:** R. Caneva (ITA). **Middle:** J. Christensen (NOR). **L. Heavy:** H. Muller (GER). **Heavy:** N. Ramm (SWE).

Amsterdam, Holland - 1928
Fly: A. Kocsis (HUN). **Bantam:** V. Tamagnini (ITA). **Feather:** B. van Klaveren (HOL). **Light:** C. Orlandi (ITA). **Welter:** R. Galataud (FRA). **Middle:** P. Toscani (ITA). **L. Heavy:** E. Pistulla (GER). **Heavy:** N. Ramm (SWE).

Budapest, Hungary - 1930
Fly: I. Enekes (HUN). **Bantam:** J. Szeles (HUN). **Feather:** G. Szabo (HUN). **Light:** M. Bianchini (ITA). **Welter:** J. Besselmann (GER). **Middle:** C. Meroni (ITA). **L. Heavy:** T. Petersen (DEN). **Heavy:** J. Michaelson (DEN).

Los Angeles, USA - 1932
Fly: I. Enekes (HUN). **Bantam:** H. Ziglarski (GER). **Feather:** J. Schleinkofer (GER). **Light:** T. Ahlqvist (SWE). **Welter:** E. Campe (GER). **Middle:** R. Michelot (FRA). **L. Heavy:** G. Rossi (ITA). **Heavy:** L. Rovati (ITA).

Budapest, Hungary - 1934
Fly: P. Palmer (GBR). **Bantam:** I. Enekes (HUN). **Feather:** O. Kaestner (GER). **Light:** E. Facchini (ITA). **Welter:** D. McCleave (GBR). **Middle:** S. Szigetti (HUN). **L. Heavy:** P. Zehetmayer (AUT). **Heavy:** G. Baerlund (FIN).
Bronze medal: P. Floyd (GBR).

Milan, Italy - 1937
Fly: I. Enekes (HUN). **Bantam:** U. Sergo (ITA). **Feather:** A. Polus (POL). **Light:** H. Nuremberg (GER). **Welter:** M. Murach (GER). **Middle:** H. Chmielewski (POL). **L. Heavy:** S. Szigetti (HUN). **Heavy:** O. Tandberg (SWE).

Dublin, Eire - 1939
Fly: J. Ingle (IRL). **Bantam:** U. Sergo (ITA). **Feather:** P. Dowdall (IRL). **Light:** H. Nuremberg (GER). **Welter:** A. Kolczyski (POL). **Middle:** A. Raadik (EST). **L. Heavy:** L. Musina (ITA). **Heavy:** O. Tandberg (SWE).
Bronze medal: C. Evenden (IRL).

Dublin, Eire - 1947
Fly: L. Martinez (ESP). **Bantam:** L. Bogacs (HUN). **Feather:** K. Kreuger (SWE). **Light:** J. Vissers (BEL). **Welter:** J. Ryan (ENG). **Middle:** A. Escudie (FRA). **L. Heavy:** H. Quentemeyer (HOL). **Heavy:** G. O'Colmain (IRL).
Silver medals: J. Clinton (SCO), P. Maguire (IRL), W. Thom (ENG), G. Scriven (ENG).
Bronze medals: J. Dwyer (SCO), A. Sanderson (ENG), W. Frith (SCO), E. Cantwell (IRL), K. Wyatt (ENG).

Oslo, Norway - 1949
Fly: J. Kasperczak (POL). **Bantam:** G. Zuddas (ITA). **Feather:** J. Bataille (FRA). **Light:** M. McCullagh (IRL). **Welter:** J. Torma (TCH). **Middle:** L. Papp (HUN). **L. Heavy:** G. di Segni (ITA). **Heavy:** L. Bene (HUN).
Bronze medal: D. Connell (IRL).

Milan, Italy - 1951
Fly: A. Pozzali (ITA). **Bantam:** V. Dall'Osso (ITA). **Feather:** J. Ventaja (FRA). **Light:** B. Visintin (ITA). **L. Welter:** H. Schelling (GER). **Welter:** Z. Chychla (POL). **L. Middle:** L. Papp (HUN). **Middle:** S. Sjolin (SWE). **L. Heavy:** M. Limage (BEL). **Heavy:** G. di Segni (ITA).
Silver medal: J. Kelly (IRL).
Bronze medals: D. Connell (IRL), T. Milligan (IRL), A. Lay (ENG).

Warsaw, Poland - 1953
Fly: H. Kukier (POL). **Bantam:** Z. Stefaniuk (POL). **Feather:** J. Kruza (POL). **Light:** V. Jengibarian (URS). **L. Welter:** L. Drogosz (POL). **Welter:** Z. Chychla (POL). **L. Middle:** B. Wells (ENG). **Middle:** D. Wemhoner (GER). **L. Heavy:** U. Nietchke (GER). **Heavy:** A. Schotzikas (URS).
Silver medal: T. Milligan (IRL).
Bronze medals: J. McNally (IRL), R. Barton (ENG).

Berlin, West Germany - 1955
Fly: E. Basel (GER). **Bantam:** Z. Stefaniuk (POL). **Feather:** T. Nicholls (ENG). **Light:** H. Kurschat (GER). **L. Welter:** L. Drogosz (POL). **Welter:** N. Gargano (ENG). **L. Middle:** Z. Pietrzykowski (POL). **Middle:** G. Schatkov (URS). **L. Heavy:** E. Schoeppner (GER). **Heavy:** A. Schotzikas (URS).

Prague, Czechoslovakia - 1957
Fly: M. Homberg (GER). **Bantam:** O. Grigoryev (URS). **Feather:** D. Venilov (BUL). **Light:** K. Pazdzior (POL). **L. Welter:** V. Jengibarian (URS). **Welter:** M. Graus (GER). **L. Middle:** N. Benvenuti (ITA). **Middle:** Z. Pietrzykowski (POL). **L. Heavy:** G. Negrea (ROM). **Heavy:** A. Abramov (URS).
Bronze medals: R. Davies (WAL), J. Morrissey (SCO), J. Kidd (SCO), F. Teidt (IRL).

Lucerne, Switzerland - 1959
Fly: M. Homberg (GER). **Bantam:** H. Rascher (GER). **Feather:** J. Adamski (POL). **Light:** O. Maki (FIN). **L. Welter:** V. Jengibarian (URS). **Welter:** L. Drogosz (POL). **L. Middle:** N. Benvenuti (ITA). **Middle:** G. Schatkov (URS). **L. Heavy:** Z. Pietrzykowski (POL). **Heavy:** A. Abramov (URS).
Silver medal: D. Thomas (ENG).
Bronze medals: A. McClean (IRL), H. Perry (IRL), C. McCoy (IRL), H. Scott (ENG).

Belgrade, Yugoslavia - 1961
Fly: P. Vacca (ITA). **Bantam:** S. Sivko (URS). **Feather:** F. Taylor (ENG). **Light:** R. McTaggart (SCO). **L. Welter:** A. Tamulis (URS). **Welter:** R. Tamulis (URS). **L. Middle:** B. Lagutin (URS). **Middle:** T. Walasek (POL). **L. Heavy:** G. Saraudi (ITA). **Heavy:** A. Abramov (URS).
Bronze medals: P. Warwick (ENG), I. McKenzie (SCO), J. Bodell (ENG).

Moscow, USSR - 1963
Fly: V. Bystrov (URS). **Bantam:** O. Grigoryev (URS). **Feather:** S. Stepashkin (URS). **Light:** J. Kajdi (HUN). **L. Welter:** J. Kulej (POL). **Welter:** R. Tamulis (URS). **L. Middle:** B. Lagutin (URS). **Middle:** V. Popenchenko (URS). **L. Heavy:** Z. Pietrzykowski (POL). **Heavy:** J. Nemec (TCH).
Silver medal: A. Wyper (SCO).

Berlin, East Germany - 1965
Fly: H. Freisdadt (GER). **Bantam:** O. Grigoryev (URS). **Feather:** S. Stepashkin (URS). **Light:** V. Barranikov (URS). **L. Welter:** J. Kulej (POL). **Welter:** R. Tamulis (URS). **L. Middle:** V. Ageyev (URS). **Middle:** V. Popenchenko (URS). **L. Heavy:** D. Poznyak (URS). **Heavy:** A. Isosimov (URS).
Silver medal: B. Robinson (ENG).
Bronze medals: J. McCluskey (SCO), K. Buchanan (SCO), J. McCourt (IRL).

Rome, Italy - 1967
Fly: H. Skrzyczak (POL). **Bantam:** N. Giju (ROM). **Feather:** R. Petek (POL). **Light:** J. Grudzien (POL). **L. Welter:** V. Frolov (URS). **Welter:** B. Nemecek (TCH). **L. Middle:** V. Ageyev (URS). **Middle:** M. Casati (ITA). **L. Heavy:** D. Poznyak (URS). **Heavy:** M. Baruzzi (ITA).
Silver medal: P. Boddington (ENG).

Bucharest, Romania - 1969
L. Fly: G. Gedo (HUN). **Fly:** C. Ciuca (ROM). **Bantam:** A. Dumitrescu (ROM). **Feather:** L. Orban (HUN). **Light:** S. Cutov (ROM). **L. Welter:** V. Frolov (URS). **Welter:** G. Meier (GER). **L. Middle:** V. Tregubov (URS). **Middle:** V. Tarasenkov (URS). **L. Heavy:** D. Poznyak (URS). **Heavy:** I. Alexe (ROM).
Bronze medals: M. Dowling (IRL), M. Piner (ENG), A. Richardson (ENG), T. Imrie (SCO).

Madrid, Spain - 1971
L. Fly: G. Gedo (HUN). **Fly:** J. Rodriguez (ESP). **Bantam:** T. Badar (HUN). **Feather:** R. Tomczyk (POL). **Light:** J. Szczepanski (POL). **L. Welter:** U. Beyer (GDR). **Welter:** J. Kajdi (HUN). **L. Middle:** V. Tregubov (URS). **Middle:** J. Juotsiavitchus (URS). **L. Heavy:** M. Parlov (YUG). **Heavy:** V. Tchernishev (URS).
Bronze medals: N. McLaughlin (IRL), M. Dowling (IRL), B. McCarthy (IRL), M. Kingwell (ENG), L. Stevens (ENG).

Belgrade, Yugoslavia - 1973
L. Fly: V. Zasypko (URS). **Fly:** C. Gruescu (ROM). **Bantam:** A. Cosentino (FRA). **Feather:** S. Forster (GDR). **Light:** S. Cutov (ROM). **L. Welter:** M. Benes (YUG). **Welter:** S. Csjef (HUN). **L. Middle:** A. Klimanov (URS). **Middle:** V. Lemechev (URS). **L. Heavy:** M. Parlov (YUG). **Heavy:** V. Ulyanich (URS).
Bronze medal: J. Bambrick (SCO).

Katowice, Poland - 1975
L. Fly: A. Tkachenko (URS). **Fly:** V. Zasypko (URS). **Bantam:** V. Rybakov (URS). **Feather:** T. Badari (HUN). **Light:** S. Cutov (ROM). **L. Welter:** V. Limasov (URS). **Welter:** K. Marjaama (FIN). **L. Middle:** W. Rudnowski (POL). **Middle:** V. Lemechev (URS). **L. Heavy:** A. Klimanov (URS). **Heavy:** A. Biegalski (POL).
Bronze medals: C. Magri (ENG), P. Cowdell (ENG), G. McEwan (ENG).

Halle, East Germany - 1977
L. Fly: H. Srednicki (POL). **Fly:** B. Blazynski (POL). **Bantam:** S. Forster (GDR). **Feather:** R. Nowakowski (GDR). **Light:** A. Rusevski (YUG). **L. Welter:** B. Gajda (POL). **Welter:** V. Limasov (URS). **L. Middle:** V. Saychenko (URS). **Middle:** I. Shaposhnikov (URS). **L. Heavy:** D. Kvachadze (URS). **Heavy:** E. Gorstkov (URS).
Bronze medal: P. Sutcliffe (IRL).

Cologne, West Germany - 1979

L. Fly: S. Sabirov (URS). **Fly:** H. Strednicki (POL). **Bantam:** N. Khrapzov (URS). **Feather:** V. Rybakov (URS). **Light.** V. Demianenko (URS). **L. Welter:** S. Konakbaev (URS). **Welter:** E. Muller (GER). **L. Middle:** M. Perunovic (YUG). **Middle:** T. Uusiverta (FIN). **L. Heavy:** A. Nikolyan (URS). **Heavy:** E. Gorstkov (URS). **S. Heavy:** P. Hussing (GER). **Bronze medal:** P. Sutcliffe (IRL).

Tampere, Finland - 1981

L. Fly: I. Mustafov (BUL). **Fly:** P. Lessov (BUL). **Bantam:** V. Miroschnichenko (URS). **Feather:** R. Nowakowski (GDR). **Light:** V. Rybakov (URS). **L. Welter:** V. Shisov (URS). **Welter:** S. Konakvbaev (URS). **L. Middle:** A. Koshkin (URS). **Middle:** J. Torbek (URS). **L. Heavy:** A Krupin (URS). **Heavy:** A. Jagupkin (URS). **S. Heavy:** F. Damiani (ITA). **Bronze medal:** G. Hawkins (IRL).

Varna, Bulgaria - 1983

L. Fly: I. Mustafov (BUL). **Fly:** P. Lessov (BUL). **Bantam:** Y. Alexandrov (URS). **Feather:** S. Nurkazov (URS). **Light:** E. Chuprenski (BUL). **L. Welter:** V. Shishov (URS). **Welter:** P. Galkin (URS). **L. Middle:** V. Laptev (URS). **Middle:** V. Melnik (URS). **L. Heavy:** V. Kokhanovski (URS). **Heavy:** A. Jagubkin (URS). **S. Heavy:** F. Damiani (ITA). **Bronze medal:** K. Joyce (IRL).

Budapest, Hungary - 1985

L. Fly: R. Breitbarth (GDR). **Fly:** D. Berg (GDR). **Bantam:** L. Simic (YUG). **Feather:** S. Khachatrian (URS). **Light:** E. Chuprenski (BUL). **L. Welter:** S. Mehnert (GDR). **Welter:** I. Akopokhian (URS). **L. Middle:** M. Timm (GDR). **Middle:** H. Maske (GDR). **L. Heavy:** N. Shanavasov (URS). **Heavy:** A. Jagubkin (URS). **S. Heavy:** F. Somodi (HUN). **Bronze medals:** S. Casey (IRL), J. Beckles (ENG).

Turin, Italy - 1987

L. Fly: N. Munchyan (URS). **Fly:** A. Tews (GDR). **Bantam:** A. Hristov (BUL). **Feather:** M. Kazaryan (URS). **Light:** O. Nazarov (URS). **L. Welter:** B. Abadjier (BUL). **Welter:** V. Shishov (URS). **L. Middle:** E. Richter (GDR). **Middle:** H. Maske (GDR). **L. Heavy:** Y. Vaulin (URS). **Heavy:** A. Vanderlijde (HOL). **S. Heavy:** U. Kaden (GDR). **Bronze medal:** N. Brown (ENG).

Athens, Greece - 1989

L. Fly: I.Mustafov (BUL). **Fly:** Y. Arbachakov (URS). **Bantam:** S. Todorov (BUL). **Feather:** K. Kirkorov (BUL). **Light:** K. Tsziu (URS). **L. Welter:** I. Ruznikov (URS). **Welter:** S. Mehnert (GDR). **L. Middle:** I. Akopokhian (URS). **Middle:** H. Maske (GDR). **L. Heavy:** S. Lange (GDR). **Heavy:** A. Vanderlijde (HOL). **S. Heavy:** U. Kaden (GDR). **Bronze Medal:** D. Anderson (SCO).

Gothenburg, Sweden - 1991

L. Fly: I. Marinov (BUL). **Fly:** I. Kovacs (HUN). **Bantam:** S. Todorov (BUL). **Feather:** P. Griffin (IRL). **Light:** V. Nistor (ROM). **L. Welter:** K. Tsziu (URS). **Welter:** R. Welin (SWE). **L. Middle:** I. Akopokhian (URS). **Middle:** S. Otke (GER). **L. Heavy:** D. Michalczewski (GER). **Heavy:** A. Vanderlijde (HOL). **S. Heavy:** E. Beloussov (URS). **Bronze medals:** P. Weir (SCO), A. Vaughan (ENG).

Bursa, Turkey - 1993

L. Fly: D. Petrov (BUL). **Fly:** R. Husseinov (AZE). **Bantam:** R. Malakhbetov (RUS). **Feather:** S. Todorov (BUL). **Light:** J. Bielski (POL). **L. Welter:** N. Suleymanogiu (TUR). **Welter:** V. Karpaclauskas (LIT). **L. Middle:** F. Vastag (ROM). **Middle:** D. Eigenbrodt (GER). **L. Heavy:** I. Kshinin (RUS). **Heavy:** G. Kandelaki (GEO). **S. Heavy:** S. Rusinov (BUL). **Bronze medals:** P. Griffin (IRL), D. Williams (ENG), K. McCormack (WAL).

Vejle, Denmark - 1996

L. Fly: D. Petrov (BUL). **Fly:** A. Pakeev (RUS). **Bantam:** I. Kovacs (HUN). **Feather:** R. Paliani (RUS). **Light:** L. Doroftei (ROM). **L. Welter:** O. Urkal (GER). **Welter:** H. Al (DEN). **L. Middle:** F. Vastag (ROM). **Middle:** S. Ottke (GER). **L. Heavy:** P. Aurino (ITA). **Heavy:** L. Krasniqi (GER). **S. Heavy:** A. Lezin (RUS). **Bronze medals:** S. Harrison (SCO), D. Burke (ENG), D. Kelly (IRL).

Minsk, Belarus - 1998

L. Fly: S. Kazakov (RUS). **Fly:** V. Sidorenko (UKR). **Bantam:** S. Danilchenko (UKR). **Feather:** R. Paliani (TUR). **Light:** K. Huste (GER). **L. Welter:** D. Simion (ROM). **Welter:** O. Saitov (RUS). **L. Middle:** F. Esther (FRA). **Middle:** Z. Erdei (HUN). **L. Heavy:** A. Lebsiak (RUS). **Heavy:** G. Fragomeni (ITA). **S. Heavy:** A. Lezin (RUS). **Silver Medals:** B. Magee (IRL), C. Fry (ENG). **Bronze medal:** C. Bessey (ENG).

Tampere, Finland - 2000

L. Fly: Valeri Sidorenko (UKR). **Fly:** Vladimir Sidorenko (UKR). **Bantam:** A. Agagueloglu (TUR). **Feather:** R. Paliani (TUR). **Light:** A. Maletin (RUS). **L. Welter:** A. Leonev (RUS). **Welter:** B. Ueluesoy (TUR). **L. Middle:** A. Catic (GER). **Middle:** Z. Erdei (HUN). **L. Heavy:** A. Lebsiak (RUS). **Heavy:** J. Chanet (FRA). **S. Heavy:** A. Lezin (RUS).

Perm, Russia - 2002

L. Fly: S. Kazakov (RUS). **Fly:** G. Balakshin (RUS). **Bantam:** K. Khatsygov (BE). **Feather:** R. Malakhbekov (RUS). **Light:** A. Maletin (RUS). **L. Welter:** D. Panayotov (BUL). **Welter:** T. Gaidalov (RUS). **L. Middle:** A. Mishin (RUS). **Middle:** O. Mashkin (UKR). **L. Heavy:** M. Gala (RUS). **Heavy:** E. Makarenko (RUS). **S. Heavy:** A. Povetkin (RUS).

Note: Gold medals were awarded to the Europeans who went the furthest in the Olympic Games of 1924, 1928 & 1932.

European Junior Champions, 1970-2003

Miskolc, Hungary - 1970

L. Fly: Gluck (HUN). **Fly:** Z. Kismeneth (HUN). **Bantam:** A. Levitschev (URS). **Feather:** Andrianov (URS). **Light:** L. Juhasz (HUN). **L. Welter:** K. Nemec (HUN). **Welter:** Davidov (URS). **L. Middle:** A. Lemeschev (URS). **Middle:** N. Anfimov (URS). **L. Heavy:** O. Sasche (GDR). **Heavy:** J. Reder (HUN). **Bronze medals:** D. Needham (ENG), R. Barlow (ENG), L. Stevens (ENG).

Bucharest, Romania - 1972

L. Fly: A. Turei (ROM). **Fly:** Condurat (ROM). **Bantam:** V. Solomin (URS). **Feather:** V. Lvov (URS). **Light:** S. Cutov (ROM). **L. Welter:** K. Pierwieniecki (POL). **Welter:** Zorov (URS). **L. Middle:** Babescu (ROM). **Middle:** V. Lemeschev (URS). **L. Heavy:** Mirounik (URS). **Heavy:** Subutin (URS). **Bronze medals:** J. Gale (ENG), R. Maxwell (ENG), D. Odwell (ENG).

Kiev, Russia - 1974

L. Fly: A. Tkachenko (URS). **Fly:** V. Rybakov (URS). **Bantam:** C. Andreikovski (BUL). **Feather:** V. Sorokin (URS). **Light:** V. Limasov (URS). **L. Welter:** N. Sigov (URS). **Welter:** M. Bychkov (URS). **L. Middle:** V. Danshin (URS). **Middle:** D. Jende (URS). **L. Heavy:** D. Dafinoiu (ROM). **Heavy:** K. Mashev (BUL). **Silver medal:** C. Magri (URS). **Bronze medals:** G. Gilbody (ENG), K. Laing (ENG).

Izmir, Turkey - 1976

L. Fly: C. Seican (ROM). **Fly:** G. Khratsov (URS). **Bantam:** M. Navros (URS). **Feather:** V. Demoianeko (URS). **Light:** M. Puzovic (YUG). **L. Welter:** V. Zverev (URS). **Welter:** K. Ozoglouz (TUR). **L. Middle:** W. Lauder (SCO). **Middle:** H. Lenhart (GER). **L. Heavy:** I. Yantchauskas (URS). **Heavy:** B. Enjenyan (URS). **Silver medal:** J. Decker (ENG). **Bronze medals:** I. McLeod (SCO), N. Croombes (ENG).

Dublin, Ireland - 1978

L. Fly: R. Marx (GDR). **Fly:** D. Radu (ROM). **Bantam:** S. Khatchatrian (URS). **Feather:** H. Loukmanov (URS). **Light:** P. Oliva (ITA). **L. Welter:** V. Laptiev (URS). **Welter:** R. Filimanov (URS). **L. Middle:** A. Beliave (URS). **Middle:** G. Zinkovitch (URS). **L. Heavy:** I. Jolta (ROM). **Heavy:** P. Stoimenov (BUL). **Silver medal:** M. Holmes (IRL), P. Hanlon (ENG), M. Courtney (ENG). **Bronze medals:** T. Thompson (IRL), J. Turner (ENG), M. Bennett (WAL), J. McAllister (SCO), C. Devine (ENG).

Rimini, Italy - 1980

L. Fly: A. Mikoulin (URS). **Fly:** J. Varadi (HUN). **Bantam:** F. Rauschning (GDR). **Feather:** J. Gladychev (URS). **Light:** V. Shishov (URS). **L. Welter:** R. Lomski (BUL). **Welter:** T. Holonics (GDR). **L. Middle:** N. Wilshire (ENG). **Middle:** S. Laptiev (URS). **L. Heavy:** V. Dolgoun (URS). **Heavy:** V. Tioumentsev (URS). **S. Heavy:** S. Kormihtsine (URS). **Bronze medals:** N. Potter (ENG), B. McGuigan (IRL), M. Brereton (IRL), D. Cross (ENG).

Schwerin, East Germany - 1982

L. Fly: R. Kabirov (URS). **Fly:** I. Filchev (BUL). **Bantam:** M. Stecca (ITA). **Feather:** B. Blagoev (BUL). **Light:** E. Chakimov (URS). **L. Welter:** S. Mehnert (GDR). **Welter:** T. Schmitz (GDR). **L. Middle:** B. Shararov (URS). **Middle:** E. Christie (ENG). **L. Heavy:** Y. Waulin (URS). **Heavy:** A. Popov (URS). **S. Heavy:** V. Aldoshin (URS). **Silver medal:** D. Kenny (ENG). **Bronze medal:** O. Jones (ENG).

Tampere, Finland - 1984

L. Fly: R. Breitbart (GDR). **Fly:** D. Berg (GDR). **Bantam:** K. Khdrian

(URS). **Feather:** O. Nazarov (URS). **Light:** C. Furnikov (BUL). **L. Welter:** W. Schmidt (GDR). **Welter:** K. Doinov (BUL). **L. Middle:** O. Volkov (URS). **Middle:** R. Ryll (GDR). **L. Heavy:** G. Peskov (URS). **Heavy:** R. Draskovic (YUG). **S. Heavy:** L. Kamenov (BUL).
Bronze medals: J. Lowey (IRL), F. Harding (ENG), N. Moore (ENG).

Copenhagen, Denmark - 1986
L. Fly: S. Todorov (BUL). **Fly:** S. Galotian (URS). **Bantam:** D. Drumm (GDR). **Feather:** K. Tsziu (URS). **Light:** G. Akopkhian (URS). **L. Welter:** F. Vastag (ROM). **Welter:** S. Karavayev (URS). **L. Middle:** E. Elibaev (URS). **Middle:** A. Kurnabka (URS). **L. Heavy:** A. Schultz (GDR). **Heavy:** A. Golota (POL). **S. Heavy:** A. Prianichnikov (URS).

Gdansk, Poland - 1988
L. Fly: I. Kovacs (HUN). **Fly:** M. Beyer (GDR). **Bantam:** M. Aitzanov (URS). **Feather:** M. Rudolph (GDR). **Light:** M. Shaburov (URS). **L. Welter:** G. Campanella (ITA). **Welter:** D. Konsun (URS). **L. Middle:** K. Kiselev (URS). **Middle:** A. Rudenko (URS). **L. Heavy:** O. Velikanov (URS). **Heavy:** A. Ter-Okopian (URS). **S. Heavy:** E. Belusov (URS).
Bronze medals: P. Ramsey (ENG), M. Smyth (WAL).

Usti Nad Labem, Czechoslovakia - 1990
L. Fly: Z. Paliani (URS). **Fly:** K. Pielert (GDR). **Bantam:** K. Baravi (URS). **Feather:** P. Gvasalia (URS). **Light:** J. Hildenbrandt (GDR). **L. Welter:** N. Smanov (URS). **Welter:** A. Preda (ROM). **L. Middle:** A. Kakauridze (URS). **Middle:** J. Schwank (GDR). **L. Heavy:** Iljin (URS). **Heavy:** I. Andrejev (URS). **S. Heavy:** W. Fischer (GDR).
Silver medal: A. Todd (ENG).
Bronze medal: P. Craig (ENG).

Edinburgh, Scotland - 1992
L. Fly: M. Ismailov (URS). **Fly:** F. Brennfuhrer (GER). **Bantam:** S. Kuchler (GER). **Feather:** M. Silantiev (URS). **Light:** S. Shcherbakov (URS). **L. Welter:** O. Saitov (URS). **Welter:** H. Kurlumaz (TUR). **L. Middle:** Z. Erdie (HUN). **Middle:** V. Zhirov (URS). **L. Heavy:** D. Gorbachev (URS). **Heavy:** L. Achkasov (URS). **S. Heavy:** A. Mamedov (URS).
Silver medals: M. Hall (ENG), B. Jones (WAL).
Bronze medals: F. Slane (IRL), G. Stephens (IRL), C. Davies (WAL).

Salonika, Greece - 1993
L. Fly: O. Kiroukhine (UKR). **Fly:** R. Husseinov (AZE). **Bantam:** M. Kulbe (GER). **Feather:** E. Zakharov (RUS). **Light:** O. Sergeev (RUS). **L. Welter:** A. Selihanov (RUS). **Welter:** O. Kudinov (UKR). **L. Middle:** E. Makarenko (RUS). **Middle:** D. Droukovski (RUS). **L. Heavy:** A. Voida (RUS). **Heavy:** Vladimir Klitschko (UKR). **S. Heavy:** A. Moiseev (RUS).
Bronze medal: D. Costello (ENG).

Sifok, Hungary - 1995
L. Fly: D. Gaissine (RUS). **Fly:** A. Kotelnik (UKR). **Bantam:** A. Loutsenko (UKR). **Feather:** S. Harrison (SCO). **Light:** D. Simon (ROM). **L. Welter:** B. Ulusoy (TUR). **Welter:** O. Bouts (UKR). **L. Middle:** O. Bukalo (UKR). **Middle:** V. Plettnev (RUS). **L. Heavy:** A. Derevtsov (RUS). **Heavy:** C. O'Grady (IRL). **S. Heavy:** D. Savvine (RUS).
Silver medal: G. Murphy (SCO).
Bronze medal: N. Linford (ENG).

Birmingham, England - 1997
L. Fly: G. Balakshine (RUS). **Fly:** K. Dzhamoloudinov (RUS). **Bantam:** A. Shaidulin (RUS). **Feather:** D. Marciukaitis (LIT). **Light:** D. Baranov (RUS). **L. Welter:** A. Mishine (RUS). **Welter:** D. Yuldashev (UKR). **L. Middle:** A. Catic (GER). **Middle:** D. Lebedev (RUS). **L. Heavy:** V. Uzelkov (UKR). **Heavy:** S. Koeber (GER). **S. Heavy:** D. Pirozhenko (RUS).
Silver medal: S. Miller (ENG).
Bronze medals: S. Burke (ENG), M. Dean (ENG), P. Pierson (ENG), M. Lee (IRE).

Rijeka, Croatia - 1999
L. Fly: Kibalyuk (UKR). **Fly:** A. Bakhtin (RUS). **Bantam:** V. Simion (ROM). **Feather:** Kiutkhukow (BUL). **Light:** Pontilov (RUS). **L. Welter:** G. Ajetovic (YUG). **Welter:** S. Nouaouria (FRA). **L. Middle:** S. Kazantsev (RUS). **Middle:** D. Tsariouk (RUS). **L. Heavy:** Alexeev (RUS). **Heavy:** Alborov (RUS). **S. Heavy:** Soukhoverkov (RUS).
Bronze medal: S. Birch (ENG).

Sarejevo, Croatia - 2001
L. Fly: A. Taratokin (RUS). **Fly:** E. Abzalimov (RUS). **Bantam:** G. Kovaljov (RUS). **Feather:** M. Hratchev (RUS). **Light:** S. Aydin (TUR). **L. Welter:** D. Mikulin (RUS). **Welter:** O. Bokalo (UKR). **L. Middle:** M. Korobov (RUS). **Middle:** I. Bogdanov (UKR). **L. Heavy:** R. Kahkijev (RUS). **Heavy:** V. Zuyev (BE). **S. Heavy:** I. Timurziejev (RUS).
Bronze medal: K. Anderson (SCO).

Warsaw, Poland - 2003
L. Fly: P. Bedak (HUN). **Fly:** A. Ganev (RUS). **Bantam:** M. Tretiak (UKR). **Feather:** A. Alexandru (ROM). **Light:** A. Aleksiev (RUS). **L. Welter:** T. Tabotadze (UKR). **Welter:** Z. Baisangurov (RUS). **Middle:** J. Machoncev (RUS). **L. Heavy:** I. Michalkin (RUS). **Heavy:** Y. Romanov (RUS). **S. Heavy:** D. Arshba (RUS).
Bronze medal: S. Smith (E), F. Gavin (E), J. O'Donnell (E), T. Jeffries (E).

Note: The age limit for the championships were reduced from 21 to 19 in 1976.

Commonwealth Champions, 1930-2002

Hamilton, Canada - 1930
Fly: W. Smith (ENG). **Bantam:** H. Mizler (ENG). **Feather:** F. Meacham (ENG). **Light:** J. Rolland (SCO). **Welter:** L. Hall (SAF). **Middle:** F. Mallin (ENG). **L. Heavy:** J. Goyder (ENG). **Heavy:** V. Stuart (ENG).
Silver medals: T. Pardoe (ENG), T. Holt (SCO).
Bronze medals: A. Lyons (SCO), A. Love (ENG), F. Breeman (ENG).

Wembley, England - 1934
Fly: P. Palmer (ENG). **Bantam:** F. Ryan (ENG). **Feather:** C. Cattarall (SAF). **Light:** L. Cook (AUS). **Welter:** D. McCleave (ENG). **Middle:** A. Shawyer (ENG). **L. Heavy:** G. Brennan (ENG). **Heavy:** P. Floyd (ENG).
Silver medals: A. Barnes (WAL), J. Jones (WAL), F. Taylor (WAL), J. Holton (SCO).
Bronze medals: J. Pottinger (WAL), T. Wells (SCO), H. Moy (ENG), W. Duncan (NIR), J. Magill (NIR), Lord D. Douglas-Hamilton (SCO).

Melbourne, Australia - 1938
Fly: J. Joubert (SAF). **Bantam:** W. Butler (ENG). **Feather:** A. Henricus (CEY). **Light:** H. Groves (ENG). **Welter:** W. Smith (AUS). **Middle:** D. Reardon (WAL). **L. Heavy:** N. Wolmarans (SAF). **Heavy:** T. Osborne (CAN).
Silver medals: J. Watson (SCO), M. Dennis (ENG).
Bronze medals: H. Cameron (SCO), J. Wilby (ENG).

Auckland, New Zealand - 1950
Fly: H. Riley (SCO). **Bantam:** J. van Rensburg (SAF). **Feather:** H. Gilliland (SCO). **Light:** R. Latham (ENG). **Welter:** T. Ratcliffe (ENG). **Middle:** T. van Schalkwyk (SAF). **L. Heavy:** D. Scott (ENG). **Heavy:** F. Creagh (NZL).
Bronze medal: P. Brander (ENG).

Vancouver, Canada - 1954
Fly: R. Currie (SCO). **Bantam:** J. Smillie (SCO). **Feather:** L. Leisching (SAF). **Light:** P. van Staden (SR). **L. Welter:** M. Bergin (CAN). **Welter:** N. Gargano (ENG). **L. Welter:** W. Greaves (CAN). **Middle:** J. van de Kolff (SAF). **L. Heavy:** P. van Vuuren (SAF). **Heavy:** B. Harper (ENG).
Silver medals: M. Collins (WAL), F. McQuillan (SCO).
Bronze medals: D. Charnley (ENG), B. Wells (ENG).

Cardiff, Wales - 1958
Fly: J. Brown (SCO). **Bantam:** H. Winstone (WAL). **Feather:** W. Taylor (AUS). **Light:** R. McTaggart (SCO). **L. Welter:** H. Loubscher (SAF). **Welter:** J. Greyling (SAF). **L. Middle:** G. Webster (SAF). **Middle:** T. Milligan (NIR). **L. Heavy:** A. Madigan (AUS). **Heavy:** D. Bekker (SAF).
Silver medals: T. Bache (ENG), M. Collins (WAL), J. Jordan (NIR), R. Kane (SCO), S. Pearson (ENG), A. Higgins (WAL), D. Thomas (ENG).
Bronze medals: P. Lavery (NIR), D. Braithwaite (WAL), R. Hanna (NIR), A. Owen (SCO), J. McClory (NIR), J. Cooke (ENG), J. Jacobs (ENG), B. Nancurvis (ENG), R. Scott (SCO), W. Brown (WAL), J. Caiger (ENG), W. Bannon (SCO), R. Pleace (WAL).

Perth, Australia - 1962
Fly: R. Mallon (SCO). **Bantam:** J. Dynevor (AUS). **Feather:** J. McDermott (SCO). **Light:** E. Blay (GHA). **L. Welter:** C. Quartey (GHA). **Welter:** W. Coe (NZL). **L. Middle:** H. Mann (CAN). **Middle:** M. Calhoun (JAM). **L. Heavy:** A. Madigan (AUS). **Heavy:** G. Oywello (UGA).
Silver medals: R. McTaggart (SCO), J. Pritchett (ENG).
Bronze medals: M. Pye (ENG), P. Benneyworth (ENG), B. Whelan (ENG), B. Brazier (ENG), C. Rice (NIR), T. Menzies (SCO), H. Christie (NIR), A. Turmel (CI).

Kingston, Jamaica - 1966
Fly: S. Shittu (GHA). **Bantam:** E. Ndukwu (NIG). **Feather:** P. Waruinge (KEN). **Light:** A. Andeh (NIG). **L. Welter:** J. McCourt (NIR). **Welter:** E. Blay (GHA). **L. Middle:** M. Rowe (ENG). **Middle:** J. Darkey (GHA). **L. Heavy:** R. Tighe (ENG). **Heavy:** W. Kini (NZL).
Silver medals: P. Maguire (NIR), R. Thurston (ENG), R. Arthur (ENG), T. Imrie (SCO).
Bronze medals: S. Lockhart (NIR), A. Peace (SCO), F. Young (NIR), J. Turpin (ENG), D. McAlinden (NIR).

Edinburgh, Scotland - 1970

L. Fly: J. Odwori (UGA). **Fly:** D. Needham (ENG). **Bantam:** S. Shittu (GHA). **Feather:** P. Waruinge (KEN). **Light:** A. Adeyemi (NIG). **L. Welter:** M. Muruli (UGA). **Welter:** E. Ankudey (GHA). **L. Middle:** T. Imrie (SCO). **Middle:** J. Conteh (ENG). **L. Heavy:** F. Ayinla (NIG). **Heavy:** B. Masanda (UGA).
Silver medals: T. Davies (WAL), J. Gillan (SCO), D. Davies (WAL), J. McKinty (NIR).
Bronze medals: M. Abrams (ENG), A. McHugh (SCO), D. Larmour (NIR), S. Oglivie (SCO), A. Richardson (ENG), T. Joyce (SCO), P. Doherty (NIR), J. Rafferty (SCO), L. Stevens (ENG).

Christchurch, New Zealand - 1974

L. Fly: S. Muchoki (KEN). **Fly:** D. Larmour (NIR). **Bantam:** P. Cowdell (ENG). **Feather:** E. Ndukwu (NIG). **Light:** A. Kalule (UGA). **L. Welter:** O. Nwankpa (NIG). **Welter:** M. Muruli (UGA). **L. Middle:** L. Mwale (ZAM). **Middle:** F. Lucas (STV). **L. Heavy:** W. Knight (ENG). **Heavy:** N. Meade (ENG).
Silver medals: E. McKenzie (WAL), A. Harrison (SCO).
Bronze medals: J. Bambrick (SCO), J. Douglas (SCO), J. Rodgers (NIR), S. Cooney (SCO), R. Davies (ENG), C. Speare (ENG), G. Ferris (NIR).

Edmonton, Canada - 1978

L. Fly: S. Muchoki (KEN). **Fly:** M. Irungu (KEN). **Bantam:** B. McGuigan (NIR). **Feather:** A. Nelson (GHA). **Light:** G. Hamill (NIR). **L. Welter:** W. Braithwaite (GUY). **Welter:** M. McCallum (JAM). **L. Middle:** K. Perlette (CAN). **Middle:** P. McElwaine (AUS). **L. Heavy:** R. Fortin (CAN). **Heavy:** J. Awome (ENG).
Silver medals: J. Douglas (SCO), K. Beattie (NIR), D. Parkes (ENG), V. Smith (ENG).
Bronze medals: H. Russell (NIR), M. O'Brien (ENG), J. McAllister (SCO), T. Feal (WAL).

Brisbane, Australia - 1982

L. Fly: A. Wachire (KEN). **Fly:** M. Mutua (KEN). **Bantam:** J. Orewa (NIG). **Feather:** P. Konyegwachie (NIG). **Light:** H. Khalili (KEN). **L. Welter:** C. Ossai (NIG). **Welter:** C. Pyatt (ENG). **L. Middle:** S. O'Sullivan (CAN). **Middle:** J. Price (ENG). **L. Heavy:** F. Sani (FIJ). **Heavy:** W. de Wit (CAN).
Silver medals: J. Lyon (ENG), J. Kelly (SCO), R. Webb (NIR), P. Hanlon (ENG), J. McDonnell (ENG), N. Croombes (ENG), H. Hylton (ENG).
Bronze medals: R. Gilbody (ENG), C. McIntosh (ENG), R. Corr (NIR).

Edinburgh, Scotland - 1986

L. Fly: S. Olson (CAN). **Fly:** J. Lyon (ENG). **Bantam:** S. Murphy (ENG). **Feather:** B. Downey (CAN). **Light:** A. Dar (CAN). **L. Welter:** H. Grant (CAN). **Welter:** D. Dyer (ENG). **L. Middle:** D. Sherry (CAN). **Middle:** R. Douglas (ENG). **L. Heavy:** J. Moran (ENG). **Heavy:** J. Peau (NZL). **S. Heavy:** L. Lewis (CAN).

Silver medals: M. Epton (ENG), R. Nash (NIR), P. English (ENG), N. Haddock (WAL), J. McAlister (SCO), H. Lawson (SCO), D. Young (SCO), A. Evans (WAL).
Bronze medals: W. Docherty (SCO), J. Todd (NIR), K. Webber (WAL), G. Brooks (SCO), J. Wallace (SCO), C. Carleton (NIR), J. Jacobs (ENG), B. Lowe (NIR), D. Denny (NIR), G. Thomas (WAL), A. Mullen (SCO), G. Ferrie (SCO), P. Tinney (NIR), B. Pullen (WAL), E. Cardouza (ENG), J. Oyebola (ENG), J. Sillitoe (CI).

Auckland, New Zealand - 1990

L. Fly: J. Juuko (UGA). **Fly:** W. McCullough (NIR). **Bantam:** S. Mohammed (NIG). **Feather:** J. Irwin (ENG). **Light:** G. Nyakana (UGA). **L. Welter:** C. Kane (SCO). **Welter:** D. Defiagbon (NIG). **L. Middle:** R. Woodhall (ENG). **Middle:** C. Johnson (CAN). **L. Heavy:** J. Akhasamba (KEN). **Heavy:** G. Onyango (KEN). **S. Heavy:** M. Kenny (NZL).
Bronze medals: D. Anderson (SCO), M. Edwards (ENG), P. Douglas (NIR).

Victoria, Canada - 1994

L. Fly: H. Ramadhani (KEN). **Fly:** P. Shepherd (SCO). **Bantam:** R. Peden (AUS). **Feather:** C. Patton (CAN). **Light:** M. Strange (CAN). **L. Welter:** P. Richardson (ENG). **Welter:** N. Sinclair (NIR). **L. Middle:** J. Webb (NIR). **Middle:** R. Donaldson (CAN). **L. Heavy:** D. Brown (CAN). **Heavy:** O. Ahmed (KEN). **S. Heavy:** D. Dokiwari (NIG).
Silver medals: S. Oliver (ENG), J. Cook (WAL), M. Renaghan (NIR), M. Winters (NIR), J. Wilson (SCO).
Bronze medals: D. Costello (ENG), J. Townsley (SCO), D. Williams (ENG).

Kuala Lumpar, Malaysia - 1998

L. Fly: S. Biki (MAS). **Fly:** R. Sunee (MRI). **Bantam:** M. Yomba (TAN). **Feather:** A. Arthur (SCO). **Light:** R. Narh (GHA). **L. Welter:** M. Strange (CAN). **Welter:** J. Molitor (CAN). **L. Middle:** C. Bessey (ENG). **Middle:** J. Pearce (ENG). **L. Heavy:** C. Fry (ENG). **Heavy:** M. Simmons (CAN). **S. Heavy:** A. Harrison (ENG).
Silver medal: L. Cunningham (NIR).
Bronze medals: G. Jones (ENG), A. McLean (ENG), C. McNeil (SCO), J. Townsley (SCO), B. Magee (NIR), K. Evans (WAL).

Manchester, England - 2002

L. Fly: M. Ali Qamar (IND). **Fly:** K. Kanyanta (ZAM). **Bantam:** J. Kane (AUS). **Feather:** H. Ali (PAK). **Light:** J. Arthur (WAL). **L. Welter:** D. Barker (ENG). **Welter:** D. Geale (AUS). **L. Middle:** J. Pascal (CAN). **Middle:** P. Miller (AUS). **L. Heavy:** J. Albert (NIG). **Heavy:** J. Douglas (CAN). **S. Heavy:** D. Dolan (ENG).
Silver medals: D. Langley (ENG), P. Smith (ENG), S. Birch (ENG).
Bronze medals: M. Moran (ENG), A. Morris (ENG), C. McEwan (SCO), A. Young (SCO), K. Evans (WAL).

David Dolan (left), the Commonwealth Games super-heavyweight champion in 2002, pictured taking the 2001 ABA heavyweight title

Les Clark

308

The Triple Hitters' Boxing Quiz (Part 8)

Compiled by Ralph Oates

QUESTIONS

1. Over how many rounds did Terry Allen outpoint Mickey Jones on 30th November 1943?
   A. Six.   B. Eight.   C. 10.

2. On 4th February 1944, Bruce Woodcock knocked out Tom Reddington in round six. Where did the contest take place?
   A. Nottingham.   B. London.   C. Manchester.

3. On 5th December 1947, Joe Louis retained his world heavyweight championship when he outpointed Jersey Joe Walcott over 15 rounds. Who was the referee for this contest?
   A. Eddie Joseph.   B. Ruby Goldstein.   C. Dave Miller.

4. On 9th March 1949, Ken Shaw retained his Scottish heavyweight title when he defeated Bert Gilroy. By which method was this achieved?
   A. Four-round knockout.   B. Eight-round stoppage.
   C. 12-round points decision.

5. Carmen Basilio and Gaby Ferland met in New Orleans on 12th April 1950 in a contest scheduled for 10 rounds. What was the result?
   A. Points win for Ferland.   B. A draw.
   C. Points win for Basilio.

6. Eddie Thomas lost his European welterweight championship to Charles Humez on 13th June 1951. By which method was this achieved?
   A. Four-round knockout.   B. Six-round stoppage.
   C. 15-round points decision.

7. On 25th June 1952, Joey Maxim retained his world light-heavyweight title when Sugar Ray Robinson retired in round 13. Such was the high temperature at the time of the contest that the referee, Ruby Goldstein, was duly overcome by the heat and was replaced before the bout came to its final conclusion. Who was the referee who took over?
   A. Ray Miller.   B. Harry Kessler.   C. Cy Gottfried.

8. On 4th September 1953, Central Area Heavyweight champion Ray Wilding stopped Billy Teasdale in round five. In which country did this contest take place?
   A. England.   B. Canada.   C. America.

9. How many times did Rocky Marciano defend his world heavyweight title in 1955?
   A. Once.   B. Twice.   C. Three times.

10. On 19th May 1957, Henry Cooper challenged Ingemar Johansson for the European heavyweight title, but failed in his attempt when knocked out in round five. In which country did this contest take place?
    A. England.   B. Denmark.   C. Sweden.

11. Which British title did Randolph Turpin not hold during his professional career?
    A. Welterweight.   B. Middleweight.
    C. Light-Heavyweight.

12. Dave Charnley failed to win the world lightweight championship on 18th April 1961, when he was outpointed by the holder, Joe Brown, over 15 rounds. Who was the referee for this contest?
    A. Frankie Van.   B. Tommy Little.   C. Jimmy Devlin.

13. On 24th May 1965, the future British, European and Commonwealth welterweight champion, Ralph Charles, stopped Bob Sempey in round four. At this stage of his career Charles was undefeated in how many professional bouts?
    A. 10.   B. 11.   C. 12.

14. Which future British and Commonwealth middleweight champion did Hugh Lynch outpoint over six rounds on 25th October 1966?
    A. Johnny Pritchett.   B. Bunny Sterling.
    C. Mark Rowe.

15. On 16th January 1967, John McCluskey won the vacant British flyweight title when he knocked out Tony Barlow in round eight. At that stage of his career, McCluskey had participated in how many professional contests?
    A. Seven.   B. Eight.   C. Nine.

16. Billy Walker failed to win the European heavyweight championship on 21st March 1967 when Karl Mildenberger stopped him in round eight. In which country did this contest take place?
    A. Italy.   B. England.   C. Germany.

17. On 14th October 1967, Howard Winstone failed in his third attempt to win the world featherweight championship when he retired in round 12 of his challenge against Vicente Saldivar in Mexico City. Who was the referee for this contest?
A. Ramon Berumen. B. George Latka. C. Ken Morita.

18. During his career, which boxer did the former British middleweight champion, Mick Leahy, not box in the professional ranks?
A. Sugar Ray Robinson. B. Nino Benvenuti.
C. Dick Tiger.

19. In which year was the former British lightweight champion, Maurice Cullen, born?
A. 1936. B. 1937. C. 1938.

20. John H. Stracey won his first eight professional bouts inside the distance. However, he was taken the distance for the first time on 12th May 1970 when he outpointed which opponent over eight rounds?
A. Ait Bouzid Elmenceur. B. Dante Pelaez.
C. David Pesenti.

21. On 31st October 1975, Jim Watt was outpointed over 12 rounds by Andre Holyk in a contest which was a final eliminator for the European lightweight championship. In which country did this bout take place?
A. England. B. France. C. Holland.

22. Ken Buchanan stopped his first three professional opponents inside the same round. Name the respective round?
A. One. B. Two. C. Three.

23. In defence of his European flyweight title on 24th February 1981, Charlie Magri stopped Enrique Rodriguez Cal. In which round?
A. One. B. Two. C. Three.

24. How many professional bouts did former world, British, European and Commonwealth light-heavy-weight champion, John Conteh, have in America?
A. Two. B. Three. C. Four.

25. Which of these boxers did not box in the southpaw stance?
A. Richard Dunn. B. Jim Watt. C. John H. Stracey.

26. James Cook retained his European Super-middle-weight title on the 1st June 1991 when challenger Mark Kaylor retired. In which round?
A. Five. B. Six. C. Seven.

27. Which one of the following did not box in America during their professional career?
A. Chris Eubank. B. Tony Sibson. C. Charlie Magri.

28. During his time in the amateur ranks, promoter, trainer and manager, Graham Moughton, boxed a number of high quality opponents. Which of the following did he not meet?
A. John H. Stracey. B. Thomas Hearns.
C. Sugar Ray Leonard.

29. Over how many rounds did Colin Dunne outpoint Phil Found on 17th May 1994?
A. Four. B. Six. C. Eight.

30. On 11th October 1996, Jason Cook made his professional debut, stopping Brian Robb. In which round?
A. Two. B. Three. C. Four.

31. Which opponent did Colin Lynes stop in the first round on 23rd July 1998?
A. Les Frost. B. Trevor Smith. C. Ram Singh.

32. In which round did William Joppy stop Roberto Duran on 28th August 1998, when defending his WBA middleweight title?
A. One. B. Two. C. Three.

33. On 10th March 2000, Nicky Cook stopped Chris Jickells in the first round. At this stage of his career, how many first round victories had Cook scored?
A. One. B. Two. C. Three.

34. In which round did Cathy Brown stop Viktoria Vargal, in a contest which took place on 31st October 2000?
A. Two. B. Three. C. Four.

35. How many bouts did former European heavyweight champion, Dick Richardson, have during his professional career?
A. 45. B. 46. C. 47.

36. In defence of his British lightweight championship on 5th May 2001, Bobby Vanzie stopped Steve Murray in round seven. Who was the referee for this contest?
A. Paul Thomas. B. Dave Parris. C. Mickey Vann.

37. On 31st July 2001, Jane Couch outpointed Shakurah Witherspoon over four rounds. In which country did this contest take place?
A. America. B. Jamaica. C. Denmark.

38. In defence of his WBU light-welterweight championship on 15th September 2001, Ricky Hatton stopped John Bailey. In which round?
    A. Five.   B. Six.   C. Seven.

39. On 20th October 2001, Audley Harrison stopped Piotr Jurczyk in round two. Where did this contest take place?
    A. Cardiff.   B. Glasgow.   C. Belfast.

40. On 19th January 2002, Wayne Alexander won the vacant European light-middleweight championship, when he stopped Paolo Pizzamiglio in three rounds. Who was the last British boxer prior to Alexander to hold this title?
    A. Herol Graham.   B. Jimmy Cable.   C. Chris Pyatt.

41. Which lady is a promoter?
    A. Annette Conroy.   B. Tania Follett.
    C. Michelle Sutcliffe.

42. On 20th April 2002, Joe Calzaghe successfully defended his WBO super-middleweight title for the 10th time when he outpointed Charles Brewer over 12 rounds. Which version of the world championship did Brewer formerly hold?
    A. WBC.   B. WBA.   C. IBF.

43. On 21st May 2002, Mark Krence lost his undefeated record when he was outpointed over six rounds by Audley Harrison. Prior to this defeat, Krence was undefeated in how many professional bouts?
    A. Nine.   B. 10.   C. 11.

44. Which promoter is associated with the St Andrew's Sporting Club?
    A. Tommy Gilmour.   B. Jonathan Feld.
    C. Joe Pyle.

45. Kevin Lear won the vacant WBU super-featherweight championship on 1st June 2002, when Michael Gomez retired in round eight. At this stage of his career, Lear was undefeated in how many professional contests?
    A. 13.   B. 14.   C. 15.

46. On 8th June 2002, Lennox Lewis retained his world heavyweight championship in Memphis, when he knocked out Mike Tyson in round eight. At this stage of his career, Lewis had participated in how many world heavyweight title bouts?
    A. 15.   B. 16.   C. 17.

47. Danny Williams retained his British and Commonwealth heavyweight titles on 17th September 2002, outpointing Keith Long over 12 rounds. In so doing, Williams also won a Lonsdale Belt outright. Who was the referee for this contest?
    A. John Keane.   B. Mickey Vann.
    C. Ian John-Lewis.

48. James Hare retained his Commonwealth welterweight title on 5th October 2002, when he stopped Farai Musiiwa. In which round?
    A. Seven.   B. Eight.   C. Nine.

49. Tony Oakey retained his WBU light-heavyweight title on 12th October 2002, when he defeated Andrei Kaersten. By which method did this happen?
    A. Four-round stoppage.   B. Six-round knockout.
    C. 12-round points decision.

50. On 19th October 2002, Scott Harrison captured the WBO version of the world featherweight title, when he outpointed Julio Pablo Chacon over 12 rounds. Prior to Harrison, who was the last British holder of the WBO featherweight championship?
    A. Colin McMillan.   B. Steve Robinson.
    C. Prince Naseem Hamed.

Directory of Ex-Boxers' Associations

by Ron Olver

BOURNEMOUTH Founded 1980. HQ: Horse & Jockey, Wimborne Road, Bournemouth. Dai Dower (P); Percy Singer (T); Dave Fry (VC); Doug Mitchell (S); Peter Fay (C), 24 Monkswell Green, Purewell, Christchurch, Dorset BH23 1MN.

CORK Founded 1973. HQ: Glen Boxing Club, Blackpool, Cork. William O'Leary (P & C); John Martin (S); Phil Murray (VC); John Donovan (T).

CORNWALL Founded 1989. HQ: Truro City Football Club. Stan Cullis (P); Jimmy Miller (T); Chris Trembath (C); Bill Matthews (S), 33 Victoria Road, St Austell, Cornwall PL25 4QF.

CROYDON Founded 1982. HQ: Ivy House Club, Campbell Road, West Croydon. Derek O'Dell (C); Richard Evans (PRO & S); Barry Penny (VC); Gilbert Allnutt (P), 37 Braemar Avenue, Thornton Heath, Croydon CR9 7RJ.

EASTERN AREA Founded 1973. HQ: Norfolk Dumpling, Cattle Market, Hall Road, Norwich. Brian Fitzmaurice (P); Ron Springall (C); Len Cooke (S & T); Clive Campling (VC), 57 Northfields, Norwich NR4 7ES.

HULL & EAST YORKSHIRE Founded 1996. HQ: The Dram Shop, George Street, Hull. Don Harrison (C); Geoff Rymer (PRO & S); Bert Smith (T), 54 St Aidan Road, Bridlington, E. Yorks.

IPSWICH Founded 1970. HQ: Loco Club, Ipswich. Alby Kingham (P); Vic Thurlow (C & T); Michael Thurlow (S), 147 Clapgate Lane, Ipswich IP3 0RF.

IRISH Founded 1973. HQ: National Boxing Stadium, South Circular Road, Dublin. Val Harris (P); Tommy Bruce (C); Tommy Butler (T); Willie Duggan (S), 175 Kimmage Road West, Dublin 6W.

KENT Founded 1997. HQ: RAFA Club, Chatham. Mick Smith (P & C); Ray Lambert (PRO); Paul Nihill, MBE (S & T), 5 Acre Close, Rochester, Kent ME1 2RE.

LEEDS Founded 1952. HQ: North Leeds WMC, Burmantofts, Lincoln Green, Leeds 9. Alan Richardson (P); Greg Steene (HP); Kevin Cunningham (C & S); Alan Alster (T); Frank Johnson (PRO), Franwyn, 7 Allenby Drive, Leeds LS11 5RP.

LEICESTER Founded 1972. HQ: Belgrave WMC, Checketts Road, Leicester. Mick Greaves (P & C); Mrs Rita Jones (T); Norman Jones (S), 60 Dumbleton Avenue, Leicester LE3 2EG.

LONDON Founded 1971. HQ; The Queen Mary College, Bancroft Road, Mile End, London E1. Stephen Powell (P); Micky O'Sullivan (C); Ron Olver (PRO); Ray Caulfield (T); Mrs Mary Powell (S), 36 St Peters Street, Islington, London N1 8JT.

MANCHESTER Founded 1968. HQ: Hat & Feathers Pub, Ancoats, Manchester. Tommy Proffitt (P); Jack Edwards (C); Kenny Baker (T); Jimmy Lewis (VC); Eddie Copeland (S), 9 Lakeside, Hadfield, Glossop, Derby SK13 1HW.

MERSEYSIDE (Liverpool) Founded 1973. HQ: Cross Keys Pub, Liverpool. Johnny Cooke (P); Terry Carson (C); Jim Boyd (VC); Jim Jenkinson (S & T), 13 Brooklands Avenue, Waterloo, Liverpool L22 3XY.

MIDLANDS EBA Founded 2002. HQ: The Castle Hill Casino, Castle Hill, Dudley. Richie Woodhall (P); Barry DeLacy (C); Martin Florey (VC); Les Potts (T); Ron Gray (P); Jerry Hjelter (S), 67 Abberley Avenue, Stourport on Severn, Worcs DY13 0LY.

NORTHAMPTON DISTRICT Founded 2001. HQ: Northampton Boys Club, Towcester Road, Northampton. Jeff Tite (P); Roy Davies (C); Keith Hall (VC); Sid Green (S & T), 8 Friars Close, Delapre, Northampton NN4 8PU.

NORTHAMPTONSHIRE Founded 1981. HQ: Cue Club, Bridge Street, Northampton. Dick Rogers (P); Gil Wilson (C); George Ward (VC); Peter Cripps (T); Mrs Pam Ward (S), 6 Derwent Close, Kings Heath, Northampton.

NORTHERN FEDERATION Founded 1974. Several member EBAs. Annual Gala. Eddie Monahan (S), 16 Braemar Avenue, Marshside, Southport.

NORTHERN IRELAND Founded 1970. HQ: Ulster Sports Club, High Street, Belfast. Gerry Hassett (P); Paddy Graham (C); Paddy Maguire (VC); Micky Hannah (T); Freddie Gilroy (PRO); Al Gibson (S), 900 Crumlin Road, Belfast.

NORTH STAFFS & SOUTH CHESHIRE Founded 1969. HQ: The Saggar Makers Bottom Knocker, Market Place, Burslem, Stoke on Trent. Tut Whalley (P); Roy Simms (VC); Les Dean (S); John Greatbach (T); Billy Tudor (C & PRO), 133 Springbank Road, Chell Heath, Stoke on Trent, Staffs ST6 6HW.

NORWICH Founded 1990. HQ: West End Retreat, Brown Street, Norwich. Les King (P); John Pipe (C); Jack Wakefield (T); Albert Howe (S), 15 Grange Close, Hoveton, Norwich NR2 8EA.

NOTTINGHAM Founded 1979. HQ: The Earl Howe, Carlton Road, Sneinton, Nottingham. Len Chorley (P); Walter Spencer (C); Walter Thomas (VC); Gary Rooksby (T); John Kinsella (PRO); Graham Rooksby (S), 42 Spinney Road, Keyworth, Notts NG12 5LN.

PLYMOUTH Founded 1982. HQ: Stoke Social Club, Devonport Road, Plymouth. Tom Pryce-Davies (C); Doug Halliday (S); Tony Penprase (VC); Arthur Willis (T); Buck Taylor (P & PRO), 15 Greenbank Avenue, St Judes, Plymouth PL4 9BT.

PRESTON Founded 1973. HQ: Barney's Piano Bar, Church Street, Preston. John Allen (P & C); Tommy Smith (T); Peter Osborne (S), 39 Prospect Place, Ashton, Preston PR2 1DL.

ST HELENS Founded 1983. HQ: Royal Naval Association, Volunteer Street, St Helens. Johnny Molloy (P); Ray Britch (C); Tommy McNamara (T); Paul Britch (S), 16 Oxley Street, Sutton, St Helens WA9 3PE.

SCOTTISH Founded 1997. HQ: Iron Horse Public House, Nile Street, Glasgow. John McCluskey (P); Andy Grant (C); Charlie Sexton (VC); Frank O'Donnell (LP); Peter Baines (T); Liam McColgan (S), 25 Dalton Avenue, Linnvale, Clydebank G81 2SH.

SHEFFIELD Founded 1974. Reformed 2002. HQ: Springwood Hotel, Sheffield. Billy Calvert (P); Peter Skinner (C); Harry Carnall (VC); Jim Daly (T); John Redfern (S), 33 Birch Avenue, Chapeltown, Sheffield S35 1RQ.

SQUARE RING Founded 1978. HQ: Snooty Fox Hotel, St Marychurch. George Pook (P); Johnny Mudge (S); Jim Banks (T); Paul King (C), 10 Pine Court Apartments, Middle Warberry Road, Torquay.

SUNDERLAND Founded 1959. HQ: River Wear Social Club, Sunderland. George Martin (P); Teddy Lynn (C); Les Simm (T & S), 21 Orchard Street, Pallion, Sunderland SR4 6QL.

SUSSEX Founded 1974. Reformed 2003. HQ: Ladies Mile Club, Hatcham, Sussex. Tommy Mellis (P); John McNeil (C); John Mercer (S); Ernie Price (PRO), 132 Amberley Drive, Hove, Sussex BN3 8JQ.

SWANSEA & SOUTH WEST WALES Founded 1983. HQ: Villiers Arms, Neath Road, Hafod, Swansea. Cliff Curvis (P); Gordon Pape (C); Ernie Wallis (T); Len Smith (S), 105 Cockett Road, Swansea SA2 0FG.

TYNESIDE Founded 1970. HQ: Pelaw Social Club, Heworth. Billy Charlton (P); Maxie Walsh (C); Harry Greenwood (VC); Malcolm Dinning (T); Alan Gordon (S), 16 Dove Court, Birtley, Chester le Street, Durham PH3 1HB.

WELSH Founded 1976. HQ: Rhydyfelin Labour Club, Pontypridd. Wynford Jones (P); Ron Bruzas (T); Don James (S), 28 Woodfield Road, Talbot Green, Pontyclun, Mid-Glamorgan. Patron - Lord Brooks. Chairman: Vacant.

WIRRAL Founded 1973. Reformed 2003. HQ: RNA Club, Birkenhead. Terry Carson (C); Pat Carry (T); Don Parr (S), 13 James Street, Prenton, Birkenhead, Merseyside CH43 5RO.

The above information is set at the time of going to press and no responsibility can be taken for any changes in officers or addresses of HQs that may happen between then and publication or changes that have not been notified to me.

ABBREVIATIONS
P - President. HP - Honorary President. LP - Life President. AP - Acting President. C - Chairman. VC - Vice Chairman. T - Treasurer. S - Secretary. PRO - Public Relations Officer and/or Press Officer.

Left to right: Ron Olver (Chairman), John Morris (the former BBBoC General Secretary) and Bernard Hart (Managing Director of the Lonsdale International Sporting Club) seen at a meeting of the Grants Committee of the BBBoC Benevolent Fund (now the Board Charity)

Obituaries

by Derek O'Dell

It is impossible to list everyone, but I have again done my best to include final tributes for as many of the well-known boxers and other familiar names within the sport who have passed away since the 2003 Yearbook was published. We honour them and remember them. Two men who died recently and who I would like to make special mention of in this summary are Bob Hope (100) and Andrew Ray (63), both actors. The London-born Hope supposedly had three contests in America as 'Packy East', before becoming a legend of the 'Big Screen', while Andrew, the son of the famous comedian, Ted Ray, shot to prominence at the age of 10 when taking the lead in the film titled 'The Mudlark'. Just like his dad, Andrew was a great fan of the sport and should be remembered as such.

ABREW Charlie *From* Edinburgh. *Died* September 2002, aged 86. Charlie boxed during the same period as his brother, Manuel, and with dark-skinned Scottish boxers being very thin on the ground in those far-off days they became very popular with the fans. A busy fighter, who would have had a much longer fistic account had it not been for the war, he started as a bantamweight in 1934 and was soon fighting 10-round contests. He beat Young McManus twice during his first year of activity, but lost a points decision to Freddie Tennant and lost just six fights out of a total of 19 during his baptismal year in the game, which shows that he was already a useful performer. He was even busier in 1935, especially in April, when he squeezed in four fights, his best win being a knockout over Bill Ewing at Edinburgh. After Freddie Tennant beat him on points in 1936, he took a break from the game for two years and came back in 1939 to lose to George Marsden. There wasn't a lot more, the war putting paid to what had been a busy career. Charlie lost his sight in his later years, but kept his interest in the game and seldom missed a meeting of the London Ex-Boxers Association.

ALBERTINA Jimmy *From* Liverpool. *Died* July 2003, aged 53. An amateur boxer with Bootle's Maple Leaf ABC in his youth, Jimmy went on to become a trainer with the Rotunda ABC and was successful enough to have guided his boys to win over 70 national titles.

AXFORD Neville *From* Bermondsey. *Died* October 2002, aged 68. A good class welter and middleweight as an amateur, having won an NABC title while with the Canterbury, Oxford and Bermondsey club, Neville was tough and showed his mettle in a bout against Jeff Beeston, when he climbed off the deck to win. He had a brief professional career, commencing in 1959 to 1961, during which he beat tough Tony Valledy, Peter Anderson, Ricky McMasters, Vernon Pellai and Gordon Mullen. There were just three defeats to smudge his copybook, but it took the likes of Tony Mancini, Billy Tarrant and George Cottle to inflict them and in each case, Neville gave a good account of himself. In recent years he became mine host at the 'Ring' public house in Blackfriars Road.

BEEKIN Ron *From* Sydney, Australia. *Died* May 2003, aged 60, following a stroke. Ron, a top Australian middleweight during the 1960s, soon ran out of opposition in his native Australia and had to campaign abroad for much of his career. It was in New Zealand in 1967 that he knocked out Kahu Mahanga and, in Tahiti a year later, he outpointed France's Pascal Di Benedetto. He also beat Lee Moto on the Lionel Rose versus Alan Rudkin undercard. However, world class Fate Davis was too good for him and beat the tough Aussie on points back in 1967. His last fight was in 1971 and although past his best he still had enough in the tank to go the distance with Fred Etuati, who had just licked world-rated Charkey Ramon.

BINGHAM Graham *From* Stoke. *Died* 4 February 2003. For many years a BBBoC inspector, Graham had recently been appointed to the Midland Area Council. An unassuming man, who carried out his duties quietly and efficiently, he was also a member of the Midlands EBA.

BINNEY Lionel *From* Sheffield. *Died* December 2002, aged around 80. The brother of Al, and a coloured boy, he was thought to have been boxing before the last war through to 1950. Men on his record include Tommy Griffiths, Billy Barnard (2), Idris Pickens, Tommy Barton, Art Benton, Danny Nagle, Billy Hill (2), Tony Hardwick, Eddie Lartey, Teddy Lewis, Tommy Blears and Dennis Pratt. After retiring from the ring, he stayed in boxing and was involved with the rise of Billy Calvert.

BONNICI Sammy *From* Stepney. Born Valleta, Malta. *Died* 21 September 2002, aged 71. Sammy's professional career would have started sooner had it not been for Army service, but it was while in uniform that he first took up the game. On demobilisation, he came under Jim Pettengell's management and got off to a good start in the professional ranks. A rangy featherweight southpaw, he had a defensive style, took very little heavy punishment, and scored most of his wins on points. In his second year as a professional, he beat some rated fighters in what was a very competitive division. Jackie Turpin, Stan Skinkiss, Don McTaggart and Freddie Hicks were outpointed against a loss to the hard-punching Johnny Butterworth. The following year saw Sammy become recognised as a title contender after beating Teddy Peckham, Bobby Boland and Allan Tanner. Later he performed overseas, where he was on the wrong end of points decisions to Alvaro Cerasini and Fred Galiana, but scored a rare stoppage victory against Marcel Ranvial in Dunkirk. At home, however, he scored fine wins

against the dangerous Alby Tissong and Boswell St Louis before packing his bags and settling in Australia, running up nine fights there before being stopped for the first time in his life by the Empire challenger, George Bracken. On the credit side, he beat Russell Sands twice and Frederico Scarponi. He was past his best at this stage, but carried on fighting for a few years and ran up a credible record before hanging up his gloves. Although wheelchair-bound in his final years, his death came suddenly, leaving a wife, two children and a grandson.

Sammy Bonnici

BRANDWOOD Harold *From* Blackburn. *Died* 28 April 2003, aged 71. Harold's interest in sport led him to become a boxing coach between 1976 and 1986. He had left his native Lancashire by this time and had settled in Henley on Thames. During the year that he started coaching, he and his son, Chris, started the Henley ABC and were actively involved in running the club until a couple of years before his death. Bad health forced him to take a back seat, but by that time he had gone on to qualify as a referee and judge and eventually became President of the Home Counties' Association, the England team manager, and a founder-member of the present Amateur Boxing Association, England Ltd. In his 20s, Harold had been a pro footballer for Scunthorpe United.

BROAD James *From* Wildwood, New Jersey, USA. *Died* 20 November 2001, aged 43. A Former NABF heavyweight champion, James Broad's death passed by unrecorded until early in 2003. By that time he'd been dead for over a year. When the USA boycotted the Moscow Olympics, James lost his chance to make a name for himself as a medallist after taking less than three minutes to flatten Marvis Frazier and looking a certainty for a place in the American squad. He kicked off his paid career in 1981 and won the NABF title from Eddie Gregg in 1984. At that stage, only two men had beaten him, his old rival, Marvis Frazier, and Art Robinson by disqualification. He'd stopped 'Bonecrusher' James Smith in four rounds in his first pro year and also beat Larry Alexander, before losing the title to Tim Witherspoon (1985). He carried on boxing until 1993, but failing eyesight eventually forced his retirement.

BURNS Barney *From* Belfast. *Died* November 2002, aged 59. A regular representative with the Irish amateur team, boxing frequently for Ulster alongside the late Jim Monaghan, Barney boxed 17 times for Ireland and once for a European team. He also contested five ABA championships, against Chris Finnegan, Willie Stack, Alan Edwards and Alan Ball, and was extremely unlucky to lose to Terry McCann in the 1968 middleweight final. Overall, Barney had 124 amateur contests and won both the Ulster and Irish Senior titles in 1964 and the Irish Senior title again in 1967.

CANETE Carlos Ruben *From* Argentina. *Died* March 2003, aged 62. Carlos was the Argentinian champion at feather and junior lightweight levels and also the holder of the South American featherweight championship, his career spanning nine years from its commencement in 1962 to his unsuccessful challenge for the world junior-lightweight title in 1969. He had to journey to Tokyo for his shot at the champion, Hiroshi Kobayashi, and it went the full 15 rounds with the Japanese still champion at the finish. A good puncher, who usually beat his foe inside the scheduled distance, of his first 23 fights only one went the distance and he scored a total of 49 stoppage wins in 89 fights. Seven were draws and losses totalled only six.

CARROLL 'Irish' Pat *From* Detroit, Michigan, USA. *Died* 21 February 2003, aged 83. Known as the 'Pride of Cork Town', being born in Louth, Ireland, Pat was a highly regarded welterweight of the early 1940s, who achieved a fair amount of fame when he and his opponent, Sammy Secreet, both badly cut, were deemed by the referee as not being fit to continue, at the same time, in the seventh round of their 12 February 1941 fight in Detroit. He had earlier beaten Secreet on points in December 1940, but while Secreet went on to become a decent fighter not much more is heard of Carroll. However, we do know that, apart from Secreet, he beat largely unknown fighters such as Johnny Zally, Oliver Johnson, Billy Noeske (2), Pat Thomas, Chinie Gauthier, Joe Doty, Johnny Ryan (2) and Kippy Dumas prior to August 1941, before drawing with Tom

Glaspy in a comeback fight on 1 January 1942. *The Ring* Magazine ratings for 1942 shows Pat listed in group seven of the welterweights.

CASSIDY Paul *From* Bournemouth. *Died* 8 October 2002, aged 56. Paul started boxing in 1968 and for a fighter of that era he was quite a busy performer, but being a heavyweight he had his share of stoppage defeats. He beat Brian Jewett, John Cullen and Rodney Parkinson, but floundered against Peter Boddington, Les Stevens, Eddie Nielson and Graham Sines. However, his winning percentage picked up considerably in 1972 and going into 1976 he'd strung together nine stoppage wins out of 11 victories, the most notable being over Guinea Roger and Dave Roden. Although losing to John L. Gardner in 1975, he outpointed Roger Tighe at Blackpool and, at his best, he could give a good account of himself against the peripheral contenders.

COLLETT Charlie *From* Hemel Hempstead. *Died* 28 June 2003, aged 82. A heavyweight who was active in the years following the war, he began in 1945 with a stoppage win over Fred Clark, whom he was destined to meet on five occasions. None went the distance, but few of Charlie's fights did. Charlie was one of those men who either got his man early or was clobbered himself. Usually, the former was the case. He was a crowd-pleaser who gave the fans action galore and he was usually too good for the fringe contenders of his day, but had mixed fortunes when he stepped up in class. On the debit side, Don Cockell, Ray Wilding, Jack Gardner and Reg Andrews beat him, but there were plenty of good wins too, Tom Benjamin, George James, Frank Ronan, Al Marson, Len Bennett, Gene Fowler and Matt Hardy all failing against him.

COREN Phil *From* London. *Died* August 2002, aged 74. A black cab driver, Phil first came to prominence when running the Box Office and doing some matchmaking for David Braitman and Ronnie Ezra, predominately at the Empress Hall, Earls Court, between 1949 and 1951. Thereafter, he became a well-known fight manager who put together a strong stable of boxers in the 1950s, right through to the 1980s, which included men such as Vincent O'Kine, Denton Ruddock, Sylvester Gordon and Alan Salter.

COSTNER George 'Sugar' *From* Cincinnati, Ohio, USA. *Died* 29 October 2002, aged 79. A classy and top-rated welterweight from Cincinnati, George fought from 1940 to 1950 and had a remarkable record of stoppage wins. He was one of the best men never to have won a championship and was unfortunate in being around at the same time as 'Sugar' Ray Robinson. It was Robinson who inflicted two of his rare stoppage defeats and they came five years apart. Jake LaMotta was too heavy for George and beat the Cincinnati man in six rounds in 1945, but the rest of his record gives an idea of just how classy this man was. He drew with Freddie Dawson, when Dawson was at his best, and claimed the scalps of two world champions in Kid

Gavilan and Ike Williams. In close on 100 fights he lost only 10, running up several series of consecutive knockout wins before his career came to an abrupt end. Having well outpointed the world lightweight champion, Ike Williams, over 10 rounds, it was discovered that he was suffering from detached retinas in both eyes and he never fought again. However, overcoming his blindness, he qualified for a degree in Business Studies at the age of 56, calling it his greatest ever victory.

CROTTY Peter *From* Clonmel, Ireland. *Died* May 2003, aged 77. Peter was a prominent Irish welterweight, who was active in the 1940s and 1950s, and a member of Clonmel ABC when the amateur ranks were bursting with talent. He had a solid punch and was good enough to represent his country in the Helsinki Olympics, his aggressive and uncompromising style making him a great favourite with the fans. Turning out for his country in 17 internationals, he was a durable fighter who could take it as well as being capable of dishing out punishment. Unfortunately, he had a penchant for drink and this affected his health in his last few years.

DAVEY Chuck *From* Detroit, Michigan, USA. *Died* 4 December 2002, aged 77. A college student, Chuck was a good southpaw boxer but lacked the ruggedness to make that final step to world-title fame. When he got his chance in 1953, Kid Gavilan was in the opposite corner and Chuck took a nine-round beating, while the Kid went home still champion. However, he had enough skills to beat three former or future world champions in Ike Williams, Rocky Graziano and Carmen Basilio, and was a solid puncher as well as a competent boxer. He retired on a winning note, beating Alan Kennedy, and became a millionaire after entering the insurance business.

DEMMINGS Doug *From* St Paul, Minnesota, USA. *Died* June 2002, aged 50. Starting in 1973, Doug put together a 31-fight record of 14 wins, 12 losses and one draw before bowing out in 1983. A middleweight, cum light-heavy, his biggest win came against Willie Featherstone, while Danny Brewer, Ray Seales, Alan Minter, Dwight Davison, Alex Blanchard and John Mugabi were among those he shared a ring with. The highlight of his career was a US fight against the great Marvin Hagler in 1978.

DEVINE Chris *From* Chesterfield. *Died* March 2003, aged 43. A good amateur with the St Thomas ABA, gaining a European Junior bronze medal in 1978, Chris turned pro in 1979 and had 23 contests, winning 13, before retiring in 1987. Beat Theo Josephs, Alex Romeo, Winston Burnett (2), Tony Tricker and Mick Cordon and met men like Roy Skeldon, Nick Jenkins, Tee Jay, Bobby Wells, Andy Straughn (2) and Lou Gent. Chris was managed by Billy Shinfield.

DUMAZEL Eddie *From* Cardiff. *Died* 15 April 2003, aged 79. Eddie was one of those busy but inconsistent featherweights operating between 1946 and 1951. He

fought in London only five times, but was very active in rings stretching from Dundee to Cirencester and to the Isle of Man. He also fought in Jamaica and campaigned in the USA. Despite winning only half his fights, he was an experienced craftsman who beat Stan Gossip, Black Bond, Jim McCann, Jackie Lucraft, Peter Guichan and Gene Caffrey. There are some honorable draws on his scoresheet too – Bernard Pugh, Tommy Burns and Hugh Mackie. On the debit side, he conceded defeat to some good-class men in Jackie Turpin, Tommy Bailey, Gus Foran, Ray Fitton, Stan Rowan and Ronnie Draper. After retirement, he held a manager's licence and, among others, he guided Dai Corp, who spoke highly of him.

Eddie Dumazel

DUSSART Kid (Augustus Dussart) *From* Liege, Belgium. *Died* 25 November 2002, aged 81. The Kid was a highly-regarded lightweight who beat our champion, Billy Thompson, for the European title in his first appearance in England. That was back in 1949, but he was an old hand at the game by then, having begun in 1940. Going into the Thompson fight, he had won, lost, and regained the

Belgian featherweight title. He had also collected the European title when beating Emile Di Cristo, before losing it to Roberto Proietti soon after, and when Thompson picked up that same title from Proietti he grabbed his chance to regain it. He was back in London three months later and forced crack Canadian, Solly Cantor, to a draw, but before the year was out the European title had returned to Proietti. He had a six-fight campaign in the USA after beating Mosh Mancini in England, but the States didn't suit him and he returned home without having scored a win. Back home, he picked up the Belgian welterweight title by stopping Emile Delmine, lost it to Harry Mino and regained it seven months later. In between these title clashes he dropped a decision to Charles Humez. He beat Wally Thom and Idrissa Dione before defeating Richard Bouchez for the Belgian middleweight championship in 1957. Following that, there were just five fights left, wins over Emilio Marconi, Jean Ruellet, Jo Janssens and Ben Buker II, and a points loss to Bruno Visintin bringing his career to a close. This busy fighter could boast of having been a champion at four different weights and, had he succeeded to win his country's bantam title at the beginning of his career, that number would have risen to five.

Kid Dussart

ESCOE Vern *From* Toronto, Canada. *Died* September 2002, aged 80. A Canadian heavyweight who campaigned in this country from 1949, he fought Jack London, Johnny Williams and Jack Gardner – all holders at some time of the British title. Gardner's first defeat came at the hands of the Canadian, who repeated his victory in 1950. Escoe had fought some big names like Archie Moore, Nate Bolden and Lee Q Murray, but he never got a shot at the Empire title and returned home to box spasmodically for a couple of years before making two unsuccessful attempts to wrest the Canadian title from Earl Walls. He resurrected his fortunes in 1953, when winning six fights against stiff opposition, but when Ezzard Charles stopped him a couple of years later his best days were over.

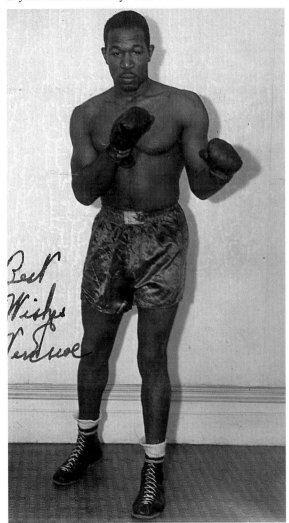

Vern Escoe

ESPINDOLA Daniel *From* Argentina. *Died* 24 November 2002, aged 25. Daniel died from a cerebral haemorrhage two days after losing on points to Fabio Oliva in a contest for the Argentinian super-bantamweight title. A former Latino and Argentinian bantamweight champion, he had an 11-5-4 record.

FAUX Jim *From* Liverpool. *Died* April 2002. Jim, with his wife Betty, formed the Merseyside Left Hook Club at a time when the ex-boxers' movement was at its strongest. They were both indefatigable workers and, despite Betty's incapacity, they travelled throughout the country to promote unity amongst the Ex-Boxers' Associations. Now that they have both passed away, a huge gap is left in the ranks of Liverpools' old-timers.

Albert Finch

FINCH Albert *From* Croydon. *Died* 23 January 2003, aged 76. Never a hard puncher, Albert relied on boxing skills and durability to see him through. He had those qualties in abundance, but had to campaign through 44 fights before getting a shot at the British middleweight title. Losing an extremely close decision to Dick Turpin, he turned the tables a year later when edging out Turpin at Nottingham and, as the British champion, he went to Belgium and held the highly-rated Cyril Delannoit to a

draw. Delannoit was one of only four men to beat Marcel Cerdan. Albert's luck ran out a couple of fights later when he lost his title to Dick Turpin's younger brother, Randolph, a man he'd outpointed two years previously. Moving up to the light-heavyweight division, he made three unsuccessful bids for British title stardom, losing to Don Cockell (1951), Alex Buxton (1954) and Ron Barton (1956), before beating Terence Murphy for the Southern Area title in 1957. He had won the same title at the middleweight limit 10 years prior to that and was proud to point out that he was never beaten for either of them.

FORSYTH Jim *From* Forest Gate, London. *Died* 6 December 2002. This popular Dublin-born MC died suddenly of a heart attack. A true amateur, he was a tireless worker for the sport he loved and never accepted payment for what he did, travelling with local amateur clubs and being a master at controlling crowds. His journeys took him all over London and the Home Counties and he also travelled to Ireland with teams of boxers, being very highly regarded as a boxing official.

FOX Jack *From* Aldgate. *Died* December 2002. Commencing in 1935, Jack fought as a pro until 1942. His known record stretches to 31 fights, during which he beat Jack Forster, Tom Casey, George Hartley and Mick McLaglen, and he was very proud that he was once considered to be good enough to spar with Len Harvey. Although his final days were spent wheelchair-bound, his sudden death still shocked the boxing fraternity, having recently married his long-term girlfriend, Gloria.

FRANSISCUS Johannes *From* Indonesia. *Died* 7 February 2003, aged 19. On 4 February 2003, the Indonesian light flyweight was stopped in the seventh round by Slamet Nizar, in what turned out to be his last contest. In becoming the 18th Indonesian boxer to die from ring-related injuries since 1948, he suffered from a cerebral haemorrhage and died in hospital three days later. Johannes had been undefeated in nine fights up to that stage.

GAVILAN Kid (Gerardo Gonzalez) *From* USA, via Cuba. *Died* 13 February 2003, aged 77. The bolo-punching Kid, one of the all-time greats, died in Miami, blind in one eye and destitute. It was a sad end to this fun-loving and extremely tough scrapper, who never lost a fight inside the distance. His greatness can be measured, strangely enough, by his two defeats against 'Sugar' Ray Robinson. They

Kid Gavilan (right) takes the welterweight title from Johnny Bratton

fought twice at the welterweight limit and there has never been a better welter than Robinson. On both occasions the decision was wafer thin. The 'Keed' was a pure boxer, not a puncher, and in his long and very distinguished career he took on the cream of talent in three weight divisions. His first 28 recorded fights took place in either his native Cuba or in Mexico City, but it is likely that there were many more that were not recorded. They were times when a man could fight every week. His incursion into the USA came in his fourth year as a professional and he twice beat Johnny Williams, who is mostly forgotten today but was a respectable performer in the 1940s. Bigger names soon followed. He lost a decision to Ike Williams, but won against him on two further occasions. His first fight with Robinson occurred in 1948 and by the time they fought again, with the welterweight crown at stake, he had twice licked Ike Williams. He held his form for years and his record is studded with contenders' names: Rocky Castellani, Beau Jack, Laurent Dauthille, Robert Villemain, George 'Sugar' Costner, Tony Janiro, etc. He grabbed the welterweight title in 1951, licking Johnny Bratton, and retained it on seven occasions against men such as Carmen Basilio and Billy Graham. He then unsuccessfully challenged Carl Olsen for the middleweight diadem, before losing the welter title to Johnny Saxton. He fought on for another five years, but his peak years had gone and he began to lose as often as he won. The Kid could still give a good account of himself, but when Yama Bahama beat him in 1958 he announced his retirement. British fight fans would remember him for his two dramatic contests against the then unbeaten Peter Waterman.

GAYFORD Jim *From* Newcastle. *Died* 15 August 2002, aged 87. Boxing under the name of Jim Bennett, and with 'Seaman' Tommy Watson in his corner, he can be traced losing to Dave Penfield at the inaugural Devonshire Club show in December 1934. Having supposedly begun boxing at the St James' Hall from the age of 13 and fighting under names such as 'Gunner Bennett' and 'Young Tucker', it is difficult to track fights down for him. As a heavyweight, he was said to have taken part in an unofficial bout with Freddie Mills at the Exeter Fair in 1939 and sparred with Larry Gains, Joe Louis and Tommy Farr. After the war, Jim became involved with several amateur boxing clubs, both judging and refereeing, and worked as the Physical Education Master at the Vickers Shipbuilders' naval yard. His nephew was Chas Chandler, of the 'Animals', a leading 'pop' group of the 1960s.

GRAY Allan *From* Roehampton. *Died* 8 March 2003. A former amateur opponent of Chris Finnegan and Mark Rowe, Allan had a credible career, the highlight of which was when he was selected to represent London Irish. It was then that he fought Finnegan. Later on, he helped to run several gyms in South London, but in recent years he concentrated on developing his son's career. Allan (junior) is the current holder of the Southern Area Light-middleweight championship.

GRAY Patsy *From* West Ham. *Died* August 2002, aged 29. An outstanding junior with West Ham ABC, Patsy won a schools title before impressively defeating Lee Hobson to take the 1988 ABA junior title. He never turned to the paid ranks, but beat quality opponents such as Marlon Thompson, Danny Oliver, Pat Wright, Nigel Philpotts and Wayne Alexander, currently a top pro, before leaving the sport.

GREAVES Gerry *From* Mold. *Died* 3 March 2002, aged 81. Reported belatedly, it was said that Gerry boxed as a pro throughout the mid to late 1930s, but although no reference was found of that he almost certainly made his reputation as a trainer when producing future pros through the Mold Athletic ABC such as Ron Hammersley and Cyril Jackson. In the 1970s, he joined the Welsh ABA's team of national coaches and in 2000 he was presented with the Sid Matthews' Community Award by the Mold Town Council for his contribution to sport in the town.

GROGAN Ron *From* Paddington. *Died* 6 December 2002, aged 77. A middleweight, Ron boxed from 1945 to 1953 during the boom years that followed the end of the war. His progress was steady, rather than spectacular, but in March 1948 he beat Jimmy Davis, drew with Bob Cleaver and twice beat Johnny Blake, before being thrown in with another contender, Alex Buxton, and being beaten on cuts in five rounds. He had only six fights in the next two years and managed to win only twice, but in 1951 and 1952 he was back in the ring with good company. He won and lost against his former foe, Jimmy Davis, and beat that tough Pole, Gene Szczap. Ron continued to win a few and to lose a few, with the names of fighters such as Wally Beckett, Gordon Hazell, Johnny Sullivan, Ronnie King, Jeff Tite, Billy Carroll and Michael Stack among those he fought that year. However, 1953 was his final year and, after back-to-back losses against Tom Meli and Pat McAteer, the time had come to hang up his gloves.

HACKETT Ron *From* Salford. *Died* January 2003, aged 73. As an amateur boxer for the Flying Angel, Salford, Ron reached the ABA semi-finals in 1950, losing to Stan Knowles. The following year, he won both the light-heavy and heavyweight classes in the Northern Counties championships, but was again beaten in the ABA semis, this time by Scotland's Marshall Bell, when opting to go for the light-heavy title. Although it was thought that he would be joining the paid ranks following this, I cannot trace any contests for him. However, as a pro referee for 29 years before becoming the Central Area Secretary, he served the professionals diligently to the last.

HASSEN Jack *From* Cloncurry, Queensland, Australia. *Died* December 2002, aged 77. Jack had it in him to become one of his country's greats, but when he knocked out Archie Kemp for the Australian lightweight title in 1949, it turned out to be the last fight that he won. Kemp died next day and the new champ couldn't bring himself to punish another man. On the way to the fight, Jack had

beaten Pierre Montane, Rudy Cruz and Andre Famechon. However, as the champion, he was stopped by Freddie Dawson and Joe Brown and lost his title to Frankie Flannery. It was only his 36th fight, but his drive and enthusiasm had gone. His final years saw him losing his last battle after putting up his gamest ever fight against Alzheimer's disease.

HAWTHORNE Stan *From* North Shields. *Died* November 2002, aged 78. One of the hardest-punching lightweights to grace British rings, Stan became 'Cock of the North' when, after running up an impressive tally of quick wins, he beat his old amateur nemesis, Billy Thompson, for the vacant Northern Area Lightweight title. However, having kayoed or stopped 22 of his 26 opponents, after five more victories he was knocked out himself by a single punch from the Belgian champion, Joseph Preys. Hawthorne ran up 11 more contests without loss before his old rival, Thompson, beat him for the vacant British title. Following the Thompson fight, Stan experienced difficulty in getting his weight down to 9st 9lbs, so he went up to welterweight, and campaigned for another couple of years before Eddie Thomas beat him in a title eliminator. While winning 60 of his 75 fights and finishing off 43 of his opponents inside the scheduled distance, only one of his defeats came via a points decision. Add to that a few seasons of booth appearances and you have a remarkable record.

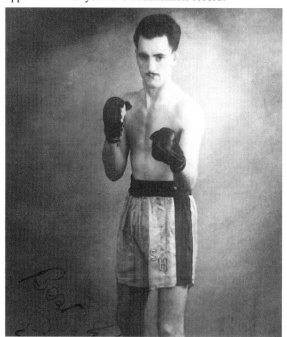

Stan Hawthorne

HAYNES Mark *From* Maidenhead. *Died* 22 February 2003, aged 40. This fine amateur star from Maidenhead ABC died while on a training run, having just taken out a professional licence under the management of Jim Evans.

HAZELGROVE Billy *From* Brighton. *Died* 11 April 2003, aged 86. As a youngster, Billy turned pro just before Neville Chamberlain declared war on Germany. Small wonder then, with Billy having so many bouts at short notice, that he lost many he could have won had training not been interrupted. However, he mixed with the very best of his day and never refused an opponent. Two world champions – Jackie Paterson and Terry Allen – beat him, as did that crack Scottish bantamweight, Peter Keenan, but there were enough good fighters who found his all-action style too much. His first win was against Les Johnson, who was a 28-fight veteran in comparison. Les had beaten Dave Kellar by a knockout and had forced Joe Curran to a draw, but Billy was too good for him and went on to lose only one of his fights that year, against none other than Pat Palmer. Fighting from 1939 to 1950, some of the other names on his record are Kid Bonsor, Sammy Reynolds, Bunty Doran, Jackie Bryce, Jimmy Gill, Jimmy Webster, Charlie Squires, Norman Lewis, Jim Warnock, Tiny Bostock and Henry Carpenter. There were small men galore in those days and the fly and bantamweight divisions oozed with talent. Billy took on them all and never refused a fight.

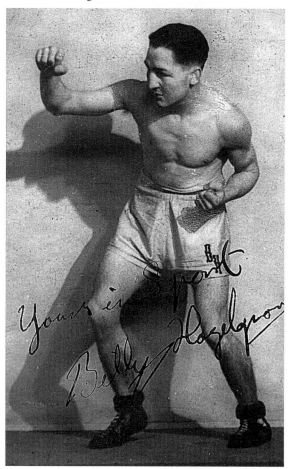

Billy Hazelgrove

HERBERT Harry *From* Bethnal Green. *Died* May 2003, aged 74, after being admitted to hospital with heart problems. A lightweight, he fought from 1949 to 1953. Harry was a good eight-round class scrapper with Johnny Butterworth, Stan Parkes, Terry Riley, Ron Greb, Jackie Horseman and Notting Hill's Roy Paine amongst his victims.

Harry Herbert

HILL Freddie *From* London. *Died* 20 April 2003, aged 82. Freddie will be remembered as one of the top trainers of his day, his base being at his gymnasium in Lavender Hill, South London, from where he conditioned such notables as Chris and Kevin Finnegan, Frankie Taylor, Billy Walker and Alan Rudkin. As an amateur, he boxed for Fitzroy Lodge ABC and although a useful performer he never won a major title. He then turned his attention to training his clubmates, his brother, Peter, being by this time the ABA middleweight champion. When he decided to go over to the paid side of the game, he and Sam Burns

established the Lavender Hill base and, thanks to Freddie's expertise, the apellation 'Lavender Hill Mob' became synonymous with quality fighters. Freddie never lost his passion for the game and was a regular face at ex-boxers' meetings.

HOLDEN Doug *From* Perth, Scotland. *Died* 7 November 2002, aged 65. A top-class amateur with the Perth Railways ABC, winning a Scottish middleweight title in 1959, Doug was proud to wear the Scottish vest on numerous occasions, taking on good men such as the much-heavier Len Hobbs and Genadi Schatkov, the European champion, among many others. Doug never turned pro and could number Bill Bannon and Tommy McGuinness among his many victims before retiring and making a success out of scrap metal.

HUGHES Winston *From* Northampton. *Died* October 2002, aged 86. A former BBBoC timekeeper and amateur referee, Winston was born in Wales and moved to London as a boy. He boxed for the London Hospital ABC before the war and during the conflict he enlisted in the RAF. A keen supporter of the Northampton boxing club, he was also a tireless charity worker and will be much missed.

KEOUGH Jackie *From* Cleveland, Ohio, USA. *Died* October 2002, aged 76. This middleweight was Randolph Turpin's last opponent before he wrested the world title from 'Sugar' Ray Robinson and boxed from 1947 to 1954. Never world-class, but an efficient and brainy boxer, he was not a puncher of note as his record shows, with a sole knockout win against Ike Stevenson in 1950. The breakdown of his record is 25 wins, 15 losses and two draws. Apart from Turpin, the other world-rated men who beat him were Rocky Castellani, Bobby Dykes, Joe Rindone and Eugene Hairston. He packed in punching for pay to become a very active referee in his local area and was a judge at the Ali versus Chuck Wepner fight in 1975. He was proud to be inducted into the Greater Cleveland Sports' Hall of Fame.

KING Ron *From* Walworth. *Died* May 2003, aged 72. A former middleweight and good journeyman fighter, Ronnie had a shaky start in the pro ranks. However, after losing his first two fights he settled down to put together another 20 fights with only two losses – one of those being on a foul after he had run up a clear points lead. Ron was a hard puncher and won only three fights on points, stopping Steve Brimah, Morley Nightingale, Bert Middleton and Jackie Allpress amongst others, but after being outpointed by Ron Grogan over eight rounds in 1952 his ambition faded.

LAKE Lennie *From* Paddington. *Died* 18 April 2003. A former boxing trainer with impressive connections to some class fighters, Lennie had one pro fight, beating Al Wilson on a foul in 1955, before working as a trainer with the late George Francis at the Wellington gym in Highgate. Trevor Cattouse, Lotte Mwale, Pat McCann, Glenn McCrory, Lou

Gent and Devon Bailey were just a few of the men he handled and through his connection with Francis he was a cornerman to John Conteh when the Liverpudlian fought Yugoslavia's Mate Parlov. He was also one of the stable that guided Jimmy Cable during Jimmy's days as British and European champion. Cable's title win over Said Skouma was voted contest of the year at our 1984 Awards Luncheon and Lennie's tactical advice was instrumental in bringing the European title home to Britain.

Lennie Lake   Philip Sharkey

LAMPERTI Gracieux *From* Corsica, France. *Died* 22 November 2002, aged 69. Gracieux boxed mainly in the area of Marseilles from 1953 to 1963, cleaning up most of the Continental opposition en-route to his aquisition of the European featherweight title, which came with a points victory over Italy's Sergio Caprari in 1959. He was the holder of the French title at the time and had some good wins to swell his record, twice outpointing Aldo Pravisani, stopping Jean Sneyers and drawing with Giordano Campari. Surprisingly, he didn't fare too well with British opposition, Teddy Peckham stopping him early in his career and Percy Lewis edging him out in a dull 12 rounder in London, although he came back to beat Lewis in his favourite Marseilles' ring. The Frenchman defended his title successfully three times before losing it to Alberto Serti and gave the world champion, Davey Moore, quite a fight before going down on points. He was approaching 30 when Howard Winstone stopped him in 1963 and ran down the curtain on his career.

Gracieux Lamperti

LEWIS Laurie *From* Blackpool. *Died* 15 May 2003, aged 76. Laurie started promoting in the early 1960s and established himself in the north with some value-for-money shows, matching Maurice Cullen with Terry Edwards for the British lightweight title in 1967. This turned out to be the last boxing promotion to be held in the famous St James' Hall in Newcastle. Later on, he joined forces with Jack Solomons to put on the Muhammad Ali versus Brian London world title fight.

LUDICK Willie *From* South Africa. *Died* 13 May 2003, aged 62. Willie held South African titles in the welterweight and middleweight divisions. What is often forgotten is that this southpaw fought and won a fight that was recognised in South Africa as being for the world welterweight crown. His credentials were impressive, having beaten Ralph Dupas, Brian Curvis and Oscar Miranda to get his chance for the 'big one' against Jean Josselin in 1966. In a bruising and bloody battle, Willie came home on points and with it gained local recognition as being world champion. His days at the top ended when Curtis Cokes twice stopped him, their first fight being for the universally recognised world title. By then, he had become too big for the welters and moved up a division, but he was nowhere near as effective as a middleweight, the tough bouts with Josselin and Cokes having taken their

toll. Although he was good enough to beat Johnny Kramer, Dick Duffy, Terry McTigue and Fabio Bettii, after Pierre Fourie stopped him with the national middleweight title at stake, Willie called it a day.

LUNNY Ray *From* San Francisco, California, USA. *Died* May 2003, aged 83. Nicknamed 'The Pride of the Mission', Ray was a hard-punching featherweight who had more than 100 fights as an amateur and professional. Turning pro in 1938, he met quite a few of the top men, beating Vern Bybee (2), George Latka, Claude Varner, Lew Feldman and Richie Fontaine, winning and losing to Richie Lemos, and being outpointed in a non-title match against Chalky Wright among his highlights. The loss at the hands of Wright was his first defeat in the paid ranks, having run up 32 straight. Retiring in 1944, after losing to Lulu Constantino and Willie Joyce, he became the boxing coach at Stanford University for nearly 25 years. He was extremely proud of his son, Ray, who was a two-time Golden Gloves champion before turning pro and later losing to Alfredo Escalera for the WBC junior-lightweight title in 1976.

McKENZIE Ian *From* Ayr. *Died* July 2003, aged 62. Ian was a former Scottish middleweight champion, having turned professional in 1961 and winning the vacant title in 1963 with an impressive win over Willie Hart. He had won 12 fights up to his ascension to the Scottish crown with only one loss to Steve Gibson to blot his copybook, but, as champion, his form seemed to desert him. He drew with Dennis Read, but lost a further nine fights before hanging up his gloves in 1967. As an amateur he represented Scotland on a number of occasions, winning a bronze medal at the 1961 European Championships, and reached the ABA welterweight final the same year, losing to Tony Lewis.

MAMBWE Patrick *From* Kitwe, Zambia. *Died* March 2003, aged 58. Turning pro in 1963, Patrick had seven bouts behind him, with one defeat, when he came to Europe in 1967 to widen his horizons. In six bouts, he lost to Glyn Davies, Tommaso Galli and Evan Armstrong, drew with Davies and Armstrong and beat Tommy O'Connor. He next surfaced in Lusaka, Zambia, outpointing John McCluskey over 10 rounds in March 1974, before winning the vacant Commonwealth flyweight title when stopping the Australian, Gwyn Jones, inside nine rounds. He didn't appear to fight again and the Commonwealth title was vacated in 1979.

MANCINI Lennie *From* London. *Died* 6 June 2003, aged 79. The elder brother of Dennie, a nephew of Alf and uncle of Tony, Lennie was born into a world of boxing and served the sport as a promoter and matchmaker. In his days as a BBBoC licence-holder, he worked alongside Mickey Duff, Tommy Gibbons, Jim Wicks and promoters, Braitman and Ezra. Everyone worth a candle in the fight game knew Lennie and it's safe to say that everyone had affection for him. He was a great collector of boxing magazines, having

a full set of *Rings*, and had in recent years had completed his run of *Boxing News*. Boxing was his main love, but he also had a wide knowledge of other sports. His collection of soccer memorabilia filled a room in his Hammersmith home and he was a font of knowledge on all aspects of sport.

MARATHE Dr Ramesh *From* Stoke. *Died* May 2003, aged 65. A long-serving Board of Control official, with a strong love for the game, Dr Marathe died of a heart attack in his hometown of Stoke on Trent.

MARTIN George *From* Hull and Bermondsey, London. *Died* July 2003, aged 68. Prior to turning pro in 1956, George had a distinguished amateur career, which started with St Mary's, Hull, where he won an ABA Youth title, before he moved down to London to win the ABA light-welter title in 1954, while boxing for the Army and the famous Fisher ABC. A pro until 1959, he beat Ray Akwei, Johnny Mann, Armand Savoie, Arthur Donnachie and Teddy Best, but lost to Billy 'Spider' Kelly in an eliminator for the British lightweight title in 1958. He then appeared to lose ambition, being beaten by Darkie Hughes, Johnny Kidd, Spike McCormick, Jimmy Brown and Dave Stone, and retired the following year.

George Martin

MARTINEZ Vince *From* Paterson, New Jersey, USA. *Died* 29 January 2003, aged 73. A good-looking, world-class welterweight, Vince met and usually beat the best men of his day yet, when his chance came to grab the vacant world title, he surprisingly lost to Virgil Akins. Few challengers have been better qualified than Vince, who had beaten Kid Gavilan (2), Lester Felton, Chico Vejar, Gil Turner, Art Aragon, Larry Baker and Peter Muller. Points losses to Tony DeMarco and Ralph Dupas marred a very impressive record, but he was a true pro, putting it down to experience and getting on with his career. Vince was technically very accomplished, but he was also a good finisher if he got an opponent in trouble, 35 of his 66 victories coming via the short route.

Vince Martinez

MATTA Hector *From* Puerto Rico. *Died* in early 2003, aged 57. A decent lightweight who started out in 1968, he is remembered in Britain for his defeat over 10 rounds at the hands of Ken Buchanan. Although his main claim to fame was in twice beating Saoul Mamby, the future WBC light-welterweight champion, and drawing with Chu Chu Malave, he was not afraid to take the big boys on, losing to men like Roberto Duran, Tony Petronelli, Esteban DeJesus, Joao Henrique, Adolfo Viruet, Wifred Benitez and Hector Camacho.

MATTHEWS Harry 'Kid' *From* Seattle, Washington, USA. *Died* 21 February 2003, aged 80. Harry was a brilliant protege of the legendary manager, Jack Hurley, who, back in the 1950s took him nearly to the summit, only to find Rocky Marciano in the way. When they met, a shot at the heavyweight championship was the prize and Matthews was expected to streak ahead on points in the early stages before succumbing to the first heavy punch that Rocky threw. However, the fight lasted less than two

rounds. As a heavyweight contender, Harry's bubble had been burst, but he is unfairly remembered for that loss alone. In a career spanning from 1937 to 1956, he had an enviable scoresheet, with victories over Al Hostak, Bernie Reynolds, Phil Muscato, Lloyd Marshall, Rex Layne, Anton Raadik and Freddie Beshore. The list goes on and on. It was one year after losing to Marciano that he lost to Don Cockell, but he was at the tail-end of his career and Don licked him twice more. Although a match over here with Johnny Williams fell through, Harry got out on a winning note when he outscored the former champ, Ezzard Charles, in his penultimate fight.

MELI Tom *From* Belfast. *Died* 14 February 2003, aged 72. A man of Italian ancestry, Tom was born in Belfast and started boxing in 1945 with the St George's ABC. He commenced pro boxing in 1948 and in his third fight created a surprise when he stopped Jackie Brown. Thereafter, he made steady progress towards the Irish middleweight championship, which he won from Jackie Wilson in 1951. Tom had established himself as a genuine fighter at this stage, having beaten Gerry McCready, the dangerous Sammy Sullivan and India's Johnny Nuttall. In 1950, and after he won his middleweight championship, he beat Bert Sanders and George Roe. Then, after Michael Stack outpointed him, he stepped up a division and took the Irish light-heavyweight title from Garnett Denny. He next lost two points decisions to Richard Armah before coming back to beat Ron Grogan, drawing with Wally Beckett and losing to Les Allen. Although still active in 1955, by then he'd relinquished his light-heavyweight crown, being a natural middleweight who did not relish conceding weight. After losing his middleweight crown to George Lavery in 1955, he called it a day.

MILLIGAN Terry *From* Belfast, Northern Ireland. *Died* June 2003, aged 73. A representative of Ireland's amateur team in the years following the war, while boxing for Short & Harland, Milligan had one of the most outstanding records of any amateur. In nearly 350 fights he tasted defeat only 13 times, having started as a featherweight and fighting through six weight divisions before retiring as a middleweight. During his remarkable career, he won six Irish Senior titles, an Empire gold medal and, at European level, a silver and bronze. He was, in total, an Irish and Ulster champion no fewer than 11 times.

MIROSCHNICHENKO Alex *From* Kostanau, Kazakhstan. *Died* May 2003, aged 39. This former Olympic bronze medallist will be remembered here for his first-round stoppage over the Bradford heavyweight, Steve Garber. As an amateur he lost to Riddick Bowe, who forced him out of the silver medal position in the Seoul Olympics of 1988, but in 22 pro fights he lost only one. His death was caused by a fall from a balcony in his apartment block.

MONAGHAN Jim *From* Derry. *Died* 18 September 2002, aged 62. Harry Doherty was a school friend of Jim Monaghan, the former Irish heavyweight, and reports as

follows. Jim was a good journeyman heavyweight who never refused a fight and, as an amateur, he fought Billy Walker and Dante Cane, while in the pro ranks he unsuccessfully challenged for the Northern Ireland title in 1966. He had some good wins against Gerry Hassett, Eric Fearon, Lloyd Walford and Rocky James, but could never get past Carl Gizzi, who beat him five times.

MOUZON Wesley *From* Philadelphia, Pennsylvania, USA. *Died* 8 July 2003, aged 75. Wesley was one of those very good fighters who were considered as 'dangerous' and therefore often avoided by men with title ambitions. Boxing out of Philadelphia, where he did the bulk of his fighting, he forced Ike Williams to a 10-round draw in only his second year of scrapping and, in that same year, he lost to Allie Stolz, who had fought for the world lightweight championship in 1942. Bob Montgomery underestimated him in 1946 and paid the price when he was kayoed in two rounds, but in a return for Montgomery's world title a couple of months later, Wesley was stopped in eight rounds. It was the last time that he tasted defeat, a detached retina putting an end to his career. He later became one of the great modern trainers and worked with Tony Thornton and Dwight Muhammed Qawi, among many others.

MUNDEN Len *From* Bristol. *Died* 3 October 2003, aged 90. An old opponent of Bruce Woodcock, Len started boxing back in the 1930s, giving his first fight as being held in 1930 at Bedminster Arcade, Bristol. "I beat Billy Davis," said Len. He would have been 17 at the time, but the first traceable fight on his record occurred in 1935 in Hackney. Although an inconsistent performer, like most big men he could either bang out a stoppage win or go under himself. He beat Plymouth's Dick Allen, George Hartley, Jack Horton, George Ward, among others, but was beaten by Canada's Packey Paul, Dom Lydon and Frank Hough. After losing his left arm in an aircrash, whilst serving in the Middle-East as a parachute instructor in the last war, Len went on to become a coach driver! Taking out a promoter's licence in the 1950s, he soon found himself subsidising this venture as Bristol turned out to be a tough area to promote in, so he became a manager and, in later years, a BBBoC inspector.

O'DONNELL Hugh *From* Herne Bay. *Died* circa 1999. One of those whose passing slipped through the net unnoticed until his son made enquiries about his father's career. Hugh, who turned pro in 1949 and was active until 1954, had his most notable win late in 1951 when he impressively beat the former ABA lightweight champion, Ronnie Latham. By this time, he had teamed up with Paddington's Tommy Ryan for a season on the booths and continued with his booth activities for many years after his last 'official' fight. Later, he became coach for the Kingston ABC, by which time he was living in that area. His last known address was in Streatham and he made infrequent appearances at ex-boxers' meetings, usually as a 'minder' to Alex Steene.

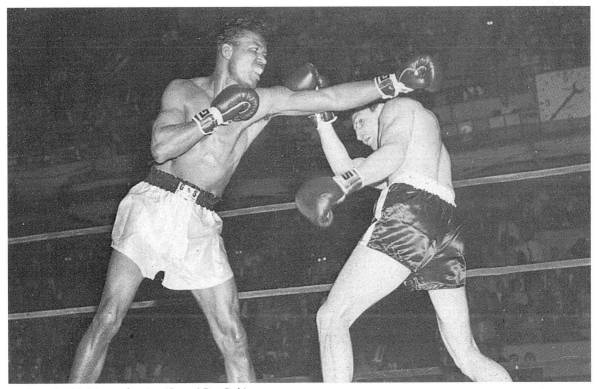

Paul Pender (right) seen beating 'Sugar' Ray Robinson

PENDER Paul *From* Brooklyn, Mass, USA. *Died* 12 January 2003, aged 72. Recognised as one of the underrated world middleweight champions who, because of fragile hands, had to rely on good boxing rather than punching, he is remembered in this country for three fights with Terry Downes, to whom he lost and regained the world middleweight championship. Having won his title from a fading 'Sugar' Ray Robinson and repeating his victory five months later, he had been lightly-regarded before this but went on to prove himself a good champion by beating Carmen Basilio and Downes. There are some notable wins on his early record, such as points victories over Ernie 'The Rock' Durando, Roy Wouters, Otis Graham and Sonny Horne and a draw with Joe Rindone. He also stopped Norman Hayes and Ted Olla before losing on points to Gene Fullmer, but came back after a year of inactivity to beat Ralph 'Tiger' Jones. It is worth noting that between his loss to Fullmer and his regaining of the middleweight crown from Downes in 1962, he was never beaten.

RILEY Terry *From* Liverpool. *Died* 23 February 2003, aged 77. After a successful amateur career with the Liverpool Star ABC, Terry turned pro. That was in July 1947 and he got off to a good start by beating Jack Crossley and Jackie Turpin, before going up into the eight-round class and losing a close points decision to Bernard Pugh. He carried on until 1953, running up a record of 48 contests with wins over name fighters like Bert Jackson, Johnny Molloy, Bernard Pugh (they met three times), Denny Dawson and Kid Tanner. He lost to Ray Fitton three times and once to Teddy Peckham, but held Gene Caffrey to a draw.

RIX Fred *From* Croydon. *Died* 14 May 2003, aged 63. A long-established amateur trainer with Sir Philip Game ABC, later managing of an impressive array of pro fighters, Fred's life was devoted to the fight game and he was instrumental in developing Frank Bruno from a novice amateur to an ABA champion. Chris Blake, the McKenzie brothers from Croydon, Pat Doherty and Frankie Lucas are just some of the many aspiring amateurs who came under his umbrella. Doherty stayed with Fred when both of them turned to the punch-for-pay side of the game. The McKenzie brothers, Duke, Dudley and Winston all paid Rix tribute. "He took me to my first domestic title", said Duke. Others in his stable were Mickey Durvan, Tony Burke and Duke's cousin, Lee McKenzie, all three becoming Southern Area champions.

RONE Brad *From* Las Vegas, Nevada, USA. *Died* 18 July 2003, aged 34. Strictly an 'opponent', Rone had lost 41 of his 51 fights but his record belies his true ability. He lost, predictably, to some big names like Michael Grant, Vaughn Bean, Orlin Norris, Hasim Rahman, Kirk Johnson and at European level, to Sinan Samil Sam. Sadly, he suffered heart problems following a loss to Billy Zumbrum and died in hospital, but had courage in abundance.

ROSA Chico *From* Hawaii. *Died* in California in 2003, aged 78. Turning pro in 1945, Chico ran up 17 straight wins, over men such as Speedy Cabanella, Rush Dalma, Henry Davis, Manny Ortega and the future world feather-weight champion, Sandy Saddler, before losing to Dado Marino in 1948. He then lost more than he won, being defeated by Charley Riley, Davis, David 'Kui Kong' Young, Glen Flanagan, Eddie Chavez and Lauro Salas, before bowing out after losing to Flash Elorde in May 1956. He also drew with Harold Dade, the former world bantamweight champion. From a boxing family, both his brother and uncle, Adolph Samuels, being boxers, he held both the Territorial bantam and featherweight titles and was recognised as a box-fighter who could tangle with the best of them.

ROZADILLA Larry *From* NYC, New York, USA. *Died* 11 January 2003, aged 72. A very experienced judge and referee, Larry formed an interest in boxing whilst in service uniform and had a very brief boxing career before going to college, where he graduated and earned his master's degree. He officiated at the Mike Tyson versus Buster Douglas fight in Tokyo and was referee in some of Roy Jones' early fights.

SADD Dick *From* Norwich. *Died* September 2002, aged 84. This elder brother of the renowned 'Ginger', Dick made a tremendous contribution not only to Norwich and District boxing, but to the sport in general. He was chairman of the local Ex-Boxers' Association, the editor of that association's newsletter and a trainer to the Norwich Boys' Club, where he developed the amateur career of Herbie Hide. Although associated with boxing for most of his life, Dick was a highly intelligent man who could have made a career for himself in the Army, but turned down a commission and returned to civilian life. His family ties were strong and he devoted his time to bringing up his six children. Also, his love was boxing and he, more than most, kept the local club going. He had a stroke in his later years, but fought his way back courageously and learned to speak again, while still managing to produce a local magazine devoted to Eastern Counties' boxing, which under his circumstances was a remarkable achievement.

SCHUTTE Abri *From* South Africa. *Died* 5 July 2003, aged 66. A leading South African judge and referee, Abri first made his name as an amateur boxer when representing his country in 1959. The following year, he won the national light-middleweight title and represented South Africa in the Rome Olympics, where he was eliminated in the early rounds by the Australian, John Bukowski. In later years, he trained under-privileged youngsters in the Soweto region.

SELPA Andres *From* Argentina. *Died* February 2003, aged 71. Andres fought from 1951 to 1968 and had a total of 190 contests. Only two of these were held outside of the South American continent, the last being a loss to Bob Foster in Washington right at the end of his outstanding

career. He contested five title fights at middle and light-heavy, winning them all, but was relieved of the Argentinian middleweight title by the Argentine Federation when he was outpointed by Eduardo Lausse in 1958. It is unfortunate for boxing that Selpa confined his activities to his own part of the world, but such was the density of boxing activity that he could earn a steady living without travelling too far. Names that stand out on his record are Chico Vejar, Carlos Monzon (they boxed a draw in January 1966, followed by a points win for Monzon two months later), Miguel Angel Paez (they met five times), Farid Salim, Fernando 'Sugar Boy Nando' Muller and Rocky Rivero. The rest of his record reads like a who's who of South American fighters.

SHAFREN Roy *From* Harrow. *Died* 27 May 2003, aged 70. After a useful career in the amateur ranks as a member of Harrow ABC, Roy was conscripted into the RAF and had several contests as their middleweight representative. With a respectable record as a simon-pure he turned professional under Les Roberts' management in 1953, having a brief career during which he beat Sid Reardon, Al Wilson (twice) and Fulham's Andy Oliver. When Sonny Quinn knocked him out with a body punch in Belfast in the summer of 1955, Roy called it a day.

Howard Sharpe

SHANNON Robert junior *From* Manchester. *Died* 22 June 2003, aged 22, from injuries suffered in a car crash. The son of the Manchester trainer of the same name, Robert became one of the country's youngest cornermen when helping his dad look after men like Wayne Rigby, Mike Holden, Michael Murray, Gary Hibbert and many others.

SHARPE Howard *From* Harlesden. *Died* 10 April 2003, aged 55. A middleweight with a punch, Howard's career reached its peak in 1972 when, as a substitute, he stopped the former champion, Mark Rowe, in the first round at the Albert Hall. It was a short-lived moment of glory, ending three weeks later when he was stopped by Don McMillan. Having arrived here from Jamaica when still in short pants, he shone at boxing and won a British Schools' title at the age of 12, but as a professional, although his power punching helped to gain him the Southern Area middleweight title, the national title eluded him.

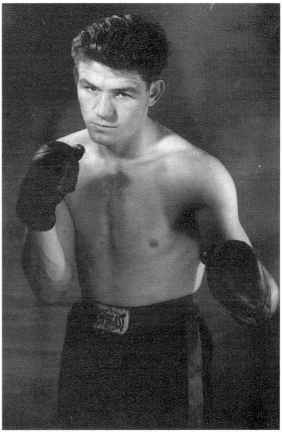

Johnny Sullivan

SULLIVAN Johnny (Johnny Hallmark) *From* Preston. *Died* 4 February 2003, aged 70. The son of 'Battling' Sullivan and the elder brother of Sammy, Johnny was the member of the family who brought it the highest honour

when he won the British middleweight title by stopping Gordon Hazell in one round in 1954. By then, he was a seasoned veteran with over 70 fights under his belt, having beaten Henry Hall, fought for the Empire title, and making one incursion into Canada and America, winning four out of his five fights there. From December 1955 he campaigned in America, but because he set his sights very high it took some time for him to settle down. World class Eduardo Lausse stopped him in Cleveland, as did Rory Calhoun, but Johnny beat Willie Troy and Jackie LaBua and dropped two decisions to Joey Giambra. Despite the number of losses on his account sheet, he'd done well in all his fights and had proved that he could give the world's best plenty to think about. He returned home and beat Arthur Howard, but when Yolande Pompee beat him, his best days were over. It was the loss of his title by disqualification to Pat McAteer that led him to fight in the States and he returned there for one more fight in 1960, but he didn't have the old spark and was beaten. At the end of a long career of nearly 100 fights, he'd proved to be a durable, tough and very popular fighter.

TAYLOR Harry *Died* 27 July 2003, aged 71. The founding editor of the *Black Country Bugle*, perhaps the finest local paper for boxing content in this country, Harry wrote under the pen-name of Frank Sayers. As an enthusiastic chronicler of Midlands' boxing history, he became an expert on bare-knuckle history and his boxing column drew comment and queries throughout the Commonwealth, leading to readers' reminiscences often revealing facts that the trade press had missed. In his 31 years with the 'Bugle', Harry did as much or more than any other man to preserve and record the history of boxing in the Black Country.

VALLADARES Jaime (Chico de Oro) *From* Ecuador. *Died* February 2003, aged 66. Jaime was another of those very experienced South-American boxers whose career seemed to go on to eternity, having started trading punches in 1952 at the age of 16 and boxing for 11 years before tasting defeat. He beat globe-trotting Don Johnson in three rounds in 1965 and later forced Carlos Teo Cruz to a draw. He also went on to draw with Hiroshi Kobayashi, but lost to the Jap when the world-junior-lightweight title was on the line. Was the feather and junior-lightweight champion of his country.

VETOUX Alexander *From* Ukraine. *Died* 22 June 2003, aged 23. Having challenged unsuccessfully for the European welterweight title against Frederic Klose a week earlier, Alexander tragically drowned while swimming with friends in the Dniepr River. In 23 fights, he had only been defeated once, by Klose, and among his victims were British fighters, Karl Taylor (3) and Howard Clarke and Ilia Spassov, Adam Skosana and Nico Welcome. A WBC Youth and WBF International champion, he was managed by Phillipe Fondu.

WARRICK Alf *From* Reading. *Died* September 2002,

aged 81. Beginning his amateur career in 1933 as a schoolboy before turning pro in 1937, any progress to be made was halted by World War Two. After the war, he turned to coaching amateurs and, among others, he trained Ken Cook at Maidenhead ABC and Gerald John at Slough, before moving on to Bracknell and Reading ABC's. Alf was firstly Vice-Chairman and then the Chairman of the Reading EBA between 1977 and 1986.

WEBBER Stan *From* Paddington. *Died* September 2002, aged 73. A lightweight, Stan turned pro in 1949, losing a four rounder on points to Terry Bullivant, but despite the poor start he was unbeaten in his first nine contests in 1952, beating men such as Wally Webb (2), George Goodsell and Arthur Carrington. He also beat Roy Groome, Maurice Murfitt and Al Sharpe before stepping out of his class against Ron Richardson, who stopped him inside two rounds. A good six-round fighter who won more than he lost, he retired in 1953.

WELLS Ken (Ken Wellstead) *From* Poole. *Died* October 2002. A lightweight, who was both an old opponent and stablemate of Harry Legge, between 1944 and 1948 they fought eight times in rings as far apart as Torquay, Kidderminster, Weymouth and the Scilly Isles. They also fought on countless occasions in the booths. Harry described Ken as a well-built fighter with a punch, but one who never took the game seriously. He was an accomplished footballer and cricketer and a counties' standard half-miler.

WILLIAMS Mac (Malcolm Williams) *From* Cardiff. *Died* February 2003. A respected manager and trainer for over 30 years, Mac had a stable of fighters who won between them one British title and 14 area championships. Being based in Wales, he was always assured of being busy, but he spread his influence beyond the borders of his native country. Ricky Porter from Shepherds Bush came under his wing at a time when his fortunes were looking bad. Mac changed all that, as Ricky went on to stop the European champion in Paris and to give Ralph Charles a sterling battle at the Albert Hall. Some of the other outstanding fighters in his charge were Des Rea, who won a British title, Steve Sims, Billy Waith and Dai Corp.

WOOD Bobby *From* Northampton. *Died* July 2003, aged 71. A lightweight who was active from 1950 to 1952, he had 26 professional contests in which he beat Laurie Henry of Jamaica, Jeff Holdsworth, Roy Groome, Ronnie Gill and Jack Sommerville, among others. He was taken from the crowd, where he was a spectator, to box Gill and won in the first round. Bobby was an early opponent of Freddie King, who was on his way to a title fight with Ronnie Clayton, and he also went the distance with hard-punching Charlie Tucker. In 1951 he dropped a decision to Reg Kray at the NSC and bowed out five months later with a good win over Tom Berry. As an amateur, he boxed for the well-known Roadmenders club, where he won an NABC title in 1948.

A Boxing Quiz with a Few Below the Belt (Part 8)

Compiled by Les Clark

QUESTIONS

1. Between 1989 and 1990, Iran Barkley contested world Middleweight titles on three occasions. Against whom and for which belts?

2. In 1995, Javier Castillejo lost his European light-middleweight title to Laurent Boudouani. Against whom did he regain it and where?

3. The first world super-middleweight title was won by Murray Sutherland. Against whom?

4. Can you name a former Argentinian world champion who retired with a record of 136 fights, 117 wins, while losing only four and drawing 14?

5. There are only three 'Father and Sons' inaugurated into the International Boxing Hall of Fame. Can you name them?

6. Gerardo Gonzalez died this year, 2003. By what name did he fight under?

7. Who did Alan Minter beat in 1978 to win the vacant European middleweight title?

8. This Italian fighter beat Shane Mosley, but lost to Vernon Forest as an amateur. As a pro he went on to beat an Englishman for a vacant European title and then won and defended the WBU title nine times. He also won and lost the IBF title. Name him?

9. Can you name the ex-pro who returned to the vest and was runner-up in the 2002 ABA finals?

10. Where would you find the following venues, which in the past have been used for British title fights – Shawfield Park, Coney Beach Arena, Premierland, Caesars Palace, The Pier Pavilion?

11. Leotis Martin, who had a great battle against Thad Spencer in England, won his last fight before retiring due to a detached retina. Who did he beat?

12. Leon Spinks beat Ali for the world title in only his eighth fight. Who was the referee for that fight?

13. How many times did Dennis Andries contest a British title?

14. Who was Angelo Dundee's first world champion?

15. Carlos DeLeon, who fought the bore draw with Johnny Nelson, also fought another British fighter. Can you name him?

16. Marvin Camel was the first world cruiserweight champion. Who did he beat to win the title?

17. Where did Montell Griffin's first bout outside the US take place and against whom?

18. What was the nickname of Darrin van Horn?

19. Who did John Conteh face in his first major title fight?

20. Who was the referee when Carmen Basilio beat Sugar Ray Robinson for the world middleweight title?

21. Which British boxer fought 24 times in world title fights, losing only five times?

22. Steve Collins defeated Sam Storey for the Irish middleweight title in 1988. In which city did this take place?

23. How many times did Dennis Andries contest world titles?

24. Richie Woodhall beat Vito Gaudiosi for the Commonwealth middleweight title. Against whom was his first defence?

25. In the 1960s there was a WBA heavyweight elimination tournament between eight fighters. Can you name them?

26. Lee Savold twice fought Bruce Woodcock. At which venues did the contests take place?

27. Primo Carnera lost his last three fights to the same man. Can you name him?

28. In 28 bouts, James J. Corbett contested the world heavyweight title on five occasions. Can you name his opponents?

29. After Max Schmeling's loss to Joe Louis for the world heavyweight title, he never again fought outside Germany. How many bouts did he have after this defeat?

30. Former world heavyweight champion Ernie Terrell's first two defeats were by the same man. Can you name him?

31. Who was the referee for Colin Jones' first British welterweight title defence against Kirkland Laing?

32. Where was Eddie Futch born?

33. Which year was amateur boxing included in the Boxing Yearbook?

34. Can you name the Liverpool middleweight whose last fight was a points win over Brendan Ingle, in defence of his Central Area middleweight title?

35. How many times did Primo Carnera fight in England?

36. Can you name the British gold medallists in the 2002 Commonwealth Games?

37. What did referees, Roland Dakin, John Coyle and Harry Gibbs, have in common?

38. This boxer beat Billy Thomas for the vacant Welsh featherweight title, successfully defended it against him two years later, but lost to Howard Winstone in a challenge for the European and British featherweight title. Can you name him?

39. Who was the heavyweight champion of the world with only one eye?

40. Can you name a British featherweight who won three titles in one fight?

41. Can you name a British heavyweight who lost to Alfredo Evangelista in a European title challenge, followed by defeats at the hands of John L. Gardner and Gordon Ferris whilst twice challenging for the vacant British heavyweight title?

42. Can you name a boxer who took part in 34 world featherweight title bouts?

43. How many 1991 ABA champions went on to win a major professional title?

44. Barry Michael faced Rocky Lockridge in 1987 at Windsor for the IBF super-featherweight title. Can you name a boxer on the undercard who, three years later, won a world title himself?

45. Which boxer broke the unbeaten run of former European champion, Jim McDonnell?

46. In 1966, Howard Winstone was the British featherweight champion. Who was rated as his number-one challenger in the Boxing News annual ratings on 31st December of that year?

47. Do you know 'Sugar' Ray Leonard's middle name?

48. The great Marvin Hagler lost only three times during his career. Can you name his conquerors?

49. How many times did Charlie Magri defend the British flyweight title?

50. Can you name the fighter who faced Chris Christensen for the vacant Danish welterweight title and, at a later date, the middleweight title, before losing on points to Pat McAteer for the British and British Empire middleweight titles?

Leading BBBoC License Holders: Names and Addresses

Licensed Promoters

Jack Bishop
76 Gordon Road
Fareham
Hants
PO16 7SS
0132 928 4708

Paul Boyce
79 Church Street
Briton Ferry
Neath
Wales
0163 981 3723

David Bradley
Aston Hall, Aston Lane
Claverley
Nr Wolverhampton
WV5 7DZ
0174 671 0287

Pat Brogan
112 Crewe Road
Haslington
Crewe
Cheshire
0127 087 4825

**Tony Burns
Promotions**
67 Peel Place
Clayhill Avenue
Ilford
Essex IG5 0PT
0208 551 3791

Roy Cameron
43 Beaulieu Close
Colindale
London
NW9 6SB
0208 205 2949

Capitol Promotions
Capitol Gymnasium
180 Longford Road
Coventry
CV6 6DR
0247 636 4237

David Casey
424 Barking Road
London E13 8HJ
0207 377 6333

Annette Conroy
144 High Street East
Sunderland
Tyne and Wear
SR1 2BL
0191 567 6871

Jane Couch
Spanorium Farm Gym
Berwick Lane
Bristol
BS35 5RX
07748 841755

**Coventry Sporting
Club**
Les Allen/Paul Carpenter
180 Longford Road
Longford
Coventry
0247 636 4237

Pat Cowdell
129a Moat Road
Oldbury, Warley
West Midlands
0121 552 8082

Denis Cross
6 Partington Street
Newton Heath
Manchester M40 2AQ
0161 205 6651

David Currivan
15 Northolt Avenue
South Ruislip
Middlesex HA4 6SS
0208 841 9933

Christine Dalton
12 Ladysmith Road
Grimsby
Lincolnshire DN32 9EF
0147 231 0288

Michael Dalton
16 Edward Street
Grimsby
South Humberside
0147 231 0288

Ronnie Davies
3 Vallensdean Cottages
Hangleton Lane
Portslade
Sussex
0127 341 6497

**Evans-Waterman
Promotions**
88 Windsor Road
Bray
Berkshire SL6 2DJ
0162 862 3640

Neil Featherby
Sportslink Promotions
Unit 6
Drayton Business Park
Taversham
Drayton
Norwich NR8 6RL
0160 386 8606

Joe Frater
The Cottage
Main Road
Grainthorpe
Louth,
Lincolnshire
0147 234 3194

Dave Garside
33 Lowthian Road
Hartlepool
Cleveland TS26 8AL
0142 929 1611
07973 792588

Johnny Griffin
0116 2262 9287
07989 215287

Jess Harding
c/o UK Industrial Pallets
Ltd
Travellers Lane
Industrial Estate
Travellers Lane
Welham Green
Hatfield
Herts AL9 7HF
0170 727 0440

Hennessy Sports
Mick Hennessy
3rd Floor, Albany House
18 Theydon Road
London E5 9NZ
0208 815 4027

Dennis Hobson
130 Handsworth Road
Sheffield
South Yorkshire
S9 4AE
0114 256 0555
07836 252429

Harry Holland
12 Kendall Close
Feltham
Middlesex
0208 867 0435

Lloyd Honeyghan
PO Box 17216
London SE17 1ZU
0795 640 5007

**Hull & District
Sporting Club**
Mick Toomey
25 Purton Grove
Bransholme
Hull HU7 4QD
0148 282 4476

Alma Ingle
26 Newman Road
Wincobank
Sheffield S9 1LP
0114 281 1277

John Ingle
20 Rockmount Road
Wincobank
Sheffield S9 1NF
0114 261 7934

Lester Jacobs
2 Radnor Road
Peckham
London SE15 6UR
0207 639 4734

Koncrete Promotions
Dave Caldwell
Castle Court
2 St John's Road
Sheffield S2 5JX
0114 275 0303

Lion Promotions
The Sport Entertainment
Media Group
Lennox Lewis/Joel
Berman/Dave Lewis
98 Cockfosters Road
Barnet
Hertfordshire EN4 0DP
0208 447 4250

Patrick Loftus
117 Rutland Road
West Bridgeford
Nottingham NG2 5DY
0115 981 0982

Paul McCausland
20 Invernook Drive
Belfast
Northern Ireland
BT41 1RW
0289 020 2355

Malcolm McKillop
14 Springfield Road
Mangotsfield
Bristol
0117 957 3567

Owen McMahon
3 Atlantic Avenue
Belfast BT15 2HN
0123 274 3535

Eugene Maloney
Maloney's Fight
Factory
516 Old Kent Road
London SE1
0207 740 2876

Matchroom
Barry Hearn
10 Western Road
Romford
Essex RM1 3JT
0170 878 2200

**John Merton
Promotions**
33 Springshaw Road
Walsingham Gate
Kent BR5 2RH
0207 232 0234

Alex Morrison
197 Swanston Street
Laird Business Park
Dalmarnock
Glasgow G40 4HW
0141 554 7777

Katherine Morrison
197 Swanston Street
Laird Business Park
Dalmarnock
Glasgow G40 4HW
0141 554 7777

National SC (Charity)
Cafe Royal
68 Regents Street
London W1R 6EL
0207 437 0144

Peacock Promotions
Anthony Bowers
Peacock Gym
Caxton Street North
Canning Town
London E16 1JR
0207 511 3799

Steve Pollard
899 Beverley High Road
Hull HU6 9NJ
0148 280 3455

Prince Promotions
John Sheppard
Prince House
172 Psalter Lane
Sheffield
South Yorkshire
SI1 8UR
0114 220 3000

Joe Pyle
36 Manship Road
Mitcham
Surrey CR4 2AZ
0208 646 7793

Glyn Rhodes
70 Oldfield Road
Stannington
Sheffield S6
0114 232 6513

Gus Robinson MBE
Stranton House
Westview Road
Hartlepool
Cleveland TS24 0BB
0142 923 4221

Christine Rushton
20 Alverley Lane
Balby
Doncaster
Yorkshire DN4 9AS
0130 231 0919

333

St Andrew's Sporting Club
Tommy Gilmour
Holiday Inn
Bothwell Street
Glasgow G2 7EN
0141 248 5461

Chris Sanigar
Bristol Boxing Gym
40 Thomas Street
St Agnes
Bristol
Avon BS2 9LL
0117 949 6699

Sports Network
Frank Warren
Centurion House
Bircherley Green
Hertford
Hertfordshire SG14 1AP
0199 250 5550

Sportsman Promotions
Frank Quinlan
Hollinthorpe Low Farm
Swillington Lane
Leeds
Yorkshire
LS26 8BZ
0113 287 0167

Kevin Spratt
8 Springfield Road
Guisley
Leeds LS20 8AL
0194 387 6229

Tara Promotions
Jack Doughty
Lane End Cottage
Golden Street
Off Buckstone Road
Shaw
Oldham OL1 8LY
01706 845753

Stephen Vaughan
c/o Lee Maloney
72 East Damswood
Road
Speke
Liverpool
L24 7RJ
07971 024704

Louis Veitch
37 Silverwood Avenue
Blackpool
FY4 3BW
0125 334 1425

Viking Promotions
Stephen Wood
Edward Street
Cambridge Industrial
Area
Salford
Manchester M7 1RL
0161 834 9496

Keith Walker
Wayside Bungalow
Selby Road
Eggborough
DN14 0LN
0197 766 2616

Geraldine Williams
Pendeen
Bodiniel Road
Bodmin
Cornwall
PL31 2PE
0120 872 575

Philip Williams
18 Queens Avenue
Sandycroft
Deeside
CH5 2PR
0124 453 9344

World Sports Organisation
Unit 5, Ella Mews
Cressy Road
London
NW3 2NH
0207 284 2133

Yorkshire Executive Sporting Club
John Celebanski
87 Crowtree Lane
Allerton
Bradford
B8 0AN
0127 482 4015

Licensed Managers

Sam Adair
Ashfield Cottage
Barnstaple
Devon
EX31 4DB
0123 747 4989

Isola Akay
129 Portnall Road
Paddington
London W9 3BN
0208 960 7724

Kofi Asante
102 Old Hospital Close
St James Drive
Balham
London SW12 8SS
0208 672 0475

Chris Aston
23 Juniper Grove Mews
Netherton
Huddersfield
West Yorkshire
HD4 7WG
0148 432 9616

Andy Ayling
Centurion House
Bircherley Green
Hertford
Hertfordshire
SG14 1AP
0199250 5550

Bruce Baker
Garden Flat
38 Lupus Street
Pimlico
London
SW1 U3EB
0207 592 0102

Robert Bannan
1c Thornton Street
Townhead, Coatbridge
North Lanarkshire
ML5 2NZ
0123 660 6736

John Baxter
53 Battenburg Road
Leicester LE3 5HB
0116 243 2325

Sam Betts
The Railway Hotel
115 Station Road
Kirkham
Lancashire PR4 2HD
0177 268 7973

Jack Bishop
76 Gordon Road
Fareham
Hants PO16 7SS
0132 928 4708

Adam Booth
31 Claireville Road
Orpington
Kent BR5 1RU
0793 295 2666

Tony Borg
39 Clarence Street
Newport
Gwent, Wales
0163 378 2824

Gerald Boustead
4 Firlands Road
Barton
Torquay
Devon TQ2 8EW
0180 332 5195

Peter Bowen
50 Newman Avenue
Lanesfield
Wolverhampton
West Midlands
WV4 6BZ
0190 282 8159

Tony Bowers
3 The Green Walk
Chingford
London
E4
0208 523 8113

Paul Boyce
Winstones
Church Street
Briton Ferry
Neath
West Glamorgan
SA11 2GJ
0163 981 3723

David Bradley
The Dovecote
Aston Hall
Claverley
WV5 7DZ
0174 671 0287

John Branch
44 Hill Way
Holly Lodge Estate
London
NE6 4EP

John Breen
Cedar Lodge
589 Antrim Road
Belfast
BT15
0123 277 0238

Mike Brennan
2 Canon Avenue
Chadwell Heath
Romford
Essex
0208 599 4588

Steve Butler
107 Cambridge Street
Normanton
West Yorkshire
WF6 1ES
0192 489 1097

Trevor Callighan
Apartment 9, Deph Brow
Skircoat Moor Road
Halifax
West Yorkshire
HX3 0GZ
0142 232 2592

Enzo Calzaghe
51 Caerbryn
Pentwynmawr
Newbridge
Gwent
South Wales
0149 524 8988

George Carman
5 Mansion Lane
Mobile Home Site
Iver
Bucks
S10 9RQ
0175 365 3096

John Celebanski
87 Crowtree Lane
Allerton
Bradford 8 0AN
01274 824015/542903

Nigel Christian
80 Alma Road
Plymouth
Devon PL3 4HU
0175 225 2753

William Connelly
72 Clincart Road
Mount Florida
Glasgow G42
0141 632 5818

Tommy Conroy
144 High Street East
Sunderland
Tyne and Wear
0191 567 6871

John Cox
11 Fulford Drive
Links View
Northampton NN2 7NX
0160 471 2107

Dave Currivan
15 Northolt Avenue
South Ruislip
Middlesex
0208 841 9933

David Davies
10 Bryngelli, Carmel
Llanelli
Dyfed SA14 7EL
0126 984 3204

John Davies
Unit 14, Rectors Yard
Rectors Lane
Penre Sandycroft
Deeside
Flintshire CH5 2DH
0124 453 8984

Ronnie Davies
3 Vallensdean Cottages
Hangleton Lane
Portslade
Sussex
0127 341 6497

Owen Delargy
133 Leamington Road
Styvechale
Coventry CV3 6GT
07970 102553

Brendan Devine
80 Fallbrook Drive
West Derby
Liverpool L12 5NA
0151 263 1179

Jack Doughty
Lane End Cottage
Golden Street
Off Buckstones Road
Shaw
Oldham OL2 8LY
01706 845753

Mickey Duff
c/o Mrs E Allen
16 Herga Court
Harrow on the Hill
Middlesex HA1 3RS
0208 423 6763

Paul Dykes
Boxing Network
International
Suites 1, 2 & 3, Lord
Lonsdale Chambers
10 Furlong Passage
Burslem
Stoke on Trent
ST6 3AY
0783 177 7310

Gwyn Evans
1 Merchistoun Road
Horndean
Portsmouth
Hants PO8 9LS
0239 259 4504

Jim Evans
88 Windsor Road
Maidenhead
Berkshire SL6 2DJ
0162 823 640

Jonathan Feld
19 The Ridgeway
London NW11 8TD

Stuart Fleet
7 Forsythia Avenue
Healing
Grimsby DN41 7JE
0147 228 0181

Tania Follett
123 Calfridus Way
Bracknell
Berkshire RG12 3HD
07930 904303

Steve Foster
62 Overdale
Swinton
Salford M27 5WE
0161 794 1723

Dai Gardiner
13 Hengoed Hall Drive
Cefn Hengoed
Mid Glamorgan
CF8 7JW
0144 381 2971

Dave Garside
33 Lowthian Road
Hartlepool
Cleveland
TS26 8AL
0142 929 1611

Jimmy Gill
69a Inham Road
Chilwell
Nottingham
NG9 4GT
0115 913 5482

Tommy Gilmour
St Andrew's Sporting
Club
Holiday Inn
Bothwell Street
Glasgow G2 7EN
0141 248 5461

Mike Goodall
Ringcraft
Unit 21
Briars Close Business
Park
Evesham
Worcestershire
WR11 4JT
0138 644 2118

Alex Gower
22 Norwood Avenue
Rush Green
Romford
Essex RM7 0QH
0170 875 3474

Billy Graham
116 Stockport Road
Mossley
Ashton under Lyme
Manchester
0145 783 5100

Lee Graham
28 Smeaton Court
50 Rockingham Street
London SE1 6PF

Johnny Griffin
0116 262 9287
07989 215287

Carl Gunns
14 Whiles Lane
Birstall
Leicester LE4 4EE
0116 267 1494

Christopher Hall
3 Dewhurst Road
Cheshunt
Hertford
EN8 9PG
07930 454731

Jess Harding
c/o UK Industrial Pallets
Ltd
Travellers Lane
Industrial Estate
Travellers Lane
Welham Green
Hatfield
Herts AL9 7HF
0170 727 0440

Tony Harris
237 Stapleford Road
Trowell
Nottingham
NG9 3QE
0115 913 6564

Pat Healy
1 Cranley Buildings
Brookes Market
Holborn
London EC1
0207 242 8121

Barry Hearn
Matchroom
10 Western Road
Romford
Essex RM1 3JT
0170 878 2200

Mick Hill
35 Shenstone House
Aldrington Road
Streatham
London SW16
0208 769 2218

Dennis Hobson
Promotions
130 Handsworth Road
Sheffield
S9 4AE
0114 256 0555

Harry Holland
12 Kendall Close
Feltham
Middlesex
0208 737 4886

Gordon Holmes
15 Robert Andrew
Close
Morley St Botolph
Wymondham
Norfolk
NR18 9AA
0195 360 7887

Lloyd Honeyghan
PO Box 17216
London
SE17 1ZU
07956 405007

Brian Hughes
41 Fold Green
Chadderton
Lancashire OL9 9DX
0161 620 2916

Geoff Hunter
6 Hawkshead Way
Winsford
Cheshire CW7 2SZ
0160 686 2162

Brendan Ingle MBE
26 Newman Road
Wincobank
Sheffield S9 1LP
0114 281 1277

Dominic Ingle
26 Newman Road
Sheffield S9 1LP
0114 281 1277

John Ingle
20 Rockmount Road
Wincobank
Sheffield S9
0114 261 7934

Derek Isaaman
179 Liverpool Road
South
Maghull
Liverpool L31 8AA
0151 526 4087

Thomas Jones
13 Planetree Road
Hale
Cheshire WA15 9JL
0161 980 2661

Freddie King
7 St Charles Road
Brentwood
Essex CM14 4TS

Brian Lawrence
50 Willow Vale
London W12
0208 723 0182

Buddy Lee
The Walnuts
Roman Bank
Leverington, Wisbech
Cambridgeshire
PE13 5AR
0194 558 3266

Daniel Lutaaya
3 Knebworth House
Union Grove
London SW8 2RS
07751 262037

Pat Lynch
Gotherington
68 Kelsey Lane
Balsall Common
Near Coventry
CV7 7GL
0167 633374

Paul McCausland
20 Invernook Drive
Belfast
Northern Ireland
BT4 1RW
0123 220 2355

Robert McCracken
16 Dusard Way
Droitwich
Worcestershire
WR9 8UX
0190 579 8976

Gary McCrory
Croftside
Low Enterprise Park
Greencroft
Stanley
Co Durham
DH9 8NN
0120 723 7117

Jim McDonnell
2 Meadway
Hillside Avenue
Woodford Green
Essex
IG8 7RF
07860 770006

Owen McMahon
3 Atlantic Avenue
Belfast BT15
0289 074 3535

Colin McMillan
60 Billet Road
Chadwell Heath
Romford
Essex
RM6 5SU
0208 597 4464

Frank Maloney
Sports Network
Centurion House
Bircherley Green
Hertfordshire
SG14 1AP
0199 250 5550

Eugene Maloney
Maloney's Fight Factory
516 Old Kent Road
London
SE1 5BA
0207 740 2876

Dennie Mancini
16 Rosedew Road
Off Fulham Palace Road
London
W6 9ET
0207 437 1526

Michael Marsden
1 North View
Roydes Lane
Rothwell
Leeds
LS26 0BQ
0113 282 5565

Terry Marsh
60 Gaynesford
Basildon
Essex SS16 5SG
0207 0152207

Tony Marshall
29 Seagull Bay Drive
Coseley
West Midlands
WV14 8AL
0121 520 3212

Tommy Miller
128 Clapton Mount
King Cross Road
Halifax
West Yorkshire
0142 236 1147

Clifton Mitchell
42 Wiltshire Road
Derby DE21 6EX
01332 295380

Alex Morrison
197 Swanston Street
Laird Business Park
Dalmarnock
Glasgow G40 4HW
0141 554 7777

Katherine Morrison
197 Swanston Street
Laird Business Park
Dalmarnock
Glasgow G40 4HW
0141 554 7777

James Murray
87 Spean Street
Glasgow G44 4DS
0141 637 7926

Bert Myers
8 Thornley Street
Burnley
Lancashire BB12 6LU
07816 966742

Trevor Nerwal
64 Wayside Cottage
Vicarage Lane
Water Orton
Birmingham B26 1RN

Paul Newman
12 Edgehill Way
Portslade
Brighton BN41 2PU
0127 341 9777

Norman Nobbs
364 Kings Road
Kingstanding
Birmingham B44 0UG
0121 355 5341

Stewart Nubley
94 Richmond Road
Kirkby in Ashfield
Nottinghamshire
NG17 7PW
0162 343 2357

Mark O'Callaghan
1 Keel Gardens
Southborough
Tunbridge Wells
Kent TN4 0JQ
0189 268 9979

Terry O'Neill
48 Kirkfield View
Colton Village
Leeds LS15 9DX
0113 225 6140

James Oyebola
194 Portnall Road
London W9
0208 930 9685

Ian Pauly
1202 Lincoln Road
Peterborough PE4 6LA
0173 357 1782

Alan Phillips
Glendowor Lodge
Coventry Road
Wolvey
Hinckley
Leicestershire
LE10 3LD

Steve Pollard
899 Beverley High Road
Hull HU6 9NJ
0148 280 9455

David Poston
2 Whitegate Road
Daisy Bank
Bliston
West Midlands
WV14 8UY
0190 249 3040

Brian Powell
138 Laurel Road
Bassaleg
Newport
Gwent NP10 8PT
0163 389 2165

Dean Powell
Lion Promotions
98 Cockfoster Road
Barnet EN4 0DP
0795 690 5741

Joe Pyle
36 Manship Road
Mitcham
Surrey CR4 2AZ
0208 395 6907

Michael Quinn
64 Warren Road
Wanstead
London E11 2NA
0208 989 0082

Howard Rainey
9 Castlebeck Drive
Sheffield S2 1NP
0114 264 4106

Paul Rees
11 Abbots Park
London Road
St Albans
Herts AL1 1TW
0172 776 7656

Glyn Rhodes
166 Oldfield Road
Stannington
Sheffield S6 6DY
0114 232 6513

Gus Robinson, MBE
Stranton House
Westview Road
Hartlepool
TS24 0BB
0142 923 4221

Mark Roe
48 Westbrooke Road
Sidcup
Kent
DA15 7PH
0208 309 9396

John Rooney
6 Coach House Mews
217 Long Lane
London SE1 4PP
0788 407 7024

John Rushton
20 Alverley Lane
Balby
Doncaster DN4 9AS
0130 231 0919

Kevin Sanders
135 Coneygree Road
Peterborough
Cambridgeshire
PE1 8LQ
0173 355 5916

Chris Sanigar
Bristol Boxing Gym
40 Thomas Street
St Agnes
Bristol BS2 9LL
0117 949 6699

Trevor Schofield
234 Doncaster Road
Barnsley
South Yorkshire
S70 1UQ
0122 629 7376

Mike Shinfield
126 Birchwood Lane
Somercotes
Derbyshire
DE55 4NE
0177 360 3124

Tony Sims
67 Peel Place
Clayhall
Ilford
Essex IG5 0PT
017931 188308

Les Southey
Oakhouse
Park Way
Hillingdon
Middlesex
0189 525 4719

Norrie Sweeney
3 Saucehill Terrace
Paisley
Scotland PA2 6SY
0141 580 0269

Wally Swift
12 Garden Close
Knowle
Solihull
West Midlands B93 92F
0156 477 5140

Glenroy Taylor
73 Aspen Lane
Northolt
Middlesex U35 6XH
0795 645 3787

Terry Toole
6 Churchwell Close
Chipping Onger
Essex CM5 9BH
0127 736 2372

Mick Toomey
25 Purton Grove
Bransholme
Hull HU7 4QD
0148 282 4476

Jack Trickett
Acton Court Hotel
187 Buxton Road
Stockport
Cheshire SK2 7AB
0161 483 6523

Stephen Vaughan
c/o Lee Maloney
72 East Damswood
Road, Speke
Liverpool L24 7RJ
0797 102 4704

Louis Veitch
37 Silverwood Avenue
Blackpool FY4 3BW
0125 334 1425

Keith Walker
Walkers Boxing
Promotions
Headland House
Suite 21-35
Spawd Bone Lane
Knottingley
West Yorks WF11 0HY
0197 763 6905

Frank Warren
Centurion House
Bircherley Green
Hertford
Hertfordshire SG14 1AP
0199 250 5550

Robert Watt
32 Downhill Street
Glasgow G11
0141 334 7465

Jack Weaver
301 Coventry Road
Hinckley
Leicestershire LE10 0NE
0145 561 9066

Malcolm Webb
51 Bedwellty Road
Aberbargoed
Bargoed
Mid Glamorgan
Wales CF81 9AX
0144 387 9118

Lee Wicks
22a Stone Close
Worthing
West Sussex
BN13 2AU
0190 369 1936

Derek V. Williams
65 Virginia Road
Surrey
CR7 8EN
0208 458 0511

Derek Williams
Pendeen
Bodiniel Road
Bodmin
Cornwall
PL31 2PE

John Williams
3a Langham Road
Tottenham
London
N15 3QX
0794 933 5787

Alan Wilton
The Bridge
42 Derryboy Road
Crossgar
BT30 9LH
0289 754 2195

Barry Winter
9 McNeill Avenue
Linnvale
Clydebank
G81 2TB
0141 952 9942

Stephen Wood
Viking Promotions
Edward Street
Cambridge Industrial
Area, Salford
Manchester M7 1RL
0161 834 9496

Tex Woodward
Spaniorum Farm
Compton Greenfield
Bristol BS12 3RX
0145 463 2448

Licensed Matchmakers

John Ashton
1 Charter Close
Kirby in Ashfield
Nottinghamshire
NG17 8PF
0162 372 1278

Neil Bowers
59 Carson Road
Canning Town
London
E16 4BD
0207 473 5631

Nigel Christian
89 Oaklands Park
Polperro Road
Looe
Cornwall
PL13 2JS

Jim Evans
88 Windsor Road
Bray
Maidenhead
Berks SL6 2DJ
0162 862 3640

Ernie Fossey
26 Bell Lane
Brookmans Park
Hatfield
Hertfordshire
0170 765 6545

John Gaynor
7 Westhorne Fold
Counthill Drive
Brooklands Road
Crumpsall
Manchester M8 4JN
0161 740 6993

Tommy Gilmour
St Andrew's SC
Holiday Inn
Bothwell Street
Glasgow G2 7EN
0141 248 5461

Roy Hilder
2 Farrington Place
Chislehurst
Kent BR7 6BE
0208 325 6156

John Ingle
20 Rockmount Road
Wincobank
Sheffield S9 1LP
0114 261 7934

Stevie James
117 Main Street
Little Harrowden
Wellingbrough
Northamptonshire
NN9 5BA
0193 322 2241

Dennie Mancini
16 Rosedew Road
Off Fulham Palace Road
Hammersmith
London W6 9ET
0207 437 1526

Tommy Miller
128 Clapton Mount
King Cross Road
Halifax
West Yorkshire
0142 236 1147

Ken Morton
3 St Quintin Mount
'Bradway'
Sheffield
S17 4PQ
0114 262 1829

Dean Powell
98 Cockfoster Road
Barnet
Herts
EN4 0DP
0208 447 4250

Richard Poxon
148 Cliffefield Road
Sheffield
S8 9BS
0114 225 7856

John Rushton
20 Averley Lane
Balby
Doncaster
South Yorkshire
0130 231 0919

Chris Sanigar
Bristol Boxing Gym
40 Thomas Street
St Agnes
Bristol BS2 9LL
07831 359978

Terry Toole
6 Churchwell Close
Chipping Onger
Essex CM5 9BH
0127 736 2372

Ian Watson
120 York Street
Jarrow
Tyne & Wear
NE32 5RY
07850 779773

John Wilson
1 Shenley Hill
Radlett
Herts
WD7 3AS
0192 385 7874

Kevin Lear (right) made a successful defence of the WBU super-featherweight title when forcing Bulgaria's Kirkor Kirkorov to retire in the seventh round

Les Clark

Licensed BBBoC Referees, Timekeepers, Ringwhips and Inspectors

Licensed Referees

Class 'B'

Billy Aird	Southern Area
Dean Bramhald	Midland Area
Mark Curry	Northern Area
Seamus Dunne	Southern Area
Christopher Kelly	Central Area
Shaun Messer	Midlands Area
David Morgan	Welsh Area
Andrew Wright	Northern Area

Class 'A'

Terence Cole	Northern Area
Lee Cook	Midlands Area
Kenneth Curtis	Southern Area
Philip Edwards	Central Area
Roddy Evans	Welsh Area
Keith Garner	Central Area
Paul Graham	Scottish Area
Michael Heatherwick	Welsh Area
Jeff Hinds	Southern Area
Al Hutcheon	Scottish Area
David Irving	Northern Ireland
Wynford Jones	Welsh Area
Phil Kane	Central Area
Victor Loughin	Scottish Area
Grant Wallis	Western Area

Class 'A' Star

John Coyle	Midlands Area
Richie Davies	Southern Area
Howard Foster	Central Area
Mark Green	Southern Area
Ian John-Lewis	Southern Area
John Keane	Midlands Area
Marcus McDonnell	Southern Area
Larry O'Connell	Southern Area
Terry O'Connor	Midlands Area
Dave Parris	Southern Area
Paul Thomas	Midlands Area
Mickey Vann	Central Area

Licensed Timekeepers

Arnold Bryson	Northern Area
Neil Burder	Welsh Area
Richard Clark	Central Area
Anthony Dunkerley	Midlands Area
Robert Edgeworth	Southern Area
Dale Elliott	Northern Ireland
Harry Foxall	Midlands Area
Eric Gilmour	Scottish Area
Gary Grennan	Central Area
Brian Heath	Midlands Area
Greg Hue	Southern Area
Jon Lee	Western Area
Michael McCann	Southern Area
Peter McCann	Southern Area
Norman Maddox	Midlands Area
Barry Pinder	Central Area

Raymond Rice	Southern Area
Colin Roberts	Central Area
James Russell	Scottish Area
David Walters	Welsh Area
Kevin Walters	Northern Area
Paul Webster	Central Area
Nick White	Southern Area

Licensed Ringwhips

Lester Arthur	Western Area
Michael Burke	Scottish Area
Steve Butler	Central Area
Ernie Draper	Southern Area
Simon Goodall	Midlands Area
Denzil Lewis	Western Area
Stuart Lithgo	Northern Area
Tommy Miller (Jnr)	Central Area
Tommy Rice	Southern Area
Sandy Risley	Southern Area
Stephen Sidebottom	Central Area
James Wallace	Scottish Area

Inspectors

Herold Adams	Southern Area
Alan Alster	Central Area
William Ball	Southern Area
Richard Barber	Southern Area
Michael Barnett	Central Area
Don Bartlett	Midlands Area
Geoff Boulter	Central Area
Fred Breyer	Southern Area
David Brown	Western Area
Walter Campbell	Northern Ireland
Harry Carroll	Welsh Area
Geoff Collier	Midlands Area
Michael Collier	Southern Area
Constantin Cotzias	Southern Area
Julian Courtney	Welsh Area
Jaswinder Dhaliwal	Midlands Area
Christopher Dolman	Midlands Area
Kevin Fulthorpe	Welsh Area
Bob Galloway	Southern Area
Paul Gooding	Northern Area
Eddie Higgins	Scottish Area
Michael Hills	Northern Area
Neil Holland	Midlands Area
Alan Honnibal	Western Area
David Hughes	Welsh Area
Francis Keenan	Northern Ireland
James Kirkwood	Scottish Area
Nicholas Laidman	Southern Area
Kevin Leafe	Central Area
Eddie Lillis	Central Area
Fred Little	Western Area
Reginald Long	Northern Area
Bob Lonkhurst	Southern Area
Paul McAllister	Northern Ireland
Sam McAughtry	Northern Ireland

Dave McAuley	Northern Ireland
Liam McColgan	Scottish Area
Billy McCrory	Northern Ireland
Gerry McGinley	Scottish Area
Paul McKeown	Northern Ireland
Neil McLean	Scottish Area
Pat Magee	Northern Ireland
Dave Porter	Southern Area
Fred Potter	Northern Area
Les Potts	Midlands Area
Suzanne Potts	Midlands Area
Steve Ray	Central Area
Bob Rice	Midlands Area
Hugh Russell	Northern Ireland
Charlie Sexton	Scottish Area
Neil Sinclair	Southern Area
Bert Smith	Central Area
Nigel Underwood	Midlands Area
David Venn	Northern Area
Phil Waites	Midlands Area
Ron Warburton	Central Area
Danny Wells	Southern Area
Andrew Whitehall	Midlands Area
Bob Williams	Southern Area
Trevor Williams	Midlands Area
Barney Wilson	Northern Ireland
Robert Wilson	Scottish Area
Fred Wright	Central Area

Dave McAuley (left) was the BBBoC's 'Fighter of the Year' in 1991   Les Clark

PROFESSIONAL BOXING PROMOTERS' ASSOCIATION

PRESENTS

THE BRITISH MASTERS CHAMPIONS

UNDER BBB OF C RULES

HEAVY:	JACKLORD JACOBS
CRUISER:	VACANT
LIGHT-HEAVY:	STEVEN SPARTACUS
SUPER-MIDDLE:	DONOVAN SMILLIE
MIDDLE:	MARTYN BAILEY
LIGHT-MIDDLE:	MATT SCRIVEN
WELTER:	VACANT
LIGHT-WELTER:	LEE McALLISTER
LIGHTWEIGHT:	DAVE STEWART
SUPER-FEATHER:	VACANT
FEATHER:	CHOI TSEVEENPUREV
SUPER-BANTAM:	FRANKIE DEMILO
BANTAM:	GARETH PAYNE
FLYWEIGHT:	DELROY SPENCER
LIGHT FLY:	VACANT

THE ONLY ALLCOMERS TITLE OPERATING IN BRITISH BOXING. OUR CHAMPIONS HAVE TO DEFEND WHEN A VALID CHALLENGE IS MADE WITH MORE THAN 30 DAYS NOTICE. TO CHALLENGE FOR OUR TITLE, PROMOTERS SHOULD APPLY TO:

THE PBPA   TEL: 020 7592 0102
P O BOX 25188   FAX: 020 7592 0087
LONDON   EMAIL: bdbaker@tinyworld.co.uk
SW1V 3WL

CHAIRMAN: Bruce Baker
GENERAL SECRETARY: Greg Steene

DIRECTORS: B. Baker, G. Steene, P. Brogan, J. Gill, J. Evans, R. Cameron, J. Griffin

MEMBERSHIP OPEN TO ALL SMALL HALL PROMOTERS

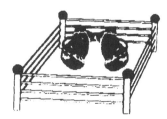

PEACOCK PROMOTIONS

PROMOTER/MANAGER: TONY BOWERS
AGENT/MATCHMAKER: ROY HILDER
TRAINERS: MARTIN BOWERS/JACKIE BOWERS/ALI FORBES/
JOHN BOSCOE/JOHN HUMPHREY SNR
SECRETARY: ALAN RITCHINGS

WE ARE VERY PROUD TO BOTH PROMOTE AND MANAGE THE FOLLOWING LIST OF PROFESSIONAL BOXERS:

JULIUS FRANCIS (37)	HEAVY	EX BRITISH & COMMONWEALTH CHAMPION	23-12-1
GARRY DELANEY (32)	CRUISER	BRITISH MASTERS CHAMPION	30-6-1
ELVIS MICHAILENKO (27)	LIGHT-HEAVY	WBA INTER-CONTINENTAL & WBF EUROPEAN CHAMPION	13-0-1
ERIK TEYMOUR (22)	SUPER-MIDDLE		12-1-0
CHRIS NEMBHARD (24)	MIDDLE		7-4-1
THOMAS DA SILVA (25)	LIGHT-MIDDLE		4-8-1
JOHN 'BOY' HUMPHREY (22)	WELTER	FORMER SOUTHERN AREA CHAMPION. FORMER UNDEFEATED BRITISH MASTERS CHAMPION	14-3-0
LUKE RUDD (21)	WELTER		2-1-0
DANIEL JAMES (26)	LIGHT-WELTER	FORMER UNDEFEATED SOUTHERN AREA CHAMPION	12-3-0
DARREN MELVILLE (27)	LIGHT-WELTER		11-2-1
SILENCE SAHEED (25)	LIGHT		2-0-1
JOHN MACKAY (21)	SUPER-BANTAM		7-3-0
BUSTER DENNIS (22)	SUPER-BANTAM		1-3-0
ROCKY DEAN (25)	BANTAM		7-1-1
JOSEPH AGBEKO (22)	BANTAM	WBF WORLD CHAMPION	21-0-0

**READY, WILLING AND ABLE
ANYTIME, ANYPLACE, ANYWHERE**

TBS SPORT MANAGEMENT LTD
Boxing Training • Management • Promotions

T Burns   **Office:** *020 85508911*
T Sims   **Fax:**   *020 8550 8915*
T Stewart   **Mobile:** *07739 617830*

Current Boxers

Steven Spartcus	*Light-Heavyweight*	*13-0-0*	*British Masters Champion*
Andrew Lowe	*Light-Heavyweight*	*11-0-0*	*Southern Area Champion*
Dave Stewart	*Lightweight*	*10-0-0*	*British Masters Champion*
Paul Halpin	*Super-Featherweight*	*12-0-1*	
Mark Alexander	*Featherweight*	*4-1-0*	
Ben Hudson	*Light-Welterweight*	*5-3-1*	
Marcus Lee	*Cruiserweight*	*2-1-0*	
Daniel Cadman	*Middleweight*	*1-0-0*	

Licensed by The British Boxing Board of Control Ltd
Registered Office: Abacus House, 68a North Street, Romford RM1 1DA
Incorporated in England: 4765859 / VAT Number: 815 1039 61

Boxers' Record Index